11-98

DATE			DATE DUE		
			JUL 05 2007	JUL 10 2009	
			JAN 21 2009		

THE NEW YORK PUBLIC LIBRARY
BOOK OF TWENTIETH-CENTURY
AMERICAN QUOTATIONS

THE NEW YORK PUBLIC LIBRARY BOOK OF TWENTIETH-CENTURY AMERICAN QUOTATIONS

edited by

STEPHEN DONADIO, JOAN SMITH, SUSAN MESNER, AND REBECCA DAVISON

A STONESONG PRESS BOOK

WARNER BOOKS

A Time Warner Company

11-92 BT 24.95

Warner Books, Inc., Time and Life Building, 1271 Avenue of the Americas, New York, NY 10020

 Time Warner Company

Printed in the United States of America

First Printing: July, 1992

10 9 8 7 6 5 4 3 2 1

A Stonesong Press Book

Design by Binns and Lubin/Martin Lubin

We are grateful to the following sources for their permission to quote certain of the lengthier selections in this work:

I Have a Dream Copyright © 1963 by Dr. Martin Luther King, Jr., copyright renewed 1991 by Coretta Scott King, reprinted by permission of the Joan Daves Agency.

Words from *Hark, When Gerald Ford Was King* reprinted by permission of William Strauss.

Houghton Mifflin Company for the essay from *New England: The Four Seasons* by Arthur Griffin. Copyright © 1980 by Arthur Griffin. Reprinted by permission of Houghton Mifflin Company. All rights reserved. The essay, entitled *Summer* is by Robert Parker.

The Twelve Steps of Alcoholics Anonymous reprinted with permission of the National Council on Alcoholism.

The Port Huron Statement, delivered in 1962 in Port Huron, Michigan, is reprinted by permission of Tom Hayden.

Library of Congress Cataloging-in-Publication Data

The New York Public Library book of twentieth-century American quotations / Stephen Donadio... [et al.].

    p.   cm.

"A Stonesong Press Book"

Includes index.

ISBN 0-446-51639-2

1. Quotations, American. I. Donadio, Stephen. II. New York Public Library

PN6081.N53 1992   91-50395

081—dc20   CIP

CONTENTS

FOREWORD

Threading your way through the maze of a great library takes the courage of Theseus and the skill of a lace-maker. Books are still the most convenient, the most portable, and in many ways the most durable carriers of speech we have. But when you deal with The New York Public Library, which has, in all its parts, some 15 million books, not to mention magazines, newspapers, maps, scrapbooks, photos, prints, and tracts pious, impious, and political, you have a lifetime's work cut out for you. A map of the contents of any library, certainly a behemoth like this one, is like an inventory of the human mind. Somewhere along these endless stacks is the phrase, the sentence, the paragraph that echoes your own thought, helps define it, or dresses it in borrowed finery. The real problem is finding that book, that passage, those words.

The New York Public Library Book of Twentieth-Century American Quotations will provide one small key to unlocking the treasures of this vast collection. Unlike many other gatherings of good sayings, this volume focuses exclusively on the thoughts and words of the modern American world. Scholar, author, student, public speaker, journalist, or even those of us who only come to dabble will find it of real use. This book is for you and me, for people who quote "by necessity, by proclivity, and by delight" (to echo Ralph Waldo Emerson) or, perhaps more humbly, for all of us who are convinced that quotation is an acceptable substitute for an original mind. Since this gathering is based exclusively on twentieth-century Americana, you will look in vain for Chaucer or even Emerson. You will find W.E.B. Dubois, Eleanor Roosevelt, Albert Einstein, and Woody Allen. Here are sayings on abstractions such as democracy, individualism, and humor, as well as more precise ones on baseball, the weather, and the Gulf War. There are marvelous quotes about government and politics, including campaign slogans. Here are the fads and fashions of television, radio, and the theater, and a solid section on "marriage, divorce, and other arrangements." I could go on, but you, the reader, will find your own way and will revel in it. Some quotes will delight you; others will leave you splenetic with rage. Some will sound despairing, and some will apply the sovereign balm of hope. One by one they may be fragments, but even a fragmented mirror can show us ourselves, our lives, our twentieth-century America.

TIMOTHY S. HEALY
President, New York Public Library

INTRODUCTION

The *New York Public Library Book of Twentieth-Century American Quotations* provides the reader with a collage of the major and minor forces and figures that have shaped this country. It includes profound insights, such as writer Waldo Frank's view of our constant quest for identity: "We go forth all to seek America. And in the seeking we create her. In the quality of our search shall be the nature of the America that we created." And it does not ignore the more ridiculous aspects of modern life: "Following a nuclear attack on the United States, the U.S. Postal Service plans to distribute Emergency Change of Address Cards." It embraces the seventh-generation American and the immigrant, the politician and the scientist, the movie star and the soldier, the historian and the novelist, the musician and the baseball player.

There is no disputing Gertrude Stein's observation that "In America everybody is, but some are more than others." Accordingly, our efforts to capture American life led us first to the historic figures in this century. Theodore Roosevelt, often remembered for his "speak softly and carry a big stick" approach to foreign policy, was also the first president to sound the alarm on environmental ravages. Margaret Sanger's manifesto on birth control is as relevant today as it was almost a century ago. Reading Martin Luther King's "I Have a Dream" speech enables us to recall the power and dignity he marshaled to confront the forces of segregation.

As significant as these people's voices are, they express only a part of the dynamism and diversity of twentieth-century America. We searched beyond the notable to find lesser known contributions. It was especially satisfying to find people who were well known within their communities but who have not been visible to the larger society. Melvin Tolson, a journalist for the Washington Herald in the 1930s and 1940s, never received much recognition in white society, yet his social commentary was profoundly relevant to all Americans. Lillian Smith, now not as well known as she should be, offers insights into racial strife and the plight of women in this country that have a clarity made sharper by the passage of time. We strove to make this book representative of the contributions of all cultures, though our efforts on this score are incomplete. If there seem to be a shortage of minority and women's voices in such categories as "Freedom" and "Justice," it is because those out of power often see these ideals not as abstract concepts but as rights granted to some and denied to others. Their cries for freedom and justice are specific to their situation and are most often categorized under "Civil Rights" or "Women."

It is also significant that "Men" is such a small category, especially compared with "Women." In countless quotations, concerning everything from "Action" to "Character" to "Success," we took the word "man" to mean both men and women, and therefore categorized the quotations according to their subject. There is no such ambiguity regarding the word "woman," and the profusion of writing about women in this century, particularly in the last thirty years, provided a mother lode of rich quotations. Still, the tension between these categories suggests we as a society have not yet reached a common language for the many dreams and ideals we hold in common.

We found much that was thoughtful, witty, eloquent, and profound in the words of people in all walks of life, each holding a piece of what America is all about. The colloquial quip and the scholarly quotation, the pronouncements of defenders of the status quo and of dissenters, commercial advertising slogans and the exhortations of political and religious leaders have all found a home in this volume. Of the more than 8,000 quotations collected, there are over 2,000 contributors, not including those taken from advertisements and anonymous sources.

Straying yet again from the conventional path,

The New York Public Library Book of Twentieth-Century American Quotations is organized into major and minor topics. Rather than a straightforward list of subjects, we chose a thematic format that more clearly reflects the complexity of forces that have shaped the United States. Two world wars and two undeclared wars, the Great Depression, the Cold War, organized movements for labor and civil rights, a new environmental awareness, changes in the family and community, class and political differences, a proliferation of new technologies, and the sexual revolution are some of the major challenges Americans have had to confront. The category "Dreams and Ideals" provided particularly fertile ground for exploring our national character. Herbert Croly, in a book that received wide attention early in the century, captured a persistent feature of our character that explains our surprise when our noble ideals produce ignoble results:

> [Americans] still believe that somehow and sometime something better will happen to good Americans than has happened to men in any other country: and this belief, vague, innocent, and uninformed though it be, is the expression of an essential constituent in our national ideal.

Though the innocence of our beliefs has been badly tarnished since Croly wrote these words in 1909, the faith in an unrealized future is still strong, as evidenced by the visceral response to Ronald Reagan's "morning in America" campaign slogan. There is often tension between promise and actuality within an idea:

> Individualism, we are entitled to say, is, if not truth, the nearest thing we have to truth, no closer thing to truth in the field of social relations having appeared on the horizon.
>
> WILLIAM F. BUCKLEY

> We reveal the fullness of our devotion to individualism by keeping it as a reward for full participation in society. For the prisoner, the chronically ill, the bedridden old and the destitute, we reserve the forced collective life.
>
> ELAINE CUMMING

There is conflict, too, among our various ideals: risk versus security, patriotism versus democracy, justice versus progress, freedom versus equality.

> Liberty and Equality are the twin ideals of American democracy. But they are not the same thing.... Many persons who would gladly die for liberty are appalled by equality. Many who are devoted to equality are puzzled and even troubled by liberty. Much of the political history of the American nation can be seen as a competition between these two ideals.
>
> DANIEL PATRICK MOYNIHAN

When viewed as a whole the "Dreams and Ideals" section throws such conflicts into greater relief. That quotation from Moynihan could easily have been categorized under either "Freedom" or "Equality." Though we chose the latter, its inclusion under the general rubric of dreams and ideals is perhaps most appropriate.

Grouping quotations under general topics also allowed us to look at twentieth-century America in an historical context, with an eye toward how our thinking as a nation has evolved. This is particularly apparent in an area like "Science and Technology," which has seen such radical changes in this century. Readers can also begin to trace Americans' views on social issues, such as civil rights or the environment, from 1900 to the present day. It is obvious, however, that some prevailing attitudes have not changed—our distrust of politicians has never wavered. At times, past and present seem tightly linked: The language of the Declaration of the National Woman's Christian Temperance Union, written in 1902, is not so dated when placed alongside the Twelve Steps of Alcoholics Anonymous. These, together with the contract developed in the latter part of the 1980s by Students Against Drunk Driving, serve as compelling evidence of how much this nation has struggled to control a substance that has given such pleasure and created so much pain.

As the examples indicate, many of the quotations are longer than those traditionally found in quotation books. In addition, we've included over twenty longer documents of historical or cultural importance. Richard Nixon's famous "I am not a crook" remark perfectly exemplifies one reason for fuller quotations. While commonly assumed to refer to his role in Watergate, the quotation in fact refers to a tax scandal in which he was embroiled in late 1973:

> I made my mistakes, but in all my years of public life I have never profited, never profited from public service. I've earned every cent. And in all of my years in public life I have never obstructed justice.... I welcome this kind of examination because people have got to know whether or not their president is a crook. Well, I'm not a crook. I've earned everything I've got.

While many quotations of historical importance are included, we attempted to find the important thought wrapped in the well-turned phrase. The words of some writers and politicians seemed especially compelling and articulate: Frances FitzGerald, Arthur Schlesinger, Jr., Woodrow Wilson, Franklin D. Roosevelt, Barbara Tuchman, Henry Steele Commager, to name a few. We found, however, that not all good writing is quotable. S.J. Perelman and Ring Lardner, for example, composed in tightly ordered patterns—lifting pearls out of their writing only breaks the string. We owe a particularly large debt to that genre of writing known as social commentary. Whether the subject is business or religion, politics or education, science or art, social commentators often hold as much sway with the public as experts in the field. Their perceptions tend to be characterized by exceptional vividness, and everything from the momentous to the mundane comes in for scrutiny. Although not unique to the United States, this country's odd milieu of naiveté and cynicism provides an environment in which social commentators thrive. It is hard to think of this century without the contributions of H.L. Mencken and Will Rogers, whose perspicacity and mordant humor have remained unforgettable.

The United States is a nation of immigrants and a magnet for many talented people, and so it was difficult at times to define "American"—as Zora Neale Hurston wrote, "Wese a mingled people." Moreover, some Americans have resided elsewhere: T.S. Eliot was born in the United States but became a naturalized British citizen—both Britain and the United States claim him. Wanda Landowska, the Polish-born harpsichordist, lived in Paris for a time but finally settled in the United States. Three countries could count her as theirs. It was necessary to devote significant time to researching the origins of contributors, which points to the tremendous cross-fertilization that has occurred in all aspects of our society. We attempted to verify the U.S. citizenship of everyone we included, but in those rare instances where we were unable to find conclusive verification, we made a determination based on the significance of a person's contribution to our national experience and the amount of time he or she had actually spent in this country. Whether spoken by recent immigrant or native American, artist or businessperson, whether written for congressional testimony or radio skit, whether dated in the first or last decade of the century, the quotations herein reflect the America we know. Here you have both a reference book and a book that invites extensive browsing, a book to stimulate memory and to produce new inquiry. In this land where the ephemeral and enduring lie familiarly side by side, The *New York Public Library Book of Twentieth-Century American Quotations* holds a mirror to both, and so to the nation's restless consciousness.

We could not have undertaken a book of this size and scope without the support and cooperation of many people. The credit for the idea of this book and all the initial work of getting it off the ground belongs to Paul Fargis of The Stonesong Press. He also provided valuable ideas for quotations and enthusiasm when our spirits were lagging. Michael Bell guided us safely through the world of database systems by designing our program and making himself available at all hours of the day and night when emergencies arose. Marilyn Johnson patiently and carefully entered the thousands of quotations into the database. We were assisted in our research by Donna Imbeninato, Linda Leehman, Joan Patterson, and Glenn Quint, who searched out quotations and verified citations.

We owe a special debt to the librarians we consulted who cheerfully gave of their time and valuable knowledge. Barbara Berliner of The New York Public Library Telephone Reference Service and

Richard Newman of The New York Public Library Publications Department were generous in their advice and the careful review of our selections and sources. Janet Reit at the University of Vermont Bailey-Howe Library was kind enough to take the time to sit down with us at the beginning of the project and guide us to time-saving reference tools. The staffs at the University of Vermont, the State Law and Reference Library, and the Midstate Regional Library were always patient as we pelted them with questions and interlibrary loan forms. Roberta Downing at the Kellogg-Hubbard Library in Montpelier was unstinting in her doggedness to find some esoteric detail we needed at a moment's notice. In addition to The New York Public Library, librarians around New England offered their aid. Wendy Thomas at Radcliffe's Schlesinger Library was especially valuable in helping us to locate quotations by women from all walks of life; the research staff at the John Fitzgerald Kennedy Library aided us in finding the source for a Kennedy quotation; and Susan Griggs at the Smith College archives sent us information about Margaret Sanger's manifesto on birth control. Finally, the staff of the Library of Congress in Washington, D.C., kindly guided us through that venerable institution's riches.

Other individuals also generously gave us valuable information or resources. Frank Deford, the sportswriter, was willing to discuss the merits of the great sportswriters of the past and to offer suggestions for contributors. Senate staff members in Edward Kennedy's (MA), Bob Doyle's (KS), Jim Jeffords' (VT), and Bob Kerry's (NE) offices provided us with critical government documents. J.J. Wilson, chair of the Women's Studies Program at Sonoma State University, and Kris Montgomery of the Women's Archive Project, helped uncover additional sources for contributions by women. Our thanks, too, go to the Vermont Public Interest Research Group staff for letting us take over their laser printer and offices until the wee hours of the morning. We want to note and thank Felice Levy, Cynthia Crippen, Teresa Mamone, Betty Binns, and Anne Milburn for their help during the editorial and production stages. Last, there should be a special round of applause for Judy Steer, the chief proofreader, and Martin Lubin for his skill and patience.

USING THIS BOOK

The *New York Public Library Book of Twentieth-Century American Quotations* is divided into forty major topics with over half having subtopics. Both main topics and subtopics are arranged alphabetically and listed in the Contents.

Many quotations cover more than one topic and could easily be placed in more than one category. To assist you in finding related quotations or finding a quotation that mentions the same subject but has a heavier emphasis on another topic, we have listed cross-references at the start of major categories. For example, there are quotations about religion and science found under both Religion and Science and Technology. "Life lessons," however, is not cross-referenced because of its broad range of topics—all the quotes in some sense instruct us. The difference here is more in tone than content.

Under most topic headings, the quotations are listed alphabetically by author's last name in chronological order. A few sections such as "Political Slogans" and "Radio Lines" are listed chronologically rather than alphabetically since most of the selections reflect a party, an era, or an anonymous voice that might have been repeated many times. Aside from the person's name, the credit line for the quotations includes either a primary or secondary source so you may check the context or find the whole passage. For the most part, the dates at the end of the sources are dates of publication or broadcast. Wherever possible we have also added the date of the actual quotation. For example:

RACHEL CARSON, acceptance speech for National Book Award, 1952, in Paul Brooks, *The House of Life: Rachel Carson at Work*, 1972.

We were not always able to determine the exact date a quotation first appeared. In those cases, we have given the approximate time (ca. 1937) or the year and/or month when they could be determined.

There is both an author and a subject index. Entries in the latter are listed under a keyword. The entries are also cross-referenced: topics that pertain to love might also be listed as:

Moral, *see also* Ethics

and then

Ethics, *see also* Moral

Each entry has the page number and an "L" or an "R" indicating whether the quotation is in the left- or right-hand column on the page.

Dead, more to say when I am — , 93R

Quotations running over onto the next page are numbered with the page on which they begin.

THE NEW YORK PUBLIC LIBRARY
BOOK OF TWENTIETH-CENTURY
AMERICAN QUOTATIONS

Age

See also **Children and Youth**; **Dreams and Ideals**—Beauty, Wisdom; **Life's Lessons**; **Popular Culture**; **Relationships**—Marriage, Divorce and Other Arrangements, Parents and Children; **Social Issues**—Health, Poverty, and Hunger

Years ago we discovered the exact point, the dead center of middle age. It occurs when you are too young to take up golf and too old to rush up to the net.

FRANKLIN P. ADAMS, *Nods and Becks*, 1944.

The man who views the world at 50 the same as he did at 20 has wasted 30 years of his life.

MUHAMMAD ALI, interview, *Playboy*, November, 1975.

Was she old? When they lit all of the candles on her birthday cake, six people were overcome with the heat.

FRED ALLEN, *Much Ado About Me*, 1956.

What do years matter, particularly if your apartment is rent-controlled?

WOODY ALLEN, *Without Feathers*, 1975.

Life is precious to the old person. He is not interested merely in thoughts of yesterday's good life and tomorrow's path to the grave. He does not want his later years to be a sentence of solitary confinement in society. Nor does he want them to be a death watch.

DR. DAVID ALLMAN, speech, "The Brotherhood of Healing," National Conference of Christians and Jews, February 12, 1958.

If this was adulthood, the only improvement she could detect in her situation was that now she could eat dessert without eating her vegetables.

LISA ALTHER, *Kinflicks*, 1977.

The gift from middle age was the ability to enjoy the moment without expecting it to last.

LISA ALTHER, *Other Women*, 1984.

When somebody says to me—which they do like every five years—"How does it feel to be over the hill," my response is, "I'm just heading up the mountain."

JOAN BAEZ, *Rolling Stone*, 1983.

A man is not old until regrets take the place of dreams.

JOHN BARRYMORE, in Gene Fowler, *Good Night, Sweet Prince*, 1943.

To me, old age is always fifteen years older than I am.

BERNARD M. BARUCH, *New York Times*, June 6, 1984.

If we crack the aging barrier, the human race will probably be faced with the greatest crisis of its existence. The nature of the crisis can be summarized by saying, who wants to be an assistant professor for 500 years?

KENNETH BOULDING, "The Prospects of Economic Abundance," *The Control of Environment*, 1967.

Perhaps one has to be very old before one learns how to be amused rather than shocked.

PEARL S. BUCK, *China, Past and Present*, 1972.

I have passed from the positive to the negative side of life, when we begin to take in sail; when we want less and not more; when the hunger for new scenes and new worlds to conquer is diminishing; when the inclination not to stir beyond one's own chimney corner is fast growing upon us.

JOHN BURROUGHS, journal entry, January 30, 1900.

One of the drawbacks of old age is that one outlives his generation and feels alone in the world. The new generations have interests of their own, and are no more in sympathy with you than you are with them. The octogenarian has no alternative but to live in the past. He lives with the dead, and they pull him down.

JOHN BURROUGHS, journal entry, April 28, 1920.

Middle age is Janus-faced. As we look back on our accomplishments and our failures to achieve the things we wanted, we look ahead to the time we have left to us.…Our children are gaining life, and our parents are losing it.

STANLEY H. CATH, *New York Times*, April 18, 1983.

The dead might as well try to speak to the living as the old to the young.
WILLA CATHER, *One of Ours*, 1922.

Death has become a private buzzword for me, warning me of the shoals of ageism before me.
BABA COOPER, "Voice on Becoming Old Women," in Jo Alexander et al., *Women and Aging*, 1986.

At twenty a man is full of fight and hope. He wants to reform the world. When he's seventy he still wants to reform the world, but he knows he can't.
CLARENCE DARROW, interview, April 18, 1936.

When a middle-age man says in a moment of weariness that he is half-dead, he is telling the literal truth.
ELMER DAVIS, "On Not Being Dead, As Reported," *By Elmer Davis*, 1964.

I have an understandable reluctance to pay much attention to the passage of time, and a certain animosity toward those who assume that if one is in his seventies he must have been a high school buddy of Abraham Lincoln.
FRED DE CORDOVA, *Johnny Came Lately*, 1988.

I'm at an age when my back goes out more than I do.
PHYLLIS DILLER, *The Joys of Aging and How to Avoid Them*, 1981.

In all the world there are no people so piteous and forlorn as those who are forced to eat the bitter bread of dependency in their old age, and find how steep are the stairs of another man's house.
DOROTHY DIX, *Dorothy Dix, Her Book*, 1926.

It may be, old age is gentle and fair...
Still I shall tremble at a gray hair.
DOROTHY DOW, "Unbeliever," *Time and Love*, 1942.

I grow old...I grow old...
I shall wear the bottoms of my trousers rolled.
T.S. ELIOT, "The Love Song of J. Alfred Prufrock," 1915.

The years between fifty and seventy are the hardest. You are always being asked to do things and yet you are not decrepit enough to turn them down.
T.S. ELIOT, *Time*, October 23, 1950.

At sixteen I was stupid, confused, insecure and indecisive. At twenty-five I was wise, self-confident, prepossessing and assertive. At forty-five I am stupid, confused, insecure and indecisive. Who would have supposed that maturity is only a short break in adolescence?
JULES FEIFFER, caption to cartoon, *Observer*, February 3, 1974.

"Age" is the acceptance of a term of years. But maturity is the glory of years.
MARTHA GRAHAM, *The Christian Science Monitor*, May 25, 1979.

An oldtimer is someone who can remember when a naughty child was taken to the woodshed instead of to a psychiatrist.
DAVID GREENBERG, *American Opinion*, November, 1975.

If you rest, you rust.
HELEN HAYES, *Washington Post*, May 7, 1990.

With age, we become responsible for what's in our heads—the character of the memories there, the music we are familiar with, the storehouse of books we have read, the people whom we can call, the scenery we know and love. Our memories become our dreams.
EDWARD HOAGLAND, *Harper's*, January, 1991.

As you become older, gradually accustom yourself to neglect.
EDGAR WATSON HOWE, *Sinner Sermons*, 1926.

After a man passes sixty, his mischief is mainly in his head.
EDGAR WATSON HOWE, *Sinner Sermons*, 1926.

I'm having a glorious old age. One of my greatest delights is that I have outlived most of my opposition.
MAGGIE KUHN, speech, Vermont state legislature, 1991.

As one grew older, he said, one learned that with enough care almost anything would keep. It was only a matter of choosing what to take care of.
BARRY LOPEZ, "The Orrery," *Winter Count*, 1981.

I promise to keep on living as though I expected to live forever. Nobody grows old by merely living a number of years. People grow old only by deserting their ideals. Years may wrinkle the skin, but to give up interest wrinkles the soul.
DOUGLAS MACARTHUR, *New York Times*, June 8, 1984.

The old woman is at the other end of that motherhood myth. She has no personhood, no desires or value of her own. She must not fight for her own issues—if she fights at all, it must be for "future generations." Her greatest joy is seen as giving all to her grandchildren. And to the extent that she no longer directly serves a man—can no longer produce his children, is no longer sexually desirable to men—she is erased more completely as grandmother than she was as mother.

BARBARA MACDONALD, speech, National Women's Studies Association Conference, June 22, 1985, in Jo Alexander et al., *Women and Aging*, 1986.

Of middle age the best that can be said is that a middle-aged person has likely learned how to have a little fun in spite of his troubles.

DON MARQUIS, *The Almost Perfect State*, 1927.

I have a bone to pick with Fate,

Come here and tell me, girlie,

Do you think my mind is maturing late,

Or simply rotted early?

OGDEN NASH, "Lines on Facing Forty," *Good Intentions*, 1937.

Middle age is when you've met so many people that every new person you meet reminds you of someone else.

OGDEN NASH, *Versus*, 1949.

And so came middle-age, for I have discovered that middle-age is not a question of years. It is that moment in life when one realizes that one has exchanged, by a series of subtle shifts and substitutes, the vague and vaporous dreams of youth for the definite and tangible realization.

KATHLEEN NORRIS, *Noon*, 1924.

How old would you be if you didn't know how old you was?

SATCHEL PAIGE, *New York Times*, June 8, 1984.

Age is nothing to a live man.

EDWARD E. PURINTON, *Independent*, April 16, 1921.

Age. Ageism. In a society rooted in a virtual cult to youth, the nature and circumstance of youth is often grossly distorted. But the nature of age is often invisible.

MARGARET RANDALL, in Jo Alexander et al., *Women and Aging*, 1986.

I have always felt that a woman has the right to treat the subject of her age with ambiguity until, perhaps, she passes into the realm of over ninety. Then it is better she be candid with herself and with the world.

HELENA RUBINSTEIN, *My Life for Beauty*, 1966.

Age puzzles me. I thought it was a quiet time. My seventies were interesting and fairly serene, but my eighties are passionate. I grow more intense as I age.

FLORIDA SCOTT-MAXWELL, *The Measure of My Days*, 1972.

There are compensations for growing older. One is the realization that to be sporting isn't at all necessary. It is a great relief to reach this stage of wisdom.

CORNELIA OTIS SKINNER, *Dithers and Jitters*, 1937.

We grow with years more fragile in body, but morally stouter, and we can throw off the chill of a bad conscience almost at once.

LOGAN PEARSALL SMITH, *Afterthoughts*, 1931.

There is more felicity on the far side of baldness than young men can possibly imagine.

LOGAN PEARSALL SMITH, *Afterthoughts*, 1931.

Most people are dead at my age. You could look it up.

CASEY STENGEL, at 85, *Sports Illustrated*, October 13, 1975.

I'll never make the mistake of being seventy again.

CASEY STENGEL, 1960, in Norman MacLean, *Casey Stengel: A Biography*, 1976.

Nothing so dates a man as to decry the younger generation.

ADLAI E. STEVENSON, speech, University of Wisconsin, Madison, October 8, 1952.

In youth, everything seems possible; but we reach a point in the middle years when we realize that we are never going to reach all the shining goals we had set for ourselves. And in the end, most of us reconcile ourselves, with what grace we can, to living with our ulcers and arthritis, our sense of partial failure, our less-than-ideal families—and even our politicians!

ADLAI E. STEVENSON, *Call to Greatness*, 1954.

Old age approaches, an awful specter of loneliness to those who have never found joy in being alone.

DOROTHY THOMPSON, *The Courage to Be Happy*, 1957.

Old elephants limp off to the hills to die; old Americans go out to the highway and drive themselves to death with huge cars.

HUNTER S. THOMPSON, *Fear and Loathing in Las Vegas*, 1972.

Old men dream dreams; young men see visions.

MELVIN B. TOLSON, "A Discussion of Hogs, Dogs, Fish, and the Declaration of Independence," *Washington Tribune*, July 22, 1939.

The first half of life consists of the capacity to enjoy without the chance; the last half consists of the chance without the capacity.

Mark Twain, letter to Edward L. Dimmitt, July 19, 1901.

Most old people...are disheartened to be living in the ailing house of their bodies, to be limited physically and economically, to feel an encumbrance to others—guests who didn't have the good manners to leave when the party was over.

Barbara Walters, *How to Talk with Practically Anybody About Practically Anything*, 1970.

Which of you is going to step up and put me out to pasture?

John Wayne, to Congressional Committee on Aging, 1977.

There's no such thing as old age, there is only sorrow.

Edith Wharton, "A First Word," *A Backward Glance*, 1934.

American Mosaic

See also **American Society; Dreams and Ideals**—Immigration; **Social Issues**—
Civil Rights, Discrimination and Racism, Poverty and Hunger

We really are 15 countries, and it's really remarkable that each of us thinks we represent the *real* America. The Midwesterner in Kansas, the black American in Durham—both are certain they are the real American.

MAYA ANGELOU, *Time*, April 24, 1978.

I had a heritage, rich and nearer than the tongue which gave it voice. My mind resounded with the words and my blood raced to the rhythms.

MAYA ANGELOU, *The Heart of a Woman*, 1981.

There was much to cry for, much to mourn, but in my heart I felt exalted knowing there was much to celebrate. Although separated from our languages, our families and customs, we had dared to continue to live. We had crossed the unknowable oceans in chains and had written its mystery into "Deep river, my home is over Jordan." Through the centuries of despair and dislocation, we had been creative, because we faced down death by daring to hope.

MAYA ANGELOU, *All God's Children Need Traveling Shoes*, 1986.

It had often been said that Black people were childish, but in America we had matured without ever experiencing the true abandon of adolescence. Those actions which appeared to be childish most often were exhibitions of bravado, not unlike humming a jazz tune while walking into a gathering of the Ku Klux Klan.

MAYA ANGELOU, *All God's Children Need Traveling Shoes*, 1986.

The white man saves the whooping crane, he saves the goose in Hawaii, but he is not saving the way of life of the Indian.

A young Blackfoot, ca. 1968, VIRGINIA IRVING ARMSTRONG, comp., *I Have Spoken: American History Through the Voices of the Indians*, 1971.

We're a great heart people.

PEARL BAILEY, *New York Post*, April 27, 1965.

[D]espite the terrorization which the Negro in America endured and endures sporadically until today, despite the cruel and totally inescapable ambivalence of his status in this country, the battle for his identity has long ago been won. He is not a visitor to the West, but a citizen there, an American.

JAMES BALDWIN, *Notes of a Native Son*, 1955.

If we do not now dare everything, the fulfillment of that prophecy, re-created from the Bible in song by a slave, is upon us: *God gave Noah the rainbow sign, No more water, the fire next time.*

JAMES BALDWIN, *The Fire Next Time*, 1963.

To be black and conscious in America is to be in a constant state of rage.

JAMES BALDWIN, in Joan Didion, *The White Album*, 1979.

To be a Jew is a destiny.

VICKI BAUM, *And Life Goes On*, 1932.

On Broadway it was still bright afternoon and the gassy air was almost motionless under the leaden spokes of sunlight, and sawdust footprints lay about the doorways of butcher shops and fruit stores. And the great, great crowd, the inexhaustible current of millions of every race and kind pouring out, pressing round, of every age, of every genius, possessors of every human secret, antique and future, in every face the refinement of one particular motive or essence—*I labor, I spend, I strive, I design, I love, I cling, I uphold, I give way, I envy, I long, I scorn, I die, I hide, I want.* Faster, much faster than any man could make the tally. The sidewalks were wider than any causeway; the street itself was immense, and it quaked and gleamed and it seemed...to throb at the last limit of endurance.

SAUL BELLOW, *Seize the Day*, 1956.

[J]ust at the moment when everyone else has become a "person," blacks have become blacks.... They continue to have the inward sentiments of separateness caused by exclusion when it no longer effectively exists. The heat is under the pot, but they do not melt as have *all* other groups.

ALLAN BLOOM, *The Closing of the American Mind*, 1987.

PROCLAMATION: TO THE GREAT WHITE FATHER AND ALL HIS PEOPLE

We, the Native Americans, re-claim the land known as Alcatraz Island in the name of all American Indians by right of discovery.

We wish to be fair and honorable in our dealings with the Caucasian inhabitants of this land, and hereby offer the following treaty:

We will purchase said Alcatraz Island for twenty-four dollars ($24) in glass beads and red cloth, a precedent set by the white man's purchase of a similar island about 300 years ago. We know that $24 in trade goods for these 16 acres is more than was paid when Manhattan Island was sold, but we know that land values have risen over the years. Our offer of $1.24 per acre is greater than the 47 cents per acre that the white men are now paying the California Indians for their land. We will give to the inhabitants of this island a portion of that land for their own, to be held in trust by the American Indian Affairs and by the bureau of Caucasian Affairs to hold in perpetuity—for as long as the sun shall rise and the rivers go down to the sea. We will further guide the inhabitants in the proper way of living. We will offer them our religion, our education, our life-ways, in order to help them achieve our level of civilization and thus raise them and all their white brothers up from their savage and unhappy state. We offer this treaty in good faith and wish to be fair and honorable in our dealings with all white men....

We feel that this so-called Alcatraz Island is more than suitable for an Indian Reservation, as determined by the white man's own standards. By this we mean that this place resembles most Indian reservations in that:

1. It is isolated from modern facilities, and without adequate means of transportation.

2. It has no fresh running water.

3. It has inadequate sanitation facilities.

4. There are no oil or mineral rights.

5. There is no industry and so unemployment is very great.

6. There are no health care facilities.

7. The soil is rocky and non-productive; and the land does not support game.

8. There are no educational facilities.

9. The population has always exceeded the land base.

10. The population has always been held as prisoners and kept dependent upon others.

Further, it would be fitting and symbolic that ships from all over the world, entering the Golden Gate, would first see Indian land, and thus be reminded of the true history of this nation. This tiny island would be a symbol of the great lands once ruled by free and noble Indians.

Proclamation of Native Americans who seized the island of Alcatraz, the old prison site, November, 1969.

The behavior of an individual is determined not by his racial affiliation, but by the character of his ancestry and his cultural environment.

Franz Boas, *Race and Democratic Society*, 1945.

The twentieth century ideals of America have been the ideals of the Jew for more than twenty centuries.

Louis D. Brandeis, "A Call to the Educated Jew," *Menorah Journal*, January, 1915.

Whatever we have been able to achieve has been the result of the inherent harmony of the inheritance which we have received from other cultures...not merely in what is called the West, but what is called the East as well.

Erwin D. Canham, in Arthur Goodfriend, *What Is America?*, 1954.

By descent, I am one fourth German, one fourth Irish, one fourth English, and another quarter French. My God! If my ancestors are permitted to look down upon me, they might perhaps upbraid me. But I am also an American!

JOSEPH G. CANNON, speech to Congress, April, 1917.

We become not a melting pot but a beautiful mosaic. Different people, different beliefs, different yearnings, different hopes, different dreams.

JIMMY CARTER, speech, Pittsburgh, Pennsylvania, October 27, 1976.

[I]t isn't a matter of black is beautiful as much as it is white is not *all* that's beautiful.

BILL COSBY, interview, *Playboy*, May, 1969.

[T]o an unrecognized extent, we're a nation of professional, religious, ethnic, and racial tribes—the Tribes of America—who maintain a fragile truce, easily and often broken. We had to conquer this continent—and its original tribes—in order to exploit its resources. But we were never able to conquer our atavistic hatreds, to accept our widely diverse pasts, to transcend them, to live together as a single people.

PAUL COWAN, Introduction, *The Tribes of America*, 1979.

[B]eing colored can be a lotta fun when ain't nobody lookin'.

OSSIE DAVIS, *Purlie Victorious*, 1961.

This country was a lot better off when the Indians were running it.

VINE DELORIA, JR., *New York Times Magazine*, March 3, 1970.

One could conclude that there are not really any Indians in American society, but that it has been infiltrated by OTHERS.

VINE DELORIA, JR., *We Talk, You Listen*, 1970.

If the attempted renovation of religious imagery is ever combined with the dominant schools of ethnic studies, the result will be the Last Supper as the gathering of the "All-American Platoon" highlighted by the contributions of each group represented. Instead of simple bread and wine, the table will be overflowing with pizza, tamales, greens, peanuts, popcorn, German sausage, and hamburgers. Everyone will feel that they have had a part in the creation of the great American Christian social order.

VINE DELORIA, JR., *We Talk, You Listen*, 1970.

One ever feels his twoness—an American, a Negro; two souls, two thoughts, two unreconciled strivings; two warring ideals in one dark body,

whose dogged strength alone keeps it from being torn asunder.

W.E.B. DU BOIS, *The Souls of Black Folk*, 1903.

We who are Indians today live in a world of confusion. This is the issue: the confusion in our lives. We are Indians, and we love the Indian ways. We are comfortable in the Indian ways. But to get along in this world the white man tells us we must be white men, that we cannot be what we were born to be.

BEN BLACK ELK, ca. 1968, in Virginia Irving Armstrong, comp., *I Have Spoken: American History Through the Voices of the Indians*, 1971.

America is woven of many strands; I would recognize them and let it so remain....Our fate is to become one, and yet many—This is not prophecy, but description.

RALPH ELLISON, *Invisible Man*, 1952.

[T]he real death of the United States will come when everyone is just alike.

RALPH ELLISON, interview, *That Same Pain, That Same Pleasure*, December, 1961.

If this nation is to obtain its destiny, there will have to be a harmonious assimilation [which] three powerful elements will defy:...the Negro,...alarmingly vitiated by venereal infection,...the Jew,...not American,...[and] the illiterate Catholic.

H.W. EVANS, Imperial Wizard, speech, KKK State Fair, Texas, 1923.

We should not want to think of America as a "melting pot," but as a great inter-racial laboratory where Americans can really begin to build the thing which the rest of the world feels that they stand for today, and that is real democracy.

MRS. CRYSTAL BIRD FAUSET, speech, Woman's Centennial Congress, November 26, 1940.

Jews in Utah, being non-Mormon, are theoretically subject to classification as Gentiles, which gave rise to the well-known remark that "Utah is the only place in the world where Jews are Gentiles."

JOHN GUNTHER, *Inside U.S.A*, 1947.

To live in Harlem is to be a Negro; to be a Negro is to participate in a culture of poverty and fear that goes far deeper than any law for or against discrimination. In this sense Harlem could well be a warning: that after the racist statutes are all struck down, after legal equality has been achieved in the schools and in the courts, there remains the profound institutionalized and abiding wrong that white America has worked on the Negro for so long.

MICHAEL HARRINGTON, *The Other America: Poverty in the United States,* 1963.

It is possible...for a culture to be overwhelmed physically but not culturally. That is what has happened to the American Indian. It is a strange kind of conquest over the white conquerors. Almost half the states have names borrowed from Indian lore, and so do thousands of cities, rivers, towns, lakes, and mountain ranges. Americans drink hooch, meet in a caucus, bury the hatchet, have clambakes, run the gauntlet, smoke the peace pipe, hold powwows, and enjoy Indian summer. Today's highways, a triumph of American technology, are concrete tracings of trails Indians pioneered and trod for tens of thousands of years.

JAMAKE HIGHWATER, *Fodor's Indian America,* 1975.

Despite the focus in the media on the affluent and the poor, the average man is neither. Despite the concentration in TV commercials on the blond, blue-eyed WASP, the real American prototype is of Italian or Irish or Polish or Greek or Lithuanian or German or Hungarian or Russian or any one of the still amazing number of national origins represented in this country—a "white ethnic," sociologists soberly call him.

LOUISE KAPP HOWE, *The White Majority,* 1970.

I am not tragically colored. There is no great sorrow dammed up in my soul, nor lurking behind my eyes. I do not mind at all. I do not belong to the sobbing school of Negrohood who hold that nature somehow has given them a lowdown dirty deal and whose feelings are all hurt about it....No, I do not weep at the world—I am too busy sharpening my oyster knife.

ZORA NEALE HURSTON, "How It Feels to Be Colored Me," *The World Tomorrow,* 1928.

Wese a mingled people.

ZORA NEALE HURSTON, *Jonah's Gourd Vine,* 1934.

I hear that melting pot stuff a lot, and all I can say is that we haven't melted.

JESSE JACKSON, interview, *Playboy,* November, 1969.

Our flag is red, white and blue, but our nation is a rainbow—red, yellow, brown, black and white—and we're all precious in God's sight. America is not like a blanket—one piece of unbroken cloth, the same color, the same texture, the same size. America is more like a quilt—many patches, many pieces, many colors, many sizes, all woven and held together by a common thread....Even in our fractured state, all of us count and all of us fit somewhere.

JESSE JACKSON, speech, Democratic National Convention, July 16, 1984.

Indians taught the white man how to survive on this continent. They showed the white settlers procedures for planting, irrigation, fertilization, cultivation, storage, and utilization. They gave the white man corn and potatoes. In return we have given you cyclamates and DDT.

EDWARD M. KENNEDY, January 26, 1970, in Thomas P. Collins and Louis M. Savary, eds., *A People of Compassion,* 1972.

Our nation is moving toward two societies, one black, one white—separate and unequal.

OTTO KERNER, JR., in the *Report of the National Advisory Commission on Civil Disorders,* 1968.

My fight is not to be a white man in a black skin, but to inject some black blood, some black intelligence into the pallid mainstream of American life, culturally, socially, psychologically, philosophically.

JOHN OLIVER KILLENS, "Explanation of the Black Psyche," *New York Times,* June 7, 1964.

Being a Negro in America means trying to smile when you want to cry. It means trying to hold on to physical life amid psychological death. It means the pain of watching your children grow up with clouds of inferiority in their mental skies. It means having your legs cut off, and then being condemned for being a cripple. It means seeing your mother and father spiritually murdered by the slings and arrows of daily exploitation, and then being hated for being an orphan.

MARTIN LUTHER KING, JR., *Where Do We Go from Here: Chaos or Community?,* 1967.

To be a Negro in America is to hope against hope.

MARTIN LUTHER KING, JR., *Where Do We Go from Here: Chaos or Community?,* 1967.

While white Americans by the thousands enjoy the romance and color of the Indians, and love to sentimentalize about them, they do not give a whoop in hell whether they live well, die in misery, or just drag along in weary, broken despair.

OLIVER LAFARGE, *Harper's Magazine,* November, 1947.

It is pre-eminently our assignment...to demonstrate to the world that peoples of diverse racial and national origins, of different backgrounds and of many cultures, can live and work together in a modern democracy.

CAREY McWILLIAMS, *Brothers Under the Skin*, 1945.

[T]olerance is not acceptance, and indifference is not assimilation.

CAREY McWILLIAMS, *Brothers Under the Skin*, 1945.

The Indian has never wanted integration, although he is too intelligent not to realize that it is inevitable.

JOSEPHINE C. MILLS, letter, March, 1964, Virginia Irving Armstrong, comp., *I Have Spoken: American History Through the Voices of the Indians*, 1971.

That the Negro American has survived at all is extraordinary—a lesser people might simply have died out, as indeed others have. That the Negro community has not only survived, but in this political generation has entered national affairs as a moderate, humane, and constructive national force, is the highest testament to the healing powers of the democratic ideal and the creative vitality of the Negro people.

DANIEL PATRICK MOYNIHAN, "The Negro Family: The Case for National Action," March, 1965.

The Negro's relationship with one another is utterly deplorable. The Negro wants to be everything but himself. He wants to be a white man. He processes his hair. Acts like a white man. He wants to integrate with the white man, but he cannot integrate with himself or with his own kind. The Negro wants to lose his identity because he does not know his own identity.

ELIJAH MUHAMMED, in E.U. Essien-Udom, *Black Nationalism*, 1962.

Why is it so important that Indians be brought into the "mainstream of American life"? What is the "mainstream of American life"? I would not know how to interpret the phrase to my people in our language. The closest I would be able to come to "mainstream" would be to say, in Indian, "a big wide river." Am I then going to tell my people that they will be "thrown into the Big, Wide River of the United States"?

EARL OLD PERSON, congressional testimony, in Vine Deloria, Jr., ed., *Of Utmost Good Faith*, 1966.

Coming to America has always been hard. Thriving in America is harder than ever. But so many things remain the same. And one of them is that the people who, generation to generation, believe America is a finished product are habitually revealed as people whose ideas would have im-

poverished this country beyond measure. It is foolish to forget where you come from, and that, in the case of the United States, is almost always somewhere else. The true authentic American is a pilgrim with a small "p" armed with little more than the phrase "I wish...."

ANNA QUINDLEN, *New York Times*, November 20, 1991.

There is no room in this country for hyphenated Americans.... The one absolutely certain way of bringing this nation to ruin, of preventing all possibility of it continuing to be a nation at all, would be to permit it to become a tangle of squabbling nationalities.

THEODORE ROOSEVELT, speech, "Americanism," New York City, October 12, 1915.

Although we prided ourselves on our political freedom, civil liberties and constitutional rights, we never believed fully in our own professions and therefore invented a melting pot to transform men into the sort of citizens who would not jeopardize the system by placing excessive demands on its tolerance. They were supposed to go in as ethnics and come out as WASPs. We have made a lot of WASPs but overlooked the cultural possibilities for other forms of Americanism and now find ourselves with the choice between enforcing allegiance to an increasingly unattractive mainstream and trying to establish the pluralism that might have been and might still be.

PETER SCHRAG, *The Vanishing American*, 1972.

[T]he crucial thing about the melting pot was that it did not happen: American politics and American social life are still dominated by the existence of sharply-defined ethnic groups.

CHARLES E. SILBERMAN, *Crisis in Black and White*, 1964.

The white man does not understand the Indian for the reason that he does not understand America. He is too far removed from its formative processes. The roots of the tree of his life have not yet grasped the rock and soil.

LUTHER STANDING BEAR, *Land of the Spotted Eagle*, 1933.

The feathered and blanketed figure of the American Indian has come to symbolize the American continent. He is the man who through centuries has been molded and sculpted by the same hand that shaped its mountains, forests, and plains, and marked the course of its rivers.

LUTHER STANDING BEAR, *Land of the Spotted Eagle*, 1933.

The pressure that has been brought to bear upon the native people, since the cessation of armed conflict, in the attempt to force conformity of custom and habit has caused a reaction more destructive than war, and the injury has not only affected the Indian, but has extended to the white population as well. Tyranny, stupidity, and lack of vision have brought about the situation now alluded to as the "Indian Problem."

LUTHER STANDING BEAR, *Land of the Spotted Eagle*, 1933.

The Jew is neither a newcomer nor an alien in this country or on this continent; his Americanism is as original and ancient as that of any race of people with the exception of the American Indian and other aborigines. He came in the caravels of Columbus, and he knocked at the gates of New Amsterdam only thirty-five years after the Pilgrim Fathers stepped ashore on Plymouth Rock.

OSCAR SOLOMON STRAUS, speech, "America and the Spirit of American Judaism," American Hebrew Congregation, New York City, January 18, 1911.

This Melting Pot of ours absorbs the second generation over a flame so high that the first is left encrusted on the rim.

JOHN TARKOV, "Fitting In," *New York Times*, July 7, 1985.

Please stop using the word "Negro".... We are the only human beings in the world with fifty-seven varieties of complexions who are classed together as a single racial unit. Therefore, we are really colored people, and that is the only name in the English language which accurately describes us.

MARY CHURCH TERRELL, letter to the editor, *Washington Post*, May 14, 1949.

Who is culturally deprived? Not the Indian.... You might say we are the only people in this melting pot who have kept their culture.

MEL THOM, in Stan Steiner, *The New Indians*, 1968.

The most common trait of all primitive peoples is a reverence for the life-giving earth, and the Native American shared this elemental ethic: The land was alive to his loving touch, and he, its son, was brother to all creatures.

STEWART L. UDALL, *The Quiet Crisis*, 1963.

It is painfully clear that the United States needs its Indians and their culture. A society increasingly homogenized and mechanized—a society headed toward ant-hill conformity and depersonalized living—desperately needs the lessons of a culture that has a deep reverence for nature, and values the simple, the authentic, and the humane.

STEWART L. UDALL, *American Way*, May, 1971.

The United States is the only place where a [foreign] accent is an asset; it is a country that actively assimilates different world cultures.

VICTOR WEISSKOPF, *The Privilege of Being a Physicist*, 1989.

[O]nly the face of Chinatown is bright. The heart of Chinatown is frustrated, perplexed, discontented, restless. It represents a "melting pot" which has "let the people down."

NATE R. WHITE, "Crisis in Chinatown," *Christian Science Monitor*, February 1, 1941.

Some Americans need hyphens in their names, because only part of them has come over; but when the whole man has come over, heart and thought and all, the hyphen drops of its own weight out of his name.

WOODROW WILSON, speech, Washington, D.C., May 16, 1914.

You cannot become thorough Americans if you think of yourselves in groups. America does not consist of groups. A man who thinks of himself as belonging to a particular national group in America has not yet become an American.

WOODROW WILSON, speech, Convention Hall, Philadelphia, Pennsylvania, May 10, 1915.

How do Negroes feel about the way they have to live? How do they discuss it when alone among themselves? I think this question can be answered in a single sentence. A friend of mine who ran an elevator once told me:

"Lawd, man! Ef it wuzn't fer them polices 'n' them ol' lynch mobs, there wouldn't be nothin' but uproar down here!"

RICHARD WRIGHT, *Black Boy*, 1937.

I think that what you should realize is that in America there are 20 million black people, all of whom are in prison. You don't have to go to Sing Sing to be in prison. If you're born in America with a black skin, you're born in prison, and the masses of black people in America today are beginning to regard our plight or predicament in this society as one of a prison inmate.

MALCOLM X, interview with Kenneth B. Clark, June, 1963.

The racial lines, which once were bitterly real, now serve nothing more than marking out a living mosaic of human beings.

ZITKALA-SA, *Atlantic Monthly*, December, 1902.

American Society

See also **American Mosaic; Culture and Civilization; Dreams and Ideals; Foreign Views; Popular Culture; Social Issues; States and Regions; Work**

The establishment is made up of little men, very frightened.

BELLA ABZUG, in Mel Ziegler, *Bella!*, 1972.

As for America, it is the ideal fruit of all your youthful hopes and reforms. Everybody is fairly decent, respectable, domestic, bourgeois, middle-class, and tiresome. There is absolutely nothing to revile except that it's a bore.

HENRY ADAMS, letter to Charles Milnes Gaskell, December 17, 1908.

American society is a sort of flat, fresh-water pond which absorbs silently, without reaction, anything which is thrown into it.

HENRY ADAMS, letter to Royal Cortissoz, September 20, 1911.

When the water of Chicago is foul, the prosperous buy water bottled at distant springs; the poor have no alternative but the typhoid fever which comes from using the city's supply. When the garbage contracts are not enforced, the well-to-do pay for private service; the poor suffer the discomfort and illness which are inevitable from a foul atmosphere.

JANE ADDAMS, "Political Reform," *Democracy and Social Ethics*, 1902.

A society which comes to fear its children is effete. A sniveling, hand-wringing power structure deserves the violent rebellion it encourages. If my generation doesn't stop cringing, yours will inherit a lawless society where emotion and muscle displace reason.

SPIRO T. AGNEW, speech, Ohio State University, June, 1968.

We have something special...a culture which we do not think of as something for the elite, but as something which is accessible to practically everybody.

FREDERICK LEWIS ALLEN, in Arthur Goodfriend, *What Is America?*, 1954.

In America, we have people who are too rich, people who are too poor, people who are hungry, people who are sick, people who are homeless, people who are imprisoned, people who are bored, people who are strung-out, people who are lonely, people who are exploited, people who lose and can't find their way, people who give up on life. America, we better live as sisters and brothers. Let us take care of our land. We cannot stand up for every other land. Stand up for ourselves.

PEARL BAILEY, *Hurry Up, America, and Spit*, 1976.

The making of an American begins at that point where he himself rejects all other ties, any other history, and himself adopts the vesture of his adopted land.

JAMES BALDWIN, *Notes of a Native Son*, 1955.

O beautiful for spacious skies,
For amber waves of grain,
For purple mountain majesties
Above the fruited plain!
America! America!
God shed His grace on thee,
And crown thy good with brotherhood
From sea to shining sea!

O beautiful for pilgrim feet,
Whose stern, impassioned stress
A thoroughfare for freedom beat
Across the wilderness!
America! America!
God mend thine every flaw,
Confirm thy soul in self-control,
Thy liberty in law!

O beautiful for heroes proved
In liberating strife,
Who more than self their country loved,
And mercy more than life!
America! America!
May God thy gold refine,
Till all success be nobleness
And every gain divine!

O beautiful for patriot dream
That sees beyond the years.
Thine alabaster cities gleam,
Undimmed by human tears!
America! America!
God shed His grace on thee,
And crown thy good with brotherhood
From sea to shining sea!

KATHARINE LEE BATES, "America the Beautiful," first
written in 1893, published in 1895, revised in 1904,
and again in 1911.

I have fallen in love with American names,
The sharp names that never get fat,
The snakeskin titles of mining claims,
The plumed war-bonnet of Medicine Hat,
Tucson and Deadwood and Lost Mule Flat....
You may bury my body in Sussex grass,
You may bury my tongue at Champmedy.
I shall not be there. I shall rise and pass.
Bury my heart at Wounded Knee.

STEPHEN VINCENT BENÉT, "American Names," 1927.

Ours is the age of substitutes; instead of language, we have jargon; instead of principles, slogans; instead of genuine ideas, bright ideas.

ERIC BENTLEY, The Dramatic Event, 1954.

Never have people been more the masters of their environment. Yet never has a people felt more deceived and disappointed. For never has a people expected so much more than the world could offer.

DANIEL J. BOORSTIN, Introduction, The Image, 1962.

[Americans] expect to eat and stay thin, to be constantly on the move and ever more neighborly...to revere God and be God.

DANIEL J. BOORSTIN, Newsweek, February 26, 1962.

In the past few decades American institutions have struggled with the temptations of politics. Professions and academic disiplines that once possessed a life and structure of their own have steadily succumbed, in some cases almost entirely, to the belief that nothing matters beyond politically desirable results, however achieved....

ROBERT BORK, The Tempting of America, 1990.

No country can touch us when it comes to heartburn and upset stomachs. This nation, under God, with liberty and justice for all, neutralizes more stomach acid in one day than the Soviet Union does in a year.

ART BUCHWALD, "Acid Indigestion," Mom, the Flag, and Apple Pie, 1976.

Americans are all too soft.

PEARL S. BUCK, The Child Who Never Grew, 1950.

A society that seduces the conscience by sweet reason is one thing, but ours is developing into a society that harpoons the conscience and tows it right into the maws of the mother vessel, there to be macerated and stuffed into a faceless can.

WILLIAM F. BUCKLEY, JR., "We Want Our Politicians to Be Hypocrites," The Jeweler's Eye, 1968.

American society is characterized by spontaneous, voluntary, non-governmental cooperation of citizens in their local communities. It is brotherhood in action.

ERWIN D. CANHAM, in Arthur Goodfriend, What Is America?, 1954.

For the first time in the history of our country the majority of our people believe that the next five years will be worse than the past five years.

JIMMY CARTER, address to the nation, July 15, 1979.

The President circles the globe seemingly handing out carte-blanche military commitment credit cards and scientists in Houston dissect dusty rocks in search of other life-forms while humans starve to death—physically, mentally and spiritually—at home and abroad.

SHIRLEY CHISHOLM, speech, Church Women United, Massachusetts, August 21, 1969.

In the culture that secretly subscribes to the piratical ethic of "every man for himself"...the logical culmination of this ethic, on a person-to-person level, is that the weak are seen as the natural and just prey of the strong. But since this dark principle violates our democratic ideals and professions, we force it underground, out of a perverse national modesty that reveals us as a nation of peep freaks who prefer the bikini to the naked body, the white lie to the black truth, Hollywood smiles and canned laughter to a soulful Bronx cheer.

ELDRIDGE CLEAVER, Soul on Ice, 1968.

This is a crazy culture. Absolutely nutty. You see it reflected everywhere you look, this desperate search—who are we, what are we, can we ever make it in the hip world? On the scene, on the go, in the know.

Judy Collins, interview, *Life*, May 2, 1969.

Loneliness seems to have become the great American disease.

John Corry, *New York Times*, April 25, 1984.

We believe we must be the family of America, recognizing that at the heart of the matter we are bound one to another.

Mario Cuomo, speech, Democratic National Convention, July 16, 1984.

The center was not holding. It was a country of bankruptcy notices and public-auction announcements and commonplace reports of casual killings and misplaced children and abandoned homes and vandals who misspelled even the four-letter words they scrawled. It was a country in which families routinely disappeared, trailing bad checks and repossession papers. Adolescents drifted from city to torn city, sloughing off both the past and the future as snakes shed their skins, children who were never taught and would never now learn the games that had held the society together. People were missing. Children were missing. Parents were missing. Those left behind filed desultory missing-persons reports, then moved on themselves.

Joan Didion, "Slouching Towards Bethlehem," *Slouching Towards Bethlehem*, 1968.

I think we are all of us a pretty milky lot, without tea-table convictions and our radicalism that keeps so consistently within the bounds of decorum....I'd like to annihilate these stupid colleges of ours, and all the nice young men therein, instillers of stodginess—every form of bastard culture, middle class snobbism.

John Dos Passos, ca. 1912, in Richard Hofstadter, *Anti-Intellectualism in American Life*, 1963.

God will save the good American, and seat him at His right hand on the Golden Throne.

Theodore Dreiser, *Life, Art, and America*, 1917.

To accept as a fact of life that a certain technology will be used for the simple reason that we know how to use it, or that we shall continue to live under a certain social system after it has become too complicated for human understanding, is tantamount to an abdication of intellectual and social responsibility.

René Dubos, *A God Within*, 1972.

[I] would rather live in Russia on black bread and vodka than in the United States at the best hotels. America knows nothing of food, love, or art.

Isadora Duncan, interview, 1922.

From Jesse James to Loeb and Leopold, from the perpetrators of the St. Valentine's Day massacre to the Lindbergh kidnapper and beyond, our celebrated delinquents have become a part of the national heritage.

F.W. Dupee, *New York Review of Books*, February 3, 1966.

Whether the middle class looks down toward the realm of less, or up toward the realm of more, there is the fear, always, of falling.

Barbara Ehrenreich, *Fear of Falling*, 1990.

The working class became, for many middle-class liberals, a psychic dumping ground for such unstylish sentiments as racism, male chauvinism, and crude materialism: a rearguard population that loved white bread and hated black people.

Barbara Ehrenreich, *Fear of Falling*, 1990.

Modern man lives increasingly in the future and neglects the present. A people who seek to do this have an insatiable demand for soothsayers and oracles to assure and comfort them about the insubstantial road they tread.

Loren Eiseley, *The Night Country*, 1971.

They [the Founding Fathers] proclaimed to all the world the revolutionary doctrine of the divine rights of the common man. That doctrine has ever since been the heart of the American faith.

Dwight D. Eisenhower, speech, Columbia University, May 30, 1954.

Recognition of the Supreme Being is the first, the most basic, expression of Americanism. Without God, there could be no American form of government, nor American way of life.

Dwight D. Eisenhower, 1955, in Lois and Alan Gordon, *American Chronicle*, 1987.

Terminal decadence.

Nora Ephron, "The New Porn," *Esquire*, March, 1976.

Sometimes I wonder if today social class, at least as we used to think of it in this country, has about as much relevance as an electric salad fork and as bright a future as a cha-cha instructor in Montana.

Joseph Epstein, "They Said You Was High-Class," *American Scholar*, Spring, 1986.

It is a bit difficult to have a serious class system when, as in this country at present, you don't have a convincing upper class.

JOSEPH EPSTEIN, "They Said You Was High-Class," *American Scholar*, Spring, 1986.

Who stole America?

LAWRENCE FERLINGHETTI, *Starting from San Francisco*, 1961.

France was a land, England was a people, but America, having about it still that quality of the idea, was harder to utter—it was the graves at Shiloh, and the tired, drawn, nervous faces of its great men, and the country boys dying in the Argonne for a phrase that was empty before their bodies withered. It was a willingness of the heart.

F. SCOTT FITZGERALD, *The Crack-Up*, 1945.

We go forth all to seek America. And in the seeking we create her. In the quality of our search shall be the nature of the America that we created.

WALDO FRANK, *Our America*, 1919.

The fundamental fact which emerges is the elimination of class warfare in the United States.

LEWIS GALANTIERE, in Arthur Goodfriend, *What Is America?*, 1954.

The family which takes its mauve and cerise, air-conditioned, power-steered and power-braked automobile out for a tour passes through cities that are badly paved, made hideous by litter, blighted buildings, billboards and posts for wires that should long since have been put underground. They pass on into a countryside that has been rendered largely invisible by commercial art.... They picnic on exquisitely packaged food from a portable icebox by a polluted stream and go on to spend the night at a park which is a menace to public health and morals. Just before dozing off on an air mattress, beneath a nylon tent, amid the stench of decaying refuse, they may reflect vaguely on the curious unevenness of their blessings. Is this, indeed, the American genius?

JOHN KENNETH GALBRAITH, *The Affluent Society*, 1976.

America does not concern itself now with Impressionism. We own no involved philosophy. The psyche of the land is to be found in its movement. It is to be felt as a dramatic force of energy and vitality. We move; we do not stand still. We have not yet arrived at the stock-taking stage.

MARTHA GRAHAM, "The American Dance," in Virginia Stewart, ed., *Modern Dance*, 1935.

Our society is an immense stamping ground for the careless production of underdeveloped and malformed human beings...[not] concerned with moral issues, with serious purposes, or with human dignity.

ROBERT HEILBRONER, 1960, in Lois and Alan Gordon, *American Chronicle*, 1987.

We are a people who do not want to keep much of the past in our heads. It is considered unhealthy in America to remember mistakes, neurotic to think about them, psychotic to dwell on them.

LILLIAN HELLMAN, *Scoundrel Time*, 1976.

An American Religion: Work, play, breathe, bathe, study, live, laugh, and love.

ELBERT HUBBARD, *The Roycroft Dictionary and Book of Epigrams*, 1923.

O, yes,

I say it plain,

America never was America to me.

And yet I swear this oath—

America will be!

LANGSTON HUGHES, "Let America Be America Again," in *The Poetry of the Negro*, 1949.

Most Americans...still see themselves primarily as a democratic people dedicated to the doctrine of free enterprise. They celebrate the founding fathers and argue that the business of America is business. They celebrate technological achievements, too, but they see these as fruits of free enterprise and democratic politics. They commonly assume that Americans are primarily dedicated to money making and business dealing. Americans rarely think of themselves as builders, a people whose most notable and character-forming achievement for almost three centuries has been to transform a wilderness into a building site. A major reason that a nation of builders does not know itself is that most of the history it reads and hears instructs otherwise.

THOMAS HUGHES, *American Genesis: A Century of Invention and Technological Enthusiasm*, 1989.

Nothing so challenges the American spirit as tackling the biggest job on earth....Americans are stimulated by the big job—the Panama Canal, Boulder Dam, Grand Coulee, Lower Colorado River developments, the tallest building in the world, the mightiest battleship.

LYNDON B. JOHNSON, speech to Congress, April 30, 1941.

I pray we are still a young and courageous nation, that we have not grown so old and so fat and so prosperous that all we can think about is to sit back with our arms around our money bags. If we choose to do that I have no doubt that the smoldering fires will burst into flame and consume us—dollars and all.

LYNDON B. JOHNSON, speech to Congress, May 7, 1947.

I cannot see why, if we have the will to do it, we can't provide for our own happiness, education, health, and environment....We're greedy but not short on the wherewithal to meet our problems.

LYNDON B. JOHNSON, in Doris Kearns, *Lyndon Johnson and the American Dream*, 1976.

Solitude is un-American.

ERICA JONG, *Fear of Flying*, 1973.

For here in America show people are the only kind of royalty we have. They are the princes and princesses, the kings and queens, of our country and their *mots* are repeated the next day over the back fence, the saloon bar, and the bridge table across the length and breadth of the republic.

NORMAN KATKOV, *The Fabulous Fanny*, 1953.

It is hard for a man who has enjoyed both the taste of our beer and the flavor of our politics to say which of these national glories has gone flatter.

MURRAY KEMPTON, *America Comes of Middle Age*, 1963.

All this wealth and space presented possibilities in America which have made the American outlook unique, and therefore inapplicable to any other society.

GEORGE F. KENNAN, *Encounter*, September, 1976.

The United States has to move very fast to even stand still.

JOHN F. KENNEDY, "Sayings of the Week," *Observer*, July 21, 1963.

The trouble with our age is all signposts and no destination.

LOUIS KRONENBERGER, *Look*, May 17, 1954.

Who would have guessed that, thanks to all the ingenious tie-ins between advertising, entertainment, the popular arts, and the great corporations, the time would come when one of the most obvious aspects of the condition of the average American man is simply this: Most of the news he hears, most of the music he listens to, and most of the drama he witnesses—in fact almost all the intellectual or artistic experience he ever has—is provided by medicine shows.

JOSEPH WOOD KRUTCH, *Human Nature and the Human Condition*, 1959.

The typical American believes that no necessity of the soul is free and that there are precious few, if any, which cannot be bought.

JOSEPH WOOD KRUTCH, "The European Visitor," *If You Don't Mind My Saying So*, 1964.

I don't think it does any harm just once in a while to acknowledge that the whole country isn't in flames, that there are people in the country besides politicians, entertainers, and criminals.

CHARLES KURALT, *American Way*, March, 1978.

Is America a religion or a state?

LEWIS H. LAPHAM, "The Lost American Empire," *Harper's*, November, 1980.

Although not a warlike people, the Americans can be aroused to battle by a sense of alarm, outrage, or moral fervor. But the martial impulse is difficult to sustain and soon fades in the absence of an obvious and dramatic enemy. They prefer to be seen not as bullies but as pals—large and friendly people who subdue their enemies not with firing squads but with cigarettes and smiles and chocolate bars.

LEWIS H. LAPHAM, "The Lost American Empire," *Harper's*, November, 1980.

We think American society is an insane anthill, and the human being has been living for, you know, hundreds of thousands of years before we had any of the things we consider so necessary in American life today. You can actually live, you can make love, you can enjoy food, you can raise children, without being a computerized mechanized American.

TIMOTHY LEARY, April 10, 1967, in William F. Buckley, Jr., *On the Firing Line*, 1989.

America is a tune. It must be sung together.

GERALD STANLEY LEE, *Crowds*, 1913.

Memory in America suffers amnesia.

MERIDEL LESUEUR, *Crusaders*, 1955.

Intellectually I know that America is no better than any other country; emotionally I know she is better than every other country.

SINCLAIR LEWIS, interview, Berlin, Germany, December 29, 1930.

We are an uprooted people, newly arrived, and *nouveau riche*. As a nation we have all the vulgarity that goes with that, all the scattering of soul.

WALTER LIPPMANN, *Drift and Mastery*, 1914.

All social classes are divided down the middle by a line which, however classless we may think we are, maintains a state of social tension. On one side of the line are men; on the other, women.

RUSSELL LYNES, *A Surfeit of Honey*, 1957.

In some ways, America had grown up to be a masterpiece of self-concern.

SHIRLEY MACLAINE, *You Can Get There from Here*, 1975.

America is a hurricane, and the only people who do not hear the sound are those fortunate if incredibly stupid and smug White Protestants who live in the center, in the serene eye of the big wind.

NORMAN MAILER, *Advertisements for Myself*, 1959.

If American men are obsessed with money, American women are obsessed with weight. The men talk of gain, the women talk of loss, and I do not know which talk is the more boring.

MARYA MANNES, *More in Anger*, 1958.

Conspicuous waste beyond the imagination of Thorstein Veblen has become the mark of American life. As a nation we find ourselves overbuilt, if not overhoused; overfed, although millions of poor people are undernourished; overtransported in overpowered cars; and also...overdefended or overdefensed.

EUGENE J. MCCARTHY, *America Revisited*, 1978.

The American character looks always as if it had just had a rather bad haircut, which gives it, in our eyes at any rate, a greater humanity than the European, which even among its beggars has an all too professional air.

MARY MCCARTHY, "America the Beautiful: The Humanist in the Bathtub," *On the Contrary*, 1961.

Those who were born in the United States take its history for granted. They take America for granted. They have seen too much democracy, too much wealth, and too much exploitation and brutality, that they take everything for granted in America. America has very little meaning to them. To them it is a wide stretch of land with an enormous wealth. To them it is New York, Hollywood; it is baseball, movies; pulp magazines and books. But to the Indians in Alaska, to the foreign born, America is a living force—a great institution that changes with society.

CAREY MCWILLIAMS, *Brothers Under the Skin*, 1945.

No one ever went broke underestimating the taste of the American public.

Attributed to H.L. MENCKEN.

Nowhere in the world is superiority more easily attained, or more eagerly admitted. The chief business of the nation, as a nation, is the setting up of heroes, mainly bogus.

H.L. MENCKEN, *Prejudices*, 1923.

There is a need for heroism in American life today.

AGNES MEYER, *Education for a New Morality*, 1957.

There's something missing in the sanitized life we lead. Something that our leaders in Washington can never supply by simple edict, something that the commercials on television never advertise because nobody's yet found a way to bottle it or box it or can it. What's missing is the touch, the warmth, the meaning of life. A four-color spread in *Time* is no substitute for it. Neither is a 30-second commercial or a reassuring Washington press conference.

HARVEY MILK, speech, fund-raising meeting, 1977.

I have never been able to look upon America as young and vital, but rather as prematurely old, as a fruit which rotted before it had a chance to ripen.

HENRY MILLER, *The Air-conditioned Nightmare*, 1945.

The Negro is the barometer of all America's institutions and values.

WHITNEY MOORE, JR., *To Be Equal*, 1964.

The real 1960s began on the afternoon of November 22, 1963....It came to seem that Kennedy's murder opened some malign trap door in American culture, and the wild bats flapped out.

LANCE MORROW, *Time*, November 14, 1983.

Ours is a society which presumes male leadership in private and public affairs. The arrangements of society facilitate such leadership and reward it.

DANIEL PATRICK MOYNIHAN, "The Negro Family: The Case for National Action," report, March, 1965.

You must understand that Americans are a warrior nation.

DANIEL PATRICK MOYNIHAN, speech to Arab leaders, September, 1990, in article by Barbara Ehrenreich, *Time*, October 17, 1990.

With all of our differences, whenever we are confronted with a threat to our security we are not then Republicans or Democrats but Americans; we are not then fifty states but the United States.

RICHARD M. NIXON, *The Challenges We Face*, 1960.

For in a time when the national focus is concentrated upon the unemployed, the impoverished and the dispossessed, the working Americans have become the forgotten Americans. In a time when the national rostrums and forums are given over to shouters and protestors and demonstrators, they have become the silent Americans.

RICHARD M. NIXON, Labor Day speech, 1968.

The American leader class has really had it in terms of their ability to lead. It's really sickening to have to receive them at the White House as I often do and to hear them whine and whimper and that's one of the reasons why I enjoy very much more receiving labor leaders and people from middle America who still have character and guts and a bit of patriotism.

RICHARD M. NIXON, diary entry, September, 1971, *The Memoirs of Richard Nixon*, 1978.

Life was a lot simpler when what we honored was father and mother rather than all major credit cards.

ROBERT ORBEN, *Wall Street Journal*, March 17, 1980.

Americans are notoriously hard to divide along class lines. With the exception of professors of sociology (who know exactly where in the upper middle class they fit) and a few billionaires—who hope they are upper-class, but have a horrible fear there may be a real aristocracy hiding somewhere in Boston or Philadelphia—most of us have only the vaguest idea what class we belong to.

NOEL PERRIN, *Third Person Rural*, 1983.

America, my country, is almost a continent and hardly yet a nation.

EZRA POUND, essay in *Patria Mia*, 1912.

We are leaning too much on government. If our forefathers did not make enough money, they worked harder, and did not run to the government for a bonus. The American stock is changing.

DAVID REED, 1924, in Lois and Alan Gordon, *American Chronicle*, 1987.

As a New World, many Americans believe their country to be the last, best hope of the world, a place of youth, of new beginnings, of booming. Even those who believe that America is, in reali-

ty, no such place of hope or virtue believe it somehow *ought to be*.

JAMES OLIVER ROBERTSON, *American Myth, American Reality*, 1980.

As the rights of the majority have been replaced by the rights of the minority, so the spiritual foundations of the nation have been replaced by an entirely secular view of man.

PAT ROBERTSON, *America's Dates with Destiny*, 1986.

Americans are getting like a Ford car—they all have the same exact parts, the same upholstering and make exactly the same noises.

WILL ROGERS, in Donald Day, ed., *Autobiography of Will Rogers*, 1949.

We don't know what we want, but we are ready to bite somebody to get it.

WILL ROGERS, in Donald Day, ed., *Autobiography of Will Rogers*, 1949.

A trait no other nation seems to possess in quite the same degree that we do—namely, a feeling of almost childish injury and resentment unless the world as a whole recognizes how innocent we are of anything but the most generous and harmless intentions.

ELEANOR ROOSEVELT, "My Day," newspaper column, November 11, 1946.

The saving grace of America lies in the fact that the overwhelming majority of Americans are possessed of two great qualities—a sense of humor and a sense of proportion.

FRANKLIN D. ROOSEVELT, speech, Savannah, Georgia, November 18, 1933.

From the very beginning our people have markedly combined practical capacity for affairs with power of devotion to an ideal. The lack of either quality would have rendered the possession of the other of small value.

THEODORE ROOSEVELT, speech, Philadelphia, Pennsylvania, November 22, 1902.

The American people abhor a vacuum.

THEODORE ROOSEVELT, speech, Cairo, Illinois, October 3, 1907.

Let's face it: Intellectual achievement and the intellectual elite are alien to the mainstream of American society. They are off to the side in a sub-section of esoteric isolation labeled "oddball," "high brow," "egghead," "double-dome."

ELMO ROPER, "Roadblocks to Bookbuying," *Publishers Weekly*, June 16, 1958.

Self-government is a form of self-control, self-limitation. It goes against our whole grain. We're [Americans] supposed to go after what we want, not question whether we really need it.

JUDITH ROSSNER, *Any Minute I Can Split*, 1972.

So far as I am aware, we are the only society that thinks of itself as having risen from savagery, identified with a ruthless nature. Everyone else believes they are descended from gods.

MARSHALL SAHLINS, *The Use and Abuse of Biology*, 1976.

I am the people—the mob—the crowd—the mass.

Do you know that all the great work of the
    world is done through me?

CARL SANDBURG, "I Am the People, the Mob," 1916.

America is a young country with an old mentality.

GEORGE SANTAYANA, *Winds of Doctrine*, 1913.

Americans are eminently prophets; they apply morals to public affairs; they are impatient and enthusiastic. Their judgments have highly speculative implications, which they often make explicit; they are men with principles, and fond of stating them. Moreover, they have an intense self-reliance; to exercise private judgment is not only a habit with them but a conscious duty.

GEORGE SANTAYANA, *Character and Opinion in the United States*, 1920.

To be an American is of itself almost a moral condition, an education, and a career.

GEORGE SANTAYANA, *Character and Opinion in the United States*, 1920.

If it were given me to look into the depths of a man's heart, and I did not find goodwill at the bottom, I should say without any hesitation, you are not an American.

GEORGE SANTAYANA, *Character and Opinion in the United States*, 1920.

The American is wonderfully alive; and his vitality, not having often found a suitable outlet, makes him appear agitated on the surface; he is always letting off an unnecessarily loud blast of incidental steam.

GEORGE SANTAYANA, *Character and Opinion in the United States*, 1920.

It is veneer, rouge, aestheticism, art museums, new theaters, etc. that make America important.

The good things are football, kindness, and jazz bands.

GEORGE SANTAYANA, letter to Van Wyck Brooks, May 22, 1927.

America is the greatest of opportunities and the worst of influences.

GEORGE SANTAYANA, *The Last Puritan*, 1935.

For some reason, self-doubt appears to thrive in our Bicentennial year.

ARTHUR SCHLESINGER, JR., 1976, in Lois and Alan Gordon, *American Chronicle*, 1987.

America is the child society *par excellence*, and possibly the only one ever politically arrived at. It is a society of all rights and no obligations, the society of deliberate wreckage and waste, the only society that ever raised gangsterism to the status of myth, and murder to the status of tragedy or politics.

KARL SHAPIRO, "To Abolish Children," *To Abolish Children and Other Essays*, 1968.

The American people never carry an umbrella. They prepare to walk in eternal sunshine.

ALFRED E. SMITH, syndicated newspaper article, 1931.

We Americans are perhaps the most flexible people on earth. Nowhere else are people so easy with each other, so free, and resilient. Nowhere is there less awe of authority, less bending to tradition, even though we acknowledge the lag of the South in these particulars. Nowhere more ingenuity and resourcefulness and energy and laughter, nowhere more genuine belief in men's capacity to get what they want, and nowhere are lines so fluid, so everchanging. Nowhere so much wealth, economic power, technological development. Nowhere such potentials for world leadership.

And yet, again and again we let the world down by our moral impotence.

LILLIAN SMITH, *Killers of the Dream*, 1949.

It seems Americans would live by a Chamber-of-Commerce Creationism that declares itself satisfied with a divinely presented Shopping Mall. The integrity and character of our own ancestors is dismissed with "I couldn't live like that" by people who barely know how to live *at all*. An ancient forest is seen as a kind of overripe garbage, not unlike the embarrassing elderly.

GARY SNYDER, "Ancient Forests of the Far West," *The Practice of the Wild*, 1990.

Discount air fares, a car in every parking space and the interstate highway system have made every place accessible—and every place alike.

RONALD STEEL, "Life in the Last 50 Years," *Esquire*, June, 1983.

They were a lost generation.

GERTRUDE STEIN, conversation with Ernest Hemingway, 1926.

In America everybody is, but some are more than others.

GERTRUDE STEIN, *Everybody's Autobiography*, 1938.

Americans have always assumed, subconsciously, that all problems can be solved; that every story has a happy ending; that the application of enough energy and good will can make everything come out right. In view of our history, this assumption is natural enough. As a people, we have never encountered any obstacle that we could not overcome.

ADLAI E. STEVENSON, *Call to Greatness*, 1954.

Ours is a warfare, not a welfare, state.

I.F. STONE, "The Rich March on Washington All the Time," *I.F. Stone's Weekly*, May 13, 1968.

Who is...the Forgotten Man? He is the clean, quiet, virtuous, domestic citizen, who pays his debts and his taxes and is never heard of out of his little circle.

WILLIAM GRAHAM SUMNER, "The Forgotten Man," *The Forgotten Man and Other Essays*, 1919.

We have no class structure, we don't even sense it, we don't know what it means....The national hero is not a prince, not a king, not a rich man—but a cowboy.

FRANK TANNENBAUM, in Arthur Goodfriend, *What Is America?*, 1954.

We take nothing for granted; we accept nothing as perfect; we define nothing as the final end.

FRANK TANNENBAUM, in Arthur Goodfriend, *What Is America?*, 1954.

The diminution of the reality of class, however socially desirable, in many respects seems to have the practical effect of diminishing our ability to see people in their differences and specialness.

LIONEL TRILLING, *The Liberal Imagination*, 1950.

Ours is not a time of self-esteem or self-confidence—as was, for instance, the nineteenth century, when self-esteem may be seen oozing from its portraits. Victorians, especially the men, pictured themselves as erect, noble, and splendidly

handsome. Our self-image looks more like Woody Allen or a character from Samuel Beckett.

BARBARA TUCHMAN, "Mankind's Better Moments," Jefferson Lecture, Washington D.C., April, 1980.

America is a vast conspiracy to make you happy.

JOHN UPDIKE, "How to Love America and Leave It at the Same Time," *Problems*, 1980.

Oh, it's home again, and home again,
  America for me!
I want a ship that's westward bound to
  plough the rolling sea,
To the blessed Land of Room Enough
  beyond the ocean bars,
Where the air is full of sunlight and the
  flag is full of stars.

HENRY VAN DYKE, "America for Me," 1909.

People are too easygoing. The American people will not stand up for their rights. They'll be violent, of course, but they will not stand up for their rights.

VIRGINIA VERONA, in article by Ursula Vils, "Fighting for Her—and Our—Rights," *Los Angeles Times*, January 5, 1975.

It is the truth: comedians and jazz musicians have been more comforting and enlightening to me than preachers and politicians or philosophers or poets or painters or novelists of my time. Historians in the future, in my opinion, will congratulate us on very little other than our clowning and our jazz.

KURT VONNEGUT, Foreword, *The Best of Bob and Ray*, 1974.

Here we are, busily preparing ourselves for a war already described as "unthinkable," bombarding our bodies with gamma rays that everybody admits are a genetical hazard, spying on each other, rewarding people on quiz programs with a hundred thousand dollars for knowing how to spell "cat," and Zwicky wants to make a hundred *new* worlds.

E.B. WHITE, in response to astrophysicist Fritz Zwicky's suggestion that 100 new planets be created, "Coon Tree," June 14, 1956, *Essays of E.B. White*, 1977.

All other nations have come into being among people whose families had lived for time out of mind on the same land where they were born. Englishmen are English, Frenchmen are French, Chinese are Chinese, while their governments come and go; their national states can be torn apart and remade without losing their nationhood. But Americans are a nation born of an idea; not a place, but the idea, created the United States Government.

THEODORE H. WHITE, *New York Times Magazine*, May, 1986.

America is not anything if it consists of each of us. It is something only if it consists of all of us.

WOODROW WILSON, speech, Pittsburgh, Pennsylvania, January 29, 1916.

Sometimes people call me an idealist. Well, that is the way I know I am an American.... America is the only idealist nation in the world.

WOODROW WILSON, speech, Sioux Falls, South Dakota, September 8, 1919.

Americans on Americans

BUSINESS LEADERS

Rockefeller made his money in oil, which he discovered at the bottom of wells. Oil was crude in those days, but so was Rockefeller. Now both are considered quite refined.

RICHARD ARMOUR, *It All Started with Columbus*, 1953.

Mr. Morgan buys his partners; I grow my own.

ANDREW CARNEGIE, in Burton J. Hendrick, *Life of Andrew Carnegie*, 1932.

[Cecil B. de Mille] held the belief that he got the best work from people when he had stripped their nerves raw, when they could no longer think, when they acted through an instinct of rage and desperation.

AGNES DE MILLE, *Dance to the Piper*, 1952.

[Cecil B. de Mille] was a phenomenally shrewd man who augmented an instinct for popular taste with bold and astonishing business coups. His success was a world success, and he enjoyed every minute of it, and it lasted. He kept sex, sadism, patriotism, real estate, religion and public relations dancing in midair like jugglers' balls for fifty years.

AGNES DE MILLE, *Speak to Me, Dance with Me*, 1973.

If there is one thing [Howard] Hughes dislikes, it is a gun to his head (generally this means a request for an appearance, or a discussion of policy), and at least one president of T.W.A., a company which, as Hughes ran it, bore an operational similarity only to the government of Honduras, departed on this note.

JOAN DIDION, "7000 Romaine, Los Angeles 38," *Slouching Towards Bethlehem*, 1968.

Andrew Carnegie started out in Pittsburgh as a tiny bobbin boy, and ended up a tiny millionaire; he was only five feet three.

ANNIE DILLARD, *An American Childhood*, 1987.

Gail Sheehy quite cleverly compared her [Dorothy Schiff] with Scheherazade, but it would be more apt, I think, to compare her with Marie Antoinette. As in let them read schlock.

NORA EPHRON, "Dorothy Schiff and the *New York Post*," *Esquire*, April, 1975.

[Samuel Goldwyn] was, as were many of the bright, rough, tough lot that first saw the potential of the motion picture camera, a man of great power. Often the power would rise to an inexplicable pitch of panic anger when he was crossed or disappointed, and could then decline within minutes to the whispered, pained moral talk of a loony clergyman whimpering that God had betrayed him.

LILLIAN HELLMAN, *Pentimento*, 1973.

[J.P.] Morgan's ruby nose added to his personal fame and with some humor he once said it "Would be impossible for me to appear on the streets without it." His nose, he remarked on another occasion, "was part of the American business structure."

STEWART HOLBROOK, *The Age of the Moguls*, 1953.

I think of Samuel Goldwyn as an American Primitive, possessed of a superior instinct for the profession in which he finally found himself. This is not to say that he was not often duped or snowed or conned. Those who retain a part of their innocence are easy prey for those who have lost all theirs.

GARSON KANIN, *Hollywood*, 1978.

It did not concern [Cecil B. de Mille] in the least that in the opinion of "serious" film makers his works were considered as artistically significant as Barnum and Bailey's Circus. He feared only one thing—that an audience might be bored.

JESSE LASKY, Jr., *Whatever Happened to Hollywood?*, 1975.

[Marcus Loew] understood the American appetite for glitter and pastry-cone architecture, for three-dimensional corn on a scale of magnificence. For some it was the essence of bad taste; for many of us it was the epitome of delightful nonsense, the best kind of corn; for others it was a temporary dreamworld accessible to anyone for seventy-five cents or less.

RUSSELL LYNES, on Loew's movie palaces, "Corn, Glorious Corn," *Architectural Digest*, 1987.

While [John D. Rockefeller's] subtle, ruminative, daring mind solved large problems by an acid process of thought, he presented to the world a front of silence which was like smooth steel.

ALLEN NEVINS, *Study in Power: John D. Rockefeller*, 1953.

He [William Randolph Hearst] had discovered that there was room at the bottom and with sensational news sensationally written and pictured, he did reach for and get the people. He was a demagogue; he was pro-labor. I cannot describe the hate of those days for Hearst except to say that it was worse than it is now.

LINCOLN STEFFENS, *The Autobiography of Lincoln Steffens*, 1931.

In practical terms Henry Ford was more of a revolutionist than Marx. Ford saw that poverty was incompatible with successful technological enterprise, that interest charges were a more parasitic burden on enterprise than profits, and that profits themselves could more securely be maintained by very small returns per unit of vast production and turnover.

DOROTHY THOMPSON, *The Courage to Be Happy*, 1957.

When I saw one of [Cecil B. de Mille's] pictures, I wanted to quit the business.

KING VIDOR, in Kevin Brownlow, *The Parade's Gone By*, 1968.

[U]ntil the moment of his death, [Andrew Carnegie] had remained to millions of his countrymen their prize showpiece of what they liked to think was the real essence of the American experience—the Americanized immigrant, the rugged individual, the self-made man, the Horatio Alger hero, the beneficent philanthropist, the missionary of secular causes, the democrat who could not only walk with but argue with kings.

JOSEPH FRAZIER WALL, *Andrew Carnegie*, 1970.

GOVERNMENT OFFICIALS AND POLITICIANS

Mr. Gingrich is a congressional Jimmy Swaggart, who condemns sin while committing hypocrisy.

BILL ALEXANDER, *Village Voice*, May 9, 1989.

[Al Smith] could make statistics sit up, beg, roll over and bark.

ANONYMOUS, in Oscar Handlin, *Al Smith and His America*, 1958.

[John J.] Pershing inspired confidence but not affection. Personal magnetism seemed lacking; he won followers and admirers but not personal worshippers. Plain in word, sane and direct in action, he applied himself to all duty and all work with a manifest purpose, not only of succeeding in what he attempted, but of surpassing, guiding and directing his followers in what was before them.

ROGER L. BULLARD, in Donald Smythe, *Guerrilla Warrior: The Early Life of John J. Pershing*, 1973.

Huey Long was no true revolutionary. Power for power's sake was his mastering god. No revolutionary but—the word is used not loosely but gingerly—a dictator. A dictator, *sui generis*, the first truly such out of the soil of America.

HODDING CARTER, "Huey Long: American Dictator," *The Aspirin Age: 1919–1941*, 1949.

[Joseph McCarthy's] name has become associated with a style of politics, "McCarthyism," notable for its crude, below-the-belt, eye-gouging, bare-knuckled partisan exploitation of anti-Communism, usually on the basis of half-truths, warmed-over "revelations," and plain lies. McCarthy was also the man with the briefcase full of incriminating documents—this appealed to a country much enamored of factuality, of the cult of hard fact. At the same time, his pugilistic flamboyance, blatant love of money, women and horseflesh, his Falstaff-like war service and mythical *machismo*, caught a cowboy nation by the gut.

DAVID CAUTE, *The Great Fear: The Anti-Communist Purge Under Truman*, 1978.

The fire-eating administrator of Federal Emergency Relief, Harry L. Hopkins, may safely be credited with spoiling the Thanksgiving Day dinners of many conservatives who had been led to believe that President Roosevelt's recent zig to the right would not be followed by a zag to the left.

DELBERT CLARK, *New York Times*, December 2, 1934.

[Geraldine Ferraro] handled it exactly like Ronald Reagan. Like him, she showed tremendous inner peace.

TONY COELHO, on Ferraro's handling of her husband's tax scandal, *Newsweek*, September 3, 1984.

A distinguished member since 1948 of the "most exclusive gentlemen's club in the world," Senator Smith reaffirms the growing realization, wisely recognized by her astute constituents, that ability and proven performance, rather than sex, provide the reasonable standards for political selection.

COLUMBIA UNIVERSITY, on awarding the Doctor of Law degree to Margaret Chase Smith of Maine, June 1, 1955.

His House colleagues still call him "Jackie One Note"—joking that if you ask him how to solve the problem of teenage pregnancy, he'll tell you to cut taxes.

MAUREEN DOWD, "Is Jack Kemp Mr. Right?" *New York Times*, June 28, 1987.

[Thomas Dewey] is just about the nastiest little man I've ever known. He struts sitting down.

LILLIAN DYKSTRA, July 8, 1952, in James Patterson, *Mr. Republican*, 1972.

He dons his war paint. He goes into his war dance. He emits war whoops. He goes forth to battle and proudly returns with the scalp of a pink dentist.

RALPH FLANDERS, on Joseph McCarthy, March 9, 1954.

Small, quick, articulate, jaunty, Frankfurter was inexhaustible in his energy, and his curiosity, giving off sparks like an overcharged electric battery.

MAX FREEDMAN, *Roosevelt and Frankfurter: Their Correspondence*, 1967.

If all women had the qualities of Margaret [Chase Smith], I'd have voted for the equal-rights amendment.

BARRY M. GOLDWATER, *Washington Post*, May 3, 1972.

North defended his character—or saved his honor, if you prefer. He didn't, he says, take a penny. He never committed adultery. He was proud of his work. His ability to present himself as a man who erred only out of concern for his family or ardor for his country was allowed to whitewash his actions. The risk is that, in this case, private morality may cover or color a far deeper public immorality.

ELLEN GOODMAN, "Oliver North: The Good, the Bad, and the Boffo," *Washington Post*, June, 1987.

I like Charlie. He's the only man in the administration who doesn't talk about God.

Reporter's comment on Secretary of Defense Charles Wilson, 1957, in Lois and Alan Gordon, *American Chronicle*, 1987.

[Robert McNamara] embodied the virtues Americans have always respected, hard work, self-sacrifice, decency, loyalty....He was, finally, the embodiment of the liberal contradictions of that era, the conflict between the good intentions and the desire to hold and use power (most of what was good in us and what was bad in us was there; the Jeffersonian democracy become a superpower).

DAVID HALBERSTAM, *The Best and the Brightest*, 1969.

McGeorge Bundy...was the finest example of a special elite, a certain breed of men whose continuity is among themselves. They are linked to one another rather than to the country; in their minds they become responsible for the country but not responsive to it.

DAVID HALBERSTAM, *The Best and the Brightest*, 1969.

Dulles was indisputably the conceptual fount, as well as the prime mover of United States foreign policy....He was the informing mind, indeed almost the sole keeper of the keys to the ramified web of understandings and relationships that constituted America's posture of categorical anti-Communism and limitless strategic concern.

TOWNSEND HOOPES, *The Devil and John Foster Dulles*, 1973.

[Henry Kissinger] believes all power begins in the White House. It is his firm belief that he and the President know what is best; the rest of us are to be patient and they will announce our destiny.

BARBARA HOWAR, *Laughing All the Way*, 1972.

It's probably better to have him [J. Edgar Hoover] inside the tent pissing out, than outside the tent pissing in.

LYNDON B. JOHNSON, *New York Times*, October 31, 1971.

All that Hubert [Humphrey] needs over there is a gal to answer the phone and a pencil with an eraser on it.

LYNDON B. JOHNSON, recalled on Johnson's death, January 22, 1973.

The secret of the Kennedy successes in politics was not money but meticulous planning and organization, tremendous effort, and the enthusiasm and devotion to family and friends.

ROSE FITZGERALD KENNEDY, *Times to Remember*, 1974.

For six days in July, Lieutenant Colonel Oliver North played so sweetly on the panpipes of the American dream that he allowed the television public to believe in any and all of its best-beloved fairy tales. The truth of what he was saying didn't matter as much as the timbre of his voice or the tears in his eyes.

LEWIS H. LAPHAM, "Landscape with Trolls," *Harper's*, September, 1987.

A four-hundred-dollar suit on old Uncle Earl would look like socks on a rooster.

EARL LONG, campaign speech, in A.J. Liebling, *The Earl of Louisiana*, 1970.

Much of what Mr. [Henry A.] Wallace calls his global thinking is, no matter how you slice it, still Globaloney.

CLARE BOOTHE LUCE, speech to Congress, February 9, 1943.

The plain fact is that Al [Smith], as a good New Yorker, is as provincial as a Kansas farmer. He is not only not interested in the great problems that heave and lather the country: he has never heard of them.

H.L. MENCKEN, July, 1927, *A Carnival of Buncombe*, 1956.

If you elect a matinee idol mayor, you're going to have a musical comedy administration.

ROBERT MOSES, on John V. Lindsay, *New York Times*, January 8, 1978.

He has mastered an essential element in political life—the art of behaving as if no one has any memory. He can contradict himself and praise men he loathes. He is, in short, a very good politician.

JACK NEWFIELD, "The Case Against Nelson Rockefeller," *Bread and Roses Too*, March, 1969.

In foreign countries people are forced by their governments to submit to their gestapos. In this country, [J. Edgar] Hoover has the voluntary support of all those who delight in gangster movies and ten-cent detective magazines.

New Republic, February 19, 1940.

Mr. [John Foster] Dulles' moral universe makes everything quite clear, too clear…self-righteousness is the inevitable fruit of simple moral judgments.

REINHOLD NIEBUHR, "The Moral World of John Foster Dulles," *New Republic*, December 1, 1958.

You really have to get to know [Thomas] Dewey to dislike him.

JAMES T. PATTERSON, *Mr. Republican*, 1972.

He knows the tax code as thoroughly as the pope knows the Lord's Prayer.

WILLIAM PROXMIRE, on Russell B. Long, November 10, 1986.

[California Supreme Court Justice] Rose Bird is a walking incendiary. Someday, she's going to walk too close to a spark.

H.L. RICHARDSON, *Newsweek*, August 9, 1982.

[Joseph] McCarthy invented the Multiple Lie— the lie with so many tiny gears and fragile connecting rods that reason exhausted itself in the effort to combat it.

RICHARD ROVERE, "The Frivolous Demagogue," *Esquire*, June, 1958.

He [Henry Kissinger] was endearing only when he wanted to be and caused even those who were most attracted to him to wonder whether he was more respectful of position than personality.

WILLIAM SAFIRE, *Before the Fall*, 1975.

[John J. Pershing] was no tin soldier and certainly no figurine saint.

DONALD SMYTHE, *Guerrilla Warrior: The Early Life of John J. Pershing*, 1973.

Like Hitler and Goebbels, [Joseph McCarthy] knows the value of ceaseless reiteration. He has their complete lack of scruple, and sets as low an estimate as they on the popular mind's capacity to remember.

I.F. STONE, "Time for a Deportation—to Wisconsin," *I.F. Stone's Weekly*, April 4, 1953.

His mind was like a soup dish, wide and shallow; it could hold a small amount of nearly anything, but the slightest jarring spilled the soup into somebody's lap.

IRVING STONE, on William Jennings Bryan, *They Also Ran*, 1945.

[Edgar J. Hoover] was a charmer. He was a brilliant chameleon. But he was also a master con man. That takes intelligence of a certain kind, an astuteness, a shrewdness. He never read anything that would broaden his mind or give depth to his thinking. I never knew him to have an intellectual or educated friend.

WILLIAM SULLIVAN, *Time*, December 22, 1975.

Clad each day in a pair of platitudes.

NORMAN THOMAS, on Thomas Dewey, in Murray B. Seidler, *Norman Thomas, Respectable Rebel*, 1961.

Hoover and the FBI were one—creator and creation. He served eight Presidents as the world's most powerful policeman. With a genius for administration and popular myth, he fashioned his career as an improbable bureaucratic morality play peopled by bad guys and G-men.
Time, May 15, 1972.

The reason that poor [George] Shultz is getting the reputation of a dull plodder...is that the right-wing wackos around the Administration keep going behind his back and accusing him of overt sanity.
CALVIN TRILLIN, "I'll Take the Low Road," King Features Syndicate, January 26, 1986.

[Michael Deaver] had, after all, become one of the three most powerful people in the White House—an impressive achievement for someone whose most serious talents were said to lie in the direction of knowing precisely which camera angle was most flattering to each of Nancy Reagan's ball gowns. He is so close to Ronald and Nancy that he is often described as being like a son to them—something that has never been said of any of their own children.
CALVIN TRILLIN, "Not Hiring Deaver," King Features Syndicate, June 22, 1986.

After [Pat] Robertson said that running for president was part of God's plan for his life...it was obviously tempting to speculate about how to explain people who think God's plan for their lives requires them to snooker Pat Robertson out of the Iowa delegation. We would have to conclude that either Robertson or the gang of delegate-grabbers got God's plan wrong, but it might be difficult to find out which one. If God filed these plans down at the courthouse, after all, we wouldn't need so many religions.
CALVIN TRILLIN, "Deity Overload," King Features Syndicate, October 12, 1986.

Why, this fellow don't know any more about politics than a pig knows about Sunday.
HARRY S TRUMAN, on Dwight D. Eisenhower, in Richard M. Nixon, *RN: Memoirs of Richard M. Nixon*, 1978.

The trouble was [Thomas Dewey had] forgot what it was like to have to work for a living and it showed on him, which is why he lost the election.
HARRY S TRUMAN, in Merle Miller, *Plain Speaking—An Oral Biography of Harry S Truman*, 1948.

I fired him because he wouldn't respect the authority of the President. That's the answer to

that. I didn't fire him because he was a dumb son of a bitch, although he was, but that's not against the law for generals. If it was, half to three-quarters of them would be in jail.
HARRY S TRUMAN, on Douglas MacArthur, in Merle Miller, *Plain Speaking*, 1974.

[John Foster] Dulles, the new Secretary of State, was a cold war extremist naturally, a drum-beater with the instincts of a bully, deliberately combative because that was the way he believed foreign relations should be conducted. Brinkmanship was his contribution, counteroffensive rather than containment was his policy, "a passion to control events" was his motor.
BARBARA TUCHMAN, *The March of Folly*, 1984.

For Brandeis was a liberal by affirmation and championed his causes not out of disinterest, but out of strong beliefs. A Jeffersonian democrat who passionately feared the "curse of bigness," he fought for the rights of states to use their police powers effectively and experimentally in order to preserve a federal system he considered essential for a democratic society.
MELVIN F. UROFSKY, *A Mind of One Piece: Brandeis and American Reform*, 1971.

Displaying a bland, even an eerie, disregard for what appeared to be the facts of the situation, he fell back on an old habit of looking ahead to the next defeat.
LOUDON WAINWRIGHT, on Harold E. Stassen, *Life*, March 20, 1964.

His magnificent earnestness was hypnotic, first of all self-hypnotic, because he lost no force of eloquence in convincing himself. The weight of all his rhetoric, of his splendid magnetic presence, of his resonant voice, fell upon the wicked who opposed his holy cause.
WILLIAM ALLEN WHITE, on William Jennings Bryan, *Masks in a Pageant*, 1928.

More power for good or evil rested for twenty-five years under Bryan's black slouch hat than under any other single contemporaneous head-piece in America.
WILLIAM ALLEN WHITE, on William Jennings Bryan, *Masks in a Pageant*, 1928.

When in a hundred years from now, courage, sheer courage based upon moral indignation, is celebrated in this country, the name of Jeannette Rankin, who stood firm in folly for her faith, will be written in monumental bronze not for what she did but for the way she did it.

WILLIAM ALLEN WHITE, Kansas *Emporia Gazette*, 1941.

In his long public life of obtrusive goodwill and usefulness, Humphrey has exhausted more people than he has persuaded. But in politics the effect sometimes is the same.

GEORGE WILL, "Hubert Humphrey: The Art of Exhaustion," September 19, 1975, *The Pursuit of Happiness, and Other Sobering Thoughts*, 1978.

After [Huey] Long, as before him, the rich were rich and the poor were poor. But the poor were left with sustaining memories of a time when the rich had known fear. The memories were better than beans and gravy, and were more than the poor usually got from government.

GEORGE WILL, "Huey Long: 'I Bet Earl Bit Him, Didn't He?'" September 3, 1975, *The Pursuit of Happiness, and Other Sobering Thoughts*, 1978.

[Patrick] Moynihan was always a minimalist about the government's ability to deliver and perform, because he was a maximalist about the nature of ethnic conflict in America.

GARRY WILLS, *Nixon Agonistes*, 1970.

MUSICIANS AND DANCERS

Elvis Presley, the Hillbilly Cat, Swivel-Hips, the King of Rock and Roll, the King of Bebop, the King of Country Music, simply, the King.

MICHAEL BANE, *Country Music*, December, 1977.

So Elvis Presley came, strumming a weird guitar and wagging his tail across the continent, ripping off fame and fortune as he scrunched his way, and, like a latter-day Johnny Appleseed, sowing seeds of a new rhythm and style in the white souls of the new white youth of America, whose inner hunger and need was no longer satisfied with the antiseptic white shows and whiter songs of Pat Boone. "You can do anything," sang Elvis to Pat Boone's white shoes, "but don't you step on my Blue Suede Shoes!"

ELDRIDGE CLEAVER, *Soul on Ice*, 1968.

If a young man at the age of twenty-three can write a symphony like that, in five years he will be ready to commit murder.

WALTER DAMROSCH, on Aaron Copland's Symphony for Organ and Orchestra, 1925, in Alan and Lois Gordon, *American Chronicle*, 1987.

The hair was a Vaseline cathedral, the mouth a touchingly uncertain sneer of allure. One, two-wham! Like a berserk blender the lusty young pelvis whirred and the notorious git-tar slammed forward with a jolt that symbolically deflowered a generation of teenagers and knocked chips off 90 million older shoulders. Then out of the half-melted vanilla face a wild black baritone came bawling in orgasmic lurches. *Whu-huh-huh-huh f'the money! Two f'the show! Three t'git riddy naa GO CAAT GO!*

BRAD DARRACH, on Elvis Presley, *Life*, Winter, 1977.

In the most evanescent of all professions she is regarded, and I believe, rightly, as an immortal. Dancers for untold generations will dance differently because of her labors.

AGNES DE MILLE, on Martha Graham, 1949.

[Joan Baez] could reach an audience in a way that neither the purists nor the more commercial folksingers seemed to be able to do. If her interest was never in the money, neither was it really in the music: she was interested instead in something that went on between her and the audience.

JOAN DIDION, "Where the Kissing Never Stops," *Slouching Towards Bethlehem*, 1968.

Joan Baez was a personality before she was entirely a person, and, like anyone to whom that happens, she is in a sense the hapless victim of what others have seen in her, written about her, wanted her to be and not to be.

JOAN DIDION, "Where the Kissing Never Stops," *Slouching Towards Bethlehem*, 1968.

If she did not invent it [modern dance]...she embodied it, propagated it, imposed a clear discipline and aesthetic on a new, inchoate art.

MARTHA DUFFY, on Martha Graham, *Time*, April 5, 1991.

What interested her was not the airiness and elevation of ballet. She made the earth her touchstone and reveled in the downward pull of gravity.

MARTHA DUFFY, on Martha Graham, *Time*, April 5, 1991.

Isadora [Duncan], who had an un-American genius for art, for organizing love, maternity, politics and pedagogy on a great personal scale, had also an un-American genius for grandeur.

JANET FLANNER, *Paris Was Yesterday*, 1927.

[Little] Richard's records all sounded as if they were made in the Saturday night uproar of a turpentine logging camp. His raw strident voice was torn from his throat in a bawling, shouting torrent that battered and scattered the words until they sounded like raving.

ALBERT GOLDMAN, "The Emergence of Rock," *New American Review*, April, 1968.

Ray Charles was the eternal Negro, a poor blind man crying out of his darkness, singing to assuage his pain.

ALBERT GOLDMAN, "The Emergence of Rock," *New American Review*, April, 1968.

Mr. [Elvis] Presley made another television appearance last night on the Milton Berle show over Channel 4...he might possibly be classified as an entertainer. Or, perhaps quite as easily as an assignment for a sociologist.

JACK GOULD, *New York Times*, June 7, 1956.

I knew she was destined for stardom the minute I saw her feet.

MARTHA GRAHAM, on Bette Davis, *The Lively Arts*, May 7, 1990.

For Elvis [Presley] there was no escape in art, since his original triumph was his very artlessness. He didn't write songs, nor did he aspire to anything more than success. Even his films were no more than a magnification of his image, a further reinforcement of the impossible perfection, which transformed him, like all our public figures, from a living presence into an all-purpose, economy-rate icon.

PETER GURNALNICK, *Country Music*, December, 1977.

[Cole] Porter deliberately chose to be a snob, at least to all appearances. He inherited money and loved it; but he made much more by himself and loved it as well. He spent freely and gained it freely; he even complained about taxes in a lighthearted vein. "My ninety-two percent, I suppose, supports some unknown government bureau," he said. He was determined to be a gay divorcé from life and never abandoned the pose.

RICHARD G. HUBLER, *The Cole Porter Story*, 1965.

Isadora [Duncan] was above everything American. Her thoughts continually turned toward this country that she loved above all others. But she could not love blindly, and America is perhaps still too young to endure criticism. Isadora saw infinite possibilities, the wide horizons, the pulsing vitality, the strength, the joy of this country, and longed to throw her vision and her wisdom at its feet. How strange it is that a country born and cradled in Revolution should so consistently turn its austere back on its greatest and most typical children.

EVA LE GALLIENNE, "Isadora Remembered," in Isadora Duncan, *The Art of the Dance*, 1928.

[Bruce Springsteen] is a national presence, his charisma co-opted by as unlikely an adherent as Ronald Reagan—even as Springsteen himself pokes relentlessly through the withered and waterless cultural underbrush of the president's new American Eden.

KURT LODER, *Rolling Stone*, 1984.

[Ted Shawn] made use of American continental themes, and employed music far beyond the contemporary dance norm—and he brought to the dance in America a dignity, a masculine purpose and a spiritual awareness such as the theatre had not known until then.

OLGA MAYNARD, *The American Ballet*, 1959.

George [Gershwin] died on July 11, 1937, but I don't have to believe that if I don't want to.

JOHN O'HARA, *Newsweek*, July 15, 1940.

Here was a great woman; a magnificent, generous, gallant, reckless, fated fool of a woman. There was never a place for her in the ranks of the terrible, slow army of the cautious. She ran ahead, where there were no paths.

DOROTHY PARKER, on Isadora Duncan, "Poor, Immortal Isadora," *The New Yorker*, January 14, 1928.

[Ellington] the magus, the wizard, the villain, the lover, the enchanter, the necromancer. He was the great conjurer of passion, emotion and soul.

GORDON PARKS, "Jazz and the Duke," *Mom, the Flag, and Apple Pie*, 1976.

[Duke] Ellington never grinned. He smiled. Ellington never shuffled. He strode. It was "Good afternoon, ladies and gentlemen," never "How y'all doin'?" At his performances we sat up high in our seats. We wanted to be seen by the whites in the audience. We wanted them to know that this elegant, handsome and awe-inspiring man playing that ever-so-fine music on that golden stage dressed in those fine clothes before that big beautiful black band was black—like us.

GORDON PARKS, "Jazz and the Duke," *Mom, the Flag, and Apple Pie*, 1976.

In these days when rock stars hatch one evening and perish the next with the mortality of mayflies, how many of those who, like myself, idolized him ever give a thought to Liberace? All of us were spellbound by his meteoric rise, hungrily followed his career, and kept his picture under our pillow, but I suppose that essentially we looked upon him as a great, gorgeous peacock who shed enchantment on our lives and then flapped off into obscurity.

S.J. PERELMAN, on Liberace, *The Last Laugh*, 1981.

Bessie's [Smith] husky voice made you remember and made you forget. She was the sobbing scop of aristocrats and common people.

MELVIN B. TOLSON, "Caviar and Cabbage," *Washington Tribune*, November 20, 1937.

Robeson is the New Negro in action. He is not a rugged individualist. He is not a snob. He does not scorn the masses. He is not concerned in rising from the ranks, but in rising with the ranks....He wants life in the arts; not sentimental romanticism.

MELVIN B. TOLSON, "Paul Robeson Rebels against Hollywood's Dollars," *Washington Tribune*, March 25, 1939.

A small, amicable, quiet man, with tremendous stores of nervous energy, [Jerome] Kern wore horn-rimmed glasses, smoked constantly, poured forth hundreds of facile tunes with a radio blaring in his ears, and modestly called himself a dull fellow with little talent and lots of luck.

WESLEY TOWNER, in Max Wilk, *They're Playing Our Song*, 1973.

If the spirit is kind to [Dwike] Mitchell, it's because he trusts it and feels that he is its servant. Often in a concert he reaches a high that borders on a religious experience. He enters a trance-like state, expending prodigious energy at the keyboard and feeling no fatigue at the end.

WILLIAM ZINSSER, *Willie and Dwike*, 1984.

[Willie Ruff] is a man on the move, a listener and a learner, a hustler and a charmer, making his own luck.

WILLIAM ZINSSER, *Willie and Dwike*, 1984.

This was no actress, no imitator of women's woes; there was no pretense. It was the real thing.

CARL VAN VECHTEN, on Bessie Smith, in John S. Wilson, "The Blues," in *Show Business Illustrated*, October 17, 1961.

PRESIDENTS

[William Taft] can be depended upon to stand for property rights whenever they come into conflict with human rights.

ANONYMOUS, *Literary Digest*, July 16, 1921.

[Herbert] Hoover isn't a stuffed shirt. But at times he can give the most convincing impersonation of a stuffed shirt you ever saw.

ANONYMOUS, in E. Lyons, *Herbert Hoover*, 1947.

To err is Truman.

A POPULAR JOKE IN 1946.

Grover Cleveland was a man of honor, courage, and integrity. He followed the right as he saw it. But he saw it through a conservative and conventional cast of mind.

DEAN ACHESON, *A Democrat Looks at His Party*, 1955.

I have a curious and apprehensive feeling as I watch JFK that he is sort of an Indian snake charmer.

DEAN ACHESON, letter to Harry S Truman, in David S. McLellan and David C. Acheson, eds., *Among Friends*, 1980.

He proved the most bewildered President in our history.

SAMUEL HOPKINS ADAMS, "The Timely Death of President Harding," *The Aspirin Age: 1919–1941*, 1949.

George Bush is just a tweedier version of Ronald Reagan.

JOHN B. ANDERSON, *New York Times Magazine*, February 17, 1980.

Looking for all the world like a benign undertaker, [McKinley] embalmed himself for posterity. Never permitting himself to be photographed in disarray, he would change his white vests, when wrinkled, several times a day.

THOMAS A. BAILEY, *Presidential Greatness*, 1966.

President McKinley, the conservative's conservative, stepped gingerly into the lukewarm water of tropical imperialism when he reluctantly scooped up the Spanish Philippines, Guam, and Puerto Rico.

THOMAS A. BAILEY, *Presidential Greatness*, 1966.

The amiable, good-natured, subthyroid Taft had the misfortune to follow the crusading, club-brandishing, hyperthyroid Roosevelt, much as a dim star follows a blazing comet. The Nation felt let down.

THOMAS A. BAILEY, *Presidential Greatness*, 1966.

A new star with a tremendous national appeal, the skill of a consummate showman.

RUSSELL BAKER, on John F. Kennedy's first televised press conference, *New York Times*, January 26, 1961.

After two years in what is usually described as the world's most difficult job, after one bullet in his lung, the oldest President in American history looked more fit then he did while running for the office. He insisted on conducting the presidency according to his own metabolism. Reagan the man was as much an anomaly in the White House as Reagan the ism was in American history.

LAURENCE I. BARRETT, *Gambling with History*, 1983.

With all the confidence of a man dialing his own telephone number.

JOHN BELL, on Taft's manner in handling crises, *The Splendid Misery*, 1960.

I too would allow that Ronald Reagan is undoubtedly a sincere man. I also believe that he is in reality what he appears to be: a simple man. His ideas, his philosophy, his perceptions, his comprehension of human affairs and society are also neatly confined to a simple framework of thought and action that permits no doubts and acknowledges no sobering complexities. No wonder his manner is that of a man with utter confidence in his own fundamentalist purity and integrity, the efficient missionary dedicated to eradicating evil. Unfortunately, in these times the simple man or the simple answer is not enough.

EDMUND G. (PAT) BROWN, *Reagan: The Political Chameleon*, 1976.

On balance, Carter was not good at public relations. He did not fire enthusiasm in the public or inspire fear in his adversaries. He was trusted, but—very unfairly—that trust was in him as a person but not in him as a leader. He had ambitious goals for this nation, both at home and abroad, and yet he did not succeed in being seen as a visionary or in captivating the nation's imagination. His personal qualities—honesty, integrity, religious conviction, compassion—were not translated in the public mind into statesmanship with a historical sweep.

ZBIGNIEW BRZEZINSKI, *Power and Principle*, 1983.

Just when you think there's nothing to write about, Nixon says, "I am not a crook." Jimmy Carter says, "I have lusted after women in my heart." President Reagan says, "I have just taken a urinalysis test, and I am not on dope."

ART BUCHWALD, speech, Grand Rapids, Michigan, *Time*, September 29, 1986.

[Reagan] was an American original, both in form and substance.

LOU CANNON, *President Reagan: The Role of a Lifetime*, 1991.

Reagan's most frequent target was Reagan. No president since Lincoln was as self-effacing, and no president in the history of the republic was as effective at self-ridicule.

LOU CANNON, *President Reagan: The Role of a Lifetime*, 1991.

Hark, when Gerald Ford was king—
We were bored with everything.
Unemployment 6 percent,
What a boring president.
Nothing major needed fixin'
So he pardoned Richard Nixon.

Capitol Steps, political satirists, lyrics by Bill Strauss and Eliana Newport, first performed in 1982.

I personally think he did violate the law, that he committed impeachable offenses. But I don't think that he thinks he did.

JIMMY CARTER, on Richard M. Nixon, to reporters after press conference, May 12, 1977.

[Ronald] Reagan is different from me in almost every basic element of commitment and experience and promise to the American people, and the Republican party now is sharply different from what the Democratic party is. And I might add parenthetically that the Republican party is sharply different under Reagan from what it was under Gerald Ford and Presidents all the way back to Eisenhower.

JIMMY CARTER, speech, Independence, Missouri, September 2, 1980.

[Richard M. Nixon] has a deeper concern for his place in history than for the people he governs. And history will not fail to note that fact.

SHIRLEY CHISHOLM, *The Good Fight*, 1973.

He is running not for election but for the history books.

GEORGE J. CHURCH, on Ronald Reagan, *Time*, September 29, 1986.

The hand of Moscow backs the Communist leaders in America…[and] aims to support FDR….I ask you to purge the man who claims to be a Democrat from the Democratic Party, and I mean Franklin Double-Crossing Roosevelt.

FATHER CHARLES COUGHLIN, 1936, in Lois and Alan Gordon, *American Chronicle*, 1987.

[Herbert Hoover] is not a complicated personality, but rather a personality of monolithic simplicity. With no reflection on anyone, it might be said that whenever and wherever Herbert Hoover has mystified people or has been misunderstood by them, nearly always it has been because he is an extremely plain man living in an extremely fancy age.

JAMES M. COX, Springfield, Ohio, *Sun*, August 10, 1949.

It would be difficult to imagine a less political and popularly ingratiating personality than that of this round, sedentary, factual-minded man who seems incapable of pretending to be anything that he does not know himself to be.

HERBERT CROLY, "Who Is Hoover?" *New Republic*, June 27, 1928.

the only man woman or child who wrote a
simple declarative sentence with seven
grammatical errors "is dead"

E.E. CUMMINGS, on Warren G. Harding, *ViVa*, 1931.

At his worst, Reagan made the denial of compassion respectable.

MARIO CUOMO, "Goodbye to the Gipper," *Newsweek*, January 9, 1989.

History buffs probably noted the reunion at a Washington party a few weeks ago of three ex-presidents: Carter, Ford, and Nixon—See No Evil, Hear No Evil, and Evil.

ROBERT J. DOLE, speech, Washington Gridiron Club, March 26, 1983.

I believe Dick Nixon to be an honest man. I am confident that he will place all the facts before the American people fairly and squarely.

DWIGHT D. EISENHOWER, statement made during the presidential campaign, September, 1952.

There was no more unlikely leader of a political revolution than this septuagenarian who had become known to the nation as a Grade B movie actor. Sometimes, he seemed more improbable as a national leader viewed at first hand than he did as a personality dimly viewed through the news media.

ROWLAND EVANS and ROBERT NOVAK, *The Reagan Revolution*, 1981.

Truman's very ordinariness has today made him something of a folk hero: a plain-speaking, straight-talking, ordinary fellow who did what he saw as his duty without turning his obligation into an opportunity for personal gain.

ROBERT H. FERRELL, *Truman: A Centenary Remembrance*, 1984.

[President] Johnson condemned his officials who worked on Vietnam to the excruciating mental task of holding reality and the official version of reality together as they moved farther and farther apart.

FRANCES FITZGERALD, *Fire in the Lake*, 1972.

I am a Ford, not a Lincoln.

GERALD R. FORD, on being sworn in as vice president, December 6, 1973.

Governor Reagan and I have one thing in common. We both played football....I played for Michigan. He played for Warner Brothers.

GERALD R. FORD, 1976, in Lois and Alan Gordon, *American Chronicle*, 1987.

He wanted everyone with him all the time, and when they weren't, it broke his heart.

MAX FRANKEL, on Lyndon Johnson, in Richard Harwood and Haynes Johnson, *Lyndon*, 1973.

[William Taft] loathed being President and being Chief Justice was all happiness for him. He fought against being President and yielded to the acceptance of that heritage because of the insistence of Mrs. Taft—very ambitious in that direction. It had always been the ambition of his life to be on the Supreme Court. Taft once said that the Supreme Court was his notion of what heaven must be like.

FELIX FRANKFURTER, *Reminiscences*, 1960.

I'm sure that President Johnson would never have pursued the war in Vietnam if he'd ever had a Fulbright to Japan, or say Bangkok, or had any feeling for what these people are like and why they acted the way they did. He was completely ignorant.

J. WILLIAM FULBRIGHT, *New York Times*, June 26, 1986.

[Lyndon Johnson was] an extraordinarily gifted President who was the wrong man from the wrong place at the wrong time under the wrong circumstances.

ERIC GOLDMAN, *The Tragedy of Lyndon Johnson*, 1969.

I wouldn't trust Nixon from here to that phone.

BARRY M. GOLDWATER, *Newsweek*, September 29, 1986.

The Great Communicator has always been an Indifferent Historian, his memory as selective as his myths. This pitch for patriotism was no belated boost for history lessons at the dinner table. To the very end, this man of Hollywood and Washington preferred a story line of anecdotes and images to a time line of facts and figures.

ELLEN GOODMAN, "Exit Ron Reagan, Stage Right," *Washington Post*, January, 1989.

He has a chance to make somebody move over on Mount Rushmore. He's working for his place on the coins and the postage stamps.

HENRY GRAFF, on Ronald Reagan, *Newsweek*, January 28, 1985.

Eisenhower was a subtle man, and no fool, though in pursuit of his objectives he did not like to be thought of as brilliant; people of brilliance, he thought, were distrusted.

DAVID HALBERSTAM, *The Best and the Brightest*, 1972.

Now look! That damned cowboy is President of the United States.

Attributed to MARK HANNA, on hearing of Theodore Roosevelt's accession to the presidency, September 14, 1901.

I can see but one word written over a head of my husband if he is elected, and the word is "Tragedy."

FLORENCE HARDING, in Robert K. Murray, *The Harding Era*, 1969.

I was more surprised to learn from the autopsy of the President that he was dying of old age at 58, if he had not been shot.

JOHN HAY, on William McKinley, letter to Henry Adams, October 21, 1901.

The presidency is a huge echo chamber magnifying every little thing he does.

STEPHEN HESS, on Ronald Reagan, *Time*, February 6, 1984.

He [Theodore Roosevelt] was very likeable, a big figure, a rather ordinary intellect, with extraordinary gifts, a shrewd and I think pretty unscrupulous politician. He played all his cards—if not more.

OLIVER WENDELL HOLMES, JR., letter to Sir Frederick Pollock, in Catherine Drinker Bowen, *Yankee from Olympus*, 1944.

In the heat of a political lifetime, Ronald Reagan innocently squirrels away tidbits of misinformation and then, sometimes years later, casually drops them into his public discourse, like gum balls in a quiche.

LUCY HOWARD, *Newsweek*, November 11, 1985.

An intellectual, [Eisenhower] bestowed upon the games of golf and bridge all the enthusiasm and perseverance that he withheld from books and ideas.

EMMET JOHN HUGHES, *The Ordeal of Power: A Political Memoir of the Eisenhower Years*, 1963.

Underneath the beautiful exterior there was an element of ruthlessness and toughness that I had trouble either accepting or forgetting.

HUBERT H. HUMPHREY, on John F. Kennedy, *The Education of a Public Man*, 1976.

Lyndon [Johnson] acts like there was never going to be a tomorrow.

CLAUDIA "LADY BIRD" JOHNSON, *New York Times Magazine*, November 29, 1964.

Gerry Ford is a nice guy, but he played too much football with his helmet off.

Attributed to LYNDON B. JOHNSON.

[Gerald Ford] can't fart and chew gum at the same time.

Attributed to LYNDON B. JOHNSON.

Jack was out kissing babies while I was out passing bills. Someone had to tend the store.

LYNDON B. JOHNSON, on John F. Kennedy, in Ralph G. Martin, *A Hero for Our Time*, 1983.

[Eisenhower] was the great tortoise upon whose back the world sat for eight years. We laughed at him; we talked wistfully about moving; and all the while we never knew the cunning beneath the shell.

MURRAY KEMPTON, "The Underestimation of Dwight D. Eisenhower," *Esquire*, September, 1967.

What extraordinary vehicles destiny selects to accomplish its designs. This man, so lonely in his hour of triumph, so ungenerous in some of his motivations, had navigated our nation through one of the most anguishing periods in its history. Not by nature courageous, he had steeled himself to conspicuous acts of rare courage. Not normally outgoing, he had forced himself to rally his people to its challenge. He had striven for a revolution in American foreign policy so that it would overcome the disastrous oscillations between overcommitment and isolation. Despised by the Establishment, ambiguous in his human perceptions, he had yet held fast to a sense of national honor and responsibility, determined to prove that the strongest free country had no right to abdicate.

HENRY KISSINGER, on Richard M. Nixon, *White House Years*, 1979.

Nixon had three goals: to win by the biggest electoral landslide in history; to be remembered as a peacemaker; and to be accepted by the "Establishment" as an equal. He achieved all these objectives at the end of 1972 and the beginning of 1973. And he lost them all two months later—partly because he turned a dream into an obsession.

HENRY KISSINGER, on Richard M. Nixon, *Years of Upheaval*, 1982.

When you meet the president, you ask yourself, "How did it ever occur to anybody that he should be governor much less president?"

HENRY KISSINGER, on Ronald Reagan, *US*, June 2, 1986.

Here is a guy who's had a stake driven through his heart. I mean, really nailed to the bottom of the coffin with a wooden stake, and a silver bullet through the forehead for good measure—and yet he keeps coming back.

TED KOPPEL, on Richard M. Nixon, *New York*, August 13, 1984.

Certainly he is not of the generation that regards honesty as the best policy. However, he does regard it as a policy.

WALTER LIPPMANN, on Richard M. Nixon, *Newsweek*, May 12, 1980.

I think everyone must feel that the brevity of his tenure of office was a mercy to him and to the country. Harding was not a bad man. He was just a slob.

ALICE ROOSEVELT LONGWORTH, *Crowded Hours*, 1933.

Though I yield to no one in my admiration for Mr. Coolidge, I do wish he did not look as if he had been weaned on a pickle.

ALICE ROOSEVELT LONGWORTH, quoting a remark made to her doctor by one of his patients, *Crowded Hours*, 1933.

Nixon was the artist who had discovered the laws of vibration in all the frozen congelations of the mediocre.

NORMAN MAILER, *St. George and the Godfather*, 1972.

What kind of President would Nixon be? Well, to begin with, he would be perhaps the hardest-driving chief executive and the most controversial since Theodore Roosevelt. There would be nothing haphazard, nothing bland about his administration, nor any doubt about its political identity.

EARL MAZO, *Richard Nixon: A Political and Personal Portrait*, 1959.

His speeches left the impression of an army of pompous phrases moving over the landscape in search of an idea; sometimes these meandering words would actually capture a straggling thought and bear it triumphantly, a prisoner in

their midst, until it died of servitude and overwork.

WILLIAM G. MCADOO, on Warren Harding's speaking style, 1920, in Ralph G. Martin, *Ballots & Bandwagons*, 1964.

We forgave, followed and accepted because we liked the way he looked. And he had a pretty wife. Camelot was fun, even for the peasants, as long as it was televised to their huts.

JOE MCGINNISS, on John F. Kennedy, *The Selling of the President 1968*, 1969.

But he [Richard M. Nixon] was like a kamikaze pilot who keeps apologizing for the attack.

MARY MCGRORY, syndicated newspaper column, November 8, 1962.

Hard on [Herbert Hoover] to go out of office to the sound of crashing banks. Like the tragic end of a tragic story....The history of H's administration is Greek in its fatality.

AGNES MEYER, diary, February 25, 1933.

Jack [Kennedy] knew how to create the kind of fun that lightened the mood of everyone around him. His innate gaiety and zest for living challenged even the most caustic, passive member of their class. His high spirits were contagious.

DAVID MICHAELIS, *The Best of Friends*, 1983.

Through his mastery of storytelling techniques, he has managed to separate his character, in the public mind, from his actions as president....He has, in short, mesmerized us with that steady gaze.

JAMES NATHAN MILLER, "Ronald Reagan and the Techniques of Deception," *Atlantic*, February, 1984.

[Nixon] bleeds people. He draws every drop of blood and then drops them from a cliff. He'll blame any person he can put his foot on.

MARTHA MITCHELL, *Los Angeles Times*, August 28, 1973.

[Lyndon] Johnson himself turned out to be so many different characters he could have populated all of *War and Peace* and still had a few people left over.

HERBERT MITGANG, review of Merle Miller's *Lyndon: An Oral Biography*, August 15, 1980.

I work for him despite his faults and he lets me work for him despite my deficiencies.

BILL MOYERS, on Lyndon B. Johnson, *New York Times*, April 3, 1966.

Hyperbole was to Lyndon Johnson what oxygen is to life.

BILL MOYERS, *New York Times*, September 11, 1975.

I think Gerald Ford will be remembered as a man who bumped his head, had a wonderful wife, and left Americans more at peace with themselves and the rest of the world than at any time since it became a world power.

DANIEL PATRICK MOYNIHAN, 1977, in Lois and Alan Gordon, *American Chronicle*, 1987.

Ronald Reagan is the most ignorant President since Warren Harding.

RALPH NADER, *Pacific Sun*, March 21, 1981.

He wouldn't commit himself to the time of day from a hatful of watches.

WESTBROOK PEGLER, on Herbert Hoover, ca. 1929, in Oliver Pilat, *Pegler: Angry Man of the Press*, 1963.

The quality of his being one with the people, of having no artificial or natural barriers between him and them, made it possible for him to be a leader without ever being, or thinking of being, a dictator.

FRANCES PERKINS, on Franklin D. Roosevelt, *The Roosevelt I Knew*, 1946.

I don't know anyone who is as vain or more selfish than Lyndon Johnson.

SAM RAYBURN, in Robert A. Caro, *The Path to Power*, 1982.

Roosevelt is my shepherd. I live in want. He maketh me to lie down on park benches. He leadeth me past still factories. He disturbeth my soul. He crooneth me into paths of destruction for his party's sake. Yea, though I walk through the shadow of Depression, I anticipate no recovery, for He is with me. His policies and diplomacies they bewilder me. He prepareth a reduction in my salary, He anointeth my small income with taxes, My expenses runneth over. Surely unemployment and poverty shall follow me all the days of my life, and I shall dwell in a mortgaged house forever.

Republican update on 23rd Psalm, in Paul F. Boller, *Presidential Campaigns*, 1940.

I doubt if Eisenhower can stand a second term and I doubt if the country can stand Nixon as President.

ELEANOR ROOSEVELT, January 20, 1956, letter to Lord Elibank, in Joseph P. Lash, *Eleanor: The Years Alone*, 1972.

McKinley has a chocolate eclair backbone.

THEODORE ROOSEVELT, ca. 1901, in Ralph G. Martin, *Ballots & Bandwagons*, 1964.

In terms of graciousness, dignity, propriety, and the kind of modest eloquence that makes guests comfortable and guests of honor glow, Nixon acting as host or master of ceremonies was the best in the business.

WILLIAM SAFIRE, *Before the Fall*, 1975.

Instinctively a conservative, bred to the value of self-reliance, Nixon adopted progressive views on social legislation after rational analysis and political education. His heart was on the right, and his head was, with FDR, "slightly left of center."

WILLIAM SAFIRE, *Before the Fall*, 1975.

He [Nixon] may be the only genuinely tragic hero in our history, his ruination caused by the flaws in his own character.

WILLIAM SAFIRE, *Before the Fall*, 1975.

I've often thought with Nixon that if he'd made the football team, his life would have been different.

ADELA ROGERS ST. JOHN, in article by Joyce Haber, *Los Angeles Times*, October 13, 1974.

Perhaps [Eisenhower's] particular contribution to the art of politics was to make politics boring at a time when the people wanted any excuse to forget public affairs.

ARTHUR SCHLESINGER, JR., *Esquire*, January, 1960.

I was cooking breakfast this morning for my kids, and I thought, "He's just like a Teflon frying pan: Nothing sticks to him."

PATRICIA SCHROEDER, on Ronald Reagan, in article by Michael Kenney, *Boston Globe*, October 24, 1984.

Nobody shoots at Santa Claus.

ALFRED E. SMITH, on Franklin D. Roosevelt, 1936.

He forever perplexes and annoys. Every time you think he is about to show the statesmanship for which his intelligence and experience have equipped him, he throws a spitball.

RONALD STEEL, on Richard M. Nixon, *New York Review of Books*, May 30, 1985.

This is a man of many masks. Who can say they have seen his real face?

ADLAI E. STEVENSON, on Richard M. Nixon, 1956.

When I suggested to [William Taft] that he occupy a Chair of Law at the University he said that he was afraid that a chair would not be adequate, but that if we would provide a Sofa of Law, it might be all right.

ANSON PHELPS STOKES, in F.C. Hicks, *William Howard Taft: Yale Professor of Law and New Haven Citizen*, 1912.

Calvin Coolidge believed that the least government was the best government; he aspired to become the least President the country had ever had; he attained his desire.

IRVING STONE, "Calvin Coolidge: A Study in Inertia," in Isabel Leighton, ed., *The Aspirin Age: 1919–1941*, 1949.

Such a little man could not have made so big a depression.

NORMAN THOMAS, on Herbert Hoover, letter to Murray B. Seidler, August 3, 1960.

They said that there is definitely a distinction between real life and the movies, despite the fact that…President [Reagan] once mentioned as an example of inspiring patriotism a heroic act that turned out to have been from a World War II bomber movie starring Dana Andrews.

CALVIN TRILLIN, "The Gipper Still Lives," King Features Syndicate, November 23, 1986.

Nixon is a shifty-eyed goddamn liar.…He's one of the few in the history of this country to run for high office talking out of both sides of his mouth at the same time and lying out of both sides.

HARRY S TRUMAN, in Leo Rosten, *Infinite Riches*, 1978.

I never think of anyone as the President but Mr. Roosevelt.

HARRY S TRUMAN, letter to Eleanor Roosevelt nearly six months after FDR's death, in Robert H. Ferrell, *Off the Record*, 1980.

The Presidency has gained too great a lead; it has bewitched the occupant, the press, and the public. While this process has been apparent from John F. Kennedy on, it took the strange transformation of good old open-Presidency Gerald R. Ford to make it clear that the villain is not the man but the office.

Hardly had he settled in the ambiance of the White House than he began to talk like Louis XIV and behave like Richard M. Nixon.

BARBARA TUCHMAN, "Defusing the Presidency," *New York Times*, September 20, 1974.

Since [John F. Kennedy's] concern was so much with the appearance of things, he was at his worst when confronted with those issues where a moral commitment might have informed his political response not only with passion but with shrewdness.

GORE VIDAL, "The Holy Family," *Reflections Upon a Sinking Ship*, 1969.

I suspect there never has been a President who could move in two different directions with less time intervening than Truman. He feels completely sincere and earnest at all times.

HENRY A. WALLACE, ca. 1948, in David Caute, *The Great Fear*, 1978.

If he was a freak, God and the times needed one.

WILLIAM ALLEN WHITE, on Theodore Roosevelt, *Masks in a Pageant*, 1928.

Of all the masks in the long pageant of the generation that has led up through politics into the White House, this face of McKinley's, this placid, kindly, unchipped mask of a kindly, dull gentleman, is a cast most typical to represent American politics; on the whole decent, on the whole dumb, and rarely reaching above the least common multiple of the popular intelligence. In McKinley our politics reached its finest flower.

WILLIAM ALLEN WHITE, *Masks in a Pageant*, 1928.

Theodore Roosevelt was a giant; an overgrown personality. He was one of those sports that, appearing once or twice in a century or in an age, work tremendous havoc or harmony, and disappear apparently without spiritual progeny.

WILLIAM ALLEN WHITE, *Masks in a Pageant*, 1928.

Figuratively, he used to come out upon the front stoop of the White House and quarrel petulantly with the American people every day.

WILLIAM ALLEN WHITE, on William H. Taft, *Masks in a Pageant*, 1928.

Lyndon Johnson came into office seeking a Great Society in America and found instead an ugly little war that consumed him.

TOM WICKER, *JFK and LBJ*, 1968.

As in all true tragedy, we see in Richard Nixon's ruination the ravages of a failing to which all men are prey.

Nixon's sin, like all sin, was a failure of restraint. It was the immoderate craving for that which, desired moderately, is a noble goal.

GEORGE WILL, "Richard Nixon: Too Many Evenings," August 8, 1974, *The Pursuit of Happiness, and Other Sobering Thoughts*, 1978.

Coolidge is a faded memory, as unromantic as old commerce statistics, relegated to that remote corner of the national consciousness reserved for quaint and faintly ridiculous characters. This does no credit to the nation which under his stewardship enjoyed a 45 percent increase in the production of ice cream.

GEORGE WILL, "Calvin Coolidge: Pickles and Ice Cream," July 2, 1975, *The Pursuit of Happiness, and Other Sobering Thoughts*, 1978.

Reagan the actor never made anyone forget Barrymore, but Reagan the President, serenely confident and not apt to panic, is going to try to make Washington forget where others found the limits of the possible.

GEORGE WILL, "No Panic in the Oval Office," February 2, 1981, *The Pursuit of Virtue and Other Tory Notions*, 1982.

People say satire is dead. It's not dead; it's alive and living in the White House. [Reagan] makes a Macy's Thanksgiving Day float look ridiculous. I think he's slowly but surely regressing into movies again. In his mind he's looking at dailies, playing dailies over and over.

ROBIN WILLIAMS, *Rolling Stone*, 1988.

[Ronald Reagan's] philosophical approach is superficial, overly simplistic, one-dimensional. What he preaches is pure economic pap, glossed over with uplifting homilies and inspirational chatter. Yet so far the guy is making it work. Appalled by what seems to me a lack of depth, I stand in awe nevertheless of his political skill. I am not sure that I have seen its equal.

JIM WRIGHT, diary entry, June 11, 1981.

PUBLIC FIGURES

[Joseph Nye Welch] dressed like a middle-aged dandy. He was unfailingly courteous and at the same time shrewd and brilliant in his rapierlike thrusts and counterthrusts. He endeared himself to millions of televiewers during the hearings and inflicted severe damage on McCarthy in numerous exchanges, where McCarthy's blunderbuss crudeness was exacerbated by his losing skirmishes with Welch.

JOHN G. ADAMS, *Without Precedent*, 1983.

Read that Father Coughlin arrived in Boston surrounded by guards with rifles and tear-gas bombs. Apparently, he isn't going to be crucified without a struggle, and from recent indications I would say the good old rampant dominie's mind is turned around to match his collar.

FRED ALLEN, in Robert Taylor, *Fred Allen—His Life and Wit*, 1936.

She's supposed to be so feminine and all. Well, she's about as feminine as a sidewalk drill.

MARYON ALLEN, on Phyllis Schlafly, *Washington Post*, July 30, 1978.

[Howard] Cosell was crazy about being in the movie [*Bananas*]. He's a tremendous ham, a cartoonlike character. He comes across that way on TV, too. He's the same way if you're eating dinner with him—he broadcasts the meal.

WOODY ALLEN, *Sports Illustrated*, May 31, 1971.

[Eugene V.] Debs has a face that looks like a death's head...as the arch "Red" talked he was bent at the hips like an old old man, his eerie face peering up and out at the crowd like a necromancer leading a charm.

ANONYMOUS, *Los Angeles Times*, September 11, 1908.

Carrie Nation was responsible for legislation that required printing the alcoholic content on the label so that sick people would know whether they were getting enough alcohol to do them any good.

RICHARD ARMOUR, *It All Started With Columbus*, 1953.

In the bedlam of tragedy, melodrama and light opera in which we live, [John] Dewey is still the master of the commonplace.

C.E. AYRES, "Dewey and His 'Studies in Logical Theory,'" in Malcolm Cowley and Bernard Smith, *Books That Changed Our Minds*, 1930.

Elijah Muhammad has been able to do what generations of welfare workers and committees and resolutions and reports and housing projects and playgrounds have failed to do: to heal and redeem drunkards and junkies, to convert people who have come out of prison and to keep them out, to make men chaste and women virtuous, and to invest both the male and the female with a poise and a serenity that hang about them like an unfailing light.

JAMES BALDWIN, *The Fire Next Time*, 1963.

If Mr. Einstein doesn't like the natural laws of the universe, let him go back to where he came from.

ROBERT BENCHLEY, 1921, in Lois and Alan Gordon, *American Chronicle*, 1987.

He couldn't Master Mind an electric bulb into a socket.

FANNY BRICE, on her husband Nick Arnstein, ca. 1915, in Norman Katkov, *The Fabulous Fanny*, 1953.

[Bernard Berenson] was supposed to have invented a trick by which one could tell infallibly the authorship of any Italian painting, and he made an enemy of every owner of a picture he would not ascribe to Raphael, Giorgione, Tintoretto or Titian. He ranked with astrologers, palmists and fortune-tellers, while he was a pet of rich collectors.

VAN WYCK BROOKS, *The Confident Years: 1885–1915*, 1952.

The author of *Soul on Ice* has become a soul on the run—an unwilling refugee from his heritage and his mission—a latter-day man without a country.

SHIRLEY CHISHOLM, on Eldridge Cleaver, speech, Church Women United, Massachusetts, August 21, 1969.

He has no intention of living in the ghetto of heaven or even its suburbs.

JAN DARGATZ, on Oral Roberts, *Boston Globe*, January 20, 1987.

If you knew him you would know why we must honor him: Malcolm was our manhood, our living, black manhood! This was his meaning to his people. And, in honoring him, we honor the best in ourselves....However much we may have differed with him or with each other about him and his value as a man, let his going from us serve only to bring us together, now....And we will know him then for what he was and is—a Prince—our own black shining Prince!—who didn't hesitate to die, because he loved us so.

OSSIE DAVIS, in Eldridge Cleaver, *Soul on Ice*, 1968.

The Eleanor Roosevelt I shall always remember was a woman of tenderness and deep sympathy, a woman with the most exquisite manners of anyone I have known—one who did what she was called upon to do with complete devotion and rare charm.

HELEN GAHAGAN DOUGLAS, *The Eleanor Roosevelt We Remember*, 1963.

[Edward] Teller preached the gospel of world government with great charm and intelligence. I concluded my weekly report to my family with the words, "He is a good example of the saying that no man is so dangerous as an idealist."

FREEMAN DYSON, *Disturbing the Universe*, 1979.

Edison was a giant. He had gigantic successes and gigantic failures. He had a giant's zest, a giant's power of recuperation and, until his last years, a giant's vision. If he had invented only the electric light bulb, he would have been noteworthy. That he also gave us the microphone,

the kinetoscope, the phonograph and scores of other devices makes him one of the greatest inventors the world has ever known. Most important, he pioneered the industrial research laboratory, this making possible the technological progress which enabled us to put a man on the moon. Whether he would have thought such a project worthwhile is doubtful. But once it was achieved, he would have been ready with a dozen ideas for turning it to good advantage. Making invention profitable was his main aim in life.

KEITH ELLIS, *Thomas Edison: Genius of Electricity*, 1974.

I had never confused Martha Mitchell with Diogenes, never thought she knew a great deal about Watergate, never found her anything but a rather frowzy, excessive, blathering woman who never (until the Watergate break-in) said anything that I found remotely sympathetic. I did not expect to find her charming, and I did not expect to find her canny, and I certainly did not expect to find her moving. All of which she was.

NORA EPHRON, "Crazy Ladies, II," *Crazy Salad, Some Things about Women*, April, 1974.

[Eugene V. Debs] was *an agitator*, born of the first national awakening of American labor. The shame of servitude and the glory of struggle were emblazoned in the mind of every worker who heard Debs.

ELIZABETH GURLEY FLYNN, *Debs, Haywood, Ruthenberg*, 1939.

The most powerful influence on modern women, in terms of both functionalism and the feminine protest, was Margaret Mead....She was, and still is, the symbol of the woman thinker in America.

BETTY FRIEDAN, *The Feminine Mystique*, 1963.

Betty Ford, First Mama, was different. From the moment she "confessed" that she shared a bed with her husband, to the morning she read his concession speech in her slow, measured and dignified manner, the woman, who was born with the impossible stage name of Betty Bloomer, played only one character: Herself.

ELLEN GOODMAN, *Boston Globe*, January 18, 1977.

[A] myriad-sided nature; a creature of poetry and practical action; a dreamer, yet a doer of the world's work; a soul of storm while diffusing sunshine—a combination of wholly opposing characteristics…I love him next to my mother.

RoSE LEE GUARD, on Samuel Gompers, in B. Mandel, *Samuel Gompers*, 1963.

Sam [Gompers] was very short and chunky with a big head that was bald in patches, resembling a child suffering with ringworm. He had small snapping eyes, a hard cruel mouth, wide with thin drooping lips, heavy jaws, a personality vain, conceited, petulant and vindictive.

"BIG BILL" HAYWOOD, *The Autobiography of William D. Haywood*, 1929.

Ken Kesey did for acid roughly what Johnny Appleseed did for trees, and probably more.

WARREN HINCKLE, "A Social History of the Hippies," *Ramparts*, March, 1967.

It would be easier to take Dr. Leary seriously if he could overcome his penchant for treating LSD as a patent snake-bite medicine.

WARREN HINCKLE, "A Social History of the Hippies," *Ramparts*, March, 1967.

[Mary McLeod Bethune] had been as relentless as a frail plant pushing aside a heavy stone. And she had impressed upon the lives of countless young the stamp of her own indomitable character. She was a mighty mother to the youth of the world.

RACKHAM HOLT, *Mary McLeod Bethune*, 1964.

She [Margaret Mead] was a patron saint of the peripheral.

JANE HOWARD, *Margaret Mead*, 1984.

From seeds of his body blossomed the flower that liberated a people and touched the soul of a nation.

JESSE JACKSON, on Martin Luther King, Sr., November 15, 1984.

[John Dewey] imparted a new freshness, a sturdy and mature optimism, to the best spirits in contemporary society. As a psychologist he opened the mind to new vistas; as a student of ethics, he projected a radiant vision of modern conduct.

ALFRED KAZIN, *On Native Grounds*, 1942.

I do not think it altogether inappropriate to introduce myself. I am the man who accompanied Jacqueline Kennedy to Paris, and I have enjoyed it.

JOHN F. KENNEDY, France, June, 1961, in Evelyn Lincoln, *My Twelve Years with John F. Kennedy*, 1965.

Mrs. [Mabel Dodge] Luhan treated her husbands and lovers like possessions of the same order as the beautiful objects with which she filled her houses. She collected people and arranged them like flowers. Her New York *salon* was only one of many; wherever she went, she loved to combine people in startling new juxtapositions.

CHRISTOPHER LASCH, *The New Radicalism in America*, 1965.

[John Dewey's] name is used as a charm within the profession and an exorcism without. This is an interesting fate for the century's most consistent foe of dogmatism.

ALBERT LYND, "Who Wants Progressive Education?" in Reginald D. Archambault, ed., *Dewey on Education, Appraisals*, 1966.

Abbie [Hoffman] had a charisma that must have come out of an immaculate conception between Fidel Castro and Groucho Marx. They went into his soul and he came out looking like an ethnic milkshake—Jewish revolutionary, Puerto Rican lord, Italian street kid, Black Panther with the old Afro haircut, even a glint of Irish gunman in the mad, green eyes.

NORMAN MAILER, Foreword, *The Best of Abbie Hoffman*, 1989.

Old man Burbank is gone. Perhaps you remember him. He was a great man in a garden. His wife often said Luther had ten green thumbs. What a witty woman she must have been! Burbank was the wizard who crossed all those fruits and vegetables until he had the poor plants in such a confused and jittery condition that they could never decide whether to enter the dining room on the meat platter or the dessert dish.

GROUCHO MARX, "Letters to Warner Brothers," *Why a Duck?* 1971.

Mrs. [Aimee Semple] McPherson has the nerve of a brass monkey and the philosophy of the Midway—"Never give a sucker an even break"—is grounded in her.

MORROW MAYO, "Aimee Rises from the Sea," *New Republic*, December 25, 1929.

One of the shameful chapters of this country was how so many of the comfortable—especially those who profited from the misery of others—abused her….But she got even in a way that was almost cruel. She forgave them.

RALPH MCGILL, in Helen Gahagan Douglas, *The Eleanor Roosevelt We Remember*, 1963.

[Bucky] Fuller's prophecies had the density of fissionable material. They were unstable with respect to polite society.

DAVID MICHAELIS, *The Best of Friends*, 1983.

There was a kind of scientific poetry in [Bucky] Fuller's diction, a childlike simplicity in his manner. He had a voice like a Marine lobsterman: axiomatic, prosaic, yet oddly lyrical.

DAVID MICHAELIS, *The Best of Friends*, 1983.

Mrs. Nation thoroughly believes in her mission. She is a harmless paranoiac animated by a compelling obsession. She does not impress me as a fanatic. The word "zealot" best describes her. Dumpy in figure, plain but neat in dress, the possessor of a soft, melodious voice, she seems to be the incarnation of motherly benevolence.

SHANNON MOUNTJOY, *Muskogee Times-Democrat*, November 10, 1907.

Lindbergh...has shown that we are *not* rotten at the core, but morally sound and sweet and good.

MARY B. MULLET, "The Biggest Thing That Lindbergh Has Done," *American*, 1927.

[Harold Ross, editor of *The New Yorker*] was an almost impossible man to work for—rude, ungracious and perpetually dissatisfied with what he read; and I admire him more than anyone I have met in professional life. Only perfection was good enough for him, and on the rare occasions he encountered it, he reviewed it with astonished suspicion.

OGDEN NASH, in James Thurber, *The Years with Ross*, 1957.

It may be that [Aimee Semple McPherson's] autobiography is set down in sincerity, frankness, and simple effort. It may be, too, that the Statue of Liberty is situated in Lake Ontario.

DOROTHY PARKER, "Our Lady and the Loudspeaker," *The New Yorker*, February 25, 1928.

It is difficult to say whether Mrs. McPherson is happier in her crackling exclamations or in her bead-curtain-and-chenille-fringe style. Presumably the lady is happy in both manners. That would make her two up on me.

DOROTHY PARKER, "Our Lady and the Loudspeaker," *The New Yorker*, February 25, 1928.

When the revolution comes, it will be everybody against [Harold] Ross.

DOROTHY PARKER, as reported by Dale Kramer, 1951.

No man spoke harder against violence. Yet few men suffered more from it than he. His worship of a higher law got him jailed, stoned and stabbed. He led us into fire hoses, police dogs and police clubs. His only armor was truth and love. Now that he lies dead from a lower law, we begin to wonder if love is enough.

GORDON PARKS, "On the Death of Martin Luther King, Jr.," *Born Black*, April, 1968.

[Eldridge] Cleaver is armored with the brutal truth of Panther history, of hard streets and tough prisons. Yet a basic naivete makes him vulnerable at times.

GORDON PARKS, "Papa Rage: A Visit with Eldridge Cleaver," *Born Black*, February, 1970.

[Al Capone is a] pleasant enough fellow to meet—socially—in a speakeasy—if the proprietor were buying Capone beer: a fervent handshaker, with an agreeable, ingratiating smile, baring a gleaming expanse of dental ivory: a facile conversationalist; fluent as to topics of the turf, the ring, the stage, the gridiron, and the baseball field; what the police reporters call "a right guy"; generous—lavishly so, if the heart that beat beneath the automatic harnessed athwart the left armpit were touched.

FRED D. PASLEY, *Al Capone, The Biography of a Self-Made Man*, 1930.

[J. Robert] Oppenheimer wanted every experience. In that sense he never focused. My own feeling is that if he had studied the Talmud and Hebrew, rather than Sanskrit, he would have been a much greater physicist. I never ran into anyone who was brighter than he was. But to be more original and profound I think you have to be more focused.

I.I. RABI, in Jeremy Bernstein, *Experiencing Science*, 1978.

Darrow's journey among the barbarians of the universe encompassed the stammering years of America's young adulthood. His presence along the way added much to the tumultuous years into which the lawyer was, as he liked to think, haphazardly thrown. In spite of his feeling that reality is grim, that futility and dread of annihilation are requisites for straight thinking, and that poverty and relentless fate haunt mankind constantly, the infinite paradox on which he built all of his work and art predicted the hope "that tomorrow will be less irksome than today."

ABE C. RAVITZ, *Clarence Darrow and the American Literary Tradition*, 1962.

The success of Cesar Chavez is the success of a Mexican-American Catholic who taught the grape pickers that they are worth more, as workers and as human beings, than the system had ordained.

PETER SCHRAG, *The Vanishing American*, 1972.

People loved [Jane Addams] and she attracted many disciples. Partly this may have been because saintly figures are always rare, and in them we sense the dimly seen possibilities of the human condition. Partly it may have been her gift for communication and capacity to identify with almost any other person. She dealt effectively with practical questions and things unseen.

ANNE FIROR SCOTT, Introduction, in Jane Addams, *Democracy and Social Ethics*, 1964.

Al Capone was to crime what J.P. Morgan was to Wall Street, the first man to exert national influence over his trade.

ANDREW SINCLAIR, in Fred D. Pasley, *Al Capone, The Biography of a Self-Made Man*, 1930.

Other demagogues in the American tradition have been hay-wagon orators, shirt-sleeve spellbinders from park bandstands and town-hall platforms. But Father Coughlin was the first to discover how he could do the whole job by remote control, be free of hecklers, be just as sure of taking up the collection, and in addition have documentary proof by letter of what his audiences wanted. He boasted many times that he knew American public opinion better than any man alive. In his limited way he was right.

WALLACE STEGNER, "The Radio Priest and His Flock," in Isabel Leighton, ed., *The Aspirin Age: 1919–1941*, 1949.

All [Samuel Gompers's] vital expressions rose and fell together as though controlled by some inner mechanism. One moment, the mobile mask would be cunningly furtive and quizzical, then intimately and wistfully kind; then again it would glow with a self-righteous passion that in retrospect seemed grotesque. It was a congenitally histrionic face, and its outlay in spiritual energy bespoke an enormous vitality.

BENJAMIN STOLBERG, in B. Mandel, *Samuel Gompers*, 1963.

I want to say a few words about an infidel, the late Clarence Darrow. He did not live the way an infidel is supposed to live; he did not die the way an infidel is supposed to die. He was a thorn in the side of the good Christians. His life of unselfishness was an everlasting challenge to the Christianity-talking followers of Jesus.

MELVIN B. TOLSON, "The Death of an Infidel," *Washington Tribune*, April 2, 1938.

If you have a spark of humanity in you, read the life of [Eugene] Debs; then see if you are worthy to unlace the shoes of a Debs.

MELVIN B. TOLSON, "The Death of an Infidel," *Washington Tribune*, April 2, 1938.

Dr. [W.E.B.] Du Bois is essentially an artist turned into a scholar by the awful alchemy of racial prejudice. He is a black John the Baptist crying in the white man's wilderness.

MELVIN B. TOLSON, "The Oldest Problem in the World," *Washington Tribune*, April 8, 1939.

[Craig] Claiborne has co-authored a cookbook of Chinese recipes, so he might even be able to speak a couple of words of Mandarin to Chairman Mao—at least if the couple of words the Chairman wanted to hear happened to be words like "bamboo shoots" or "black mushrooms" or "hot and spicy."

CALVIN TRILLIN, "Mao and Me," *Alice, Let's Eat*, 1978.

Little wonder that the last years of [Bernard Berenson's] life had become so precious to him that, as he said, he would willingly stand at "street corners hat in hand begging passers-by to drop their unused minutes in it."

JOHN WALKER, Introduction, in Hanna Kiel, ed., *The Bernard Berenson Treasury*, 1962.

[Woody] Hayes, like bouillabaisse, is an acquired taste. But in an age of plastic politicans, professors professing the day's flaccid consensus, and tradesmen who can't do their jobs, Hayes is a glorious anachronism.

GEORGE WILL, "Woody Hayes: Kulturkampf in Columbus," November 19, 1974, *The Pursuit of Happiness, and Other Sobering Thoughts*, 1978.

Mrs. [Mary Baker] Eddy does not so deceive us for a little while, making life seem all the sadder afterward. She permanently proves that nobody, except by willful self-delusion, can possibly be unhappy.

EUGENE WOOD, *Atlantic Monthly*, October, 1901.

[To hear Eugene Debs] was to listen to a hammer riveting a chamber in Hell for the oppressors of the poor.

ART YOUNG, *On My Way*, 1928.

At the age of ten, young Alva's mind was an electric thunderstorm rushing through the fields of truth.

J. LEWIS YOUNG, *Edison & His Phonography*, 1970.

SHOW PEOPLE

I don't think that Jack Benny has an enemy in the world. He is the best-liked actor in show business. He is the only comedian I know who dies laughing at all of the other comedians.

FRED ALLEN, *Treadmill to Oblivion*, 1954.

The little girl laughter that erupts unexpectedly mid-sentence should not lure any observer into believing her to be childish, nor should the direct glance encourage any to feel that she is a hardened sophisticate. She is an honest, hard-working woman who has developed an unusual amount of caring and courage. Oprah [Winfrey] is making her journey at what might seem to be a dizzying pace, but it is her pace. She has set her own tempo.

MAYA ANGELOU, *Ms.*, January/February, 1989.

Fred Allen delivers [his jokes] in a flat voice like the wit of the senior dormitories. He is not merely an ingratiating comedian, but a deft one, with an extraordinary talent for making his points at a skimming pace.

BROOKS ATKINSON, *New York Times*, May, 1929.

The newest and in some ways most scarifyingly funny proponent of significance...to be found in a nightclub these days is Lenny Bruce, a sort of abstract expressionist stand-up comedian paid $1750 a week to vent his outrage on the clientele.

New York Times, May, 1959.

[Lenny] Bruce stands up against all limitations on the flesh and spirit, and someday they are going to crush him for it.

New York Post, March, 1964.

When Jack Benny has a party, you not only bring your own scotch, you bring your own rocks.

GEORGE BURNS, *Living It Up; or, They Still Love Me in Altoona!*, 1976.

Carol Channing's personality is bigger than life. To her, everything is show business. If she goes to the bathroom, it's an exit—when she comes out, it's an entrance. When she and Charlie go to bed at night she's so full of show business that Charlie has to keep applauding her until she falls asleep. And in the morning if he doesn't give her a standing ovation, she won't get up!

GEORGE BURNS, *Living It Up; or, They Still Love Me in Altoona!*, 1976.

Nobody ever dominated a theater like [Al] Jolson. And nobody was ever as quick to admit it as he was, either.

GEORGE BURNS, *All My Best Friends*, 1989.

[Jimmy Durante] spoke, and sang, in an unmistakable voice that sounded like gravel being mixed in a food processor, and he fought a life-long battle with the English language.

GEORGE BURNS, *All My Best Friends*, 1989.

This was some great act this guy had; Jack Benny carried a violin that he didn't play, a cigar he didn't smoke, and he was funniest when he said nothing.

GEORGE BURNS, *All My Best Friends*, 1989.

That was one of the main characteristics of Fanny, that the worst thing that could happen to her was to be mistaken for a sucker. The truth was that she was probably the biggest sucker the world has ever known. She had the acclaim of all of America: here was a woman who was up in the money; here was a woman who had jewels, fine clothes, furs, beautiful homes, everything she could want. But she always had some guy around to break her heart.

EDDIE CANTOR, in Norman Katkov, *The Fabulous Fanny*, 1953.

Sophie's [Tucker] entirely a night-club singer. Her style and material are hardly what you'd want at a Holy Name breakfast. But in the night clubs she's queen, she has no inhibitions and needs none, she sings the words we used to write on the sidewalks of New York. And you *hear* her.

EDDIE CANTOR, *Take My Life*, 1957.

[Fanny Brice] was like a liontamer when she walked on stage, and the audience were the beasts to be subdued.

GEORGE CUKOR, in Norman Katkov, *The Fabulous Fanny*, 1953.

[Marilyn Monroe] was very courageous—you know the book *Twelve Against the Gods*? Marilyn was like that, she had to challenge the gods at every turn, and eventually she lost.

GEORGE CUKOR, in Gavin Lambert, *On Cukor*, 1972.

If [Marilyn Monroe] was a victim of any kind, she was a victim of friends.

GEORGE CUKOR, in Gavin Lambert, *On Cukor*, 1972.

I tell you this neither in a spirit of self-revelation nor as an exercise in total recall, but simply to demonstrate that when John Wayne rode through my childhood, and perhaps through yours, he determined forever the shape of certain of our dreams.

JOAN DIDION, "John Wayne: A Love Song," *Slouching Towards Bethlehem*, 1968.

Timid? As timid as a buzzsaw.

GEORGE ELLS, on Hedda Hopper, *Hedda & Louella*, 1966.

He was the Bobby Fischer of locks.

DANIEL MARK EPSTEIN, "The Case of Harry Houdini," *Star of Wonder*, 1986.

[Jack Benny] may be the only great comedian in history who isn't associated with a single witticism. He got his biggest laughs with two exclamations—"Now cut that out!" and "Well!"

GARY GIDDINS, "'This Guy Wouldn't Give You the Parsley off His Fish,'" *Grand Street*, 1986.

Easily, Fred Astaire danced down staircases, on balconies and rooftops, in a living room, a ballroom, a garden. Easily, he danced on a wedding cake, on roller skates and on the ceiling. He kept his sweat offscreen.

ELLEN GOODMAN, "Fred Astaire: He Made It Look Easy," *Washington Post*, June, 1987.

[Houdini] was no master-manipulator of cards and coins, in spite of his ambition to be remembered as a wizard of dexterity. But he did manipulate life and circumstance and the imagination of men.

WILLIAM GRESHAM, *Houdini*, 1959.

Chaplin and Keaton developed wit and ingenuity the way other men develop muscles.

MOLLY HASKELL, *From Reverence to Rape: The Treatment of Women in the Movies*, 1973.

[Marilyn Monroe] catered to these fantasies and played these roles because she was afraid that if she stopped—which she did once and for all with sleeping pills—there would turn out to be nothing there, and therefore nothing to love. She was never permitted to mature into a warm, vibrant woman, or fully use her gifts for comedy, despite the signals and flares she kept sending up. Instead, she was turned into a figure of mockery in the parts she played and to the men she played with.

MOLLY HASKELL, *From Reverence to Rape: The Treatment of Women in the Movies*, 1974.

Mr. [John] Drew's face could only have belonged to an actor of his time. No senator, general, or emperor would have dared to look so classically

pre-arranged. He was larger than life—a Victorian overstatement like the Albert Memorial.

HELEN HAYES, *On Reflection, An Autobiography*, 1968.

Tallulah [Bankhead] was sitting in a large group giving the monologue she always thought was conversation.

LILLIAN HELLMAN, *Pentimento*, 1973.

For some people, [Bela Lugosi] was the embodiment of dark, mysterious forces, a harbinger of evil from the world of shadow. For others he was merely a ham actor appearing in a type of film unsuitable for children and often unfit for adults.

ARTHUR LENNIG, *The Count*, 1974.

If [Bela] Lugosi chews the scenery at times, he chews with grandiose vigor, and often that chewing provides our only nourishment. This much can be said; he is never dull. When he is on the screen, the film moves, and when he is not, the film is generally a species of the "undead."

ARTHUR LENNIG, *The Count*, 1974.

Like two other interdependent young rogues— Tom Sawyer and Huckleberry Finn—[Dan] Aykroyd and [John] Belushi understood that romance was the secret of friendship. The romantic sensibility they shared became the invisible bond of a highly visible, multimedia, comedy team.

DAVID MICHAELIS, *The Best of Friends*, 1983.

Humphrey Bogart was a brilliant smoker. He taught generations how to hold a cigarette, how to inhale, how to squint through the smoke. But as a kisser, Bogart set an awful example. His mouth addressed a woman's lips with the quivering nibble of a horse closing in on an apple.

LANCE MORROW, "Changing the Gestures of Passion," *Fishing in the Tiber*, 1988.

I loved [Groucho Marx's] lightning transitions of thought, his ability to detect pretentiousness and bombast, and his genius for disembowelling the spurious and hackneyed phrases that litter one's conversation.

S.J. PERELMAN, *The Last Laugh*, 1981.

What [Fred Allen] actually did was literally to stop the show whenever he was on the stage. It was Allen versus the rest of the company, and usually Allen won.

STEVEN RATHBURN, *Chicago Sun*, ca. 1928.

The Marx brothers were dedicated to deflation, not disintegration. They were quick-relief-pill dispensers, not cancer surgeons. Complete antidisestablishmentarians.

RICHARD SHEPARD, Preface, in Richard J. Anobile, ed., *Why a Duck?*, 1971.

Harpo, who never said a word, was the literalist of deed, a clown who, with pristine amicability, invariably ended up handing his leg over the arm of the men of pretension.

RICHARD SHEPARD, Preface, in Richard J. Anobile, ed., *Why a Duck?*, 1971.

[The Marx Brothers] can make you laugh,... and if you're half the worried, beset, polluted, traffic-jammed, debt-ridden, family-bugged citizen that I suspect you are, laughter is not something that you can toss off lightly.

RICHARD SHEPARD, Preface, in Richard J. Anobile, ed., *Why a Duck?*, 1971.

SPORTS FIGURES

[Knute] Rockne wanted nothing but "bad losers." Good losers get into the habit of losing.

GEORGE E. ALLEN, *Presidents Who Have Known Me*, 1950.

All weekend the country watched other losing coaches standing on sidelines eating their livers in deference to the official cant that it doesn't matter whether you win or lose. Not Woody [Hayes]. With what can only be called fool's courage, considering his age and physical condition, he responded like an Ahab determined to put one last harpoon into the white whale that was destroying him.

RUSSELL BAKER, *New York Times*, January 6, 1978.

He was a hard out.

YOGI BERRA, on Jackie Robinson, *New York Times*, October 25, 1972.

There was no way Jack [Nicklaus] could have made that putt, because I was standing right behind him mentally clutching his club.

PETE BROWN, *Sports Illustrated*, February 16, 1970.

But you couldn't ever mess up [Johnny] Unitas, he was different, he was cold. He never even acknowledged you were there. You could be yelling at him and he never even looked at you. He had no reaction at all. At least not until he completed the pass. Then he gave you that smile. That damn smile.

DICK BUTKUS, *New York Times*, January 30, 1979.

In what other country would this saga of Jesse Owens come true? American Negro youth ventures onto the stage occupied prominently by a Nazi dictator and steals the spotlight from him for a little while. The bright glow of romance hovers over such a feat.

The Crisis, September, 1926.

Just to think about [Dick Butkus] was intimidating. I'd come up over the ball and instead of thinking: "I'm going to take three steps at a 45-degree angle and cut him off and I'm going to knock his knees out from under him," I'd wonder: "What's he going to do to me now? Where is he?"

BILL CURRY, *New York Times Book Review*, July 31, 1977.

His best weapon is his chin.

RICHIE GIACHETTI, on Vito Antuofermo, *New York Times*, March 16, 1980.

I saw a young kid of an outfielder I can't believe. He can run, hit to either field, and has a real good arm. Don't ask any questions. You've got to get this boy.

NEW YORK GIANTS SCOUT'S REPORT, on Willie Mays, 1951, in Lois and Alan Gordon, *American Chronicle*, 1987.

Everyone says that he [Bjorn Borg] can't volley because his ground strokes are so good. He has learned how to volley. It is not textbook, but who cares. It is such hard work playing against him. So many balls come back. It's like taking too many body punches. You are tired by the end.

BRIAN GOTTFRIED, *New York Times*, July 4, 1980.

Seriously, coach [Vince] Lombardi is very fair. He treats us all like dogs.

HENRY JORDAN, *New York Times*, February 24, 1977.

He [Jim Thorpe] was the greatest athlete who ever lived. Lovely fellah. What he had was natural ability. There wasn't anything he couldn't do. All he had to see is someone doin' something and he tried it...and he'd do it better. He had brute strength...stamina...endurance. A lot of times, like in the decathlon, he didn't know what he was doing. He didn't know the right way to throw the javelin or the discus but it didn't matter. He just went there and threw it further than anyone else.

ABEL KIVIAT, *New York Times*, October 17, 1982.

There isn't enough mustard in the world to cover Reggie Jackson.

DAROLD KNOWLES, on famous "hotdog" label given to Jackson, *Sports Illustrated*, January 24, 1977.

He talks very well for a guy who's had two fingers in his mouth all his life.

GENE MAUCH, on Don Drysdale as sports announcer, *New York Times*, June 25, 1979.

After watching [Bill] Bradley play several times, even when he was eighteen, it seemed to me that I had been watching all the possibilities of the game that I had ever imagined, and then some. His play was integral. There was nothing missing.

JOHN MCPHEE, *A Sense of Where You Are*, 1965.

When he [Jack Nicklaus] plays well, he wins. When he plays badly, he finishes second. When he plays terrible, he finishes third.

JOHNNY MILLER, *Sports Illustrated*, September 10, 1973.

To me, and to many sports fans around the world, Muhammad Ali has always been the champion. No fighter withstood his fire. His crown was wrested by a primitive law that sets man upon man for death. He refused that law for what he felt was a higher one.

GORDON PARKS, postscript to "Redemption of a Champion," *Born Black*, 1970.

[Jimmy Connors is] an animal as a competitor with a good nose for blood...more savage than anyone since Gonzalez. The vulgarness—the cursing, the finger, the stroking of his racket like he was masturbating—that's all part of it.

GENE SCOTT, *New York Times Magazine*, April 10, 1977.

Throwing a fastball by Henry Aaron is like trying to sneak the sun past a rooster.

CURT SIMMONS, *Sports Illustrated*, November 19, 1973.

When you tackle [Earl] Campbell, it reduces your I.Q.

PETE WYSOCKI, *New York Times*, November 5, 1979.

VISUAL ARTISTS

Mr. Stieglitz is very kind to us, providing these frequent fillips to our interest. There is none else in New York who strikes the same note. It sounds to us shrill and piercing above the heavy rhythms of the Avenue.

ELIZABETH LUTHER CARY, *New York Times*, April 12, 1912.

[Edward] Hopper's chief subject matter was the physical face of America. His attitude toward the native scene was not simple. He once said to me, speaking of his early years, that after France this country seemed "a chaos of ugliness." No artist was more aware of the architectural disorder and monotony of our cities, the dreariness of our suburbs, the rawness of our countryside, ravaged by industry and high-speed transportation. But beneath this awareness lay a deep emotional attachment.

LLOYD GOODRICH, *Edward Hopper*, 1971.

What is thought to be [Jackson] Pollock's bad taste is in reality simply his willingness to be ugly in terms of contemporary taste. In the course of time this ugliness will become a new standard of beauty.

CLEMENT GREENBERG, *The Nation*, April 13, 1946.

Although one of his long-standing fantasies was to open a house of prostitution, the fantasy role he chose for himself was that of cashier.

JESSE KORNBLUTH, on Andy Warhol, *New York*, March 9, 1987.

Giving a camera to Diane Arbus is like putting a live grenade in the hands of a child.

NORMAN MAILER, *Newsweek*, October 22, 1984.

It was as though he had cut up the sky, melted down a flower garden, tossed in some jewels and made it into glass.

HUGH MCKEAN, *The Lost Treasures of Louis Comfort Tiffany*, 1980.

[His] special triumph is in the conviction his countrymen share that the mythical world he evokes actually exists.

WRIGHT MORRIS, on Norman Rockwell, *Time*, July 7, 1986.

He paints the astonishingly complicated loneliness of the limbo hours in a coffee shop, like a glass-hulled boat trapped in the black ice of the city, lit by a slice of yellow light like stale lemon pie, and full of the sadness of a gray fedora, a red dress and a clean coffee urn.

Newsweek, on *Nighthawks* by Edward Hopper, May 29, 1967.

Rockwell Kent is probably the most versatile man alive. Now that I have written this and have remembered Kent's activities, the sentence looks like an understatement. He is so multiple a person as to be multifarious; sometimes (in spite of the physical evidence) I suspect he is not a person at all, but an Organization—possibly The Rockwell Kent Joint and Associated Enterprises, Inc. I have known him as a painter, pamphleteer, poet (in private), politician (a poor one), propagandist, lecturer, explorer, architect (he redesigned my home in the Adirondacks), grave-digger, farmer, illustrator, Great Dane-breeder, type-designer, zylographer ("wood-engraver" to the uninitiated), friend, and general stimulator. In all these capacities he has been publicized; he has even attained legendary proportions.

LOUIS UNTERMEYER, "Kent—the Writer," *Demcourier*, 1937.

WRITERS

Miss Lillian Hellman evidently knows the box where the fruitcake is hidden in the dramaturgic pantry, for she fills her plays with good, rich raisins and solid theatrical fare—a little indigestible, possibly, but awfully, awfully good.

ROBERT BENCHLEY, *The New Yorker*, December 23, 1939.

[Peter] Arnett became a soldier's reporter, following the Vietnamese troops into the paddies and jungles when few other journalists bothered. "He was like Kilroy," one of them recalls. "Wherever you went, Arnett was there."

MALCOLM W. BROWNE, "The Military vs. the Press," *New York Times Magazine*, March 3, 1991.

[It] isn't writing at all—it's typing.

TRUMAN CAPOTE, on Jack Kerouac, TV interview with David Susskind, "Open End," 1959.

[Jack Kerouac] was a man whose life was directed by what he felt under his skin, not inside his head.

ANN CHARTERS, *Kerouac*, 1973.

There in Oxford [Mississippi], [William] Faulkner performed a labor of imagination that has not been equaled in our time, and a double labor: first, to invent a Mississippi county that was like a mythical kingdom, but was complete and living in all its details; second, to make his story of Yoknapatawpha County stand as a parable or legend of all the Deep South.

MALCOLM COWLEY, *A Second Flowering*, 1973.

And one must bear in mind that with Langston Hughes Harlem is both place and symbol. When he depicts the hopes, the aspirations, the frustrations, and the deep-seated discontent of the New York ghetto, he is expressing the feelings of Negroes in black ghettos throughout America.

ARTHUR P. DAVIS, "The Harlem of Langston Hughes' Poetry," in Seymour L. Gross and John Edward Hardy, eds., *Images of the Negro in American Literature*, 1966.

It was the ponderous battering ram of his novels that opened the way through the genteel reticences of American nineteenth-century fiction for what seemed to me to be a truthful description of people's lives. Without [Theodore] Dreiser's treading out a path for naturalism none of us would have had a chance to publish even.

JOHN DOS PASSOS, *The Best Times*, 1966.

[e.e. cummings's] mind was essentially extemporaneous. His fits of poetic fury were like the maenadic seizures described in Greek lyrics.

JOHN DOS PASSOS, *The Best Times*, 1966.

I exaggerate, but it did seem sometimes that wind, rain, work, and mockery were his tailors.

WALKER EVANS, on James Agee, *Let Us Now Praise Famous Men*, 1941.

Like many born writers who are floating in the illusory amplitude of their youth, [James] Agee did a great deal of writing in the air. Often you had the impulse to gag him and tie a pen to his hand. That wasn't necessary; he was an exception among talking writers. He wrote—devotedly and incessantly.

WALKER EVANS, *Let Us Now Praise Famous Men*, 1941.

Even those who call Mr. Faulkner our greatest literary sadist do not fully appreciate him, for it is not merely his characters who have to run the gauntlet but also his readers.

CLIFTON FADIMAN, *The New Yorker*, April 21, 1934.

Miss [Gertrude] Stein was a past master in making nothing happen very slowly.

CLIFTON FADIMAN, *The Selected Writings of Clifton Fadiman*, 1955.

As a matter of fact [Sherwood] Anderson is a man of practically no ideas—but he is one of the very best and finest writers in the English language today. God, he can write.

F. SCOTT FITZGERALD, letter to Maxwell Perkins, June 1, 1925.

[Theodore] Dreiser may be as great as Michelangelo, or Tolstoi or Wagner, or less great or more. When you are beside a mountain you can't see its relative importance.

FORD MADOX FORD, "Portrait of Dreiser," in Alfred Kazin and Charles Shapiro, eds., *The Stature of Theodore Dreiser*, 1955.

Norman Mailer is one of the leading spectator sports in America.

MERV GRIFFIN, May, 1968, in Jack Newfield, *Bread and Roses Too*, 1971.

Charlie MacArthur was a card, all right, the wildest in the deck—changeable and always welcome—the joker who could magically fill an inside straight for anyone but himself.

HELEN HAYES, *On Reflection, An Autobiography*, 1968.

The wit was never as attractive as the comment, often startling, always sudden, as if a curtain had opened and you had a brief and brilliant glance into what you would never have found for yourself.

LILLIAN HELLMAN, on Dorothy Parker, *An Unfinished Woman*, 1969.

He's teaching me to write, and I'm teaching him to box.

ERNEST HEMINGWAY, 1922, on Ezra Pound, in Carlos Baker, *Ernest Hemingway—A Life Story*, 1969.

[Ezra] Pound's crazy. All poets are....They have to be. You don't put a poet like Pound in the loony bin. For history's sake we shouldn't keep him there.

ERNEST HEMINGWAY, in an article by Leonard Lyons, *New York Post*, January 24, 1957.

Old Corndrinking Mellifluous.

ERNEST HEMINGWAY, on William Faulkner, in Carlos Baker, *Ernest Hemingway—A Life Story*, 1922.

Emerson, Longfellow, Lowell, Holmes—I knew them all and all the rest of our sages, poets, seers, critics, humorists; they were like one another and like other literary men; but Clemens was sole, incomparable, the Lincoln of our literature.

WILLIAM DEAN HOWELLS, *My Mark Twain*, 1910.

Henry Adams, snob, scholar, and misanthrope....

ALFRED KAZIN, *On Native Grounds*, 1942.

But if Mencken had never lived, it would have taken a whole army of assorted philosophers, monologists, editors, and patrons of the new writing to make up for him. As it was, he not only rallied all the young writers together and imposed his skepticism upon the new generation, but also brought a new and uproarious gift for high comedy into a literature that had never been too quick to laugh.

ALFRED KAZIN, *On Native Grounds*, 1942.

He [Van Wyck Brooks] was a Ruskin come alive in New York in 1915, a sensitive, dynamic, brilliant young American who had found his standards in the great Victorian critics of materialism.

ALFRED KAZIN, *On Native Grounds*, 1942.

He launched a massive attack on everything this country held inviolate, on most of what it held self-evident. He showed how our politics was dominated by time-servers and demagogues, our religion by bigots, our culture by puritans. He showed how the average citizen, both in himself and in the way he let himself be pulled around by the nose, was a boob.

LOUIS KRONENBERGER, "H.L. Mencken," in Malcolm Cowley, ed., *After the Genteel Tradition*, 1964.

Henry Adams offers to his fellow Americans the richest and most challenging image of what they are, what they have been, and what they may be.

J.C. LEVENSON, *The Mind and Art of Henry Adams*, 1957.

Morris Bishop was *always* unpredictable in his choice of subjects when it came to verse. Which is why I take it for truth that one day in Ithaca he set out to buy a loaf of bread...and returned wearing a new beret and driving a new white Jaguar.

DAVID McCORD, *The Best of Bishop*, 1980.

Sexual congress in a Mailer novel is always a matter of strenuous endeavor, rather like mountain climbing—a matter of straining after achievement.

KATE MILLETT, *Sexual Politics*, 1969.

[Norman] Mailer's sexual journalism reads like the sporting news grafted onto a series of war dispatches.

KATE MILLETT, *Washington Post*, July 30, 1970.

[E]very so often [Don Marquis] would turn on some particular fog of hooey and cut it with a blade that would divide floating silk. With a magic that seemed like that of Alice going through the mirror, suddenly we saw the whole furniture of affairs from the other side.

CHRISTOPHER MORLEY, Introduction, *The Best of Don Marquis*, 1939.

Maya's story conveys a deep mythological truth about suffering and redemption, about the journey a person takes into the experience and knowledge of self, where any potential gift anyone has to share with the world lies waiting to be discovered.

BILL MOYERS' INTERVIEW WITH MAYA ANGELOU, Public Affairs Television, 1989.

The presence alone of Faulkner in our midst makes a great difference in what the writer can and cannot permit himself to do. Nobody wants his mule and wagon stalled on the same tracks the Dixie Limited is roaring down.

FLANNERY O'CONNOR, "Some Aspects of the Grotesque in Southern Fiction," in Sally and Robert Fitzgerald, eds., *Mystery and Manners*, 1969.

Upton Sinclair is his own King Charles' head. He cannot keep himself out of his writings, try though he may; or, by this time, try though he doesn't. Let him start off upon an essay on a subject miles away from his own concerns, and in half a minute there he'll be, popping up between the sentences with a tale of some old but still throbbing grievance, or of some recent wrong that has been worked upon him.

DOROTHY PARKER, "The Socialist Looks at Literature," *The New Yorker*, December 10, 1927.

Dashiell Hammett is as American as a sawed-off shotgun. He is as immediate as a special extra. Brutal he is, but his brutality, for what he must write, is clean and necessary, and there is in his work none of the smirking and swaggering savageries of a Hecht or a Bodenheim.

DOROTHY PARKER, "Oh, Look—A Good Book," *The New Yorker*, April 25, 1931.

I dared not yip it out loud, much less offer it up in print. But now, what with a series of events that have made me callous to anything that may later occur, I have become locally known as the What-the-Hell Girl of 1931. In that, my character, I may say that to me [Theodore] Dreiser is a dull, pompous, dated, and darned near ridiculous writer. All right. Go on and bring on your lightning bolts.

DOROTHY PARKER, "Words, Words, Words," *The New Yorker*, May 30, 1931.

With his great bulk, there was a spirit that was solid and delicate, giant-like and gentle. [Heywood Broun] was a gallant knight who smiled at his own gallantries and his own generosities.

EDWARD G. ROBINSON, in John L. Lewis, *Heywood Broun as He Seemed to Us*, 1940.

Not a word. Not a word about that misguided woman.

JOHN D. ROCKEFELLER, on Ida Tarbell's *The History of the Standard Oil Company*, in Ida M. Tarbell, *All in a Day's Work*, 1939.

[F. Scott Fitzgerald] was our darling, our genius, our fool. Let the young people consider his untypical case with admiration but great caution;

with qualms and a respect for fate, without fatalism. He was young to the bitter end.

PAUL ROSENFELD, "F. Scott Fitzgerald," *Men Seen: Twenty-Four Modern Authors*, 1925.

He is a poet of place, creating wonder from common things, finding miraculous the true apprehension of the ordinary experience.

GRACE SCHULMAN, "Mark Van Doren as an American," *The Nation*, October 15, 1973.

He lent himself to anecdote. Because of this, and because his personal qualities were large in scale and included a formidable charm and magnetism, the serious and inspired work that he did as an editor tended at times to be lost sight of.

WILLIAM SHAWN, on Harold Ross, in Brendan Gill, *Here at The New Yorker*, 1975.

Humorists are often unhappy men and satirists downright miserable, but S.J. Perelman was a cheery soul who, when he flew into one of his exalted rages, seemed to have the gift of tongues.

PAUL THEROUX, Introduction, in S.J. Perelman, *The Last Laugh*, 1981.

A satirist seems a sour and forbidding figure—a mocker, a pessimist, a grudge-bearer, a smirker, something of a curmudgeon, perhaps with a streak of cruelty, who, in inviting the reader to jeer at his victim, never misses a trick or withholds a nudge.

PAUL THEROUX, Introduction, in S.J. Perelman, *The Last Laugh*, 1981.

[Edna St. Vincent Millay's] elements were surely fire and water: she was self-consuming, and self-drowned.

DOROTHY THOMPSON, *The Courage to Be Happy*, 1957.

He resigned the way other men went home to dinner.

JAMES THURBER, on Alexander Woollcott, *The Years with Ross*, 1957.

He loved to make everybody mad, and used insults the way other people use simple declarative sentences.

JAMES THURBER, on Alexander Woollcott, *The Years with Ross*, 1957.

[Thomas] Wolfe is one of the men whose life and work keep me from committing suicide. No man has pictured so vividly an iron steed thundering across a continent, moving through the illimitable reaches of Time.

MELVIN B. TOLSON, "Fellow Travelers in Dixie," *Washington Tribune*, September 2, 1939.

Mr. [Richard] Wright has faith in the Negro underdog. He does not scorn Sambo and Aunt Hagar. His attitude is antipodally different from that of our 2x4 upper-class Negro snobs. Mr. Wright is not interested in "The Talented Tenth." He is concerned with black humanity. There is a sermon in *Native Son* for every Negro preacher in America. There is a lesson in it for every Negro teacher.

MELVIN B. TOLSON, "Richard Wright, the Negro
Emancipator: His Tribute to the *Washington Tribune*,"
Washington Tribune, April 6, 1940.

Tarbell is remembered as the journalist who bested the robber barons in a fair fight and scotched the reptilian principle of special privilege that they had attempted to substitute for the historic American principle of equal opportunity.

MARY E. TOMKINS, *Ida M. Tarbell*, 1974.

Muckraking crusader for the middle class, liberated New Woman who yet remained womanly, promoter of the values of Old America, and a person of unquestioned integrity, she was a sort of national maiden aunt.

MARY E. TOMKINS, *Ida M. Tarbell*, 1974.

Right off, it must be noted that only a total egotist could have written a book which has no subject other than Henry Miller in all his sweet monotony. Like shadows in a solipsist's daydream, the other characters flit through the narrative, playing straight to the relentless old exhibitionist whose routine has not changed in nearly half a century.

GORE VIDAL, "The *Sexus* of Henry Miller," *Book Week*,
August 1, 1965.

Religion, as generally practiced by the Americans of [H.L. Mencken's] day, he saw as a Great Wall of China designed to keep civilization out while barbarism might flourish within the gates. He himself was a resolute breacher of the Great Wall, and to the extent that some civilization has got through, he is one of the few Americans we can thank. Plainly, so clear and hard a writer would not be allowed in the mainstream press of today, and those who think that they would like him back would be the first to censor and censure him.

GORE VIDAL, "The Essential Mencken," *The Nation*,
August 26/September 2, 1991.

[Van Wyck Brooks's] career was one long sustained attempt to realize a community of art and letters working and located at the very heart of American civilization. During his lifetime American literature came of age, and it did so to the accompaniment of his voice exhorting writers to meet their responsibility with courage and dignity—and with pride in their membership in a great communty.

JAMES R. VITELLI, *Van Wyck Brooks*, 1969.

Since Miriam sang of deliverance and triumph by the Red Sea, the Semitic race has had no braver singer.

JOHN GREENLEAF WHITTIER, in H.E. Jacob, *The World of
Emma Lazarus*, 1949.

Poe gave the sense for the first time in America that literature is *serious*, not a matter of courtesy but of truth.

WILLIAM CARLOS WILLIAMS, "Edgar Allan Poe," *In the
American Grain*, 1925.

He [John Dos Passos] is perhaps the first really important writer to have succeeded in using colloquial American for a novel of the highest artistic seriousness.

EDMUND WILSON, review of *The 42nd Parallel*, *The New
Republic*, 1930.

Mr. [Logan Pearsall] Smith, with his dear eccentric spinsters with whom he loves to take tea and about whom, after their deaths, he writes droll but unsympathetic memoirs, with his rummaging in old English country houses for hitherto unpublished documents of mild antiquarian interest, is the ghost of James's Passionate Pilgrim, himself a little spectral in his prime, the last and faintest incarnation of Eliot's Mr. Prufrock, who has forgotten even the eagles and the trumpets and the mermaids riding seaward on the waves.

EDMUND WILSON, *The Bit Between My Teeth*, 1965.

In my opinion Carl Sandburg is the worst thing that has happened to Lincoln since Booth shot him.

EDMUND WILSON, letter to John Dos Passos, April 30,
1953, in *Letters on Literature and Politics: 1912–1972*,
1977.

[Henry] Adams, in brief, did not care for truth, unless it was amusing; for he was a modern nihilist, and hence a hedonist or nothing.

YVOR WINTERS, *The Anatomy of Nonsense*, 1943.

The Arts

See also **Americans on Americans**—Musicians and Dancers, Show People, Visual Artists, Writers; **The Human Condition**—Creativity, Imagination, Perception, Talent; **Popular Culture**; **Science and Technology**; **Social Issues**—Censorship, Pornography and Obscenity; **Work**—Architects, Artists, Writers

True art selects and paraphrases, but seldom gives a verbatim translation.

THOMAS BAILEY ALDRICH, "Leaves from a Notebook," *Ponkapog Papers*, 1903.

Art distills sensation and embodies it with enhanced meaning in memorable form—or else it is not art.

JACQUES BARZUN, *The House of Intellect*, 1959.

Pop art is the inedible raised to the unspeakable.

LEONARD BASKIN, *Publishers Weekly*, April 5, 1965.

Black art has always existed. It just hasn't been looked for in the right places.

ROMARE BEARDEN, interview, *Encore*, October, 1972.

Art is the soul of a people.

ROMARE BEARDEN, interview, *Encore*, October, 1972.

Art strives for form, and hopes for beauty.

GEORGE BELLOWS, in Stanley Walker, *City Editor*, 1934.

Art obeys the opposite of Gresham's law: Quality drives out quantity.

DANIEL BOORSTIN, *Hidden History*, 1987.

There is no known device for artistic contraception.

DANIEL BOORSTIN, *Hidden History*, 1987.

Life is a copycat and can be bullied into following the master artist who bids it come to heel.

HEYWOOD BROUN, "Nature the Copycat," *It Seems to Me*, 1935.

I don't know anything about art, but I know what I like.

Popular saying, in Gelett Burgess, *Are You a Bromide?*, 1907.

What was any art but a mould in which to imprison for a moment the shining elusive element which is life itself—life hurrying past us and running away, too strong to stop, too sweet to lose.

WILLA CATHER, *The Song of the Lark*, 1915.

Religion and art spring from the same root and are close kin. Economics and art are strangers.

WILLA CATHER, *On Writing*, 1949.

The truest expression of a people is in its dances and its music.

AGNES DE MILLE, "Do I Hear a Waltz?" *New York Times Magazine*, May 11, 1975.

Art is the stored honey of the human soul, gathered on wings of misery and travail.

THEODORE DREISER, *Life, Art and America*, 1917.

No poet, no artist of any art, has his complete meaning alone. His significance, his appreciation, is the appreciation of his relation to the dead poets and artists.... You must set him, for contrast and comparison, among the dead.

T.S. ELIOT, "Tradition and the Individual Talent," *The Sacred Wood*, 1919.

Life is as the sea, art a ship in which man conquers life's crushing formlessness, reducing it to a course, a series of swells, tides and wind currents inscribed on a chart.

RALPH ELLISON, *Shadow and Act*, 1964.

We look too much to museums. The sun coming up in the morning is enough.

RALPH ELLISON, interview, *Ebony*, November, 1975.

Among the most truly responsible for all people are artists and revolutionaries, for they most of all are prepared to pay with their lives.

ANNE FREMANTLE, Introduction, in Fred C. Giffin, ed., *Woman as Revolutionary*, 1973.

I usually start with a repulsive character and go on from there.

CHESTER GOULD, on his Dick Tracy cartoons, *New York Daily News*, December 18, 1955.

We rely upon the poets, the philosophers, and the playwrights to articulate what most of us can only feel, in joy or sorrow. They illuminate the thoughts for which we only grope; they give us the strength and balm we cannot find in ourselves. Whenever I feel my courage wavering I rush to them. They give me the wisdom of acceptance, the will and resilience to push on.

HELEN HAYES, *A Gift of Joy*, 1965.

I cry out for order and find it only in art.

HELEN HAYES, *On Reflection, An Autobiography*, 1968.

[W]hat is necessary for art in America, as in any land, is first an appreciation of the great ideas native to the country and then the achievement of the masterly freedom in expressing them. Take any American and develop his mind and soul and heart to the fullest by the right work and the right study, and then let him find through this training the utmost freedom of expression, a fluid technique which will respond to every inspiration and enthusiasm which thrills him, and without question his art will be characteristically American, whatever the subject.

ROBERT HENRI, in Hershel B. Chipp, ed., *Theories of Modern Art*, 1909.

Art is a staple of mankind—never a by-product of elitism. So urgent, so utterly linked with the pulse of feeling that it becomes the singular sign of life when every other aspect of civilization fails....Like hunger and sex, it is a disposition of the human cell—a marvelous fiction of the brain which recreates itself as something as mysterious as *mind*. Art is consistent with every aspect of every day in the life of every people.

JAMAKE HIGHWATER, *Fodor's Indian America*, 1975.

Art *is* an act of attempted justice and its responsible exercise stirs the ultimate issues when it cannot decide them.

WILLIAM ERNEST HOCKING, *Strength of Men and Nations*, 1959.

Art is not a thing: it is a way.

ELBERT HUBBARD, *One Thousand and One Epigrams*, 1911.

Great art is an instant arrested in eternity.

JAMES GIBBONS HUNEKER, *The Pathos of Distance*, 1913.

Art is nothing more than the shadow of humanity.

ATTRIBUTED TO HENRY JAMES.

In art economy is always beauty.

HENRY JAMES, "The Altar of the Dead," *Prefaces*, 1907–1909.

It is art that *makes* life, makes interest, makes importance, for our consideration and application of these things, and I know of no substitute whatever for the force and beauty of its process.

HENRY JAMES, letter to H.G. Wells, July 10, 1915.

Art is the window to man's soul. Without it, he would never be able to see beyond his immediate world; nor could the world see the man within.

CLAUDIA ("LADY BIRD") JOHNSON, speech, Museum of Modern Art, New York City, *New York Times*, May 25, 1964.

Irresponsibility is part of the pleasure of all art, it is the part the schools cannot recognize.

PAULINE KAEL, "Movies as Opera," *Going Steady*, 1968.

[A]dvertising determines what is accepted as art.

PAULINE KAEL, *Kiss Kiss Bang Bang*, 1968.

True art is eternal, but it is not stationary.

OTTO H. KAHN, *Of Many Things*, 1926.

Art changes all the time, but it never "improves." It may go down, or up, but it never improves as technology and medicine improve.

ALFRED KAZIN, "Art on Trial," *Harper's*, October, 1967.

We must never forget that art is not a form of propaganda; it is a form of truth.

JOHN F. KENNEDY, speech, Amherst College, Massachusetts, October 26, 1963.

Art must unquestionably have a social value; that is, as a potential means of communication it must be addressed, and in comprehensible terms, to the understanding of mankind.

ROCKWELL KENT, *It's Me O Lord*, 1955.

Art is the objectification of feeling.

SUSANNE K. LANGER, *Mind, An Essay on Human Feeling*, 1967.

Art cannot disdain the gift of the natural irony, of a transfiguring imagination, or rhapsodic Biblical speech, of dynamic musical swing, of cosmic emotion such as only the gifted pagans knew, of a return to nature, not by way of the forced and worn formula of Romanticism, but through the closeness of an imagination that has never broken kinship with nature. Art must accept such gifts, and revaluate the giver.

ALAIN LOCKE, on need to recognize black artists, "Negro Youth Speaks," *The New Negro*, 1969.

Art is the desire of a man to express himself, to record the reactions of his personality to the world he lives in.

AMY LOWELL, *Tendencies in Modern American Poetry*, 1917.

[A]lthough art is regarded, at least among the business class, as a thing of unusual merit, art in the homes is highly standardized and used almost entirely as furniture.

ROBERT S. LYND and HELEN MERRELL LYND, *MIDDLETOWN: A STUDY IN CONTEMPORARY AMERICAN CULTURE*, 1929.

Music and art and poetry attune the soul to God because they induce a kind of contact with the Creator and Ruler of the Universe.

THOMAS MERTON, *No Man Is an Island*, 1955.

Art teaches nothing, except the significance of life.

HENRY MILLER, "Reflections on Writing," *The Wisdom of the Heart*, 1941.

As a result of the poverty of modern life, we are confronted with the circumstance that art is more interesting than life.

ROBERT MOTHERWELL, 1944, in Herschel B. Chipp, ed., *Theories of Modern Art*, 1968.

Art is much less important than life, but what a poor life without it!

ROBERT MOTHERWELL, letter to Frank O'Hara, 1965.

Art is a reaching out into the ugliness of the world for vagrant beauty and the imprisoning of it in a tangible dream.

GEORGE JEAN NATHAN, *The Critic and the Drama*, 1922.

Great art is as irrational as great music. It is mad with its own loveliness.

GEORGE JEAN NATHAN, *The House of Satan*, 1926.

To speak of morals in art is to speak of legislature in sex. Art is the sex of the imagination.

GEORGE JEAN NATHAN, "Art," *American Mercury*, July, 1926.

I am for an art that is political-erotical-mystical, that does something other than sit on its ass in a museum.

CLAES OLDENBURG, *Store Days*, 1967.

I think art, literature, fiction, poetry, whatever it is, makes justice in the world. That's why it almost always has to be on the side of the underdog.

GRACE PALEY, in Harriet Shapiro, "Grace Paley: Art Is on the Side of the Underdog," *Ms.*, March, 1974.

Art is a form of catharsis.

DOROTHY PARKER, *Sunset Gun*, 1928.

Good art weathers the ages because once in so often a man of intelligence commands the mass to adore it.

EZRA POUND, *Imaginary Letters*, 1930.

In an atmosphere of liberty, artists and patrons are free to think the unthinkable and create the audacious; they are free to make both horrendous mistakes and glorious celebrations.

RONALD REAGAN, speech to recipients of National Medal of Arts, *Newsweek*, May 13, 1985.

Nothing is so poor and melancholy as an art that is interested in itself and not in its subject.

GEORGE SANTAYANA, *The Life of Reason*, 1905–1906.

The vitality of a new movement in art or letters can be pretty accurately gauged by the fury it arouses.

LOGAN PEARSALL SMITH, *Afterthoughts*, 1931.

The art of our era is not art, but technology. Today Rembrandt is painting automobiles; Shakespeare is writing research reports; Michelangelo is designing more efficient bank lobbies.

HOWARD SPARKS, *The Petrified Truth*, 1969.

Now the Negro Problem is this: It is the question whether a youthful people living in the midst of an old and moribund civilization shall die with it or find themselves able to shake loose from its complexities and build their own culture on its ruins....This condition of doubt will find its esthetic expression in dissonances of sound and color, and such explosive comedy and tragedy as results from the struggles of a passionate people to escape the restraints of the Calvinist version of the Ten Commandments.

LEWIS THEOPHILUS, *Messenger*, July, 1926.

He knows all about art, but he doesn't know what he likes.

JAMES THURBER, *The New Yorker*, November 4, 1939.

All art requires courage.

ANNE TUCKER, *The Woman's Eye*, 1973.

Art is like baby shoes. When you coat them with gold, they can no longer be worn.

JOHN UPDIKE, "Alphonse Peintre," *Assorted Prose*, 1965.

ARCHITECTURE

The lobbies of the new hotels and the Pan American Building exhale a chill as from the unopened Pharaonic tombs....And in their marble labyrinths there is an evil presence that hates warmth and sunlight.

RUSSELL BAKER, *New York Times*, May 19, 1964.

There isn't much wrong with most of those summerhouses that a really good hurricane wouldn't cure [and] when it comes it may do for the Hamptons what Mrs. O'Leary's cow did for Chicago.

PETER BLAKE, "Summerhouses: Eyefuls and Eyesores," *New York*, August 24, 1970.

When they built this building they were afraid to say that beauty is truth for fear that it wouldn't be by the time it was completed.

DANIEL J. BOORSTIN, on the Library of Congress' 1980 Madison Building, *New York Times*, July 8, 1983.

The American dwelling house has been throughout our culture our greatest architectural distinction....American buildings, in respect of the comforts they offer, convenience, general livability, are far ahead of buildings produced anywhere else in the world.

JOHN ELY BURCHARD, in Arthur Goodfriend, *What Is America?*, 1954.

As a symbol, the tower, in its heyday, was vertical, silent, lonely and aspiring. It pointed toward the future. It was the architectural equivalent of tall Gary Cooper or the Lone Ranger, stalking the great American plain. The tavern and the marketplace, by contrast, are horizontal, noisy, social, matter-of-fact links with the past. They are precisely the gabby, confused, culture-bound community that Coop and the Lone Ranger always disdained to join.

ROBERT CAMPBELL, "Why Tall Buildings Are Held in Low Esteem These Days," *Boston Globe*, February 10, 1991.

The Solomon R. Guggenheim Museum...is a war between architecture and painting in which both come out badly maimed.

JOHN CANADAY, *New York Times*, October 21, 1959.

[A] mass of Victorian wiles and granite...that resembles a battleship in the rain and a wedding cake in the sun.

FRANCIS X. CLINES, on Old Executive Office Building in Washington, D.C., *New York Times*, May 17, 1985.

My job is to create an environment that relaxes morality.

ROBERT DiLEONARDO, on Atlantic City casinos, *Wall Street Journal*, January 10, 1983.

Let architects sign of aesthetics that bring
Rich clients in hordes to their knees;
Just give me a home, in a great circle dome
Where stresses and strains are at ease.

R. BUCKMINSTER FULLER, lines for tune of "Home on the Range," *Time*, June 10, 1964.

My ideas have undergone a processs of emergence by emergency. When they are needed badly enough, they are accepted.

R. BUCKMINSTER FULLER, on geodesic domes, *Time*, June 10, 1964.

It is the theater God would have built if he had the money.

HENRY GELDZAHLER, on preservation of Radio City Music Hall, *New York Times*, April 2, 1978.

A suburban mall turned vertical.

PAUL GOLDBERGER, on Marriott Marquis Hotel in Times Square, *New York Times*, August 31, 1985.

A noble space, unlike any other of our time, for it is both strong and delicate....It seems to call at once for a Boeing 747 and for a string quartet.

PAUL GOLDBERGER, on Jacob K. Javits Convention Center, *New York Times*, March 31, 1986.

Architecture begins where engineering ends.

WALTER GROPIUS, to Harvard Department of Architecture, in Paul Heyer, ed., *Architects on Architecture*, 1978.

Concrete is, essentially, the color of bad weather.

WILLIAM HAMILTON, *Gourmet*, December, 1986.

The architectural profession gave the public 50 years of modern architecture and the public's response has been 10 years of the greatest wave of historical preservation in the history of man.

GEORGE E. HARTMAN, in article by Barbara Gamarekian, "New Game in Town: Facademanship," *New York Times*, August 31, 1983.

An excellent job with a dubious undertaking, which is like saying it would be great if it wasn't awful.

ADA LOUISE HUXTABLE, on Marcel Breuer's design for an office tower above Grand Central Terminal, *New York Times*, June 20, 1968.

The building is a national tragedy...a cross between a concrete candy box and a marble sarcophagus in which the art of architecture lies buried.

ADA LOUISE HUXTABLE, on John F. Kennedy Center for the Performing Arts in Washington, D.C., *New York Times*, September 6, 1971.

No matter what an architect may be at home, he becomes a monumentalist when he comes to Washington.

ADA LOUISE HUXTABLE, "The National Gallery: Breaking the Role of Mediocrity," July 11, 1971, *Kicked a Building Lately?*, 1976.

This is born-dead, neo-penitentiary modern.

ADA LOUISE HUXTABLE, "The Hirshhorn Museum," October 6, 1974, *Kicked a Building Lately?*, 1976.

All architecture is shelter, all great architecture is the design of space that contains, cuddles, exalts, or stimulates the person in that space.

PHILIP JOHNSON, speech, Columbia University, 1975, *Philip Johnson: Writings*, 1979.

A great building...must begin with the unmeasurable, must go through measurable means when it is being designed and in the end must be unmeasurable.

LOUIS KAHN, on architecture for academia, *Fortune*, May, 1963.

Consider...the momentous event in architecture when the wall parted and the column became.

LOUIS KAHN, in John Lobell, *Between Silence and Light*, 1979.

The bungalow had more to do with how Americans live today than any other building that has gone remotely by the name of architecture in our history.

RUSSELL LYNES, *The Domesticated Americans*, 1963.

I don't think you understand just what my work has been here. The decorative part was all done by a New York firm. My work was structural.

JULIA MORGAN, on rebuilding of the Fairmont Hotel following 1906 earthquake, *San Francisco Call*, 1907.

I venture to predict that long after the public has wearied of Frank Lloyd Wright's inverted oatmeal dish and silo·with awkward cantilevering, their jaundiced skin and the ingenious spiral ramp leading down past the abstractions which mirror the tortured maladjustments of our times, the Metropolitan will still wear well.

ROBERT MOSES, on Guggenheim and Metropolitan museums, *New York Times*, May 21, 1959.

We want and deserve tin-can architecture in a tin-horn culture. And we will probably be judged not by the monuments we build but by those we have destroyed.

New York Times editorial, on demolition of Pennsylvania Station, October 30, 1963.

The building has all the requisites of a great aunt. She is neither very pretty nor elegant, but she has enduring qualities of character.

RICHARD OULAHAN, on Old Executive Office Building in Washington, D.C., *Smithsonian*, March, 1986.

It is not an individual act, architecture. You have to consider your client. Only out of that can you produce great architecture. You can't work in the abstract.

I.M. PEI, *Washington Post*, May 14, 1978.

It's like saying trousers with two legs is a design cliché.

JOHN PORTMAN, on criticism of his use of cavernous atriums, *New York Times*, October 12, 1985.

A real building is one on which the eye can light and stay lit.

EZRA POUND, *The Dial*, 1923.

We live in the time of the colossal upright oblong.

CARL SANDBURG, to Chicago Dynamic Committee, *Life*, November 4, 1957.

I realized that architecture was made for people who go about on their feet, that that is what architecture is made for.

GERTRUDE STEIN, "Raoul Dufy," *Harper's Bazaar*, December, 1949.

The dialogue between client and architect is about as intimate as any conversation you can have, because when you're talking about building a house, you're talking about dreams.

ROBERT A.M. STERN, *New York Times*, January 13, 1985.

In Hollywood's heyday the films were only celluloid, but the cinemas that showed them were marbled citadels of fantasy and opulence.

Time magazine, May 5, 1980.

I would have you a man of sense as well as sensibility. You will find goodness and truth everywhere you go. If you have to choose, choose truth. For that is closest to Earth. Keep close to Earth, my boy: in that lies strength. Simplicity of heart is just as necessary to an architect as for a farmer or a minister if the architect is going to build great buildings.

ANN WRIGHT, to her son Frank Lloyd Wright, in Frank Lloyd Wright, *An Autobiography*, 1932.

No house should ever be *on* a hill or *on* anything. It should be *of* the hill. Belonging to it. Hill and house should live together each the happier for the other.

FRANK LLOYD WRIGHT, *An Autobiography*, 1932.

Architecture is life, or at least it is life itself taking form and therefore it is the truest record of life as it was lived in the world yesterday, as it is lived today or ever will be lived.

FRANK LLOYD WRIGHT, *An Organic Architecture*, 1970.

DANCE

Ballet is woman.

GEORGE BALANCHINE, *Time*, February 6, 1978.

You see a little bit of [Fred] Astaire in everybody's dancing.

GEORGE BALANCHINE, *Time*, December 28, 1987.

I think of dance as a constant transformation of life itself.

MERCE CUNNINGHAM, *The Dancer and the Dance*, 1985.

The basic thing about dancing is the energy, and an amplification of it which comes through the rhythm, and if you lose that you end up in decoration.

MERCE CUNNINGHAM, *The Dancer and the Dance*, 1985.

It's difficult to talk about dance. It's not so much intangible as evanescent.

MERCE CUNNINGHAM, *The Dancer and the Dance*, 1985.

The truest expression of a people is in its dances and its music. Bodies never lie.

AGNES DE MILLE, "Do I Hear a Waltz?" *New York Times Magazine*, May 11, 1975.

Dance today is terrifying.

AGNES DE MILLE, *Los Angeles Times Calendar*, June 11, 1978.

Ballet is in the habit of using the fantasy gifts of serious composers and painters without depreciating them. It is by nature a form of poetic theater.

EDWIN DENBY, "Ballet—The American Position," April, 1947, *Looking at the Dance*, 1968.

I think one reason people like ballet is that nobody on stage says a foolish word all evening and just now that alone is an intense relief.

EDWIN DENBY, "Five Centuries of Ballet," April 23, 1944, *Looking at the Dance*, 1968.

Dancing produces few masterpieces and those few are ephemeral. They can't be stored away; they depend on virtuoso execution, sometimes even on unique interpreters. They exist only in conjunction with music, stage architecture and decoration, in transitory highly expensive performances. It is difficult to see the great dance effects as they happen, to see them accurately, catch them so to speak in flight and hold them fast in memory.

EDWIN DENBY, "The Critic," Winter, 1947, *Looking at the Dance*, 1968.

If we seek the real source of the dance, if we go to nature, we find that the dance of the future is the dance of the past, the dance of eternity, and has been and will always be the same.

ISADORA DUNCAN, "The Dance of the Future," ca. 1902, *The Art of the Dance*, 1928.

Nothing is more revealing than movement.

MARTHA GRAHAM, "The American Dance," in Virginia Steward, ed., *Modern Dance*, 1935.

We look at the dance to impart the sensation of living in an affirmation of life, to energize the spectator into keener awareness of the vigor, the mystery, the humor, the variety, and the wonder of life. This is the function of the American dance.

MARTHA GRAHAM, "The American Dance," in Virginia Steward, ed., *Modern Dance*, 1935.

Dance is a song of the body. Either of joy or pain.

MARTHA GRAHAM, *The Christian Science Monitor*, May 25, 1979.

And we love to dance—especially that new one called the Civil War Twist. The Northern part of you stands still while the Southern part tries to secede.

DICK GREGORY, *From the Back of the Bus*, 1962.

Dance is the most beautiful metaphor of existence in the world.

ERICK HAWKINS, *New York Times*, July 1, 1979.

Twentieth-century dance moved far from the traditional concepts of form and order. Its tenet was freedom, and its prerogatives were the inventions of new styles, forms, motifs and costumes.

OLGA MAYNARD, *The American Ballet*, 1959.

As Americans, we dance not only in obedience to the *danse d'école* of the Classic style but in the ballroom, on the street, and in ways which we have invented ourselves. It has become obvious that we are representative of America when we dance, and that often our dancing is the most eloquent and joyous converse our country holds with foreigners.

OLGA MAYNARD, *The American Ballet*, 1959.

American ballet had no endowment other than wit and energy, and no support except the charity of its patrons. It had a past bankrupted by a frivolous attitude toward dance, and no possibility of a future, unless it could establish itself in the theatre. It was without an academic standard of teaching and performance, and it had no company as a base of operations. There was no such patron of princely estate as had lavished dowries on ballet elsewhere. And the United States government proffered no state subsidy.

OLGA MAYNARD, *The American Ballet*, 1959.

The pioneers of modern dance were rebels, and rebels, by definition, must have antagonists. They found theirs in emptiness, the empty conventions of ballet and the simulated revels of show dancing.

JOSEPH H. MAZO, *Prime Movers: The Makers of Modern Dance in America*, 1977.

For almost three quarters of a century in American dance, the most intense, individual pursuit of dance expression has been going on, an almost prodigal invention that often has spent itself leaving no real relics....The security and status that have benefited European dancers have thrown them into an almost complete paralysis of choreographic imagination, but the perilous existence that keeps American dancers outsiders has kept them free. They haven't had to please anyone, repeat their past successes, reinforce societal norms, or refrain from shocking people. They have been free to dance.

MARCIA B. SIEGEL, *The Shapes of Change: Images of American Dance*, 1979.

Dancing is like bank robbery, it takes split-second timing.

TWYLA THARP, *Ms.*, October, 1976.

LITERATURE

The writer has a grudge against society, which he documents with accounts of unsatisfying sex, unrealized ambition, unmitigated loneliness, and a sense of local and global distress. The square, overpopulation, the bourgeois, the bomb and the cocktail party are variously indentified as sources of the grudge. There follows a little obscenity here, a dash of philosophy there, considerable whining overall, and a modern satirical novel is born.

RENATA ADLER, "Salt into Old Scars," *Toward a Radical Middle*, June 22, 1963.

A man is known by the company his mind keeps.

THOMAS BAILEY ALDRICH, "Leaves from a Notebook," *Ponkapog Papers*, 1903.

Poetry is not concerned with telling people what to do, but with extending our knowledge of good and evil, perhaps making the necessity for action more urgent and its nature more clear, but only leading us to the point where it is possible for us to make a rational and moral choice.

W.H. AUDEN and J. GARRETT, Introduction, *The Poet's Tongue*, 1935.

A good heavy book holds you down. It's an anchor that keeps you from getting up and having another gin and tonic.

ROY BLOUNT, JR., "Reading and Nothingness, Of Proust in the Summer Sun," *New York Times*, June 2, 1985.

The principle of literature is devotion to the particulars of life.

CAROL BLY, "A Gentle Education for Us All," *Letters from the Country*, 1981.

What is important—what lasts—in another language is not what is said but what is written. For the essence of an age, we look to its poetry and its prose, not its talk shows.

PETER BRODIE, *New York Times*, July 18, 1984.

Self-expression must pass into communication for its fulfillment.

PEARL S. BUCK, "In Search of Readers," in Helen Hull, ed., *The Writer's Book*, 1950.

There are only two or three human stories, and they go on repeating themselves as fiercely as if they had never happened before.

WILLA CATHER, *O Pioneers!*, 1913.

Every fine story must leave in the mind of the sensitive reader an intangible residuum of pleasure, a cadence, a quality of voice that is exclusively the writer's own, individual, unique.

WILLA CATHER, *Not Under Forty*, 1936.

Literature is a transmission of power. Text books and treatises, dictionaries and encyclopedias, manuals and books of instruction—they are communications; but literature is a power line, and the motor, mark you, is the reader.

CHARLES P. CURTIS, *A Commonplace Book*, 1957.

The Lord created Heaven and Earth and, as an immediate afterthought, writers.

FRED DE CORDOVA, *Johnny Came Lately*, 1988.

The poets were among the first to realize the hollowness of a world in which love is made to seem as standardized as plumbing, and death is actually a mechanized industry.

BABETTE DEUTSCH, "Poetry at the Mid-Century," in Helen Hull, ed., *The Writer's Book*, 1950.

Fiction keeps its audience by retaining the world as its subject matter. People like the world. Many people actually prefer it to art and spend their days by choice in the thick of it.

ANNIE DILLARD, *Living by Fiction*, 1983.

A book of fiction was a bomb. It was a land mine you wanted to go off. You wanted it to blow your whole day.

ANNIE DILLARD, *An American Childhood*, 1987.

In my own experience of the appreciation of poetry I have always found that the less I knew about the poet and his work, before I began to read it, the better.

T.S. ELIOT, *Dante*, 1929.

Literature is not, in itself, a means of solving problems; these can be solved only by action, by social and political action.

JAMES T. FARRELL, *Harper's Magazine*, October, 1954.

Art is simpler than people think because there is so little to write about. All the moving things are eternal in man's history and have been written before, and if a man writes hard enough, sincerely enough, humbly enough, and with the unalterable determination never, never, to be quite satisfied with it he will repeat them, because art like poverty takes care of its own, shares its bread.

WILLIAM FAULKNER, in Michael Millgate, "Faulkner: The Problem of Point of View," in L.W. Wagner, ed., *William Faulkner, Four Decades of Criticism*, 1973.

Poetry is a way of taking life by the throat.

ROBERT FROST, *Vogue*, March 15, 1963.

Poetry is the renewal of words forever and ever. Poetry is that by which we live forever and ever

unjaded. Poetry is that by which the world is never old.

ROBERT FROST, letter to R.P.T. Coffin, February 24, 1938, in Laurance Thompson, ed., *Selected Letters of Robert Frost*, 1964.

American literature, in order to be great, must be national, and in order to be national, must deal with conditions peculiar to our own land and climate. Every genuinely American writer must deal with the life he knows best and for which he cares the most.

HAMLIN GARLAND, *A Son of the Middle Border*, 1917.

I permit myself to think that American literature should somehow be considered quite apart from its effect on the sale of underwear or safety razors. . . . [not as] a narrow rill of text meandering down a wide plain of advertising.

HAMLIN GARLAND, May, 1924, in Jean Holloway, *Hamlin Garland*, 1960.

Reading is a joy, but not an unalloyed joy. Books do not make life easier or more simple, but harder and more interesting.

HARRY GOLDEN, *So What Else Is New?*, 1964.

A people's literature is the great textbook for real knowledge of them. The writings of the day show the quality of the people as no historical reconstruction can.

EDITH HAMILTON, Preface, *The Roman Way*, 1932.

For every book that survives the merciless judgment of time, there are nine hundred and ninety-nine rotting unread in libraries and nine thousand and ninety-nine that were never written in the first place.

MICHAEL HARRINGTON, *Fragments of the Century*, 1973.

Orr was crazy and he could be grounded. All he had to do was ask: and as soon as he did he would no longer be crazy and would have to fly more missions. Or be crazy to fly more missions and sane if he didn't, but if he was sane he had to fly them. If he flew them he was crazy, didn't have to; but if he didn't want to he was sane and had to.

JOSEPH HELLER, *Catch-22*, 1961.

He knew everything about literature except how to enjoy it.

JOSEPH HELLER, *Catch-22*, 1961.

All modern American literature comes from one book by Mark Twain called *Huckleberry Finn*.

ERNEST HEMINGWAY, *Green Hills of Africa*, 1935.

One is always a fool disliking a classic. Like disliking a nation one visits, it's the result of a blind spot, which goes away and leaves one embarrassed.

EDWARD HOAGLAND, "In Hazelton and Flying North," *Notes from the Century Before: A Journal from British Columbia*, 1969.

A poem is no place for an idea.

EDGAR WATSON HOWE, *Country Town Sayings*, 1911.

Does it afflict you to find your books wearing out? I mean literally....The mortality of all inanimate things is terrible to me, but that of books most of all.

WILLIAM DEAN HOWELLS, letter to Charles Eliot Norton, April 6, 1903.

Poetry is the bill and coo of sex.

ELBERT HUBBARD, *The Roycroft Dictionary and Book of Epigrams*, 1923.

Literature: The art of saying a thing by saying something else just as good.

ELBERT HUBBARD, *The Roycroft Dictionary and Book of Epigrams*, 1923.

As long as mixed grills and combination salads are popular, anthologies will undoubtedly continue in favor.

ELIZABETH JANEWAY, in Helen Hull, ed., *The Writer's Book*, 1950.

In this nadir of poetic repute, when the only verse that most people read from one year's end to the next is what appears on greeting cards, it is well for us to stop and consider our poets.... Poets are the leaven in the lump of civilization.

ELIZABETH JANEWAY, in Helen Hull, ed., *The Writer's Book*, 1950.

Literature is my Utopia. Here I am not disfranchised. No barrier of the senses shuts me out from the sweet, gracious discourse of my book friends. They talk to me without embarrassment or awkwardness.

HELEN KELLER, *The Story of My Life*, 1902.

When power leads man toward arrogance, poetry reminds him of his limitations. When power narrows the areas of man's concerns, poetry reminds him of the richness and diversity of his existence. When power corrupts, poetry cleanses, for art establishes the basic human truths which must serve as the touchstone of our judgment.

JOHN F. KENNEDY, speech, Amherst College, Massachusetts, October 26, 1963.

Until I feared I would lose it, I never loved to read. One does not love breathing.

HARPER LEE, *To Kill a Mockingbird*, 1960.

All books are either dreams or swords,

You can cut, or you can drug, with words.

AMY LOWELL, *Sword Blades and Poppy Seed*, 1914.

A poem should not mean

But be.

ARCHIBALD MACLEISH, *Ars Poetica*, 1926.

Every novel was suckled at the breast of older novels, and great mothers are often prolific of anemic offspring.

JOHN MACY, *The Spirit of American Literature*, 1913.

Literature exists for the sake of the people—to refresh the weary, to console the sad, to hearten the dull and downcast, to increase man's interest in the world, his joy of living, and his sympathy in all sorts of conditions of man.

M.T. MANTON, dissenting U.S. Court of Appeals opinion, *United States v. One Book Called "Ulysses,"* 1934.

Poetry has done enough when it charms, but prose must also convince.

H.L. MENCKEN, *Prejudices*, 1922.

Poetry is a comforting piece of fiction set to more or less lascivious music.

H.L. MENCKEN, *Prejudices*, 1922.

The people must grant a hearing to the best poets they have else they will never have better.

HARRIET MONROE, in Hope Stoddard, *Famous American Women*, 1970.

A book is the only place in which you can examine a fragile thought without breaking it, or explore an explosive idea without fear it will go off in your face....It is one of the few havens remaining where a man's mind can get both provocation and privacy.

EDWARD P. MORGAN, *Clearing the Air*, 1963.

When you sell a man a book you don't sell him just twelve ounces of paper and ink and glue— you sell him a whole new life.

CHRISTOPHER MORLEY, *Parnassus on Wheels*, 1917.

There is no such thing as a dirty theme. There are only dirty writers.

GEORGE JEAN NATHAN, *Testament of a Critic*, 1931.

As sheer casual reading matter, I still find the English dictionary the most interesting book in our language.

ALBERT JAY NOCK, *Memoirs of a Superfluous Man*, 1943.

The two worst sins of bad taste in fiction are pornography and sentimentality. One is too much sex and the other too much sentiment.

FLANNERY O'CONNOR, letter to Eileen Hall, March 10, 1956, in Sally Fitzgerald, ed., *The Habit of Being: Letters of Flannery O'Connor*, 1979.

The novel is an art form and when you use it for anything other than art, you pervert it.

FLANNERY O'CONNOR, letter to Father John McCown, May 9, 1956, in Sally Fitzgerald, ed., *The Habit of Being: Letters of Flannery O'Connor*, 1979.

There isn't a story written that isn't about blood and money. People and their relationship to each other is the blood, the family. And how they live, the money of it.

GRACE PALEY, in Harriet Shapiro, "Grace Paley: Art Is on the Side of the Underdog," *Ms.*, March, 1974.

We needed, and we needed badly, a book about Harlem Negroes by a Negro. White men can write, and have written, Heaven knows, such tales, but one never loses consciousness, while reading them, of the pallor of the authors' skins.

DOROTHY PARKER, "The Compleat Bungler," *The New Yorker*, March 17, 1928.

[We] can confidently say of American fiction that, while it may not be national, and may not be great, it will have at least the negative virtue of being clean.

BLISS PERRY, *A Study of Prose Fiction*, 1902.

It took me quite a while to realize that there were fashions in literary criticism and that they shifted and changed much like the fashions in women's hats.

ANN PETRY, "The Novel as Social Criticism," in Helen Hull, ed., *The Writer's Book*, 1950.

Literature is news that stays news.

EZRA POUND, *How to Read*, 1931.

Poetry atrophies when it gets too far from music.

EZRA POUND, *How to Read*, 1931.

Great literature is simply language charged with meaning to the utmost degree possible.

EZRA POUND, *How to Read*, 1931.

No man understands a deep book until he has seen and lived at least part of its contents.

EZRA POUND, *The ABC of Reading*, 1934.

Books, I say, are truly alchemical agents; for they, more than other of man's creations, have the power of transforming something common (meaning you and me as we are most of the time) into something precious (meaning you and me as God meant us to be).

LAWRENCE CLARK POWELL, *The Alchemy of Books*, 1954.

More often than prose or mathematics, poetry is received in a hostile spirit, as if its publication were an affront to the reader.

MICHAEL ROBERTS, *The Faber Book of Modern Verse*, 1936.

There must always be some pretentiousness about literature, or else no one would take its pains or endure its disappointments.

PAUL ROSENFELD, "F. Scott Fitzgerald," *Men Seen: Twenty-Four Modern Authors*, 1925.

Bad writing is in fact a rank feverish unnecessary slough. Good writing is a dyke, in which there is a leak for every one of our weary hands.

PAUL ROSENFELD, "F. Scott Fitzgerald," *Men Seen: Twenty-Four Modern Authors*, 1925.

Fiction, it seems, even living fiction, excuses just about anything.

HARRIET ROSENSTEIN, *Ms.*, July, 1974.

Poetry is the journal of a sea animal living on land, wanting to fly in the air. Poetry is a search for syllables to shoot at the barriers of the unknown and the unknowable. Poetry is a phantom script telling how rainbows are made and why they go away.

CARL SANDBURG, "Poetry Considered," *Atlantic Monthly*, March, 1923.

Poetry is the achievement of the synthesis of hyacinths and biscuits.

CARL SANDBURG, "Poetry Considered," *Atlantic Monthly*, March, 1923.

The degree in which a poet's imagination dominates reality is, in the end, the exact measure of his importance and dignity.

GEORGE SANTAYANA, *The Life of Reason*, 1905–1906.

To turn events into ideas is the function of literature.

GEORGE SANTAYANA, *Little Essays*, 1920.

Literature is the memory of humanity.

ISAAC BASHEVIS SINGER, *U.S. News & World Report*, November 6, 1978.

People say that life is the thing, but I prefer reading.

LOGAN PEARSALL SMITH, *Afterthoughts*, 1931.

Our novelists are the declared enemies of their society. There has hardly been a serious or important novel in this century that did not repudiate in part or in whole American technological culture for its commercialism, its vulgarity, and the way in which it has dirtied a clean continent and a clean dream.

WALLACE STEGNER, "The Wilderness Idea," in David Brower, ed., *Wilderness: America's Living Heritage*, 1960.

Poetry must resist the intelligence almost successfully.

WALLACE STEVENS, "Adagia," *Opus Posthumous*, 1957.

Vigorous writing is concise. A sentence should contain no unnecessary words, a paragraph no unnecessary sentences, for the same reason that a drawing should have no unnecessary lines and a machine no unnecessary parts. This requires not that the writer make all his sentences short, or that he avoid all detail and treat his subjects only in outline, but that every word tell.

WILLIAM STRUNK, JR., *The Elements of Style*, 1918.

[Humorists] lead, as a matter of fact, an existence of jumpiness and apprehension. They sit on the edge of the chair of Literature. In the house of Life they have the feeling that they have never taken off their overcoats.

JAMES THURBER, Preface, *My Life and Hard Times*, 1973.

The original of Walter Mitty is every other man I have ever known. When the story was printed... twenty-two years ago six men from around the country...wrote and asked me how I got to know them so well.

JAMES T. THURBER, letter to Mrs. Robert Blake, April 7, 1961.

As part of my research for *An Anthology of Authors' Atrocity Stories About Publishers*, I conducted a study (employing my usual controls) that showed the average shelf life of a trade book to be somewhere between [that of] milk and [that of] yogurt.

CALVIN TRILLIN, *Uncivil Liberties*, 1982.

To be a bestseller is not necessarily a measure of quality, but it *is* a measure of communication.

BARBARA TUCHMAN, speech, American Historical Association, December, 1966.

Temples fall, statues decay, mausoleums perish, eloquent phrases declaimed are forgotten, but good books are immortal.

WILLIAM VERNON, sermon, Western University, Quindaro, Kansas, 1900.

Fiction reveals truths that reality obscures.

JESSAMYN WEST, *Reader's Digest*, April, 1973.

I don't know which is more discouraging, literature or chickens.

E.B. WHITE, letter to James Thurber, November 18, 1938.

I think there is no such thing as a long poem. If it is long it isn't a poem; it is something else. A book like *John Brown's Body*, for instance, is not a poem—it is a series of poems tied together with cord. Poetry is intensity, and nothing is intense for long.

E.B. WHITE, "Poetry," November, 1939, *One Man's Meat*, 1944.

The essayist is a self-liberated man, sustained by the childish belief that everything he thinks about, everything that happens to him, is of general interest.

E.B. WHITE, Foreword, *Essays of E.B. White*, 1977.

The essayist arises in the morning and, if he has work to do, selects his garb from an unusually extensive wardrobe: he can pull on any sort of shirt, be any sort of person, according to his mood or his subject matter—philosopher, scold, jester, raconteur, confidant, pundit, devil's advocate, enthusiast.

E.B. WHITE, Foreword, *Essays of E.B. White*, 1977.

I was always keenly aware that literature demands not only all one can give it but also all one can get other people to give it.

EDMUND WILSON, letter to T.S. Matthews, 1960, *Letters on Literature and Politics 1912–1972*, 1977.

I would never read a book if it were possible for me to talk half an hour with the man who wrote it.

WOODROW WILSON, speech, Princeton University, ca. 1900.

MUSIC

Music was my refuge. I could crawl into the space between notes and curl my back to loneliness.

MAYA ANGELOU, *Gather Together in My Name*, 1974.

Always in the black spirituals there's that promise that things are going to be better, by and by.

MAYA ANGELOU, interview with Bill Moyers, Public Affairs Television, 1989.

All music is folk music. I ain't never heard a horse sing a song.

Louis Armstrong, *New York Times*, July 7, 1971.

Music is my mistress, and she plays second fiddle to no one.

Louis Armstrong, in Duke Ellington, *Music Is My Mistress*, 1973.

There is hardly any money interest in the realm of art, and music will be here when money is gone.

Louis Armstrong, in Duke Ellington, *Music Is My Mistress*, 1973.

What I like about music is its ability to be convincing, to carry an argument through successfully to the finish, though the terms of the argument remain unknown quantities.

John Ashbery, *New York Times Magazine*, May 23, 1976.

Music, not being made up of objects nor referring to objects, is intangible and ineffable; it can only be, as it were, inhaled by the spirit: the rest is silence.

Jacques Barzun, *Pleasures of Music*, 1951.

There's this mood about the music, a kind of need to be moving. You just can't set it down and hold it. You just can't keep the music unless you move with it.

Sidney Bechet, in article by Nat Hentoff, *Jazz Is*, 1976.

Einstein said that "the most beautiful experience we can have is the mysterious." Then why do so many of us try to explain the beauty of music, thus apparently depriving it of its mystery?

Leonard Bernstein, *The Unanswered Question*, 1976.

I know what these people want; I have seen them pick up my violin and turn it over in their hands. They may not know it themselves, but they want music, not by the ticketful, the purseful, but music as it should be had, music at home, a part of daily life, a thing as necessary, as satisfying, as the midday meal. They want to *play*. And they are kept back by the absurd, the mistaken, the wicked notion that in order to play an instrument one must be possessed by that bogey called Talent.

Catherine Drinker Bowen, *Friends and Fiddlers*, 1934.

My message to the world is "Let's swing, sing, shout, make noise! Let's not mimic death before our time comes! Let's be wet and noisy."

Mel Brooks, interview, *New York Times*, March 30, 1975.

A rock concert is in fact a rite involving the evocation and transmutation of energy.

William Burroughs, *Crawdaddy*, 1975.

When we separate music from life we get art.

John Cage, *Silence*, 1961.

Let no one imagine that in owning a recording he has the music. The very practice of music is a celebration that we own nothing.

John Cage, *Silence*, 1961.

It is better to make a piece of music than to perform one, better to perform one than to listen to one, better to listen to one than to misuse it as a means of distraction, entertainment, or acquisition of "culture."

John Cage, *Silence*, 1961.

One must be disinterested, accept that a sound is a sound and a man is a man, give up illusions about ideas of order, expressions of sentiment, and all the rest of our inherited aesthetic claptrap.

John Cage, in Marshall McLuhan, *The Medium Is the Message: An Inventory of Effects*, 1967.

If you can sell green toothpaste in this country, you can sell opera.

Sarah Caldwell, *New York Times Magazine*, October 5, 1975.

Thus it came to pass that jazz multiplied all over the face of the earth and the wriggling of bottoms was tremendous.

Peter Clayton and Peter Gammond, *14 Miles on a Clear Night*, 1966.

The greatest moments of the human spirit may be deduced from the greatest moments in music.

Aaron Copland, radio address, "Music as an Aspect of the Human Spirit," 1954.

What's swinging in words? If a guy makes you pat your foot and if you feel it down your back, you don't have to ask anybody if that's good music or not. You can always feel it.

Miles Davis, *Down Beat*, November 2, 1955.

No composer has yet caught the rhythm of America—it is too mighty for the ears of most. But some day it will gush forth from the great stretches of earth, rain down from the vast sky spaces of stars, and the American will be expressed in some mighty music that will shape its chaos to Harmony.

Isadora Duncan, "I See America Dancing," *The Art of the Dance*, 1927.

Playing "bop" is like playing Scrabble with all the vowels missing.
DUKE ELLINGTON, *Look*, August 10, 1954.

The artist must say it without saying it.
DUKE ELLINGTON, *Music Is My Mistress*, 1973.

Commercial rock-and-roll music is a brutalization of one stream of contemporary Negro church music...an obscene looting of a cultural expression.
RALPH ELLISON, *Shadow and Act*, 1964.

Music is the only language in which you cannot say a mean or sarcastic thing.
JOHN ERSKINE, *Reader's Digest*, April, 1934.

[Jazz is] the expression of protest against law and order, the bolshevik element of license striving for expression in music.
ANNE SHAW FAULKNER, "Does Jazz Put the Sin in Syncopation?" *Ladies' Home Journal*, August, 1921.

Jazz without the beat, most musicians know, is a telephone yanked from the wall; it just can't communicate.
LEONARD FEATHER, *Show*, January, 1962.

The word jazz in its progress toward respectability has meant first sex, then dancing, then music. It is associated with a state of nervous stimulation, not unlike that of big cities behind the lines of a war.
F. SCOTT FITZGERALD, "Echoes of the Jazz Age," November, 1931, *The Crack-up*, 1956.

Jazz I regard as an American folk music; not the only one, but a very powerful one which is probably in the blood and feeling of the American people more than any other style of folk music.
GEORGE GERSHWIN, "The Relation of Jazz to American Music," in Henry Cowell, ed., *American Composers on American Music*, 1933.

The [popular] song of today is machine-made, machine-played, machine-heard. It is a formula....It obeys every rule laid down...in search of speed, pep and punch. It builds up a musical literature of escape, of wish fulfillment, of vicarious sex experience, of whoopee. It is in itself a tonal aphrodisiac, providing a limited but effective vocabulary of love for a vast audience whose conceptions—and executions—of *love* are, if limited, effective.
-ISAAC GOLDBERG, *Tin Pan Alley*, 1930.

Ragtime is something that music did to the Negro and that the Negro did to music. It

began...in the restless feet of the black; it rippled through his limbs, and communicated itself to every instrument upon which he could lay his hands.
ISAAC GOLDBERG, *Tin Pan Alley*, 1930.

Rock was born in a flashback, a celluloid loop doubled back inside a time machine. The date was 1954; the place was Cleveland, Ohio; the occasion, the first broadcast of Negro race records to an audience of white teen-agers.
ALBERT GOLDMAN, "The Emergence of Rock," *New American Review*, April, 1968.

The Blues, the most convenient harmonic progression ever discovered...the most hackneyed, overplayed, obvious musical effect in the world, and yet in some curious way at times the most compelling.
BENNY GREEN, *This Is Jazz*, 1960.

Rock is a corruption of Rhythm and Blues which was a dilution of the blues, so that today's mass-marketed noise is a vulgarization of a vulgarization.
BENNY GREEN, notes for a Joe Turner record album, 1976.

The best way to get to knowing any bunch of people is to go and listen to their music.
WOODY GUTHRIE, *Woody Sez*, 1975.

Banality and self-deception are so integral a part of patriotic music that even in the few successful examples of the genre we must learn to avert our ears in embarrassment at times....How easy it is to produce when propaganda is the muse.
DONAL HENAHAN, *New York Times*, August 15, 1976.

When people hear good music, it makes them homesick for something they never had, and never will have.
EDGAR WATSON HOWE, *Country Town Sayings*, 1911.

Music is the only one of the arts that cannot be prostituted to a base use.
ELBERT HUBBARD, *The Roycroft Dictionary and Book of Epigrams*, 1923.

A dark man shall see dark days. Bop comes out of them dark days. That's why Bop is mad, wild, frantic, crazy—and not to be dug unless you've seen dark days, too. Folks who ain't suffered much cannot play Bop, neither appreciate it. They think Bop is nonsense like you. They think it's just *crazy* crazy. They do not know Bop is also MAD crazy, SAD crazy, FRANTIC WILD CRAZY—

beat out of somebody's head! That's what Bop is. Them young colored kids who started it, they know what Bop is.

Langston Hughes, *Simple Takes a Wife*, 1953.

Music remains the only art, the last sanctuary, wherein originality may reveal itself in the face of fools and not pierce their mental opacity.

James G. Huneker, *Iconoclasts*, 1905.

Blues are the songs of despair, but gospel songs are the songs of hope.

Mahalia Jackson, with Evan McLoud Wylie, *Moving On Up*, 1966.

It started with the moans and groans of the people in the cotton fields. Before it got the name of soul, men were sellin' watermelons and vegetables on a wagon drawn by a mule, hollerin' "watermellllon!" with a cry in their voices. And the man on the railroad track layin' crossties—everytime they hit the hammer it was with a sad feelin', but with a beat. And the Baptist preacher—he the one who had the soul—he give out the meter, a long and short meter, and the old mothers of the church would reply. This musical thing has been here since America been here. This is trial and tribulation music.

Mahalia Jackson, *Time*, June 28, 1968.

It is from the blues that all that may be called American music derives its most distinctive characteristic.

James Weldon Johnson, *Black Manhattan*, 1930.

Ghetto blacks..."speak jazz" (or blues or gospel) as their native tongue as Italians "speak opera."

Frank Kofsky, *Black Nationalism and the Revolution in Music*, 1970.

Music hath alarums to wild the civil breast.

Tuli Kupferberg, *When the Mode of the Music Changes*, 1968.

The tragedy in the interpretation of music of the past lies in the fact that it is confined to concert halls, congresses of musicology, or conservatory classes....Music needs air, sunlight, and liberty to be alive. It is only then that it will impart to us surprising secrets.

Wanda Landowska, *Landowska on Music*, 1964.

Music is our myth of the inner life.

Susanne Langer, *Philosophy in a New Key*, 1942.

The kids today are quite right about the music their parents listened to: most of it was trash. The parents are quite right about what their young listen to: most of it is trash too.

Gene Lees, "Rock," *High Fidelity*, November, 1967.

In his music [the Negro] gave voice to the character and quality of his existence, to his rage and the infinite variations of joy, lust, languor, growl, cramp, pinch, scream and despair of his orgasm. For jazz is orgasm.

Norman Mailer, *The White Negro*, 1957.

I want to hear screaming and hollering and kicking and biting. That's what the world's about today....Life is a bit chaotic, and I think jazzmen should express something of the way life is lived.

Charlie Mariano, *Down Beat Yearbook*, 1967.

Ragtime is a type of music substantially new in musical history....I am sure that many a native composer could save his soul if he would open his ears to this folk music of the American city.

Hiram K. Moderwell, *New Republic*, October 16, 1915.

Music is a form of spiritual carbon dating.

Lance Morrow, "They're Playing Ur-Song," *Fishing in the Tiber*, 1988.

I care not who writes the laws of a country so long as I may listen to its songs.

George Jean Nathan, *The World in Falseface*, 1923.

Music is your own experience, your thoughts, your wisdom. If you don't live it, it won't come out of your horn.

Charlie Parker, in Nat Shapiro and Nat Hentoff, *Hear Me Talkin' to Ya*, 1955.

Music rots when it gets too far from the dance.

Ezra Pound, *How to Read*, 1931.

If music could be translated into human speech, it would no longer need to exist.

Ned Rorem, "Composer and Performance," *Music from Inside Out*, 1967.

Music exists—not on canvas nor yet on the staff—only in motion. The good listener will hear it as the present prolonged.

Ned Rorem, "Pictures and Pieces," *Music from Inside Out*, 1967.

To the social-minded, a definition for Concert is: that which surrounds an intermission.

Ned Rorem, *The Final Diary*, 1974.

Drum on your drums, batter on your banjos,
  sob on the long cool winding
    saxophones.

Go to it, O jazzmen.

CARL SANDBURG, "Jazz Fantasia," *Smoke and Steel*, 1920.

Songs are like people, animals, plants. They have genealogies, pedigrees, thoroughbreds, cross-breeds, mongrels, strays, and often a strange lovechild.

CARL SANDBURG, *The American Songbag*, 1927.

A musical education is necessary for musical judgment. What most people relish is hardly music; it is rather a drowsy revery relieved by nervous thrills.

GEORGE SANTAYANA, "Reason in Art," *The Life of Reason*, 1905–1906.

Music has always had its own syntax, its own vocabulary and symbolic means. Indeed, it is with mathematics the principal language of the mind when the mind is in a condition of non-verbal feeling.

GEORGE STEINER, *Language and Silence*, 1958.

Music is feeling, then, not sound.

WALLACE STEVENS, "Peter Quince at the Clavier," 1923, in *The Collected Poems of Wallace Stevens*, 1954.

The trouble with music appreciation in general is that people are taught to have too much respect for music; they should be taught to love it instead.

IGOR STRAVINSKY, *New York Times Magazine*, September 27, 1964.

Music is indivisible. The dualism of feeling and thinking must be resolved to a state of unity in which one thinks with the heart and feels with the brain.

GEORGE SZELL, *Time*, February 22, 1963.

The great American music of the future will be a music to which America will listen and respond. But it will not be the music of Sitting Bull or Booker T. Washington—or even George. It will... like all great music, belong to the world. And the world will not be curious regarding the name and address of the composer.

DEEMS TAYLOR, *Of Men and Music*, 1937.

I don't give a damn about "The Missouri Waltz" but I can't say it out loud because it's the song of Missouri. It's as bad as "The Star-Spangled Banner" so far as music is concerned.

HARRY S TRUMAN, *Time*, February 10, 1958.

Bop is the shorthand of jazz, an epigram made by defying the platitude of conventional harmony; it performs a post-mortem on the dissected melody. The chastity of this music is significant. It shuns climaxes of feeling, and affirms nothing but disintegration.

KENNETH TYNAN, *The Observer*, May 8, 1955.

THEATER

The motion-picture theaters, on the other hand, were cathedrals that made the vaudeville theaters look like privies.

FRED ALLEN, *Much Ado About Me*, 1956.

Vaudeville could not vouch for the honesty, the integrity, or the mentality of the individuals who collectively made up the horde the medium embraced. All the human race demands of its members is that they be born. That is all vaudeville demanded.

FRED ALLEN, *Much Ado About Me*, 1956.

Dig. The only honest art form is laughter, comedy. You can't fake it, Jim. Try to fake three laughs in an hour—ha ha ha ha ha—they'll take you away, man. You can't.

LENNY BRUCE, ca. 1960, in John Cohen, ed., *The Essential Lenny Bruce*, 1967.

There was never anything like vaudeville. Except for the big stars, being in vaudeville meant doing three shows a day and five shows on Saturday and Sunday, often to half-filled houses. It meant carrying your whole life around in a steamer trunk, spending most of your time on trains or in hotel rooms so small that your shadow had to wait for you outside, cooking over illegal hot plates that had to be snuck into the hotel or eating in one-arm joints or all-night hash houses; it meant never being able to save any money and always being worried about being cancelled or getting the next booking, and it meant never, ever being home for any holidays and rarely seeing your family unless they were part of the act...but only if you were very lucky. I think that to most of us, probably the only thing that was worse than working in vaudeville was not working in vaudeville.

GEORGE BURNS, *All My Best Friends*, 1989.

When you are away from old Broadway you are only camping out.

GEORGE M. COHAN, in Fred J. Ringel, *America as Americans See It*, 1932.

Theater people are always pining and agonizing because they're afraid that they'll be forgotten. And in America they're quite right. They will be.

AGNES DE MILLE, in Jane Howard, "The Grande Dame of Dance," *Life*, November 15, 1963.

Generally speaking, the American theater is the aspirin of the middle classes.

WOLCOTT GIBBS, *More in Sorrow*, 1958.

It is best in the theatre to act with confidence no matter how little right you have to it.

LILLIAN HELLMAN, *Pentimento*, 1973.

One can play comedy; two are required for melodrama; but a tragedy demands three.

ELBERT HUBBARD, *The Roycroft Dictionary and Book of Epigrams*, 1923.

Everything in life is theatre.

MARGO JONES, *New York Times*, July 26, 1955.

Satire is what closes on Saturday night.

GEORGE S. KAUFMAN, in Robert E. Drennan, *The Algonquin Wits*, 1968.

The most alarming thing about the contemporary American theater is the absolute regularity of its march toward extinction.

WALTER KERR, *How Not to Write a Play*, 1955.

Comedians on the stage are invariably suicidal when they get home.

ELSA LANCHESTER, *Charles Laughton and I*, 1938.

Coughing in the theater is not a respiratory ailment. It is a criticism.

ALAN JAY LERNER, *The Street Where I Live*, 1978.

In all ages the drama, through its portrayal of the acting and suffering spirit of man, has been more closely allied than any other art to his deeper thoughts concerning his nature and his destiny.

LUDWIG LEWISOHN, *The Modern Drama*, 1915.

The theater is no place for painful speculation; it is a place for diverting representation.

H.L. MENCKEN, *Prejudices*, 1919.

Great drama is the reflection of a great doubt in the heart and mind of a great, sad, gay man.

GEORGE JEAN NATHAN, *Materia Critica*, 1924.

Drama—what literature does at night.

GEORGE JEAN NATHAN, *The Testament of a Critic*, 1931.

The basis of the dramatic form of entertainment is the emotional catharsis experienced by the audience....We've kept a little stardust in our mundane lives by identifying with make-believe characters in make-believe adventures in the house of illusion— the theatre.

RONALD REAGAN, *Where's the Rest of Me?*, 1965.

Success in show business depends on your ability to make and keep friends.

SOPHIE TUCKER, with Dorothy Giles, *Some of These Days*, 1945.

VISUAL ARTS

Sometimes I do get to places just when God's ready to have somebody click the shutter.

ANSEL ADAMS, in *American Way*, October, 1974.

Not everybody trusts paintings but people believe photographs.

ANSEL ADAMS, recalled on his death, April 22, 1984.

There is nothing worse than a brilliant image of a fuzzy concept.

ANSEL ADAMS, recalled on his death, April 22, 1984.

You don't take a photograph, you make it.

ANSEL ADAMS, *Time*, December 31, 1984.

It's in trying to direct the traffic between Artiface [sic] and Candor, without being run over, that I'm confronted with the questions about photography that matter most to me.

RICHARD AVEDON, *New York Times*, December 27, 1985.

All pictures are unnatural. All pictures are sad because they're about dead people. Paintings you don't think of in a special time or with a special event. With photos I always think I'm looking at something dead.

DAVID BAILEY, *International Herald Tribune*, November 15, 1985.

Painting, n. The art of protecting flat surfaces from the weather and exposing them to the critic.

AMBROSE BIERCE, *The Devil's Dictionary*, 1906.

Much harmless and much helpful enjoyment is given by the humble popularizer of art; and if we insist sufficiently upon the adjective humble we may go far as to say that he or she provides the best means of stimulating the intelligent but unlearned public to having thoughts and opinions of their own in matters of art.

ELIZABETH LUTHER CARY, "Art Critics & Art Interpreters," *Putnam's Monthly*, December, 1907.

Distortion may be used in ways not literary but supremely moving to the aesthetic sense. To take a bit of nature and twist and pull it into harmony with the fine design of which it is to be part requires great skill and gives great pleasure, if the artist keeps in mind that, after all, it is a bit of nature and the essential of its original should not be denied.

ELIZABETH LUTHER CARY, "Casual Impressions of Modernism," *American Magazine of Art*, August, 1930.

Murals in restaurants are on a par with the food in museums.

PETER DE VRIES, *Madder Music*, 1977.

To my mind the old masters are not art; their value is in their scarcity.

THOMAS A. EDISON, *Golden Book*, April, 1931.

[I]t is light that counts above everything. Not colored light, but color that gives off light—radiance.

The supreme gift, after light, is scale.

HELEN FRANKENTHALER, in Frank O'Hara, *Robert Motherwell*, 1965.

A picture that is beautiful or that works looks as if it was all made at one stroke. I don't like to see the trail of a brushstroke or a drip of paint.

HELEN FRANKENTHALER, from film *Painters Painting*, 1972.

Whether the *artist* works directly from nature, from memory, or from fantasy, nature is always the source of his creative impulses.

HANS HOFFMANN, 1948, in Herschel B. Chipp, ed., *Theories of Modern Art*, 1968.

Landscape...is to American painting what sex and psychoanalysis are to the American novel.

ROBERT HUGHES, *Time*, December 30, 1985.

A painting [is] a symbol for the universe. Inside it, each piece relates to the other. Each piece is only answerable to the rest of that little world. So, probably in the total universe, there is that kind of total harmony, but we get only little tastes of it.

CORITA KENT, *Newsweek*, December 17, 1984.

[Pop art is] the use of commercial art as a subject matter in painting....It was hard to get a painting that was despicable enough so that no one would hang it....The one thing everyone hated was commercial art; apparently they didn't hate that enough either.

ROY LICHTENSTEIN, 1964, in Lois and Alan Gordon, *American Chronicle*, 1987.

It terrified me to have an idea that was solely mine to be no longer a part of my mind, but totally public.

MAYA LIN, on her design for Vietnam Veterans Memorial in Washington, D.C., *National Geographic*, May, 1985.

Pop art is an American phenomenon that departs from the cliché of big, bold, raw America that became current when Abstract Expressionism triumphed internationally.

LUCY LIPPARD, *Pop Art*, 1966.

The camera shall take its place as the greatest and by all measurements the most convincing reporter of contemporary life.

ARCHIBALD MACLEISH, telegram to Henry Luce, June 29, 1936, in Vicki Goldberg, *Margaret Bourke-White: A Biography*, 1986.

I would say to a person who thinks he wants to paint, Go and look at the way a bird flies, a man walks, the sea moves. There are certain laws, certain formulae. You have to know them. They are nature's laws and you have to follow them just as nature follows them. You find the laws and you fill them in in your pictures and you discover that they are the same laws as in the old pictures. You don't create the formulae....You see them.

JOHN MARIN, 1937, in Herschel B. Chipp, ed., *Theories of Modern Art*, 1968.

It may be that the deep necessity of art is the examination of self-deception.

ROBERT MOTHERWELL, *New York Times*, November 17, 1985.

I see no reason for painting anything that can be put into any other form as well.

GEORGIA O'KEEFFE, letter to William M. Milliken, November 1, 1930, in *Georgia O'Keeffe*, 1976.

The idea of an isolated American painting... seems absurd to me just as the idea of creating a purely American mathematics or physics would seem absurd....An American is an American and his painting would naturally be qualified by that fact, whether he wills it or not. But the basic problems of contemporary painting are independent of any country.

JACKSON POLLOCK, 1944, in Herschel B. Chipp, ed., *Theories of Modern Art*, 1968.

[Mosaic is] not painting with stones and not sculpture, but an art the essential quality of which is luminosity....[M]osaics do not belong to a time but a human need of exceptional duration, a need for a new variety of flower, for the spirit of man who has in his heart a stone, the universe.

Jeanne Reynal, in Dore Ashton et al., *The Mosaics of Jeanne Reynal*, 1969.

The function of art is no longer to satisfy wants, including intellectual wants, but to serve as a stimulus to further creation. The Sistine Chapel is valuable not for the feelings it aroused in the past but for the creative acts it will instigate in the future. Art comes into being through a chain of inspiration.

Harold Rosenberg, in Douglas Davis, *Artculture*, 1977.

Whatever the moral claims made on behalf of photography, its main effect is to convert the world into a department store or museum-without-walls in which every subject is depreciated into an article of consumption, promoted into an item for aesthetic appreciation.

Susan Sontag, *On Photography*, 1977.

Cameras began duplicating the world at that moment when the human landscape started to undergo a vertiginous rate of change: while an untold number of forms of biological and social life are being destroyed in a brief span of time, a device is available to record what is disappearing.

Susan Sontag, *On Photography*, 1977.

People robbed of their past seem to make the most fervent picture takers, at home and abroad.

Susan Sontag, *On Photography*, 1977.

Recently, photography has become almost as widely practiced an amusement as sex and dancing—which means that, like every mass art form, photography is not practiced by most people as an art. It is mainly a social rite, a defense against anxiety, and a tool of power.

Susan Sontag, *On Photography*, 1977.

Photography records the gamut of feelings written on the human face, the beauty of the earth and skies that man has inherited and the wealth and confusion man has created.

Edward Steichen, *Time*, April 7, 1961.

When that shutter clicks, anything else that can be done afterward is not worth consideration.

Edward Steichen, recalled on his death, March 25, 1973.

A painting is like a man. If you can live without it, then there isn't much point in having it.

Lila Acheson Wallace, recalled on her death, May 8, 1984.

Business

See also **Dreams and Ideals**—Excellence, Leadership, Opportunity; **Economics;**
Ethics and Morality; Government and Politics—Domestic Policy; **The Human**
Condition—Ambition, Competitiveness, Creativity, Greed, Ingenuity,
Materialism, Talent, Toughness; **Language and Discourse**—Jargon,
Doublespeak and Obfuscation; **Popular Culture; Social Issues**—Crime and
Punishment, Environment and Pollution, Labor; **Sports; Work**—Businesspeople

When business is good it pays to advertise; when business is bad you've got to advertise.

ANONYMOUS.

Bureaucracy is nothing more than a hardening of an organization's arteries.

WILLIAM P. ANTHONY, *Managing Incompetence*, 1981.

There are many highly successful businesses in the United States. There are also many highly paid executives. The policy is not to intermingle the two.

NORMAN AUGUSTINE, "Augustine's 13th Law," *Augustine's Laws*, 1986.

The last 10 percent of performance generates one-third of the cost and two-thirds of the problems.

NORMAN AUGUSTINE, "Augustine's 15th Law," *Augustine's Laws*, 1986.

Corporation, n. An ingenious device for obtaining individual profit without individual responsibility.

AMBROSE BIERCE, *The Devil's Dictionary*, 1906.

Honey, if there's a part of the human body to exploit you might as well get onto it.

BILL BLASS, on his line of feminine-hygiene spray, March, 1973, in Nora Ephron, *Crazy Salad: Some Things about Women*, 1975.

Business leaders today can't shrink from their obligation to set a moral example.

WILLARD C. BUTCHER, speech, New Orleans, May 15, 1987.

The skyline of an American city today is virtually a bar graph of power and money in the business community at a given moment.

ROBERT CAMPBELL, "Why Tall Buildings Are Held in Low Esteem These Days," *Boston Globe*, February 10, 1991.

A foolish American myth has it that the rich and super-rich are entrepreneurial Daniel Boones who decry the restraints of government and, as rugged individualists, fare forth to wrest fame and fortune from other like-minded souls. With some notable exceptions nothing could be farther from the truth. In the main the rich are the clever and adroit who understand the purposes and functions of government and bend it to their purposes. Government becomes a device which they use to expand their fortunes, then hide behind to make certain their gains remain intact.

HARRY M. CAUDILL, *A Darkness at Dawn*, 1976.

The private business corporation is the dominant institution in American economic life. In its distinctively American form, it is probably more responsible for our economic performance than any other single feature. Without its limited liability feature, the large aggregations of capital which have revolutionized our economic life through mechanized mass production would have been impossible.

EVANS CLARK, in Arthur Goodfriend, *What Is America?*, 1954.

The business of America is business.

CALVIN COOLIDGE, 1924, in Lois and Alan Gordon, *American Chronicle*, 1987.

Like the Church, companies also have priests. They are the designated worriers of the corporations and the guardians of the culture's values.

TERRENCE E. DEAL and ALLEN A. KENNEDY, *Corporate Cultures*, 1982.

Modern industry needs visionary heroes more than ever before, not only to build new worlds, but also to invent better mousetraps.

TERRENCE E. DEAL and ALLAN A. KENNEDY, *Corporate Cultures*, 1982.

One aspect of modern life which has gone far to stifle men is the rapid growth of tremendous corporations. Enormous spiritual sacrifices are made in the transformation of shopkeepers into employees....The disppearance of free enterprise has led to a submergence of the individual in the impersonal corporation in much the same manner as he has been submerged in the state in other lands.

WILLIAM O. DOUGLAS, speech, Fordham University Alumni Association, February 9, 1939.

No one who has to earn a living can shake the dust of business off his feet, nor is that necessary for what used to be called salvation. For most of us complete integrity, in the sense of one-hundred per cent consecration to elevated objectives, is an unattainable luxury and pharisaism to boot.

CARL DREHER, "What Business Kills," *Harper's Magazine*, June, 1936.

The three-martini lunch is the epitome of American efficiency. Where else can you get an earful, a bellyful and a snootful at the same time?

GERALD R. FORD, speech, National Restaurant Association, Chicago, May 28, 1978.

There are two ways of making money—one at the expense of others, the other by service to others. The first method does not "make" money, does not create anything; it only "gets" money—and does not always succeed in that.

HENRY FORD, "Success," *Forum*, October, 1928.

What qualities...characterize today's bizkids?... [S]elf-confidence, ingenuity, an interest in finding practical solutions to real problems—and a poet's belief that if the first effort doesn't pay off, the world won't end.

PETER FUHRMAN, *Forbes*, April 27, 1987.

These men of the technostructure are the new and universal priesthood. Their religion is business success; their test of virtue is growth and profit. Their bible is the computer printout; their communion bench is the committee room. The sales force carries their message to the world, and a message is what it is often called.

JOHN KENNETH GALBRAITH, *The Age of Uncertainty*, 1977.

In the business world, everyone is paid in two coins: cash and experience. Take the experience first; the cash will come later.

HAROLD GENEEN, *Managing*, 1984.

In the business world, everyone is always working at legitimate cross purposes, governed by self interest.

HAROLD GENEEN, *Managing*, 1984.

No one can possibly achieve any real and lasting success or get rich in business by being a conformist.

J. PAUL GETTY, *International Herald Tribune*, January 10, 1961.

The meek shall inherit the earth, but not the mineral rights.

J. PAUL GETTY, in Robert Lenzner, *The Great Getty*, 1985.

Entrepreneurship is the last refuge of the trouble-making individual.

JAMES K. GLASSMAN, *Washington Monthly*, October, 1976.

Read through the course catalog of an average business school. Sit through the local success seminar. You hear a whole lot more about process than about product.

ELLEN GOODMAN, "The Joy of the Business of Sex," *Washington Post*, October, 1986.

Inequality of knowledge is the key to a sale.

DEIL O. GUSTAFSON, on selling real estate, *Newsweek*, May 20, 1974.

It's easy to make good decisions when there are no bad options.

ROBERT HALF, *Robert Half on Hiring*, 1985.

As a small business-person, you have no greater leverage than the truth.

PAUL HAWKEN, *Inc.*, August, 1987.

The greater the "risk," usually the worse the idea.

ROBERT HELLER, *The Super Managers*, 1984.

The notion that a business is clothed with a public interest and has been devoted to the public use is little more than a fiction intended to beautify what is disagreeable to the sufferers.

OLIVER WENDELL HOLMES, JR., *Tyson v. Banton*, 1927.

People want economy and they will pay any price to get it.

LEE IACOCCA, *New York Times*, October 13, 1974.

Are we going to be a services power? The double-cheeseburger-hold-the-mayo kings of the whole world?

LEE IACOCCA, speech, Japan Society of New York, *Fortune*, July 7, 1986.

Price-cutting and rebating, collecting information of the trade of competitors, the operation of companies under other names to obviate prejudice or secure an advantage, or for whatever reason, are all legitimate methods of competition....

There is no rule of fairness or reasonableness which regulates competition.

JOHN G. JOHNSON and JOHN G. MILBURN, brief for
Standard Oil Company, St. Louis, Missouri, 1909.

Business is like sex. When it's good, it's very, very good; when it's not so good, it's still good.

GEORGE KATONA, *Wall Street Journal*, April 9, 1969.

Men always try to keep a woman out of business so they won't find out how much fun it really is.

VIVIEN KELLEMS, in Gloria Swanson, "Unforgettable
Vivien Kellems," *Reader's Digest*, October, 1975.

Most businessmen have a romantic image of themselves as protectors of the status quo, and very few of them understand that the capitalist spirit is a revolutionary one.

LEWIS H. LAPHAM, "Eskimo Economics," *Harper's*,
December, 1980.

The conservative ethos presumes an attitude of moderation and magnanimity (i.e., a willingness to restrain one's primitive appetites in the interest of civilization), but what corporation can afford to conduct its affairs on so admirable a premise?

LEWIS H. LAPHAM, "Eskimo Economics," *Harper's*,
December, 1980.

Ford has saved America from a social crisis.... When the alcohol was taken [away],...the flivver was needed to replace it.

SAMUEL M. LAUGHLIN, 1924, in Lois and Alan Gordon,
American Chronicle, 1987.

A man's success in business today turns upon his power of getting people to believe he has something that they want.

GERALD STANLEY LEE, *Crowds*, 1913.

The trouble with research is that it tells you what people were thinking about yesterday, not tomorrow. It's like driving a car using a rearview mirror.

BERNARD LOOMIS, *International Herald Tribune*, October
9, 1985.

American businessmen strive to make a mass commodity out of almost everything that used to be a class commodity.

FREDERICK MARTIN, in Arthur Goodfriend, *What Is
America?*, 1954.

Meanwhile, the empty forms of social behavior survive inappropriately in business situations. We all know that when a business sends its customers "friendly reminders," it really means business.

JUDITH MARTIN, *Common Courtesy*, 1985.

If you're going to make rubber tires, you should go to Malaya and see the damn rubber trees.

FRITZ MAYTAG, *Harvard Business Review*, July/August,
1986.

Perhaps the most revolting character that the United States ever produced was the Christian businessman.

H.L. MENCKEN, *Minority Report*, 1956.

Businesses are, in reality, quasi-religious sects. When you go to work in one you embrace *a new faith*. And if they are really big businesses, you progress from faith to a kind of mystique. Belief in the product, preaching the product, in the end the product becomes the focus of a transcendental experience. Through "the product" one communes with the vast forces of life, nature, and history that are expressed in business.

THOMAS MERTON, *Conjectures of a Guilty Bystander*,
1968.

Being in the microcomputer business is like going 55 miles an hour 3 feet from a cliff.

GEORGE MORROW, *Fortune*, April 14, 1986.

For almost 70 years the life insurance industry has been a smug sacred cow feeding the public a steady line of sacred bull.

RALPH NADER, testimony to U.S. Senate subcommittee,
New York Times, May 19, 1974.

Bureaucracy defends the status quo long past the time when the quo has lost its status.

LAURENCE J. PETER, *San Francisco Chronicle*, January 29,
1978.

Competence always contains the seeds of incompetence.

LAURENCE J. PETER, *Why Things Go Wrong*, 1985.

If you don't know where you are going, you will probably end up somewhere else.

LAURENCE J. PETER and RAYMOND HULL, *The Peter Principle*,
1969.

Are we going to guarantee businessmen against their own incompetence?

WILLIAM PROXMIRE, on Chrysler bailout, 1979, in Lois and
Alan Gordon, *American Chronicle*, 1987.

Among the nations of the earth today America stands for one idea: *Business*.

EDWARD E. PURINTON, *Independent*, April 16, 1921.

What is the finest game? Business. The soundest science? Business. The truest art? Business. The fullest education? Business. The fairest opportunity? Business. The cleanest philanthropy? Business. The sanest religion? Business.

EDWARD E. PURINTON, *Independent*, April 16, 1921.

A Holding Company is a thing where you hand an accomplice the goods while the policeman searches you.

WILL ROGERS, in Donald Day, ed., *The Autobiography of Will Rogers*, 1949.

I hold it to be our duty to see that the wage worker, the small producer, the ordinary consumer, shall get their fair share of the benefit of business prosperity. But it either is or ought to be evident to everyone that business has to prosper before anybody can get any benefit from it.

THEODORE ROOSEVELT, speech, Ohio Constitutional Convention, February 1, 1912.

Apparently, identity consultant companies are often hired these days by a corporation's CEO to change the corporation's name into something that will sound flashy enough on Wall Street to make the CEO's stock options worth something. Anyone who wants to impress Wall Street obviously has to get rid of any suggestion that the corporation is connected with the stodgy and outmoded process of actually producing goods rather than fiddling with balance sheets.

CALVIN TRILLIN, "UNISYS Revealed," King Features Syndicate, December 7, 1986.

All business sagacity reduces itself in the last analysis to a judicious use of sabotage.

THORSTEIN VEBLEN, *An Inquiry into the Nature of Peace and the Terms of Its Perpetuation*, 1917.

Business has to do with the intangibles of ownership and only indirectly with the tangible facts of workmanship.

THORSTEIN VEBLEN, *Absentee Ownership and Business Enterprise in Recent Times*, 1923.

I never varied from the managerial rule that the worst possible thing we could do was to lie dead in the water of any problem. Solve it. Solve it quickly, solve it right or wrong. If you solved it wrong, it would come back and slap you in the face and then you could solve it right. Lying dead in the water and doing nothing is a comfortable alternative because it is without risk, but it is an absolutely fatal way to manage a business.

THOMAS J. WATSON, JR., *Fortune*, 1977.

What is good for the country is good for General Motors, and what's good for General Motors is good for the country.

CHARLES ERWIN WILSON, testifying before Senate Armed Forces Committee, 1952.

We have witnessed in modern business the submergence of the individual within the organization, and yet the increase to an extraordinary degree of the power of the individual, of the individual who happens to control the organization. Most men are individuals no longer so far as their business, its activities, or its moralities are concerned. They are not units but fractions.

WOODROW WILSON, speech, Chattanooga, Tennessee, August 31, 1910.

Business underlies everything in our national life, including our spiritual life. Witness the fact that in the Lord's Prayer, the first petition is for daily bread. No one can worship God or love his neighbor on an empty stomach.

WOODROW WILSON, speech in New York City, May 23, 1912.

ADVERTISING AND MARKETING

Time spent in the advertising business seems to create a permanent deformity like the Chinese habit of foot-binding.

DEAN ACHESON, in David S. McLellan and David C. Acheson, eds., *Among Friends*, 1980.

To me, an advertising agency is 85 per cent confusion and 15 per cent commission. A vice-president in an advertising agency is a "molehill man." A molehill man is a pseudo-busy executive who comes to work at 9 A.M. and finds a molehill on his desk. He has until 5 P.M. to make this molehill into a mountain.

FRED ALLEN, *Treadmill to Oblivion*, 1954.

[Christ] would be a national advertiser today, I am sure, as He was a great advertiser in His own day. He thought of His life as business.

BRUCE BARTON, 1924, in Lois Alan and Gordon, *American Chronicle*, 1987.

The deeper problems connected with advertising come less from the unscrupulousness of our "deceivers" than from our pleasure in being deceived, less from the desire to seduce than from the desire to be seduced.

DANIEL J. BOORSTIN, *The Image*, 1962.

Doing business without advertising is like winking at a girl in the dark. You know what you are doing, but nobody else does.

STUART HENDERSON BRITT, *New York Herard Tribune*, October 30, 1956.

Sex! What is that but *life*, after all? We're all of us selling sex, because we're all selling life.

ALVIN CHERESKIN, in article by Kennedy Fraser, "Gorgeous As It Gets," *The New Yorker*, September 15, 1986.

Advertising is what you do when you can't go see somebody. That's all it is.

FAIRFAX CONE, *Christian Science Monitor*, March 20, 1963.

Mass demand has been created almost entirely through the development of advertising.... Advertising ministers to the spiritual side of trade....It is a great power...part of the greater work of the regeneration and redemption of mankind.

CALVIN COOLIDGE, ca. 1926, in Ben H. Bagdikian, *The Media Monopoly*, 1983.

The first law in advertising is to avoid the concrete promise...and cultivate the delightfully vague.

JOHN CROSBY, *New York Herald Tribune*, August 18, 1947.

We grew up founding our dreams on the infinite promise of American advertising. I *still* believe that one can learn to play the piano by mail and that mud will give you a perfect complexion.

ZELDA FITZGERALD, *Save Me the Waltz*, 1932.

You know why Madison Avenue advertising has never done well in Harlem? We're the only ones who know what it means to *be* brand X.

DICK GREGORY, *From the Back of the Bus*, 1962.

Once you get the right image the details aren't that important. Over analyzing reduced the myth. A big insight we learned during this period was that you didn't have to explain why. That's what advertising was all about.

ABBIE HOFFMAN, *Soon to Be a Motion Picture*, 1980.

Folks with their wits about them knew that advertisements were just a pack of lies—you had only to look at the claims of patent medicines!

FRANCES PARKINSON KEYES, *Blue Camellia*, 1957.

The trouble with us in America isn't that the poetry of life has turned to prose, but that it has turned to advertising copy.

LOUIS KRONENBERGER, "The Spirit of the Age," *Company Manners*, 1954.

[The advertiser] is the overrewarded court jester and court pander at the democratic court.

JOSEPH WOOD KRUTCH, "Permissive Exploitation," *Human Nature and the Human Condition*, 1959.

Advertising is a valuable economic factor because it is the cheapest way of selling goods, particularly if the goods are worthless.

SINCLAIR LEWIS, *New York Times*, April 18, 1943.

Hollywood has its Oscars. Television has its Emmys. Broadway has its Tonys. And advertising has its Clios. And its Andys, Addys, Effies and Obies. And 117 other assorted awards. And those are just the big ones.

JOANNE LIPMAN, "Ad Creators Collect Prizes Ad Nauseam, Almost Ad Infinitum," *Wall Street Journal*, March 26, 1987.

Who's kidding whom? What's the difference between Giant and Jumbo? Quart and *full* quart? Two-ounce and *big* two-ounce? What does Extra Long mean? What's a *tall* 24-inches? And what busy shopper can tell?

MARYA MANNES, "New Bites by a Girl Gadfly," *Life*, June 12, 1964.

Advertising treats all products with the reverence and the seriousness due to sacraments.

THOMAS MERTON, *Conjectures of a Guilty Bystander*, 1968.

The most important word in the vocabulary of advertising is TEST. If you pretest your product with consumers, and pretest your advertising, you will do well in the marketplace.

DAVID OGILVY, *Confessions of an Advertising Man*, 1963.

The consumer isn't a moron; she is your wife. You insult her intelligence if you assume that a mere slogan and a few vapid adjectives will persuade her to buy anything.

DAVID OGILVY, *Confessions of an Advertising Man*, 1963.

Ninety-nine percent of advertising doesn't sell much of anything.

DAVID OGILVY, *Chicago Tribune*, January 4, 1984.

In the field of marketing,...the trend toward selling [has] reached something of a nadir with the unveiling...of so-called subliminal projection. That is the technique designed to flash messages past our conscious guard.

VANCE PACKARD, *The Hidden Persuaders*, 1958.

Market research can establish beyond the shadow of a doubt that the egg is a sad and sorry product and that it obviously will not continue to sell. Because after all, eggs won't stand up by themselves, they roll too easily, are too easily broken, require special packaging, look alike, are difficult to open, won't stack on the shelf.

ROBERT PLISKIN, speech, National Packaging Forum, October 16, 1963.

It is our job to make women unhappy with what they have.

B. EARL PUCKETT, recalled on his death, *Newsweek*, February 23, 1976.

Strategy and timing are the Himalayas of marketing. Everything else is the Catskills.

AL RIES and JACK TROUT, *Marketing Warfare*, 1986.

The question about those aromatic advertisements that perfume companies are having stitched into magazines these days is this: under the freedoms guaranteed by the First Amendment, is smelling up the place a constitutionally protected form of expression?

CALVIN TRILLIN, "Confessions of a Crank," King Features Syndicate, November 16, 1986.

It took at least 200 people, in 5 states, 4 months to turn out a Ford Thunderbird commercial that lasted 90 seconds.

JOAN WALKER, *New York Herald Tribune*, July 5, 1964.

Commercial society regards people as bundles of appetites, a conception that turns human beings inside out, leaving nothing to be regarded as inherently private. Commercial society finds unintelligible the idea that anything—an emotion, activity, or product—is too "intimately personal" for uninhibited commercial treatment.

GEORGE WILL, "Privacy in the Republic of Appetites," August 6, 1975, *The Pursuit of Happiness, and Other Sobering Thoughts*, 1978.

As advertising blather becomes the nation's normal idiom, language becomes printed noise.

GEORGE WILL, "Personality Against Character," July 1, 1976, *The Pursuit of Happiness, and Other Sobering Thoughts*, 1978.

ADVERTISING SLOGANS

Skim milk does not come from skinny cows.

Alba

I can't believe I ate the whole thing!

Alka-Seltzer

Plop, plop, fizz fizz, oh what a relief it is!

Alka-Seltzer

Grapes, like children, need love and affection.

Almaden

Rest, keep warm and drink liquids.

American Airlines ad for vacations, 1973.

If man were meant to fly, God would have lowered the fares.

American Coach Lines

Don't leave home without it.

American Express credit card.

A, B, C, D, E,...

Your public library has arranged these in ways that make you cry, giggle, laugh, love, hate, wonder, ponder and understand.

American Library Association, 1961.

Reach out and touch someone.

American Telephone & Telegraph (AT&T), 1982.

From the Sahara to the Ritz

In a tent of Bedouin on the Sands of Sahara, or over the counter of the Ritz in London, as fare on a junk in Hong Kong, or on an American Pullman.... American Travelers Cheques

American Travelers Cheques, 1922.

See America at see level.

Amtrak

Anita Nose Adjuster—shapes while you sleep. (Write for Free Booklet "Happy Days.")

Anita Nose Adjuster

If you can't decide between a Shepherd, a Setter, or a Poodle, get them all.... Adopt a mutt.

ASPCA

We try harder.

Avis Car Rental

It's in the bag.

Ballantine beer

The price of food has gone up more in the month than the banana has in 10 years.

Banana Corporation of America

Upstairs, Downstairs, all about the House... The New Telephone Convenience.

Bell System

Nothing else you use so often does so much yet costs so little. And the more you use it the more valuable it becomes.

Bell Telephone

Enough to make your hair curl.
Best's Exclusive Lamp Curl, 1946.

Now your kids don't have to miss Monday Night Football because they're studying for a Tuesday morning exam.
Betamax, Sony

Victory won't wait for the nation that's late.
Big Ben clocks

Which orange juice tastes better than just-squeezed?—Birds Eye, guaranteed or money back.
Birds Eye foods

Tell someone you love about V.D. The health business, we're not in it for the money.
Blue Cross/Blue Shield health insurance, 1970.

Do you want a shape like a bra?

Or do you want a shape like a woman?
Body Bra by Warner's

At thirty every woman reaches a crossroads. Will she develop—or merely age?
Boncilla Beautifier, the Clasmic Clay, 1923.

America's Bookstore.
Book-of-the-Month Club

Today the discriminating family finds it absolutely necessary to own two or more motor cars.
Buick

Equal Pay
Equal Time
Bulova Accutron, for men and women, 1974.

The mainspring in a Bulova is made to last 256 years or 146 leather straps—whichever comes first.
Bulova Watches

Have it your way.
Burger King

So creamy it's almost fattening.
Burma Shave

What this commercial is trying to sell you won't make your breath any sweeter, your clothes any whiter or your acid indigestion any better. It'll just make you more human.
Business Committee for the Arts, 1972.

Nothing comes between me and my Calvins.
Calvin Klein jeans

You are in a Beauty Contest Every Day of your Life.
Camay soap

For Digestion's Sake—Smoke Camels.
Camel cigarettes

Experience is the best teacher...in choosing a cigarette.

Your T-zone will tell you why.

More doctors smoke Camels than any other cigarette.
Camel cigarettes

Now they whisper *to* her...not about her.
Cashmere Bouquet soap

Come to the Central Park Zoo Cafeteria. Let the animals watch you eat for a change.
Central Park Zoo

Please don't squeeze the Charmin.
Charmin toilet tissue

See the USA in your Chevrolet.
Chevrolet

The road isn't built that can make it breathe hard!
Chevrolet

How strong is the Chiquita name?

How many banana commercials can you sing?
Chiquita Banana Company

Isn't that a lot for a bottle of Scotch? Yes.
Chivas Regal

Are your friends living beyond your means?
Chivas Regal

If enough people would stop smoking and start drinking, we could get out of ashtrays and into vermouth.
Cinzano

Stop right now and forget everything you ever knew about being a blonde. Up to now you could never be any of these delicate blondes.
Clairol

Does she or doesn't she?
Clairol

If I've only one life, let me live it as a blonde!
Clairol

Vacation is a world where there are no locks on the doors or the mind or the body.
Club Med

The pause that refreshes.
Coca-Cola

It's the real thing.
Coca-Cola

Have a Coke and a smile.
Coca-Cola

Don't spread the cold....Spread the word.
Coldene cold tablets

Your client is a poor, rejected stepchild, whose best friends are dwarfs. Can you insure her against poisoned apples?
Continental Insurance Company

One of the Soviet Georgia's senior citizens thought Dannon was an excellent yogurt. She ought to know. She's been eating yogurt for 137 years.
Dannon

How to please a Dictator.
Dictaphone

On watch 24 hours a day, DEW (that's Distant Early Warning) will probe the polar sky with radar. The DEW line will stand between you and a sneak attack over the top of the world.
Douglas Aircraft

Better things for better living through chemistry.
Du Pont

Where hearts are gay
There's Blond Dubonnet.
Dubonnet

Fly now. Shovel later.
Eastern Airlines

Einstein's Theory of Relativity: give strangers the same price you give relatives.
Einstein-Moomjy Carpets

Please do not have a fit in the fitting room. Your fashion life begins there.
FLORENCE EISEMAN, manufacturer of children's clothing, in *The New Yorker*, March 19, 1966.

Winged Victory—a new lipstick with matching nail polish.
Elizabeth Arden

167 days of foggy, foggy dew can't claim all the credit for beautiful English complexions.
Elizabeth Arden

Dick and Jane is dead.
Encyclopaedia Britannica, 1970.

Wishful Thinning
Enhance by Lily of France, 1967.

STOP TRIPLE "O"
   Stop Breath Odor
   Stop Body Odor
   Stop Other Personal Odors
Ennds chlorophyll tablets, 1952.

The unwashables. Take 'em for a ride.
Evan-Picone

Farewell to the ugly cigarette.
Eve

When there's no tomorrow.
Federal Express

A day without orange juice is like a day without sunshine.
Florida Citrus Commission

No hits and misses. No dibs, dabs, and splatters.
5-Day Deodorant Pads

Ford has a better idea.
Ford

'Twas the night before Christmas—the children
   were dreaming
Of a Ford in their future—smart, swanky and
   gleaming.
Ford

Here's spaghetti sauce with meat—the way Italians make it.
Franco-American canned spaghetti, 1954.

Should a Tough Man Make a Tender Turkey?
Frank Perdue Poultry

Extinct is forever.
Friends of Animals

When Cathy Cole and Peggy Burton saw Joan Emery's new floor, they couldn't believe their feet.
GAF Softstep vinyl floors

Progress is our most important product.
General Electric

THERE ARE NO WHITES WORKING AT G.E.

No blacks either. Just people. And we need more.

General Electric

Shall the man work—or shall you?…Back of every great step in women's progress from a drudge to a free citizen has been some labor-saving invention.

General Electric clothes washer, 1924.

Do you arise irked with life? Are you prone to snap at loved ones? Our strong, hearty breakfast coffee will change all this! Breakfast becomes a spirited, even hilarious affair.

General Foods gourmet foods, 1958.

Riddle: What's college?

That's where girls who are above cooking and sewing go to meet a man they can spend their lives cooking and sewing for.

Gimbel's ad for campus clothes, 1952.

Try walking into Merrill Lynch and asking for Mr. Lynch.

Goldberg-Pollen

No wonder the English have kept cool for 192 years.

Gordon's gin

Know the Bomb's True Dangers. Know the Steps You Can Take to Escape Them!

Government pamphlet

Roar, Boys, Roar

It tastes like more

What a flavor

Zippity-zow—it's grand—and HOW.

Grape-Nuts Flakes

I feel like a Guinness.

I wish you were.

Guinness

Don't be an e.s.s.*

Wear smart *seamless* stockings by Hanes

*eternal seam straightener!

Hanes

Can Head & Shoulders stop dandruff?

Can Wilt Chamberlain stuff?

Head & Shoulders shampoo

What food these morsels be!

Heinz fresh cucumber pickles, 1938.

Chapped hands are cold company.

Hines honey and almond cream, 1936.

Better gas mileage. A Civic responsibility.

Honda

Many Happy Returns.

IBM Electric Typewriters

Look for the union label.

International Ladies' Garment Workers' Union.

Husbands are funny. You know I really think they are more sentimental than we are. Deep down in their hearts they wish that they could keep us fresh and lovely as we were on our wedding day right to our very fingertips.

Ivory Snow

Only the brave deserve the fair

and the fair deserve JAEGER.

Jaeger Sportswear

Scotch and the Single Girl.

J&B

It sits as lightly on a heavy meal as it does on your conscience.

Jell-O

The King and Queen Might Eat Thereof

And Noblemen Besides.

Jell-O

If all the world were Jell-O

And whipped cream filled the sea,

Then the only spoon from here to the moon

Would have to belong to me.

Jell-O

What the well-dressed man is wearing this year.

Jockey shorts, 1971.

Look your best while you wear your least.

Jockey shorts

The best seat in the house.

Jockey underwear

If you want to impress someone, put him on your Black list.

Johnny Walker Black

Honor thy self

Johnny Walker Black

Buy a bucket of chicken and have a barrel of fun.

Kentucky Fried Chicken

Well—Shut my Mouth
I shut my mouth on a Kleenex tissue
To give my lipstick that neat, natural look.
These days it's a crime to stain a towel.
Kleenex

Don't put a cold in your pocket!—Use Kleenex Tissues.
Kleenex

Just what the doctor ordered.
L&M cigarettes

Betcha can't eat just one.
Lay's potato chips

Have you ever had a bad time in Levi's?
Levi's

You don't have to be Jewish to love Levy's.
Levy's Rye bread

Gee, I wish I had a nickel.
Life Savers

It is found wherever noble things are valued.
Lincoln

Nice toys don't kill.
Lionel Trains

Lipton's gets into more hot water than anything.
Lipton tea

Often a bridesmaid
but never a bride
—For Halitosis, Use Listerine
Listerine mouthwash

Air Power is Peace Power—Lockheed.
Lockheed Aircraft

Taking the "if" out of "gift."
Lord & Taylor

Do you inhale? Of course you do! Lucky Strike has dared to raise this vital question *because* certain impurities concealed in even the finest, mildest tobacco leaves are removed by Luckies' famous purifying process.
Lucky Strike cigarettes, 1932.

I wanna give 'em away but Mrs. Muntz won't let me. She's crazy.
MADMAN MUNTZ, Los Angeles used-car dealer, 1946.

I dreamed I stopped traffic in my Maidenform bra.
Maidenform

I dreamed I went shopping in my Maidenform bra.
Maidenform

The milk chocolate melts in your mouth—not in your hand.
M&Ms

He was a first-name kind of guy. He was everybody's kind of guy.... He was God's kind of guy.
Ad for film *A Man Called Peter.*

At last. A pickle that bites back.
Marcus Valley pickles

We sell more cars than Ford, Chrysler, Chevrolet, and Buick combined.
Matchbox toy cars

To bring the wolves out—Riding Hood Red.
Max Factor

Good to the last drop.
Maxwell House Coffee, first said by TEDDY ROOSEVELT, 1929.

Our repairmen are the loneliest guys in town.
Maytag appliances

You deserve a break today.
McDonald's

One in a billion.
McDonald's

Where was Moses When the Lights Went Out?—Groping for a pack of Meccas.
Mecca cigarettes

When the rubbers are rapid and the finessing is frantic.
Menthol-cooled Spuds

A child is someone who passes through your life and then disappears into an adult.
Metropolitan Life Insurance

No matter what what's-his-name says, I'm the prettiest and Lite's the greatest.
JOE FRAZIER for Miller Beer, 1978

Only 1 out of 25 men is color blind. The other 24 just dress that way.
Mohara suits

Any melon worth its salt...
Morton

Has your girl turned into a refrigerator? If her air is arctic, try...MUM.
Mum deodorant

Our readers knew Henry [Kissinger] was getting married before Henry did.
National Enquirer

Open wide and say ahhh.
National Library Week

Why be color-blind?…This fall more than 2/3 of nighttime programming will be in color.
NBC

Play it again, Sam.
New York State Lottery

All the news that's fit to print.
New York Times

Amusing "stocking present." Lifelike figure, in washable-rubberoid, smiles, lolls tongue, says "Peace" when tilted. Exclusive, patented mechanism makes teeth snap unexpectedly when doll is approached too closely, inflicting small, powerful bites. (Disinfectant and first-aid kit included.)
Nikita Doll

The cat who doesn't act finicky soon loses control of his owner.
9-Lives cat food

In 1944 you won the war together. Isn't it worth $1.50 to spend five minutes with him again?
Northwestern Bell

Our summer sale began Oct. 4, 1923.
Ohrbach's

We're tobacco men…not medicine men. Old Gold cures just one thing. The World's Best Tobacco.
Old Gold cigarettes

The thrill of Roses
Spiced with excitement
Speaking of love.
Old Spice toiletries

Pass the Ammunition
Oldsmobile workers have been doing it for nearly two years. Backing up our fighting men with volume production of fire-power.
Oldsmobile

The Other Pill
One-a-Day multiple vitamins plus iron, 1967.

Dancing pleats that won't sit out.
Orlon

All that glitters is not Pabst
Pabst beer

Thousands of man are denying their wives Packard Six cars.
Packard

Give your baby something you never had as a baby. A drier bottom.
Pampers

Live today. Tomorrow will cost more.
Pan American World Airways

We will sell no wine before its time.
Paul Masson

Trichinosis, encephalitis, scarlet fever, amoebiasis, jungle rot. We think you'll find them more challenging than the sniffles.
Peace Corps

In 1962, the starving residents of an isolated Indian village received 1 plow and 1,700 pounds of seeds. They ate the seeds.
Peace Corps

I seem to be Achilles…but, my dear, it happens to be *your* heel that is my vulnerable spot. Such slenderness! Such grace! One look and I am slain.
Peacock Shoes

Sandals being what they are, toes now compete with fingers.
Peggy Sage liquid polish

Come alive!
You're in the Pepsi generation.
Pepsi-Cola

When they [the enemy] find the Pepsi-Cola bottles are empty, their morale will go down another 10 points.
Pepsi-Cola

Pepsi-Cola hits the spot,
12 full ounces, that's a lot,
Twice as much for a nickel too
Pepsi-Cola is the Drink for you!
Nickel, nickel, nickel, nickel
Trickle, trickle, trickle, trickle…
Pepsi-Cola

Where will you be when your laxative starts to work?
Phospho-Soda buffered laxative, 1969.

Nothin' says lovin' like somethin' from the oven.
Pillsbury

The world's most pleasant alarm clock!
Pillsbury pancake flour

It is common knowledge today that intestinal putrefaction causes brain fatigue, often reducing efficiency 50 per cent and more.
Pillsbury's health bran

It won't let you stop. Suddenly you see a picture everywhere you look....
Polaroid's SX-70

She who Prizes Beauty Must Obey Nature's Law!

Faulty Elimination is the greatest enemy that
    beauty knows. It plays havoc with the
    complexion,
    brings sallow skin, dull and listless eyes.

Everybody

Everyday

Eat Post's Bran Flakes, as an ounce of Prevention
Post's bran flakes

It costs a lot to bring a hero home.

Get ready to buy Victory Bonds.
Public service ad

The More Women at War

The Sooner We'll Win
Public service ad

I quit school when I were sixteen.
Public service ad

Act your age—today is Election Day. If you're over 21, make sure you vote.
Public service ad

If your son is old enough to shave, he's old enough to get syphilis.
Public service ad

If you won't hire her, don't complain about supporting her.
Public service ad

If someone's selling you sacks of diet pills, he's not in business for your health.
Public service ad

May the Force Be with You. Best Wishes from the Boston Police Relief Association.
Public service ad

Children can't protect themselves from the people they love.
Public service ad

If 2,225,000 Americans were starving to death, this ad would be a lot bigger. Feed Cambodia.
Public service ad

If you choose the wrong executor for your estate, you might as well take it with you.
Putnam Trust

Does it make sense to jump out of a warm bed into a cold cereal?
Quaker Oats

All you add is love.
Ralston Purina

The greatest tragedy is indifference.
Red Cross

Replique will not turn you into a sultry sex siren.

It will not transform you into a simple, unsullied
    ingenue.

Replique is for women who are interesting to
    begin with.
Replique

She's wearing Cherry Coke...one of Revlon's colors of the hour.
Revlon

Go with the grain.

Rice. A great eating idea whose time has come.
Rice industry

How do you spell relief? R-O-L-A-I-D-S.
Rolaids

Some girls have developed a lot more than just their minds.
Roxanne swimsuits

Tasty uranium burger, 45 cents.
Salt Lake City Fast Food Store.

Women: Stand up for your right to sit down at dinner time.
Salton hottray

If you have a son 10 years old, you'd better start worrying. Help Unsell the War.
SANE

One fiddler you won't have to pay.
Sanka coffee

Serutan...It's natures, spelled backwards.
Serutan tonic

Even a Policeman can get Stuck in Traffic.
Talon zipper

Natural lips win with Dick Powell.
Tangee lipstick

I'd rather fight than switch.
Tareyton cigarettes

You can trust your car to the man who wears the star.
Texaco

I'm fighting for my right to boo the Dodgers!
Texaco

Christmas is a time to believe in things you can't see.
3M Company Scotch Tape

You don't watch it, or think about it. You read, go out of the room, answer the phone, do anything you like, leave it as long as you want....

No turning. No burning.
Toastmaster

Which twin has the Toni?
Toni permanents

Fighting Red—new brave lipstick color by Tussey.
Tussey cosmetics

Sight for Soaring Eyes.
TWA

More Jobs Through Science
Union Carbide and Carbon

Fly the friendly skies of United.
United Air Lines

Bananas broiled with bacon
—guaranteed to start conversation.
United Fruit Company

A mind is a terrible thing to waste.
United Negro College Fund.

Be all that you can be.
United States Army

Some of our best men are women.
United States Army

If you think asparagus has a lot of iron, you don't know beans.
Van Camp's Pork and Beans, 1979.

You've come a long way, baby.
Virginia Slims cigarettes.

Vogue—[for] the overwhelming minority.
Vogue

If it wasn't in VOGUE
It wasn't in vogue.
Vogue

Relieves gas pains.
Volkswagen

While in Europe, pick up an ugly European.
Volkswagen

If gas pains persist, try Volkswagen.
Volkswagen

Small wonder.
Volkswagen

Play off your fat...get thin to music.
Wallace Reducing records

The daily diary of the American dream.
Wall Street Journal

The corset department is obsolete. The slimwear department is here.
Warner's

Where's the beef?
Wendy's

Covers a Multitude of Chins.
Williams' shaving cream

Winston tastes good like a cigarette should.
Winston cigarettes

Ring around the collar.
Wisk laundry detergent

Let your fingers do the walking.
Yellow Pages

BIGNESS

Bigness is still the curse.
Louis D. Brandeis, December 7, 1940, in Alfred Lief, ed., *The Brandeis Guide to the Modern World*, 1941.

We believe that there is one economic lesson which our twentieth century experience has demonstrated conclusively—that America can no more survive and grow without big business than it can survive and grow without small business...the two are interdependent. You cannot strengthen one by weakening the other, and you cannot add to the stature of a dwarf by cutting off the legs of a giant.

BENJAMIN FRANKLIN FAIRLESS, testimony before House Subcommittee on Study of Monopoly Power of the Committee on the Judiciary, April 26, 1950.

Where are the corporate entrepreneurs? The answer is: There are none.

HAROLD GENEEN, *Managing*, 1984.

The Americans burn incense before [democracy], but they are themselves ruled by the Boss and the Trust.

WILLIAM RALPH INGE, *Outspoken Essays*, 1919.

The frontiers run between markets and spheres of commerical interest, not along the boundaries of sovereign states. If a company is large enough and rich enough (commanding assets worth several billion dollars and employing more people than lived in fourteenth-century Venice), the company, of necessity, conducts its own foreign policy. In part, this is because the nation-state can make good on so few of its promises.

LEWIS H. LAPHAM, "After 1984," *Harper's*, September, 1988.

The simple opposition between the people and big business has disappeared because the people themselves have become so deeply involved in big business.

WALTER LIPPMANN, speech, Academy of Political Science, March 25, 1931, in Ronald Steel, *Walter Lippmann and the American Century*, 1980.

The biggest corporation, like the humblest private citizen, must be held to strict compliance with the will of the people.

THEODORE ROOSEVELT, speech, Cincinnati, Ohio, 1902.

The great corporations which we have grown to speak of rather loosely as trusts are the creatures of the state, and the state not only has the right to control them, but it is in duty bound to control them whenever the need of such control is shown.

THEODORE ROOSEVELT, speech, Providence, Rhode Island, August 23, 1902.

We demand that big business give people a square deal; in return we must insist that when any one engaged in big business honestly endeavors to do right, he shall himself be given a square deal.

THEODORE ROOSEVELT, *Autobiography*, 1913.

Neither the tenuous things of the human spirit nor the gross material needs of human life can come in contact with this business enterprise [Big Business] in such a way as to deflect its course from the line of least resistance, which is the line of greatest present gain within the law.

THORSTEIN VEBLEN, *Absentee Ownership and Business Enterprise in Recent Times*, 1923.

BOSSES AND WORKERS

It will certainly be embarrassing to have our age written down triumphant in the matter of inventions, in that our factories were filled with intricate machines, the result of advancing mathematical and mechanical knowledge in relation to manufacturing processes, but defeated in that it lost its head over the achievement and forgot the men.

JANE ADDAMS, "Educational Methods," *Democracy and Social Ethics*, 1902.

It was once rumored that fledgling executives walked around their offices backwards so they wouldn't have to face an issue.

FRED ALLEN, *Treadmill to Oblivion*, 1954.

Being in your own business is working 80 hours a week so that you can avoid working 40 hours a week for someone else.

RAMONA E. F. ARNETT, speech, Boston, Massachusetts, 1973.

If a sufficient number of management layers are superimposed on top of each other, it can be assured that disaster is not left to chance.

NORMAN AUGUSTINE, "Augustine's 26th Law," *Augustine's Laws*, 1986.

A good manager is a man who isn't worried about his own career but rather the careers of those who work for him.

H.S.M. BURNS, in Osborn Elliott, *Men at the Top*, 1959.

The employer puts his money into...business and the workman his life. The one has as much right as the other to regulate that business.

CLARENCE DARROW, *Railroad Trainman*, November, 1909.

Businesses want plans and controls. The new workers want options and individual treatment. Indeed, this may be the ultimate challenge that women initiate in the workplace.

ELLEN GOODMAN, "Mommy Track or Trough?" *Washington Post*, March, 1989.

A corporation prefers to offer a job to a man who already has one....To obtain entry into paradise, in terms of employment, you should be in a full state of grace.

ALAN HARRINGTON, *Life in the Crystal Palace*, 1959.

We have created an industrial order geared to automatism, where feeble-mindedness, native or acquired, is necessary for docile productivity in the factory; and where a pervasive neurosis is the final gift of the meaningless life that issues forth at the other end.

LEWIS MUMFORD, "The Fulfillment of Man," *The Conduct of Life*, 1951.

In a hierarchy, every employee tends to rise to his level of incompetence; the cream rises until it sours.

LAURENCE J. PETER, *The Peter Principle*, 1969.

No business which depends for existence on paying less than living wages to its workers has any right to continue in this country. By business I mean the whole of commerce as well as the whole of industry; by workers I mean all workers—the white-collar class as well as the man in overalls; and by living wages I mean more than a bare subsistence level—I mean the wages of decent living.

FRANKLIN D. ROOSEVELT, statement, June 16, 1933.

It's been clear for years, after all, that in the world of huge corporations there's nothing more lucrative than being fired well.

CALVIN TRILLIN, "Corporate Triumphs," King Features Syndicate, September 28, 1986.

PROFIT AND PRODUCTION

We were fairly arrogant, until we realized the Japanese were selling quality products for what it cost us to make them.

PAUL A. ALLAIRE, *New York Times*, February 21, 1988.

It costs a lot to build bad products.

NORMAN AUGUSTINE, "Augustine's 12th Law," *Augustine's Laws*, 1986.

Knowledge is the only instrument of production that is not subject to diminishing returns.

JOHN BATES CLARK, "Overhead Costs in Modern Industry," *Journal of Political Economy*, October, 1927.

Civilization and profits go hand in hand.

CALVIN COOLIDGE, speech, New York City, November 27, 1920.

The reins may be held loosely or tightly, but they are always in the business man's hands. Whether it is automobiles or radio receivers or books or film, the stuff can be made only as good as profit considerations will permit, and no more of it will be made than that. When the quality is poor or mediocre the cause, nine times out of ten, is not technical incompetence, but financial hamstringing. That the instinct for workmanship survives under such conditions is a psychological marvel.

CARL DREHER, "What Business Kills," *Harper's*, June, 1936.

We have learned that productivity is a social if not a moral principle, and not just a business principle; that increased productivity must contribute to a greater income of the masses, to greater job security of the workers, to greater satisfaction of the consumer...and that it is not enough for it to contribute to profits.

PETER F. DRUCKER, in Arthur Goodfriend, *What Is America?*, 1954.

Humans must breathe, but corporations must make money.

ALICE EMBREE, "Media Images I: Madison Avenue Brainwashing—The Facts," in Robin Morgan, ed., *Sisterhood Is Powerful*, 1970.

So the question is, do *corporate executives*, provided they stay within the law, have responsibilities in their business activities other than to make as much money for their stockholders as possible? And my answer to that is, no they do not.

MILTON FRIEDMAN, *Chemtech*, February, 1974.

In the matter of betterment of the masses... America has set the pace. America has found out how you do these things in the way of production and how you get them to the largest number of people at the cheapest price.

LEWIS GALANTIERE, in Arthur Goodfriend, *What Is America?*, 1954.

Consumer wants can have bizarre, frivolous, or even immoral origins, and an admirable case can still be made for a society that seeks to satisfy them. But the case cannot stand if it is the process of satisfying wants that creates the wants. For then the individual who urges the importance of production to satisfy these wants is precisely in the position of the onlooker who applauds the efforts of the squirrel to keep abreast of the wheel that is propelled by his own efforts.

JOHN KENNETH GALBRAITH, *The Affluent Society*, 1976.

American society has tried so hard and so ably to defend the practice and theory of production for profits and not primarily for use that now it has succeeded in making its jobs and products profitable and useless.

PAUL GOODMAN, *Growing Up Absurd*, 1960.

Any jackass can draw up a balanced budget on paper.

LANE KIRKLAND, *U.S. News & World Report*, May 19, 1980.

You think that the only thing that counts is the bottom line! What a presumptuous thing to say. The bottom line is in heaven.

EDWIN LAND, speech, Polaroid shareholders annual meeting, 1977.

You don't need an M.B.A. from Harvard to figure out how to lose money.

ROYAL LITTLE, *Best of Business Quarterly*, 1987.

Junk bonds are the Holy Grail for hostile takeovers.

ROGER MILLER, *New York Times*, April 14, 1985.

The paramount goal of the United States is to guard the rights of the individual, and to enlarge his opportunity....This is the goal. This is the object of everything we are working at: to produce things for consumers.

President's Council of Economic Advisors report, 1960.

We must accelerate obsolescence....Basic utility cannot be the foundation of a prosperous apparel industry.

B.E. PUCKETT, 1950, in Lois and Alan Gordon, *American Chronicle*, 1987.

Profits may be obtained either by producing what consumers want or by making consumers want what one is actually producing.

HENRY SIMONS, *Economic Policy for a Free Society*, 1948.

Children and Youth

See also **Age**; **Education**; **Holidays**; **Relationships**—Family, Friendship, Parents and Children; **Social Issues**—Drugs and Alcohol, Health, Poverty and Hunger, Violence

Boys naturally look on all force as an enemy, and generally find it so.
HENRY ADAMS, *The Education of Henry Adams*, 1918.

Young men have a passion for regarding their elders as senile.
HENRY ADAMS, *The Education of Henry Adams*, 1918.

In every child who is born, under no matter what circumstances, and of no matter what parents, the potentiality of the human race is born again.
JAMES AGEE, with Walker Evans, *Let Us Now Praise Famous Men*, 1941.

The young have no depth perception in time. Ten years back or 10 years forward is an eternity.
ROBERT C. ALBERTS, *New York Times*, November 17, 1974.

It is ominous for the future of a child when the discipline he receives is based on the emotional needs of the disciplinarian rather than on any consideration of the child's own needs.
GORDON W. ALLPORT, *Personality and Social Encounter: Prejudice in Modern Perspective*, 1960.

Children's talent to endure stems from their ignorance of alternatives.
MAYA ANGELOU, *I Know Why the Caged Bird Sings*, 1970.

At fifteen life had taught me undeniably that surrender, in its place, was as honorable as resistance, especially if one had no choice.
MAYA ANGELOU, *I Know Why the Caged Bird Sings*, 1970.

To be left alone on the tightrope of youthful unknowing is to experience the excruciating beauty of full freedom and the threat of eternal indecision.
MAYA ANGELOU, *I Know Why the Caged Bird Sings*, 1970.

When you're young, the silliest notions seem the greatest achievements.
PEARL BAILEY, *The Raw Pearl*, 1968.

As I vaguely recalled from my own experience, adolescence was a time when you firmly believed that sex hadn't been invented until the year you started high school, when the very idea that anything interesting might have happened during your parents' lifetime was unthinkable.
RUSSELL BAKER, "Life with Mother," in William Zinsser, ed., *Inventing the Truth*, 1987.

It seems to be typical of life in America, where opportunities, real and fancied, are thicker than anywhere else on the globe, that the second generation has no time to talk to the first.
JAMES BALDWIN, *Notes of a Native Son*, 1955.

I had lost something in youth and made money instead.
STEPHEN VINCENT BENÉT, *James Shore's Daughter*, 1934.

I never felt that there was anything enviable in youth. I cannot recall that any of us, as youths, admired our condition to excess or had a desire to prolong it.
BERNARD BERENSON, *Rumor and Reflection*, 1952.

Childhood, n. The period of human life intermediate between the idiocy of infancy and the folly of youth—two removes from the sin of manhood and three from the remorse of age.
AMBROSE BIERCE, *The Devil's Dictionary*, 1906.

At 19, everything is possible and tomorrow looks friendly.
JIM BISHOP, *New York Journal-American*, May 9, 1961.

In general my children refused to eat anything that hadn't danced on TV.
ERMA BOMBECK, *Motherhood: The Second Oldest Profession*, 1983.

It is one of the surprising things about youth that it can so easily be the most conservative of all ages.
RANDOLPH BOURNE, *Youth and Life*, 1913.

The average child is an almost non-existent myth. To be normal one must be peculiar in some way or another.
HEYWOOD BROUN, *Sitting in the World*, 1924.

If our American way of life fails the child, it fails us all.

PEARL S. BUCK, *Children for Adoption*, 1964.

The young do not know enough to be prudent, and therefore they attempt the impossible—and achieve it, generation after generation.

PEARL S. BUCK, *The Goddess Abides*, 1972.

Have you slugged your kid today?

Bumper sticker on car of ALFRED S. REGNERY, nominee for director of Office of Juvenile Justice and Delinquency Prevention, *Newsweek*, May 2, 1983.

Adolescence is just one big walking pimple.

CAROL BURNETT, on "Donahue," October 16, 1986.

Children can stand vast amounts of sternness. They rather expect to be wrong and are quite used to being punished. It is injustice, inequity and inconsistency that kill them.

ROBERT F. CAPON, *Bed and Board*, 1965.

If a child is to keep alive his inborn sense of wonder, he needs the companionship of at least one adult who can share it, rediscovering with him the joy, excitement and mystery of the world we live in.

RACHEL CARSON, *The Sense of Wonder*, 1965.

I was the kind of kid who didn't like to admit she'd lost her faith for fear of hurting God's feelings.

CHRIS CHASE, *How to Be a Movie Star, or a Terrible Beauty Is Born*, 1968.

Will Your Child Learn to Multiply Before She Learns to Subtract?

Children's Defense Fund poster on teen pregnancies, 1986.

Young people should remain idealistic all their lives. If you have to choose between being Don Quixote and Sancho Panza, for heaven's sake, be the Don.

RAMSEY CLARK, *The Detroit News*, April 28, 1978.

The sins of the fathers are visited upon the heads of their children—but only if the children continue in the evil deeds of the fathers.

ELDRIDGE CLEAVER, *Soul on Ice*, 1968.

As soon as I stepped out of my mother's womb on to dry land, I realized that I had made a mistake—that I shouldn't have come—but the trouble with children is that they are not returnable.

QUENTIN CRISP, *The Naked Civil Servant*, 1966.

Babies are unreasonable; they expect far too much of existence. Each new generation that comes takes one look at the world, thinks wildly, "Is *this* all they've done to it?" and bursts into tears.

CLARENCE DAY, "Odd Countries," *The Crow's Nest*, 1921.

The hatred of the youth culture for adult society is not a disinterested judgment but a terror-ridden refusal to be hooked into the...ecological chain of birthing, growing, and dying. It is the demand, in other words, to remain children.

MIDGE DECTER, *The New Chastity and Other Arguments Against Women's Liberation*, 1972.

From one end of this country to another in each of the comfortable suburbs and fashionable neighborhoods that have been settled by members of the "new class," are to be found people of my age huddling together from time to time... asking one another [what] has gone wrong with the children?

MIDGE DECTER, *Liberal Parents, Radical Children*, 1975.

The college undergraduate is lots of things—many of them as familiar, predictable, and responsible as the bounce of a basketball, and others as startling (and occasionally as disastrous) as the bounce of a football.

JOHN SLOAN DICKEY, "Conscience and the Undergraduate," *Atlantic*, April, 1955.

Our children are growing up now in an ethically polluted nation where substance is being sacrificed daily for shadow.

MARIAN WRIGHT EDELMAN, speech, Howard University, May 12, 1990.

The years between eighteen and twenty-two were not given to us to be frittered away in contemplation of future tax shelters and mortgage payments. In fact, it is almost a requirement of developmental biology that these years be spent in erotic reverie, metaphysical speculation, and schemes for universal peace and justice. Sometimes, of course, we lose sight of the heroic dreams of youth later on, as overdue bills and carburetor problems take their toll. But those who never dream at all start to lose much more—their wit, empathy, perspective, and, for lack of a more secular term, their immortal souls.

BARBARA EHRENREICH, "Premature Pragmatism," *The Worst Years of Our Lives*, 1986.

O Youth: Do you know that yours is not the first generation to yearn for a life of beauty and freedom? Do you know that all your ancestors felt as you do—and fell victim to trouble and hatred? Do you know, also, that your fervent wishes can only find fulfillment if you succeed in attaining love and understanding of men, and animals, and plants, and stars, so that every joy becomes your joy and every pain your pain? Open your eyes, your heart, your hands, and avoid the poison your forebears so greedily sucked in from History. Then will all the earth be your fatherland, and all your work and effort spread forth blessings.

ALBERT EINSTEIN, album entry, Caputh, Germany, 1932.

Fortunately for us and our world, youth is not easily discouraged. Youth with its clear vista and boundless faith and optimism is uninhibited by the thousands of considerations that always bedevil man in his progress. The hopes of the world rest on the flexibility, vigor, capacity for new thought, and the fresh outlook of the young.

DWIGHT D. EISENHOWER, speech, Gettysburg College, May 27, 1946.

Now once more the belt is tight and we summon the proper expression of horror as we look back at our wasted youth. Sometimes, though, there is a ghostly rumble among the drums, an asthmatic whisper in the trombones that swings me back into the early twenties when we drank wood alcohol and every day in every way grew better and better, and there was a first abortive shortening of the skirts, and girls all looked alike in sweater dresses, and people you didn't want to know said "Yes, we have no bananas," and it seemed only a question of a few years before the older people would step aside and let the world be run by those who saw things as they were—and it all seems rosy and romantic to us who were young then, because we will never feel quite so intensely about our surroundings any more.

F. SCOTT FITZGERALD, "Echoes of the Jazz Age," November, 1931, The Crack-up, 1945.

Youth has one great element in its favor—it can live in the future.

HENRY FORD, "Success," Forum, October, 1928.

Youths have a tremendous advantage over their elders in possessing the power of vision without the drawback of retrospect.

HENRY FORD, "Success," Forum, October, 1928.

In a world as empirical as ours, a youngster who does not know what he is good *at* will not be sure what he is good *for*.

EDGAR Z. FRIEDENBERG, The Vanishing Adolescent: Emotional Development in Adolescence, 1959.

Adults are obsolete children and the hell with them.

THEODOR GEISEL (DR. SEUSS), Time, May 7, 1979.

Noticed, studied, commented on, and incessantly interfered with; forced into miserable self-consciousness by this unremitting glare; our little ones grow up permanently injured in character by this lack of one of humanity's most precious rights—privacy.

CHARLOTTE PERKINS GILMAN, "Two Callings," The Home, 1910.

An empty larder is something you come to expect when you live through the locust phase of adolescence.

ELLEN GOODMAN, "Nething to Eat," Washington Post, August, 1986.

Think about how hard it is for kids to shock the sort of elders who once played in college productions of Hair. Imagine rebelling against today's parents who accept rebellion as a normal stage of life. Try being outrageous in front of a teacher who refuses to notice that you have waxed your eyebrows off and are wearing black lipstick on the upper lip and white on the lower.

ELLEN GOODMAN, "Understanding Madonna," Washington Post, June 1985.

Their intolerance is breath-taking. Do your thing means do their thing.

PAUL GOODMAN, New Reformation, 1970.

As for boys and girls, it is one of the sorriest mistakes to talk down to them: almost always your lad of fifteen thinks more simply, more fundamentally than you do; and what he accepts as good coin is not facts or precepts, but feelings and convictions.

DAVID GRAYSON, The Friendly Road, 1913.

The number-one thing young people in America—indeed, young people around the world—have going for them is their sense of honesty, morality, and ethics. Young people refuse to accept the lies and rationalizations of the established order.

DICK GREGORY, Dick Gregory's Political Primer, 1972.

Misery is when you make your bed and then your mother tells you it's the day she's changing the sheets.

SUZANNE HELLER, Misery, 1964.

Grown people were always on the edge of telling you something valuable and then withdrawing it, a form of bully-teasing.

Lillian Hellman, *Pentimento*, 1973.

Kids today live with awful nightmares: AIDS will wipe us out; the polar ice cap will melt; the nuclear bomb will go off at any minute. Even the best tend to believe we are hopeless to affect matters.... Young people are detached from history, the planet and, most important, the future.

Abbie Hoffman, speech to jury during trial on trespassing charges, April 15, 1987.

Mom and Pop were just a couple of kids when they got married. He was eighteen, she was sixteen, and I was three.

Billie Holiday, *Lady Sings the Blues*, 1958.

I can't stand children. The little crumb-crushers eat you out of house and home and never say, "Dog, kiss my foot."

Billie Holiday, in Maya Angelou, *The Heart of a Woman*, 1981.

For we like children who are a little afraid of us, docile, deferential children, though not, of course, if they are so obviously afraid that they threaten our image of ourselves as kind, lovable people whom there is no reason to fear.

John Holt, *How Children Fail*, 1982.

Children need love, especially when they do not deserve it.

Harold S. Hulbert, *Reader's Digest*, May, 1949.

Our Gilded Youths should be packed off to coal and iron mines, to freight trains, to fishing fleets in December, to dishwashing and clothes-washing, to road building and tunnel making, according to their choice, to get the childishness knocked out of them, and to come back into society with healthier sympathies and sobererer ideas.

William James, "The Moral Equivalent of War," 1910.

All children are potential victims, dependent upon the world's good will.

Sally Kempton, "Cutting Loose," *Esquire*, July, 1970.

If I can leave a single message with the younger generation, it is to lash yourself to the mast, like Ulysses if you must, to escape the siren calls of complacency and indifference.

Edward M. Kennedy, speech, June 4, 1978, in Henry Steele Commager, ed., *Our Day and Generation*, 1979.

What the vast majority of American children need is to stop being pampered, stop being indulged, stop being chauffeured, stop being catered to. In the final analysis it is not what you do for your children but what you have taught them to do for themselves that will make them successful human beings.

Ann Landers, *Ann Landers Says Truth Is Stranger...*, 1968.

I have begun to suspect that American society has little liking for its children, that more often than not children find themselves cast in the role of expensive enemies.

Lewis H. Lapham, "The Spoils of Childhood," *Baltimore Sun*, August, 1984.

We have kept our children so busy with "useful" and "improving" activities that we are in danger of raising a generation of young people who are terrified of silence, of being alone with their own thoughts.

Eda J. Le Shan, *The Conspiracy Against Childhood*, 1967.

Every generation must go further than the last or what's the use in it?

Meridel Le Sueur, *Salute to Spring*, 1940.

Children ask better questions than do adults. "May I have a cookie?" "Why is the sky blue?" and "What does a cow say?" are far more likely to elicit a cheerful response than "Where's your manuscript?" "Why haven't you called?" and "Who's your lawyer?"

Fran Lebowitz, *Metropolitan Life*, 1974.

The high IQ has become the American equivalent of the Legion of Honor, positive proof of the child's intellectual aristocracy.... It has become more important to be a smart kid than a good kid or even a healthy kid.

Sam Levenson, *Everything but Money*, 1966.

We still put a blight on the "illegitimate" child, though we have never defined how he differs from ordinary children.

Ben B. Lindsey and Wainwright Evans, *The Revolt of Modern Youth*, 1925.

I am for children first, because I am for Society first, and the children of today are the Society of tomorrow. I insist, therefore, on the right of the child to be born, and that there be no "illegitimate" children.

Ben B. Lindsey and Wainwright Evans, *The Revolt of Modern Youth*, 1925.

Youth condemns; maturity condones.

AMY LOWELL, *Tendencies in Modern American Poetry*, 1917.

A truly appreciative child will break, lose, spoil, or fondle to death any really successful gift within a matter of minutes.

RUSSELL LYNES, "The Art of Accepting," *Vogue*, 1952.

The teenagers ain't all bad. I love 'em if nobody else does. There ain't nothin' wrong with young people. Jus' quit lyin' to 'em.

JACKIE "MOMS" MABLEY, *Newsday*, April 6, 1967.

If a child shows himself incorrigible, he should be decently and quietly beheaded at the age of twelve, lest he grow to maturity, marry, and perpetuate his kind.

DON MARQUIS, *The Almost Perfect State*, 1927.

In point of fact, we are all born rude. No infant has ever appeared yet with the grace to understand how inconsiderate it is to disturb others in the middle of the night.

JUDITH MARTIN, *Common Courtesy*, 1985.

A young man must let his ideas grow, not be continually rooting them up to see how they are getting on.

WILLIAM MCFEE, *Harbours of Memory: The Idea*, 1921.

In those days, people did not think it was important for girls to read. Some people thought much reading gave girls brain fever.

ANN MCGOVERN, *The Secret Soldier*, 1975.

Even very recently, the elders could say: "You know I have been young, and *you* can never have been old." But today's young people can reply: "You have never been young in the world I am young in, and you never can be...." This break between generations is wholly new: it is planetary and universal.

MARGARET MEAD, *Culture and Commitment*, 1970.

To cease to be loved is for the child practically synonymous with ceasing to live.

KARL A. MENNINGER, *A Psychiatrist's World*, 1959.

The children are always the chief victims of social chaos.

AGNES MEYER, *Out of These Roots*, 1953.

Childhood Is the Kingdom Where Nobody Dies.

EDNA ST. VINCENT MILLAY, poem title, *Wine from These Grapes*, 1934.

Show me the man who has enjoyed his schooldays and I will show you a bully and a bore.

ROBERT MORLEY, *Robert Morley: Responsible Gentleman*, 1966.

We have become the first society in history in which children are the poorest group in the population.

DANIEL MOYNIHAN, *Commentary*, November, 1985.

The commonest axiom of history is that every generation revolts against its fathers and makes friends with its grandfathers.

LEWIS MUMFORD, *The Brown Decades*, 1931.

It's time we let kids grow up naturally. Suppose they don't grow up to be athletic superstars. That isn't so terrible. Let them find their own interests and their own levels. Let them be kids instead of forcing them to play being adults.

JOE PATERNO, *Mainliner*, April, 1976.

Nature makes boys and girls lovely to look upon so they can be tolerated until they acquire some sense.

WILLIAM LYON PHELPS, *Essays on Things*, 1930.

My father had always said that there are four things a child needs—plenty of love, nourishing food, regular sleep, and lots of soap and water—and after those, what he needs most is some intelligent neglect.

IVY BAKER PRIEST, *Green Grows Ivy*, 1958.

Where are you going, my little one, little one,
Where are you going, my baby, my own?
Turn around and you're two,
Turn around and you're four,
Turn around and you're a young girl going out
  of my door.

MALVINA REYNOLDS, "Turn Around," 1958.

It's a family joke that when I was a tiny child I turned from the window out of which I was watching a snowstorm, and hopefully asked, "Momma, do we believe in winter?"

PHILIP ROTH, *Portnoy's Complaint*, 1969.

If you really want to hear all about it, the first thing you'll probably want to know is where I was born and what my lousy childhood was like and how my parents were occupied and all before they had me, and all that David Copperfield kind of crap, but I don't feel like going into it, if you want to know the truth.

J.D. SALINGER, *The Catcher in the Rye*, 1951.

A baby is God's opinion that the world should go on.

CARL SANDBURG, *Remembrance Rock*, 1948.

Children don't read to find their identity, to free themselves from guilt, to quench the thirst for rebellion or to get rid of alienation. They have no use for psychology. They detest sociology. They still believe in God, the family, angels, devils, witches, goblins, logic, clarity, punctuation, and other such obsolete stuff....When a book is boring, they yawn openly. They don't expect their writer to redeem humanity, but to leave to adults such childish illusions.

ISAAC BASHEVIS SINGER, speech on receiving Nobel Prize for Literature, 1978.

The denunciation of the young is a necessary part of the hygiene of older people, and greatly assists in the circulation of their blood.

LOGAN PEARSALL SMITH, *Afterthoughts*, 1931.

I am a student. Please do not fold, spindle, or mutilate me.

Free speech slogan, 1964.

Childhood is a prison sentence of twenty-one years.

THOMAS SZASZ, *The Second Sin: Childhood*, 1973.

A child becomes an adult when he realizes that he has a right not only to be right but also to be wrong.

THOMAS SZASZ, *The Second Sin: Childhood*, 1973.

Healthy children are, among other things, little animals, who only slowly evolve (if they ever do) into civilized human beings....Children are not naturally "good," according to any standards ever set by a civilized society. They are natural barbarians.

DOROTHY THOMPSON, *The Courage To Be Happy*, 1957.

If men do not keep on speaking terms with children, they cease to be men, and become merely machines for eating and for earning money.

JOHN UPDIKE, "A Foreword for Younger Readers," *Assorted Prose*, 1965.

Until the rise of American advertising, it never occurred to anyone anywhere in the world that the teenager was a captive in a hostile world of adults.

GORE VIDAL, *Rocking the Boat*, 1962.

Don't trust anyone over 30.

Slogan of the 1960s attributed to DAVID WEINBERGER, in Jerry Rubin, *Growing (Up) at 37*, 1976.

To grown people a girl of fifteen and a half is a child still; to herself she is very old and very real; more real, perhaps, than ever before or after.

MARGARET WIDDEMER, *The Boardwalk: The Changeling*, 1919.

I have been slow to understand that the contrariness of the "terrible twos" is the bloody-mindedness of little people trying to get a grip on their partially formed selves. I used to think that a two-year-old's father needs only what a Washington columnist needs, the ability to look perfectly grave no matter what nonsense is being spoken to him. But I no longer think that what two-year-olds say is nonsense.

GEORGE WILL, "Gorilla in the Kitchen," October 17, 1976, *The Pursuit of Happiness, and Other Sobering Thoughts*, 1978.

Americans are predisposed to believe too much in environmental determinism. They are inclined to regard infants as malleable bundles of "potential"—clay on which determined parents, handbooks in hand, can work wonders.

In the "nature versus nurture" argument, Americans are can-do optimists who believe that skilled nurturing is all-important in shaping individuals. The United States is a manufacturing nation that sometimes seems to regard children as raw material from which ever-better products can be manufactured as know-how increases.

GEORGE WILL, "Perils of Parenting," February 13, 1977, *The Pursuit of Happiness, and Other Sobering Thoughts*, 1978.

They are the most selfish people I know. They just terrify me. They are acting out a society I'd like to live in as an orangutan.

WILLIAM APPLEMAN WILLIAMS, on young adherents to New Left movement, *New York Times*, November 20, 1967.

You cannot have ecstasy and divine vision without bitterness and despair, and both of these are the property of youth....For the young are not always lighthearted; youth bears a heavy heart. The earth quakes beneath his tread; the stars are combined against him; he is the battleground for a menagerie which is ready to spring at his throat. And when in the midst of these disasters he finds a moment of calm or freedom, his heart goes up like a rocket to the farthest reaches of the sky.

EDMUND WILSON, letter to Christian Gauss, April 25, 1922.

We are the people our parents warned us against.

Youth movement slogan, ca. 1965.

Culture and Civilization

See also **American Mosaic; American Society; The Arts; Dreams and Ideals; Ethics and Morality; History and Tradition; The Human Condition; Language and Discourse; Popular Culture; Religion and Spirituality; Science and Technology; War and Peace**

Civilization is a method of living, an attitude of equal respect for all men.

JANE ADDAMS, speech, Honolulu, Hawaii, 1933.

Civilization is the lamb's skin in which barbarism masquerades.

THOMAS BAILEY ALDRICH, "Leaves from a Notebook," *Ponkapog Papers,* 1903.

A scientific culture is one in which the structure of the atom is studied and comes to be more or less vaguely known; it is also a culture in which a winning racehorse is named Correlation and in which the matching pieces of a woman's suit are sold as "coordinates"; it is a culture in which the photograph of the diffraction of electrons by zinc oxide resembles a prevailing mode of painting, and in which a polished roller bearing or a magnified diagram of the male hormone, when colored, can be used as a decoration in the home.

JACQUES BARZUN, *Science: The Glorious Entertainment,* 1964.

In matters pertaining to the care of life there has been no marked gain over Greek and Roman antiquity.

MARY RITTER BEARD, *Understanding Women,* 1931.

Modern culture is defined by this extraordinary freedom to ransack the world storehouse and to engorge any and every style it comes upon. Such freedom comes from the fact that the axial principle of modern culture is the expression and remaking of the "self" in order to achieve self-realization and self-fulfillment. And in its search, there is a denial of any limits or boundaries to experience. It is a reaching out for all experience; nothing is forbidden, all is to be explored.

DANIEL BELL, *Cultural Contradictions of Capitalism,* 1976.

American cultural traditions define personality, achievement, and the purpose of human life in ways that leave the individual suspended in glorious, but terrifying, isolation. These are limitations of our culture, of the categories and ways of thinking we have inherited, not limitations of individuals...who inhabit this culture.

ROBERT BELLAH ET AL., *Habits of the Heart,* 1985.

No man ever looks at the world with pristine eyes. He sees it edited by a definite set of customs and institutions and ways of thinking.

RUTH BENEDICT, *Patterns of Culture,* 1934.

The acquiring of culture is the developing of an avid hunger for knowledge and beauty.

JESSE LEE BENNETT, *On Culture and a Liberal Education,* 1922.

The true worth of a race must be measured by the character of its womanhood.

MARY MCLEOD BETHUNE, speech, "A Century of Progress of Negro Women," June 3, 1933, Chicago Women's Federation, in Gerda Lerner, ed., *Black Women in White America,* 1973.

Home building, home decoration and furnishing, *home making,* in fact, is the most outstanding phase of modern civilization.

EDWARD BOK, "The American Home, the Joyous Adventure," *American Home,* January, 1929.

A civilization based purely on agriculture was a civilization which never went hungry. But a raucous and ruthless civilization, dependent on the churning of the "devil machines" within brick walls, was vulnerable to every sensitive wind that blew from Wall Street.

TAYLOR CALDWELL, *This Side of Innocence,* 1946.

In this era of affluence and permissiveness, we have, in all but cultured areas, bred a nation of overprivileged youngsters, saturated with vitamins, television and plastic toys. But they are nurtured from infancy on a Dick-and-Jane literary and artistic level; and the cultural drought, as far as entertainment is concerned, sets in when they are between six and eight.

JUDITH CRIST, *The Private Eye, the Cowboy and the Very Naked Girl,* 1968.

If the public is given a chance to discriminate, the tendency is always upward.

OLIN DOWNES, in Arthur Goodfriend, *What Is America?,* 1954.

Our civilization is still in the middle stage: scarcely beast, in that it is no longer wholly guided by instinct; scarcely human, in that it is not yet wholly guided by reason.

THEODORE DREISER, *Sister Carrie,* 1900.

Civilizations commonly die from the excessive development of certain characteristics which had at first contributed to their success.

RENÉ DUBOS, *A God Within,* 1972.

Civilizations commmonly behave as if they became intoxicated with their technological and social proficiency and lost critical sense in dealing with their own creations.

RENÉ DUBOS, *A God Within,* 1972.

No civilization professes openly to be unable to declare its destination. In an age like our own, however, there comes a time when individuals in increasing numbers unconsciously seek direction and taste despair.

LOREN EISELEY, *The Night Country,* 1971.

The great advances of civilization, whether in architecture or painting, in science and literature, in industry or agriculture, have never come from centralized government.

MILTON FRIEDMAN, *Capitalism and Freedom,* 1962.

In the nineteenth century the problem was that God is dead; in the twentieth century the problem is that man is dead.

ERICH FROMM, *The Sane Society,* 1955.

The great problem that we have in the United States is the problem that would face any society in which the greatest proportion of people had been given the purchasing power with which to satisfy whatever instincts they had for cultural objects.... In a free society, the market is solicited by all kinds of people—manufacturers, printers of comic books, Wheatsu-Teetsu producers, etc.

LEWIS GALANTIERE, in Arthur Goodfriend, *What Is America?,* 1954.

The civilization malaise, in a word, reflects the inability of a civilization directed to material improvement—higher incomes, better diets, miracles of medicine, triumphs of applied physics and chemistry—to satisfy the human spirit.

ROBERT L. HEILBRONER, *An Inquiry into the Human Prospect,* 1980.

Culture is only culture when the owner is not aware of its existence. Capture culture, hog-tie it, and clap your brand upon it, and you find the shock has killed the thing you loved. You can brand a steer, but you cannot brand deer.

ELBERT HUBBARD, *The Roycroft Dictionary and Book of Epigrams,* 1923.

Men who sit back and pride themselves on their culture haven't any to speak of.

ELBERT HUBBARD, *The Roycroft Dictionary and Book of Epigrams,* 1923.

Culture is simply how one lives and is connected to history by habit.

LEROI JONES, "The Legend of Malcolm X," *Home,* 1966.

All of us confront limits of body, talent, temperament. But that is not all. We are, all of us, also constrained by our time, our place, our civilization. We are bound by the culture we have in common, that culture which distinguishes us from other people in other times and places. Cultural constraints condition and limit our choices, shaping our characters with their imperatives.

JEANE KIRKPATRICK, speech, Georgetown University, May 24, 1981.

Human history, if you read it right, is the record of the efforts to tame Father. Next to striking a fire and the discovery of the wheel, the greatest triumph of what we call civilization was the domestication of the human male.

MAX LERNER, "The Revolt of the American Father," *The Unfinished Country,* 1959.

I have tried to show that contemporary society is a repressive society in all its aspects, that even the comfort and the prosperity, the alleged political and moral freedom, are utilized for repressive ends.

HERBERT MARCUSE, in Lois and Alan Gordon, *American Chronicle,* 1987.

Chief among our gains must be reckoned this possibility of choice, the recognition of many possible ways of life, where other civilizations have recognized only one. Where other civilizations give a satisfactory outlet to only one temperamental type, be he mystic or soldier, businessman or artist, a civilization in which there are many standards offers a possibility of satisfctory adjustment to individuals of many different temperamental types, of diverse gifts and varying interests.

MARGARET MEAD, *Coming of Age in Samoa*, 1928.

[T]he most cooperative, most stable societies that I know are not patriarchal and they are not matriarchal, but they are societies in which both men and women work together, and they are societies in which women are very sure they are women and are not trying to be imitation men while they are being citizens.

MARGARET MEAD, speech, Woman's Centennial Congress, November 26, 1940.

We must recognize that beneath the superficial classifications of sex and race the same potentialities exist, recurring generation after generation, only to perish because society has no place for them.

MARGARET MEAD, *Male and Female*, 1948.

It is human nature to imagine that our present reality is squalid, diminished, an ignominious comedown from better days when household appliances lasted and workers worked, and manners were exquisite and marriages endured, and wars were just, and honor mattered, and you could buy a decent tomato. The lament for vanished standards is an old art form: besieged gentility cringes, indignant and vulnerable, full of memories, before a present that behaves like Stanley Kowalski: crude, loud, upstart, and stupid as a fist.

LANCE MORROW, "Excellence," *Fishing in the Tiber*, 1988.

The world of culture—man's achievement—exists within the world of grace—God's Kingdom.

REINHOLD NIEBUHR, *Christ and Culture*, 1951.

The adjustment of modern religion to the "mind" of modern culture inevitably involved capitulation to its thin "soul."

REINHOLD NIEBUHR, *An Interpretation of Chrisian Ethics*, 1935.

The present age is demented. It is possessed by a sense of dislocation, a loss of personal identity, an alternating sentimentality and rage which, in an individual patient, could be characterized as dementia.

WALKER PERCY, in Clifton Fadiman, ed., *Living Philosophies*, 1990.

It has been demonstrated many times that a culture can survive misinformation and false opinion. It has not yet been demonstrated whether a culture can survive if it takes the measure of the world in twenty-two minutes. Or if the value of its news is determined by the number of laughs it provides.

NEIL POSTMAN, *Amusing Ourselves to Death*, 1985.

People who cannot recognize a palpable absurdity are very much in the way of civilization.

AGNES REPPLIER, *In Pursuit of Laughter*, 1936.

No civilization can become world-wide and enduring if a white skin is the indispensable passport to justice and distinction. This would exclude...the majority of mankind.

CHARLES VICTOR ROMAN, *Science and Christian Ethics*, 1913.

Society is like the air, necessary to breathe, but insufficient to live on.

GEORGE SANTAYANA, *Little Essays*, 1920.

The preservation of civilization and culture is now one with the preservation of religion.

FULTON J. SHEEN, *The Woman*, 1951.

One can judge a civilization by the way it treats its women.

HELEN FOSTER SNOW, "Bound Feet and Straw Sandals," *Women in Modern China*, 1967.

We came, therefore (and with many Western thinkers before us), to suspect civilization may be overvalued.

GARY SNYDER, 1966, in Lois and Alan Gordon, *American Chronicle*, 1987.

Camp is the answer to the problem: how to be a dandy in an age of mass culture. Camp asserts...there is a good taste of bad taste...[for example] The *Enquirer*..."Swan Lake"...Shoedsack's "King Kong"...Jayne Mansfield...Victor Mature...Bette Davis...Art Nouveau.

SUSAN SONTAG, "Notes on Camp," 1964.

True, the white man brought great change. But the varied fruits of his civilization, though highly colored and inviting, are sickening and deadening. And if it be the part of civilization to maim, rob, and thwart, then what is progress?

LUTHER STANDING BEAR, *Land of the Spotted Eagle*, 1933.

[T]rue civilization lies in the dominance of self and not in the dominance of other man.

LUTHER STANDING BEAR, *Land of the Spotted Eagle*, 1933.

The Law of Raspberry Jam: The wider any culture is spread, the thinner it gets.

ALVIN TOFFLER, *The Culture Consumers*, 1964.

Beyond all plans and programs, true conservation is ultimately something of the mind—an ideal of men who cherish their past and believe in the future. Our civilization will be measured by its fidelity to this ideal as surely as by its art and poetry and system of justice. In our perpetual search for abundance, beauty, and order we manifest both our love for the land and our sense of responsibility toward future generations.

STEWART L. UDALL, *The Quiet Crisis*, 1963.

The lack of awareness of sense and purpose has led culture to become increasingly shallow.

VICTOR WEISSKOPF, *The Joy of Insight*, 1991.

Men and women are biological facts. Ladies and gentlemen—*citizens*—are social artifacts, works of political art. They carry the culture that is sustained by wise laws, and traditions of civility. At the end of the day we are right to judge a society by the character of the people it produces. That is why statecraft is, inevitably, soulcraft.

GEORGE WILL, Introduction, *The Pursuit of Happiness, and Other Sobering Thoughts*, 1978.

A few suits of clothes, some money in the bank, and a new kind of fear constitute the main differences between the average American today and the hairy men with clubs who accompanied Attila to the city of Rome.

PHILIP WYLIE, *Generation of Vipers*, 1942.

Few there are who have paused to question whether real life or long-lasting death lies beneath this semblance of civilization.

ZITKALA-SA, *Atlantic Monthly*, March, 1900.

Death

See also **Age**; **The Human Condition**—Fear; **Life's Lessons**; **Religion and Spirituality**; **Social Issues**—Health, Violence; **War and Peace**

Death not merely ends life, it also bestows upon it a silent completeness, snatched from the hazardous flux to which all things human are subject.

ELIZABETH ARDEN, *The Life of the Mind*, 1978.

If there be anything in me that is of permanent worth and service to the universe, the universe will know how to preserve it. Whatsoever in me is not of permanent worth and service, neither can nor should be preserved.

HORACE JAMES BRIDGES, in Joseph Fort Newton, "Concerning God," *My Idea of God*, 1926.

[Walt] Whitman once said to me that he would as soon hope to argue a man into good health as to argue him into a belief of immortality. He said he *knew* it was so without proof; but I never could light my candle at his great torch.

JOHN BURROUGHS, in Clara Barrus, *Life and Letters of John Burroughs*, 1925.

"You should not be discouraged; one does not die of a cold," the priest said to the bishop.

The old man smiled. "I shall not die of a cold, my son. I shall die of having lived."

WILLA CATHER, *Death Comes for the Archbishop*, 1927.

Death is not the enemy; living in constant fear of it is.

NORMAN COUSINS, *The Healing Heart*, 1983.

Death gives life its fullest reality.

ANTHONY DALLA VILLA, eulogy for Andy Warhol, St. Patrick's Cathedral, New York City, April 1, 1987.

When we abandon the thought of immortality we at least have cast out fear. We gain a certain dignity and self-respect. We regard our fellow travelers as companions in the pleasures and tribulations of life....We gain kinship with the world.

CLARENCE DARROW, *The Story of My Life*, 1932.

The passing years bring with them a great number of disadvantages—death being of one of the most hazardous.

FRED DE CORDOVA, *Johnny Came Lately*, 1988.

Loss grew as you did, without your consent; your losses mounted beside you like earthworm castings. No willpower could prevent someone's dying.

ANNIE DILLARD, *An American Childhood*, 1987.

Man, tree, and flower are supposed to die; but the fact remains that God's universe is spiritual and immortal.

MARY BAKER EDDY, *Science and Health*, 1908.

In reality, man never dies.

MARY BAKER EDDY, *Science and Health*, 1908.

To die is poignantly bitter, but the idea of having to die without having lived is unbearable.

ERICH FROMM, *Man for Himself*, 1947.

Death? Why this fuss about death? Use your imagination, try to visualize a world *without* death!...Death is the essential condition of life, not an evil.

CHARLOTTE PERKINS GILMAN, *The Living of Charlotte Perkins Gilman*, 1935.

It's funny the way most people love the dead. Once you are dead, you are made for life.

JIMI HENDRIX, *Rolling Stone*, December 2, 1976.

There is need for some kind of make-believe in order to face death unflinchingly. To our real, naked selves there is not a thing on earth or in heaven worth dying for.

ERIC HOFFER, *The True Believer*, 1951.

The sanest and best of us are of one clay with lunatics and prison inmates, and death finally runs the robustest of us down.

WILLIAM JAMES, *The Varieties of Religious Experience*, 1902.

The strong lean upon death as on a rock.

ROBINSON JEFFERS, "Gale in April," 1930.

And God said, Go down, Death, go down;

Go down to Savannah, Georgia,

Down to Yamacraw,

And find Sister Caroline.

She's borne the burden and the heat of the day,

She's labored long in my vineyard,

And she's tired—

She's weary—

Go down, Death, and bring her to me.

JAMES WELDON JOHNSON, "Go Down, Death," *American Mercury*, April, 1927.

To me death is not a fearful thing. It's living that's cursed.

JIM JONES, Jonestown, Guyana, November 18, 1978.

Death is not the cessation of life, but an incident in it. It is but the "narrows," to use the Psalmist's striking expression, through which the soul passes on its fateful voyage.

MORRIS JOSEPH, *Judaism as Creed and Life*, 1903.

Watching a peaceful death of a human being reminds us of a falling star; one of a million lights in a vast sky that flares up for a brief moment only to disappear into the endless night forever.

ELISABETH KÜBLER-ROSS, *On Death and Dying*, 1969.

As you know, most of your fellow countrymen choose to look upon death as a mistake—an accident distinctly un-American.

LEWIS H. LAPHAM, "The Senior Practitioner," speech, Northwestern Medical School, June, 1987.

O death where is thy sting? O grave where is thy victory? Where, indeed? Many a badly stung survivor, faced with the aftermath of some relative's funeral, has ruefully conceded that the victory has been won hands down by a funeral establishment—in disastrously unequal battle.

JESSICA MITFORD, *The American Way of Death*, 1963.

All victory ends in the defeat of death. That's sure. But does defeat end in the victory of death? That's what I wonder!

EUGENE O'NEILL, *Mourning Becomes Electra*, 1931.

Guns aren't lawful;

Nooses give;

Gas smells awful;

You might as well live.

DOROTHY PARKER, "Resume," *Enough Rope*, 1927.

Dying

Is an art, like everything else.

I do it exceptionally well.

I do it so it feels like hell,

I do it so it feels real.

I guess you could say I've a call.

SYLVIA PLATH, "Lady Lazarus," *Ariel*, 1961.

He said he was dying of fast women, slow horses, crooked cards and straight whiskey.

KENNETH REXROTH, on his father, *An Autobiographical Novel*, 1966.

I shall have more to say when I am dead.

EDWIN ARLINGTON ROBINSON, "John Brown," *The Three Taverns*, 1920.

Pile the bodies high at Austerlitz and Waterloo.

Shovel them under and let me work—

I am the grass; I cover all.

CARL SANDBURG, "Grass," *Cornhuskers*, 1918.

Nothing can be meaner than the anxiety to live on, to live on anyhow and in any shape; a spirit with any honor is not willing to live except in its own way, and a spirit with any wisdom is not over-eager to live at all.

GEORGE SANTAYANA, *Winds of Doctrine*, 1913.

Everybody has got to die, but I have always believed an exception would be made in my case. Now what?

WILLIAM SAROYAN, last words telephoned to Associated Press, 1981.

Dying seems less sad than having lived too little.

GLORIA STEINEM, *Outrageous Acts and Everyday Rebellions*, 1983.

[F]unerals are always occasions for pious lying. A deep vein of superstition and a sudden touch of kindness always lead people to give the departed credit for more virtues than he possessed.

I.F. STONE, "We All Had a Finger on That Trigger," *I.F. Stone's Weekly*, December 9, 1963.

Death is not a sudden-all-at-once affair; cells go down in sequence, one by one. You can, if you like, recover great numbers of them many hours after the lights have gone out, and grow them out in cultures. It takes hours, even days, before the irreversible word finally gets around to all the provinces.

LEWIS THOMAS, "The Long Habit," *The Lives of a Cell*, 1974.

People and societies who cannot see any purpose in their existence beyond the material and the tangible must live chartlessly, and must live in spiritual misery, because they cannot overcome the greatest fact and mystery of human life, next to birth, which is death.

DOROTHY THOMPSON, *The Courage To Be Happy*, 1957.

Funerals are pretty compared with death.

TENNESSEE WILLIAMS, *A Streetcar Named Desire*, 1947.

It's a blessing to die for a cause, because you can so easily die for nothing.

ANDREW YOUNG, interview, *Playboy*, July, 1977.

Dreams and Ideals

There is no force so democratic as the force of an ideal.

CALVIN COOLIDGE, speech, New York City, November 27, 1920.

They [Americans] still believe that somehow and sometime something better will happen to good Americans than has happened to men in any other country: and this belief, vague, innocent, and uninformed though it be, is the expression of an essential constituent in our national ideal.

HERBERT CROLY, *The Promise of American Life*, 1909.

The fulfillment of the American promise was considered inevitable because it was based upon a combination of self-interest and the natural goodness of human nature.

HERBERT CROLY, *The Promise of American Life*, 1909.

There has always been that divergence between our official and our unofficial heroes. It is impossible to think of Howard Hughes without seeing the apparently bottomless gulf between what we say we want and what we do want, between what we officially admire and secretly desire, between, in the largest sense, the people we marry and the people we love.

JOAN DIDION, "7000 Romaine, Los Angeles 38," *Slouching Towards Bethlehem*, 1968.

Ideas are indeed the most dangerous weapons in the world.

WILLIAM O. DOUGLAS, *An Almanac of Liberty*, 1954.

Dear Posterity,

If you have not become more just, more peaceful, and generally more rational than we are (or were)—why then, the Devil take you.

Having, with all respect, given utterance to this pious wish,

I am (or was),

Your,

Albert Einstein

ALBERT EINSTEIN, ca. 1936, in Timothy Ferris, "The Other Einstein," *A Passion to Know: 20 Profiles in Science*, 1985.

I believe that man will not merely endure; he will prevail. He is immortal, not because he alone among creatures has an inexhaustible voice, but because he has a soul, a spirit capable of compassion and sacrifice and endurance.

WILLIAM FAULKNER, Nobel Prize acceptance speech, Stockholm, Sweden, December 10, 1950.

If a man hasn't discovered something that he will die for, he isn't fit to live.

MARTIN LUTHER KING, Jr., speech, Detroit, Michigan, June 23, 1963.

I unconsciously decided that, even if it wasn't an ideal world, it should be and so painted only the ideal aspects of it—pictures in which there are no drunken slatterns or self-centered mothers... only foxy grandpas who played baseball with the kids and boys who fished from logs and got up circuses in the backyard.

NORMAN ROCKWELL, *Washington Post*, May, 1972.

We observe today not a victory of party but a celebration of freedom—symbolizing an end as well as a beginning—signifying renewal as well as change. For I have sworn before you and Almighty God the same solemn oath our forebears prescribed nearly a century and three-quarters ago.

The world is very different now. For man holds in his mortal hands the power to abolish all forms of human poverty and all forms of human life. And yet the same revolutionary beliefs for which our forebears fought are still at issue around the globe—the belief that the rights of man come not from the generosity of the state but from the hand of God.

We dare not forget today that we are the heirs of that first revolution. Let the word go forth from this time and place, to friend and foe alike, that the torch has been passed to a new generation of Americans—born in this century, tempered by war, disciplined by a hard and bitter peace, proud of our ancient heritage—and unwilling to witness or permit the slow undoing of those human rights to which this nation has always been committed, and to which we are committed today at home and around the world.

Let every nation know, whether it wishes us well or ill, that we shall pay any price, bear any burden, meet any hardship, support any friend, oppose any foe to assure the survival and the success of liberty.

This much we pledge—and more.

To those old allies whose cultural and spiritual origins we share, we pledge loyalty of faithful friends. United, there is little we cannot do in a host of cooperative ventures. Divided, there is little we can do—for we dare not meet a powerful challenge at odds and split asunder.

To those new states whom we welcome to the ranks of the free, we pledge our word that one form of colonial control shall not have passed away merely to be replaced by a far more iron tyranny. We shall not always expect to find them supporting our view. But we shall always hope to find them strongly supporting their own freedom—and to remember that, in the past, those who foolishly sought power by riding the back of the tiger ended up inside.

To those people in the huts and villages of half the globe struggling to break the bonds of mass misery, we pledge our best efforts to help them help themselves, for whatever period is required—not because the Communists may be doing it, not because we seek their votes, but because it is right. If a free society cannot help the many who are poor, it cannot save the few who are rich.

To our sister republics south of the border, we offer a special pledge—to convert our good words into good deeds—in a new alliance for progress—to assist free men and free governments in casting off the chains of poverty. But this peaceful revolution of hope cannot become the prey of hostile powers. Let all our neighbors know that we shall join with them to oppose aggression or subversion anywhere in the Americas. And let every other power know that this hemisphere intends to remain the master of its own house.

To that world assembly of sovereign states, the United Nations, our last best hope in an age where the instruments of war have far outpaced the instruments of peace, we renew our pledge of support—to prevent it from becoming merely a forum for invective—to strengthen its shield of the new and the weak—and to enlarge the area in which its writ may run.

Finally, to those nations who would make themselves our adversary, we offer not a pledge but a request: that both sides begin anew the quest for peace, before the dark powers of destruction unleashed by science engulf all humanity in planned or accidental self-destruction.

We dare not tempt them with weakness. For only when our arms are sufficient beyond doubt can we be certain beyond doubt that they will never be employed.

But neither can two great and powerful groups of nations take comfort from our present course—both sides overburdened by the cost of modern weapons, both rightly alarmed by the steady spread of the deadly atom, yet both racing to alter that uncertain balance of terror that stays the hand of mankind's final war.

So let us begin anew—remembering on both sides that civility is not a sign of weakness, and sincerity is always subject to proof. Let us never negotiate out of fear. But let us never fear to negotiate.

Let both sides explore what problems unite us instead of belaboring those problems which divide us.

Let both sides, for the first time, formulate serious and precise proposals for the inspection and control of arms—and bring the absolute power to destroy other nations under the absolute control of all nations.

Let both sides seek to invoke the wonders of science instead of its terrors. Together let us explore the stars, conquer the deserts, eradicate disease, tap the ocean depths, and encourage the arts and commerce.

Let both sides unite to heed in all corners of the earth the command of Isaiah—to "undo the heavy burdens...[and] let the oppressed go free."

And if a beachhead of cooperation may push back the jungle of suspicion, let both sides join in creating a new endeavor, not a new balance of power, but a new world of law, where the strong are just and the weak secure and the peace preserved.

All this will not be finished in the first one hundred days. Nor will it be finished in the first one thousand days, nor in the life of this administration, nor even perhaps in our lifetime on this planet. But let us begin.

In your hands, my fellow citizens, more than mine, will rest the final success or failure of our course. Since this country was founded, each generation of Americans has been summoned to give testimony to its national loyalty. The graves of young Americans who answered the call to service surround the globe.

Now the trumpet summons us again—not as a call to bear arms, though arms we need—not as a call to battle, though embattled we are—but a call to bear the burden of the long twilight struggle, year in and year out, "rejoicing in hope, patient in tribulation"—a struggle against the common enemies of man: tyranny, poverty, disease, and war itself.

Can we forge against these enemies a grand and global alliance, North and South, East and West, that can assure a more fruitful life for all mankind? Will you join in that historic effort?

In the long history of the world, only a few generations have been granted the role of defending freedom in its hour of maximum danger. I do not shrink from this responsibility—I welcome it. I do not believe that any of us would exchange places with any other people or any other generation. The energy, the faith, the devotion which we bring to this endeavor will light our country and all who serve it—and the glow from that fire can truly light the world.

And so, my fellow Americans: ask not what your country can do for you—ask what you can do for your country.

My fellow citizens of the world: ask not what America will do for you, but what together we can do for the freedom of man.

Finally, whether you are citizens of America or citizens of the world, ask of us here the same high standards of strength and sacrifice which we ask of you. With a good conscience our only sure reward, with history the final judge of our deeds, let us go forth to lead the land we love, asking His blessing and His help, but knowing that here on earth God's work must truly be our own.

JOHN F. KENNEDY, inaugural address, January 20, 1961

An ideal cannot wait for its realization to prove its validity.

GEORGE SANTAYANA, *The Life of Reason*, 1905–1906.

Science and technology revolutionize our lives, but memory, tradition and myth frame our response. Expelled from individual consciousness by the rush of change, history finds its revenge by stamping the collective unconscious with habits, values, expectations, dreams. The dialectic between past and future will continue to form our lives.

ARTHUR M. SCHLESINGER, JR., "The Challenge of Change," *New York Times Magazine*, July 27, 1986.

The American dream has always depended on the dialogue between the present and the past. In our architecture, as in all our other arts—indeed, as in our political and social culture as a whole—ours has been a struggle to formulate and sustain a usable past.

ROBERT A.M. STERN, *Pride of Place*, 1986.

If the outside world could be made aware of the inner commitments by which we are guided, it would understand our motivations better and be less prone to accept the distortions and falsehoods that arise from our dealings with other peoples.

FRANK TANNENBAUM, in Arthur Goodfriend, *What Is America?* 1954.

AFFLUENCE

Without the free spirit, affluence is only a form of slavery to undisciplined desires.

KENNETH BOULDING, "Where Do We Go From Here, If Anywhere?" *Beasts, Ballads, and Bouldingisms*, 1961.

The fault in the vision of our national future possessed by the ordinary American does not consist in the expectation of some continuity of achievement. It consists rather in the expectation that the familiar benefits will continue to accumulate automatically.

HERBERT CROLY, *The Promise of American Life*, 1909.

The promise of American life is to be fulfilled not merely by a maximum amount of economic freedom but by a certain measure of discipline; not merely by the abundant satisfaction of individual desires but by a large measure of individual subordination and self-denial. And this necessity of subordinating the satisfaction of individual desires to the fulfillment of a national purpose is

attached particularly to the absorbing occupation of the American people—the occupation, viz.: of accumulating wealth.

HERBERT CROLY, *The Promise of American Life*, 1909.

Affluence was seen as a general condition, attached to no particular persons or groups. It hung over the entire landscape like a bright, numbing haze, a kind of smog with no known source or cure.

BARBARA EHRENREICH, *Fear of Falling*, 1990.

Affluence, abetted by the ancient tradition of gender inequality, was reducing the middle class to a race of sleepwalkers.

BARBARA EHRENREICH, *Fear of Falling*, 1990.

We have limited the area of the so-called luxury goods. There are few things possessed by the rich which are not also the possession of the family of the worker.

LEWIS GALANTIERE, in Arthur Goodfriend, *What Is America?*, 1954.

We've grown unbelievably prosperous, and we maunder along in a stupor of fat.

ERIC GOLDMAN, 1960, in Lois and Alan Gordon, *American Chronicle*, 1987.

The human race has had long experience and a fine tradition in surviving adversity. But now we face a task for which we have little experience, the task of surviving prosperity.

ALAN GREGG, *New York Times*, November 4, 1956.

To the achievement of the tangible goods we enjoy we have devoted almost the whole of our intelligence and our energy, and because the questions answered and the problems solved here centered [on] the achievement of power or the creation of wealth, man is now a creature more powerful and more wealthy than ever before.

JOSEPH WOOD KRUTCH, *Human Nature and the Human Condition*, 1959.

The politics of the Fifties were...the politics of fatigue...[and student] apathy probably unexampled in history....[We chose] to invest not in people but in things.

ARTHUR SCHLESINGER, JR., "The Mood in Politics," 1960.

It's better to have a society where all of us have something than to have one in which a few of us have all.

MELVIN B. TOLSON, "Tigers and Lions and Men," *Washington Tribune*, July 27, 1940.

BEAUTY

Character contributes to beauty. It fortifies a woman as her youth fades. A mode of conduct, a standard of courage, discipline, fortitude and integrity can do a great deal to make a woman beautiful.

JACQUELINE BISSET, *Los Angeles Times*, May 16, 1974.

[I]t is the spirit that knows Beauty, that has music in its soul and the color of sunsets in its headkerchiefs; that can dance on a flaming world and make the world dance, too. Such is the soul of the Negro.

W.E.B. DU BOIS, *Dusk of Dawn*, 1940.

Beauty, what is that? There are phalanxes of beauty in every comic show. Beauty neither buys food nor keeps up a home.

MAXINE ELLIOTT, 1908.

One of the few advantages to not being beautiful is that one usually gets better-looking as one gets older; I am, in fact, at this very moment gaining my looks.

NORA EPHRON, "On Never Having Been a Prom Queen," August, 1972, *Crazy Salad: Some Things about Women*, 1975.

There isn't an ugly girl in America who wouldn't exchange her problems for the problems of being beautiful; I don't believe there's a beautiful girl anywhere who would honestly prefer not to be.

NORA EPHRON, "On Never Having Been a Prom Queen," August, 1972, *Crazy Salad: Some Things about Women*, 1975.

It isn't just older women who get depressed checking out the before and after portraits of women who injected collagen into their laugh lines. The baby-boom generation of women, raised on youth and fitness, has turned forty, facing a future of Optifast, aerobics and sunblock.

ELLEN GOODMAN, "Barbara Bush: The Silver Fox," January, 1989, *Making Sense*, 1989.

Reared as we were in a youth- and beauty-oriented society, we measured ourselves by our ornamental value.

JANET HARRIS, *The Prime of Ms. America*, 1975.

Beauty is not an easy thing to measure. It does not show up in the gross national product, in a weekly paycheck, or in profit-and-loss statements. But these things are not ends in themselves. They are a road to satisfaction and plea-sure and the good life. Beauty makes its own direct contribution to these final ends. Therefore it is one of the most important components of our true national income, not to be left out simply because statisticians cannot calculate its worth.

LYNDON B. JOHNSON, special message to Congress, February 8, 1965.

I'm tired of all this nonsense about beauty being only skin-deep. That's deep enough. What do you want—an adorable pancreas?

JEAN KERR, "Mirror, Mirror, on the Wall, I Don't Want to Hear One Word Out of You," *The Snake Has All the Lines*, 1960.

Beauty in all things—no, we cannot hope for that; but some place set apart for it.

EDNA ST. VINCENT MILLAY, "Invocation to the Muses," *Make Bright the Arrows*, 1940.

It's nice to be included in people's fantasies, but you also like to be accepted for your own sake.

MARILYN MONROE, 1955, in Lois and Alan Gordon, *American Chronicle*, 1987.

What's beautiful is all that counts, pal. That's *all* that counts.

JACK NICHOLSON, *Rolling Stone*, 1986.

There are no ugly women, only lazy ones.

HELENA RUBINSTEIN, *My Life for Beauty*, 1966.

It's not that I don't want to be a beauty, that I don't yearn to be dripping with glamor. It's just that I can't see how any woman can find time to do to herself all the things that must apparently be done to make herself beautiful and, having once done them, how anyone without the strength of mind of a foreign missionary can keep up such a regime.

CORNELIA OTIS SKINNER, "The Skin Game," *Dithers and Jitters*, 1937.

Suppose I'm not so cute when I grow up as I am now?

SHIRLEY TEMPLE, 1936, in Lois and Alan Gordon, *American Chronicle*, 1987.

CHANGE

If we learn the art of yielding what must be yielded to the changing present we can save the best of the past.

DEAN ACHESON, speech, Law Club of Chicago, January 22, 1937.

Controversial proposals, once accepted, soon become hallowed.

DEAN ACHESON, speech, Independence, Missouri, March 31, 1962.

The need for change bulldozed a road down the center of my mind.

MAYA ANGELOU, *I Know Why the Caged Bird Sings*, 1969.

Why this reluctance to make the change? We fear the process of reeducation! Adults have invested endless hours of learning in growing accustomed to inches and miles; to February's twenty-eight days; to "night" and "debt" with their silent letters; to qwertyuiop; and to all the rest. To introduce something altogether new would mean to begin all over, to become ignorant again, and to run the old, old risk of failing to learn.

ISAAC ASIMOV, *Machines That Think*, 1983.

We must change in order to survive.

PEARL BAILEY, *Hurry Up, America, & Spit*, 1976.

Great cultural changes begin in affectation and end in routine.

JACQUES BARZUN, *The House of Intellect*, 1959.

Each new season grows from the leftovers from the past. That is the essence of change, and change is the basic law.

HAL BORLAND, "Autumn's Clutter," *Sundial of the Seasons*, 1964.

We must adjust to changing times and still hold to unchanging principles.

JIMMY CARTER, quoting his high school teacher Julia Coleman, inaugural address, January 20, 1977.

When great changes occur in history, when great principles are involved, as a rule the majority are wrong. The minority are usually right.

EUGENE V. DEBS, speech, trial for sedition, Cleveland, Ohio, September 12, 1918.

There is no force so powerful as an idea whose time has come.

EVERETT DIRKSEN, speech on civil rights bill, U.S. Senate, 1964.

Mankind passes from the old to the new on a human bridge formed by those who labor in the three principal arts—agriculture, manufacture, transportation.

HENRY FORD, "Success," *Forum*, October, 1928.

Most of the change we think we see in life
Is due to truths being in and out of favor.

ROBERT FROST, "The Black Cottage," *North of Boston*, 1914.

To ask for overt renunciation of a cherished doctrine is to expect too much of human nature. Men do not repudiate the doctrines and dogmas to which they have sworn their loyalty. Instead they rationalize, revise, and re-interpret them to meet new needs and new circumstances, all the while protesting that their heresy is the purest orthodoxy.

J. WILLIAM FULBRIGHT, *Old Myths and New Realities*, 1964.

Reform must come from within, not from without. You cannot legislate for virtue.

JAMES CARDINAL GIBBONS, speech, Baltimore, Maryland, September 13, 1909.

A new town was only the same town in a different place.

SUSAN GLASPELL, "His Smile," *The Pictorial Review*, 1921.

The ultimate end of all revolutionary social change is to establish the sanctity of human life, the dignity of man, the right of every human being to liberty and well-being.

EMMA GOLDMAN, *My Disillusionment in Russia*, 1925.

A movement seeking to remodel social life, to create another industrial revolution, to purge sex relations of barter and property, to set up a new type of home and family relation, must necessarily shake all established things, creating conscious disturbance and distress where now habit blinds us to the existence of danger and evil....It must be prepared to meet opposition.

TERESA BILLINGTON GREIG, *The Woman Rebel*, March, 1914.

We accept the verdict of the past until the need for change cries out loudly enough to force upon us a choice between the comforts of further inertia and the irksomeness of action.

LEARNED HAND, speech, Supreme Judicial Court of Massachussets, November 21, 1942.

Even in slight things the experience of the new is rarely without some stirring of foreboding.

ERIC HOFFER, *The Ordeal of Change*, 1963.

The status quo sits on society like fat on cold chicken soup and it's quite content to be what it is. Unless someone comes along to stir things up there just won't be change.

ABBIE HOFFMAN, speech, University of South Carolina, September 16, 1987.

The history of mankind is one long record of giving revolution another trial, and limping back at last to sanity, safety, and work.

EDGAR WATSON HOWE, *Preaching from the Audience,* 1926.

Life is either a daring adventure or nothing. To keep our faces toward change and behave like free spirits in the presence of fate is strength undefeatable.

HELEN KELLER, *Let Us Have Faith,* 1940.

Progress is a nice word. But change is its motivator. And change has its enemies.

ROBERT F. KENNEDY, "Federal Power and Local Poverty," *The Pursuit of Justice,* 1964.

Times don't change. Men do.

SAM LEVENSON, *You Don't Have To Be in Who's Who To Know What's What,* 1979.

When reform becomes impossible, revolution becomes imperative.

KELLY MILLER, *The Negro in the New World Order,* 1919.

One thing that is new is the prevalence of newness, the changing scale and scope of change itself, so that the world alters as we walk in it.

J. ROBERT OPPENHEIMER, *The Dynamics of Change,* 1967.

Success breeds conservatism, and that means a love affair with the status quo and an aversion to change.

FRANK POPOFF, *New York Times,* November 22, 1987.

Most new things are not good, and die an early death; but those which push themselves forward and by slow degrees force themselves on the attention of mankind are the unconscious productions of human wisdom, and must have honest consideration, and must not be made the subject of unreasoning prejudice.

THOMAS BRACKETT REED, *North American Review,* December, 1902.

Revolutions appeal to those who have not; they have to be imposed on those who have.

GILBERT SELDES, *Against Revolution,* 1932.

How can we live without our lives? How will we know it's us without our past? No. Leave it. Burn it.

They sat and looked at it and burned it into their memories. How'll it be not to know what land's outside the door? How if you wake up in the night and know—and *know* the willow tree's not

there? Can you live without the willow tree? Well, no, you can't. The willow tree is you.

JOHN STEINBECK, *The Grapes of Wrath,* 1939.

What current leaders and theoreticians define as revolution is usually little more than taking over the army and the radio stations.

GLORIA STEINEM, *Ms.,* September, 1979.

Our constitutional system has provided a vehicle for continuous revolution....We can absorb very great shocks without seriously affecting either the stability or the inner sense of security of the nation.

FRANK TANNENBAUM, in Arthur Goodfriend, *What Is America?,* 1954.

I had the benefit of people who knew they had to walk a straighter line, climb a taller mountain, and carry a heavier load. They took all that segregation and prejudice would allow them *and* at the same time fought to remove those awful barriers.

CLARENCE THOMAS, speech, Savannah State College, June 9, 1985.

Since we live in a changing universe, why do men oppose change?...If a rock is in the way, the root of a tree will change its direction. The dumbest animals try to adapt themselves to changed conditions. Even a rat will change its tactics to get a piece of cheese.

MELVIN B. TOLSON, "Does Human Nature Change? We Are Not Born Human Beings," *Washington Tribune,* April 1, 1939.

Americans have been conditioned to respect newness, whatever it costs them.

JOHN UPDIKE, *A Month of Sundays,* 1975.

All experience shows that even smaller technological changes than those now in the cards profoundly transform political and social relationships. Experience also shows that those transformations are not *a priori* predictable and that most contemporary "first guesses" concerning them are wrong. For all these reasons, one should take neither present difficulties nor presently proposed reforms too seriously....To ask in advance for a complete recipe would be unreasonable. We can specify only the human qualities required: patience, flexibility, intelligence.

JOHN VON NEUMANN, *Fortune,* June, 1955.

Our own revolution has ended the need for revolution forever.

WILLIAM C. WESTMORELAND, speech, Daughters of the American Revolution, in Daniel Berrigan, *America Is Hard to Find*, 1972.

Many of the commonest assumptions, it seems to me, are arbitrary ones: that the new is better than the old, the untried superior to the tried, the complex more advantageous than the simple, the fast quicker than the slow, the big greater than the small, and the world as remodeled by Man the Architect functionally sounder and more agreeable than the world as it was before he changed everything to suit his vogues and his conniptions.

E.B. WHITE, "Coon Tree," June 14, 1956, *Essays of E.B. White*, 1977.

There is a time for departure even when there's no certain place to go.

TENNESSEE WILLIAMS, *Camino Real*, 1953.

DEMOCRACY

We slowly learn that life consists of processes as well as results, and that failure may come quite as easily from ignoring the adequacy of one's method as from selfish or ignoble aims. We are thus brought to a conception of Democracy not merely as a sentiment which desires the well-being of all men, nor yet as a creed which believes in the essential dignity and equality of all men, but as that which affords a rule of living as well as a test of faith.

JANE ADDAMS, Introduction, *Democracy and Social Ethics*, 1902.

This is the penalty of a democracy,—that we are bound to move forward or retrograde together.

JANE ADDAMS, "Political Reform," *Democracy and Social Ethics*, 1902.

This will be a land of liberty, they said in the beginning, and as they hacked the forest, drove their ploughshares deep into the earth, and spread their herds across the ranges, they sang of the land of the free that they were making. All that they finally built upon this continent is founded in that faith—that here there would be opportunity and independence and security for any man.

Those things are the power and the hope of this democracy. And they have sprung, very largely,

from the goodness of our land, its capacity to produce rewardingly. Yet with astonishing improvidence, Americans have plundered the resource that made it possible to realize their dream.

HUGH HAMMOND BENNETT, *Soil Conservation*, 1939.

Vote, n. The instrument and symbol of a freeman's power to make a fool of himself and a wreck of his country.

AMBROSE BIERCE, *The Devil's Dictionary*, 1906.

For the Founders, minorities are in general bad things, mostly identical to factions, selfish groups which have no concern as such for the common good....The Founders wished to achieve a national majority concerning the fundamental rights and then prevent that majority from using that power to overturn those fundamental rights. In 20th Century social science, however, the common good disappeared and along with it the negative view of minorities. The very idea of majority...is done away with in order to protect the minorities.

ALLAN BLOOM, *The Closing of the American Mind*, 1987.

Democracy is Government by Squawk.

KENNETH BOULDING, "Parity, Charity, and Clarity," *Michigan Daily*, October 16, 1955.

They [the makers of the Constitution] conferred, as against the government, the right to be let alone—the most comprehensive of rights and the right most valued by civilized men.

LOUIS D. BRANDEIS, Supreme Court opinion, *Olmstead* v. *United States*, 1928.

When we define democracy now it must still be as a thing hoped for but not seen.

PEARL S. BUCK, speech, House of Representatives, January 16, 1941.

For our democracy has been marred by imperialism, and it has been enlightened only by individual and sporadic efforts at freedom.

PEARL S. BUCK, speech, "Freedom for All," New York, March 14, 1942.

The experience of democracy is like the experience of life itself—always changing, infinite in its variety, sometimes turbulent and all the more valuable for having been tested by adversity.

JIMMY CARTER, speech, Indian Parliament, January 2, 1978.

[T]he woman suffrage movement in the United States was a movement of the spirit of the Revolution which was striving to hold the nation to the ideals which won independence.

CARRIE CHAPMAN CATT and NETTIE ROGERS SHULER, *Woman Suffrage and Politics*, 1923.

As there were no black Founding Fathers, there were no founding mothers—a great pity on both counts.

SHIRLEY CHISHOLM, *Congressional Record*, Joint Resolution 264, August 10, 1970.

Democracy is perhaps the most promiscuous word in the world of public affairs.

BERNARD CRICK, *In Defence of Politics*, 1964.

The essential nature of a democracy compels it to insist that individual power of all kinds, political, economic, or intellectual, shall not be perversely and irresponsibly exercised.

HERBERT CROLY, *The Promise of American Life*, 1909.

Let's face it: however old-fashioned and out of date and devaluated the word is, we like the way of living provided by democracy.

EVE CURIE, speech, American Booksellers Association, New York, April 9, 1940.

If there is one conclusion to which human experience unmistakably points it is that democratic ends demand democratic methods for their realization.

JOHN DEWEY, *Freedom and Culture*, 1939.

The struggle for democracy has to be maintained on as many fronts as culture has aspects: political, economic, international, educational, scientific and artistic, religious.

JOHN DEWEY, *Freedom and Culture*, 1939.

Cooperation—called fraternity in the classic French formula—is as much a part of the democratic ideal as is personal initiative. That cultural conditions were allowed to develop (markedly so in the economic phase) which subordinated cooperativeness to liberty and equality serves to explain the decline in the two latter.

JOHN DEWEY, *Freedom and Culture*, 1939.

Resort to military force is a first sure sign that we are giving up the struggle for the democratic way of life, and that the Old World has conquered morally as well as geographically—succeeding in imposing upon us its ideals and methods.

JOHN DEWEY, *Freedom and Culture*, 1939.

As believers in democracy we have not only the right but the duty to question existing mecha-

nisms of, say, suffrage and to inquire whether some functional organization would not serve to formulate and manifest public opinion better than the existing methods. It is not irrelevant to the point that a score of passages could be cited in which Jefferson refers to the American Government as an *experiment*.

JOHN DEWEY, *Freedom and Culture*, 1939.

We have advanced far enough to say that democracy is a way of life. We have yet to realize that it is a way of personal life and one which provides a moral standard for personal conduct.

JOHN DEWEY, *Freedom and Culture*, 1939.

A vigorous democracy—a democracy in which there are freedom from want, freedom from fear, freedom of religion, and freedom of speech—would never succumb to communism or any other ism.

HELEN GAHAGAN DOUGLAS, speech to Congress, March 26, 1946, *A Full Life*, 1982.

As men and women of character and of faith in the soundness of democratic methods, we must work like dogs to justify that faith.

DWIGHT D. EISENHOWER, letter to Mamie Doud Eisenhower, September 15, 1942.

Democracy is not brute numbers; it is a genuine union of true individuals...the essence of democracy is creating. The technique of democracy is group organization.

MARY PARKER FOLLETT, *The New State*, 1918.

The price of democratic survival in a world of aggressive totalitarianism is to give up some of the democratic luxuries of the past.

J. WILLIAM FULBRIGHT, "American Foreign Policy in the 20th Century Under an 18th-Century Constitution," *Cornell Law Quarterly*, Fall, 1961.

We are inclined to confuse freedom and democracy, which we regard as moral principles, with the way in which they are practiced in America—with capitalism, federalism, and the two-party system, which are not moral principles but simply the preferred and accepted practices of the American people.

J. WILLIAM FULBRIGHT, *Old Myths and New Realities*, 1964.

In democracies where the citizens may read, hear or say what they like, the leaders are no better and no worse than the followers. So perhaps, if we cannot blame the leaders because the job of peacemaking is a sorry mess, we can only blame ourselves.

MARTHA GELLHORN, "They Talked of Peace," December, 1946, *The Face of War*, 1988.

Democracy must first be safe for America before it can be safe for the world.

EMMA GOLDMAN, "Address to the Jury," *Mother Earth*, July, 1917.

In the United States, the Constitution is a health chart left by the Founding Fathers which shows whether or not the body politic is in good health. If the national body is found to be in poor health, the Founding Fathers also left a prescription for the restoration of health called the Declaration of Independence.

DICK GREGORY, *Dick Gregory's Political Primer*, 1972.

We hear about constitutional rights, free speech, and the free press. Every time I hear those words I say to myself, "That man is a Red, that man is a Communist." You never heard a real American talk in that manner.

FRANK HAGUE, speech, Jersey City Chamber of Commerce, January 12, 1938.

Democracy, it must be emphasized, is a practical necessity and not just a philosophic value.

MICHAEL HARRINGTON, *Toward a Democratic Left*, 1968.

As the histories of ancient and modern democracies illustrate, the pressure of political movement in times of war, civil commotion, or general anxiety pushes in the direction of authority, not away from it.

ROBERT L. HEILBRONER, *An Inquiry into the Human Prospect*, 1980.

Voting is a civic sacrament.

THEODORE M. HESBURGH, *Reader's Digest*, October, 1984.

Democracy is not tolerance. Democracy is a prescribed way of life erected on the premise that all men are created equal.

CHESTER HIMES, *If You're Scared, Go Home!*, 1944.

I grew up with the idea that democracy is not something you believe in, or a place you hang your hat, but it's something you do. You participate. If you stop doing it, democracy crumbles and falls apart.

ABBIE HOFFMAN, speech during trial on trespassing charges, April 15, 1987.

The Constitution was based on the old English law that a man's home is his castle. It was designed essentially to protect individuals from government intrusion. That is a good deal for men who own castles.

ABBIE HOFFMAN, speech, University of South Carolina, September 16, 1987.

If the Constitution is to be construed to mean what the majority at any given period in history wish the Constitution to mean, why a written Constitution and deliberate processes of amendment?

FRANK J. HOGAN, speech, American Bar Association, July 10, 1939.

In contrast to totalitarianism, democracy can face and live with the truth about itself.

SIDNEY HOOK, *New York Times Magazine*, September 30, 1951.

I swear to the Lord
   I still can't see

Why Democracy means
   Everybody but me.

LANGSTON HUGHES, "The Black Man Speaks," *Jim Crow's Last Stand*, 1943.

The death of democracy is not likely to be an assassination from ambush. It will be a slow extinction from apathy, indifference, and undernourishment.

ROBERT M. HUTCHINS, *Great Books*, 1954.

It is the common failing of totalitarian regimes that they cannot really understand the nature of our democracy. They mistake dissent for disloyalty. They mistake restlessness for a rejection of policy. They mistake a few committees for a country. They misjudge individual speeches for public policy.

LYNDON B. JOHNSON, speech, San Antonio, Texas, September 29, 1967.

"We, the people." It is a very eloquent beginning. But when that document was completed on the seventeenth of September in 1787 I was not included in that "We, the people." I felt somehow for many years that George Washington and Alexander Hamilton just left me out by mistake. But through the process of amendment, interpretation, and court decision I have finally been included in "We, the people."

BARBARA JORDAN, speech to Congress, July 25, 1974.

And so the chauvinists of all times and places go their appointed way: plucking the easy fruits, reaping the little triumphs of the day at the expense of someone else tomorrow, deluging in noise and filth anyone who gets in their way, dancing their reckless dance on the prospects for human progress, drawing the shadow of a great doubt over the validity of democratic institutions. And until peoples learn to spot the fanning of mass emotions and the sowing of bitterness, suspicion, and intolerance as crimes in themselves—as perhaps the greatest disservice that can be done to the cause of popular government—this sort of thing will continue to occur.

GEORGE F. KENNAN, *American Diplomacy, 1900–1950,* 1951.

We, the people, are the boss, and we will get the kind of political leadership, be it good or bad, that we demand and deserve.

JOHN F. KENNEDY, *Profiles in Courage,* 1955.

Although most governments in the world are, as they always have been, autocracies of one kind or another, no idea holds greater sway in the mind of educated Americans than the belief that it is possible to democratize governments, anytime, anywhere, under any circumstances.

JEANE KIRKPATRICK, "Dictatorship and Double Standards," *Commentary,* November, 1979.

A nation riven by factions, in which the minority has no hope of ever becoming a majority, or in which some group knows it is perpetually outcast, will seem oppressive to its members, whatever the legal pretensions.

HENRY KISSINGER, *White House Years,* 1979.

The practice of democracy means that I, one person, one humble person, nevertheless feel some responsibility if the officials for whose election I was responsible go too far out of line.

CLYDE K.M. KLUCKHOHN, in Arthur Goodfriend, *What Is America?,* 1954.

The one thing that doesn't abide by majority rule is a person's conscience.

HARPER LEE, *To Kill a Mockingbird,* 1960.

Cure the evils of Democracy by the evils of Fascism! Funny therapeutics! I've heard of their curing syphilis by giving the patient malaria, but I've never heard of their curing malaria by giving the patient syphilis.

SINCLAIR LEWIS, *It Can't Happen Here,* 1935.

On the whole, with scandalous exceptions, Democracy has given the ordinary worker more dignity than he ever had.

SINCLAIR LEWIS, *It Can't Happen Here,* 1935.

Democracy, which began by liberating man politically, has developed a dangerous tendency to enslave him through the tyranny of majorities and the deadly power of their opinion.

LUDWIG LEWISOHN, *The Modern Drama,* 1915.

Whether happiness or unhappiness, freedom or slavery, in short whether good or evil results from an improved environment depends largely upon how the change has been brought about, upon the methods by which the physical results have been reached, and in what spirit and for what purpose the fruits of that change are used. Because a higher standard of living, a greater productiveness and a command over nature are not good in and of themselves does not mean that we cannot make good of them, that they cannot be a source of inner strength.

DAVID E. LILIENTHAL, *TVA: Democracy on the March,* 1944.

A democracy which fails to concentrate authority in an emergency inevitably falls into such confusion that the ground is prepared for the rise of a dictator.

WALTER LIPPMANN, *New York Herald Tribune,* February 24, 1933.

The most popular man under a democracy is not the most democratic man, but the most despotic man. The common folk delight in the exactions of such a man. They like him to boss them. Their natural gait is the goosestep.

H.L. MENCKEN, *Prejudices,* 1920.

Democracy is the theory that the common people know what they want, and deserve to get it good and hard.

H.L. MENCKEN, "Sententiae," *The Vintage Mencken,* 1955.

Only a country that is rich and safe can afford to be a democracy, for democracy is the most expensive and nefarious kind of government ever heard of on earth.

H.L. MENCKEN, *Minority Report,* 1956.

We have forgotten that democracy must live as it thinks and think as it lives.

AGNES MEYER, Introduction, *Journey Through Chaos,* 1943.

The unhealthy gap between what we preach in America and what we often practice creates a moral dry rot that eats at the very foundation of our democratic ideals and values.

WHITNEY MOORE, JR., *To Be Equal,* 1964.

Citizen participation [is] a device whereby public officials induce nonpublic individuals to act in a way the officials desire.

DANIEL PATRICK MOYNIHAN, *The Public Interest*, Fall, 1969.

Man's capacity for justice makes democracy possible, but man's inclination to injustice makes democracy necessary.

REINHOLD NIEBUHR, *The Children of Light and the Children of Darkness*, 1944.

It seems to me very important to the idea of democracy—to the country and to the world eventually—that all men and women stand equal under the sky.

GEORGIA O'KEEFFE, letter to Eleanor Roosevelt, February 10, 1944, *Georgia O'Keeffe*, 1976.

One has the right to be wrong in a democracy.

CLAUDE PEPPER, *Congressional Record*, May 27, 1946.

The armored horseman brought in the feudal system. The gun restored democracy.

JAMES R. RANDOLPH, "Can We Go to Mars?" *Scientific American*, 1928.

We all have a large stake in preserving our democracy, but I maintain that those without power in our society, the black, the brown, the poor of all colors, have the largest stake—not because we have the most to lose, but because we have worked the hardest, and given the most, for what we have achieved.

CHARLES B. RANGEL, *Congressional Record*, July, 1974.

Democracy is not a fragile flower: still, it needs cultivating.

RONALD REAGAN, speech, British Parliament, June 8, 1982.

Democracy can thrive only when it enlists the devotion of those whom Lincoln called the common people. Democracy can hold that devotion only when it adequately respects their dignity by so ordering society as to assure to the masses of men and women reasonable security and hope for themselves and for their children.

FRANKLIN D. ROOSEVELT, speech, Democratic National Convention, Chicago, Illinois, July 19, 1940.

The first requisite of a good citizen in this Republic of ours is that he shall be able and willing to pull his weight.

THEODORE ROOSEVELT, speech, New York City, November 11, 1902.

Universal suffrage, to justify itself, must be based on universal service. It is only you and your kind who have the absolute clear title to the management of the Republic.

THEODORE ROOSEVELT, speech to soldiers at Camp Upton, November 18, 1917.

There is no tyranny so hateful as a vulgar and anonymous tyranny. It is all-permeating, all-thwarting; it blasts every budding novelty and sprig of genius with its omnipresent and fierce stupidity. Such a headless people has the mind of a worm and the claws of a dragon.

GEORGE SANTAYANA, *The Life of Reason*, 1905–1906.

The democratic conscience recoils before anything that savors of privilege; and lest it should concede an unmerited privilege to any pursuit or person, it reduces all things as far as possible to the common denominator of quantity.

GEORGE SANTAYANA, *Character and Opinion in the United States*, 1920.

One of the reasons that democracy has worked so well for so long in America is that we have had a wide ownership of land in the hands of a great many people. That contribution is today very definitely threatened.

MRS. RAYMOND SAYRE, speech, Woman's Centennial Congress, November 26, 1940.

For most Americans the Constitution had become a hazy document, cited like the Bible on ceremonial occasions but forgotten in the daily transactions of life.

ARTHUR M. SCHLESINGER, JR., *The Imperial Presidency*, 1973.

Democracy cannot survive where there is such uniformity that everyone wears exactly the same intellectual uniform or point of view. Democracy implies diversity of outlook, a variety of points of view on politics, economics, and world affairs. Hence the educational ideal is not uniformity but unity, for unity allows diversity of points of view regarding the good means to a good end.

FULTON J. SHEEN, *The Wit and Wisdom of Bishop Fulton J. Sheen*, 1968.

All the ills of democracy can be cured by more democracy.

ALFRED E. SMITH, speech, Albany, New York, June 27, 1933.

Democracy appears to me potentially a higher form of political organization than any kind of dictatorship. But if it turns out that in America, which could afford a decent living for everyone, the comfortable majority is willing to condone the misery and abuse of a minority for an indefinite period, the exploitation by the majority becomes as repugnant as exploitation by an oligarchy, and democracy loses half its supposed superiority.

BENJAMIN SPOCK, *Decent and Indecent*, 1968.

The right of revolution does not exist in America. We had a revolution 140 years ago which made it unnecessary to have any other revolution in this country....One of the many meanings of democracy is that it is a form of government in which the right of revolution has been lost.

State manual for elementary schools, in ROBERT S. LYND and HELEN MERRELL LYND, *Middletown*, 1921.

I hunted far enough to suspect that the Fathers of the Republic who wrote our Sacred Constitution of the United States not only did not, but did not want to, establish a democratic government.

LINCOLN STEFFENS, *The Autobiography of Lincoln Steffens*, 1931.

We intended to know why, if democracy were so precious as to demand the nation's blood and treasure for its achievement abroad, its execution at home was so undesirable.

DORIS STEVENS, *Jailed for Freedom*, 1920.

By "America," I suppose we all think of not just the real estate or inhabitants of the United States, but also of the idea that we who live here share and cherish in common—the concept of government by the free consent of the governed as the only tolerable system of management of human affairs.

ADLAI E. STEVENSON, "War, Weakness, and Ourselves," *Look*, November, 1954.

If we do justice at the polls to our own conscience and sense of responsibility, then alone can we do justice to the nation we love; then alone can we make our beloved land a symbol and shrine of hope and faith for all free men.

ADLAI E. STEVENSON, speech, New York City, October 30, 1954.

If a fascist movement ever triumphs in America it will undoubtedly triumph in the name of our most popular slogan—Democracy—and under the leadership of some such "friend of the common people" as the late Huey Long.

LILLIAN SYMES, "Fascism for America—Threat or Scarehead," *Harper's*, June, 1939.

To believe that the democratic psychology is immune to fascist barbarism is to forget our own shameful hysterias during our comparatively easygoing participation in the last World War. Some of those incidents—including the whipping of German farmers, the torture of conscientious objectors, the beating and imprisonment of Socialists, all the mob violence and psychopathic witch-hunting of 1917–1920—are worth recalling in these days. We recovered our sanity of course after 1920, because our economic order was still healthy enough to regain its balance. In 1939 we are living in another world.

LILLIAN SYMES, "Fascism for America—Threat or Scarehead," *Harper's*, June, 1939.

There can be no democracy without economic equality.

MELVIN B. TOLSON, "The Merry-Go-Round and the Ferris Wheel of History," *Washington Tribune*, October 19, 1940.

Democracy—what infamy is committed in thy name?

MELVIN B. TOLSON, "The Buzzards in the Senate of the U.S.A.," *Washington Tribune*, November 28, 1942.

Secrecy and a free, democratic government don't mix.

HARRY S TRUMAN, in Merle Miller, *Plain Speaking: An Oral Biography of Harry S Truman*, 1974.

The century on which we are entering can be and must be the century of the common man.

HENRY A. WALLACE, speech, May 8, 1942.

Democracy is the recurrent suspicion that more than half of the people are right more than half of the time.

E.B. WHITE, *The Wild Flag*, 1946.

Liberal democracy is government that rests lightly upon people. It has existed rarely, and only during the two centuries of rapid economic growth in the West. It probably has been made possible by that growth, by the belief that a rising tide raises all boats, a belief that dampens the worst social conflicts. And viewed against the backdrop of history, our experience of liberal democracy has been, as Saul Bellow says, "brief as a bubble."

GEORGE WILL, "Governing Appetite," April 18, 1977, *The Pursuit of Happiness, and Other Sobering Thoughts*, 1978.

Democracy is a political, not a social concept.

GEORGE WILL, "Freedom, True and False," May 29, 1978, *The Pursuit of Virtue and Other Tory Notions*, 1982.

The beauty of a democracy is that you never can tell when a youngster is born what he is going to do with himself, and that no matter how humbly he is born, no matter where he is born, no matter what circumstances hamper him at the outset, he has got a chance to master the minds and lead the imaginations of the whole country.

WOODROW WILSON, speech, Chamber of Commerce, Columbus, Ohio, December 10, 1915.

I am all kinds of a democrat, so far as I can discover—but the root of the whole business is this, that I believe in the patriotism and energy and initiative of the average man.

WOODROW WILSON, speech, Philadelphia, Pennsylvania, June 29, 1916.

A democracy cannot long endure with the head of a God and the tail of a demon.

JOSEPHINE SILONE YATES, *The Voice of the Negro*, July, 1904.

DESTINY

We Americans cannot save the world. Even Christ failed at that. We Americans have our hands full trying to save ourselves.

EDWARD ABBEY, "Down the River with Henry Thoreau," *Words From the Land*, 1981.

As long as Americans believed they were able to fulfill a noble national promise merely by virtue of maintaining intact a set of political institutions and by the vigorous individual pursuit of private ends, their allegiance to their national fulfillment remained more a matter of words than of deeds.

HERBERT CROLY, *The Promise of American Life*, 1909.

No trumpets sound when the important decisions of our life are made. Destiny is made known silently.

AGNES DE MILLE, *Dance to the Piper*, 1952.

Neither a wise man nor a brave man lies down on the tracks of history to wait for the train of the future to run over him.

DWIGHT D. EISENHOWER, speech, *Time*, October 6, 1952.

Americans see history as a straight line and themselves standing at the cutting edge of it as representatives for all mankind. They believe in the future as if it were a religion; they believe that there is nothing they cannot accomplish, that solutions wait somewhere for all problems, like brides.

FRANCES FITZGERALD, *Fire in the Lake*, 1972.

The transformations of this century are not merely a matter of historic events; there is no day on which history will leap from necessity to freedom. There is rather a molecular process, composed of millions and even billions of personal decisions, whereby men and women assert their will to take control of their own destiny.

MICHAEL HARRINGTON, *Fragments of the Century*, 1973.

This nation, this generation, in this hour has man's first chance to build a Great Society, a place where the meaning of man's life matches the marvels of man's labor.

LYNDON B. JOHNSON, speech, Democratic National Convention, August, 1964.

Prophecy today is hardly the romantic business that it used to be. The old tools of the trade, like the sword, the hair shirt, and the long fast in the wilderness, have given way to more contemporary, mundane instructions of doom—the book, the picket and the petition, the sit-in...at City Hall.

JANE KRAMER, "The Ranks and Rungs of Mrs. Jacobs' Ladder," *Off Washington Square*, 1963.

To me Americanism means...an imperative duty to be nobler than the rest of the world.

MEYER LONDON, speech to Congress, January 18, 1916.

History is not kind to idlers. The time is long past when America's destiny was assured simply by an abundance of national resources and inexhaustible human enthusiasm, and by our relative isolation from the malignant problems of older civilizations. The world is indeed one global village. We live among determined, well-educated and strongly motivated competitors. We compete with them for international standing and markets, not only with products but also with the ideas of our laboratories and neighborhood workshops. America's position in the world may once have been reasonably secure with only a few exceptionally well-trained men and women. It is no longer.

National Commission on Excellence in Education, *A Nation at Risk*, 1983.

I have long believed there was a divine plan that placed this land here to be found by people of a special kind, that we have a rendezvous with destiny. Yes, there is a spirit moving in this land and a hunger in the people for a spiritual revival. If the task I seek should be given to me, I would pray only that I could perform it in a way that would serve God.

RONALD REAGAN, campaign letter, 1976, in Helene von Damm, *Sincerely, Ronald Reagan*, 1976.

We have to move ahead, but we are not going to leave *anyone* behind.

RONALD REAGAN, speech, Republican National Convention, July, 1980.

We live in an age of revolution and explosion: exploding bombs, exploding population, revolutionary wars, revolutionary wants. In such an age, we have only two choices, no more. We shall learn to be masters of circumstance—or we shall be its victims.

NELSON A. ROCKEFELLER, *Unity, Freedom and Peace: A Blueprint for Tomorrow*, 1968.

There is a mysterious cycle in human events. To some generations much is given. Of others much is expected. This generation of Americans has a rendezvous with destiny.

FRANKLIN D. ROOSEVELT, speech, Democratic National Convention, June, 1936.

Destiny is something men select; women achieve it only by default or stupendous suffering.

HARRIET ROSENSTEIN, book review, *Ms.*, July, 1974.

For national purpose is not something that is enshrined in monuments or preserved in historic documents. It acquires meaning as part of an ongoing process; its certification lies, not in rhetoric, but in performance.

ARTHUR M. SCHLESINGER, JR., *Esquire*, January, 1960.

In America the recurring dreams of centuries could be realized: This was the new garden, the American was the new Adam; the new Jerusalem was at hand. We were the last children of the Renaissance.

PETER SCHRAG, *The Vanishing American*, 1972.

DISSENT

A spirit of national masochism prevails, encouraged by an effete corps of impudent snobs who characterize themselves as intellectuals.

SPIRO T. AGNEW, on Vietnam War protestors at Moratorium Day demonstration, October 20, 1969.

The point of nonviolence is to build a floor, a strong new floor, beneath which we can no longer sink. A platform which stands a few feet above napalm, torture, exploitation, poison gas, A and H bombs, the works. Give man a decent place to stand.

JOAN BAEZ, *Daybreak*, 1966.

I love America more than any other country in the world, and, exactly for this reason, I insist on the right to criticize her perpetually.

JAMES BALDWIN, *Notes of a Native Son*, 1955.

Criticism and dissent are the indispensable antidote to major delusions.

ALAN BARTH, *The Loyalty of Free Men*, 1951.

Like the other defendants, I am an American and a Christian insofar as I face my country and humanity under the Declaration of Independence and the Gospel. As a democratic man, I must cling to a tradition of protest going back to our birth as a nation—traditions which brightened our finest hours as people. Jefferson, Washington, Madison, Thoreau, Emerson, Whitman, and Twain; they also stand in the dock today; they judge you as you judge me. They judge our uses of political power, our racism, our neglect of the poor, our courts serving the interests of war. I do not hesitate to assert that were these men alive today, they would disobey as I have disobeyed and be convicted as I am convicted.

DANIEL BERRIGAN, "Statement at Sentencing," *Prison Journals*, May 24, 1968.

Unlike lions and dogs, we are a dissenting animal. We need to dissent in the same way that we need to travel, to make money, to keep a record of our time on earth and in dream, and to leave a permanent mark. Dissension is a drive, like those drives.

CAROL BLY, "Extended *vs.* Nuclear Families," *Letter from the Country*, 1981.

There is no stopping the world's tendency to throw off imposed restraints, the religious authority that is based on the ignorance of the many, the political authority that is based on the knowledge of a few.

VAN WYCK BROOKS, *From a Writer's Notebook*, 1957.

The framers of the Declaration of Independence prophesied that uprisings would occur "in the course of human events," if people are denied those inalienable rights to which the "laws of nature and of nature's God entitle them." Reread their prophecy....If that's Red, then the writers of the Declaration of Independence were very

Red. They told Americans not to stand injustice after "patient sufferance."

NANNIE HELEN BURROUGHS, "Declaration of 1776 Is Cause of Harlem Riot," *The Afro-American*, April 13, 1935.

The "flatfoot mentality" insists that any individual or organization that wants to change *anything* in our present system is somehow subversive of "the American way," and should be under continuous surveillance.

TONI CARABILLO, "The 'Flatfoot Mentality,'" *Hollywood NOW News*, August, 1975.

If our democracy is to flourish, it must have criticism; if our government is to function it must have dissent.

HENRY STEELE COMMAGER, *Freedom, Loyalty, Dissent*, 1954.

Men in authority will always think that criticism of their policies is dangerous. They will always equate their policies with patriotism, and find criticism subversive.

HENRY STEELE COMMAGER, *Freedom and Order*, 1966.

As long as the world shall last there will be wrongs, and if no man objected and no man rebelled, those wrongs would last forever.

CLARENCE DARROW, speech to jury, Chicago, Illinois, 1920, in Arthur Weinberg, *Attorney for the Damned*, 1957.

The objector and the rebel who raises his voice against what he believes to be the injustice of the present and the wrongs of the past is the one who hunches the world along.

CLARENCE DARROW, speech to jury, Chicago, Illinois, 1920, in Arthur Weinberg, *Attorney for the Damned*, 1957.

The right to revolt has sources deep in our history.

WILLIAM O. DOUGLAS, *An Almanac of Liberty*, 1954.

The answer, my friend, is blowin' in the wind.

Bob Dylan, "Blowin' in the Wind," 1963

To all of them, professors and pundits, the student movement demanded, in so many words (and sometimes in these very words): Why should we listen to you? What do you know about American society compared to a black woman on welfare, a Southern sharecropper, or, for that matter, a Vietnamese peasant whose village has just been devastated by American firepower? What is your vaunted objectivity but a mask for privilege, your expertise but an excuse for power?

BARBARA EHRENREICH, *Fear of Falling*, 1990.

Never do anything against conscience, even if the state demands it.

ALBERT EINSTEIN, in Virgil G. Hinshaw, *Albert Einstein: Philosopher-Scientist*, 1949.

Here in America we are descended in blood and in spirit from revolutionaries and rebels—men and women who dared to dissent from accepted doctrine. As their heirs, may we never confuse honest dissent with disloyal subversion.

DWIGHT D. EISENHOWER, speech, Columbia University, May 31, 1954.

[I despise people who] go to the gutter on either the right or the left and hurl rocks at those in the center.

DWIGHT D. EISENHOWER, *Time*, October 25, 1963.

Political agitation, by the passions it arouses or the convictions it engenders, may in fact stimulate men to the violation of law. Detestation of existing policies is easily transformed into forcible resistance of the authority which puts them in execution, and it would be folly to disregard the causal relation between the two. Yet to assimilate agitation, legitimate as such, with direct incitement to violent resistance, is to disregard the tolerance of all methods of political agitation which in normal times is a safeguard of free government.

LEARNED HAND, opinion, *Masses Publishing Co. v. Patten*, 1917.

The widespread fear that radicalism [in the 1960s] would displace our conventional values or institutions was only a sign of our insecurity, not a reaction to an actual threat.

ROBERT L. HEILBRONER, *An Inquiry into the Human Prospect*, 1980.

I cannot and will not cut my conscience to fit this year's fashions.

LILLIAN HELLMAN, letter to House Committee on Un-American Activities, May 19, 1952.

Youth in its protest must be heard.

WALTER HICKEL, 1970, in Lois and Alan Gordon, *American Chronicle*, 1987.

If there is any principle of the Constitution that more imperatively calls for attachment than any other it is the principle of free thought—not free thought for those who agree with us but freedom for the thought that we hate.

OLIVER WENDELL HOLMES, JR., opinion, *United States v. Schwimmer*, 1929.

Freedom to differ is not limited to things that do not matter much. That would be a mere shadow of freedom. The test of its substance is the right to differ as to things that touch the heart of the existing order.

ROBERT JACKSON, opinion, *West Virginia State Board v. Barnette*, 1943.

It is time to call together the daring and unreconciled. It is time to march again.

EDWARD M. KENNEDY, speech, AFL-CIO convention, Massachusetts, October 6, 1971, in Thomas P. Collins and Louis M. Savary, eds., *A People of Compassion*, 1972.

Nonviolent action, the Negro saw, was the way to supplement, not replace, the progress of change. It was the way to divest himself of passivity without arraying himself in vindictive force.

MARTIN LUTHER KING, JR., *Why We Can't Wait*, 1964.

If you don't like the president, it costs you 90 bucks to fly to Washington to picket. If you don't like the governor, it costs you 60 bucks to fly to Albany to picket. If you don't like me, 90 cents.

EDWARD KOCH, *New York Times*, January 20, 1984.

Every compulsion is put upon writers to become safe, polite, obedient, and sterile. In protest, I declined election to the National Institute of Arts and Letters some years ago, and now I must decline the Pulitzer Prize.

SINCLAIR LEWIS, letter, 1926.

The dissenter is every human being at those moments of his life when he resigns momentarily from the herd and thinks for himself.

ARCHIBALD MACLEISH, "In Praise of Dissent," *New York Times Book Review*, December 16, 1956.

With the pride of the artist, you must blow against the walls of every power that exists the small trumpet of your defiance.

NORMAN MAILER, *The Deer Park*, 1955.

It doesn't take a majority to make a rebellion; it takes only a few determined leaders and a sound cause.

H.L. MENCKEN, *Prejudices*, 1926.

The radical of the thirties came out of a system that had stopped and the important job was to organize new production relations which would start up again. The sixties radical opened his eyes to a system pouring its junk over everybody, or nearly everybody, and the problem was to stop just that, to escape being overwhelmed by a mindless, goalless flood which marooned each individual on his little island of commodities.

ARTHUR MILLER, Introduction, *Kesey's Garage Sale*, 1973.

If conscience is regarded as imperative, then compliance with its dictates commends a society not to forgive, but to celebrate, its conscientious citizens.

LIANE NORMAN, "Selective Conscientious Objection," *The Center Magazine*, May/June, 1972.

I am not for a return of that definition of liberty under which for many years a free people were being gradually regimented into the service of the privileged few.

FRANKLIN D. ROOSEVELT, Fireside Chat, September 30, 1934.

The government, in an organized fashion, had executed some demonstrators on a command.

WILLIAM SAFIRE, on killings at Kent State University, *Before the Fall*, 1975.

Freedom of speech and press...does not protect disturbances to the public peace or the attempt to subvert the government. It does not protect publications or teachings which tend to subvert or imperil the government, or to impede or hinder it in the performance of its governmental duties.

EDWARD TERRY SANFORD, opinion, *Gitlow v. People of New York*, 1925.

There is a time when the operation of the machine becomes so odious, makes you so sick at heart that you can't take part; you can't even tacitly take part, and you've got to put your bodies upon the levers, upon all the apparatus and you've got to make it stop. And you've got to indicate to the people who run it, to the people who own it, that unless you're free the machine will be prevented from working at all.

MARIO SAVIO, speech, University of California, Berkeley, 1964.

Extremism bent upon polarization of our people is increasingly forcing upon the American people the narrow choice between anarchy and repression. And make no mistake about it, if that narrow choice has to be made, the American people, even with reluctance and misgiving, will choose repression.

MARGARET CHASE SMITH, on Vietnam War protests and reaction of Congress, *New York Times*, June 2, 1970.

We are people of this generation, bred in at least modest comfort, housed now in universities, looking uncomfortably to the world we inherit.

When we were kids the United States was the wealthiest and strongest country in the world; the only one with the atom bomb, the least scarred by modern war, an initiator of the United Nations that we thought would distribute Western influence throughout the world. Freedom and equality for each individual, government of, by, and for the people—these American values were found good, principles by which we could live as men. Many of us began maturing in complacency.

As we grew, however, our comfort was penetrated by events too troubling to dismiss. First, the permeating and victimizing fact of human degradation, symbolized by the Southern struggle against racial bigotry, compelled most of us from silence to activism. Second, the enclosing fact of the Cold War, symbolized by the presence of the Bomb, brought awareness that we ourselves, and our friends, and millions of abstract "others" we knew more directly because of our common peril, might die at any time. We might deliberately ignore, or avoid, or fail to feel all other human problems, but not these two, for these were too immediate and crushing in their impact, too challenging in the demand that we as individuals take the responsibility for encounter and resolution.

While these and other problems either directly oppressed us or rankled our consciences and became our own subjective concern, we began to see complicated and disturbing paradoxes in our surrounding America. The declaration "all men are created equal…" rang hollow before the facts of Negro life in the South and the big cities of the North. The proclaimed peaceful intentions of the United States contradicted its economic and military investments in the Cold War status quo.

We witnessed, and continue to witness, other paradoxes. With nuclear energy whole cities can easily be powered, yet the dominant nation-states seem more likely to unleash destruction greater than that incurred in all wars of human history. Although our own technology is destroying old and creating new forms of social organization, men still tolerate meaningless work and idleness. While two-thirds of mankind suffers undernourishment, our own upper classes revel amidst superfluous abundance. Although world population is expected to double in forty years, the nations still tolerate anarchy as a major principle of international conduct and uncontrolled exploitation governs the sapping of the earth's physical resources. Although mankind desperately needs revolutionary leadership, America rests in national stalemate, its goals ambiguous and tradition-bound instead of informed and clear, its democratic system apathetic and manipulated rather than "of, by, and for the people."

Not only did tarnish appear on our image of American virtue, not only did disillusion occur when the hypocrisy of American ideals was discovered, but we began to sense that what we had originally seen as the American Golden Age was actually the

---

For some reason, too deep to fathom, men contend more furiously over the road to heaven, which they cannot see, than over their visible walks on earth.

WALTER PARKER STACY, in Sam J. Ervin, Jr., *Humor of a Country Lawyer*, 1983.

Thinking implies disagreement; and disagreement implies nonconformity; and nonconformity implies heresy; and heresy implies disloyalty—so, obviously, thinking must be stopped.

ADLAI E. STEVENSON, *Call to Greatness*, 1954.

Do not…regard the critics as questionable patriots. What were Washington and Jefferson and Adams but profound critics of the colonial status quo?

ADLAI E. STEVENSON, "The Hard Kind of Patriotism," *Harper's*, July, 1963.

In the heat of conflicting views and interests, men often debate eloquently over spurious issues, and leap to doubtful remedies.

PAUL S. TAYLOR, "Good-by to the Homestead Farm," *Harper's*, May, 1941.

decline of an era. The worldwide outbreak of revolution against colonialism and imperialism, the entrenchment of totalitarian states, the menace of war, overpopulation, international disorder, supertechnology—these trends were testing the tenacity of our own commitment to democracy and freedom and our abilities to visualize their application to a world in upheaval.

Our work is guided by the sense that we may be the last generation in the experiment with living. But we are a minority—the vast majority of our people regard the temporary equilibriums of our society and world as eternally functional parts. In this is perhaps the outstanding paradox: we ourselves are imbued with urgency, yet the message of our society is that there is no viable alternative to the present. Beneath the reassuring tones of the politicians, beneath the common opinion that America will "muddle through," beneath the stagnation of those who have closed their minds to the future, is the pervading feeling that there simply are no alternatives, that our times have witnessed the exhaustion not only of Utopias, but of any new departures as well. Feeling the press of complexity upon the emptiness of life, people are fearful of the thought that at any moment things might be thrust out of control. They fear change itself, since change might smash whatever invisible framework seems to hold back chaos for them now. For most Americans, all crusades are suspect, threatening. The fact that each individual sees apathy in his fellows perpetuates the common reluctance to organize for change. The dominant institutions are complex enough to blunt the minds of their potential critics, and entrenched enough to swiftly dissipate or entirely repel the energies of protest and reform, thus limiting human expectancies. Then, too, we are a materially improved society, and by our own improvements we seem to have weakened the case for further change.

Some would have us believe that Americans feel contentment amidst prosperity—but might it not better be called a glaze above deeply felt anxieties about their role in the new world? And if these anxieties produce a developed indifference to human affairs, do they not as well produce a yearning to believe that there *is* an alternative to the present, that something *can* be done to change circumstances in the school, the workplaces, the bureaucracies, the government? It is to this latter yearning, at once the spark and engine of change, that we direct our present appeal. The search for truly democratic alternatives to the present, and a commitment to social experimentation with them, is a worthy and fulfilling human enterprise, one which moves us and, we hope, others today. On such a basis do we offer this document of our convictions and analysis: as an effort in understanding and changing the conditions of humanity in the late twentieth century, an effort rooted in the ancient, still unfulfilled conception of man attaining determining influence over his circumstances of life.

"The Port Huron Statement," manifesto for Students for a Democratic Society (SDS), 1962.

Discussion in America means dissent.

JAMES THURBER, "The Duchess and the Bugs," *Lanterns and Lances,* 1961.

In a nation blessed with more scholars than scholarly subjects, no rabble-rouser can escape being studied as a "spokesman."

GEORGE WILL, "Democracy as Vaudeville," April 20, 1975, *The Pursuit of Happiness, and Other Sobering Thoughts,* 1978.

Those who are most deeply committed to the American system are most critical of it; they are filled with "a divine discontent."

HENRY M. WRISTON, in Arthur Goodfriend, *What Is America?,* 1954.

Come into the streets on Nov. 5, election day. Vote with your feet. Rise up and abandon the creeping meatball! Demand the bars be open. Make music and dance at every red light. A festival of life in the streets and parks throughout the world. The American election represents death, and we are alive.

Yippie manifesto for election day demonstrations, 1968.

EQUALITY

Equality is the result of human organization. We are not born equal.

HANNAH ARENDT, *The Origins of Totalitarianism*, 1973.

In America, equality means simply that no handicap is imposed by society upon any child to prevent him from realizing the best that is in him.

ELLIOT V. BELL, in Arthur Goodfriend, *What Is America?*, 1954.

In our egalitarian democracy...we have just about empowered a branch of the government, the FHA, to specify the size and shape of the typical American suburban master bedroom in which all Americans are thus created equal.

PETER BLAKE, *God's Own Junkyard*, 1963.

No poor, rural, weak, or black person should ever again have to bear the additional burden of being deprived of the opportunity for an education, a job, or simple justice.

JIMMY CARTER, inaugural address as governor of Georgia, January 12, 1971.

[To] blot out of every law book in the land, to sweep out of every dusty courtroom, to erase from every judge's mind that centuries-old precedent as to women's inferiority and dependence and need for protection; to substitute for it at one blow the simple new precedent of equality, that is a fight worth making if it takes ten years.

CRYSTAL EASTMAN, letter to the editor, "Feminists Must Fight," *The Nation*, November 12, 1924.

What I don't understand is that with so many of us stuck with these clichéd feminine/masculine, submissive/dominant, masochistic/sadistic fantasies, how are we ever going to adjust fully to the less thrilling but more desirable reality of equality?

NORA EPHRON, "Fantasies," July, 1972, *Crazy Salad: Some Things About Women*, 1975.

True equality can only mean the right to be uniquely creative.

ERIK H. ERIKSON, *The Woman in America*, 1965.

A society that puts equality...ahead of freedom will end up with neither equality nor freedom.

MILTON FRIEDMAN and ROSE FRIEDMAN, *Free To Choose*, 1979.

Just as modern mass production requires the standardization of commodities, so the social process requires standardization of man, and this standardization is called equality.

ERICH FROMM, *The Art of Loving*, 1956.

Let us either stop our pretence before the nations of the earth of being a republic and having "equality before the law" or else let us become the republic that we pretend to be.

HELEN H. GARDNER, brief submitted to House and Senate Judiciary Committees, *History of Woman Suffrage*, 1914.

Senator, I am one of them. You do not seem to understand who I am. I am a black woman, the daughter of a dining-car worker....If my life has any meaning at all, it is that those who start out as outcasts can wind up as being part of the system.

PATRICIA ROBERTS HARRIS, reply to William Proxmire regarding her defense of interests of the poor, January 24, 1977.

The struggle for equal opportunity in America is the struggle for America's soul. The ugliness of bigotry stands in direct contradiction to the very meaning of America.

HUBERT H. HUMPHREY, *Beyond Civil Rights—A New Day of Equality*, 1968.

A good many observers have remarked that if equality could come at once the Negro would not be ready for it. I submit that the white American is even more unprepared.

MARTIN LUTHER KING, JR., *Where Do We Go From Here: Chaos or Community?*, 1967.

The passion for equality...is always dangerous to liberty because it is a passion for power: the power to impose one's ideal of justice-as-equality on other people.

IRVING KRISTOL, "Thoughts on Equality and Egalitarianism," *Income Redistribution*, 1976.

I believe that the only hope for satisfying the American idea of equality of treatment in this society—being recognized as "being as good as anyone else"—is reestablishing the dualism of the commercial and the personal realms. By not separating trade and society in the lives of individuals, we force people to take total identity from their jobs, and therefore rob them of any realm in which human beings could and should have full equality in our society.

JUDITH MARTIN, *Common Courtesy*, 1985.

Liberty and Equality are the twin ideals of American democracy. But they are not the same thing....Many persons who would gladly die for liberty are appalled by equality. Many who are devoted to equality are puzzled and even troubled by liberty. Much of the political history of the American nation can be seen as a competition between these two ideals.

DANIEL PATRICK MOYNIHAN, "The Negro Family: The Case for National Action," March, 1965.

On the road to equality there is no better place for blacks to detour around American values than in forgoing its example in the treatment of its women and the organization of its family life.

ELEANOR HOLMES NORTON, "For Sadie and Maude," in Robin Morgan, ed., *Sisterhood Is Powerful*, 1970.

Equality is not when a female Einstein gets promoted to assistant professor: Equality is when a female schlemiel moves ahead as fast as a male schlemiel.

EWALD B. NYQUIST, *New York Times*, October 9, 1975.

Unless man is committed to the belief that all of mankind are his brothers, then he labors in vain and hypocritically in the vineyards of equality.

ADAM CLAYTON POWELL, *Keep the Faith, Baby!*, 1967.

I am an aristocrat; I love liberty, I hate equality.

JOHN RANDOLPH, in Russell Kirk, *John Randolph of Roanoke*, 1951.

No one can make you feel inferior without your consent.

ELEANOR ROOSEVELT, *This Is My Story*, 1937.

Supporting the Equal Rights Amendment is like trying to kill a fly with a sledge hammer. You don't kill the fly, but you end up breaking the furniture....We cannot reduce women to equality. Equality is a step down for most women.

PHYLLIS SCHLAFLY, *Boston Globe*, July 16, 1974.

There is nothing much to be "taught" about equality—you either believe it or you don't. But there is much that can be taught about rights and about liberty, including the basic stuff: that a right derives from a responsibleness, and that men become free as they become willing to accept restrictions on their acts. These are elementary concepts, of course, but an awful lot of

youngsters seem to emerge from high school and even from college without acquiring them. Until they *are* acquired, the more subtle, intricate, and delicate problems of civil rights and freedom are largely incomprehensible.

E.B. WHITE, letter to Robert M. Hutchins, January 4, 1957.

The Constitution does not provide for first and second class citizens.

WENDELL L. WILLKIE, *An American Program*, 1944.

Goddammit, look! We live here and they live there. We black and they white. They got things and we ain't. They do things and we can't. It's just like living in jail.

RICHARD WRIGHT, *Native Son*, 1940.

EXCELLENCE

The sad truth is that excellence makes people nervous.

SHANA ALEXANDER, *The Feminist Eye: Neglected Kids—The Bright Ones*, 1970.

Man transcends death by finding meaning in his life....It is the burning desire for the creature to count....What man really fears is not so much extinction, but extinction with *insignifiance*.

ERNEST BECKER, in Thomas Peters and Robert Waterman, Jr., *In Search of Excellence*, 1982.

We expect to be inspired by mediocre appeals to "excellence," to be made literate by illiterate appeals for literacy.

DANIEL J. BOORSTIN, *The Image*, 1962.

These are the days when men of all social disciplines and all political faiths seek the comfortable and the accepted; when the man of controversy is looked upon as a disturbing influence; when originality is taken to be a mark of instability; and when, in minor modification of the scriptural parable, the bland lead the bland.

JOHN KENNETH GALBRAITH, *The Affluent Society*, 1976.

The society which scorns excellence in plumbing because plumbing is a humble activity and tolerates shoddiness in philosophy because it is an exalted activity will have neither good plumbing nor good philosophy. Neither its pipes nor its theories will hold water.

JOHN W. GARDNER, *Excellence: Can We Be Equal and Excellent Too?*, 1971.

Inefficiency seems to be running rampant in our world, and our only hope lies in the fact that the wicked so often share this lack of dedication to a job well done.

HELEN HAYES, *On Reflection, An Autobiography*, 1968.

Pride in workmanship is a sentimental memory, a residue of Victorianism that, along with self-reliance, perseverance, and honesty, form what is now considered the very squarest of life's foundations.

HELEN HAYES, *On Reflection, An Autobiography*, 1968.

Some men are born mediocre, some men achieve mediocrity, and some men have mediocrity thrust upon them. With Major Major it had been all three.

JOSEPH HELLER, *Catch-22*, 1961.

Help your children understand that excellence in education cannot be achieved without intellectual and moral integrity coupled by hard work and commitment.

National Commission on Excellence in Education, *A Nation at Risk*, 1983.

It isn't evil that's ruining the earth, but mediocrity. The crime is not that Nero played while Rome burned, but that he played badly.

NED ROREM, *The Final Diary*, 1974.

Excellence costs a great deal.

MAY SARTON, *The Small Room*, 1961.

If you don't do it excellently, don't do it at all. Because if it's not excellent, it won't be profitable or fun, and if you're not in business for fun or profit, what the hell are you doing there?

ROBERT TOWNSEND, *Farther Up the Organization*, 1984.

FREEDOM

Liberty Is Always Unfinished Business.

American Civil Liberties Union, title of annual report, 1955–56.

Freedom is perhaps the most resonant, deeply held American value. In some ways, it defines the good in both personal and political life. Yet freedom turns out to mean being left alone by others, not having other people's values, ideas, or styles of life forced upon one, being free of arbitrary authority in work, family, and political life. What it is that one might do with that free-

dom is much more difficult for Americans to define.

ROBERT BELLAH ET AL., *Habits of the Heart*, 1985.

Freedom, n. Exemption from the stress of authority in a beggarly half dozen of restraint's infinite multitude of methods. A political condition that every nation supposes itself to enjoy in virtual monopoly. Liberty. The distinction between freedom and liberty is not accurately known; naturalists have never been able to find a living specimen of either.

AMBROSE BIERCE, *The Devil's Dictionary*, 1906.

Liberty, n. One of Imagination's most precious possessions.

AMBROSE BIERCE, *The Devil's Dictionary*, 1906.

I am for the First Amendment from the first word to the last. I believe it means what it says.

HUGO BLACK, interview, American Jewish Congress, April 14, 1962.

An unconditional right to say what one pleases about public affairs is what I consider to be the minimum guarantee of the First Amendment.

HUGO BLACK, opinion, *New York Times Company v. Sullivan*, 1964.

[F]reedom often means little more than the effective coordination of humanity in the achievement of economic ends.

MURRAY BOOKCHIN, *The Ecology of Freedom*, 1982.

Men born to freedom are naturally alert to repel invasion of their liberty by evil-minded rulers. The greater dangers to liberty lurk in insidious encroachment by men of zeal, well-meaning but without understanding.

LOUIS D. BRANDEIS, opinion, *Olmstead v. United States*, 1928.

Fear of serious injury cannot alone justify suppression of free speech and assembly. Men feared witches and burned women. It is the function of speech to free men from the bondage of irrational fears.

LOUIS D. BRANDEIS, opinion, *Whitney v. California*, 1927.

Experience should teach us to be most on our guard to protect liberty when the government's purposes are beneficent. Men born to freedom are naturally alert to repel invasion of their liberty by evil-minded rulers. The greatest dangers to liberty lurk in insidious encroachment by men of zeal, well-meaning but without understanding.

LOUIS D. BRANDEIS, opinion, *Olmstead v. United States*, 1928.

Free speech is about as good a cause as the world has ever known. But like the poor, it is always with us and gets shoved aside in favor of things which seem at some given moment more vital.

HEYWOOD BROUN, "The Miracle of Debs," *New York World*, October 23, 1926.

None who have always been free can understand the terrible fascinating power of the hope of freedom to those who are not free.

PEARL S. BUCK, *What America Means to Me*, 1943.

We are so concerned to flatter the majority that we lose sight of how very often it is necessary, in order to preserve freedom for the minority, let alone for the individual, to face that majority down.

WILLIAM F. BUCKLEY, JR., "We Want Our Politicians To Be Hypocrites," October 17, 1964, *The Jeweler's Eye*, 1968.

Freedom of expression is the matrix, the indispensable condition, of nearly every other form of freedom.

BENJAMIN CARDOZO, opinion, *Palko* v. *Connecticut*, 1937.

Our American values are not luxuries but necessities—not the salt in our bread but the bread itself. Our common vision of a free and just society is our greatest source of cohesion at home and strength abroad—greater than the bounty of our material blessings.

JIMMY CARTER, speech, January 14, 1981.

There are two kinds of restrictions upon human liberty—the restraint of law and that of custom. No written law has ever been more binding than unwritten custom supported by popular opinion.

CARRIE CHAPMAN CATT, speech, "For the Sake of Liberty," February, 1900, in Susan B. Anthony and Ida Husted, eds., *History of Woman Suffrage*, 1902.

Freedom is not a luxury that we can indulge in when at last we have security and prosperity and enlightenment; it is, rather, antecedent to all of these, for without it we can have neither security nor prosperity nor enlightenment.

HENRY STEELE COMMAGER, *Freedom, Loyalty, Dissent*, 1954.

The justification and the purpose of freedom of speech is not to indulge those who want to speak their minds. It is to prevent error and discover truth. There may be other ways of detecting error and discovering truth than that of free discussion, but so far we have not found them.

HENRY STEELE COMMAGER, *Freedom and Order*, 1966.

We cannot have a society half slave and half free; nor can we have thought half slave and half free.

If we create an atmosphere in which men fear to think independently, inquire fearlessly, express themselves freely, we will in the end create the kind of society in which men no longer care to think independently or to inquire fearlessly. If we put a premium on conformity we will, in the end, get conformity.

HENRY STEELE COMMAGER, *Freedom and Order*, 1966.

Liberty like charity must begin at home.

JAMES BRYANT CONANT, speech, "Our Unique Heritage," Harvard College, June 30, 1942.

Every generation must wage a new war for freedom against new forces that seek through new devices to enslave mankind.

Conference for Progressive Political Action, Platform, 1924.

You can only protect your liberties in this world by protecting the other man's freedom. You can only be free if I am free.

CLARENCE DARROW, speech to jury, Chicago, Illinois, 1920, in Arthur Weinberg, *Attorney for the Damned*, 1957.

We know that the road to freedom has always been stalked by death.

ANGELA DAVIS, "Tribute to George Jackson," *Daily World*, August 25, 1971.

I realize that...there are certain limitations placed upon the right of free speech. I must be exceeding careful, prudent, as to what I say, and even more careful and prudent as to how I say it. I may not be able to say all I think, but I am not going to say anything I do not think.

EUGENE V. DEBS, speech, Canton, Ohio, June 16, 1918.

To say that a man is free to choose to walk while the only walk he can take will lead him over a precipice is to strain words as well as facts.

JOHN DEWEY, *Human Nature and Conduct*, 1922.

The problem of freedom and of democratic institutions is tied up with the question of what kind of culture exists; with the necessity of free culture for free political institutions.

JOHN DEWEY, *Freedom and Culture*, 1939.

That we have made a hero of Howard Hughes tells us something interesting about ourselves, something only dimly remembered, tells us that the secret point of money and power in America is neither the things that money can buy nor power for power's sake (Americans are uneasy with their possessions, guilty about power, all of which is difficult for Europeans to perceive because they are themselves so truly materialistic, so versed in the uses of power), but absolute personal freedom, mobility, privacy. It is the instinct which drove America to the Pacific, all through the nineteenth century, the desire to be able to find a restaurant open in case you want a sandwich, to be a free agent, live by one's own rules.

JOAN DIDION, "7000 Romaine, Los Angeles 38,"
Slouching Towards Bethlehem, 1968.

It is not easy to be free men, for to be free you must afford freedom to your neighbor, regardless of race, color, creed, or national origin, and that sometimes, for some, is very difficult.

HELEN GAHAGAN DOUGLAS, speech to Congress, 1945.

The Fifth Amendment is an old friend and a good friend. It is one of the great landmarks in man's struggle to be free of tyranny, to be decent and civilized.

WILLIAM O. DOUGLAS, *An Almanac of Liberty,* 1954.

Liberty trains for liberty. Responsibility is the first step in responsibility.

W.E.B. DU BOIS, *John Brown,* 1909.

The cost of liberty is less than the price of repression.

W.E.B. DU BOIS, *John Brown,* 1909.

Freedom always entails danger.

W.E.B. DU BOIS, "Freedom to Learn," *Midwest Journal,*
Winter, 1949.

In my youth I stressed freedom, and in my old age I stress order. I have made the great discovery that liberty is a product of order.

WILL DURANT, *Time,* August 13, 1965.

Don't put no constrictions on da people. Leave 'em ta hell alone.

JIMMY DURANTE, in Nelson A. Rockefeller, *Unity, Freedom and Peace: A Blueprint for Tomorrow,* 1968.

Freedom has its life in the hearts, the actions, the spirit of men and so it must be daily earned and refreshed—else like a flower cut from its life-giving roots, it will wither and die.

DWIGHT D. EISENHOWER, speech, English Speaking Union,
London, 1944.

Systems political or religious or racial or national will not just respect us because we practice freedom, they will fear us because we do.

WILLIAM FAULKNER, *Harper's,* June, 1956.

We cannot choose freedom established on a hierarchy of degrees of freedom, on a caste system of equality like military rank. We must be free not because we claim freedom, but because we practice it.

WILLIAM FAULKNER, *Harper's,* June, 1956.

[L]iberty is a living thing that passes from one generation to the next....The greatest enemy of a living thing is not its enemies but its friends who wish to cling to its antiquated form.

HARRY EMERSON FOSDICK, *The Power To See It Through,*
1935.

Freedom is a rare and delicate plant. Our minds tell us, and history confirms, that the great threat to freedom is the concentration of power. Government is necessary to preserve our freedom, it is an instrument through which we can exercise our freedom; yet by concentrating power in political hands, it is also a threat to freedom.

MILTON FRIEDMAN, *Capitalism and Freedom,* 1962.

Freedom is a tenable objective only for responsible individuals.

MILTON FRIEDMAN and ROSE FRIEDMAN, *Free To Choose,*
1979.

Before every free conscience in America is subpoenaed, please speak up!

JUDY GARLAND, ca. 1947, in Anne Edwards, *Judy Garland,*
1975.

I would remind you that extremism in the defense of liberty is no vice. And let me remind you also that moderation in the pursuit of justice is no virtue.

BARRY M. GOLDWATER, speech, Republican National
Convention, San Francisco, California, July 16, 1964.

The freedom of speech and the freedom of the press have not been granted to the people in order that they may say the things which please, and which are based upon accepted thought, but the right to say the things which displease, the right to say the things which may convey the new and yet unexpected thoughts, the right to say things, even though they do a wrong.

SAMUEL GOMPERS, speech, Bucks Stove case, 1908,
Seventy Years of Life and Labor, 1925.

I hold a jail more roomy in the expression of my judgment and convictions than would be the whole world if I were to submit to repression and be denied the right to express myself.

SAMUEL GOMPERS, *Seventy Years of Life and Labor,* 1925.

Everyone appears to be noticing only the statue's torch and not the manacles on her ankles.

ROGER L. GREEN, on centennial of Statue of Liberty, *New York Times*, May 30, 1986.

The spirit of liberty is the spirit which is not too sure that it is right; the spirit of liberty is the spirit which seeks to understand the minds of other men and women; the spirit of liberty is the spirit which weighs their interests alongside its own without bias; the spirit of liberty remembers that not even a sparrow falls to earth unheeded; the spirit of liberty is the spirit of Him who, nearly two thousand years ago, taught mankind that lesson it has never learned, but has never quite forgotten: that there is a kingdom where the least shall be heard and considered side by side with the greatest.

LEARNED HAND, speech, "The Spirit of Liberty," New York City, May 21, 1944.

A society in which men recognize no check upon their freedom soon becomes a society where freedom is the possession of only a savage few.

LEARNED HAND, speech, "The Spirit of Liberty," New York City, May 21, 1944.

Liberty lies in the hearts of men and women; when it dies there, no constitution, no law, no court can save it.

LEARNED HAND, speech, "The Spirit of Liberty," New York City, May 21, 1944.

Ruin is the destination toward which all men rush, each pursuing his own best interest in a society that believes in the freedom of the commons. Freedom in a commons brings ruin to all.

GARRETT HARDIN, "The Tragedy of the Commons," *Science*, December 13, 1968.

The liberty of the citizen to do as he likes so long as he does not interfere with the liberty of others to do the same, which has been a shibboleth from some well-known writers, is interfered with by school laws, by the Post Office, by every state or municipal institution which takes his money for purposes thought desirable, whether he likes it or not.

OLIVER WENDELL HOLMES, JR., opinion, *Lochner* v. *New York*, 1905.

The most stringent protection of free speech would not protect a man in falsely shouting fire in a theater and causing a panic.

OLIVER WENDELL HOLMES, JR., opinion, *Schenck* v. *United States*, 1919.

All life is an experiment. Every year if not every day we have to wager our salvation upon some prophecy based upon imperfect knowledge.

OLIVER WENDELL HOLMES, JR., opinion, *Abrams* v. *United States*, 1919.

Liberty is a beloved discipline.

GEORGE C. HOMANS, *The Human Group*, 1950.

Free speech does not live many hours after free industry and free commerce die.

HERBERT HOOVER, speech, New York City, October 22, 1928.

I express many absurd opinions. But I am not the first man to do it; American freedom consists largely in talking nonsense.

EDGAR WATSON HOWE, *Preaching from the Audience*, 1926.

Liberty: 1. A password in universal use, and hence of no value. 2. The slogan of a party or sect that seeks to enslave some other party or sect.

ELBERT HUBBARD, *The Roycroft Dictionary and Book of Epigrams*, 1923.

There is no freedom on earth or in any star for those who deny freedom to others.

ELBERT HUBBARD, *The Roycroft Dictionary and Book of Epigrams*, 1923.

Poverty curtails individual freedom. So do illiteracy, prejudice, lack of education, inability to obtain the basic needs of life.

HUBERT H. HUMPHREY, *The Cause Is Mankind*, 1964.

No official, high or petty, can prescribe what shall be orthodox in politics, nationism, religion, or other matters of opinion, or force citizens to confess by word or act their faith therein.

ROBERT H. JACKSON, opinion, *West Virginia Board of Education* v. *Barnette*, 1943.

We are reluctant to admit that we owe our liberties to men of a type that today we hate and fear—unruly men, disturbers of the peace, men who resent and denounce what Whitman called "the insolence of elected persons"—in a word, free men....Freedom is always purchased at a great price, and even those who are willing to pay it have to admit that the price is great.

GERALD W. JOHNSON, *American Freedom and the Press*, 1958.

Lift every voice and sing

Till earth and heaven ring,

Ring with the harmonies of Liberty;

Let our rejoicing rise

High as the listening skies,

Let it resound loud as the rolling sea.

Sing a song full of the faith that the dark past has taught us,

Sing a song full of the faith that the present has brought us,

Facing the rising sun of our new day begun,

Let us march on till victory is won.

JAMES WELDON JOHNSON, *Lift Every Voice and Sing*, 1900.

Emancipation was a Proclamation but not a fact.

LYNDON B. JOHNSON, in Martin Luther King, Jr., *Why We Can't Wait*, 1963.

A man is either free or he is not. There cannot be any apprenticeship for freedom.

LEROI JONES, "Tokenism: 300 Years for Five Cents," *Home*, 1966.

Those who bewail the loss of personal liberty have not learned one of the essentials of a democracy. They should know that no one has the personal liberty in a republic to do what the majority has properly declared shall not be done.

WESLEY LIVSEY JONES, speech, U.S. Senate, February 22, 1919.

The deadliest foe of democracy is not autocracy but liberty frenzied. Liberty is not foolproof. For its beneficent working it demands self-restraint.

OTTO KAHN, speech, University of Wisconsin, January 14, 1918.

The path we have chosen for the present is full of hazards, as all paths are....The cost of freedom is always high, but Americans have always paid it. And one path we shall never choose, and that is the path of surrender, or submission.

JOHN F. KENNEDY, speech announcing blockade of Cuba to stop delivery of Soviet missiles, October 22, 1962.

Man is man because he is free to operate within the framework of his destiny. He is free to deliberate, to make decisions, and to choose between alternatives. He is distinguished from animals by his freedom to do evil or to do good and to walk the high road of beauty or tread the low road of ugly degeneracy.

MARTIN LUTHER KING, JR., *The Measures of Man*, 1959.

Tyranny and anarchy are alike incompatible with freedom, security, and the enjoyment of opportunity.

JEANE KIRKPATRICK, speech, Third Committee of United Nations General Assembly, November 24, 1981.

The defense of freedom is finally grounded in an appreciation of its value. No government, no foreign policy, is more important to the defense of freedom than are the writers, teachers, communication specialists, researchers—whose responsibility it is to document, illustrate, and explain the human consequences of freedom and unfreedom.

JEANE KIRKPATRICK, speech, Committee for the Free World, Washington, D.C., January 23, 1982.

Freedom's just another word for nothin' left to lose

Nothin' ain't worth nothin' but it's free.

KRIS KRISTOFFERSON and FRED FOSTER, song, "Me and Bobby McGee," 1969.

The revolutionists did not succeed in establishing human freedom; they poured the new wine of belief in equal rights for all men into the old bottle of privilege for some; and it soured.

SUZANNE LaFOLLETTE, *Concerning Women*, 1926.

[R]eal freedom is not a matter of the shifting of advantage from one sex to the other or from one class to another. Real freedom means the disappearance of advantage, and primarily of economic advantage.

SUZANNE LaFOLLETTE, *Concerning Women*, 1926.

Often those who seek only license for their plundering, cry "liberty." In the guise of this Old American ideal, men of vast economic domain would destroy what little liberty remains to those who toil. The liberty we seek is different. It is liberty for common people—freedom from economic bondage, freedom from the oppressions of the vast bureaucracies of great corporations; freedom to regain again some human initiative, freedom that arises from economic security and human self-respect.

JOHN L. LEWIS, speech, First Constitutional Convention of the Committee for Industrial Organization, November 14, 1938.

Private property was the original source of freedom. It still is its main bulwark.

WALTER LIPPMANN, *The Good Society*, 1937.

We, of all peoples in the world, have matched the freedom of our continent with the freedom of our souls and lived—until now at least—in the image of generosity. It is the first quality the rest of the world has always praised us for, and our history is blazoned with gestures of humanity and altruism that have served as models for the less fortunate and the less free. Why then should we now constrict ourselves out of fear: fear of being suckers, fear of being "soft," fear of being outraced by others?

MARYA MANNES, "The Handsome Heart," *But Will It Sell?*, 1964.

[F]reedom to criticize is held to compensate for the freedom to err—this is the American system....One is assured, gently, that one has the freedom to criticize, as though this freedom, *in itself*, as it attaches to a single individual, counterbalanced the unjust law on the books.

MARY McCARTHY, "No News, or What Killed the Dog," *The Reporter*, July, 1952.

Liberty, as it is conceived by current opinion, has nothing inherent about it; it is a sort of gift or trust bestowed on the individual by the state pending *good behavior*.

MARY McCARTHY, speech, "The Contagion of Ideas," Summer, 1952.

Today we are not put up on the platforms and sold at the courthouse square. But we are forced to sell our strength, our time, our souls during almost every hour that we live. We have been freed from one kind of slavery only to be delivered into another.

CARSON McCULLERS, *The Heart Is a Lonely Hunter*, 1940.

Coercion, after all, merely captures man. Freedom captivates him.

ROBERT S. McNAMARA, speech, American Society of Newspaper Editors, *New York Times*, May 19, 1966.

A superficial freedom to wander aimlessly here or there, to taste this or that, to make a choice of distractions (in Pascal's sense) is simply a sham. It claims to be a freedom of "choice" when it has evaded the basic task of discovering who it is that chooses.

THOMAS MERTON, *Love and Living*, 1979.

Our best hope, both of a tolerable political harmony and of an inner peace, rests upon our ability to observe the limits of human freedom even while we responsibly exploit its creative possibilities.

REINHOLD NIEBUHR, *The Structure of Nations and Empires*, 1959.

It is a mistake to base one's hopes for happiness upon the enforcement of security and equality. *In principle*, both desires are insatiable....No individual or society is secure in a world of emergent probability and sin....To exercise liberty is to take risks, to embrace uncertainties.

MICHAEL NOVAK, *The Spirit of Democratic Capitalism*, 1982.

As long as men are free to ask what they must, free to say what they think, free to think what they will, freedom can never be lost, and science can never regress.

J. ROBERT OPPENHEIMER, *Life*, October 10, 1949.

Freedom is an internal achievement rather than an external adjustment.

ADAM CLAYTON POWELL, *Keep the Faith, Baby!*, 1967.

We have plenty of freedom in this country but not a great deal of independence.

JOHN W. RAPER, *What This World Needs*, 1954.

There can be no greater good than the quest for peace, and no finer purpose than the preservation of freedom.

RONALD REAGAN, speech to Congress on Geneva summit meeting, November 21, 1985.

Freedom in contemporary society finds its most powerful (because most ubiquitous) symbol in the automobile, its operation by individual Americans (thereby assuring them of both freedom and mobility) and its operation in defiance of visibly established laws and authority (a *proof* of individual liberty).

JAMES OLIVER ROBERTSON, *American Myth, American Reality*, 1980.

Freedom is a hard-bought thing.

PAUL ROBESON, *Here I Stand*, 1958.

Freedom breeds freedom. Nothing else does.

ANNE ROE, *The Making of a Scientist*, 1952.

A society in which everyone works is not necessarily a free society and may indeed be a slave society; on the other hand, a society in which there is widespread economic insecurity can turn freedom into a barren and vapid right for millions of people.

ELEANOR ROOSEVELT, speech, "The Struggle for Human Rights," Paris, September 27, 1948.

Freedom of conscience, of education, of speech, of assembly are among the very fundamentals of democracy and all of them would be nullified should freedom of the press ever be successfully challenged.

FRANKLIN D. ROOSEVELT, letter to W.N. Hardy, September 4, 1940.

We look forward to a world founded upon four essential human freedoms. The first is freedom of speech and expression everywhere in the world. The second is freedom of every person to worship God in his own way everywhere in the world. The third is freedom from want...everywhere in the world. The fourth is freedom from fear...anywhere in the world.

FRANKLIN D. ROOSEVELT, speech to Congress, January 6, 1941.

The basic freedom of the world is woman's freedom.

MARGARET SANGER, *Woman and the New Race*, 1920.

The individual freedoms destroyed by the increase in national authority have been in the main the freedom to deny black Americans their elementary rights as citizens, the freedom to work little children in mills...the freedom to pay starvation wages...the freedom to...pollute the environment—all freedoms that, one supposes, a civilized country can readily do without.

ARTHUR M. SCHLESINGER, JR., *The Cycles of American History*, 1986.

Privacy is absolutely essential to maintaining a free society. The idea that is at the foundation of the notion of privacy is that the citizen is not the tool or the instrument of government—but the reverse....If you have no privacy, it will tend to follow that you have no political freedom, no religious freedom, no freedom of families to make their own decisions [regarding having children]. All these freedoms tend to reinforce one another.

BENNO C. SCHMIDT, JR., interview, *The Christian Science Monitor*, December 5, 1986.

Who ever walked behind anyone to freedom? If we can't go hand in hand, I don't want to go.

HAZEL SCOTT, in Margo Jefferson, "Great (Hazel) Scott!" *Ms.*, November, 1974.

There's only one free person in this society, and he is white and male.

HAZEL SCOTT, in Margo Jefferson, "Great (Hazel) Scott!" *Ms.*, November, 1974.

The eternal idea of Justice makes no one just, as the eternal Right makes no one righteous. In a certain sense, we are less free than freeable; we

make ourselves free. Before truth and righteousness and freedom can become mature, they require training, discipline, trial, and the awful possibility of failure.

The whole purpose of freedom is to train minds to use freedom rightly.

FULTON J. SHEEN, *The Wit and Wisdom of Bishop Fulton J. Sheen*, 1968.

Freedom does not mean the right to do whatever we please, but rather to do whatever we ought.... The right to do whatever we *please* reduces freedom to a physical power and forgets that freedom is a moral power.

FULTON J. SHEEN, *The Wit and Wisdom of Bishop Fulton J. Sheen*, 1968.

There is no "slippery slope" toward loss of liberties, only a long staircase where each step downward must first be tolerated by the American people and their leaders.

ALAN K. SIMPSON, *New York Times*, September 26, 1982.

Freedom unexercised may become freedom forfeited.

MARGARET CHASE SMITH, speech, Westbrook Junior College, Portland, Maine, June 7, 1953.

Liberty is the right of any person to stand up anywhere and say anything whatsoever that everybody thinks.

LINCOLN STEFFENS, *Autobiography*, 1931.

My definition of a free society is a society where it is safe to be unpopular.

ADLAI E. STEVENSON, speech, Detroit, Michigan, October 7, 1952.

A hungry man is not a free man.

ADLAI E. STEVENSON, speech, September 6, 1952.

If our freedom means ease alone, if it means shirking the hard disciplines of learning, if it means evading the rigors and rewards of creative activity, if it means more expenditure on advertising than education, if it means in the schools the steady cult of the trivial and the mediocre, if it means—worst of all—indifference, or even contempt for all but athletic excellence, we may keep for a time the forms of free society, but its spirit will be dead.

ADLAI E. STEVENSON, speech, National School Boards Association, San Francisco, California, January 26, 1959.

Freedom is not an ideal, it is not even a protection, if it means nothing more than freedom to stagnate, to live without dreams, to have no greater aim than a second car and another television set—and this in a world where half our fellow men have less than enough to eat.

ADLAI E. STEVENSON, "Putting First Things First," *Foreign Affairs*, January, 1960.

If I want to be free from any other man's dictation, I must understand that I can have no other man under my control.

WILLIAM GRAHAM SUMNER, "The Forgotten Man," *The Forgotten Man and Other Essays*, 1919.

When I say liberty I do not simply mean what is referred to as "free enterprise." I mean liberty of the individual to think his own thoughts and live his own life as he desires to think and to live; the liberty of the family to decide how they wish to live, what they want to eat for breakfast and for dinner, and how they wish to spend their time; liberty of a man to develop his ideas and get other people to teach those ideas, if he can convince them that they have some value to the world; liberty of every local community to decide how its children shall be educated; how its local services shall be run, and who its local leaders shall be; liberty of a man to choose his own occupation; and liberty of a man to run his own business as he thinks it ought to be run, as long as he does not interfere with the right of other people to do the same thing.

ROBERT A. TAFT, *A Foreign Policy for Americans*, 1951.

He who would save liberty must put his trust in democracy.

NORMAN THOMAS, *Saturday Review of Literature*, June 7, 1930.

It is not the fact of liberty but the way in which liberty is exercised that ultimately determines whether liberty itself survives.

DOROTHY THOMPSON, "What Price Liberty," *Ladies' Home Journal*, May, 1958.

When liberty is taken away by force it can be restored by force. When it is relinquished voluntarily by default it can never be recovered.

DOROTHY THOMPSON, "New Caspar Milquetoasts," *Ladies' Home Journal*, August, 1958.

Of all forms of government and society, those of free men and women are in many respects the most brittle. They give the fullest freedom for activities of private persons and groups who often identify their own interests, essentially selfish, with the general welfare.

DOROTHY THOMPSON, "On the Record," May, 1958.

For in the end, freedom is a personal and lonely battle; and one faces down fears of today so that those of tomorrow might be engaged.

ALICE WALKER, "Choosing To Stay at Home: Ten Years After the March on Washington," *In Search of Our Mothers' Gardens*, 1973.

The greatest right in the world is the right to be wrong.

HARRY WEINBERGER, New York *Evening Post*, April 10, 1917.

I hold that it would be improper for any committee or any employer to examine my conscience. They wouldn't know how to get into it, they wouldn't know what to do when they got in there, and I wouldn't let them in anyway. Like other Americans, my acts and my words are open to inspection—not my thoughts or my political affiliation.

E.B. WHITE, letter to *New York Herald Tribune*, November 29, 1947.

You can have no wise laws nor free enforcement of wise laws unless there is free expression of the wisdom of the people—and, alas, their folly with it. But if there is freedom, folly will die of its own poison, and the wisdom will survive.

WILLIAM ALLEN WHITE, *The Editor and His People*, 1924.

Liberty is the only thing you cannot have unless you are willing to give it to others.

WILLIAM ALLEN WHITE, speech, "A Free Press in a Machine Age," University of Pennsylvania, May 2, 1938.

Happiness must be achieved through liberty rather than in spite of liberty.

WENDELL WILLKIE, speech, Republican National Convention, August 17, 1940.

The only soil in which liberty can grow is that of a united people. We must have faith that the welfare of one is the welfare of all. We must know that the truth can only be reached by the expression of our free opinions, without fear and without rancor....We must learn to abhor those disruptive pressures, whether religious, political, or economic, that the enemies of liberty employ.

WENDELL WILLKIE, speech, Republican National Convention, August 17, 1940.

America is not a mere body of traders; it is a body of free men. Our greatness is built upon our freedom—is moral, not material. We have a great ardor for gain; but we have a deep passion for the rights of man.

WOODROW WILSON, speech, New York City, December 6, 1911.

I would rather belong to a poor nation that was free than to a rich nation that had ceased to be in love with liberty. We shall not be poor if we love liberty.

WOODROW WILSON, speech, Mobile, Alabama, October 27, 1912.

Freedom exists only where the people take care of the government.

WOODROW WILSON, speech, New York City, September 4, 1912.

Liberty has never come from the government. Liberty has always come from the subjects of it. The history of liberty is a history of resistance. The history of liberty is a history of limitations of governmental power, not the increase of it.

WOODROW WILSON, speech, New York Press Club, September 9, 1912.

Liberty does not consist…in mere declarations of the rights of man. It consists in the translation of those declarations into definite actions.

WOODROW WILSON, speech, July 4, 1914.

I have always summed up for myself individual liberty and business liberty and every other kind of liberty in the phrase that is common in the sporting world—"A free field and no favor."

WOODROW WILSON, speech, Electric Railway Association, Washington D.C., January 29, 1915.

Freedom belongs to the strong.

RICHARD WRIGHT, Long Black Song, 1936.

To think that the bell does not toll for academic freedom or freedom of the press if economic freedom is shackled is a dangerous illusion.

WALTER WRISTON, Time, August 13, 1979.

FRONTIER

[F]or a transitory enchanted moment man must have held his breath in the presence of this continent, compelled into an aesthetic contemplation he neither understood nor desired, face to face for the last time in history with something commensurate [with] his capacity for wonder.

F. SCOTT FITZGERALD, The Great Gatsby, 1925.

We stand today on the edge of a new frontier—the frontier of the 1960s—a frontier of unknown opportunities and perils—a frontier of unfulfilled hopes and threats.

JOHN F. KENNEDY, speech, Democratic National Convention, July 15, 1960.

If we could stop thinking of ourselves as omnipotent, perhaps we could relocate the frontier to that point in time when men can sense, but cannot quite see, the looming shape of the future. Suppose, for instance, that the frontier could be understood as being always and everywhere present—as near at hand as the wish to murder, cheat, steal, lie, and generally conduct ourselves in a manner unbecoming in an ape.

LEWIS H. LAPHAM, "Econometrics," Washington Post, March, 1983.

Wheeler-dealerism is an extension of the frontier ethos, refined and transplanted to an urban context; and while only a few of us are wheeler-dealers most of us practice symbolic frontiersmanship in some form or fashion.

LARRY MCMURTRY, In a Narrow Grave: Essays on Texas, 1968.

The shuttle crew, spectacularly democratic (male, female, black, white, Japanese American, Catholic, Jewish, Protestant), was the best of us, Americans thought, doing the best of things Americans do. The mission seemed symbolically immaculate, the farthest reach of a perfectly American ambition to cross frontiers. And it simply vanished in the air.

LANCE MORROW, on Challenger explosion, Fishing in the Tiber, 1988.

Frontiers and lines are powerful symbols for Americans….When Americans felt themselves or their beliefs threatened, they drew a line and dared their enemies to cross it.

JAMES OLIVER ROBERTSON, American Myth, American Reality, 1980.

From the beginning America was a place to be discovered.

PETER SCHRAG, The Vanishing American, 1972.

Could that last American frontier be an amusement park?

NICHOLAS VON HOFFMAN, "America on the Run," Spectator, September 23, 1978.

GREATNESS

They are fresh out of heroes in the Eighties.

JOAN BAEZ, Rolling Stone, 1983.

If you would be accounted great by your contemporaries, be not too much greater than they.

AMBROSE BIERCE, Collected Works, 1909–1912.

In the last half century we have misled ourselves, not only about how much novelty the world contains, but about men themselves, and how much greatness can be found among them. One of the oldest of man's visions was the flash of divinity in the great man. He seemed to appear for reasons men could not understand, and the secret of his greatness was God's secret. His generation thanked God for him as for the rain, for the Grand Canyon or the Matterhorn, or for being saved from wreck at sea.

DANIEL BOORSTIN, *Hidden History*, 1987.

Two centuries ago when a great man appeared, people looked for God's purpose in him; today we look for his press agent.

DANIEL BOORSTIN, *Hidden History*, 1987.

We live amidst funny, terrifying paradoxes, in which our most unbending heroes may simply not know where to find their ankles.

GARY COMSTOCK, "Grandma's Backbone, Dougie's Ankle," in Michael Martone, ed., *A Place of Sense*, 1988.

It is frequently the tragedy of the great artist, as it is of the great scientist, that he frightens the ordinary man.

LOREN EISELEY, *The Night Country*, 1971.

Behind almost every great man there stands either a good parent or a good teacher.

GILBERT HIGHET, *Man's Unconquerable Mind*, 1954.

Not until the game is over and all of the chips have been counted can you calculate a man's winnings or losses. And not until he stands against the perspective of history can you correctly measure his stature.

JIMMY HOFFA, *The Trials of Jimmy Hoffa*, 1970.

Little minds are interested in the extraordinary; great minds in the commonplace.

ELBERT HUBBARD, *The Roycroft Dictionary and Book of Epigrams*, 1923.

We must not measure greatness from the mansion down, but from the manger up.

JESSE JACKSON, speech, Democratic National Convention, San Francisco, California, July 17, 1984.

The people are tired of greatness.

WALTER LIPPMANN, analyzing mood of 1920s, in Michael V. DiSalle, *Second Choices*, 1966.

In the years to come...what will determine whether Senator Kennedy or I, if I am elected, was a great President? It will not be our ambi-tion...because greatness is not something that is written on a campaign poster. It will be determined to the extent that we represent the deepest ideals, the highest feelings and faith of the American people. In other words, the next President as he leads America in the free world can be only great as the American people are great.

RICHARD M. NIXON, presidential debate with John F. Kennedy, 1960, in Fawn Brodie, *Richard Nixon: The Shaping of His Character*, 1981.

America is too great for small dreams.

RONALD REAGAN, speech to Congress, January 1, 1984.

Shouldn't we stop worrying whether someone likes us and decide once again we're going to be respected in the world?

RONALD REAGAN, 1979, in Lois and Alan Gordon, *American Chronicle*, 1987.

We can't all be heroes because somebody has to sit on the curb and clap as they go by.

ATTRIBUTED TO WILL ROGERS.

When you cease to make a contribution you begin to die.

ELEANOR ROOSEVELT, February 19, 1960, in Joseph P. Lash, *Eleanor: The Years Alone*, 1972.

To stand upon the ramparts and die for our principles is heroic, but to sally forth to battle and win for our principles is something more than heroic.

FRANKLIN D. ROOSEVELT, speech, Democratic National Convention, June, 1928.

There has been something crude and heartless and unfeeling in our haste to succeed and be great. Our thought has been "Let every man look out for himself, let every generation look out for itself," while we reared giant machinery which made it impossible that any but those who stood at the levers of control should have a chance to look out for themselves. We had not forgotten our morals. We remembered well enough that we had set up a policy which was meant to serve the humblest as well as the most powerful, with an eye single to the standards of justice and fair play, and remembered it with pride. But we were very heedless and in a hurry to be great.

WILLIAM SAFIRE, *Before the Fall*, 1975.

Strength, the American way, is not manifested by threats of criminal prosecution or police state methods. Leadership is not manifested by coercion, even against the resented. Greatness is not manifested by unlimited pragmatism, which places such a high premium on the end justifying *any* means and *any* methods.

MARGARET CHASE SMITH, speech, National Republican Women's Conference, April 16, 1962.

It is an easy matter, requiring little thought, generosity or statesmanship to push a weak man down when he is struggling to get up. Anyone can do that. Greatness, generosity, statesmanship are shown in stimulating, encouraging every individual in the body politic to make of himself the most useful, intelligent and patriotic citizen possible.

BOOKER T. WASHINGTON, interview, *The Atlanta Constitution*, 1906, in Howard Brotz, ed., *Negro Social and Political Thought: 1850–1920*, 1966.

Greatness, generally speaking, is an unusual quantity of a usual quality grafted upon a common man.

WILLIAM ALLEN WHITE, on Theodore Roosevelt, *Masks in a Pageant*, 1928.

I do not believe that America is securely great because she has great men in her now. America is great in proportion as she can make sure of having great men in the next generation. She is rich, that is to say, if those unborn children see the sun in a day of opportunity, see the sun when they are free to exercise their energies as they will. If they open their eyes in a land where there is no special privilege, then we shall come into a new era of American greatness and American liberty; but if they open their eyes in a country where they must be employees or nothing,... where all the conditions of industry are determined by small groups of men, then they will see an America such as the founders of this Republic would have wept to think of.

WOODROW WILSON, in W.B. Hale, *The New Freedom*, 1913.

IMMIGRATION

So at last I was going to America! Really, really going, at last! The boundaries burst. The arch of heaven soared. A million suns shone out for every star. The winds rushed in from outer space, roaring in my ears, "America! America!"

MARY ANTIN, *The Promised Land*, 1912.

Immigrant, n. An unenlightened person who thinks one country better than another.

AMBROSE BIERCE, *The Devil's Dictionary*, 1906.

The immigrants made a voyage not only across the sea, but across time to land at Ellis Island. It was a journey from a Europe and a way of life that had not changed for hundreds of years to an America that was changing too rapidly to know its own nature.

DAVID M. BROWNSTONE ET AL., *Island of Hope, Island of Tears*, 1979.

[Ellis Island] was a nexus, a whirlpool of forces, people, contending ideas. A place where the long-growing, deeply felt idea of a free and open America came into sharp and irreconcilable conflict with an equally old and strong tradition of bigotry in America.

DAVID M. BROWNSTONE ET AL., *Island of Hope, Island of Tears*, 1979.

Why should I fear the fires of Hell? I have been through Ellis Island.

Inscription on wall at Ellis Island, in David M. Brownstone Et al., *Island of Hope, Island of Tears*, 1979.

Foreigners ourselves, and mostly unable to speak English, we had Americanized the system of providing clothes for the American woman of moderate or humble means....We had done away with prohibitive prices and greatly improved the popular taste. Indeed, the Russian Jew had made the average American girl a "tailor-made" girl.

ABRAHAM CAHAN, *The Rise of David Levinsky*, 1917.

Once I thought to write a history of the immigrants in America. Then I discovered that the immigrants *were* American history.

OSCAR HANDLIN, *The Uprooted*, 1951.

What has become of the descendants of the irresponsible adventurers, the scapegrace sons, the bond servants, the redemptionists and the indentured maidens, the undesirables, and even the criminals, which made up, not all, of course, but nevertheless a considerable part of, the earliest emigrants to these virgin countries? They have become the leaders of the thought of the world, the vanguard in the march of progress, the inspirers of liberty, the creators of national prosperity, the sponsors of universal education and enlightenment.

WILLIAM RANDOLPH HEARST, testimony to American Crime Study Commission, May 19, 1929.

But how does one bend toward another culture without falling over, how does one strike an elastic balance between rigidity and self-effacement? How does one stop reading the exterior signs of a foreign tribe and step into the inwardness, the viscera of their meanings? Every anthropologist understands the difficulty of such a feat; and so does every immigrant.

EVA HOFFMAN, *Lost in Translation*, 1989.

The pervasiveness of identity-talk is the kind of second-stage question that emigres—those who have the leisure and the curiosity to attend to such matters—confront, after the initial culture shock and culture thrill wear off....After the immigrant's dendrites stop standing on end from the vividness of first impressions, comes this other, more elusive strangeness—the strangeness of glimpsing internal landscapes that are arranged in different formations as well.

EVA HOFFMAN, *Lost in Translation*, 1989.

This was the secret of America: a nation of people with the fresh memory of old traditions who dared to explore new frontiers, people eager to build lives for themselves in a spacious society that did not restrict their freedom of choice and action.

JOHN F. KENNEDY, *A Nation of Immigrants*, 1964.

The *continuous* immigration of the nineteenth and early twentieth centuries was...central to the whole American faith. It gave every old American a standard by which to judge how far he had come and every new American a realization of how far he might go. It reminded every American, old and new, that change is the essence of life, and that American society is a process, not a conclusion.

JOHN F. KENNEDY, *A Nation of Immigrants*, 1964.

When I was a boy it was a dream, an incredible place where tolerance was natural and personal freedom unchallenged. Even when I learned later that America, too, had massive problems, I could never forget what an inspiration it had been to the victims of persecution, to my family, and to me during cruel and degrading years.

HENRY KISSINGER, *White House Years*, 1979.

The United States once went on the notion that all men are created equal, and admitted everybody....But we found we were becoming an insane asylum....Unless the U.S. adopts this biologic principle [of racial differences] they will be flooded over by people of inferior stock because of their greater fecundity.

HARRY H. LAUGHLIN, speech on exclusionary immigration law, 1924, in Lois and Alan Gordon, *American Chronicle*, 1987.

We are a nation of immigrants. It is immigrants who brought to this land the skills of their hands and brains to make of it a beacon of opportunity and of hope for all men.

HERBERT H. LEHMAN, testimony to House Subcommittee on Immigration and Naturalization, July 2, 1947.

The great social adventure of America is no longer the conquest of the wilderness but the absorption of fifty different peoples.

WALTER LIPPMANN, "Some Necessary Iconoclasm," *A Preface to Politics*, 1914.

Yes, we have a good many poor tired people here already, but we have plenty of mountains, rivers, woods, lots of sunshine and air, for tired people to rest in. We have Kansas wheat and Iowa corn and Wisconsin cheese for them to eat, Texas cotton for them to wear. So give us as many as come—we can take it, and take care of them.

MARY MARGARET McBRIDE, *America for Me*, 1941.

For years there has been a marked tendency on the part of students of immigration to dissociate the movement of immigrants across the Pacific from the movement of immigrants across the Atlantic. Our "immigration problem," as such, was associated almost exclusively with the movement across the Atlantic. It became associated, in our minds, with Ellis Island, the Statue of Liberty, and the doctrine of the Melting Pot. Conversely, the movement across the Pacific became associated with an entirely different set of symbols. We came to associate it with the Yellow Peril, the Chinese Must Go!, and Japanese Picture Brides.

CAREY McWILLIAMS, *Brothers Under the Skin*, 1945.

Politics aside, two other elements had entered our lives which effectively tipped the scales in favor of emigration: the Process Server and my hundred pounds.

JESSICA MITFORD, "Emigration," *Daughters and Rebels*, 1960.

Our people have moved from lower to higher position in the social structure....It is not unusual in the United States for an immigrant to be a member of the Senate, to be Mayor of New York City, Governor or a great industrialist.

FRANK TANNENBAUM, in Arthur Goodfriend, *What Is America?*, 1954.

I remember as a child people used to say to me, "In America you'd find gold in the streets." The streets of gold! And as a child I said to myself,

"Gee, we're in America. Now I can go out in the streets and pick up gold."

ARNOLD WEISS, ca. 1912, in David M. Brownstone Et al., *Island of Hope, Island of Tears*, 1979.

INDIVIDUALISM

I'm a ragged individualist.

Attributed to JANE ACE, in Goodman Ace, *The Fine Art of Hypochondria*, 1966.

If I smashed the traditions it was because I knew no traditions.

MAUDE ADAMS, in Ada Patterson, *Maude Adams: A Biography*, 1907.

I don't mind being different. I don't want to be Jim-Crowed to a back seat because I'm black and I don't want to be ushered to a front seat because I'm not white so they can "palaver" over me.

MARY MCLEOD BETHUNE, in Emma Gelders Steine, *Mary McLeod Bethune*, 1957.

Ours is an individualistic society, indeed, and the state must do for the individual what the family does for the older civilizations.

PEARL S. BUCK, *The Child Who Never Grew*, 1950.

Individualism, we are entitled to say, is, if not truth, the nearest thing we have to truth, no closer thing to truth in the field of social relations having appeared on the horizon.

WILLIAM F. BUCKLEY, JR., *God and Man at Yale*, 1951.

We reveal the fullness of our devotion to individualism by keeping it as a reward for full participation in society. For the prisoner, the chronically ill, the bedridden old and the destitute, we reserve the forced collective life.

ELAINE CUMMING, "Allocation of Care to the Mentally Ill, American Style," in Mayer N. Sald, ed., *Organizing for Community Welfare*, 1967.

The trouble with the sacred Individual is that he has no significance, except as he can acquire it from others, from the social whole.

BERNARD DEVOTO, "The Easy Chair," *Harper's*, May, 1941.

The individual is the central, rarest, most precious capital resource of our society.

PETER F. DRUCKER, in Arthur Goodfriend, *What Is America?*, 1954.

Human diversity makes tolerance more than a virtue; it makes it a requirement for survival.

RENÉ DUBOS, *Celebrations of Life*, 1981.

Any power must be an enemy of mankind which enslaves the individual by terror and force, whether it arises under the Fascist or the Communist flag. All that is valuable in human society depends upon the opportunity for development accorded to the individual.

ALBERT EINSTEIN, statement, England, September 15, 1933.

So much of learning to be an American is learning not to let your individuality become a nuisance.

EDGAR Z. FRIEDENBERG, "The Impact of the School," *The Vanishing Adolescent*, 1959.

It is one thing to decry the rat race...that is the good and honorable work of moralists. It is quite another thing to quit the rat race, to drop out, to refuse to run any further—that is the work of the individualist. It is offensive because it is impolite; it makes the rebuke personal; the individualist calls not his or her behavior into question, but mine.

PAUL GRUCHOW, *Our Sustainable Table*, 1990.

Individualism is rather like innocence; there must be something unconscious about it.

LOUIS KRONENBERGER, *Company Manners*, 1954.

Non-conformism is a major, perhaps the only, sin of our time.

ROBERT LINDNER, "Homosexuality and the Contemporary Scene," *Must You Conform?*, 1956.

Perhaps Western values, for the past five hundred years, had been a human distortion, perhaps competition was simply not compatible with harmony, not conducive to human happiness, perhaps the competitive urge came only from the exaggerated emphasis on the individual. Maybe the individual was simply not as important as the group.

SHIRLEY MACLAINE, *You Can Get There from Here*, 1975.

Once you permit those who are convinced of their own superior rightness to censor and silence and suppress those who hold contrary opinions, just at that moment the citadel has been surrendered. For the American citadel is a man. Not man in general. Not man in the abstract. Not the majority of men. But man. *That* man. *His* worth. *His* uniqueness.

ARCHIBALD MACLEISH, speech, Wellesley College, 1951, in "Parting Shots: A Century of Commencement Speeches," *Saturday Review*, May 12, 1979.

[I]f a man is not faithful to his own individuality, he cannot be loyal to anything.

CLAUDE MCKAY, *A Long Way from Home*, 1937.

The man who walks alone is soon trailed by the F.B.I.

WRIGHT MORRIS, *A Bill of Rites, A Bill of Wrongs, A Bill of Goods*, 1967.

Behind the concept of equality is a belief in individualism born of historic forces that are peculiarly American—the conditions of colonization and frontier life on this continent.

ALLAN NEVINS, in Arthur Goodfriend, *What Is America?*, 1954.

Men are created different; they lose their social freedom and their individual autonomy in seeking to become like each other.

DAVID RIESMAN, "Autonomy and Utopia," *The Lonely Crowd*, 1950.

In the past we have admitted the right of the individual to injure the future of the Republic for his own present profit. In fact there has been a good deal of a demand for unrestricted individualism, for the right of the individual to injure the future of all of us for his own temporary and immediate profit. The time has come for a change. As a people we have the right and the duty, second to none other but the right and duty of obeying the moral law, of requiring and doing justice, to protect ourselves and our children against the wasteful development of our natural resources, whether that waste is caused by the actual destruction of such resources or by making them impossible of development hereafter.

THEODORE ROOSEVELT, speech, national conference on conservation, 1908.

To have one's individuality completely ignored is being pushed quite out of life. Like being blown out as one blows out a light.

EVELYN SCOTT, *Escapade*, 1913.

Self-expression can be wrong as well as right.... When self-expression is identified with irrational surrender to lower instincts, it ends by making the person a slave to those passions. Self-denial is not a renunciation of freedom; it is rather the taming of what is savage and base in our nature for what is higher and better. It is a release from imprisonment by our lusts and passions.

FULTON J. SHEEN, *The Wit and Wisdom of Bishop Fulton J. Sheen*, 1968.

One day our descendants will think it incredible that we paid so much attention to things like the amount of melanin in our skin or the shape of our eyes or our gender instead of the unique identities of each of us as complex human beings.

FRANKLIN THOMAS, in Gloria Steinem, *Outrageous Acts and Everyday Rebellions*, 1983.

The white man's civilization with its inhuman economic competition and rugged individualism has produced millions of physical and mental wrecks. It has produced enough vices to fill Dante's hell. Nine-tenths of the people who reach forty are suffering from shattered nerves. Husbands and wives fuss continually from maladjustments growing out of our national mess-up.

MELVIN B. TOLSON, "Masses of Negroes Are Ahead of Whites!" *Washington Tribune*, August 19, 1939.

History shows that a minority group has an opportunity of raising its status only during a period of social awakening. As long as the vast majority of Americans believed in the theory and practice of rugged individualism, it was inevitable that the Negro should remain a John the Baptist crying in the white man's wilderness.

MELVIN B. TOLSON, "I Am Thankful for the Great Depression," *Washington Tribune*, October 7, 1939.

"Self-government" is primarily a personal morality in America, not a political philosophy....Thus does our individualism reduce social problems, always, to the level of private morality, to things outside the scope of legislation.

GARRY WILLS, *Nixon Agonistes*, 1970.

JUSTICE

It is easy to be popular. It is not easy to be just.

ROSE BIRD, *Boston Globe*, December 25, 1982.

Justice, though due to the accused, is due to the accuser also. The concept of fairness must not be strained till it is narrowed to a filament. We are to keep the balance true.

BENJAMIN CARDOZO, opinion, *Snyder v. Commonwealth of Massachusetts*, 1934.

When a just cause reaches its flood tide...whatever stands in the way must fall before its overwhelming power.

CARRIE CHAPMAN CATT, speech, "Is Woman Suffrage Progressing?" Stockholm, Sweden, 1911.

If every man and woman and child in the world had a chance to make a decent, fair, honest living, there would be no jails, and no lawyers and no courts.

CLARENCE DARROW, speech to prisoners, Cook County Jail, 1902.

There is no such thing as justice—in or out of court.

CLARENCE DARROW, interview, *New York Times*, April 19, 1936.

Justice, I think, is the tolerable accommodation of the conflicting interests of society, and I don't believe there is any royal road to attain such accommodations concretely.

LEARNED HAND, in Philip Hamburger, *The Great Judge*, 1946.

If we are to keep our democracy, there must be one commandment: Thou shalt not ration justice.

LEARNED HAND, speech, New York Legal Aid Society, February 16, 1951.

It is still in the lap of the gods whether a society can succeed which is based on "civil liberties and human rights" conceived as I have tried to describe them; but of one thing at least we may be sure: the alternatives that have so far appeared have been immeasurably worse.

LEARNED HAND, "A Fanfare for Prometheus," in Irving F. Dilliard, *The Spirit of Liberty*, 1955.

Beyond the limits of his confining skin, no man can own any *thing*. "Property" refers not to things owned but to the rights granted by society; they must periodically be re-examined in the light of social justice.

GARRETT HARDIN, *Exploring New Ethics for Survival*, 1972.

Many of the ugly pages of American history have been obscured and forgotten....America owes a debt of justice which it has only begun to pay. If it loses the will to finish or slackens in its determination, history will recall its crimes and the country that would be great will lack the most indispensable element of greatness—justice.

MARTIN LUTHER KING, JR., *Where Do We Go from Here: Chaos or Community?*, 1967.

The Negroes of America had taken the President, the press and the pulpit at their word when they spoke in broad terms of freedom and justice. But the absence of brutality and unregenerate evil is not the presence of justice. To stay murder is not the same thing as to ordain brotherhood.

MARTIN LUTHER KING, JR., *Where Do We Go from Here: Chaos or Community?*, 1967.

Injustice is relatively easy to bear; what stings is justice.

H.L. MENCKEN, *Prejudices*, 1922.

One of the things that make a Negro unpleasant to white folks is the fact that he suffers from their injustice. He is thus a standing rebuke to them.

H.L. MENCKEN, *Minority Report*, 1956.

Oh, Elizabeth, your justice would freeze beer!

ARTHUR MILLER, *The Crucible*, 1953.

Any modern community which establishes a tolerable justice is the beneficiary of the ironic triumph of the wisdom of common sense over the foolishness of its wise men.

REINHOLD NIEBUHR, *The Irony of American History*, 1952.

Justice cannot be for one side alone, but must be for both....

ELEANOR ROOSEVELT, newspaper column, "My Day," October 15, 1947.

Fairness is what justice really is.

POTTER STEWART, *Time*, October 20, 1958.

If it had not been for these things, I might have lived out my life talking at street corners to scorning men. I might have died, unmarked, unknown, a failure. Now we are not a failure. This is our career and our triumph. Never in our full life could we hope to do such work for tolerance, for justice, for man's understanding of men as now we do by accident. Our words—our lives—our pains—nothing! The taking of our lives—lives of a good shoemaker and a poor fish-peddler—all! The last moment belongs to us—that agony is our triumph.

BARTOLOMEO VANZETTI, statement on the death sentences imposed on him and Nicola Sacco, April 9, 1927.

Justice has nothing to do with expediency. Justice has nothing to do with any temporary standard whatever. It is rooted and grounded in the fundamental instincts of humanity.

WOODROW WILSON, speech, Washington, D.C., February 26, 1916.

LEADERSHIP

Leadership should be born out of the understanding of the needs of those who would be affected by it.

MARIAN ANDERSON, *New York Times*, July 22, 1951.

In our country, leadership has to establish itself. It is not taken for granted. It is not the inherent right of any caste. It does not proceed from generation to generation. It must prove itself.

ERWIN D. CANHAM, in Arthur Goodfriend, *What Is America?*, 1954.

We don't need any more leadership training; we need some followership training.

MAUREEN CAROLL, speech, University Research, management, February 15, 1985.

People are more easily led than driven.

DAVID HAROLD FINK, *Release from Nervous Tension*, 1943.

Uncertainty will always be part of the taking-charge process.

JOHN J. GABARRO, *The Dynamics of Taking Charge*, 1987.

Leadership cannot really be taught. It can only be learned.

HAROLD GENEEN, *Managing*, 1984.

Jingshen is the Mandarin word for spirit and vivacity. It is an important word for those who would lead, because above all things, spirit and vivacity set effective organizations apart from those that will decline and die.

JAMES L. HAYES, *Memos for Management: Leadership*, 1983.

Charlatanism of some degree is indispensable to effective leadership.

ERIC HOFFER, *The True Believer*, 1951.

Leadership has a harder job to do than just choose sides. It must bring sides together.

JESSE JACKSON, "Face the Nation," April 9, 1988.

The only real training for leadership is leadership.

ANTONY JAY, *Management and Machiavelli*, 1968.

The genius of a good leader is to leave behind him a situation which common sense, without the grace of genius, can deal with successfully.

WALTER LIPPMANN, "Roosevelt Has Gone," *New York Times*, April 14, 1945.

The art of leading, in operations large or small, is the art of dealing with humanity, of working diligently on behalf of men, of being sympathetic with them, but equally, of insisting that they make a square facing toward their own problems.

S.L.A. MARSHALL, *Men Against Fire*, 1947.

I start with the premise that the function of leadership is to produce more leaders, not more followers.

RALPH NADER, *Time*, November 8, 1976.

You take people as far as they will go, not as far as you would like them to go.

JEANNETTE RANKIN, Prologue, in Hannah Josephson, *Jeannette Rankin: First Lady in Congress*, 1974.

I'm really glad that our young people missed the Depression and missed the great big war. But I do regret that they missed the leaders that I knew—leaders who told us when things were tough and that we'd have to sacrifice, and that these difficulties might last for a while. They didn't tell us things were hard for us because we were different, or isolated, or special interests. They brought us together, and they gave us a sense of national purpose.

ANN W. RICHARDS, Democratic National Convention, July 18, 1988.

I wouldn't make the slightest concession for moral leadership. It's much overrated.

DEAN RUSK, in David Halberstam, *The Best and the Brightest*, 1962.

Leadership is not manifested by coercion, even against the resented.

MARGARET CHASE SMITH, speech, National Republican Women, April 16, 1962.

Whether a man is burdened by power or enjoys power; whether he is trapped by responsibility or made free by it; whether he is moved by other people and outer forces or moves them—this is of the essence of leadership.

THEODORE H. WHITE, *The Making of the President, 1960*, 1961.

LEISURE

I think the only reason you should retire is if you can find something you enjoy doing more than what you're doing now. I happen to be in love with show business, and I can't think of anything I'd enjoy more than that. So I guess I've been retired all my life.

GEORGE BURNS, *Living It Up; or, They Still Love Me in Altoona!*, 1976.

It takes application, a fine sense of value, and a powerful community spirit for a people to have serious leisure, and this has not been the genius of the Americans.

PAUL GOODMAN, *Growing Up Absurd*, 1960.

The moral and spiritual forces of our country do not lose ground in the hours we are busy on our jobs; their battle is the leisure time. We are organizing the production of leisure. We need better organization of its consumption.

HERBERT HOOVER, *Memoirs II*, 1950.

Use of the automobile has apparently been influential in spreading the "vacation" habit. The custom of having each summer a respite, usually of two weeks, from getting-a-living activities, with pay unabated, is increasingly common among the business class, but it is as yet very uncommon among the workers.

ROBERT S. LYND and HELEN MERRELL LYND, *Middletown: A Study in Contemporary American Culture*, 1929.

Leisure and the cultivation of human capacities are inextricably interdependent.

MARGARET MEAD, *Redbook*, December, 1963.

The mass production of distraction is now as much a part of the American way of life as the mass production of automobiles.

C. WRIGHT MILLS, "The Unity of Work and Leisure," *Power, Politics and People*, 1963.

Freedom from worries and surcease from strain are illusions that always inhabit the distance.

EDWIN WAY TEALE, "April 3," *Circle of the Seasons*, 1953.

So far I've found that most high-level executives prefer the boardroom to the Bahamas. They don't really enjoy leisure time; they feel their work is their leisure.

WILLIAM THEOBALD, *American Way*, February 5, 1985.

OPPORTUNITY

The American dream, I think, was that within this system every man could become an owner.... It has been said that every soldier of Napoleon carried in his knapsack a marshal's baton, and in the early days of this century it seems to have been thought that every young American carried in his lunch box a roll of ticker tape.

DEAN ACHESON, speech, Law Club of Chicago, January 22, 1937.

I don't know anything about luck. I've never banked on it, and I'm afraid of people who do. Luck to me is something else: hard work—and realizing what is opportunity and what isn't.

LUCILLE BALL, in Eleanor Harris, *The Real Story of Lucille Ball*, 1954.

For this is what America is all about. It is the uncrossed desert and the unclimbed ridge. It is the star that is not reached and the harvest that is sleeping in the unplowed ground.

LYNDON B. JOHNSON, inaugural address, January 20, 1965.

Problems are only opportunities in work clothes.

HENRY J. KAISER, recalled on his death, August 24, 1967.

Luck is what happens when preparation meets opportunity.

DARRELL ROYAL, in James A. Michener, *Sports in America*, 1976.

PATRIOTISM

The belief that if the meanest man in the republic is deprived of his rights, then every man in the republic is deprived of his rights, is the only patriotism.

JANE ADDAMS, speech, Union League Club, Chicago, Illinois, 1903.

Patriot, n. One to whom the interests of a part seem superior to those of the whole. The dupe of statesmen and the tool of conquerors.

AMBROSE BIERCE, *The Devil's Dictionary*, 1906.

Patriotism, n. Combustible rubbish ready to the torch of any one ambitious to illuminate his name. In Dr. Johnson's famous dictionary patriotism is defined as the last resort of a scoundrel. With all due respect to an enlightened but inferior lexicographer I beg to submit that it is the first.

AMBROSE BIERCE, *The Devil's Dictionary*, 1906.

What this country needs—what every country needs occasionally—is a good hard bloody war to revive the vice of patriotism on which its existence as a nation depends.

AMBROSE BIERCE, letter, February 15, 1911.

Who are the really disloyal? Those who inflame racial hatreds, who sow religious and class dissensions. Those who subvert the Constitution by violating the freedom of the ballot box. Those who make a mockery of majority rule by the use of the filibuster. Those who impair democracy by denying equal educational facilities. Those who frustrate justice by lynch law or by making a farce of jury trials. Those who deny freedom of speech and of the press and of assembly. Those who demand special favors against the interest of the commonwealth. Those who regard public office merely as a source of private gain. Those who would exalt the military over the civil.

Those who for selfish and private purposes stir up national antagonisms and expose the world to the ruin of war.

HENRY STEELE COMMAGER, *Freedom, Loyalty, Dissent*, 1954.

When Dr. Johnson defined patriotism as the last refuge of a scoundrel, he ignored the enormous possibilities of the word reform.

ROSCOE CONKLING, in David M. Jordan, *Roscoe Conkling of New York*, 1971.

Patriotism is easy to understand in America. It means looking out for yourself by looking out for your country.

CALVIN COOLIDGE, speech, Northampton, Massachusetts, May 30, 1923.

You can't prove you're an American by waving Old Glory.

HELEN GAHAGAN DOUGLAS, *A Full Life*, 1982.

Nationalism is an infantile disease. It is the measles of mankind.

ALBERT EINSTEIN, to George Sylvester Viereck, 1921.

Of all ennobling sentiments, patriotism may be the most easily manipulated. On the one hand, it gives powerful expression to what is best in a nation's character: a commitment to principle, a willingness to sacrifice, a devotion to the community by the choice of the individual. But among its toxic fruits are intolerance, belligerence and blind obedience, perhaps because it blooms most luxuriantly during times of war.

NANCY GIBBS, *Time*, February 11, 1991.

To be radical is, in the best and only decent sense of the word, patriotic.

MICHAEL HARRINGTON, *Fragments of the Century*, 1973.

What we need are critical lovers of America—patriots who express their faith in their country by working to *improve* it.

HUBERT H. HUMPHREY, *Beyond Civil Rights: A New Day of Equality*, 1968.

I look upon the world as my fatherland....I look upon true patriotism as the brotherhood of man and the service of all to all.

HELEN KELLER, *New York Call*, December 20, 1915.

There are things a man must not do even to save a nation.

MURRAY KEMPTON, "To Save a Nation," *America Comes of Middle Age*, 1963.

National patriotism is civic pride writ large.

ROBERT S. LYND and HELEN MERRELL LYND, *Middletown: A Study in Contemporary American Culture*, 1929.

Whenever you hear a man speak of his love for his country it is a sign that he expects to be paid for it.

H.L. MENCKEN, "Sententiae," *The Vintage Mencken*, 1955.

At its truest, American patriotism has a sort of abstraction about it that makes it uniquely difficult and valuable: it is a devotion not to a specific physical place, gene pool, cuisine, or cultural tradition, but to a political and social vision, a promise and the idea of freedom—an idea not much honored elsewhere in the world or in history. At its worst, American patriotism degenerates into a coarse form of national self-congratulation.

LANCE MORROW, "The Return of Patriotism," *Fishing in the Tiber*, 1988.

Patriotism is often an arbitrary veneration of real estate above principles.

GEORGE JEAN NATHAN, *Testament of a Critic*, 1931.

There can be no fifty-fifty Americanism in this country. There is room here for only 100% Americanism, only for those who are Americans and nothing else.

THEODORE ROOSEVELT, speech, State Republican Convention, Saratoga, New York, July 19, 1918.

The man who loves other countries as much as his own stands on a level with the man who loves other women as much as he loves his own wife.

THEODORE ROOSEVELT, speech, New York City, September 6, 1918.

I don't know much about patriotism but I know what I like. The U.S. Constitution. I like that. The sight of fellow citizens doing something generous and valuable for one another. The knowledge that we belong to a system dedicated to equal stature and equal changes. Such things make me and most feel good about our country.

ROGER ROSENBLATT, *Life*, April, 1991.

Patriotism is just loyalty to friends, people, families.

ROBERT SANTOS, in Al Santoli, *Everything We Had: An Oral History of the Vietnam War by Thirty-three American Soldiers Who Fought It*, 1981.

I feel this do-or-die, my-country-right-or-wrong kind of patriotism is not merely out of place in a nuclear armed world, it is criminal egotism on a monstrous scale. The world won't be safe until people in all countries recognize it for what it is and, instead of cheering the leader who talks that way, impeach him.

BENJAMIN SPOCK, *Decent and Indecent*, 1968.

I venture to suggest that patriotism is not a short and frenzied outburst of emotion but the tranquil and steady dedication of a lifetime.

ADLAI E. STEVENSON, speech, American Legion Convention, August 27, 1952.

The typical American patriot really feels that repugnance to "fascism, communism, and other foreign isms" about which the editorial writers and politicians have become so eloquent—even though his social instincts may be identical with those of his fellows abroad. He also considers himself unimpeachably democratic—even when he is breaking up a labor meeting in New Jersey or helping to lynch a Negro in the South.

LILLIAN SYMES, "Fascism for America—Threat or Scarehead," *Harper's*, June, 1939.

There would never be a moment, in war or in peace, when I wouldn't trade all the patriots in the country for one tolerant man. Or when I wouldn't swap the vitamins in a child's lunchbox for a jelly of magnanimity.

E.B. WHITE, "Coon Hunt," November, 1941, *One Man's Meat*, 1944.

You're not supposed to be so blind with patriotism that you can't face reality. Wrong is wrong, no matter who does it or who says it.

MALCOLM X, *Malcolm X Speaks*, 1965.

POWER

The effect of power and publicity on all men is the aggravation of self, a sort of tumor that ends by killing the victim's sympathies.

HENRY ADAMS, *The Education of Henry Adams*, 1907.

In every community there is a class of people profoundly dangerous to the rest. I don't mean the criminals. For them we have punitive sanctions. I mean the leaders. Invariably the most dangerous people seek the power.

SAUL BELLOW, *Herzog*, 1964.

We are in jail, we insist, because we would neither remain silent nor passive before the pathology of naked power, which rules our country and dominates half the world, which shamelessly wastes resources as well as people, which leaves in its wake racism, poverty, foreign exploitation, and war. In face of this we felt, free men cannot remain free and silent, free men cannot confess their powerlessness by doing nothing.

DANIEL BERRIGAN and PHILIP BERRIGAN, in Daniel Berrigan, *America Is Hard To Find*, 1972.

Power intoxicates men. It is never voluntarily surrendered. It must be taken from them.

JAMES F. BYRNES, *New York Times*, May 15, 1956.

We are sojourners and strangers in this nation that rewards those who succumb to the temptation of the desert.

JOAN B. CAMPBELL, *Sojourners*, August/September, 1991.

Power politics is the diplomatic name for the law of the jungle.

ELY CULBERTSON, *Must We Fight Russia?*, 1946.

As children of this particular enlightened class, you were expected one day to be manning a more than proportional share of the positions of power and prestige in this society. It was at least partly to this end that we brought you up.

MIDGE DECTER, *Liberal Parents, Radical Children*, 1975.

The power to do good is also the power to do harm; those who control the power today may not tomorrow; and, more important, what one man regards as good, another may regard as harm.

MILTON FRIEDMAN, *Capitalism and Freedom*, 1962.

Concentrated power is not rendered harmless by the good intentions of those who create it.

MILTON FRIEDMAN, *Capitalism and Freedom*, 1962.

The lust for power is not rooted in strength but in weakness.

ERICH FROMM, *Escape from Freedom*, 1941.

The first step toward liberation for *any* group is to use the power in hand....And the power in hand is the vote.

HELEN GAHAGAN DOUGLAS, in Lee Israel, "Helen Gahagan Douglas," *Ms.*, October, 1973.

[Power is] exerted energy and capacity for action. When followed by the word structure, it refers to a group which includes America's most wealthy and influential citizens. When prefixed by the word black, it creates terror in the minds of the power structure.

DICK GREGORY, *Dick Gregory's Political Primer*, 1972.

I am the law.

FRANK HAGUE, 1937, in Lois and Alan Gordon, *American Chronicle*, 1987.

Now I can go back to being ruthless again.

ROBERT F. KENNEDY, on winning race for U.S. Senate,
Esquire, April, 1965.

Power at its best is love implementing the demands of justice. Justice at its best is love correcting everything that stands against love.

MARTIN LUTHER KING, JR., *Where Do We Go from Here:
Chaos or Community?*, 1967.

Power...is not an end in itself, but is an instrument that must be used toward an end.

JEANE KIRKPATRICK, speech, National Urban League,
Washington, D.C., July 20, 1981.

We are making the price of power much too high in this society. I worry that we are making the conditions of public life so tough that nobody except people really obsessed with power will be willing finally to pay that price. That would be tragic from the point of view of public well-being.

JEANE KIRKPATRICK, *Newsweek*, September 3, 1984.

Power is the great aphrodisiac.

HENRY KISSINGER, *New York Times*, January 19, 1971.

Power should not be concentrated in the hands of so few, and powerlessness in the hands of so many.

MAGGIE KUHN, "How to Fight Age Bias," *Ms.*, June,
1975.

Goodness, armed with power, is corrupted; and pure love without power is destroyed.

REINHOLD NIEBUHR, *Beyond Tragedy*, 1938.

Men and nations must use their power with the purpose of making it an instrument of justice and a servant of interests broader than their own.

REINHOLD NIEBUHR, *The Irony of American History*, 1952.

Isolation from reality is inseparable from the exercise of power.

GEORGE REEDY, in Arthur M. Schlesinger, Jr., *The Imperial
Presidency*, 1973.

The power to define the situation is the ultimate power.

JERRY RUBIN, *Growing (Up) at 37*, 1976.

We in America are fighting the money power; but if men can elsewhere get the power without money, what do they care about money? Power is what men seek, and any group that gets it will abuse it.

LINCOLN STEFFENS, to Upton Sinclair, *Exposé*, February,
1956.

Power can be taken, but not given. The process of the taking is empowerment in itself.

GLORIA STEINEM, *Ms.*, July, 1978.

Most of us, consciously or unconsciously, are discontented with the nature rather than with the use of the human faculty; deep in our assumption lies the hope and the belief that humanity will end its career by developing virtues which will be admirable exactly because we cannot now conceive them. The past has been a weary failure, the present cannot matter, for it is but a step forward to the final judgment; we look to the future when the best of the works of man will seem but the futile and slightly disgusting twitchings of primeval creatures; thus, in the name of a superior and contemptuous posterity, we express our self-hatred—and our desire for power.

LIONEL TRILLING, *E.M. Forster*, 1943.

Power in defense of freedom is greater than power in behalf of tyranny and oppression.

MALCOLM X, speech, New York City, 1965.

PROGRESS

Like an ox-cart driver in monsoon season or the skipper of a grounded ship, one must sometimes go forward by going back.

JOHN BARTH, *New York Times*, September 16, 1984.

In recent years we have come to understand what progress is. It is the total replacement of nature by an artificial technology. Progress is the absolute destruction of the real world in favor of a technology that creates a comfortable way of life for a few fortunately situated people.

VINE DELORIA, JR., *We Talk, You Listen*, 1970.

In the long run, the only limits to the technological growth of a society are internal. A society has always the option of limiting its growth, either by conscious decision or by stagnation or by disinterest. A society in which these internal limits are absent may continue its growth forever.

FREEMAN DYSON, *Disturbing the Universe*, 1979.

I hold to the relay race theory of history: progress in human affairs depends on accepting, generation after generation, the individual duty to oppose the evils of the time.

MARTHA GELLHORN, "Conclusion," *The Face of War*,
1988.

Our central problem arises from a deep conflict between the processes of material progress and the ideals of "progressive" government and culture. Equality, bureaucratic rationality, predictability, sexual liberation, political "populism," and the pursuit of pleasure—all the values of advanced culture—are quite simply inconsistent with the disciplines and investments of economic and technical advance. The result is that all modern governments pretend to promote economic growth but in practice doggedly obstruct it.

GEORGE GILDER, *Wealth and Poverty*, 1981.

There can be no conquest to the man who dwells in the narrow and small environment of a groveling life, and there can be no vision to the man the horizon of whose vision is limited by the bounds of self. But the great things of the world, the great accomplishments of the world, have been achieved by men who had high ideals and who have received great visions. The path is not easy, the climbing is rugged and hard, but the glory at the end is worthwhile.

MATT HENSON, lecture notes, 1909, in William Loren Katz, ed., *Eyewitness: The Negro in American History*, 1967.

The concept of progress acts as a protective mechanism to shield us from the terrors of the future.

FRANK HERBERT, *Dune*, 1965.

The slogan of progress is changing from the full dinner pail to the full garage.

HERBERT HOOVER, speech, New York City, October 22, 1928.

Our progress as a nation can be no swifter than our progress in education....The human mind is our fundamental resource.

JOHN F. KENNEDY, message to Congress, February 20, 1961.

Today, the notion of progress in a single line without goal or limit seems perhaps the most parochial notion of a very parochial century.

LEWIS MUMFORD, *Technics and Civilization*, 1934.

Trends, like horses, are easier to ride in the direction they are already going.

JOHN NAISBITT, Introduction, *Megatrends*, 1984.

Progress might have been all right once, but it's gone on too long.

OGDEN NASH, *Reader's Digest*, February, 1975.

The viewpoint that progress must be slow is rooted in the idea that democratic rights, as far as Negroes are concerned, are not inalienable and self-evident as they are for white Americans.

PAUL ROBESON, *Here I Stand*, 1958.

The country needs and, unless I mistake its temper, the country demands bold, persistent experimentation. It is common sense to take a method and try it; if it fails, admit it frankly and try another. But above all, try something.

FRANKLIN D. ROOSEVELT, speech, Oglethorpe University, Atlanta, Georgia, May 22, 1932.

All progress has resulted from people who took unpopular positions.

ADLAI E. STEVENSON, speech, Princeton University, New Jersey, March 22, 1954.

Life means progress, and progress means suffering.

HENDRIK WILLEM VAN LOON, *Tolerance*, 1925.

That's the old American way—if you get a good thing, then overdo it.

PHIL WALDEN, *Rolling Stone*, July 1, 1976.

RISK

Our whole way of life today is dedicated to the removal of risk. Cradle to grave we are supported, insulated, and isolated from the risks of life—and if we fall, our government stands ready with Band-Aids of every size.

SHIRLEY TEMPLE BLACK, speech, Texas, June, 1967, in Rodney G. Minott, *The Sinking of the Lollipop*, 1968.

It's too bad that one has to conceive of sports as being the only arena where risks are, [for] all of life is risk exercise. That's the only way to live more freely, and more interestingly.

WILLIAM SLOANE COFFIN, JR., *Once to Every Man*, 1977.

Security is mostly a superstition. It does not exist in nature, nor do the children of men as a whole experience it. Avoiding danger is no safer in the long run than outright exposure. Life is either a daring adventure, or nothing.

HELEN KELLER, *The Open Door*, 1957.

Oddly enough, a gambler never entertains the thought of loss. He can't afford to. No one who has never gambled can possibly understand the projects, plans, dreams a gambler can create on the turn of a card or the chance of a horse going to the post.

BELLE LIVINGSTONE, *Belle Out of Order*, 1959.

Go for the moon. If you don't get it, you'll still be heading for a star.

WILLIS REED, quoting one of his high school coaches, in Bill Bradley, *Life on the Run*, 1976.

Our father made money in lumber and naval stores for the excitement of making and losing it—not for what money can buy nor the security which it sometimes gives.

LILLIAN SMITH, *Killers of the Dream*, 1949.

The right stuff was not bravery in the simple sense of being willing to risk your life (by riding on top of a Redstone or Atlas rocket). Any fool could do that (and many fools would no doubt volunteer, given the opportunity), just as any fool could throw his life away in the process. No, the idea (as all *pilots* understood) was that a man should have the ability to go up in a hurtling piece of machinery and put his hide on the line and have the moxie, the reflexes, the experience, the coolness, to pull it back at the last yawning moment.

TOM WOLFE, *The Right Stuff*, 1979.

Those who misrepresent the normal experiences of life, who decry being controversial, who shun risk, are the enemies of the American way of life, whatever the piety of their vocal professions and the patriotic flavor of their platitudes.

HENRY M. WRISTON, *Wall Street Journal*, June 1, 1960.

SECURITY

The insurance policy was a guarantee that, no matter how many necessities a person had to forego all through life, death was something to which he could look forward.

FRED ALLEN, *Much Ado About Me*, 1956.

Security is a feeling that there is a larger and more enduring life surrounding, appreciating, upholding the individual, and guaranteeing that his efforts and sacrifice will not be in vain.

CHARLES H. COOLEY, *Social Progress*, 1908.

This is the Hartford heresy. Economic, material security, life insurance, endowments, annuities take the place of a providential destiny, so that ultimate values are not built upon a rock whose name is Peter, but upon a rock whose name is Prudential.

WILLIAM T. COSTELLO, *Address*, December, 1948.

You're a star on the stage, in pictures, on TV. You make a fortune every week. Trade papers, magazines, and Barbara Walters all report your popularity. You live in a mansion, your wife loves you, and your children are clean, decent, and don't do drugs. You have every reason to be happy and secure. But it's one to ten that you're insecure.

FRED DE CORDOVA, *Johnny Came Lately*, 1988.

In the long course of history, having people who understand your thought is much greater security than another submarine.

J. WILLIAM FULBRIGHT, *The New Yorker*, May 10, 1958.

There are one hundred men seeking security to one able man who is willing to risk his fortune.

J. PAUL GETTY, *International Herald Tribune*, January 10, 1961.

Social security depends on *personal* security. And *personal* security depends on *spiritual* security. Spiritual security is primary, in the sense that every other kind of security stems from it. Without spiritual security, there just can't be any other kind of lasting security.

JOHN E. LARGE, *The Small Needle of Doctor Large*, 1962.

There is no security on this earth; there is only opportunity.

DOUGLAS MACARTHUR, in Courtney Whitney, *MacArthur: His Rendezvous with History*, 1955.

An overemphasis on temporal security is a compensation for a loss of the sense of eternal security.

FULTON J. SHEEN, *Peace of Soul*, 1949.

Everybody knows if you are too careful you are so occupied in being careful that you are sure to stumble over something.

GERTRUDE STEIN, *Everybody's Autobiography*, 1937.

The preservation of peace and the improvement of the lot of all people require us to have faith in the rationality of humans. If we have this faith and if we pursue understanding, we have not the promise but at least the possibility of success. We should not be misled by promises. Humanity in all its history has repeatedly escaped disaster by a hair's breadth. Total security has never been available to anyone. To expect it is unrealistic; to imagine that it can exist is to invite disaster.

EDWARD TELLER, *The Pursuit of Simplicity*, 1980.

From his cradle to his grave a man never does a single thing which has any first and foremost object save one—to secure peace of mind, spiritual comfort, for himself.

MARK TWAIN, *What Is Man?*, 1906.

Security is a kind of death.

TENNESSEE WILLIAMS, *Esquire*, September, 1971.

A guidance counselor who has made a fetish of security, or who has unwittingly surrendered his thinking to economic determinism, may steer a youth away from his dream of becoming a poet, an artist, a musician or any other of thousands of things, because it offers no security, it does not pay well, there are no vacancies, it has no "future."

HENRY M. WRISTON, *Wall Street Journal*, June 1, 1960.

SPACE

Space, room, expanse—that is America; green space, fertile land; and man, migrant man, only the traveler there.

HAL BORLAND, *New York Times*, July 24, 1955.

Space has a spiritual equivalent and can heal what is divided and burdensome in us. My grandchildren will probably use space shuttles for a honeymoon trip or to recover from heart attacks, but closer to home we might also learn how to carry space inside ourselves in the effortless way we carry our skins. Space represents sanity, not a life purified, dull, or "spaced out" but one that might accommodate intelligently any idea or situation.

GRETEL EHRLICH, *The Solace of Open Spaces*, 1985.

The distances, in America, are still the salient thing. The large facts of geographic distances and the smaller facts of the distances between apartments and offices and houses inform the most intimate distances between us. In the distended and foreshortened perspectives of the American spaces, others tend to become puzzling Others—and so do our own selves, which grow in strangeness and uncertainty in direct proportion to the opaqueness of those around us. There are so many strangers, in America.

EVA HOFFMAN, *Lost in Translation*, 1989.

They may be America's last pioneers, urban nomads in search of wide open *interior* spaces.

CATHLEEN McGUIGAN, "The Soho Syndrome: Artists Are Revitalizing City Neighborhoods," *Newsweek*, September 22, 1986.

In the United States there is more space where nobody is than where anybody is. That is what makes America what it is.

GERTRUDE STEIN, *The Geographical History of America*, 1936.

Time and space—time to be alone, space to move about—these may well become the great scarcities of tomorrow.

EDWIN WAY TEALE, *Autumn Across America*, 1956.

TRUTH

I had rather starve and rot and keep the privilege of speaking the truth as I see it, than of holding all the offices that capital has to give from the presidency down.

BROOKS ADAMS, *The Degradation of the Democratic Dogma*, 1919.

The truth that makes men free is for the most part the truth which men prefer not to hear.

HERBERT AGAR, *A Time for Greatness*, 1942.

Truth has a way of shifting under pressure.

CURTIS BOK, *Saturday Review*, February 13, 1954.

For truth there is no deadline.

HEYWOOD BROUN, *The Nation*, December 30, 1939.

When I'm interested in a truth, it's really a *truth* truth, one hundred percent. And that's a terrible kind of truth to be interested in.

LENNY BRUCE, ca. 1960, in John Cohen, ed., *The Essential Lenny Bruce*, 1967.

The most casual student of history knows that, as a matter of fact, truth does *not* necessarily vanquish. What is more, truth can *never* win unless it is promulgated. Truth does not carry within itself an antitoxin to falsehood. The cause of truth must be championed, and it must be championed dynamically.

WILLIAM F. BUCKLEY, JR., *God and Man at Yale*, 1951.

To [William Jennings] Bryan, truth lay only in holy scripture, and scripture comprised two books: the Bible and the Constitution of the United States.

ALISTAIR COOKE, *America*, 1973.

Chase after the truth like all hell and you'll free yourself, even though you never touch its coat-tails.

CLARENCE DARROW, *Voltaire*, 1916.

If men can ever learn to accept their truths as not final, and if they can ever learn to build on something better than dogma, they may not be found saying, discouragedly, every once in so often, that every civilization carries in it the seeds of decay.

CLARENCE DAY, *This Simian World*, 1920.

The truth has always been dangerous to the rule of the rogue, the exploiter, the robber. So the truth must be ruthlessly suppressed.

EUGENE V. DEBS, speech, Canton, Ohio, June 16, 1918.

The greatest and most immediate danger of white culture...is its fear of the Truth, its childish belief in the efficacy of lies as a method of human uplift.

W.E.B. DU BOIS, *Dusk of Dawn*, 1940.

Truth is what stands the test of experience.

ALBERT EINSTEIN, *Out of My Later Years*, 1950.

Whoever undertakes to set himself up as judge in the field of Truth and Knowledge is shipwrecked by the laughter of the gods.

ALBERT EINSTEIN, *Ideas and Opinions*, 1954.

The majority of the people are naturally straddlers. They are not in the world to pioneer but to be as happy as possible. If pioneering in a cause brings discomfort, they would rather not be among the pioneers. They would rather stand on the sidelines and, in the combat between truth and error, wait and see which proves the stronger. Though they may have a lazy faith that truth at last will win, they do not wish to lend a premature support.

HENRY FORD, "Success," *Forum*, October, 1928.

That's not a lie, it's a terminological inexactitude.

ALEXANDER HAIG, TV interview, 1983.

A society committed to the search for truth must give protection to, and set a high value upon, the independent and original mind, however angular, however rasping, however socially unpleasant it may be; for it is upon such minds, in large measure, that the effective search for truth depends.

CARYL P. HASKINS, *New York Times*, December 9, 1963.

Legends die hard. They survive as truth rarely does.

HELEN HAYES, *On Reflection, An Autobiography*, 1968.

When men have realized that time has upset many fighting faiths, they may come to believe even more than they believe the very foundations of their own conduct that the ultimate good desired is better reached by free trade in ideas—that the best test of truth is the power of the thought to get itself accepted in the competition of the market, and that truth is the only ground upon which their wishes safely can be carried out.

OLIVER WENDELL HOLMES, JR., opinion, *Abrams v. United States*, 1919.

A lie travels by the Marconi route, while Truth goes by slow freight and is often ditched at the first water-tank.

ELBERT HUBBARD, *The Roycroft Dictionary and Book of Epigrams*, 1923.

Truth, in its struggles for recognition, passes through four distinct stages. First, we say it is damnable, dangerous, disorderly, and will surely disrupt society. Second, we declare it is heretical, infidelic, and contrary to the Bible. Third, we say it is really a matter of no importance either one way or the other. Fourth, we aver that we have always upheld and believed it.

ELBERT HUBBARD, *The Roycroft Dictionary and Book of Epigrams*, 1923.

Live truth instead of professing it.

ELBERT HUBBARD, *The Roycroft Dictionary and Book of Epigrams*, 1923.

Truth lies at the end of a circle.

ELBERT HUBBARD, *The Roycroft Dictionary and Book of Epigrams*, 1923.

All truths cannot be equally important. It is true that a finite whole is greater than any of its parts. It is also true, in the common-sense use of the word, that the New Haven telephone book is smaller than that of Chicago. The first truth is infinitely more fertile and significant than the second.

ROBERT M. HUTCHINS, *The Higher Learning in America*, 1936.

There is no worse lie than a truth misunderstood by those who hear it.

WILLIAM JAMES, *The Varieties of Religious Experience*, 1902.

The truth of an idea is not a stagnant property in it. Truth *happens* to an idea. It *becomes* true, is *made* true by events. Its verity *is* in fact an event, a process: the process namely of its verifying itself, its veri-*fication*. Its validity is the process of its valid-*ation*.

WILLIAM JAMES, *Pragmatism: Lecture VI*, 1907.

But it's the truth even if it didn't happen.

KEN KESEY, *One Flew Over the Cuckoo's Nest*, 1962.

Our reliance in this country is on the inquiring, individual human mind....Not the truth but the man: not the truth as the state sees the truth or as the church sees the truth or as the majority sees the truth or as the mob sees the truth, but the truth as the man sees it, as the man finds it, for himself as man.

ARCHIBALD MACLEISH, *Freedom Is the Right to Choose*, 1951.

Man has no nobler function than to defend the truth.

RUTH MCKENNEY, letter to George Seldes, in George Seldes, ed., *The Great Quotations*, 1960.

The ideals of yesterday are the truths of today.

WILLIAM MCKINLEY, speech, Cincinnati, Ohio, September 1, 1901.

All the durable truths that have come into the world within historic times have been opposed as bitterly as if they were so many waves of smallpox, and every individual who has welcomed and advocated them, absolutely without exception, has been denounced and punished as an enemy of the race.

H.L. MENCKEN, *Smart Set*, June, 1920.

Nine times out of ten, in the arts as in life, there is actually no truth to be discovered; there is only error to be exposed.

H.L. MENCKEN, *Prejudices*, 1922.

The smallest atom of truth represents some man's bitter toil and agony; for every ponderable chunk of it there is a brave truth-seeker's grave upon some lonely ash-dump and a soul roasting in hell.

H.L. MENCKEN, *Prejudices*, 1922.

Truth is the strong compost in which beauty may sometimes germinate.

CHRISTOPHER MORLEY, *Inward Ho!*, 1923.

Half-truths to which men are accustomed are so much easier to pass than the golden mintage they rarely encounter!

CHRISTOPHER MORLEY, *Religio Journalistici*, 1924.

It is neither possible for man to know the truth fully nor to avoid the error of pretending that he does.

REINHOLD NIEBUHR, *Human Destiny*, 1943.

The truth is America's most potent weapon. We cannot enlarge upon the truth. But we can and must intensify our efforts to make that truth more shining.

RICHARD M. NIXON, *The Challenges We Face*, 1960.

Let us begin by committing ourselves to the truth—to see it as it is, and tell it like it is—to find the truth, to speak the truth, and to live the truth.

RICHARD M. NIXON, presidential nomination acceptance speech, 1968.

The People have a right to the Truth as they have a right to life, liberty and the pursuit of happiness. It is *not* right that they be exploited and deceived with false views of life, false characters, false sentiment, false morality, false history, false philosophy, false emotions, false heroism, false notions of self-sacrifice, false views of religion, of duty, of conduct and manners.

FRANK NORRIS, *The Responsibilities of the Novelist*, 1903.

The best of us only pass from one inaccuracy to another, and so do the worst, but on the whole, the last inaccuracy is nearer the truth than the old one.

THOMAS BRACKETT REED, in Samuel Walker McCall, *The Life of Thomas Brackett Reed*, 1914.

The truth survives, the untruth perishes. Men have but little capacity for the recognition of truth at first sight, and of a hundred things which seem plausible, it is fortunate if one be true. Hence it is well that all things should be held at arm's length and stand the scrutiny of our prejudices and interests, of our religion and our skepticism.

THOMAS BRACKETT REED, in Samuel Walker McCall, *The Life of Thomas Brackett Reed*, 1914.

Truth is a jewel which should not be painted over; but it may be set to advantage and shown in a good light.

GEORGE SANTAYANA, *The Life of Reason*, 1905–1906.

We shall seek the truth and endure the consequences.

CHARLES SEYMOUR, in William F. Buckley, Jr., *God and Man at Yale*, 1951.

As scarce as truth is, the supply has always been in excess of the demand.

HENRY WHEELER SHAW, *Rocky Mountain News*, June 5, 1980.

Man may burn his brother at the stake, but he cannot reduce truth to ashes; he may murder his fellow man with a shot in the back, but he does not murder justice; he may slay armies of men, but as it is written, "Truth beareth off the victory."

ADLAI E. STEVENSON, speech, Alton, Illinois, November 9, 1952.

The truth is often unpopular and the contest between agreeable fancy and disagreeable fact is unequal. For, in the vernacular, we Americans are suckers for good news.

ADLAI E. STEVENSON, *New York Times*, June 9, 1958.

You can prove almost anything with the evidence of a small enough segment of time. How often, in any search for truth, the answer of the minute is positive, the answer of the hour qualified, the answers of the year contradictory!

EDWIN WAY TEALE, "January 6," *Circle of the Seasons*, 1953.

As a rule people are afraid of truth. Each truth we discover in nature or social life destroys the crutches on which we used to lean.

ERNST TOLLER, *Saturday Review of Literature*, May 20, 1944.

I never give 'em hell. I just tell the truth and they think it's hell.

HARRY S TRUMAN, *Look*, April 3, 1956.

There would seem to be a law operating in human experience by which the mind once suddenly aware of a verity for the first time immediately invents it again.

AGNES SLIGH TURNBALL, *The Golden Journey*, 1955.

WISDOM

To know one's self is wisdom, but to know one's neighbor is genius.

MINNA ANTRIM, *Naked Truth and Veiled Allusions*, 1902.

The world has achieved brilliance without wisdom, power without conscience. Ours is a world of nuclear giants and ethical infants.

OMAR BRADLEY, speech, Boston, Massachusetts, November 10, 1948.

God pity the man or the nation wise in proverbs...for there is much error gone into the collecting of such a store.

KENNETH BURKE, *Towards a Better Life*, 1932.

Wisdom is not to be obtained from textbooks, but must be coined out of human experience in the flame of life.

MORRIS RAPHAEL COHEN, *A Dreamer's Journey*, 1949.

A word to the wise ain't necessary—it's the stupid ones who need the advice.

BILL COSBY, *Fat Albert's Survival Kit*, 1975.

To have lived long does not necessarily imply the gathering of much wisdom and experience. A man who has pedaled twenty-five thousand miles on a stationary bicycle has not circled the globe. He has only garnered weariness.

PAUL ELDRIDGE, *Horns of Glass*, 1943.

Wisdom: A term Pride uses when talking of Necessity.

ELBERT HUBBARD, *The Roycroft Dictionary and Book of Epigrams*, 1923.

Wise Man: One who sees the storm coming before the clouds appear.

ELBERT HUBBARD, *The Roycroft Dictionary and Book of Epigrams*, 1923.

To know when to be generous and when firm— this is wisdom.

ELBERT HUBBARD, *The Roycroft Dictionary and Book of Epigrams*, 1923.

Every man is a damn fool for at least five minutes every day. Wisdom consists in not exceeding the limit.

ELBERT HUBBARD, *The Roycroft Dictionary and Book of Epigrams*, 1923.

He dares to be a fool, and that is the first step in the direction of wisdom.

JAMES G. HUNEKER, *Pathos of Distance*, 1913.

The next year, the next decade, in all likelihood the next generation, will require more bravery and wisdom on our part than any period in our history. We will be face to face, every day, in every part of our lives and times, with the real issue of our age—the issue of survival.

JOHN F. KENNEDY, speech, Milwaukee, Wisconsin, March 11, 1959, in James MacGregor Burns, *John Kennedy: A Political Profile*, 1960.

I do not believe that sheer suffering teaches. If suffering alone taught, all the world would be wise, since everyone suffers. To suffering must be added mourning, understanding, patience, love, openness and the willingness to remain vulnerable.

ANNE MORROW LINDBERGH, *Time*, February 5, 1973.

It requires wisdom to understand wisdom; the music is nothing if the audience is deaf.

WALTER LIPPMANN, *A Preface to Morals*, 1929.

The older I grow the more I distrust the familiar doctrine that age brings wisdom.

H.L. MENCKEN, *Prejudices*, 1922.

In the collective life of man, at least, most evil arises because finite men involved in the flux of time pretend that they are not so involved. They make claims of virtue, of wisdom, and of power which are beyond their competence as creatures. These pretensions are the source of evil, whether they are expressed by kings and emperors or by commissars and revolutionary statesmen.

REINHOLD NIEBUHR, *The Structure of Nations and Empires*, 1959.

Nine-tenths of wisdom consists in being wise in time.

THEODORE ROOSEVELT, speech, Lincoln, Nebraska, June 14, 1917.

Wisdom comes by disillusionment.

GEORGE SANTAYANA, *The Life of Reason*, 1905–1906.

Old places and old persons in their turn, when spirit dwells in them, have an intrinsic vitality of which youth is incapable; precisely the balance and wisdom that comes from long perspectives and broad foundations.

GEORGE SANTAYANA, *My Host the World*, 1953.

Knowledge alone is not enough. It must be leavened with magnanimity before it becomes wisdom.

ADLAI E. STEVENSON, *Call to Greatness*, 1954.

What is always needed in the appreciation of art, or life, is the larger perspective. Connections made, or at least attempted, where none existed before, the straining to encompass in one's glance at the varied world the common thread, the unifying theme through immense diversity, a fearlessness of growth, of search, of looking, that enlarges the private and the public world. And yet, in our particular society, it is the narrowed and narrowing view of life that often wins.

ALICE WALKER, "Saving the Life That Is Your Own," 1976, *In Search of Our Mothers' Gardens*, 1983.

Economics

See also **Americans on Americans**—Business Leaders, Public Figures; **Business**; **Ethics and Morality**; **Government and Politics**—Domestic Policy, Political Philosophies; **Science and Technology**; **Social Issues**—Labor, Poverty and Hunger; **War and Peace**; **Work**

Once demystified, the dismal science [of economics] is nothing less than the study of power.
RICHARD J. BARNET, *New York Times*, September 16, 1973.

Corruption is the market economy operating in political life.
KENNETH BOULDING, "Economic Libertarianism," *Beasts, Ballads, and Bouldingisms*, 1965.

Economics without sociology is almost skeletal; especially since becoming mathematized it has lost contact with the real world. It deals too much with *x* and *y* and not enough with English sheep and French wine, local carpenters and wide-ranging truck drivers.
KENNETH BOULDING, *Administrative Science Quarterly*, December, 1973.

As the economy gets better, everything else gets worse.
ART BUCHWALD, *Time*, January 31, 1972.

The American economic system is far from perfect...its greatest defect is its striking instability; its proclivity to booms and depressions.
EVANS CLARK, in Arthur Goodfriend, *What Is America?*, 1954.

Machines and computers are now so efficient that they are eliminating the ability and opportunity of most people to compete economically. Whether we like it or not we have undertaken to remove ourselves from the economic equation that was designed to support American society.
VINE DELORIA, JR., *We Talk, You Listen*, 1970.

It is possible to regard the present emphasis upon economic factors as a sort of intellectual revenue taken upon its earlier all but total neglect.
JOHN DEWEY, *Freedom and Culture*, 1939.

In the economic field the new system of direct economic management proceeds beyond the fight between sound-money and easy-money advocates into a sphere where money becomes a mere instrument of economic policy....The system of direct economic management goes beyond capitalism and socialism into a sphere in which private property and private profits cease altogether to be the constitutive elements of the social structure and become subsidiary.
PETER DRUCKER, "Must a War Economy Be Permanent?" *Harper's*, May, 1941.

In all recorded history there has not been one economist who had to worry about where the next meal was coming from.
PETER F. DRUCKER, *New York Times*, May 16, 1976.

We now know that anything which is economically right is also morally right; there can be no conflict between good economics and good morals.
HENRY FORD, in C.E. Hudson, *Christian Morals*, 1945.

In economics, hope and faith coexist with great scientific pretension and also a deep desire for respectability.
JOHN KENNETH GALBRAITH, *New York Times Magazine*, June 7, 1970.

If ignorance paid dividends, most Americans could make a fortune out of what they don't know about economics.
LUTHER H. HODGES, *Wall Street Journal*, March 14, 1962.

You ought to shoot all the economists and elect a couple of historians.
ERNEST HOLLINGS, *New York Times*, June 8, 1983.

We've had trickle-down economics in the country for ten years now, and most of us aren't even damp yet.
MOLLY IVINS, *Mother Jones*, January/February, 1991.

In 1980, Mr. George Bush, a man with reasonable access to Mr. Reagan, did an analysis of Mr. Reagan's economic plan. Mr. George Bush concluded that Reagan's plan was "voodoo economics." He was right.

JESSE JACKSON, speech, Democratic National
Convention, July 16, 1984.

Innovating economies expand and develop. Economies that do not add new kinds of goods and services, but continue only to repeat old work, do not expand much nor do they, by definition, develop.

JANE JACOBS, *The Economy of Cities*, 1969.

The instinct of ownership is fundamental in man's nature.

WILLIAM JAMES, *The Varieties of Religious Experience*, 1902.

The idea behind Reaganomics is this: A rising tide lifts all yachts.

WALTER MONDALE, *Time*, September 3, 1984.

An economist is a man that can tell you…what can happen under any given condition, and his guess is liable to be as good as anybody else's too.

WILL ROGERS, in Adam Smith, *Paper Money*, 1981.

I am for gold dollars as against baloney dollars.

ALFRED E. SMITH, interview on gold standard, New York
City, November 24, 1933.

When you earn it and spend it you know the difference between three dollars and a million dollars, but when you say it and vote it, it all sounds the same.

GERTRUDE STEIN, *Saturday Evening Post*, June 13, 1936.

As we deliver economic security, we undercut the implicit assumptions of capitalism, democracy, and individual initiative.

LESTER C. THUROW, *The Zero-Sum Society*, 1980.

Intractable problems are usually not intractable because there are no solutions, but because there are no solutions without severe side effects….It is only when we demand a solution with no costs that there are no solutions.

LESTER C. THUROW, *The Zero-Sum Society*, 1980.

Verily what bishops are to the English, bankers are to Americans.

MABEL ULRICH, "A Doctor's Diary, 1904–1932,"
Scribner's, June, 1933.

The instability of the economy is equaled only by the instability of economists.

JOHN HENRY WILLIAMS, *New York Times*, June 2, 1956.

It is easier to pick up dornicks than diamonds, but harder to get high prices for them.

EUGENE WOOD, *Atlantic Monthly*, October, 1901.

CAPITALISM

Capitalism without bankruptcy is like Christianity without hell.

FRANK BORMAN, *US*, April 21, 1986.

If you can only cover costs, capitalism is irrelevant.

ERNEST F. COOKE, classroom remark, University of
Baltimore, 1983.

I am ready to concede that the capitalistic system is not fool-proof.

JOHN W. DAVIS, speech to the Liberty League, 1934, in
Lois and Alan Gordon, *American Chronicle*, 1987.

The fall of capitalism began when it made razor blades that would get dull in a month instead of those that would easily last 10 years at the same cost.

W.E.B. DU BOIS, "As the Crow Flies," *Crisis*, January,
1933.

America's technology has turned in upon itself; its corporate form makes it the servant of profits, not the servant of human needs.

ALICE EMBREE, "Media Images I: Madison Avenue
Brainwashing—The Facts," in Robin Morgan, ed.,
Sisterhood Is Powerful, 1970.

History suggests that capitalism is a necessary condition for political freedom. Clearly it is not a sufficient condition.

MILTON FRIEDMAN, *Capitalism and Freedom*, 1962.

Economic arrangements play a dual role in the promotion of a free society. On the one hand, freedom in economic arrangements is itself a component of freedom broadly understood, so economic freedom is an end in itself. In the second place, economic freedom is also an indispensable means toward the achievement of political freedom.

MILTON FRIEDMAN, *Capitalism and Freedom*, 1962.

When I began to examine just how wealth is created, it seemed to me plain that it arises not from taking, but from *giving*. People get rich by giving rather than by taking, and this seemed to me to be a very important perception, because the reason for the crisis in capitalism today, it seems to me, is not its practical achievements, but rather the perception of its moral character.

GEORGE GILDER, January 5, 1981, in William F. Buckley,
Jr., *On the Firing Line*, 1989.

The old traditions—the calculus of loss and gain, the cult of efficiency, the assumption that the most profitable use of a resource is the best use— are not only unnecessary, they are profoundly anti-social as well.

MICHAEL HARRINGTON, *Toward a Democratic Left*, 1968.

The stress on personal achievement, the relentless pressure for advancement, the acquisitive drive that is touted as the Good Life—all this may be, in the end, the critical weakness of capitalist society, although providing so much of the motor force of its economy.

ROBERT L. HEILBRONER, *An Inquiry into the Human Prospect*, 1980.

Capitalism disarms socialism by incorporating some of its elements within itself.

ROBERT L. HEILBRONER, *An Inquiry into the Human Prospect*, 1980.

It's universally wrong to steal from your neighbor, but once you get beyond the one-to-one level and pit the individual against the multinational conglomerate, the federal bureaucracy, the modern plantation of agro-business, or the utility company, it becomes strictly a value judgment to decide exactly who is stealing from whom. One person's crime is another person's profit. Capitalism *is* license to steal; the government simply regulates who steals and how much.

ABBIE HOFFMAN, "Steal This Author: Introduction," *The Best of Abbie Hoffman*, 1989.

I am aware that there are many who wince at a distinction between property and persons—who hold both sacrosanct. My views are not so rigid. A life is sacred. Property is intended to serve life, and no matter how much we surround it with rights and respect, it has no personal being. It is part of the earth man walks on; it is not man.

MARTIN LUTHER KING, JR., *The Trumpet of Conscience*, 1967.

Capitalism delivers many good things but, on the whole, economic equality is not one of them.... Rather, capitalism has always stood for equality of economic opportunity, reasonably understood to mean the absence of official barriers to economic opportunity.

IRVING KRISTOL, "The Capitalist Concept of Justice," *Ethics, Free Enterprise, and Public Policy*, 1978.

The genius of capitalism consists precisely in its lack of morality. Unless he is rich enough to hire his own choir, a capitalist is a fellow who, by definition, can ill afford to believe in anything other than the doctrine of the bottom line. Deprive a capitalist of his God-given right to lie and cheat and steal, and the poor sap stands a better than even chance of becoming one of the abominable wards of the state from whose grimy fingers the Reagan Administration hopes to snatch the ark of democracy.

LEWIS H. LAPHAM, "Moral Dandyism," *Harper's*, July, 1985.

If you mean by capitalism the God-given right of a few big corporations to make all the decisions that will affect millions of workers and consumers and to exclude everyone else from discussing and examining those decisions, then the unions are threatening capitalism.

MAX LERNER, "A Look at the Books and a Share of the Pie," *Actions and Passions*, 1949.

What's been forgotten is that those people of the Tenderloin and Hunters Point, those people in the streets, are the customers, certainly potential ones, and they must be treated as such. Government cannot ignore them and neither can business ignore them. What sense is there in making products if the would-be customer can't afford them? It's not alone a question of price, it's a question of ability to pay. For a man with no money, $.99 reduced from $1.29 is still a fortune.

HARVEY MILK, speech, fund-raising meeting, 1977.

I believe, I have always believed, and I will always believe in private enterprise as the backbone of economic well-being in America.

FRANKLIN D. ROOSEVELT, speech, Chicago, Illinois, October 14, 1936.

If we are brought face to face with the naked issue of either keeping or totally destroying a prosperity in which the majority share, but in which some share improperly, why, as sensible men, we must decide that it is a great deal better that some people should prosper too much than that no one should prosper enough.

THEODORE ROOSEVELT, speech, Fitchburg, Massachusetts, September 2, 1902.

The road of capitalism is full of ruts and bumps. Why damn Mr. Roosevelt for the road?

MELVIN B. TOLSON, "A Discussion of Hogs, Dogs, Fish, and the Declaration of Independence," *Washington Tribune*, July 22, 1939.

I wrote to *Forbes* magazine...to say that its motto, "Capitalist Tool," sounded like something a Russian premier might shout at an American president over the hot line in a moment of complete exasperation—as in "You've wiped out Rumania by mistake, you capitalist tool!"

CALVIN TRILLIN, "The Motto-Maker's Art," *The Nation*, February 23, 1985.

In public services, we lag behind all the industrialized nations of the West, preferring that the public money go not to the people but to big business. The result is a unique society in which we have free enterprise for the poor and socialism for the rich.

GORE VIDAL, "Edmund Wilson, Tax Dodger," *Reflections Upon a Sinking Ship*, 1969.

Our whole economy hangs precariously on the assumption that the higher you go the better off you are, and that unless more stuff is produced in 1958 than was produced in 1957, more deer killed, more automatic dishwashers installed, more out-of-staters coming into the state, more heads aching so they get the fast fast fast relief from a pill, more automobiles sold, you are headed for trouble, living in danger and maybe in squalor.

E.B. WHITE, "A Report in January," January 30, 1958, *Essays of E.B. White*, 1977.

The material success of capitalism—to which we owe the marble in our lives—has been made possible by habits of discipline that were reinforced by hardships of life in the Connecticut and Minnesota and Oregon trail mud. But abundance subverts such habits. And the dynamic of our abundance produces—indeed requires—a constant increase in consumption, and in appetites. This dynamic generates a culture of self-indulgence. Such a culture is incompatible with self-government, which is, after all, about governing the self.

GEORGE WILL, "Personality Against Character," July 1, 1976, *The Pursuit of Happiness, and Other Sobering Thoughts*, 1978.

You show me a capitalist, I'll show you a bloodsucker.

MALCOLM X, *Malcolm X Speaks*, 1965.

DEBT

I can remember when people actually talked about reducing the debt. There were two things wrong with that concept: It was too easy to understand and we couldn't do it. So we began to talk about reducing the deficit. Reducing, that is, the annual amount by which the debt increases.

ROY BLOUNT, JR., *New York Times*, January 13, 1991.

Washington's spending is giving me the jitters. The Administration tosses out billions and billions as if they were pennies. Not a word of concern is voiced over the ultimate outcome, over how this or the next generation will be able to liquidate the bill. A federal debt of $100 billion—one hundred thousand millions—looms.

B.C. FORBES, *Forbes*, March 1, 1941.

Debt cannot be used as a substitute for growth or progress, and when progress has been limited, debt also has become limited as a solution for the problems of industrial or national maturity.

ROY HELTON, "Debt Threatens Democracy," *Harper's*, June, 1939.

Christmas is a time when kids tell Santa what they want and adults pay for it. Deficits are when adults tell the government what they want—and their kids pay for it.

RICHARD LAMM, to National League of Cities, Seattle, Washington, December 10, 1985.

When your bank account is so overdrawn that it is positively photographic, steps must be taken.

DOROTHY PARKER, "Home Is the Sailor," *The New Yorker*, January 24, 1931.

The deficit is big enough to take care of itself.

RONALD REAGAN, *Newsweek*, November 21, 1988.

The debt of this Nation is greater than it has ever been in our history. We fought a world war on less debt than the Republicans have built up in the last eight years. You know, it's kind of like that brother-in-law who drives a flashy new car but he's always borrowing money from you to make the payments.

ANN W. RICHARDS, speech, Democratic National Convention, July 18, 1988.

If the nation is living within its income, its credit is good. If in some crisis it lives beyond its income for a year or two it can usually borrow temporarily on reasonable terms. But if, like the spendthrift, it throws discretion to the winds, is willing to make no sacrifice at all in spending, extends its taxing to the limit of the people's power to pay, and continues to pile up deficits, it is on the road to bankruptcy.

FRANKLIN D. ROOSEVELT, speech, Pittsburgh, Pennsylvania, October 19, 1932.

Let us have the courage to stop borrowing to meet continuing deficits. Stop the deficits.

FRANKLIN D. ROOSEVELT, radio address, July 30, 1932.

Any government, like any family, can for a year spend a little more than it earns. But you and I know that a continuance of that habit means the poorhouse.

FRANKLIN D. ROOSEVELT, radio address, July 30, 1932.

Solvency is entirely a matter of temperament and not of income.

LOGAN PEARSALL SMITH, *Afterthoughts*, 1931.

You want 21 percent risk free? Pay off your credit cards.

ANDREW TOBIAS, *American Way*, November, 1982.

Today any man who owes $25,000 has arrived. His material worries will disappear. He will find that he can command the best of everything, and head waiters will have a special bow for him. He has put himself in a situation in which his creditors have a vested interest in him. They cannot afford to let him down.

ELI WALLACH, *How To Be Deliriously Happy*, 1950.

DEPRESSION AND INFLATION

[I]t turned out to be the first outbreak of a wasting economic fever which, through long years of depression, debilitated an entire nation, deprived it of the use of its productive strength, and created want in the midst of plenty. The public discovered that "sound" business thinking had been mostly superstition. Respectable theories of the functions of the state had to be abandoned. A hesitant Federal Government was forced, step by step, into a dominant role in the operation of our economy, against every American habit and tradition.

THURMAN ARNOLD, on crash of 1929, "The Crash—and What It Meant," *The Aspirin Age: 1919 to 1941*, 1949.

Steel prices cause inflation like wet sidewalks cause rain.

ROGER BLOUGH, *Forbes*, August 1, 1967.

[The Wall Street crash] doesn't mean that there will be any general or serious business depression....For six years American business has been diverting a substantial part of its attention, its energies and its resources to the speculative game....Now that irrelevant, alien and hazardous adventure is over. Business has come home again, back to its job, providentially unscathed, sound in wind and limb, financially stronger than ever before.

Business Week, November 2, 1929.

This year, when we all needed something to take our minds off our troubles, miniature golf did it....If we cannot find bread, we are satisfied with the circus.

ELMER DAVIS, *Harper's*, 1930.

The breakdown in which we are living is the breakdown of the particular romance known as business,...the revelation that the elated excitement of the romantic adventure has to be paid for with an equal depression.

JOHN DEWEY, 1932, in Lois and Alan Gordon, *American Chronicle*, 1987.

These really are good times, but only a few know it. If this period of convalescence through which we have been passing must be spoken of as a depression, it is far and away the finest depression that we have ever had.

HENRY FORD, ca. 1930, in Arthur Zipser and George Novack, eds., *Who's Hooey: Nitwitticisms of the Notable*, 1932.

Men who lost their jobs dropped out of sight. They were quiet; and you had to know just when and where to find them: at night, for instance, on the edge of town huddling for warmth around a bonfire, or even the municipal incinerator; at dawn, picking over the garbage dump for scraps of food or salvageable clothing.

Fortune, 1932.

Men have been swindled by other men on many occasions. The autumn of 1929 was, perhaps, the first occasion when men succeeded on a large scale in swindling themselves.

JOHN KENNETH GALBRAITH, *The Great Crash, 1929*, 1955.

One can relish the varied idiocy of human action during a panic to the full, for, while it is a time of great tragedy, nothing is being lost but money.

JOHN KENNETH GALBRAITH, *The Great Crash, 1929*, 1955.

Inflation might be called prosperity with high blood pressure.

ARNOLD H. GLASOW, *Reader's Digest*, September, 1966.

Inflation has...become the cruelest tax, destroying the value of the dollar and adding new costs to every purchase.

ELLA GRASSO, Connecticut gubernatorial inaugural address, January 3, 1979.

We are obviously all hurt by inflation. Everybody is hurt by inflation. If you really wanted to examine who percentage-wise is hurt the most in

They used to tell me I was building a dream,

And so I followed the mob

When there was earth to plough or guns to bear

I was always there right on the job.

They used to tell me I was building a dream

With peace and glory ahead

Why should I be standing in line

Just waiting for bread?

Once I built a railroad, made it run,

Made it race against time.

Once I built a railroad,

Now it's done

Brother, can you spare a dime?

Once I built a tower, to the sun.

Brick and rivet and lime,

Once I built a tower,

Now it's done,

Brother, can you spare a dime?

Once in khaki suits

Gee, we looked swell

Full of that Yankee Doodle-de-dum.

Half a million boots went sloggin' thru Hell,

I was the kid with the drum.

Say, don't you remember, they called me Al

It was Al all the time

Say, don't you remember I'm your Pal!

Buddy, can you spare a dime?

E.Y. (YIP) HARBURG, song that became anthem of the Depression, "Brother, Can You Spare a Dime?" 1928, first performed October 5, 1932.

their incomes, it is the Wall Street brokers. I mean their incomes have gone down the most.
ALAN GREENSPAN, conference on inflation, Washington, D.C., September 19, 1974.

You gotta realize, my people have never known what job security is. For instance, come another recession and the economy has to tighten its belt—who do you think's gonna be the first notch?
DICK GREGORY, *From the Back of the Bus*, 1962.

[A] descent from respectability...must be numbered in the millions. This is what we have accomplished with our bread lines and soup kitchens,... defeated, discouraged, hopeless men and women cringing and bowing as they come to ask for public aid....It is a spectacle of national degeneration. This is the fundamental tragedy for America.
JOSEPH L. HEFFERNAN, *Atlantic Monthly*, 1932.

[W]hen we look back to the 1930s, we discover that many economists and statesmen knew how the Great Depression could be cured. It would require enough government expenditure to offset the inadequate flow of private spending, and enough social support to restore public morale and household buying power. The trouble was

that such measures were "impossible" to take because they would have been regarded as tantamount to socialism. Capitalism might have been saved but only by surrendering to the enemy.
ROBERT L. HEILBRONER, *An Inquiry into the Human Prospect*, 1980.

I have no fears for the future of our country. It is bright with hope.
HERBERT HOOVER, inaugural address, March 4, 1929.

[This] has been a twelvemonth of unprecedented advance, of wonderful prosperity....If there is any way of judging the future by the past, this new year may well be one of felicitation and hopefulness.
HERBERT HOOVER, 1929, in Lois and Alan Gordon, *American Chronicle*, 1987.

Any lack of confidence in the economic future of the basic strength of business in the United States is foolish.
HERBERT HOOVER, inaugural address, March 4, 1929.

While the crash only took place six months ago, I am convinced we have passed the worst.
HERBERT HOOVER, 1930, in Lois and Alan Gordon, *American Chronicle*, 1987.

They are playing politics at the expense of human misery.

HERBERT HOOVER, on congressmen sponsoring bills for relief of unemployed, December 9, 1930.

[T]he depression brought everybody down a peg or two. And the Negroes had but a few pegs to fall.

LANGSTON HUGHES, on end of Harlem Renaissance in 1931, *The Big Sea*, 1940.

When future historians look back on our way of curing inflation...they'll probably compare it to bloodletting in the Middle Ages.

LEE IACOCCA, *Fortune*, June 27, 1983.

I see nothing in the present situation that is either menacing or warrants pessimism. During the winter months there may be some slackness or unemployment, but hardly more than at this season each year.

ANDREW W. MELLON, 1930, in Lois and Alan Gordon, *American Chronicle*, 1987.

I don't know anything about any depression.

J.P. MORGAN, JR., ca. 1930, in Arthur Zipser and George Novack, eds., *Who's Hooey: Nitwitticisms of the Notable*, 1933.

Wall Street's brokerages were overflowing with a new type of speculator,...the inexperienced—the "suckers,"...men who had been attracted by newspaper stories of the big, easy profits to be made in a tremendous bull market.

The Nation, 1928.

But with the slow menace of a glacier, depression came on. No one had any measure of its progress; no one had any plan for stopping it. Everyone tried to get out of its way.

FRANCES PERKINS, *People at Work*, 1934.

Inflation is as violent as a mugger, as frightening as an armed robber and as deadly as a hit man.

RONALD REAGAN, *Los Angeles Times*, October 20, 1978.

A recession is when your neighbor loses his job. A depression is when you lose yours.

RONALD REAGAN, in Lou Cannon, *Reagan*, 1982.

If we can "boondoggle" ourselves out of this depression, that word is going to be enshrined in the hearts of the American people for years to come.

FRANKLIN D. ROOSEVELT, speech, New Jersey State Emergency Council, Newark, January 18, 1936.

Wall Street Lays an Egg.

SIME SILVERMAN, news headline following stock market crash, *Variety*, October, 1929.

The present depression is one of abundance, not of scarcity....The cause of the trouble is that a small class has the wealth, while the rest have the debts.

The remedy is to give the workers access to the means of production, and let them produce for themselves, not for others,...the American way.

UPTON SINCLAIR, "The Epic Plan for California," *The Nation*, 1934.

Mellon pulled the whistle,

Hoover rang the bell,

Wall Street gave the signal

And the country went to hell.

Song of the "Bonus Marchers," 1932.

It required the Great Depression to open the eyes of the American people to the economic, cultural, social, political, and spiritual values inherent in a great democracy. For this I am thankful. As a distinctly finite being, man learns only through tragic experiences. Progress and Pain are Siamese twins.

MELVIN B. TOLSON, "I Am Thankful for the Great Depression," *Washington Tribune*, October 7, 1939.

FINANCIAL INSTITUTIONS

If stock market experts were so expert, they would be buying stock, not selling advice.

NORMAN AUGUSTINE, "Augustine's 22nd Law," *Augustine's Laws*, 1986.

The last two years were just too disgusting a spectacle. Pigs gorging themselves at the trough... you know it won't last.

PETER F. DRUCKER, on Wall Street speculation, in Ellen Goodman, "Wall Street and Main Street," *Washington Post*, October, 1987.

A bank is a place that will lend you money if you can prove that you don't need it.

BOB HOPE, in Alan Harrington, "The Tyranny of Forms," *Life in the Crystal Palace*, 1959.

For several years now the speculators on Wall Street have been giving regularly scheduled lessons in the arts of pillage and extortion. Hardly a day passes but that some undervalued oil or communications company doesn't fall prey

I am certain that my fellow Americans expect that on my induction into the Presidency I will address them with a candor and a decision which the present situation of our Nation impels. This is preeminently the time to speak the truth, the whole truth, frankly and boldly. Nor need we shrink from honestly facing conditions in our country today. This great Nation will endure as it has endured, will revive and will prosper. So, first of all, let me assert my firm belief that the only thing we have to fear is fear itself—nameless, unreasoning, unjustified terror which paralyzes needed efforts to convert retreat into advance. In every dark hour of our national life a leadership of frankness and vigor has met with that understanding and support of the people themselves which is essential to victory. I am convinced that you will again give the support to leadership in these critical days.

In such a spirit on my part and on yours we face our common difficulties. They concern, thank God, only material things. Values have shrunken to fantastic levels; taxes have risen; our ability to pay has fallen; government of all kinds is faced by serious curtailment of income; the means of exchange are frozen in the currents of trade; the withered leaves of industrial enterprise lie on every side; farmers find no markets for their produce; the savings of many years in thousands of families are gone.

More important, a host of unemployed citizens face the grim problem of existence, and an equally great number toil with little return. Only a foolish optimist can deny the dark realities of the moment.

Yet our distress comes from no failure of substance. We are stricken by no plague of locusts. Compared with the perils which our forefathers conquered because they believed and were not afraid, we have still much to be thankful for. Nature still offers her bounty and human efforts have multiplied it. Plenty is at our doorsteps, but a generous use of it languishes in the very sight of the supply. Primarily this is because the rulers of the exchange of mankind's goods have failed, through their own stubbornness and their own incompetence, have admitted their failure, and abdicated. Practices of the unscrupulous money changers stand indicted in the court of public opinion, rejected by the hearts and minds of men....

Happiness lies not in the mere possession of money; it lies in the joy of achievement, in the thrill of creative effort. The joy and moral stimulation of work no longer must be forgotten in the mad chase of evanescent profits. These dark days will be worth all they cost us if they teach us that our true destiny is not to be ministered unto but to minister to ourselves and to our fellow men....

Our greatest primary task is to put people to work. This is no unsolvable problem if we face it wisely and courageously. It can be accomplished in part by direct recruiting by the Government itself, treating the task as we would treat the emergency of a war, but at the same time, through this employment, accomplishing greatly needed projects to stimulate and reorganize the use of our natural resources.

Hand in hand with this we must frankly recognize the overbalance of population in our industrial centers and, by engaging on a national scale in a redistribution, endeavor to provide a better use of the land for those best fitted for the land. The task can be helped by definite efforts to raise the values of agricultural products and with this the power to purchase the output of our cities. It can be helped by preventing realistically the tragedy of the growing loss through foreclosure of our small homes and our farms. It can be helped by insistence that the Federal, State, and local governments act forthwith on the demand that their cost be drastically reduced. It can be helped by the unifying of relief activities which today are often scattered, uneconomical, and unequal. It can be helped by national planning for and supervision of all forms of transportation and of communications and other utilities which have a definitely public character. There are many ways in which it can be helped, but it can never be helped merely by talking about it. We must act and act quickly.

Finally, in our progress toward a resumption of work we require two safeguards against a return of the evils of the old order; there must be a strict supervision of all banking and credits and investments; there must be an end to speculation with other people's money, and there must be provision for an adequate but sound currency.

These are the lines of attack. I shall presently urge upon a new Congress in special session detailed measures for their fulfillment, and I shall seek the immediate assistance of the several States. Through this program of action we address ourselves to putting our own national house in order and making income balance outgo....

In the field of world policy I would dedicate this Nation to the policy of the good neighbor—the neighbor who resolutely respects himself and, because he does so, respects the rights of others—the neighbor who respects his obligations and respects the sanctity of his agreements in and with a world of neighbors.

If I read the temper of our people correctly, we now realize as we have never realized before our interdependence on each other; that we cannot merely take but we must give as well; that if we are to go forward, we must move as a trained and loyal army willing to sacrifice for the good of a common discipline, because without such discipline no progress is made, no leadership becomes effective. We are, I know, ready and willing to submit our lives and property to such discipline, because it makes possible a leadership which aims at a larger good. This I propose to offer, pledging that the larger purposes will bind upon us all as a sacred obligation with a unity of duty hitherto evoked only in time of armed strife.

With this pledge taken, I assume unhesitatingly the leadership of this great army of our people dedicated to a disciplined attack upon our common problems.

Action in this image and to this end is feasible under the form of government which we have inherited from our ancestors. Our Constitution is so simple and practical that it is possible always to meet extraordinary needs by changes in emphasis and arrangement without loss of essential form. This is why our constitutional system has proved itself the most superbly enduring political mechanism the modern world has produced. It has met every stress of vast expansion of territory, of foreign wars, of bitter internal strife, of world relations.

It is to be hoped that the normal balance of executive and legislative authority may be wholly adequate to meet the unprecedented task before us. But it may be that an unprecedented demand and need for undelayed action may call for temporary departure from that normal balance of public procedure.

I am prepared under my constitutional duty to recommend the measures that a stricken nation in the midst of a stricken world may require. These measures, or such other measures as the Congress may build out of its experience and wisdom, I shall seek, within my constitutional authority, to bring to speedy adoption.

But in the event that the Congress shall fail to take one of these two courses, and in the event that the national emergency is still critical, I shall not evade the clear course of duty that will then confront me. I shall ask the Congress for the one remaining instrument to meet the crisis—broad Executive power to wage a war against the emergency, as great as the power that would be given to me if we were in fact invaded by a foreign foe.

For the trust reposed in me I will return the courage and the devotion that befit the time. I can do no less.

FRANKLIN D. ROOSEVELT, inaugural address, March 4, 1933.

to Ivan Boesky, T. Boone Pickens, or the Bass brothers.

Lewis H. Lapham, "Boiling the Whale," *Harper's*, April, 1985.

This is the twilight of the banks. It would be a more cheerful spectacle if we could envision the dawn of the institutions that will replace them.

Martin Mayer, *The Money Bazaars*, 1984.

Will you please tell me what you do with all the vice presidents a bank has? I guess that's to get you more discouraged before you can see the president. Why, the United States is the biggest business institution in the world and they only have one vice president and nobody has ever found anything for him to do.

Will Rogers, speech, International Bankers Association, 1922.

TAXATION

Dear Mr. President, Internal Revenue regulations will turn us into a nation of bookkeepers. The life of every citizen is becoming a business. This, it seems to me, is one of the worst interpretations of the meaning of human life history has ever seen. Man's life is not a business.

Saul Bellow, *Herzog*, 1964.

Tariff, n. A scale of taxes on imports, designed to protect the domestic producer against the greed of his consumer.

Ambrose Bierce, *The Devil's Dictionary*, 1906.

Expense accounts are tax deductible. The swindle-sheet's a cheat right down the line. It's stealing—but it's socially acceptable. In fact, it's now a mainstay of our economic life. Most restaurants and theatres would close down in a matter of weeks without it.

Eddie Cantor, *The Way I See It*, 1959.

There is one difference between a tax collector and a taxidermist—the taxidermist leaves the hide.

Mortimer Caplin, *Time*, February 1, 1963.

Collecting more taxes than is absolutely necessary is legalized robbery.

Calvin Coolidge, *New York Times*, March 6, 1955.

If Patrick Henry thought that taxation without representation was bad, he should see how bad it is with representation.

Farmer's Almanac, 1966.

But I would say that one of the great civilizing influences of my lifetime and indeed of the whole period since 1913 has been the leveling effect of the progressive income tax. If the progressive income tax had not been inaugurated—incidentally, by a Republican President, President Taft—the extremes of income that would have developed would have been an enormously disturbing influence in the economy; and perhaps that tax is the single most important conserving and conservative force in the modern society. One of the things that best helps the poor and the deprived to bear life is to hear the occasional screams of the rich.

John Kenneth Galbraith, January 7, 1982, in William F. Buckley, Jr., *On the Firing Line*, 1989.

Man is not like other animals in the ways that are really significant: animals have instincts, we have taxes.

Erving Goffman, *New York Times*, February 12, 1969.

We don't pay taxes. The little people pay taxes.

Attributed to Leona Helmsley, *Time*, July 24, 1989.

A democracy has to punish itself to pay its obligations. It has to be the operator that wields the knife on its own body. Few surgeons would care to amputate their own feet, no matter how good a local anaesthetic was at hand. There are some things which personal human nature recoils from. So do men in democracies recoil from self-punishment through taxation. The strength of our democracy and its greatest danger lie in our biennial stated election. Under the American system no political party, whether local or national, can impose a serious increase in general taxes and hope to remain in office after the ensuing election. In that fact lies the one serious flaw in the armor of democracy. There is the heel of our modern Achilles.

Roy Helton, "Debt Threatens Democracy," *Harper's*, June, 1939.

Taxes are what we pay for civilized society.

Oliver Wendell Holmes, Jr., opinion, *Compania de Tabocas v. Collector*, 1904.

The power to tax is not the power to destroy while this court sits.

Oliver Wendell Holmes, Jr., opinion, *Panhandle Oil Co. v. Mississippi*, 1930.

[T]he IRS has stolen from me over the past 20 years because I am single. It is unconstitutional to impose a penalty tax of 40 percent on me because I have no husband.

VIVIEN KELLEMS, in Gloria Swanson, "Unforgettable Vivien Kellems," *Reader's Digest*, October, 1975.

I hold in my hand 1,379 pages of tax simplification.

DELBERT L. LATTA, *U.S. News & World Report*, December 23, 1985.

[A tax loophole is] something that benefits the other guy. If it benefits you, it is tax reform.

RUSSELL B. LONG, recalled on his retirement, *Time*, November 10, 1986.

As the Chinese poet, Ah Ling, put it (in the wastebasket):

The more the moolah

You make in your racket,

The quicker you go

In a higher bracket.

GROUCHO MARX, *Many Happy Returns*, 1942.

I'm a middle-bracket person with a middle-bracket spouse

And we live together gaily in a middle-bracket house.

We've a fair-to-middlin' family; we take the middle view;

So we're manna sent from heaven to internal revenue.

PHYLLIS McGINLEY, "The Chosen Peoples," *Times Three: 1932–1960*, 1960.

I don't think meals have any business being deductible. I'm for separation of calories and corporations.

RALPH NADER, *Wall Street Journal*, July 15, 1985.

Even Albert Einstein reportedly needed help on his 1040 form.

RONALD REAGAN, address to the nation, May 28, 1985.

The Income Tax has made more Liars out of the American people than golf has.

WILL ROGERS, "Helping the Girls with Their Income Taxes," *The Illiterate Digest*, 1924.

Taxes, after all, are the dues that we pay for the privileges of membership in an organized society.

FRANKLIN D. ROOSEVELT, speech, Worcester, Massachusetts, October 21, 1936.

Few people realize that our present tax and welfare structure is such as to encourage the wealthy to speculate and the poor to vegetate.

I.F. STONE, "The Rich March on Washington All the Time," *I.F. Stone's Weekly*, May 13, 1968.

The state and municipality go to great expense to support policemen and sheriffs and judicial officers, to protect people against themselves, that is, against the results of their own folly, vice, and recklessness. Who pays for it? Undoubtedly the people who have not been guilty of folly, vice, or recklessness.

WILLIAM GRAHAM SUMNER, "The Forgotten Man," *The Forgotten Man and Other Essays*, 1919.

No Taxation without Depreciation.

CALVIN TRILLIN, suggested motto for rich against Reagan's flat-tax plan, "The Motto-Maker's Art," *The Nation*, February 23, 1985.

WEALTH AND MONEY

Money isn't everything, but lack of money isn't anything.

FRANKLIN P. ADAMS, in Robert E. Drennan, *The Algonquin Wits*, 1968.

Where there is money, there is fighting.

MARIAN ANDERSON, in Kosti Vehanen, *Marian Anderson: A Portrait*, 1941.

It's a lot tougher to get up in the morning when you start wearing silk pajamas.

EDDIE ARCARO, *Sports Illustrated*, May 13, 1972.

Nothing that costs only a dollar is worth having.

ELIZABETH ARDEN, *Chicago Tribune*, June 25, 1978.

Wealth and economic well-being, we have asserted, are the fruits of freedom, while we should have been the first to know that this kind of "happiness"...has been an unmixed blessing only in this country, and it is a minor blessing compared with the truly political freedoms, such as freedom of speech and thought, of assembly and association, even under the best conditions. Economic growth may one day turn out to be a curse rather than a good, and under no conditions can it either lead into freedom or constitute a proof for its existence.

HANNAH ARENDT, *On Revolution*, 1963.

Each dollar is a soldier that does your bidding.

VINCENT ASTOR, in Harvey O'Connor, *The Astors*, 1941.

It seems to be a law in American life that whatever enriches us anywhere except in the wallet inevitably becomes uneconomic.

RUSSELL BAKER, "Observer," *New York Times*, March 24, 1968.

[M]oney, it turned out, was exactly like sex; you thought of nothing else if you didn't have it and thought of other things if you did.

JAMES BALDWIN, "The Black Boy Looks at the White Boy," *Nobody Knows My Name*, 1961.

We can have democracy in this country or we can have wealth in a few hands, but we can't have both.

LOUIS D. BRANDEIS, *Labor*, October 17, 1941.

Well, I'd say I lost a few million here and there.

CAB CALLOWAY, *American Way*, March, 1977.

Pity the poor millionaire, for the way of the philanthropist is hard.

ANDREW CARNEGIE, letter to *Independent*, July 26, 1913.

The control of manufacturing, mining, and transportation industries is to an increasing degree passing into the hands of great corporations through stock ownership, and control of credit is centralized in a comparatively small number of enormously powerful financial institutions. The financial institutions are in turn dominated by a very small number of powerful financiers.

Report of Commission on Industrial Relations, "The Concentration of Wealth and Influence," 1915.

A moderate addiction to money may not always be hurtful; but when taken in excess it is nearly always bad for the health.

CLARENCE DAY, "Improving the Lives of the Rich," *The Crow's Nest*, 1921.

I am absolutely convinced that no wealth in the world can help humanity forward, even in the hands of the most devoted worker in this cause. The example of great and pure personages is the only thing that can lead us to fine ideas and noble deeds. Money only appeals to selfishness and always irresistibly tempts its owners to abuse it.

ALBERT EINSTEIN, *The World as I See It*, 1934.

Let me tell you about the very rich. They are different from you and me. They possess and enjoy early, and it does something to them, makes them soft where we are hard, and cynical where we are trustful, in a way that, unless you were born rich, it is very difficult to understand. They think, deep in their hearts, that they are better than we are because we had to discover the compensations and refuges of life for ourselves. Even when they enter deep into our world or sink below us, they still think that they are better than we are. They are different.

F. SCOTT FITZGERALD, "The Rich Boy," *All the Sad Young Men*, 1926.

There are two fools in this world. One is the millionaire who thinks that by hoarding money he can somehow accumulate real power, and the other is the penniless reformer who thinks that if only he can take the money from one class and give it to another, all the world's ills will be cured.

HENRY FORD, *My Life and Work*, 1923.

The hold which controllers of money are able to maintain on productive forces is seen to be more powerful when it is remembered that, although money is supposed to represent the real wealth of the world, there is always much more wealth than there is money, and real wealth is often compelled to wait upon money, thus leading to that most paradoxical situation—a world filled with wealth but suffering want.

HENRY FORD, *My Life and Work*, 1923.

Money, after all, is extremely simple. It is a part of our transportation system. It is a simple and direct method of conveying goods from one person to another. Money is in itself most admirable. It is essential. It is not intrinsically evil. It is one of the most useful devices in social life. And when it does what it was intended to do, it is all help and no hindrance.

HENRY FORD, *My Life and Work*, 1923.

Money is like an arm or a leg—use it or lose it.

HENRY FORD, interview, *New York Times*, November 8, 1931.

There's only so much money to go around. If people can't spend it in six days, they sure aren't going to spend it in seven.

JOHN FREIJE, on blue laws, Montpelier, Vermont, *Times Argus*, February 11, 1991.

Wealth is not without its advantages and the case to the contrary, although it has often been made, has never proved widely persuasive.

JOHN KENNETH GALBRAITH, *The Affluent Society*, 1958.

If you can count your money, you don't have a billion dollars.

J. PAUL GETTY, *International Herald Tribune*, January 10, 1961.

The central event of the twentieth century is the overthrow of matter. In technology, economics, and the politics of nations, wealth in the form of physical resources is steadily declining in value and significance. The powers of mind are everywhere ascendant over the brute force of things.

GEORGE GILDER, *Microcosm*, 1989.

One of the precious things the rich can buy in America is "out." If people have enough money, it appears, they can buy out of consensus-building, buy out of community, buy out of compromising, buy out of, around or over the common will.

ELLEN GOODMAN, "A Private Foreign Policy," *Washington Post*, May, 1987.

What I know about money, I learned the hard way—by having had it.

MARGARET HALSEY, *The Folks at Home*, 1952.

Wealth is something you acquire so you can share it, not keep it.

LADONNA HARRIS, on Indian values, *New York Times*, October 27, 1980.

Let us distinguish between the creation of wealth for the community and the extortion of wealth from the community.

WILLIAM RANDOLPH HEARST, editorial, March 28, 1918.

The rich are not rich because they eat filet mignon or own yachts....The rich are rich because they can afford to buy other people's time. They can hire other people to make their beds, tend their gardens, and drive their cars.

CHRISTOPHER JENCKS, ET AL., *Inequality: A Reassessment of the Effects of Family and Schooling in America*, 1972.

Wealth is the means, and people are the ends. All our material riches will avail us little if we do not use them to expand the opportunities of our people.

JOHN F. KENNEDY, State of the Union address, January 11, 1962.

Misplaced emphasis occurs...when you think that everything is going well because your car drives so smoothly, and your new suit fits you so well, and those high-priced shoes you bought make your feet feel so good; and you begin to believe that these things, these many luxuries all around, are the really important matters of your life.

MARTIN LUTHER KING, SR., *Daddy King*, 1980.

In our culture we make heroes of the men who sit on top of a heap of money, and we pay attention not only to what they say in their field of competence, but to their wisdom on every other question in the world.

MAX LERNER, "The Epic of Model T," *Actions and Passions*, 1949.

I cried all the way to the bank.

LIBERACE, *An Autobiography*, 1973.

Puzzler: The average cost of a new automobile—$600—is almost as much as the average income.

Life, 1934.

We live in a welfare state which seeks to put a floor below which no one sinks but builds no ceiling to prevent man from rising.

HENRY CABOT LODGE, JR., September 18, 1959.

For both working and business class no other accompaniment of getting a living approaches in importance the money received for their work. It is more this future, instrumental aspect of work, rather than the intrinsic satisfactions involved, that keeps Middletown working so hard as more and more of the activities of living are coming to be strained through the bars of the dollar sign.

ROBERT S. LYND and HELEN MERRELL LYND, *Middletown: A Study in Contemporary American Culture*, 1929.

Money bears the same relation to social solutions that water does to blood.

NORMAN MAILER, *New York Times Magazine*, May 18, 1965.

Hollywood's queens and kings lived far more luxuriously than most of the reigning families in Europe. Most of them tossed their money around as though they manufactured it themselves in the cellar. They went in for solid gold bathtubs, chauffeur-driven Rolls Royces, champagne for breakfast and caviar every fifteen minutes. It was the kind of world that today only exists in the pages of movie magazines and for the sons of a few Latin American dictators.

GROUCHO MARX, *Groucho and Me*, 1959.

The most valuable of all human possessions, next to a superior and disdainful air, is the reputation of being well to do.

H.L. MENCKEN, *Prejudices*, 1922.

Much work is merely a way to make money; much leisure is merely a way to spend it.

C. WRIGHT MILLS, "Diagnosis of Our Moral Uneasiness," *Power, Politics and People*, 1963.

Money is like manure. If you spread it around, it does a lot of good, but if you pile it up in one place, it stinks like hell.

CLINT W. MURCHISON, recalled by Clint Murchison, Jr., *Time*, June 16, 1961.

Certainly there are lots of things in life that
    money won't buy, but it's very funny—

Have you ever tried to buy them without
    money?

OGDEN NASH, "The Terrible People," *Happy Days*, 1933.

Americans want action for their money. They are fascinated by its self-reproducing qualities.

PAULA NELSON, *The Joy of Money*, 1975.

Money does not pay for anything, never has, never will. It is an economic axiom as old as the hills that goods and services can be paid for only with goods and services.

ALBERT JAY NOCK, *Memoirs of a Superfluous Man*, 1943.

Money never remains just coins and pieces of paper. It is constantly changing into the comforts of daily life. Money can be translated into the beauty of living, a support in misfortune, an education, or future security. It also can be translated into a source of bitterness.

SYLVIA PORTER, *Sylvia Porter's Money Book*, 1975.

If a man saves $15 a week and invests in good common stocks,...at the end of 20 years, he will have at least $80,000 and...$400 a month. He will be rich. And because income can do that, I am firm in my belief that anyone not only can be rich, but ought to be rich.

JOHN T. RASKOB, in Lois and Alan Gordon, *American Chronicle*, 1987.

God gave me my money.

JOHN D. ROCKEFELLER, SR., in John Thomas Flynn, *God's Gold: The Story of Rockefeller and His Times*, 1932.

This concentration of wealth and power has been built upon other people's money, other people's business, other people's labor. Under this concentration independent business was allowed to exist only by sufferance. It has been a menace to the social system as well as to the economic system which we call American democracy.

FRANKLIN D. ROOSEVELT, speech, October 14, 1936.

Probably the greatest harm done by vast wealth is the harm that we of moderate means do ourselves when we let the vices of envy and hatred enter deep into our own natures.

THEODORE ROOSEVELT, speech, Providence, Rhode Island, August 23, 1902.

If you rub up against money long enough, some of it may rub off on you.

DAMON RUNYON, "A Very Honorable Guy," *Furthermore*, 1938.

Money is power, freedom, a cushion, the root
    of all evil, the sum of blessings....

Money breeds money,

Money rules the world.

CARL SANDBURG, *The People, Yes*, 1936.

Wealth must justify itself in happiness.

GEORGE SANTAYANA, *The Life of Reason*, 1905–1906.

The American talks about money because that is the symbol and measure he has at hand for success, intelligence, and power; but, as to money itself, he makes, loses, spends, and gives it away with a very light heart.

GEORGE SANTAYANA, *Character and Opinion in the United States*, 1920.

Too long we have reckoned our resources in terms of illusion. Money, even gold, is but a metrical device...not the substance of wealth. Our capital is the accumulation of material and energy with which we can work. Soil, water, minerals, vegetables and animal life—these are the basis of our existence and the measure of our future.

PAUL B. SEARS, *This Is Our World*, 1937.

There is no principle involved in my holdout. Only money.

O.J. SIMPSON, *Sports Illustrated*, July 28, 1969.

Resources, people and ideas are all that exist; so some combination of them must be the source of wealth [of a society]. At least one of them must change if we are to get more wealth. Which of these has been changing to increase our wealth? Not the original resources; they are fixed. Not the people; their fundamental characteristics [have not changed]....The big change is ideas.... It must be that ideas are responsible for the increase in average wealth.

MAX SINGER, *Passage to a Human World*, 1987.

"Community learning" is the key part of the learning process that enables a country to become wealthy. We are wealthy because we work in a society that has developed (learned) a culture and a system that supports high and growing productivity.

MAX SINGER, *Passage to a Human World,* 1987.

All money is a matter of belief.

ADAM SMITH, *Paper Money,* 1981.

My life is a bubble; but how much solid cash it costs to keep that bubble floating!

LOGAN PEARSALL SMITH, *Afterthoughts,* 1931.

It is the wretchedness of being rich that you have to live with rich people.

LOGAN PEARSALL SMITH, *All Trivia,* 1933.

American business does not see the worker as a coolie to be driven, but as a consumer to be satisfied. For an American wealth is not something to be hoarded but to be spent.

DOROTHY THOMPSON, *The Courage To Be Happy,* 1957.

Alice's Law of Compensatory Cashflow...holds that any money not spent on a luxury one considered even briefly is the equivalent of windfall income and should be spent accordingly. If you decide, for instance, that buying a five-hundred-dollar color television set would be, all things considered, an act of lunacy and the final step toward complete financial collapse, you have an extra five hundred dollars that you "saved" on the television set available to spend on something else.

CALVIN TRILLIN, "Fly Frills to Miami," *Alice, Let's Eat,* 1978.

You can be young without money but you can't be old without it.

TENNESSEE WILLIAMS, *Cat on a Hot Tin Roof,* 1955.

The people of this country are not jealous of fortunes, however great, which have been built up by the honest development of great enterprises, which have been actually earned by business energy and sagacity; they are jealous only of speculative wealth, of the wealth which has been piled up by no effort at all, but only by shrewd wits playing on the credulity of others, taking advantage of the weakness of others, trading in the necessities of others. This is "predatory wealth."

WOODROW WILSON, speech, "Law or Personal Power," New York City, April 13, 1908.

Education

See also **Children and Youth**; **Dreams and Ideals**—Excellence, Leadership, Truth, Wisdom; **The Human Condition**—Intelligence; **Knowledge**; **Religion and Spirituality**—Religion and Government; **Social Issues**—Civil Rights; **Work**—Educators

From cradle to grave this problem of running order through chaos, direction through space, discipline through freedom, unity through multiplicity, has always been, and must always be, the task of education.

HENRY ADAMS, *The Education of Henry Adams*, 1907.

The chief wonder of education is that it does not ruin everybody concerned in it, teachers and taught.

HENRY ADAMS, *The Education of Henry Adams*, 1907.

Education is to get where you can start to learn.

GEORGE AIKEN, *New York Times*, January 29, 1967.

Real education should educate us out of self into something far finer—into selflessness which links us with all humanity.

NANCY ASTOR, *My Two Countries*, 1923.

Teaching is not a lost art, but the regard for it is a lost tradition.

JACQUES BARZUN, *Newsweek*, December 5, 1955.

A good education is not so much one which prepares a man to succeed in the world, as one which enables him to sustain failure.

BERNARD IDDINGS BELL, *Life*, October 16, 1950.

Erudition, n. Dust shaken out of a book into an empty skull.

AMBROSE BIERCE, *The Devil's Dictionary*, 1906.

Education is learning what you didn't know you didn't know.

GEORGE BOAS, "The Century of the Child," *The American Scholar*, 1938.

If you think education is expensive, try ignorance.

DEREK BOK, *Poughkeepsie Journal*, March 26, 1978.

Parochial education...cannot be said to meet the requirements of a democracy that rests upon a community of shared educational experience.

WILLIAM CLAYTON BOWER, *Church and State in Education*, 1944.

[They] realized that education was not a thing of one's own to do with what one pleases—that it was not a personal privilege to be merely enjoyed by the possessor—but a precious treasure transmitted; a sacred trust to be held, used and enjoyed, and if possible strengthened—then passed on to others upon the same trust.

LOUIS D. BRANDEIS, speech, Menora Conference, Harvard University, 1914.

It's an insane tragedy that 700,000 people get a diploma each year and can't read the damned diploma.

WILLIAM E. BROCK, to Senate Committee on Labor and Human Resources, *New York Times*, January 14, 1987.

What our time needs is mystery....There is a hex on us, the specters in books, the authority of the past; and to exorcise these ghosts is the great work of magical self-liberation....What education does is to put a series of filters over your awareness so that year by year...you experience less and less.

NORMAN O. BROWN, 1961, in Lois and Alan Gordon, *American Chronicle*, 1987.

We conclude that in the field of public education the doctrine of "separate but equal" has no place. Separate educational facilities are inherently unequal. Therefore, we hold that the plaintiffs and others similarly situated for whom the actions have been brought are, by reason of the segregation complained of, deprived of the equal protection of the laws guaranteed by the Fourteenth Amendment.

Brown v. Board of Education, May 17, 1954.

Today, education is perhaps the most important function of state and local governments. Compulsory school attendance laws and the great expenditures for education both demonstrate our recognition of the importance of education to our democratic society. It is required in the performance of our most basic public responsibilities, even service in the armed forces. It is the very foundation of good citizenship. Today it is a principal instrument in awakening the child to cultural values, in preparing him for later professional training, and in helping him to adjust normally to his environment. In these days, it is doubtful that any child may reasonably be expected to succeed in life if he is denied the opportunity of an education. Such an opportunity, where the state has undertaken to provide it, is a right which must be made available to all on equal terms.

Brown v. Board of Education, May 17, 1954.

The proper education for democracy should produce young men and women equally eager for marriage and for work and the development to be found in both.

PEARL S. BUCK, speech to U.S. House of Representatives, January 16, 1941.

Geography is where it's at.

BUMPER STICKER.

I take a very old-fashioned view of the importance of spelling and grammar. I don't care tuppence for imaginative stories that are badly spelt in poorly constructed sentences with no observable punctuation.

ROBERT BURCHFIELD, "A Conversation with Robert Burchfield," *U.S. News & World Report,* December 15, 1980.

The acceptance of women as authority figures or as role models is an important step in female education....It is this process of identification, respect, and then self-respect that promotes growth.

JUDY CHICAGO, *Through the Flower: My Struggle as a Woman Artist,* 1975.

A number of people who are essentially ignorant now have degrees and diplomas to certify they are educated. These people either know how ignorant they are, and thus realize education is a fraud, or they go around saying they are just as good as everybody else. Ignorance is curable. Stupidity is not.

JOHN CIARDI, *Waco Tribune-Herald,* March 18, 1976.

American education needs training for character.

SEYMOUR COHEN, *Affirming Life,* 1987.

Educational writers are always blaming subjects instead of men, looking for some galvanic theme or method which when applied by a man without any gift for teaching to a mind without

any capacity for learning will somehow produce intellectual results.

FRANK MOORE COLBY, *The Colby Essays,* 1926.

The forcing of Latin, geometry, and algebra in a certain kind of manner into a certain kind of head is not education; it is persecution.

FRANK MOORE COLBY, *The Colby Essays,* 1926.

The tradition of scholarship as a separate and rather exalted department of life has never taken a firm hold on American culture...art and scholarship are bogus unless they derive from life directly.

HENRY S. COMMAGER, in Arthur Goodfriend, *What Is America?,* 1954.

Each generation of Americans has outstripped its parents in education, in literacy, and in economic attainment. For the first time in the history of our country, the educational skills of one generation will not surpass, will not equal, will not even approach, those of their parents.

PAUL COPPERMAN, in National Commission on Excellence in Education, *A Nation at Risk,* 1983.

Respect for the fragility and importance of an individual life is still the first mark of the educated man.

NORMAN COUSINS, *Saturday Review,* 1954.

Education tends to be diagrammatic and categorical, opening up no sluices in the human imagination on the wonder or beauty of their unique estate in the cosmos. Little wonder that it becomes so easy for our young to regard human hurt casually or to be uninspired by the magic of sensitivity.

NORMAN COUSINS, *Saturday Review,* 1965.

The educational process has no end beyond itself; it is its own end.

JOHN DEWEY, *Democracy and Education,* 1916.

What then is education when we find actual satisfactory specimens of it in existence? In the first place, it is a process of development, of growth. And it is the *process* and not merely the result that is important.

JOHN DEWEY, "The Need for a Philosophy of Education," in Joseph Ratner, ed., *Education Today,* 1940.

All education is a continuous dialogue—questions and answers that pursue every problem to the horizon. That is the essence of academic freedom.

WILLIAM O. DOUGLAS, *Wisdom,* October, 1956.

Education has become too important to be left to educators.

PETER F. DRUCKER, *The Age of Discontinuity,* 1968.

Education and work are the levers to uplift a people. Work alone will not do it unless inspired by the right ideals and guided by intelligence. Education must not simply teach work—it must teach Life.

W.E.B. DU BOIS, *The Negro Problem,* 1903.

It is the trained, living human soul, cultivated and strengthened by long study and thought, that breathes the real breath of life into boys and girls and makes them human, whether they be black or white, Greek, Russian, or American.

W.E.B. DU BOIS, *The Negro Problem,* 1903.

One might say that the American trend of education is to reduce the senses almost to nil.

ISADORA DUNCAN, *My Life,* 1926.

Education is that which remains, if one has forgotten everything he learned in school.

ALBERT EINSTEIN, *Out of My Later Years,* 1950.

The aim [of education] must be the training of independently acting and thinking individuals, who, however, see in the service of the community their highest life problem.

ALBERT EINSTEIN, *Out of My Later Years,* 1950.

By academic freedom I understand the right to search for truth and to publish and teach what one holds to be true. This right implies also a duty: one must not conceal any part of what one has recognized to be true.

ALBERT EINSTEIN, letter, March 13, 1954.

It does not necessarily follow that a scholar in the humanities is also a humanist—but it should. For what does it avail a man to be the greatest expert on John Donne if he cannot hear the bell tolling?

MILTON S. EISENHOWER, "The Need for a New American," *The Educational Record,* October, 1963.

Most Americans do value education as a business asset, but not as the entrance into the joy of intellectual experience or acquaintance with the best that has been said and done in the past. They value it not as an experience, but as a tool.

W.H.P. FAUNCE, letter to Abraham Flexner, January 16, 1928.

Nations have recently been led to borrow billions for war; no nation has ever borrowed large-ly for education. Probably no nation is rich enough to pay for both war and civilization. We must make our choice; we cannot have both.

ABRAHAM FLEXNER, *Universities,* 1930.

The prevailing philosophy of education tends to discredit hard work.

ABRAHAM FLEXNER, *Universities,* 1930.

There is little or no intellectual challenge or discipline involved in merely learning to adjust.

BETTY FRIEDAN, *The Feminine Mystique,* 1963.

That we have not made any respectable attempt to meet the special educational needs of women in the past is the clearest possible evidence of the fact that our educational objectives have been geared exclusively to the vocational patterns of men.

BETTY FRIEDAN, *The Feminine Mystique,* 1963.

Education is the ability to listen to almost anything without losing your temper or your self-confidence.

ROBERT FROST, *Reader's Digest,* April, 1960.

Education doesn't change life much. It just lifts trouble to a higher plane of regard.

ROBERT FROST, *Quote,* July 9, 1961.

The ability to think straight, some knowledge of the past, some vision of the future, some skill to do useful service, some urge to fit that service into the well-being of the community—these are the most vital things education must try to produce.

VIRGINIA GILDERSLEEVE, *Many a Good Crusade,* 1954.

The philosophic aim of education must be to get one out of his isolated class and into one humanity.

PAUL GOODMAN, *Compulsory Mis-education,* 1964.

To be able to be caught up into the world of thought—that is educated.

EDITH HAMILTON, *Saturday Evening Post,* September 27, 1958.

The right to impart instruction, harmless in itself or beneficial to those who receive it, is a substantial right of property.

JOHN MARSHALL HARLAN, opinion, *Berea College* v. *Kentucky,* 1908.

Why do most Americans look up to education and look down upon educated people? (Our national schizophrenia.)

SYDNEY HARRIS, column, *Detroit Free Press,* April 2, 1981.

The end product of education, yours and mine and everybody's, is the total pattern of reactions and possible reactions we have inside ourselves.

S.I. HAYAKAWA, "How Words Change Our Lives," *Saturday Evening Post*, December 27, 1958.

Ideas move fast when their time comes.

CAROLYN HEILBRUN, *Toward a Recognition of Androgyny*, 1973.

The invention of IQ did a great disservice to creativity in education....Individuality, personality, originality, are too precious to be meddled with by amateur psychiatrists whose patterns for a "wholesome personality" are inevitably their own.

JOEL H. HILDEBRAND, *New York Times*, June 16, 1964.

We have ignored cultural literacy in thinking about education....We ignore the air we breathe until it is thin or foul. Cultural literacy is the oxygen of social intercourse.

E.D. HIRSCH, JR., *Cultural Literacy: What Every American Needs To Know*, 1987.

If the past cannot teach the present and the father cannot teach the son, then history need not have bothered to go on, and the world has wasted a great deal of time.

RUSSELL HOBAN, *The Lion of Boaz-Jachin and Jachin-Boaz*, 1973.

We need education in the obvious more than investigation of the obscure.

OLIVER WENDELL HOLMES, JR., speech, New York City, February 15, 1913.

I look for a day when education will be like the landscape, free for all. Beauty and truth should be free to every one who has the capacity to absorb. The private school, the private library, the private art gallery, the exclusive college, have got to go. We want no excellence that is not for all.

ELBERT HUBBARD, *Note Book*, 1927.

Education is what you learn in books, and nobody knows you know it but your teacher.

VIRGINIA CARY HUDSON, *O Ye Jigs & Juleps!*, 1962.

The history of scholarship is a record of disagreements.

CHARLES EVANS HUGHES, speech, Washington, D.C., May 7, 1936.

Academic freedom is simply a way of saying that we get the best results in education and research if we leave their management to people who know something about them.

ROBERT M. HUTCHINS, *Higher Learning in America*, 1936.

We do not know what education can do for us, because we have never tried it.

ROBERT M. HUTCHINS, *The Atomic Bomb versus Civilization*, 1945.

The policy of the repression of ideas cannot work and never has worked. The alternative to it is the long, difficult road of education. To this the American people have been committed.

ROBERT M. HUTCHINS, testimony to Illinois Seditious Activities Investigation Commission, April 21, 1949.

When we talk of our political goals, we admit the right of every man to be a ruler. When we talk of our educational program, we see no inconsistency in saying that only a few have the capacity to get the education that rulers ought to have.

ROBERT M. HUTCHINS, *The Conflict in Education in a Democratic Society*, 1953.

The aim of education is the knowledge not of facts but of values.

WILLIAM RALPH INGE, *The Church in the World*, October, 1932.

It is one of the paradoxes of our time that modern society needs to fear...only the educated man.

ROBERT H. JACKSON, in William F. Buckley, Jr., *God and Man at Yale*, 1951.

I wonder if I had had an education I should have been more or less a fool than I am.

ALICE JAMES, in Leon Edel, ed., *Diary*, 1964.

Education is not a problem. Education is an opportunity.

LYNDON B. JOHNSON, speech, William Jewell College, November 9, 1961.

We just must not, we just cannot afford the great waste that comes from the neglect of a single child.

LYNDON B. JOHNSON, speech, National Conference on Education Legislation, March 1, 1965.

Education by means of pre-fabricated ideas is propaganda.

MORDECAI M. KAPLAN, *Reconstructionist*, April, 1950.

The most important function of education at any level is to develop the personality of the individual and the significance of his life to himself and to others. This is the basic architecture of a life; the rest is ornamentation and decoration of the structure.

GRAYSON KIRK, *Quote*, January 27, 1963.

The right to interfere with the rights of others is no part of academic freedom.

GRAYSON KIRK, *New York Times*, June 6, 1965.

If we watch ourselves honestly, we shall often find that we have begun to argue against a new idea even before it has been completely stated.

ARTHUR KOESTLER, *The Act of Creation*, 1964.

What are we educating women for? To raise this question is to face the whole problem of women's role in society. We are uncertain about the end of women's education precisely because the status of women in our society is fraught with contradictions and confusion.

MIRRA KOMAROVSKY, *Women in the Modern World*, 1953.

There is no common faith, no common body of principle, no common body of knowledge, no common moral and intellectual discipline....We have established a system of education in which we insist that while everyone must be educated, yet there is nothing in particular that an educated man must know.

WALTER LIPPMANN, speech, American Association for Advancement of Science, December 29, 1940.

We are quite rich enough to defend ourselves, whatever the cost. We must now learn that we are quite rich enough to educate ourselves as we need to be educated.

WALTER LIPPMANN, *Citizens and Their Schools*, 1952.

This thing, education, appears to be desired frequently not for its specific content but as a symbol—by the working class as an open sesame that will mysteriously admit their children to a world closed to them, and by the business class as a heavily sanctioned aid in getting on further economically or socially in the world.

ROBERT S. LYND and HELEN MERRELL LYND, *Middletown: A Study in Contemporary American Culture*, 1929.

[W]hile education slowly pushes its tents closer to the practical concerns of the local life, the latter are forever striking camp and removing deeper into the forest.

ROBERT S. LYND and HELEN MERRELL LYND, *Middletown: A Study in Contemporary American Culture*, 1929.

Our chief aim of any true system of education must be to impart to the individual the courage to play the game against any and all odds, the nerve to walk into the ambushes of existence, the hardiness to face the most despicable truth about himself and not let it daunt him permanently; it must armour him with an ultimate carelessness.

DON MARQUIS, *The Almost Perfect State*, 1927.

There is only one sound method of moral education. It is teaching people to think.

EVERETT DEAN MARTIN, *The Meaning of a Liberal Education*, 1926.

The danger of education, I have found, is that it so easily confuses means with ends. Worse than that, it quite easily forgets both and devotes itself merely to the mass production of uneducated graduates—people literally unfit for anything except to take part in an elaborate and completely artificial charade which they and their contemporaries have conspired to call "life."

THOMAS MERTON, *Love and Living*, 1980.

A man with his belly full of the classics is an enemy of the human race.

HENRY MILLER, *Tropic of Cancer*, 1934.

In an information society, education is no mere amenity; it is the prime tool for growing people and profits.

JOHN NAISBITT and PATRICIA ABURDENE, *Re-inventing the Corporation*, 1985.

It is a woeful mistake to suppose that the educated are kinder or more tolerant: education creates vested interests, and renders the beneficiaries acutely jealous and very vocal.

LEWIS BERNSTEIN NAMIER, *Conflicts*, 1943.

Part of what is at risk is the promise first made on this continent: All, regardless of race or class or economic status, are entitled to a fair chance and to the tools for developing their individual powers of mind and spirit to the utmost. This promise means that all children by virtue of their own efforts, competently guided, can hope to attain the mature and informed judgment needed to secure gainful employment and to manage their own lives, thereby serving not only their own interests but also the progress of society itself.

National Commission on Excellence in Education, *A Nation at Risk*, 1983.

A high level of shared education is essential to a free, democratic society and to the fostering of a common culture, especially in a country that prides itself on pluralism and individual freedom.

National Commission on Excellence in Education, *A Nation at Risk*, 1983.

If an unfriendly foreign power had attempted to impose on America the mediocre educational performance that exists today, we might well have viewed it as an act of war.

National Commission on Excellence in Education, *A Nation at Risk*, 1983.

That's what education means—to be able to do what you've never done before.

George Herbert Palmer, *Life of Alice Freeman Palmer*, 1908.

Real education must ultimately be limited to men who INSIST on knowing, the rest is mere sheep-herding.

Ezra Pound, *ABC of Reading*, 1934.

When we look at the troubled state of the present world...one thing becomes manifest. This is the failure of recent educational practice to prepare men in terms of heart and will to prevent the strife, misunderstanding, and willfulness that now arises.

Nathan M. Pusey, *Religion and Freedom of Thought*, 1954.

Education is not the means of showing people how to get what they want. Education is an exercise by means of which enough men, it is hoped, will learn to want what is worth having.

Ronald Reagan, *Sincerely, Ronald Reagan*, 1976.

The papers today say that illiteracy has decreased. The more that learn how to read the less learn how to make a living. That's one thing about a little education. It spoils you for actual work. The more you know the more you think somebody owes you a living.

Will Rogers, September 4, 1931, in Donald Day, ed., *The Autobiography of Will Rogers*, 1949.

A democratic form of government, a democratic way of life, presupposes free public education over a long period; it presupposes also an education for personal responsibility that too often is neglected.

Eleanor Roosevelt, "Let Us Have Faith in Democracy," *Land Policy Review*, January, 1942.

The gains of education are never really lost. Books may be burned and cities sacked, but truth, like the yearning for freedom, lives in the hearts of humble men.

Franklin D. Roosevelt, speech, Democratic National Convention, June 27, 1936.

One of the reasons, perhaps the major reason, why education has made so little progress in comparison with other cultural endeavors over the last thousand years is that much of it has been, and still is, aloof from practical, or even intelligent, purpose.

Dagobert D. Runes, *Letter to My Teacher*, 1961.

I would argue that a man or woman who cannot speak or write clearly cannot think and reason cogently either.

John C. Sawhill, speech, "Higher Education in the 80's: Beyond Retrenchment," American Association of Higher Education, Washington, D.C., March 6, 1980.

True education makes for inequality; the inequality of individuality, the inequality of success; the glorious inequality of talent, of genius, for inequality, not mediocrity, individual superiority, not standardization, is the measure of the progress of the world.

Felix E. Schelling, *Pedagogically Speaking*, 1929.

I am not an educational theorist but I think I know what an educated man looks like. He is thoroughly inoculated against humbug, thinks for himself and tries to give his thoughts, in speech or on paper, some style.

Alan Simpson, *Newsweek*, July 1, 1963.

Education is what survives when what has been learnt has been forgotten.

B.F. Skinner, "Education in 1984," *New Scientist*, May 21, 1964.

One of the ultimate advantages of an education is simply coming to the end of it.

B.F. Skinner, *The Technology of Teaching*, 1968.

Teaching kids to count is fine, but teaching them what counts is best.

Bob Talbert, *Detroit Free Press*, April 5, 1982.

Teaching has ruined more American novelists than drink.

Gore Vidal, in Beverly Kempton, "Conversations with Gore Vidal," *Oui*, April, 1975.

Every human being has four hungers; the hunger of the loins, the hunger of the belly, the hunger of the mind, the hunger of the soul. You can get by a long time on the loins and the belly, but there is a good deal of evidence that even the meanest of men eventually crave something for the mind and soul.

James Webb, in Arthur Goodfriend, *What Is America?*, 1954.

COLLEGES AND UNIVERSITIES

The colleges have long been full of the best ethical teaching....But while the teaching has included an ever-broadening range of obligation and has insisted upon the recognition of the claims of human brotherhood, the training has been singularly individualistic; it has fostered ambitions for personal distinction, and has trained the faculties almost exclusively in the direction of intellectual accumulation.

JANE ADDAMS, "Filial Relations," *Democracy and Social Ethics*, 1907.

An inviolable refuge from tryanny should be found in the university. It should be an *intellectual experience station*, where new ideas may germinate and where their fruit, though still distasteful to the community as a whole, may be allowed to ripen until finally, perchance, it may become part of the accepted international food of the nation or of the world.

Declaration of First Committee on Academic Freedom of American Association of University Professors, 1915.

It takes most men five years to recover from a college education, and to learn that poetry is as vital to thinking as knowledge.

BROOKS ATKINSON, "August 31," *Once Around the Sun*, 1951.

The school's obligation is to follow established principles and to uphold warranted knowledge as against the views commonly held in the marketplace. The competition is between scientific and critical beliefs, on the one hand, and popular emotional beliefs, on the other.

I.B. BERKSON, *The Ideal and the Community*, 1958.

Equalizing opportunity through universal higher education subjects the whole population to the intellectual mode natural only to a few. It violates the fundamental egalitarian principle of respect for the differences between people.

CAROLINE BIRD, *The Case Against College*, 1975.

The big advantage of getting your college money in cash now is that you can invest it in something that has a higher return than a diploma.

CAROLINE BIRD, *The Case Against College*, 1975.

A liberal-arts education is supposed to provide you with a value system, a standard, a set of ideas, not a job.

CAROLINE BIRD, *The Case Against College*, 1975.

By consenting to play an active or "positive," a participatory, role in society, the university has become inundated and saturated with the backflow of society's "problems." Preoccupied with questions of Health, Sex, Race, War, academics make their reputations and their fortunes and the university has become society's conceptual warehouse of often harmful influences.

ALLAN BLOOM, *The Closing of the American Mind*, 1987.

At best, more college presidents are running something that is somewhere between a faltering corporation and a hotel.

LEON BOTSTEIN, *Center*, March, 1977.

The association only with men of one's own class, such as the organization of college life today fosters, is simply fatal to any broad understanding of life. The refusal to make the acquaintance while in college of as many as possible original, self-dependent personalities, regardless of race and social status, is morally suicidal.

RANDOLPH BOURNE, *Youth and Life*, 1913.

The atmosphere of libraries, lecture rooms and laboratories is dangerous to those who shut themselves up in them too long. It separates us from reality like a fog.

ALEXIS CARREL, *Reflections on Life*, 1950.

A university studies politics, but it will not advocate fascism or communism. A university studies military tactics, but it will not promote war. A university studies peace, but it will not organize crusades of pacifism. It will study every question that affects human welfare, but it will not carry a banner in a crusade for anything except freedom of learning.

LOTUS DELAT COFFMAN, *Journal of the American Association of University Women*, 1936.

He who enters a university walks on hallowed ground.

JAMES BRYANT CONANT, *Notes on the Harvard Tercentenary*, 1936.

What is the purpose of a college or university? It is to educate and train, to prepare its student body for the great tasks of life....The last thing in the world a college or university should be concerned with is being number one in football or basketball if the price one pays for that is the corruption of character and the undermining of true student morale on campus.

HOWARD COSELL, *Like It Is*, 1974.

College ain't so much where you been as how you talk when you get back.

OSSIE DAVIS, *Purlie Victorious*, 1961.

I learned three important things in college—to use a library, to memorize quickly and visually, to drop asleep at any time given a horizontal surface and fifteen minutes. What I could not learn was to think creatively on schedule.

AGNES DE MILLE, *Dance to the Piper*, 1952.

I am not impressed by the Ivy League establishments. Of course they graduate the best—it's all they'll take, leaving to others the problem of educating the country. They will give you an education the way the banks will give you money—provided you can prove to their satisfaction that you don't need it.

PETER DE VRIES, *The Vale of Laughter*, 1967.

All men cannot go to college but some men must; every isolated group or nation must have its yeast, must have for the talented few centers of training where men are not so mystified and befuddled by the hard and necessary toil of earning a living, as to have no aims higher than their bellies, and no God greater than Gold.

W.E.B. DU BOIS, *The Negro Problem*, 1903.

The function of the university is not simply to teach bread-winning, or to furnish teachers for the public schools or to be a center of polite society; it is, above all, to be the organ of that fine adjustment between real life and the growing knowledge of life, an adjustment which forms the secret of civilization.

W.E.B. DU BOIS, *The Souls of Black Folk*, 1903.

And this goddamned school is antifemale, they look down on women, especially women my age. It's a goddamned monastery that's been invaded by people in skirts and the men who run it only hope that the people in skirts are pseudomen, so they won't disturb things, won't insist that feeling is as important as thinking and body as important as mind.

MARILYN FRENCH, *The Women's Room*, 1977.

If you feel that you have both feet planted on level ground, then the university has failed you.

ROBERT GOHEEN, speech, Princeton University, June 23, 1961.

If Carlyle could define a university as a collection of books, Socrates might have defined it as a conversation about wisdom.

A. WHITNEY GRISWOLD, *Essays on Education*, 1954.

Why is it that the boy or girl who on June 15 receives his degree, eager, enthusiastic, outspoken, idealistic, reflective, and independent, is on the following Sept. 15, or even June 16...dull, uninspiring, shifty, pliable and attired in a double-breasted, blue serge suit? The answer must lie in the relative weakness of the higher education, compared with the forces that make everybody think and act like everybody else.

ROBERT M. HUTCHINS, speech, University of Chicago, February 12, 1951.

Our colleges ought to have lit up in us a lasting relish for the better kind of man, a loss of appetite for mediocrities.

WILLIAM JAMES, "The Social Value of the College-Bred," *Memories and Studies*, 1911.

What the colleges...should at least try to give us is a general sense of what, under various disguises, *superiority* has always signified and may still signify. The feeling for a good human job anywhere, the admiration of the really admirable, the disesteem of what is cheap and trashy and impermanent—this is what we call the critical sense, the sense for ideal values. It is the better part of what men know as wisdom.

WILLIAM JAMES, *Memories and Studies*, 1911.

I find that the three major administrative problems on a campus are sex for the students, athletics for the alumni, and parking for the faculty.

CLARK KERR, speech, University of Washington, *Time*, November 17, 1958.

A university anywhere can aim no higher than to be as British as possible for the sake of the undergraduates, as German as possible for the sake of the public at large—and as confused as possible for the preservation of the whole uneasy balance.

CLARK KERR, lecture, "The Uses of the University," Harvard University, *New York Times*, April 26, 1963.

"An investigation into Sex" is now offered at Dartmouth. "Analogues to the LSD Experience" can now be studied at Penn. "Guerilla Warfare" is being examined by DePauw students. Stanford undergraduates are studying "American Youth in Revolt," and "The Origins and Meaning of Black Power" is a course at Brooklyn College. Has higher education finally caught up with the times?

RALPH KEYES, "The Free Universities," 1967.

I enjoy learning things, but a university is the last place in the world to learn anything.

CHARLES KOWAL, *Time*, October 27, 1975.

Does a college education pay? Does it pay to feed in pork trimmings at five cents a pound in the hopper and draw out nice, cunning, little "country" sausages at the other end? Does it pay to take a steer that's been running loose on the range and living on cactus and petrified wood till he's just a bunch of barb-wire and sole-leather, and feed him corn till he's just a solid hunk of porterhouse steak and oleo oil?

GEORGE HORACE LORIMER, *Letters from a Self-Made Merchant to His Son*, 1902.

This idea that going to college is one of the inherent rights of man seems to have obtained a baseless foothold in the minds of many of our people.

ABBOTT LAWRENCE LOWELL, speech, Haverford College, April 17, 1931.

My job is to bore you and let the hardness of your seat and the warmth of your robe prepare you for what is to come.

WILLIAM H. McNEILL, speech, Bard College, May 26, 1984.

No man should escape our universities without knowing how little he knows.

J. ROBERT OPPENHEIMER, in J.H. Raleigh, *Partisan Review*, Summer, 1967.

When we exchanged the short undergraduate gown for the B.A.–M.A. gown and hood, we put on more than an emblem of brief scholastic achievement. We put on the mantle of humility before great learning; we put on the love of learning and belief in its significance; we put on the responsibility to us all that great teachers had given us, the duty not to let the torch go out unheeded.

VIRGINIA RIDLEY, "American Girl at Oxford," *Christian Science Monitor*, October 21, 1958.

College is always on the road to somewhere else.

TOM ROBBINS, *Bookviews*, February, 1978.

The college was not founded to give society what it wants. Quite the contrary.

MAY SARTON, *The Small Room*, 1961.

The pyramid has been supplanted by the shelf theory of education: courses are arranged like bottles on a shelf. It does not make a great deal of difference what is in the bottles. Each bottle stands for a prescribed number of hours in the classroom; at the end of four years, if one can collect enough bottles, one brings them to the dean; the dean counts them, but he, too, ignores

what is in them. If a sufficient number are presented, generally 120 bottles, the college, which has succeeded in pulling the wool over the student's eyes, celebrates its success by giving him a sheepskin.

FULTON J. SHEEN, *The Wit and Wisdom of Bishop Fulton J. Sheen*, 1968.

It is possible to get an education at a university. It has been done; not often, but the fact that a proportion, however small, of college students do get a start in interested, methodical study proves my thesis.

LINCOLN STEFFENS, *Autobiography*, 1931.

What a blessed place this would be if there were no undergraduates!...No waste of good brains in cramming bad ones.

LESLIE STEPHEN, in Jacques Barzun, *The American University*, 1968.

[There has been a] triumph of ideology over ideas in American higher education: the fragmentation and incoherence in the curriculum; the nihilism that passes for the humanities: the politicization of both scholarship and the classroom; and the darkening shadow of intolerance and intimidation reflected in official attempts to limit free speech.

CHARLES SYKES, *The Hollow Men: Politics and Corruption in Higher Education*, 1990.

What then is the nature of the danger facing higher education? It is that *it is in the Western tradition* that we find the origins of democratic society, of the focus on individual worth and human dignity, and of aspirations for human freedom. It is the fountainhead of our language, our culture, our aesthetics, our religions, and our ethical systems. To lose that legacy through a curriculum of enforced cultural amnesia is to deconstruct an entire civilization. One would expect that its preservation would be the primary concern of the academy.

CHARLES SYKES, *The Hollow Men: Politics and Corruption in Higher Education*, 1990.

Touch a university with hostile hands and the blood you draw is prompt, copious, and real.

DIANE TRILLING, on campus unrest in 1960s, *We Must March, My Darlings*, 1977.

The use of a university is to make young gentlemen as unlike their fathers as possible.

WOODROW WILSON, speech, Pittsburgh, Pennsylvania, October 24, 1914.

LEARNING AND LEARNERS

What one knows is, in youth, of little moment; they know enough who know how to learn.

HENRY ADAMS, *The Education of Henry Adams*, 1907.

Children, taught either years beneath their intelligence or miles wide of relevance to it, or both: their intelligence becomes hopelessly bewildered, drawn off its centers, bored, or atrophied. Carry it foward a few years and recognize how soft-brained an American as against a European "college graduate" is.

JAMES AGEE, with Walker Evans, *Let Us Now Praise Famous Men*, 1941.

Experience has no text books nor proxies. She demands that her pupils answer her roll-call personally.

MINNA ANTRIM, *Naked Truth and Veiled Allusions*, 1902.

Experience is a good teacher, but she sends in terrific bills.

MINNA ANTRIM, *Naked Truth and Veiled Allusions*, 1902.

[Education] is where we decide whether we love our children enough not to expel them from our world and leave them to their own devices, not to strike from their hands their chance of undertaking something new, something unforseen by us, but to prepare them in advance for the task of renewing a common world.

HANNAH ARENDT, *Between Past and Present*, 1961.

The test and the use of man's education is that he finds pleasure in the exercise of his mind.

JACQUES BARZUN, "Science vs the Humanities," *Saturday Evening Post*, May 3, 1958.

Learning, n. The kind of ignorance distinguishing the studious.

AMBROSE BIERCE, *The Devil's Dictionary*, 1906.

[A student] wants to feel that the instructor is not simply passing on dead knowledge in the form that it was passed on to him, but that he has assimilated it and has read his own experience into it, so that it has come to mean more to him than almost anything in the world.

RANDOLPH BOURNE, *Youth and Life*, 1913.

There is no adequate defense, except stupidity, against the impact of a new idea.

PERCY W. BRIDGMAN, *The Intelligent Individual and Society*, 1938.

A new idea is delicate. It can be killed by a sneer or a yawn; it can be stabbed to death by a quip and worried to death by a frown on the right man's brow.

CHARLES BROWER, *Advertising Age*, August 10, 1959.

Any subject can be effectively taught in some intellectually honest form to any child at any stage of development.

JEROME BRUNER, *The Process of Education*, 1960.

Any place that anyone young can learn something useful from someone with experience is an educational institution.

AL CAPP, *The Hardhat's Bedtime Story Book*, 1971.

Children who are treated as if they are uneducable almost invariably become uneducable.

KENNETH B. CLARK, *Dark Ghetto*, 1965.

Students...who wish to keep growing need education for surprise.

SEYMOUR COHEN, *Affirming Life*, 1987.

I was thinking that we all learn by experience, but some of us have to go to summer school.

PETER DE VRIES, *The Tunnel of Love*, 1954.

Genuine ignorance is...profitable because it is likely to be accompanied by humility, curiosity, and open-mindedness; whereas ability to repeat catch-phrases, cant terms, familiar propositions, gives the conceit of learning and coats the mind with varnish water-proof to new ideas.

JOHN DEWEY, *Democracy and Education*, 1916.

I behaved in school like a half-wild animal who comes up to the common trough to get food, but sneaks off with it to his own den where he has gamier morsels of his own and his own ways of devouring them.

MAX EASTMAN, *Enjoyment of Living*, 1948.

When you reread a classic you do not see more in the book than you did before; you see more in *you* than there was before.

CLIFTON FADIMAN, *Any Number Can Play*, 1957.

What is learned in high school, or for that matter, anywhere at all, depends far less on what is taught than on what one actually experiences in the place.

EDGAR Z. FRIEDENBERG, *The Dignity of Youth and Other Atavisms*, 1965.

The trouble with most men of learning is that their learning goes to their heads.

ISAAC GOLDBERG, *Reflex*, December, 1927.

No one has yet fully realized the wealth of sympathy, kindness and generosity hidden in the soul of the child. The effort of every true educator should be to unlock that treasure—to stimulate the child's impulses and call for the best and noblest tendencies.

EMMA GOLDMAN, *Living My Life*, 1931.

There *is* only one curriculum, no matter what the method of education: what is basic and universal in human experience and practice, the underlying structure of culture.

PAUL GOODMAN, *Growing Up Absurd*, 1960.

Teachers may say, "But reading must be difficult, or so many children wouldn't have trouble with it." I say it is *because* we assume that it is so difficult that so many children have trouble with it. Our anxieties, our fears, and the ridiculous things we do to "simplify" what is simple enough already, *cause* most of the trouble.

JOHN HOLT, *How Children Learn*, 1967.

[We] can best understand learning as growth, an expanding of ourselves into the world around us. We can also see that there is no difference between living and learning, that living *is* learning, that it is impossible, and misleading, and harmful to think of them as being separate.

JOHN HOLT, *What Do I Do Monday?*, 1970.

It is hard to convince a high-school student that he will encounter a lot of problems more difficult than those of algebra and geometry.

EDGAR W. HOWE, *Country Town Sayings*, 1911.

An idea, to be suggestive, must come to the individual with the force of a revelation.

WILLIAM JAMES, *The Varieties of Religious Experience*, 1911.

Education in the long run is an affair that works itself out between the individual student and his opportunities. Methods of which we talk so much play but a minor part. Offer the opportunities, leave the student to his natural reaction on them, and he will work out his personal destiny, be it a high one or a low one.

WILLIAM JAMES, speech, "Stanford's Ideal Destiny," Stanford University, 1906.

When I was a boy...we didn't wake up with Vietnam and have Cyprus for lunch and the Congo for dinner.

LYNDON B. JOHNSON, to Conference on Educational Legislation, March 1, 1965.

There is less energy or interest left for fraternities, hazing, and the tribal rites of student culture; there is less room for experimentation, risk-taking, making mistakes, and taking false tacks.... [Most students] must work far harder in college than their parents ever thought of working.

KENNETH KENISTON, *Youth and Dissent: The Rise of a New Opposition*, 1966.

Liberty without learning is always in peril and learning without liberty is always in vain.

JOHN F. KENNEDY, speech, Vanderbilt University, March 18, 1963.

We are not asking our children to do their own best but to be *the* best. Education is in danger of becoming a religion based on fear; its doctrine is to compete. The majority of our children are being led to believe that they are doomed to failure in a world which has room only for those at the top.

EDA J. LE SHAN, *The Conspiracy Against Childhood*, 1967.

To learn is to change. Education is a process that changes the learner.

GEORGE B. LEONARD, *Education and Ecstasy*, 1968.

The least of the work of learning is done in classrooms.

THOMAS MERTON, *Love and Living*, 1980.

Learning is the indispensable investment required for success in the "information age" we are entering.

National Commission on Excellence in Education, *A Nation at Risk*, 1983.

In a free world, if it is to remain free, we must maintain, with our lives if need be, but surely by our lives, the opportunity for a man to learn anything.

J. ROBERT OPPENHEIMER, *Journal of the Atomic Scientists*, 1956.

Learning is discovering that something is possible.

FRITZ PERLS, *Omni*, November, 1979.

It is impossible to withhold education from the receptive mind, as it is impossible to force it upon the unreasoning.

AGNES REPPLIER, *Times and Tendencies*, 1931.

If we value independence, if we are disturbed by the growing conformity of knowledge, of values, of attitudes, which our present system induces, then we may wish to set up conditions of learning which make for uniqueness, for self-direction, and for self-initiated learning.

CARL R. ROGERS, *On Becoming a Person*, 1961.

When you stop learning, stop listening, stop looking and asking questions, always new questions, then it is time to die.

LILLIAN SMITH, "Bridges to Other People," *Redbook*, September, 1969.

Education is a private matter between the person and the world of knowledge and experience, and has little to do with school or college.

LILLIAN SMITH, "Bridges to Other People," *Redbook*, September, 1969.

I could undertake to be an efficient pupil if it were possible to find an efficient teacher.

GERTRUDE STEIN, "Q.E.D.," 1903, *Fernhurst, Q.E.D., and Other Early Writings*, 1972.

The perfect method of learning is analogous to infection. It enters and spreads.

LEO STEIN, *Journey into the Self*, 1950.

I always loved learning and hated school.

I.F. STONE, "In Defence of the Campus Rebels," *I.F. Stone's Weekly*, May 19, 1969.

Most of the most important experiences that truly educate cannot be arranged ahead of time with any precision.

HAROLD TAYLOR, "The Private World of the Man with a Book," *Saturday Review*, January 7, 1961.

Our young people must be exposed to science both because it is useful and because it is fun. Both of these qualities should be taken at a truly high value.

EDWARD TELLER, *Conversations on the Dark Secrets of Physics*, 1991.

One may receive the information but miss the teaching.

JEAN TOOMER, *Definitions and Aphorisms, XXXVII*, 1931.

I didn't do very well in math—I could never seem to persuade the teacher that I hadn't meant my answers literally.

CALVIN TRILLIN, "Geography Lesson," King Features Syndicate, September 21, 1986.

This is the great vice of academicism, that it is concerned with ideas rather than with thinking.

LIONEL TRILLING, *The Liberal Imagination: The Sense of the Past*, 1950.

Youngsters and adults cannot learn if information is pressed into their brains. You can teach only by creating interest, by creating an urge to know. Knowledge has to be sucked into the brain, not pushed into it. First, one must create a state of mind that craves knowledge, interest and wonder.

VICTOR WEISSKOPF, *The Privilege of Being a Physicist*, 1989.

It's what you learn after you know it all that counts.

JOHN WOODEN, *They Call Me Coach*, 1973.

SCHOOLS

[A] realistic high school counselor teaches kids to get ready for disappointment.

CAROL BLY, "To Unteach Greed," *Letters from the Country*, 1981.

The shrewd guess, the fertile hypothesis, the courageous leap to a tentative conclusion—these are the most valuable coins of the thinker at work. But in most schools guessing is heavily penalized and is associated somehow with laziness.

JEROME BRUNER, *The Process of Education*, 1960.

Our schools are still set up as though every mother were at home all day and the whole family needed the summer to get the crops in.

SIDNEY CALLAHAN, *Reader's Digest*, October, 1972.

Education don't come by bumping against the school-house.

SELWYN GURNEY CHAMPION, *Racial Proverbs*, 1938.

Schools are now asked to do what people used to ask God to do.

JEROME CRAMER, *Time*, June 16, 1980.

This school was on top of a hill so that God could see everything that went on. It looked like a cross between a prison and a church and it was.

QUENTIN CRISP, *The Naked Civil Servant*, 1966.

We might cease thinking of school as a place, and learn to believe that it is basically relationships between children and adults, and between children and other children. The four walls and the principal's office would cease to loom so hugely as the essential ingredients.

GEORGE DENNISON, *The Lives of Children*, 1969.

To me the worst thing seems to be for a school principally to work with the methods of fear, force and artificial authority. Such treatment destroys sound sentiments, the sincerity and the self-confidence of the pupil. It produces the submissive subject.

ALBERT EINSTEIN, *Out of My Later Years*, 1950.

Schools exploit you because they tap your power and use it to perpetuate society's trip, while they teach you not to respect your own....Schools petrify society because their method, characterized by coercion from the top down, works against any substantial social change. Students are coerced by teachers, who take orders from administrators, who do the bidding of those stalwarts of the status quo on the board of education or the board of trustees. Schools petrify society because students, through them, learn to adjust unquestioningly to institutions.

JERRY FARBER, *The Student as Nigger*, 1971.

The school imprisons children physically, intellectually, and morally, in order to direct the development of their faculties in the paths desired. It deprives them of contact with nature, in order to model them after its own pattern.

FRANCISCO FERRER, *The Modern School*, ca. 1909.

The teaching of reading—all over the United States, in all the schools, in all the text books—is totally wrong and flies in the face of all logic and common sense. Johnny couldn't read...for the simple reason that nobody ever showed him how. Johnny's only problem was that he was unfortunately exposed to an ordinary American school.

RUDOLF FLESCH, *Why Johnny Can't Read*, 1955.

We call our schools free because we are not free to stay away from them until we are sixteen years of age.

ROBERT FROST, Introduction, *Collected Poems*, 1939.

The school is a place or institution for teaching and learning.

Underneath this definition in every standard dictionary is another definition: School is a large number of fish of the same kind swimming together in the same direction.

HARRY GOLDEN, *Ess, Ess, Mein Kindt*, 1966.

It is one thing when business is interested in young people as students. Quite another when they are interested in students as consumers. It is one thing when the marketplace supports the schools. Quite another when the schools become a marketplace.

ELLEN GOODMAN, "Commercials in the Classroom," March, 1989, *Making Sense*, 1989.

One of the things that is manifestly wrong with our school system is our thoughtless practice of hiring and assigning the youngest and the least

experienced teachers for the lowest classes, when it should be quite the other way around.

SYDNEY HARRIS, *Detroit Free Press*, July 15, 1981.

The massive failure in basic skills—particularly reading and writing—is nothing short of scandalous.

FRED M. HECHINGER, *New York Times*, 1977.

In American society, the university is traditionally considered to be a psychosocial moratorium, an ivory tower where you withdraw from the problems of society and the world around you to work on important things like your career and your marriage.

ABBIE HOFFMAN, speech, University of South Carolina, September 16, 1987.

Academic education is the act of memorizing things read in books, and things told by college professors who got their education mostly by memorizing things read in books.

ELBERT HUBBARD, *Note Book*, 1927.

A kind of state-supported baby-sitting service.

GERALD KENNEDY, on schools, *Time*, April 11, 1960.

If the schools and universities have failed in their task over the last two decades, it is because their employers (i.e., the society as a whole) neither wished nor expected them to succeed. What in heaven's name did the society want with people who knew how to think?

LEWIS H. LAPHAM, "Multiple Choice," *Washington Post*, February, 1982.

The schools are in terrible shape....What has long been an ignored material problem, Sputnik has made a recognized crisis. [The] spartan Soviet system is producing many students better equipped to cope with the technicalities of the Space Age.

Editorial, *Life*, 1958.

The school, like the factory, is a thoroughly regimented world.

ROBERT S. LYND and HELEN MERRELL LYND, *Middletown: A Study in Contemporary American Culture*, 1929.

What the school wants first from any child, whatever the psychologists say, is that he gets his work done—if only because children who don't work tend to employ their spare time by making mischief.

MARTIN MAYER, *The Schools*, 1961.

In pursuit of an educational program to suit the bright and the not-so-bright we have watered down a rigid training for the elite until we now have an educational diet in many of our public high schools that nourishes neither the classes nor the masses.

AGNES MEYER, *Out of These Roots*, 1953.

The New York school system was at that time [early 1900s] wonderful in many respects. For example, it took these immigrant boys and turned them into Republicans. We became very patriotic.

I.I. RABI, in Jeremy Bernstein, *Experiencing Science*, 1978.

The ladder was there "from the gutter to the university," and for those stalworth enough to ascend it, the schools were a boon and a path out of poverty.

DIANE RAVITCH, *The Great School Wars*, 1974.

I am beginning to suspect all elaborate and special systems of education. They seem to me to be built upon the supposition that every child is a kind of idiot who must be taught to think.

Whereas, if the child is left to himself, he will think more and better.

ANNE SULLIVAN, in Helen Keller, *The Story of My Life*, 1903.

When I was a boy on the Mississippi River there was a proposition in a township there to discontinue public schools because they were too expensive. An old farmer spoke up and said if they stopped the schools they would not save anything, because every time a school was closed a jail had to be built.

MARK TWAIN, speech, Public Education Association, New York, November 23, 1900.

The Founding Fathers...in their wisdom decided that children were an unnatural strain on parents. So they provided jails called schools, equipped with tortures called an education. School is where you go between when your parents can't take you and industry can't take you.

JOHN UPDIKE, *The Centaur*, 1963.

Ethics and Morality

See also **American Society; Business; Government and Politics**—Political Philosophies, Scandals; **Law and Justice; Science and Technology; Sports; War and Peace**

It is well to remind ourselves, from time to time, that "Ethics" is but another word for "righteousness," that for which many men and women of every generation have hungered and thirsted, and without which life becomes meaningless.

JANE ADDAMS, Introduction, *Democracy and Social Ethics*, 1902.

An exaggerated personal morality is often mistaken for a social morality, and until it attempts to minister to a social situation its total inadequacy is not discovered. To attempt to attain a social morality without a basis of democratic experience results in the loss of the only possible corrective and guide, and ends in an exaggerated individual morality but not in social morality at all.

JANE ADDAMS, "Industrial Amelioration," *Democracy and Social Ethics*, 1902.

When the entire moral energy of an individual goes into the cultivation of personal integrity, we all know how unlovely the result may become; the character is upright, of course, but too coated over with the result of its own endeavor to be attractive.

JANE ADDAMS, "Political Reform," *Democracy and Social Ethics*, 1902.

Charity, as if it didn't have enough trouble in this day and age, will always be suspected of morbidity—sado-masochism, perversity of some sort. All higher or moral tendencies lie under suspicion of being rackets. Things we simply honor with old words, but betray or deny in our very nerves.

SAUL BELLOW, *Herzog*, 1964.

If I'm elected, at the end of four years or eight years I hope people will say, "You know, Jimmy Carter made a lot of mistakes, but he never told me a lie."

JIMMY CARTER, interview with Bill Moyers, May 6, 1976.

When morality comes up against profit, it is seldom that profit loses.

SHIRLEY CHISHOLM, *Unbought and Unbossed*, 1970.

It is a duty we cannot shirk to point to the true ideal, to chastity, to a single standard of morals for men and women.

JOSEPHUS DANIELS, memorandum to U.S. naval commanders, February 27, 1915.

People are very inclined to set moral standards for others.

ELIZABETH DREW, *The New Yorker*, February 16, 1987.

To justify Christian morality because it provides a foundation of morality, instead of showing the necessity of Christian morality from the truth of Christianity, is a very dangerous inversion.

T.S. ELIOT, *The Idea of a Christian Society*, 1940.

[Americans] are an obsessively moral people, but our morality is a team morality.

EDGAR Z. FRIEDENBERG, "The Impact of the School," *The Vanishing Adolescent*, 1959.

Only science can hope to keep technology in some sort of moral order.

EDGAR Z. FRIEDENBERG, "The Impact of the School," *The Vanishing Adolescent*, 1959.

There is much cant in American moralism and not a little inconsistency.

J. WILLIAM FULBRIGHT, speech to U.S. Senate, March 25, 1964.

The biggest lesson I learned from Vietnam is not to trust [our own] government statements. I had no idea until then that you could not rely on [them].

J. WILLIAM FULBRIGHT, *New York Times*, April 30, 1985.

Corruption of politics has nothing to do with the morals, or the laxity of morals, of various political personalities. Its cause is altogether a material one.

EMMA GOLDMAN, "The Tragedy of Women's Emancipation," *Anarchism and Other Essays*, 1911.

The new [bio] technology allows us to imitate the act of creation in a laboratory petri dish. But it has devised no biogenetic way to resolve everyday human conflicts. We are left to sweep up after the new technology.

ELLEN GOODMAN, "A Custody Fight for an Egg," *Washington Post*, March, 1989.

We are at ease with a moral judgment made against someone's private sin—lust or greed. We are much less comfortable judging someone's public ethic—those decisions that can lead to such outcomes as aggression, the abuse of the environment, the neglect of the needy.

ELLEN GOODMAN, "A Price Tag on Ethics," *Washington Post*, April, 1989.

America will tolerate the taking of human life without giving it a second thought. But don't misuse a household pet.

DICK GREGORY, *The Shadow That Scares Me*, 1968.

There are two classes of moralists: those who seek to improve the quality of other people's lives, and those who are content to improve their own.

PAUL GRUCHOW, *Our Sustainable Table*, 1990.

Nothing is so terrifying as a demonstration of principle.

PAUL GRUCHOW, *Our Sustainable Table*, 1990.

Moral perfection in death is a luxury most men can do without.

GARRETT HARDIN, *Exploring New Ethics for Survival*, 1972.

We were brought up with the value that as we sow, so shall we reap. We discarded the idea that anything we did was its own reward.

JANET HARRIS, *The Prime of Ms. America*, 1975.

It doesn't pay well to fight for what we believe in.

LILLIAN HELLMAN, *Watch on the Rhine*, 1941.

I did what my conscience told me to, and you can't fail when you do that.

ANITA HILL, interview, "60 Minutes," CBS-TV, February 2, 1992.

When there is a lack of honor in government, the morals of the whole people are poisoned.

HERBERT HOOVER, *New York Times*, August 9, 1964.

When a fellow says it hain't the money but the principle o' the thing, it's th' money.

KIN HUBBARD, *Hoss Sense and Nonsense*, 1926.

There are plenty of recommendations on how to get out of trouble cheaply and fast. Most of them come down to this: Deny your responsibility.

LYNDON B. JOHNSON, Democratic fund-raiser, September 30, 1967.

[Conscience] is the voice of our ideal self, our complete self, our real self, laying its call upon the will.

RUFUS JONES, *The Nature and Authority of Conscience*, 1920.

Personal virtue is a good in itself, but it is not a sufficient means to the end of good government.

JEANE KIRKPATRICK, speech, Washington, D.C., September 29, 1982.

To "play the game" is the current version of accepting the universe, and protest is blasphemy; the good man has given place to the "good sport."

FRANK H. KNIGHT, "The Ethics of Competition," *Quarterly Journal of Economics*, August, 1923.

A scientist...shouldn't be asked to judge the economic and moral value of his work. All we should ask the scientist to do is find the truth—and then not keep it from anyone.

ARTHUR KORNBERG, *San Francisco Examiner & Chronicle*, December 19, 1971.

Post-Watergate morality, by which anything left private is taken as presumptive evidence of wrongdoing.

CHARLES KRAUTHAMMER, "Pietygate: School for Scandal," *Time*, September 10, 1984.

He was nimble in the calling of selling houses for more than people could afford to pay.

SINCLAIR LEWIS, *Babbitt*, 1922.

Morality, if it is not fixed by custom and authority, becomes a mere matter of taste determined by the idiosyncrasies of the moralist.

WALTER LIPPMANN, *A Preface to Morals*, 1929.

It is never right to compromise with dishonesty.

HENRY CABOT LODGE, JR., conversation with Republican leaders, 1952, in Richard Norton Smith, *Thomas E. Dewey and His Times*, 1982.

Morality is not an imposition removed from life and reason; it is a compendium of the minimum of sacrifices necessary for man to live in company with other men, without suffering too much or causing others to suffer.

GINA LOMBROSO, *The Tragedies of Progress*, 1931.

I know what I have done, and Your Honor knows what I have done....Somewhere between my ambition and my ideals, I lost my ethical compass.

JEB STUART MAGRUDER, Watergate investigation, *Time*, June 3, 1974.

Science by itself has no moral dimension. But it does seek to establish truth. And upon this truth morality can be built.

WILLIAM H. MASTERS, *Life*, June 24, 1966.

Every generation has the privilege of standing on the shoulders of the generation that went before; but it has no right to pick the pockets of the first-comer.

BRANDER MATTHEWS, *Recreations of an Anthologist*, 1904.

Conscience is the inner voice which warns us that someone may be looking.

H.L. MENCKEN, "Sententiae," *The Vintage Mencken*, 1955.

We create an environment where it is alright to hate, to steal, to cheat, and to lie if we dress it up with symbols of respectability, dignity and love.

WHITNEY MOORE, JR., *To Be Equal*, 1964.

I owe the public nothing.

JOHN PIERPONT MORGAN, in Matthew Josephson, *The Robber Barons*, 1934.

Science cannot resolve moral conflicts, but it can help to more accurately frame the debates about those conflicts.

HEINZ PAGELS, *The Dreams of Reason*, 1988.

Morality, including political morality, has to do with the definition of right *conduct*, and this not simply by way of the ends of action. *How* we do *what* we do is as important as our goals.

PAUL RAMSEY, *War and the Christian Conscience*, 1961.

We do many things at the federal level that would be considered dishonest and illegal if done in the private sector.

DONALD T. REGAN, *New York Times*, August 25, 1986.

Conscience is the voice of values long and deeply infused into one's sinew and blood.

ELLIOT L. RICHARDSON, *Life* Special Report, 1973.

I learned years ago not to doze off or leave my wallet lying around in the presence of people who tell me that they are more moral than others.

CARL T. ROWAN, "In the Name of Morality," *Washington Star*, October 17, 1980.

A mental possession of ours which enables us to pass some sort of judgment, correct or mistaken, upon moral questions as they arise...your conscience is simply that ideal of life which constitutes your moral personality.

JOSIAH ROYCE, *The Philosophy of Loyalty*, 1908.

Science cannot stop while ethics catches up... and nobody should expect scientists to do all the thinking for the country.

ELVIN STACKMAN, *Life*, January 9, 1950.

You are so afraid of losing your moral sense that you are not willing to take it through anything more dangerous than a mud-puddle.

GERTRUDE STEIN, "Q.E.D.," 1903, *Fernhurst, Q.E.D., and Other Early Writings*, 1972.

It is a paradox of the acquisitive society in which we now live that although private morals are regulated by law, the entrepreneur is allowed considerable freedom to use—and abuse—the public in order to make money. The American pursuit of happiness might be less desperate if the situation were reversed.

GORE VIDAL, "A Manifesto," *Esquire*, October, 1968.

In civilized life, law floats in a sea of ethics.

EARL WARREN, *New York Times*, November 12, 1962.

Our whole free dynamic society's future depends upon a continued growth of our sense of responsibility and morality in direct proportion to the increase in our material wealth.

WALTER H. WHEELER, in Arthur Goodfriend, *What Is America?*, 1954.

Political principles are like split needles. They make it risky to step or sit.

GEORGE WILL, "Government by 'The People,'" October 18, 1976, *The Pursuit of Happiness, and Other Sobering Thoughts*, 1978.

Food and Drink

See also **Children and Youth, Holidays; Popular Culture**—Fads and Fashions, Life-styles; **Social Issues**—Health, Poverty and Hunger; **Work**—Homemakers

You eat it, usually sitting in a booth in a bare, plain restaurant, with a mural of Vesuvio on the wall, a jukebox, and a crowded bar. The customers are Italian families, Bohemians, lovers, and—if a college is nearby—students and faculty members.
On pizza, *Atlantic Monthly*, 1949.

The French fried potato has become an inescapable horror in almost every public eating place in the country. "French fries," say the menus, but they are not French fries any longer. They are a furry-textured substance with the taste of plastic wood.
RUSSELL BAKER, "Observer," *New York Times*, February 22, 1968.

You can't drown yourself in drink. I've tried: you float.
JOHN BARRYMORE, conversation with playwright Ashton Stevens, in Gene Fowler, *Good Night, Sweet Prince*, 1943.

Food is our common ground, a universal experience.
JAMES BEARD, *Beard on Food*, 1974.

Let's get out of these wet clothes and into a dry martini.
ROBERT BENCHLEY, in Robert E. Drennan, *The Algonquin Wits*, 1968.

Wine, n. Fermented grape-juice known to the Women's Christian Temperance Union as "liquor," sometimes as "rum." Wine, madam, is God's next best gift to man.
AMBROSE BIERCE, *The Devil's Dictionary*, 1906.

Chili's a lot like sex: When it's good it's great, and even when it's bad, it's not so bad.
BILL BOLDENWECK, *American Way*, June, 1982.

I doubt whether the world holds for any one a more soul-stirring surprise than the first adventure with ice-cream.
HEYWOOD BROUN, "Holding a Baby," *Seeing Things at Night*, 1921.

Drunkenness is a joy reserved for the gods: so men do partake of it impiously, and so they are very properly punished for their audacity.
JAMES BRANCH CABELL, *Jurgen*, 1919.

Food, one assumes, provides nourishment; but Americans eat it fully aware that small amounts of poison have been added to improve its appearance and delay its putrefaction.
JOHN CAGE, "Indeterminacy," *Silence*, 1961.

Eat plenty of garlic. This guarantees you twelve hours of sleep—alone—every night, and there's nothing like rest to give you shining orbs (poetic), peepers (colloquial) or lamps (slang). A diet of potatoes and garlic leaves you oodles of time for reading *Roget's Thesaurus in Dictionary Form* too.
CHRIS CHASE, *How To Be a Movie Star, or A Terrible Beauty Is Born*, 1968.

Fake food—I mean those patented substances chemically flavored and mechanically bulked out to kill the appetite and deceive the gut—is unnatural, almost immoral, a bane to good eating and good cooking.
JULIA CHILD, *Julia Child and Company*, 1978.

I just hate health food.
JULIA CHILD, *San Francisco*, August, 1983.

Man is born to eat.
CRAIG CLAIBORNE, *Craig Claiborne's Kitchen Primer*, 1969.

I'm at the age where food has taken the place of sex in my life. In fact, I've just had a mirror put over my kitchen table.
RODNEY DANGERFIELD, *New York*, May 5, 1980.

[Whiskey] doesn't sustain life, but, whin taken hot with wather, a lump iv sugar, a piece iv lemon peel, and just th' dustin' iv the nutmeg-grater, it makes life sustainable.
FINLEY PETER DUNNE, *Mr. Dooley's Philosophy*, 1900.

Alcohol is nicissary f'r a man so that now an' thin he can have a good opinion iv himself, ondisturbed be th' facts.
FINLEY PETER DUNNE, "Mr. Dooley on Alcohol," *Chicago Tribune*, April 26, 1914.

Cheese—milk's leap toward immortality.
CLIFTON FADIMAN, *Any Number Can Play*, 1957.

There is no such thing as bad whiskey. Some whiskeys just happen to be better than others. But a man shouldn't fool with booze until he's fifty; then he's a damn fool if he doesn't.

WILLIAM FAULKNER, in J.R. Cofield, "Many Faces, Many Moods," in James W. Webb and A. Wigfall Green, *William Faulkner of Oxford*, 1965.

Roast Beef, Medium, is not only a food. It is a philosophy. Seated at Life's Dining Table, with the menu of Morals before you, your eye wanders a bit over the entrees, the hors d'oeuvres, and the things *a la* though you know that Roast Beef, Medium, is safe and sane, and sure.

EDNA FERBER, *Roast Beef, Medium*, 1911.

I exercise extreme self-control. I never drink anything stronger than gin before breakfast.

W.C. FIELDS, in Robert Lewis Taylor, *W.C. Fields, His Follies and Fortunes*, 1949.

I never drank anything stronger than beer before I was twelve.

W.C. FIELDS, in Robert Lewis Taylor, *W.C. Fields, His Follies and Fortunes*, 1949.

The advantages of whiskey over dogs are legion. Whiskey does not need to be periodically wormed, it does not need to be fed, it never requires a special kennel, it has no toenails to be clipped or coat to be stripped. Whiskey sits quietly in its special nook until you want it. True, whiskey has a nasty habit of running out, but then so does a dog.

W.C. FIELDS, in Ronald J. Fields, *W.C. Fields by Himself*, 1973.

A complete lack of caution is perhaps one of the true signs of a real gourmet: he has no need for it, being filled as he is with a God-given and intelligently self-cultivated sense of gastronomical freedom.

M.F.K. FISHER, "C Is for Cautious," *An Alphabet for Gourmets*, 1949.

The agribusiness moguls end up spending enormous time and energy in order to create and distribute a strain of corn suitable for starching shirts, a cantaloupe useful for bowling and an entire orange shotput collection. We have more and more fruits and vegetables whose only claim to life is their shelf life. Color them plastic.

ELLEN GOODMAN, "Time and the Tomato," *Washington Post*, August, 1987.

All happiness depends on a leisurely breakfast.

JOHN GUNTHER, *Newsweek*, April 14, 1958.

I decided to stop drinking with creeps.
I decided to drink only with friends.
I've lost 30 pounds.

ERNEST HEMINGWAY, *American Way*, August, 1974.

There is something in the red of a raspberry pie that looks as good to a man as the red in a sheep looks to a wolf.

EDGAR WATSON HOWE, *Sinner Sermons*, 1926.

Wine: An infallible antidote to commonsense and seriousness; an excuse for deeds otherwise unforgivable.

ELBERT HUBBARD, *The Roycroft Dictionary and Book of Epigrams*, 1923.

A salad is not a meal. It is a style.

FRAN LEBOWITZ, *Metropolitan Life*, 1974.

Technological innovation has done great damage not only to reading habits but also to eating habits. Food is now available in such unpleasant forms that one frequently finds smoking between courses to be an aid to the digestion.

FRAN LEBOWITZ, *Metropolitan Life*, 1974.

Breakfast cereals that come in the same colors as polyester leisure suits make oversleeping a virtue.

FRAN LEBOWITZ, *Metropolitan Life*, 1974.

Thoroughly distasteful as synthetic foods might be, one cannot help but accord them a certain value when confronted with the health food buff. One is also ever mindful of the fact that the aficionado of whole food is a frequent champion of excessive political causes.

FRAN LEBOWITZ, *Metropolitan Life*, 1974.

Men do not knowingly drink for the effect alcohol produces on the body. What they drink for is the brain-effect; and if it must come through the body, so much the worse for the body.

JACK LONDON, *John Barleycorn*, 1913.

Only a rank degenerate would drive 1,500 miles across Texas without eating a chicken fried steak.

LARRY MCMURTRY, *In a Narrow Grave: Essays on Texas*, 1968.

I've made it a rule never to drink by daylight and never to refuse a drink after dark.

H.L. MENCKEN, *New York Post*, September 18, 1945.

Americans can eat garbage, provided you sprinkle it liberally with ketchup, mustard, chili sauce, Tabasco sauce, cayenne pepper, or any other condiment which destroys the original flavor of the dish.

HENRY MILLER, "The Staff of Life," *Remember to Remember*, 1947.

You can travel fifty thousand miles in America without once tasting a piece of good bread.

HENRY MILLER, "The Staff of Life," *Remember to Remember*, 1947.

There aint gonna be no whiskey; there aint
  gonna be no gin;
There aint gonna be no highball to put the
  whiskey in;
There aint gonna be no cigarettes to make
  folks pale and thin;
But you can't take away the tendency to sin,
  sin, sin.

VAUGHN MILLER, "There Ain't Gonna Be No Whiskey," 1919.

Candy
  is dandy
But liquor
  is quicker.

OGDEN NASH, "Reflection on Ice-Breaking," 1931, *I Wouldn't Have Missed It*, 1975.

I say it's spinach and I say the hell with it.

New Yorker cartoon of child refusing to eat broccoli, 1928.

I get no kick from champagne.
Mere alcohol doesn't thrill me at all.

COLE PORTER, song, "I Get a Kick Out of You," *Anything Goes*, 1934.

Drink the first. Sip the second slowly. Skip the third.

KNUTE ROCKNE, in Jerry Brondfield, *Rockne*, 1976.

There are two things that will be believed of any man whatsoever, and one of them is that he has taken to drink.

BOOTH TARKINGTON, *Penrod*, 1914.

It's a naive domestic Burgundy without any breeding, but I think you'll be amused by its presumption.

JAMES THURBER, cartoon caption, *The New Yorker, Men, Women and Dogs*, 1944.

Seeing is deceiving. It's eating that's believing.

JAMES THURBER, *Further Fables for Our Time*, 1956.

My tongue is smiling.

ABIGAIL TRILLIN, ca. 1975, in Calvin Trillin, *Alice, Let's Eat*, 1978.

The sort of shrimp hidden under a pound and a half of batter on what Midwestern menus call "French-fried butterfly shrimp" could as easily be turnips.

CALVIN TRILLIN, "Confessions of a Crab Eater," *Alice, Let's Eat*, 1978.

Canned crabmeat tastes like Styrofoam.

CALVIN TRILLIN, "Confessions of a Crab Eater," *Alice, Let's Eat*, 1978.

Yes, I'll admit that I was relieved to find that there were still some pigeons left in the squares of San Francisco; it had occurred to me that since my previous visit, every last one of them might have been snatched up, smoked, and thrown on a bed of radicchio.

CALVIN TRILLIN, on California cuisine, "My Life in Wine," *The Nation*, April 27, 1985.

You've probably been wondering how they figure out just how many calories there are in, say, a four-ounce Italian sausage. I've been wondering the same thing. You may have been wondering about it for the same reason I've been wondering about it: maybe they're wrong. Maybe calculating calories is a science that is about as exact as handicapping horses.

CALVIN TRILLIN, "Calories May Not Count," King Features Syndicate, July 13, 1986.

Working solely from the evidence of what's presented to someone who orders Surf 'n' Turf in an American restaurant—a slab of red meat and a shellfish claw—I deducted that a surfnturf might be a tiny aquatic Hereford.

CALVIN TRILLIN, "Secrets of the Deep," King Features Syndicate, August 24, 1986.

Cooking is like love. It should be entered into with abandon or not at all.

HARRIET VAN HORNE, *Vogue*, October, 1956.

Foreign Views on Americans

The following quotations are from people who have observed the society and culture from outside and given their insights on the American character

Among the things Americans invented or improved is the poker game, financial shenanigans, the art of stock exchange speculation, the rackets, and...ingenious petty swindles.

LUIGI BARZINI, "Reflections 1972," 1972.

After 20 annual visits, I am still surprised each time to return to see this giant asparagus bed of alabaster and rose and green skyscrapers.

CECIL BEATON, on New York City, *It Gives Me Great Pleasure*, 1955.

Americans have an abiding belief in their ability to control reality by purely material means...airline insurance replaces the fear of death with the comforting prospect of cash.

CECIL BEATON, *It Gives Me Great Pleasure*, 1955.

Americans are not materialistic in the money sense: they are too generous and wasteful, too idealistic for that. Yet this idealism is curiously lacking in the spiritual values.

CECIL BEATON, *It Gives Me Great Pleasure*, 1955.

More and more in American restaurants, advertising has taken over the menu. You are sold on the meal before you have even started.

CECIL BEATON, *It Gives Me Great Pleasure*, 1955.

America is still the best hope. But the Americans themselves will have to be the best hope too.

JORGE LUIS BORGES, *Time*, July 5, 1976.

A people that has licked a more formidable enemy than Germany or Japan, primitive North America...a country whose national motto has been "root, hog, or die."

DENIS WILLIAM BROGAN, *The American Character*, 1944.

Any well-established village in New England or the Northern Middle West could afford a town drunkard, a town atheist, and a few Democrats.

DENIS WILLIAM BROGAN, *The American Character*, 1944.

The combination of a hatred of war and militarism with an innocent delight in playing soldiers is one of the apparent contradictions of American life that one has to accept.

DENIS WILLIAM BROGAN, *The American Character*, 1944.

The American idea of religion is that religion is very much this-worldly; that it is less a philosophical picture, it is a view of your duty here and now...of good works...of service.

DENIS WILLIAM BROGAN, in Arthur Goodfriend, *What Is America?*, 1954.

The American race seems to have developed two classes, and only two, the upper-middle, and the lower-middle.

RUPERT BROOKE, *Letters from America*, 1916.

The action of America upon the nerves and emotions of Europe is that of a power whose strength is known, but whose future course can only be guessed at. In a flash, she has expanded from a stay-at-home republic into a venturesome empire.

SYDNEY BROOKS, *Atlantic Monthly*, November, 1901.

America, on one level, is a great old-movie museum.

ANTHONY BURGESS, "David Susskind Show," January 4, 1976.

J.F.D. [John Foster Dulles] the wooliest type of useless pontificating American....Heaven help us!

ALEXANDER CADOGAN, diary entry, July 13, 1942.

The jean! The jean is the destructor! It is a dictator! It is destroying creativity. The jean must be stopped!

PIERRE CARDIN, *People*, June 28, 1976.

America is so terribly grim in spite of all that material prosperity....Compassion and the old neighborliness are gone, people stand by and do nothing when friends and neighbors are attacked, libeled and ruined.

CHARLES CHAPLIN, 1953, in Lois and Alan Gordon, *American Chronicle*, 1987.

America has a new delicacy, a coarse, rank refinement.

G.K. CHESTERTON, *Charles Dickens*, 1906.

There is nothing the matter with Americans except their ideals. The real American is all right; it is the ideal American who is all wrong.

G.K. CHESTERTON, *New York Times*, February 1, 1931.

I might express it somewhat abruptly by saying that most Americans are born drunk, and really require a little wine or beer to sober them. They have a sort of permanent intoxication from within, a sort of invisible champagne....Americans do not need to drink to inspire them to do anything, though they do sometimes, I think, need a little for the deeper and more delicate purpose of teaching them how to do nothing.

G.K. CHESTERTON, *New York Times*, June 28, 1931.

Meeting Franklin Roosevelt was like opening your first bottle of champagne: knowing him was like drinking it.

WINSTON CHURCHILL, recalled on his death, January 24, 1965.

I always seem to get inspiration and renewed vitality by contact with this great novel land of yours which sticks up out of the Atlantic.

WINSTON CHURCHILL, to Richard M. Nixon, Washington D.C., 1954, *RN: Memoirs of Richard Nixon*, 1978.

You simply cannot hang a millionaire in America.

BOURKE COCKRAN, in Shane Leslie, *American Wonderland*, 1936.

It is all part of the America tragedy—that, in the one remaining country where necessities are cheap, where a room and food and wine and clothes and cigarettes and travel are within everyone's reach, to be poor is still disgraceful. The American way of life is one of the most effective the world has known, but about the end of life Americans are more in the dark than any people since the Gauls of Tacitus.

CYRIL CONNOLLY, "American Injection," *Ideas and Places*, 1947.

Newport [Rhode Island] had once been a haven for religious dissenters out of Massachusetts and later a capital port of the slave trade. One hundred years after the Declaration that "all men are created equal," there began to gather in Newport a colony

of the rich, determined to show that some Americans were conspicuously more equal than others.

ALISTAIR COOKE, *America*, 1973.

Where the West begins depends when you asked the question. In the nineteenth century Charles Dickens got no farther than St. Louis, nine hundred miles short even of the Rockies. He went home convinced he had seen the West, and he declared it to be a fraud.

ALISTAIR COOKE, *America*, 1973.

As always, the British especially shudder at the latest American vulgarity, and then they embrace it with enthusiasm two years later.

ALISTAIR COOKE, *American Way*, March, 1975.

It would be difficult to tear myself away from these splendid visions of hope; and yet I know their wiles. In America, life also ebbs away in the effort to survive.

SIMONE DE BEAUVOIR, *America Day by Day*, 1953.

This is the source of the sadness that I often felt when with them [Americans]. This world full of generous promise crushes them, and its splendor soon appears barren, for no one controls it.

SIMONE DE BEAUVOIR, *America Day by Day*, 1953.

There is and has long been—perhaps this is something of a boast on my part, but I say it as I feel it—there has been a special bond between New York and me....How often, at difficult moments, I looked to New York, I listened to New York, to find out what you were thinking and feeling here, and always I found a comforting echo.

CHARLES DE GAULLE, *New York Times*, April 27, 1960.

Roosevelt, a false witness; Truman, a merchant; Eisenhower, I am told that on the golf links he is better [with a putter] than he is with the long shots and that doesn't surprise me; Kennedy, the style of a hairdresser's assistant—he combed his way through problems; Johnson, a truck driver or a stevedore—or a legionnaire.

CHARLES DE GAULLE, *Time*, February, 1969.

[John Kennedy] died as a soldier under fire, doing his duty in the service of his country.

CHARLES DE GAULLE, 1963, in Lois and Alan Gordon, *American Chronicle*, 1987.

The American language differs from English in that it seeks the top of expression while English seeks its lowly valleys.

SALVADOR DE MADARIAGA, *Americans*, 1930.

The United States brags about its political system, but the president says one thing during the election, something else when he takes office, something else at midterm and something else when he leaves.

DENG XIAOPING, in John F. Burns, "Deng Asserts Ties to West Are Vital to Fight Poverty," *New York Times*, January 2, 1985.

Is the U.S. a great power—or merely a large country?

Editorial, *Dong-A Ilbo* (South Korean newspaper), February, 1968.

The thing that impresses me most about America is the way parents obey their children.

DUKE OF WINDSOR, *Look*, March 5, 1957.

From the moment of its discovery...America has been, sometimes quite literally, the creation of European wishful thinking.

J. MARTIN EVANS, *America: The View From Europe*, 1976.

The Americans provide themselves with the best-equipped kitchens in the world, but when the weather permits—or as often as not, when it does not permit—they abandon them, to cook and eat in conditions of unspeakable discomfort, by a method of which the masters could be counted on a single hand.

HENRY FAIRLIE, "An American Ordeal—The Barbecue," *Manchester Guardian Weekly*, August 1, 1976.

The true mark of American society is an informality which itself forms its own patterns and codes. Although the outsider at first cannot detect it, there is a rhythm to American life. This rhythm is a constant improvisation, a flexibility that will accommodate the wishes and whims of every member of a group. No voice in an American family takes precedence over the rest.

HENRY FAIRLIE, "An American Ordeal—The Barbecue," *Manchester Guardian Weekly*, August 1, 1976.

The American aversion to meals...is not really an aversion to food. As every statistic shows, Americans consume vast quantities of food. They merely parcel their food into things that can be eaten with the hand.

HENRY FAIRLIE, "An American Ordeal—The Barbecue," *Manchester Guardian Weekly*, August 1, 1976.

America is rather like life. You can usually find in it what you look for....It will probably be interesting, and it is sure to be large.

E.M. FORSTER, "The United States," *Two Cheers for Democracy*, 1951.

What distinguishes America is not its greater or lesser goodness, but simply its unrivalled power to do that which is good or bad.

MARK FRANKLAND, *London Observer*, November 6, 1977.

Americans have always been eager for travel, that being how they got to the New World in the first place.

OTTO FRIEDRICH, *Time*, April 22, 1985.

Any time, anywhere around the world, that a man sets out a few rows of chairs, hangs up a white sheet, turns down the lights, switches on a projector, and keeps a few hundred of his fellow men enthralled for a couple of hours, the Americans will be gratefully saluted for having invented it—the best, the biggest, the most delightful business of them all: show business.

DAVID FROST, *The Americans*, 1970.

What the United States does best is to understand itself. What it does worst is understand others.

CARLOS FUENTES, *Time*, June 16, 1986.

All benefits have been poured out upon America and America is using them as a cheerful prodigal; America is conscious of her good fortune and that is why she can afford the manifestation of pride which is called democracy.

W.L. GEORGE, *Hail Columbia!*, 1923.

The whole trend of American civilization is toward stressing the human factor; indeed, the word "human" (in the sense of "friendly") is used in no other part of the English-speaking countries.

W.L. GEORGE, *Hail Columbia!*, 1923.

America delights in tradition, and destroys it as she goes. She hates the thing she respects, burns the god that she worships.

W.L. GEORGE, *Hail Columbia!*, 1923.

American hospitality will explain the difference between watermelon, honeydew, and casaba, while English hospitality consists of letting the lunch lie about for you to eat if you like.

W.L. GEORGE, *Hail Columbia!*, 1923.

I judge that the American is more interested in getting drunk than in drinking.

GIUSEPPE GIACOSA, *Impressioni d'America*, 1908.

The most characteristic thing in America, mechanical America, is that it can make poetry out of material things. America's poetry is not in literature, but in architecture.

OLIVER ST. JOHN GOGARTY, *As I Was Going Down Sackville Street*, 1937.

The glass-walled office skyscrapers soar into the clear air, transparent by day, an illuminated fairyland by night....It seems as if such transparency has also a symbolic significance. It is a demonstration to all the world that nothing wrong, nothing subversive is going on inside this glass case, everything is quite literally open and above board....[These buildings] are shining symbols of the soaring, aspiring, transparent integrity which Americans like to think—and not without justification—is their most praiseworthy characteristic.

GEOFFREY GORER, *The American People*, 1964.

We have all learnt America in picture theatres; and it is distinctly unfortunate that we have learnt it wrong.

PHILIP GUEDALLA, *Conquistador*, 1927.

The Americans do not build walls around their houses. The humblest pedestrian going afoot through the suburbs of Philadelphia, Indianapolis, or any other city, sees not only the houses but anything in the way of a view which lies beyond them.

JAMES HANNEY, *From Dublin to Chicago*, 1914.

My American friends have gained insights about the human mechanism they may never have come by if they had not needed to ask the most rudimentary questions about love and anger and sex. Their explorations are a road to a new, instead of an ancestral, wisdom—a wisdom that may be awkward and ungainly, as youthful wisdom is, but that is required in a world whose social, if not physical, frontiers are still fluid and open and incompletely charted.

EVA HOFFMAN, *Lost in Translation*, 1989.

On my visits to America I discovered that the old Marxist dictum "From each according to his abilities, to each according to his needs," was probably more in force in America, that holy of holies of capitalism, than in any other country in the world.

FELIX HOUPHOUET-BOIGNY, *Newsweek*, August 9, 1965.

Those who remain will be a few insane or semi-insane soldiers who had escaped the furnace of battle...to tell generations about the harm inflicted on them by Bush's insistence on aggression and his false pride and empty arrogance.

INA, Iraqi news agency, *Boston Globe*, December 26, 1990.

The Americans burn incense before it [democracy], but they are themselves ruled by the Boss and the Trust.

WILLIAM RALPH INGE, "Our Present Discontents," *Outspoken Essays: First Series*, 1919.

California is a tragic country—like Palestine, like every Promised Land.

CHRISTOPHER ISHERWOOD, *Exhumations*, 1966.

Though a man of decisive mind in immediate issues, General Eisenhower is far too easily swayed and diverted to be a great commander-in-chief.

IAN JACOB, diary entry, December 12, 1942.

Every Westerner has, in a sense, two countries: the country of his heart, his origin, his language, his ancestors, and one that is the sure foundation of his political reality. Those fatherlands are many, but this foundation is today only one: The United States of America.

KARL JASPERS, *The Future of Mankind*, 1961.

All I would ask of Americans is that you go on being yourselves—valiant without being fanatical, individualistic without being foolhardy, skeptical without being cynical, open-minded without being indecisive, generous without being naive, patriotic without being nationalistic, and good without being perfect!

PETER JAY, *New York Times*, October 12, 1977.

Americans...are not only hospitable in emergency but radiant. The most lavishly helpful people in the world, accepting the burden of nuisances as if they were bunches of hothouse flowers, all the more delightful because unexpected.

PAMELA HANSFORD JOHNSON, *Night and Silence: Who Is Here?*, 1963.

The most amazing feature of American life is its boundless publicity. Everybody has to meet everybody, and they even seem to enjoy this enormity.

C.G. JUNG, *The Complications of American Psychology*, 1930.

America is fundamentally the land of the overrated child.

HERMANN KEYSERLING, *America Set Free*, 1929.

We have beaten you to the moon, but you have beaten us in sausage making.

NIKITA S. KHRUSHCHEV, Des Moines, Iowa, 1959, in Lois and Alan Gordon, *American Chronicle*, 1987.

When I was a graduate student at Harvard, I learned about showers and central heating. Ten years later, I learned about breakfast meetings. These are America's three contributions to civilization.

MERVYN A. KING, *New York Times*, March 4, 1987.

When I first arrived in the States a shrewd American said to me: "A European coming to America for the first time, should skip New York and fly directly to Kansas. Start from the Middle. The East will only mislead you."

LORD KINROSS, *The Innocents at Home*, 1959.

California is a queer place—in a way, it has turned its back on the world, and looks into the void Pacific. It is absolutely selfish, very empty, but not false, and at least, not full of false effort.

D.H. LAWRENCE, letter to J.M. Murphy, September 24, 1923.

Perhaps you have to be born an Englishwoman to realize how much attention American men shower on women and how tremendously considerate all the nice ones among them are of a woman's wishes.

GERTRUDE LAWRENCE, *A Star Danced*, 1945.

The Americans are a queer people; they can't rest.

STEPHEN LEACOCK, in Fred J. Ringel, *America as Others See It*, 1932.

The American sign of civic progress is to tear down the familiar and erect the monstrous.

SHANE LESLIE, *American Wonderland*, 1936.

I don't think they're brash, that's a stereotype from the past, the Americans these days are cool and shut off, they've got glass or ice between them and the rest of the world.

DORIS LESSING, *Golden Notebook*, 1962.

America is the last abode of romance and other medieval phenomena.

ERIC LINKLATER, *Juan in America*, 1931.

"There won't be any revolution in America," said Isadore. Niktin agreed. "The people are all too clean. They spend all their time changing their shirts and washing themselves. You can't feel fierce and revolutionary in a bathroom."

ERIC LINKLATER, *Juan in America*, 1931.

In this realm of Mammon and Moloch everything has a value—except human life.

COUNT VAY DE VAYA UND ZU LUSKOD, *Inner Life of the United States*, 1908.

Work in the United States is everything, and everything has become work.

COUNT VAY DE VAYA UND ZU LUSKOD, *Inner Life of the United States*, 1908.

[New York is] humanity in microcosm, reflecting the infinite variety as well as the infinite capacity for good or evil of the human race.

DIOSDADO MACAPAGAL, on visit to United States, 1964.

It is a peculiar business, the American attitude to Antiquity. Of all the citizens of the world there is no one so alive as the American to the values of modernity, so fertile in experiment, so feverish in the search for something new. There is nothing, from Architecture to Contract Bridge, from the Immortality of the Soul to the Ventilation of Railroad-Cars, from Golf to God that he does not pounce upon and examine critically to see if it cannot be improved. And then, having pulled it to pieces, mastered its fundamental theory, and reassembled it in a novel and efficient design, he laments bitterly because it is not old.

A.G. MACDONELL, *A Visit to America*, 1935.

Americans seem sometimes to believe that if you are a thinker you must be a frowning bore, because thinking is so damn serious.

JACQUES MARITAIN, *Reflections on America*, 1958.

Congress is so strange. A man gets up to speak and says nothing. Nobody listens—and then everybody disagrees.

BORIS MARSHALOV, *Reader's Digest*, March, 1941.

The Americans, who are the most efficient people on earth...have invented so wide a range of pithy and hackneyed phrases that they can carry on an amusing and animated conversation without giving a moment's reflection to what they are saying and so leave their minds free to consider the more important matters of big business and fornication.

W. SOMERSET MAUGHAM, *Cakes and Ale*, 1930.

When you consider how indifferent Americans are to the quality and cooking of the food they put into their insides, it cannot but strike you as peculiar that they should take such pride in the mechanical appliances they use for its excretion.

W. SOMERSET MAUGHAM, *A Writer's Notebook*, 1949.

Things on the whole move much faster in America; people don't *stand for election*, they *run for office*. If a person says he's *sick*, it doesn't mean regurgitating; it means *ill*. *Mad* means angry, not *insane*. Don't ask for the left-luggage; it's called a check-room. A nice joint means a good pub, not roast meat.

JESSICA MITFORD, *Daughters and Rebels*, 1960.

From seeing *The Petrified Forest*, I gathered that Americans often made love under tables while gangster bullets whizzed through the air.

JESSICA MITFORD, "Emigration," *Daughters and Rebels*, 1960.

Americans relate all effort, all work, and all of life itself to the dollar. Their talk is of nothing but dollars. The English seldom sit happily chatting for hours on end about pounds. In England, public business is its own reward, nobody would go into Parliament in order to become rich, neither do riches bring public appointments.

NANCY MITFORD, *Noblesse Oblige*, 1956.

A European soldier, [Europeans complained in World War II] when he steals, will steal a package or even a carton of cigarettes. But Americans, nothing but a whole train and all of its contents will do!

ASHLEY MONTAGU, *The American Way of Life*, 1967.

There are men in America who on perceiving a green field or a meadow begin to slaver at the gills and, like Uriah Heep, start washing their hands with invisible soap at the contemplation of the thought, nay, the beautific vision, of a glorious development at the site.

ASHLEY MONTAGU, *The American Way of Life*, 1967.

In a land in which the tough guy is admired, politeness is widely considered to be effeminate.

ASHLEY MONTAGU, *The American Way of Life*, 1967.

Privacy is a reservation of civilized life which Americans do not cherish.

ASHLEY MONTAGU, *The American Way of Life*, 1967.

The United States is the greatest single achievement of European civilization.

ROBERT BALMAIN MOWAT, *The United States of America*, 1938.

[College students]...think that they, by being Americans, and well-to-do, bring privilege to what they touch....This vanity is becoming an empty caste arrogance. Ignorant people in preppy clothes are more dangerous to America than oil embargoes.

V.S. NAIPAUL, *New York Times*, December 21, 1981.

Americans don't have friends, they have interests.

Panamanian government official, "All Things Considered," National Public Radio, December 19, 1990.

America knew what it would be....For more than three centuries, the word "American" designated a man who was defined not by what he had done, but by what he would do.

OCTAVIO PAZ, "A Literature of Foundations," *Tri Quarterly*, 1968.

When something happens in America, the media cover every detail of the event: a Mafia scandal in New Jersey, with political implications; illegal betting on football games; the financial wheeling and dealing of a former secretary to the Senate Majority. There is never any "Mr. X." Names are given, and photographs, and details about the crime, and the amounts of money involved.

JEAN-FRANÇOIS REVEL, *Without Marx or Jesus*, 1970.

It is impossible to read in America, except in the train, because of the telephone. Everyone has a telephone, and it rings all day and most of the night. This makes conversation, thinking, and reading out of the question, and accordingly these activities are somewhat neglected.

BERTRAND RUSSELL, *Impressions of America*, 1924.

In America...where law and custom alike are based upon the dreams of spinsters.

BERTRAND RUSSELL, *Marriage and Morals*, 1929.

The Russians can give you arms, but only the United States can give you a selection.

ANWAR EL-SADAT, *Newsweek*, January 13, 1975.

You have set up in New York harbor a monstrous idol which you call Liberty. The only thing that remains to complete that monument is to put on its pedestal the inscription written by Dante on the gate of Hell: "All hope abandon, ye who enter here."

GEORGE BERNARD SHAW, speech, Academy of Political Science, New York City, April 11, 1933.

I have spoken at...election meetings. I have heard all the cheers and heard the candidates talking, and...I have seen the profound feeling, and the older I get, the more I feel [campaigning] to be, as part of a government of the country, something entirely intolerable and disgraceful to human nature.

GEORGE BERNARD SHAW, speech, Academy of Political Science, New York City, April 11, 1933.

You are very much afraid of dictators, and you arrived at a state of society in which every ward boss was a dictator, and in which every financier was in his way a dictator, and every man who represented big business was a dictator and they had no responsibility.

GEORGE BERNARD SHAW, speech, Academy of Political Science, New York City, April 11, 1933.

[The Constitution] was a charter of anarchism. It was not really a Constitution at all. It was not an instrument of government; it was a guarantee to a whole nation that they never could be governed at all. And that is exactly what they wanted....The ordinary man...is an anarchist. He wants to do as he likes.

GEORGE BERNARD SHAW, speech, Academy of Political Science, New York City, April 11, 1933.

The real thing with which you are corrupting the world is the anarchism of Hollywood. There you put a string of heroes in front of people and all of them are anarchists, and the one answer to anything annoying or to any breach of the law or to any expression which he considers unmanly, is to give the other person a sock in the jaw. I wonder you don't prosecute the people who produce these continual strings of gentlemen who, when they are not kissing the heroine, are socking the jaw of somebody else. It is a criminal offense to sock a person in the jaw.

GEORGE BERNARD SHAW, speech, Academy of Political Science, New York City, April 11, 1933.

"[S]he happens to belong to a type [of American woman] I frequently met—it goes to lectures. And entertains afterwards....Amazing, their energy," he went on. "They're perfectly capable of having three or four children, running a house, keeping abreast of art, literature and music—superficially of course, but good lord, that's something—and holding down a job into the bargain. Some of them get through two or three husbands as well, just to avoid stagnation."

DODIE SMITH, I Capture the Castle, 1948.

To American productivity, without which this war would have been lost.

JOSEPH STALIN, toast, Teheran, Iran, 1943, in Lois and Alan Gordon, American Chronicle, 1987.

Washington isn't a city, it's an abstraction.

DYLAN THOMAS, in John Malcolm Brinnin, Dylan Thomas in America, 1956.

America is a large friendly dog in a small room. Every time it wags its tail it knocks over a chair.

ARNOLD TOYNBEE, July 14, 1954.

Here I was in New York, city of prose and fantasy, of capitalist automatism, its streets a triumph of cubism, its moral philosophy that of the dollar. New York impressed me tremendously because, more than any other city in the world, it is the fullest expression of our modern age.

LEON TROTSKY, My Life, 1930.

Living next to you is in some ways like sleeping with an elephant. No matter how friendly and even-tempered is the beast, if I can call it that, one is affected by every twitch and grunt.

PIERRE ELLIOTT TRUDEAU, on relations with United States, New York Times, March 26, 1969.

That impersonal insensitive friendliness that takes the place of ceremony in that land of waifs and strays.

EVELYN WAUGH, The Loved One, 1948.

Thank you for sending Catch-22. I am sorry that the book fascinates you so much. It has many passages quite unsuitable to a lady's reading. It suffers not only from indelicacy but from prolixity....You may quote me as saying: "This exposure of corruption, cowardice and incivility of American officers will outrage all friends of your country (such as myself) and greatly comfort your enemies."

EVELYN WAUGH, letter to Nina Bourne, 1961.

That tall Liberty with its spiky crown that stands in New York Harbor and casts an electric flare upon the world, is, in fact, the liberty of property, and there she stands at the Zenith.

H.G. WELLS, "The Future in America," 1906.

American cities are being littered with a disorder of unsystematized foundations and picturesque [architectural] legacies, much as I find my nursery floor littered with abandoned toys and battles and buildings when the children are in bed after a long wet day.

H.G. WELLS, "The Future in America," 1906.

America is still, by virtue of its great Puritan tradition and in the older sense of the word, an intensely moral land. Most lusts here are strongly curbed, by public opinion, by training and tradition. But the lust of acquisition has not been curbed but glorified.

H.G. WELLS, "The Future in America," 1906.

Every time Europe looks across the Atlantic to see the American eagle, it observes only the rear end of an ostrich.

H.G. WELLS, America, 1907.

One comes to the United States—always, no matter how often—to see the future. It's what life in one's own country will be like, five, ten, twenty years from now.

EHUD YONAY, New York Times, November 26, 1972.

America is God's Crucible, the great Melting-Pot where all the races of Europe are melting and reforming.

ISRAEL ZANGWILL, The Melting Pot, 1908.

Government and Politics

See also **Americans on Americans**—Government Officials and Politicians, Presidents; **Business**; **Dreams and Ideals**—Democracy, Equality, Freedom, Justice, Leadership, Patriotism, Power; **Economics**; **Education**; **Ethics and Morality**; **Foreign Views on Americans**; **Journalism and the Media**; **Law and Justice**; **Religion and Spirituality**—Government and Religion; **Science and Technology**; **Social Issues**; **War and Peace**; **Work**—Government Officials and Politicians

But the establishment is made up of little men, very frightened.

BELLA ABZUG, May 5, 1971, in Mel Ziegler, *Bella!*, 1972.

If we get a government that reflects more of what this country is really about, we can turn the country—and the economy—around.

BELLA ABZUG, in article by Claire Safran,
"Impeachment," *Redbook*, April, 1974.

Knowledge of human nature is the beginning and end of political education.

HENRY ADAMS, *The Education of Henry Adams*, 1907.

Modern politics is, at bottom, a struggle not of men but of forces.

HENRY ADAMS, *The Education of Henry Adams*, 1907.

Only in time of fear is government thrown back to its primitive and sole function of self-defense and the many interests of which it is the guardian become subordinated to that.

JANE ADDAMS, "Woman, War and Suffrage," November 6, 1915.

The idea of public interest becomes a fiction used to describe an amalgam which is shaped and reshaped in the furnace of [interest group] conflicts.

ARTHUR F. BENTLEY, *The Process of Government*, 1908.

Politics, n. A strife of interests masquerading as a contest of principles. The conduct of public affairs for private advantage.

AMBROSE BIERCE, *The Devil's Dictionary*, 1906.

Except for national defense, the Federal Government is almost unnecessary in this country!... If

it disappeared, we would not notice it in Colorado for weeks!

KENNETH BOULDING, *Beasts, Ballads, and Bouldingisms*, 1975.

Politics, where fat, bald, disagreeable men, unable to be candidates themselves, teach a president how to act on a public stage.

JIMMY BRESLIN, *Table Money*, 1986.

Too bad that all the people who know how to run the country are busy driving taxicabs and cutting hair.

GEORGE BURNS, *Life*, December, 1979.

Government is a contrivance of human wisdom to provide for human wants. People have the right to expect that these wants will be provided for by this wisdom.

JIMMY CARTER, inaugural address as governor of Georgia, January 12, 1971.

To keep from gravitating toward genocidal conflict, we must stop demanding perpetual progress. For quite nonpolitical reasons, governments and politicians cannot achieve the paradise they habitually promise. Political leaders who continue to dangle before their constituents enticing carrots that are becoming unattainable hasten the erosion of faith in political processes. Circumstances have ceased to be what they were when the once-New World's myth of limitlessness made sense.

WILLIAM R. CATTON, JR., "On the Dire Destiny of Human Lemmings," in Michael Tobias, ed., *Deep Ecology*, 1985.

[Politics] is a beautiful fraud that has been imposed on the people for years, whose practitioners exchange gilded promises for the most valuable thing their victims own: their votes. And who benefits most? The lawyers.

SHIRLEY CHISHOLM, *Unbought and Unbossed*, 1970.

Allow the state to invade the areas of thought, of education, of the press, of religion, of association, and we will have statism....Those who fear statism, as all who are rooted in American history and tradition fear it, must resolutely oppose it where it is most dangerous, precisely in the realm of the mind and the spirit of men. For if once we get a government strong enough to control men's minds, we will have a government strong enough to control everything.

HENRY STEELE COMMAGER, *Freedom and Order*, 1966.

Autocratic government, not self-government, has been the prevailing state of mankind. It needs to be remembered that the record of past history is the record, not of the success of republics, but of their failure.

CALVIN COOLIDGE, speech, "The Destiny of America," Northampton, Massachusetts, May 30, 1923.

It is fair to ask whether people who have demonstrated they cannot be trusted to safeguard the wealth and resources of the American people should be trusted to safeguard the national security.

NORMAN COUSINS, *Pathology of Power*, 1987.

There are seasons in Washington when it is even more difficult than usual to find out what is going on in the government. Possibly it is because nothing is going on, although a great many people seem to be working at it.

DOROTHY SALISBURY DAVIS, *Old Sinners Never Die*, 1959.

I think politics is an instrument of the Devil. Just that clear. I think politics is what kills; it doesn't bring anything alive. Politics is corrupt; I mean, anybody knows that.

BOB DYLAN, *Rolling Stone*, 1984.

My life is a mixture of politics and war. The latter is bad enough—but I've been trained for it! The former is straight and unadulterated venom! But I have to devote lots of my time, and much more of my good disposition, to it.

DWIGHT D. EISENHOWER, letter to Mamie Doud Eisenhower, September 27, 1943.

Politics...excites all that is selfish and ambitious in man.

DWIGHT D. EISENHOWER, letter to Sid Richardson, June 20, 1951.

Politics is not the art of the possible. It consists in choosing between the disastrous and the unpalatable.

JOHN KENNETH GALBRAITH, *Ambassador's Journal*, 1969.

Nothing is so admirable in politics as a short memory.

JOHN KENNETH GALBRAITH, *A Guide to the 99th Congress*, 1985.

The government's like a mule, it's slow and it's sure; it's slow to turn, and it's sure to turn the way you don't want it.

ELLEN GLASGOW, *The Voice of the People*, 1900.

The experience of Russia, more than any theories, has demonstrated that *all* government, whatever its forms or pretenses, is a dead weight that paralyzes the free spirit and activities of the masses.

EMMA GOLDMAN, *My Disillusionment in Russia*, 1923.

What we are witnessing is the "dumbing ground" of politics.

ELLEN GOODMAN, "Is This a Campaign or a Comic Strip?" *Washington Post*, September, 1988.

There are no generalizations in American politics that vested selfishness cannot cut through.

JOHN GUNTHER, *Inside U.S.A*, 1947.

The whole flavor and quality of the American representative government turns to ashes on the tongue, if one regards the government as simply an inferior and rather second-rate sort of corporation.

MARGARET HALSEY, *The Folks at Home*, 1952.

What is politics but persuading the public to vote for this and support that and endure these for the promise of those?

GILBERT HIGHET, "The Art of Persuasion," *Vogue*, January, 1951.

[T]he cocktail party remains a vital Washington institution, the official intelligence system.

BARBARA HOWAR, *Laughing All the Way*, 1973.

The government is mainly an expensive organization to regulate evildoers, and tax those who behave; government does little for fairly respectable people except annoy them.

EDGAR WATSON HOWE, *Notes for My Biographer*, 1926.

It's a terribly hard job to spend a billion dollars and get your money's worth.

GEORGE M. HUMPHREY, *Look*, February 23, 1954.

To the extent that the United States was governed by anyone during the decades after World War II, it was governed by the President acting with the support and cooperation of key individuals and groups in the executive office, the federal bureaucracy, Congress, and the more important businesses, banks, law firms, foundations, and media, which constitute the private sector's "Establishment."

SAMUEL HUNTINGTON, Trilateral Commission report, "The Governability of Democracies," 1976.

The oldest rule in politics is "You dance with them that brung you." Second oldest is "Money is the mother's milk of politics."

MOLLY IVINS, *Mother Jones*, January, 1991.

The best politics is no politics.

HENRY M. JACKSON, speech, American Bar Association, Chicago, Illinois, February 3, 1980.

I seldom think of politics more than 18 hours a day.

LYNDON B. JOHNSON, *A Guide to the 99th Congress*, 1985.

A man can take a little bourbon without getting drunk, but if you hold his mouth open and pour in a quart, he's going to get sick on it.

LYNDON B. JOHNSON, on political persuasion, "Love It or Loathe It, Here's the Wit and Wisdom of LBJ," *People*, February 2, 1987.

If you're going to play the game properly, you'd better know every rule.

BARBARA JORDAN, *Ebony*, February, 1975.

The stakes…are too high for government to be a spectator sport.

BARBARA JORDAN, speech, Harvard University, June 16, 1977.

There is rarely political risk in supporting the President and rarely political advantage in disagreement—unless and until a particular policy appears a failure.

NICHOLAS D. KATZENBACH, *New York Times Book Review*, February 18, 1973.

Politics is property.

MURRAY KEMPTON, in Norman Mailer, *Miami and the Siege of Chicago*, 1968.

Politics is like football. If you see daylight, go through the hole.

JOHN F. KENNEDY, ca. 1960, in Joseph Alsop, syndicated column, April 3, 1964.

Politics is the process of getting along with the querulous, the garrulous and the congenitally unlovable.

MARILYN MOATS KENNEDY, "Playing Office Politics," *Newsweek*, September 16, 1985.

Everyone is for more openness [in government] and an end to secrecy.

HENRY KISSINGER, in Richard Valeriani, *Travels with Henry*, 1979.

If we insist that public life be reserved for those whose personal history is pristine, we are not going to get paragons of virtue running our affairs. We will get the very rich, who contract out the messy things in life; the very dull, who have nothing to hide and nothing to show; and the very devious, expert at covering their tracks and ambitious enough to risk their discovery.

CHARLES KRAUTHAMMER, "Pietygate: School for Scandal," *Time*, September 10, 1984.

No system of government can hope long to survive the cynical disregard of both law and principle which government in America regularly exhibits.

SUZANNE LAFOLLETTE, "What Is To Be Done," *Concerning Women*, 1926.

I have not been able to convince myself that one policy, one party, one class, or one set of tactics, is as fertile as human need.

WALTER LIPPMANN, *Drift and Mastery*, 1914.

In relation to society and government it may be repeated that new ideas are rare; in regard to the latter, perhaps not more than two really large and new ideas have been developed in as many millenniums.

HENRY CABOT LODGE, speech, Schenectady, New York, June 9, 1915.

The kind of thing I'm good at is knowing every politician in the state and remembering where he itches. And I know where to scratch him.

EARL LONG, in article by A. J. Liebling, "The Great State," *The New Yorker*, June 4, 1960.

The man who pulls the plow gets the plunder in politics.

HUEY P. LONG, speech to U.S. Senate, January 30, 1934.

In a political fight, when you've got nothing in favor of your side, start a row in the opposition camp.

HUEY P. LONG, in T. Harry Williams, *Huey Long*, 1969.

I really think that it's better to retire, in Uncle Earl's terms, when you still have some snap left in your garters.

RUSSELL B. LONG, on Earl Long, *New York Times*, March 18, 1985.

For once let us try to think about a political convention without losing ourselves in housing projects of fact and issue. Politics has its virtues, all too many of them—it would not rank with baseball as a topic of conversation if it did not satisfy a great many things—but one can suspect that its secret appeal is close to nicotine. Smoking cigarettes insulates one from one's life, one does not feel as much, often happily so, and politics quarantines one from history; most of the people who nourish themselves in the political life are in the game not to make history but to be diverted from the history which is being made.

NORMAN MAILER, *Esquire*, November, 1960.

Politics is the art of looking for trouble, finding it everywhere, diagnosing it incorrectly, and applying the wrong remedies.

GROUCHO MARX, recalled on his death, August 19, 1977.

Ideas are great arrows, but there has to be a bow. And politics is the bow of idealism.

BILL MOYERS, *Time*, October, 1965.

The single most exciting thing you encounter in government is competence, because it's so rare.

DANIEL PATRICK MOYNIHAN, *New York Times*, March 2, 1976.

Whenever government's interests become by definition more substantial than the humanity of its citizens, the drift toward government by divine right gathers momentum.

LIANE NORMAN, "Selective Conscientious Objection," *The Center Magazine*, May/June, 1972.

Perhaps it is the expediency in the political eye that blinds it.

VIRGILIA PETERSON, *A Matter of Life and Death*, 1961.

If the hogs of the nation are ten times more important than the children, it is high time that women should make their influence felt.

JEANNETTE RANKIN, campaign speech on federal government appropriation of $300,000 to study fodder for hogs and only $30,000 to study children's needs, 1916.

I must say acting was good training for the political life which lay ahead for us.

NANCY REAGAN, *Nancy*, 1980.

Politics I supposed to be the second-oldest profession. I have come to realize that it bears a very close resemblance to the first.

RONALD REAGAN, *Los Angeles Herald-Examiner*, March 3, 1978.

Government is not the solution, it's the problem.

RONALD REAGAN, presidential inaugural address, 1981.

Grand ideas of government—lofty abstract principles, even the wisest constitutions and laws—depend for their very life and meaning on the willingness of citizens and leaders to apply them and to improve them.

NELSON A. ROCKEFELLER, *The Future of Federalism*, 1962.

Politics is the life blood of democracy. To call politics "dirty" is to call democracy "dirty."

NELSON A. ROCKEFELLER, *The Future of Federalism*, 1962.

Politics, of course, requires sweat, work, combat, and organization. But these should not be ugly words for any free people.

NELSON A. ROCKEFELLER, *The Future of Federalism*, 1962.

If we ever pass out as a great nation, we ought to put on our tombstone "America died of the delusion that she had moral leadership."

WILL ROGERS, in Donald Day, ed., *Autobiography of Will Rogers*, 1949.

The New Left was a series of epiphanies.

MICHAEL ROGIN, in Todd Gitlin, *The Sixties*, 1987.

The moment a mere numerical superiority by either states or voters in this country proceeds to ignore the needs and desires of the minority, and for their own selfish purpose or advancement, hamper or oppress that minority, or debar them in any way from equal privileges and equal rights—that moment will mark the failure of our constitutional system.

FRANKLIN D. ROOSEVELT, radio broadcast, March 2, 1930.

Our Constitution is so simple and practical that it is possible always to meet extraordinary needs by changes in emphasis and arrangement without loss of essential form. That is why our constitutional system has proved itself the most superbly enduring political mechanism the modern world has produced.

FRANKLIN D. ROOSEVELT, first presidential inaugural address, March 4, 1933.

The government is us; we are the government, you and I.

THEODORE ROOSEVELT, speech, Asheville, North Carolina, September 9, 1902.

I learned in business that you had to be very careful when you told somebody that's working for you to do something, because the chances were very high he'd do it. In government, you don't have to worry about that.

GEORGE P. SHULTZ, *New York Times*, October 14, 1984.

Nothing ever gets settled in this town...a seething debating society in which the debate never stops, in which people never give up, including me. And so that's the atmosphere in which you administer.

GEORGE P. SHULTZ, to House investigating committee, *New York Times*, December 9, 1986.

We mean by "politics" the people's business—the most important business there is.

ADLAI E. STEVENSON, speech, Chicago, Illinois, November 19, 1955.

Since the beginning of time, governments have been mainly engaged in kicking people around. The astonishing achievement in modern times in the Western world is the idea that the citizen should do the kicking.

ADLAI E. STEVENSON, *What I Think*, 1956.

Our government collaborates abroad with the worst enemies of humanity and liberty. It wastes our substance on useless proliferation of military hardware that can never buy security no matter how high the pile. It learns no lessons, employs no wisdom, and corrupts all who succumb to Potomac fever.

BARBARA TUCHMAN, "On Our Birthday—America as Idea," *Newsweek*, July 12, 1976.

Mankind, it seems, makes a poorer performance of government than of almost any other human activity.

BARBARA TUCHMAN, *The March of Folly*, 1984.

Wooden-headedness, the source of self-deception, is a factor that plays a remarkably large role in government. It consists in assessing a situation in terms of preconceived fixed notions while ignoring or rejecting any contrary signs. It is acting according to wish while not allowing oneself to be deflected by the facts.

BARBARA TUCHMAN, *The March of Folly*, 1984.

Aware of the controlling power of ambition, corruption and emotion, it may be that in the search for wiser government we should look for the test of character first.

BARBARA TUCHMAN, *The March of Folly*, 1984.

The older you get the more you realize that gray isn't such a bad color. And in politics you work with it or you don't work at all.

AGNES SLIGH TURNBULL, *The Golden Journey*, 1955.

To know that the lady in Dayton is afraid to walk the streets alone at night, to know that she has a mixed view about blacks and civil rights because before moving to the suburbs she lived in a neighborhood that became all black, to know that her brother-in-law is a policeman, to know that she does not have the money to move again if her new neighborhood deteriorates, to know that she is deeply distressed because her son goes to a community college where LSD has been found on campus—to know all this is the beginning of contemporary political wisdom.

BEN WATTENBERG AND RICHARD SCAMMON, *The Real Majority*, 1969.

Politics in America is the binding secular religion.

THEODORE H. WHITE, *Time*, December 29, 1986.

[T]he system was set and institutionalized. It was as respectable as the Constitution, and the Constitution was held up before the eyes of innocent children as the inspiration and defense of the system. Money controlled caucuses; caucuses controlled conventions; conventions nominated candidates; candidates became officials; officials were controlled by politics; politics was owned by business.

WILLIAM ALLEN WHITE, *Masks in a Pageant*, 1928.

Politics I conceive to be nothing more than the science of the ordered progress of society along the lines of greatest usefulness and convenience to itself.

WOODROW WILSON, in an address to the Pan-American Scientific Congress, Washington, D.C, January 6, 1916.

CAMPAIGN AND POLITICAL SLOGANS

The following are in chronological, not alphabetical, order.

We'll stand pat!

REPUBLICAN CAMPAIGN SLOGAN (MCKINLEY), 1900.

Four more years of the dull dinner pail.

REPUBLICAN PARTY, campaign slogan (McKinley), 1900.

McKinley drinks soda water, Bryan drinks rum; McKinley is a gentleman, Bryan is a bum.

REPUBLICAN CAMPAIGN SLOGAN (MCKINLEY), 1900.

No Crown of Thorns, No Cross of Gold.
DEMOCRATIC CAMPAIGN SLOGAN (BRYAN), 1900.

Same Old Flag and Victory—Stand Pat.
REPUBLICAN CAMPAIGN SLOGAN (T. ROOSEVELT), 1904.

Get on the Raft with Taft.
REPUBLICAN CAMPAIGN SLOGAN (TAFT), 1908.

Bill-a-Gain.
REPUBLICAN CAMPAIGN SLOGAN (TAFT), 1912.

You are working, not fighting.
DEMOCRATIC CAMPAIGN SLOGAN (WILSON), 1916.

He Kept Us Out of War.
DEMOCRATIC CAMPAIGN SLOGAN (WILSON), 1916.

Back to Normalcy.
REPUBLICAN CAMPAIGN SLOGAN (HARDING), 1920.

Cox and Cocktails.
DEMOCRATIC CAMPAIGN (COX), 1920.

Convict No. 9653 for President.
SOCIALIST CAMPAIGN SLOGAN (DEBS), 1920.

Keep Cool with Coolidge.
REPUBLICAN CAMPAIGN SLOGAN (COOLIDGE), 1924.

A Chicken in Every Pot.
REPUBLICAN CAMPAIGN SLOGAN (HOOVER), 1928.

Hoover and Happiness or Smith and Soup Houses? Which Shall It Be?
REPUBLICAN CAMPAIGN SLOGAN (HOOVER), 1928.

4 Out of 5 Democrats
    Contain harmful Acids
—Insist on Hoover
    Accept no Substitute
POLITICAL AD

Now you can have a Roosevelt

in your White House at Surprisingly Low Cost
    the Candidate with the Monitor Top
Protected from either Dryness or Wetness
Silent—no Whirring Noises about Prohibition.
    Keep Regular with Roosevelt
POLITICAL AD

If you are Wet, vote for Smith,
If you are Dry, vote for Garner,
—If you don't know what you are,
    Vote for Roosevelt.
DEMOCRATIC CAMPAIGN SLOGAN (F.D. ROOSEVELT), 1932.

Who But Hoover?
REPUBLICAN CAMPAIGN SLOGAN (HOOVER), 1932.

Life, Liberty, and Landon.
REPUBLICAN CAMPAIGN SLOGAN (LANDON), 1936.

No man is good three times.
REPUBLICAN CAMPAIGN SLOGAN (REFERRING TO F.D. ROOSEVELT), 1940.

Two Good Terms Deserve a Rest.
REPUBLICAN CAMPAIGN SLOGAN (WILKIE), 1940.

Let's Re-Re-Re-Elect Roosevelt.
DEMOCRATIC CAMPAIGN SLOGAN (F.D. ROOSEVELT), 1944.

Had Enough?
REPUBLICAN CAMPAIGN SLOGAN (DEWEY), 1944.

I Like Ike.
REPUBLICAN CAMPAIGN SLOGAN (EISENHOWER), 1952.

You Never Had It So Good.
DEMOCRATIC CAMPAIGN SLOGAN (STEVENSON), 1952.

Communism, Corruption, and Korea.
REPUBLICAN CAMPAIGN SLOGAN (EISENHOWER), 1952.

I Still Like Ike.
REPUBLICAN CAMPAIGN SLOGAN (EISENHOWER), 1956.

We Need Adlai Badly.
DEMOCRATIC CAMPAIGN SLOGAN (STEVENSON), 1956.

We're Madly for Adlai.
DEMOCRATIC CAMPAIGN SLOGAN (STEVENSON), 1956.

Everything's booming but the guns.
REPUBLICAN CAMPAIGN SLOGAN (EISENHOWER), 1956.

I'M VOTING
FOR
NIXON
NO GIVE AWAYS!
Remember Yalta?
NO APOLOGIES!
Remember the Summit?
NO PIE IN THE SKY!
Remember, ITS YOUR MONEY
JACK WILL PLAY POKER WITH
REPUBLICAN CAMPAIGN SLOGAN (NIXON), 1960.

Experience Counts.
REPUBLICAN CAMPAIGN SLOGAN (NIXON), 1960.

New Frontier.
DEMOCRATIC CAMPAIGN SLOGAN (KENNEDY), 1960.

All the Way with LBJ.
DEMOCRATIC CAMPAIGN SLOGAN (JOHNSON), 1964.

In Your Heart You Know He's Right.
REPUBLICAN CAMPAIGN SLOGAN (GOLDWATER), 1964.

A Choice Not an Echo.

REPUBLICAN CAMPAIGN SLOGAN (GOLDWATER), 1964.

Nixon's the One.

REPUBLICAN CAMPAIGN SLOGAN (NIXON), 1968.

Nixon: Now More Than Ever.

REPUBLICAN CAMPAIGN SLOGAN (NIXON), 1972.

Come Home, America.

DEMOCRATIC CAMPAIGN SLOGAN (MCGOVERN), 1972.

Grits and Fritz.

DEMOCRATIC CAMPAIGN SLOGAN (CARTER-MONDALE), 1976.

Get the Government Off Our Backs.

REPUBLICAN CAMPAIGN SLOGAN (REAGAN), 1980.

Don't Blame Me I Didn't Vote for Him.

BUMPER STICKER, referring to the election of Ronald
Reagan as president, ca. 1982.

It's Morning in America Again.

REPUBLICAN CAMPAIGN SLOGAN (REAGAN), 1984.

Leadership for the '90s.

DEMOCRATIC CAMPAIGN SLOGAN (DUKAKIS), 1988.

CONGRESS

Congress is a very *unrepresentative* institution.
Not only from an economic class point of view,
but from *every* point of view—sex, race, age,
vocation. Some people say this is because the
political system tends to homogenize everything,
that a Congressman by virtue of the fact that he
or she represents a half million people has to
appeal to all sorts of disparate groups. I don't
buy that at all. These men in Congress don't represent a homogeneous point of view. They represent their *own* point of view—by reason of their
sex, background and class.

BELLA ABZUG, in Mel Ziegler, *Bella!*, 1972.

You can't have a Congress that responds to the
needs of the workingman when there are practically no people here who represent him.

BELLA ABZUG, *Redbook*, April, 1974.

Can any of you seriously say the Bill of Rights
could get through Congress today? It wouldn't
even get out of committee.

F. LEE BAILEY, *Newsweek*, April 17, 1967.

Senator, n. The fortunate bidder in an auction of
votes.

AMBROSE BIERCE, *The Devil's Dictionary*, 1906.

[Congress] is an institution designed only to
react, not to plan or lead.

JIMMY BRESLIN, *How the Good Guys Finally Won*, 1975.

If we in the Senate would stop calling each other
"distinguished," we might have ten working
days a year.

EDWARD W. BROOKE, *Reader's Digest*, April, 1972.

It's strictly the schoolboy syndrome [and] seems
to last well into adulthood.

ELLIOTT CARROLL, on senatorial tradition of carving
initials on desks, *New York Times*, March 17, 1985.

There needs to be a change in the U.S. Congress.
When one sees what is happening in our country today, one knows that government cannot be
run on seniority alone.

SHIRLEY CHISHOLM, *Chicago Daily News*, February 22,
1969.

The seniority system keeps a handful of old
men...in control of the Congress. These old
men stand implacably across the paths that
could lead us toward a better future. But worse
than they, I think, are the majority of members
of both Houses who continue to submit to the
senility system.

SHIRLEY CHISHOLM, *Unbought and Unbossed*, 1970.

Exhaustion and exasperaton are frequently the
handmaidens of legislative decision.

BARBER B. CONABLE, JR., *Time*, October 22, 1984.

[Congress is] functioning the way the Founding
Fathers intended—not very well. They understood that if you move too quickly, our democracy will be less responsible to the majority.

BARBER B. CONABLE, JR., *Time*, October 22, 1984.

Face it: Here you've got American government at
its visual best: the marble, the columns, the
rotundas, the sweeping staircases. You've got
goals, you've got commitments, you've got aspirations and inspirations....But have you got a
place to sit?

CONGRESSIONAL MANAGEMENT FOUNDATION, report on
overcrowding of legislative offices, *New York Times*,
November 12, 1984.

The great object for us to seek here, for the Constitution identifies the vice-presidency with the
Senate, is to continue to make this chamber, as it
was intended by the fathers, the citadel of liberty.

CALVIN COOLIDGE, inaugural address as vice president,
March 4, 1921.

ARTICLE XVI
February 3, 1913

The Congress shall have power to lay and collect taxes on incomes, from whatever source derived, without apportionment among the several States, and without regard to any census or enumeration.

ARTICLE XVII
April 8, 1913

SECTION 1. The Senate of the United States shall be composed of two Senators from each State, elected by the people thereof, for six years; and each Senator shall have one vote. The electors in each State shall have the qualifications requisite for electors of the most numerous branch of the State legislatures.

SECTION 2. When vacancies happen in the representation of any State in the Senate, the executive authority of such State shall issue writs of election to fill such vacancies: *Provided*, That the legislature of any State may empower the executive thereof to make temporary appointments until the people fill the vacancies by election as the legislature may direct.

SECTION 3. This amendment shall not be so construed as to affect the election or term of any Senator chosen before it becomes valid as part of the Constitution.

ARTICLE XVIII
January 16, 1919

SECTION 1. After one year from the ratification of this article the manufacture, sale, or transportation of intoxicating liquors within, the importation thereof into, or the exportation thereof from the United States and all territory subject to the jurisdiction thereof for beverage purposes is hereby prohibited.

SECTION 2. The Congress and the several States shall have concurrent power to enforce this article by appropriate legislation.

SECTION 3. This article shall be inoperative unless it shall have been ratified as an amendment to the Constitution by the legislatures of the several States, as provided in the Constitution, within seven years from the date of the submission hereof to the States by the Congress.

ARTICLE XIX
August 18, 1920

SECTION 1. The right of citizens of the United States to vote shall not be denied or abridged by the United States or by any State on account of sex.

SECTION 2. Congress shall have power to enforce this article by appropriate legislation.

ARTICLE XX
January 23, 1933

SECTION 1. The terms of the President and Vice President shall end at noon on the 20th day of January, and the terms of Senators and Representatives at noon on the 3rd day of January, of the years in which such terms would have ended if this article had not been ratified; and the terms of their successors shall then begin.

SECTION 2. The Congress shall assemble at least once in every year, and such meeting shall begin at noon on the 3rd day of January, unless they shall by law appoint a different day.

SECTION 3. If, at the time fixed for the beginning of the term of the President, the President elect shall have died, the Vice President elect shall become President. If a President shall not have been chosen before the time fixed for the beginning of his term, or if the President elect shall have failed to qualify, then the Vice President elect shall act as President until a President shall have qualified; and the Congress may by law provide for the case wherein neither a President elect nor a Vice President elect shall have qualified, declaring who shall then act as President, or the manner in which one who is to act shall be selected, and such person shall act accordingly until a President or Vice President shall have qualified.

SECTION 4. The Congress may by law provide for the case of the death of any of the persons from whom the House of Representatives may choose a President whenever the right of choice shall have devolved upon them, and for the case of the death of any of the persons from whom the Senate may choose a Vice President whenever the right of choice shall have devolved upon them.

SECTION 5. Sections 1 and 2 shall take effect on the 15th day of October following the ratification of this article.

SECTION 6. This article shall be inoperative unless it shall have been ratified as an amendment to the Constitution by the legislatures of three-fourths of the several States within seven years from the date of its submission.

ARTICLE XXI
December 5, 1933

SECTION 1. The eighteenth article of amendment to the Constitution of the United States is hereby repealed.

SECTION 2. The transportation or importation into any State, Territory, or possession of the United States for delivery or use therein of intoxicating liquors, in violation of the laws thereof, is hereby prohibited.

SECTION 3. This article shall be inoperative unless it shall have been ratified as an amendment to the Constitution by conventions in the several States, as provided in the Constitution, within seven years from the date of the submission hereof to the States by the Congress.

ARTICLE XXII
February 27, 1951

SECTION 1. No person shall be elected to the office of the President more than twice, and no person who has held the office of President, or acted as President, for more than two years of a term to which some other person was elected President shall be elected to the office of the President more than once. But this article shall not apply to any person holding the office of President when this article was proposed by the Congress, and shall not prevent any person who may be holding the office of Presi-

dent, or acting as President, during the term within which this article becomes operative from holding the office of President or acting as President during the remainder of such term.

SECTION 2. This article shall be inoperative unless it shall have been ratified as an amendment to the Constitution by the legislatures of three-fourths of the several States within seven years from the date of its submission to the States by the Congress.

ARTICLE XXIII
March 29, 1961

SECTION 1. The District constituting the seat of Government of the United States shall appoint in such manner as the Congress may direct:

A number of electors of President and Vice President equal to the whole number of Senators and Representatives in Congress to which the District would be entitled if it were a State, but in no event more than the least populous State; they shall be in addition to those appointed by the States, but they shall be considered, for the purposes of the election of President and Vice President, to be electors appointed by a State; and they shall meet in the District and perform such duties as provided by the twelfth article of amendment.

SECTION 2. The Congress shall have power to enforce this article by appropriate legislation.

ARTICLE XXIV
January 23, 1964

SECTION 1. The right of citizens of the United States to vote in any primary or other election for President or Vice President, for electors for President or Vice President, or for Senator or Representative in Congress, shall not be denied or abridged by the United States or any State by reason of failure to pay any poll tax or other tax.

SECTION 2. The Congress shall have power to enforce this article by appropriate legislation.

ARTICLE XXV
February 10, 1967

SECTION 1. In case of the removal of the President from office or of his death or resignation, the Vice President shall become President.

SECTION 2. Whenever there is a vacancy in the office of the Vice President, the President shall nominate a Vice President who shall take office upon confirmation by a majority vote of both Houses of Congress.

SECTION 3. Whenever the President transmits to the President pro tempore of the Senate and the Speaker of the House of Representatives his written declaration that he is unable to discharge the powers and duties of this office, and until he transmits to them a written declaration to the contrary, such powers and duties shall be discharged by the Vice President as Acting President.

SECTION 4. Whenever the Vice President and a majority of either the principal officers of the executive departments or of such other body as Congress may by law provide, transmit to the President pro tempore of the Senate and the Speaker of the House of Representatives their written declaration that the President is unable to discharge the powers and duties of his office, the Vice President shall immediately assume the powers and duties of the office as Acting President.

Thereafter, when the President transmits to the President pro tempore of the Senate and the Speaker of the House of Representatives his written declaration that no inability exists, he shall resume the powers and duties of his office unless the Vice President and a majority of either the principal officers of the executive department or of such other body as Congress may by law provide, transmit within four days to the President pro tempore of the Senate and the Speaker of the House of Representatives their written declaration that the President is unable to discharge the powers and duties of his office. Thereupon Congress shall decide the issue, assembling within forty-eight hours for that purpose if not in session. If the Congress, within twenty-one days after receipt of the latter written declaration, or, if Congress is not in session, within twenty-one days after Congress is required to assemble, determines by two-thirds vote of both Houses that the President is unable to discharge the powers and duties of his office, the Vice President shall continue to discharge the same as Acting President; otherwise, the President shall resume the powers and duties of his office.

ARTICLE XXVI
July 1, 1971

SECTION 1. The right of citizens of the United States who are 18 years of age or older, to vote shall not be denied or abridged by the United States or by any State on account of age.

SECTION 2. The Congress shall have power to enforce this article by appropriate legislation.

CONSTITUTIONAL AMENDMENTS IN TWENTIETH CENTURY.

On Capitol Hill Congress runs by an internal clock: Legislative days are not counted the way calendar days are, and the seasons are marked not by the earth's orbit but by whether Congress is in session or not.

RICHARD CORRIGAN, "Technology Focus," *National Journal*, October 25, 1986.

Sure the people are stupid: the human race is stupid. Sure Congress is an inefficient instrument of government. But the people are not stupid enough to abandon representative government for any other kind, including government by the guy who knows.

BERNARD DE VOTO, "Sometimes They Vote Right Too," *The Easy Chair*, 1955.

We favor an amendment to the Federal Constitution providing for election of United States senators by the direct vote of the people.

DEMOCRATIC PARTY, plank in platform, 1900.

If you're hanging around with nothing to do and the zoo is closed, come over to the Senate. You'll get the same kind of feeling and you won't have to pay.

ROBERT J. DOLE, *New York Times*, May 9, 1985.

Insofar as it represents a genuine reconciliation of differences, a consensus is a fine thing; insofar as it represents a concealment of differences, it is a miscarriage of democratic procedure.

J. WILLIAM FULBRIGHT, speech to U.S. Senate, October 22, 1965.

We have the power to do any damn fool thing we want to do, and we seem to do it about every 10 minutes.

J. WILLIAM FULBRIGHT, *Time*, February 4, 1952.

It is Congress that voters mistrust, not their own congressmen.

PETER GOLDMAN, *Newsweek*, November 6, 1978.

I look at the Senators and pray for the country.

EDWARD EVERETT HALE, in Van Wyck Brooks, *New England: Indian Summer*, 1940.

What can you expect from that zoo?

JOHN F. KENNEDY, recalled in *U.S. News & World Report*, July 22, 1968.

I've had a tough time learning how to act like a congressman. Today I accidentally spent some of my own money.

JOSEPH P. KENNEDY III, *Newsweek*, February 9, 1987.

They say women talk too much. If you have worked in Congress you know that the filibuster was invented by men.

CLARE BOOTHE LUCE, *New York Times*, June 28, 1971.

Give us clear vision, that we may know where to stand and what to stand for—because unless we stand for something, we shall fall for anything.

PETER MARSHALL, Senate prayer, 1947.

The Senate is the last primitive society in the world. We still worship the elders of the tribe and honor the territorial imperative.

ATTRIBUTED TO EUGENE J. MCCARTHY.

Congress—these, for the most part, [are] illiterate hacks whose fancy vests are spotted with gravy and whose speeches, hypocritical, unctuous and slovenly, are spotted also with the gravy of political patronage.

MARY MCCARTHY, *On the Contrary*, 1961.

In that hearing, we didn't hear anything.

JAMES A. MCCLURE, on lack of leaks from closed hearing, *New York Times*, January 24, 1987.

Eighty percent were hypocrites, 80 percent liars, 80 percent serious sinners…except on Sundays. There is always boozing and floozying.…I don't have enough time to tell you everybody's name.

WILLIAM "FISHBAIT" MILLER, "60 Minutes," CBS-TV, April 24, 1977.

Today's public opinion, though it may appear as light as air, may be tomorrow's legislation—for better or for worse.

EARL NEWSOM, newsletter, American Petroleum Institute, Winter, 1963.

We're half the people; we should be half the Congress.

JEANNETTE RANKIN, calling for more women in public office, *Newsweek*, February 14, 1966.

I do strive to think well of my fellow man, but no amount of striving can give me confidence in the wisdom of a congressional vote.

AGNES REPPLIER, in Emma Repplier, *Agnes Repplier, A Memoir*, 1957.

Talking about stopping War, I will bet any man in the United States five thousand even that there ain't a man in this country that can draw up a bill that the Senate themselves won't go to war over while they are arguing it.

WILL ROGERS, newspaper column, July 22, 1923.

The U.S. Senate may not be the most refined and deliberative body in existence but they got the most unique rules. Any member can call anybody in the world anything he can think of and they can't answer him, sue him, or fight him. Our constitution protects aliens, drunks and U.S. Senators. There ought to be one day (just one) where there is an open season on Senators.

WILL ROGERS, newspaper column, March 6, 1935.

This country has come to feel the same when Congress is in session as we do when the baby gets hold of a hammer. It's just a question of how much damage he can do with it before we can take it away from him.

WILL ROGERS, in Donald Day, ed., *The Autobiography of Will Rogers*, 1949.

I could study all my life and not think up half the amount of funny things they can think of in one session of Congress. Besides my jokes don't do anybody any harm. You don't have to pay attention to them. But every one of the jokes those birds make is a LAW and hurts somebody (generally everybody).

WILL ROGERS, in Donald Day, ed., *The Autobiography of Will Rogers*, 1949.

Never blame a legislative body for not doing something. When they do nothing, they don't hurt anybody. When they do something is when they become dangerous.

WILL ROGERS, in Richard Ketchum, *Will Rogers: His Life and Times*, 1973.

You see, they have two of these bodies—Senate and House. That is for the convenience of visitors. If there is nothing funny happening in one, there is sure to be in the other; and in case one body passes a good bill, why, the other can see it in time and kill it.

WILL ROGERS, in *New York Times* article, January 28, 1984.

Give a member of Congress a junket and a mimeograph machine and he thinks he is Secretary of State.

DEAN RUSK, *Time*, May 6, 1985.

[T]he Senate is a club of prima donnas intensely self-oriented—99 kings and one queen—dedicated to their own personal accommodation.

MARGARET CHASE SMITH, on Senate's unwillingness to address chronic absenteeism, *New York Times*, December 21, 1971.

We do not elect our wisest and best men to represent us....In general, we elect men of the type that subscribes to only one principle—to get reelected.

TERRY M. TOWNSEND, speech, New York City, January 30, 1940.

I believe if we introduced the Lord's Prayer here, senators would propose a large number of amendments to it.

HENRY WILSON, in Leon A. Harris, *The Fine Art of Political Wit*, 1964.

DIPLOMACY

Force can only overcome other force. When it has done this, it has spent itself and other means of influencing conduct have to be employed.

DEAN ACHESON, *A Democrat Looks at His Party*, 1955.

I take it as clear that, where an important purpose of diplomacy is to further enduring good relations between states, the methods—the modes of conduct—by which relations between states are carried on must be designed to inspire trust and confidence. To achieve this result, the conduct of diplomacy should conform to the same moral and ethical principles which inspire trust and confidence when followed by and between individuals.

DEAN ACHESON, speech, Amherst College, December 9, 1964, in Eugene McCarthy, *The Limits of Power*, 1967.

There is no room for the quick-draw artist in the diplomatic arena; the stakes are always too high and the penalties too dear.

EDMUND G. BROWN, *Reagan: The Political Chameleon*, 1976.

American diplomacy is easy on the brain but hell on the feet.

CHARLES G. DAWES, speech, Washington, D.C., June 2, 1931.

The ability to get to the verge without getting into the war is the necessary art....If you are scared to go to the brink, you are lost.

JOHN FOSTER DULLES, in article by James Shepley, "How Dulles Averted War," *Life*, January 16, 1956.

There are few ironclad rules of diplomacy but to one there is no exception. When an official reports that talks were useful, it can safely be concluded that nothing was accomplished.

JOHN KENNETH GALBRAITH, "The American Ambassador," *Foreign Service Journal*, June, 1969.

Let us never negotiate out of fear, but let us never fear to negotiate.

JOHN F. KENNEDY, inaugural address, January 20, 1961.

The statesman's duty is to bridge the gap between his nation's experience and his vision.

HENRY KISSINGER, *Years of Upheaval*, 1982.

For a diplomat to think that rival and unfriendly powers cannot be brought to a settlement is to forget what diplomacy is all about. There would be little for diplomats to do if the world consisted of partners, enjoying political intimacy, and responding to common appeals.

WALTER LIPPMANN, *The Cold War*, 1947.

The reason that diplomacy is so stilted is that its purpose is to head off the most natural social relation between countries in economic or ideological conflict, namely war.

JUDITH MARTIN, *Common Courtesy*, 1985.

The favorite cliché of those who advocate summit talks regardless of the circumstances is, "Talking is always better than fighting." This, however, is not the only choice. Talking is not better than not talking when you do not know what you are going to talk about.

RICHARD M. NIXON, *The Challenges We Face*, 1960.

Mr. Dulles has just frightened most of our allies to death with a statement that there is an art in actually threatening war and coming to the brink but retreating from the brink.

ELEANOR ROOSEVELT, letter to Gus Ranis, January 23, 1956, in Joseph P. Lash, *Eleanor: The Years Alone*, 1972.

Diplomacy, for example, is not the art of asserting ever more emphatically that attitudes should not be what they clearly are. It is not the repudiation of actuality, but the recognition of actuality, and the use of actuality to advance our national interests.

ADLAI E. STEVENSON, *Call to Greatness*, 1954.

The central tenet of statesmanship in a democracy is that unless the people understand it and participate in it, no long-term program can endure.

ADLAI E. STEVENSON, speech, Newark, New Jersey, May 5, 1959.

The world organization debates disarmament in one room and, in the next room, moves the knights and pawns that make national arms imperative. This is not justice and law, and this is not light. It is not new forms. The U.N. is modern in intent, old-fashioned in shape.

E.B. WHITE, "Sootfall and Fallout," October 18, 1956, *Essays of E.B. White*, 1977.

Once the Xerox copier was invented, diplomacy died.

ANDREW YOUNG, interview, *Playboy*, July, 1977.

DOMESTIC POLICY

The American farmer is entitled not only to tariff schedules on his products but to protection from substitutes therefor.

PLANK IN REPUBLICAN PLATFORM, 1932.

Before we give you billions more, we want to know what you've done with the trillion you've got.

LES ASPIN, letter to Caspar Weinberger, *New York Times*, February 5, 1985.

I cannot understand how we can put together all those programs for sending food across the oceans when at home we have people who are slowly starving to death. We could use less foreign aid and more home aid.

PEARL BAILEY, *Pearl's Kitchen*, 1973.

Read my lips: no new taxes.

GEORGE BUSH, press conference, 1988.

Take back your protection; we are now men, and we can beat the world at the manufacture of steel.

ANDREW CARNEGIE, testimony at Ways and Means Committee hearing on tariffs, December 21, 1908.

Whatever America hopes to bring to pass in the world must first come to pass in the heart of America.

DWIGHT D. EISENHOWER, inaugural address, January 20, 1953.

I could have spoken from Rhode Island where I have been staying....But I felt that, in speaking from the house of Lincoln, of Jackson, and of Wilson, my words would better convey both the sadness I feel in the action I was compelled today to take and the firmness with which I intend to pursue this course until the orders of the federal court at Little Rock can be executed without unlawful interference.

DWIGHT D. EISENHOWER, speech on sending troops to enforce integration in Little Rock, Arkansas, September 24, 1957.

The pervasive nature of pollution, its disregard of political boundaries including state lines, the national character of the technical, economic and political problems involved, and the recognized Federal responsibilities for administering vast public lands which can be changed by pollution, for carrying out large enterprises which can produce pollutants, for preserving and improving the nation's natural resources, all make it mandatory that the Federal Government assume leadership and exert its influence in pollution abatement on a national scale.

ENVIRONMENT POLLUTION PANEL, *Restoring the Quality of Our Environment*, 1965.

We don't need a President who cuts taxes for the rich and nutrition programs for the poor and calls that progress.

GERALDINE FERRARO, *Boston Globe*, September 9, 1984.

Six million people have been pushed into poverty by this administration, which operates on the theory of survival of the richest.

GERALDINE FERRARO, *Boston Globe*, September 9, 1984.

If Walter Mondale is President, you can be sure that he'll be taking polluters to court and not to lunch.

GERALDINE FERRARO, *Boston Globe*, September 9, 1984.

Welfare is hated by those who administer it, mistrusted by those who pay for it and held in contempt by those who receive it.

PETER C. GOLDMARK, JR., *New York Times*, May 24, 1977.

America's present need is not heroics but healing; not nostrums but normalcy; not revolution but restoration; not surgery but serenity.

WARREN G. HARDING, campaign speech, 1920.

The New Deal will bring them [the Communist party] within striking distance of the overthrow of the American form of government and the substitution therefore of a communist state.

ARTHUR SEARS HENNING, *Chicago Tribune*, 1935.

While politicians carry on about the sanctity of the American family, we learn...that in the scale of national priorities our children and families really come last.

LOUISE KAPP HOWE, *The White Majority*, 1970.

We cannot use a double standard for measuring our own and other people's policies. Our demands for democratic practices in other lands will be no more effective than the guarantee of those practiced in our own country.

HUBERT H. HUMPHREY, speech, July 14, 1948.

The Great Society is a place where every child can find knowledge to enrich his mind and to enlarge his talents....It is a place where the city of man services not only the needs of the body and the demands of commerce but the desire for beauty and the hunger for community....It is a place where men are more concerned with the quality of their goals than the quantity of their goods.

LYNDON B. JOHNSON, speech, Ann Arbor, Michigan, May 22, 1964.

A rich harvest in a hungry land is impressive. The sight of healthy children is impressive. These—not mighty arms—are the achievements which the American nation believes to be impressive.

LYNDON B. JOHNSON, speech, Johns Hopkins University, April 7, 1965.

I knew from the start if I left a woman I really loved—the Great Society—in order to fight that bitch of a war...then I would lose everything at home. My hopes...my dreams.

LYNDON B. JOHNSON, in Doris Kearns, *Lyndon Johnson and the American Dream*, 1976.

We need President Reagan to make AIDS a moon-shot issue.

STEPHEN JOSEPH, *New York*, March 23, 1987.

The issue of race has been too much talked about....We may need a period in which Negro progress continues and racial rhetoric fades,...[a policy of] benign neglect.

DANIEL PATRICK MOYNIHAN, 1970, in Lois and Alan Gordon, *American Chronicle*, 1987.

President Reagan was elected on the promise of getting government off the backs of the people and now he demands that government wrap itself around the waists of the people.

RALPH NADER, on proposed legislation requiring air bags or automatic seat belts in all automobiles, *New York Times*, July 12, 1984.

This administration is not sympathetic to corporations, it is indentured to corporations.

RALPH NADER, *Washington Post*, October 4, 1972.

Prohibition most dramatically revealed America's ever-restless, tireless experimentation, its inexhaustible will to try something new in the hope of something better.

ALLAN NEVINS, in Arthur Goodfriend, *What Is America?*, 1954.

Move over, $7,000 coffeepots! Stand aside, $400 hammers! We now have the $792 doormat!

WILLIAM PROXMIRE, *New York Times*, October 4, 1985.

I think we should keep the grain and export the farmers.

RONALD REAGAN, speech on farm crisis, Washington Gridiron Club, March 23, 1985.

As long as there are guns, the individual that wants a gun for a crime is going to have one and going to get it. The only person who's going to be penalized and have difficulty is the law-abiding citizen, who then cannot have [it] if he wants protection—the protection of a weapon in his home, for home protection.

RONALD REAGAN, interview on his support for removal of gun controls, White House, March 22, 1986.

I propose to create a civilian conservation corps to be used in simple work, not interfering with normal employment, and confining itself to forestry, the prevention of soil erosion, flood control and similar projects. I call your attention to the fact that this type of work is of definite, practical value, not only through the prevention of great present financial loss, but also as a means of creating future national wealth.

FRANKLIN D. ROOSEVELT, message to Congress, 1933.

The money changers have fled from their high seats in the temple of our civilization. We may now restore that temple to the ancient truths. The measure of the restoration lies in the extent to which we apply social values more noble than mere monetary profit. Happiness lies not in the mere possession of money; it lies in the joy of achievement, in the thrill of creative effort.

FRANKLIN D. ROOSEVELT, inaugural address, March 4, 1933.

Not only our future economic soundness but the very soundness of our democratic institutions depends on the determination of our government to give employment to idle men. The people of America are in agreement in defending their liberties at any cost, and the first line of that defense lies in the protection of economic security.

FRANKLIN D. ROOSEVELT, Fireside Chat, April 14, 1938.

If one works for years at becoming a pitiful, helpless giant, one might just succeed.

JAMES SCHLESINGER, 1979.

The American people want to preserve their American heritage, and they have the quaint belief that public lands belong to them as much as to the people of the state where the lands are located.

JOHN F. SEIBERLING, New York Times, July 15, 1984.

Socialism is the public ownership of the means of production, and no one is proposing that. But as we use the word, it seems to be any government authority we do not like. Of course, things we like—tariffs, subsidies, mail concessions, support prices, tax write-offs, depletion allowances and government aids to particular groups—are rarely denounced as "socialism" except perhaps by the group's competitors.

ADLAI E. STEVENSON, paper delivered to National Business Conference, Harvard Business School, June 6, 1959.

This may be the last presidential election America will have. The New Deal is to America what the early phase of Nazism was to Germany and the early phase of fascism to Italy.

MARK SULLIVAN, Buffalo Evening News, 1935.

The impulse—and the propaganda—to *postpone* the consideration of our internal problems until

after we have "saved Democracy" from the enemy abroad may lead to the defeat of Hitler and the triumph of Fascism at home.

LILLIAN SYMES, "Fascism for America—Threat or Scarehead?" Harper's, June, 1939.

We cannot afford to destroy at home the very liberty which we must sell to the rest of the world—as the basis for progress and happiness.

ROBERT A. TAFT, A Foreign Policy for Americans, 1951.

[I]t remains true that to-day the working farmers are a great bulwark of democracy and curb upon dictatorship. Small wonder, then, that new sharp shifts in status of farmers cause men deep concern, that they begin to voice dim fears and to speak and to write vaguely of an alternative of "peasants on our farms or revolution on our land"; of "revolt" by men "denied the privilege of making an honest living for [their] family"; of "the rich finding themselves on the shelf"; of diminished incentive for our farm "boys sent out to fight."

PAUL S. TAYLOR, "Good-by to the Homestead Farm," Harper's, May, 1941.

Government will remain big, active, and expensive under President Thomas E. Dewey.

Wall Street Journal, October, 1948.

EXECUTIVE BRANCH

In Britain the government has to come down in front of Parliament every day to explain its actions, but here the President never answers directly to Congress.

BELLA ABZUG, in Mel Ziegler, Bella!, 1972.

Is America less of a nation than Iceland? Is America less of a nation than Denmark? Is America less of a nation than England? If those countries are man enough to elect a woman, I think America can do so as well.

BELLA ABZUG, on possible presidential candidacy of Pat Schroeder, New York Times, August 22, 1987.

Young man, I have lived in this house many years and seen the occupants of that White House across the square come and go, and nothing that you minor officials or the occupants of that house can do will affect the history of the world for long.

HENRY ADAMS, to Franklin Roosevelt, in Richard Hofstadter, The American Political Tradition, 1948.

The presidency is a young man's job. He rides herd on one hundred and eighty million people. That's it—physical gig. So big industry and educators continually have told me—especially big business—that a young president, even a thirty-year-old president, is better.

Because, here's the parallel: You want to take a chance on a man over fifty-five when Mutual of Omaha won't? That's just for a policy—this is the presidency. Rayburn is seventy-eight, and Allstate would kick him in the keester, man. So what a paradox that is. It's a young man's gig.

LENNY BRUCE, ca. 1960, in John Cohen, ed., *The Essential Lenny Bruce*, 1967.

We have entered the era of the "imperial" former presidency with lavish libraries, special staffs and benefits, around-the-clock Secret Service protection for life and other badges of privilege.

LAWTON CHILES, on legislation to cut cost of presidential perquisites, *Wall Street Journal*, July 27, 1984.

I think the American people want a solemn ass as a President. And I think I'll go along with them.

CALVIN COOLIDGE, to Ethel Barrymore, ca. 1924, *Time*, May 16, 1955.

Perhaps one of the most important accomplishments of my administration has been minding my own business.

CALVIN COOLIDGE, news conference, 1929.

When I was a boy I was told that anybody could become President; I'm beginning to believe it.

ATTRIBUTED TO CLARENCE DARROW.

The White House is another world. Expediency is everything.

JOHN DEAN, in article by Mary McGrory, *New York Post*, June 18, 1973.

Unlike presidential administrations, problems rarely have terminal dates.

DWIGHT D. EISENHOWER, State of the Union address, January 12, 1961.

No one should ever sit in this office over 70 years old, and that I know.

DWIGHT D. EISENHOWER in 1961, *Newsweek*, March 2, 1987.

I personally believe the Vice President of the United States should never be a nonentity. I believe he should be used. I believe he should have a very useful job.

DWIGHT D. EISENHOWER, in Nelson A. Rockefeller, *Unity, Freedom and Peace: A Blueprint for Tomorrow*, 1968.

The Constitution is larger than the executive branch.

DANIEL ELLSBERG, 1971, in Lois and Alan Gordon, *American Chronicle*, 1987.

Executive poppycock.

SAM ERVIN, 1973, in Lois and Alan Gordon, *American Chronicle*, 1987.

Vice President—it has such a nice ring to it!

GERALDINE A. FERRARO, *New York Times*, July 13, 1984.

Let me assure the distinguished Vice President of the United States that I have absolutely no designs on his job.

GERALD R. FORD, speech, Washington Gridiron Club, 1968.

To me the Presidency and the Vice Presidency were not prizes to be won but a duty to be done.

GERALD R. FORD, *A Time to Heal*, 1979.

A spare tire on the automobile of government.

JOHN NANCE GARNER, on the office of vice president, June 19, 1934.

Every president needs an SOB—and I'm Nixon's.

H.R. HALDEMAN, August 30, 1973.

My God, this is a hell of a job! I have no trouble with my enemies. I can take care of my enemies all right. But my damn friends, my goddamn friends....They're the ones that keep me walking the floor nights!

WARREN G. HARDING, to William Allen White, in White's *Autobiography*, 1946.

I believe that the people want an ordinary man as President, being a little tired of supermen....I believe that they want a little peace and quiet and rest from agitation and sensationalism and loud talk and back talk...and they sort of believe I want these reliefs myself. Make no mistake, the people of this country are as sound at heart as a good red apple, and always after a little emotionalism, they come back to the same, sane ways of business and government. You won't think I'm indulging in big talk, will you, if I say that is where I believe I fit in.

WARREN G. HARDING, interview, *New York Herald*, October 31, 1920, in Ralph G. Martin, *Ballots & Bandwagons*, 1964.

It would be supremely dangerous if a President were to believe in the myth of his own omnipotence. Fortunately, a new President is soon disabused.

ROBERT T. HARTMANN, *Palace Politics: An Inside Account of the Ford Years*, 1980.

In the Middle Ages it was the fashion to wear hair shirts to remind oneself of trouble and sin. Many years ago I concluded that a few hair shirts were part of the mental wardrobe of every man. The President differs from other men in that he has a more extensive wardrobe.

HERBERT HOOVER, speech, Washington, D.C., December 14, 1929.

There are only two occasions when Americans respect privacy, especially in Presidents. Those are prayer and fishing.

HERBERT HOOVER, *New York Herald Tribune*, May 19, 1947.

The Vice President will be and is what the President wants him to be.

HUBERT H. HUMPHREY, in Michael V. DiSalle, *Second Choice*, 1966.

I know I've got a heart big enough to be President. I know I've got guts enough to be President. But I wonder whether I've got intelligence and ability to be President—I wonder if any man does.

LYNDON B. JOHNSON, in Hugh Sidey, *A Very Personal Presidency: Lyndon Johnson in the White House*, 1968.

All I have I would have given gladly not to be standing here today.

LYNDON B. JOHNSON, first presidential address to Congress, November 27, 1963.

Now there are many, many people who can recommend and advise, and a few of them consent, but there is only one who has been chosen by the American people to decide.

LYNDON B. JOHNSON, speech, Omaha, Nebraska, June 30, 1966.

The presidency has made every man who occupied it, no matter how small, bigger than he was: and no matter how big, not big enough for its demands.

LYNDON B. JOHNSON, *New York Times*, March 26, 1972.

When things haven't gone well for you, call in a secretary or a staff man and chew him out. You will sleep better and they will appreciate the attention.

LYNDON B. JOHNSON, "Love It or Loathe It, Here's the Wit and Wisdom of LBJ," *People*, February 2, 1987.

I'm the only President you've got.

LYNDON B. JOHNSON, 1964, in Lois and Alan Gordon, *American Chronicle*, 1987.

The American Presidency is a formidable, exposed, and somewhat mysterious institution.

ATTRIBUTED TO JOHN F. KENNEDY.

To state the facts frankly is not to despair [for] the future nor indict the past. The prudent heir takes careful inventory of his legacies and gives a faithful accounting to those whom he owes an obligation of trust.

JOHN F. KENNEDY, on outgoing administrations, State of the Union address, January 30, 1961.

When I ran for the Presidency of the United States, I knew that this country faced serious challenges, but I could not realize, nor could any man realize who does not bear the burdens of this office, how heavy and constant would be those burdens.

JOHN F. KENNEDY, address to the nation on Berlin crisis, July 25, 1961.

The President...is rightly described as a man of extraordinary powers. Yet it is also true that he must wield those powers under extraordinary limitations—and it is these limitations which so often give the problem of choice its complexity and even poignancy. Lincoln, Franklin Roosevelt once remarked, "was a sad man because he couldn't get it all at once. And nobody can."

JOHN F. KENNEDY, Foreword, in Theodore C. Sorenson, *Decision-Making in the White House*, 1963.

I had plenty of problems when I came into office. But wait until the fellow who follows me sees what he will inherit.

JOHN F. KENNEDY, in Hugh Sidey, *John F. Kennedy, President: A Reporter's Inside Story*, 1963.

Frankly, I don't mind not being president. I just mind that someone else is.

EDWARD M. KENNEDY, speech, Washington Gridiron Club, March 22, 1986.

Everybody has a chance to become President of the United States. I'll sell mine for a quarter.

LAWRENCE LEE, 1934, in Lois and Alan Gordon, *American Chronicle*, 1987.

This is a most Presidential country. The tone and example set by the President have a tremendous effect on the quality of life in America. The President is like the conductor of a big symphony orchestra—and a new conductor can often get different results with the same score and the same musicians.

WALTER LIPPMANN, in article by William Attwood, *Look*, April 25, 1961.

If you are very active as Vice President, everyone in America knows your name. But that is your only property. It is not the same thing as real power—more like being a movie star.

NORMAN MAILER, *Miami and the Siege of Chicago*, 1968.

The Vice President of the United States is like a man in a cataleptic state: he cannot speak: he cannot move; he suffers no pain; and yet he is perfectly conscious of everything that is going on about him.

ATTRIBUTED TO THOMAS R. MARSHALL, ca. 1913.

There were once two brothers. One ran away to sea. The other was elected Vice President and neither was heard of again.

THOMAS R. MARSHALL, in Dick Gregory, *Dick Gregory's Political Primer*, 1972.

I don't think that you can lead from a position of vacillation. If you are going to lead, you've got to decide in advance whether the issue is one that you feel is worth fighting about. If it isn't, then you take no position at all. But if it is worth fighting about, you've got to take a clear-cut position and get all of the advantage that comes from being out in front.

RICHARD M. NIXON, in Earl Mazo, *Richard Nixon: A Political and Personal Portrait*, 1959.

Certainly in the next 50 years we shall see a woman president, perhaps sooner than you think. A woman can and should be able to do any political job that a man can do.

RICHARD M. NIXON, to League of Women Voters, Washington, D.C., April 16, 1969.

Under the doctrine of separation of powers, the manner in which the president personally exercises his assigned executive powers is not subject to questioning by another branch of government.

RICHARD M. NIXON, White House statement, March 12, 1973.

When the president does it, that means that it is not illegal.

RICHARD M. NIXON, TV interview with David Frost, May 4, 1977.

What kind of world view the American President has, how well he understands the uses of power and the nuances of diplomacy, whether he has a strategic vision and the will and shrewdness to carry it out—all these are vital, even indispensable, elements.

RICHARD M. NIXON, *The Real War*, 1980.

In Hollywood, if you didn't sing or dance, you would end up as an after-dinner speaker, so they made me an after-dinner speaker.

RONALD REAGAN, in Hedrick Smith et al., *Reagan the Man, the President*, 1980.

We'll all do the job as if there will never be another election. In other words...we'll take no actions or make no decisions that are based on how they might bear on or affect an election. Whatever we do will be based on what we believe, to the best of our ability, is best for the people of this country.

RONALD REAGAN, speech, first Cabinet meeting, March 30, 1981, in Rowland Evans and Robert Novak, *The Reagan Revolution*, 1981.

I've often wondered how some people in positions of this kind...manage without having had any acting experience.

RONALD REAGAN, interview with Barbara Walters, ABC-TV, March 24, 1986.

I have come to the conclusion that the 22nd Amendment [limiting the presidency to two terms] was a mistake. Shouldn't the people have the right to vote for someone as many times as they want to vote for him?

RONALD REAGAN, interview with Barbara Walters, ABC-TV, March 24, 1986.

Since I came to the White House I got two hearing aids, a colon operation, skin cancer, a prostate operation and I was shot. The damn thing is, I've never felt better in my life.

RONALD REAGAN, speech, Washington Gridiron Club, March 28, 1987.

There is far less to the presidency, in terms of essential activity, than meets the eye. A president moves through his days surrounded by literally hundreds of people whose relationship to him is that of a doting mother to a spoiled child. Whatever he wants is brought to him immediately—food, drink, helicopters, airplanes, people, in fact, everything but relief from his political problems.

GEORGE REEDY, *The Twilight of the Presidency*, 1970.

[The presidency] is preeminently a place of moral leadership.

FRANKLIN D. ROOSEVELT, in article by Anne O'Hare McCormick, *New York Times*, September 11, 1932.

It is the duty of the President to propose and it is the privilege of the Congress to dispose.

FRANKLIN D. ROOSEVELT, press conference, July 23, 1937.

I have a very definite philosophy about the Presidency. I think it should be a very powerful office, and I think the President should be a very strong man who uses without hesitation every power that the position yields; but because of this fact I believe that he should be sharply watched by the people [and] held to a strict accountability by them.

THEODORE ROOSEVELT, letter to Henry Cabot Lodge, July 19, 1908.

Oh, if I could only be President and Congress, too, for just ten minutes.

THEODORE ROOSEVELT, to Franklin D. Roosevelt, recalled in letter from FDR to Robert M. Ashburn, August 18, 1928.

A President's ability to govern depends partially on his equity in public opinion, partially on his relations with Congress, and largely on his willingness to impose his will on his own Executive Branch.

WILLIAM SAFIRE, Before the Fall, 1975.

The American democracy must discover a middle ground between making the President a czar and making him a puppet. The problem is to devise means of reconciling a strong and purposeful Presidency with equally strong and purposeful forms of democratic control. Or, to put it succinctly, we need a strong Presidency—but a strong Presidency *within the Constitution*.

ARTHUR M. SCHLESINGER, JR., The Imperial Presidency, 1973.

I have come to the conclusion that the major part of the work of a President is to increase the gate receipts of expositions and fairs and bring tourists into the town.

WILLIAM HOWARD TAFT, in Archibald W. Butt, Taft and Roosevelt, 1930.

Last night the moon, the stars and all the planets fell on me. If you fellows pray, pray for me.

HARRY S TRUMAN, to reporters on day after succeeding to the presidency, April 13, 1945.

In my opinion eight years as President is enough and sometimes too much for any man to serve in that capacity. There is a lure in power. It can get into a man's blood just as gambling and lust for money have been known to do.

HARRY S TRUMAN, memorandum, April 16, 1950.

The President of the United States is two people—he's the President and he's a human being.

HARRY S TRUMAN, speech, National Association of Broadcasters, November 14, 1950.

A President needs political understanding to *run* the government, but he may be *elected* without it.

HARRY S TRUMAN, Memoirs, 1955.

The opportunities afforded by the Vice Presidency, particularly the Presidency of the Senate, do not come—they are there to be seized. Here is one instance in which it is the man who makes the office, not the office the man.

HARRY S TRUMAN, Years of Decision, 1955.

Well all the President is, is a glorified public relations man who spends his time flattering, kissing, and kicking people to get them to do what they are supposed to do anyway.

HARRY S TRUMAN, letter to Mary Jane Truman, November 14, 1947, in Robert H. Ferrell, Off the Record, 1958.

Expansion of the Presidency in the twentieth century has dangerously altered the careful tripartite balance of governing powers established by the Constitution. The office has become too complex and its reach too extended to be trusted to the fallible judgment of any one individual. In today's world no one man is adequate for the reliable disposal of power that can affect the lives of millions—which may be one reason lately for the notable nonemergence of great men.

BARBARA TUCHMAN, "Should We Abolish the Presidency?" New York Times, February 13, 1973.

The American Presidency has become a greater risk than it is worth. The time has come to consider seriously the substitution of Cabinet government or some form of shared executive power.

BARBARA TUCHMAN, "Defusing the Presidency," New York Times, September 20, 1974.

Unless drastic reforms are made, we must accept the fact that every four years the United States will be up for sale, and the richest man or family will buy it.

GORE VIDAL, Postscript, "The Holy Family," Reflections Upon a Sinking Ship, June 6, 1968.

I wouldn't want a professional actor to be President of the United States, no matter how nice or bright he is because he's spent his entire life being moved about like a piece of furniture. He's used to being used....I couldn't imagine an actor as president, I could imagine a director. After all, he's a hustler, a liar, a cheat—plainly presidential.

GORE VIDAL, American Film, April, 1977.

It is an entirely personal office. What the President of today decides becomes the issue of tomorrow. He calls the dance.

THEODORE H. WHITE, *The Making of the President, 1960,* 1961.

From 40 to 60 percent of the Presidential office is not in administration but in morals, politics, and spiritual leadership....As President of the United States and servant of God, he has much more to do than to run a desk at the head of the greatest corporation in the world. He has to guide a people in the greatest adventure ever undertaken on the planet.

WILLIAM ALLEN WHITE, *Selected Letters,* 1947.

There never has been a great inarticulate President.

GEORGE WILL, "Democracy as Vaudeville," April 20, 1975, *The Pursuit of Happiness, and Other Sobering Thoughts,* 1978.

FOREIGN POLICY

The CIA is nothing more than the secret police of American capitalism, plugging up leaks in the political dam night and day so that shareholders of U.S. companies operating in poor countries can continue enjoying their rip-off.

PHILIP AGEE, *Time,* August 4, 1975.

What is lawful about a foreign policy which allows economic control of whole continents, which tells the Third World, as it tells our black people, "You'll make it sometime, but only under our system, at the pace we decide, by dole, by handout, by seamy charity, by delayed justice." Don't try it any other way!

DANIEL BERRIGAN, "Statement at Sentencing," *Prison Journals,* May 24, 1968.

Mr. President, the times call for candor. The Philippines are ours forever....And just beyond the Philippines are China's illimitable markets. We will not retreat from either....We will not renounce our part in the mission of our race, trustee, under God, of the civilization of the world....

It has been charged that our conduct of the war has been cruel. Senators, it has been the reverse....Senators must remember that we are not dealing with Americans or Europeans. We are dealing with Orientals.

ALBERT BEVERIDGE, speech to Congress on crushing Filipino rebellion, January 9, 1900.

In the judgment of this government, loans by American bankers to any foreign nation at war are inconsistent with the true spirit of neutrality.

WILLIAM JENNINGS BRYAN, statement to press, August 15, 1914.

For the mass public, it is easier to understand problems if they are reduced to black/white dichotomies. It is easier to understand policies if they are attached to individuals who are simplistically labeled as hawks or doves. Yet in today's world any attempt to reduce its complexities to a single set of ideological propositions, to a single personality, or to a single issue is in itself a distortion. Such a distortion also raises the danger that public emotions could become so strong as to make the management of a genuinely complex foreign policy well-nigh impossible.

ZBIGNIEW BRZEZINSKI, *Power and Principle,* 1983.

Among the nations of the world, only the United States of America has both the moral standing and the means to back it up. We are the only nation on this earth that could assemble the forces of peace.

GEORGE BUSH, in article by James Reston, *New York Times Magazine,* June 16, 1991.

Human rights is the soul of our foreign policy, because human rights is the very soul of our sense of nationhood.

JIMMY CARTER, ceremony commemorating 30th anniversary of UN Declaration of Human Rights, White House, December 6, 1978.

Aggression unopposed becomes a contagious disease.

JIMMY CARTER, on Soviet intervention in Afghanistan, address to nation, January 4, 1980.

America did not invent human rights. In a very real sense...human rights invented America.

JIMMY CARTER, farewell address, January 14, 1981.

Americans think of themselves collectively as a huge rescue squad on twenty-four-hour call to any spot on the globe where dispute and conflict may erupt.

ELDRIDGE CLEAVER, *Soul on Ice,* 1968.

Only when a menaced country has the whole-hearted support of its people and the will to resist to the limit of its resources should we consider an appeal for help.

J. LAWTON COLLINS, *War in Peacetime: The History and Lessons of Korea,* 1969.

The League [of Nations] exists as a foreign agency. We hope it will be helpful. But the United States sees no reason to limit its own freedom and independence of action by joining it.

CALVIN COOLIDGE, message to Congress, December 6, 1923.

Our government offers no objection to the carrying on of commerce by our citizens with the people of Russia. Our government does not propose, however, to enter into relations with another regime which refuses to recognize the sanctity of international obligations. I do not propose to barter away for the privilege of trade any of the cherished rights of humanity. I do not propose to make merchandise of any American principles.

CALVIN COOLIDGE, message to Congress, December 6, 1923.

Ultimately, the danger is not that military spending no longer is the adjunct of foreign policy, but that foreign policy becomes the adjunct of military spending.

NORMAN COUSINS, *Pathology of Power*, 1987.

We assert that no nation can long endure half republic and half empire, and we warn the American people that imperialism abroad will lead quickly and inevitably to despotism at home.

DEMOCRATIC PARTY PLATFORM PLANK, 1900.

The Democratic party favors the League of Nations as the surest…means of maintaining the peace of the world.

DEMOCRATIC PARTY PLATFORM PLANK, 1920.

We shall not make Britain's mistake. Too wise to try to govern the world, we shall merely own it. Nothing can stop us.

LUDWELL DENNY, *America Conquers Britain*, 1930.

You'll never run it without an iron fist. There isn't any other way. You've got to find a guy who won't be too much of a burglar. Let him steal a little and share the rest with the people. That makes sense to me.

EVERETT DIRKSEN, on U.S. policy in Latin America, in Neil MacNeil, *Dirksen: Portrait of a Public Man*, 1970.

Limited policies inevitably are defensive policies, and defensive policies inevitably are losing policies.

JOHN FOSTER DULLES, *War or Peace*, 1950.

We look on the world as a whole. We cannot be weak anywhere without creating danger everywhere.

JOHN FOSTER DULLES, in Andrew H. Berding, *Dulles on Diplomacy*, 1965.

If the United Nations once admits that international disputes can be settled by using force, then we will have destroyed the foundation of the organization and our best hope of establishing a world order.

DWIGHT D. EISENHOWER, on Israel's invasion of Egypt, address to nation, February 20, 1957.

In most communities it is illegal to cry "fire" in a crowded assembly. Should it not be considered serious international misconduct to manufacture a general war scare in an effort to achieve local political aims?

DWIGHT D. EISENHOWER, on Middle East crisis, address to U.N. General Assembly, August 13, 1958.

We are handicapped by policies based on old myths rather than current realities.

J. WILLIAM FULBRIGHT, speech to U.S. Senate, March 27, 1964.

The men in Washington seem unable to accept that there are more poor people than rich people in the world. They do not recognize that poor people, in the late twentieth century, cannot endure poverty and disease and ignorance forever.

MARTHA GELLHORN, "Wars in Central America," *The Face of War*, 1988.

The essence of good foreign policy is constant re-examination.

DAVID HALBERSTAM, *The Best and the Brightest*, 1969.

To America, China was a special country, different from other countries.…For the American missionaries loved China; it was, by and large, more exciting than Peoria, had a better life style and did not lack for worthy pagans to be converted; add to that the special quality of China, a great culture, great food, great charm, and the special relationship was cemented. The Chinese were puritanical, clean, hard-working, reverent, cheerful, all the virtues Americans most admired. And so a myth had grown up, a myth not necessarily supported by the facts, of the very special U.S.–China relationship.

DAVID HALBERSTAM, on China before Communist takeover, *The Best and the Brightest*, 1969.

The open door.

JOHN HAY, reference to trade policy just negotiated with China, January 2, 1900.

I don't know of any foreign leader that was ever assassinated by the CIA....There were always discussions of everything...things that may not be acceptable to the American people.

RICHARD HELMS, 1975, in Lois and Alan Gordon,
American Chronicle, 1987.

Protectionism is the ally of isolationism, and isolationism is the Dracula of American foreign policy.

WILLIAM G. HYLAND, speech, Washington University, St.
Louis, Missouri, *New York Times*, May 17, 1987.

If you let a bully come in your front yard, he'll be on your porch the next day and the day after that he'll rape your wife in your own bed.

LYNDON B. JOHNSON, in Walter Isaacson and Evan
Thomas, *The Wise Men*, 1986.

The best thing we can do if we want the Russians to let us be Americans is to let the Russians be Russian.

GEORGE F. KENNAN, "U.S.–Soviet Relations: The First 50
Years," WNET-TV, April 17, 1984.

[The lesson of Vietnam is] we must throw off the cumbersome mantle of world policeman and limit our readiness to areas where our interests are truly in danger.

EDWARD KENNEDY, 1975, in Lois and Alan Gordon,
American Chronicle, 1987.

Today we stand as the world's pre-eminent power. But there are signs that beneath the burnished steel of our remarkable weapons, America's underlying strength is rusting away.

EDWARD M. KENNEDY, speech to the Coalition for
Democratic Values, Chantilly, Virginia, January 26,
1991.

We cannot expect that all nations will adopt like systems, for conformity is the jailer of freedom and the enemy of growth.

JOHN F. KENNEDY, speech to U.N. General Assembly,
September 25, 1961.

Acting on our own, by ourselves, we cannot establish justice throughout the world; we cannot ensure its domestic tranquility, or provide for its common defense, or promote its general welfare, or secure the blessings of liberty to ourselves and our posterity. But joined with other free nations, we can do all this and more.

JOHN F. KENNEDY, speech, Philadelphia, Pennsylvania,
July 4, 1962, in J. William Fulbright, *Old Myths and
New Realities*, 1964.

Those who make peaceful revolution impossible will make violent revolution inevitable.

JOHN F. KENNEDY, to Latin American diplomats, White
House, March 12, 1962.

Domestic policy can only defeat us; foreign policy can kill us.

JOHN F. KENNEDY, in Arthur M. Schlesinger, Jr., *The
Imperial Presidency*, 1973.

A government is not legitimate merely because it exists.

JEANNE KIRKPATRICK, on Sandinista government in
Nicaragua, *Time*, June 17, 1985.

No foreign policy—no matter how ingenious—has any chance of success if it is born in the minds of a few and carried in the hearts of none.

HENRY KISSINGER, speech, International Platform
Association, August 2, 1973.

No nation has a monopoly of justice or virtue, and none has the capacity to enforce its own conceptions globally.

HENRY KISSINGER, in Richard Valeriani, *Travels with Henry*,
1979.

Revolutions conducted in the name of liberty more often than not refine new tools of authority.

HENRY KISSINGER, *White House Years*, 1979.

Most foreign policies that history has marked highly, in whatever country, have been originated by leaders who were opposed by experts.

HENRY KISSINGER, *Years of Upheaval*, 1982.

The American temptation [is] to believe that foreign policy is a subdivision of psychiatry.

HENRY KISSINGER, speech, University of South Carolina,
Time, June 17, 1985.

I maintain that Congress has the right and the duty to declare the object of the war, and the people have the right and the obligation to discuss it.

ROBERT M. LaFOLLETTE, SR., speech to U.S. Senate,
October 6, 1917.

Consistently and without noteworthy exception, the use of covert military action in support of American foreign policy has ended in failure or catastrophe. Whenever the United States embarks on one of those splendid little adventures so dear to the hearts of the would-be Machiavels in the White House or on the National Security Council, the patrol boats sink and the wrong tyrant seizes the palace and the radio station.

LEWIS H. LAPHAM, "Derring-Do," *Harper's*, February, 1988.

Some of the more fatuous flag-waving Americans are in danger of forgetting that you can't extract gratitude as you would extract a tooth; that unless friendship is freely given, it means nothing and less than nothing.

MAX LERNER, "How Grateful Should Europe Be?" *Actions and Passions*, 1949.

An alliance is like a chain. It is not made stronger by adding weak links to it. A great power like the United States gains no advantage and it loses prestige by offering, indeed peddling, its alliances to all and sundry. An alliance should be hard diplomatic currency, valuable and hard to get, and not inflationary paper from the mimeograph machine in the State Department.

WALTER LIPPMANN, *New York Herald Tribune*, August 5, 1952.

We have a habit of trying to get our fingers into every corner of the globe. I think we do that too often, sometimes too heavily, and perhaps a little restraint in the other direction might be beneficial in the years ahead.

MIKE MANSFIELD, speech to U.S. Senate, July, 1966, in Eugene McCarthy, *The Limits of Power*, 1967.

Our policy is directed not against any country or doctrine but against hunger, poverty, desperation and chaos. Its purpose should be the revival of a working economy in the world so as to permit the emergence of political and social conditions in which free institutions can exist.

GEORGE C. MARSHALL, on plan for European recovery from World War II, speech, Harvard University, *New York Times*, June 5, 1947.

Today our potential foreign obligations are almost unlimited. We have moved from a position of isolation and rejection of world responsibility to a position of isolated, almost singular responsibility for the whole world.

EUGENE J. MCCARTHY, *The Limits of Power*, 1967.

America today is more isolated than it has been since the heyday of isolationism, not by our withdrawal from the world but by the withdrawal of most of the world from us.

EUGENE J. MCCARTHY, *The Year of the People*, 1969.

Neither conscience nor sanity itself suggests that the United States is, should or could be the global gendarme.

ROBERT S. MCNAMARA, *New York Times*, May 19, 1966.

It's hard to imagine anything that would give our allies more cause to consider us unreliable

than that we say one thing in public and secretly do another.

GEORGE J. MITCHELL, Iran-Contra hearings, July 13, 1987.

Everywhere new hopes are rising for a world no longer overshadowed by fear, and want and war.

RICHARD M. NIXON, on SALT signing, 1972, in Lois and Alan Gordon, *American Chronicle*, 1987.

Am I wrong in listening to women who live in Nicaragua and follow the Sermon on the Mount? Or am I supposed to just sit here and believe generals?

THOMAS P. "TIP" O'NEILL, on testimony of Maryknoll nuns against U.S. aid to contras, in Jimmy Breslin, *New York Daily News*, June 29, 1986.

We have to put a shingle outside our door saying "Superpower Lives Here," no matter what the Soviets do, even if they evacuate from Eastern Europe.

COLIN POWELL, on eve of Panama invasion, in Michael T. Klare, "Policing the Gulf and the World," *The Nation*, October 15, 1990.

We built it, we paid for it, it's ours, and we're going to keep it.

RONALD REAGAN, on Panama Canal, speech, Texas, 1976.

My fellow Americans: I'm pleased to tell you today that I've signed legislation that will outlaw Russia forever. We begin bombing in five minutes.

RONALD REAGAN, joking while testing microphone, August 11, 1984.

The Republican party maintains the traditional American policy of noninterference in the political affairs of other nations. This government has definitely refused membership in the League of Nations and to assume any obligations under the convenant of the League.

REPUBLICAN PARTY PLATFORM PLANK, 1928.

This is the devilish thing about foreign affairs: they are foreign and will not always conform to our whim.

JAMES RESTON, *New York Times*, December 16, 1964.

We are revolutionaries, we Americans—although we abhor revolutions which are not made by our rules.

JAMES OLIVER ROBERTSON, *American Myth, American Reality*, 1980.

There's the one thing no Nation can ever accuse us of and that is Secret Diplomacy. Our Foreign dealings are an Open Book, generally a Check Book.

WILL ROGERS, in Donald Day, ed., *The Autobiography of Will Rogers*, 1949.

I just wish we knew a little less about his urethra and a little more about his arms sales to Iran.

ANDY ROONEY, "60 Minutes," CBS-TV, January 11, 1987.

There is a small articulate minority in this country which advocates changing our national symbol which is the eagle to that of the ostrich and withdrawing from the United Nations.

ELEANOR ROOSEVELT, speech, Democratic National Convention, July 22, 1952.

Our real battlefield today is Asia and our real battle is the one between democracy and communism.... We have to prove to the world and particularly to downtrodden areas of the world which are the natural prey to the principles of communist economics that democracy really brings about happier and better conditions for the people as a whole.

ELEANOR ROOSEVELT, memo to Harry S Truman, December 28, 1948, in Joseph P. Lash, *Eleanor: The Years Alone*, 1972.

In the field of world policy I would dedicate this nation to the policy of the good neighbor.

FRANKLIN D. ROOSEVELT, inaugural address, March 4, 1933.

There is a homely old adage which runs: "Speak softly and carry a big stick; you will go far." If the American nation will speak softly and yet build and keep at a pitch of the highest training a thoroughly efficient navy, the Monroe Doctrine will go far.

THEODORE ROOSEVELT, speech, Minnesota State Fair, September 2, 1901.

Damn the law! I want the [Panama] canal built.

ATTRIBUTED TO THEODORE ROOSEVELT, 1903.

There is a secret agreement between the United States and the Soviet Union...a simple but lucid treaty holding that when one side does something particularly fatheaded and self-destructive the other will respond by shooting itself in the foot within a period of from 17 to 30 days.

A.M. ROSENTHAL, *New York Times*, December 14, 1986.

We've got so much in the intelligence budget it makes you gag—who are we going to spy on—Albania?

PAT SCHROEDER, *New York Times Magazine*, July 1, 1990.

In America, getting on in the world means getting out of the world we have known before.

ELLERY SEDGWICK, *The Happy Profession*, 1946.

What a foreign policy we have. Our house is on fire in the Mideast, so we go down the Caribbean block, sneak in the back door of another burning house and kick Castro's dog. I can't say if dog kicking will endear us to Latin America, or stop houses from burning, but it seems to make Americans feel better.

IAN SHOALES, "Grenada," *I Gotta Go*, November, 1983.

What course a man will follow, or a nation, is set in no small measure by his basic creed, by what he really thinks about the true nature of the human being—his personality, his freedom, his destiny, his relation to others and to the rest of the universe.

EDMUND W. SINNOTT, in Arthur Goodfriend, *What Is America?*, 1954.

The new world order has a new rich odor.

SLOGAN DURING THE GULF WAR, 1991.

You take a fraction of reality and expand on it. It's very seldom totally at odds with the facts.... It's shaving a piece of reality off.

FRANK SNEPP, *Christian Science Monitor*, February 26, 1985.

We Americans can't seem to get it that you can't commit rape a little.

LINCOLN STEFFENS, on U.S. intervention in Mexico in 1914, *The Autobiography of Lincoln Steffens*, 1931.

No administration can conduct a sound foreign policy when the future sits in judgment on the past and officials are held accountable as dupes, fools or traitors for anything that goes wrong.

ADLAI E. STEVENSON, *Call to Greatness*, 1954.

Just being an American nowadays is not always comfortable. In the sensitive new areas some will denounce American aid as imperialism; but if it is not forthcoming we are denounced for indifference or discrimination. And sometimes if we stand correctly aloof from the local political scene we are accused of supporting reaction and the status quo. But if we don't keep our hands off and indicate some preference for policies or politicians then we are denounced for interfering. We are damned if we do and damned if we don't—at least now and then.

ADLAI E. STEVENSON, *Call to Greatness*, 1954.

We should be careful and discriminating in all the advice we give. We should be especially careful in giving advice that we would not think of following ourselves. Most of all, we ought to avoid giving counsel which we don't follow when it damages those who take us at our word.

ADLAI E. STEVENSON, lecture, University of Texas, September 28, 1955.

With the unlocking of the atom, mankind crossed one of the great watersheds of history. We have entered uncharted lands. The maps of strategy and diplomacy by which we guided ourselves until yesterday no longer reveal the way. Fusion and fission revolutionized the entire foundation of human affairs.

ADLAI E. STEVENSON, speech, General Federation of Women's Clubs, Philadelphia, Pennsylvania, May 24, 1955.

We cannot be any stronger in our foreign policy—for all the bombs and guns we may heap up in our arsenals—than we are in the spirit which rules inside the country. Foreign policy, like a river, cannot rise above its source.

ADLAI E. STEVENSON, speech, New Orleans, December 4, 1954, *What I Think*, 1956.

We can't behave towards people as superiors or inferiors....There isn't this feeling of status which defines permanently the relationship of one man to another.

We have a commitment to live and let live...a commitment to the idea that another people has the same right as we to live their own life as we have to live ours.

FRANK TANNENBAUM, in Arthur Goodfriend, *What Is America?*, 1954.

To the American people, it is inconceivable that military security can rest upon injustice, upon power, upon the ill-gotten fruits of imperialism and oppression.

FRANK TANNENBAUM, *The American Tradition in Foreign Policy*, 1955.

The struggle for liberty and self-government does not equate with the right of every rebel movement to commit ghastly crimes—to slaughter women and children in their beds; to organize guerilla bands to plunder, loot, and pillage; to torture and mutilate captives and prisoners.

DOROTHY THOMPSON, *The Courage To Be Happy*, 1957.

Now that Reagan has said that the [Nicaraguan] *contras* are the moral equivalent of the Founding Fathers, which one do you think is the most like Benjamin Franklin?

CALVIN TRILLIN, "Still Truly Needy," *The Nation*, May 18, 1985.

Everything was blamed on Castro. Mudslides in California. The fact that you can't buy a decent tomato anymore. Was there an exceptionally high pollen count in Massapequa, Long Island, one day? It was Castro, exporting sneezes.

CALVIN TRILLIN, "Castro Forgotten, Alas," King Features Syndicate, May 18, 1986.

I believe that it must be the policy of the United States to support free peoples who are resisting attempted subjugation by armed minorities or by outside pressures.

TRUMAN DOCTRINE, 1947.

The release of atomic energy constitutes a new force too revolutionary to consider in the framework of old ideas.

HARRY S TRUMAN, message to Congress, October 3, 1945.

The Marshall Plan will go down in history as one of America's greatest contributions to the peace of the world.

HARRY S TRUMAN, *Memoirs*, 1955.

In April 1917 the illusion of isolation was destroyed. America came to the end of innocence, and of the exuberant freedom of bachelor independence. That the responsibilities of world power have not made us happier is no surprise. To help ourselves manage them, we have replaced the illusion of isolation with a new illusion of omnipotence.

BARBARA TUCHMAN, "How We Entered World War I," *New York Times Magazine*, May 5, 1967.

Just because some of us can read and write and do a little math, that doesn't mean we deserve to conquer the universe.

KURT VONNEGUT, *Hocus Pocus*, 1990.

The danger of war is much less from communism than imperialism, whether it be of the U.S. or England.

HENRY A. WALLACE, Madison Square Garden, 1946, in Lois and Alan Gordon, *American Chronicle*, 1987.

We may well be unable to afford to be the world's policeman, but neither can we afford to fail to live up to the responsibilities that the accidents of a bountiful land and a beneficent fate have placed upon us.

WILLIAM C. WESTMORELAND, *A Soldier Reports*, 1976.

The foreign relations of the United States actually and potentially affect the state of the Union to a degree not widely realized and hardly surpassed by any other factor in the welfare of the whole nation. The position of the United States in the moral, intellectual, and material relations of the family of nations should be a matter of vital interest to every patriotic citizen. The national prosperity and power impose upon us duties which we cannot shirk if we are to be true to our ideals. The tremendous growth of the export trade of the United States has already made that trade a very real factor in the industrial and commercial prosperity of the country. With the development of our industries, the foreign commerce of the United States must rapidly become a still more essential factor in its economic welfare.

Whether we have a farseeing and wise diplomacy and are not recklessly plunged into unnecesssary wars, and whether our foreign policies are based upon an intelligent grasp of present-day world conditions and a clear view of the potentialities of the future, or are governed by a temporary and timid expediency or by narrow views befitting an infant nation, are questions in the alternative consideration of which we must convince any thoughtful citizen that no department of national polity offers greater opportunity for promoting the interests of the whole people on the one hand, or greater chance on the other of permanent national injury, than that which deals with the foreign relations of the United States.

The fundamental foreign policies of the United States should be raised high above the conflict of partisanship and wholly dissociated from differences as to domestic policy. In its foreign affairs the United States should present to the world a united front. The intellectual, financial, and industrial interests of the country and the publicist, the wage earner, the farmer, and citizen of whatever occupation must cooperate in a spirit of high patriotism to promote that national solidarity which is indispensable to national efficiency and to the attainment of national ideals....

The diplomacy of the present administration has sought to respond to modern ideas of commercial intercourse. This policy has been characterized as substituting dollars for bullets. It is one that appeals alike to idealistic humanitarian sentiments, to the dictates of sound policy and strategy, and to legitimate commercial aims. It is an effort frankly directed to the increase of American trade upon the axiomatic principle that the government of the United States shall extend all proper support to every legitimate and beneficial American enterprise abroad....

There exists in the world today a gigantic reservoir of good will toward us, the American people.
WENDELL WILLKIE, *One World*, 1943.

We have earned the slogan "Yanks, go home!"
EDMUND WILSON, Preface, *Europe Without Baedeker*, 1967.

Very well, we strike hands with our true comrades, the Communist Party.
EDMUND WILSON, 1932, in Lois and Alan Gordon,
American Chronicle, 1987.

No nation is fit to sit in judgment upon any other nation.
WOODROW WILSON, speech, New York City, April 20, 1915.

America cannot be an ostrich with its head in the sand.
WOODROW WILSON, speech, Des Moines, Iowa,
February 1, 1916.

There must be, not a balance of power, but a community of power; not organized rivalries, but an organized common peace.
WOODROW WILSON, speech to U.S. Senate, January 22,
1917.

A general association of nations must be formed under specific covenants for the purpose of affording mutual guarantees of political independence and territorial integrity to great and small states alike.
WOODROW WILSON, speech to Congress, last of
Fourteen Points, January 8, 1918.

Ours is become a nation too great to offend the least, too mighty to be unjust to the weakest, too lofty and noble to be ungenerous to the poorest and lowliest.
STEPHEN WISE, speech, July 4, 1905.

It is not possible to make to the Congress a communication upon the present foreign relations of the United States so detailed as to convey an adequate impression of the enormous increase in the importance and activities of those relations. If this government is really to preserve to the American people that free opportunity in foreign markets which will soon be indispensable to our prosperity, even greater efforts must be made. Otherwise the American merchant, manufacturer, and exporter will find many a field in which American trade should logically predominate preempted through the more energetic efforts of other governments and other commercial nations....

Congress should fully realize the conditions which obtain in the world as we find ourselves at the threshold of our middle age as a nation. We have emerged full grown as a peer in the great concourse of nations. We have passed through various formative periods. We have been self-centered in the struggle to develop our domestic resources and deal with our domestic questions. The nation is now too mature to continue in its foreign relations those temporary expedients natural to a people to whom domestic affairs are the sole concern.

In the past, our diplomacy has often consisted, in normal times, in a mere assertion of the right to international existence. We are now in a larger relation with broader rights of our own and obligations to others than ourselves. A number of great guiding principles were laid down early in the history of this government. The recent task of our diplomacy has been to adjust those principles to the conditions of today, to develop their corollaries, to find practical applications of the old principles expanded to meet new situations. Thus are being evolved bases upon which can rest the superstructure of policies which must grow with the destined progress of this nation.

The successful conduct of our foreign relations demands a broad and a modern view. We cannot meet new questions nor build for the future if we confine ourselves to outworn dogmas of the past and to the perspective appropriate at our emergence from colonial times and conditions. The opening of the Panama Canal will mark a new era in our international life and create new and worldwide conditions which, with their vast correlations and consequences, will obtain for hundreds of years to come. We must not wait for events to overtake us unawares. With continuity of purpose we must deal with the problems of our external relations by a diplomacy modern, resourceful, magnanimous, and fittingly expressive of the high ideals of a great nation.

WILLIAM HOWARD TAFT, message to Congress, December 3, 1912.

GOVERNMENT BUREAUCRACY

I will undoubtedly have to seek what is happily known as gainful employment, which I am glad to say does not describe holding public office.

DEAN ACHESON, on retirement as secretary of state, *Time*, December 22, 1952.

The greatest mistake I made was not to die in office.

DEAN ACHESON, on hearing funeral eulogies for John Foster Dulles, March 27, 1959.

The most important aspect of the relationship between the president and the secretary of state is that they both understand who is president.

DEAN ACHESON, interview with Dean Rusk, NBC-TV, March 26, 1969.

Some insomniacs take this or that potion. Our favorite soporific is the announcement by some official that this or that department will be run without regard to politics.

FRANKLIN P. ADAMS, *Nods and Becks*, 1944.

Bureaucracies are designed to perform public business. But as soon as a bureaucracy is established, it develops an autonomous spiritual life and comes to regard the public as its enemy.

BROOKS ATKINSON, "September 9," *Once Around the Sun*, 1951.

Regulations grow at the same rate as weeds.

NORMAN AUGUSTINE, *Augustine's Laws*, 1986.

Consul, n. In American politics, a person who having failed to secure an office from the people is given one by the Administration on condition that he leave the country.

AMBROSE BIERCE, *The Devil's Dictionary*, 1906.

Most bureaucratic regulations look like Chinese to me—and I can read Chinese.

W. MICHAEL BLUMENTHAL, *Washingtonian*, August, 1977.

There is nothing wrong with the United States that a dose of smaller and less intrusive government will not cure.

MILTON FRIEDMAN AND ROSE FRIEDMAN, *Tyranny of the Status Quo*, 1984.

The CIA over the years has given many virtuoso performances in the theater of geopolitical romance. It employs a repertory company of mimes and fantasts capable of believing almost any nonsense told to them in a paranoid whisper by almost anybody with a conspiracy theory to sell. The chronicle of the agency's exploits reads like a series of comic improvisations on a text by Pirandello or Molière.

LEWIS H. LAPHAM, "Going South," *Harper's*, September, 1986.

When it comes to an important portion of American ambassadorial appointments, we are still in the era of the Charge of the Light Brigade.

WILLIAM B. MACOMBER, on campaign donations in exchange for ambassadorial appointments, *New York Times*, November 20, 1984.

When considering regulations, half of what is published is probably 50 percent incorrect. The rest is 75 percent wrong.

NORMAN MAILER, in *Management* magazine, 1987.

The only thing that saves us from the bureaucracy is its inefficiency.

ATTRIBUTED TO EUGENE MCCARTHY.

Bureaucracy, the rule of no one, has become the modern form of despotism.

MARY MCCARTHY, "The Vita Activa," *The New Yorker*, October 18, 1958.

Any change is resisted because bureaucrats have a vested interest in the chaos in which they exist.

RICHARD M. NIXON, to Peter Flanigan, 1969, in William Safire, *Before the Fall*, 1975.

I beg each and every one of you to develop a passionate and public hatred for bureaucracy. Become a nuisance!

TOM PETERS, speech, U.S. Navy Civil Engineer Corps Officer School, December, 1986.

Bureaucracy does not take kindly to being assailed and isn't above using a few low blows and a knee to the groin when it fights back. Knowing this, I have become extremely cautious in dealing with government agencies.

RONALD REAGAN, *Where's the Rest of Me?*, 1965.

I have always stated that the nearest thing to eternal life we'll ever see on this earth is a government program.

RONALD REAGAN, speech, American Society of Newspaper Editors, April 9, 1986, in Lou Cannon, *President Reagan: The Role of a Lifetime*, 1991.

You don't have to be from Waco to know that when the Pentagon makes crooks rich and doesn't make America strong, that it's a bum deal.

ANN W. RICHARDS, Democratic National Convention, July 18, 1988.

The measurement of one gestation period of an original thought in a bureaucracy is still pending.

HUGH SIDEY, *Time*, November 29, 1976.

The effect of the American Presidency with its power of appointment in the Executive branch is overbearing. Advisers find it hard to say no to the President or to dispute policy because they know that their status, their invitation to the next White House meeting, depends on staying in line.

BARBARA TUCHMAN, *The March of Folly*, 1984.

There is something about a bureaucracy that does not like a poem.

GORE VIDAL, "Preface," *Sex, Death and Money*, 1968.

Government expands to absorb revenue and then some.

TOM WICKER, in article by Harold Faber, *New York Times Magazine*, March 17, 1968.

THE JUDICIARY

The judiciary must not take on the coloration of whatever may be popular at the moment. That is where society will indeed lose its way. Our role is very limited in that we are guardians of rights, and we have to tell people things they often do not like to hear.

ROSE BIRD, *Boston Globe*, December 25, 1982.

It's always the minorities who aren't a part of the mainstream who define what the limits of the state, or the limits of the majority, are going to be. And as a result, the courts are the ones who step in. My role isn't to be politically smart. My role is to do what's right under the constitution. And if that's politically unpopular, so be it.

ROSE BIRD, *The Nation*, January 18, 1986.

A great many academic theorists state explicitly, and some judges seem easily persuaded, that elected legislators and executives are not adequate to decide the moral issues that divide us, and that judges should therefore take their place. But when Americans are morally divided, it is appropriate that our laws reflect that fact....Our popular institutions, the legislative and executive branches, were structured to provide safety, to achieve compromise when we are divided, to slow change, to dilute absolutisms....They are designed, in short, to do the very things that abstract generalizations about moral principles and the just society tend to bring into contempt.

ROBERT BORK, *The Tempting of America*, 1990.

When courts are viewed as political bodies, we may expect judicial confirmations that are increasingly bitter. We may also expect a constitutional law that lurches suddenly in one direction or another as one faction or another gains the upper hand, a constitutional law that is seen as too crucial a political weapon to be left to nonpolitical judges, and certainly too important to be left to the actual Constitution.

ROBERT BORK, *The Tempting of America*, 1990.

Judges are the weakest link in our system of justice, and they are also the most protected.

ALAN M. DERSHOWITZ, *Newsweek*, February 20, 1978.

How long we shall continue to blunder along without the aid of unpartisan and authoritative scientific assistance in the administration of justice, no one knows; but all fair persons not conventionalized by provincial legal habits of mind ought, I should think, to unite to effect some such change.

LEARNED HAND, opinion, *Parke, Davis & Co. v. H.K. Mulford Co.*, 1911.

It is of course true that any kind of judicial legislation is objectionable on the score of the limited interests which a Court can represent, yet there are wrongs which in fact legislatures can-

not be brought to take an interest in, at least not until the Courts have acted.

LEARNED HAND, letter to Louis D. Brandeis, January 22, 1919.

I do not think the United States would come to an end if we [the Supreme Court] lost our power to declare an act of Congress void.

OLIVER WENDELL HOLMES, JR., speech, New York City, February 15, 1913.

May God twist my tripes, if I string out the obvious for the delectation of fools!

OLIVER WENDELL HOLMES, JR., on delivering longer opinions, ca. 1911, in Catherine Drinker Bowen, *Yankee from Olympus*, 1944.

The judicial system is the most expensive machine ever invented for finding out what happened and what to do about it.

IRVING R. KAUFMAN, *Time*, May 5, 1980.

The [Supreme] Court's only armor is the cloak of public trust; its sole ammunition, the collective hopes of our society.

IRVING R. KAUFMAN, "Keeping Politics Out of the Court," *New York Times*, December 9, 1984.

[A Supreme Court] decision does not establish a "supreme law of the land" that is binding on all persons and parts of government, henceforth and forevermore.

EDWIN MEESE III, speech, Tulane University, *New York Times*, October 23, 1986.

Our judges have been, on the whole, both able and upright public servants....But their whole training and the aloofness of their position on the bench prevent their having, as a rule, any real knowledge of, or understanding sympathy with, the lives and needs of the ordinary hard-working toiler.

THEODORE ROOSEVELT, speech, Santiago, Chile, November 22, 1913.

Putting a black robe on a man doesn't make him give just decisions, any more than putting a suit on a monkey makes him a man.

MELVIN B. TOLSON, "Big Fish Eat Little Fish—and the Color of the Fish Doesn't Count," *Washington Tribune*, May 13, 1939.

Greed vs. greed makes for the kind of lawsuits that are settled between the lawyers as soon as both sides decide to take what they can get. Principle vs. principle is a holy war, and no holy war has ever been settled out of court.

BILL VEECK, *Thirty Tons a Day*, 1972.

MCCARTHYISM

We're about as much in favor of Communism as J. Edgar Hoover.

HUMPHREY BOGART AND LAUREN BACALL, 1948, in Lois and Alan Gordon, *American Chronicle*, 1987.

We've had a long Winter, and not only in terms of weather. Humankind has achieved a kind of mass cabin fever. Life has been a serious matter, so serious that we got to forgetting that man can make a very funny fool of himself being serious.

And taking other foolish men seriously. It has become a political crime, somehow, to laugh at some of the performers.

HAL BORLAND, on U.S. Senate Subcommittee on Internal Security, *New York Times*, April 11, 1954.

A generation of workers learned to conform or to move on. Those who moved on learned how to change their identities, to migrate, to lose their trackers, to resurface as immaculate Americans. But in the process careers were ruined beyond retrieve, marriages broke up, children were alien-

---

Tonight as we celebrate the one hundred and forty-first birthday of one of the greatest men in American history, I would like to be able to talk about what a glorious day today is in the history of the world. As we celebrate the birth of this man, who with his whole heart and soul hated war, I would like to be able to speak of peace in our time, of war being outlawed, and of worldwide disarmament. These would be truly appropriate things to be able to mention as we celebrate the birthday of Abraham Lincoln.

Five years after a world war has been won, men's hearts should anticipate a long peace, and men's minds should be free from the heavy weight that comes with war. But this is not such a period—for this is not a period of peace. This is a time of the "cold war." This is a time when all the world is split into two vast, increasingly hostile armed camps—a time of a great armaments race. Today we can almost physically hear the mutterings and rumblings of an invigorated god of war. You can see it, feel it, and hear it all the way from the hills of Indochina, from the shores of Formosa, right over into the very heart of Europe itself.

The one encouraging thing is that the "mad moment" has not yet arrived for the firing of the gun or the exploding of the bomb which will set civilization about the final task of destroying itself. There is still a hope for peace if we finally decide that no longer can we safely blind our eyes and

close our ears to those facts which are shaping up more and more clearly. And that is that we are now engaged in a showdown fight—not the usual war between nations for land areas or other material gains but a war between two diametrically opposed ideologies....

The real, basic difference...lies in the religion of immoralism—invented by Marx, preached feverishly by Lenin, and carried to the unimaginable extremes by Stalin. This religion of immoralism, if the Red half of the world wins—and well it may—this religion of immoralism will more deeply wound and damage mankind than any conceivable economic or political system.

Karl Marx dismissed God as a hoax, and Lenin and Stalin have added in clear-cut, unmistakable language their resolve that no nation, no people who believe in a God can exist side by side with their communistic state....

Today we are engaged in a final, all-out battle between communistic atheism and Christianity. The modern champions of communism have selected this as the time. And, ladies and gentlemen, the chips are down—they are truly down....

Ladies and gentlemen, can there be anyone here tonight who is so blind as to say that the war is not on? Can there be anyone who fails to realize that the Communist world has said, "The time is now"—that this is the time for the show-down between the democratic Christian world and the

ated and abused, fathers sat for hours, stunned, staring blankly at the wall.

David Caute, *The Great Fear: The Anti-Communist Purge Under Truman and Eisenhower*, 1978.

It was the Truman administration that manured the soil from which the prickly cactus called McCarthy suddenly and awkwardly shot up.

David Caute, *The Great Fear: The Anti-Communist Purge Under Truman and Eisenhower*, 1978.

Such pip-squeaks as Nixon and McCarthy are trying to get us so frightened of Communism that we'll be afraid to turn out the lights at night.

Helen Gahagan Douglas, speech, 1950, in Lee Israel, "Helen Gahagan Douglas," *Ms.*, October, 1973.

The junior senator from Wisconsin, by his reckless charges, has so preyed upon the fears and hatreds and prejudices of the American people that he has started a prairie fire which neither he nor anyone else may be able to control.

J. William Fulbright, speech to U.S. Senate, November 30, 1954.

Communist atheistic world? Unless we face this fact, we shall pay the price that must be paid by those who wait too long....

At war's end we were physically the strongest nation on earth and, at least potentially, the most powerful intellectually and morally. Ours could have been the honor of being a beacon in the desert of destruction, a shining, living proof that civilization was not yet ready to destroy itself. Unfortunately, we have failed miserably and tragically to arise to the opportunity.

The reason why we find ourselves in a position of impotency is not because our only powerful, potential enemy has sent men to invade our shores, but rather because of the traitorous actions of those who have been treated so well by this nation. It has not been the less fortunate or members of minority groups who have been selling this nation out, but rather those who have had all the benefits that the wealthiest nation on earth has had to offer—the finest homes, the finest college education, and the finest jobs in government we can give.

This is glaringly true in the State Department. There the bright young men who are born with silver spoons in their mouths are the ones who have been worst....

In my opinion the State Department, which is one of the most important government departments, is thoroughly infested with Communists.

I have in my hand fifty-seven cases of individuals who would appear to be either card-carrying members or certainly loyal to the Communist Party, but who nevertheless are still helping to shape our foreign policy.

One thing to remember in discussing the Communists in our government is that we are not dealing with spies who get thirty pieces of silver to steal the blueprints of a new weapon. We are dealing with a far more sinister type of activity because it permits the enemy to guide and shape our policy....

Actually, ladies and gentlemen, one of the important reasons for the graft, the corruption, the dishonesty, the disloyalty, the treason in high government positions—one of the most important reasons why this continues—is a lack of moral uprising on the part of the 140 million American people. In the light of history, however, this is not hard to explain.

It is the result of an emotional hangover and a temporary moral lapse which follows every war. It is the apathy to evil which people who have been subjected to the tremendous evils of war feel. As the people of the world see mass murder, the destruction of defenseless and innocent people, and all of the crime and lack of morals which go with war, they become numb and apathetic. It has always been thus after war. However, the morals of our people have not been destroyed. They still exist. This cloak of numbness and apathy has only needed a spark to rekindle them. Happily, this spark has finally been supplied....

Joseph R. McCarthy, speech, Wheeling, West Virginia, February 9, 1950.

I would like to speak briefly and simply about a serious national condition. It is a national feeling of fear and frustration that could result in national suicide and the end of everything that we Americans hold dear. It is a condition that comes from the lack of effective leadership either in the legislative branch or the executive branch of our Government. That leadership is so lacking that serious and responsible proposals are being made that national advisory commissions be appointed to provide such critically needed leadership.

I speak as briefly as possible because too much harm has already been done with irresponsible words of bitterness and selfish political opportunism. I speak as simply as possible because the issue is too great to be obscured by eloquence. I speak simply and briefly in the hope that my words will be taken to heart.

Mr. President, I speak as a Republican. I speak as a woman. I speak as a United States Senator. I speak as an American.

The United States Senate has long enjoyed world-wide respect as the greatest deliberative body in the world. But recently that deliberative character has too often been debased to the level of a forum of hate and character assassination sheltered by the shield of congressional immunity.

It is ironical that we Senators can in debate in the Senate, directly or indirectly, by any form of words, impute to any American who is not a Senator any conduct or motive unworthy or unbecoming an American—and without that non-Senator American having any legal redress against us—yet if we say the same thing in the Senate about our colleagues we can be stopped on the grounds of being out of order.

It is strange that we can verbally attack anyone else without restraint and with full protection, and yet we hold ourselves above the same type of criticism here on the Senate floor. Surely the United States Senate is big enough to take self-criticism and self-appraisal. Surely we should be able to take the same kind of character attacks that we "dish out" to outsiders.

I think that it is high time for the United States Senate and its members to do some real soul searching and to weigh our consciences as to the manner in which we are performing our duty to the people of America and the manner in which we are using or abusing our individual powers and privileges.

I think it is high time that we remembered that we have sworn to uphold and defend the Constitution. I think it is high time that we remembered that the Constitution, as amended, speaks not only of the freedom of speech but also of trial by jury instead of trial by accusation.

Whether it be a criminal prosecution in court or a character prosecution in the Senate, there is little practical distinction when the life of a person has been ruined.

Those of us who shout the loudest about Americanism in making character assassinations are all too frequently those who, by our own words and acts, ignore some of the basic principles of Americanism—

Before every free conscience in America is subpoenaed, please speak up.

JUDY GARLAND, 1947, in Lois and Alan Gordon, *American Chronicle*, 1987.

I well know from my own experience how essential it is for the survival of our democracy that scholars and teachers should have freedom of the mind to pursue truth "with clear eyes unafraid." Now our witchhunters are trying to drive students and teachers into conformity with a rigid concept of Americanism defined by ignorant and irresponsible politicians. If we do not check this movement, we shall become a totalitarian state like the Fascist and Communist models and our colleges and universities will produce frightened rabbits instead of scholars with free minds.

VIRGINIA GILDERSLEEVE, "The Inescapable Desert," *Many a Good Crusade*, 1954.

Joe McCarthy was over the land.

LILLIAN HELLMAN, *Pentimento*, 1973.

Truth made you a traitor as it often does in a time of scoundrels.

LILLIAN HELLMAN, *Scoundrel Time*, 1976.

The right to criticize.

The right to hold unpopular beliefs.

The right to protest.

The right of independent thought.

The exercise of these rights should not cost one single American citizen his reputation or his right to a livelihood nor should he be in danger of losing his reputation or livelihood merely because he happens to know someone who holds unpopular beliefs. Who of us does not? Otherwise none of us could call our souls our own. Otherwise thought control would have set in.

The American people are sick and tired of being afraid to speak their minds lest they be politically smeared as Communists or Fascists by their opponents. Freedom of speech is not what it used to be in America. It has been so abused by some that it is not exercised by others.

The American people are sick and tired of seeing innocent people smeared and guilty people whitewashed. But there have been enough proved cases, such as the Amerasia case, the Hiss case, the Coplon case, the Gold case, to cause nationwide distrust and strong suspicion that there may be something to the unproved, sensational accusations....

As a woman, I wonder how the mothers, wives, sisters, and daughters feel about the way in which members of their families have been politically mangled in Senate debate—and I use the word "debate" advisedly.

As a United States Senator, I am not proud of the way in which the Senate has been made a publicity platform for irresponsible sensationalism. I am not proud of the reckless abandon in which unproved charges have been hurled from this side of the aisle. I am not proud of the obviously staged, undignified countercharges which have been attempted in retaliation from the other side of the aisle.

I do not like the way the Senate has been made a rendezvous for vilification, for selfish political gain at the sacrifice of individual reputations and national unity. I am not proud of the way we smear outsiders from the floor of the Senate and hide behind the cloak of congressional immunity and still place ourselves beyond criticism on the floor of the Senate.

As an American, I am shocked at the way Republicans and Democrats alike are playing directly into the Communist design of "confuse, divide, and conquer." As an American, I do not want a Democratic administration whitewash or cover-up any more than I want a Republican smear or witch hunt.

As an American, I condemn a Republican Fascist just as much as I condemn a Democrat Communist. I condemn a Democrat Fascist just as much as I condemn a Republican Communist. They are equally dangerous to you and me and to our country. As an American, I want to see our Nation recapture the strength and unity it once had when we fought the enemy instead of ourselves.

MARGARET CHASE SMITH, speech to U.S. Senate, June 1, 1950.

You can't help smelling them [the Reds].

RUPERT HUGHES, 1947, in Lois and Alan Gordon, American Chronicle, 1987.

Are they going to scare us into silence?

FREDRIC MARCH, 1947, in Lois and Alan Gordon, American Chronicle, 1987.

McCarthyism is Americanism with its sleeves rolled.

JOSEPH R. MCCARTHY, theme for reelection to U.S. Senate, 1952, in Richard H. Rovere, Senator Joe McCarthy, 1959.

How can we account for our present situation unless we believe that men high in this government are concerting to deliver us to disaster? This must be the product of a great conspiracy, a conspiracy on a scale so immense as to dwarf any previous venture in the history of man. A conspiracy of infamy so black that, when it is finally exposed, its principals shall be forever deserving of the maledictions of all honest men.

JOSEPH R. MCCARTHY, speech to U.S. Senate, June 14, 1951, in Richard Hofstadter, The Paranoid Style in American Politics, 1965.

While I cannot take the time to name all the men in the State Department who have been named as members of the Communist Party and members of a spy ring, I have here in my hand a list of 205 that were known to the Secretary of State as being members of the Communist Party and who nevertheless are still working and shaping policy in the State Department.

JOSEPH R. McCARTHY, speech, Wheeling, West Virginia,
February 9, 1950, in David Halberstam, *The Best and the Brightest*, 1969.

Last night I discussed Communists in the State Department. I stated that I had the names of 57 card-carrying members of the Communist Party....Now, I want to tell the Secretary this: If he wants to call me tonight at the Utah Hotel, I will be glad to give him the names of those 57 card-carrying members.

JOSEPH R. McCARTHY, speech, February 10, 1950, in Fred
J. Cook, *The Nightmare Decade*, 1971.

You can't fight Communism with perfume.

JOSEPH R. McCARTHY, 1952, in Lois and Alan Gordon,
American Chronicle, 1987.

I'd like to see them all in Russia....A taste of Russia would cure them [the Reds].

ADOLPHE MENJOU, 1947, in Lois and Alan Gordon,
American Chronicle, 1987.

If none of us ever read a book that was "dangerous," had a friend who was "different," or joined an organization that advocated "change," we would all be just the kind of people Joe McCarthy wants. Whose fault is that? Not really [McCarthy's]. He didn't create this situation of fear. He merely exploited it, and rather successfully.

EDWARD R. MURROW, "See It Now," CBS-TV, March 7, 1954.

No one can terrorize a whole nation, unless we are all his accomplices.

EDWARD R. MURROW, "See It Now," CBS-TV, March 7,
1954.

Adlai [is] the appeaser...who got his Ph.D. from Dean Acheson's College of Cowardly Communist Containment.

RICHARD M. NIXON, 1952, in Lois and Alan Gordon,
American Chronicle, 1987.

Came postwar Hollywood, when McCarthy's tumbrels rolled and the mournful cry of the fink—"Bring out your dead heresies"—resounded through the streets.

S.J. PERELMAN, *The Last Laugh*, 1981.

The Communist plan for Hollywood was remarkably simple. It was merely to take over the motion picture business. Not only for its profits, as the hoodlums had tried—but also for a grand worldwide propaganda base.

RONALD REAGAN, *Where's the Rest of Me?*, 1965.

Once they get movies throttled, how long before we're told what we can say...into a radio microphone?

FRANK SINATRA, 1947, in Lois and Alan Gordon, *American Chronicle*, 1987.

The struggle against demagoguery scarcely fits the St. George-against-the-dragon myth....Our democratic St. George goes out rather reluctantly with armor awry.

NORMAN THOMAS, on 30th anniversary of U.S. Senate's
censure of McCarthy, *New York Times*, December 2,
1984.

Until this moment, Senator [McCarthy], I think I never really gauged your cruelty or your recklessness.

If it were in my power to forgive you for your reckless cruelty I would do so. I like to think that I am a gentle man, but your forgiveness will have to come from someone other than me.

Let us not assassinate this lad further, Senator. You have done enough. Have you no sense of decency, sir, at long last? Have you left no sense of decency?

JOSEPH NYE WELCH, to House Un-American Activities
Committee, 1954.

PARTIES AND ELECTIONS

For five weeks I traveled across beautiful autumnal America. It was like a booby hatch for the criminally insane....At various stops along the route there were campaigning politicans clamoring for use of the electric chair, the gallows or the gas chamber as devices for restoring public civility. Everywhere one was confronted with what seemed like a national obsession for more and more security.

RUSSELL BAKER, in Howard Zinn, *The Twentieth Century*,
1982.

Vote for the man who promises least; he'll be the least disappointing.

BERNARD BARUCH, in Meyer Berger, *Meyer Berger's New
York*, 1960.

Truman? I never can remember that name.

JOHN W. BRICKER, speech, 1944.

This is the first convention of the space age—where a candidate can promise the moon and mean it.

DAVID BRINKLEY, on 1960 Democratic National
Convention, *Newsweek*, March 13, 1961.

Without the thousands of women volunteers, the American [political] party system would not work. It would break down in a confusion of unanswered letters, unmade phone calls, unkept appointments, unwritten speeches and unheld meetings.

SHIRLEY CHISHOLM, statement to subcommittee of House
Committee on Education and Labor, July 1, 1970.

The difference between Democrats and Republicans has always been measured in courage and confidence. The Republicans believe the wagon train will not make it to the frontier unless some of our old, some of our young, and some of our weak are left behind by the side of the trail. The strong will inherit the land! We Democrats believe that we can make it all the way with the whole family intact.

MARIO CUOMO, speech, Democratic National
Convention, San Francisco, California, July 16, 1984.

We must get the American public to look past the glitter, beyond the showmanship, to the reality, the hard substance of things. And we'll do it...not so much with speeches that will bring people to their feet as with speeches that bring people to their senses.

MARIO CUOMO, speech, Democratic National
Convention, San Francisco, California, July 16, 1984.

You campaign in poetry. You govern in prose.

MARIO CUOMO, *New Republic*, April 8, 1985.

The convention will be deadlocked, and after the other candidates have gone their limit, some twelve or fifteen men, worn out and bleary-eyed for lack of sleep, will sit down, about two o'clock in the morning, around a table in a smoke-filled room in some hotel, and decide the nomination. When that time comes, Harding will be selected.

HARRY M. DAUGHERTY, accurate prediction of circumstances
of Harding's presidential nomination, 1920.

We cannot have jobs and opportunities if we surrender our freedom to Government control.... We can have both opportunity and security within the framework of a free society.

THOMAS E. DEWEY, speech, 1944.

Voting is the most basic essential of citizenship and I think that any man or woman in this country who fails to avail himself or herself of that right should hide in shame. I truly wish there were some sort of badge of dishonor that a non-voter would have to wear.

INDIA EDWARDS, *Pulling No Punches*, 1977.

It'll play in Peoria.

JOHN EHRLICHMAN, in William Safire, *Before the Fall*, 1968.

In the strongest language you can command you can state that I have no political ambitions at all. Make it even stronger than that if you can.

DWIGHT D. EISENHOWER, , speech, Abilene, Kansas, June
22, 1945, *Eisenhower Speaks*, 1948.

A rigged convention is one with the other man's delegates in control. An open convention is when your delegates are in control.

JAMES A. FARLEY, *Convention and Election Almanac*, 1964.

You don't go through a bloodbath like this and then walk away from it.

GERALDINE FERRARO, *Newsweek*, September 3, 1984.

Today is the first day of the rest of the campaign.

GERALDINE FERRARO, *Newsweek*, September 3, 1984.

Hell, I never vote *for* anybody, I always vote *against*.

W.C. FIELDS, in Robert Lewis Taylor, *W.C. Fields, His
Follies and Fortunes*, 1949.

By now, we have accepted the campaign as performance. We have become sophisticated about thirty-second bites. We know that candidates fly from market to market instead of city to city. We've seen Presidents sold like products; we know what goes on the political screen.

ELLEN GOODMAN, "Voters and Viewers," *Washington
Post*, March, 1988.

In most places in the country, voting is looked upon as a right and a duty, but in Chicago it's a *sport*. In Chicago not only *your* vote counts, but all kinds of other votes—kids, dead folks, and so on.

DICK GREGORY, *Dick Gregory's Political Primer*, 1972.

When it comes to persuading the electorate, there is currently nothing more important to a candidate than a wife, kids, and the right kind of animals. Dogs are great assets to candidates, and the feeling seems to be engendered that if a dog loves the candidate, he can't be all that bad.

DICK GREGORY, *Dick Gregory's Political Primer*, 1972.

There are two major kinds of promises in politics: the promises made by candidates to the voters and the promises made by the candidates to persons and groups able to deliver the vote. Promises falling into the latter category are loosely called "patronage," and promises falling into the former category are most frequently called "lies."

DICK GREGORY, *Dick Gregory's Political Primer*, 1972.

Political promises are much like marriage vows. They are made at the beginning of the relationship between candidate and voter, but are quickly forgotten. When voters catch a candidate breaking political promises, they try to overlook it.

DICK GREGORY, *Dick Gregory's Political Primer*, 1972.

The apathy of the modern voter is the confusion of the modern reformer.

LEARNED HAND, speech, Washington, D.C., March 8, 1932.

We drew to a pair of deuces and filled.

WARREN G. HARDING, on hearing of his nomination for president, June 12, 1920.

A crucial feature of the political apparatus in America is that greater differences are harbored within each major party than the differences existing between them.

TOM HAYDEN, Port Huron Statement, 1962.

Honor is not the exclusive property of any political party.

HERBERT HOOVER, *Christian Science Monitor*, May 21, 1964.

I've always voted for Roosevelt as President. My father always voted for Roosevelt as President.

BOB HOPE, 1944, in Lois and Alan Gordon, *American Chronicle*, 1987.

My constituency is the desperate, the damned, the disinherited, the disrespected and the despised.

JESSE JACKSON, speech, Democratic National Convention, San Francisco, California, July 17, 1984.

I cast my bread on the waters long ago. Now it's time for you to send it back to me—toasted and buttered on both sides.

JESSE JACKSON, to black voters, January 30, 1984.

A political convention is just not a place where you can come away with any trace of faith in human nature.

MURRAY KEMPTON, *America Comes of Middle Age*, 1963.

The ignorance of one voter in a democracy impairs the security of all.

JOHN F. KENNEDY, speech, Vanderbilt University, Nashville, Tennessee, May 18, 1963.

[Democrats] can't get elected unless things get worse—and things won't get worse unless they get elected.

JEANE KIRKPATRICK, *Time*, June 17, 1985.

Look, I don't even agree with *myself* at times.

JEANE KIRKPATRICK, on leaving Democratic Party to register as Republican, NBC-TV, April 3, 1985.

We cannot encourage a process that has a political saliva test administered by candidates.

WILLIAM KOVACH, on allowing campaign managers to veto proposed panelists for presidential debates, *Time*, October 22, 1984.

A three-year diet of rubber chicken and occasional crow.

CHARLES KRAUTHAMMER, on presidential campaigns, "The Appeal of Ordeal," *Time*, May 14, 1982.

I've never belonged to any political party for more than fifteen minutes.

FIORELLO H. LAGUARDIA, in John Gunther, *Inside U.S.A.*, 1947.

Why do good public servants break with political parties? It's so simple. The political people never ask you to do anything that's right—and that's what you're going to do anyway! No. What they want you to do is all the things that are wrong.

FIORELLO H. LAGUARDIA, in John Gunther, *Inside U.S.A.*, 1947.

The effort to calculate exactly what the voters want at each particular moment leaves out of account the fact that when they are troubled the thing the voters most want is to be told what to want.

WALTER LIPPMANN, "The Bogey of Public Opinion," *Vanity Fair*, December, 1931.

There exists...some kind of rule which in a democratic society limits what the voters will stand for in the way of sacrifice for the public good—the public good which is not immediately, obviously, and directly to their own personal advantage.

WALTER LIPPMANN, column, *New York Herald Tribune*, December 29, 1966.

And it is here, under this oak where Evangeline waited for her lover, Gabriel, who never came. This oak is an immortal spot, made so by Longfellow's poem, but Evangeline is not the only one who has waited here in disappointment. Where are the schools that you have waited for your children to have, that have never come? Where are the roads and highways that you send your money to build, that are no nearer now than before? Where are the institutions to care for the sick and the disabled? Evangeline wept bitter tears in her disappointment, but it lasted through only one lifetime. Your tears in this country, around this oak, have lasted for generations. Give me the chance to dry the tears of those who still weep here!

HUEY P. LONG, speech, 1927, in T. Harry Williams, *Huey Long*, 1969.

What they [direct primaries] actually appear to have accomplished is a confusion and vast expenditure of money that have proved to be, if not worse, at all events no better, than the old way of selecting candidates.

ALICE ROOSEVELT LONGWORTH, *Crowded Hours*, 1933.

A person's political party is usually determined, like his religion, by his family, and it is difficult for any one unfamiliar with this culture to picture the intense emotional concern that follows the accident of birth into one or the other camp.

ROBERT S. LYND AND HELEN MERRELL LYND, *Middletown: A Study in Contemporary American Culture*, 1929.

The Democrats were going to nominate a man who, no matter how serious his political dedication might be, was indisputably and willy-nilly going to be seen as a great box-office actor, and the consequences of that were staggering.

NORMAN MAILER, "Superman Comes to the Supermarket," 1960.

A political convention is after all not a meeting of a corporation's board of directors; it is a fiesta, a carnival, a pig-rooting, horse-snorting, band-playing, voice-screaming medieval get-together of greed, practical lust, compromised idealism, career-advancement, meeting, feud, vendetta, conciliation, of rabble-rousers, fist fights (as it used to be), embraces, drunks (again as it used to be) and collective rivers of animal sweat.

NORMAN MAILER, *Some Honorable Men: Political Conventions, 1960–1972*, 1976.

Running those poor steers back and forth in the heat is ridiculous.... What they ought to do is put the steers in the convention hall and run the delegates.

STANLEY MARCUS, on efforts to project Western image during Republican National Convention, Dallas, Texas, *New York Times*, August 28, 1984.

The unwritten rule of the bandwagon is simply that a front runner must always keep the front runner position, always make some gain, great or slight, on each succeeding ballot. To slip back

even slightly is generally fatal. And, once a bandwagon front runner gets passed by another candidate, he is almost always out. It is just about that simple and that deadly.

RALPH G. MARTIN, *Ballots & Bandwagons*, 1964.

Handshaking is friendly until your hands bleed. Confetti looks festive until you're forced to spit out mouthfuls hurled directly into your face. Applause is wonderful until you can hardly hear yourself speak. A crush of screaming women is flattering until they tear your clothes.

RALPH G. MARTIN, *A Hero for Our Time*, 1983.

The campaign kickoff was so dismal that it needed a plastic surgeon instead of a press agent to put a face on it.

JANE MAYER, on Mondale-Ferraro presidential campaign, *Wall Street Journal*, September 11, 1984.

Have you ever tried to split sawdust?

EUGENE J. MCCARTHY, reply to charge that he divided Democratic Party, NBC-TV, October 23, 1969.

The whole campaign was a tragic case of mistaken identity.

GEORGE MCGOVERN, on his unsuccessful 1972 presidential campaign, *New York Times*, May 6, 1973.

I'm 1000% for Tom Eagleton, and I have no intention of dropping him from the ticket.

GEORGE MCGOVERN, 1972, in Lois and Alan Gordon, *American Chronicle*, 1987.

There is always some basic principle that will ultimately get the Republican party together. If my observations are worth anything, that basic principle is the cohesive power of public plunder.

A.J. MCLAURIN, speech to U.S. Senate, May, 1906.

We heard from the abortionists and we heard from the people who looked like Jacks, acted like Jills and had the odors of Johns.

GEORGE MEANY, on 1972 Democratic National Convention, *Wall Street Journal*, July 11, 1984.

All the great patriots now engaged in edging and squirming their way towards the presidency of the Republic run true to form. This is to say they are all extremely wary, and all more or less palpable frauds. What they want, primarily, is the job; the necessary equipment of unescapable issues, immutable principles and soaring ideals can wait until it becomes more certain which way the mob will be whooping.

H.L. MENCKEN, on 1920 primaries, *On Politics*, 1956.

I don't want to spend the next two years in Holiday Inns.

WALTER F. MONDALE, on withdrawal from 1976
campaign, November 21, 1974.

In our system, at about 11:30 on election night, they just push you off the edge of the cliff—and that's it. You might scream on the way down, but you're going to hit the bottom, and you're not going to be in elective office.

WALTER F. MONDALE, on losing to Reagan in 1984, *New York Times*, March 4, 1987.

Any party which takes credit for the rain must not be surprised if its opponents blame it for the drought.

DWIGHT W. MORROW, in a campaign speech, October, 1930.

In the pageant of unity [at the Democratic National Convention], one speaker after another recited a Whitmanesque litany of races and classes and minorities and interests and occupations—or unemployments. Some speakers, in fact, made the nation sound like an immense ingathering of victims—terrorized senior citizens, forsaken minorities, Dickensian children—warmed by the party's Frank Capra version of America: Say, it's a wonderful life!

LANCE MORROW, "All Right, What Kind of People Are We?" *Time*, July 30, 1984.

People vote like it is. Ronald Reagan is a vote to return to the company store.

JACK NICHOLSON, *Rolling Stone*, 1986.

The Democrats let it all out and love to shout and laugh and have fun. The Republicans have fun but they don't want people to see it. The Democrats, even when they are not having fun, like to appear to be having fun.

RICHARD M. NIXON, diary entry, 1973.

I wouldn't bet the farm on it, but I'd bet the main house. I wouldn't even bet the outhouse on Mondale.

RICHARD M. NIXON, on Reagan's chances of defeating Mondale in 1984, *Time*, May 21, 1984.

The secret is to always let the other man have your way.

CLAIBORNE PELL, on first political campaign, *New York Times*, February 3, 1987.

There were so many candidates on the platform that there were not enough promises to go around.

RONALD REAGAN, on Democratic presidential primary debate in New Hampshire, February 6, 1984.

This election is a contest between those who are satisfied with what they have, and those who know we can do better. That's what this election is really all about. It's about the American dream—those who want to keep it for the few, and those who know it must be nurtured and passed along.

ANN W. RICHARDS, Democratic National Convention, July 18, 1988.

The Republicans have their splits right after election and Democrats have theirs just before an election.

WILL ROGERS, newspaper column, December 29, 1930.

Politics has got so expensive that it takes lots of money to even get beat with.

WILL ROGERS, newspaper column, June 28, 1931.

I pledge you, I pledge myself, to a new deal, for the American people. Let us all here assembled constitute ourselves prophets of a new order of competence and courage. This is more than a political campaign; it is a call to arms.

FRANKLIN D. ROOSEVELT, acceptance of presidential nomination, 1932, in Lois and Alan Gordon, *American Chronicle*, 1987.

I wish in this campaign to do...whatever is likely to produce the best results for the Republican ticket. I am as strong as a bull moose and you can use me up to the limit.

THEODORE ROOSEVELT, letter to Mark Hanna, June 27, 1900.

The old parties are husks, with no real soul within either, divided on artificial lines, boss-ridden and privilege-controlled, each a jumble of incongruous elements, and neither daring to speak out wisely and fearlessly on what should be said on the vital issues of the day.

THEODORE ROOSEVELT, speech, Progressive Party convention, Chicago, Illinois, August 6, 1912.

The advance planning and sense stimuli employed to capture a $10 million cigarette or soap market are nothing compared to the brainwashing and propaganda blitzes used to ensure control of the largest cash market in the world: the Executive Branch of the United States Government.

PHYLLIS SCHLAFLY, *A Choice Not an Echo*, 1964.

The 1972 campaign may well come out of a political museum full of relics from 1932 and 1936; our politics will then become as camp as our entertainment.

PETER SCHRAG, *The Vanishing American*, 1972.

The problems seem so easy out there on the stump. Deficits shrink with a rhetorical flourish.

HUGH SIDEY, "Talking Peace and Pork Chops," *Time*, January 23, 1984.

There are enough mistakes of the Democrats for the Republicans to criticize constructively without resorting to political smears....Freedom of speech is not what it used to be in America.

MARGARET CHASE SMITH, *Declaration of Conscience*, 1972.

When people keep telling you that you can't do a thing, you kind of like to try it.

MARGARET CHASE SMITH, announcement of presidential candidacy, *Time*, February 7, 1964.

Someone asked me, as I came in, down on the street, how I felt and I was reminded of a story that a fellow townsman of ours used to tell— Abraham Lincoln. They asked him how he felt once after an unsuccessful election. He said he felt like a little boy who had stubbed his toe in the dark. He said that he was too old to cry, but it hurt too much to laugh.

ADLAI E. STEVENSON, on his defeat in presidential election, November 5, 1952.

An election is both a selection and rejection; it is a choosing up of sides. It matters greatly whether reason or passion guides our choice. Reason will enlighten and elevate our understanding and it will discover in controversy the springs of a new unity. But passion will poison the political atmosphere in which the nation must meet the tests of the future.

ADLAI E. STEVENSON, speech, Indianapolis, Indiana, September 18, 1954.

The idea that you can merchandise candidates for high office like breakfast cereal—that you can gather votes like box tops—is, I think, the ultimate indignity to the democratic process.

ADLAI E. STEVENSON, speech, Democratic National Convention, August 18, 1956.

When a country is denied a choice on the most burning issue of the time, the war in Vietnam, then the two-party system has become a one-party rubber stamp. This is the first and essential point to be made in the wake of the Democratic and Republican conventions. The Establishment and the military have locked the ballot boxes.

I.F. STONE, "When a Two-Party System Becomes a One-Party Rubber Stamp," *I.F. Stone's Weekly*, September 9, 1968.

I am widely known in the field...for once having furnished a candidate for mayor of Buffalo with the campaign slogan "Never Been Indicted."

CALVIN TRILLIN, "The Motto-Maker's Art," *The Nation*, February 23, 1985.

Republicans are...bloodsuckers with offices in Wall Street, princes of privilege, plunderers.

HARRY S TRUMAN, whistle-stop speech, 1948.

I'll mow 'em down, Alben. I'll give 'em Hell.

HARRY S TRUMAN, to Vice President Barkley (overheard), 1948, in Lois and Alan Gordon, *American Chronicle*, 1987.

In America, where the electoral process is drowning in commercial techniques of fund-raising and image-making, we may have completed a circle back to a selection process as unconcerned with qualifications as that which made Darius King of Persia.

BARBARA TUCHMAN, reference to selection of Darius chosen because his horse was first to neigh at sunrise, *The March of Folly*, 1984.

The difference between a national Democrat and an Alabama Democrat is like the difference between a Communist and a non-Communist.

GEORGE WALLACE, *New York Times Magazine*, April 24, 1966.

A candidate could easily commit political suicide if he were to come up with an unconventional thought during a presidential tour.

E.B. WHITE, "Sootfall and Fallout," October 18, 1956, *Essays of E.B. White*, 1977.

No bands play on election day, no troops march, no guns are readied, no conspirators gather in secret headquarters. The noise and the blare, the bands and the screaming, the pageantry and oratory of the long fall campaign, fade on election day. All the planning is over, all effort spent. Now the candidates must wait.

THEODORE H. WHITE, *The Making of the President, 1960*, 1961.

All dressed up, with nowhere to go.

WILLIAM ALLEN WHITE, on Progressive Party after Theodore Roosevelt retired from presidential competition, 1916.

Celebrity, not mastery, is the fruit of victory.

GEORGE WILL, on Carter White House, "The Denim Presidency," March 6, 1978, *The Pursuit of Virtue and Other Tory Notions*, 1982.

Free elections are created by free men, not vice versa. The machinery of election will not call up, establish, or guarantee political freedom. The belief that it will reveals our trust in "the market," our belief that *competition* of itself makes excellence prevail.

GARRY WILLS, *Nixon Agonistes*, 1970.

Each election year is a revelation—in the way the electorate is consulted, wooed, or baffled; in the way issues are chosen, presented, or evaded; in the demands and promises made, compromises struck, strains felt tacitly or voiced. The nation at once celebrates and mourns itself.

GARRY WILLS, *Nixon Agonistes*, 1970.

POLITICAL PHILOSOPHIES

Liberals! They're not leaders! If they were real leaders they'd understand that their style of politicking and self-aggrandizement is what's destroying the capacity of any of us to get anywhere.

BELLA ABZUG, in Mel Ziegler, *Bella!*, 1972.

A liberal is a man who leaves the room when the fight starts.

HEYWOOD BROUN, in Robert E. Drennan, *The Algonquin Wits*, 1968.

All I want is the same thing you want. To have a nation with a government that is as good and honest and decent and competent and compassionate and as filled with love as are the American people.

JIMMY CARTER, speech, Sacramento, California, May 20, 1976.

A simple and a proper function of government is just to make it easy for us to do good and difficult for us to do wrong.

JIMMY CARTER, acceptance speech, Democratic National Convention, New York City, July 15, 1976.

A strong nation, like a strong person, can afford to be gentle, firm, thoughtful, and restrained. It can afford to extend a helping hand to others. It's a weak nation, like a weak person, that must behave with bluster and boasting and rashness and other signs of insecurity.

JIMMY CARTER, speech, New York City, October 14, 1976.

If you fear making anyone mad, then you ultimately probe for the lowest common denominator of human achievement.

JIMMY CARTER, to Future Farmers of America, Kansas City, November 9, 1978.

For this generation, ours, life is nuclear survival, liberty is human rights, the pursuit of happiness is a planet whose resources are devoted to the physical and spiritual nourishment of its inhabitants.

JIMMY CARTER, farewell address, January 14, 1981.

The governments of the past could fairly be characterized as devices for maintaining in perpetuity the place and position of certain privileged classes, without any ultimate protection for the rights of the people. The Government of the United States is a device for maintaining in perpetuity the rights of the people, with the ultimate extinction of all privileged classes.

CALVIN COOLIDGE, speech, Philadelphia, Pennsylvania, September 25, 1924.

The principal business of government is to further and promote human strivings.

WILBUR L. CROSS, interview, *New York Times*, March 29, 1931.

We believe that while survival of the fittest may be a good working description of the process of evolution, a government of humans should elevate itself to a higher order, one which fills the gaps left by chance or a wisdom we don't understand.

MARIO CUOMO, speech, Democratic National Convention, July 16, 1984.

I have one yardstick by which I test every major problem—and that yardstick is: Is it good for America?

DWIGHT D. EISENHOWER, on farm bill veto, address to nation, April 16, 1956.

A government big enough to give you everything you want is a government big enough to take from you everything you have.

GERALD R. FORD, speech to Congress, August 12, 1974.

To the free man, the country is the collection of individuals who compose it, not something over and above them. He is proud of a common heritage and loyal to common traditions. But he regards government as a means, an instrumentality, neither a grantor of favors and gifts, nor a master or god to be blindly worshipped and served. He recognizes no national goal except as it is the consensus of the goals the citizens severally serve. He recognizes no national purpose except as it is the consensus of the purposes for which the citizens severally strive.

MILTON FRIEDMAN, *Capitalism and Freedom*, 1962.

Economic freedom is an essential requisite for political freedom. By enabling people to cooperate with one another without coercion or central direction, it reduces the area over which political power is exercised.

MILTON FRIEDMAN AND ROSE FRIEDMAN, *Free To Choose*, 1980.

Sooner or later—and perhaps sooner than many of us expect—an ever bigger government would destroy both the prosperity that we owe to the free market and the human freedom proclaimed so eloquently in the Declaration of Independence.

MILTON FRIEDMAN AND ROSE FRIEDMAN, *Free To Choose*, 1980.

A liberal is a man who is willing to spend somebody else's money.

CARTER GLASS, interview, Associated Press, September 24, 1938.

None of us here in Washington knows all or even half of the answers. You people out there in the fifty states had better understand that. If you love your country, don't depend on handouts from Washington for your information. If you cherish your freedom, don't leave it all up to BIG GOVERNMENT.

BARRY M. GOLDWATER, *Why Not Victory?*, 1962.

In order to qualify as an American liberal a man had to favor compulsory FEPC, regard Taft-Hartley as completely evil, believe in the total wickedness of Generalissimo Chiang Kai-shek, take his political economics from John Maynard Keynes, and look to Washington for the answers to all problems.

JOSEPH C. HARSCH, *The Reporter*, September, 1952.

One cannot have political power without political obedience; one cannot have strong government without a sense of national identification.

ROBERT L. HEILBRONER, *An Inquiry into the Human Prospect*, 1980.

No matter how noble the objectives of a government, if it blurs decency and kindness, cheapens human life, and breeds ill will and suspicion—it is an evil government.

ERIC HOFFER, *The Passionate State of Mind*, 1954.

During 150 years we have [built] up a form of self-government and a social system which is peculiarly our own. It differs essentially from all others in the world. It is the American system. It is just as definite and positive a political and social system as has ever been developed on earth. It is founded upon a particular conception of self-government in which decentralized local responsibility is the very base. Further than this, it is founded upon the conception that only through ordered liberty, freedom and equal opportunity to the individual will his initiative and enterprise spur on the march of progress. And in our insistence upon equality of opportunity has our system advanced beyond all the world.

HERBERT HOOVER, speech, 1928.

Liberalism is a force truly of the spirit, a force proceeding from the deep realization that economic freedom cannot be sacrificed if political freedom is to be preserved.

HERBERT HOOVER, speech, 1928.

You cannot extend the mastery of the government over the daily working life of a people without at the same time making it the master of the people's souls and thoughts. Every expansion of government in business means that government in order to protect itself from the political consequences of its errors and wrongs is driven irresistibly without peace to greater and greater control of the nation's press and platform. Free speech does not live many hours after free industry and free commerce die.

HERBERT HOOVER, speech, New York City, October 22, 1928.

Even if governmental conduct of business could give us more efficiency instead of less efficiency, the fundamental objection to it would remain unaltered and unabated. It would destroy political equality. It would increase rather than decrease abuse and corruption. It would stifle initiative and invention. It would undermine the development of leadership. It would cramp and cripple the mental and spiritual energies of our people. It would extinguish equality and opportunity. It would dry up the spirit of liberty and progress.

HERBERT HOOVER, speech, New York City, October 22, 1928.

I not only believe majority rule is just, I believe it is best. All men know more than a few; all experience is better than new and untried theory.

EDGAR WATSON HOWE, *Success Easier Than Failure*, 1917.

A Conservative: One who is opposed to the things he is in favor of.

ELBERT HUBBARD, *The Roycroft Dictionary and Book of Epigrams*, 1923.

We are the standard-bearers in the only really authentic revolution, the democratic revolution against tyrannies. Our strength is not to be measured by our military capacity alone, by our industry, or by our technology. We will be remembered, not for the power of our weapons, but for the power of our compassion, our dedication to human welfare.

HUBERT H. HUMPHREY, *The Cause Is Mankind*, 1964.

Order is the first responsibility of government; without it, there can be no justice and no progress. Those who imply that continued rioting and disruption will lead to social progress are very wrong; such behavior leads instead to hardening resistance to progress, and to repression.

HUBERT H. HUMPHREY, *Beyond Civil Rights: A New Day of Equality*, 1968.

Creeping off college campuses, where liberal fascists find it easy to intimidate undergraduates, the noxious gestalt of "politically correct thinking" is emerging as the left's agenda for the '90s. This ideological sweet treat is based on familiar Marxist lines of racism, feminism and socialism, buttered with a pat of anti-capitalist environmentalism. To be Politically Correct, a devotee must slavishly humor in thought, word, and deed the rigid orthodoxy of this cult of victimization or else be threatened with an *ism* dagger.

PAUL IZZO, "In Quayle's Corner," *The Quayle Quarterly*, Winter/Spring, 1991.

The next Administration must do more than provide comfort for the comfortable.

EDWARD M. KENNEDY, Democratic National Convention, Atlanta, Georgia, July 19, 1988.

Helping citizens to do more should not become an excuse for government doing less, or cutting vital social programs to the bone. Survival of the fittest is unacceptable social policy. We do not intend to permit the noble Democratic ideal of empowerment to become just a fancy Republican word for the same old Republican neglect.

EDWARD M. KENNEDY, speech to the Coalition for Democratic Values, Chantilly, Virginia, January 26, 1991.

When at some future date the high court of history sits in judgment on each one of us—recording whether in our brief span of service we fulfilled our responsibilities to the state—our success or failure, in whatever office we may hold, will be measured by the answers to four questions—were we truly men of courage...were

we truly men of judgment...were we truly men of integrity...were we truly men of dedication?

JOHN F. KENNEDY, to Massachusetts legislature, *New York Times*, January 10, 1961.

Despite the repeated attempts of worthy people to persuade Americans that racial, sexual and ethnic quotas are necessary to achieve social justice, large majorities of citizens firmly and properly reject the argument. These opponents insist that quotas are incompatible with equal opportunity, fairness, and the principle of reward based in merit. Both political parties know how unpopular quotas are, and each claims that it, too, rejects the concept.

JEANE KIRKPATRICK, *Washington Post*, June 24, 1991.

Governments can encourage the cultivation of private virtue. They can provide a framework in which we may pursue virtue (or happiness), but they cannot make us virtuous (or happy), and the effort to use the coercive power of government for that purpose not only fails to produce private morality, it undermines public morality as well.

JEANE KIRKPATRICK, speech, Washington, D.C., September 29, 1982.

It is perfectly true that that government is best which governs least. It is equally true that that government is best which provides most.

WALTER LIPPMANN, "The Red Herring," *A Preface to Politics*, 1914.

Only the insider can make the decisions, not because he is inherently a better man, but because he is so placed that he can understand and can act.

WALTER LIPPMANN, "Insiders and Outsiders," *New Republic*, November 13, 1915.

You must not complicate your government beyond the capacity of its electorate to understand it. If you do, it will escape all control, turn corrupt and tyrannical, lose the popular confidence, offer real security to no man, and in the end it will let loose all the submerged antagonisms within the state.

WALTER LIPPMANN, *Atlantic Monthly*, October, 1924.

To those who charge that liberalism has been tried and found wanting, I answer that the failure is not in the idea, but in the course of recent history. The New Deal was ended by World War II. The New Frontier was closed by Berlin and Cuba almost before it was opened. And the Great Society lost its greatness in the jungles of Indochina.

GEORGE McGOVERN, lecture, Oxford University, *New York Times*, January 22, 1973.

America is still a government of the naive, for the naive, and by the naive. He who does not know this, nor relish it, has no inkling of the nature of his country.

CHRISTOPHER MORLEY, *Inward Ho!*, 1923.

Somehow liberals have been unable to acquire from life what conservatives seem to be endowed with at birth: namely, a healthy skepticism of the powers of government agencies to do good.

DANIEL PATRICK MOYNIHAN, *New York Post*, May 14, 1969.

Participatory Democracy.

NEW LEFT SLOGAN, ca. 1960.

We find it almost as difficult as the communists to believe that anyone could think ill of us, since we are as persuaded as they that our society is so essentially virtuous that only malice could prompt criticism of any of our actions.

REINHOLD NIEBUHR, *The Irony of American History*, 1952.

No, radicals aren't rioting on America's college campuses. Why should they?

There's no reason to riot when your radical philosophy is preached in the classroom and those with opposing views are denied a chance to air them....

You and I can't afford to let the left brainwash our young people with lies and propaganda.

JAMES QUAYLE, fund-raising letter for Young America Foundation, 1991.

Asking one of the states to surrender part of her sovereignty is like asking a lady to surrender part of her chastity.

JOHN RANDOLPH, in Russell Kirk, *John Randolph of Roanoke*, 1951.

Something the liberal will have to explain and stand trial for is his inability to see the Communist as he truly is and not as some kind of Peck's Bad Boy of liberalism who is basically all right but just a bit overboard and rough-edged. This ideological myopia is even true of some who have met the Reds in philosophical combat and who should have learned something from crossing swords.

RONALD REAGAN, *Where's the Rest of Me?*, 1965.

Sadly I have come to realize that a great many so-called liberals aren't liberal—they will defend to the death your right to agree with them.

RONALD REAGAN, *Where's the Rest of Me?*, 1965.

This absorption of revenue by all levels of government, the alarming rate of inflation and the rising toll of unemployment all stem from a single source: the belief that government, particularly the federal government, has the answer to our ills, and that the proper method of dealing with social problems is to transfer power from the private to the public sector, and within the public sector from state and local governments to the ultimate power center in Washington. This collectivist, centralizing approach, whatever name or party label it wears, has created our economic problems.

RONALD REAGAN, speech, Chicago Executives Club, September 26, 1975.

I'm sure everyone feels sorry for the individual who has fallen by the wayside or who can't keep up in our competitive society, but my own compassion goes beyond that to those millions of unsung men and women who get up every morning, send the kids to school, go to work, try to keep up the payments on their house, pay exorbitant taxes to make possible compassion for the less fortunate, and as a result have to sacrifice many of their own desires and dreams and hopes. Government owes them something better than always finding a new way to make them share the fruit of their toils with others.

RONALD REAGAN, *Sincerely, Ronald Reagan*, 1976.

In this present crisis, government is not the solution to our problem. Government is the problem.

RONALD REAGAN, on inflation and unemployment, inaugural address, January 20, 1981.

My belief has always been...that wherever in this land any individual's constitutional rights are being unjustly denied, it is the obligation of the federal government—at point of bayonet if necessary—to restore that individual's constitutional rights.

RONALD REAGAN, press conference, May 17, 1983.

Government exists to protect us from each other. We can't afford the government it would take to protect us from ourselves.

RONALD REAGAN, in Laurence I. Barrett, *Gambling with History—Reagan in the White House*, 1983.

Republicans believe every day is the Fourth of July, but Democrats believe every day is April 15.

RONALD REAGAN, *New York Times*, October 10, 1984.

For the average American, the message is clear. Liberalism is no longer the answer. It is the problem.

RONALD REAGAN, 1979, in Lois and Alan Gordon,
American Chronicle, 1987.

The trend of Democracy is toward socialism, while the Republican party stands for a wise and regulated individualism. Socialism would destroy wealth; Republicanism would prevent its abuse. Socialism would give to each an equal right to take; Republicanism would give to each an equal right to earn. Socialism would offer an equality of possession which would soon leave no one anything to possess; Republicanism would give equality of opportunity.

REPUBLICAN PARTY platform plank, 1908.

I thought it would help if Presidents and other leaders told the truth, and mentioned the word "sacrifice" once in a while. I didn't think we should amend the Constitution to conform to every popular whim of the day, or try to police the bedrooms of the American people. I thought it was unwise to corner dictators and other wild beasts, and since Presidents were not immortal, I favored Vice Presidents that were as reliable as a spare tire. I was for a longer school year because I was more interested in smart kids than "smart bombs," and I was for voluntary national service by young people to help in the overburdened, overexpensive hospitals, and for a national anthem that anybody could sing, drunk or sober.

JAMES RESTON, *New York Times Magazine*, June 16, 1991.

Now, we Democrats believe that America is still the country of fair play, that we can come out of a small town or a poor neighborhood and have the same chance as anyone else, and it doesn't matter whether we are black or Hispanic or disabled or women.

ANN W. RICHARDS, Democratic National Convention,
July 18, 1988.

Whereas a tightly centralized government tends, by its disproportionate weight and power, to stifle diversity and creativity in both the public and private sectors, a federal system provides room for both infinite variety and creativity in all sectors of national life. This is equally true for political organizations, philanthropic associations, social institutions, or economic enterprises.

NELSON A. ROCKEFELLER, *The Future of Federalism*, 1962.

America is not just a power; it is a promise. It is not enough for our country to be extraordinary in might; it must be exemplary in meaning. Our

honor and our role in the world finally depend on the living proof that we are a just society.

NELSON A. ROCKEFELLER, *Unity, Freedom and Peace: A Blueprint for Tomorrow*, 1968.

Taxes are paid in the sweat of every man who labors because they are a burden on production and can be paid only by production. If excessive, they are reflected in idle factories, tax-sold farms, and, hence, in hordes of the hungry tramping the streets and seeking jobs in vain. Our workers may never see a tax bill, but they pay in deductions from wages, in increased cost of what they buy or (as now) in broad cessation of employment.

FRANKLIN D. ROOSEVELT, speech, Pittsburgh,
Pennsylvania, October 19, 1932.

The economic royalists complain that we seek to overthrow the institutions of America. What they really complain of is that we seek to take away their power. Our allegiance to American institutions requires the overthrow of this kind of power. In vain they seek to hide behind the flag and the Constitution. In their blindness they forget what the flag and the Constitution stand for.

FRANKLIN D. ROOSEVELT, speech, Democratic National
Convention, Philadelphia, Pennsylvania, June 27, 1936.

The only sure bulwark of continuing liberty is a government strong enough to protect the interests of the people, and a people strong enough and well enough informed to maintain its sovereign control over its government.

FRANKLIN D. ROOSEVELT, radio address, April 14, 1938.

A radical is a man with both feet firmly planted—in the air. A conservative is a man with two perfectly good legs who...has never learned to walk forward. A reactionary is a somnambulist walking backward. But a liberal is a man who uses his legs and his hands at the behest—at the command—of his head.

FRANKLIN D. ROOSEVELT, radio address, October 26,
1939.

Everything is un-American that tends either to government by a plutocracy, or government by a mob. To divide along the lines of section or caste or creed is un-American. All privilege based on wealth, and all enmity to honest men merely because they are wealthy, are un-American— both of them equally so. Americanism means the virtues of courage, honor, justice, truth, sincerity, and hardihood—the virtues that made America.

The things that will destroy America are prosperity-at-any-price, peace-at-any-price, safety-first instead of duty-first, the love of soft living, and the get-rich-quick theory of life.

THEODORE ROOSEVELT, letter to S. Stanwood Menken, January 10, 1917.

There is a possibility for genuine radicalism in America—aggressive, contentious, often threatening—and that lies in the recognition that the liberal failed in his de-facto disregard for pluralism and his excessive emphasis on economic security at the expense of all other things.

PETER SCHRAG, *The Vanishing American*, 1972.

The Left will bring the carrot and the Right will bring the stick.

PETER SCHRAG, *The Vanishing American*, 1972.

If there is any possibility for an effective coalition among anti-establishment groups—kids, black people, hardhats, Italians, Poles—it will be in a populist cause directed *against* depersonalizing corporations and institutions and not necessarily in behalf of an all-absorbing whole. It will, in short, be urban ethnic politics on a national scale. Coalition politics and not consensus politics. The rallying cry: "Don't take no shit from nobody." It is a slogan everybody will understand.

PETER SCHRAG, *The Vanishing American*, 1972.

He who walks in the middle of the road gets hit from both sides.

GEORGE P. SHULTZ, in Richard M. Nixon, *The Memoirs of Richard Nixon*, 1978.

No matter how thin you slice it, it's still baloney.

ALFRED E. SMITH, on Franklin Roosevelt's New Deal, 1936.

Communism is the corruption of a dream of justice.

ADLAI E. STEVENSON, speech, Urbana, Illinois, 1951.

Let's talk sense to the American people. Let's tell them the truth, that there are no gains without pains.

ADLAI E. STEVENSON, speech, Chicago, Illinois, July 26, 1952.

But I do not think that Communism as a belief, apart from overt and illegal actions, can be successfully combatted by police methods, persecution, war or a mere anti spirit. The only force that can overcome an idea and a faith is another and better idea and faith, positively and fearlessly upheld.

DOROTHY THOMPSON, *Ladies' Home Journal*, October, 1954.

A favorite excuse of the conservative is this: "The time is not ripe."

This statement is a feather bed in which the conservative sleeps from the cradle to the grave unless he is rudely awakened by a strike, a revolution, or war.

MELVIN B. TOLSON, "The Negro and Radicalism," *Washington Tribune*, August 12, 1939.

Every segment of our population and every individual has the right to expect from our government a fair deal.

HARRY S TRUMAN, message to Congress, 1949.

Hamilton and Jefferson were, first, men of extraordinary brillance and, second, they believed passionately in their own theory of government....The collision between Jefferson and Hamilton struck real sparks. Each was a sort of monster driven by vanity, but each was also an intellectual philosopher of government, and each thought he was creating a perfect or perfectable system of government. Our politicians have not thought about such matters for half a century.

GORE VIDAL, "A Conversation with Myself," Book-of-the-Month Club *News*, November, 1973.

Modern government—spending more than it taxes, subsidizing and regulating and conferring countless other blessings—is a mighty engine for the stimulation of consumption. Every government benefit creates a constituency for the expansion of the benefit, so the servile state inflames more appetites than it slakes. It has fostered a perverse entrepreneurship, the manipulation of government—public power—for private purposes. It has eroded society's disciplining sense of the true costs of things.

GEORGE WILL, "Cool-Hand Jerry Brown," November 10, 1975, *The Pursuit of Happiness, and Other Sobering Thoughts*, 1978.

Marxism is the opium of the intellectuals.

EDMUND WILSON, *Letters on Literature and Politics 1912–1972*, 1977.

A radical is one of whom people say "He goes too far." A conservative, on the other hand, is one who "doesn't go far enough." Then there is the reactionary, "one who doesn't go at all." All these terms are more or less objectionable, wherefore we have coined the term "progressive." I should say that a progressive is one who insists upon recognizing new facts as they present themselves—one who adjusts legislation to these new facts.

WOODROW WILSON, speech, Kansas Society of New York, New York City, January 29, 1911.

The firm basis of government is justice, not pity.

WOODROW WILSON, inaugural address, March 4, 1913.

One cool judgment is worth a thousand hasty counsels. The thing to do is to supply light and not heat.

WOODROW WILSON, speech, Pittsburgh, Pennsylvania, January 29, 1916.

He was learning for himself the truth of the saying "A liberal is a conservative who has been arrested."

TOM WOLFE, *The Bonfire of the Vanities*, 1987.

SCANDALS

I never said I had no idea about most of the things you said I said I had no idea about.

ELLIOTT ABRAMS, Iran-Contra hearings, June 3, 1987.

Nixon: A Credit to His Race.

BUMPER STICKER, Watergate period, 1973.

I was hoping you fellows wouldn't ask me about that.

ALEXANDER BUTTERFIELD, on White House taping system, 1973, in Lois and Alan Gordon, *American Chronicle*, 1987.

We have a cancer within, close to the presidency, that is growing.

JOHN DEAN, to Richard M. Nixon during Watergate, 1973, in Lois and Alan Gordon, *American Chronicle*, 1987.

If the national security is involved, *anything goes*. There are no rules. There are people so lacking in roots about what is proper and what is improper that they don't know there's anything wrong in breaking into the headquarters of the opposition party.

HELEN GAHAGAN DOUGLAS, in Lee Israel, "Helen Gahagan Douglas," *Ms.*, October, 1973.

People say I've had brushes with the law. That's not true. I've had brushes with overzealous prosecutors.

EDWIN W. EDWARDS, on 12th grand jury probe in decade, *Time*, October 22, 1983.

I think we ought to let him hang there. Let him twist slowly, slowly in the wind.

JOHN EHRLICHMAN, to John Dean about L. Patrick Gray on Watergate tapes, March, 1973.

Divine right went out with the American Revolution and doesn't belong to the White House aides. What meat do they eat that makes them grow so great?

SAM ERVIN, news conference during Watergate investigation, *Time*, April 16, 1973.

I'm not going to let anybody come down at night like Nicodemus and whisper something in my ear that no one else can hear. That is not executive privilege; it is poppycock.

SAM ERVIN, during Watergate hearings, *U.S. News & World Report*, May 28, 1973.

The burglars who broke into the Democratic National Committee were in effect breaking into the home of every American.

SAM ERVIN, 1973, in Lois and Alan Gordon, *American Chronicle*, 1987.

My fellow Americans, our long national nightmare is over.

GERALD R. FORD, on succeeding Nixon as president, August 9, 1974.

The political lesson of Watergate is this: Never again must America allow an arrogant, elite guard of political adolescents to by-pass the regular party organization and dictate the terms of a national election.

GERALD R. FORD, on Committee for the Re-election of the President, *New York Times*, March 31, 1974.

It's beginning to be like the Teapot Dome. There's a smell to it; let's get rid of the smell.

BARRY M. GOLDWATER, on Watergate, 1973, in Lois and Alan Gordon, *American Chronicle*, 1987.

In Washington it is an honor to be disgraced... you have to have *been* somebody to fall.

MEG GREENFIELD, *Newsweek*, June 2, 1986.

I'm the only American alive or dead who presided unhappily over the removal of a vice president and a president.

ALEXANDER M. HAIG, JR., on service at White House during Nixon's presidency, March 24, 1987.

Once the toothpaste is out of the tube, it's hard to get it back in.

H.R. HALDEMAN, 1972, in Lois and Alan Gordon, *American Chronicle*, 1987.

The National Security Council did as it pleased—trading weapons for hostages, ignoring whatever laws it didn't care to understand, furnishing the President with the lies that he obligingly and uncomprehendingly read into the television cameras.

LEWIS H. LAPHAM, on Iran-Contra scandal, "Fade to Black," *Harper's*, May, 1987.

Watergate is the great liberal illusion that you can have public virtue without private morality.

CLARE BOOTHE LUCE, *Parade*, April 21, 1974.

Well, I wouldn't call it a vote of confidence.

JOSEPH R. MCCARTHY, on Senate resolution of condemnation, December, 1954.

Every tree in the forest will fall.

JAMES MCCORD, on Watergate, 1973, in Lois and Alan Gordon, *American Chronicle*, 1987.

When people ask if the United States can afford to place on trial the president, if the system can stand impeachment, my answer is, "Can we stand anything else?"

GEORGE MCGOVERN, on proposed impeachment of Nixon, *San Francisco Examiner*, November 29, 1973.

All that crap, you're putting it in the paper? It's all been denied. [*Washington Post* publisher] Katie Graham's gonna get her tit caught in a big fat wringer if that's published.

JOHN MITCHELL, on Watergate, 1972, in Lois and Alan Gordon, *American Chronicle*, 1987.

Pat and I have the satisfaction that every dime that we've got is honestly ours. I should say this, that Pat doesn't have a mink coat. But she does have a respectable Republican cloth coat, and I always tell her that she would look good in anything.

RICHARD M. NIXON, "Checkers" speech, on acceptance of money from wealthy constituents while serving in U.S. Senate, September 23, 1952.

I don't give a shit what happens. I want you all to stonewall it, let them plead the Fifth Amendment, cover-up or anything else, if it'll save it—save the plan. That's the whole point.

RICHARD M. NIXON, to John Dean, John Ehrlichman, Robert Haldeman, and John Mitchell in president's office, Executive Office Building, Watergate tapes, March 22, 1973.

This office is a sacred trust and I am determined to be worthy of that trust.

RICHARD M. NIXON, televised speech on presidency, April 30, 1973.

I made my mistakes, but in all my years of public life I have never profited, never profited from public service. I've earned every cent. And in all of my years in public life I have never obstructed justice....I welcome this kind of examination because people have got to know whether or not their President is a crook. Well, I'm not a crook. I've earned everything I've got.

RICHARD M. NIXON, response to newspaper editors' questions about tax returns, Orlando, Florida, November 17, 1973.

I have never been a quitter. To leave office before my term is completed is opposed to every instinct in my body. But as president I must put the interests of America first....Therefore, I shall resign the presidency effective at noon tomorrow.

RICHARD M. NIXON, address to nation, August 8, 1974.

I brought myself down. I impeached myself by resigning.

RICHARD M. NIXON, TV interview with David Frost, May 4, 1977.

When the President does it, that means that it is not illegal.

RICHARD M. NIXON, TV interview with David Frost, May 20, 1977.

What really hurts is if you try to cover it up....I can categorically say that no one on the present White House staff, no one in this administration, presently employed, was involved in this very bizarre incident.

RICHARD M. NIXON, on Watergate break-in, 1972, in Lois and Alan Gordon, *American Chronicle*, 1987.

There can be no whitewash at the White House.

RICHARD M. NIXON, 1973, in Lois and Alan Gordon, *American Chronicle*, 1987.

I don't think there is another person in America that wants to tell this story as much as I do.

OLIVER L. NORTH, testimony to House committee investigating arms sales to Iran, December 10, 1986.

I came here to tell you the truth, the good, the bad and the ugly.

OLIVER L. NORTH, testimony at Iran-Contra hearings after being granted limited immunity, July 7, 1987.

As a black American, I have been especially struck by the poetic justice of the discovery of the Watergate burglars by a black man. Black people were not considered by the Founding Fathers of this nation when they undertook to issue the Declaration of Independence in the name of freedom. Although a black man was among the first to fall in the American Revolution and blacks fought alongside the revolutionary heroes for freedom, we were not included when citizenship was defined in the Constitution. We have spent the one hundred and ninety-eight year history of this nation trying to become covered by the guarantees of freedom and equality contained in the Constitution. We therefore value, perhaps to a greater extent than most Americans, the guarantees of freedom and equality expressed in the Constitution and the structure of government which provides, through democratic participation, for the will of the people to prevail.

CHARLES B. RANGEL, *Congressional Record,* July, 1974.

The crimes to which Richard M. Nixon was a willing accessory threatened the system of law and justice, and for this alone they are impeachable offenses; but more fundamentally, this President has undermined the very basis of our government. If we do not impeach him for this, then we will be accessories to his crime and jointly responsible for raising the Presidency above the law.

CHARLES B. RANGEL, *Congressional Record,* July, 1974.

I can't type. I can't file. I can't even answer the phone.

ELIZABETH RAY, to House Ethics Committee hearing on misuse of government funds, 1976.

My father was a slave, and my people died to build this country, and I am going to stay and have a piece of it just like you.

PAUL ROBESON, statement to the House Un-American Activities Committee, June 12, 1956.

The corruption that shocks us in public affairs we practice in our private concerns. There is no essential difference between the pull that gets your wife into society or for your book a favorable notice and that which gets a heeler into office, a thief out of jail, and a rich man's son on the board of directors.

LINCOLN STEFFENS, Introduction, *The Shame of the Cities,* 1904.

I'm not going to comment on a third-rate burglary attempt.

RON ZIEGLER, on Watergate, 1972, in Lois and Alan Gordon, *American Chronicle,* 1987.

History and Tradition

See also **American Mosaic; American Society; Dreams and Ideals—**
Change, Greatness; **Holidays; Knowledge; Popular Culture**—Fads and
Fashions, Life-styles

History is a tangled skein that one may take up
at any point, and break when one has unravelled
enough.
HENRY ADAMS, *The Education of Henry Adams*, 1907.

History does not unfold: it piles up.
ROBERT M. ADAMS, *Bad Mouth*, 1977.

With the loss of tradition we have lost the thread
which safely guided us through the vast realms
of the past, but this thread was also the chain
fettering each successive generation to a prede-
termined aspect of the past. It could be that only
now will the past open up to us with unexpected
freshness and tell us things that no one as yet
had ears to hear.
HANNAH ARENDT, in Carl J. Frederich, *Nomos I, Authority*,
1958.

In the context of the Negro problem neither
whites nor blacks, for excellent reasons of their
own, have the faintest desire to look back; but I
think that the past is all that makes the present
coherent, and further, that the past will remain
horrible for exactly as long as we refuse to assess
it honestly.
JAMES BALDWIN, *Notes of a Native Son*, 1955.

1. Whom the gods would destroy, they first make
mad with power. 2. The mills of God grind slowly, but they grind exceedingly small. 3. The bee
fertilizes the flower it robs. 4. When it is dark
enough, you can see the stars.
CHARLES A. BEARD, four lessons of history, *Reader's Digest*
February, 1941.

It's always seemed to me...that legends and
yarns and folktales are as much a part of the real
history of a country as proclamations and provi-
sos and constitutional amendments.
STEPHEN VINCENT BENET, in Charles A. Fenton, *Stephen
Vincent Benét: The Life and Times of an American Man of
Letters*, 1958.

History, n. An account mostly false, of events
mostly unimportant, which are brought about by
rulers mostly knaves, and soldiers mostly fools.
AMBROSE BIERCE, *The Devil's Dictionary*, 1906.

Historian, n. A broad-gauge gossip.
AMBROSE BIERCE, *The Devil's Dictionary*, 1906.

History is the torch that is meant to illuminate
the past to guard us against the repetition of our
mistakes of other days. We cannot join in the
rewriting of history to make it conform to our
comfort and convenience.
CLAUDE G. BOWERS, Introduction, in F. Jay Taylor, *The
United States and the Spanish Civil War*, 1956.

History selects its heroes and its villains, and few
of us resist participation either at the parade or
at the guillotine.
WILLIAM F. BUCKLEY, JR., *The Jeweler's Eye*, 1968.

If past history was all there was to the game, the
richest people would be librarians.
WARREN BUFFETT, *Washington Post*, April 17, 1988.

The history of every century begins in the heart
of a man or a woman.
WILLA CATHER, *O Pioneers!*, 1913.

You cannot subjugate a man and recognize his
humanity, his history and his personality; so,
systematically, you must take this away from
him. You begin by telling lies about this man's
role in history.
JOHN HENRIK CLARKE, speech, Jewish Currents
Conference, New York City, February 15, 1969.

The devaluation of the past has become one of
the most important symptoms of our cultural
crisis. A denial of the past embodies the despair
of a society that cannot face the future.
SEYMOUR COHEN, *Affirming Life*, 1987.

History is a vast early warning system.
NORMAN COUSINS, *Saturday Review*, April 15, 1978.

Tradition! We scarcely know the word any more. We are afraid to be either proud of our ancestors or ashamed of them. We scorn nobility in name and in fact. We cling to a bourgeois mediocrity which would make it appear we are all Americans, made in the image and likeness of George Washington, all of a pattern, all prospering if we are good, and going down in the world if we are bad.

DOROTHY DAY, *The Long Loneliness*, 1952.

No man can live one way in the present and then retire and become a different sort of man. He will be whatever his history has made of him while he was living his history.

VINE DELORIA, JR., in Stan Steiner, *The New Indians*, 1968.

I breathed the air of history all unaware, and walked oblivious through its littered layers.

ANNIE DILLARD, *An American Childhood*, 1987.

History repeats itself in the large because human nature changes with geological leisureliness.

WILL AND ARIEL DURANT, *The Lessons of History*, 1968.

History is the transformation of tumultuous conquerors into silent footnotes.

PAUL ELDRIDGE, *Maxims for a Modern Man*, 1965.

The past is never dead. It's not even past.

WILLIAM FAULKNER, *Requiem for a Nun*, 1951.

The national myth is that of creativity and progress, of a steady climbing upward into power and prosperity, both for the individual and for the country as a whole. Americans see history as a straight line and themselves standing at the cutting edge of it as representatives for all mankind.

FRANCES FITZGERALD, *Fire in the Lake*, 1972.

History is bunk.

HENRY FORD, spoken on witness stand in his libel suit against the *Chicago Tribune*, July, 1919.

There is no inevitability in history except as men make it.

FELIX FRANKFURTER, in article by J.M. Brown, *Saturday Review*, October 30, 1954.

"History" is not a divine force; it is the instrument of those who make it.

J. WILLIAM FULBRIGHT, *Old Myths and New Realities*, 1964.

History is written by the winners.

ALEX HALEY, interview with David Frost, April 20, 1972.

History is bright and fiction dull with homely men who have charmed women.

O. HENRY, "Next to Reading Matter," *Roads of Destiny*, 1909.

Upon this point a page in history is worth a volume of logic.

OLIVER WENDELL HOLMES, JR., opinion, *Trust Co. v. Eisner*, 1921.

History is principally the inaccurate narration of events which ought not to have happened.

ERNEST ALBERT HOOTEN, *Twilight of Man*, 1939.

The historian, essentially, wants more documents than he can really use; the dramatist only wants more liberties than he can really take.

HENRY JAMES, *The Novels and Tales of Henry James*, 1907.

History is a bath of blood.

WILLIAM JAMES, *Memories and Studies*, 1911.

If every nation gets the government it deserves, every generation writes the history which corresponds with its view of the world.

ELIZABETH JANEWAY, *Between Myth and Morning*, 1974.

We have not formed the right theory of History until we see History itself as a spiritual drama, moving toward a significant denouement and at the same time a process which has meaning and value as it goes on.

RUFUS JONES, *The Eternal Gospel*, 1938.

Western man wrote his history as if it were the history of the entire human race. I hope that colored men all over the world have not watched Western man too long to commit the fatal folly of writing history with a colored pencil.

JOHN OLIVER KILLENS, "Explanation of the Black Psyche," *New York Times*, June 7, 1964.

History is a better guide than good intentions.

JEANE KIRKPATRICK, "Dictatorship and Double Standards," *Commentary*, November, 1979.

History is not, of course, a cookbook offering pretested recipes. It teaches by analogy, not by maxims. It can illuminate the consequences of actions in comparable situations, yet each generation must discover for itself what situations are in fact comparable.

HENRY KISSINGER, *White House Years*, 1979.

If history teaches anything it is that there can be no peace without equilibrium and no justice without restraint.

HENRY KISSINGER, *White House Years*, 1979.

The history of an oppressed people is hidden in the lies and the agreed-upon myth of its conquerors.

MERIDEL LE SUEUR, *Crusaders*, 1955.

The mark of the historic is the nonchalance with which it picks up an individual and deposits him in a trend, like a house playfully moved in a tornado.

MARY McCARTHY, "My Confession," *On the Contrary*, 1961.

History must always be taken with a grain of salt. It is, after all, not a science but an art.

PHYLLIS McGINLEY, "Aspects of Sanctity," *Saint Watching*, 1969.

The history of the world is the history of a privileged few.

HENRY MILLER, *Sunday After the War*, 1944.

America was discovered accidentally by a great seaman who was looking for something else; when discovered it was not wanted; and most of the exploration for the next fifty years was done in the hope of getting through or around it. America was named after a man who discovered no part of the New World. History is like that, very chancy.

SAMUEL ELIOT MORISON, *The Oxford History of the American People*, 1965.

Difficulty is the excuse history never accepts.

EDWARD R. MURROW, speech, 1959, London Guildhall, in A. M. Sperber, *Murrow*, 1986.

History is a realm in which human freedom and natural necessity are curiously intermingled.

REINHOLD NIEBUHR, *The Structure of Nations and Empires*, 1959.

There is no reason to repeat bad history.

ELEANOR HOLMES NORTON, in Robin Morgan, ed., *Sisterhood Is Powerful*, 1970.

If we forget what we did, we won't know who we are.

RONALD REAGAN, in Ellen Goodman, "Exit Ron Reagan, Stage Right," January, 1989, *Making Sense*, 1989.

A lot of history is just dirty politics cleaned up for the consumption of children and other innocents.

RICHARD REEVES, column, *Detroit Free Press*, November 4, 1982.

Our history is the history of a majority of the species, yet the struggles of women for a "human" status have been relegated to footnotes to the sidelines. Above all, women's relationships with women have been denied or neglected as a force in history.

ADRIENNE RICH, *Working It Out*, 1977.

You cannot walk the middle of the road holding hands with tradition on one side and modernism on the other. You have to make a choice.

ALVIN E. ROLLAND, *School and Community*, May, 1962.

I tell you the past is a bucket of ashes.

CARL SANDBURG, "Prairie," *Cornhuskers*, 1918.

The only antidote to a shallow knowledge of history is a deeper knowledge, the knowledge which produces not dogmatic certitude but diagnostic skill, not clairvoyance but insight.

ARTHUR M. SCHLESINGER, JR., *The Bitter Heritage: Vietnam and American Democracy, 1941–1966*, 1967.

Far from offering a short cut to clairvoyance, history teaches us that the future is full of surprises and outwits all our certitudes. For the study of history issues not in scientific precision nor in moral finality but in irony.

ARTHUR M. SCHLESINGER, JR., *The Bitter Heritage: Vietnam and American Democracy, 1941–1966*, 1967.

History, by putting crisis in perspective, supplies the antidote to every generation's illusion that its own problems are uniquely oppressive.

ARTHUR M. SCHLESINGER, JR., "The Challenge of Change," *New York Times Magazine*, July 27, 1986.

Ever since I could remember I'd wished I'd been lucky enough to be alive at a great time—when something big was going on, like the crucifixion. And suddenly I realized I was.

BEN SHAHN, 1932, in Lois and Alan Gordon, *American Chronicle*, 1987.

The chief value of history, if it is critically studied, is to break down the illusion that peoples are very different.

LEO STEIN, *Journey into the Self*, 1950.

The future is, of course, unknown. By contrast, the past is wrongly known. History, most often, is recorded with a great amount of undeniable and systematic distortion.

EDWARD TELLER, *The Pursuit of Simplicity*, 1980.

Historians are the biggest liars in the world. They may get the facts, but when they get through interpreting the facts and perverting the facts, it would take God's X-ray to find the grain of truth.

When the exceptional historian comes along, you have a poet.

MELVIN B. TOLSON, "Is the White Man Worse Than the Negro?" *Washington Tribune*, January 29, 1938.

In dealing with history, leave the "if's" out.

MELVIN B. TOLSON, "*Gone With the Wind* Is More Dangerous Than *Birth of a Nation*," *Washington Tribune*, March 23, 1940.

Men make history and not the other way round. In periods where there is no leadership, society stands still. Progress occurs when courageous, skillful leaders seize the opportunity to change things for the better.

HARRY S TRUMAN, *This Week*, February 22, 1959.

The only thing new in the world is the history you don't know.

HARRY S TRUMAN, in Merle Miller, *Plain Speaking: An Oral Biography of Harry S Truman*, 1982.

What his imagination is to the poet, facts are to the historian. His exercise of judgment comes in their selection, his art in their arrangement. His method is narrative. His subject is the story of man's past. His function is to make it known.

BARBARA TUCHMAN, "When Does History Happen?" *New York Times Book Review*, March 8, 1964.

Without invoking the spectre of conspiracy, I say that there has been among whites a planned destruction of the past—or at any rate, all of it that did not illustrate the national mythology.

FREDERICK W. TURNER III, Introduction, in Virginia Irving Armstrong, comp., *I Have Spoken: American History Through the Voices of the Indians*, 1971.

It has become the fact of...school children to guess that there must have been yet another kind of history, a deep, dark, subterranean stream of history running all this time under the bright ribbon of that version of the continental past they were given in their formative years.

FREDERICK W. TURNER III, Introduction, in Virginia Irving Armstrong, comp., *I Have Spoken: American History Through the Voices of the Indians*, 1971.

There is no History waiting for us like some giant and architecturally perfect edifice that we will at long last discover in the tangled growth of an intellectual forest. History does not exist for us until and unless we dig it up, interpret it, and put it together. Then the past comes alive, or, more accurately, it is revealed for what it has always been—a part of the present.

FREDERICK W. TURNER III, Introduction, in Virginia Irving Armstrong, comp., *I Have Spoken: American History Through the Voices of the Indians*, 1971.

The history of the world is the record of a man in quest of his daily bread and butter.

HENDRIK WILLEM VAN LOON, *The Story of Mankind*, 1921.

The past is only the present become invisible and mute; and because it is invisible and mute, its memoried glances and its murmurs are infinitely precious. We are tomorrow's past.

MARY WEBB, Foreword, *Precious Bane*, 1924.

History must stay open, it is all humanity.

WILLIAM CARLOS WILLIAMS, "The Virtue of History," *In the American Grain*, 1925.

To study ancient civilizations is to get a complete image of how society develops, succeeds and fades. There are few philosophical, moral or even scientific problems that have not been debated by ancient writers at one time or another. So we get a blueprint of the direction of mankind and what mankind can and cannot do under different circumstances.

MARGUERITE YOURCENAR, "Ancient History Lesson: Our Problems Are Nothing New," *U.S. News & World Report*, July 28, 1980.

Holidays

See also **History and Tradition**

From the sepulcher at sunrise to the fashion parade on Fifth Avenue is the boorish measure of our denial of Christ—from innocent wonder to cynical worldliness.

BROOKS ATKINSON, "March 28," *Once Around the Sun*, 1951.

I have always been subconsciously embarrassed by the "function" of Christmas and New Years—the spirit of "loving kindness," that is presumed to come to a head like a boil once a year, when it has been magnificently concealed up to that moment!

JOHN BARRYMORE, diary entry, December 31, 1925, in Gene Fowler, *Good Night, Sweet Prince.*

Our children await Christmas presents like politicians getting election returns; there's the Uncle Fred precinct and the Aunt Ruth district still to come in.

MARCELENE COX, *Ladies' Home Journal*, December, 1950.

Happiness is too many things these days for anyone to wish it on anyone lightly. So let's just wish each other a bileless New Year and leave it at that.

JUDITH CRIST, "1966 at Its Worst: The Dishonor Roll," *The Private Eye, the Cowboy and the Very Naked Girl*, January 1, 1967.

It is possible, indeed almost too easy, to be eloquently sentimental about large groups of assorted relatives who gather for Christmas or Thanksgiving or some such festival, and eat and drink and gossip and laugh together.

M.F.K. FISHER, "F Is for Family," *An Alphabet for Gourmets*, 1949.

One doesn't forget the rounded wonder in the eyes of a boy as he comes bursting upstairs on Christmas morning and finds the two-wheeler or the fire truck of which for weeks he scarcely dared dream.

MAX LERNER, *The Unfinished Country*, 1959.

Between the constant repetition of "White Christmas" and "Jingle Bells" on station WPAT and the increasing frenzy of the Saks and Gimbels newspaper ads as these fucking holidays draw near, I have been in a zombie-like state for weeks, totally incapable of rational thought or action.

S.J. PERELMAN, letter to Paul Theroux, 1976.

Ever since Eve gave Adam the apple, there has been a misunderstanding between the sexes about gifts.

NAN ROBERTSON, on Christmas shopping, *New York Times*, November 28, 1957.

Let us, on the day set aside for this purpose, give thanks to the Ruler of the universe for the strength which He has vouchsafed us to carry on our daily labors and for the hope that lives within us of the coming of a day when peace and the productive activities of peace shall reign on every continent.

FRANKLIN D. ROOSEVELT, Thanksgiving Day proclamation, October 31, 1939.

Fir balsam is like no other cargo; even a workaday truck is exalted and wears a consecrated look when carrying these aromatic dumplings to the hungry dwellers in cities.

E.B. WHITE, "Home-coming," December 10, 1955, *Essays of E.B. White*, 1977.

The Human Condition

See also **The Arts; Children and Youth; Death; Dreams and Ideals; Ethics and Morality; Food and Drink; Knowledge; Language and Discourse—** Gossip; **Life's Lessons; Men; Nature**—Human Beings and Nature; **Psychology; Relationships; Religion and Spirituality; Women; Work**

ACTION

For action is indeed the sole medium of expression for ethics.

JANE ADDAMS, "Political Reform," *Democracy and Social Ethics*, 1902.

The true men of action in our time, those who transform the world, are not the politicians and statesmen, but the scientists.

W.H. AUDEN, *The Dyer's Hand*, 1962.

Action is the antidote to despair.

JOAN BAEZ, *Rolling Stone*, 1983.

To act is to be committed, and to be committed is to be in danger.

JAMES BALDWIN, *The Fire Next Time*, 1963.

Only by his action can a man make (himself/his life) whole.... You are responsible for what you have done and the people whom you have influenced. IN THE END IT IS ONLY THE WORK THAT COUNTS.

MARGARET BOURKE-WHITE, notes, ca. 1965, in Vicki Goldberg, *Margaret Bourke-White: A Biography*, 1986.

Fate proceeds inexorably...only upon the passive individual, the passive people.

PEARL S. BUCK, speech to Nobel Prize winners, New York, December 10, 1942.

"Men of action," whose minds are too busy with the day's work to see beyond it...are essential men, we cannot do without them, and yet we must not allow all our vision to be bound by the limitations of "men of action."

PEARL S. BUCK, *What America Means to Me*, 1943.

We all like people who do things, even if we only see their faces on a cigar-box lid.

WILLA CATHER, *Song of the Lark*, 1915.

The trouble with Reason is that it becomes meaningless at the exact point where it refuses to act.

BERNARD DeVOTO, "The Easy Chair," *Harper's*, May, 1941.

Actions speak louder than words—but not so often.

FARMER'S ALMANAC, 1966.

To dispose a soul to action we must upset its equilibrium.

ERIC HOFFER, *The Ordeal of Change*, 1964.

Once one has experienced LSD, existential revolution, fought the intellectual game-playing of the individual in society, of one's identity, one realizes that action is the only reality; not only reality but morality as well.

ABBIE HOFFMAN, *Revolution for the Hell of It*, 1968.

Words are not of any great importance in times of economic disturbance. It is action that counts.

HERBERT HOOVER, speech to business, labor, and industrial leaders, November 15, 1929.

Sick or well, blind or seeing, bound or free, we are here for a purpose and however we are situated, we please God better with useful deeds than with many prayers or pious resignation.

HELEN KELLER, *My Religion*, 1927.

The biggest sin is sitting on your ass.

FLORYNCE R. KENNEDY, in article by Gloria Steinem, *Ms.*, March, 1973.

When action grows unprofitable, gather information; when information grows unprofitable, sleep.

URSULA K. LeGUIN, *The Left Hand of Darkness*, 1969.

Any genuine philosophy leads to action and from action back to wonder, to the enduring fact of mystery.

HENRY MILLER, *The Wisdom of the Heart*, 1941.

I feel that this award was not made to me as a man, but to my work—a life's work in the agony and sweat of the human spirit, not for glory and least of all for profit, but to create out of the materials of the human spirit something which did not exist before. So this award is only mine in trust. It will not be difficult to find a dedication for the money part of it commensurate with the purpose and significance of its origin. But I would like to do the same with the acclaim too, by using this moment as a pinnacle from which I might be listened to by the young men and women already dedicated to the same anguish and travail, among whom is already that one who will someday stand where I am standing.

Our tragedy today is a general and universal physical fear so long sustained by now that we can even bear it. There are no longer problems of the spirit. There is only the question: When will I be blown up? Because of this, the young man or woman writing today has forgotten the problems of the human heart in conflict with itself which alone can make good writing because only that is worth writing about, worth the agony and the sweat.

He must learn them again. He must teach himself that the basest of all things is to be afraid; and, teaching himself that, forget it forever, leaving no room in his workshop for anything but the old verities and trusts of the heart, the old universal truths lacking which any story is ephemeral and doomed—love and honor and pity and pride and compassion and sacrifice. Until he does so, he labors under a curse. He writes not of love but of lust, of defeats in which nobody loses anything of value, of victories without hope and, worst of all, without pity or compassion. His griefs grieve on no universal bones, leaving no scars. He writes not of the heart but of the glands.

Until he relearns these things, he will write as though he stood among and watched the end of man. I decline to accept the end of man. It is easy enough to say that man is immortal simply because he will endure; that when the last ding-dong of doom has clanged and faded from the last worthless rock hanging tideless in the last red and dying evening, that even then there will still be one more sound: that of his puny, inexhaustible voice, still talking.

I refuse to accept this. I believe that man will not merely endure: he will prevail. He is immortal, not because he alone among creatures has an inexhaustible voice, but because he has a soul, a spirit capable of compassion and sacrifice and endurance. The poet's, the writer's duty is to write about these things. It is his privilege to help man endure by lifting his heart, by reminding him of the courage and pity and sacrifice which have been the glory of his past. The poet's voice need not merely be the record of man; it can be one of the props, the pillars to help him endure and prevail.

WILLIAM FAULKNER, Nobel Prize acceptance speech, December 10, 1950.

You must do the things you think you cannot do.
ELEANOR ROOSEVELT, *You Learn By Living*, 1960.

Rhetoric is a poor substitute for action, and we have trusted only to rhetoric. If we are really to be a great nation, we must not merely talk, we must act big.
THEODORE ROOSEVELT, *The Metropolitan*, September, 1917.

We know what a person thinks not when he tells us what he thinks, but by his actions.
ISAAC BASHEVIS SINGER, *New York Times Magazine*, November 26, 1978.

One of the basic causes for all the trouble in the world today is that people talk too much and think too little. They act too impulsively without thinking. I always try to think before I talk.
MARGARET CHASE SMITH, speech, Westbrook Junior College, Portland, Maine, June 7, 1953.

The question is: Who will get to heaven first— the man who talks or the man who acts?
MELVIN B. TOLSON, "The Death of an Infidel," *Washington Tribune*, April 2, 1938.

What makes Christ's teachings difficult is that they obligate us to do something about them.

JOHN J. WADE, *Conquering with Christ*, 1942.

Caution is the confidential agent of selfishness.

WOODROW WILSON, speech, Chicago, Illinois, February 12, 1909.

ADVERSITY

Calamity, n. A more than commonly plain and unmistakable reminder that the affairs of this life are not of our own ordering. Calamities are of two kinds: misfortune to ourselves, and good fortune to others.

AMBROSE BIERCE, *The Devil's Dictionary*, 1906.

Misfortune, n. The kind of fortune that never misses.

AMBROSE BIERCE, *The Devil's Dictionary*, 1906.

It is in suffering that we are withdrawn from the bright superficial film of existence, from the sway of time and mere things, and find ourselves in the presence of a profounder truth.

YVES M. CONGAR, *God, Man and the Universe*, 1950.

Survival is nothing more than recovery.

DIANNE FEINSTEIN, *Boston Globe*, May 29, 1983.

I'm like an old tin can in an alley. Anyone who walks by can't resist kicking it.

M. DONALD GRANT, on continuing criticism of baseball fans after Seaver trade, *New York Times*, July 21, 1977.

I have always known that when trouble comes I must face it fast and move with speed, even though the speed is thoughtless and sometimes damaging.

LILLIAN HELLMAN, *Pentimento*, 1973.

No man can smile in the face of adversity and mean it.

EDGAR WATSON HOWE, *Country Town Sayings*, 1911.

If pleasures are greatest in anticipation, just remember that this is also true of trouble.

ELBERT HUBBARD, *The Roycroft Dictionary and Book of Epigrams*, 1923.

When trouble comes, wise men take to their work; weak men take to the woods.

ELBERT HUBBARD, *The Roycroft Dictionary and Book of Epigrams*, 1923.

Tragedy is a tool for the living to gain wisdom, not a guide by which to live.

ROBERT F. KENNEDY, speech, March 18, 1968.

there is always
a comforting thought
in time of trouble when
it is not our trouble

DON MARQUIS, "comforting thoughts," *archy does his part*, 1935.

People don't ever seem to realize that doing what's right's no guarantee against misfortune.

WILLIAM MCFEE, *Casuals of the Sea*, 1916.

It is extraordinary how many emotional storms one may weather in safety if one is ballasted with ever so little gold.

WILLIAM MCFEE, *Casuals of the Sea*, 1916.

He's not the finest character that ever lived. But he's a human being, and a terrible thing is happening to him. So attention must be paid. He's not to be allowed to fall into his grave like an old dog. Attention, attention must be finally paid to such a person.

ARTHUR MILLER, *Death of a Salesman*, 1949.

Death and taxes and childbirth! There's never any convenient time for any of them!

MARGARET MITCHELL, *Gone with the Wind*, 1936.

Don't get hung up on a snag in the stream, my dear. Snags alone are not so dangerous—it's the debris that clings to them that makes the trouble. Pull yourself loose and go on.

ANNE SHANNON MONROE, *Singing in the Rain*, 1926.

One of the tendencies of our age is to use children's suffering to discredit the goodness of God....In this popular pity, we mark our gain in sensibility and our loss in vision. If other ages felt less, they saw more.

FLANNERY O'CONNOR, *A Memoir of Mary Ann*, 1961.

They sicken of the calm, who know the storm.

DOROTHY PARKER, "Fair Weather," *Sunset Gun*, 1928.

To be brave in misfortune is to be worthy of manhood; to be wise in misfortune is to conquer fate.

AGNES REPPLIER, "Strayed Sympathies," *Under Dispute*, 1924.

66 is the path of a people in flight, refugees from dust and shrinking land, from the thunder of tractors and shrinking ownership, from the desert's slow northward invasion, from the twisting winds that howl up out of Texas, from the

floods that bring no richness to the land and steal what little richness is there. From all of these the people are in flight, and they come into 66 from the tributary side roads, from the wagon tracks and the rutted country roads. 66 is the mother road, the road of flight.

JOHN STEINBECK, *The Grapes of Wrath*, 1939.

A sad soul can kill you quicker, far quicker, than a germ.

JOHN STEINBECK, *Travels with Charley*, 1962.

I guess this means they fired me. I'll never make the mistake of being 70 years old again.

CASEY STENGEL, *New York Times*, July 25, 1978.

When you are down and out, something always turns up—and it is usually the noses of your friends.

ORSON WELLES, *New York Times*, April 1, 1962.

AMBITION

Children, you must remember something. A man without ambition is dead. A man with ambition but no love is dead. A man with ambition and love for his blessings here on earth is ever so alive.

PEARL BAILEY, *Talking to Myself*, 1971.

Ambition. n. An overmastering desire to be vilified by enemies while living and made ridiculous by friends when dead.

AMBROSE BIERCE, *The Devil's Dictionary*, 1906.

Women who seek to be equal to men lack ambition.

BUMPER STICKER.

When you reach for the stars, you may not quite get one, but you won't come up with a handful of mud either.

LEO BURNETT, *Reader's Digest*, January, 1985.

We specialize in the wholly impossible.

NANNIE HELEN BURROUGHS, motto, National Training School for Girls, Washington, D.C., ca. 1909, in Gerda Lerner, ed., *Black Women in White America*, 1972.

Ambition is a commendable attribute, without which no man succeeds. Only inconsiderate ambition imperils.

WARREN G. HARDING, speech, Washington, D.C., May 3, 1922.

It takes a certain level of aspiration before one can take advantage of opportunities that are clearly offered.

MICHAEL HARRINGTON, *The Other America*, 1962.

Every nation has a prominent citizen who builds a pyramid.

EDGAR WATSON HOWE, *Sinner Sermons*, 1926.

The trouble with being number one in the world—at anything—is that it takes a certain mentality to attain that position in the first place, and that is something of a driving, perfectionist attitude, so that once you do achieve number one, you don't relax and enjoy it.

BILLIE JEAN KING, *Billie Jean*, 1982.

Ambition is more interesting than greed, and always has been.

RUSSELL LYNES, "On Collecting," *Architectural Digest*, 1980.

The world is an oyster, but you don't crack it open on a mattress.

ARTHUR MILLER, *Death of a Salesman*, 1949.

I had no ambition to make a fortune. Mere money-making has never been my goal. I had an ambition to build.

JOHN D. ROCKEFELLER, in Allen Nevins, *Study in Power: John D. Rockefeller*, 1953.

[Inherited wealth is] as certain death to ambition as cocaine is to morality.

WILLIAM K. VANDERBILT, interview, 1905.

CHARACTER

I'm the foe of moderation, the champion of excess. If I may lift a line from a die-hard whose identity is lost in the shuffle, "I'd rather be strongly wrong than weakly right."

TALLULAH BANKHEAD, *Tallulah*, 1952.

During my eighty-seven years I have witnessed a whole succession of technological revolutions. But none of them has done away with the need for character in the individual or the ability to think.

BERNARD M. BARUCH, *Baruch: My Own Story*, 1957.

Sports do not build character. They reveal it.

HEYWOOD HALE BROUN, in James A. Michener, *Sports in America*, 1976.

The dismal fact is that self-respect has nothing to do with the approval of others—who are, after all, deceived easily enough; has nothing to do with reputation, which, as Rhett Butler told Scarlett O'Hara, is something people with courage can do without.

JOAN DIDION, "On Self-Respect," *Slouching Towards Bethlehem*, 1968.

My mind is as open as a forty-acre field, but that doesn't mean I'm going to change it.

EVERETT DIRKSEN, in Neil MacNeil, *Dirksen: Portrait of a Public Man*, 1970.

Life is not a static thing. The only people who do not change their minds are incompetents in asylums, who can't, and those in cemeteries.

EVERETT DIRKSEN, in Neil MacNeil, *Dirksen: Portrait of a Public Man*, 1970.

Character isn't inherited. One builds it daily by the way one thinks and acts, thought by thought, action by action. If one lets fear or hate or anger take possession of the mind, they become self-forged chains.

HELEN GAHAGAN DOUGLAS, speech, Marlboro College, 1975, *A Full Life*, 1982.

Decency—generosity—cooperation—assistance in trouble—devotion to duty; these are the things that are of greater value than surface appearances and customs.

DWIGHT D. EISENHOWER, letter to Mamie Doud Eisenhower, June 11, 1943.

Lee took the blame. "It was all my fault," he said to Pickett's troops. That's quite different from some people I know.

SAM ERVIN, 1973, in Lois and Alan Gordon, *American Chronicle*, 1987.

He believed in character, he wanted to jump back a whole generation and trust in character again as the eternally valuable element. Everything else wore out.

F. SCOTT FITZGERALD, 1931, "Babylon Revisited," *Babylon Revisited*, 1960.

It is all one to me if a man comes from Sing Sing or Harvard. We hire a man, not his history.

ATTRIBUTED TO HENRY FORD.

Old age and sickness bring out the essential characteristics of a man.

FELIX FRANKFURTER, *Felix Frankfurter Reminisces*, 1960.

Humility is not my forte, and whenever I dwell for any length of time on my own shortcomings, they gradually begin to seem mild, harmless, rather engaging little things, not at all like the staring defects in other people's characters.

MARGARET HALSEY, *With Malice Toward Some*, 1938.

Many people have character who have nothing else.

DON HEROLD, *Chicago Sun-Times*, July 14, 1979.

God will not look you over for medals, degrees or diplomas, but for scars.

ELBERT HUBBARD, *One Thousand and One Epigrams*, 1911.

If in my high moments, I have done some good, offered some service, shed some light, healed some wounds, rekindled some hope, or stirred someone from apathy and indifference, or in any way along the way helped somebody, then this campaign has not been in vain....If in my low moments, in word, deed or attitude, through some error of temper, taste or tone, I have caused anyone discomfort, created pain or revived someone's fears, that was not my truest self....I am not a perfect servant. I am a public servant doing my best against the odds. As I develop and serve, be patient. God is not finished with me yet.

JESSE JACKSON, speech, Democratic National Convention, July 16, 1984.

The good Lord endowed me with a wonderful constitution, twenty hours a day; I was plenty sturdy and tough, I had reasonable perception and astuteness, I was not a temple of wisdom or a fountain of justice, but I could comprehend things. No one ever said I was a goddamn boob, no one from Bobby [Kennedy] up or down ever said that.

LYNDON B. JOHNSON, in Doris Kearns, *Lyndon Johnson and the American Dream*, 1976.

Character cannot be developed in ease and quiet. Only through experience of trial and suffering can the soul be strengthened, vision cleared, ambition inspired, and success achieved.

HELEN KELLER, *Helen Keller's Journal*, 1938.

Where is the moral strength within us? The qualities of character that we attribute in stories to our children of the American heroes that have gone before us?

EDWARD M. KENNEDY, speech, Jefferson-Jackson Day Dinner, Denver, Colorado, April 5, 1968, in Thomas P. Collins and Louis M. Savary, eds., *A People of Compassion*, 1972.

Turning the other cheek is a kind of moral jiujitsu.

GERALD STANLEY LEE, *Crowds*, 1913.

Underneath this flabby exterior is an enormous lack of character.

OSCAR LEVANT, *The Memoirs of an Amnesiac*, 1965.

I don't have a warm personal enemy left. They've all died off. I miss them terribly because they helped define me.

CLARE BOOTHE LUCE, "The Dick Cavett Show," July 21, 1981.

You must believe in yourself, my son, or no one else will believe in you. Be self-confident, self-reliant, and even if you don't make it, you will know you have done your best. Now, go to it.

MARY HARDY MACARTHUR, in Douglas MacArthur, *Reminiscences*, 1964.

If an individual wants to be a leader and isn't controversial, that means he never stood for anything.

RICHARD M. NIXON, *Dallas Times-Herald*, December 10, 1978.

"Sincerity" is considered the international credit card of acceptance.... No matter how deeply in debt the user may be or how the card is misused, "sincerity" will erase all suspicion and validate all actions.

CHARLES SWINDOLL, *The Quest for Character*, 1987.

Three things ruin a man. Power, money, and women. I never wanted power. I never had any money, and the only woman in my life is up at the house right now.

HARRY S TRUMAN, in article by Mary McGrory, *New York Post*, December 29, 1972.

The best index to a person's character is (a) how he treats people who can't do him any good, and (b) how he treats people who can't fight back.

ABIGAIL VAN BUREN, newspaper column, "Dear Abby," May 16, 1974.

COMPETITIVENESS

Champions aren't made in gyms. Champions are made from something they have deep inside them—a desire, a dream, a vision. They have to have last-minute stamina, they have to be a little faster, they have to have the skill and the will. But the will must be stronger than the skill.

MUHAMMAD ALI, *The Greatest*, 1975.

Every time you win, you're reborn; when you lose, you die a little.

GEORGE ALLEN, in James A. Michener, *Sports in America*, 1976.

Competitions are for horses, not artists.

BÉLA BARTÓK, *Saturday Review*, August 25, 1962.

I don't meet competition. I crush it.

CHARLES REVSON, *Time*, June 16, 1958.

A competitive world has two possibilities for you. You can lose. Or, if you want to win, you can change.

LESTER C. THUROW, interview, "60 Minutes," CBS-TV, February 7, 1988.

Our civilization is competitive—heartlessly competitive. Therefore, old cars must compete with new cars, old businesses with new businesses, old women with young women.

MELVIN B. TOLSON, "Henpecked Husband: Comedy or Tragedy," *Washington Tribune*, January 20, 1940.

Did you know, throughout the cosmos they found intelligent life forms that play to play. We are the only ones that play to win. Explains why we have more than our share of losers.

JANE WAGNER, *The Search for Intelligent Life in the Universe*, performed by Lily Tomlin, 1986.

Competition is not at all an idea of getting hold of what the other fellow has, beating him down, stepping on his neck, and climbing over him. It stems from the desire of the individual somehow to prove his own worth, his own potential.

WALTER H. WHEELER, in Arthur Goodfriend, *What Is America?*, 1954.

CONCEIT

Conceit is God's gift to little men.

BRUCE BARTON, *Coronet*, September, 1958.

The world is made up for the most part of morons and natural tyrants, sure of themselves, strong in their own opinions, never doubting anything.

CLARENCE DARROW, "Personal Liberty," 1928.

We're a great people. We are that. And the best of it is, we know we are.

FINLEY PETER DUNNE, *Mr. Dooley Remembers*, 1963.

God knows how many things a man misses by becoming smug and assuming that matters will take their natural course.

LOREN EISELEY, "The Fire Apes," *The Star Thrower*, 1949.

Out of disbelief [in God] we have impudently assumed that all of life is now subject to our own will. And the disasters that have come from willing what cannot be willed have not at all brought us to some modesty about our presumptions.

LESLIE FARBER, in an article by Melvin Maddocks, "Can Therapists Be Running Out of Talk?" *Christian Science Monitor*, May 14, 1986.

You gotta say this for the white race—its self-confidence knows no bounds. Who else could go to a small island in the South Pacific where there's no poverty, no crime, no unemployment, no war and no worry—and call it a "primitive society"?

DICK GREGORY, *From the Back of the Bus*, 1962.

It is an undeniable privilege of every man to prove himself right in the thesis that the world is his enemy; for if he reiterates it frequently enough and makes it the background of his conduct he is bound eventually to be right.

GEORGE F. KENNAN, "The Sources of Soviet Conduct," *Foreign Affairs*, July, 1947.

Egotism is the anesthetic that dulls the pain of stupidity.

FRANK LEAHY, *Look*, January 10, 1955.

There were always two sides to every argument—his and the wrong side.

M.S. MICHEL, *The X-ray Murders*, 1942.

When someone is coming down with egomania, there must be symptoms that an alert diagnostician can spot: model-dating, maybe, or cosmetic surgery, or a tendency to name things after oneself.

CALVIN TRILLIN, "Diseases of the Mighty," *The Nation*, October 19, 1985.

Early in life I had to choose between honest arrogance and hypocritical humility. I chose honest arrogance and have seen no occasion to change.

FRANK LLOYD WRIGHT, recalled on his death, April 8, 1959.

CONDUCT

To offer the complexities of life as an excuse for not addressing oneself to the simpler, more manageable (trivial) aspects of daily existence is a perversity often indulged in by artists, husbands, intellectuals—and critics of the Women's Movement.

BARBARA GRIZZUTI HARRISON, *Unlearning the Life: Sexism in School*, 1973.

I do not love my neighbor as myself, and apologize to no one. I treat my neighbor as fairly and politely as I hope to be treated, but there is no law in nature or common sense ordering me to go beyond that.

EDGAR WATSON HOWE, *Success Easier Than Failure*, 1917.

It is an open question whether any behavior based on fear of eternal punishment can be regarded as ethical or should be regarded as merely cowardly.

MARGARET MEAD, *Redbook*, February, 1971.

To do *exactly as your neighbors* do is the only sensible rule.

EMILY POST, *Etiquette*, 1922.

One must think like a hero to behave like a merely decent human being.

MAY SARTON, *Journal of a Solitude*, 1973.

To me the phrase, "Act like you have some sense," probably spoken by at least one Black woman to every Black child who ever lived, is a cryptic warning that says volumes about keeping your feet on the ground and your ass covered.

BARBARA SMITH, Introduction, *Home Girls*, 1983.

Good breeding consists in concealing how much we think of ourselves and how little we think of the other person.

MARK TWAIN, *Mark Twain's Notebook*, 1935.

I believe in the brotherhood of man, all men, but I don't believe in brotherhood with anybody who doesn't want brotherhood with me. I believe in treating people right, but I'm not going to waste my time trying to treat somebody right who doesn't know how to return that treatment.

MALCOLM X, speech, New York City, December 12, 1964.

COURAGE

Bravery is the capacity to perform properly even when scared half to death.

OMAR BRADLEY, in Joe Garagiola, *Baseball Is a Funny Game*, 1960.

It is easy enough to praise men for the courage of their convictions. I wish I could teach the sad young of this mealy generation the courage of their confusions.

JOHN CIARDI, *Saturday Review*, June 2, 1962.

If Rosa Parks had not refused to move to the back of the bus, you and I might never have heard of Dr. Martin Luther King.

RAMSEY CLARK, on effectiveness of individual protests, *New York Times*, April 14, 1987.

Courage takes many forms. There is physical courage, there is moral courage. Then there is a still higher type of courage—the courage to brave pain, to live with it, to never let others know of it and to still find joy in life; to wake up in the morning with an enthusiasm for the day ahead.

HOWARD COSELL, *Like It Is*, 1974.

This republic was not established by cowards; and cowards will not preserve it.

ELMER DAVIS, speech, Harvard University, 1953, *But We Were Born Free*, 1954.

This will remain the land of the free only so long as it is the home of the brave.

ELMER DAVIS, *But We Were Born Free*, 1954.

Courage is the price that Life exacts for granting peace.

AMELIA EARHART, *Courage*, 1927.

Of course I realized there was a measure of danger. Obviously I faced the possibility of not returning when first I considered going. Once faced and settled there really wasn't any good reason to refer to it [the "Friendship" flight] again.

AMELIA EARHART, *20 Hours: 40 Minutes—Our Flight in the Friendship*, 1928.

Courage calls to courage everywhere, and its voice cannot be denied.

MILLICENT GARRETT FAWCETT, *The Women's Victory—and After*, 1920.

Show me a hero and I will write you a tragedy.

F. SCOTT FITZGERALD, "Notebooks," *The Crack-up*, 1945.

If people bring so much courage to this world the world has to kill them to break them, so of course it kills them. The world breaks every one and afterward many are strong at the broken places. But those that will not break it kills. It kills the very good and the very gentle and the very brave impartially. If you are none of these you can be sure it will kill you too but there will be no special hurry.

ERNEST HEMINGWAY, *A Farewell to Arms*, 1929.

I'd rather give my life than be afraid to give it.

LYNDON B. JOHNSON, press conference, November 25, 1963.

There is plenty of courage among us for the abstract but not for the concrete.

HELEN KELLER, *Let Us Have Faith*, 1940.

Physical courage is never in short supply in a fighting army. Moral courage sometimes is.

MATTHEW B. RIDGWAY, *The Korean War*, 1967.

We cannot afford to accumulate a deficit in the books of human fortitude.

FRANKLIN D. ROOSEVELT, speech, Democratic National Convention, Philadelphia, Pennsylvania, June 27, 1936.

It takes far less courage to kill yourself than it takes to make yourself wake up one more time. It's harder to stay where you are than to get out.

JUDITH ROSSNER, *Nine Months in the Life of an Old Maid*, 1969.

Moral cowardice that keeps us from speaking our minds is as dangerous to this country as irresponsible talk. The right way is not always the popular and easy way. Standing for right when it is unpopular is a true test of moral character.

MARGARET CHASE SMITH, speech, Westbrook Junior College, Portland, Maine, June 7, 1953.

It you're scared, just holler and you'll find it ain't so lonesome out there.

JOE SUGDEN, in Joe Garagiola, *Baseball Is a Funny Game*, 1960.

A man can be physically courageous and morally craven.

MELVIN B. TOLSON, "Paul Robeson Rebels Against Hollywood's Dollars," *Washington Tribune*, March 25, 1939.

CREATIVITY

I really believe there are things nobody would see if I didn't photograph them.

DIANE ARBUS, *Diane Arbus*, 1972.

But I'm not original. The only way I could truly say I was original is if I created the English language. I did, man, but they don't believe me.

LENNY BRUCE, ca. 1960, in John Cohen, ed., *The Essential Lenny Bruce*, 1967.

Without creative personalities able to think and judge independently, the upward development of society is as unthinkable as the development of the individual personality without the nourishing soil of the community.

ALBERT EINSTEIN, *Ideas and Opinions*, 1954.

The creative individual is someone upon whom mysterious rays have converged and are again reflected, not necessarily immediately, but in the course of years.

LOREN EISELEY, "The Last Neanderthal," *The Star Thrower*, 1964.

Directly stated, the evolution of the entire universe—stars, elements, life, man—is a process of drawing something out of nothing, out of the utter void of nonbeing. The creative element in the mind of man—that latency which can conceive gods, carve statues, move the heart with the symbols of great poetry, or devise the formulas of modern physics—emerge in as mysterious a fashion as those elementary particles which leap into momentary existence in great cyclotrons, only to vanish again like infinitesimal ghosts.

LOREN EISELEY, *The Night Country*, 1971.

Every nation, every race, has not only its own creative, but its own critical turn of mind; and is even more oblivious of the shortcomings and limitations of its critical habits than of those of its creative genius.

T.S. ELIOT, "Tradition and the Individual Talent," *The Sacred Wood*, 1919.

By artist I mean of course everyone who has tried to create something which was not here before him, with no other tools and material than the uncommerciable ones of the human spirit.

WILLIAM FAULKNER, speech, New York City, January 25, 1955.

Creativity varies inversely with the number of cooks involved in the broth.

BERNICE FITZ-GIBBON, *Macy's, Gimbels and Me*, 1967.

I look for what needs to be done....After all, that's how the universe designs itself.

R. BUCKMINSTER FULLER, *Christian Science Monitor*, November 3, 1964.

All men are creative but few are artists.

PAUL GOODMAN, *Growing Up Absurd*, 1960.

Could Hamlet have been written by a committee, or the Mona Lisa painted by a club? Could the New Testament have been composed as a conference report? Creative ideas do not spring from groups. They spring from individuals. The divine spark leaps from the finger of God to the finger of Adam, whether it takes ultimate shape

in a law of physics or a law of the land, a poem or a policy, a sonata or a mechanical computer.

A. WHITNEY GRISWOLD, speech, Yale University, June 9, 1957.

Creativity always dies a quick death in rooms that house conference tables.

BRUCE HERSCHENSOHN, *New York Times*, April 2, 1975.

Every creative act requires elimination and simplification. Simplification results from a realization of what is essential.

HANS HOFFMANN, 1948, in Herschel B. Chipp, ed., *Theories of Modern Art*, 1968.

Man, like Deity, creates in his own image.

ELBERT HUBBARD, *The Note Book*, 1927.

Human salvation lies in the hands of the creatively maladjusted.

MARTIN LUTHER KING, JR., *Strength to Love*, 1963.

The American Way is so restlessly creative as to be essentially destructive; the American Way is to carry common sense itself almost to the point of madness.

LOUIS KRONENBERGER, "Last Thoughts," *Company Manners*, 1954.

Artistic temperament...sometimes seems a battleground, a dark angel of destruction and a bright angel of creativity wrestling.

MADELEINE L'ENGLE, *A Severed Wasp*, 1982.

For me, the creative process, first of all, requires a good nine hours of sleep at night. Second, it must not be pushed by the need to produce practical applications.

WILLIAM N. LIPSCOMB, JR., *New York Times*, December 7, 1977.

Let a human being throw the energies of his soul into the making of something, and the instinct of workmanship will take care of his honesty.

WALTER LIPPMANN, "The Changing Focus," *A Preface to Politics*, 1914.

Inspiring visions rarely (I'm tempted to say never) include numbers.

TOM PETERS, *Thriving on Chaos*, 1987.

It is providential that the youth or man of inventive mind is not "blessed" with a million dollars. The mind is sharper and keener in seclusion and uninterrupted solitude. Originality thrives in seclusion free of outside influences beating upon us to cripple the creative mind. Be alone—that is the secret of invention: be alone, that is when ideas are born.

Nikola Tesla, in Thomas P. Hughes, *American Genesis: A Century of Invention and Technological Enthusiasm,* 1989.

What marks the artist is his power to shape the material of pain we all have.

Lionel Trilling, "Art and Neurosis," *The Liberal Imagination,* 1950.

Helped are those who create anything at all, for they shall relive the thrill of their own conception, and realize a partnership in the creation of the Universe that keeps them responsible and cheerful.

Alice Walker, *The Temple of My Familiar,* 1989.

Most forms of human creativity have one aspect in common: the attempt to give some sense to the various impressions, emotions, experiences, and actions that fill our lives, and thereby to give some meaning and value to our existence.... The crisis of our time in the Western world is that the search for meaning has become meaningless for many of us.

Victor Weisskopf, *The Privilege of Being a Physicist,* 1989.

CYNICISM

Cynic, n. A blackguard whose faulty vision sees things as they are, not as they ought to be.

Ambrose Bierce, *The Devil's Dictionary,* 1906.

Privatism is the mood of being uncommitted to anything, of taking no part in anything, of being primarily devoted to personal gratification. Privatism is a modern word, but it reflects a frame of mind that is as old as time. The rabbis taught, "When the community is in distress, one should not say, 'I will go home, eat and drink, and peace will be upon my soul.'"

Seymour Cohen, *Affirming Life,* 1987.

A cynic is not merely one who reads bitter lessons from the past; he is one who is prematurely disappointed in the future.

Sydney J. Harris, *On the Contrary,* 1962.

Cynicism is an unpleasant way of saying the truth.

Lillian Hellman, *The Little Foxes,* 1939.

[I]n rejecting secrecy I had also rejected the road to cynicism.

Catherine Marshall, *Christy,* 1967.

It is only the cynicism that is born of success that is penetrating and valid.

George Jean Nathan, "Cynicism," *Monks Are Monks,* 1929.

The worst cynicism: a belief in luck.

Joyce Carol Oates, *Do with Me What You Will,* 1970.

The only deadly sin I know is cynicism.

Henry L. Stimson, *On Active Service in Peace and War,* 1948.

Sacredness of human life! The world has never believed it! It has been with life that we settled our quarrels, won wives, gold and land, defended ideas, imposed religions. We have held that a death toll was a necessary part of every human achievement, whether sport, war, or industry. A moment's rage over the horror of it, and we have sunk into indifference.

Ida Tarbell, *New Ideals in Business,* 1914.

The novelists' failure is a consequence, I believe, of the historical experience of the twentieth century, which since the First World War has been one of man's cumulative disillusionment in himself. The idea of progress was the greatest casualty of that war, and its aftermath was cynicism.

Barbara Tuchman, speech, "The Historian's Opportunity," American Historical Association, December, 1966.

I worry no matter how cynical you become, it's never enough to keep up.

Jane Wagner, *The Search for Intelligent Life in the Universe,* performed by Lily Tomlin, 1986.

DELUSIONS, ILLUSIONS, AND FANTASY

The mere attempt to examine my own confusion would consume volumes.

James Agee with Walker Evans, *Let Us Now Praise Famous Men,* 1941.

Illusion is the dust the devil throws in the eyes of the foolish.

Minna Antrim, *Naked Truth and Veiled Allusions,* 1902.

The making of illusions which flood our experience has become the business in America, some of its most honest and most necessary and most respectable business. I am thinking not only of advertising and public relations and political rhetoric, but of all the activities which purport to inform and comfort and improve and educate and elevate us: the work of our best journalists, our most enterprising book publishers, our most energetic manufacturers and merchandisers, our most successful entertainers, our best guides to world travel, and our most influential leaders in foreign relations. Our every effort to satisfy our extravagant expectations simply makes them more extravagant and makes our illusions more attractive.

DANIEL J. BOORSTIN, *The Image*, 1962.

Demanding more than the world can give us, we require that something be fabricated to make up for the world's deficiency. This is only one example of our demand for illusions.

DANIEL J. BOORSTIN, *Hidden History*, 1987.

If a democratic country escapes the blight of outright repression it is susceptible to the subtler disease of wishful thinking.

WILLIAM H. CHAMBERLIN, "The Malady of Wishful Thinking," *Harper's*, May, 1941.

Most of our platitudes notwithstanding, self-deception remains the most difficult deception. The tricks that work on others count for nothing in that very well lit alley where one keeps assignations with oneself: no winning smiles will do here, no prettily drawn lists of good intentions.

JOAN DIDION, "On Self-Respect," *Slouching Towards Bethlehem*, 1968.

When I examine myself and my methods of thought, I come close to the conclusion that the gift of fantasy has meant more to me than my talent for absorbing positive knowledge.

ALBERT EINSTEIN, recalled on 100th anniversary of his birth, February 18, 1979.

Now he has departed from this strange world a little ahead of me. That means nothing. People like us, who believe in physics, know that the distinction between past, present and future is only a stubbornly persistent illusion.

ALBERT EINSTEIN, letter of condolence on death of Michele Besso, 1955, in Freeman Dyson, *Disturbing the Universe*, 1979.

Human kind
Cannot bear very much reality.

T.S. ELIOT, "Burnt Norton," *Four Quartets*, 1935.

Fantasies are more than substitutes for unpleasant reality; they are also dress rehearsals, plans. All acts performed in the world begin in the imagination.

BARBARA GRIZZUTI HARRISON, "Talking Dirty," *Ms.*, October, 1973.

I think I have always known about my memory: I know when it is to be trusted and when some dreams or fantasy entered on the life, and the dream, the need of dream, led to distortion of what happened.

LILLIAN HELLMAN, *Pentimento*, 1973.

Fantasy is the only truth.

ABBIE HOFFMAN, *Revolution for the Hell of It*, 1968.

The happy ending is our national belief.

MARY MCCARTHY, "America the Beautiful: The Humanist in the Bathtub," *On the Contrary*, 1961.

Fantasy discourages reality, particularly in that reality is, in itself, discouraging.

JOAN PATTERSON, in conversation, June 19, 1991.

Everything we do not know anything about always looks big. The human creature is imaginative. If he sees a tail disappearing over a fence, he images the whole beast and usually images the wrong beast....Whenever we take a trip into the realms of fancy, we see a good many things that never were.

THOMAS BRACKETT REED, in Samuel Walker McCall, *The Life of Thomas Brackett Reed*, 1914.

If we ever pass out as a great nation we ought to put on our tombstone "America died from a delusion that she had moral leadership."

WILL ROGERS, in Donald Day, ed., *The Autobiography of Will Rogers*, 1949.

I learned to believe in freedom, to glow when the word *democracy* is used, and to practice slavery from morning to night. I learned it the way all of my southern people learn it: by closing door after door until one's mind and heart and conscience are blocked off from each other and from reality.

LILLIAN SMITH, *Killers of the Dream*, 1949.

The men who start out with the notion that the world owes them a living generally find that the world pays its debt in the penitentiary or the poorhouse.

WILLIAM GRAHAM SUMNER, "Earth Hunger," *Earth Hunger and Other Essays*, 1913.

Disillusion comes only to the illusioned. One cannot be disillusioned of what one never put faith in.

DOROTHY THOMPSON, *The Courage To Be Happy*, 1957.

DUTY

Duty, n. That which sternly impels us in the direction of profit, along the line of desire.

AMBROSE BIERCE, *The Devil's Dictionary*, 1906.

[S]ervice is the rent each of us pays for living— the very purpose of life and not something you do in your spare time or after you have reached your personal goals.

MARIAN WRIGHT EDELMAN, speech, Howard University, May 12, 1990.

No man can always be right. So the struggle is to do one's best; to keep the brain and conscience clear; never to be swayed by unworthy motives or inconsequential reasons, but to strive to unearth the basic factors involved and then do one's duty.

DWIGHT D. EISENHOWER, letter to Mamie Doud Eisenhower, February 15, 1943.

Pressed into service means pressed out of shape.

ROBERT FROST, "The Self-Seeker," *North of Boston*, 1914.

The first duty of a human being is to assume the right functional relationship to society—more briefly, to find your real job, and do it.

CHARLOTTE PERKINS GILMAN, *The Living of Charlotte Perkins Gilman*, 1935.

The burning conviction that we have a holy duty toward others is often a way of attaching our drowning selves to a passing raft. What looks like giving a hand is often a holding on for dear life.

ERIC HOFFER, *The True Believer*, 1951.

I declare my belief that it is not your duty to do anything that is not to your own interest. Whenever it is unquestionably your duty to do a thing, then it will benefit you to perform that duty.

EDGAR WATSON HOWE, *Country Town Sayings*, 1911.

What better fate for a man than to die in the performance of his duty?

DOUGLAS MACARTHUR, reply to complaint that he was working his men to death, ca. 1946, in William Manchester, *American Caesar*, 1978.

If a sense of duty tortures a man, it also enables him to achieve prodigies.

H.L. MENCKEN, *Prejudices*, 1919.

Battle is the most magnificent competition in which a human being can indulge. It brings out all that is best; it removes all that is base. All men are afraid in battle. The coward is the one who lets his fear overcome his sense of duty. Duty is the essence of manhood.

GEORGE S. PATTON, message to troops, 1943.

A sense of duty is moral glue, constantly subject to stress.

WILLIAM SAFIRE, *New York Times*, May 23, 1986.

The paths of glory at least lead to the grave, but the paths of duty may not get you anywhere.

JAMES THURBER, "The Patient Bloodhound," *Fables for Our Time*, 1943.

Duties are not performed for duty's *sake*, but because their *neglect* would make the man *uncomfortable*. A man performs but *one* duty—the duty of contenting his spirit, the duty of making himself agreeable to himself.

MARK TWAIN, *What Is Man?*, 1906.

The worst of doing one's duty was that it apparently unfitted one for doing anything else.

EDITH WHARTON, *The Age of Innocence*, 1920.

There is no question what the roll of honor in America is. The roll of honor consists of the names of men who have squared their conduct by ideals of duty.

WOODROW WILSON, speech, Washington, D.C., February 27, 1916.

EVIL

Some men wish evil and accomplish it
But most men, when they work in that machine
Just let it happen somewhere in the wheels.
The fault is no decisive villainous knife
But the dull saw that is the routine mind.

STEPHEN VINCENT BENÉT, *John Brown's Body*, 1928.

If men were basically evil, who would bother to improve the world instead of giving it up as a bad job at the outset?

VAN WYCK BROOKS, *From a Writer's Notebook*, 1958.

Those who set in motion the forces of evil cannot always control them afterwards.

CHARLES WADDELL CHESTNUTT, *The Marrow of Tradition*, 1901.

Evil is here in the world, not because God wants it or uses it here, but because He knows not how at the moment to remove it; or knowing, has not the skill or power to achieve His end. Evil, therefore, is a fact not to be explained away, but to be accepted; and accepted not to be endured, but to be conquered. It is a challenge neither to our reason nor to our patience, but to our courage.

JOHN HAYNES HOLMES, "A Struggling God," in Joseph Fort Newton, *My Idea of God*, 1926.

No man is justified in doing evil on the ground of expediency.

THEODORE ROOSEVELT, *The Strenuous Life*, 1900.

Evil is obvious only in retrospect.

GLORIA STEINEM, *Outrageous Acts and Everyday Rebellions*, 1983.

Those who corrupt the public mind are just as evil as those who steal from the public purse.

ADLAI E. STEVENSON, speech, Albuquerque, New Mexico, September 12, 1952.

There is no evil in the atom; only in men's souls.

ADLAI E. STEVENSON, speech, Hartford, Connecticut, September 18, 1952.

FAME

I'm the world champion but I don't feel any different than that fan over there. I'll still walk in the ghettoes, answer questions, kiss babies. I didn't marry a blonde or go nude in the movies. I'll never forget my people.

MUHAMMAD ALI, after Zaire fight, 1974, *Sports Illustrated*, November 11, 1974.

A celebrity is a person who works hard all his life to become well known, then wears dark glasses to avoid being recognized.

FRED ALLEN, *Treadmill to Oblivion*, 1954.

My arrival in New York created as much commotion as the advent of another flounder at the Fulton Fish Market.

FRED ALLEN, *Much Ado About Me*, 1956.

Fame always brings loneliness. Success is as ice cold and lonely as the north pole.

VICKI BAUM, *Grand Hotel*, 1931.

The real trap of fame is its irresistibility.

INGRID BENGIS, "Monroe According to Mailer," *Ms.*, October, 1973.

Famous, adj. Conspicuously miserable.

AMBROSE BIERCE, *The Devil's Dictionary*, 1906.

The very agency which first makes the celebrity in the long run inevitably destroys him....There is not even any tragedy in the celebrity's fall, for he is a man returned to his proper anonymous station.

DANIEL J. BOORSTIN, *The Image*, 1962.

My esteem in this country has gone up substantially. It is very nice now [that] when people wave at me, they use all their fingers.

JIMMY CARTER, 1978, in Lois and Alan Gordon, *American Chronicle*, 1987.

It would be fun to be a star, if you could do it anonymously. It's the thought of people's encasing my toenail parings in plastic that makes me wonder if I'm up to the demands of the big time.

CHRIS CHASE, *How To Be a Movie Star, or A Terrible Beauty Is Born*, 1968.

There's been a disappearance of fame and an emergence of celebrities. Little McEnroe earns 10 times as much as the Chief Justice of the United States, and will be forgotten as soon as he stops playing. You hear an announcer saying at a tennis match, "On this serve rests $40,000." Imagine saying that about a sonata performed by Serkin.

HENRY STEELE COMMAGER, *New York Times*, October 26, 1982.

Next to Sinatra, I have the most hostile press in America. I have been called a company pimp, a prostitute and a man with no trace of decency or morality. I have been vilified by people I have never even seen.

HOWARD COSELL, *TV Guide*, October 1, 1975.

Fame creates its own standard. A guy who twitches his lips is just another guy with a lip twitch—unless he's Humphrey Bogart.

SAMMY DAVIS, JR., *Yes I Can*, 1965.

I never said, "I want to be alone." I only said, "I want to be *left* alone." There is all the difference.

GRETA GARBO, in John Bainbridge, *Garbo*, 1955.

Stardom can be a gilded slavery.

HELEN HAYES, *On Reflection, An Autobiography*, 1968.

It is a mark of many famous people that they cannot part with their brightest hour: what worked once must always work.

LILLIAN HELLMAN, "Theatre," *Pentimento*, 1973.

You never feel that you have fame. It's always in back of you.

KATHARINE HEPBURN, "Dick Cavett Show," ABC-TV, April 4, 1975.

I'm the only person of distinction who's ever had a depression named for him.

HERBERT HOOVER, in Richard Norton Smith, *An Uncommon Man*, 1984.

Fame is delightful, but as collateral it does not rank high.

ELBERT HUBBARD, *The Roycroft Dictionary and Book of Epigrams*, 1923.

One of the reasons that so many people who achieve fame and fortune don't find happiness is because, almost by definition, if you reach that high estate you are going to find yourself surrounded by the lowest hangers-on in the world. It is not that you get cut off from the real people; you just get cut off from the good people. And pretty soon, if you don't watch out, you can start to turn into a creep yourself.

BILLIE JEAN KING, *Billie Jean*, 1982.

The nice thing about being a celebrity is that when you bore people, they think it's their fault.

HENRY KISSINGER, *Reader's Digest*, April, 1985.

I've been on a calendar, but never on time.

MARILYN MONROE, *Look*, January 16, 1962.

A sex symbol becomes a thing. I hate being a thing.

MARILYN MONROE, in Jeremy Pascall and Clive Jeavons, *A Pictorial History of Sex in the Movies*, 1975.

Fame improves some people. Except for certain saints and others with inner resources, there is nothing ennobling about obscurity.

LANCE MORROW, "The Perils of Celebrity," *Fishing in the Tiber*, 1988.

Leave me alone. I'm a lineman. I want to be obscure.

DENNIS NELSON, *Sports Illustrated*, November 19, 1973.

The problem of fame is that you get frozen in one frame and nothing you do can alter the name.

JERRY RUBIN, *Growing (Up) at 37*, 1976.

At the London airport a few years ago I was interviewed for 10 minutes before I discovered the interviewer thought I was Tallulah Bankhead. And Miss Bankhead had already been dead for three months—if you can believe the *New York Times*.

GLORIA SWANSON, *American Way*, June, 1973.

Celebrities used to be found in clusters, like oysters—and with much the same defensive mechanisms.

BARBARA WALTERS, *How To Talk with Practically Anybody About Practically Anything*, 1970.

Just when you think you're getting famous, somebody comes along and makes you look like a warm-up act for amateur night....Pope Paul VI [for example, just arrived]. Talk about advance PR—I mean for centuries.

ANDY WARHOL, *Popism*, 1966.

FEAR

Anxiety is the space between the "now" and the "then."

RICHARD ABELL, *Own Your Own Life*, 1976.

Tell us your phobias and we will tell you what you are afraid of.

ROBERT BENCHLEY, "Phobias," *My Ten Years in a Quandary, and How They Grew*, 1936.

Fear tastes like a rusty knife and do not let her into your house.

JOHN CHEEVER, *The Wapshot Chronicle*, 1957.

There is an almost paranoid fear eating at the guts of all Americans. Black-White, Male-Female, Young-Old represent schisms between us. Racial Polarization, the Generation Gap and Virginia Slims are all brand names for products that may become lethal.

SHIRLEY CHISHOLM, speech, Church Women United, Massachusetts, August 21, 1969.

And I will show you something different from either

Your shadow at morning striding behind you

Or your shadow at evening rising to meet you;

I will show you fear in a handful of dust.

T.S. ELIOT, *The Waste Land*, 1922.

Avoiding danger is no safer in the long run than outright exposure. The fearful are caught as often as the bold.

HELEN KELLER, *Let Us Have Faith*, 1940.

Fear and risk are different creatures. What some of us fear most—poison in our drinking water, radiation in our air, pesticides on our food—pose hardly any real risk, while some we fear least—

driving, drinking and smoking—kill many hundreds of thousands each year.

H.W. Lewis, *Technological Risk*, 1990.

The more I traveled the more I realized that fear makes strangers of people who would be friends.

Shirley MacLaine, *Don't Fall Off the Mountain*, 1970.

Fear, born of the stern matron Responsibility, sits on one's shoulders like some heavy imp of darkness, and one is preoccupied and, possibly, cantankerous.

William McFee, "The Crusaders," *Harbours of Memory*, 1921.

The one permanent emotion of the inferior man is fear—fear of the unknown, the complex, the inexplicable. What he wants beyond everything else is safety.

H.L. Mencken, *Prejudices*, 1920.

Fear can infect us early in life until eventually it cuts a deep groove of apprehension in all our thinking. To counteract it, let faith, hope and courage enter your thinking. Fear is strong, but faith is stronger yet.

Norman Vincent Peale, *Have a Great Day—Every Day*, 1985.

I would like...to see us take hold of ourselves, look at ourselves and cease being afraid.

Eleanor Roosevelt, *New York Times*, October 12, 1954.

For many years we have suckled on fear and fear alone, and there is no good product of fear. Its children are cruelty and deceit and suspicion germinating in our darkness. And just as surely as we are poisoning the air with our test bombs, so are we poisoned in our souls by fear, faceless, stupid sarcomic terror.

John Steinbeck, *Once There Was a War*, 1958.

It may be well to remember that in the United States—as the history of our red-baiting practices indicates—the exploitation of popular fear may easily become a racket.

Lillian Symes, "Fascism for America—Threat or Scarehead?" *Harper's*, June, 1939.

The most destructive element in the human mind is fear. Fear creates aggressiveness; aggressiveness engenders hostility; hostility engenders fear—a disastrous circle.

Dorothy Thompson, *The Courage To Be Happy*, 1957.

Fear is a noose that binds until it strangles.

Jean Toomer, *Definitions and Aphorisms, XVI*, 1931.

Years ago, I discovered that I could keep the plane I was flying on from crashing by refusing to adjust my watch to the new time zone until we were on the ground, and I have used that method ever since.

Calvin Trillin, "Fly Frills to Miami," *Alice, Let's Eat*, 1978.

The people of the United States are at the present time dominated and driven by two kinds of officially propagated fear: fear of the Soviet Union and fear of the income tax.

Edmund Wilson, *The Cold War and the Income Tax*, 1963.

GREED

A fool bolts pleasure, then complains of moral indigestion.

Minna Antrim, *Naked Truth and Veiled Allusions*, 1902.

each generation wastes a little more

of the future with greed and lust for riches

Don Marquis, "what the ants are saying," *the lives and times of archy and mehitabel*, 1950.

What most people don't seem to realize is that there is just as much money to be made out of the wreckage of a civilization as from the upbuilding of one.

Margaret Mitchell, *Gone with the Wind*, 1936.

One of the weaknesses of our age is our apparent inability to distinguish our needs from our greeds.

Don Robinson, *Reader's Digest*, 1963.

Greed is finally being recognized as a virtue... the best engine of betterment known to man.

William Safire, in Wendell Berry, *Home Economics*, 1987.

If unlimited private indulgence means that there are not enough resources left for national defense or for education or medical care or decent housing or intelligent community planning, then in a sane society private indulgence can no longer be unlimited.

Arthur Schlesinger, Jr., *Esquire*, January, 1960.

There is a crime here that goes beyond denunciation. There is a sorrow here that weeping cannot symbolize. There is a failure here that topples all our success. The fertile earth, the straight tree rows, the sturdy trunks, and the ripe fruit. And children dying of pellagra must die because a profit cannot be taken from an orange....

[I]n the eyes of the hungry there is a growing wrath. In the souls of the people the grapes of wrath are filling and growing heavy, growing heavy for the vintage.

JOHN STEINBECK, *The Grapes of Wrath*, 1939.

[T]he enemy is single selfishness and compulsive greed. I do not think the enemy was born yesterday, or that he grew to manhood forty years ago; or that he suffered sickness and collapse in 1929, or that we began without the enemy, and that our vision faltered, that we lost the way, and suddenly were in his camp. I think the enemy is old as Time, and evil as Hell, and that he has been here with us from the beginning. I think he stole our earth from us, destroyed our wealth, and ravaged and despoiled our land. I think he took our people and enslaved them, that he polluted the fountains of our life, took unto himself the rarest treasures of our own possession, took our bread and left us with a crust, and, not content, for the nature of the enemy is insatiate—tried finally to take from us the crust.

I think the enemy comes to us with the face of innocence and says to us:

"I am your friend."

THOMAS WOLFE, "Credo," *You Can't Go Home Again*, 1940.

HAPPINESS/SADNESS

I am one of those people who just can't help getting a kick out of life—even when it's a kick in the teeth.

POLLY ADLER, *A House Is Not a Home*, 1953.

Misery no longer loves company. Nowadays it insists upon it.

RUSSELL BAKER, *Washingtonian*, November, 1978.

At the age of five I had become a skeptic and began to sense that any happiness that came my way might be the prelude to some grim cosmic joke.

RUSSELL BAKER, *Growing Up*, 1982.

The trouble is not that we are never happy—it is that happiness is so episodical.

RUTH BENEDICT, in Margaret Mead, *An Anthropologist at Work*, 1951.

Happiness, n. An agreeable sensation arising from contemplating the misery of another.

AMBROSE BIERCE, *The Devil's Dictionary*, 1906.

Happiness? A good cigar, a good meal, a good cigar and a good woman—or a bad woman; it depends on how much happiness you can handle.

GEORGE BURNS, NBC-TV, October 16, 1984.

[T]hat is happiness; to be dissolved into something complete and great.

WILLA CATHER, *My Antonia*, 1918.

We have lived through the era when happiness was a warm puppy, and the era when happiness was a dry martini, and now we have come to the era when happiness is "knowing what your uterus looks like."

NORA EPHRON, "Vaginal Politics," *Crazy Salad, Some Things about Women*, December, 1972.

Happiness means quiet nerves.

W.C. FIELDS, in Robert Lewis Taylor, *W.C. Fields, His Follies and Fortunes*, 1949.

I am glad you are happy—but I never believe much in happiness. I never believe in misery either. Those are things you see on the stage or the screen or the printed page, they never really happen to you in life.

F. SCOTT FITZGERALD, letter, Frances Scott Fitzgerald, August 8, 1933, in Andrew Turnbull, *The Letters of F. Scott Fitzgerald*, 1963.

Happiness Makes Up in Height for What It Lacks in Length.

ROBERT FROST, poem title, 1942.

I'm sure the way to be happy is to live well beyond your means!

RUTH GORDON, *The Leading Lady*, 1948.

Amos Lowen taught his daughters carefully that poor was a curse word, and that if money couldn't buy happiness—a point he never conceded—there were still plenty of other selections.

LOIS GOULD, *Necessary Objects*, 1972.

People need joy quite as much as clothing. Some of them need it far more.

MARGARET COLLIER GRAHAM, *Gifts and Givers*, 1906.

Perhaps there is no happiness in life so perfect as the martyr's.

O. HENRY, "The Country of Elusion," *The Trimmed Lamp*, 1907.

The search for happiness is one of the chief sources of unhappiness.

ERIC HOFFER, *The Passionate State of Mind*, 1954.

Happiness is a habit—cultivate it.

ELBERT HUBBARD, *The Roycroft Dictionary and Book of Epigrams*, 1923.

If you suffer, thank God!—it is a sure sign that you are alive.

ELBERT HUBBARD, *The Roycroft Dictionary and Book of Epigrams*, 1923.

How to gain, how to keep, how to recover happiness is in fact for most men at all times the secret motive of all they do, and of all they are willing to endure.

WILLIAM JAMES, *The Varieties of Religious Experience*, 1902.

No matter how dull, or how mean, or how wise a man is, he feels that happiness is his indisputable right.

HELEN KELLER, *Optimism*, 1903.

Actually, happiness is just as silly as glory for a chief cultural value, and the pursuit of it should never have been put into the Declaration of Independence.

JOHN LEONARD, "Dad," *Mom, the Flag, and Apple Pie*, 1976.

Kissing your hand may make you feel very, very good but a diamond and sapphire bracelet lasts forever.

ANITA LOOS, *Gentlemen Prefer Blondes*, 1925.

Happiness, to some elation,

Is to others, mere stagnation.

AMY LOWELL, "Happiness," *Sword Blades and Poppy Seeds*, 1911.

Puritanism—the haunting fear that someone, somewhere, may be happy.

H.L. MENCKEN, "Sententiae," *The Vintage Mencken*, 1955.

The pursuit of happiness, which American citizens are obliged to undertake, tends to involve them in trying to perpetuate the moods, tastes and aptitudes of youth.

MALCOLM MUGGERIDGE, "Women of America," *The Most of Malcolm Muggeridge*, 1966.

There is only one way to achieve happiness
    on this terrestrial ball,

And that is to have either a clear conscience,
    or none at all.

OGDEN NASH, "Interoffice Memorandum," *I'm a Stranger Here Myself*, 1938.

Happiness is desired by all men; and moments of it are probably attained by most men. Only moments of it can be attained because happiness is the inner concomitant of neat harmonies of body, spirit and society; and these neat harmonies are bound to be infrequent.

REINHOLD NIEBUHR, *The Irony of American History*, 1952.

Where's the man could ease a heart

Like a satin gown?

DOROTHY PARKER, "The Satin Dress," *Enough Rope*, 1926.

Happiness is a way-station between two little and too much.

CHANNING POLLOCK, *Mr. Moneypenny*, 1928.

I'm just as happy as if I had good sense.

GRACE PRIMMER, in conversation, ca. 1945.

Why is life different when the singing stops?

JAMES REEVES, *The Idiom of the People*, 1958.

When one has a famishing thirst for happiness, one is apt to gulp down diversions wherever they are offered. The necessity of draining the dregs of life before the wine is savored does not cultivate a discriminating taste.

ALICE CALDWELL RICE, *Calvary Alley*, 1918.

Happiness is a Warm Puppy.

CHARLES M. SCHULZ, title of a book, 1962.

She has built her memory on a scaffold of regrets.

SANDRA SCOFIELD, "Loving Leo," in Jo Alexander et al., *Women and Aging*, 1986.

A happy woman is one who has no cares at all; a cheerful woman is one who has cares but doesn't let them get her down.

BEVERLY SILLS, in an interview on "60 Minutes," CBS-TV, 1975.

Some people are more turned on by money than they are by love....In one respect they're alike. They're both wonderful as long as they last.

ABIGAIL VAN BUREN, "Dear Abby" newspaper column, April 26, 1974.

Too much of a good thing can be wonderful.

MAE WEST, in Joseph Weintraub, *The Wit and Wisdom of Mae West*, 1967.

Modern Americans travel light, with little philosophic baggage other than a fervent belief in their right to the pursuit of happiness.

GEORGE WILL, Introduction, *The Pursuit of Happiness, and Other Sobering Thoughts*, 1978.

Happy days are here again,

The skies above are clear again.

Let us sing a song of cheer again,

Happy days are here again!

JACK YELLEN, "Happy Days Are Here Again," from the musical comedy *Chasing Rainbows* (used in Franklin D. Roosevelt's presidential campaign of 1936), 1929.

HATE

You lose a lot of time hating people.

MARIAN ANDERSON, *New York Times*, April 18, 1965.

To be loved is to be fortunate, but to be hated is to achieve distinction.

MINNA ANTRIM, *Naked Truth and Veiled Allusions*, 1902.

Hatred, which could destroy so much, never failed to destroy the man who hated and this was an immutable law.

JAMES BALDWIN, *Notes of a Native Son*, 1955.

I tell you there is such a thing as creative hate!

WILLA CATHER, *The Song of the Lark*, 1915.

I have honestly never gone in for hating. My temporary bitternesses toward people have all been ended by what Freud called an inferiority complex and Christ called "Let him without sin—" I remember the day he said it. We were just like that then; we tossed up for who was going to go through with it—and he lost.

F. SCOTT FITZGERALD, letter to Ernest Hemingway, June 1, 1934, in Matthew J. Bruccoli, *Scott and Ernest*, 1978.

We do not usually look for allies when we love. Indeed, we often look on those who love with us as rivals and trespassers. But we always look for allies when we hate.

ERIC HOFFER, *The True Believer*, 1951.

Like an unchecked cancer, hate corrodes the personality and eats away its vital unity. Hate destroys a man's sense of values and his objectivity. It causes him to describe the beautiful as ugly and the ugly as beautiful, and to confuse the true with the false and the false with the true.

MARTIN LUTHER KING, JR., *Strength To Love*, 1963.

Darkness cannot drive out darkness; only light can do that. Hate cannot drive out hate; only love can do that. Hate multiplies hate, violence multiplies violence, and toughness multiplies toughness in a descending spiral of destruction....The chain reaction of evil—hate begetting hate, wars producing more wars—must be broken, or we shall be plunged into the dark abyss of annihilation.

MARTIN LUTHER KING, JR., *Strength To Love*, 1963.

Man can be the most affectionate and altruistic of creatures, yet he's potentially more vicious than any other. He is the only one who can be persuaded to hate millions of his own kind whom he has never seen and to kill as many as he can lay his hands on in the name of his tribe or his God.

BENJAMIN SPOCK, *Decent and Indecent*, 1970.

Hate is still the main enemy of the human race, the fuel that heats the furnaces of genocide.

I.F. STONE, "When a Two-Party System Becomes a One-Party Rubber Stamp," *I.F. Stone's Weekly*, September 9, 1968.

One of the most time-consuming things is to have an enemy.

E.B. WHITE, "A Report in January," January 30, 1958, *Essays of E.B. White*, 1977.

HOPE

When hope is taken away from people moral degeneration follows swiftly after.

PEARL S. BUCK, letter to *New York Times*, November 15, 1941.

All this drudgery will kill me if once in a while I cannot hope something, for somebody! If I cannot sometimes see a bird fly and wave my hand to it.

WILLA CATHER, *The Song of the Lark*, 1915.

If a man like Malcolm X could change and repudiate racism, if I myself and other former Muslims can change, if young whites can change, then there is hope for America.

ELDRIDGE CLEAVER, "The White Race and Its Heroes," *Soul on Ice*, 1968.

He's a man way out there in the blue, riding on a smile and a shoeshine. And when they start not smiling back—that's an earthquake....A salesman is got to dream, boy. It comes with the territory.

ARTHUR MILLER, "Requiem," *Death of a Salesman*, 1949.

Nothing that is worth anything can be achieved in a lifetime; therefore we must be saved by hope.

REINHOLD NIEBUHR, *The Irony of American History*, 1952.

Hope, like faith, is nothing if it is not courageous; it is nothing if it is not ridiculous.

THORNTON WILDER, *The Eighth Day*, 1967.

HUMOR

Humor is a delicate shrub, with the passing hectic flush of its time. The current topic variety is especially subject to early frosts, as is also the dialectic species.

THOMAS BAILEY ALDRICH, "Leaves from a Notebook," *Ponkapog Papers*, 1903.

Sheer madness is, of course, the highest possible brow in humor.

ROBERT BENCHLEY, 1926, in Walter Blair and Hamlin Hill, *America's Humor*, 1978.

Laughter, n. An interior convulsion, producing a distortion of the features and accompanied by inarticulate noises. It is infectious and, though intermittent, incurable. Liability to attacks of laughter is one of the characteristics distinguishing man from the animals.

AMBROSE BIERCE, *The Devil's Dictionary*, 1906.

Wit, n. The salt with which the American humorist spoils his intellectual cookery by leaving it out.

AMBROSE BIERCE, *The Devil's Dictionary*, 1906.

Witticism, n. A sharp and clever remark, usually quoted and seldom noted; what the Philistine is pleased to call a "joke."

AMBROSE BIERCE, *The Devil's Dictionary*, 1906.

Wit is a treacherous dart. It is perhaps the only weapon with which it is possible to stab oneself in one's own back.

GEOFFREY BOCCA, *The Woman Who Would Be Queen*, 1954.

Being a funny person does an awful lot of things to you. You feel that you mustn't get serious with people. They don't expect it from you, and they don't want to see it. You're not entitled to

be serious, you're a clown, and they only want you to make them laugh.

FANNY BRICE, in Norman Katkov, *The Fabulous Fanny*, 1952.

Tragedy is if I cut my finger. Comedy is if I walk into an open sewer and die.

MEL BROOKS, in article by Kenneth Tynan, *The New Yorker*, October 30, 1978.

Sometimes I look at life in the fun mirror at a carnival. I see myself as a profound, incisive wit, concerned with man's inhumanity to man. Then I stroll to the next mirror and I see a pompous, subjective ass whose humor is hardly spiritual.

I see traces of Mephistopheles. All my humor is based upon destruction and despair. If the whole world were tranquil, without disease and violence, I'd be standing on the breadline right in back of J. Edgar Hoover and—who's another real heavyweight?—Dr. Jonas Salk.

LENNY BRUCE, ca. 1960, in John Cohen, ed., *The Essential Lenny Bruce*, 1967.

Men will confess to treason, murder, arson, false teeth, or a wig. How many of them will own up to a lack of humor?

FRANK COLBY, *The Colby Essays*, 1926.

How very gracious is the straight man!—or, in this case, the straight girl. She spreads before her friend a gift-wrapped, beribboned gag line he can claim for his own, if only he will pick it up instead of pausing to contemplate what a nitwit he's talking to.

ANNIE DILLARD, *An American Childhood*, 1987.

Humor is one of God's most marvelous gifts. Humor gives us smiles, laughter, and gaiety. Humor reveals the roses and hides the thorns. Humor makes our heavy burdens light and smooths the rough spots in our pathways. Humor endows us with the capacity to clarify the obscure, to simplify the complex, to deflate the pompous, to chastise the arrogant, to point a moral, and to adorn a tale.

SAM ERVIN, *Humor of a Country Lawyer*, 1983.

For reasons I have never understood, Alexandria, Virginia, is screamingly funny to Washingtonians, while the great city of Oakland never fails to get a chuckle out of San Franciscans. And Bismarck, North Dakota, is funny anywhere in the United States.

W.C. FIELDS, ca. 1930, in Robert Lewis Taylor, *W.C. Fields, His Follies and Fortunes*, 1949.

ALLEN: Here comes a man down the street wearing bulldog Wedgies. Pardon me, sir.

CLAGHORN: Claghorn's the name. Senator Claghorn, that is. Stand aside, son! Don't hold me up! Ah'm busier than a flute player's upper lips durin' a rendition of William Tell.

ALLEN: You're busy?

CLAGHORN: Ah'm checkin' on that Hoover Report.

ALLEN: What *is* that Hoover Report, Senator?

CLAGHORN: Herby made a list of things he forgot to fix when he was President. He's givin' the list to little old Harry so's Harry can fix 'em now.

ALLEN: Fine.

CLAGHORN: Herby says the Army and the Navy is wastin' money. The Army's throwin' money around like the taxpayer was the enemy. Ah found one item: the Army spent two billion dollars for fly swatters to send to Alaska. When the fly swatters got up there they found there wasn't no flies in Alaska.

ALLEN: They sent the fly swatters back?

CLAGHORN: Not the Army, son! The Army spent four billion dollars more to raise flies to ship to Alaska so's they could use them fly swatters. That's how the Army works, son!

ALLEN: I see. What else have you been up to, Senator?

CLAGHORN: Me and Harry opened up the baseball season. Harry threw out the first ball.

ALLEN: Did the President enjoy participating?

CLAGHORN: He sure did. The way things are goin' Harry'll play ball with anybody. He couldn't wait to throw that first ball out to the Washington team, son. It was the first time this year the Senators took anything from Harry!

ALLEN: Governor Dewey went to the Yankee game.

CLAGHORN: Ah seen his pitcher in the paper, son! At first Ah didn't recognize Governor Dewey with that mustache. Ah thought it was some man eatin' a Hershey bar sideways.

ALLEN: I read that Mr. Dewey is going to Europe.

CLAGHORN: He's doin' the smart thing, son!

ALLEN: Going to Europe?

CLAGHORN: Comin' back, Dewey's goin' to enter the country as an immigrant and start all over!

FRED ALLEN, **radio skit, "Claghorn on Washington Politics," ca. 1927.**

I never saw anything funny that wasn't terrible. If it causes pain, it's funny; if it doesn't, it isn't. I try to hide the pain with embarrassment, and the more I do that, the better they like it. But that doesn't mean they are unsympathetic. Oh no, they laugh often with tears in their eyes.

W.C. FIELDS, in Walter Blair and Hamlin Hill, *America's Humor*, 1978.

Where humor is concerned, there are no standards—no one can say what is good or bad, although you can be sure that everyone will. Only a very foolish man will use a form of language that is wholly uncertain in its effect. And that is the nature of humor.

JOHN KENNETH GALBRAITH, *Annals of an Abiding Liberal*, 1979.

Wit that is kindly is not very witty.

EDGAR WATSON HOWE, *Sinner Sermons*, 1926.

Humor is laughing at what you haven't got when you ought to have it.

LANGSTON HUGHES, *The Book of Negro Humor*, 1966.

Humor is when the joke is on you but hits the other fellow first—before it boomerangs.

LANGSTON HUGHES, *The Book of Negro Humor*, 1966.

Wit, at its best, consists in the terse intrusion into an atmosphere of serene mental habit of some uncompromising truth.

PHILANDER JOHNSON, "Colyumists' Confessional," *Everybody's Magazine*, May, 1920.

The first thing any comedian does on getting an unscheduled laugh is to verify the state of his buttons; the second is to look around and see if a cat has walked out on the stage.

ALVA JOHNSTON, in Robert Lewis Taylor, *W.C. Fields, His Follies and Fortunes*, 1949.

Humor simultaneously wounds and heals, indicts and pardons, diminishes and enlarges; it constitutes inner growth at the expense of outer gain, and those who possess and honestly practice it make themselves more through a willingness to make themselves less.

LOUIS KRONENBERGER, *Company Manners*, 1954.

Ultimately, all jokes, parables, lies, and in fact all fictions and fables of whatever sort are simply the decorative showcases of their tellers' anxieties, their repressions, and generally of their neuroses.

GERSHON LEGMAN, *No Laughing Matter*, 1982.

The political cartoon is a sort of pictorial breakfast food. It has the cardinal asset of making the beginning of the day sunnier.

JOHN T. MCCUTCHEON, *New York Times*, December 3, 1975.

Laughter is man's most distinctive emotional expression. Man shares the capacity for love and hate, anger and fear, loyalty and grief, with other living creatures. But humor, which has an intellectual as well as an emotional element, belongs to man.

MARGARET MEAD, *Redbook*, March, 1963.

It always withers in the presence of the messianic delusion, like justice and truth in front of patriotic passion.

H.L. MENCKEN, on sense of humor, *Prejudices*, 1919.

Among animals, *one* has a sense of humor. Humor saves a few steps, it saves years.

MARIANNE MOORE, "The Pangolin," 1941.

Nothing disturbs, or surprises, man so much as the discrepancy between his professions and his actual behavior; in that discrepancy lies the mother lode of intellectual comedy.

CHRISTOPHER MORLEY, Introduction, *The Best of Don Marquis*, 1939.

Wit has truth in it; wisecracking is simply calisthenics with words.

DOROTHY PARKER, *Paris Review*, Summer, 1956.

People who cannot recognize a palpable absurdity are very much in the way of civilization.

AGNES REPPLIER, *In Pursuit of Laughter*, 1936.

Humour brings insight and tolerance. Irony brings a deeper and less friendly understanding.

AGNES REPPLIER, *In Pursuit of Laughter*, 1936.

On the preservation of the Comic Spirit depends in some measure the ultimate triumph of civilization. Science may carry us to Mars, but it will leave the earth peopled as ever by the inept.

AGNES REPPLIER, *In Pursuit of Laughter*, 1936.

If you don't count some of Jehovah's injunctions, there are no humorists I can recall in the Bible.

MORDECAI RICHLER, *The Best of Modern Humor*, 1983.

There is not one female comic who was beautiful as a little girl.

JOAN RIVERS, in article by Lydia Lane, *Los Angeles Times*, May 10, 1974.

Humor has been a fashioning instrument in America, cleaving its way through the national life, holding tenaciously to the spread elements of that life. Its mode has often been swift and coarse and ruthless, beyond art and beyond established civilization. It has engaged in warfare against the established heritage, against the bonds of pioneer existence. Its objective—the unconscious objective of a disunited people—has seemed to be that of creating fresh bonds, a new unity, the semblance of a society and the rounded completion of an American type.

CONSTANCE ROURKE, *American Humor*, 1931.

Everything is funny as long as it is happening to somebody else.

WILL ROGERS, *The Illiterate Digest*, 1924.

A comedian can only last till he either takes himself serious or his audience takes him serious.

WILL ROGERS, newspaper column, June 28, 1931.

The reason that there are so few women comics is that so few women can bear being laughed at.

ANNA RUSSELL, *London Sunday Times*, August 25, 1957.

There has lately been an inversion of roles between humor and society. Society is riddled with comedy, often lethal but funny nonetheless, and humor has become purposeful and serious, often deadly but unfunny nonetheless.

RICHARD SHEPARD, Preface, in Richard J. Anobile, ed., *Why a Duck?*, 1971.

We [America] are a nation that has always gone in for the loud laugh, the wow, the belly laugh and the dozen other labels for the roll-'em-in-the-aisles of gagerissimo.

JAMES THURBER, "The Quality of Mirth," *New York Times,*
February 21, 1960.

Wit is the only wall

Between us and the dark.

MARK VAN DOREN, "Wit," *A Winter Diary and Other
Poems,* 1935.

Although every American has a sense of humor—it is his birthright and encoded somewhere in the Constitution—few Americans have ever been able to cope with wit or irony, and even the simplest jokes often cause unease, especially today when every phrase must be examined for covert sexism, racism, ageism.

GORE VIDAL, "The Essential Mencken," *The Nation,*
August 26/September 2, 1991.

It's hard to be funny when you have to be clean.

MAE WEST, in Joseph Weintraub, *The Wit and Wisdom of
Mae West,* 1967.

Whatever else an American believes or disbelieves about himself, he is absolutely sure he has a sense of humor.

E.B. WHITE, "Some Remarks on Humor," *Essays of E.B.
White,* 1977.

I think the stature of humor must vary some with the times. The court fool in Shakespeare's day had no social standing and was no better than a lackey, but he did have some artistic standing and was listened to with considerable attention, there being a well-founded belief that he had the truth hidden somewhere about his person. Artistically he stood probably higher than the humorist of today, who has gained social position but not the ear of the mighty.

E.B. WHITE, "Some Remarks on Humor," *Essays of E.B.
White,* 1977.

IMAGINATION

We have learned as common knowledge that much of the insensibility and hardness of the world is due to the lack of imagination which prevents a realization of the experiences of other people.

JANE ADDAMS, Introduction, *Democracy and Social Ethics,*
1902.

Imagination has always had powers of resurrection that no science can match.

INGRID BENGIS, "Monroe According to Mailer," *Ms.,*
October, 1973.

A mind risks real ignorance for the sometimes paltry prize of an imagination enriched. The trick of reason is to get the imagination to seize the actual world—if only from time to time.

ANNIE DILLARD, *An American Childhood,* 1987.

We are often like rivers: careless and forceful, timid and dangerous, lucid and muddied, eddying, gleaming, still. Lovers, farmers, and artists have one thing in common, at least—a fear of "dry spells," dormant periods in which we do no blooming, internal droughts only the waters of imagination and psychic release can civilize.

GRETEL EHRLICH, *The Solace of Open Spaces,* 1985.

Imagination continually frustrates tradition; that is its function.

JOHN PFEIFFER, *New York Times,* March 29, 1979.

Like a chrysalis, we're emerging from the economy of the Industrial Revolution—an economy confined to and limited by the Earth's physical resources—into...an era in which there are no bounds on human imagination and the freedom to create is the most precious natural resource.

RONALD REAGAN, speech, Moscow State University, May
31, 1988.

In imagination, not in perception, lies the substance of experience, while knowledge and reason are but its chastened and ultimate form.

GEORGE SANTAYANA, *The Life of Reason,* 1905–1906.

The great scientists have been occupied with values—it is only their vulgar followers who think they are not. If scientists like Descartes, Newton, Einstein, Darwin, and Freud don't "look deeply into experience," what do they do? They have imaginations as powerful as any poet's and some of them were first-rate writers as well. How do you draw the line between *Walden* and *The Voyage of the Beagle*? The product of the scientific imagination is a new vision of relations—like that of the artistic imagination.

EDMUND WILSON, letter to Allen Tate, July 20, 1931,
Letters on Literature and Politics, 1912–1972, 1977.

INDEPENDENCE

I would rather choose to be a plumber or a peddler in the hope of finding that modest degree of independence still available under present circumstances.

ALBERT EINSTEIN, letter acknowledging award of membership card in plumbers' union, November, 1954.

You don't need a lot of bureaucrats looking over your shoulder and telling you how to run your life or how to run your business. We are a people who declared our independence 200 years ago, and we are not about to lose it now to paper shufflers and computers.

GERALD R. FORD, speech, Chicago, Illinois, August 25, 1975.

My apple trees will never get across

And eat the cones under his pines, I tell him.

He only says, "Good fences make good

neighbors."

ROBERT FROST, "Mending Wall," *North of Boston*, 1914.

It's easy to be independent when you've got money. But to be independent when you haven't got a thing—that's the Lord's test.

MAHALIA JACKSON, with Evan McLoud Wylie, *Movin' On Up,* 1966.

Passivity is *the* dragon that every woman has to murder in her quest for independence.

JILL JOHNSTON, *Lesbian Nation*, 1973.

Neither the clamor of the mob nor the voice of power will ever turn me by the breadth of a hair from the course I make out for myself, guided by such knowledge as I can obtain, and controlled and directed by a solemn conviction of right and duty.

ROBERT M. LAFOLLETTE, SR., speech to U.S. Senate, October 6, 1917.

So live that you can look any man in the eye and tell him to go to hell.

ATTRIBUTED TO ENGINEER WORKING ON PANAMA CANAL, used by John D. Rockefeller, Jr., speech, Dartmouth College, June, 1930.

[T]he trick in living against the grain of your closest associates is in hanging on grimly but good-humoredly to your own identity.

WILLIAM SAFIRE, *Before the Fall*, 1975.

What I was in love with...was the prospect of independence.

JONAS SALK, in Richard Carter, *Breakthrough: The Saga of Jonas Salk,* 1965.

Jefferson's Declaration of Independence is a practical document for the use of practical men. It is not a thesis for philosophers, but a whip for tyrants; it is not a theory of government, but a program of action.

WOODROW WILSON, speech, Indianapolis, Indiana, April 13, 1911.

INGENUITY

The Machine brought endless novelty into the world. There was hardly an activity of daily life that some device could not make more interesting—or at least more complicated. The carving knife and the toothbrush were simple tools long in use. But American inventiveness and American love of novelty would produce in time the electric knife and the electric toothbrush. And what would come next?

DANIEL J. BOORSTIN, *Hidden History*, 1987.

There is nothing mysterious about originality, nothing fantastic. Originality is merely the step beyond.

LOUIS DANZ, *Dynamic Dissonance in Nature and the Arts*, 1952.

In trying to make something new, half the undertaking lies in discovering whether it can be done. Once it has been established that it can, duplication is inevitable.

HELEN GAHAGAN DOUGLAS, *A Full Life*, 1982.

Little of beauty has America given the world save the rude grandeur God himself stamped on her bosom; the human spirit in this new world has expressed itself in vigor and ingenuity rather than in beauty.

W.E.B. DU BOIS, *The Souls of Black Folk*, 1903.

I am proud of the fact that I never invented weapons to kill.

THOMAS ALVA EDISON, *New York Times*, June 8, 1915.

Significant inventions are not mere accidents.... Happenstance usually plays a part, to be sure, but there is much more to invention than the popular notion of a bolt out of the blue. Knowledge in depth and in breadth are virtual prerequisites. Unless the mind is thoroughly changed beforehand, the proverbial spark of genius, if it should manifest itself, probably will find nothing to ignite.

PAUL FLORY, in Roylston Roberts, *Serendipity*, 1989.

I just invent, then wait until man comes around to needing what I've invented.

R. BUCKMINSTER FULLER, *Time*, June 10, 1964.

God forgives those who invent what they need.

LILLIAN HELLMAN, *The Little Foxes*, 1936.

A man likes marvelous things; so he invents them, and is astonished.

EDGAR WATSON HOWE, *Sinner Sermons*, 1926.

All Wrigley had was an idea. He was the first man to discover that American jaws must wag. So why not give them something to wag against?

WILL ROGERS, on invention of chewing gum, *The Illiterate Digest*, 1924.

"Inventive man" has invented nothing—nothing "from scratch." If he has produced a machine that in motion overcomes the law of gravity, he learned the essentials from the observation of birds. If his gardens produce flowers and fruits once unknown, the flowers are all refinements by cross-fertilization of the original flowers of the woods and the fields, and the original fruits of the soil.

DOROTHY THOMPSON, *The Courage To Be Happy*, 1957.

Your world...you have created it for yourself, it is real to yourself, and therefore real to us....It is for you to discover yourself in a world where, alone and free, you may dream the possible dream: that the wondrous is real, because that is how you feel it to be, how you wish it to be... and how you wish it into being.

DIANA VREELAND, *D.V.*, 1984.

INTELLIGENCE

I've always felt that a person's intelligence is directly reflected by the number of conflicting points of view he can entertain simultaneously on the same topic.

LISA ALTHER, *Kinflicks*, 1977.

For a long time I have hunted for a good definition of an intellectual. I wanted something simple and inclusive, not just an indirect way of bestowing my approval. But the more I tried to be fair, the more the exceptions and qualifications swamped the idea beneath them. Then one day while strap-hanging and scanning my homeward-bound fellow workers, it came over me in a flash: an intellectual is a man who carries a briefcase.

JACQUES BARZUN, *God's Country and Mine*, 1954.

Let it be clear...that our concern is not with intelligence but with Intellect, which is the form intelligence takes in the artificial products we call learning. As knowledge is to intelligence, so learning is to Intellect.

JACQUES BARZUN, *The House of Intellect*, 1959.

I am convinced that the world is not a mere bog in which men and women trample themselves in the mire and die. Something magnificent is taking place here amid the cruelties and tragedies, and the supreme challenge to intelligence is that of making the noblest and best in our curious heritage prevail.

CHARLES A. BEARD, in Will Durant, *On the Meaning of Life*, 1932.

The intellectual is a middle-class product; if he is not born into the class he must soon insert himself into it, in order to exist. He is the fine nervous flower of the bourgeoisie.

LOUISE BOGAN, *Solicited Criticism: Some Notes on Popular and Unpopular Art*, 1955.

There's no guarantee that high IQ people produce better people or a better society. It is not the retarded kids of the world who produce the wars and destruction.

DANIEL CALLAHAN, *Time*, March 10, 1980.

Curiosity is free-wheeling intelligence....It endows the people who have it with a generosity in argument and a serenity in their own mode of life which springs from the cheerful willingness to let life take the forms it will.

ALISTAIR COOKE, "The Art of Curiosity," *Vogue*, January, 1953.

It is always the task of the intellectual to "think otherwise." This is not just a perverse idiosyncrasy. It is an absolute essential feature of a society.

HARVEY COX, *The Secular City*, 1966.

To think is to differ.

CLARENCE DARROW, Scopes trial, Dayton, Tennessee, July 13, 1925.

Intelligence is not something possessed once for all. It is in constant process of forming, and its retention requires constant alertness in observing consequences, an open-minded will to learn and courage in re-adjustment.

JOHN DEWEY, *Reconstruction in Philosophy*, 1920.

Mankind likes to think in terms of extreme opposites. It is given to formulating its beliefs in terms of *Either-Ors*, between which it recognizes no intermediate possibilities. When forced to recognize that the extremes cannot be acted upon, it is still inclined to hold that they are all right in theory but that when it comes to practical matters circumstances compel us to compromise.

JOHN DEWEY, *Experience and Education*, 1938.

We should take care not to make the intellect our god; it has, of course, powerful muscles, but no personality.

ALBERT EINSTEIN, *Out of My Later Years*, 1950.

The intellect has little to do on the road to discovery. There comes a leap in consciousness, call it intuition or what you will, and the solution comes to you, and you don't know how or why.

ALBERT EINSTEIN, *Forbes*, September 15, 1974.

With the stones we cast at them, geniuses build new roads for us.

PAUL ELDRIDGE, *Maxims for a Modern Man*, 1965.

Intellectual ability without the more human attributes is admirable only in the same way as the brilliance of a child chess prodigy.

T.S. ELIOT, *Notes Towards the Definition of Culture*, 1948.

[T]he test of a first-rate intelligence is the ability to hold two opposed ideas in the mind at the same time, and still retain the ability to function. One should, for example, be able to see that things are hopeless and yet be determined to make them otherwise.

F. SCOTT FITZGERALD, 1936, *The Crack-up*, 1945.

The scholar is not The Intellectual. He is Man Thinking. Man Thinking is not the member of a race apart. He is the citizen performing the function appointed for all citizens in a civilized state, a function without which there would be no civilized state. He is Everyman purposefully apprehending the meaning of things.

A. WHITNEY GRISWOLD, *Liberal Education and the Democratic Ideal: Better Men and Better Mousetraps*, 1959.

Scratch an intellectual and you find a would-be aristocrat who loathes the sight, the sound and the smell of common folk.

ERIC HOFFER, *First Things, Last Things*, 1970.

Intellect...is a critical, creative, and contemplative side of minds. Whereas intelligence seeks to grasp, manipulate, reorder, adjust, intellect examines, ponders, wonders, theorizes, criticizes, imagines. Intelligence will seize the immediate meaning in a situation and evaluate it. Intellect evaluates evaluations, and looks for the meanings of situations as a whole.

RICHARD HOFSTADTER, *Anti-intellectualism in American Life*, 1963.

It is ironic that the United States should have been founded by intellectuals; for throughout most of our political history the intellectual has been for the most part either an outsider, a servant, or a scapegoat.

RICHARD HOFSTADTER, *Anti-intellectualism in American Life*, 1963.

Genius is the ability to act wisely without precedent—the power to do the right thing the first time.

ELBERT HUBBARD, *The Roycroft Dictionary and Book of Epigrams*, 1923.

I had no reason to doubt that brains were suitable for a woman. And as I had my father's kind of mind which was also his mother's—I learned that the mind is not sex-typed.

MARGARET MEAD, *Blackberry Winter*, 1972.

One of the functions of intelligence is to take account of the dangers that come from trusting solely to the intelligence.

LEWIS MUMFORD, *The Transformations of Man*, 1956.

It is not depravity that afflicts the human race so much as a general lack of intelligence.

AGNES REPPLIER, *In Pursuit of Laughter*, 1936.

Genius...is the capacity to see ten things where the ordinary man sees one, and where the man of talent sees two or three, *plus* the ability to register that multiple perception in the material of his art.

EZRA POUND, *Jefferson and/or Mussolini*, 1935.

The life of reason is no fair reproduction of the universe, but the expression of man alone.

GEORGE SANTAYANA, *The Life of Reason*, 1905–1906.

It takes a lot of time to be a genius, you have to sit around so much doing nothing, really doing nothing.

GERTRUDE STEIN, *Everybody's Autobiography*, 1937.

Genius seems to be the faculty of having faith in everything, and especially oneself.

ARTHUR STRINGER, *The Devastator*, 1944.

A mind truly cultivated never feels that the intellectual process is complete until it can reproduce in some media the thing which it has absorbed.

IDA TARBELL, *The Ways of a Woman*, 1914.

The kind of intelligence a genius has is a different sort of intelligence. The thinking of a genius does not proceed logically. It leaps with great ellipses. It pulls knowledge from God knows where.

DOROTHY THOMPSON, *The Courage To Be Happy*, 1957.

The fact that man knows right from wrong proves his *intellectual* superiority to the other creatures; but the fact that he can *do* wrong proves his *moral* inferiority to any creatures that *cannot.*

MARK TWAIN, *What Is Man?*, 1906.

Men are not narrow in their intellectual interests by nature; it takes special and vigorous training to accomplish that end.

JACOB VINER, *Scholarship in Graduate Training*, 1953.

A great many people think that polysyllables are a sign of intelligence.

BARBARA WALTERS, *How to Talk with Practically Anybody About Practically Anything*, 1970.

Americans have always had an ambivalent attitude toward intelligence. When they feel threatened, they want a lot of it, and when they don't they regard the whole thing as somewhat immoral.

VERNON A. WALTERS, *Silent Missions*, 1978.

Genius is no snob. It does not run after titles or seek by preference the high circles of society.

WOODROW WILSON, speech, Hodgenville, Kentucky, September 4, 1916.

LOVE

The fate of love is that it always seems too little or too much.

AMELIA E. BARR, *The Belle of Bowling Green*, 1904.

I never liked the men I loved, and never loved the men I liked.

FANNY BRICE, in Norman Katkov, *The Fabulous Fanny*, 1953.

So blind is life, so long at last is sleep,

And none but Love to bid us laugh or weep.

WILLA CATHER, "Evening Song," *April Twilights*, 1903.

Love is not enough. It must be the foundation, the cornerstone—but not the complete structure. It is much too pliable, too yielding.

BETTE DAVIS, *The Lonely Life*, 1962.

So long as little children are allowed to suffer, there is no true love in this world.

ISADORA DUNCAN, "Memoirs," *This Quarter*, Autumn, 1929.

I don't want to live—I want to love first, and live incidentally.

ZELDA FITZGERALD, letter to F. Scott Fitzgerald, 1919, in Nancy Milford, *Zelda*, 1970.

Earth's the right place for love: I don't know where it's likely to go better.

ROBERT FROST, "Birches," 1916.

Love, the strongest and deepest element in all life, the harbinger of hope, of joy, of ecstasy; love, the defier of all laws, of all conventions; love, the freest, the most powerful molder of human destiny; how can such an all-compelling force be synonymous with that poor little State- and Church-begotten weed, marriage?

EMMA GOLDMAN, "Marriage and Love," *Anarchism and Other Essays*, 1911.

Love is man's natural endowment, but he doesn't know how to use it. He refuses to recognize the power of love because of his love of power.

DICK GREGORY, *The Shadow That Scares Me*, 1968.

The truth [is] that there is only one terminal dignity—love. And the story of a love is not important—what is important is that one is capable of love. It is perhaps the only glimpse we are permitted of eternity.

HELEN HAYES, *Guideposts*, January, 1960.

To be loved is very demoralizing.

KATHARINE HEPBURN, "Dick Cavett Show," April 4, 1975.

We cannot permit love to run riot; we must build fences around it, as we do around pigs.

EDGAR WATSON HOWE, *Preaching from the Audience*, 1926.

I'll believe it when girls of twenty with money marry male paupers, turned sixty.

ELBERT HUBBARD, *The Roycroft Dictionary and Book of Epigrams*, 1923.

Love goes to those who are deserving—not to those who set snares for it and who lie in wait. The life of strife and contest never wins.

ELBERT HUBBARD, *The Roycroft Dictionary and Book of Epigrams*, 1923.

Love, we say, is life; but love without hope and faith is agonizing death.

ELBERT HUBBARD, *The Roycroft Dictionary and Book of Epigrams*, 1923.

The love we give away is the only love we keep.

ELBERT HUBBARD, *Note Book*, 1927.

Love doesn't just sit there, like a stone, it has to be made, like bread; re-made all the time, made new.

URSULA K. LEGUIN, *The Lathe of Heaven*, 1971.

Love is a force....It is not a result; it is a cause. It is not a product. It is a power, like money, or steam or electricity. It is valueless unless you can give something else by means of it.

ANNE MORROW LINDBERGH, *Locked Rooms and Open Doors*, 1974.

The emotion of love, in spite of the romantics, is not self-sustaining; it endures only when the lovers love many things together, and not merely each other.

WALTER LIPPMANN, *A Preface to Morals*, 1929.

Love, in reason's terms, answers nothing. We say that *Amor vincit omnia* but in truth love conquers nothing—certainly not death—certainly not chance.

ARCHIBALD MACLEISH, *Time*, December 22, 1958.

He drew a circle that shut me out—
Heretic, rebel, a thing to flout.
But Love and I had the wit to win:
We drew a circle that took him in!

EDWIN MARKHAM, "Outwitted," *The Shoes of Happiness and Other Poems*, 1915.

Love is born of faith, lives on hope, and dies of charity.

GIAN CARLO MENOTTI, notes for opera *Maria Golovin*, 1958.

Anyone who regards love as a deal made on the basis of "needs" is in danger of falling into a purely quantitative ethic. If love is a deal, then who is to say that you should not make as many deals as possible?

THOMAS MERTON, *Love and Living*, 1980.

This have I known always: Love is no more
Than the wide blossom which the wind assails,
Than the great tide that treads the shifting shore,
Strewing fresh wreckage gathered in the gales;
Pity me that the heart is slow to learn
What the swift mind beholds at every turn.

EDNA ST. VINCENT MILLAY, "Pity Me Not," *The Harp-Weaver and Other Poems*, 1923.

What I cannot love, I overlook. Is that real friendship?

ANAÏS NIN, "San Francisco," *The Diary of Anaïs Nin*, 1974.

Love is an expression and assertion of self-esteem, a response to one's own values in the person of another. One gains a profoundly personal, selfish joy from the mere existence of the person one loves. It is one's own personal, selfish happiness that one seeks, earns, and derives from love.

AYN RAND, *The Virtue of Selfishness*, 1964.

Love that's wise
Will not say all it means.

EDWIN ARLINGTON ROBINSON, *Tristram*, 1927.

I wonder why love is so often equated with joy when it is everything else as well. Devastation, balm, obsession, granting and receiving excessive value, and losing it again. It is recognition, often of what you are not but might be. It sears and it heals. It is beyond pity and above law. It can seem like truth.

FLORIDA SCOTT-MAXWELL, *The Measure of My Days*, 1972.

Love means not ever having to say you're sorry.

ERICH SEGAL, *Love Story*, 1970.

Sometimes love is stronger than a man's convictions.

ISAAC BASHEVIS SINGER, *New York Times Magazine*, November 26, 1978.

Platonic love is love from the neck up.

THYRA SAMTER WINSLOW, in article by James Simpson, *Interview*, August 19, 1952.

MATERIALISM

Materialism is decadent and degenerate only if the spirit of the nation has withered and if individual people are so unimaginative that they wallow in it.

BROOKS ATKINSON, "January 22," *Once Around the Sun*, 1951.

Every generation of Americans has wanted more material wealth, more luxury for the next generation. In my opinion the time has come when we must hope our children and their children ad infinitum will want from life more than material success. They must have enough of that to ensure a roof, clothing, food and some recreation, but, if we are to survive for another two hundred years, we must change our way of life.

INDIA EDWARDS, *Pulling No Punches*, 1977.

We live in a world of things, and our connection with them is that we know how to manipulate or consume them.

Erich Fromm, *The Sane Society*, 1955.

You have to decide whether you want to make money or make sense, because the two are mutually exclusive.

R. Buckminster Fuller, speech, 1947, *Critical Path*, 1981.

The steady pressure to consume, absorb, participate, receive, by eye, ear, mouth, and mail involves a cruelty to intestines, blood pressure, and psyche unparalleled in history. We are being killed with kindness. We are being stifled with cultural and material joys.

Herbert Gold, *The Age of Happy Problems*, 1962.

Man must choose whether to be rich in things or in the freedom to use them.

Ivan Illich, *Deschooling Society*, 1971.

In a consumer society there are inevitably two kinds of slaves: the prisoners of addiction and the prisoners of envy.

Ivan Illich, *Tools for Conviviality*, 1973.

The materialistic idealism that governs American life, that on the one hand makes a chariot of every grocery wagon, and on the other a mere hitching post of every star, lets every man lead a very enticing double life.

Louis Kronenberger, *Company Manners*, 1954.

[W]e are materialists—generous materialists—in the very simple sense that we believe everything worth having can be had if we are willing to spend enough money to get it.

Joseph Wood Krutch, *Human Nature and the Human Condition*, 1959.

To a throng of aging infants, the consumer society holds out the promise of eternal youth, of an enchanted mirror in which the customer can see himself reflected in the transfiguring light of immortality.

Lewis H. Lapham, "The Spoils of Childhood," Baltimore *Sun*, August, 1984.

I like to go to Marshall Field's in Chicago just to see how many things there are in the world that I do not want.

Mother Mary Madeleva, *My First Seventy Years*, 1959.

While styling themselves an exclusive elite of wealth and cultivation, the aspirants to a new American nobility are dependent for their suc-cess and values upon the mass market and leveling consumerism.

Debora Silverman, *Selling Culture*, 1985.

The truth of the matter is we have become more interested in designer jeans and break dancing than we are in obligations and responsibilities.

Clarence Thomas, speech, Savannah State College, June 9, 1985.

This country can seduce God. Yes, it has that seductive power—the power of dollarism.

Malcolm X, *Malcolm X Speaks*, 1965.

OPTIMISM/PESSIMISM

If you think you can, you can. And if you think you can't, you're right.

Mary Kay Ash, *New York Times*, October 20, 1985.

We [Americans] cheerfully assume that in some mystic way love conquers all, that good outweighs evil in the just balances of the universe and that at the eleventh hour something gloriously triumphant will prevent the worst before it happens.

Brooks Atkinson, "January 22," *Once Around the Sun*, 1951.

Life—the way it really is—is a battle not between Bad and Good, but between Bad and Worse.

Joseph Brodsky, *New York Times*, October 1, 1972.

Every day, in every way, things are getting worse and worse.

William F. Buckley, *National Review*, July 2, 1963.

The optimist proclaims that we live in the best of all possible worlds; and the pessimist fears this is true.

James Branch Cabell, *The Silver Stallion*, 1926.

An optimist, in the atomic age, is a person who thinks the future is uncertain.

Russell Crouse and Howard Lindsay, play, *State of the Union*, 1948.

It is not solutions that make ideas attractive. It is unsolved possibilities. The thing we all feel about America is that the possibilities are always unsolved.

Russell W. Davenport, in Arthur Goodfriend, *What Is America?*, 1954.

The outstanding characteristic of America is the refusal of Americans to accept defects in their society as irremediable.

LEWIS GALANTIERE, in Arthur Goodfriend, *What Is America?*, 1954.

It's simpler to be an optimist and it's a sensible defense against the uncertainties and abysses which otherwise confront us prematurely—we can die a dozen deaths and then usually we find that the outcome is not one we predicted, neither so "bad" nor so "good," but one we hadn't taken into consideration.

EDWARD HOAGLAND, "Home Is Two Places," *Commentary*, February, 1970.

Many of the optimists in the world don't own a hundred dollars, and because of their optimism never will.

EDGAR WATSON HOWE, "The Blessing of Business," 1918.

Cheer up, the worst is yet to come.

PHILANDER CHASE JOHNSON, "Shooting Stars," *Everybody's Magazine*, May, 1920.

Probably no nation in modern times has suffered so frequently or so greatly as the United States from recurrent periods of exaggerated optimism and unrealistic interpretation of its economic situation.

VIRGIL JORDAN, *North American Review*, 1930.

The American, by nature, is optimistic. He is experimental, an inventor and a builder who builds best when called upon to build greatly.

JOHN F. KENNEDY, speech, Washington, D.C., January 1, 1960.

One day nearer the grave, Thurber.

M.B. "BILL" LEVICK, greeting to James Thurber at *The New Yorker*, in James Thurber, *The Years with Ross*, 1957.

Rosiness is not a worse windowpane than gloomy gray when viewing the world.

GRACE PALEY, *Enormous Changes at the Last Minute*, 1960.

In these times you have to be an optimist to open your eyes when you awake in the morning.

CARL SANDBURG, *New York Post*, September 9, 1960.

PERCEPTION

Genius is the talent for seeing things straight. It is seeing things in a straight line without any bend or break or aberration of sight, seeing them as they are, without any warping of vision. Flawless mental sight! That is genius.

MAUDE ADAMS, in Ada Patterson, *Maude Adams: A Biography*, 1907.

Mentally bifocal.

PEARL BUCK, on being the product of two cultures, recalled on her death, *New York Times*, March 7, 1973.

The Miracles of the Church seem to me to rest not so much upon faces or voices or healing power coming suddenly near to us from afar off, but upon our perceptions being made finer, so that for a moment our eyes can see and our ears can hear what is there about us always.

WILLA CATHER, *Death Comes for the Archbishop*, 1927.

If we are to perceive all the implications of the new, we must risk, at least temporarily, ambiguity and disorder.

J.J. GORDON, *Creative Computing*, October, 1983.

Every idea is an incitement. It offers itself for belief and, if believed, it is acted on unless some other belief outweighs it, or some failure of energy stifles the movements at its birth.

OLIVER WENDELL HOLMES, JR., opinion, *Gitlow v. People of New York*, 1925.

An idea, to be suggestive, must come to the individual with the force of a revelation.

WILLIAM JAMES, *The Varieties of Religious Experience*, 1902.

We have met the enemy and he is us.

WALT KELLY, comic strip, *Pogo*, ca. 1950.

The perceptions of any people wash over the land like a flood, leaving ideas hung up in the brush, like pieces of damp paper to be collected and deciphered. No one can tell the whole story.

BARRY LOPEZ, "The Country of the Mind," *Arctic Dreams*, 1986.

It isn't the oceans which cut us off from the world—it's the American way of looking at things.

HENRY MILLER, "Letter to Lafayette," *The Air-Conditioned Nightmare*, 1945.

If you are sure you understand everything that is going on, you are hopelessly confused.

WALTER MONDALE, *Poughkeepsie Journal*, March 26, 1978.

Competence, like truth, beauty and contact lenses, is in the eye of the beholder.

LAURENCE J. PETER AND RAYMOND HULL, *The Peter Principle*, 1969.

The worm's eye point of view.

Ernie Pyle, *Here Is Your War*, 1943.

[The earth] is so small and so fragile and such a precious little spot in that universe that you can block it out with your thumb, and you realize that on that small spot, that little blue and white thing, is everything that means anything to you—all of history and music and poetry and art and death and birth and love.

Russell Schweikart, *Peace: A Dream Unfolding*, 1986.

Religion...sex...race...money...avoidance rites...malnutrition...dreams—no part of these can be looked at and clearly seen without looking at the whole of them. For, as a painter mixes colors and makes of them new colors, so religion is turned into something different by race, and segregation is colored as much by sex as by skin pigment, and money is no longer a coin but a lost wish wandering through a man's whole life.

Lillian Smith, *Killers of the Dream*, 1949.

Rose is a rose is a rose is a rose.

Gertrude Stein, "Sacred Emily," 1913.

One man's "simple" is another man's "huh?"

David Stone, *Omni*, May, 1979.

Honor wears different coats to different eyes.

Barbara Tuchman, *The Guns of August*, 1962.

I made some studies, and reality is the leading cause of stress amongst those in touch with it. I can take it in small doses, but as a life-style I found it too confining.

Jane Wagner, *The Search for Intelligent Life in the Universe*, performed by Lily Tomlin, 1986.

PERSEVERANCE

Whatever I engage in, I must push inordinately.

Andrew Carnegie, diary entry, in Matthew Josephson, *The Robber Barons*, 1934.

Even the woodpecker owes his success to the fact that he uses his head and keeps pecking away until he finishes the job he starts.

Coleman Cox, *Perseverance*, ca. 1922.

I never did anything worth doing by accident, nor did any of my inventions come by accident; they came by work.

Attributed to Thomas A. Edison.

Man is not made for defeat.

Ernest Hemingway, *The Old Man and the Sea*, 1952.

There is no failure except in no longer trying.

Elbert Hubbard, *Note Book*, 1927.

Winning isn't everything, but wanting to win is.

Vince Lombardi, *Esquire*, November, 1962.

It's easy to have faith in yourself and have discipline when you're a winner, when you're number one. What you got to have is faith and discipline when you're not a winner.

Vince Lombardi, in Tom Dowling, *Coach: A Season with Lombardi*, 1970.

I think, perhaps, as I look back at those who shaped my own life—and there are a great deal of similarities between the game of football and the game of politics—that I learned a great deal from a football coach who not only taught his players how to win but also taught them that when you lose you don't quit, that when you lose you fight harder the next time.

Richard M. Nixon, *Public Papers*, July 30, 1971.

I know of no higher fortitude than stubbornness in the face of overwhelming odds.

Louis Nizer, *My Life in Court*, 1962.

Anybody can do just about anything with himself that he really wants to and makes up his mind to do. We are capable of greater things than we realize. How much one actually achieves depends largely on: 1. Desire. 2. Faith. 3. Persistent Effort. 4. Ability. But if you are lacking the first three factors, your ability will not balance out the lack. So concentrate on the first three and the results will amaze you.

Norman Vincent Peale, *Have a Great Day—Every Day*, 1985.

The black man continues on his way. He plods wearily no longer—he is striding freedom road with the knowledge that if he hasn't got the world in a jug, at least he has the stopper in his hand.

Adam Clayton Powell, Jr., "Black Power: A Form of Godly Power," *Keep the Faith, Baby!*, 1967.

There was, I thought, something both wonderful and goofy about all this persistent American determination to reform the world. It reminded me of the little signs that used to hang in some of the service stores in Dayton, Ohio, when I was a boy. I forget the exact words, but they promised to do anything "possible" by tomorrow but conceded that the "impossible" might take a few days longer. This was the spirit that had conquered the American continent, survived the great economic depression of the 30's, helped restore Western Europe and Japan after World War II and survived the cold war with the Soviet Union for almost half a century.

JAMES RESTON, *New York Times Magazine*, June 16, 1991.

Although there are countless alumni of the school of hard knocks, there has not yet been a move to accredit that institution.

SONYA RUDIKOFF, "Women and Success," *Commentary*, October, 1974.

PREJUDICE

What *is* prejudice? An opinion, which is not based upon reason; a judgment, without having heard the argument; a feeling, without being able to trace from whence it came.

CARRIE CHAPMAN CATT, speech, National American Woman Suffrage Association, February, 1902.

[L]aws will not eliminate prejudice from the hearts of human beings. But that is no reason to allow prejudice to continue to be enshrined in our laws to perpetuate injustice through inaction.

SHIRLEY CHISHOLM, Joint Resolution 264, *Congressional Record*, August 10, 1970.

Any discrimination based simply on race or color is barbarous, we care not how hallowed it be by custom, expedience or prejudice.

W.E.B. DU BOIS, The Niagara Movement Declaration of Principles, Niagara Falls, New York, 1905.

I am free of all prejudice. I hate everyone equally.

W.C. FIELDS, in article by Jerome Beatty, Jr., *The Saturday Review*, January 28, 1967.

If a man calls me a nigger, he is calling me something I am not. The nigger exists only in his own mind; therefore his mind is the nigger. I must feel sorry for such a man.

DICK GREGORY, *The Shadow That Scares Me*, 1968.

I try not to be prejudiced, but do not make much headway against it.

EDGAR WATSON HOWE, *Sinner Sermons*, 1926.

The tendency of the casual mind is to pick out or stumble upon a sample which supports or defies its prejudices, and then to make it the representative of a whole class.

WALTER LIPPMANN, *Public Opinion*, 1929.

What generally passes for "thought" among the majority of mankind is the time one takes out to rearrange one's prejudices.

CLARE BOOTHE LUCE, *Today's Woman*, April, 1946.

We might as well give up the fiction

That we can argue any view.

For what in me is pure Conviction

Is simple Prejudice in you.

PHYLLIS MCGINLEY, "Note to My Neighbor," *Times Three: 1932–1960*, 1960.

The ignorant are always prejudiced and the prejudiced are always ignorant.

CHARLES VICTOR ROMAN, *Science and Christian Ethics*, ca. 1912.

Knowing that bitterness is a poor bent key to use to unlock the old rusty door of human failure, I wanted her to begin her search for these answers with sympathy for those who had not found them.

LILLIAN SMITH, on South's history of slavery and racism, *Killers of the Dream*, 1949.

I deplore any action which denies artistic talent an opportunity to express itself because of prejudice against race origin.

BESS TRUMAN, in an article by Helen Weigel Brown, *Liberty*, June 9, 1945.

SUCCESS

It is possible that an individual may be successful, largely because he conserves all his powers for individual achievement and does not put any of his energy into the training which will give him the ability to act with others. The individual acts promptly, and we are dazzled by his success while only dimly conscious of the inadequacy of his code.

JANE ADDAMS, "Industrial Amelioration," *Democracy and Social Ethics*, 1902.

Eighty percent of success is showing up.

WOODY ALLEN, in Thomas J. Peters and Robert H. Waterman, *In Search of Excellence*, 1982.

Success, n. The one unpardonable sin against one's fellows.

AMBROSE BIERCE, *The Devil's Dictionary*, 1906.

A winner is someone who recognizes his Godgiven talents, works his tail off to develop them into skills, and uses these skills to accomplish his goals.

LARRY BIRD, *Bird on Basketball*, 1986.

What is known as success assumes nearly as many aliases as there are those who seek it.

STEPHEN BIRMINGHAM, *Holiday*, March, 1961.

[T]ransitory success [is] dangerous. It's like a heavy rainstorm. It can do damage or it can do good, permitting something to grow.

BILL BRADLEY, in John McPhee, *A Sense of Where You Are*, 1965.

The winning team like the conquering army claims everything in its path and seems to say that only winning is important. Yet like getting into a college of your choice or winning an election or marrying a beautiful mate, victory is fraught with as much danger as glory. Victory has very narrow meanings and, if exaggerated or misused, can become a destructive force.

BILL BRADLEY, *Life on the Run*, 1976.

It takes twenty years to make an overnight success.

EDDIE CANTOR, *New York Times*, October 20, 1963.

I have found some of the best reasons I ever had for remaining at the bottom simply by looking at the men at the top.

FRANK COLBY, *The Colby Essays*, 1926.

I don't know the key to success, but the key to failure is trying to please everybody.

BILL COSBY, *Ebony*, June, 1977.

[W]ho were the mad and who the sane?....People sold themselves for jobs, for the pay check, and if they only received a high enough price, they were honored. If their cheating, their theft, their lies, were of colossal proportions, if it were successful, they met with praise, not blame.

DOROTHY DAY, *The Long Loneliness*, 1952.

Try not to become a man of success but rather try to become a man of value.

ALBERT EINSTEIN, *Life*, May 2, 1955.

Stress management, as it is known, became dear to the hearts of all those whose most punishing worries did not often include how to get food and how to keep alive.

GLORIA EMERSON, Prologue, *Some American Men*, 1985.

You can't steal second base and keep one foot on first.

UNIDENTIFIED JUNIOR EXECUTIVE, in Derek Evans and David Fulwiler, *Who's Nobody in America*, 1981.

Here was a new generation...dedicated more than the last to the fear of poverty and the worship of success; grown up to find all gods dead, all wars fought, all faiths in man shaken.

F. SCOTT FITZGERALD, *This Side of Paradise*, 1920.

The victor belongs to the spoils.

F. SCOTT FITZGERALD, *The Beautiful and Damned*, 1922.

I remember riding a taxi one afternoon between very tall buildings under a mauve and rosy sky; I began to bawl because I had everything I wanted and knew I would never be so happy again.

F. SCOTT FITZGERALD, 1932, *The Crack-up*, 1945.

Premature success gives one an almost mystical conception of destiny as opposed to will power—at its worst the Napoleonic delusion.

F. SCOTT FITZGERALD, *The Crack-up*, 1945.

The whole secret of a successful life is to find out what it is one's destiny to do, and then do it.

HENRY FORD, "Success," *Forum*, October, 1928.

Man's main task in life is to give birth to himself.

ERICH FROMM, *Man for Himself*, 1947.

No one can possibly achieve any real and lasting success or "get rich" in business by being a conformist.

J. PAUL GETTY, in Robert Lenzner, *The Great Getty*, 1985.

Being champion is all well and good, but you can't eat a crown.

ALTHEA GIBSON, on retirement from tennis, *So Much To Live For*, 1968.

This is the day of instant genius. Everybody starts at the top, and then has the problem of staying there. Lasting accomplishment, however, is still achieved through a long, slow climb and self-discipline.

HELEN HAYES, *On Reflection, An Autobiography*, 1968.

He was a self-made man who owed his lack of success to nobody.

JOSEPH HELLER, *Catch-22*, 1961.

It is a deep-seated belief on the part of almost all Americans that their success will be better assured as they help to build the success of others.

PAUL G. HOFFMAN, in Arthur Goodfriend, *What Is America?*, 1954.

When a man succeeds, he does it in spite of everybody, and not with the assistance of everybody.

EDGAR WATSON HOWE, *Country Town Sayings*, 1911.

In order to stand success you must be of a very stern fiber, with all the gods on your side.

ELBERT HUBBARD, *The Roycroft Dictionary and Book of Epigrams*, 1923.

Success: A subtle contrivance of Nature for bringing about a man's defeat.

ELBERT HUBBARD, *The Roycroft Dictionary and Book of Epigrams*, 1923.

Success consists in the climb.

ELBERT HUBBARD, *The Roycroft Dictionary and Book of Epigrams*, 1923.

All success consists in this: You are doing something for somebody—benefiting humanity—and the feeling of success comes from the consciousness of this.

ELBERT HUBBARD, *The Roycroft Dictionary and Book of Epigrams*, 1923.

A failure is a man who has blundered, but is not able to cash in on the experience.

ELBERT HUBBARD, *The Roycroft Dictionary and Book of Epigrams*, 1923.

Behind every man who achieves success

Stand a mother, a wife, and the IRS.

ETHEL JACOBSON, *Reader's Digest*, April, 1973.

The moral flabbiness born of the exclusive worship of the bitch-goddess SUCCESS. That—with the squalid cash interpretation put on the word success—is our national disease.

WILLIAM JAMES, letter to H.G. Wells, September 11, 1906.

He said he'd bring home the bacon, and the honey boy has gone and done it.

"TINY" JOHNSON, when Jack Johnson knocked out Jim Jeffries, July 4, 1910.

I don't believe I'll ever get credit for anything I do in foreign affairs, no matter how successful it is, because I didn't go to Harvard.

LYNDON B. JOHNSON, to Hugh Sidey, in Walter Isaacson and Evan Thomas, *The Wise Men*, 1986.

[S]uccess, for women, is always partly failure.

ERICA JONG, "The Artist as Housewife," in Francine Klagsbrun, ed., *The First Ms. Reader*, 1973.

Success, recognition, and conformity are the bywords of the modern world where everyone seems to crave the anesthetizing security of being identified with the majority.

MARTIN LUTHER KING, JR., *Strength to Love*, 1963.

Despite the success cult, men are most deeply moved not by the reaching of the goal but by the grandness of effort involved in getting there—or failing to get there.

MAX LERNER, "Man's Belief in Himself," *The Unfinished Country*, 1959.

The greatest accomplishment is not in never falling, but in rising again after you fall.

VINCE LOMBARDI, in Jerry Kramer, *Instant Replay*, 1968.

The real demon is success—the anxieties engendered by this quest are relentless, degrading, corroding. What is worse, there is no end to this escalation of desire.

MARYA MANNES, "The Roots of Anxiety in Modern Women," *Journal of Neuropsychiatry*, May, 1964.

I must admit that I personally measure success in terms of the contributions an individual makes to her or his fellow human beings.

MARGARET MEAD, *Redbook*, November, 1978.

If I had a message to my contemporaries, I said, it was surely this: Be anything you like, be madmen, drunks, and bastards of every shape and form, but at all costs avoid one thing: success.

THOMAS MERTON, *Love and Living*, 1980.

If you have learned only how to be a success, your life has probably been wasted. If a university concentrates on producing successful people, it is lamentably failing in its obligation to society and to the students themselves.

THOMAS MERTON, *Love and Living*, 1980.

Be nice to people on your way up because you'll meet 'em on your way down.

ATTRIBUTED TO WILSON MIZNER.

One goes through school, college, medical school and one's internship learning little or nothing about goodness but a good deal about success.

ASHLEY MONTAGU, *Northwestern University Alumni News*, Summer, 1975.

In America, the land of the permanent revolution, ulcers and cancer often become, for the men at the top, the contemporary equivalent of the guillotine.

TED MORGAN, *New York Times*, July 13, 1986.

There is only one success—to be able to spend your life in your own way.

CHRISTOPHER MORLEY, *Where the Blue Begins*, 1922.

Success has cost Americans something of their energetic desire. And those Americans not yet successful (the struggling, the underclass) are apt to aim at ease, not excellence: the confusion contaminates character and disables ambition.

LANCE MORROW, "Excellence," *Fishing in the Tiber*, 1988.

Whether you succeed or not is irrelevant—There is no such thing—Making your unknown known is the important thing—And keeping the unknown always beyond you.

GEORGIA O'KEEFFE, letter to Sherwood Anderson, 1923, in *Georgia O'Keeffe*, 1976.

The way to success: First have a clear goal, not a fuzzy one. Sharpen this goal until it becomes specific and clearly defined in your conscious mind. Hold it there until, by a process of spiritual and intellectual osmosis...it seeps into your unconscious. Then you will have it because it has you. Surround this goal constantly with positive thoughts and faith. Give it positive follow-through. That is the way success is achieved.

NORMAN VINCENT PEALE, *Have a Great Day—Every Day*, 1985.

The ultimate of being successful is the luxury of giving yourself the time to do what you want to do.

LEONTYNE PRICE, interview, *Newsday*, February 1, 1976.

The man who never tells an unpalatable truth "at the wrong time" (the right time has yet to be discovered) is the man whose success in life is fairly well assured.

AGNES REPPLIER, *Under Dispute*, 1923.

The worst tragedy that could have befallen me was my success. I knew right away that I was through—cast out.

JONAS SALK, in Richard Carter, *Breakthrough: The Saga of Jonas Salk*, 1965.

Later on I learned, especially in school, to value "success" and to hide "failure" so that I wouldn't be scolded or ridiculed. That wasn't the way I had started out, when *both* were interesting and failure was sometimes more interesting than success because it raised more questions.

BARRY STEVENS, *Person to Person*, 1967.

Success to me is having ten honeydew melons and eating only the top half of each one.

BARBRA STREISAND, *Life*, September 20, 1963.

All my life people have said I wasn't going to make it.

TED TURNER, TV interview, 1984.

Success is more a function of consistent common sense than it is of genius.

AL WANG, *Boston Magazine*, December, 1986.

I have learned that success is to be measured not so much by the position that one has reached in life as by the obstacles which he has overcome while trying to succeed.

BOOKER T. WASHINGTON, *Up from Slavery*, 1901.

It makes a great deal of difference in the life of a race, as it does in the life of an individual, whether the world expects much or little of that individual or of that race.

BOOKER T. WASHINGTON, "The Intellectuals and the Boston Mob," 1911, in Howard Brotz, ed., *Negro Social and Political Thought: 1850–1920*, 1966.

You have to want it [success] bad. You can find geniuses on any skid row and average intellects as presidents of banks. It's what pushes you from inside.

CHARLEY WINNER, in Rick Telander, *Joe Namath and the Other Guys*, 1976.

SUPERIORITY

There never has been one like me before, and there never will be one like me again.

HOWARD COSELL, *TV Guide*, June 24, 1967.

The planes at LaGuardia had better not fly too low when I'm at bat.

GEORGE FOSTER, *Sunday News Magazine*, April 14, 1982.

What a sense of superiority it gives one to escape reading some book which everyone else is reading.

ALICE JAMES, *Diary*, 1964.

The capacity to admire others is not my most fully developed trait.

HENRY KISSINGER, *The White House Years*, 1979.

In our society to admit inferiority is to be a fool, and to admit superiority is to be an outcast. Those who are in reality superior in intelligence can be accepted by their fellows only if they pretend they are not.

MARYA MANNES, *More in Anger*, 1958.

My greatest strength is that I have no weaknesses.

JOHN MCENROE, *New York Times*, June 20, 1979.

Never let your inferiors do you a favor. It will be extremely costly.

H.L. MENCKEN, "Sententiae," *The Vintage Mencken*, 1955.

If men cease to believe that they will one day become gods then they will surely become worms.

HENRY MILLER, *The Colossus of Maroussi*, 1941.

The best way to win an argument is to begin by being right.

JILL RUCKELSHAUS, *Saturday Evening Post*, March 3, 1973.

If I only had a little humility, I would be perfect.

TED TURNER, *New York Times*, September 19, 1977.

He had only one vanity; he thought he could give advice better than any other person.

MARK TWAIN, "The Man That Corrupted Hadleyburg," 1900.

Superiority and inferiority are individual, not racial or national.

PHILIP WYLIE, *Generation of Vipers*, 1942.

TALENT

Sympatica is the touchstone that leads to talent's highest altitude.

MINNA ANTRIM, *Naked Truth and Veiled Allusions*, 1902.

There are two kinds of talents, man-made talent and God-given talent. With man-made talent you have to work very hard. With God-given talent, you just touch it up once in a while.

PEARL BAILEY, *Newsweek*, December 4, 1967.

I think that knowing what you can *not* do is more important than knowing what you can do. In fact, that's good taste.

LUCILLE BALL, in Eleanor Harris, *The Real Story of Lucille Ball*, 1954.

An idea can turn to dust or magic, depending on the talent that rubs against it.

WILLIAM BERNBACH, *New York Times*, October 6, 1982.

We are destroying talent. The price of occupational success is made so high for women that barring exceptional luck only the unusually talented or frankly neurotic can afford to succeed. Girls size up the bargain early and turn it down.

CAROLINE BIRD, *Born Female*, 1968.

We are told that talent creates its own opportunities. But it sometimes seems that intense desire creates not only its own opportunities, but its own talents.

ERIC HOFFER, *The Passionate State of Mind*, 1954.

Everyone has talent. What is rare is the courage to follow the talent to the dark place where it leads.

ERICA JONG, *Los Angeles Times*, February 3, 1978.

All of us do not have equal talent, but all of us should have an opportunity to develop our talents.

JOHN F. KENNEDY, speech, San Diego State College, June 16, 1963.

If the talent or individuality is there, it should be expressed. If it doesn't find its way out into the air, it can turn inward and gnaw like the fox at the Spartan boy's belly.

SHIRLEY MACLAINE, *Don't Fall Off the Mountain*, 1970.

America is a cruel soil for talent.

NORMAN MAILER, *Advertisements for Myself*, 1959.

A career is born in public—talent in privacy.

MARILYN MONROE, in Gloria Steinem, "Marilyn: The Woman Who Died Too Soon," Francine Klagsbrun, ed., *The First Ms. Reader*, 1972.

You cannot define talent. All you can do is build the greenhouse and see if it grows.

WILLIAM P. STEVEN, *Time*, August 23, 1963.

We start with gifts. Merit comes from what we make of them.

JEAN TOOMER, *Definitions and Aphorisms, VI*, 1931.

What the voters envisioned when Ronald Reagan mentioned old-fashioned values was Ted Mack presiding over an America where anybody had the freedom to develop the talent to play "Tea for Two" on the Venetian blinds.

CALVIN TRILLIN, "Doing My Talent," *The Nation*, December 15, 1984.

TOUGHNESS

From the moment that the starting gate opens until my horse hits the wire, I'm a man competing against men. But by the time I get to the winner's circle to have my picture taken, I'm reaching for my false eyelashes and I'm all girl. After scratching my way from the Oklahoma bushes to the big time and busting my ass and being on the critical list three times, I don't have to put on any acts to prove I'm tough. All I have to do is win.

MARY BACON, *Newsweek*, June 3, 1974.

Toughness doesn't have to come in a pinstripe suit.

DIANNE FEINSTEIN, June 4, 1984.

Do it the hard way!

RUBE GOLDBERG, motto, ca. 1910.

He was not a man to leave things alone when the toothache of blind contention was upon him.

LILLIAN HELLMAN, *Pentimento*, 1973.

We must combine the toughness of the serpent and the softness of the dove, a tough mind and a tender heart.

MARTIN LUTHER KING, JR., *Strength to Love*, 1963.

There are some people, you know, they think the way to be a big man is to shout and stomp and raise hell—and then nothing ever really happens. I'm not like that...I never shoot blanks.

RICHARD M. NIXON, *Look*, October 19, 1971.

I'll probably do better in the next four years, having gone through a few crises in the White House. I confront tough problems without flapping. Actually, I have a reputation for being the coolest person in the room. I've trained myself to be that.

RICHARD M. NIXON, 1973, in Lois and Alan Gordon, *American Chronicle*, 1987.

The Eskimos are a gentle people. I like gentle people, because there are so many in the world who are not gentle. Sometimes in a big city I just sit all day in my room, with my head down, afraid to go out and talk to tough people. I expect Eskimos have spells like that too.

ERNIE PYLE, *Home Country*, 1947.

Hang tough.

EXPRESSION POPULARIZED BY NARCOTICS TREATMENT CENTER IN CALIFORNIA IN EARLY 1960s, in William Safire, *Before the Fall*, 1975.

Human Environments

See also **Nature**; **Social Issues**—Poverty and Hunger; **Science and Technology**; **Work**—Architects, Farmers and Ranchers, Homemakers

I look forward to an America which will not be afraid of grace and beauty, which will protect the beauty of our natural environment, which will preserve the great old American houses and squares and parks of our national past and which will build handsome and balanced cities for our future.

JOHN F. KENNEDY, speech, Amherst College, Massachusetts, October 26, 1963.

COMMUNITY

The neighborhood was a current, a circular field of motion. Much coming and going. Everything stood still, yet everything revolved (by the hour, the day, the season, the year) and came back to you. You departed and returned. And you were the same but different.

NORBERT BLEI, *Neighborhood*, 1987.

Neighborhood people kept a trained eye on passing life from behind the curtains and Venetian blinds of the front windows of their house facing the street and both sidewalks. Many times, day and night, someone would be watching someone pass by, something going on in or across the street. It wasn't being nosy or a busybody so much as the real need to turn one's back periodically on the household with all its demands, frustrations, sameness, and look out the window to see what was going on in the world. Sometimes to even imagine what might be going on.

NORBERT BLEI, *Neighborhood*, 1987.

There is little lonelier than small-town life when small talk is the principal means of peace.

CAROL BLY, "Enemy Evenings," *Letters from the Country*, 1981.

A painful fact of American life is that people from small towns are afraid of directness.

CAROL BLY, "Enemy Evenings," *Letters from the Country*, 1981.

If we are to survive as an institution and perhaps even as a society, then we have to find a way to move from caucuses to community and that is not terribly easy in our society.

JOAN B. CAMPBELL, speech, New York Regional Association of Grantmakers, May 2, 1991.

What is a house but a bigger skin, and a neighborhood map but the world's skin ever expanding?

ANNIE DILLARD, *An American Childhood*, 1987.

True belonging is born of relationships not only to one another but to a place of shared responsibilities and benefits. We love not so much what we have acquired as what we have made and whom we have made it with.

ROBERT FINCH, "Scratching," *The Primal Place*, 1983.

If we are willing to face it, all of the ugly signs are there to see. It seems that we have lost hold of our communities. It seems as though our country is pulling apart into separate peoples who do not know one another.

EDWARD M. KENNEDY, speech, Denver, Colorado, April 5, 1968, in Thomas P. Collins and Louis M. Savary, eds., *A People of Compassion*, 1972.

Late commuters, lost among identical rows of houses along identical street blocks, sometimes reported a sense of panic like bewildered children suddenly turned loose in a house of mirrors.

P. KIMBALL, on Levittown, New York, 1952, in Lois and Alan Gordon, *American Chronicle*, 1987.

I still love to go back to Mitchell [his home town] and wander up and down those streets. It just kind of reassures me again that there is a place that I know thoroughly, where the roots are deep. There are the big old cottonwood trees, the big American elms, the little roadways in and out of town that have always been there—without much work ever done on them—the parks. There are not lots of high schools; there's one. There aren't a lot of libraries; there's the Carnegie Library. Each one of the stores always had its personality—Mr. Becker, who ran a clothing store— and the three movie theaters—each had a distinct character. At one drugstore you got malted milks, you went to another for sodas. Everything had a place, a specific definition.

GEORGE MCGOVERN, *Life*, 1972.

Let's make no mistake about this: The American Dream starts with the neighborhoods. If we wish to rebuild our cities, we must first rebuild our neighborhoods. And to do that, we must understand that the quality of life is more important than the standard of living. To sit on the front steps—whether it's a veranda in a small town or a concrete stoop in a big city—and talk to our neighbors is infinitely more important than to huddle on the living-room lounger and watch a make-believe world in not-quite living color.

HARVEY MILK, speech, fund-raising meeting, 1977.

Living together is an art.

WILLIAM PICKENS, speech, meeting of Congregationalists, Oak Park, Illinois, November 2, 1932.

A neighborhood is where, when you go out of it, you get beat up.

PUERTO RICAN LABOR OFFICE WORKER, in Murray Kempton, "Group Dynamics," *America Comes of Middle Age*, 1963.

In summer, when doorstep life dominates, the natural quality of the neighborhood comes out.

MARY KINGSBURY SIMKHOVITCH, *Neighborhood*, 1938.

HOME

Be it ever so humble, there's no place like home for wearing what you like.

GEORGE ADE, "The Good Fairy of the Eighth Ward," *Forty Modern Fables*, 1901.

My home is in whatever town I'm booked.

POLLY ADLER, *A House Is Not a Home*, 1953.

Sometimes I think that those of us who are now in our thirties were born into the last generation to carry the burden of "home," to find in family life the source of all tension and drama.

JOAN DIDION, "On Going Home," *Slouching Towards Bethlehem*, 1968.

Home is the place to do the things you want to do. Here we eat just when we want to. Breakfast and luncheon are extremely moveable feasts. It's terrible to allow conventional habits to gain a hold on a whole household; to eat, sleep and live by clock ticks.

ZELDA FITZGERALD, interview, *Baltimore Sun*, 1923.

"Home is the place where, when you have
  to go there,
They have to take you in."

ROBERT FROST, "The Death of the Hired Man," *North of Boston*, 1914.

It takes a heap o' livin' in a house t' make it home.

EDGAR A. GUEST, "Home," *The Collected Verse of Edgar A. Guest*, 1934.

Goethe once said, "He is happiest, king or peasant, who finds happiness at home." And Goethe knew—because he never found it.

ELBERT HUBBARD, *The Roycroft Dictionary and Book of Epigrams*, 1923.

Through my college years, topping that ridge had always given me a great sense of being home, but time had diminished the emotion and I had begun to suspect that home was less a place than an empty page.

LARRY MCMURTRY, *In a Narrow Grave: Essays on Texas*, 1968.

A home is not a mere transient shelter: its essence lies in its permanence, in its capacity of accretion and solidification, in its quality of representing, in all its details, the personalities of the people who live in it.

H.L. MENCKEN, *Prejudices*, 1926.

What the Nation must realize is that the home, when both parents work, is non-existent. Once we have honestly faced that fact, we must act accordingly.

AGNES MEYER, "Living Conditions of the Woolworker," *Washington Post*, April 10, 1943.

Houses are like sentinels in the plain, old keepers of the weather watch. There, in a very little while, wood takes on the appearance of great age.

N. SCOTT MOMADAY, *The Way to Rainy Mountain*, 1969.

To be an American is to aspire to a room of one's own.

NEW YORK TIMES, "Dream House," April 19, 1987.

Home ought to be our clearinghouse, the place from which we go forth lessoned and disciplined, and ready for life.

KATHLEEN NORRIS, *Home*, 1928.

I have been very happy with my homes, but homes really are no more than the people who live in them.

NANCY REAGAN, *Nancy*, 1980.

Everyone has, I think, in some quiet corner of his mind, an ideal home waiting to become a reality.

PAIGE RENSE, Foreword, *Designers' Own Homes*, 1984.

"You can't go home again" is the expression of the fear that home is always changing, never stable, all too mortal (and that the individual is, too), *and* it is a warning to the individual that society, the hometown, the cozy rural small-town community, can destroy all freedom.

JAMES OLIVER ROBERTSON, *American Myth, American Reality*, 1980.

There were no floors, no walls, no ceilings, no windows and the plumbing was nonexistent. Of course, I fell in love.

DAVID UTZ, on renovating a loft, *New York Times*, July 8, 1982.

A man without a home can't be lost.

KURT VONNEGUT, *Breakfast of Champions*, 1974.

Everybody's always talking about people breaking into houses…but there are more people in the world who want to break out of houses.

THORNTON WILDER, *The Matchmaker*, 1955.

RURAL LIFE

Certainly life in western Minnesota must be about as untroublesome as life anywhere in the twentieth century. It is only luck; we haven't ourselves done anything, psychically or morally, to protect us from the coarsening of life that comes with more population.

CAROL BLY, "Bruno Bettelheim: Three Ideas to Try in Madison, Minnesota," 1973, *Letters from the Country*, 1981.

Living with cities, we forget how lost are cities in the vast green that reaches the length and breadth of America. Technological our economy may be, but still the great factory is the green leaf, the blade of grass or corn, the leaf of tree.

HAL BORLAND, *New York Times*, July 24, 1955.

A big ranch is a miniature society. Its demise has the impact of a bankruptcy in a small town: another hundred people out of work and a big chunk of the town's business is suddenly gone. A ranch offers more than jobs; whole families are taken in, their needs attended to: housing, food, schools, even a graveyard plot for those who

died on the job or liked the place so much they wanted to be buried there.

GRETEL EHRLICH, *The Solace of Open Spaces*, 1985.

As I look back over my life on that Iowa farm the song of the reaper fills a large place in my mind. We were all worshipers of wheat in those days. The men thought and talked of little else between seeding and harvest, and you will not wonder at this if you have known and bowed before such abundance as we then enjoyed. Deep as the breast of a man, wide as the sea, heavy-headed, supple-stocked, many-voiced, full of multitudinous secrets, whispered colloquies—a meeting place of winds and of sunlight—our fields ran to the world's end.

HAMLIN GARLAND, *Son of the Middle Border*, 1917.

There are a great many pseudo-ranches in Texas and they don't vary enough to justify much investigation. Some just have more telephones than others.

LARRY MCMURTRY, *In a Narrow Grave: Essays on Texas*, 1968.

A farm is an irregular patch of nettles, bounded by short-term notes, containing a fool and his wife who didn't know enough to stay in the city.

S.J. PERELMAN, *Acres and Pains*, 1947.

There is a vast deal of make-believe in the carefully nurtured sentiment for country life, and the barefoot boy, and the mountain girl.

AGNES REPPLIER, *Times and Tendencies*, 1931.

A man who has spent much time and money in dreary restaurants moodily chewing filet of sole on the special luncheon is bound to become unmanageable when he discovers that he can produce the main dish course directly, at the edge of his own pasture, by a bit of trickery on a fine morning.

E.B. WHITE, "Salt Water Farm," January, 1939, *One Man's Meat*, 1944.

Anything can happen at a county agricultural fair. It is the perfect human occasion, the harvest of the fields and of the emotions. To the fair come the man and his cow, the boy and his girl, the wife and her green tomato pickle, each anticipating victory and the excitement of being separated from his money by familiar devices. It is at a fair that man can be drunk forever on liquor, love, or fights; at a fair that your front pocket can be picked by a trotting horse looking for sugar, and your hind pocket by a thief looking for his fortune.

E.B. White, "Fall," September, 1941, *One Man's Meat*, 1944.

In the country, one excuse is as good as another for a bit of fun, and just because a fire has grown cold is no reason for a fireman's spirit to sag.

E.B. White, "Home-coming," December 10, 1955, *Essays of E.B. White*, 1977.

URBAN LIFE

A city has values as well as slums, excitement as well as conflict...a personality that has not yet been obliterated by its highways and gas stations.

Charles Abrams, *The City Is the Frontier*, 1965.

A city...is the pulsating product of the human hand and mind, reflecting man's history, his struggle for freedom, creativity, genius—and his selfishness and errors.

Charles Abrams, *The City Is the Frontier*, 1965.

A city is in many respects a great business corporation, but in other respects it is enlarged housekeeping.... May we not say that city housekeeping has failed partly because women, the traditional housekeepers, have not been consulted as to its multiform activities?

Jane Addams, "Utilization of Women in City Government," *Newer Ideals of Peace*, 1907.

With eight or nine exceptions...American cities differ from one another only herein, that some of them are built more with brick than with wood, and others more with wood than with brick. In all else they are alike, both great and small.

James Bryce, *The American Commonwealth*, 1914.

If a large city can, after intense intellectual efforts, choose for its mayor a man who merely will not steal from it, we consider it a triumph of the suffrage.

Frank Moore Colby, "On Seeing Ten Bad Plays," *The Colby Essays*, 1926.

The real illness of the American city today, and especially of the deprived groups within it, is voicelessness.

Harvey Cox, *The Secular City*, 1966.

Our cities are polarized. Architecturally, they consist of formless masses or tremendous statements. We build the impressive, overtly costly behemoths of the affluent commerical society while abandoned housing, without replacement, turns into architectural and sociological disaster by the mile. Building is for the rich.

Ada Louise Huxtable, "Architecture in the 1970s," April 11, 1971, *Kicked a Building Lately?*, 1976.

But look what we have built...low-income projects that become worse centers of delinquency, vandalism and general social hopelessness than the slums they were supposed to replace.... Cultural centers that are unable to support a good bookstore. Civic centers that are avoided by everyone but bums.... Promenades that go from noplace to nowhere and have no promenaders. Expressways that eviscerate great cities. This is not the rebuilding of cities. This is the sacking of cities.

Jane Jacobs, *The Death and Life of Great American Cities*, 1961.

Great cities are not like towns, only larger. They differ from towns and suburbs in basic ways, and one of these is that cities are, by definition, full of strangers.

Jane Jacobs, *The Death and Life of Great American Cities*, 1961.

When you look at a city, it's like reading the hopes, aspirations and pride of everyone who built it.

Hugh Newell Jacobsen, *New York Times*, May 31, 1984.

The city as a center where, any day in any year, there may be a fresh encounter with a new talent, a keen mind or a gifted specialist—this is essential to the life of a country. To play this role in our lives a city must have a soul—a university, a great art or music school, a cathedral or a great mosque or temple, a great laboratory or scientific center, as well as the libraries and museums and galleries that bring past and present together. A city must be a place where groups of women and men are seeking and developing the highest things they know.

Margaret Mead, *Redbook*, August, 1978.

To qualify as a city, any collection of people must have an orchestra, a large library, a system of parks, a transportation system, a university and, yes, a public stadium in which to gather and a professional team to play there. If a town doesn't have these things, it's got no right to call itself a city.

James A. Michener, quoting an unidentified New Yorker, *Sports in America*, 1976.

There are no moats around our cities that keep the problems in. What happens in New York or San Francisco will eventually happen in San Jose. It's just a matter of time. And like the flu, it usually gets worse the further it travels.

HARVEY MILK, speech at fund-raising meeting, 1977.

The cities will not be saved by the people who feel condemned to live in them, who can hardly wait to move to Marin or San Jose—or Evanston or Westchester. The cities will be saved by the people who like it here. The people who prefer the neighborhood stores to the shopping mall, who go to the plays and eat in the restaurants and go to the discos and worry about the education the kids are getting even if they have no kids of their own.

That's not just the city of the future; it's the city of today. It means new directions, new alliances, new solutions for ancient problems. The typical American family with two cars and 2.2 kids doesn't live here anymore. It hasn't for years. The demographics are different now and we all know it. The city is a city of singles and young marrieds, the city of the retired and the poor, the city of many colors who speak in many tongues.

HARVEY MILK, speech at fund-raising meeting, 1977.

American cities have ever been filled with unfamiliar people, acting in unfamiliar ways, at once terrified and threatening.

DANIEL PATRICK MOYNIHAN, *American Heritage*, February, 1969.

Forget the damned motor car and build the cities for lovers and friends.

LEWIS MUMFORD, *My Work and Days*, 1979.

There are almost no beautiful cities in America, though there are many beautiful parts of cities, and some sections that are glorious without being beautiful, like downtown Chicago. Cities are too big and too rich for beauty; they have outgrown themselves too many times.

NOEL PERRIN, *Third Person Rural*, 1983.

Are not the cities of today expressions of the romance of colossal achievement? Love blossoms as freely in the shadow of a skyscraper, as ever it did in an Arcadian field of long ago.... These are the good, new days. Color and romance are everywhere.

REDBOOK, 1931.

No rural community, no suburban community, can ever possess the distinctive qualities that city dwellers have for centuries given to the world.

AGNES REPPLIER, "Town and Suburb," *Eight Decades*, 1937.

Cities have their indispensable purposes, and their charms, not the least of which is that you can be alone in a crowd. But that kind of living alone is an acquired taste, and not for the weak or unfortunate. They are apt to learn that no city's institutions can provide protective supports like those of an extended family or real community.

GEORGE WILL, "On Her Own in the City," September 19, 1976, *The Pursuit of Happiness, and Other Sobering Thoughts*, 1978.

Journalism and Media

See also **Americans on Americans**—Writers; **The Arts**—Literature; **Business**—Advertising and Marketing; **Dreams and Ideals**—Dissent; **Ethics and Morality**; **Government and Politics**—Parties and Elections; **Language and Discourse**; **Popular Culture**—Radio, Television; **Science and Technology**—Communications; **Social Issues**—Censorship; **Work**—Writers

I don't believe in taking the kinds of risks that are going to get myself or my colleagues killed. But I am prepared to step across the unknown, to weigh the odds against the ultimate story.

PETER ARNETT, in article by Malcolm W. Browne, "The Military vs. the Press," *New York Times Magazine*, February, 1991.

To talk of the educational value of the newspaper is like talking about the educational value of horse-trading, or of the stock exchange.

JOHN BURROUGHS, journal entry, December 12, 1911.

The sovereign press for the most part acknowledges accountability to no one except its owners and publishers.

ZECHARIAH CHAFEE, JR., "The Press Under Pressure," *Nieman Reports*, April, 1948.

If a glance at an editorial page of a newspaper shows what is meant by untested opinions put forth in the garb of the general principles of sound judgment, the items of the news columns illustrate what is meant by a multitude of diverse unrelated facts.

JOHN DEWEY, *Freedom and Culture*, 1939.

Aside from the fact that the press may distract with trivialities or be an agent in support of the hidden interest of a group or class (all in the name of public interest), the wide-world present scene is such that individuals are overwhelmed and emotionally confused by publicized reverbation of isolated events.

JOHN DEWEY, *Freedom and Culture*, 1939.

I, like every soldier of America, will die for the freedom of the press, even for the freedom of newspapers that call me everything that is a good deal less than being a gentleman.

DWIGHT D. EISENHOWER, press conference, Moscow, August 14, 1945.

The message of the media is the commercial.

ALICE EMBREE, "Media Images I: Madison Avenue Brainwashing—The Facts," in Robin Morgan, ed., *Sisterhood Is Powerful*, 1970.

Now I think the networks should pay everyone. Hard news sources, soft news sources, everyone. It will serve to remind us that, at this point at least, there is no reason to confuse television news with journalism.

NORA EPHRON, on TV coverage of Vietnam War, "Bob Haldeman and CBS," *Esquire*, July, 1975.

Every so often, I manage to get through a day without reading the *New York Times*. This is an extremely risky thing to do—you never know whether the day you skip the *Times* will turn out to be the one day when some fascinating article will appear and leave you to spend the rest of your life explaining to friends who bring it up that you missed it. Fortunately, this rarely happens.

NORA EPHRON, "The New Porn," *Esquire*, March, 1976.

Every news story should, without any sacrifice of probity or responsibility, display the attributes of fiction, of drama. It should have structure and conflict, problem and denouement, rising action and falling action, a beginning, a middle and an end. These are not only the essentials of drama; they are the essentials of narrative.

REUVEN FRANK, NBC News memorandum, in Edward Jay Epstein, *News from Nowhere*, 1963.

Journalism is a means; and I now think that the act of keeping the record straight is valuable in itself. Serious, careful, honest journalism is essential, not because it is a guiding light but because it is a form of honorable behavior, involving the reporter and the reader.

MARTHA GELLHORN, Introduction, 1959, *The Face of War*, 1988.

Accurate or not, manipulated or not, television dominates our perception of events and dictates the cast of characters, long before its impact can be restrained by more cautious reports in the next day's newspapers.

DANIEL GOLDEN, *Boston Globe*, January 20, 1991.

Journalism is in fact history on the run.

THOMAS GRIFFITH, *The Waist-High Culture*, 1959.

[I]f a high official said something, then it was news, if not fact, and the role of the reporter was to print it straight without commenting, without assaulting the credibility of the incredulous; that was objectivity.

DAVID HALBERSTAM, on media's role in early days of McCarthy's accusations, *The Best and the Brightest*, 1969.

The hand that rules the press, the radio, the screen, and the far-spread magazine rules the country.

LEARNED HAND, memorial address for Justice Brandeis, December 21, 1942.

According to American principle and practice the public is the ruler of the State, and in order to rule rightly it should be informed correctly.

WILLIAM RANDOLPH HEARST, *New York Journal-American*, November 11, 1954.

The idea that the media is there to educate us, or to inform us, is ridiculous because that's about tenth or eleventh on their list. The first purpose of the media is to sell us shit, things we don't need. One moment it'll be "don't do drugs" and ten minutes later it's Miller time.

ABBIE HOFFMAN, speech, University of South Carolina, September 16, 1987.

The relationship between Government and the press in the nation's capital is so intimate as to be almost incestuous. Where newspapers in other parts of the world see it as their responsibility to lay a mine field for authority to walk through, the pundits and bureau chiefs of Washington's press corps often seem to regard it as their business instead to lay out a red carpet.

ANTHONY HOWARD, in Eugene J. McCarthy, *The Year of the People*, 1969.

Public opinion is the judgment of the incapable many opposed to that of the discerning few.

ELBERT HUBBARD, *The Roycroft Dictionary and Book of Epigrams*, 1923.

It may be true, and I suspect it is, that the mass of people everywhere are normally peace-loving and would accept many restraints and sacrifices in preference to the monstrous calamities of war. But I also suspect that what purports to be public opinion in most countries that consider themselves to have popular government is often not really the consensus of the feelings of the mass of the people at all but rather the expression of the interests of special highly vocal minorities— politicians, commentators, and publicity-seekers of all sorts: people who live by their ability to draw attention to themselves and die, like fish out of water, if they are compelled to remain silent.

GEORGE F. KENNAN, *American Diplomacy, 1900–1950*, 1951.

Even though we never like it, and even though we wish they didn't write it, and even though we disapprove, there isn't any doubt at all that we could not do the job at all in a free society without a very, very active press.

JOHN F. KENNEDY, "Conversation with President Kennedy," *Public Papers*, December 17, 1962.

In order to fuel the engines of publicity the media suck so much love and adulation out of the atmosphere that unknown men must gasp for breath.

LEWIS H. LAPHAM, "Shooting Stars," *Harper's*, June, 1981.

The press makes sculptures in snow; its truth dwells in the concrete fact and the fleeting sound of the human voice.

LEWIS H. LAPHAM, "Sculpture in Snow," *Harper's*, August, 1981.

Journalism, like history, has no therapeutic value; it is better able to diagnose than to cure, and it provides society with a primitive means of psychoanalysis that allows the patient to judge the distance between fantasy and reality.

LEWIS H. LAPHAM, "Sculpture in Snow," *Harper's*, August, 1981.

When distant and unfamiliar and complex things are communicated to great masses of people, the truth suffers a considerable and often a radical distortion. The complex is made over into the simple, the hypothetical into the dogmatic, and the relative into an absolute.

WALTER LIPPMANN, *The Public Philosophy*, 1955.

Writing for a newspaper is like running a revolutionary war; you go into battle not when you are ready but when action offers itself.

NORMAN MAILER, *The Presidential Papers*, 1963.

Newspapers have two great advantages over television. They can be used by men as barriers against their wives. It is still the only effective screen against the morning features of the loved one, and, as such, performs a unique human service. The second advantage is that you can't line a garbage pail with a television set—it's usually the other way around.

MARYA MANNES, speech, Women's National Press Club, 1960.

All successful newspapers are ceaselessly querulous and bellicose. They never defend anyone or anything if they can help it; if the job is forced upon them, they tackle it by denouncing someone or something else.

H.L. MENCKEN, *Prejudices*, 1919.

A newspaper is a device for making the ignorant more ignorant and the crazy crazier.

H.L. MENCKEN, *A Mencken Chrestomathy*, 1949.

MARTIANS BUILD TWO IMMENSE CANALS IN TWO YEARS.

NEW YORK TIMES, August 27, 1911.

You won't have Nixon to kick around anymore, because, gentlemen, this is my last press conference.

RICHARD M. NIXON, California, November 7, 1962.

The press is the enemy.

RICHARD M. NIXON, comment on the press, as remembered by William Safire, *Before the Fall*, 1975.

The media are far more powerful than the President in creating public awareness and shaping public opinion, for the simple reason that the media always have the last word.

RICHARD M. NIXON, *The Memoirs of Richard Nixon*, 1978.

Our Presidents *want* publicity, but above all, they want results. We should applaud rather than condemn them when they resist the insatiable demands of the media in order to do the job they were elected to do.

RICHARD M. NIXON, *The Real War*, 1980.

In America, public opinion is the leader.

FRANCES PERKINS, *People at Work*, 1934.

Nothing less than the highest ideals, the most scrupulous anxiety to do right, the most accurate knowledge of the problems it has to meet, and a sincere sense of moral responsibility will save journalism from a subservience to business interests, seeking selfish ends, antagonistic to public welfare.

JOSEPH PULITZER, "The College of Journalism," *North American Review*, 1904.

The mass media are the wholesalers; the peer-groups, the retailers of the communications industry.

DAVID RIESMAN, "Storytellers as Tutors," *The Lonely Crowd*, 1950.

All I know is what I see in the papers.

WILL ROGERS, ca. 1928.

It is very difficult to have a free, fair and honest press anywhere in the world....As a rule, papers are largely supported by advertising, and that immediately gives the advertisers a certain hold over the medium which they use.

ELEANOR ROOSEVELT, *If You Ask Me*, 1946.

The men with the muckrakes are often indispensable to the well-being of society; but only if they know when to stop raking the muck, and look upward to the celestial crown above them, to the crown of worthy endeavor. There are beautiful things above and round about them; and if they gradually grow to feel that the whole world is nothing but muck, their power of usefulness is gone.

THEODORE ROOSEVELT, speech, Washington, D.C., April 14, 1906.

In our country I am inclined to think that almost, if not quite, the most important profession is that of the newspaperman, including the man of the magazines, especially the cheap magazines, and the weeklies.

THEODORE ROOSEVELT, speech, Milwaukee, Wisconsin, September 7, 1910.

The sources of information are the springs from which democracy drinks.

ADLAI E. STEVENSON, speech, Cincinnati, Ohio, October 19, 1956.

Newspapers, television networks, and magazines have sometimes been outrageously abusive, untruthful, arrogant, and hypocritical. But it hardly follows that elimination of a strong and independent press is the way to eliminate abusiveness, untruth, arrogance, or hypocrisy from government itself.

POTTER STEWART, speech, Yale University Law School, 1974.

There are only two forces that can carry light to all corners of the globe—the sun in the heavens and the Associated Press.

MARK TWAIN, speech, Associated Press, New York City, September 18, 1906.

Women, wampum, and wrongdoing are always news.

STANLEY WALKER, *City Editor*, 1938.

Vietnam was the first war ever fought without any censorship. Without censorship, things can get terribly confused in the public mind.

WILLIAM C. WESTMORELAND, *Time*, April 5, 1982.

I have yet to see a piece of writing, political or non-political, that doesn't have a slant. All writing slants the way a writer leans, and no man is born perpendicular, although many men are born upright. The beauty of the American free press is that the slants and the twists and the distortions come from so many directions, and the special interests are so numerous, the reader must sift and sort and check and countercheck in order to find out what the score is.

E.B. WHITE, "Bedfellows," February 6, 1956, *Essays of E.B. White*, 1977.

Knowledge

See also **Dreams and Ideals**—Wisdom; **Education**; **History and Tradition**

Understanding, and action proceeding from understanding and guided by it, is the one weapon against the world's bombardment, the one medicine, the one instrument by which liberty, health, and joy may be shaped or shaped toward, in the individual, and in the race.

JAMES AGEE, with Walker Evans, *Let Us Now Praise Famous Men*, 1941.

Can we actually "know" the universe? My God, it's hard enough finding your way around in Chinatown.

WOODY ALLEN, *Getting Even*, 1966.

Ignorance is a *right*! Education is eroding one of the few democratic freedoms remaining to us.

CHRISTOPHER ANDREA, *Christian Science Monitor*, February 21, 1980.

At the same time that the information which is required to use and maintain modern products is increasingly dramatically, the human ability to comprehend that information is decreasing catastrophically.

NORMAN AUGUSTINE, "Augustine's 129th Law," *Augustine's Laws*, 1986.

There's a period of life when we swallow a knowledge of ourselves and it becomes either good or sour inside.

PEARL BAILEY, *The Raw Pearl*, 1968.

Most of the arguments to which I am a party fall somewhat short of being impressive, owing to the fact that neither I nor my opponent knows what we are talking about.

ROBERT BENCHLEY, *Benchley—or Else!*, 1947.

I have tried to know absolutely nothing about a great many things, and I have succeeded fairly well.

ROBERT BENCHLEY, *Rocky Mountain News*, April 23, 1980.

[It was] an initiation into the love of learning, of learning how to learn, that was revealed to me by my [Boston Latin School] masters as a matter of interdisciplinary cognition—that is, learning to know something by its relation to something else.

LEONARD BERNSTEIN, *New York Times*, November 22, 1984.

It is the appreciation of beauty and truth, the striving for knowledge, which makes life worth living.

MORRIS RAPHAEL COHEN, *A Dreamer's Journey*, 1959.

A modern commentator made the observation that there are those who seek knowledge about everything and understand nothing. It is wonder—not mere curiosity—a sense of enchantment, of respect for the mysteries of love for the other, that is essential to the difference between a knowing that is simply a gathering of information and techniques and a knowing that seeks insight and understanding. It is wonder that reveals how intimate is the relationship between knowledge of the other and knowledge of the self, between inwardness and outwardness.

SEYMOUR COHEN, *Affirming Life*, 1987.

Neither wealth nor knowledge can provide effective ways to deal with human excesses.

RENÉ DUBOS, *A God Within*, 1972.

We often speak of the ignorance of the past; but our distant forefathers were no more ignorant than we. They were grinding the grist of experience through the mills of the mind and were discovering what was good and what was bad for them. That is all we are doing.

HENRY FORD, "Success," *Forum*, October, 1928.

Knowledge fills a large brain; it merely inflates a small one.

SYDNEY HARRIS, *Detroit Free Press*, January 7, 1982.

Ignorance per se is not nearly as dangerous as ignorance of ignorance.

SYDNEY HARRIS, *Pieces of Eight*, 1982.

No knowledge is so easily found as when it is needed.

ROBERT HENRI, *The Art Spirit*, 1923.

Wonder, rather than doubt, is the root of knowledge.

ABRAHAM HESCHEL, *Man Is Not Alone*, 1951.

If a hypothesis offers *no* way to prove itself true or false, it is not useful scientifically. It should be thrown away; it is a belief. Knowledge advances on the wings of testable ideas, not beliefs.

MAHLON HOAGLAND, *Toward the Habit of Truth*, 1990.

Far more crucial than what we know or do not know is what we do not want to know.

ERIC HOFFER, *The Passionate State of Mind*, 1954.

Knowledge is the distilled essence of our intuitions, corroborated by experience.

ELBERT HUBBARD, *Note Book*, 1927.

Our knowledge grows *in spots*. The spots may be large or small, but the knowledge never grows all over: some old knowledge always remains what it was....Our minds grow in spots; and like grease-spots, the spots spread. But we let them spread as little as possible: we keep unaltered as much of our old knowledge, as many of our old prejudices and beliefs, as we can. We patch and tinker more than we renew.

WILLIAM JAMES, *Pragmatism*, 1907.

We can add to our knowledge, but we cannot at will subtract from it.

ARTHUR KOESTLER, *Arrow in the Blue*, 1970.

What man knows is everywhere at war with what he wants.

JOSEPH WOOD KRUTCH, *The Modern Temper*, 1929.

If we would have new knowledge, we must get a whole world of new questions.

SUSANNE K. LANGER, *Philosophy in a New Key*, 1957.

Penetrating so many secrets, we cease to believe in the unknowable. But there it sits nevertheless, calmly licking its chops.

H.L. MENCKEN, *Minority Report: Notebooks*, 1956.

Sin, guilt, neurosis—they are one and the same, the fruit of the tree of knowledge.

HENRY MILLER, *The Wisdom of the Heart: Creative Death*, 1941.

In expanding the field of knowledge we but increase the horizon of ignorance.

HENRY MILLER, *The Wisdom of the Heart*, 1941.

Knowledge, learning, information, and skilled intelligence are the new raw materials of international commerce and are today spreading throughout the world as vigorously as miracle drugs, synthetic fertilizers and blue jeans did earlier.

NATIONAL COMMISSION ON EXCELLENCE IN EDUCATION, *A Nation at Risk*, 1983.

To an earlier age knowledge was power, merely that and nothing more; to us it is life and the *summum bonum*.

CHARLES S. PEIRCE, *Annual Report*, Smithsonian Institution, June 30, 1900.

We live in a time of such rapid change and growth of knowledge that only he who is in a fundamental sense a scholar—that is, a person who continues to learn and inquire—can hope to keep pace, let alone play the role of guide.

NATHAN M. PUSEY, *The Age of the Scholar*, 1963.

We're drowning in information and starving for knowledge.

RUTHERFORD D. ROGERS, *New York Times*, February 25, 1985.

Everybody is ignorant, only on different subjects.

WILL ROGERS, *The Illiterate Digest*, 1924.

He [the American] seems to bear lightly the sorrowful burden of human knowledge. In a word, he is young.

GEORGE SANTAYANA, *Character and Opinion in the United States*, 1920.

His had been an intellectual decision founded on his conviction that if a little knowledge was a dangerous thing, a lot was lethal.

TOM SHARPE, *Porterhouse Blues*, 1974.

Like sex, knowledge is good if used in the service of life and love.

LILLIAN SMITH, *Killers of the Dream*, 1949.

We know nothing important. In the essentials we are still as wholly a mystery to ourselves as Adam was to himself.

BOOTH TARKINGTON, *Looking Forward*, 1926.

It is often claimed that knowledge multiplies so rapidly that nobody can follow it. I believe this is incorrect. At least in science it is not true. The main purpose of science is simplicity and as we understand more things, everything is becoming simpler. This, of course, goes contrary to what everybody accepts.

EDWARD TELLER, *Conversations on the Dark Secrets of Physics*, 1991.

In the United States there is a firmly established custom of sending researchers around the country to prove to ourselves how dumb we are.

CALVIN TRILLIN, "Geography Lesson," King Features Syndicate, September 21, 1986.

It does not seem as if knowledge has done the best thing for humanity. In the time of wisdom, I respected my brother's dream and he respected mine.

JOHN TRUEDELL, in Kay Boyle, "A Day on Alcatraz with the Indians," *Words That Must Somehow Be Said*, 1969.

Only the curious will learn and only the resolute overcome the obstacles to learning. The quest quotient has always excited me more than the intelligence quotient.

EUGENE S. WILSON, *Reader's Digest*, April, 1968.

This is what knowledge really is. It is finding out something for oneself with pain, with joy, with exultancy, with labor, and with all the little ticking, breathing moments of our lives, until it is ours as that only is ours which is rooted in the structure of our lives.

THOMAS WOLFE, *The Web and the Rock*, 1939.

Ignorance is not bliss—it is oblivion.

PHILIP WYLIE, *Generation of Vipers*, 1942.

Language and Discourse

See also **American Society; Americans on Americans**—Writers; **The Arts**—Literature; **Business**—Advertising and Marketing, Advertising Slogans; **Education; Government and Politics**—Campaign and Political Slogans; **Popular Culture**—Manners and Etiquette; **Science and Technology**—Communications; **Social Issues**—Censorship, Pornography and Obscenity; **Work**—Writers

English, n. A language so haughty and reserved that few writers succeed in getting on terms of familiarity with it.

AMBROSE BIERCE, *The Enlarged Devil's Dictionary*, 1967.

The English language is in very good shape. It is changing in its own undiscoverable way, but it is not going rotten like a plum dropping off a tree.

ROBERT BURCHFIELD, "A Conversation with Robert Burchfield," *U.S. News & World Report*, December 15, 1980.

Words are what hold society together.

STUART CHASE AND MARION T. CHASE, *Power of Words*, 1954.

Some of mankind's most terrible misdeeds have been committed under the spell of certain magic words or phrases.

JAMES BRYANT CONANT, speech, Harvard University, June, 1934.

No man ever made a great speech on a mean subject.

ATTRIBUTED TO EUGENE V. DEBS.

If the word has the potency to revive and make us free, it has also the power to bind, imprison and destroy.

RALPH ELLISON, unpublished essay, *Twentieth-Century Fiction and the Black Mask of Humanity*, 1946, reprinted in *Confluence*, December 1953.

Language is a living thing. We can feel it changing. Parts of it become old: they drop off and are forgotten. New pieces bud out, spread into leaves, and become big branches, proliferating.

GILBERT HIGHET, *Explorations: Changing Words*, 1971.

Words can destroy. What we call each other ultimately becomes what we think of each other, and it matters.

JEANE KIRKPATRICK, speech, "Israel as Scapegoat," Anti-Defamation League, February 11, 1982.

A people's speech is the skin of its culture.

MAX LERNER, *America as a Civilization*, 1957.

When an age is in throes of profound transition, the first thing to disintegrate is language.

ROLLO MAY, *Power and Innocence*, 1972.

Language makes culture, and we make a rotten culture when we abuse words.

CYNTHIA OZICK, "We Are the Crazy Lady and Other Feisty Feminist Fables," in Francine Klagsbrun, ed., *The First Ms. Reader*, 1972.

Only where there is language is there world.

ADRIENNE RICH, "The Demon Lover," *Leaflets*, 1969.

Every immigrant who comes here should be required within five years to learn English or leave the country.

THEODORE ROOSEVELT, *Kansas City Star*, April 27, 1918.

They sing. They hurt. They teach. They sanctify. They were man's first, immeasurable feat of magic. They liberated us from ignorance and our barbarous past.

LEO ROSTEN, *The Many Worlds of L*E*O R*O*S*T*E*N: The Power of Words*, 1964.

Language, like all art, becomes pale with years; words and figures of speech lose their contagious and suggestive power.

GEORGE SANTAYANA, *The Life of Reason*, 1905–1906.

Language is the soul of intellect, and reading is the essential process by which that intellect is cultivated beyond the commonplace experiences of everyday life.

CHARLES SCRIBNER, JR., *Publishers Weekly*, March 30, 1984.

Language is learned in the house and in the fields, not at school.

GARY SNYDER, "The Etiquette of Freedom," *The Practice of the Wild*, 1990.

I personally think we developed language because of our deep inner need to complain.

JANE WAGNER, *The Search for Intelligent Life in the Universe*, performed by Lily Tomlin, 1986.

COMMUNICATION

You can taste a word.

PEARL BAILEY, *Newsweek*, December 4, 1967.

The search is for the just word, the happy phrase, that will give expression to the thought, but somehow the thought itself is transfigured by the phrase when found.

BENJAMIN CARDOZO, *The Growth of the Law*, 1924.

Words are chameleons, which reflect the color of their environment.

LEARNED HAND, opinion, *Commissioner v. National Carbide*, 1948.

It's all in the ear of the beholder.

TOM HAYDEN, *Boston Globe*, September 24, 1979.

Never impose your language on people you wish to reach.

ABBIE HOFFMAN, *Revolution for the Hell of It*, 1968.

Recognizing the limited time span of someone staring at a lighted square in their living room, I trained for the one-liner, the retort jab, or sudden knock-out put-ons.

ABBIE HOFFMAN, *Soon to Be a Motion Picture*, 1980.

A word is not a crystal, transparent and unchanging, it is the skin of a living thought and may vary greatly in color and content according to the circumstances and time in which it is used.

OLIVER WENDELL HOLMES, JR., opinion, *Towne v. Eisner*, January 7, 1918.

We have to face the fact that either all of us are going to die together or we are going to learn to live together and if we are to live together we have to talk.

ELEANOR ROOSEVELT, in article by A. David Gurewitsch, *New York Times*, October 15, 1960.

To communicate, put your thoughts in order; give them a purpose; use them to persuade, to instruct, to discover, to seduce.

WILLIAM SAFIRE, *Reader's Digest*, December, 1987.

One must be chary of words because they turn into cages.

VIOLA SPOLIN, in article by Barry Hyams, *Los Angeles Times*, May 26, 1974.

Precision of communication is important, more important than ever, in our era of hair-trigger balances, when a false, or misunderstood word may create as much disaster as a sudden thoughtless act.

JAMES THURBER, *Lanterns and Lances: Friends, Romans, Countrymen, Lend Me Your Muffs*, 1961.

Human beings live—literally live, as if life is equated with the mind—by symbols, particularly words, because the brain is constructed to process information almost exclusively in their terms.

EDWARD O. WILSON, *Biophilia*, 1984.

CONVERSATION

For parlor use the vague generality is a life-saver.

GEORGE ADE, "The Wise Piker," *Forty Modern Fables*, 1901.

She had learnt...that it was impossible to discuss issues civilly with a person who insisted on referring to himself as "we."

LISA ALTHER, *Kinflicks*, 1977.

Words mean more than what is set down on paper. It takes the human voice to infuse them with shades of deeper meaning.

MAYA ANGELOU, *I Know Why the Caged Bird Sings*, 1970.

Repartee is what you wish you'd said.

HEYWOOD BROUN, in Robert E. Drennan, *The Algonquin Wits*, 1968.

Too much agreement kills a chat.

ELDRIDGE CLEAVER, "A Day in Folsom Prison," *Soul on Ice*, 1968.

Talk ought always to run obliquely, not nose to nose with no chance of mental escape.

FRANK MOORE COLBY, "Simple Simon," *The Colby Essays*, 1926.

He pronounced some of his words as if they were corks being drawn out of bottles.

WINSTON GRAHAM, *Reader's Digest*, November, 1981.

One has to grow up with good talk in order to form the habit of it.

HELEN HAYES, with Lewis Funke, *A Gift of Joy*, 1965.

[T]he distinction between men's and women's language is a symptom of a problem in our culture, not the problem itself. Basically it reflects the fact that men and women are expected to have different interests and different roles, hold different types of conversations, and react differently to other people.

ROBIN LAKOFF, *Language and Woman's Place*, 1975.

Years ago, I tried to top everybody, but I don't anymore. I realized it was killing conversation. When you're always trying for a topper you aren't really listening. It ruins communication.

GROUCHO MARX, *The Groucho Phile*, 1976.

We do not talk—we bludgeon one another with facts and theories gleaned from cursory readings of newspapers, magazines, and digests.

HENRY MILLER, "The Shadows," *The Air-Conditioned Nightmare*, 1945.

There is no such thing as a worthless conversation, providing you know what to listen for. And questions are the breath of life for a conversation.

JAMES NATHAN MILLER, *Reader's Digest*, September, 1965.

It is not what we learn in conversation that enriches us. It is the elation that comes of swift contact with tingling currents of thought.

AGNES REPPLIER, "The Luxury of Conversation," *Compromises*, 1904.

GOSSIP

The idea of strictly minding our own business is moldy rubbish. Who could be so selfish?

MYRTIE LILLIAN BARKER, *I Am Only One*, 1963.

What people say behind your back is your standing in the community in which you live.

EDGAR WATSON HOWE, *Sinner Sermons*, 1926.

Gossip is only the lack of a worthy theme.

ELBERT HUBBARD, *The Roycroft Dictionary and Book of Epigrams*, 1923.

Men have always detested women's gossip because they suspect the truth: their measurements are being taken and compared.

ERICA JONG, *Fear of Flying*, 1973.

Gossip is the opiate of the oppressed.

ERICA JONG, *Fear of Flying*, 1973.

Gossip, unlike river water, flows both ways.

MICHAEL KORDA, *Reader's Digest*, June, 1976.

If you haven't got anything nice to say about anybody, come sit next to me.

ALICE ROOSEVELT LONGWORTH, motto embroidered on a cushion.

From the morning of the first individual folly of the race, gossip has been the normal nattering background noise of civilization: Molly Goldberg at her kitchen window, Voltaire at the water cooler. To say that gossip has been much condemned is like saying that sex has sometimes been held in low esteem. It is true, but it misses some of the fun of the thing.

LANCE MORROW, "The Morals of Gossip," *Fishing in the Tiber*, 1988.

Gossip is news running ahead of itself in a red satin dress.

LIZ SMITH, *American Way*, September 3, 1985.

Gossip, even when it avoids the sexual, bears around it a faint flavor of the erotic.

PATRICIA MEYER SPACKS, *New York Times*, September 1, 1985.

GRAMMAR

If you take hyphens seriously you will surely go mad.

JOHN BENBOW, *Manuscript and Proof*, 1937.

The approach to English grammar in the 20th century—the move toward a kind of logical, mathematical description of the language—has been a disaster, leaving children totally at sea. Schoolmasters are also confused and don't know what to teach. The upshot is that, by some estimates, about 15 percent of all Americans are now functionally illiterate.

ROBERT BURCHFIELD, "A Conversation with Robert Burchfield," *U.S. News & World Report*, December 15, 1980.

Would you convey my compliments to the purist who reads your proofs and tell him or her that I write in a sort of brokendown patois which is something like the way a Swiss waiter talks, and that when I split an infinitive, God damn it, I split it so it will stay split.

RAYMOND CHANDLER, letter to Edward Weeks, January 18, 1947.

Congress is really the home of the split infinitive, where it finds its finest fruition. This is the place where the dangling participle is certainly nourished. This is the home of the broken sentence.

EVERETT DIRKSEN, in Neil MacNeil, *Dirksen: Portrait of a Public Man*, 1970.

I give you a new definition of a sentence: A sentence is a sound in itself on which other sounds called words are strung.

ROBERT FROST, letter to John T. Bartlett, February 22, 1914, *Selected Letters of Robert Frost*, 1964.

There is no such thing as good and bad (or correct and incorrect, grammatical and ungrammatical, right or wrong) in language.

ROBERT A. HALL, JR., *Linguistics and Your Language*, 1950.

Invention in language should no more be discouraged than should invention in mechanics. Grammar is the grave of letters.

ELBERT HUBBARD, *Note Book*, 1927.

A period is to let the writer know he has finished his thought and he should stop there if he will only take the hint.

ART LINKLETTER, *A Child's Garden of Misinformation*, 1965.

A period is a stop sign. A semicolon is a rolling stop sign; a comma is merely an amber light.

ANDREW J. OFFUTT, in *Writer's Digest*, July, 1978.

As far as I'm concerned, "whom" is a word that was invented to make everyone sound like a butler.

CALVIN TRILLIN, "Whom Says So?" *The Nation*, June 8, 1985.

JARGON, DOUBLESPEAK, AND OBFUSCATION

No one means all he says, and yet very few say all they mean, for words are slippery and thought is viscous.

HENRY ADAMS, *The Education of Henry Adams*, 1907.

Euphemisms, like fashions, have their day and pass, perhaps to return at another time. Like the guests at a masquerade ball, they enjoy social approval only so long as they retain the capacity for deception.

FREDA ADLER, *Sisters in Crime*, 1975.

Simply stated, it is sagacious to eschew obfuscation.

NORMAN AUGUSTINE, "Augustine's 65th Law," *Augustine's Laws*, 1986.

I have received memos so swollen with managerial babble that they struck me as the literary equivalent of assault with a deadly weapon.

PETER BAIDA, "Management Babble," *American Heritage*, April, 1985.

Incomprehensible jargon is the hallmark of a profession.

KINGMAN BREWSTER, speech to British Institute of Management, December 13, 1977.

Perhaps our greatest responsibility is to repledge our continuing devotion to perpetuating a legacy of language in an age when the spoken word is suspected as "a glib and oily art," manipulative doublespeak; when the written word—badly written, of course—is unread; and when "vibrations" are alleged to be, not inarticulate throbbing, but true communication where every sentence begins with "I feel" and ends with "you know."

PAUL CUBETA, *Christian Science Monitor*, August 2, 1976.

Drugspeak is at once damning and forgiving. The subtext is the excuse as well as the admission that "I can't help myself." The way that notion has crept into our everyday conversation, infesting our criticism and self-criticism, undermines the sense that average people are in control of their own lives.

ELLEN GOODMAN, "Nancy's No Clothes Junkie," *Washington Post*, October, 1988.

When speech is divorced from speaker and word from meaning, what is left is just ritual, language as ritual.

ELLEN GOODMAN, "Ghostwriters in the Sky," *Washington Post*, February, 1986.

Words are not pebbles in alien juxtaposition.

LEARNED HAND, opinion, *NLRB v. Federbush Co., Inc.*, 1941.

Professional jargon is unpleasant. Translating it into English is a bore. I narrow-mindedly outlawed the word "unique." Practically every press release contains it. Practically nothing ever is.

FRED HECHINGER, *New York Herald Tribune*, August 5, 1956.

All our words from loose using have lost their edge.

ERNEST HEMINGWAY, *Death in the Afternoon*, 1932.

I for one appreciate a good form letter, having worked on Capitol Hill and learned several dozen cordial ways to say nothing.

CARRIE JOHNSON, "Judging American Business by Its Writing Habits," *New York Times*, July 14, 1984.

It's the kind of language used extensively in the educational profession. Long words and complex sentences are intended to add importance to something unimportant.

JACK MABLEY, *Detroit Free Press*, November 2, 1981.

Napalm has become "Incinderjell," which makes it sound like Jell-O. And defoliants are referred to as weed-killers—something you use in your driveway. The resort to euphemism denotes, no doubt, a guilty conscience or—the same thing nowadays—a twinge in the public-relations nerve.

MARY MCCARTHY, *Vietnam*, 1967.

One of our defects as a nation is a tendency to use what have been called "weasel words." When a weasel sucks eggs the meat is sucked out of the egg. If you use a "weasel word" after another there is nothing left of the other. You can have universal training, or you can have voluntary training, but when you use the word "voluntary" to qualify the word "universal" you are making a "weasel word"; it has sucked all the meaning out of "universal."

THEODORE ROOSEVELT, on Woodrow Wilson's phrase "universal voluntary military training," speech, St. Louis, Missouri, May 31, 1916.

"Wild and Free." An American dream-phrase loosing images: a long-maned stallion racing across the grasslands, a V of Canada Geese high and honking, a squirrel chattering and leaping limb to limb overhead in an oak. It also sounds like an ad for a Harley-Davidson. Both words, profoundly political and sensitive as they are, have become consumer baubles.

GARY SNYDER, "The Etiquette of Freedom," *The Practice of the Wild*, 1990.

More has been screwed up on the battlefield and misunderstood in the Pentagon because of a lack of understanding of the English language than any other single factor.

JOHN W. VESSEY, JR., *New York Times*, July 15, 1984.

USAGE

Expletive deleted.

TERM USED TO REPLACE VULGARITY IN TRANSCRIPTS OF WHITE HOUSE RECORDINGS OF CONVERSATIONS RELATED TO WATERGATE AFFAIR, released April 30, 1974.

In fact, when you really hate [someone], what's the vernacular we use? "*Screw* you, mister!" If you were taught it was a sweet Christian act of procreation, it was the nicest thing we can do for each other, you'd use the term correctly and say, "*Unscrew* you, mister."

LENNY BRUCE, ca. 1960, in John Cohen, ed., *The Essential Lenny Bruce*, 1967.

Words, like men, grow individuality; their character changes with years and with use.

FREDERICK E. CRANE, *Adler v. Deegan*, 1929.

You can be a little ungrammatical if you come from the right part of the country.

ROBERT FROST, *The Atlantic*, January, 1962.

Nouns and verbs are almost pure metal; adjectives are cheaper ore.

MARIE GILCHRIST, in article by Leonora Speyer, "On the Teaching of Poetry," *The Saturday Review of Literature*, 1946.

I'm glad you like adverbs—I adore them; they are the only qualifications I really much respect.

HENRY JAMES, letter to Bethan Edwards, January 5, 1912.

NOTICE TO PERFORMERS

Don't say "slob" or "son-of-a-gun" or "hully gee" on this stage unless you want to be cancelled peremptorily. Do not address anyone in the audience in any manner. If you have not the ability to entertain Mr. Keith's audiences without risk of offending them, do the best you can. Lack of talent will be less open to censure than would be an insult to a patron. If you are in doubt as to the character of your act, consult the local manager before you go on the stage, for if you are guilty of uttering anything sacrilegious or even suggestive, you will be immediately closed and will never again be allowed in a theatre where Mr. Keith is in authority.

PAUL KEITH, ca. 1918, in Fred Allen, *Much Ado About Me*, 1956.

An abstract noun neither smiles nor sings nor tells bedtime stories. The promise of human feeling on the part of any institution—whether a bank or an infantry regiment—debases the language and props up the effigy to whom George Orwell gave the name "Big Brother."

LEWIS H. LAPHAM, "Nouns and Pronouns," *Harper's*, January, 1989.

There have been times when her sedulously tortuous style, her one-word sentences and her curiously compounded adjectives, drive me into an irritation that is only to be relieved by kicking and screaming.

DOROTHY PARKER, "Re-enter Miss Hurst, Followed by Mr. Tarkington," *The New Yorker*, January 28, 1928.

I wouldn't touch a superlative again with an umbrella.

DOROTHY PARKER, "Excuse It, Please," *The New Yorker*, February 18, 1928.

Good swearing is used as a form of punctuation, not necessarily as a response to pain or insult, and is utilized by experts to lend a sentence a certain zest, like a sprinkling of paprika.

GEORGE PLIMPTON, *Paper Lion*, 1965.

Slang is a language that rolls up its sleeves, spits on its hands and goes to work.

CARL SANDBURG, *New York Times*, February 13, 1959.

But why wasn't I born, alas, in an age of Adjectives; why can one no longer write of silver-shedding Tears and moon-tailed Peacocks, of elo-quent Death, of the Negro and star-enamelled Night?

LOGAN PEARSALL SMITH, *More Trivia: Adjectives*, 1921.

A people who are prosperous and happy, optimistic and progressive, will produce much slang; it is a case of play; they amuse themselves with the language.

WILLIAM GRAHAM SUMNER, A.G. KELLER, AND M.R. DAVID, *The Science of Society*, 1927.

An average English word is four letters and a half. By hard, honest labor I've dug all the large words out of my vocabulary and shaved it down till the average is three and a half....I never write "metropolis" for seven cents, because I can get the same money for "city." I never write "policeman," because I get the same price for "cop." I never write "valetudinarian" at all, for not even hunger and wretchedness can humble me to the point where I will do a word like that for seven cents; I wouldn't do it for fifteen.

MARK TWAIN, speech, Associated Press, New York City, September 18, 1906.

"Give us this day our daily bread" is probably the most perfectly constructed and useful sentence ever set down in the English language.

P.J. WINGATE, *Wall Street Journal*, August 8, 1977.

Law and Justice

See also **Dreams and Ideals**—Justice; **Ethics and Morality; Government and Politics**—Congress, Domestic Policy, The Judiciary, Political Philosophies; **Social Issues**—Censorship, Civil Rights; **Work**—Judges and Lawyers

Intellectual and spiritual leaders hailed the cause of civil rights and gave little thought to where the civil disobedience road might end. But defiance of the law, even for the best reasons, opens a tiny hole in the dike and soon a trickle becomes a flood....And while no thinking person denies that social injustice exists, no thinking person can condone any group, for any reason, taking justice into its own hands. Once this is permitted, democracy dies; for democracy is sustained through one great premise: the premise that civil rights are balanced by civil responsibilities.

SPIRO T. AGNEW, in Robert Marsh, *Agnew, the Unexplained Man*, 1971.

Bulls do not win bull fights; people do.

People do not win people fights; lawyers do.

NORMAN AUGUSTINE, "Augustine's 10th Law," *Augustine's Laws*, 1986.

There is never a deed so foul that something couldn't be said for the guy; that's why there are lawyers.

MELVIN BELLI, *Los Angeles Times*, December 18, 1981.

Lawful, adj. Compatible with the will of a judge having jurisdiction.

AMBROSE BIERCE, *The Devil's Dictionary*, 1906.

The term "rule of law," like the phrases "love of God" and "brotherhood of man," is a short and simple expression of one of the few most sublime concepts that the mind and spirit of man has yet achieved.

GEORGE H. BOLDT, speech, Law Day USA, Tacoma, Washington, 1958.

Crime is contagious. If the government becomes a lawbreaker, it breeds contempt for law.

LOUIS D. BRANDEIS, opinion, *Olmstead v. U.S*, 1928.

The law is not an end in itself, nor does it provide ends. It is preeminently a means to serve what we think is right.

WILLIAM J. BRENNAN, opinion, *Roth v. United States*, 1957.

Clearly, police officers cannot break the law to enforce it.

REESE BROWN, "All Things Considered," National Public Radio, April 17, 1991.

Now the problem I had in understanding the law was because of the language of the law. Instead of taking each word and finding out the case that the word related to, once in a while I got lazy and I would apply common sense. And then I got really screwed up.

LENNY BRUCE, ca. 1960, in John Cohen, ed., *The Essential Lenny Bruce*, 1967.

Even an attorney of moderate talent can postpone doomsday year after year, for the system of appeals that pervades American jurisprudence amounts to a legalistic wheel of fortune, a game of chance, somewhat fixed in the favor of the criminal, that the participants play interminably....But at intervals the wheel does pause to declare a winner—or, though with increasing rarity, a loser.

TRUMAN CAPOTE, *In Cold Blood*, 1965.

The best trained, most technically skilled and ethically most responsible lawyers are reserved for the upper reaches of business and society. This leaves the least competent, least well-trained, and least ethical lawyers to the lower-income individuals.

JEROME E. CARLIN, *Lawyer's Ethics*, 1966.

No written law has ever been more binding than unwritten custom supported by popular opinion.

CARRIE CHAPMAN CATT, speech on woman suffrage, U.S. Senate, February 13, 1900.

It is indisputably clear...that the Justice Department was simply wrong as a matter of law in advising that [Muhammad] Ali's beliefs were not religiously based and were not sincerely held.

CLAY A.K.A. ALI v. U.S., 1971.

Jurisprudence, in effect, is a special branch of the science of transcendental nonsense.

FELIX S. COHEN, *Transcendental Nonsense and the Functional Approach*, 1935.

I don't want to know what the law is, I want to know who the judge is.

Roy Cohn, in article by Tom Wolfe, *New York Times Book Review*, April 3, 1988.

If you pass a bad law you find out and correct it; some damage is done but not irreparable damage; the same group who passed the laws say, "Come, we made fools of ourselves and we will now repeal that law."

Henry S. Commager, in Arthur Goodfriend, *What Is America?*, 1954.

Late every night in Connecticut, lights go out in the cities and towns, and citizens by tens of thousands proceed zestfully to break the law....And, of course, there is always a witness to the crime—but as though to make the law completely unenforceable, Connecticut forbids spouses from testifying against one another.

On Connecticut law on birth control, *Time*, March 10, 1961.

Men speak of natural rights, but I challenge anyone to show where in nature any rights existed or were recognized until there was established for their declaration and protection a duly promulgated body of corresponding laws.

Calvin Coolidge, vice-presidential nomination acceptance speech, Republican National Convention, July 27, 1920.

One with the law is a majority.

Calvin Coolidge, vice-presidential nomination acceptance speech, Republican National Convention, July 27, 1920.

Free government has no greater menace than disrespect for authority and continual violation of law. It is the duty of a citizen not only to observe the law but to let it be known that he is opposed to its violation.

Calvin Coolidge, message to Congress, December 6, 1923.

Bias and prejudice are attitudes to be kept in hand, not attitudes to be avoided.

Charles Curtis, *A Commonplace Book*, 1957.

All sides in a trial want to hide at least some of the truth.

Alan M. Dershowitz, *U.S. News & World Report*, August 9, 1982.

It is seldom appropriate for one group within society to seek to insert their moral beliefs, however profoundly held, into a document designed for people of fundamentally differing views.

Robert Drinan, on Supreme Court ruling on abortion, *American Herald*, March 25, 1974.

Our Constitution works. Our great republic is a government of laws, not of men.

Gerald R. Ford, on succeeding Richard M. Nixon as president, August 9, 1974.

The concept of property is fundamental to our society, probably to any workable society. Operationally, it is understood by every child above the age of three. Intellectually, it is understood by almost no one.

Consider the slogan, "property rights vs. human rights." Its rhetorical force comes from the implication that property rights are the rights of property and human rights are the rights of humans; humans are more important than property...; consequently human rights take precedence over property rights.

But property rights are not the rights of property; they are the rights of humans in regard to property.

David Friedman, *The Machinery of Freedom*, 1978.

When the law contradicts what most people regard as moral and proper, they will break the law—whether the law is enacted in the name of a noble ideal...or in the naked interest of one group at the expense of another. Only fear of punishment, not a sense of justice and morality, will lead people to obey the law.

When people start to break one set of laws, the lack of respect for the law inevitably spreads to all laws, even those that everyone regards as moral and proper—laws against violence, theft, and vandalism.

Milton Friedman and Rose Friedman, *Free to Choose*, 1980.

Perhaps there are women who want to be biological entrepreneurs. Perhaps there are some who want to market their genes, to hire their wombs to an absentee owner. But the one right we don't need is the right to sign away our rights.

Ellen Goodman, "Baby M III: The Right to Give Away Your Rights," *Washington Post*, March, 1987.

If a state has the right to tell man and man how to behave sexually with each other, it has the right to tell man and woman. If homosexuals have no privacy in bed, then neither do heterosexuals. If a legislature can criminalize oral sex, it can criminalize any other practice considered "deviant" by any political majority. Never on Sunday?

Ellen Goodman, "Homosexual Crimes," *Washington Post*, July, 1986.

There is something monstrous in commands couched in invented and unfamiliar language; an alien master is worst of all. The language of the law must not be foreign to those who are to obey it.

LEARNED HAND, speech, Washington, D.C., May 11, 1929.

If the prosecution of crime is to be conducted with so little regard for that protection which centuries of English law have given to the individual, we are indeed at the dawn of a new era; and much that we have deemed vital to our liberties is a delusion.

LEARNED HAND, opinion, *United States* v. *Di Re*, 1947.

Expedience, not justice, is the rule of contemporary American law.

ABBIE HOFFMAN, "The Crime of Punishment," *Square Dancing in the Ice Age*, 1981.

Great cases like hard cases make bad law. For great cases are called great not by reason of their real importance in shaping the law of the future but because of some accident of immediate overwhelming interest which appeals to the feelings and distorts the judgment. These immediate interests exercise a kind of hydraulic pressure which makes what previously was clear seem doubtful, and before which even well-settled principles of law will bend.

OLIVER WENDELL HOLMES, JR., opinion, *Northern Securities Company* v. *United States*, 1904.

Every opinion tends to become a law.

OLIVER WENDELL HOLMES, JR., opinion, *Lochner* v. *New York*, 1905.

General propositions do not decide concrete cases.

OLIVER WENDELL HOLMES, JR., opinion, *Lochner* v. *New York*, 1905.

While there still is doubt, while opposite convictions still keep a battlefront against each other, the time for law has not come.

OLIVER WENDELL HOLMES, JR., speech, New York City, February 15, 1913.

It is our duty to declare lynch law as little valid when practiced by a regularly drawn jury as when administered by one elected by a mob intent on death.

OLIVER WENDELL HOLMES, JR., opinion, *Frank* v. *Mangum*, 1915.

Mob law does not become due process of law by securing the assent of a terrorized jury.

OLIVER WENDELL HOLMES, JR., opinion, *Frank* v. *Mangum*, 1915.

Pretty much all law consists in forbidding men to do some things that they want to do.

OLIVER WENDELL HOLMES, JR., opinion, *Adkins* v. *Children's Hospital*, 1922.

If the law is upheld only by government officials, then all law is at an end.

HERBERT HOOVER, message to Congress, 1929.

Laws that do not embody public opinion can never be enforced.

ELBERT HUBBARD, *The Roycroft Dictionary and Book of Epigrams*, 1923.

Law: 1. A scheme for protecting the parasite and prolonging the life of the rogue, averting the natural consequences which would otherwise come to them. 2. The crystallization of public opinion.

ELBERT HUBBARD, *The Roycroft Dictionary and Book of Epigrams*, 1923.

Liberty is not the mere absence of restraint, it is not a spontaneous product of majority rule, it is not achieved merely by lifting underprivileged classes to power, nor is it the inevitable by-product of technological expansion. It is achieved only by a rule of law.

ROBERT H. JACKSON, *The Supreme Court in the American System of Government*, 1955.

A rioter with a Molotov cocktail in his hands is not fighting for civil rights any more than a Klansman with a sheet on his back and mask on his face. They are both more or less what the law declares them: lawbreakers, destroyers of constitutional rights and liberties and ultimately destroyers of a free America.

LYNDON B. JOHNSON, to White House Conference on Equal Employment Opportunity held during rioting in Watts, Los Angeles, August 20, 1965.

Every form of bigotry can be found in ample supply in the legal system of our country. It would seem that Justice (usually depicted as a woman) is indeed blind to racism, sexism, war, and poverty.

FLORYNCE R. KENNEDY, in Robin Morgan, ed., *Sisterhood Is Powerful*, 1970.

It may be true that the law cannot make a man love me, but it can keep him from lynching me, and I think that's pretty important.

MARTIN LUTHER KING, JR., *Wall Street Journal*, November 13, 1962.

Laws are felt only when the individual comes into conflict with them.

SUZANNE LaFOLLETTE, "The Beginnings of Emancipation," *Concerning Women*, 1926.

The law does not exist for the lawyers though there are some of us who seem to think that it does. The law is for all the people and the lawyers are only its ministers.

ROBERT A. LEFLAR, speech, American Judicature Society,
Wall Street Journal, May 27, 1971.

The contempt for law and the contempt for the human consequences of lawbreaking go from the bottom to the top of American society.

MARGARET MEAD, in article by Claire Safran,
"Impeachment," *Redbook*, April, 1974.

It is a further irony that our legal ethic prosecutes those who are forced (economically or psychologically) to offer themselves for sale as objects, but condones the act of buying persons as objects.

KATE MILLETT, *The Prostitution Papers*, 1971.

You have the right to remain silent; anything you say can be held against you in a court of law; you have the right to the presence of an attorney to assist you prior to questioning and to be with you during questioning, and if you cannot afford an attorney, you have the right to have an attorney appointed for you prior to questioning.

MIRANDA WARNING, *Miranda v. Miranda*, June 13, 1966.

The law must be stable, but it must not stand still.

ROSCOE POUND, *Introduction to the Philosophy of Law*, 1922.

Law is experience developed by reason and applied continually to further experience.

ROSCOE POUND, *Christian Science Monitor*, April 24, 1963.

We have the means to change the laws we find unjust or onerous. We cannot, as citizens, pick and choose the laws we will or will not obey.

RONALD REAGAN, on dismissing striking air traffic
controllers, to United Brotherhood of Carpenters and
Joiners, Chicago, Illinois, September 3, 1981.

There was the whole rule of law to consider… the whole fabric of society.

NELSON A. ROCKEFELLER, 1971, in Lois and Alan Gordon,
American Chronicle, 1987.

We are always saying let the law take its course, but what we mean is "Let the law take our course."

WILL ROGERS, February 19, 1935, in Donald Day, ed.,
The Autobiography of Will Rogers, 1949.

It is difficult to make our material condition better by the best law, but it is easy enough to ruin it by bad laws.

THEODORE ROOSEVELT, speech, Providence, Rhode Island,
August 23, 1902.

No man is above the law and no man is below it; nor do we ask any man's permission when we require him to obey it. Obedience to the law is demanded as a right, not asked as a favor.

THEODORE ROOSEVELT, message to Congress, January, 1904.

No people is wholly civilized where a distinction is drawn between stealing an office and stealing a purse.

THEODORE ROOSEVELT, presidential acceptance speech,
Chicago, Illinois, June 22, 1912.

A single revolutionary spark may kindle a fire that, smoldering for a time, may burst into a sweeping and destructive conflagration. It cannot be said that the state is acting arbitrarily or unreasonably when, in the exercise of its judgment as to the measures necessary to protect the public peace and safety, it seeks to extinguish the spark without waiting until it has enkindled the flame or blazed into the conflagration.

Edward Terry Sanford, opinion, Gitlow v. People of
New York, 1925.

Law reform is far too serious a matter to be left to the legal profession.

LESLIE SCARMAN, to New York City Bar Association,
Record, January, 1955.

Law is a reflection and a source of prejudice. It both enforces and suggests forms of bias.

DIANE B. SCHULDER, "Does the Law Oppress Women?"
Robin Morgan, ed., *Sisterhood Is Powerful*, 1970.

When a people lose respect for one bad law, it is but a short step before they include the good laws with the bad and are shortly in rebellion against all law.

OSCAR W. UNDERWOOD, *Drifting Sands of Party Politics*, 1928.

Defining immorality is of course not an easy task, though English judges and American state legislatures seem not to mind taking it on.

GORE VIDAL, "Sex and the Law," *Partisan Review*, Summer, 1965.

It is the spirit and not the form of law that keeps justice alive.

EARL WARREN, *Fortune*, November, 1955.

In civilized life, law floats in a sea of ethics.

EARL WARREN, *New York Times*, November 12, 1962.

What we seek is the reign of law, based upon the consent of the governed and sustained by the organized opinion of mankind.

WOODROW WILSON, on League of Nations, speech,
July 4, 1918.

[The law] is designed to protect the power and privilege of those who write the law and to ward off any values or vision that threatens it.

ANDREW YOUNG, *New York Times*, August 7, 1976.

Life's Lessons

Money is not everything, but it is better than having one's health.

WOODY ALLEN, *Without Feathers*, 1975.

Self-pity in its early stages is as snug as a feather mattress. Only when it hardens does it become uncomfortable.

MAYA ANGELOU, *Gather Together in My Name*, 1974.

Experience is a good teacher, but she sends in terrific bills.

MINNA ANTRIM, *Naked Truth and Veiled Allusions*, 1902.

Golden fetters hurt as cruelly as iron ones.

MINNA ANTRIM, *Naked Truth and Veiled Allusions*, 1902.

In any age, life confronts all but the most obtuse with a set of impossible demands; it is an action to be performed without rehearsal or respite; it is a very confused spectacle to be sorted out and charted; it is a mystery, not indeed to be solved, but to be restated according to some vision, however imperfect. These demands bear down with redoubled force in times of decay and deconstruction, because guiding customs and conventions are in disarray. At first, this loosening of rules looks like liberation, but it is illusory. A permissive society acts liberal or malignant erratically; seeing which, generous youth turns cynic or rebel of principle.

JACQUES BARZUN, in Clifton Fadiman, ed., *Living Philosophies*, 1990.

There is nothing final about a mistake, except its being taken as final.

PHYLLIS BOTTOME, *Strange Fruit*, 1928.

Never pick a fight with anyone who buys ink by the barrel.

JIM BRADY, 1981, in Norman Augustine, *Augustine's Laws*, 1986.

Every great mistake has a halfway moment, a split second when it can be recalled and perhaps remedied.

PEARL S. BUCK, *What America Means to Me*, 1942.

If decisions were a choice between alternatives, decisions would come easy. Decision is the selection and formulation of alternatives.

KENNETH BURKE, *Towards a Better Life*, 1932.

We know life is futile. A man who considers that his life is of very wonderful importance is awfully close to a padded cell.

CLARENCE DARROW, lecture, University of Chicago, 1929.

The first and great commandment is, Don't let them scare you.

ELMER DAVIS, *But We Were Born Free*, 1954.

I have learned in the great University of Hard Knocks a philosophy that no woman who has had an easy life ever acquires. I have learned to live each day as it comes, and not to borrow trouble by dreading tomorrow. It is the dark menace of the future that makes cowards of us.

DOROTHY DIX, *Dorothy Dix, Her Book*, 1926.

Sometimes when you get in a fight with a skunk, you can't tell who started it.

LLOYD DOGGETT, *Time*, November 5, 1984.

Life is a God-damned, stinking, treacherous game, and nine hundred and ninety-nine men out of every thousand are bastards.

THEODORE DREISER, quoting an unidentified newspaper editor, *A Book About Myself*, 1922.

Only a life lived for others is the life worth while.

ALBERT EINSTEIN, *New York Times*, June 20, 1932.

Listen, you son of a bitch, life isn't all a goddamn football game! You won't always get the girl! Life is rejection and pain and loss.

FREDERICK EXLEY, *A Fan's Notes*, 1977.

Modern life is confusing—no "Ms take" about it.

GERALDINE A. FERRARO, *New York Times*, July 13, 1984.

Most people hew the battlements of life from compromise, erecting their impregnable keeps from judicious submissions, fabricating their philosophical drawbridges from emotional retractions and scalding marauders in the boiling oil of sour grapes.

ZELDA FITZGERALD, *Save Me the Waltz*, 1932.

It is easier to live through someone else than to become complete yourself.

BETTY FRIEDAN, *The Feminine Mystique*, 1963.

There are only three things worthwhile—fighting, drinking, and making love.

KATHERINE GEROULD, "The Tortoise," *Vain Oblations*, 1914.

Our lives are littered with mid-course corrections. A full half of us divorced. Many of the women have had career paths that look like games of Chutes and Ladders. We have changed directions and priorities again and again. But our "mistakes" become crucial parts, sometimes the best parts, of the lives we have made.

ELLEN GOODMAN, "Reunion of the Ungeneration," *Washington Post*, June, 1988.

Bromidic though it may sound, some questions *don't* have answers, which is a terribly difficult lesson to learn.

KATHERINE GRAHAM, in Jane Howard, "The Power That Didn't Corrupt," *Ms.*, October, 1974.

Don't hurry, don't worry. You're only here for a short visit. So be sure to stop and smell the flowers.

WALTER HAGEN, *New York Times*, May 22, 1977.

Reality was such a jungle—with no signposts, landmarks, or boundaries.

HELEN HAYES, *On Reflection, An Autobiography*, 1968.

I decided long ago never to look at the right hand of the menu or the price tag of clothes—otherwise I would starve, naked.

HELEN HAYES, *Washington Post*, May 7, 1990.

Those most dedicated to the future are not always the best prophets.

ELINOR HAYS, *Morning Star*, 1961.

The world is a fine place and worth fighting for.

ERNEST HEMINGWAY, *For Whom the Bell Tolls*, 1940.

Life is made up of sobs, sniffles, and smiles, with sniffles predominating.

O. HENRY, "The Gift of the Magi," *The Four Million*, 1906.

Without discipline, there's no life at all.

KATHARINE HEPBURN, on "Dick Cavett Show," April 4, 1975.

Life is an end in itself, and the only question as to whether it is worth living is whether you have enough of it.

OLIVER WENDELL HOLMES, JR., speech, Boston, Massachusetts, 1900.

Life is a romantic business. It is painting a picture, not doing a sum.

OLIVER WENDELL HOLMES, JR., letter to Oswald Ryan, June 5, 1911.

A good scare is worth more to a man than good advice.

EDGAR WATSON HOWE, *Country Town Sayings*, 1922.

Common sense is compelled to make its way without the enthusiasm of anyone; all admit it grudgingly.

EDGAR WATSON HOWE, *The Indignations of E.W. Howe*, 1933.

Life is just one damn thing after another.

ELBERT HUBBARD, *The Roycroft Dictionary and Book of Epigrams*, 1923.

Do not take life too seriously—you will never get out of it alive.

ELBERT HUBBARD, *The Roycroft Dictionary and Book of Epigrams*, 1923.

Experience is the name every one gives his mistakes.

ELBERT HUBBARD, *The Roycroft Dictionary and Book of Epigrams*, 1923.

The greatest mistake you can make in life is to be continually fearing that you will make one.

ELBERT HUBBARD, *Note Book*, 1927.

The early tire gits the roofin' tack.

KIN HUBBARD, *Abe Martin's Broadcast*, 1930.

Live all you can; it's a mistake not to. It doesn't so much matter what you do in particular so long as you have your life.

HENRY JAMES, *The Ambassadors*, 1903.

The philosophic climate of our time inevitably forces its own clothing on us.

WILLIAM JAMES, *The Varieties of Religious Experience*, 1902.

Don't throw a monkey-wrench into the machinery.

PHILANDER CHASE JOHNSON, "Shooting Stars," *Everybody's Magazine*, May, 1920.

Forgive your enemies, but never forget their names.

ATTRIBUTED TO JOHN F. KENNEDY.

Pick battles big enough to matter, small enough to win.

JONATHAN KOZOL, *On Being a Teacher*, 1981.

Life has its heroes and its villains, its soubrettes and its ingenues, and all roles may be acted well.

JOSEPH WOOD KRUTCH, *The Modern Temper*, 1929.

There is nothing more innately human than the tendency to transmute what has become customary into what has been divinely ordained.

SUZANNE LAFOLLETTE, "The Beginnings of Emancipation," *Concerning Women*, 1926.

Living on Earth has always been a dangerous way to spend your time.

ANNE LAMOTT, *Rosie*, 1983.

Experience is a hard teacher because she gives the test first, the lesson afterwards.

VERNON SANDERS LAW, "How to Be a Winner," *This Week*, August 14, 1960.

Where do consequences lead? Depends on the escort?

STANISLAW LEM, *Holiday*, September, 1963.

Money is only money, beans tonight and steak tomorrow. So long as you can look yourself in the eye.

MERIDEL LESUEUR, *Crusaders*, 1955.

One cannot collect all the beautiful shells on the beach.

ANNE MORROW LINDBERGH, *A Gift from the Sea*, 1955.

Life is a loom, weaving illusion.

VACHEL LINDSAY, "The Chinese Nightingale," 1917.

I have a simple philosophy. Fill what's empty. Empty what's full. And scratch where it itches.

ALICE ROOSEVELT LONGWORTH, in Peter Russell and Leonard Ross, *The Best*, 1974.

Never trust a man who combs his hair straight from his left armpit.

ALICE ROOSEVELT LONGWORTH, on Douglas MacArthur, in Michael Teague, *Mrs. L: Conversations with Alice Roosevelt Longworth*, 1981.

It may be necessary temporarily to accept a lesser evil, but one must never label a necessary evil as good.

MARGARET MEAD, *Redbook*, November, 1978.

The basic fact about human existence is not that it is a tragedy, but that it is a bore.

H.L. MENCKEN, *Prejudices*, 1926.

Unrest of spirit is a mark of life.

KARL MENNINGER, *This Week*, October 16, 1958.

The best advice one can offer to both press and public is the suggestion Ronald Reagan himself gave to students in Chicago..."Don't let me get away with it. Check me out. Don't be the sucker generation."

JAMES NATHAN MILLER, "Ronald Reagan and the Techniques of Deception," *Atlantic Monthly*, February, 1984.

Death and taxes and childbirth! There's never any convenient time for any of them!

MARGARET MITCHELL, *Gone with the Wind*, 1936.

Life's under no obligation to give us what we expect. We take what we get and are thankful it's no worse than it is.

MARGARET MITCHELL, *Gone with the Wind*, 1936.

Life is a foreign language; all men mispronounce it.

CHRISTOPHER MORLEY, *Thunder on the Left*, 1925.

Only when a man is safely ensconced under six feet of earth, with several tons of...granite upon his chest, is he in a position to give advice with any certainty, and then he is silent.

A. EDWARD NEWTON, *The Amenities of Book-Collecting and Kindred Affections*, 1918.

We do not live to extenuate the miseries of the past nor to accept as uncurable those of the present.

FAIRFIELD OSBORN, *The Limits of the Earth*, 1953.

Moral: In saying what is obvious, never choose cunning. Yelling works better.

CYNTHIA OZICK, "We Are the Crazy Lady and Other Feisty Feminist Fables," in Francine Klagsbrun, ed., *The First Ms. Reader*, 1972.

Don't look back, somebody might be gaining on you.

SATCHEL PAIGE, ca. 1920, *Sunday News Magazine*, April 6, 1980, ca. 1920.

Bewildered is the fox who lives to find that grapes beyond reach can be *really* sour.

DOROTHY PARKER, "Not Even Funny," *The New Yorker*, March 18, 1933.

The squeaky wheel doesn't always get greased; it often gets replaced.

JOHN PEERS, *1,001 Logical Laws*, 1979.

You start by saying no to requests. Then if you have to go to yes, OK. But if you start with yes, you can't go to no.

MILDRED PERLMAN, *New York Times*, December 1, 1975.

The thing that must survive you is not just the record of your practice, but the principles that are the basis of your practice.

BERNICE JOHNSON REAGON, "Coalition Politics: Turning the Century," *Home Girls*, 1983.

Never invest your money in anything that eats or needs repainting.

BILLY ROSE, *New York Post*, October 26, 1957.

An awful lot of life on this planet is one man's assessment of the other.

WALT W. ROSTOW, in Hugh Sidey, *John F. Kennedy, President: A Reporter's Inside Story*, 1963.

A life without surrender is a life without commitment.

JERRY RUBIN, *Growing (Up) at 37*, 1976.

That life is worth living is the most necessary of assumptions, and, were it not assumed, the most impossible of conclusions.

GEORGE SANTAYANA, "Reason in Common Sense," *The Life of Reason*, 1905–1906.

There is no cure for birth and death save to enjoy the interval.

GEORGE SANTAYANA, "War Shrines," *Soliloquies in England and Later Soliloquies*, 1922.

Even without wars, life is dangerous.

ANNE SEXTON, "Hurry Up Please It's Time," *The Death Notebooks*, 1974.

There are two things to aim at in life: first to get what you want; and, after that, to enjoy it. Only the wisest of mankind achieve the second.

LOGAN PEARSALL SMITH, *Afterthoughts*, 1931.

It is awfully important to know what is and what is not your business.

GERTRUDE STEIN, "What Is English Literature," 1934, in Patricia Meyerowitz, ed., *Gertrude Stein: Writings and Lectures 1909–1945*, 1974.

Ninety percent of everything is crap.

"STURGEON'S LAW," Theodore Sturgeon, in Robert Forward and Joel Davis, *Mirror Matter*, 1988.

It is better to ask some of the questions than to know all the answers.

JAMES THURBER, "The Scotty Who Knew Too Much," *Fables for Our Time*, 1940.

We learn the rope of life by untying its knots.

JEAN TOOMER, *Definitions and Aphorisms, LI*, 1931.

Study men, not historians.

HARRY S TRUMAN, in Robert H. Ferrell, *Off the Record*, 1980.

Always do right—this will gratify some and astonish the rest.

MARK TWAIN, message to Young People's Society, Greenpoint Presbyterian Church, Brooklyn, New York, February 16, 1901.

Life is like an overlong drama through which we sit being nagged by the vague memories of having read the reviews.

JOHN UPDIKE, *The Coup*, 1978.

People who fight fire with fire usually end up with ashes.

ABIGAIL VAN BUREN, newspaper column, "Dear Abby," March 7, 1974.

People do not wish to appear foolish; to avoid the appearance of foolishness, they were willing actually to remain fools.

ALICE WALKER, "One Child of One's Own: A Meaningful Digression Within the Work(s)," *In Search of Our Mothers' Gardens*, 1979.

Life is better than death, I believe, if only because it is less boring, and because it has fresh peaches in it.

ALICE WALKER, speech, Grace Cathedral, San Francisco, March 16, 1982, in Barbara Smith, ed., *Home Girls*, 1983.

It is better to be looked over than overlooked.

MAE WEST, in Joseph Weintraub, *The Wit and Wisdom of Mae West*, 1967.

My advice to you is not to inquire why or whither, but just enjoy your ice cream while it's on your plate—that's my philosophy.

THORNTON WILDER, *The Skin of Our Teeth*, 1942.

The cost of living is going up and the chance of living is going down.

FLIP WILSON, in Eric Lax, *On Being Funny*, 1975.

Men

See also **American Society; Americans on Americans; Children and Youth; Dreams and Ideals; Relationships; Social Issues**—Violence; **Women**

Man forgives woman anything save the wit to outwit him.

MINNA ANTRIM, *Naked Truth and Veiled Allusions*, 1902.

We are living at an important and fruitful moment now, for it is clear to men that the images of adult manhood given by the popular culture are worn out; a man can no longer depend on them. By the time a man is thirty-five he knows that the images of the right man, the tough man, the true man which he received in high school do not work in life.

ROBERT BLY, Preface, *Iron John*, 1990.

My ancestors wandered lost in the wilderness for 40 years because even in biblical times, men would not stop to ask for directions.

ELAYNE BOOSLER, *Time*, Fall, 1990.

Men build bridges and throw railroads across deserts, and yet they contend successfully that the job of sewing on a button is beyond them. Accordingly, they don't have to sew buttons.

HEYWOOD BROUN, "Holding a Baby," *Seeing Things at Night*, 1921.

But chicks don't know that guys are like dogs. You know, you take a dog, you beat the shit out of him—POW! POW!—but he'll keep coming back. Ladies are like cats. You yell at a cat *once*—Siamese cat—*phsst*! They're gone.

LENNY BRUCE, ca. 1960, in John Cohen, ed., *The Essential Lenny Bruce*, 1967.

Male culture is dominated by the concept of hierarchy, as anyone can attest who's sat through a weekend of football on television.

ROBERT CAMPBELL, "Why Tall Buildings Are Held in Low Esteem These Days," *Boston Globe*, February 10, 1991.

It is no more right for all men to govern all women than it was for one man to govern one woman. It is no more right for men to govern women than it was for one man to govern other men.

CARRIE CHAPMAN CATT, speech, National American Woman Suffrage Association, February, 1902.

Maleness remains a recessive genetic trait like color-blindness and hemophilia, with which it is linked. The suspicion that maleness is abnormal and the Y chromosome is an accidental mutation boding no good for the race is strongly supported by the recent discovery by geneticists that congenital killers and criminals are possessed of not one but *two* Y chromosomes, bearing a double dose, as it were, of genetically undesirable maleness.

ELIZABETH GOULD DAVIS, *The First Sex*, 1971.

The American male at the peak of his physical powers and appetites, driving 160 big white horses across the scenes of an increasingly open society, with weekend money in his pocket and with little prior exposure to trouble and tragedy, personifies "an accident going to happen."

JOHN SLOAN DICKEY, "Conscience and the Undergraduate," *Atlantic*, April, 1955.

[T]here's nowhere for [the marginal man] to put that pride except into the politics of gesture: the macho stance, the 75-mph takeoff down the expressway, and, eventually, maybe, the drawn gun.

BARBARA EHRENREICH, "Angry Young Men," *Utne Reader*, May/June 1991.

The iconic myth surrounding him is built on American notions of heroism: the index of a man's value as measured in *physical courage*. Such ideas have perverted manliness into a self-absorbed race for cheap thrills.

GRETEL EHRLICH, *The Solace of Open Spaces*, 1985.

Every twelve-year-old boy knows what must be done to make it as a man, what it will cost him to be an American: the lessons seep through the skin forever. Money must be made, nothing is as masculine as this.

GLORIA EMERSON, Prologue, *Some American Men*, 1985.

Once I believed, as who did not, that Americans always had a freer hand, could take life in larger, more rapid steps, although, as they used to say, it was a man's world, I had no way of understanding there might be penalties for them to pay. Even now what many women most dislike about men—their hardness; their lack of the generous, quick response; the distance they keep; their faces that so often seem shut; the things they find difficult to say; their tendency to tell women when a decision is required, "We'll see"—is often the result of the old stances they are certain they must assume. In a country whose insistence on delusion seems without clear limits, the old definition of masculinity still persists. And it persists because of hidden permission and unspoken expections.

GLORIA EMERSON, Prologue, Some American Men, 1985.

Whatever they may be in public life, whatever their relations with men, in their relations with women, all men are rapists, and that's all they are. They rape us with their eyes, their laws, and the codes.

MARILYN FRENCH, The Women's Room, 1977.

If a number of single American men suffer from what the pop psychologists call the Peter Pan syndrome, it may be biology that has destined them for Never-Never Land. There is, for some, rooted in...lifelong fertility, the sense that as fatherhood is open-ended so is life. It allows some men to postpone so much, even maturity.

ELLEN GOODMAN, "Men-O-Pause," Washington Post, November, 1986.

We will no longer be led only by that half of the population whose socialization, through toys, games, values and expectations, sanctions violence as the final assertion of manhood, synonymous with nationhood.

WILMA SCOTT HEIDE, NOW Official Biography, 1971.

The natural man has a difficult time getting along in this world. Half the people think he is a scoundrel because he is not a hypocrite.

EDGAR WATSON HOWE, Sinner Sermons, 1926.

Behind every man who achieves success

Stand a mother, a wife and the IRS.

ETHEL JACOBSON, Reader's Digest, April, 1973.

If you had to work in the environment of Washington, D.C., as I do, and watch those men who are so imprisoned and so confined by their 18th-century thought patterns, you would know that if anybody is going to be liberated, it's men who must be liberated in this country.

BARBARA JORDAN, speech, International Women's Year Conference, Austin, Texas, November 10, 1975.

It's hard for men to find the best strategy for campaigning against a woman. It's like hitting a marshmallow. Either you appear too aggressive or as though you can't handle it.

NANCY KASSENBAUM, New York Times, September 9, 1984.

Women speak because they wish to speak, whereas a man speaks only when driven to speech by something outside himself—like, for instance, he can't find any clean socks.

JEAN KERR, "How to Talk to a Man," The Snake Has All the Lines, 1960.

As men became the primary cog in industrial production, they lost touch with the earth and the parts of themselves that needed the earth to survive. Men by the millions—who long prided themselves on their husbandry of family, community, and land—were forced into a system whose ultimate goal was to turn one man against another in the competitive "jungle" of industrialized society. As the industrial revolution advanced, men lost not only their independence and dignity, but also the sense of personal creativity and responsibility associated with individual crafts and small-scale farming.

ANDREW KIMBRELL, "A Time for Men to Pull Together," Utne Reader, May/June 1991.

Man *qua* thinker may delight in the intricacies of psychology, but man *qua* lover has not learned to feel in its terms.

JOSEPH WOOD KRUTCH, "The Genesis of a Mood," The Modern Temper, 1929.

He had grown up in a country run by politicians who sent the pilots to man the bombers to kill the babies to make the world safe for children to grow up in.

URSULA K. LEGUIN, The Lathe of Heaven, 1971.

[For American men] maintaining one's lawn is more important than maintaining one's friendships.

LARRY LETICH, "Do You Know Who Your Friends Are?" Utne Reader, May/June 1991.

Women, it's true, make human beings, but only men can make men.

MARGARET MEAD, Male and Female, 1948.

Women want mediocre men, and men are working to be as mediocre as possible.

MARGARET MEAD, Quote Magazine, May 15, 1958.

The male form of a female liberationist is a male liberationist—a man who realizes the unfairness of having to work all his life to support a wife and children so that someday his widow may live in comfort, a man who points out that commuting to a job he doesn't like is just as oppressive as his wife's imprisonment in a suburb, a man who rejects his exclusion, by society and most women, from participation in childbirth and the engrossing, delightful care of young children—a man, in fact, who wants to relate himself to people and the world around person.

MARGARET MEAD, *Redbook*, August, 1975.

Men have a much better time of it than women. For one thing, they marry later. For another thing, they die earlier.

H.L. MENCKEN, *A Mencken Chrestomathy*, 1949.

There is one unmistakable lesson in American history: a community that allows a large number of young men to grow up in broken families, dominated by women, never acquiring any stable relationship to male authority, never acquiring any set of rational expectations about the future—that community asks for and gets chaos. Crime, violence, unrest, disorder—most particularly the furious, unrestrained lashing out at the whole social structure—that is not only to be expected; it is very near to inevitable. And it is richly deserved.

DANIEL PATRICK MOYNIHAN, *Family and Nation*, 1965.

Perhaps the time has come for a new agenda. Women, after all, are not a big problem. Our society does not suffer from burdensome amounts of empathy and altruism, or a plague of nurturance. The problem is men—or more accurately, maleness.... Men are killing themselves doing all the things that our society wants them to do. At every age they're dying in accidents, they're being shot, they drive cars badly, ride the tops of elevators, they're two-fisted drinkers. And violence against women is incredibly pervasive. Maybe it's men's raging hormones, [or]...because they're trying to be a *man*.

"GUNS AND DOLLS," *Newsweek*, May 28, 1990.

The average American male stands five feet nine inches...158 pounds, prefers brunettes, baseball, beefsteak, and French fried potatoes, and thinks the ability to run a home smoothly and efficiently is the most important quality in a wife.

READER'S DIGEST, 1954.

I have no hostility towards men. Some of my best friends are men. I married a man, and my father was a man.

JILL RUCKELSHAUS, in article by Frederic A. Birmingham, *Saturday Evening Post*, March 3, 1973.

It takes a woman twenty years to make a man of her son, and another woman twenty minutes to make a fool of him.

HELEN ROWLAND, *Reflections of a Bachelor Girl*, 1903.

The average man takes all the natural taste out of his food by covering it with ready-made sauces, and all the personality out of a woman by covering her with his ready-made ideals.

HELEN ROWLAND, *A Guide to Men*, 1922.

I was about half in love with her by the time we sat down. That's the thing about girls. Every time they do something pretty, even if they're not much to look at, or even if they're sort of stupid, you fall half in love with them, and then you never know *where* the hell you are.

J.D. SALINGER, *Catcher in the Rye*, 1951.

Warriors and toilers: those seemed, in my boyhood vision, to be the chief destinies for men.

SCOTT RUSSELL SANDERS, "The Men We Carry in Our Minds," *Utne Reader*, May/June 1991.

The young man who has not wept is a savage, and the old man who will not laugh is a fool.

GEORGE SANTAYANA, *Dialogues in Limbo*, 1925.

That common cold of the male psyche, fear of commitment.

RICHARD SCHICKEL, *Time*, November 29, 1983.

Things are so easy to make in this Age of Production. Men are so hard to grow.

LILLIAN SMITH, *Killers of the Dream*, 1949.

What is the use of being a little boy if you are going to grow up to be a man.

GERTRUDE STEIN, *Everybody's Autobiography*, 1937.

Early to rise and early to bed makes a male healthy and wealthy and dead.

JAMES THURBER, "The Shrike and the Chipmunks," *Fables for Our Time*, 1940.

A man, it seems, may be intellectually in complete sympathy with a woman's aims. But only about ten percent of him is his intellect—the other ninety his emotions.

MABEL ULRICH, "A Doctor's Diary, 1904–1932," *Scribner's Magazine*, June, 1933.

What is it that distinguishes the American Man from his counterparts in other climes; what *is* it that makes him so special? He is quietly affirmative. He is trustworthy, loyal, helpful, friendly, courteous, kind, obedient, cheerful, thrifty, brave, clean, and reverent.

JOHN UPDIKE, "Anywhere Is Where You Hang Your Hat," *Assorted Prose*, 1965.

A healthy male adult bore consumes each year one and a half times his own weight in other people's patience.

JOHN UPDIKE, "Confessions of a Wild Bore," *Assorted Prose*, 1965.

There is hardly an American male of my generation who has not at one time or another tried to master the victory cry of the great ape as it issued from the androgynous chest of Johnny Weissmuller, to the accompaniment of thousands of arms and legs snapping during attempts to swing from tree to tree in the backyards of the Republic.

GORE VIDAL, "The Waking Dream: Tarzan Revisited," *Esquire*, December, 1963.

I think we're a kind of desperation. We're sort of a maddening luxury. The basic and essential human is the woman, and all that we're doing is trying to brighten up the place. That's why all the birds who belong to our sex have prettier feathers—because males have got to try and justify their existence. Look how little we do to keep the race going.

ORSON WELLES, interview with David Frost, *The Americans*, 1970.

A man in the house is worth two in the street.

MAE WEST, *Belle of the Nineties*, 1934.

There is a period near the beginning of every man's life when he has little to cling to except his unmanageable dream, little to support him except good health, and nowhere to go but all over the place.

E.B. WHITE, "The Years of Wonder," March 13, 1961, *Essays of E.B. White*, 1977.

Nature

See also **Government and Politics**—Domestic Policy; **Human Environments**; **Science and Technology**; **Social Issues**—Environment and Pollution; **States and Regions**

Everything in nature invites us constantly to be what we are.

GRETEL EHRLICH, *The Solace of Open Spaces*, 1985.

In America nature is autocratic, saying "I am not arguing, I am telling you."

ERIK H. ERIKSON, *Childhood and Society*, 1950.

Nature is not affected by finance. If someone offered you ten thousand dollars to let them touch you on your eyeball without you blinking, you would never collect the money. At the very last moment, Nature would force you to blink your eye. Nature will protect her own.

DICK GREGORY, *The Shadow That Scares Me*, 1968.

Nature: The Unseen Intelligence which loved us into being, and is disposing of us by the same token.

ELBERT HUBBARD, *The Roycroft Dictionary and Book of Epigrams*, 1923.

Nature has no one distinguishable ultimate tendency with which to feel a sympathy.

WILLIAM JAMES, *The Varieties of Religious Experience*, 1902.

What nature delivers to us is never stale. Because what nature creates has eternity in it.

ISAAC BASHEVIS SINGER, in article by Richard Burgh, *New York Times Magazine*, November 26, 1978.

EVOLUTION

Evolution is fascinating to watch. To me it is most interesting when one can observe the evolution of a single man.

SHANA ALEXANDER, "Evolution of a Rebel Priest," *The Feminine Eye*, 1970.

A man is the sum of his ancestors; to reform him you must begin with a dead ape and work downward through a million graves. He is like the lower end of a suspended chain; you can sway him slightly to the right or the left, but remove him slightly to the right or the left, but remove your hand and he falls into line with the other links.

AMBROSE BIERCE, *Collected Works*, 1911.

One of the odd things about evolution is why it has gone on so long, because you would have thought that any decent world would have stopped with the amoeba. It's an extraodinarily satisfying organism and we've been going into what you might call pathological complexity ever since, ending up, of course, with the Federal Reserve System.

KENNETH BOULDING, "The World as an Economic Region," *Regional Economic Policy*, 1974.

There are no shortcuts in evolution.

LOUIS D. BRANDEIS, speech, Boston, Massachusetts, April 22, 1904.

There is no more reason to believe that man descended from some inferior animal than there is to believe that a stately mansion has descended from a small cottage.

WILLIAM JENNINGS BRYAN, Dayton, Tennessee, July 28, 1925.

All the ills from which America suffers can be traced back to the teaching of evolution. It would be better to destroy every other book ever written, and save just the first three verses of Genesis.

WILLIAM JENNINGS BRYAN, 1923, in Richard Hofstadter, *Anti-Intellectualism in American Life*, 1963.

[Evolution theory is a] program of infidelity masquerading under the name of science.

WILLIAM JENNINGS BRYAN, 1923, in Richard Hofstadter, *Anti-Intellectualism in American Life*, 1963.

As to modesty and decency, if we are simians we have done well, considering: but if we are something else—fallen angels—we have indeed fallen far.

CLARENCE DAY, *This Simian World*, 1920.

It was the failures who had always won, but by the time they won they had come to be called successes. This is the final paradox, which men call evolution.

LOREN EISELEY, "The Inner Galaxy," *The Star Thrower*, 1964.

Any careful study of living things, whether wolves, bears or man, reminds one of the same direct truth; also of the clarity of the fact that evolution itself is obviously not some process of drowning beings clutching at straws and climbing from suffering and travail and virtual expiration to tenuous, momentary survival. Rather, evolution has been a matter of days well-lived, chameleon strength, energy, zappy sex, sunshine stored up, inventiveness, competitiveness, and the whole fun of busy brain cells.

EDWARD HOAGLAND, "Thoughts on Returning to the City
After Five Months on a Mountain Where the Wolves
Howled," *Red Wolves and Black Bears*, 1976.

If you believe in evolution...you can trace all of our lower back problems to the time when the first hominid stood erect.

HUGO A. KEIM, "That Aching Back," *Time*, July 14, 1980.

Darwin had proved scientifically what Americans had long believed, that America was the cutting edge of the evolutionary process, the most progressive representative of all humanity.

JAMES OLIVER ROBERTSON, *American Myth, American Reality*, 1980.

It is disturbing to discover in oneself these curious revelations of the validity of the Darwinian theory. If it is true that we have sprung from the ape, there are occasions when my own spring appears not to have been very far.

CORNELIA OTIS SKINNER, *The Ape in Me*, 1959.

If evolution was worth its salt, by now it should've evolved something better than survival of the fittest. Yeah, I told 'em I think a better idea would be survival of the wittiest. At least, that way, the creatures that didn't survive could've died *laughing*.

JANE WAGNER, *The Search for Intelligent Life in the
Universe*, performed by Lily Tomlin, 1986.

FAUNA

Nothing wholly admirable ever happens in this country except the migration of birds.

BROOKS ATKINSON, "March 23," *Once Around the Sun*, 1951.

A dog teaches a boy fidelity, perseverance, and to turn around three times before lying down.

ROBERT BENCHLEY, Introduction, *Artemus Ward, His Book*,
1964.

We need another and a wiser and perhaps a more mystical concept of animals....In a world older and more complete than ours they move finished and complete, gifted with extensions of the senses we have lost or never attained, living by voices we shall never hear. They are not brethren, they are not underlings; they are other nations, caught with ourselves in the net of life and time, fellow prisoners of the splendour and travail of the earth.

HENRY BESTON, *The Outermost House*, 1928.

Man, n. An animal so lost in rapturous contemplation of what he thinks he is as to overlook what he undubitably ought to be. His chief occupation is extermination of other animals and his own species, which, however, multiplies with such insistent rapidity as to infest the whole habitable earth and Canada.

AMBROSE BIERCE, *The Devil's Dictionary*, 1906.

The owl, that bird of onomatopoetic name, is a repetitious question wrapped in feathery insulation especially for Winter delivery.

HAL BORLAND, "Questioner," *Sundial of the Seasons*,
1964.

The ability to make love frivolously is the thing which distinguishes human beings from the beasts.

HEYWOOD BROUN, in Robert E. Drennan, *The Algonquin
Wits*, 1968.

Over increasingly large areas of the United States, spring now comes unheralded by the return of the birds, and the early mornings are strangely silent where once they were filled with the beauty of bird song.

RACHEL CARSON, *The Silent Spring*, 1962.

The Dodo never had a chance. He seems to have been invented for the sole purpose of becoming extinct and that was all he was good for.

WILL CUPPY, *How to Become Extinct*, 1941.

Animals give us their constant, unjaded faces and we burden them with our bodies and civilized ordeals.

GRETEL EHRLICH, *The Solace of Open Spaces*, 1985.

Of all the animals on earth, man has shown himself to be the most cruel and brutal. He is the only animal that will create instruments of death for his own destruction. Man is the only animal on all the earth that has ever been known to burn its young as a sacrifice to appease the wrath of some imaginary deity. He is the only one that will build homes, towns, and cities at such a cost in sacrifice and suffering and turn around and destroy them in war.

ATTRIBUTED TO "AN AMERICAN HILL-COUNTRY PHILOSOPHER" BY J. WILLIAM FULBRIGHT, *Old Myths and New Realities*, 1964.

Cats seem to go on the principle that it never does any harm to ask for what you want.

JOSEPH WOOD KRUTCH, "February," *The Twelve Seasons*, 1949.

A human being: an ingenious assembly of portable plumbing.

CHRISTOPHER MORLEY, *Human Being*, 1932.

A door is what a dog is perpetually on the wrong side of.

OGDEN NASH, "A Dog's Best Friend Is His Illiteracy," *The Private Dining Room*, 1953.

Pigs get a bad press. Pigs are regarded as selfish and greedy—as living garbage pails. Pigs are the villains in George Orwell's *Animal Farm*. Pigs have little mean eyes. There is truth in this account—not that it's entirely the fault of the pigs. For perhaps five thousand generations pigs have been deliberately bred to be gluttonous.... Do the same thing with human beings for five thousand generations, and it would be interesting to see what kind of people resulted.

NOEL PERRIN, *Second Person Rural*, 1980.

Ants are so much like human beings as to be an embarrassment. They farm fungi, raise aphids as livestock, launch armies into war, use chemical sprays to alarm and confuse enemies, capture slaves, engage in child labor, exchange information ceaselessly. They do everything but watch television.

LEWIS THOMAS, *The Lives of a Cell*, 1974.

When you consider the size of an individual termite, photographed standing alongside his nest, he ranks with the New Yorker and shows a better sense of organization than a resident of Los Angeles.

LEWIS THOMAS, *The Lives of a Cell*, 1974.

Man loves the dog because the dog is fool enough to trust Man. On the other hand, the cat obeys the Scriptures: "Put not thy trust in things." The cat is like the wise man: he trusts a principle; not a man of principle.

MELVIN B. TOLSON, "Tigers and Lions and Men," *Washington Tribune*, July 27, 1940.

Dogs' lives are too short. Their only fault, really.

AGNES SLIGH TURNBULL, *The Flowering*, 1972.

As a thinker and planner the ant is the equal of any savage race of men; as a self-educated specialist in several arts she is the superior of any savage race of men; and in one or two high mental qualities she is above the reach of any man, savage or civilized.

MARK TWAIN, *What Is Man?*, 1906.

The best thing about animals is that they don't talk much.

THORNTON WILDER, *The Skin of Our Teeth*, 1942.

FLORA

Our attitude toward plants is a singularly narrow one. If we see any immediate utility in a plant we foster it. If for any reason we find its presence undesirable or merely a matter of indifference, we may condemn it to destruction forthwith.

RACHEL CARSON, *The Silent Spring*, 1962.

I like trees because they seem more resigned to the way they have to live than other things do.

WILLA CATHER, *O Pioneers!*, 1913.

They [trees] hang on from a past no theory can recover. They will survive us. The air makes their music. Otherwise they live in savage silence, though mites and nematodes and spiders teem at their roots, and though the energy with which they feed on the sun and are able to draw water sometimes hundreds of feet up their trunks and into their twigs and branches calls for a deafening volume of sound.

JOHN HAY, "Living with Trees," *The Undiscovered Country*, 1981.

There is that in the glance of a flower which may at times control the greatest of creation's braggart lords.

JOHN MUIR, *A Thousand-Mile Walk to the Gulf*, 1916.

The forests of America, however slighted by man, must have been a great delight to God, because they were the best He ever planted.

JOHN MUIR, in John Gunther, *Inside U.S.A.*, 1947.

A tree is a tree—how many more do you need to look at?

RONALD REAGAN, speech, Western Wood Products Association, September 12, 1965.

The redwoods, once seen, leave a mark or create a vision that stays with you always....It's not only their unbelievable stature, nor the color which seems to shift and vary under your eyes, no, they are not like any trees we know, they are ambassadors from another time.

JOHN STEINBECK, *Travels with Charley*, 1962.

As an instrument of planetary home repair, it is hard to imagine anything as safe as a tree.

JONATHAN WEINER, *The Next One Hundred Years*, 1990.

HUMAN BEINGS AND NATURE

Nature is not easy to live with. It is hard to have rain on your cut hay, or floodwater over your cropland, or coyotes in your sheep; it is hard when nature does not respect your intentions, and she never does exactly respect them. Moreover, such problems belong to all of us, to the human lot. Humans who do not experience them are exempt only because they are paying (or underpaying) other humans such as farmers to deal with nature on their behalf.

WENDELL BERRY, 1985, "Preserving Wildness," *Home Economics*, 1987.

When the Pleiades and the wind in the grass are no longer a part of the human spirit, a part of very flesh and bone, man becomes, as it were, a kind of cosmic outlaw, having neither the completeness and integrity of the animal nor the birthright of a true humanity.

HENRY BESTON, Foreword, *The Outermost House*, 1928.

Some people are like ants. Give them a warm day and a piece of ground and they start digging. There the similarity ends. Ants keep on digging. Most people don't. They establish contact with the soil, absorb so much vernal vigor that they can't stay in one place, and desert the fork or spade to see how the rhubarb is coming and whether the asparagus is yet in sight.

HAL BORLAND, *New York Times*, April 27, 1947.

One of the emptiest of man's boasts is that he has mastered his environment, this earth on which he lives. Spring after Spring he sees the floods come, sometimes minor, sometimes major and disastrous, but always water overflowing and invading land that man doesn't want flooded. And despite dams, dikes, diversion channels and all manner of controls, the streams from brook to river still have their way, and about all that

man can do when the floods come is issue warnings and help people get out of the way of the water.

HAL BORLAND, *New York Times*, April 10, 1960.

The people cannot conquer the river; it cannot shake them from its bank. It is like an endless war wherein first one side and then the other is victorious.

JUANITA BROOKS, "The Water's In," *Harper's*, May, 1941.

If I were to name the three most precious resources of life, I should say books, friends, and nature; and the greatest of these, at least the most constant and always at hand, is nature.

JOHN BURROUGHS, "The Art of Seeing Things," *Leaf and Tendril*, 1908.

We are rooted to the air through our lungs and to the soil through our stomachs. We are walking trees and floating plants.

JOHN BURROUGHS, "The Grist of the Gods," *Leaf and Tendril*, 1908.

Rocks do not recommend the land to the tiller of the soil, but they recommend it to those who reap a harvest of another sort—the artist, the poet, the walker, the student and lover of all primitive open-air things.

JOHN BURROUGHS, "The Friendly Rocks," *Under the Apple Trees*, 1916.

Here were the imponderable processes and forces of the cosmos, harmonious and soundless. Harmony, that was it!....The universe was a cosmos, not a chaos; man was as rightfully a part of that cosmos as were the day and night.

RICHARD E. BYRD, on flying over the North Pole, 1928, in Lois and Alan Gordon, *American Chronicle*, 1987.

Only within the moment of time represented by the present century has one species—man—acquired significant power to alter the nature of his world.

RACHEL CARSON, *The Silent Spring*, 1962.

The "control of nature" is a phrase conceived in arrogance, born of the Neanderthal age of biology and philosophy, when it was supposed that nature exists for the convenience of man.

RACHEL CARSON, *The Silent Spring*, 1962.

To be head-taut with the stars around you, foot secure on soil and stone, to know your direction and return through outer signs, is as new as it is ancient. We are still people of the planet, with all its original directions waiting in our being.

JOHN HAY, "Homing," *The Undiscovered Country*, 1981.

Farming, like mining or house-building or any construction, is one way humans use land; it is no more "natural" a land use than oil-drilling.

JANET KAUFFMAN, "Letting Go: The Virtue of Vacant Ground," in Michael Martone, ed., *A Sense of Place,* 1988.

The wild is a place to be tamed. It is an arrogant designation of priority—make the world over for humans. Americans, seeing landscape from the beginning as real estate, are scrupulous about dealing in it, and in prosperous areas all over the country, a fierce moral judgment falls on "waste" places, scrubland, even the vacant lots in developments, where the ragweed's got a good hold. For God's sake, do something with it! everybody says.

JANET KAUFFMAN, "Letting Go: The Virtue of Vacant Ground," in Michael Martone, ed., *A Sense of Place,* 1988.

Get you off the skin of this world.

STEPHEN KING AND PETER STRAUB, *The Talisman,* 1984.

The cockroach and the birds were both here long before we were. Both could get along very well without us, although it is perhaps significant that of the two the cockroach would miss us more.

JOSEPH WOOD KRUTCH, "November," *The Twelve Seasons,* 1949.

Conservation is a state of harmony between men and land.

ALDO LEOPOLD, *A Sand County Almanac,* 1949.

Man's role is uncertain, undefined, and perhaps unnecessary.

MARGARET MEAD, *Male and Female,* 1948.

The Kiowas are a summer people; they abide the cold and keep to themselves, but when the season turns and the land becomes warm and vital they cannot hold still; an old love of going returns upon them.

N. SCOTT MOMADAY, *The Way to Rainy Mountain,* 1969.

It is unfair to blame man too fiercely for being pugnacious; he learned the habit from Nature.

CHRISTOPHER MORLEY, *Inward Ho!,* 1923.

Everybody needs beauty as well as bread, places to play in and pray in, where Nature may heal and cheer and give strength to body and soul alike.

JOHN MUIR, *The Yosemite,* 1912.

Man is that curious creature who, though partly determined and limited by the necessities of nature, also possesses a rational freedom which enables him to harness the forces of nature in the world and to transmute the natural appetites and drives in his own nature so that he can conceive ends and entertain ambitions which exceed the limits which pure nature sets for all her creatures except man.

REINHOLD NIEBUHR, *The Structure of Nations and Empires,* 1959.

Whatever life is (and nobody can define it) it is something forever changing shape, fleeting, escaping us into death. Life is indeed the only thing that can die, and it begins to die as soon as it is born, and never ceases dying. Each of us is constantly experiencing cellular death. For the renewal of our tissues means a corresponding death of them, so that death and rebirth become, biologically, right and left hand of the same thing. All growing is at the same time a dying away from that which lived yesterday.

DONALD CULROSS PEATTIE, *The Road of a Naturalist,* 1941.

Man's unique reward...is that while animals survive by adjusting themselves to their background, man survives by adjusting his background to himself.

AYN RAND, *For the New Intellectual,* 1961.

Man is distinctly more aggressive, cruel, and relentless than any of the other apes.

BENJAMIN SPOCK, *Decent and Indecent,* 1970.

We simply need that wild country available to us, even if we never do more than drive to its edge and look in. For it can be a means of reassuring ourselves of our sanity as creatures, a part of the geography of hope.

WALLACE STEGNER, "The Wilderness Idea," in David Brower, ed., *Wilderness: America's Living Heritage,* 1960.

Nature is neutral. Man has wrested from nature the power to make the world a desert or to make the deserts bloom. There is no evil in the atom; only in men's souls.

ADLAI E. STEVENSON, speech, Hartford, Connecticut, September 18, 1952.

Watching television, you'd think we lived at bay, in total jeopardy, surrounded on all sides by human-seeking germs, shielded against infection and death only by a chemical technology that enables us to keep killing them off.

LEWIS THOMAS, "Germs," *The Lives of a Cell,* 1974.

My attraction for mosquitoes is so great that people who have some reason to walk near stagnant ponds or swampy marshes sometimes ask me along as a means of drawing off attackers, the way a quarterback who intends to pass might first send a decoy halfback into the line without the ball in the hope of having him jumped on by the opposition's largest and most vicious linemen.

CALVIN TRILLIN, "Fear of Chiggers," King Features Syndicate, August 31, 1986.

My heart and I lie small upon the earth like a grain of throbbing sand.

ZITKALA-SA, *Atlantic Monthly*, December, 1902.

LAND

Though we have established the right of individuals to own pieces of land, the implication has always been that this was a trust—not an absolute right. And judging by the manner in which that trust has been abused by many of its present, private owners, a review of this arrangement may be in order.

PETER BLAKE, *God's Own Junkyard*, 1964.

No people has inherited a more naturally beautiful land than we: within an area representing a mere 6 per cent of the land surface of the globe we can point to mountain ranges as spectacular as those of the Dolomites and to jungles as colorful as those of the Amazon valley; to lake-studded forests as lovely as those of Finland and to rolling hills as gentle as those around Salzburg; to cliffs that rival those of the French Riviera and to sandy beaches that are unexcelled even by the shores of Jutland; in short, to about as varied and thrilling a geography as has ever been presented to man.

PETER BLAKE, *God's Own Junkyard*, 1964.

When Indians speak of the continent they yielded, they are not referring only to the loss of some millions of acres in real estate. They have in mind that the land supported a universe of things they knew, valued, and loved.

DECLARATION OF INDIAN PURPOSE, American Indian Conference, Chicago, Illinois, June, 1961.

Where Indian people had had a reverence for the productiveness of the land, whites wanted to make the land support their way of life whether it was suited to do so or not.

VINE DELORIA, JR., *We Talk, You Listen*, 1970.

The bare, uncompromising face of the land is too much for us to behold, and so we clothe it in myth, sentiment, and imposed expectations.

ROBERT FINCH, "Into the Maze," *The Primal Place*, 1983.

I suppose that those who go to islands like this one are a hard-core subspecies of summer people. Water is the last line of defense against malls and modernism. The ocean may be a saline preservative against change. Those who choose islands choose also to believe that the fog can protect their refuge the way the mists and magic protected Brigadoon.

ELLEN GOODMAN, "Hometowns," *Washington Post*, August, 1985.

We have an arsenal of ideas about land use possibly as dangerous to human life on the planet as the use of nuclear arms.

JANET KAUFFMAN, "Letting Go: The Virtue of Vacant Ground," in Michael Martone, ed., *A Sense of Place*, 1988.

Much has been written about the beauty, the stillness, the terror of the desert but little about its flies.

BELLE LIVINGSTONE, *Belle Out of Order*, 1959.

The land is like poetry: it is inexplicably coherent, it is transcendent in its meaning, and it has the power to elevate a consideration of human life.

BARRY LOPEZ, "The Country of the Mind," *Arctic Dreams*, 1986.

Throughout our history, our greatest resource has been our land—forests and plains, mountains and marshlands, rivers and lakes. Our land has sustained us. It has given us a love of freedom, a sense of security, and courage to test the unknown.

RICHARD M. NIXON, message to Congress, 1970.

Night comes to the desert all at once, as if someone turned off the light.

JOYCE CAROL OATES, "Interior Monologue," *The Wheel of Love and Other Stories*, 1969.

The Grand Canyon is carved deep by the master hand; it is the gulf of silence, widened in the desert; it is all time inscribing the naked rock; it is the book of earth.

DONALD CULROSS PEATTIE, *The Road of a Naturalist*, 1941.

The only people who feel they belong to the land, and so to each other, are the people we call Indian. They are the people who made the wilderness their own.

RICHARD RHODES, *Playboy*, January, 1972.

SEASONS

Ah, summer, what power you have to make us suffer and like it.

RUSSELL BAKER, *New York Times*, June 27, 1965.

To see a hillside white with dogwood bloom is to know a particular ecstasy of beauty, but to walk the gray Winter woods and find the buds which will resurrect that beauty in another May is to partake of continuity.

HAL BORLAND, *New York Times*, November 28, 1948.

There is this about a chill November: It makes one appreciate a fireside. And there is this about a hearth: It calls for small company, for companionship.

HAL BORLAND, *New York Times*, November 25, 1951.

There are two seasonal diversions that can ease the bite of any winter. One is the January thaw. The other is the seed catalogues.

HAL BORLAND, *New York Times*, January 19, 1958.

Summer is a promissory note signed in June, its long days spent and gone before you know it, and due to be repaid next January.

HAL BORLAND, *New York Times*, June 18, 1961.

In winter, consciousness looks like an etching.

GRETEL EHRLICH, *The Solace of Open Spaces*, 1985.

On the winter solstice it is thirty-four degrees below zero and there is very little in the way of daylight. The deep ache of this audacious Arctic air is also the ache in our lives made physical.

GRETEL EHRLICH, *The Solace of Open Spaces*, 1985.

April is the cruellest month, breeding

Lilacs out of the dead land, mixing

Memory and desire, stirring

Dull roots with spring rain.

T.S. ELIOT, *The Waste Land*, 1922.

Summer is the time when one sheds one's tensions with one's clothes, and the right kind of day is jeweled balm for the battered spirit. A few

of those days and you can become drunk with the belief that all's right with the world.

ADA LOUISE HUXTABLE, *New York Times*, September 29, 1977.

February, when the days of winter seem endless and no amount of wistful recollecting can bring back any air of summer.

SHIRLEY JACKSON, *Raising Demons*, 1956.

A solitary maple on a woodside flames in single scarlet, recalls nothing so much as the daughter of a noble house dressed for a fancy ball, with the whole family gathered round to admire her before she goes.

HENRY JAMES, *The American Scene*, 1907.

The most serious charge which can be brought against New England is not Puritanism but February.

JOSEPH WOOD KRUTCH, *The Twelve Seasons*, 1949.

Spring has many American faces. There are cities where it will come and go in a day and counties where it hangs around and never quite gets there....Summer is drawn blinds in Louisiana, long winds in Wyoming, shade of elms and maples in New England.

ARCHIBALD MACLEISH, "Sweet Land of Liberty," *Collier's*, July 8, 1955.

Despite March's windy reputation, winter isn't really blown away: it is washed away. It flows down all the hills, goes swirling down the valleys and spills out to sea. Like so many of this earth's elements, winter itself is soluble in water.

NEW YORK TIMES, March 17, 1964.

There seems to be so much more winter than we need this year.

KATHLEEN NORRIS, *Bread into Roses*, 1936.

I'm always this way in the Spring. Sunk in Springtime: or Take Away Those Violets. I hate the filthy season. Summer makes me drowsy, Autumn makes me sing. Winter's pretty lousy, but I hate Spring. They know how I feel. They know what Spring makes out of me. Just a Thing That Was Once a Woman, that's all I am in the Springtime. But do they do anything about it? Oh, no. Not they. Every year, back Spring comes, with the nasty little birds yapping their fool heads off, and the ground all mucked up with arbutus. Year after year after year. And me not able to sleep, on account of misery. All right, Spring. Go ahead and laugh your girlish laughter, you big sap. Funny, isn't it? People with melancholic insomnia are screams, aren't they? You just go on and laugh yourself simple. That's the girl!

DOROTHY PARKER, "Ethereal Mildness," *The New Yorker*, March 24, 1928.

Summer in New England is earned. We accomplish it through proud endurance. And we accept it as proper wage for the winter we have once again outlasted. Fish are jumping, quail whistle about us, school is out. And while living may not, in fact, be easy, the cinch of limitation is loosened. We know it will tighten in a while. We know, perhaps better than others, the implacable alternations of life—in the effulgence of July, we do not forget January. This is the moral condition of New England. The alternate contraction and relaxation of our spiritual frame has made us sinewy (and stiff, perhaps). We are grateful. We do not long for endless summer. We know that death is the mother of beauty, and we know that only those who have stood beside the frozen water and shivered in the wind can take the full measure of sunlight and locust hum and fish moving in the deep eddied pools beneath the falls.

ROBERT B. PARKER, in Arthur Griffin, *New England: The Four Seasons*, 1980.

Children hold spring so tightly in their brown fists—just as grownups, who are less sure of it, hold it in their hearts.

E.B. WHITE, "A Report in Spring," May 10, 1957, *Essays of E.B. White*, 1977.

No matter what changes take place in the world, or in me, nothing ever seems to disturb the face of spring.

E.B. WHITE, "A Report in Spring," May 10, 1957, *Essays of E.B. White*, 1977.

I prefer winter and fall, when you feel the bone structure in the landscape—the loneliness of it— the dead feeling of winter. Something waits beneath it—the whole story doesn't show.

ANDREW WYETH, in Richard Meryman, *The Art of Andrew Wyeth*, 1973.

WATER

You have probably accepted water as one of the free gifts of nature, like sunshine or air, or as one of the essentials, like electricity, which comes to you for a small monthly fee.

JUANITA BROOKS, "The Water's In," *Harper's*, May, 1941.

The ocean is a place of paradoxes.

RACHEL CARSON, "Under Sea," *Atlantic Monthly*, September, 1937.

To stand at the edge of the sea, to sense the ebb and the flow of the tides, to feel the breath of a mist moving over a great salt marsh, to watch the flight of shore birds that have swept up and down the surf lines of the continents for untold thousands of years, to see the running of the old eels and the young shad to the sea, is to have knowledge of things that are as nearly eternal as any earthly life can be.

RACHEL CARSON, Foreword, *Under the Sea-Wind*, 1941.

In an age when man has forgotten his origins and is blind even to his most essential needs for survival, water along with other resources has become the victim of his indifference.

RACHEL CARSON, *The Silent Spring*, 1962.

The Mississippi meanders down the spine of America.

BOB DODSON, CBS-TV, August 26, 1984.

A river seems a magic thing. A magic, moving, living part of the very earth itself—for it is from the soil, both from its depth and from its surface, that a river has its beginning.

LAURA GILPIN, *The Rio Grande*, 1949.

The best thing to do with water is to use a lot of it.

PHILIP JOHNSON, on designing fountains, *The New Yorker*, July 9, 1966.

What's in the Great Salt Lake?... Salt. Eight billion tons of salt, worth about fifty billion dollars. Also gypsum, magnesium, lithium, sulfur, boron, and potash.... Swimmers like the Great Salt Lake. Nonswimmers are absolutely knocked out by it because they can't sink. There is no record of anybody ever having gone swimming and drowned in the Great Salt Lake. The best life preserver, they say, is a ten-pound weight tied to your feet, to keep your feet down and your head up.

CHARLES KURALT, *Dateline America*, 1979.

Rivers perhaps are the only physical features of the world that are at their best from the air.

ANNE MORROW LINDBERGH, *North to the Orient*, 1935.

WEATHER

Fog is a unique blend of mood and weather. It is not really weather at all, as rain is, or sunshine. And it is no more palpable than any mood. You feel it on your face and in your hair, as well as in your mind. Yet it creeps in, silently, and it blows away like smoke; and it lies like an emotion over the land. Sun may sliver it into brilliance, and shadow may darken it into unwonted desolation. But there it is, fog, atmospheric moisture still uncertain in destination, not quite weather and not altogether mood, yet partaking of both.

HAL BORLAND, *New York Times*, September 24, 1945.

And when I say heat, I mean the kind that thickens the whites of eggs left in the coop and that makes the lizards, scurrying from the shelter of one little bush to another, flip over on their backs and blow their toes.

JUANITA BROOKS, "The Water's In," *Harper's*, May, 1941.

The rain had returned and the wind increased, a mixture that made the air look like a shattering mirror.

TRUMAN CAPOTE, "A Day's Work," *Music for Chameleons*, 1980.

The wind shows us how close to the edge we are.

JOAN DIDION, "Los Angeles Notebook," *Slouching Towards Bethlehem*, 1968.

Thunder does all the barking, but it's lightning that bites.

ART LINKLETTER, *A Child's Garden of Misinformation*, 1965.

Americans are weather junkies. They monitor it the way a hypochondriac listens to his own breathing and heartbeat in the middle of the night.

LANCE MORROW, "The Art of Weathercasting," *Fishing in the Tiber*, 1988.

The substance of the winds is too thin for human eyes, their written language is too difficult for human minds, and their spoken language mostly too faint for the ears.

JOHN MUIR, *A Thousand-Mile Walk to the Gulf*, 1916.

Withering heat, rushing out of the furnace of the prairie dust bowl, blasted crops, sucked up rivers and lakes, and transformed the nation—from the Rockies to the Atlantic—into a vast simmering cauldron.

Newsweek, 1936.

This is Methodist weather—sprinkling. We Baptists prefer total immersion.

ADAM CLAYTON POWELL, JR., *New York Times*, September 21, 1964.

Thank heavens, the sun has gone in, and I don't have to go out and enjoy it.

LOGAN PEARSALL SMITH, *Afterthoughts*, 1931.

I've lived in good climate, and it bores the hell out of me. I like weather rather than climate.

JOHN STEINBECK, *Travels with Charley*, 1962.

Thunder is good, thunder is impressive; but it is lightning that does the work.

MARK TWAIN, letter, 1908.

I got a letter from a lightning rod company this morning trying to put the fear of God in me, but with small success. Lightning seems to have lost its menace. Compared to what is going on on earth today, heaven's firebrands are penny fireworks with wet fuses.

E.B. WHITE, "Removal," July, 1938, *One Man's Meat*, 1944.

It was so cold I almost got married.

SHELLEY WINTERS, *New York Times*, April 29, 1956.

WILDERNESS

Going to the woods and the wild place has little to do with recreation, and much to do with creation. For the wilderness is the creation in its pure state, its processes unqualified by the doings of people. A man in the woods comes face to face with the creation, of which he must begin to see himself a part—a much less imposing part than he thought.

WENDELL BERRY, "The Journey's End," *Recollected Essays, 1965–1980*, 1981.

Saving marshlands and redwoods does not need biological justification any more than does opposing callousness and vandalism. The cult of wilderness is not a luxury; it is a necessity for the protection of humanized nature and for the preservation of mental health.

RENÉ DUBOS, *A God Within*, 1972.

Never did we plan the morrow, for we had learned that in the wilderness some new and irresistible distraction is sure to turn up each day before breakfast.

ALDO LEOPOLD, *A Sand County Almanac*, 1949.

I am glad I shall never be young without wild country to be young in. Of what avail are forty freedoms without a blank spot on the map?

ALDO LEOPOLD, *A Sand County Almanac*, 1949.

We each wish in our different ways for some insurance against the disappearance of wild relationships here. These dreams of preservation for the very things that induce a sense of worth in human beings must have been dreamt seven thousand years ago on the Euphrates. They are dreams one hopes are dreamt on the Potomac but suspects may not be, dreams of respectful human participation in a landscape, generation after generation.

BARRY LOPEZ, *Crossing Open Ground*, 1989.

Yellowstone, it seemed to me, was the top of the world, a region of deep lakes and dark timber, canyons and waterfalls. But, beautiful as it is, one might have the sense of confinement there. The skyline in all directions is close at hand, the high wall of the woods and deep cleavages of shade. There is a perfect freedom in the mountains, but it belongs to the eagle and the elk, the badger and the bear.

N. SCOTT MOMADAY, *The Way to Rainy Mountain*, 1969.

The clearest way into the Universe is through a forest wilderness.

JOHN MUIR, *John of the Mountains*, 1938.

Something will have gone out of us as a people if we ever let the remaining wilderness be destroyed; if we permit the last virgin forests to be turned into comic books and plastic cigarette cases; if we drive the few remaining members of the wild species into zoos or to extinction; if we pollute the last clear air and dirty the last clean streams and push our paved roads through the last of the silence, so that never again will Americans be free in their own country from the noise, the exhausts, the stinks of human and automotive waste. . . . We need wilderness preserved—as much of it as is still left, and as many kinds—because it was the challenge against which our character as a people was formed.

WALLACE STEGNER, "The Wilderness Idea," in David Brower, ed., *Wilderness: America's Living Heritage*, 1960.

The long fight to save wild beauty represents democracy at its best. It requires citizens to practice the hardest of virtues—self-restraint.

EDWIN WAY TEALE, "February 2," *Circle of the Seasons*, 1953.

Popular Culture

See also **American Society; Americans on Americans**—Show People; **The Arts; Business**—Advertising Slogans; **Children and Youth; Culture and Civilization; Food and Drink; History and Tradition; Holidays; Journalism and Media; Language and Discourse**—Conversation, Gossip, Jargon, Doublespeak, and Obfuscation; **Psychology; Relationships; Social Issues**—Censorship, Drugs and Alcohol; **Sports**

FADS AND FASHIONS

The feeling about time and what to do with it has changed. What has become of those long hours when we brushed our hair, fooled with our nails, tried for the most effective place of a beauty spot? Fashion is one of the great sacrifices of the jet age—there just isn't time to play at it.

BETTINA BALLARD, *In My Fashion*, 1960.

Fashions are born and they die too quickly for anyone to learn to love them.

BETTINA BALLARD, *In My Fashion*, 1960.

When in doubt wear red.

BILL BLASS, December 31, 1982.

A best-seller was a book which somehow sold well simply because it was selling well.

DANIEL J. BOORSTIN, *The Image*, 1962.

Glamour is what makes a man ask for your telephone number. But it also is what makes a woman ask for the name of your dressmaker.

LILLY DACHE, *Woman's Home Companion*, July, 1955.

Nutrition is a young subject; it has been kicked around like a puppy that cannot take care of itself. Food faddists and crackpots have kicked it pretty cruelly.... They seem to believe that unless food tastes like Socratic hemlock, it cannot build health. Frankly, I often wonder what such persons plan to do with good health in case they acquire it.

ADELLE DAVIS, *Let's Eat Right to Keep Fit*, 1954.

Give feminine fashions time enough and they will starve all the moths to death.

DETROIT FREE PRESS, June, 1925.

These days there are those who would topple the tiptop, claiming that haute couture—the business of made-to-order clothes—is a colossally expensive, expendable luxury.

CARRIE DONOVAN, *New York Times Magazine*, August l8, 1991.

A woman who doesn't wear lipstick feels undressed in public. Unless she works on a farm.

MAX FACTOR, *Time*, June 16, 1958.

The original mini [skirt] was probably brought down, literally, by three things: December, January and February. Now the same designers want to see if women will once again prove their allegiance with a badge of frostbite.

ELLEN GOODMAN, "A Miniskirt Attack," *Washington Post*, April, 1987.

I get uncomfortable when we turn ideas into trends, when we trivialize concepts and values into games of "ins" and "outs." When ideology, literacy and civil rights are treated like racquetball, nouvelle cuisine and new-wave music, it's time to write a post-script to the era: Label it post-cerebral.

ELLEN GOODMAN, "A Postscript for the Post-Yuppies," *Washington Post*, July, 1985.

Skirts couldn't get any shorter and remain legal.

AMY GREENE, *American Way*, June, 1970.

American interiors tend to have no happy medium between execrable taste and what is called "good taste" and is worn like a wart.

MARGARET HALSEY, *With Malice Toward Some*, 1938.

You are only as good as the people you dress.

HALSTON, 1972, in Lois and Alan Gordon, *American Chronicle*, 1987.

Those obsessed with health are not healthy: the first requisite of good health is a certain calculated carelessness about oneself.

SYDNEY J. HARRIS, *Last Things First*, 1961.

The trouble is, once one has managed to achieve a style that indicates one's status group and expresses one's personality, then a whole herd of Bloomingdale's rack-slappers comes along and copies it, and then one has to start all over.

MOLLY IVINS, *New York Times*, August 15, 1976.

I think there's something incredibly sexy about a woman wearing her boyfriend's T-shirt and underwear.

CALVIN KLEIN, *People*, December 24, 1984.

The figure of the enthusiast who has just discovered jogging or a new way to fix tofu can be said to stand or, more accurately, to tremble on the threshold of conversion, as the representative American.

LEWIS H. LAPHAM, "The Complete American," *Harper's*, November, 1981.

For those of you fortunate enough to have your lack of awareness extend into the realm of advertising, mood jewelry is jewelry that tells you your feelings via a heat-sensitive stone. And although one would think that stones would have quite enough to do, what with graves and walls and such, it seems that they have now taken on the job of informing people that they are nervous.

FRAN LEBOWITZ, *Metropolitan Life*, 1974.

While clothes with pictures and/or writing on them are not entirely an invention of the modern age, they are an unpleasant indication of the general state of things. The particular general state of things that I am referring to is the general state of things that encourages people to express themselves through their clothing....I mean, be realistic. If people don't want to listen to *you*, what makes you think they want to hear from your sweater?

FRAN LEBOWITZ, *Metropolitan Life*, 1974.

A great many people in Los Angeles are on strict diets that restrict their intake of synthetic foods. The reason for this appears to be a widely held belief that organically grown fruit and vegetables make the cocaine work faster.

FRAN LEBOWITZ, *Social Studies*, 1983.

The trench coat is the only thing that has kept its head above water.

JACK LIPMAN, *Wall Street Journal*, October 11, 1984.

Girls fight with clothes in competition for a mate as truly as the Indians of the Northwest coast fight with the potlatch for social prestige.

ROBERT S. LYND AND HELEN MERRELL LYND, *Middletown: A Study in Contemporary American Culture*, 1929.

If fascism ever comes to America, it will come as a fad dressed in lovebeads and hyped by *Esquire* magazine.

JACK NEWFIELD, Introduction, *Bread and Roses Too*, 1971.

[There has been] a change for the worse during the past year in feminine dress, dancing, manners, and general moral standards. [We] should realize the serious ethical consequences of immodesty in girls' dress.

PITTSBURGH OBSERVER, 1922.

In the beginning, it looked quite elegant, but like a lot of trends, it soon became a fashion made by the wrong people, including guys with big bellies wearing gold chains.

FRED PRESSMAN, on Nehru jackets, *Wall Street Journal*, June 27, 1984.

Many people who wouldn't hurt a fly have annexed to fashion the imagery of torture—the thongs and spikes and metal studs—hence reducing it to the frivolous and transitory.

PHYLLIS ROSE, "Tools of Torture: An Essay on Beauty and Pain," *The Atlantic*, October, 1986.

To call a fashion wearable is the kiss of death. No new fashion worth its salt is ever wearable.

EUGENIA SHEPPHARD, *New York Herald Tribune*, January 13, 1960.

You can buy your clothes pretorn a la *Flash Dance*; you can dress for success; you can dress to please the opposite sex, to please the same sex, to dress *like* the opposite sex—nobody cares anymore.

IAN SHOALES, "The Body," *I Gotta Go*, July 2, 1984.

Today the hip thing to do is get high on your body. Running huge distances is supposed to provide a feeling of euphoria and elation. There are entire magazines devoted to running, which the runner pores over for types of shoes, in the same way a sophisticate sniffs through a wine list. Only in rich America can severely monklike behavior turn into self-indulgence.

IAN SHOALES, "Sophistication," *I Gotta Go*, May 14, 1984.

We use up cute fads in this country the way we use up Kleenex....Maybe when we buy a little fuzzy stuffed puppy with a tag, "I Wuv Oo," it's a kind of psychic sneeze, a way to rid the collective unconscious of consciousness-blocking mucus.

IAN SHOALES, "Cute," *I Gotta Go*, February 22, 1985.

Our society and its institutions are diseased. So we call in quacks of all sorts. Dale Carnegie comes along with *How to Win Friends and Influ-*

ence People. So we buy a million copies containing his bunk. A dusky mulatto with showbutton eyes and straight hair puts on an Oriental costume; and we pay four bits when he tells us how to win success and love. Somebody starts a chain letter that ends in the outhouse.

MELVIN B. TOLSON, "The Negro and Radicalism," *Washington Tribune*, August 12, 1939.

The talk shows are stuffed full of sufferers who have regained their health—congressmen who suffered through a serious spell of boozing and skirt-chasing, White House aides who were stricken cruelly with overweening ambition, movie stars and baseball players who came down with acute cases of wanting to trash hotel rooms while under the influence of recreational drugs. Most of them have found God, or at least a publisher.

CALVIN TRILLIN, "Diseases of the Mighty," *The Nation*, October 19, 1985.

Here we've been accepting the best-dressed list all these years as if it were the scientific findings of an expert panel that went around calibrating people's lapels and testing the sharpness of their trouser creases against day-old bread and checking the lumps in their jacket pockets for Italian sausage sandwiches. Here my wife has for years been saying things like, "Maybe if you'd dress a little more like Cesar Romero, you'd be on the Fashion Foundation of America's list of best-dressed men yourself"—or thinking such things, at least, when she said something like, "You're not really going to go out of the house wearing that jacket, are you?"

CALVIN TRILLIN, "Calories May Not Count," King Features Syndicate, July 13, 1986.

The rush of power to the head is not as becoming as a new hat.

HELEN VAN SLYKE, *New York Times*, August 28, 1963.

I have gained and lost the same ten pounds so many times over and over again my cellulite must have déjà vu.

JANE WAGNER, *The Search for Intelligent Life in the Universe*, performed by Lily Tomlin, 1986.

I am *sick* of being the victim of trends I reflect but don't even understand.

JANE WAGNER, *The Search for Intelligent Life in the Universe*, performed by Lily Tomlin, 1986.

I don't know how I functioned before this seminar, Bob. I learned "desktop gardening," "office isometrics" and "power dressing," a new fashion trend where you wear something around the neck that looks sort of like a scarf and sort of like a tie and sort of like a ruffle and doesn't threaten anyone, because you don't look good in it.

JANE WAGNER, *The Search for Intelligent Life in the Universe*, performed by Lily Tomlin, 1986.

Today, accountants look like Shakespearean actors, space salesmen look like art directors, hair stylists wear short hair, clothes designers dress conservatively,...an orthodontist comes on like a cowboy....Everybody's into reverse role-playing.

JOHN WEITZ, 1975, in Lois and Alan Gordon, *American Chronicle*, 1987.

Today we are a nation which in the midst of the severe recent recession still managed to spend millions on "pet rocks." And today we are spending hundreds of millions on citizen band radios for the joy of talking to total strangers in a jargon unsuited for communicating thoughts unrelated to driving.

GEORGE WILL, "Personality Against Character," July 1, 1976, *The Pursuit of Happiness, and Other Sobering Thoughts*, 1978.

Once it was power that created style. But now high styles come from low places, from people who have no power,...who are marginal, who carve out worlds for themselves in the nether depths, in tainted 'undergrounds.'

TOM WOLFE, "Girl of the Year," 1965.

LIFE-STYLES

Hippies are more than just people who walk down Haight Street with beads, bells, long hair, stoned on drugs. They are a concept, an act of rejection, a militant vanguard, a hope for the future.

BERKELEY BARB, October 26, 1967.

The youth rebellion is a worldwide phenomenon that has not been seen before in history. I do not believe they will calm down and be ad execs at thirty as the Establishment would like us to believe.

WILLIAM BURROUGHS, 1968, in Lois and Alan Gordon, *American Chronicle*, 1987.

Of course the activists—not those whose thinking had become rigid, but those whose approach to revolution was imaginatively anarchic—had long ago grasped the reality which still eluded the press: we were seeing something important.

We were seeing the desperate attempt of a handful of pathetically unequipped children to create a community in a social vacuum.

JOAN DIDION, "Slouching Towards Bethlehem,"
Slouching Towards Bethlehem, 1968.

The Beats were the true radicals of the fifties, not in any conventional political sense but for the depth of their critique of America's desperate materialism.

BARBARA EHRENREICH, *Fear of Falling*, 1990.

Anyone who believed that his or her life would be qualitatively transformed by a walnut television console or wall-to-wall carpeting, as the advertisements insisted, would have to confront the failure of these objects every day. They were the dead residue of ambition, hope, effort, hardened into lame, unloving objects.

BARBARA EHRENREICH, *Fear of Falling*, 1990.

Whenever I get married, I start buying *Gourmet* magazine. I think of it as my own personal bride's disease.

NORA EPHRON, "Gourmet Magazine," *Esquire*,
December, 1976.

Gourmet gives you a full-page color picture of an incredibly serious rack of lamb persillé sitting on a somber Blue Canton platter by Mottahedeh Historic Charleston Reproductions sitting on a stiff eighteenth-century English mahogany table from Charles Deacon & Son—and it's no wonder I never cook anything from this magazine: the pictures are so reverent I almost feel I ought to pray to them.

NORA EPHRON, "Gourmet Magazine," *Esquire*,
December, 1976.

Our family was not so much socially uninteresting as socially uninterested. If life is in some sense a status race, my parents never noticed the flag drop.

JOSEPH EPSTEIN, "They Said You Was High Class,"
American Scholar, Spring, 1986.

The decisive moment in the defeat of upper-class, capital-S Society may have come when, in newspapers all over the nation, what used to be called the Society page was replaced by the Style section.

JOSEPH EPSTEIN, "They Said You Was High Class,"
American Scholar, Spring, 1986.

The country is fed up with radical causes…the unisex movement…the departure from basic decency, from the philosophy of the monogamous home.

JERRY FALWELL, 1978, in Lois and Alan Gordon, *American Chronicle*, 1987.

Scarcely had the staider citizens of the republic caught their breaths when the wildest of all generations, the generation which had been adolescent during the confusion of the War, brusquely shouldered my contemporaries out of the way and danced into the limelight. This was the generation whose girls dramatized themselves as flappers, the generation that corrupted its elders and eventually overreached itself less through lack of morals than through lack of taste. May one offer in exhibit the year 1922!

F. SCOTT FITZGERALD, *The Crack-up*, 1945.

The restlessness approached hysteria. The parties were bigger. The shows were bigger. The pace was faster,…the buildings higher, the morals looser.

F. SCOTT FITZGERALD, 1926, in Lois and Alan Gordon,
American Chronicle, 1987.

The most important thing about a TV set is to get it back against something and not out in the middle of a room where it's like a somber fellow making electronic judgments on you.

BRUCE JAY FRIEDMAN, *The Lonely Guy's Book of Life*, 1978.

Values are not trendy items that are casually traded in. Those whose values were warmed in the cauldron of the sixties don't see Yuppie and Yippie as two choices of the eighties, but as two warnings. They are warnings about the importance of growing up and the dangers of giving up. Warnings about the difficulty of living a daily life that is both moral and practical.

ELLEN GOODMAN, "The Sixties: Love It or Leave It?"
Washington Post, April, 1989.

Out on the streets I couldn't tell the Vietnam veterans from the rock and roll veterans. The Sixties had made so many casualties, its war and its music had run power off the same circuit for so long they didn't even have to fuse. The war primed you for lame years while rock and roll turned more lurid and dangerous than bullfighting, rock stars started falling like second lieutenants; ecstasy and death and (of course and for sure) life, but it didn't seem so then. What I'd thought of as two obsessions were really only one, I don't know how to tell you how complicated that made my life. Freezing and burning

and going down again into the sucking mud of the culture, hold on tight and move real slow.
MICHAEL HERR, *Dispatches*, 1977.

There [in Haight-Ashbury], in a daily street-fair atmosphere, upwards of 15,000 unbonded girls and boys interact in a tribal love-seeking, free-winging, acid-based society, where if you are a hippie and you have a dime, you can put it in a parking meter and lie down in the street for an hour's sunshine.
WARREN HINCKLE, "Social History of the Hippies," *Ramparts*, March, 1967.

Led by men like Ginsberg and Ferlinghetti, the early beats weighed America by its words and deeds, and found it pennyweight. They took upon themselves the role of conscience for the machine. They rejected all values and when, in attempting to carve a new creative force, they told America to "go fuck itself," America reacted, predictably, with an obscenity trial.
WARREN HINCKLE, "A Social History of the Hippies," *Ramparts*, March, 1967.

The crisis of the happy hippie ethic is precisely this: it is all right to turn on, but it is not enough to drop out.
WARREN HINCKLE, "A Social History of the Hippies," *Ramparts*, March, 1967.

In [the] commercial sense, the hippies have not only accepted assimilation (the beats fought it, and lost), they have swallowed it whole.
WARREN HINCKLE, "A Social History of the Hippies," *Ramparts*, March, 1967.

Hippiedom is more than a choice of lifestyle. It's an apolitical systemcide.
CHUCK HOLLANDER, *Time*, July 7, 1967.

The mind-cure principles are beginning so to pervade the air that one catches their spirit second hand. One hears of "The Gospel of Relaxation," of the "Don't Worry Movement," of people who repeat to themselves "Youth, health, vigor!" when dressing in the morning.
WILLIAM JAMES, *The Varieties of Religious Experience*, 1900.

John Clellan Holmes...and I were sitting around trying to think up the meaning of the Lost Generation and the subsequent existentialism and I said, "You know, this is really a beat generation," and he leapt up and said, "That's it, that's right!"
JACK KEROUAC, *Playboy*, June, 1959.

He had a massive stroke. He died with his tie on. Do you think that could be our generation's

equivalent of that old saying about dying with your boots on?
STEPHEN KING, *The Stand*, 1990.

If I could turn you on, if I could drive you out of your wretched mind, if I could tell you, I would let you know.
R.D. LAING, *Politics of Experience*, 1967.

[This is a time of] hedonism,...narcissism,...cult of the self.
CHRISTOPHER LASCH, *New York Review of Books*, 1976.

If you take the game of life seriously, if you take your nervous system seriously, if you take your sense organs seriously, if you take the energy process seriously, you must turn on, tune in, and drop out.
TIMOTHY LEARY, *Politics of Ecstasy*, 1966.

What you have when everyone wears the same playclothes for all occasions, is addressed by nickname, expected to participate in Show and Tell, and bullied out of any desire for privacy, is not democracy; it is kindergarten.
JUDITH MARTIN, *Common Courtesy*, 1985.

Don't trust anyone over thirty.
NEW LEFT SLOGAN, 1960s.

Far out!
1960s EXPRESSION.

Bohemia is a state of mind inhabited by those who, whether or not they are creative or particularly intellectual, like to stand on the margins and scoff at the Babbitts.
VANCE PACKARD, *The Status Seekers*, 1959.

The hippies were taught by their parents, their neighbors, their tabloids and their college professors that faith, instinct and emotion are superior to reason—and obeyed. They were taught that material concerns are evil, that the State or the Lord will provide, that the Lilies of the Field do not toil—and they obeyed. They were taught that love, indiscriminate love, for one's fellow-men is the highest virtue—and they obeyed. They were taught that the merging of one's self with a herd, a tribe or a community is the noblest way for men to live—and they obeyed. There isn't a single basic principle of the Establishment which they do not share—there isn't a belief which they have not accepted.
AYN RAND, "Apollo and Dionysus," *The New Left*, 1968.

[The counterculture stands against] the final consolidation of a technocratic totalitarianism in which we shall find ourself ingeniously adapted to an existence wholly estranged from anything that has ever made the life of man an interesting adventure.

THEODORE ROSZAK, *The Making of a Counterculture*, 1969.

READ THIS BOOK STONED

The Youth International Revolution will begin with a mass breakdown of authority.... Tribes of long hairs, blacks, armed women, workers, peasants and students will take over.... The White House will become one big commune.... The Pentagon will be replaced with an LSD experimental farm.... To steal from the rich is a sacred and religious act.

JERRY RUBIN, *Do It*, 1969.

Should we, perhaps, see the development of the commune movement in another light, as a less expensive form of summer camp for a growing population—post-adolescent, post-industrial, post-Christian and unemployed?

SONYA RUDIKOFF, *Commentary*, 1974.

Transcendental Meditation is the McDonald's of the meditation business. Or maybe the Howard Johnson's.

ADAM SMITH, *Powers of Mind*, 1975.

On the Road from the City of Skepticism, I had to pass through the Valley of Ambiguity.

ADAM SMITH, *Powers of Mind*, 1975.

You are all a lost generation.

GERTRUDE STEIN, in Ernest Hemingway, *The Sun Also Rises*, 1926.

The trouble with the lost generation is that it doesn't get lost enough.

JAMES THURBER, *Credos and Curios*, 1962.

Any survey-taker is aware that it could be dangerous to offend yuppies by asking too many personal questions, since all of them have a racquetball racquet on their person at all times.

CALVIN TRILLIN, "To Catch a Wonk," *The Nation*, November 9, 1985.

It's the Me Decade.

TOM WOLFE, *New York*, 1976.

All the things I really like to do are either immoral, illegal, or fattening.

ALEXANDER WOOLLCOTT, in Robert F. Drennan, *The Algonquin Wits*, 1968.

MANNERS AND ETIQUETTE

I am continually fascinated at the difficulty intelligent people have in distinguishing what is controversial from what is merely offensive.

NORA EPHRON, "Barney Collier's Book," *Esquire*, January, 1976.

There is a great difference in my mind between innocence in this gourmand interpretation, and ignorance. The one presupposes the other, and yet a truly innocent cook or host is never guilty of the great sin of pretension, while many an ignorant one errs hideously in this direction.

M.F.K. FISHER, "I is for Innocence," *An Alphabet for Gourmets*, 1949.

Alone...and so am I, if a choice must be made between most people I know and myself. This misanthropic attitude is one I am not proud of, but it is firmly there, based on my increasing conviction that sharing food with another human being is an intimate act that should not be indulged in lightly.

M.F.K. FISHER, "A is for dining Alone," *An Alphabet for Gourmets*, 1949.

Public smoking, like public spitting, is becoming a socially unacceptable habit.

ELLEN GOODMAN, "In Search of Fresh Lungs," *Washington Post*, April, 1988.

In society it is etiquette for ladies to have the best chairs and get handed things. In the home the reverse is the case. That is why ladies are more sociable than gentlemen.

VIRGINIA GRAHAM, *Say Please*, 1949.

It is one of the strange American changes in custom that the drunks of my day often hit each other, but never in the kind of bar fight that so often happens now with knives. In those days somebody hit somebody, and when that was finished one of them offered his hand and it would have been unheard of to refuse.

LILLIAN HELLMAN, *Pentimento*, 1973.

Rudeness is the weak man's imitation of strength.

ERIC HOFFER, *The Passionate State of Mind*, 1955.

The first quality of a good education is good manners—and some people flunk the course.

HUBERT H. HUMPHREY, remark to hecklers at San Fernando Valley State College, *Connecticut Sunday Herald*, January 1, 1967.

Applesauce.

So's your anchovie.

Banana oil.

Chew to the line.

Let the hips fall where they will.

LADY'S REPLIES TO UNWANTED ADVANCES, *Life*, 1926.

There is a truism about manners that can be stated didactically: Each generation believes that the manners of the generation that follows it have gone to hell in a hand basket.

RUSSELL LYNES, "On Good Behavior," *Architectural Digest*, 1986.

The praise of injudicious friends frequently fosters bad mannerisms.

ELISABETH MARBURY, *My Crystal Ball*, 1923.

Private houses are treated by their guests as public accommodations, or worse. A restaurant may be entitled to demand reservations, but a private invitation is not only not thought worth the bother of a reply, but considered an entitlement to bring along one's own guests. If the Second Coming were scheduled for next week, my mail would be full of letters asking, "Can I bring a date?"

JUDITH MARTIN, *Common Courtesy*, 1985.

From its birth, America has badly needed a way to express equality, individual freedom, social mobility, and the dignity of labor in the language of human social behavior (which is what etiquette is).

JUDITH MARTIN, *Common Courtesy*, 1985.

It is astonishing to Miss Manners that so many people presume that the gentle art of manners is based on a preoccupation with money. Etiquette, it is widely believed, consists of forms of behavior requiring fortunes in silverware, evening clothing, and unwieldly vehicles. Most people feel they need etiquette only on occasions when they are spending a great deal of money— putting on a wedding, for example. Otherwise, they can apparently make do with rudeness. Dear, dear. You can imagine how upsetting Miss Manners finds this. She doesn't know which offends her more—people who seek to demonstrate their genuineness by eschewing manners or those who are scrambling to learn them to serve their social ambitions. They all end up rude. The truth is that there is very little relationship between manners and money. Certainly,

Miss Manners has never noticed any preponderance of politeness on the part of the rich.

JUDITH MARTIN, *Miss Manners' Guide for the Turn of the Millennium*, 1989.

Those who have mastered etiquette, who are entirely, impeccably right, would seem to arrive at a point of exquisite dullness.

DOROTHY PARKER, "Mrs. Post Enlarges on Etiquette," *The New Yorker*, December 31, 1927.

You know how you ought to be with men? You should always be aloof, you should never let them know you like them, you must on no account let them feel that they are of any importance to you, you must be wrapped up in your own concerns, you may never let them lose sight of the fact that you are superior, you must be, in short, a regular stuffed chemise. And if you could see what I've been doing!

DOROTHY PARKER, "Wallflower's Lament," *The New Yorker*, November 17, 1928.

Civilization has taught us to eat with a fork, but even now if nobody is around we use our fingers.

WILL ROGERS, January 20, 1935, in Donald Day, ed., *The Autobiography of Will Rogers*, 1949.

When we're dressing to go to someone's house for dinner, Alice often tries to persuade me that there are ways of showing appreciation to the hostess other than having thirds.

CALVIN TRILLIN, "Dinner with Friends," *Alice, Let's Eat*, 1978.

There are a lot of ways wars can end—a truce, a surrender, the complete destruction of the planet—but there's no established way to end a correspondence.

CALVIN TRILLIN, "Whom Says So?" *The Nation*, June 8, 1985.

Good manners have much to do with the emotions. To make them ring true, one must feel them, not merely exhibit them.

AMY VANDERBILT, *New Complete Book of Etiquette*, 1963.

One face to the world, another at home makes for misery.

AMY VANDERBILT, *New Complete Book of Etiquette*, 1963.

Don't confuse being stimulating with being blunt.

BARBARA WALTERS, *How to Talk with Practically Anybody About Practically Anything*, 1970.

MOVIE LINES

There just isn't room for two doctors and two vampires in one small town.
Max Adrian, *Dr. Terror's House of Horrors*, 1967.

Remember wherever you go, there you are.
Peter Weller, *The Adventures of Buckaroo Bonzi*, 1984.

I wanted to marry her when I saw the moonlight shining on the barrel of her father's shotgun.
Eddie Albert, *Oklahoma*, 1955.

I suppose you know you have a wonderful body. I'd like to do it in clay.
Lola Albright, *Champion*, 1949.

I used to—used to make obscene phone calls to her—collect—and she used to accept the charges all the time.
Woody Allen, *Take the Money and Run*, 1969.

I hate the beach. I hate the sun. I'm pale and I'm red-headed. I don't tan—I stroke!
Woody Allen, *Play It Again, Sam*, 1972.

Life is divided into the horrible and the miserable. Those are the two categories. The horrible would be like, you know, terminal cases, and blind, and crippled. I don't know how they get through life. It's amazing to me. And the miserable is everyone else. So you should be thankful you're miserable.
Woody Allen, *Annie Hall*, 1977.

Hey, don't knock masturbation. It's sex with someone I love.
Woody Allen, *Annie Hall*, 1977.

Very stupid to kill the only servant in the house. Now we don't even know where to find the marmalade.
Judith Anderson, *And Then There Were None*, 1945.

Personally, Veda's convinced me that alligators have the right idea. They eat their young.
Eve Arden, *Mildred Pierce*, 1945.

Just because you're paranoid doesn't mean they aren't after you.
Alan Arkin, *Catch-22*, 1970.

Oh, my God! Someone's been sleeping in my dress!
Beatrice Arthur, *Maude*, 1974.

Look, I can understand the temptation of a young man over here—but a grandfather! Really,

Colonel Plummer, you should have your brakes relined.
Jean Arthur, *A Foreign Affair*, 1948.

If I'd have forgotten myself with that girl, I'd remember it.
Fred Astaire, *Top Hat*, 1935.

If you want anything, just whistle. You know how to whistle don't you? Steve? Just put your lips together and blow.
Lauren Bacall, *To Have and Have Not*, 1944.

First the hunt, then the revels!
Leslie Banks, *The Most Dangerous Game*, 1932.

Kill, then love! When you have known that, you have known everything.
Leslie Banks, *The Most Dangerous Game*, 1932.

Killers kill, squealers squeal.
Jean-Paul Belmondo, *Breathless*, 1959.

Why don't you get out of that wet coat and into a dry martini?
Robert Benchley, *The Major and the Minor*, 1942.

Play it, Sam. Play "As Time Goes By!"
Ingrid Bergman, *Casablanca*, 1942.

I don't know how to kiss, or I would kiss you. Where do the noses go?
Ingrid Bergman, *For Whom the Bells Toll*, 1943.

Did anyone ever tell you that you have a dishonest face—for a priest, I mean?
Ingrid Bergman, *The Bells of St. Mary's*, 1945.

I know you have a civil tongue in your head—I sewed it there myself.
Whit Bissell, *Teenage Frankenstein*, 1957.

As long as they've got sidewalks, you've got a job.
Joan Blondell, *Footlight Parade*, 1933.

Your idea of fidelity is not having more than one man in bed at the same time.
Dirk Bogarde, *Darling*, 1965.

I stick my neck out for nobody.
Humphrey Bogart, *Casablanca*, 1942.

I came to Casablanca for the waters.
But we're in the middle of the desert!
I was misinformed.
Humphrey Bogart and Claude Rains, *Casablanca*, 1942.

She tried to sit on my lap while I was standing up.

Humphrey Bogart, *The Big Sleep*, 1946.

What is it?

The stuff that dreams are made of.

Ward Bond and Humphrey Bogart, *The Maltese Falcon*, 1941.

I could'a been a contender. I could'a had class and been somebody. Real class. Instead of a bum, let's face it, which is what I am.

Marlon Brando, *On the Waterfront*, 1954.

Get up you scum suckin' pig.

Marlon Brando, *One-Eyed Jacks*, 1961.

I like my convictions undiluted, same as I do my bourbon.

George Brent, *Jezebel*, 1938.

Cameron's so tight if you stuck a piece of coal up his ass in two weeks you'd have a diamond.

Matthew Broderick, *Ferris Bueller's Day Off*, 1986.

Are we having fun yet?

Carol Burnett, *Four Seasons*, 1981.

Just because you have good manners doesn't mean I suddenly turn into Dale Evans.

Ellen Burstyn, *Alice Doesn't Live Here Anymore*, 1975.

Martha and I are merely exercising, that's all. We're merely walking what's left of our wits. Don't pay any attention.

Richard Burton, *Who's Afraid of Virginia Woolf?*, 1966.

I'm sorry, Pepe. He thought you were going to escape.

And so I have, my friend.

Joseph Calleia and the dying Charles Boyer, *Algiers*, 1938.

Honey, will you get me a Tab? My mouth is so dry they could shoot *Lawrence of Arabia* in it.

Dyan Cannon, *The Last of Sheila*, 1973.

Why do we always expect them to come in metal ships?

Veronica Cartwright, *Invasion of the Body Snatchers*, 1978.

You don't understand…every night when the moon is full, I turn into a wolf.

You and fifty million other guys!

Lon Chaney and Lou Costello, *Abbott and Costello Meet Frankenstein*, 1948.

Take him to the tower and teach him the error of false pride.

Eduardo Ciannelli, *Gunga Din*, 1939.

See them down there, coiling and wiggling, sticking their pretty tongues out.

Eduardo Ciannelli, peering into a snake pit, *Gunga Din*, 1939.

I've distilled everything to one simple principle—win or die.

Glenn Close, *Dangerous Liaisons*, 1988.

You have no idea what a long-legged gal can do without doing anything.

Claudette Colbert, *The Palm Beach Story*, 1942.

If I see your eyes, I might forget to be kind.

Ronald Coleman, *The Prisoner of Zenda*, 1937.

If you want to call me that, smile.

Gary Cooper, *The Virginian*, 1929.

People all say that I've had a bad break, but today—today I consider myself the luckiest man on the face of the earth.

Gary Cooper, *The Pride of the Yankees*, 1942.

It's no good. I've got to go back. They're making me run. I've never run from anyone before.

Gary Cooper, *High Noon*, 1952.

I'm a ba-a-a-a-ad boy!

Lou Costello, ca. 1940.

I wouldn't take you if you were covered in diamonds—upside down!

Joan Crawford, *The Female on the Beach*, 1955.

Sometimes I sing and dance around my house in my underwear. That doesn't make me Madonna.

Joan Cusack, *Working Girl*, 1988.

Go out there and be so swell you'll make me hate you.

Bebe Daniels, to Ruby Keeler, *42nd Street*, 1933.

Ya can't learn to be real. It's like learning to be a midget. It's not something you can learn.

Jeff Daniels, *The Purple Rose of Cairo*, 1985.

I'd like to kiss you, but I just washed my hair.

Bette Davis, *Cabin in the Cotton*, 1931.

The only fun I get is feeding the goldfish, and they only eat once a day!

Bette Davis, *Bordertown*, 1935.

Yes, I killed him. And I'm glad, I tell you. Glad, glad, glad!

Bette Davis, *The Letter*, 1941.

Don't hurt that fly—that's Old Tom—they named a gin after him. That fly followed me out here from the show.... He used to drive the chariot races in the flea circus.... One afternoon in a small town outside of Hoosic Falls, when I was ignominiously dragged off to the local bastille and placed in durance vile at the behest of a blackguard regarding the loss of his silver timepiece,... Old Tom, feeling he was implicated—remembering the adage—"Time Flies"... stuck his left hind leg into the Governor's inkwell, dragged it above the dotted line, forging the Governor's signature. The Governor's secretary, unware of the hoax, inadvertently picked up the document, gave it to a messenger and sent it to the warden, who released me with profuse apologies. I love that fly.

W.C. FIELDS, *The Bank Dick*, 1940.

I guess you are sort of attractive in a corn-fed sort of way. You can find yourself a poor girl falling for you if—well, if you threw in a set of dishes.

BETTE DAVIS, *The Man Who Came to Dinner*, 1941.

There comes a time in every woman's life when the only thing that helps is a glass of champagne.

BETTE DAVIS, *Old Acquaintance*, 1943.

What a dump!

BETTE DAVIS, *Beyond the Forest*, 1949.

Now don't shoot the sheriff, it's against the law.

BRIAN DENNEHY, *Silverado*, 1985.

You better watch your ass or these guys'll shoot it off.

BRIAN DENNEHY, *Silverado*, 1985.

It took more than one man to change my name to Shanghai Lily.

MARLENE DIETRICH, *Shanghai Express*, 1932.

Greed is good! Greed is right! Greed works! Greed will save the U.S.A!

MICHAEL DOUGLAS, *Wall Street*, 1987.

No matter where you go or what you do, you're gonna die.

OLYMPIA DUKAKIS, *Moonstruck*, 1987.

I wouldn't go on living with you if you were dipped in platinum.

IRENE DUNNE, *The Awful Truth*, 1937.

Attention must finally be paid to such a man! He's not to be allowed to fall into his grave like an old dog. Attention—attention must be paid!

MILDRED DUNNOCK, *Death of a Salesman*, 1951.

The only reason you're still living is that I never kissed you.

CHARLES DURNING, *Tootsie*, 1982.

I love the smell of napalm in the morning—it smells like victory.

ROBERT DUVALL, *Apocalypse Now*, 1979.

Too many girls follow the line of least resistance. Yeah, but a good line is hard to resist.

HELEN JEROME EDDY, AND MAE WEST, *Klondike Annie*, 1936.

Your dream prince, reporting for duty!

NELSON EDDY, *Rose Marie*, 1936.

E.T. phone home.

E.T., *E.T. The Extra-Terrestrial*, 1982.

Never give a sucker an even break.

W.C. FIELDS, *Poppy*, 1932.

It ain't a fit night out for man or beast.

W.C. FIELDS, *The Fatal Glass of Beer*, 1933.

She drove me to drink. That's the one thing I'm indebted to her for.

W.C. FIELDS, *Never Give a Sucker an Even Break*, 1941.

You've all suffered from their cruelty—the ear loppings, the beatings, the blindings and hot irons, the burning of our farms and homes, the mistreatment of our women. It's time to put an end to this!

ERROL FLYNN, *The Adventures of Robin Hood*, 1938.

I jes trying to get on without shovin' anybody, that's all.

HENRY FONDA, *The Grapes of Wrath*, 1940.

He has every characteristic of a dog except loyalty.

HENRY FONDA, *The Best Man*, 1964.

Men have paid $200 for me, and here you are, turning down a freebie. You could get a perfectly good dishwasher for that.

JANE FONDA, *Klute*, 1971.

With Nixon in the White House, good health seemed to be in bad taste.

JANE FONDA, *California Suite*, 1978.

A good night's rest'll do you a lot of good. Besides, you got nothing to worry about: the walls of Jericho will protect you from the big bad wolf.

CLARK GABLE, *It Happened One Night*, 1934.

I'll take my chances against the law. You'll take yours against the sea.

CLARK GABLE, *Mutiny on the Bounty*, 1935.

Frankly, my dear, I don't give a damn!

CLARK GABLE, *Gone with the Wind*, 1939.

Gimme a visky with a chincher ale on the side—and don't be stingy, baby.

GRETA GARBO, *Anna Christie*, 1930.

I am Mata Hari, my own master!

GRETA GARBO, *Mata Hari*, 1932.

I vant to be left alone.

GRETA GARBO, *Grand Hotel*, 1932.

I always look well when I'm near death.

GRETA GARBO, *Camille*, 1936.

I'm afraid of nothing, except being bored.

GRETA GARBO, *Camille*, 1936.

The arrangement of the features of your face is not entirely repulsive to me.

GRETA GARBO, *Ninotchka*, 1939.

When I die, in the newspapers they'll write that the sons of bitches of this world have lost their leader.

VINCENT GARDENIA, *Bang the Drum Slowly*, 1973.

Toto, I have a feeling we're not in Kansas anymore.

JUDY GARLAND, *The Wizard of Oz*, 1939.

Toto, we're home…home…and this is my room, and you're all here…and I'm not going to leave here ever, ever, again…because I love you all, and, oh, Aunt Em…there's no place like home!

JUDY GARLAND, *The Wizard of Oz*, 1939.

Anyone who wants to get out of combat isn't really crazy, so I can't ground him.

JACK GILFORD, *Catch-22*, 1970.

I don't want to kill you and you don't wanna die.

DANNY GLOVER, *Silverado*, 1985.

You're slipping, Red. I used to be frightened of that look—the withering glance of the goddess.

CARY GRANT, to Katharine Hepburn, *The Philadelphia Story*, 1940.

Insanity runs in my family. It practically gallops.

CARY GRANT, *Arsenic and Old Lace*, 1944.

I'll get you, my pretty, and your little dog, too!

MARGARET HAMILTON, *The Wizard of Oz*, 1939.

Another fine mess you've got us in, Stanley.

OLIVER HARDY, frequent admonition to Stan Laurel, ca. 1930.

Would you be shocked if I put on something more comfortable?

JEAN HARLOW, *Hell's Angels*, 1930.

I was reading a book the other day…the guy said machinery is going to take the place of every profession.

Oh, my dear, that's something you'll never have to worry about.

JEAN HARLOW AND MARIE DRESSLER, *Dinner at Eight*, 1933.

Armies have marched over me.

RITA HAYWORTH, *Fire Down Below*, 1957.

The calla lilies are in bloom again.

KATHARINE HEPBURN, *Stage Door*, 1937.

You may as well go to perdition in ermine. You're sure to come back in rags.

KATHARINE HEPBURN, *Stage Door*, 1937.

I know he's a good man—you know he's a good man. My bad days are when he knows he's a good man.

KATHARINE HEPBURN, *The State of the Union*, 1948.

Nature, Mr. Allnut, is what we are put into this world to rise above.

KATHARINE HEPBURN, *The African Queen*, 1951.

Mrs. Robinson, you're trying to seduce me, aren't you?

DUSTIN HOFFMAN, *The Graduate*, 1967.

You give me powders, pills, baths, injections, and enemas—when all I need is love.

WILLIAM HOLDEN, *The Bridge on the River Kwai*, 1957.

Tell me why it is that every man who seems attractive these days is either married or barred on a technicality.

CELESTE HOLM, *Gentleman's Agreement*, 1946.

Once I tried to let a smile be my umbrella. I got awful wet.

CELESTE HOLM, *Gentleman's Agreement*, 1947.

Living, I'm worth nothing to her. But dead, I can buy her the tallest cathedrals, golden vineyards and dancing in the streets. One well-directed bullet will accomplish all that.

LESLIE HOWARD, *The Petrified Forest*, 1936.

Buried three of 'em. Good women, bad diets.

ARTHUR HUNNICUTT, *Harry and Tonto*, 1974.

A soul? A soul is nothing. Can you see it? Smell it? Touch it? No!

WALTER HUSTON, *All That Money Can Buy*, 1941.

Pearl, you're curved in the flesh of temptation. Resistance is going to be a darn sight harder for you than for females protected by the shape of sows.

WALTER HUSTON, *Duel in the Sun*, 1946.

We have one simple rule here: Be kind.

SAM JAFFE, *Lost Horizon*, 1937.

Crime is a left-handed form of human endeavor.

SAM JAFFE, *The Asphalt Jungle*, 1950.

Wait a minute, wait a minute, you ain't heard nothin' yet! Wait a minute, I tell you. You ain't heard nothin' yet! Do you want to hear "Toot, Toot, Tootsie"?

AL JOLSON, *The Jazz Singer*, 1927.

You go. We belong dead.

BORIS KARLOFF, *Bride of Frankenstein*, 1935.

Oh, I see…the pellet with the poison's in the flagon with the dragon, the vessel with the pestle has the brew that is true.

DANNY KAYE, *The Court Jester*, 1956.

Science proved relationships don't last. We get on each other's nerves.…You don't believe in science, or political systems, or God. What do you believe in?
Sex and death. Things which come once in a lifetime. At least after death, you're not nauseous.

DIANE KEATON AND WOODY ALLEN, *Sleeper*, 1973.

That's quite a dress you almost have on.

GENE KELLY, *An American in Paris*, 1951.

Hello, Devil. Welcome to Hell.

GENE KELLY, *Inherit the Wind*, 1960.

Do you think it will ever take the place of night baseball?

DEBORAH KERR, *An Affair to Remember*, 1957.

There are worse things than chastity, Mr. Shannon.

Yes—lunacy and death.

DEBORAH KERR AND RICHARD BURTON, *The Night of the Iguana*, 1964.

I hope your fingers aren't tickling my ivory-handled Colt.

KEVIN KLINE, *Silverado*, 1985.

Why did you put your head in the oven?
Oh, I don't know, Meg…I'm havin' a bad day—it's been a real bad day.

JESSICA LANGE AND SISSY SPACEK, *Crimes of the Heart*, 1986.

Am I a king or a breeding bull?

CHARLES LAUGHTON, *The Private Life of Henry VIII*, 1933.

I do not like to be interrupted in the middle of an insult.

CHARLES LAUGHTON, *The Paradine Case*, 1947.

As God is my witness—as God is my witness—they're not going to lick me! I'm going to live through this, and, when it's all over I'll never be hungry again—no, nor any of my folks!—if I have to lie, steal, cheat or kill! As God is my witness, I'll never be hungry again.

VIVIEN LEIGH, *Gone with the Wind*, 1939.

I have always depended on the kindness of strangers.

VIVIEN LEIGH, *A Streetcar Named Desire*, 1947.

People who are very beautiful make their own laws.

VIVIEN LEIGH, *The Roman Spring of Mrs. Stone*, 1961.

Captain, it is I—Ensign Pulver—and I just threw your stinking palm tree overboard. Now, what's all this crud about no movie tonight?

JACK LEMMON, *Mr. Roberts*, 1955.

Now you've done it! Now you've done it!…You've torn off one of my chests.

JACK LEMMON, *Some Like It Hot*, 1959.

You don't understand, Osgood…I'm a man!
Well, nobody's perfect.

JACK LEMMON AND JOE E. BROWN, *Some Like It Hot*, 1959.

It's not a pretty face, I grant you, but underneath its flabby exterior is an enormous lack of character.

OSCAR LEVANT, *An American in Paris*, 1951.

Susan's growing pains are rapidly becoming a major disease.

MYRNA LOY, *The Bachelor and the Bobby Soxer*, 1947.

I refuse to endanger the health of my children in a house with less than three bathrooms.

MYRNA LOY, *Mr. Blandings Builds His Dream House*, 1948.

Ay yam—Drak-ku-lah....Ay bid you velcome!
BELA LUGOSI, *Dracula*, 1931.

Well, I suppose we'll have to feed the duchess. Even vultures have to eat.
SHIRLEY MacLAINE, *The Children's Hour*, 1962.

A man's gotta dream; it comes with the territory.
FREDRIC MARCH, *Death of a Salesman*, 1952.

What we have here is a failure to communicate.
STROTHER MARTIN, *Cool Hand Luke*, 1967.

Just think—tonight, tonight when the moon is sneaking around the clouds I'll be sneaking around you.
GROUCHO MARX, *The Cocoanuts*, 1929.

Be free, my friends. One for all and all for me—me for you and three for five and six for a quarter.
GROUCHO MARX, *The Cocoanuts*, 1929.

You go Uruguay and I'll go mine.
GROUCHO MARX, *Animal Crackers*, 1930.

One morning I shot an elephant in my pajamas. How he got into my pajamas I'll never know.
GROUCHO MARX, *Animal Crackers*, 1930.

And you can say it was a real love match. We married for money.
GROUCHO MARX, *Monkey Business*, 1931.

That's what I always say. Love flies out the door when money come innuendo.
GROUCHO MARX, *Monkey Business*, 1931.

Look at me: I worked my way up from nothing to a state of extreme poverty.
GROUCHO MARX, *Monkey Business*, 1931.

Do you suppose I could buy back my introduction to you?
GROUCHO MARX, *Monkey Business*, 1931.

Why don't you bore a hole in yourself and let the sap run out?
GROUCHO MARX, *Horse Feathers*, 1932.

You've got the brain of a four-year-old boy, and I bet he was glad to get rid of it.
GROUCHO MARX, *Horse Feathers*, 1932.

Don't look now, but there's one man too many in this room and I think it's you.
GROUCHO MARX, *Horse Feathers*, 1932.

I suggest we give him ten years in Leavenworth or eleven years in Twelveworth.

I tell you what I'll do. I'll take five and ten in Woolworth.
GROUCHO MARX AND CHICO MARX, *Duck Soup*, 1933.

Let joy be unconfined. Let there be dancing in the streets, drinking in the saloons, and necking in the park.
GROUCHO MARX, *A Night at the Opera*, 1935.

Don't point that beard at me, it might go off.
GROUCHO MARX, *A Day at the Races*, 1937.

I bet your father spent the first year of your life throwing rocks at the stork.
GROUCHO MARX, *At the Circus*, 1939.

I told you 158 times I cannot stand little notes on my pillow. "We are out of corn flakes. F.U." It took me three hours to figure out F.U. was Felix Unger. It's not your fault, Felix: it's a rotten combination, that's all.
WALTER MATTHAU, *The Odd Couple*, 1968.

If you've got anything on your chest besides your chin, you'd better get it off.
WALTER MATTHAU, *The Odd Couple*, 1968.

How 'bout coming up to my place for a spot of heavy breathing?
WALTER MATTHAU, *Pete 'n' Tillie*, 1972.

Are you eating a tomato, or is that your nose?
CHARLIE McCARTHY (EDGAR BERGEN), to W.C. Fields, *You Can't Cheat an Honest Man*, 1939.

He has a heart of gold—only harder.
ADOLPHE MENJOU, *A Star Is Born*, 1937.

I'm being marked down? I've been kidnapped by K-Mart!
BETTE MIDLER, *Ruthless People*, 1986.

Somewhere, sometime, there may be the bullet or the wrong bottle waiting for Josiah Boone. Why worry when or where?
THOMAS MITCHELL, *Stagecoach*, 1939.

A kiss on the hand might feel very good, but a diamond tiara is forever.
MARILYN MONROE, *Gentlemen Prefer Blondes*, 1953.

She's got those eyes that run up and down men like a searchlight.
DENNIE MOORE on Joan Crawford, *The Women*, 1939.

That's it, baby. If you've got it, flaunt it.
ZERO MOSTEL, *The Producers*, 1967.

How could this happen? I was so careful. I picked the wrong play, the wrong director, the wrong cast—where did I go right?

ZERO MOSTEL, *The Producers*, 1968.

Not only is an innocent man crying out for justice; but more, much more—a great nation is in desperate danger of forfeiting her honor!

PAUL MUNI, *The Life of Emile Zola*, 1937.

Fat man, you shoot a great game of pool.

PAUL NEWMAN, *The Hustler*, 1961.

I am not part of your luggage. Whatever I am, I am not part of your luggage.

PAUL NEWMAN, *Sweet Bird of Youth*, 1962.

The only question I ever ask any woman is: "What time is your husband coming home?"

PAUL NEWMAN, *Hud*, 1963.

Now all you have to do is hold the chicken, bring me the toast, give me a check for the chicken salad sandwich—and you haven't broken any rules.

JACK NICHOLSON, *Five Easy Pieces*, 1970.

They was giving 10,000 watts a day, and you know, I'm hot to trot. The next woman takes me out is going to light up like a pinball machine and pay off in silver dollars.

JACK NICHOLSON, *One Flew Over the Cuckoo's Nest*, 1975.

The white woman stays with me.

WARNER OLAND, *Shanghai Express*, 1932.

Live? I can't go on *live*!! I'm a movie-star—not an actor!

PETER O'TOOLE, *My Favorite Year*, 1982.

My father made him an offer he couldn't refuse.

AL PACINO, *The Godfather*, 1972.

Mother—what's the phrase?—isn't quite herself today.

ANTHONY PERKINS, *Psycho*, 1960.

You're just walkin' around to save funeral expenses.

VALERIE PERRINE, *The Electric Horseman*, 1979.

How in the hell would I know why there are Nazis? I don't know how this can opener works.

LEO POSTREL, *Hannah and Her Sisters*, 1986.

I've got to get more steps. I need more steps. I've got to get higher…higher!

WILLIAM POWELL, *The Great Ziegfeld*, 1936.

Fifty—the age of youth, the youth of old age.

WILLIAM POWELL, *Mr. Peabody and the Mermaid*, 1948.

We'll start with a few murders. Big men. Little men. Just to show we make no distinction.

CLAUDE RAINS, *The Invisible Man*, 1932.

Someday, when things are tough, maybe you can ask the boys to go in there and win just one for the Gipper.

RONALD REAGAN, *Knute Rockne—All American*, 1940.

He's very progressive. He has all sorts of ideas about artificial insemination and all that sort of thing. He breeds all over the world.

DEBBIE REYNOLDS, *The Pleasure of His Company*, 1961.

Your wife is safe with Tonetti—he prefers spaghetti.

ERIK RHODES, *The Gay Divorcee*, 1934.

If there's anything worse than a woman living alone, it's a woman saying she likes it.

THELMA RITTER, *Pillow Talk*, 1959.

This is your neighbor speaking. I'm sure I speak for all of us when I say that something must be done about your garbage cans in the alley here. *It is definitely second-rate garbage*! Now, by next week, I want to see a better class of garbage. I want to see champagne bottles and caviar cans. I'm sure you're all behind me on this, so let's snap it up and get on the ball.

JASON ROBARDS, *A Thousand Clowns*, 1965.

Mother of Mercy, is this the end of Rico?

EDWARD G. ROBINSON, dying words, *Little Caesar*, 1930.

Why are you wearing those clothes?
Because I just went gay all of a sudden.

MAY ROBSON on seeing Cary Grant in a woman's robe, *Bringing Up Baby*, 1938.

Cynthia…oh, she'll let you kiss her whenever you want. She doesn't want to swim. She doesn't want to play tennis, go for walks. All she wants to do is kiss you. I'm a nervous wreck!

MICKEY ROONEY, *Love Finds Andy Hardy*, 1938.

Believe you me, if it didn't take men to make babies I wouldn't have anything to do with any of you!

GENA ROWLANDS, *Lonely Are the Brave*, 1962.

His mother and father together are like a bad car wreck.

CHRIS SARANDON, *Dog Day Afternoon*, 1975.

It's the only disease you don't look forward to being cured of.

EVERETT SLOANE, on old age, *Citizen Kane*, 1941.

I've aged, Sidney. There are new lines in my face. I look like a brand-new, steel-belted radial tire.

MAGGIE SMITH, *California Suite*, 1978.

Why did you two ever get married?

Ah, I don't know. It was raining, and we were in Pittsburgh.

BARBARA STANWYCK AND HELEN BRODERICK, *The Bride Walks Out*, 1936.

I've met some hardboiled eggs, but you—you're twenty minutes.

JAN STERLING, *Ace in the Hole*, 1951.

I've wrestled with reality for 35 years, and I'm happy, Doctor, I finally won out over it.

JIMMY STEWART, to psychiatrist, *Harvey*, 1950.

May I ask you a personal question: Do you smile all the time?

BARBRA STREISAND, *The Way We Were*, 1973.

I'm not living with you. We occupy the same cage, that's all.

ELIZABETH TAYLOR, *Cat on a Hot Tin Roof*, 1958.

I swear, if you existed, I'd divorce you.

ELIZABETH TAYLOR, *Who's Afraid of Virginia Woolf?*, 1966.

Now, look, Whitey. In a pinch I can be tougher than you are, and I guess maybe this is the pinch.

SPENCER TRACY, *Boys Town*, 1938.

You see her face? A real honest face. Only disgusting thing about her.

SPENCER TRACY, *Pat and Mike*, 1952.

You're not too bright. I like that in a man.

KATHLEEN TURNER, *Body Heat*, 1981.

Chivalry is not only dead, it's decomposing.

RUDY VALLEE, *The Palm Beach Story*, 1942.

Well, I'll tell you the truth now. I ain't a real cowboy, but I am one helluva stud.

JON VOIGHT, *Midnight Cowboy*, 1969.

Some people are better off dead—like your wife and my father, for instance.

ROBERT WALKER, *Strangers on a Train*, 1951.

We women are so much more sensible! When *we* tire of ourselves, we change the way we do our hair, or hire a new cook. Or redecorate the house. I suppose a man could do over his office, but he never thinks of anything so simple. No, dear, a man has only one escape from his old self—to see a different self in the mirror of some woman's eyes.

LUCILE WATSON, *The Women*, 1939.

Never apologize and never explain—it's a sign of weakness.

JOHN WAYNE, *She Wore a Yellow Ribbon*, 1949.

Sometimes I wonder whose side God's on.

JOHN WAYNE, *The Longest Day*, 1963.

Out here, due process is a bullet.

JOHN WAYNE, *The Green Berets*, 1968.

Fill your hand, you son of a bitch!

JOHN WAYNE, *True Grit*, 1969.

It's lavish, but I call it home.

CLIFTON WEBB, *Laura*, 1944.

You know, I've never been able to understand why, when there's so much space in the world, people would deliberately choose to live in the Middle West.

CLIFTON WEBB, *The Razor's Edge*, 1946.

I hate the dawn. The grass always looks as though it's been left out all night.

CLIFTON WEBB, *The Dark Corner*, 1946.

In Italy for thirty years under the Borgias they had warfare, terror, murder, bloodshed—they produced Michelangelo, Leonardo da Vinci, and the Renaissance. In Switzerland they had brotherly love, five hundred years of democracy and peace, and what did that produce? The cuckoo clock.

ORSON WELLES, *The Third Man*, 1949.

Come up and see me sometime.

MAE WEST, *Diamond Lil*, 1932.

Goodness, what beautiful diamonds!

Goodness had nothing to do with it, dearie.

MAE WEST AND CHECK-OUT GIRL, *Night After Night*, 1932.

Beulah, peel me a grape.

MAE WEST, *I'm No Angel*, 1933.

It's not the men in my life, but the life in my men.

MAE WEST, *I'm No Angel*, 1933.

Is that a gun in your pocket or are you just glad to see me?

MAE WEST, *She Done Him Wrong*, 1933.

Why don't you come up sometime 'n' see me...I'm home every evening.

MAE WEST, *She Done Him Wrong*, 1933.

Don't these big empty houses scare you?

Not me, I was in vaudeville.

NYDIA WESTMAN AND BOB HOPE, *The Cat and the Canary,*
1939.

You know what I do with squealers? I let 'em
have it in the belly so they can roll around for a
long time thinking it over.

RICHARD WIDMARK, *Kiss of Death,* 1947.

Would you take your clammy hand off my chair?
You have the touch of a love-starved cobra.

MONTY WOOLLEY, *The Man Who Came to Dinner,* 1941.

There can only be one winner, folks, but isn't
that the American way?

GIG YOUNG, *They Shoot Horses Don't They?,* 1970.

MOVIES

I...doubt that film can ever argue effectively
against its own material: that a genuine anti-war
film, say, can be made on the basis of even the
ugliest battle scenes....No matter what filmmak-
ers intend, film always argues yes. People have
been modeling their lives after films for years,
but the medium is somehow unsuited to moral
lessons, cautionary tales or polemics of any kind.
If you want to make a pacifist film, you must
make an exemplary film about peaceful men.

RENATA ADLER, "The Movies Make Heroes of Them All,"
January 7, 1968, *A Year in the Dark: A Year in the Life of
a Film Critic,* 1971.

Though films become more daring sexually, they
are probably less sexy than they ever were. There
haven't been any convincing love scenes or
romances in the movies for a while. (Nobody
even seems to neck in theaters anymore.)...
When the mechanics and sadism quotients go
up, the movie love interest goes dead, and the
film just lies there, giving a certain amount of
offense.

RENATA ADLER, "Temper, Misogyny, and Couples in
Theaters," October 13, 1968, *A Year in the Dark: A Year
in the Life of a Film Critic,* 1971.

Won't the new "Suggested for Mature Audience"
protect our youngsters from such films? I don't
believe so. I know many forty-five-year-old men
with the mentalities of six-year-olds, and my
feeling is that they should not see such pictures,
either.

SHIRLEY TEMPLE BLACK, *McCall's,* January, 1967.

Hollywood...scripts...a medium where both
syntax and the language itself were subjected to
horrid mutilation by young men who thought of
themselves as writers and who proved it by the
enormous salaries they received from those higher up who were even less knowledgeable of the
mother tongue.

BESSIE BREUER, *The Actress,* 1955.

Moving pictures need sound as much as
Beethoven symphonies need lyrics.

CHARLES CHAPLIN, 1928, in Lois and Alan Gordon,
American Chronicle, 1987.

In this lovely land of corrugated cartons and
plastic bags, we want our entertainment packaged as neatly as the rest of our consumer goods:
an attractive label on the outside, a complete
and accurate detailing of contents there or on
the inside, no loose ends, no odd parts, nothing
left out.

JUDITH CRIST, *The Private Eye, the Cowboy and the Very
Naked Girl,* 1968.

Movies suddenly become "film" and "cinema,"
an "art form" and terribly chic....Film criticism
becomes the means whereby a stream of young
intellectuals could go straight from the campus
film society into the professionals' screening
room without managing to get a glimpse of the
real world in between.

JUDITH CRIST, *The Private Eye, the Cowboy and the Very
Naked Girl,* 1968.

We went three and four afternoons a week, sat
on folding chairs in the darkened Quonset hut
which served as a theater, and it was there, that
summer of 1943 while the hot wind blew outside, that I first saw John Wayne. Saw the walk,
heard the voice. Heard him tell the girl in a picture called *War of the Wildcats* that he would
build her a house, "at the bend in the river
where the cottonwoods grow." As it happened I
did not grow up to be the kind of woman who is
the heroine in a Western, and although the men
I have known have had many virtues and have
taken me to live in many places I have come to
love, they have never been John Wayne, and
they have never taken me to that bend in the
river where the cottonwoods grow. Deep in that
part of my heart where the artificial rain forever
falls, that is still the line I wait to hear.

JOAN DIDION, "John Wayne: A Love Song," *Slouching
Towards Bethlehem,* 1968.

G means the hero gets the girl. R means the villain gets the girl. And X means everybody gets the girl.

KIRK DOUGLAS, *Parade*, December 30, 1990.

For the entire state of Georgia, having the premiere of *Gone With the Wind* on home ground was like winning the Battle of Atlanta 75 years late.

ANNE EDWARDS, *Road to Tara*, 1983.

The lowest action trash is preferable to wholesome family entertainment. When you clean them up, when you make movies respectable, you kill them.

PAULINE KAEL, *Going Steady*, 1968.

Movies have been doing so much of the same thing—in slightly different ways—for so long that few of the possibilities of this great hybrid art have yet been explored.

PAULINE KAEL, *Going Steady*, 1968.

Good movies make you care, make you believe in possibilities again.

PAULINE KAEL, *Going Steady*, 1968.

Art is still what teachers and ladies and foundations believe in, it's civilized and refined, cultivated and serious, cultural, beautiful. European, Oriental: it's what America isn't, and it's especially what American movies are not.

PAULINE KAEL, "Movies as Opera," *Going Steady*, 1968.

If big film directors are to get credit for doing badly what others have been doing brilliantly for years with no money, just because they've put it on a big screen, then businessmen are greater than poets and theft is art.

PAULINE KAEL, "Movies as Opera," *Going Steady*, 1968.

The words "Kiss Kiss Bang Bang," which I saw on an Italian movie poster, are perhaps the briefest statement imaginable of the basic appeal of movies.

PAULINE KAEL, *Kiss Kiss Bang Bang*, 1968.

For 50 cents we took the middle-class man out of his home and gave him an environment that only the Church had given before.

S. CHARLES LEE, on motion-picture palaces of 1930s, *Newsweek*, September 10, 1979.

The cynics are always with us—those who say Hollywood cannot face reality, that everything must be glossed over and made unreal. What the cynics do not realize is that dreams are often more real than reality. There is a reality beyond that which we see and touch and feel. There exists within man a groping toward an idealistic extension of himself; an undefeatable belief that life can be pleasanter than it may be at the moment, a staunch conviction that there are possibilities beyond his own narrow horizons. The movie with the fairytale, Cinderella, happy-ending plot brings joy because it also brings hope.

MERVYN LEROY, 1953, in Richard Dyer MacCann, *Film and Society*, 1964.

The legitimate theatre is in a panic...[with] talking pictures...all their seats at the same price.... Get it? The rich man stands in line with the poor.

LLOYD LEWIS, *New Republic*, 1929.

"Childish" is the word with which the intelligentsia once branded Hollywood. And yet, those movies, which depicted Life as life can never be, were fairy tales for the adult. Today there are no fairy tales for us to believe in, and this is possibly a reason for the universal prevalence of mental crack-up. Yes, if we were childish in the past, I wish we could be children once again.

ANITA LOOS, *No Mother to Guide Her*, 1961.

We have a little catch phrase in our family which somehow fits almost everyone in the movie colony: "Spare no expense to make everything as economical as possible."

FRANCES MARION, "1914 Through 1924," *Off with Their Heads*, 1972.

The picture is so essentially Spanish that I want everyone in the theater...to eat garlic during the performance.

FRED NIBLO, on *Blood and Sand*, 1922, in Lois and Alan Gordon, *American Chronicle*, 1987.

I often ask myself these days as I shell out four dollars, stumble over people's feet in the murk, and gingerly settle down on the slag of their popcorn just what sort of will-o'-the-wisp I'm still pursuing. Surely anyone marinated by sixty-five years' exposure to the silver screen, mile upon mile of acetate etched with the hallucinations of ribbon clerks and debauched waitresses, would be much better off at home sipping hot cocoa and reading Pascal's *Pensées* in his nightgown—they now have nightgowns embroidered with Pascal's thoughts—yet there I sit, slack-jawed, a grizzled prospector still avid for whatever nuggets might turn up in the sludge.

S.J. PERELMAN, *The Last Laugh*, 1981.

I believe that "the unexamined life is not worth living"—and what a glorious medium film is on which to conduct our examinations!

ELEANOR PERRY, in "Rebirth," by Kay Loveland and Estelle Changas, in Richard Corliss, ed., *The Hollywood Screenwriters*, 1972.

Movies have a surface realism which tends to disguise fantasy and makes it seem true....It is this quality of realness which makes the escape into the world of movies so powerful, bringing with it conscious and unconscious absorption of the screenplay's values and ideas.

HORTENSE POWDERMAKER, 1950, in Richard Dyer MacCann, *Film and Society*, 1964.

[I]nstead of the usual "Why can't we make movies more like real life?" I think a more pertinent question is "Why can't real life be more like the movies?" A movie is a series of climaxes—little glimpses of high spots and low spots—and in the end there is the great climax, and the darkness, and no concern for the years of dying embers and the utter monotony ahead....

It isn't what the movies put in that makes them so wonderful—it's what they leave out.

ERNIE PYLE, 1947, in Richard Dyer MacCann, *Film and Society*, 1964.

We talk of the worth, the service, the entertaining power, the community value, the recreative force, the educational influence, the civilizing and commerical possibilities of the motion picture. And everyone has, singularly enough, neglected to mention its rarest and subtlest beauty:

Silence....

The value of silence in art is its stimulation to the imagination....The talking picture will be made practical, but it will never supersede the motion picture without sound.

JAMES R. QUIRK, *Photoplay*, May, 1921.

To be completely candid, I think most movies nowadays are trash, and many strike me as unhealthy. The explicit sex, pointless violence, and crude language appeal only to our lowest instincts. They have taken away our idealism, our sense of fun and joy. It's chic to be cynical and tear our heroes down. What has happened to us? And what are we doing to our young people?

NANCY REAGAN, *Nancy*, 1980.

There is only one thing that can kill the Movies and that is education.

WILL ROGERS, *Autobiography*, 1926.

You can't spring a new plot on an audience the first time and expect it to go. It takes a Movie audience years to get on to a new plot.

WILL ROGERS, in Donald Day, ed., *The Autobiography of Will Rogers*, 1949.

Movies have always been a form of popular culture that altered the way women looked at the world and reflected how men intended to keep it.

MARJORIE ROSEN, *Popcorn Venus*, 1973.

Studios, purporting to ease the anguish of Depression reality, transformed movies into the politics of fantasy, the great black-and-white opiate of the masses.

MARJORIE ROSEN, *Popcorn Venus*, 1973.

After twenty years of being only in its infancy, the moving picture which gave some promise of an interesting adult life has suddenly gone senile—and garrulous. It is talking at the top of its voice, talking to itself, talking in its sleep. Terrified of...radio broadcasting, it has incorporated radio itself.

GILBERT SELDES, "The Movies Commit Suicide," *Vanity Fair*, 1928.

The motion pictures present our customs and our daily life more distinctly than any other medium and, therefore, if we were to come back a thousand years from today and tried to find some form of expression that would more clearly, more perfectly explain how we live today, it would have to be the motion picture, because there is no medium of today that so universally must please as great a number of people....

IRVING THALBERG, 1929, in Richard Dyer MacCann, *Film and Society*, 1964.

They'll wear toilet seats around their necks if you give 'em what they want to see.

BILL THOMAS, on 3-D glasses, 1952, in Lois and Alan Gordon, *American Chronicle*, 1987.

All Americans born between 1890 and 1945 wanted to be movie stars.

GORE VIDAL, "Scott's Case," *New York Review of Books*, May 1, 1980.

Who the hell wants to hear actors talk?

HARRY M. WARNER, ca. 1927, in Don Atyeo and Jonathan Green, *Don't Quote Me*, 1981.

RADIO SHOW LINES

The following are in chronological, not alphabetical, order.

Holy mackerel, Andy.
"Amos 'n' Andy," 1929.

There will be a brief pause...while we throw at you Mrs. Pennyfeather's Personal Service for Perturbed People."
Announcer, "The Cuckoo Hour," 1930.

So long...until tomorrow.
Lowell Thomas, 1930.

Who's the little chatterbox?
The one with pretty auburn locks?
Who can it be? It's Little Orphan Annie.
Announcer, "Little Orphan Annie," 1931.

Time...marches on! As it must to all men, death came this week to...
Announcer, "The March of Time," 1931.

How *do* you *do*?
Eddy Cantor, "The Eddy Cantor Show," 1931.

Now, cut that out.
Anaheim, Azusa, and Cu-ca-monga.
Jack Benny, "The Jack Benny Show," 1932.

Good evening, Mr. and Mrs. America, and all the ships at sea.
Walter Winchell, 1932.

Be good to yourself!
Announcer, "Breakfast Club," 1933.

...dedicated to the mothers and fathers of the younger generation and their bewildering offspring.
Announcer, "One Man's Family," 1933.

...[the story of a woman] who sets out to prove... romance can live...at thirty-five.
Announcer, "The Romance of Helen Trent," 1933.

You're a hard man, McGee.
"Fibber McGee and Molly," 1935.

...the story of...what it means to be the wife of a famous Broadway star—dream sweetheart of a million other women.
Announcer, "Backstage Wife," 1935.

The wheel of fortune goes 'round and 'round and where she stops nobody knows.
Major Bowes, "Major Bowes and His Original Amateur Hour," 1934.

Drawn by the magnetic force of the fantastic metropolis,...great trains rush toward the gigantic stage on which are played a thousand dramas daily!
Announcer, "Grand Central Station," 1937.

Can this girl from a mining town in the West find happiness as the wife of a wealthy and titled Englishman?
Announcer, "Our Gal Sunday," 1937.

Britt Reid, daring young publisher, matches wits with the underworld....He hunts the biggest...of all game. Public enemies who try to destroy our America.
Announcer, "The Green Hornet," 1938.

Wake up, America. It's time to stump the experts.
Announcer, "Information Please!" 1938.

I'm speaking from the roof of the Broadcasting Building, New York City. The bells you hear are ringing to warn people to evacuate the city as the Martians approach.
Announcer, Orson Welles' "The War of the Worlds," Mercury Radio Theatre, 1938.

...able to leap tall buildings at a single bound!... It's a bird! It's a plane! It's Superman!
Announcer, "Superman," 1940.

Now it's time to close the door of the Inner Sanctum.
Announcer, "Inner Sanctum," 1941.

...where the elite meet to eat. Archie, the manager, speaking.
Archie, "Duffy's Tavern," 1941.

If I dood it, I gets a whipping.
Red Skelton, "The Red Skelton Show," 1941.

Hey Abbott! I'm a ba-a-a-d boy.
Lou Costello, "Abbott and Costello," 1942.

It pays to be ignorant, to be dumb, to be dense, to be ignorant.
It pays to be ignorant,
Just like me!
Theme song, "It Pays to Be Ignorant," 1942.

Pancho: Cisco, the sheriff and hees posse...they are comeeng closer.
Cisco: This way, Pancho. Vámonos.
"Cisco Kid," 1943.

Pardon me for talking in your face, Señorita.
"The Judy Canova Show," 1943.

RADIO

Radio could not survive because it was a by-product of advertising. Ability, merit and talent were not requirements of writers and actors working in the industry. Audiences had to be attracted, for advertising purposes, at any cost and by any artifice....When television belatedly found its way into the home, after stopping off too long at the tavern, the advertisers knew they had a more potent force available for their selling purposes. Radio was abandoned like the bones at a barbecue.

FRED ALLEN, *Treadmill to Oblivion*, 1954.

Radio in the 30's was a calm and tranquil medium. Oleaginous-voiced announcers smoothly purred their commercial copy into the microphones enunciating each lubricated syllable. Tony Wons was cooing his soothing poems. Bedtime stories were popular. Radio was one unruffled day from Cheerio in the early morning through to Music to Read By at midnight. Radio was fraught with politeness.

FRED ALLEN, *Treadmill to Oblivion*, 1954.

[R]adio will serve to make the concept of Peace on Earth, Good Will Toward Man a reality.

JAMES J. HARBORD, 1925, *Foreign Affairs*, January, 1944.

One of the chief pretenders to the throne of God is radio itself, which has acquired a sort of omniscience. I live in a strictly rural community, and people here speak of "The Radio" in the large sense, with an over-meaning. When they say "The Radio" they don't mean a cabinet, an electrical phenomenon, or a man in a studio, they refer to a pervading and somewhat godlike presence which has come into their lives and homes.

E.B. WHITE, "Sabbath Morn," February, 1939.

TELEVISION

Television is a triumph of equipment over people, and the minds that control it are so small that you could put them in a gnat's navel with room left over for two caraway seeds and an agent's heart.

FRED ALLEN, *CoEvolution Quarterly*, Winter, 1977.

Because of television, history will never again be quite the same. By putting the viewer on the scene at the moment that news is made or shortly thereafter, television is transforming history

from something we read about into something that happens to us, involves us and becomes a permanent part of us through our participation.

1968 ANNUAL REPORT TO SHAREHOLDERS OF CBS, in Martin Mayer, *About Television*, 1972.

The single biggest problem of television is that everyone talks so much.

ROONE ARLEDGE, *Time*, August 22, 1977.

If the proverb is true that prison is college for crime, I believe for young disturbed adolescents, TV is a preparatory school for delinquency.

RALPH S. BANAY, testimony before U.S. Senate, April 6, 1955, in Richard Dyer MacCann, *Film and Society*, 1964.

Children who have been taught, or conditioned, to listen passively most of the day to the warm verbal communication coming from the TV screen, to the deep emotional appeal of the so-called TV personality, are often unable to respond to real persons because they arouse so much less feeling than the skilled actor. Worse, they lose the ability to learn from reality because life experiences are more complicated than the ones they see on the screen, and there is no one who comes in at the end to explain it all. The "TV child"...gets discouraged when he cannot grasp the meaning of what happens to him....If, later in life, this block of solid inertia is not removed, the emotional isolation from others that starts in front of TV may continue.... This being seduced into passivity and discouraged about facing life actively on one's own is the real danger of TV.

BRUNO BETTELHEIM, in Martin Mayer, *About Television*, 1972.

Along with the constant newness of everything and the ceaseless moving from place to place, first radio, then television, have assaulted and overturned the privacy of the home, the real American privacy, which permitted the development of a higher and more independent life within democratic society. Parents can no longer control the atmosphere of the home and have lost even the will to do so. With great subtlety and energy, television enters not only the room, but also the tastes of old and young alike, appealing to the immediately pleasant and subverting whatever does not conform to it.

ALLAN BLOOM, *The Closing of the American Mind*, 1987.

Nothing is real unless it happens on television.

DANIEL J. BOORSTIN, *New York Times*, February 19, 1978.

Fight Prime Time, Read a Book.

BUMPER STICKER.

My husband runs what is called an educational television network. You must have seen some of the wonderful work they put on. Who else gives you a close look at gum surgery? Just as you're sitting down to dinner?

CHRIS CHASE, *How to Be a Movie Star, or A Terrible Beauty Is Born*, 1968.

Television is business, and business is America.

BILL COSBY, *Ebony*, September, 1966.

While theoretically and technically television may be feasible, commercially and financially I consider it an impossibility, a development of which we need waste little time dreaming.

LEE DEFOREST, in Norman Augustine, *Augustine's Laws*, 1926.

Television has the power to transmit the experience itself.

REUVEN FRANK, *Television*, February 15, 1988.

After all, not one couch potato has ever come down with tennis elbow. Not one has ever had a shin splint. Maybe one or two got stiff fingers from pressing the TV remote, but they haven't suffered a single major injury. Except, of course, to their pride.

ELLEN GOODMAN, "The Rise of the Couch Potato," *Washington Post*, December, 1987.

[T]he future of television constitutes a genuine challenge to the resiliency of the free-enterprise system. The test that lies ahead is whether the profit motive can survive without compromising cultural values that are just as vital to a well-rounded society. What appears tomorrow on television's twenty-one-inch screen is not a narrow matter of electronics or show business; it also will be a reflection of democracy in action, one way or another.

JACK GOULD, in Richard Dyer MacCann, *Film and Society*, 1964.

The convictions of Hollywood and television are made of boiled money.

LILLIAN HELLMAN, *An Unfinished Woman*, 1969.

Television has done much for psychiatry by spreading information about it, as well as contributing to the need for it.

ALFRED HITCHCOCK, *Alfred Hitchcock Presents*, ca. 1960.

Television has brought back murder into the home—where it belongs.

ALFRED HITCHCOCK, *The Observer*, December 19, 1965.

The widely held belief that television experienced a golden age which was destroyed by a tyranny of ratings and the philistinism of a profit philosophy is one of the many myths of broadcasting. There was a time in the early fifties when television was filled with a heady excitement, and recollections of it invite us to indulge ourselves in nostalgia. But that this brief period was television's apotheosis is denied not only by discerning critics but by the very men who were responsible for programming at the time.

ROY HUGGINS, in Richard Dyer MacCann, *Film and Society*, 1964.

In an automobile civilization, which was one of constant motion and activity, there was almost no time to think; in a television one, there is small desire.

LOUIS KRONENBERGER, *Company Manners*, 1954.

Television won't matter in your lifetime or mine.

REX LAMBERT, *The Listener*, 1936.

The more I see of television, the more I dislike and defend it. Television is not for me but for many others who do like it, but who have no time for many things that I like. It seems to me that television is: the literature of the illiterate, the culture of the lowbrow, the wealth of the poor, the privilege of the underprivileged, and the exclusive club of the excluded masses.

LEE LOEVINGER, in Martin Mayer, *About Television*, 1972.

Each day a few more lies eat into the seed with which we are born, little institutional lies from the print of newspapers, the shock waves of television, and the sentimental cheats of the movie screen.

NORMAN MAILER, "First Advertisement for Myself," *Advertisements for Myself*, 1959.

Television pollutes identity.

NORMAN MAILER, *St. George and the Godfather*, 1972.

It is television's primary damage that it provides ten million children with the same fantasy, ready-made and on a platter.

MARYA MANNES, *More in Anger*, 1958.

If the television craze continues with the present level of programs, we are destined to have a nation of morons.

DANIEL MARSH, 1950, in Lois and Alan Gordon, *American Chronicle*, 1987.

Ours has been called the jet age, the atomic age, the space age. It is also, I submit, the television age. And just as history will decide whether the leaders of today's world employed the atom to destroy the world or rebuild it for mankind's benefit, so will history decide whether today's broadcasters employed their powerful voice to enrich the people or debase them.

NEWTON MINOW, speech, National Association of Broadcasters, May 9, 1961.

I invite you to sit down in front of your television set when your station goes on the air and stay there without a book, magazine, newspaper, profit-and-loss sheet, or rating book to distract you—and keep your eyes glued to that set until the station signs off. I can assure you that you will observe a vast wasteland.

NEWTON MINOW, speech, National Association of Broadcasters, May 9, 1961.

The power of instantaneous sight and sound is without precedent in mankind's history. This is an awesome power. It has limitless capabilities for good—and for evil.

NEWTON MINOW, speech, National Association of Broadcasters, May 9, 1961.

Man does not live by ratings alone.

NEWTON MINOW, 1962, in Lois and Alan Gordon, *American Chronicle*, 1987.

Television can be a distorting mirror.

EDWIN R. NEWMAN, *Television*, February 15, 1988.

I don't like what the light box has done to America at night—turned everybody into a fucking pinball-machine moth. If they had just outlawed these light boxes, the world would simply look bigger.

JACK NICHOLSON, *Rolling Stone*, 1986.

I used to pride myself on being impervious to the sentimentalities of soap opera, but when that loveliest of English actresses, Rachel Gurney, of *Upstairs, Downstairs*, perished on the *Titanic*, I wept so convulsively and developed such anorexia that I had to be force-fed.

S.J. PERELMAN, *The Last Laugh*, 1981.

Television's strongest point is that it brings personalities into our hearts, not abstractions into our heads.

NEIL POSTMAN, *Amusing Ourselves to Death*, 1985.

Entertainment is the supra-ideology of all discourse on television. No matter what is depicted or from what point of view, the overarching pre-

sumption is that it is there for our amusement and pleasure.

NEIL POSTMAN, *Amusing Ourselves to Death*, 1985.

It is probable that television drama of high caliber and produced by first-rate artists will materially raise the level of dramatic taste of the nation.

DAVID SARNOFF, "The Future of Television," *Popular Mechanics*, 1939.

[A] nation that can't tell the difference between their television screens and their lives deserves everything that happens to them.

IAN SHOALES, "TV Violence," *I Gotta Go*, October 1, 1984.

Instances of people harmed by television will not be found in averages or statistics but in hospitals and prisons.

HARRY SKORNIA, 1965, in Martin Mayer, *About Television*, 1972.

There is no boredom or misery to equal the pursuit of distraction alone. We do not slip into happiness. It is strenuously sought and earned. A nation glued to the television screen is not simply at a loss before the iron pioneers of the new collective society. It isn't even having a good time.

ADLAI E. STEVENSON, speech, National School Boards Association, San Francisco, California, January 26, 1959.

There are days when any electrical appliance in the house, including the vacuum cleaner, seems to offer more entertainment possibilities than the TV set.

HARRIET VAN HORNE, *New York World-Telegram and Sun*, June 7, 1957.

Senator McCarthy and television came into prominence together, and it is a nice irony that a medium so perfectly made to order for a demagogue should have proved to be the means of his undoing, thanks as much to [Edward R.] Murrow and [Fred] Friendly as to the Senator's own extraordinary capers.

GORE VIDAL, "Public Television: A Meditation," *Reflections Upon a Sinking Ship*, 1969.

I hate television. I hate it as much as peanuts. But I can't stop eating peanuts.

ORSON WELLES, *New York Herald Tribune*, October 12, 1956.

I believe television is going to be the test of the modern world, and that in this new opportunity to see beyond the range of our vision we shall discover either a new and unbearable disturbance of the general peace or a saving radiance in the sky. We shall stand or fall by television—of that I am quite sure.

E.B. WHITE, 1938, in Martin Mayer, *About Television*, 1972.

Chewing gum for the eyes.

ATTRIBUTED TO FRANK LLOYD WRIGHT.

[Television] won't be able to hold onto any market it captures after the first six months. People will soon get tired of staring at a plywood box every night.

DARRYL F. ZANUCK, in Gabe Essoe, *The Book of Movie Lists*, 1981.

TELEVISION SHOW LINES

The following are in chronological, not alphabetical, order.

One man's theft is another man's justice.

ALAN ALDA, *M*A*S*H*, 1970s.

This recipe is certainly silly. It says to separate eggs, but it doesn't say how far to separate them.

GRACIE ALLEN, *The George Burns and Gracie Allen Show*, 1950s.

I want it *all*.

BEA ARTHUR, *Maude*, 1970s.

I guess being a mother sometimes interferes with logic.

BARBARA BILLINGSLEY, *Leave It to Beaver*, 1950s–1960s.

Send me your poor, your deadbeats, your filthy…all of them free to live together in peace and harmony in their little, separate sections where they feel safe, and break your head if you go in there.

ARCHIE BUNKER, *All in the Family*, 1971.

With credit, you can buy everything you can't afford.

EDITH BUNKER, *All in the Family*, 1978.

Some parents get better children than they deserve.

RAYMOND BURR, *Perry Mason*, 1950s–1970s.

Well, I certainly don't believe God's a woman, because if He were, men would be the ones walking around wearing high heels, taking Midol, and having their upper lips waxed.

DIXIE CARTER, *Designing Women*, 1980s–1990s.

If it weren't for art, there wouldn't be any science.

ANGELA CARTWRIGHT, *Lost in Space*, 1960s.

Why do they call them tellers? They never tell you anything. They just ask questions. And why do they call it interest? It's boring. And another thing—how come the Trust Department has all their pens chained to the table?

NICHOLAS COLASANTO, *Cheers*, 1980s.

There is a passion in the human heart called aspiration. It flares with a noble flame, and by its light Man has traveled from the caves of darkness to outer space. But when this passion called aspiration becomes lust, when its flame is fanned by greed and private hunger, then aspiration becomes ambition—by which sin the angels fell.

THE CONTROL VOICE, *The Outer Limits* (TV), 1960s,.

I am your father. I brought you into this world and I can take you out.

BILL COSBY, *The Cosby Show*, 1980s–1990s.

That shows how long we've been married. Now you kiss me to calm me down.

JOAN DAVIS, *I Married Joan*, 1950s.

Don't start comparing yourself with me. It will only make you crazy.

RON GLASS, *Barney Miller*, 1970s–1980s.

There's nothing more sophomoric than men contemplating their own hormones.

SHARON GLESS, *Cagney & Lacey*, 1980s.

When you're a lawman and you're dealing with people, you do a whole lot better if you go not so much by the book but by the heart.

ANDY GRIFFITH, *The Andy Griffith Show*, 1960s.

I tell ya—you take all the gray-suited lawyers, you round 'em up and put them on a boat to Indochina, and you wouldn't have no more problems with the criminal justice system in this country.

CHARLES HAID, *Hill Street Blues*, 1980s.

The first thing I remember liking that liked me back was food.

VALERIE HARPER, *Rhoda*, 1970s.

I moved to Minneapolis, where it was cold….I figured I'd keep better.

VALERIE HARPER, *Rhoda*, 1970s.

There are no bad children, there are only stingy fathers.

DWAYNE HICKMAN, *The Many Loves of Dobie Gillis*, 1960s.

There's nothing to be afraid of. You have a stomach ache, you go to a doctor, right? You have a toothache, you go to a dentist. You have primary and secondary ego diffusion, you got to go to a psychiatrist.

JUDD HIRSCH, *Taxi*, 1980s–1970s.

Actually, I have no regard for money. Aside from its purchasing power, it's completely useless as far as I'm concerned.

ALFRED HITCHCOCK, *Alfred Hitchcock Presents*,
1950s–1960s.

I seem to have lost some weight and I don't wish to mar my image. I cannot reveal exactly how much weight. I can only say that had I lost ten more pounds, I would have had to file a missing persons report.

ALFRED HITCHCOCK, *Alfred Hitchcock Presents*,
1950s–1960s.

Aristotle once said that a play should have a beginning, a middle, and an end. But what did he know? Today, a play must have a first half, a second half, and a station break.

ALFRED HITCHCOCK, *Alfred Hitchcock Presents*,
1950–1960s.

I love my bladder. It keeps me warm, it keeps me company, it keeps my pants up.

JACK KLUGMAN, *The Odd Couple*, 1970s–1980s.

There's a standard formula for success in the entertainment medium, and that is: Beat it to death if it succeeds.

ERNIE KOVACS, *The Ernie Kovacs Show*, 1950s.

You can always find something on the evening news to take your mind off life.

LOUISE LASSER, "Mary Hartman, Mary Hartman," 1977.

If brains were money, you'd need to take out a loan to buy a cup of coffee.

SHELLEY LONG, *Cheers*, 1980s.

Rob, every man makes a fool of himself over a woman sooner or later, and I think the sooner the better.

FRED MACMURRAY, *My Three Sons*, 1960s.

[To a young man who wants to be a cop] "Listen to me, son…let me give you the hard facts. When you put on that uniform you're a marked man—marked by the supercritical eyes of the public, marked by the guns of every hoodlum you chase into a corner. You work around the clock, half your life in darkness, and you sleep the other half…away from God's good sunshine. You're strictly a second-class citizen. You can't enter controversial subjects in public, you can't enter a political campaign, you can't even write a letter to the editor. You make one mistake, you're a headline."

JOHN MCINTIRE, *Naked City*, 1950s–1960s.

Heeeeeere's Johnny.

ED MCMAHON, *The Tonight Show*, 1854–1990s.

Home is where the computer is.

JACK MERCER, *The Adventures of Felix the Cat*, 1960s.

He's not fat, he's just short for his weight.

AGNES MOOREHEAD, *Bewitched*, 1960s–1970s.

He's not man enough to pull on stretch socks.

AGNES MOOREHEAD, *Bewitched*, 1960s–1970s.

You can fool some of the people all of the time, and all of the people some of the time, but *you can't fool Mom*!

CAPTAIN PENNY, WEWS-TV, Cleveland, Ohio, 1980s.

Be true to your teeth and they won't be false to you.

SOUPY SALES, *The Soupy Sales Show*, 1950s–1960s.

A suburban junior high school cafeteria is like a microcosm of the world. The goal is to protect yourself, and safety comes in groups. You had your cool kids, you had your smart kids, you had your greasers. And in those days, of course, you had your hippies. In effect, in junior high school, who you are is defined less by who you are than who is the person next to you.

FRED SAVAGE, *The Wonder Years*, 1980s–1990s.

Sex in the hands of public educators is not a pretty thing.

FRED SAVAGE, *The Wonder Years*, 1980s–1990s.

How do you like my luck? Every time opportunity knocks I ain't got enough money to open the door.

PHIL SILVERS, *The Phil Silvers Show*, 1950s.

Where would Al Capone be today if he didn't take chances?

PHIL SILVERS, *The Phil Silvers Show*, 1950s.

I don't like being afraid. It scares me.

LORETTA SWIT, *M*A*S*H*, 1970s.

There shouldn't be heart attacks…or cancer, or anything like that. There should just be a certain age where ya have to turn your life in—like a library book. You pack a bag. You go—and that's that.

BETTY WHITE, *The Golden Girls*, 1980s–1990s.

Why do they call it rush hour when nothing moves?

ROBIN WILLIAMS, *Mork and Mindy*, 1970s–1980s.

We have nothing to fear but sanity itself.

ROBIN WILLIAMS, *Mork and Mindy*, 1970s–1980s.

Those little lines around your mouth, those crow's feet around your eyes, the millimeter your derriere has slipped in the last decade—they're just nature's way of telling you that you've got nine holes left to play, so get out here and have a good time.

BRUCE WILLIS, *Moonlighting*, 1980s.

Money can't buy happiness....But then, happiness can't buy government-insured C.D.'s.

BRUCE WILLIS, *Moonlighting*, 1980s.

Psychology

See also **The Human Condition; Life's Lessons; Men; Relationships; Social Issues**—Health; **Women**

As a whole part of "psychological education" it needs to be remembered that a neurosis can be valuable; also that "adjustment" to a sick and insane environment is of itself not "health" but sickness and insanity.

JAMES AGEE, with Walker Evans, *Let Us Now Praise Famous Men*, 1941.

What a surprise to find you could shift the contents of your head like rearranging furniture in a room.

LISA ALTHER, *Other Women*, 1984.

Asking questions in therapy would be so helpful if anyone ever answered them accurately. But no one ever does.

VIRGINIA MAE AXLINE, *Dibs: In Search of Self*, 1965.

In today's highly complex society it takes years of training in rationalization, accommodation and compromise to qualify for the good jobs; with the really big payoffs you need to retain a first-class psychiatrist in today's world.

RUSSELL BAKER, *New York Times*, March 21, 1968.

I have three phobias which, could I mute them, would make my life as slick as a sonnet, but as dull as ditch water: I hate to go to bed, I hate to get up, and I hate to be alone.

TALLULAH BANKHEAD, *Tallulah*, 1952.

Mad, adj. Affected with a high degree of intellectual independence; not conforming to standards of thought, speech and action derived by the conformants from study of themselves; at odds with the majority; in short, unusual. It is noteworthy that persons are pronounced mad by officials destitute of evidence that they themselves are sane.

AMBROSE BIERCE, *The Devil's Dictionary*, 1906.

The mad truth: the boundary between sanity and insanity is a false one....The proper posture is to listen and learn from lunatics as in former times.

NORMAN O. BROWN, *Love's Body*, 1966.

The lunatic asylum of the solar system.

SAMUEL PARKES CADMIN, on planet Earth, speech, New York City, November 17, 1935.

I've got a momma who joined the Peace Corps and went to India when she was sixty-eight. I've got one sister [Ruth], who's a Holy Roller preacher, another sister [Gloria], who...rides a motorcycle. So that makes me the only sane person in the family.

JIMMY CARTER, 1976, in Lois and Alan Gordon, *American Chronicle*, 1987.

Psychiatry's chief contribution to philosophy is the discovery that the toilet is the seat of the soul.

ALEXANDER CHASE, *Perspectives*, 1966.

Plagued by anxiety, troubled by worry, the psychological individual of our decade seeks only "peace of mind." It appears to represent the best way of coping with life's tensions. There is a pathological need to fill the hollow of our inner being. As we do not have a sufficient sense of selfhood, there must be a constant reaffirmation of our existence by seeing ourselves in others.

SEYMOUR COHEN, *Affirming Life*, 1987.

Fads run their course through the mob like the measles....One of the latest is psychonanalysis.

FRANK CRANE, *Current Opinion*, ca. 1920.

I think we are well advised to keep on nodding terms with the people we used to be, whether we find them attractive company or not. Otherwise they turn up unannounced and surprise us, come hammering on the mind's door at 4 a.m. of a bad night and demand to know who deserted them, who betrayed them, who is going to make amends.

JOAN DIDION, "On Keeping a Notebook," *Slouching Towards Bethlehem*, 1968.

It's a waste of time to read books on child psychology written by adults unless we are willing to check every page by what children know about the psychology of parents.

JOHN ERSKINE, *The Complete Life*, 1943.

The scars left from the child's defeat in the fight against irrational authority are to be found at the bottom of every neurosis.

ERICH FROMM, *Man for Himself*, 1947.

The man who once cursed his fate, now curses himself—and pays his psychoanalyst.

JOHN W. GARDNER, *No Easy Victories*, 1968.

There can be no proper interpretation of yourself to others if you are confused about yourself.... The first job is to get some clarity of understanding about yourself, what you are, and where you are going.

HARRY D. GIDEONESE, in Arthur Goodfriend, *What Is America?*, 1954.

The invention of I.Q. did a great disservice to creativity in education....Individuality, personality, originality, are too precious to be meddled with by amateur psychiatrists whose patterns for a "wholesome personality" are inevitably their own.

JOEL HILDEBRAND, speech, "Education for Creativity in the Sciences," *New York Times*, June 16, 1963.

Analysis requires that the psychiatrist be the recipient of unreserved self-avowal....If science is a partial judge of life, if science is omitting the moral ingredient, omits an essential part of true judgment, then confession to the scientist must by its own logic be incomplete.

WILLIAM ERNEST HOCKING, *Science and the Idea of God*, 1944.

Concern should drive us into action and not into a depression.

KAREN HORNEY, *Self-Analysis*, 1942.

Fortunately [psycho]analysis is not the only way to resolve inner conflicts. Life itself will still remain a very effective therapist.

KAREN HORNEY, *Our Inner Conflicts*, 1945.

It is hard to fight an enemy who has outposts in your head.

SALLY KEMPTON, "Cutting Loose," *Esquire*, July, 1970.

We believe that all men somehow possess a divine potentiality....We reject the tired dualism that seeks God and human potentialities in denying the joys of the senses.

GEORGE B. LEONARD, 1967, in Lois and Alan Gordon, *American Chronicle*, 1987.

When I was in therapy I saw such parallels between the two things—prostitution and psychiatry—kinds of therapy.

KATE MILLETT, *The Prostitution Papers*, 1971.

All the art of analysis consists in saying a truth only when the other person is ready for it, has been prepared for it by an organic process of gradation and evolution.

ANAÏS NIN, *The Diary of Anaïs Nin*, April, 1932.

The business of psychology is to tell us what actually goes on in the mind. It cannot possibly tell us whether the beliefs are true or false.

HASTINGS RASHDALL, *Philosophy and Religion*, 1909.

If parapsychology deals with all the personality manifestations that are beyond explanation by physics, then by definition it should claim the entire spiritual order of reality.

J.B. RHINE, *New World of the Mind*, 1953.

There is something operative in man that transcends the laws of matter and, therefore, by definition, a nonphysical or spiritual law is made manifest....This new world of the mind, represented and perhaps only suggested by the psi operations already identified, may very well, through further exploration, expand into an order of significance for a spiritual universe beyond the dreams of religion's own prophets and mystics.

J.B. RHINE, *New World of the Mind*, 1953.

I have come to feel that the only learning which significantly influences behavior is self-discovered, self-appropriated learning.

CARL R. ROGERS, *On Becoming a Person*, 1961.

In psychoanalysis as in art, God resided in the details, the discovery of which required enormous patience, unyielding seriousness, and the skill of an acrobat—walking a tightrope over memory and speculation, instinct and theory, feeling and denial.

JUDITH ROSSNER, *August*, 1983.

A lot of people, especially this one psychoanalyst guy they have here, keeps asking me if I'm going to apply myself when I go back to school in September. It's such a stupid question, in my opinion. I mean, how do you know what you're going to do till you do it?

J.D. SALINGER, *The Catcher in the Rye*, 1951.

Sanity is a madness put to good use.

GEORGE SANTAYANA, *Little Essays*, 1920.

A large part of the popularity and persuasiveness of psychology comes from its being a sublimated spiritualism: a secular, ostensibly scientific way of affirming the primacy of "spirit" over matter.

Susan Sontag, *Illness as Metaphor*, 1978.

There is no psychology; there is only biography and autobiography.

Thomas Szasz, *The Second Sin*, 1973.

As the internal-combustion engine runs on gasoline, so the person runs on self-esteem: if he is full of it, he is good for a long run; if he is partly filled, he will soon need to be refueled; and if he is empty, he will come to a stop.

Thomas Szasz, *The Second Sin*, 1973.

Psychiatrists are the new monks, their offices the secular monasteries against whose walls come to wail, while seeking to be shriven, the guilt-ridden, the sinner, the troubled-in-mind.

Alexander Theroux, "The Psychiatrist," *Mom, the Flag, and Apple Pie*, 1976.

I do not have a psychiatrist and I do not want one, for the simple reason that if he listened to me long enough, he might become disturbed.

James Thurber, *Credos and Curios*, 1962.

Psychotherapy, unlike castor oil, which will work no matter how you get it down, is useless when forced on an uncooperative patient.

Abigail Van Buren, "Dear Abby" newspaper column, July 11, 1974.

Trying to define yourself is like trying to bite your own teeth.

Alan Watts, *Life*, April 21, 1961.

Relationships

Apparently, it is the nature of all human relationships to aspire to be permanent. To propose temporariness as a goal in such relationships is to bring them under the rule of aims and standards that prevent them from beginning. Neither marriage, nor kinship, nor friendship, nor neighborhood can exist with a life expectancy that is merely convenient.

WENDELL BERRY, 1985, "Men and Women in Search of Common Ground," *Home Economics*, 1975.

If homosexuality were the normal way, God would have made Adam and Bruce.

ANITA BRYANT, *New York Times*, 1977.

The basic discovery about any people is the discovery of the relationship between its men and women.

PEARL S. BUCK, *Of Men and Women*, 1941.

Kindness and intelligence don't always deliver us from the pitfalls and traps: there are always failures of love, of will, of imagination. There is no way to take the danger out of human relationships.

BARBARA GRIZZUTI HARRISON, "Secrets Women Tell Each Other," *McCall's*, August, 1975.

Relationships, casual or intimate, are frequently played out as they might be in theatre, heightened, dramatized, staged with echoes of past dialogue and gestures that corrupt the spontaneity.

HELEN HAYES, *On Reflection, An Autobiography*, 1968.

Were our knowledge of human relationships a hundredfold more reliable than it is now, it would still be foolish to seek ready-made solutions for problems of living in the index of a book.

MIRRA KOMAROVSKY, *Women in the Modern World*, 1953.

Many of our problems with anger occur when we choose between having a relationship and having a self.

HARRIET GOLDHOR LERNER, *The Dance of Anger*, 1985.

People come into our lives and then they go out again. The extropy law, as applied to human relations. Sometimes in their passing, though, they register an unimagined and far-reaching influence....There is no scientific way to discern such effects, but memory believes before knowing remembers. And the past lives coiled within the present, beyond sight, beyond revocation, lifting us up or weighing us down, sealed away—almost completely—behind walls of pearl.

DAVID QUAMMEN, "Chambers of Memory," *Words from the Land*, 1986.

It's the little questions from women about tappets that finally push men over the edge.

PHILIP ROTH, *Letting Go*, 1962.

FAMILY

Families mean support and an audience to men. To women, they just mean more work.

ANONYMOUS, in article by Gloria Steinem, *Ms.*, September, 1981.

[The family:] The only preserving and healing power counteracting any historical, intellectual or spiritual crisis no matter what depth.

RUTH NANDA ANSHEN, ed., *The Family: Its Function*, 1959.

I worry about people who get born nowadays, because they get born into such tiny families—sometimes into no family at all. When you're the only pea in the pod, your parents are likely to get you confused with the Hope Diamond.

RUSSELL BAKER, "Life with Mother," William Zinsser, ed., *Inventing the Truth*, 1987.

We need a better family life to make us better servants of the people. So those of you living in sin, I hope you get married. And those of you who have left your spouses, go back home.

JIMMY CARTER, 1977, in Lois and Alan Gordon, *American Chronicle*, 1987.

No actor ever had a happy home life. If the affection of those near and dear could have warmed him, he wouldn't have gone out looking to soak up the heat of the multitudes, begging for love from faceless strangers.

Chris Chase, *How To Be a Movie Star, or A Terrible Beauty Is Born*, 1968.

How many different things a family can be—a nest of tenderness, a jail for the heart, a nursery of souls. Families name us and define us, give us strength, give us grief. All our lives we struggle to embrace or escape their influence. They are magnets that both hold us close and drive us away.

George Howe Colt, *Life*, April, 1991.

[Family] bonds are formed less by moments of celebration and of crisis than by the quiet, undramatic accretion of minutiae—the remark on the way out the door, the chore undone, the unexpected smile.

George Howe Colt, *Life*, April, 1991.

The dear little wife at home, John,

With ever so much to do,

Stitches to set and babies to pet,

And so many thoughts of you—

The beautiful household fairy,

Filling your heart with light—

Whatever you meet today, John,

Go cheerily home tonight.

Mary Lowe Dickinson, "The Dear Little Wife at Home," 1901.

Some people are your relatives but others are your ancestors, and you choose the ones you want to have as ancestors. You create yourself out of those values.

Ralph Ellison, *Time*, March 27, 1964.

It is my conviction that the family is God's basic unit in society. God's most important unit in society. No wonder then...we are in a holy war for the survival of the family. Before a nation collapses the families of that nation must go down first. What is a local church? Nothing but a congregation of families.

Jerry Falwell, December 2, 1979.

The cold truth is that family dinners are more often than not an ordeal of nervous indigestion, preceded by hidden resentment and ennui and accompanied by psychosomatic jitters.

M.F.K. Fisher, "F Is for Family," *An Alphabet for Gourmets*, 1949.

Total commitment to family and total commitment to career is possible, but fatiguing.

Muriel Fox, in article by Barbara Jordan Moore, *New Woman*, October, 1971.

Each suburban wife struggled with it alone. As she made the beds, shopped for groceries, matched slipcover material, ate peanut butter sandwiches with her children, chauffeured Cub Scouts and Brownies, lay beside her husband at night—she was afraid to ask even of herself the silent question—"Is this all?"

Betty Friedan, *The Feminine Mystique*, 1963.

Woman no longer wants to be a party to the production of a race of sickly, feeble, decrepit, wretched human beings, who would have neither the strength nor moral courage to throw off the yoke of poverty and slavery.

Emma Goldman, *The Woman Rebel*, March, 1914.

The craze for genealogy...is connected with the epidemic for divorce....If we can't figure out who our living relatives are, then maybe we'll have more luck with the dead ones.

Jane Howard, *Families*, 1979.

It has long been my belief that in times of great stress, such as a four-day vacation, the thin veneer of family wears off almost at once, and we are revealed in our true personalities....

Shirley Jackson, *Raising Demons*, 1956.

Today's family is built like a pyramid; with all the intrafamilial rivalries, tensions, jealousies, angers, hatreds, loves and needs focused on the untrained, vulnerable, insecure, young, inexperienced and incompetent paternal apex...about whose incompetence our vaunted educational system does nothing.

Lawrence Kubie, *Newsweek*, March 7, 1960.

The care of children, even from the period when their cognitive powers first emerge, is infinitely better left to the best-trained practitioners of both sexes who have chosen it as a vocation, rather than to harried and all too frequently unhappy persons with little time or taste for the work of educating minds however young or beloved....The family, as that term is presently understood, must go.

Kate Millett, *Sexual Politics*, 1969.

Every generation revolts against its fathers and make friends with its grandfathers.

Lewis Mumford, *The Brown Decades*, 1931.

The average family exists only on paper and its average budget is a fiction, invented by statisticians for the convenience of statisticians.

SYLVIA PORTER, *Sylvia Porter's Money Book*, 1975.

The family is one of nature's masterpieces.

GEORGE SANTAYANA, *The Life of Reason*, 1905–1906.

If a grandmother wants to put her foot down, the only safe place to do it these days is in a note book.

FLORIDA SCOTT-MAXWELL, *The Measure of My Days*, 1972.

It sometimes happens, even in the best of families, that a baby is born. This is not necessarily cause for alarm. The important thing is to keep your wits about you and borrow some money.

ELINOR GOULDING SMITH, *The Complete Book of Absolutely Perfect Baby and Child Care*, 1957.

FRIENDSHIP

Friendship needs a certain parallelism of life, a community of thought, a rivalry of aim.

HENRY ADAMS, *The Education of Henry Adams*, 1907.

Acquaintance, n. A person whom we know well enough to borrow from, but not well enough to lend to. A degree of friendship called slight when its object is poor or obscure, and intimate when he is rich or famous.

AMBROSE BIERCE, *The Devil's Dictionary*, 1906.

Friendship, n. A ship big enough to carry two in fair weather, but only one in foul.

AMBROSE BIERCE, *The Devil's Dictionary*, 1906.

Only solitary men know the full joys of friendship. Others have their family; but to a solitary and an exile his friends are everything.

WILLA CATHER, *Shadows on the Rock*, 1931.

I pretind ivry man is honest, and I believe none iv them ar-re. In that way I keep me friends an' save me money.

FINLEY PETER DUNNE, "The Christmas Spirit," *American Magazine*, December, 1906.

I have no trouble with my enemies. But my goddam friends,...they are the ones that keep me walking the floor nights.

WARREN G. HARDING, in David L. Cohn, *The Fabulous Democrats*, 1923.

Probably no man ever had a friend he did not dislike a little; we are all so constituted by nature no one can possibly entirely approve of us.

EDGAR WATSON HOWE, *The Indignations of E.W. Howe*, 1933.

Your friend is the man who knows all about you, and still likes you.

ELBERT HUBBARD, *The Roycroft Dictionary and Book of Epigrams*, 1923.

WHEN ARE YOU COMING BACK AND WHY PLEASE ANSWER

RING LARDNER, telegram, 1933, in F. Scott Fitzgerald, *The Crack-up*, 1945.

I'm a controversial figure. My friends either dislike me or hate me.

OSCAR LEVANT, Introduction, *Artemus Ward, His Book*, 1964.

The richer your friends, the more they will cost you.

ELISABETH MARBURY, *My Crystal Barr*, 1923.

A man of active and resilient mind outwears his friendships just as certainly as he outwears his love affairs, his politics and his epistemology.

H.L. MENCKEN, *Prejudices*, 1922.

Their belief in one another seeks no results.

DAVID MICHAELIS, *The Best of Friends*, 1983.

The loneliest woman in the world is a woman without a close woman friend.

TONI MORRISON, speech, Sarah Lawrence College, Bronxville, New York, 1978.

Love demands infinitely less than friendship.

GEORGE JEAN NATHAN, "Attitude Toward Love and Marriage," *The Autobiography of an Attitude*, 1925.

Friends are generally of the same sex, for when men and women agree, it is only in the conclusions; their reasons are always different.

GEORGE SANTAYANA, *The Life of Reason*, 1905–1906.

A friend's only gift is himself....To praise the utility of friendship, as the ancients so often did, and to regard it as a political institution justified, like victory or government, by its material results, is to lose one's moral bearings....We are not to look now for what makes friendships useful, but for whatever may be found in friendship that may lend utility to life.

GEORGE SANTAYANA, *The Life of Reason*, 1905–1906.

To cement a new friendship, especially between foreigners or persons of a different social world, a spark with which both were secretly charged must fly from person to person, and cut across the accidents of place and time.

GEORGE SANTAYANA, *Persons and Places: The Middle Span*, 1945.

Good friends are good for your health.

IRWIN SARASON, *New York Times*, August 27, 1985.

MARRIAGE, DIVORCE, AND OTHER ARRANGEMENTS

I read about divorce, and I can't see why two people can't get along together in harmony, and I see two people and I can't see how either of them can live with the other.

FRANKLIN P. ADAMS, *Nods and Becks*, 1944.

The women who take husbands not out of love but out of greed, to get their bills paid, to get a fine house and clothes and jewels; the women who marry to get out of a tiresome job, or to get away from disagreeable relatives, or to avoid being called an old maid—these are whores in everything but name. The only difference between them and my girls is that my girls gave a man his money's worth.

POLLY ADLER, *A House Is Not a Home*, 1953.

When two people marry they become in the eyes of the law one person, and that one person is the husband!

SHANA ALEXANDER, Introduction, *State-by-State Guide to Women's Legal Rights*, 1975.

I married beneath me. All women do.

NANCY ASTOR, in Marjorie P. Weiser and Jean S. Arbeiter, *Womanlist*, 1981.

Alimony is the most exorbitant of all stud-fees, and the worst feature of it is that you pay it retroactively.

JOHN BARRYMORE, in Gene Fowler, *Good Night, Sweet Prince*, 1943.

Marriage always demands the greatest understanding of the art of insincerity possible between two human beings.

VICKI BAUM, *And Life Goes On*, 1932.

They stood before the altar and supplied
The fire themselves in which their fat was fried.

AMBROSE BIERCE, *The Devil's Dictionary*, 1906.

Divorce, n. A resumption of diplomatic relations and rectification of boundaries.

AMBROSE BIERCE, in Ernest J. Hopkins, *The Enlarged Devil's Dictionary*, 1967.

Married. It was like a dream come true for Donna. Just think, soon her little girl would have unpaid bills, unplanned babies, calls from the bank and sub-standard housing. All the things a mother dreams of for her child.

ERMA BOMBECK, *Motherhood: The Second Oldest Profession*, 1983.

Marriage is not just spiritual communion and passionate embraces; marriage is also three-meals-a-day and remembering to carry out the trash.

JOYCE BROTHERS, "When Your Husband's Affection Cools," *Good Housekeeping*, May, 1972.

If you're going to break up with your old lady and you live in a small town, make sure you don't break up at three o'clock in the morning. Because you're screwed—there's nothing to do. You sit in the car all night, parked somewhere. Yeah. So make it about nine in the morning, so you can go to the five-and-ten, bullshit around, worry her a little, then come back at seven in the night, you know?

LENNY BRUCE, in John Cohen, ed., *The Essential Lenny Bruce*, 1967.

It is very difficult and expensive to undo after you are married the things that your mother and father did to you while you were putting your first six birthdays behind you.

BUREAU OF SOCIAL HYGIENE STUDY, 1928.

They make a business out of [marriage]. When you work too hard at a business you get tired; and when you get tired you get grouchy; and when you get grouchy you start fighting; and when you start fighting you're out of business.

GEORGE BURNS, *Living It Up; or They Still Love Me in Altoona!*, 1976.

People marry through a variety of other reasons, and with varying results; but to marry for love is to invite inevitable tragedy.

JAMES BRANCH CABELL, *The Cream of the Jest*, 1917.

The very fact that we make such a to-do over golden weddings indicates our amazement at human endurance. The celebration is more in the nature of a reward for stamina.

ILKA CHASE, *Free Admission*, 1948.

So many persons who think divorce a panacea for every ill find out, when they try it, that the remedy is worse than the disease.

DOROTHY DIX, *Dorothy Dix, Her Book*, 1926.

Any intelligent woman who reads the marriage contract, and then goes into it, deserves all the consequences.

ISADORA DUNCAN, *My Life*, 1927.

I believe, as a wage-earning woman, that if I make the great sacrifice of strength and health and even risk my life, to have a child, I should certainly not do so if, on some future occasion, the man can say that the child belongs to him by law and he will take it from me and I shall see it only three times a year!

ISADORA DUNCAN, *My Life*, 1927.

The love we have in our youth is superficial compared to the love that an old man has for his old wife.

WILL DURANT, *New York Times*, November 6, 1975.

Men often marry their mothers.

EDNA FERBER, *Cimarron*, 1929.

Your life has been a disappointment, as mine has been too. But we haven't gone through this sweat for nothing.

F. SCOTT FITZGERALD, letter to Zelda Fitzgerald, October 6, 1939, *The Letters of F. Scott Fitzgerald*, 1963.

If divorce has increased by one thousand percent, don't blame the women's movement. Blame the obsolete sex roles on which our marriages were based.

BETTY FRIEDAN, speech, New York City, January 20, 1974.

Husbands are like fires. They go out when unattended.

ZSA ZSA GABOR, *Newsweek*, March 28, 1960.

A man in love is incomplete until he has married. Then he's finished.

ZSA ZSA GABOR, *Newsweek*, March 28, 1960.

Don't tell me marriage is still a safe haven any place in America. Well, maybe among the Amish.

HERBERT GOLD, *A Walk on the West Side*, 1981.

It is this slavish acquiescence to a man's superiority that has kept the marriage institution seemingly intact for so long a period. Now that woman is coming into her own, now that she is actually growing aware of herself as a being outside of the master's grace, the sacred institution of marriage is gradually being undermined, and no amount of sentimental lamentation can stay it.

EMMA GOLDMAN, "Marriage and Love," *Anarchism and Other Essays*, 1911.

The institution of marriage makes a parasite of woman, an absolute dependent. It incapacitates her for life's struggle, annihilates her social consciousness, paralyzes her imagination, and then imposes its gracious protection, which is in reality a snare, a travesty on human character.

EMMA GOLDMAN, "Marriage and Love," *Anarchism and Other Essays*, 1911.

Marriage is like a war. There are moments of chivalry and gallantry that attend the victorious advances and strategic retreats, the birth or death of children, the momentary conquest of loneliness, the sacrifice that ennobles him who makes it. But mostly there are the long dull sieges, the waiting, the terror and boredom. Women understand this better than men; they are better able to survive attrition.

HELEN HAYES, *On Reflection, An Autobiography*, 1968.

Marriage today must...be concerned not with the inviolable commitment of constancy and unending passion, but with the changing patterns of liberty and discovery.

CAROLYN HEILBRUN, "Marriage Is the Message," *Ms.*, August, 1974.

If men knew how women pass the time when they are alone, they'd never marry.

O. HENRY, "Memoirs of a Yellow Dog," *The Four Million*, 1906.

The great leveler nowadays is divorce; almost everybody thinks about it, whether because we expect to be happy all the time—daily, weekly— or because we want the smell of brimstone in lives made too affluent and easy.

EDWARD HOAGLAND, "Other Lives," *Harper's*, July, 1973.

Sometimes it's worse to win a fight than to lose.

BILLIE HOLIDAY, *Lady Sings the Blues*, 1956.

I believe that we all should wise up and recognize that a marriage is a small business and that married couples are business partners.

DAVID HOPKINSON, *American Way*, May 14, 1985.

A man should be taller, older, heavier, uglier, and hoarser than his wife.

EDGAR WATSON HOWE, *Country Town Sayings*, 1911.

A honeymoon is a good deal like a man laying off to take an expensive vacation, and coming back to a different job.

EDGAR WATSON HOWE, *Sinner Sermons*, 1926.

The trouble with many married people is that they are trying to get more out of marriage than there is in it.

ELBERT HUBBARD, *The Roycroft Dictionary and Book of Epigrams*, 1923.

Marriage: A legal or religious ceremony by which two persons of the opposite sex solemnly agree to harass and spy on each other for ninety-nine years, or until death do them join.

ELBERT HUBBARD, *The Roycroft Dictionary and Book of Epigrams*, 1923.

Bigamy is having one husband too many. Monogamy is the same.

ERICA JONG, *Fear of Flying*, 1974.

Marrying a man is like buying something you've been admiring for a long time in a shop window. You may love it when you get it home, but it doesn't always go with everything else in the house.

JEAN KERR, "The Ten Worst Things About a Man," *The Snake Has All the Lines*, 1958.

Being divorced is like being hit by a Mack truck—if you survive you start looking very carefully to the right and left.

JEAN KERR, *Mary, Mary*, 1963.

Love is moral even without legal marriage, but marriage is immoral without love.

ELLEN KEY, *The Woman Rebel*, April, 1914.

When one hears the argument that marriage should be indissoluble for the sake of children, one cannot help wondering whether the protagonist is really such a firm friend of childhood, or whether his concern for the welfare of children is merely so much protective coloration for a constitutional and superstitious fear of change.

SUZANNE LAFOLLETTE, "Women and Marriage," *Concerning Women*, 1926.

For man, marriage is regarded as a station; for women, as a vocation.

SUZANNE LAFOLLETTE, "Women and Marriage," *Concerning Women*, 1926.

All married couples should learn the art of battle as they should learn the art of making love. Good battle is objective and honest—never vicious or cruel. Good battle is healthy and constructive, and brings to a marriage the principle of equal partnership.

ANN LANDERS, *Ann Landers Says Truth Is Stranger...*, 1968.

College women in general have greater difficulty in marrying....Men still want wives who will bolster their egos rather than detract from them.

PAUL H. LANDIS, *Your Marriage and Family Living*, 1954.

What counts in making a happy marriage is not so much how compatible you are, but how you deal with incompatibility.

GEORGE LEVINGER, in article by Daniel Goleman, "Marriage Research Reveals Ingredients of Happiness," *New York Times*, April 16, 1985.

She had become so dully habituated to married life that in her full matronliness she was as sexless as an anemic nun.

SINCLAIR LEWIS, *Babbitt*, 1922.

Marriage is tough, because it is woven of all these various elements, the weak and the strong. "In loveness" is fragile for it is woven only with the gossamer threads of beauty. It seems to me absurd to talk about "happy" and "unhappy" marriages.

ANNE MORROW LINDBERGH, *War Within and Without*, 1980.

I have always believed that the key to a happy marriage was the ability to say with a straight face, "Why, I don't know what you're worrying about. I thought you were very funny last night, and I'm sure everybody else did, too." Perhaps the greatest rudenesses of our time come not from the callousness of strangers, but from the solicitousness of intimates who believe that their frank criticisms are always welcome, and who feel free to "be themselves" with those they love, which turns out to mean being their worst selves, while saving their best behavior for strangers.

JUDITH MARTIN, *Common Courtesy*, 1985.

I played Santa Claus many times, and if you don't believe it, check out the divorce settlements awarded my wives.

GROUCHO MARX, *The Groucho Phile*, 1976.

Some people claim that marriage interferes with romance. There's no doubt about it. Anytime you have a romance, your wife is bound to interfere.

GROUCHO MARX, *The Groucho Phile*, 1976.

Who are happy in marriage? Those with so little imagination that they cannot picture a better state, and those so shrewd that they prefer quiet slavery to hopeless rebellion.

H.L. MENCKEN, *Prejudices*, 1920.

For one American husband who maintains a chorus girl in Levantine luxury around the corner, there are hundreds who are as true to their oaths, year in and year out, as so many convicts in the deathhouse.

H.L. MENCKEN, *In Defense of Women*, 1922.

Alimony—The ransom that the happy pay to the devil.

H.L. MENCKEN, "Sententiae," *The Vintage Mencken*, 1955.

Adultery is the application of democracy to love.

H.L. MENCKEN, "Sententiae," *The Vintage Mencken*, 1955.

With children no longer the universally accepted reason for marriage, marriages are going to have to exist on their own merits.

ELEANOR HOLMES NORTON, in Robin Morgan, ed., *Sisterhood Is Powerful*, 1970.

Love means giving one's self to another person fully, not just physically. When two people really love each other, this helps them to stay alive and grow. One must really be loved to grow. Love's such a precious and fragile thing that when it comes we have to hold on tightly. And when it comes, we're very lucky because for some it never comes at all. If you have love, you're wealthy in a way that can never be measured. Cherish it.

NANCY REAGAN, *Nancy*, 1980.

When you see what some girls marry, you realize how they must hate to work for a living.

HELEN ROWLAND, *Reflections of a Bachelor Girl*, 1903.

A husband is what is left of the lover after the nerve has been extracted.

HELEN ROWLAND, *The Rubaiyat of a Bachelor*, 1915.

Marriage is the only thing that affords a woman the pleasure of company and the perfect sensation of solitude at the same time.

HELEN ROWLAND, "The World in Epigram," F.P. Adams, D. Taylor, and J. Bechdolt, eds., *The Book of Diversion*, 1925.

I think every woman's entitled to a middle husband she can forget.

ADELA ROGERS ST. JOHN, in article by Joyce Haber, "She's Had the Last Word for Sixty Years," *Los Angeles Times*, October 13, 1974.

Marriage is like pantyhose. It all depends on what you put into it.

PHYLLIS SCHLAFLY, *Boston Globe*, July 16, 1974.

Successful marriage is an art that can only be learned with difficulty. But it gives pride and satisfaction, like any other expertness that is hard won....I would say that the surest measure of a man's or woman's maturity is the harmony, style, joy, dignity he creates in his marriage, and the pleasure and inspiration he provides for his spouse. An immature person may achieve great success in a career but never in marriage.

BENJAMIN SPOCK, *Decent and Indecent*, 1968.

A nagging woman is a bird beating her wings against the cage of matrimony.

MELVIN B. TOLSON, "Henpecked Husband: Comedy or Tragedy," *Washington Tribune*, January 20, 1940.

What a holler would ensue if people had to pay the minister as much to marry them as they have to pay a lawyer to get them a divorce.

CLAIRE TREVOR, *New York Journal-American*, October 12, 1960.

In recent years it has become common to hear people all over the country speak of long-term marriage in a tone of voice that assumes it to be inextricably intertwined with the music of Lawrence Welk.

CALVIN TRILLIN, "Old Marrieds," *The Nation*, August 3, 1985.

The best part of married life is the fights. The rest is merely so-so.

THORNTON WILDER, *The Matchmaker*, 1954.

Take my wife...please!

HENNY YOUNGMAN.

PARENTS AND CHILDREN

Most fathers would rather see their sons dead than either cultivated or devout.

LOUIS AUCHINCLOSS, *The Rector of Justin*, 1964.

There must be such a thing as a child with average ability, but you can't find a parent who will admit that it is his child....Start a program for gifted children, and every parent demands that his child be enrolled.

THOMAS D. BAILEY, *Wall Street Journal*, December 17, 1962.

The best thing that could happen to motherhood already has. Fewer women are going into it.

VICTORIA BILLINGS, *The Woman's Book*, 1974.

When a father, absent during the day, returns home at six, his children receive only his temperament, not his teaching.

ROBERT BLY, *Iron John*, 1990.

There are to us no ties at all just in being a father. A son is distinctly an acquired taste. It's the practice of parenthood that makes you feel that, after all, there may be something in it.

HEYWOOD BROUN, *Pieces of Hate*, 1922.

Discipline is a symbol of caring to a child. He needs guidance. If there is love, there is no such thing as being too tough with a child. A parent must also not be afraid to hang himself. If you have never been hated by your children, you have never been a parent.

BETTE DAVIS, *The Lonely Life*, 1962.

All they wished for her was that she should turn herself into a little replica of them.

MIDGE DECTER, *Liberal Parents/Radical Children*, 1975.

Mother-and-daughter blood conspires in the old mammalian office. Father-and-son blood vies in the ancient phallic enmity.

PETER DE VRIES, "Requiem for a Noun, or Intruder in the Dusk," *Without a Stitch in Time*, 1950.

Thou shalt not belittle your child.

FITZHUGH DODSON, *How to Parent*, 1973.

Parents have become so convinced that educators know what is best for children that they forget that they themselves are really the experts.

MARIAN WRIGHT EDELMAN, in article by Margie Cassady, "Society's Pushed-Out Children," *Psychology Today*, June, 1975.

[W]hile everything else in our lives has gotten simpler, speedier, more microwavable and user-friendly, child-raising seems to have expanded to fill the time no longer available for it.

BARBARA EHRENREICH, "Stop Ironing the Diapers," *The Worst Years of Our Lives*, 1989.

No culture on earth outside of mid-century suburban America has ever deployed one woman per child without simultaneously assigning her such major productive activities as weaving, farming, gathering, temple maintenance, and tent building. The reason is that full-time, one-on-one child-raising is not good for women *or* children.

BARBARA EHRENREICH, "Stop Ironing the Diapers," *The Worst Years of Our Lives*, 1989.

A mother is not a person to lean on but a person to make leaning unnecessary.

DOROTHY CANFIELD FISHER, *Her Son's Wife*, 1926.

Female biology, women's "biological careerline," may be changeless…but the nature of the human relationship to biology *has* changed.

BETTY FRIEDAN, *The Feminine Mystique*, 1963.

The father is always a Republican toward his son, and his mother's always a Democrat.

ROBERT FROST, in George Plimpton, ed., *Writers at Work*, 1963.

I believe the most stirring moment in the experience of a parent comes on the day he leaves the child in school for the first time. This can be so sharp an experience that, where there are two or three children, this ritual has to be alternated between parents.

HARRY GOLDEN, *Only in America*, 1950.

The adult world is…built on the shifting grounds of friendship and competition. The double message of this society and economy are to get along and get ahead. We want our children to fit in and to stand out. We rarely address the conflict between these goals.

ELLEN GOODMAN, "Old Friendship and Competition," *Washington Post*, April, 1986.

What do you do with all the antennae of motherhood when they become obsolete? What do you do with the loose wires that dangle after eighteen years of intimate connection to your own child? What use is there for the expertise of motherhood that took so long to acquire?

ELLEN GOODMAN, "Caravan to College," *Washington Post*, September, 1986.

There is no shower for a woman when she completes the trimester of her life spent as a full-time mother. There is no midwife to help that woman deliver a healthy adult.

ELLEN GOODMAN, "Post-Child Mothering," *Washington Post*, May, 1988.

There's nothing so sad as a 55-year-old orphan.

ELLA GRASSO, on her parents' deaths, *Boston Globe*, November 10, 1974.

I decided that Whistler's Mother was going to seem like Medea when compared to the perfection of my motherhood. I studied the character and started to draw my portrait—half Olympia and half Mary Cassatt.

HELEN HAYES, *On Reflection, An Autobiography*, 1968.

Parents, however old they and we may grow to be, serve among other things to shield us from a sense of our doom. As long as they are around, we can avoid the fact of our mortality; we can still be innocent children.

JANE HOWARD, *A Different Woman*, 1973.

If there were no schools to take the children away from home part of the time, the insane asylum would be filled with mothers.

EDGAR WATSON HOWE, *Country Town Sayings*, 1911.

No parent was ever very comfortable with a child after it had reached twenty-five.

EDGAR WATSON HOWE, *Sinner Sermons*, 1926.

One reason why corporal punishment is popular is that a big person can hit a little person with relative safety. Many parents, it seems, give up corporal punishment when their children are old enough to make a stiff defence or counter-attack.

ARTHUR T. JERSILD, *Educational Psychology*, 1942.

The real menace in dealing with a five-year-old is that in no time at all you begin to sound like a five-year-old.

JEAN KERR, *Please Don't Eat the Daisies: How to Get the Best of Your Children*, 1957.

God knows that a mother needs fortitude and courage and tolerance and flexibility and patience and firmness and nearly every other brave aspect of the human soul. But because I happen to be a parent of almost fiercely maternal nature, I praise *casualness*. It seems to me the rarest of virtues. It is useful enough when children are small. It is important to the point of necessity when they are adolescents.

PHYLLIS MCGINLEY, *McCall's*, May, 1959.

What the world needs is not romantic lovers who are sufficient unto themselves, but husbands and wives who live in communities, relate to other people, carry on useful work and willingly give time and attention to their children.

MARGARET MEAD, *Redbook*, 1965.

The secret cruelties that parents visit upon their children are past belief.

KARL A. MENNINGER, *A Psychiatrist's World*, 1959.

More than in any other human relationship, overwhelmingly more, motherhood means being instantly interruptible, responsive, responsible.

TILLIE OLSEN, *Silences: When Writers Don't Write*, 1965.

My child looked at me and I looked back at him in the delivery room, and I realized that out of a sea of infinite possibilities it had come down to this: a specific person, born on the hottest day of the year, conceived on a Christmas Eve, made by his father and me miraculously from scratch.

ANNA QUINDLEN, *New York Times*, March 13, 1986.

Helping your eldest to pick a college is one of the greatest educational experiences of life—for the parents. Next to trying to pick his bride, it's the best way to learn that your authority, if not entirely gone, is slipping fast.

SALLY RESTON AND JAMES RESTON, *Saturday Evening Post*, May 5, 1956.

Biological *possibility* and desire are not the same as biological *need*. Women have child-bearing equipment. For them to choose not to use the equipment is no more blocking what is instinctive than it is for a man who, muscles or no, chooses not to be a weightlifter.

BETTY ROLLIN, "Motherhood: Who Needs It?" *Look*, May 16, 1971.

Willful sterility is, from the standpoint of the nation, from the standpoint of the human race, the one sin for which the penalty is national death, race death; a sin for which there is no atonement....No man, no woman, can shirk the primary duties of life, whether for love of ease and pleasure, or for any other cause, and retain his or her self-respect.

THEODORE ROOSEVELT, message to Congress, December 3, 1906.

Without the means to prevent, and to control the timing of conception, economic and political rights have limited meaning for women. If women cannot plan their pregnancies, they can plan little else in their lives.

ALICE ROSSI, "The Right to One's Body," *The Feminist Papers*, 1973.

When motherhood becomes the fruit of a deep yearning, not the result of ignorance or accident, its children will become the foundation of a new race.

MARGARET SANGER, *Women and the New Race*, 1920.

Bringing up a family should be an adventure, not an anxious discipline in which everybody is constantly graded for performance.

MILTON R. SAPIRSTEIN, *Paradoxes of Everyday Life*, 1955.

It is not enough for parents to understand children. They must accord children the privilege of understanding them.

MILTON R. SAPIRSTEIN, *Paradoxes of Everyday Life*, 1955.

There's a time when you have to explain to your children why they're born, and it's a marvelous thing if you know the reason by then.

HAZEL SCOTT, in Margo Jefferson, "Great (Hazel) Scott!" *Ms.*, November, 1974.

No matter how old a mother is she watches her middle-aged children for signs of improvement.

FLORIDA SCOTT-MAXWELL, *The Measure of My Days*, 1972.

It doesn't matter who my father was; it matters who I remembered he was.

ANNE SEXTON, *A Small Journal*, January 1, 1972.

Sometimes I have grown tired of hearing Mom blamed for all that is wrong with her sons and daughters. After all, we might well ask, who started the grim mess?

LILLIAN SMITH, *Killers of the Dream*, 1949.

It seems to me that we are doing things we do not want to do for kids who do not really want to have them done.

ROBERT PAUL SMITH, "Let Your Kids Alone," *Life*, January 27, 1958.

I have no sympathy with the old idea that children owe such immense gratitude to their parents that they can never fulfill their obligations to them. I think the obligation is all on the other side. Parents can never do too much for their children to repay them for the injustice of having brought them into the world, unless they have insured them high moral and intellectual gifts, fine physical health, and enough money and education to render life something more than one careless struggle for necessaries.

ELIZABETH CADY STANTON, diary entry, in Theodore Stanton and Harriet Stanton Blatch, *Elizabeth Cady Stanton*, 1922.

It's clear that most American children suffer too much mother and too little father.

GLORIA STEINEM, *New York Times*, August 26, 1971.

Childbirth is more admirable than conquest, more amazing than self-defense, and as courageous as either one.

GLORIA STEINEM, *Ms.*, April, 1981.

Parenthood remains the greatest single preserve of the amateur.

ALVIN TOFFLER, *Future Shock*, 1970.

Parents of young children should realize that few people, and maybe no one, will find their children as enchanting as they do.

BARBARA WALTERS, *How to Talk with Practically Anybody About Practically Anything*, 1970.

It's a wonderful feeling when your father becomes not a god but a man to you—when he comes down from the mountain and you see he's this man with weaknesses. And you love him as this whole being, not as a figurehead.

ROBIN WILLIAMS, *Rolling Stone*, 1988.

There are no illegitimate children—only illegitimate parents.

LEON R. YANKWICH, opinion, *Zipkin v. Mozon*, June, 1928.

ROMANCE

Romance cannot be put into quantity production—the moment love becomes casual, it becomes commonplace.

FREDERICK LEWIS ALLEN, *Only Yesterday*, 1931.

The face of a lover is an unknown, precisely because it is invested with so much of oneself. It is a mystery, containing, like all mysteries, the possibility of torment.

JAMES BALDWIN, *Another Country*, 1962.

Love is a delightful day's journey. At the farther end kiss your companion and say farewell.

AMBROSE BIERCE, *Collected Works*, 1909–1912.

I am Tarzan of the Apes. I want you. I am yours. You are mine. We will live here together always in my house. I will bring you the best fruits, the tenderest deer, the finest meats that roam the jungle. I will hunt for you. I am the greatest of the jungle hunters. I will fight for you. I am the mightiest of the jungle fighters. You are Jane Porter, I saw it in your letter. When you see this you will know that it is for you and that Tarzan of the Apes loves you.

EDGAR RICE BURROUGHS, *Tarzan of the Apes*, 1914.

The true beloveds of this world are in their lover's eyes lilacs opening, ship lights, school bells, a landscape, remembered conversations, friends, a child's Sunday, lost voices, one's favorite suit, autumn and all seasons, memory, yes, it being the earth and water of existence, memory.

TRUMAN CAPOTE, *Other Voices, Other Rooms*, 1948.

So many of the conscious and unconscious ways men and women treat each other have to do with romantic and sexual fantasies that are deeply ingrained, not just in society but in literature. The [women's] movement may manage to clean up the mess in society, but I don't know whether it can ever clean up the mess in our minds.

NORA EPHRON, "Fantasies," July, 1972, *Crazy Salad: Some Things about Women*, 1975.

If a woman doesn't chase a man a little, she doesn't love him.

EDGAR WATSON HOWE, *Sinner Sermons*, 1926.

Love affairs have always greatly interested me, but I do not greatly care for them in books or moving pictures. In a love affair I wish to be the hero, with no audience present.

EDGAR WATSON HOWE, *Sinner Sermons*, 1926.

Lovers are fools, but Nature makes them so.

ELBERT HUBBARD, *The Roycroft Dictionary and Book of Epigrams*, 1923.

Love is like playing checkers. You have to know which man to move.

JACKIE "MOMS" MABLEY, interview, *Black Stars*, May, 1973.

In an age where the lowered eyelid is merely a sign of fatigue, the delicate game of love is pining away.

MARYA MANNES, "A Plea for Flirtation," *But Will It Sell?*, 1964.

To be in love is merely to be in a state of perceptual anesthesia—to mistake an ordinary young man for a Greek god or an ordinary young woman for a goddess.

H.L. MENCKEN, *Prejudices*, 1919.

A man always remembers his first love with special tenderness. But after that he begins to bunch them.

H.L. MENCKEN, "Sententiae," *The Vintage Mencken*, 1955.

Romantic love is the privilege of emperors, kings, soldiers and artists; it is the butt of democrats, traveling salesmen, magazine poets, and the writers of American novels.

GEORGE JEAN NATHAN, *Testament of a Critic*, 1931.

Love is only half the illusion; the lover, but not his love, is deceived.

GEORGE SANTAYANA, *The Life of Reason*, 1905–1906.

Love is the strange bewilderment which overtakes one person on account of another person.

JAMES THURBER AND E.B. WHITE, *Is Sex Necessary?*, 1929.

He was reminded of Marta, who often said she would find a male companion just as soon as she figured out what she needed one for.

SCOTT TUROW, *The Burden of Proof*, 1990.

Love is much nicer to be in than an automobile accident, a tight girdle, a higher tax bracket, or a holding pattern over Philadelphia.

JUDITH VIORST, "What IS This Thing Called Love?" *Redbook*, February, 1975.

Will you love me in December as you do in
   May,
Will you love me in the good old fashioned
   way?
When my hair has all turned gray,
Will you kiss me then and say,
That you love me in December as you do in
   May?

JAMES J. WALKER, "Will You Love Me in December As You Do in May?" verse set to music by Ernest R. Ball, 1905.

SEX

Modern men and women are obsessed with the sexual; it is the only realm of primordial adventure still left to most of us. Like apes in a zoo, we spend our energies on the one field of play remaining; human lives otherwise are pretty well caged in by the walls, bars, chains, and locked gates of our industrial culture.

EDWARD ABBEY, "Down the River with Henry Thoreau," *Words From the Land*, 1981.

Never play cards with any man named "Doc."
Never eat at any place called "Mom's."
And never, never, no matter what else you do in your whole life, never sleep with anyone whose troubles are worse than your own.

NELSON ALGREN, in H.E.F. Donahue, *Conversations with Nelson Algren*, 1964.

Be good. And if you can't be good, be careful. And if you can't be careful, name it after me.

ANONYMOUS.

Lemme tell you something. If you believe there is a God, a God that made your body, and yet you think that you can do anything with that body that's dirty, then the fault lies with the manufacturer.

LENNY BRUCE, in John Cohen, ed., *The Essential Lenny Bruce*, 1967.

My concept? You can't do *anything* with anybody's body to make it dirty to me. Six people, eight people, one person—you can do only one thing to make it dirty: kill it. Hiroshima was dirty. Chessman was dirty.

LENNY BRUCE, in John Cohen, ed., *The Essential Lenny Bruce*, 1967.

A kiss is now attestedly a quite innocuous performance, with nothing very fearful about it one way or the other. It even has its pleasant side.

JAMES BRANCH CABELL, *Jungle*, 1919.

You're not just sleeping with one person, you're sleeping with everyone *they* ever slept with.

THERESA CRENSHAW, *Men, Women, Sex and AIDS*, NBC-TV, January 13, 1987.

The act of sex, gratifying as it may be, is God's joke on humanity. It is man's last desperate stand at superintendency.

BETTE DAVIS, *The Lonely Life*, 1962.

Women's Liberation calls it enslavement but the real truth about the sexual revolution is that it has made of sex an almost chaotically limitless and therefore unmanageable realm in the life of women.

MIDGE DECTER, *The New Chastity and Other Arguments Against Women's Liberation*, 1972.

Society considers the sex experiences of a man as attributes of his general development, while similar experiences in the life of a woman are looked upon as a terrible calamity, a loss of honor and of all that is good and noble in a human being.

EMMA GOLDMAN, "The Traffic in Women," *Anarchism and Other Essays*, 1911.

For most Americans, the sexual revolution was not a vast national orgy of swingers. There was never widespread approval of adultery or promiscuity. The revolution—*evolution* is a better word—appeared rather as a massive questioning of the double standard and the sexual constraints we grew up with.

ELLEN GOODMAN, "Sex Education: A Curriculum of Fear," *Washington Post*, October, 1986.

I know how easy it is...for a girl to be tempted to foresake her chastity...especially in these times when human life is uncertain,...especially still if

the boy is in uniform. Our salvation...lies within us, in a hard-boiled code of wartime morals.

BONITA GRANVILLE, 1943, in Lois and Alan Gordon, *American Chronicle*, 1987.

Quite a few women told me, one way or another, that they thought it was sex, not youth, that's wasted on the young.

JANET HARRIS, *The Prime of Ms. America*, 1975.

If there is any one thing that a man should do in private, it is his loving.

EDGAR WATSON HOWE, *Country Town Sayings*, 1911.

The zipless fuck is the purest thing there is. And it is rarer than the unicorn. And I have never had one.

ERICA JONG, *Fear of Flying*, 1973.

Nothing could be more grotesquely unjust than a code of morals, reinforced by laws, which relieves men from responsibility for irregular sexual acts, and for the same acts drives women to abortion, infanticide, prostitution and self-destruction.

SUZANNE LAFOLLETTE, "Women and Marriage," *Concerning Women*, 1926.

Women complain about sex more often than men. Their gripes fall into two major categories: (1) Not enough, (2) Too much.

ANN LANDERS, *Ann Landers Says Truth Is Stranger...*, 1968.

When the Sexual Revolution began, I tried to enlist. But all I got was a series of humiliating rejections.

That was from the men. From the women came nothing but hysterical laughter.

GROUCHO MARX, in Richard J. Anobile, ed., *Why a Duck?*, 1971.

Sex is a natural function. You can't make it happen, but you can teach people to let it happen.

WILLIAM H. MASTERS, *New York Times*, October 29, 1984.

When things don't work well in the bedroom, they don't work well in the living room either.

WILLIAM H. MASTERS, NBC-TV, June 23, 1986.

Custom controls the sexual impulse as it controls no other.

MARGARET SANGER, interview, *American Mercury*, 1924.

Granted, the sexual revolution went too far, information-wise. When you find phrases like "suck face" as a euphemism for "kiss" it sort of takes the zing out of intimate personal contact.

IAN SHOALES, "Single in the '80s," *I Gotta Go*, May 12, 1984.

Copulation is...dangerous immediately after a meal and during the two and three hours which the first digestion needs, or having finished a rapid walk or any other violent exercise. In the same way, if the mental faculties are excited by some mental effort, by a theater party or a dance, rest if necessary, and it is advisable to defer amatory experience till the next morning.

BERNARD S. TALMEY, *Love: A Treatise on the Science of Sex-Attraction*, 1919.

In its slow way, our society is beginning to shed many of its superstitions about the sexual act. The idea that there is no such thing as "normality" is at last penetrating the tribal consciousness, although the religiously inclined still regard non-procreative sex as "unnatural," while the statistically inclined regard as "normal" only what the majority does.

GORE VIDAL, Afterword, *The City and the Pillar Revised*, 1965.

When women go wrong, men go right after them.

MAE WEST, in Joseph Weintraub, *The Wit and Wisdom of Mae West*, 1967.

It is no longer enough to be lusty. One must be a sexual gourmet.

GEORGE WILL, "The Ploy of Sex," January 29, 1974, *The Pursuit of Happiness, and Other Sobering Thoughts*, 1978.

Sex is the Tabasco sauce which an adolescent national palate sprinkles on every course in the menu.

MARY DAY WINN, *Adam's Rib*, 1931.

Religion and Spirituality

See also **American Society; Death; Education; Ethics and Morality; Life's Lessons; Science and Technology; Work**—Clergy

I do occasionally envy the person who is religious naturally, without being brainwashed into it or suckered into it by all the organized hustles. Just like having an ear for music or something. It would just never occur to such a person for a second that the world isn't about something.
WOODY ALLEN, *Rolling Stone*, 1987.

Religion tends to speak the language of the heart, which is the language of friends, lovers, children, and parents.
EDWARD SCRIBNER AMES, "My Conception of God," in Joseph Fort Newton, ed., *My Idea of God*, 1926.

One miracle is just as easy to believe as another.
WILLIAM JENNINGS BRYAN, Scopes trial, Dayton, Tennessee, July 21, 1925.

Joy in the universe, and keen curiosity about it all—that has been my religion.
JOHN BURROUGHS, journal entry, February 18, 1910.

The miracles of the church seem to me to rest not so much upon faces or voices or healing power coming suddenly near to us from afar off, but upon our perceptions being made finer, so that for a moment our eyes can see and our ears can hear what is there about us always.
WILLA CATHER, *Death Comes for the Archbishop*, 1927.

The starting point of the religious experience is wonder.
SEYMOUR COHEN, *Affirming Life*, 1987.

All human beings have an innate need to hear and tell stories and to have a story to live by...religion, whatever else it has done, has provided one of the main ways of meeting this abiding need.
HARVEY COX, *The Seduction of the Spirit*, 1973.

It is only when civilization is mature, when society becomes self-conscious and the struggle for bare survival is slackened, that the spiritual needs of man's nature exert their full power.
CHRISTOPHER DAWSON, *God and the Supernatural*, 1920.

"I don't know," I said. "I'd like to do something more religious. Explore America in the screaming night. You know. Yin and yang in Kansas. That scene."
DON DELILLO, *Americana*, 1971.

Religion has shifted to take in every change of the winds, so that its obedience to American culture and political trends is apparent. As life styles have changed, so has the theology of the churches. Manifest destiny became social gospel with barely a backward glance.
VINE DELORIA, JR., *We Talk, You Listen*, 1970.

By dipping us children in the Bible so often, they hoped, I think, to give our lives a serious tint, and to provide us with quaintly magnificent snatches of prayer to produce as charms while, say, being mugged for our cash or jewels.
ANNIE DILLARD, *An American Childhood*, 1987.

Religious experiences which are as real as life to some may be incomprehensible to others.
WILLIAM O. DOUGLAS, opinion, *United States v. Ballard*, 1944.

If I were personally to define religion I would say that it is a bandage that man has invented to protect a soul made bloody by circumstance.
ATTRIBUTED TO THEODORE DREISER.

It was the experience of mystery—even if mixed with fear—that engendered religion.
ALBERT EINSTEIN, *Living Philosophies*, 1931.

What is the meaning of human life, or of organic life altogether? To answer this question at all implies a religion. Is there any sense then, you ask, in putting it? I answer, the man who regards his own life and that of his fellow creatures as meaningless is not merely unfortunate but almost disqualified for life.

ALBERT EINSTEIN, *The World as I See It*, 1934.

Any religion...is for ever in danger of petrifaction into mere ritual and habit, though ritual and habit be essential to religion.

T.S. ELIOT, *Selected Essays*, 1927.

Religious faith is not a storm cellar to which men and women can flee for refuge from the storms of life. It is, instead, an inner spiritual strength which enables them to face those storms with hope and serenity. Religious faith has the miraculous power to lift ordinary human beings to greatness in seasons of stress.

SAM ERVIN, *Humor of a Country Lawyer*, 1983.

Religion is more like a response to a friend than it is like obedience to an expert.

AUSTIN FARRAR, *Saving Belief*, 1964.

Nothing in human life, least of all in religion, is ever right until it is beautiful.

HARRY EMERSON FOSDICK, *As I See Religion*, 1932.

The fact that astronomies change while the stars abide is a true analogy of every realm of human life and thought, religion not least of all. No existent theology can be a final formulation of spiritual truth.

HARRY EMERSON FOSDICK, *The Living of These Days*, 1956.

No priestcraft can longer make man content with misery here in the hope of compensation hereafter.

G. STANLEY HALL, *Senescence*, 1922.

A religious man is a person who holds God and man in one thought at one time, at all times, who suffers harm done to others, whose greatest passion is compassion, whose greatest strength is love and defiance of despair.

ABRAHAM JOSHUA HESCHEL, *New York Journal-American*, April 5, 1963.

The Indian...sees his music as indistinct from his dancing and his dancing as indistinct from his worship and his worship as indistinct from his living.

JAMAKE HIGHWATER, *Fodor's Indian America*, 1975.

The enduring value of religion is in its challenge to aspiration and hope in the mind of man.

ERNEST MARTIN HOPKINS, in Will Durant, *On the Meaning of Life*, 1932.

Religion is not an intelligence test, but a faith.

EDGAR WATSON HOWE, *Sinner Sermons*, 1926.

Primitive societies without religion have never been found.

WILLIAM HOWELLS, *The Heathens*, 1948.

Religions are many and diverse, but reason and goodness are one.

ELBERT HUBBARD, *The Roycroft Dictionary and Book of Epigrams*, 1923.

Religion, whatever it is, is a man's total reaction upon life.

WILLIAM JAMES, *The Varieties of Religious Experience*, 1902.

The highest flights of charity, devotion, trust, patience, bravery to which the wings of human nature have spread themselves have been flown for religious ideals.

WILLIAM JAMES, *The Varieties of Religious Experience*, 1902.

Religion, in short, is a monumental chapter in the history of human egotism.

WILLIAM JAMES, *The Varieties of Religious Experience*, 1902.

Religion is not an opiate, for religion does not help people to forget, but to remember. It does not dull people. It does not say *Take*, but *Give*.

BEDE JARRETT, *The Catholic Mother*, 1956.

I can see, and that is why I can be happy, in what you call the dark, but which to me is golden. I can see a God-made world, not a manmade world.

HELEN KELLER, documentary, *The Unconquered*, 1955.

As soon as religion becomes prosaic or perfunctory art appears somewhere else.

SUSANNE K. LANGER, *Feeling and Form*, 1953.

It is, I think, an error to believe that there is any need of religion to make life seem worth living.

SINCLAIR LEWIS, in Will Durant, *On the Meaning of Life*, 1932.

As a social and as a personal force, religion has become a dependent variable. It does not originate; it reacts. It does not denounce; it adapts. It does not set forth new models of conduct and sensibility; it imitates. Its rhetoric is without deep appeal; the worship it organizes is without piety. It has become less a revitalization of the spirit in permanent tension with the world than a respectable distraction from the sourness of life.

C. WRIGHT MILLS, *The Nation*, March 8, 1958.

The divorce of the practical and relative world of daily living from the astronomical sense of the high religions is surely one of the ultimate causes of the breakdown that has been going on so fast in our own generation.

LEWIS MUMFORD, *Faith for Living*, 1940.

Nothing which is true or beautiful or good makes complete sense in any immediate context of history; therefore we must be saved by faith.

REINHOLD NIEBUHR, *The Irony of American History*, 1952.

The final test of religious faith...is whether it will enable men to endure insecurity without complacency or despair, whether it can so interpret the ancient verities that they will not become mere escape hatches from responsibilities but instruments of insights into what civilization means.

REINHOLD NIEBUHR, *Saturday Evening Post*, July 23, 1960.

[D]on't pray when it rains if you don't pray when the sun shines.

LEROY [SATCHEL] PAIGE, *New York Post*, October 4, 1959.

Where life is colorful and varied, religion can be austere or unimportant. Where life is appallingly monotonous, religion must be emotional, dramatic and intense. Without the curry, boiled rice can be very dull.

C. NORTHCOTE PARKINSON, *East and West*, 1963.

Religion in its humility restores man to his only dignity, the courage to live by grace.

GEORGE SANTAYANA, *Dialogues in Limbo*, 1925.

Religion isn't yours firsthand until you doubt it right down to the ground.

FRANCIS B. SAYRE, *Life*, April 2, 1965.

When the American poor turn to religion, as most of them do, they turn not to faith in revolution, but to a more radical revolt against faith in their fellow man.

HERBERT WALLACE SCHNEIDER, *Religion in the 20th Century*, 1952.

Doubt is part of all religion. All the religious thinkers were doubters.

ISAAC BASHEVIS SINGER, *New York Times*, December 3, 1978.

Man is a spiritual being in that—unless he is badly corrupted—he responds powerfully to non-material stimuli: the beauty in nature or in art, the trust of children, the needs of helpless people, the death of a friend even though long absent.

BENJAMIN SPOCK, *Decent and Indecent*, 1970.

Some of us worship in churches, some in synagogues, some on golf courses.

ADLAI E. STEVENSON, 1952, in Lois and Alan Gordon, *American Chronicle*, 1987.

Spiritual truth is truth in whatever age, but the tasks of its service change as society changes.

DOROTHY THOMPSON, *The Courage to Be Happy*, 1957.

Being religious means asking passionately the question of the meaning of our existence and being willing to receive answers, even if the answers hurt.

PAUL TILLICH, *Saturday Evening Post*, June 14, 1958.

Religion, like water, may be free, but when they pipe it to you, you've got to help pay for the piping. And the piper!

ABIGAIL VAN BUREN, "Dear Abby," newspaper column, April 28, 1974.

"One sacred memory from childhood is perhaps the best education," said Feodor Dostoevski. I believe that, and I hope that many Earthling children will respond to the first human footprint on the moon as a sacred thing. We need sacred things.

KURT VONNEGUT, *Wampeters, Foma, and Granfalloons*, 1974.

A religious awakening which does not awaken the sleeper to love has roused him in vain.

JESSAMYN WEST, *The Quaker Reader*, 1962.

The acute delight Americans have always got from denying themselves joy and maiming others that they might be "saved" from some obliquity of moral carriage is only lately understood. One step further and it leads to persecutions. The world is made to eat, not leave, that the spirit may be full, not empty.

WILLIAM CARLOS WILLIAMS, "The Virtue of History," *In the American Grain*, 1925.

ARMAGEDDON

Hurry, my children, hurry. They will start parachuting out of the air. They'll torture our children. Lay down your life with dignity. Let's get gone. Let's get gone.

JIM JONES, People's Temple, Guyana, 1978.

I think the world is going to blow up in seven years. The public is entitled to a good time during those seven years.

HENRY LUCE, 1960, in article by Bob Arnebeck, "Stumbling to Tomorrow," *Washington Post Magazine*, December 26, 1982.

I sometimes believe we're heading very fast for Armageddon right now.

RONALD REAGAN, in article by James L. Franklin, "The Religious Right and the New Apocalypse," *Boston Globe*, May 2, 1982.

I do not know how many future generations we can count on before the Lord returns.

JAMES WATT, in article by James L. Franklin, *Boston Globe*, May 2, 1982.

I have read the Book of Revelation and, yes, I believe the world is going to end—by an act of God, I hope—but every day I think that time is running out.

CASPAR WEINBERGER, interview, *New York Times*, August 23, 1982.

ATHEISM AND AGNOSTICISM

I do not consider it an insult, but rather a compliment to be called an agnostic. I do not pretend to know where many ignorant men are sure—that is all that agnosticism means.

CLARENCE DARROW, Scopes trial, Dayton, Tennessee, July 13, 1925.

I don't believe in God because I don't believe in Mother Goose.

CLARENCE DARROW, speech, Toronto, Canada, 1930.

A dead atheist is someone who's all dressed up with no place to go.

JAMES DUFFEY, *New York Times*, August 21, 1964.

I have never known a thinking man who did not believe in God....Everyone who reflects at all believes, in one way or another, in God....To me it is unthinkable that a real atheist should exist at all.

ROBERT A. MILLIKAN, *World's Work*, April, 1926.

An atheist is a man who has no invisible means of support.

FULTON J. SHEEN, *Look*, December 14, 1955.

BELIEF

It is wanting to know the end that makes us believe in God, or witchcraft, believe, at least, in something.

TRUMAN CAPOTE, *Other Voices, Other Rooms*, 1948.

Bryan: I believe that everything in the Bible should be accepted as it is given here.

Darrow: But when you read that Jonah swallowed the whale—or that the whale swallowed Jonah—do you literally interpret it?

Bryan: Yes sir.... If the Bible said so.

CLARENCE DARROW, cross-examination of William Jennings Bryan, Scopes trial, Dayton, Tennessee, 1925.

And this I do believe above all, especially in times of greater discouragement, that I must BELIEVE—that I must believe in my fellow men—that I must believe in myself—that I must believe in God—if life is to have any meaning.

MARGARET CHASE SMITH, in Edward R. Murrow, ed., *This I Believe:* 1954.

What do I believe? As an American I believe in generosity, in liberty, in the rights of man. These are social and political faiths that are part of me, as they are, I suppose, part of all of us. Such beliefs are easy to express. But part of me too is my relation to all life, my religion. And this is *not* so easy to talk about. Religious experience is highly intimate and, for me, ready words are not at hand.

ADLAI E. STEVENSON, speech, Libertyville, Illinois, May 21, 1954.

In religion and politics people's beliefs and convictions are in almost every case gotten at second-hand, and without examination, from authorities who have not themselves examined the questions at issue but have taken them at second-hand from other non-examiners, whose opinions about them were not worth a brass farthing.

MARK TWAIN, *Mark Twain's Autobiography*, 1959.

EVANGELISTS AND REVIVALISTS

Work for the Lord, pay is small, retirement benefits are out of this world.

A SIGN OUTSIDE CHUCK MEYER'S HOUSE OF TELEVISION, Phoenix, Arizona, in Bill Bradley, *Life on the Run*, 1976.

The tendency of the revivalist was to oversimplify theological issues and the ultimate result was to render the faith devoid of content.

W.S. HUDSON, *The Great Tradition of the American Churches*, 1953.

Inherent in revivalism is the temptation to stress results and to justify whatever produces them.

W.S. HUDSON, *The Great Tradition of the American Churches*, 1953.

For a town whose opera house rarely had the spider webs dusted out, whose citizens depended for theater on the annual play given by the high school, and for gaiety on a minstrel show and a circus each winter, the big tent was a magnet which drew not only the rural folks but the most literate and wealthy from Main Street.

LILLIAN SMITH, on turn-of-the-century Southern revivals, *Killers of the Dream*, 1949.

Camp meetings and revivals are the South's past, and once were a heroic part of that past. Today, though often cheapened and vulgarized to the point of obscenity, they are still part of the South's present. Guilt was then and is today the biggest crop raised in Dixie, harvested each summer just before cotton is picked.

LILLIAN SMITH, *Killers of the Dream*, 1949.

The passing of the religious revival from the American scene has deprived our churches... of what has been for at least a century the one most familiar means of recruiting the ranks of members.

WILLIARD L. SPERRY, *Religion in America*, 1946.

Who would have the balls to say, "God will take me away unless I get $8 million"? As if God's a large man named Vinnie, going, *"Where the fuck's the money?"* They're selling the promise of hope on the strength that there's no such word as *audit* in the Bible. The Lord was not audited. Jesus did not have an accountant, even though *he* was Jewish.

ROBIN WILLIAMS, *Rolling Stone*, 1988.

FAITHS

You don't have to be dowdy to be a Christian.

TAMMY FAYE BAKKER, *Newsweek*, June 8, 1987.

The Christian opposition to Russia and Communism must not be identified with the capitalistic opposition which now generates so much emotion in the United States.

JOHN C. BENNETT, *Perspectives on a Troubled Decade*, 1950.

We claim to be Christian, but that is a claim never really verified or completed. It is rather a process of becoming, since man is by definition one who becomes himself—a painful but glorious process, as history tells us.

DANIEL BERRIGAN, "Statement at Sentencing," *Prison Journals*, May 24, 1968.

Christian, n. One who believes that the New Testament is a divinely inspired book admirably suited to the spiritual needs of his neighbor. One who follows the teachings of Christ in so far as they are not inconsistent with a life of sin.

AMBROSE BIERCE, *The Devil's Dictionary*, 1906.

The Catholic wife is under great pressure....If she uses contraceptives, she is called wicked by her parish priest. If she follows the advice of her priest and refrains from sexual intercourse, she is called cold by her husband. If she doesn't take steps, she is called mad by society at large.

ANNE BIEZANEK, *New York Times*, May 21, 1964.

Christ and Moses standing in the back of St. Pat's, looking around. Confused, Christ is, at the grandeur of the interior, the baroque interior, the rococo baroque interior. Because his route took him through Spanish Harlem, and he was wondering what the hell fifty Puerto Ricans were doing living in one room when that stained glass window is worth ten G's a square foot.

LENNY BRUCE, in John Cohen, ed., *The Essential Lenny Bruce*, 1967.

It is always easier to believe than to deny. Our minds are naturally affirmative.

JOHN BURROUGHS, *The Light of Day*, 1900.

The trouble with born-again Christians is that they are an even bigger pain the second time around.

HERB CAEN, *San Francisco Chronicle*, July 20, 1981.

[Jesus'] ministry was clearly defined, and the alternatives to the illusion and temptations of the desert were spelled out. A choice was made—life abundant, full, and free for all. Make no mistake about it, the day that choice was made, Jesus became suspect. That day in the temple he sealed the fate already prepared for him. How was the world to understand one who rejected an offer of power and control?

JOAN B. CAMPBELL, *Sojourners*, August–September, 1991.

Is Christianity dying? Is the religion that gave morals, courage, and art to Western civilization suffering slow decay through the spread of knowledge, the widening of astronomic, geographical, and historical horizons, the realization of evil in history and the soul, the decline of faith in an afterlife and of trust in the benevolent guidance of the world? If this is so, it is the basic event of modern times, for the soul of a civilization is its religion, and it dies with its faith.

WILL DURANT, *The Age of Reason Begins*, 1961.

I would no more quarrel with a man because of his religion than I would because of his art.

MARY BAKER EDDY, "Harvest," *The Independent*, November, 1906.

No one is without Christianity, if we agree on what we mean by the word. It is every individual's individual code of behavior by means of which he makes himself a better human being than his nature wants to be, if he followed his nature only.

WILLIAM FAULKNER, interview, *Writers at Work: First Series*, 1958.

It sometimes seems that the inheritors of the zeal of the early Christians are not Catholics but Communists.

JAMES M. GILLIS, *This Our Day*, 1949.

Heaven: The Coney Island of the Christian imagination.

ELBERT HUBBARD, *The Roycroft Dictionary and Book of Epigrams*, 1923.

The heresy of one age becomes the orthodoxy of the next.

HELEN KELLER, *Optimism*, 1903.

The most important thing about me is that I am a Catholic. It's a superstructure within which you can work, like a sonnet.

JEAN KERR, *Time*, April 14, 1961.

When men can no longer be theists, they must, if they are civilized, become humanists.

WALTER LIPPMANN, *A Preface to Morals*, 1929.

I consider myself 40 percent Catholic and 60 percent Baptist...but I'm in favor of *every* religion, with the possible exception of snake-chunking. Anybody that so presumes on how he stands with Providence that he will let a snake bite him, I say he deserves what he's got coming to him.

EARL LONG, *The New Yorker*, June 4, 1960.

No man is a Christian who cheats his fellows, perverts the truth, or speaks of a "clean bomb," yet he will be the first to make public his faith in God.

MARYA MANNES, *More in Anger*, 1958.

It is easier to believe than to doubt.

EVERETT DEAN MARTIN, *The Meaning of a Liberal Education*, 1926.

Christian endeavor is notoriously hard on female pulchritude.

H.L. MENCKEN, "The Aesthetic Recoil," *American Mercury*, July, 1931.

The chief contribution of Protestantism to human thought is its massive proof that God is a bore.

H.L. MENCKEN, *Minority Report*, 1956.

Mormons invented themselves just as other religious and ethnic groups invented themselves. But Mormons did so in such a singularly impressive way that we will probably always remain baffled as to how exactly it happened.

LAURENCE MOORE, *New York Times*, July 21, 1985.

Men insist most vehemently upon their certainties when their hold upon them has been shaken. Frantic orthodoxy is a method for obscuring doubt.

REINHOLD NIEBUHR, *Does Civilization Need Religion?*, 1927.

The 11 o'clock hour on Sunday is the most segregated hour in American life.

JAMES A. PIKE, *Life*, obituary, September 19, 1969.

No one can say that Christianity has failed. It has never been tried.

ADAM CLAYTON POWELL, JR., "Black Man's Burden," *Marching Blacks*, 1945.

The brute necessity of believing something so long as life lasts does not justify any belief in particular.

GEORGE SANTAYANA, *Scepticism and Animal Faith*, 1923.

For Catholics before Vatican II, the land of the free was pre-eminently the land of Sister Says—except, of course, for Sister, for whom it was the land of Father Says.

WILFRID SHEED, *Frank and Maisie: A Memoir with Parents*, 1985.

In other religions, one must be purified before he can knock at the door; in Christianity, one knocks on the door as a sinner, and He Who answers to us heals.

FULTON J. SHEEN, *Peace of Soul*, 1949.

The Jewish people have been in exile for 2,000 years; they have lived in hundreds of countries, spoken hundreds of languages and still they kept their old language, Hebrew. They kept their Aramaic, later their Yiddish; they kept their books; they kept their faith.

ISAAC BASHEVIS SINGER, *New York Times*, November 26, 1978.

To believe in something not yet proved and to underwrite it with our lives; it is the only way we can leave the future open. Man, surrounded by facts, permitting himself no surprise, no intuitive flash, no great hypothesis, no risk, is in a locked cell. Ignorance cannot seal the mind and imagination more securely.

LILLIAN SMITH, *The Journey*, 1954.

When the Lakota heart was filled with high emotion, he danced. When he felt the benediction of the warming rays of the sun, he danced. When his blood ran hot with success of the hunt or chase, he danced. When his heart was filled with pity for the orphan, the lonely father, or bereaved mother, he danced. All the joys and exaltations of life, all his gratefulness and thankfulness, all his acknowledgments of the mysterious power that guided life, and all his aspirations for a better life, culminated in one great dance—the Sun Dance.

LUTHER STANDING BEAR, *Land of the Spotted Eagle*, 1933.

It is the maturest fruit of Christian understanding to understand that Christianity, as such, is of no avail.

PAUL TILLICH, *The New Being*, 1955.

The only test of a Christian is this: How does he treat the poor? How does he treat the lame, the halt, and the blind?

MELVIN B. TOLSON, "The Death of an Infidel," *Washington Tribune*, April 2, 1938.

One thing I have no worry about is whether God exists. But it has occurred to me that God has Alzheimer's and has forgotten we exist.

JANE WAGNER, *The Search for Intelligent Life in the Universe*, performed by Lily Tomlin, 1986.

To make Christianity conform fully to the modern rational mood, it would have to cease to be Christianity.

BARBARA WARD, *Way*, January–February, 1963.

GOD

Not only is there no God, but try getting a plumber on weekends.

WOODY ALLEN, "My Philosophy," *The New Yorker*, December 27, 1969.

How can I believe in God when just last week I got my tongue caught in the roller of an electric typewriter?

WOODY ALLEN, "Selections from the Allen Notebooks," *Without Feathers*, 1975.

We must recognize that the death of God is a historical event: God has died in our time, in our history, in our existence.

THOMAS J. ALTIZER, *Time*, October 22, 1965.

People see God every day, they just don't recognize him.

PEARL BAILEY, *New York Times*, November 26, 1967.

God is the Celebrity-Author of the World's Best Seller. We have made God into the biggest celebrity of all, to contain our own emptiness.

DANIEL J. BOORSTIN, *The Image*, 1962.

Every day people are straying away from the church and going back to God. Really.

LENNY BRUCE, "Religions Inc.," in John Cohen, ed., *The Essential Lenny Bruce*, 1967.

I think there are innumerable gods. What we on earth call God is a little tribal God who has made an awful mess.

WILLIAM S. BURROUGHS, *Paris Review*, Fall, 1965.

What rubbish has been written about being masters of our fate and captains of our souls and creators of an ideal commonwealth! Such talk bowed God out of His universe, and put men on the throne.

HENRY SLOANE COFFIN, *Joy in Believing*, 1956.

It is the creative potential itself in human beings that is the image of God.

MARY DALY, *Beyond God the Father*, 1973.

When man substituted God for the Great Goddess he at the same time substituted authoritarian for humanistic values.

ELIZABETH GOULD DAVIS, *The First Sex*, 1971.

Natural Theology says not only look up and look out—it also says look down and look in, and you will find the proofs of the reality of God in the depth of your own nature.

CHRISTOPHER DAWSON, *Religion and Culture*, 1947.

The white man has lost his soul. But he is so small-minded that he has confused his soul with God.

VINE DELORIA, JR., in Stan Steiner, *The New Indians*, 1968.

It is the final proof of God's omnipotence that he need not exist in order to save us.

PETER DE VRIES, *Mackeral Plaza*, 1958.

The greatest question of our time is not communism vs. individualism, not Europe vs. America, not even the East vs. the West; it is whether men can bear to live without God.

WILL DURANT, *On the Meaning of Life*, 1932.

I find in the universe so many forms of order, organization, system, law, and adjustment of means to ends, that I believe in a cosmic intelligence and I conceive God as the life, mind, order, and law of the world.

WILL DURANT, in Edward R. Murrow, ed., *This I Believe*, 1954.

Men in the nineteenth century were sad that they could no longer believe in God; they are more deeply saddened now by the fact that they can no longer believe in man.

IRWIN EDMAN, *Candle in the Dark*, 1939.

I am waiting for them to prove that God is really American.

LAWRENCE FERLINGHETTI, *A Coney Island of the Mind*, 1958.

The God who deliberately sends sickness and death as a punishment for our sins—that God has died. The God who took all the joy out of Sunday and draped it in black, that God, I am glad to say, has died. It is not so much that He died as that He changed his name and thereafter was quite different for us.... He may have withdrawn for a while to teach us how to get along without Him.... Yet once in a while the clouds break through and He appears when we least expect Him.

THEODORE FERRIS, *New York Herald Tribune*, November 7, 1965.

Whatever may be true of men's creed, nothing is clearer than the fact that the personality and the sovereignty of God are not a large factor in the practical life and thought of our age.

CHARLES W. GARMAN, *Letters, Lectures, Addresses*, 1909.

Seem like God don't see fit to give the black man nothing but dreams—but He did give us children to make them dreams seem worthwhile.

LORRAINE HANSBERRY, *A Raisin in the Sun*, 1959.

Good God, how much reverence can you have for a Supreme Being who finds it necessary to include such phenomena as phlegm and tooth-decay in His divine system of Creation?

JOSEPH HELLER, *Catch-22*, 1961.

I didn't know what she was saying when she moved her lips in a Baptist church or a Catholic cathedral or, less often, in a synagogue, but it was obvious that God could be found anywhere.

LILLIAN HELLMAN, *An Unfinished Woman*, 1969.

God will not look you over for medals, degrees, or diplomas, but for scars.

ELBERT HUBBARD, *The Roycroft Dictionary and Book of Epigrams*, 1923.

The God whom science recognizes must be a God of universal laws exclusively, a God who does a wholesale, not a retail business. He cannot accommodate his processes to the convenience of individuals.

WILLIAM JAMES, *Varieties of Religious Experience*, 1902.

I myself believe that the evidence for God lies primarily in inner personal experiences.

WILLIAM JAMES, *Pragmatism*, 1907.

The prince of darkness may be a gentleman, as we are told he is, but whatever the God of earth and heaven is, He can surely be no gentleman. His menial services are needed in the dust of our human trials, even more than his dignity is needed in the empyrean.

WILLIAM JAMES, *Pragmatism*, 1907.

God has been replaced, as he has all over the West, with respectability and air conditioning.

LEROI JONES, "What Does Nonviolence Mean?" *Home*, 1966.

The God who answers special prayers, the God who blesses cannon, the God who is the man upstairs, the God who is "my co-pilot" is very much dead, for this God never existed except in some wild imaginations. But to say that God is dead because some people have a very human concept of God is only to say, if we are truthful, that this particular idea of God is dead.

WALTER DONALD KRING, *New York Herald Tribune*, November 7, 1965.

God is what man finds that is divine in himself. God is the best way man can behave in the ordinary occasions of life, and the farthest point to which man can stretch himself.

MAX LERNER, "Seekers and Losers," *The Unfinished Country*, 1959.

Often God has to shut a door in our face, so that He can subsequently open the door through which He wants us to go.

CATHERINE MARSHALL, *A Man Called Peter*, 1951.

If there were no other proof of the infinite patience of God with men, a very good one could be found in His toleration of the pictures that are painted of Him and of the noise that proceeds from musical instruments under the pretext of being in His "honor."

THOMAS MERTON, in E.S. Skillin, ed., *The Commonweal Reader*, 1950.

There are many who stay away from church these days because you hardly ever mention God any more.

ARTHUR MILLER, *The Crucible*, 1953.

Natural religion...finds a God who is majestic, but not majestic enough to threaten human self-esteem.

REINHOLD NIEBUHR, *Do the State and Nation Belong to God or Man?*, 1937.

While there is almost no religion operating in race relations, there is plenty of God.

J. SAUNDERS REDDING, *On Being a Negro*, 1951.

God's life...sees the plan fulfilled through all the manifold lives.

JOSIAH ROYCE, *The World and the Individual*, 1900.

[Act of God:] a term applied to unexpected fires, wrecks, eruptions of volcanoes and other catastrophes in which lives and property are destroyed. This term is freely used as advertising for the church by Christian clergymen and laymen, but was doubtless invented by atheists as a libel on the Deity.

GEORGE SAMUEL SCHUYLER, "Shafts and Darts," *The Messenger*, February, 1927.

Many souls fail to find God because they want a religion which will remake society without remaking themselves.

FULTON J. SHEEN, *Peace of Soul*, 1949.

I am sustained by a sense of the worthwhileness of what I am doing; a trust in the good faith of the process which created and sustains me. That process I call God.

UPTON SINCLAIR, *What God Means to Me*, 1935.

By positing God it inhibits man from laying claim to being God. It prevents his becoming less than man through the arrogance of claiming to be more.

MILTON STEINBERG, *A Believing Jew*, 1951.

In general the churches, visited by me too often on weekdays...bore for me the same relation to God that billboards did to Coca-Cola; they promoted thirst without quenching it.

JOHN UPDIKE, *A Month of Sundays*, 1975.

I think it pisses God off if you walk by the color purple in a field somewhere and don't notice it.

ALICE WALKER, *The Color Purple*, 1982.

Individual man owes his first allegiance and responsibility only to God. We do not accept the notion that the State is higher than man.

WALTER H. WHEELER, in Arthur Goodfriend, *What Is America?*, 1954.

We're all of us guinea pigs in the laboratory of God. Humanity is just a work in progress.

TENNESSEE WILLIAMS, *Camino Real*, 1953.

All your Western theologies, the whole mythology of them, are based on the concept of God as a senile delinquent.

TENNESSEE WILLIAMS, *The Night of the Iguana*, 1961.

Life is too short to understand God altogether, especially nowadays.

HELEN YGLESIAS, *How She Died*, 1972.

GUILT

Everyone in daily life carries such a heavy, mixed burden on his own conscience that he is reluctant to penalize those who have been caught.

BROOKS ATKINSON, "February 28," *Once Around the Sun*, 1951.

Guilt: the gift that keeps on giving.

ERMA BOMBECK, in article by John Skow, *Time*, July 2, 1984.

I am suspicious of guilt in myself and in other people; it is usually a way of not thinking, or of announcing one's own fine sensibilities the better to be rid of them fast.

LILLIAN HELLMAN, *Scoundrel Time*, 1976.

Not wishing to be other than they are, the blameless ones, in their self-love, cannot conceive the real alternative: another self, cleansed of guilt and freed from folly, capable of renewal.

LEWIS MUMFORD, *The Conduct of Life*, 1951.

Belief in Some One's right to punish you is the fate of all children in Judaic-Christian culture. But nowhere else, perhaps, have the rich seedbeds of Western homes found such a growing climate for guilt as is produced in the South by the combination of a warm moist evangelism and racial segregation.

LILLIAN SMITH, *Killers of the Dream*, 1949.

RELIGION AND GOVERNMENT

We repeat and again reaffirm that neither a state nor the Federal Government can constitutionally force a person "to profess a belief or disbelief in any religion." Neither can constitutionally pass laws or impose requirements which aid all religions as against non-believers, and neither can aid those religions based on a belief in the existence of God as against those religions founded on different beliefs.

HUGO L. BLACK, opinion, *Torcaso v. Watkins*, 1961.

The parents have a right to say that no teacher paid by their money shall rob their children of faith in God and send them back to their homes skeptical, or infidels, or agnostics, or atheists.

WILLIAM JENNINGS BRYAN, Scopes trial, Dayton, Tennessee, July 16, 1925.

The "wall" of separation between Church and State, as it is conceived by most "absolute separationists" in America, is not really a constitutional concept. It is rather a private doctrine (of militant secularism in some cases, of one version of Christian theology in others) which a minority of Americans seem intent on imposing on all.

WILLIAM CLANCY, *Religion and the Free Society*, 1958.

American Christianity has been the captive of the State since the inception of the Republic.

VINE DELORIA, JR., *We Talk, You Listen*, 1970.

From this day forward, the millions of our schoolchildren will daily proclaim in every city and town, every village and rural schoolhouse, the dedication of our nation and our people to the Almighty.

DWIGHT D. EISENHOWER, on signing law that included "under God" in Pledge of Allegiance, June 14, 1954.

Our government makes no sense unless it is founded in a deeply felt religious faith and I don't care what it is.

DWIGHT D. EISENHOWER, 1952, in Lois and Alan Gordon, *American Chronicle*, 1987.

The idea [that] religion and politics don't mix was invented by the Devil to keep Christians from running their own country. If any place in the world we need Christianity, it's in Washington. And that's why preachers long since need to get over that intimidation forced upon us by liberals, that if we mention anything about politics, we are degrading our ministry.

JERRY FALWELL, sermon, July 4, 1976.

We're not a political people. We've just been preaching the issues. We're trying to be the moral conscience of the nation. I don't equate America with Christianity. I don't wrap the cross in a flag.

JERRY FALWELL, news conference. Washington, D.C., January 27, 1981.

For thirty years, the Bible-believing Christians of America have been largely absent from the executive, legislative, and judicial branches of both federal and local government.

JERRY FALWELL, in William R. Goodman, Jr., and James J.H. Price, *Jerry Falwell: An Unauthorized Profile*, 1981.

Religious factions will go on imposing their will on others unless the decent people connected to them recognize that religion has no place in public policy.

BARRY M. GOLDWATER, speech, 1981.

The Congress should at once submit an amendment to the Constitution which establishes the right to religious devotion in all governmental agencies—national, state or local.

HERBERT HOOVER, *New York Times*, July 1, 1962.

When churches succumb to the pressures of secular life and fail to exhibit a distinctive quality of faith and life, the separation of church and state...loses its point.

W.S. HUDSON, *The Great Tradition of the American Churches*, 1953.

The day that this country ceases to be free for irreligion it will cease to be free for religion—except for the sect that can win political power.

ROBERT H. JACKSON, opinion, *Zorach v. Clauson*, 1952.

I hope that no American...will waste his franchise and throw away his vote by voting either for me or against me solely on account of my religious affiliation. It is not relevant.

JOHN F. KENNEDY, *Time*, July 25, 1960.

I believe in an America where the separation of church and state is absolute—where no Catholic prelate would tell the President (should he be a Catholic) how to act and no Protestant minister would tell his parishioners for whom to vote—where no church or church school is granted any public funds or political preference—and where no man is denied public office merely because his religion differs from the President who might appoint him or the people who might elect him.

JOHN F. KENNEDY, speech, Greater Houston Ministerial Association, Houston, Texas, September 12, 1960.

The church must be reminded that it is not the master or the servant of the state, but rather the conscience of the state. It must be the guide and the critic of the state, and never its tool. If the church does not recapture its prophetic zeal, it will become an irrelevant social club without moral or spiritual authority.

MARTIN LUTHER KING, JR., *Strength to Love*, 1963.

We're in the hands of the state legislature and God, but at the moment, the state legislature has more to say than God.

EDWARD KOCH, *New York Times*, June 27, 1986.

The wall of separation ensures the government's freedom from religion and the individual's freedom of religion. The second probably cannot flourish without the first.

LEONARD W. LEVY, *The Establishment Clause: Religion and the First Amendment*, 1986.

Modern governments are not merely neutral as between rival churches. They draw to themselves much of the loyalty which was once given to the churches.

WALTER LIPPMANN, *A Preface to Morals*, 1929.

The God-given rights of parents are not understood or are ignored by our secularist educators and by many school administrators who, in the delusion of sovereignty, act as though they, not the parents, have complete control of the education of the child.

JOHN T. MCNICHOLAS, *No Wall Between God and Child*, 1947.

We will be a better country when each religious group can trust its members to obey the dictates of their own religious faith without assistance from the legal structure of the country.

MARGARET MEAD, *Redbook*, February, 1963.

Although he's regularly asked to do so, God does not take sides in American politics.

GEORGE J. MITCHELL, Iran-Contra hearings, July 13, 1987.

With us, separation of church and state was never intended to mean separation of religion from society.

JAMES A. PIKE, *New York Times*, July 13, 1962.

[We seek] a constitutional amendment to permit voluntary school prayer. God should never have been expelled from America's classrooms in the first place.

RONALD REAGAN, State of the Union address, January 25, 1983.

The Founding Fathers unfailingly recognized a clear and elemental distinction which appears to elude the mind of the present Court—between religion as a well nigh universal concern of men and the several specific forms and institutions of "organized religion."

HENRY P. VAN DUSEN, letter, *New York Times*, July 7, 1963.

SCIENCE AND RELIGION

If we take science as our sole guide, if we accept and hold fast that alone which is verifiable, the old theology must go.

JOHN BURROUGHS, *The Light of Day*, 1900.

To pursue science is not to disparage the things of the spirit. In fact, to pursue science rightly is to furnish a framework on which the spirit may rise.

VANNEVAR BUSH, speech, Massachusetts Institution of Technology, October 5, 1953.

Professional scientists today live under a taboo against mixing science and religion.

FREEMAN DYSON, *Disturbing the Universe*, 1979.

The cosmic religious experience is the strongest and noblest force behind the driving force of scientific research.

ALBERT EINSTEIN, *Cosmic Religion*, 1931.

Science without religion is lame, religion without science is blind.

ALBERT EINSTEIN, *Out of My Later Years*, 1950.

It seems hard to sneak a look at God's cards. But that he plays dice and uses "telepathic" methods (as the present quantum theory requires of him) is something that I cannot believe for a single moment.

ALBERT EINSTEIN, letter to Cornelius Lanczos, February 14, 1938, in Helen Dukas and Banesh Hoffman, *Albert Einstein: The Human Side*, 1979.

Where there is the necessary technical skill to move mountains, there is no need for the faith that moves mountains.

ERIC HOFFER, *The Passionate State of Mind*, 1954.

It [science] has nothing to say, and can have nothing to say, on the question of ultimate realities of an eternal order which are essential to a spiritual religion.

RUFUS M. JONES, *A Preface to Christian Faith in a New Age*, 1932.

The world of poetry, mythology, and religion represents the world as man would like to have it, while science represents the world as he gradually comes to discover it.

JOSEPH WOOD KRUTCH, *The Modern Temper*, 1929.

Technology is not in itself opposed to spirituality and to religion. But it presents a great temptation.

THOMAS MERTON, *Conjectures of a Guilty Bystander*, 1968.

The general tendency of scientific discovery has been to weaken not only religious but ethical values.

REINHOLD NIEBUHR, *Christian Century*, April 22, 1926.

Religion belongs to that realm that is inviolable before the law of causation and therefore closed to science.

MAX PLANCK, *Where Is Science Going?*, 1932.

How could science be any enemy of religion when God commanded man to be a scientist the day He told him to rule the earth and subject it?

FULTON J. SHEEN, *The Life of All Living*, 1929.

SIN

In his heart, he knows your wife.

BUMPER STICKER, following Jimmy Carter's *Playboy* interview, 1976.

I have looked upon a lot of women with lust. I've committed adultery in my heart many times.

JIMMY CARTER, interview, *Playboy*, 1976.

"When I'm in normal health, I'm a Presbyterian, but just now I feel that even the wicked get worse than they deserve."

WILLA CATHER, *One of Ours*, 1922.

I read about an Eskimo hunter who asked the local missionary priest, "If I did not know about God and sin, would I go to hell?" "No," said the priest, "not if you did not know." "Then why," asked the Eskimo earnestly, "did you tell me?"

ANNIE DILLARD, *Pilgrim at Tinker Creek*, 1974.

If we had more hell in the pulpit, we would have less hell in the pew.

BILLY GRAHAM, *New York Herald Tribune*, May 25, 1964.

Fashions in sin change.

LILLIAN HELLMAN, *Watch on the Rhine*, 1941.

Who are those who will eventually be damned? Oh, the others, the others, the others!

ELBERT HUBBARD, *The Roycroft Dictionary and Book of Epigrams*, 1923.

The only sure-enough sinner is the man who congratulates himself that he is without sin.

ELBERT HUBBARD, *The Roycroft Dictionary and Book of Epigrams*, 1923.

I had a dream that I was in purgatory and I ran across Bill Madlock with the ugliest woman I've ever seen. He explained that was his penance for all the sins he committed on earth. Then I saw George Steinbrenner with Bo Derek. I couldn't believe it. George Steinbrenner with Bo Derek? Until somebody explained. "You don't understand. This is Bo Derek's penance."

TOMMY LASORDA, *New York Daily News*, February 7, 1982.

Religions generally put regulations about eating, dress, and washing in the same category as opportunities for sinning that promise considerably more fun.

JUDITH MARTIN, *Common Courtesy*, 1985.

Sin…has been made not only ugly but passé. People are no longer sinful, they are only immature or underprivileged or frightened or, more particularly, sick.

PHYLLIS MCGINLEY, "In Defense of Sin," *The Province of the Heart*, 1959.

In some crude sense, which no vulgarity, no humor, no overstatement can quite extinguish, the physicists have known sin, and this is a knowledge which they cannot lose.

J. ROBERT OPPENHEIMER, 1949, in Lois and Alan Gordon, *American Chronicle*, 1987.

Whatever the theologians thought about this most cruel of human ideas, which grew through the centuries into a dragon that devoured the minds of the children of Christendom, to me as a child the Unpardonable Sin had to do with one's forbidden dreams.

LILLIAN SMITH, *Killers of the Dream*, 1949.

Well, there's a Book that says we're all sinners and I at least chose a sin that's made quite a few people happier than they were before they met me.

SALLY STANFORD, *The Lady of the House*, 1966.

Repentance is…not only a realization of failure, not only a burst of contrition for having failed the good, not only a readiness to admit this failure freely…but also a determination not to fail the good again.

DOUGLAS V. STEERE, *Door into Life*, 1948.

Science and Technology

See also **American Society; Dreams and Ideals**—Change, Risk; **Ethics and Morality; The Human Condition**—Creativity, Imagination, Ingenuity; **Religion and Spirituality**—Science and Religion; **War and Peace; Work**—Scientists

That which today calls itself science gives us more and more information, an indigestible glut of information, and less and less understanding.

EDWARD ABBEY, "Down the River with Henry Thoreau," *Words From the Land*, 1981.

If the human race wants to go to hell in a basket, technology can help it get there by jet. It won't change the desire or the direction, but it can greatly speed the passage.

CHARLES M. ALLEN, speech, "Unity in a University," Wake Forest University, Winston-Salem, North Carolina, April 25, 1967.

The machine [herded] men into towns and cities, the age of the factory....Men all began to dress alike, eat the same foods, read the same kind of newspapers and books. Minds began to be standardized as were the clothes men wore.

SHERWOOD ANDERSON, 1926, in Lois and Alan Gordon, *American Chronicle*, 1987.

Every answer given arouses new questions. The progress of science is matched by an increase in the hidden and mysterious.

LEO BAECK, *Judaism and Science*, 1949.

It is not clear to anyone, least of all the practitioners, how science and technology in their headlong course do or should influence ethics and law, education and government, art and social philosophy, religion and the life of the affections. Yet science is an all-pervasive energy, for it is at once a mode of thought, a source of strong emotion, and a faith as fanatical as any in history.

JACQUES BARZUN, *Science: The Glorious Entertainment*, 1964.

For the educated, the authority of science rested on the strictness of its method; for the mass, it rested on its powers of explanation.

JACQUES BARZUN, *Science: The Glorious Entertainment*, 1964.

Once regarded as the herald of enlightenment in all spheres of knowledge, science is now increasingly seen as a strictly instrumental system of control. Its use as a means of social manipulation and its role in restricting human freedom now parallel in every detail its use as a means of natural manipulation.

MURRAY BOOKCHIN, *The Ecology of Freedom*, 1982.

Just as the American's love affair with his land produced pioneering adventures and unceasing excitement in the conquest of the continent, so too his latter-day romance with the Machine produced pioneering adventures—of a new kind...there were no boundaries to a machine-made world.

DANIEL BOORSTIN, *Hidden History*, 1987.

Consider the wheelbarrow. It may lack the grace of an airplane, the speed of an automobile, the initial capacity of a freight car, but its humble wheel marked out the path of what civilization we still have. Particularly that phase of civilization which leads down Main Street, through the front gate, around the house and into the back garden.

HAL BORLAND, *New York Times*, April 27, 1947.

DNA was the first three-dimensional Xerox machine.

KENNETH BOULDING, "Energy and the Environment," *Beasts, Ballads, and Bouldingisms*, 1976.

We have grasped the mystery of the atom and rejected the Sermon on the Mount.

OMAR BRADLEY, speech, Boston, Massachusetts, November 10, 1948.

That is the essence of science: ask an impertinent question, and you are on the way to the pertinent answer.

JACOB BRONOWSKI, *The Ascent of Man*, 1973.

We landed on the Sea of Tranquility, in the cool of the early lunar morning, when the long shadows would aid our perception.

The sun was only ten degrees above the horizon, while the earth turned through nearly a full day during our stay. The sun at Tranquility Base rose barely eleven degrees—a small fraction of the monthlong lunar day. There was a peculiar sensation of the duality of time—the swift rush of events that characterizes all our lives—and the ponderous parade which makes the aging of the universe.

Both kinds of time were evident—the first by the routine events of the flight—whose planning and execution were detailed to fractions of a second—the latter by rocks around us, unchanged throughout the history of man—whose three-billion-year-old secrets made them the treasures we sought.

The plaque on the "Eagle" which summarized our hopes bears this message:

Here men from the planet Earth first set foot upon the moon July 1969 A.D.

We came in peace for all mankind whose nineteen hundred and sixty-nine years had constituted the majority of the ages of Pisces—a twelfth of the great year that is measured by the thousand generations the precession of the earth's axis requires to scribe a giant circle in the heavens.

In the next twenty centuries, the age of Aquarius of the great year, the age for which our young people have such high hopes, humanity may begin to understand its most baffling mystery—where are we going? The earth is, in fact, traveling many thousands of miles per hour in the direction of the constellation Hercules—to some unknown destination in the cosmos. Man must understand his universe in order to understand his destiny.

Mystery, however, is a very necessary ingredient in our lives.

Mystery creates wonder and wonder is the basis for man's desire to understand. Who knows what mysteries will be solved in our lifetime, and what new riddles will become the challenge of the new generations? Science has not mastered prophesy. We predict too much for next year yet far too little for the next ten. Responding to challenge is one of democracy's great strengths. Our successes in space lead us to hope that this strength can be used in the next decade in the solution of many of our planet's problems.

Several weeks ago I enjoyed the warmth of reflection on the true meaning of the spirit of Apollo.

I stood in the highlands of this nation, near the Continental Divide, introducing to my sons the wonders of nature, and pleasures of looking for deer and elk.

In their enthusiasm for the view they frequently stumbled on the rocky trails. But when they looked only to their footing, they did not see the elk. To those of you who have advocated looking high we owe our sincere gratitude, for you have granted us the opportunity to see some of the grandest views of the Creator.

To those of you who have been our honest critics, we also thank, for you have reminded us that we dare not forget to watch the trail. We carried on Apollo 11 two flags of this Union that had flown over the Capitol, one over the House of Representatives, one over the Senate.

It is our privilege to return them now in these halls which exemplify man's highest purpose—to serve one's fellow man.

We thank you, on behalf of all the men of Apollo, for giving us the privilege of joining you in serving—for all mankind.

Neil A. Armstrong, speech to Congress,
September 16, 1969.

To treat your facts with imagination is one thing, to imagine your facts is quite another.

JOHN BURROUGHS, journal entry, October 24, 1907.

Often a liberal antidote of experience supplies a sovereign cure for a paralyzing abstraction built upon a theory.

BENJAMIN N. CARDOZO, *The Paradoxes of Legal Science*, 1928.

We live in a scientific age, yet we assume that knowledge of science is the prerogative of only a small number of human beings, isolated and priestlike in their laboratories. This is not true. The materials of science are the materials of life itself. Science is part of the reality of living; it is the what, the how and the why for everything in our experience.

RACHEL CARSON, speech, 1952, in Paul Brooks, *The House of Life: Rachel Carson at Work*, 1972.

Science is wonderfully equipped to answer the question "How?" but it gets terribly confused when you ask the question "Why?"

ERWIN CHARGAFF, *Columbia Forum*, Summer, 1969.

As soon as questions of will or decision or reason or choice of action arise, human science is at a loss.

NOAM CHOMSKY, TV interview, *Listener*, March 30, 1978.

Science is triumphant with far-ranging success, but its triumph is somehow clouded by growing difficulites in providing for the simple necessities of human life on the earth.

BARRY COMMONER, *Science and Survival*, 1966.

Despite the dazzling successes of modern technology and the unprecedented power of modern military systems, they suffer from a common and catastrophic fault. While providing us with a bountiful supply of food, with great industrial plants, with high-speed transportation, and with military weapons of unprecedented power, they threaten our very survival.

BARRY COMMONER, *Science and Survival*, 1966.

The gap between brute power and human need continues to grow, as the power fattens on the same faulty technology that intensifies the need.

BARRY COMMONER, *The Closing Circle: Nature, Man, and Technology*, 1972.

In recent times, modern science has developed to give mankind, for the first time in the history of the human race, a way of securing a more abundant life which does not simply consist in taking away from someone else.

KARL TAYLOR COMPTON, speech, American Philosophical Society, 1938.

Take the so called standard of living. What do most people mean by "living"? They don't mean living. They mean the latest and closest plural approximation to singular prenatal passivity which science, in its finite but unbounded wisdom, has succeeded in selling their wives.

E.E. CUMMINGS, Introduction, *Poems*, 1954.

Every great advance in science has issued from a new audacity of imagination.

JOHN DEWEY, *The Quest for Certainty*, 1929.

Science through its physical technological consequences is now determining the relations which human beings, severally and in groups, sustain to one another. If it is incapable of developing moral techniques which will also determine these relations, the split in modern culture goes so deep that not only democracy but all civilized values are doomed.

JOHN DEWEY, *Freedom and Culture*, 1939.

Putting on the spectacles of science in expectation of finding the answer to everything looked at signifies inner blindness.

J. FRANK DOBIE, *The Voice of the Coyote*, 1949.

Most of the dangerous aspects of technological civilization arise, not from its complexities, but from the fact that modern man has become more interested in the machines and industrial goods themselves than in their use to human ends.

RENÉ DUBOS, *A God Within*, 1972.

Natural science has outstripped moral and political science. That is too bad; but it is a fact, and the fact does not disappear because we close our eyes to it.

JOHN FOSTER DULLES, *War or Peace*, 1950.

Every science begins as philosophy and ends as art.

WILL DURANT, *The Story of Philosophy*, 1926.

Science and technology, like all original creations of the human spirit, are unpredictable. If we had a reliable way to label our toys good and bad, it would be easy to regulate technology wisely. But we can rarely see far enough ahead to know which road leads to damnation. Whoever concerns himself with big technology, either to push it forward or to stop it, is gambling in human lives.

FREEMAN DYSON, *Disturbing the Universe*, 1979.

Why does this magnificent applied science which saves work and makes life easier bring us so little happiness? The simple answer runs: Because we have not yet learned to make sensible use of it.

ALBERT EINSTEIN, speech, California Institute of Technology, February, 1931.

The whole of science is nothing more than a refinement of everyday thinking.

ALBERT EINSTEIN, "Physics and Reality," 1936.

Concern for man himself and his fate must always form the chief interest of all technical endeavors....Never forget this in the midst of your diagrams and equations.

ALBERT EINSTEIN, in Robert S. Lynd, *Knowledge for What?*, 1939.

Science can only ascertain what *is*, but not what *should be*, and outside of its domain value judgments of all kinds remain necessary.

ALBERT EINSTEIN, *Out of My Later Years*, 1950.

In the end, science as we know it has two basic types of practitioners. One is the educated man who still has a controlled sense of wonder before the universal mystery, whether it hides in a snail's eye or within the light that impinges on that delicate organ. The second kind of observer is the extreme reductionist who is so busy stripping things apart that the tremendous mystery has been reduced to a trifle, to intangibles not worth troubling one's head about.

LOREN EISELEY, "Science and the Sense of the Holy," *The Star Thrower*, 1978.

Science, in the very act of solving problems, creates more of them.

ABRAHAM FLEXNER, *Universities*, 1930.

The danger of the past was that men became slaves. The danger of the future is that men may become robots.

ERICH FROMM, *The Sane Society*, 1955.

Science has radically changed the conditions of human life on earth. It has expanded our knowledge and our power but not our capacity to use them with wisdom.

J. WILLIAM FULBRIGHT, *Old Myths and New Realities*, 1964.

It is a commonplace of modern technology that problems have solutions before there is knowledge of how they are to be solved.

JOHN KENNETH GALBRAITH, *The New Industrial State*, 1967.

[By 1940] the relativity theory will be considered a joke.

GEORGE FRANCIS GILETTE, in Martin Gardner, *Fads and Fallacies in the Name of Science*, 1929.

Once upon a time we were just plain people. But that was before we began having relationships with mechanical systems. Get involved with a machine and sooner or later you are reduced to a factor.

ELLEN GOODMAN, "The Human Factor," *Washington Post*, January, 1987.

In all human activities, it is not ideas or machines that dominate; it is people. I have heard people speak of "the effect of personality on science." But this is a backward thought. Rather, we should talk about the effect of science on personalities. Science is not the dispassionate analysis of impartial data. It is the human, and thus passionate, exercise of skill and sense on such data. Science is not an exercise in objectivity, but, more accurately, an exercise in which objectivity is prized.

PHILIP HILTS, *Scientific Temperaments: Three Lives in Contemporary Science*, 1982.

As children we all possess a natural, uninhibited curiosity, a hunger for explanation, which seems to die slowly as we age—suppressed, I suppose, by the high value we place on conformity and by the need not to appear ignorant. It betokens a conviction that somehow science is innately incomprehensible. It precludes reaching deeper, thereby denying the profound truth that understanding enriches experience, that explanation vastly enhances the beauty of the natural world in the eye of the beholder.

MAHLON HOAGLAND, *Toward the Habit of Truth*, 1990.

It is often the scientist's experience that he senses the nearness of truth when...connections are envisioned. A connection is a step toward simplification, unification. Simplicity is indeed often the sign of truth and a criterion of beauty.

MAHLON HOAGLAND, *Toward the Habit of Truth*, 1990.

One machine can do the work of fifty ordinary men. No machine can do the work of one extraordinary man.

ELBERT HUBBARD, *The Roycroft Dictionary and Book of Epigrams*, 1923.

Equipped with his five senses, man explores the universe around him and calls the adventure Science.

EDWIN POWELL HUBBLE, *The Nature of Science*, 1954.

Modern technology was made in America.

THOMAS HUGHES, *American Genesis: A Century of Invention and Technological Enthusiasm*, 1989.

By 1900 [Americans] had reached the promised land of the technological world, the world as artifact. In doing so they had acquired traits that have become characteristically American. A nation of machine makers and system builders, they became imbued with a drive for order, system, and control.

THOMAS HUGHES, *American Genesis: A Century of Invention and Technological Enthusiasm*, 1989.

It's as important an event as would be the transfer of the Vatican from Rome to the New World. The Pope of Physics has moved and the United States will now become the center of the natural sciences.

PAUL LANGEVIN, on Albert Einstein's move to Princeton, New Jersey, from Germany in 1933, in Robert Jungk, *Brighter than a Thousand Suns*, 1958.

Without meaning to belittle the wonders of science, I do not think they can absolve mankind of suffering, desire, madness, and death.

LEWIS H. LAPHAM, speech, "The Senior Practitioner," Northwestern Medical School, June, 1987.

It is a curious paradox that aversion of future harm seems more important than the promise of future benefit. That was not always true. Those who are unwilling to invent in the future haven't earned one.

H.W. LEWIS, *Technological Risk*, 1990.

The machine that frees a man's back of drudgery does not thereby make his spirit free. Technology has made us more productive, but it does not necessarily enrich our lives. Engineers can build us great dams, but only great people make a valley great. There is no technology of goodness. Men must make themselves spiritually free.

DAVID E. LILIENTHAL, *TVA: Democracy on the March*, 1944.

You cannot endow even the best machine with initiative; the jolliest steamroller will not plant flowers.

WALTER LIPPMANN, "Routineer and Inventor," *A Preface to Politics*, 1914.

The history of America is a history of gigantic engineering feats and colossal mechanical construction.

LOUIS LOZOWICK, in Thomas Hughes, *American Genesis: A Century of Invention and Technological Enthusiasm*, 1989.

Significant advances in science often have a peculiar quality: they contradict obvious, commonsense opinions.

S.E. LURIA, *A Slot Machine, A Broken Test Tube: An Autobiography*, 1984.

Everyone knows that in research there are no final answers, only insights that allow one to formulate new questions.

S.E. LURIA, *A Slot Machine, A Broken Test Tube: An Autobiography*, 1984.

[T]he world of science may be the only existing participatory democracy.

S.E. LURIA, *A Slot Machine, A Broken Test Tube: An Autobiography*, 1984.

Science, at bottom, is really anti-intellectual. It always distrusts pure reason, and demands the production of objective fact.

H.L. MENCKEN, *Minority Report: Notebooks*, 1956.

Isn't it strange that as technology advances, the quality of life frequently declines?

HARVEY MILK, speech, fund-raising meeting, 1977.

By his very success in inventing labor-saving devices, modern man has manufactured an abyss of boredom that only the privileged classes in earlier civilizations have ever fathomed.

LEWIS MUMFORD, "The Challenge to Renewal," *The Conduct of Life*, 1951.

What it is important to realize is that automation...is an attempt to exercise control, not only of the mechanical process itself, but of the human being who once directed it: turning him from an active to a passive agent, and finally eliminating him altogether.

LEWIS MUMFORD, "The Myth of the Machine," *The Pentagon of Power*, 1970.

For those of us who have thrown off the myth of the machine, the next move is ours: for the gates of the technocratic prison will open automatically, despite their rusty ancient hinges, as soon as we choose to walk out.

LEWIS MUMFORD, "The Myth of the Machine," *The Pentagon of Power*, 1970.

Modern technology has lost its magic. No longer do people stand in awe, thrilled by the onward rush of science, the promise of a new day. Instead, the new is suspect. It arouses our hostility as much as it used to excite our fancy. With each breakthrough there are recurrent fears and suspicion. How will the advance further pollute our lives; modern technology is not merely what it first appears to be. Behind the white coats, the disarming jargon, the elaborate instrumentation, and at the core of what has often seemed an automatic process, one finds what Dorothy found in Oz: modern technology is human after all.

DAVID NOBLE, in Rita Arditti, Pat Brennan, and Steve Cavrak, eds., "Corporate Roots of American Science," *Science and Liberation*, 1980.

The open society, the unrestricted access to knowledge, the unplanned and uninhibited association of men for its furtherance—these are what may make a vast, complex, ever growing, ever changing, even more specialized and expert technological world, nevertheless a world of human community.

J. ROBERT OPPENHEIMER, *Science and the Common Understanding*, 1953.

Both the man of science and the man of art live always at the edge of mystery, surrounded by it. Both, as the measure of their creation, have always had to do with the harmonization of what is new with what is familiar, with the balance between novelty and synthesis, with the struggle to make partial order in total chaos.... This cannot be an easy life.

J. ROBERT OPPENHEIMER, lecture, ca. 1954, in Robert Jungk, *Brighter than a Thousand Suns*, 1958.

Science will never be able to reduce the value of a sunset to arithmetic. Nor can it reduce friendship to a formula. Laughter and love, pain and loneliness, the challenge of accomplishment in living, and the depth of insight into beauty and truth: these will always surpass the scientific mastery of nature.

LOUIS ORR, speech, American Medical Association, June 6, 1960.

I'm not afraid of facts, I welcome facts *but a congeries of facts is not equivalent to an idea.* This is the essential fallacy of the so-called "scientific" mind. People who mistake facts for ideas are incomplete thinkers; they are gossips.

CYNTHIA OZICK, "We Are the Crazy Lady and Other Feisty Feminist Fables," Francine Klagsbrun, ed., *The First Ms. Reader*, 1972.

Science provides a vision of reality seen from the perspective of reason, a perspective that sees the vast order of the universe, living and nonliving matter, as a material system governed by rules that can be known by the human mind. It is a powerful vision, formal and austere but strangely silent about many of the questions that deeply concern us. Science shows us what exists but not what to do about it.

HEINZ PAGELS, *The Dreams of Reason*, 1988.

It was a *wonderful* mess at that time. Wonderful! Just great! It was so *confusing*—physics at its best, when everything is confused and you know something important lies just around the corner.

ABRAHAM PAIS, on particle physics in early 1950s, in Robert Crease and Charles Mann, *The Second Creation: Makers of the Revolution in 20th-Century Physics*, 1985.

Either we've seen the birth of the universe, or we've seen a pile of pigeon shit.

ARNO PENZIAS, 1956, in Roylston Roberts, *Serendipity*, 1989.

One geometry cannot be more true than another; it can only be more *convenient*. Geometry is not true, it is advantageous.

ROBERT M. PIRSIG, *Zen and the Art of Motorcycle Maintenance*, 1974.

Traditional scientific method has always been at the very *best*, 20-20 hindsight. It's good for seeing where you've been.

ROBERT M. PIRSIG, *Zen and the Art of Motorcycle Maintenance*, 1974.

It is only in science, I find, that we can get outside ourselves. It's realistic, and to a great degree verifiable, and it has this tremendous stage on which it plays. I have the same feeling—to a certain degree—about some religious expressions... but only to a certain degree. For me, the proper study of mankind is *science*, which also means that the proper study of mankind is man.

I.I. RABI, in Jeremy Bernstein, *Experiencing Science*, 1978.

With science I felt I could grab on to actual things and try to understand them. And then they turned out to be so extraordinarily *mysterious*! Newton's laws of motion, the laws of the electromagetic field, relativity—they're so far removed from experience, but yet there it is. It's a measure of all the other things that I look at. It gives you an approach to the human race, apart from these inherited things of nationality and whatnot, which you can't take very seriously. That's what science was for me—a citadel. I know some place where I can find out things which are *so*, and not trivial. Far from trivial.

I.I. RABI, in Robert Crease and Charles Mann, *The Second Creation: Makers of the Revolution in 20th-Century Physics*, 1986.

There is a lurking fear that some things are "not meant" to be known, that some inquiries are too dangerous for human beings to make.

CARL SAGAN, *Broca's Brain*, 1979.

A machine is not a genie, it does not work by magic, it does not possess a will, and [Norbert] Wiener to the contrary, nothing comes out which has not been put in, barring of course, an infrequent case of malfunctioning....The "intentions" which the machine seems to manifest are the intentions of the human programmer, as specified in advance, or they are subsidiary intentions derived from these, following rules specified by the programmer....The machine will not and cannot do any of these things until it has been instructed as to how to proceed....To believe otherwise is either to believe in magic or to believe that the existence of man's will is an illusion and that man's actions are as mechanical as the machine's.

ARTHUR L. SAMUEL, *Science*, September 16, 1960.

The real problem is not whether machines think but whether men do.

B.F. SKINNER, *Contingencies of Reinforcement*, 1969.

Technology, while adding daily to our physical ease, throws daily another loop of fine wire around our souls. It contributes hugely to our mobility, which we must not confuse with freedom. The extensions of our senses, which we find so fascinating, are not adding to the discrimination of our minds, since we need increasingly to take the reading of a needle on a dial to discover whether we think something is good or bad, or right or wrong.

ADLAI E. STEVENSON, "My Faith in Democratic Capitalism," *Fortune*, October, 1955.

Mystics always hope that science will some day overtake them.

BOOTH TARKINGTON, *Looking Forward*, 1926.

If there ever was a misnomer, it is "exact science." Science has always been full of mistakes. The present day is no exception. And our mistakes are good mistakes; they require a genius to correct them. Of course, we do not see our own mistakes.

EDWARD TELLER, *Conversations on the Dark Secrets of Physics*, 1991.

Our technological powers increase, but the side effects and potential hazards also escalate.

ALVIN TOFFLER, *Future Shock*, 1970.

That great, growing engine of change—technology.

ALVIN TOFFLER, *Future Shock*, 1970.

Technology feeds on itself. Technology makes more technology possible.

ALVIN TOFFLER, *Future Shock*, 1970.

Each new machine or technique, in a sense, changes all existing machines and techniques, by permitting us to put them together into new combinations. The number of possible combinations rises exponentially as the number of new machines or techniques rises arithmetically. Indeed, each new combination may, itself, be regarded as a new super-machine.

ALVIN TOFFLER, *Future Shock*, 1970.

I want to change the way people think about their everyday lives. How you think is going to affect who you marry, what kind of relationship you establish, whether and in what manner you reproduce. That's day-to-day thinking, right? But they don't even teach courses on that stuff.... Life *is* intrinsically biological. It's absurd not to use our best biological concept.

ROBERT TRIVERS, in Roger Bingham, "Robert Trivers: Biologist of Behavior," *A Passion to Know: 20 Profiles in Science*, 1985.

[S]cience seldom proceeds in the straightforward logical manner imagined by outsiders. Instead, its steps forward (and sometimes backward) are often very human events in which personalities and cultural traditions play major roles.... [Science moves with] the spirit of an adventure characterized both by youthful arrogance and by the belief that the truth, once found, would be simple as well as pretty.

JAMES D. WATSON, *The Double Helix*, 1968.

Specialization has gotten out of hand. There are more branches in the tree of knowledge than there are in the tree of life. A petrologist studies rocks; a pedologist studies soils. The first one sieves the soil and throws away the rocks. The second one picks up the rocks and brushes off the soil. Out in the field, they bump into each other only like Laurel and Hardy, by accident, when they are both backing up.

JONATHAN WEINER, *The Next One Hundred Years*, 1990.

But science and technology are only one of the avenues toward reality: others are equally needed to comprehend the full significance of our existence. Indeed, these other avenues are necessary for the prevention of thoughtless and inhuman abuses of the results of science.

VICTOR WEISSKOPF, *The Privilege of Being a Physicist,* 1989.

Science is an important part of the humanities because it is based on an essential human trait: curiosity about the how and why of our environment. We must foster wonder, joy of insight.

VICTOR WEISSKOPF, *The Privilege of Being a Physicist,* 1989.

The history of physics shows that deeper insights into the nature of things are best achieved with distance from daily experience.

VICTOR WEISSKOPF, *The Privilege of Being a Physicist,* 1989.

Some people maintain that scientific insight has eliminated the need for meaning. I do not agree. The scientific worldview established the notion that there is a sense and purpose in the development of the universe when it recognized the evolution from the primal explosion to matter, life, and humanity. In humans, nature begins to recognize itself.

VICTOR WEISSKOPF, *The Joy of Insight,* 1991.

The same system that produced a bewildering succession of new-model, style-obsolescent autos and refrigerators can also produce an endless out-pouring of new-model, style-obsolescent science.

HARVEY WHEELER, *New York Times,* August 11, 1975.

The goal is to understand the plan of creation, period.

JOHN WHEELER, in Dennis Overbye, "John Wheeler: Messenger at the Gates of Time," *A Passion to Know: 20 Profiles in Science,* 1985.

The audaciously destructive tendencies of our species run deep and are poorly understood. They are so difficult to probe and manage as to suggest an archaic biological origin. We run a risk if we continue to diagnose them as by-products of history and suppose that they be erased with simple economic and political remedies.

EDWARD O. WILSON, *Biophilia,* 1984.

Important science is not just any similarity glimpsed for the first time. It offers analogues that map the gateways to unexplored terrain.

EDWARD O. WILSON, *Biophilia,* 1984.

To a considerable degree science consists in originating the maximum amount of information with the minimum expenditure of energy. Beau-

ty is the cleanness of line in such formulations, along with symmetry, surprise, and congruence with other prevailing beliefs.

EDWARD O. WILSON, *Biophilia,* 1984.

As a builder of accelerators, I could thrill to what appeared to me to be a medieval physicist responding to a very challenging physical problem. I saw the similarity between the cathedral and the accelerator. The one structure was intended to reach a soaring height in space; the other is intended to reach a comparable height in energy.

ROBERT WILSON, in Philip Hilts, "Robert Wilson: Lord of the Rings," *A Passion to Know: 20 Profiles in Science,* 1985.

SUCCESS FOUR FLIGHTS THURSDAY MORNING ALL AGAINST TWENTY-ONE MILE WIND STARTED FROM LEVEL WITH ENGINE POWER ALONE AVERAGE SPEED THROUGH AIR THIRTY-ONE MILES LONGEST 59 SECONDS INFORM PRESS HOME CHRISTMAS.

ORVILLE AND WILBUR WRIGHT, telegram to their father from Kitty Hawk, North Carolina, December 17, 1903.

We did not know how to make the theory fit experiment. It was our judgment, however, that the beauty of the idea alone merited attention.

CHEN NING YANG, in Robert Crease and Charles Mann, *The Second Creation: Makers of the Revolution in 20th-Century Physics,* 1985.

COMMUNICATIONS

The computer is only a fast idiot, it has no imagination; it cannot originate action. It is, and will remain, only a tool to man.

AMERICAN LIBRARY ASSOCIATION STATEMENT ON UNIVAC COMPUTER EXHIBITED AT NEW YORK WORLD'S FAIR, 1964.

If arithmetical skill is the measure of intelligence, then computers have been more intelligent than all human beings all along. If the ability to play chess is the measure, then there are computers now in existence that are more intelligent than any but a very few human beings. However, if insight, intuition, creativity, the ability to view a problem as a whole and guess the answer by the "feel" of the situation, is a measure of intelligence, computers are very unintelligent indeed. Nor can we see right now how this deficiency in computers can be easily remedied, since human beings cannot program a computer to be intuitive or creative for the very good reason that we do not know what we ourselves do when we exercise these qualities.

ISAAC ASIMOV, *Machines That Think*, 1983.

One of the most feared expressions in modern times is "The computer is down."

NORMAN AUGUSTINE, "Augustine's 94th Law," *Augustine's Laws*, 1986.

The technology of so-called mass communication seemingly extended the reach of ideas, but actually dulled public attention by excess and abolished the capacity of quick, common response. In short, the gains produced by the ideal of diffusion proved, as might have been expected, diffuse.

JACQUES BARZUN, *Science: The Glorious Entertainment*, 1964.

The computer is in some ways a grand machine in the Western mechanical-dynamic tradition and in other ways a tool-in-hand from the ancient craft tradition....A machine is characterized by sustained, autonomous action....A tool, unlike a machine, is not self-sufficent or autonomous in action. It requires the skill of a craftsman and, when handled with skill, permits him to reshape the world in his way....However, the computer is not really a tool-in-hand; it is designed to extend the human brain rather than the hand, to allow the manipulation of mathematical and logical symbols at high speed. Yet it can be used with a kind of mental dexterity and reminds us of the craftsman's hand.

DAVID J. BOLTER, *Turing's Man*, 1984.

The computer...has given us continuously compounded interest at banks, easier airplane reservations, and a large quantity of unread Ph.D. theses.

KENNETH BOULDING, "Toward a Modest Society," *Economic Perspectives of Boulding and Samuelson*, 1971.

I have travelled the length and breadth of this country, and talked with the best people in business administration. I can assure you on the highest authority that data processing is a fad and won't last out the year.

EDITOR WHO REJECTED IDEA OF BOOK ON DATA PROCESSING, ca. 1957, in Christopher Cerf and Victor Navasky, *The Experts Speak*, 1984.

Man is about to be an automaton; he is identifiable only in the computer. As a person of worth and creativity, as a being with an infinite poten-

tial, he retreats and battles the forces that make him inhuman.

The dissent we witness is a reaffirmation of faith in man; it is protest against living under rules and prejudices and attitudes that produce the extremes of wealth and poverty and that make us dedicated to the destruction of people through arms, bombs, and gases, and that prepare us to think alike and be submissive objects for the regime of the computer.

WILLIAM O. DOUGLAS, *Points of Rebellion*, 1970.

Throughout my childhood, it was clear that [phone] lines were not for conversation but for announcements. We were as likely to reach out and touch someone by telephone as we were to communicate by using a cattle prod. Casual phoning was as rare as casual sex.

ELLEN GOODMAN, "Casual Phoning and the College Student," *Washington Post*, February, 1989.

Man is still the most extraordinary computer of all.

JOHN F. KENNEDY, speech, May 21, 1963.

Call Waiting. One of Miss Manners' least favorite devices, this is like a child screaming for attention while one is on the telephone. It is possible that the scream is "There's a fire in the kitchen," but demands to pay attention to a ringing telephone while you are already on the telephone constitute the rude policy of "Last come, first served."

JUDITH MARTIN, *Miss Manners' Guide for the Turn of the Millennium*, 1989.

Well I'll tell you what a phone is for. It's for not looking someone in the eyeball and saying I love you.

LOUISE MATTAGE, "Getting There," in Jo Alexander et al., *Women and Aging*, 1986.

A computer with as many vacuum tubes as a man has neurons in his head would require the Pentagon to house it, Niagara's power to run it, and Niagara's waters to cool it.

WARREN S. MCCULLOCH, in Robert Lindner, *Must You Conform?*, 1956.

The life-efficiency and adaptability of the computer must be questioned. Its judicious use depends upon the ability of its human employers quite literally to keep their own heads, not merely to scrutinize the programming but to reserve for themselves the right of ultimate decision. No automatic system can be intelligently run by automatons—or by people who dare not assert human intuition, human autonomy, human purpose.

LEWIS MUMFORD, "The Myth of the Machine," *The Pentagon of Power*, 1970.

If anything could testify to the magical powers of the priesthood of science and their technical acolytes, or declare unto mankind the supreme qualifications for absolute rulership held by the Divine Computer, this new invention alone should suffice. So the final purpose of life in terms of the megamachine at last becomes clear: it is to furnish and process an endless quantity of data, in order to expand the role and ensure the domination of the power system.

LEWIS MUMFORD, "The Myth of the Machine," *The Pentagon of Power*, 1970.

There is no reason for any individual to have a computer in their home.

KEN OLSON, Convention of the World Future Society, 1977, in Christopher Cerf and Victor Navasky, *The Experts Speak*, 1984.

Today, communication itself is the problem. We have become the world's first overcommunicated society. Each year we send more and receive less.

AL RIES, with Jack Trout, *Positioning: The Battle for Your Mind*, 1980.

Everybody gets so much information all day long that they lose their common sense.

GERTRUDE STEIN, "Reflection on the Atomic Bomb," in Robert A. Goldwin, ed., Readings in World Politics, 1959.

I do not worry much about the computers that are wired to help me find a friend among fifty thousand. If errors are made, I can always beg off with a headache. But what of the vaster machines that will be giving instructions to cities, to nations? If they are programmed to regulate human behavior according to today's view of nature, we are surely in for apocalypse.

LEWIS THOMAS, "An Earnest Proposal," *The Lives of a Cell*, 1974.

Humans, if they are machines at all, are vastly general-purpose machines and...they understand communications couched in natural languages (e.g., English) that lack, by very far, the precision and unambiguousness of ordinary programming languages.

JOSEPH WEIZENBAUM, *Computer Power and Human Reason*, 1984.

There is a myth that computers are today making important decisions of the kind that were earlier made by people. Perhaps there are isolated examples of that here and there in our society. But the widely believed picture of managers typing questions of the form "What shall we do now?" into their computers and then waiting for their computers to "decide" is largely wrong. What is happening instead is that people have turned the processing of information on which decisions must be based over to enormously complex computer systems. They have, with few exceptions, reserved for themselves the right to make decisions based on the outcome of such computing processes.

JOSEPH WEIZENBAUM, *Computer Power and Human Reason*, 1984.

Render unto man the things which are man's and unto the computer the things which are the computer's. This would seem the intelligent policy to adopt when we employ men and computers together in common undertakings. It is a policy as far removed from that of the gadget worshipper as it is from the man who sees only blasphemy and the degradation of man in the use of any mechanical adjuvants whatever to thoughts. What we need now is an independent study of systems involving both human and mechanical elements. This system should not be prejudiced either by a mechanical or antimechanical bias.

NORBERT WIENER, *God and Golem, Inc.*, 1964.

ENERGY

Behind the black portent of the new atomic age lies a hope which, seized upon with faith, can work our salvation. If we fail, then we have damned every man to be the slave of fear.

BERNARD BARUCH, speech, United Nations Atomic Energy Commission, June 14, 1946.

[I save energy] by asking my servants not to turn on the self-cleaning oven after seven in the morning.

BETSY BLOOMINGDALE, *Esquire*, January, 1982.

Society cannot continue to live on oil and gas. Those fossil fuels represent nature's savings accounts which took billions of years to form.

R. BUCKMINSTER FULLER, 1977, in Lois and Alan Gordon, *American Chronicle*, 1987.

Nuclear powered vacuum cleaners will probably be a reality within 10 years.

ALEX LEWYT, *New York Times*, June 10, 1955.

Atomic energy bears the same duality that has faced man from time immemorial, a duality expressed in the Book of Books thousands of years ago: "See, I have set before thee this day life and good and death and evil...therefore choose life."

DAVID E. LILIENTHAL, in Edward R. Murrow, ed., *This I Do Believe*, 1949.

[B]y 1980 all "power" (electric, atomic, solar) is likely to be virtually costless.

HENRY LUCE, *The Fabulous Future*, 1956.

There isn't a gasoline shortage. There's a driving surplus.

JOHN O'LEARY, *Time*, June 25, 1979.

All the waste in a year from a nuclear power plant can be stored under a desk.

RONALD REAGAN, *Burlington Free Press*, February 15, 1980.

[I]t can be taken for granted that before 1980 ships, aircraft, locomotives and even automobiles will be atomically fuelled.

DAVID SARNOFF, *The Fabulous Future: America in 1980*, 1955.

It took us eighteen months to build the first nuclear power generator; it now takes twelve years; that's progress.

EDWARD TELLER, in Milton Friedman and Rose Friedman, *Free To Choose*, 1979.

MEDICINE

The use of fetuses as organ and tissue donors is a ticking time bomb of bioethics.

ARTHUR CAPLAN, in article by Joe Levine, "Help from the Unborn," *Time*, January 12, 1987.

Thousands upon thousands of persons have studied disease. Almost no one has studied health.

ADELLE DAVIS, *Let's Eat Right To Keep Fit*, 1954.

It is simply absurd that without modern science painless childbirth does not exist as a matter of course.

ISADORA DUNCAN, *My Life*, 1927.

In the biotech revolution, it is the human body, not iron or steel or plastic, that's at the source. Are the biocapitalists going to be allowed to dig without consent into our genetic codes, then market them?

ELLEN GOODMAN, "Spleen for Sale," *Washington Post*, July, 1988.

In medicine, as in statecraft and propaganda, words are sometimes the most powerful drugs we can use.

SARA MURRAY JORDAN, *New York Times*, November 23, 1959.

The very success of medicine in a material way may now threaten the soul of medicine.

WALTER MARTIN, speech, "Medicine and the Public Welfare," American Medical Association, June 23, 1954.

The [doctor] has been taught to be interested not in health but in disease. What the public is taught is that health is the cure for disease.

ASHLEY MONTAGU, *New York Times*, September 30, 1975.

You must remember that nothing happens quite by chance. It's a question of accretion of information and experience...it's just chance that I happened to be here at this particular time when there was available and at my disposal the great experience of all the investigators who plodded along for a number of years.

JONAS SALK, on discovery of polio vaccine, in Richard Carter, *Breakthrough: The Saga of Jonas Salk*, 1965.

Surgery is the red flower that blooms among the leaves and thorns that are the rest of medicine.

RICHARD SELZER, *Letters to a Young Doctor*, 1982.

The next major explosion is going to be when genetics and computers come together. I'm talking about an organic computer—about biological substances that can function like semiconductors.

ALVIN TOFFLER, *New York Times*, February 21, 1988.

They are babies in waiting, life on ice.

CLAUDIA WALLIS, on frozen sperm cells, "Quickening Debate over Life on Ice," *Time*, July 2, 1984.

Clearly, if disease is man-made, it can also be man-prevented. It should be the function of medicine to help people die young as late in life as possible.

ERNST WUNDER, *New York Times*, September 30, 1975.

MILITARY HARDWARE

Science, which gave us this dread power, shows that it *can* be made a giant help to humanity, but science does *not* show us how to prevent its baleful use. So we have been appointed to obviate that peril by finding a meeting of the minds and the hearts of our people. Only in the will of mankind lies the answer.

BERNARD BARUCH, from plan presented to U.N. Atomic Energy Commission, June 14, 1946.

If we fight a war and win it with H-bombs, what history will remember is *not* the ideals we were fighting for but the method we used to accomplish them.

HANS BETHE, *Scientific American*, ca. 1950, in Robert Jungk, *Brighter than a Thousand Suns*, 1958.

With the monstrous weapons man already has, humanity is in danger of being trapped in this world by its moral adolescents. Our knowledge of science has already outstripped our capacity to control it. We have many men of science, too few men of God.

OMAR BRADLEY, speech, Boston, Massachusetts, November 10, 1948.

I went over the complete inventory of U.S. nuclear warheads, which is really a sobering experience.

JIMMY CARTER, diary entry, December 28, 1977.

Perhaps the quintessential symbol of society's anomalies is the neutron bomb. The distinctive feature of this weapon is that it will expunge life but spare property. It does, however, have this virtue: it is an open autobiographical statement. It is a confession of values. It identifies the hierarchy of things society believes are worth saving: the inanimate ahead of the animate, property ahead of people.

NORMAN COUSINS, *The Healing Heart*, 1983.

It may be possible to set up a nuclear reaction in uranium by which vast amounts of power could be released....This new phenomenon would also lead to the construction of...extremely powerful bombs of a new type.

ALBERT EINSTEIN, letter to Franklin D. Roosevelt, 1939.

Science has brought forth this danger, but the real problem is in the minds and hearts of men.

ALBERT EINSTEIN, on nuclear bomb, *New York Times Magazine*, June 23, 1946.

Radioactive poisoning of the atmosphere and hence annihilation of any life on earth has been brought within the range of technical possibilities. The ghostlike character of this development [the hydrogen bomb] lies in its apparently compulsory trend. Every step appears as the unavoidable consequence of the proceding one. In the end there beckons more and more clearly general annihilation.

ALBERT EINSTEIN, 1947, in Robert Jungk, *Brighter than a Thousand Suns*, 1958.

Thirty seconds after the explosion came, first the air blast pressing hard against people and things, to be followed almost immediately by the strong, sustained awesome roar which warned of doomsday and made us feel that we puny things were blasphemous to dare tamper with the forces heretofore reserved to the Almighty.

THOMAS FARRELL, official report on first atom bomb test, Alamogordo, New Mexico, July 16, 1945.

The President just plain old believed in an impenetrable shield around the United States. While a galaxy of scientists protested, he clapped for this Tinkerbell and we paid $12 billion.

ELLEN GOODMAN, on Star Wars program, "Science and the Stars," *Washington Post*, May, 1988.

It's like having a cobra in the nursery with your grandchildren....You get rid of the cobra or you won't have any grandchildren.

THEODORE M. HESBURGH, on nuclear weapons, "60 Minutes," CBS-TV, March 14, 1982.

Here's the thing that is top secret. Our scientists...[since] Hiroshima and Nagasaki have been trying to make what is known as a super-bomb,...a thousand times the effect of that terrible bomb. That's the secret, the big secret.

LOUIS JOHNSON, 1949, in Lois and Alan Gordon, *American Chronicle*, 1987.

The problem posed by the discovery and development of nuclear weaponry has proved to be one too large for the normal political system of this country.

GEORGE F. KENNAN, Introduction, in Norman Cousins, *Pathology of Power*, 1987.

Only technology has permitted us to put a city to the sword without quite realizing what we are doing.

JOSEPH WOOD KRUTCH, "If You Don't Mind My Saying So," *The American Scholar*, Summer, 1967.

This is the biggest fool thing we have ever done....The [atomic] bomb will never go off, and I speak as an expert in explosives.

WILLIAM LEAHY, to Harry S Truman, in Norman Augustine, *Augustine's Laws*, 1986.

It is part of the general pattern of misguided policy that our country is now geared to an arms industry which was bred in an artificially induced psychosis of war hysteria and nurtured upon an incessant propaganda of fear.

DOUGLAS MACARTHUR, speech, Michigan state legislature, May 15, 1952.

We knew the world would not be the same.

J. ROBERT OPPENHEIMER, on first atom bomb test, Alamogordo, New Mexico, July 16, 1945.

The atomic bomb...made the prospect of future war unendurable. It has led us up those last few steps to the mountain pass; and beyond there is a different country.

J. ROBERT OPPENHEIMER, in Richard Rhodes, *The Making of the Atomic Bomb*, 1987.

It is the Edsel of the 1980s. It is overpriced, it has been oversold, it will not perform as advertised.

GERRY E. STUDDS, on the Strategic Defense Initiative, *New York Times*, June 21, 1985.

During 1943 and part of 1944 our greatest worry was the possibility that Germany would perfect an atomic bomb before the invasion of Europe.... In 1945, when we ceased worrying about what the Germans might do to us, we began to worry about what the government of the United States might do to other countries.

LEO SZILARD, in Robert Jungk, *Brighter than a Thousand Suns*, 1958.

It is necessary to provide every person in the U.S. with a shelter.

EDWARD TELLER, 1959, in Lois and Alan Gordon, *American Chronicle*, 1987.

The experience of the scientists who have worked on the atomic bomb has indicated that in any investigation of this kind the scientist ends by putting unlimited powers in the hands of the people whom he is least inclined to trust with their use. It is perfectly clear also that to disseminate information about a weapon in the present state of our civilization is to make it practically certain that that weapon will be used.

NORBERT WIENER, in Robert Jungk, *Brighter than a Thousand Suns*, 1958.

SPACE EXPLORATION

Contact light.

NEIL ARMSTRONG, first words to NASA on landing on moon, July 20, 1969.

Houston, Tranquility Base here. The Eagle has landed.

NEIL ARMSTRONG, first report from moon, July 20, 1969.

That's one small step for a man, one giant leap for mankind.

NEIL ARMSTRONG, on becoming first person to stand on moon, July 20, 1969.

Reaching the Moon by three-man vessels in one long bound from Earth is like casting a thin thread across space. The main effort, in the coming decades, will be to strengthen this thread; to make it a cord, a cable, and, finally, a broad highway.

ISAAC ASIMOV, "The Coming Decades in Space," *The Beginning and the End*, 1977.

Man must have bread and butter, but he must also have something to lift his heart. This program is clean. We are not spending the money to kill people. We are not harming the environment. We are helping the spirit of man. We are unlocking secrets billions of years old.

FAROUK EL BAZ, "Skylab: Next Great Moment in Space," *American Way*, April, 1973.

Exploration is really the essence of the human spirit.

FRANK BORMAN, speech to Congress, *New York Times*, January 10, 1969.

It is in the long run essential to the growth of any new and high civilization that small groups of people can escape from their neighbors and from their governments, to go and live as they please in the wilderness. A truly isolated, small, and creative society will never again be possible on this planet.

FREEMAN DYSON, *Disturbing the Universe*, 1979.

There are three reasons why, quite apart from scientific considerations, mankind needs to travel in space. The first reason is garbage disposal; we need to transfer industrial processes into space so that the earth may remain a green and pleasant place for our grandchildren to live in. The second reason is to escape material impoverishment; the resources of this planet are finite, and we shall not forgo forever the abundance of solar energy and minerals and living space that are spread out all around us. The third reason is our spiritual need for an open frontier. The ultimate purpose of space travel is to bring to humanity, not only scientific discoveries and an occasional spectacular show on television, but a real expansion of our spirit.

FREEMAN DYSON, *Disturbing the Universe*, 1979.

The American satellite ought to be called Civil Servant. It won't work and you can't fire it.

JOKE, 1957.

We believe that when men reach beyond this planet, they should leave their national differences behind them.

JOHN F. KENNEDY, news conference, Washington, D.C., February 21, 1962.

[The Russian sputnik is] an outer-space raspberry to a decade of American pretensions that the American way of life is a gilt-edge guarantee of our national security.

CLARE BOOTHE LUCE, 1958, in Lois and Alan Gordon, *American Chronicle*, 1987.

Interplanetary communication is one of the persistent dreams of the inhabitants of this oblate spheroid on which we move, breathe, and suffer for lack of beer. There seems to be a feeling in many quarters that if we could get speech with the Martians, let us say, we might learn from them something to our advantage.

DON MARQUIS, "The Almost Perfect State," *The Best of Don Marquis*, 1927.

The creative conquest of space will serve as a wonderful substitute for war.

JAMES S. MCDONNELL, *Time*, March 31, 1967.

Our exploration of the planets represents a triumph of imagination and will for the human race. The events of the last twenty years are perhaps too recent for us to adequately appreciate their proper historical significance. We can, however, appraise the scientific significance of these voyages of exploration: They have been nothing less than revolutionary both in providing a new picture of the nature of the solar system, its likely origin and evolution, and in giving us a new perspective on our own planet Earth.

NASA ADVISORY COMMITTEE, report of Solar System Exploration Committee, *Planetary Exploration Through Year 2000: A Core Program*, 1983.

This is the greatest week in the history of the world since the Creation.

RICHARD M. NIXON, to Apollo 11 crew aboard USS *Hornet*, July 24, 1969.

It will free man from the remaining chains, the chains of gravity which still tie him to this planet.

WERNHER VON BRAUN, on importance of space travel, February 10, 1958.

What is it that makes a man willing to sit up on top of an enormous Roman candle, such as a Redstone, Atlas, Titan or Saturn rocket, and wait for someone to light the fuse?

TOM WOLFE, *The Right Stuff*, 1979.

TRANSPORTATION

The automobile is technologically more sophisticated than the bundling board, but the human motives in their uses are sometimes the same.

CHARLES M. ALLEN, speech, Wake Forest University, Winston-Salem, North Carolina, April 25, 1967.

Except the American woman, nothing interests the eye of American man more than the automobile, or seems so important to him as an object of esthetic appreciation.

A.H. BARR, JR., on pop art incorporating pieces of old autos, 1963.

[Sputnik is] a hunk of iron anybody could launch.

LAWSON BENNETT, 1957, in Lois and Alan Gordon, *American Chronicle*, 1987.

One did not "hop" a plane. One took a long slow ride to an airport, and argued for hours with ticket agents who seemed to have been hired five minutes ago for what they supposed to be another job; and if one survived that, one got to Chicago only to join a "stack" over the airfield there, and then either died of boredom or crashed into a plane that thought it was in the stack over Newark.

AMANDA CROSS, *In the Last Analysis*, 1966.

Motorists have exhibited the one worse attitude than defiance of law—indifference to it.

FREDERICK DWIGHT, "Automobiles: The Other Side of the Shield," *Independent*, December 3, 1908.

High-powered cars might with greater logic be regarded as morphine and cocaine are. Possessions and the ability to use them, when combined with an inborn passion, create a temptation that many are unable to resist.

FREDERICK DWIGHT, "Automobiles: The Other Side of the Shield," *Independent*, December 3, 1908.

I remain oppressed by the thought that the venture into space is meaningless unless it coincides with a certain interior expansion, an ever-growing universe within, to correspond with the far flight of the galaxies our telescopes follow from without.

LOREN EISELEY, "The Inner Galaxy," *The Star Thrower*, 1964.

If the public wants to lower its standard of living by driving a cheap crowded car, we'll make it.

GENERAL MOTORS EXECUTIVE, 1958, in Lois and Alan Gordon, *American Chronicle*, 1987.

It was quite a day. I don't know what you can say about a day when you see four beautiful sunsets. . . . This is a little unusual, I think.

JOHN GLENN, 1962, in Lois and Alan Gordon, *American Chronicle*, 1987.

The actual building of roads devoted to motor cars is not for the near future, in spite of the many rumors to that effect.

Harper's Weekly, August 2, 1902.

[I]ndeed train travel is that, without the fast-forward thrust of a jet engine in back of your seat throwing your thoughts ahead to your destination. Instead, you fussily settle in, the sweet-sour piquancy of your departure unmarred by emergency-escape rehearsals and the sensations of a sardine being catapulted into the clouds.

EDWARD HOAGLAND, *Harper's*, January, 1991.

I wanted to see New York . . . so I tried to see how fast I could do it in.

HOWARD HUGHES, on breaking cross-country flight record, 1936, in Lois and Alan Gordon, *American Chronicle*, 1987.

Whither goest thou, America, in thy shiny car in the night?

JACK KEROUAC, *On the Road*, 1957.

His motor car was poetry, tragedy, love and heroism.

SINCLAIR LEWIS, *Babbitt*, 1922.

Travelers are always discoverers, especially those who travel by air. There are no signposts in the sky to show a man has passed that way before.

There are no channels marked. The flier breaks each second into new uncharted seas.

ANNE MORROW LINDBERGH, *North to the Orient*, 1935.

I have seen the science I worshiped, and the aircraft I loved, destroying the civilization I expected them to serve.

CHARLES A. LINDBERGH, *Time*, May 26, 1967.

People on horses look better than they are. People in cars look worse than they are.

MARYA MANNES, *More in Anger*, 1958.

The car has become a secular sanctuary for the individual, his shrine to the self, his mobile Walden Pond.

EDWARD McDONAGH, *Time*, May 10, 1963.

In the space age, man will be able to go around the world in two hours—one for flying and the other to get to the airport.

NEIL H. McELROY, *Look*, February 18, 1958.

The sketches. They are indeed exciting; they have quality, and the toucan tones lend tremendous allure—confirmed by the wheels. Half the magic—sustaining effects of this kind. Looked at upside down, furthermore, there is a sense of fish buoyancy. Immediately your word impeccable sprang to mind. Might it be a possibility? The Impeccable. In any case, the baguette lapidary glamor you have achieved certainly spurs the imagination. Car-innovation is like launching a ship—"drama."

MARIANNE MOORE, letter to Ford Motor Company regarding name for new car, eventually named Edsel, *The New Yorker*, 1957.

Our national flower is the concrete cloverleaf.

LEWIS MUMFORD, *Quote*, October 8, 1961.

We are the first nation in the history of the world to go to the poorhouse in an automobile.

WILL ROGERS, 1931, in Lois and Alan Gordon, *American Chronicle*, 1987.

Take most people, they're crazy about cars . . . and if they get a brand-new car already they start thinking about trading it in for one that's even newer. I don't even like *old* cars. I mean they don't even interest me. I'd rather have a goddam horse. A horse is at least *human*, for God's sake.

J.D. SALINGER, *Catcher in the Rye*, 1951.

[Before man reaches the moon] your mail will be delivered within hours from New York to California, to England, to India or to Australia by guided missiles.... We stand on the threshold of rocket mail.

ARTHUR E. SUMMERFIELD, AP wire report, January 23, 1959.

You define a good flight by negatives: you didn't get hijacked, you didn't crash, you didn't throw up, you weren't late, you weren't nauseated by the food. So you are grateful.

PAUL THEROUX, *The Old Patagonian Express*, 1979.

The last Model T was built in 1927, and the car is fading from what scholars call the American scene—which is an understatement, because to a few million people who grew up with it, the old Ford practically *was* the American scene.

E.B. WHITE, "Farewell My Lovely!" 1936, *Essays of E.B. White*, 1977.

It was over in a blink of an eye, that moment when aviation stirred the modern imagination. Aviation was transformed from recklessness to routine in Lindbergh's lifetime. Today the riskiest part of air travel is the drive to the airport, and airlines use a barrage of stimuli to protect passengers from ennui.

GEORGE WILL, "Charles Lindbergh, Craftsman," May 15, 1977, *The Pursuit of Happiness, and Other Sobering Thoughts*, 1978.

Social Issues

See also **American Mosaic; American Society; Economics; Education; Ethics and Morality; Government and Politics**—Domestic Policy, Parties and Elections, Political Philosophies; **The Human Condition**—Competitiveness, Greed, Ingenuity, Materialism, Prejudice; **Journalism and Media; Law and Justice; Relationships; Science and Technology; War and Peace**

ABORTION

One does not need to be a pious Roman Catholic or, indeed, a Catholic at all, to reject the arbitrary claim that human life begins at three months after conception. Everyone knows that an embryo in the womb is genetically complete at conception; there is no obvious reason to think it any less human than the teen-ager who, we suspect, will prove more nearly human when he leaves home.

BERNARD AVISHAI, *New York Times*, February 8, 1985.

The states are not free, under the guise of protecting maternal health or potential life, to intimidate women into continuing pregnancies.

HARRY A. BLACKMUN, opinion, *Roe* v. *Wade*, January 22, 1973.

Controversy over the meaning of our nation's most majestic guarantees frequently has been turbulent....Abortion raises moral and spiritual questions over which honorable persons can disagree sincerely and profoundly. But those disagreements did not then and do not now relieve us of our duty to apply the Constitution faithfully.

HARRY A. BLACKMUN, opinion, *Roe* v. *Wade*, January 22, 1973.

America is embarked on a rampage against life, potentially far more extensive, and already far sicker, than any of the great genocides of history. This genocide has many weapons: government life-prevention campaigns, sterilization, proposals for genetic manipulation, euthanasia. But the most flagrant at the moment—because the killing is direct and lawful—is abortion.

L. BRENT BOZELL, *New York Times*, October 14, 1970.

Society's attitude seems to be "You've had your pleasure, now pay the price." What is more immoral, granting an abortion or forcing a young girl—some of them as young as 14 or 15—to assume the responsibility of an adult while she is still a child?

SHIRLEY CHISHOLM, speech to U.S. House of Representatives, December 3, 1969.

Though I would march myself into blisters for a woman's right to exercise the option of motherhood, I discovered there in the waiting room that I was not the modern woman I thought I was.

JANE DOE, *New York Times*, May 14, 1976.

This is our choice, for biology will never have an answer to that strange and cabalistic question of when a fetus becomes a person. Potential persons are lost every day as a result of miscarriage, contraception, or someone's simple failure to respond to a friendly wink. What we can answer, with a minimum of throat clearing and moral agonizing, is the question of when women themselves will finally achieve full personhood; and that is when we have the right, unquestioned and unabrogated, to *choose* not to be pregnant when we decide not to be pregnant.

BARBARA EHRENREICH, "Their Dilemma and Mine," *The Worst Years of Our Lives*, 1985.

In most of the antiabortion literature I have seen, women are so invisible that an uninformed reader might conclude that fetuses reside in artificially warm tissue culture flasks or similar containers. It must be enormously difficult for the antiabortionist to face up to the fact that real fetuses can only survive inside women, who, unlike any kind of laboratory appartus, have thoughts, feelings, aspirations, responsibilities and, very often, checkbooks.

BARBARA EHRENREICH, *New York Times*, February 7, 1985.

I believe the soul begins at conception. At that moment life begins.

JERRY FALWELL, sermon, February 26, 1978.

Where is our Nation going? Abortion is stripping us of the value of life. We are killing off the next generation and destroying our consciousness in the process.

JERRY FALWELL, sermon, February 26, 1978.

Legalized abortion is the first "giant step" being taken in this new campaign which promotes death as a solution to solve social problems.

GARY GERGEL, *Abortion in America*, 1980.

There has been, moreover, an increasing indication in decisions of the Supreme Court of the United States that as a secular matter a women's liberty and right of privacy extends to family, marriage and sex matters and may well include the right to remove an unwanted child at least in early stages of pregnancy.

GERHARD GESELL, opinion, *U.S. v. Shirley A. Boyd*, 1987.

The emphasis must be not on the right to abortion but on the right to privacy and reproductive control.

RUTH BADER GINSBERG, in article by Susan Edmiston, "Portia Faces Life—The Trials of Law School," *Ms.*, April, 1974.

Abortion almost always symbolizes failure—the failure of a contraceptive, of a relationship, of a family, of a dream, even of a social system. Government need not add an extra lash to the whip.

SOMA GOLDEN, *New York Times*, March 17, 1978.

The ironic fact is that those who favor legalization of abortion share a common goal with those who don't—the elimination of all abortions.

DR. ALAN F. GUTTMACHER, *Planned Parenthood,* 1972.

We don't eliminate the problems that people have simply by eliminating the people.

HOUSTON RIGHT-TO-LIFE PAMPHLET, ca. 1985.

The real problem with abortion is that it is destined to remain a permanently unsettled issue; a subject about which responsible human beings can entertain quite different beliefs. The only fair conclusion, then, is that no solution seems possible now.

CHARLES KELBLEY, *Newsweek*, December 16, 1985.

If men could get pregnant, abortion would be a sacrament.

FLORYNCE R. KENNEDY, in article by Gloria Steinem, *Ms.*, March, 1973.

For those who call themselves "pro-life," there is little room for balance when one's ideology admits only one value—fetal life—as worthy of consideration.

FRANCES KISSLING, "A Nation Divided," *Boston Globe*, April 30, 1989.

Opposition to abortion has now become the spearhead of political fanaticism.

LAWRENCE LADER, *New York Times*, January 11, 1978.

Abortion is a toxic side-effect of the human condition. Would that society *could* ensure that there be no *mis*conceptions. But that is utopian. Mindless nature has the task of compelling the survival of species—rabbits and whales and human beings. Those who can, breed.

INA S. MOORE, *New York Times*, May 16, 1981.

I read not long ago about a teen-ager who said she meant to have an abortion but spent the money on clothes instead; now she has a baby who turns out to be a lot more trouble than a toy. The people who had out those execrable little pictures of dismembered fetuses at abortion clinics seem to forget the extraordinary pain children may endure after they are born when they are unwanted, even hated or simply tolerated.

I believe that in a contest between the living and the almost living, the latter must, if necessary, give way to the will of the former.

ANNA QUINDLEN, *New York Times*, March 13, 1991.

I don't know anyone who has had an abortion who has not been haunted by it. If there is one thing I find intolerable about most of the so-called right-to-lifers, it is that they try to portray abortion rights as something that feminists thought up on a slow Saturday over a light lunch. That is nonsense.

ANNA QUINDLEN, *New York Times*, March 13, 1991.

[I]n this pampered nation where Cabbage Patch dolls get more love and attention than human beings, it's hard for me to take a debate on abortion seriously.

IAN SHOALES, "Abortion," *I Gotta Go*, January 29, 1985.

AUSCHWITZ, DACHAU, AND MARGARET SANGER: THREE OF A KIND

SIGN AT RIGHT-TO-LIFE CONVENTION, 1979.

I must...mourn that, for nearly two decades now, abortion-rights advocacy has been injecting powerful doses of the "individual autonomy" ideology into the veins of the public debate, overwhelming our feminist collaborative and cooperative ideal with a dinning chant of "I—

me—mine! My body, my right, myself!" This emphasis on physical, social, sexual autonomy has not only weakened many of women's traditional attachments (pair-bonding to a man, mother-bonding to a baby), it has also dissolved much of the old solidarity between women. Remember "Sisterhood Is Powerful"? Remember "Women United Can Never Be Defeated"? Dissolved, defeated by the bitter divisiveness of the abortion campaign.

JULI LOESCH WILEY, *Boston Globe*, April 30, 1989.

Society is so beautifully sentimental on the subject of murder. Abortion is looked upon as murder. But do those who make our Christian laws ever hesitate to kill children born or unborn when there is a sufficient profit in the act?

The Woman Rebel, editorial, "Into the Valley of Death— For What?" April, 1914.

CENSORSHIP

As we see censorship it is a stupid giant traffic policeman answering "Yes" to "Am I my brother's copper?" He guards a one-way street and his semaphore has four signs, all marked "STOP."

FRANKLIN P. ADAMS, *Nods and Becks*, 1944.

Like the course of the heavenly bodies, harmony in national life is a resultant of the struggle between contending forces. In frank expression of conflicting opinion lies the greatest promise of wisdom in governmental action; and in suppression lies ordinarily the greatest peril.

LOUIS D. BRANDEIS, opinion, *Gilbert v. Minnesota*, 1928.

In some respects the life of a censor is more exhilarating than that of an emperor. The best the emperor can do is to snip off the heads of men and women, who are mere mortals. The censor can decapitate ideas which but for him might have lived forever.

HEYWOOD BROUN, *Pieces of Hate*, 1922.

And you know why we got this—this is really weird—the censorship? It's motivated by bad early toilet training.

LENNY BRUCE, in John Cohen, ed., *The Essential Lenny Bruce*, 1967.

If you check the records, there's not one citizen who bought a dirty book. Every case has been initiated by the police department.

LENNY BRUCE, in John Cohen, ed., *The Essential Lenny Bruce*, 1967.

The fact is that censorship has always defeated its own purpose, for it creates in the end the kind of society that is incapable of exercising real discretion, incapable of doing an intelligent and honest job, and this guarantees a steady intellectual and cultural decline.

HENRY S. COMMAGER, in Arthur Goodfriend, *What Is America?*, 1954.

Restriction of free thought and free speech is the most dangerous of all subversions. It is the one un-American act that could most easily defeat us.

WILLIAM O. DOUGLAS, speech, on receiving the Lauterbach Award, Author's Guild, December 3, 1952.

Don't join the book burners. Don't think you are going to conceal faults by concealing evidence that they ever existed.

DWIGHT D. EISENHOWER, speech, Dartmouth College, June 14, 1953.

Where there is official censorship it is a sign that speech is serious. Where there is none, it is pretty certain that the official spokesmen have all the loud-speakers.

PAUL GOODMAN, *Growing Up Absurd*, 1960.

Books won't stay banned. They won't burn. Ideas won't go to jail. In the long run of history, the censor and the inquisitor have always lost. The only sure weapon against bad ideals is better ideas. The source of better ideas is wisdom. The surest path of wisdom is a liberal education.

ALFRED WHITNEY GRISWOLD, *Essays on Education*, 1954.

The problem of freedom in America is that of maintaining a competition of ideas, and you do not achieve that by silencing one brand of idea.

MAX LERNER, "The Muzzling of the Movies," *Actions and Passions*, 1949.

At present our notion of preserving what we think to be the truth is to gag all who do not think it's the truth. We win our arguments by forbidding argument.

BEN B. LINDSEY AND WAINWRIGHT EVANS, *The Revolt of Modern Youth*, 1925.

Censors are necessary, increasingly necessary, if America is to avoid having a vital literature.

DON MARQUIS, *Prefaces: Foreword to a Literary Censor's Autobiography*, 1919.

What nonsense! No one was ever seduced by books? Since the invention of writing, people have been seduced by the power of the word into all kinds of virtues, follies, conspiracies and

gallantries. They have been converted to religion, urged into sin and lured into salvation.
PHYLLIS MCGINLEY, *Ladies' Home Journal*, July, 1961.

Censorship strikes at the taproot of our free society.
NEWTON MINOW, speech, National Association of Broadcasters, May 9, 1961.

There is no such thing as a dirty theme. There are only dirty writers.
GEORGE JEAN NATHAN, *The Testament of a Critic*, 1931.

It is the American conviction that direct governmental control of cultural activities is uncongenial to government, and tends to restrict the free expression of such interests and activities on the part of the people.
NORMAN HOLMES PEARSON, in Arthur Goodfriend, *What Is America?*, 1954.

Pornography is in the groin of the beholder.
CHARLES REMBAR, *The End of Obscenity*, 1968.

We all know that books burn—yet we have the greater knowledge that books cannot be killed by fire. People die, but books never die. No man and no force can abolish memory.
FRANKLIN D. ROOSEVELT, message to American Booksellers Association, April 23, 1942.

Obscenity has no objective existence. It is neither a quality that inheres in or emanates from a book, picture or play. On the contrary, obscenity is wholly an attitude or predisposition of the viewing and accusing mind, which is only delusionally read into, or ascribed to, that which is accused of being obscene.
THEODORE SCHROEDER, *A Challenge to Sex Censors*, 1938.

[In San Antonio] the main question is: Should books on the public library shelves whose authors are either identified as Communists or suspected of Communist sympathies be branded with a red stamp?
STANLEY WALKER, "Book Branding," 1953, in Lois and Alan Gordon, *American Chronicle*, 1987.

I am beginning to feel a little more like an author now that I have had a book banned. The literary life, in this country, begins in jail.
E.B. WHITE, letter to Stanley Hart White, on Army and Navy banning of *One Man's Meat*, June, 1944.

The meaning of the word "obscene" as legally defined by the Courts is: tendency to stir the sex impulses or to lead to sexually impure and lustful thoughts....Whether a particular book would tend to excite such impulses and thoughts must be tested by the Court's opinion as to its effect on a person with average sex instincts....It is only with normal persons that the law is concerned.
JOHN M. WOOLSEY, opinion, *United States* v. *One Book Called "Ulysses,"* December 5, 1933.

CIVIL RIGHTS

I am not elevating women to sainthood, nor am I suggesting that all women are good and all men are bad. Women have screamed for war. Women, like men, have stoned black children going to integrated schools. Women have been and are prejudiced, narrow-minded, reactionary, even violent. *Some* women. They, of course, have a right to vote and a right to run for office. I will defend that right, but I will not support them or vote for them.
BELLA ABZUG, speech, National Women's Political Caucus, Washington, D.C., July 10, 1971.

Foremost among the barriers to equality is the system which ignores the mother's service to Society in making a home and rearing children. The mother is still the uncharted servant of the future, who receives from her husband, at *his* discretion, a share in *his* wages.
KATHARINE ANTHONY, *The Endowment of Motherhood*, 1920.

We are going to have to decide what kind of people we are—whether we obey the law only when we approve of it or whether we obey it no matter how distasteful we may find it.
HARRY S. ASHMORE, on integration of Little Rock High School, Arkansas, *Gazette*, September 4, 1957.

My feets is tired, but my soul is rested.
BLACK WOMAN DURING BUS BOYCOTT, Montgomery, Alabama, ca. 1955, in Martin Luther King, Jr., "Letter from a Birmingham Jail," April 16, 1963.

I cannot emphasize one point too strongly. The white South is as united as 30,000,000 people can be in its insistence upon segregation. Federal action cannot change them. It will be tragic for the South, the Negro, and the nation itself if the government should enact and attempt to enforce any laws or Supreme Court decisions that would open the South's public schools and public gathering places to the Negro.
HODDING CARTER, *Atlanta Journal*, September 3, 1948.

Only a fool would say the Southern pattern of separation of the races can, or should be, overthrown.
EDITORIAL, *Atlanta Constitution*, September 26, 1948.

Freedom Now!
Civil rights movement slogan, ca. 1960.

Sensible and responsible women do not want to vote. The relative positions to be assumed by man and woman in the working out of our civilization were assigned long ago by a higher intelligence than ours.
Grover Cleveland, *Ladies' Home Journal*, April, 1905.

The Negro revolt is not aimed at winning friends but at winning freedom, not interpersonal warmth but institutional justice.
Harvey Cox, *The Secular City*, 1966.

The fact that Indian rights to land is guaranteed by the Constitution of the United States, over four hundred treaties, and some six thousand statutes seems irrelevant to a people hungry for land and dedicated to law and order.
Vine Deloria, Jr., *We Talk, You Listen*, 1970.

We repudiate the monstrous doctrine that the oppressor should be the sole authority as to the rights of the oppressed.
W.E.B. Du Bois, The Niagara Movement Declaration of Principles, Niagara Falls, New York, 1905.

Section 1 Equality of rights under the law shall not be denied or abridged by the United States or by any State on account of sex. *Section 2* The Congress shall have the power to enforce, by appropriate legislation, the provisions of this article. *Section 3* This amendment shall take effect two years after the date of ratification.
Proposed Equal Rights Amendment, 1972.

ERA would nullify any laws that make any distinction between men and women. When the good Lord created the earth, he didn't have the advice of Gloria Steinem or Bella Abzug.
Sam Ervin, 1978, in Lois and Alan Gordon, *American Chronicle*, 1987.

What we succeeded in doing in the Sixties was in dealing with the constitutional issue of rights. We've won that battle.... [Now] we're dealing with real equality.
James Farmer, 1976, in Lois and Alan Gordon, *American Chronicle*, 1987.

[W]oman's participation in political life...would involve the domestic calamity of a deserted home and the loss of the womanly qualities for which refined men adore women and marry them....Doctors tell us, too, that thousands of children would be harmed or killed before birth by the injurious effect of untimely political excitement on their mothers.
Henry T. Finck, on women's suffrage, *Independent*, January 31, 1901.

This is not a bedroom war. This is a political movement.
Betty Friedan, on women's rights, 1970, in Lois and Alan Gordon, *American Chronicle*, 1987.

The right to vote, or equal civil rights, may be good demands, but true emancipation begins neither at the polls nor in the courts. It begins in woman's soul.
Emma Goldman, "Woman Suffrage," *Anarchism and Other Essays*, 1911.

Civil Rights: What black folks are given in the U.S. on the installment plan, as in civil-rights bills. Not to be confused with *human rights*, which are the dignity, stature, humanity, respect, and freedom belonging to all people by right of their birth.
Dick Gregory, *Dick Gregory's Political Primer*, 1972.

There are those who say to you—we are rushing this issue of civil rights. I say we are 172 years late.
Hubert H. Humphrey, speech, Democratic National Convention, July 14, 1948.

Until justice is blind to color, until education is unaware of race, until opportunity is unconcerned with the color of men's skins, emancipation will be a proclamation but not a fact.
Lyndon B. Johnson, speech, Gettysburg, Pennsylvania, May 30, 1963.

We have talked long enough in this country about equal rights....It is time now to write the next chapter—and to write it in the books of law.
Lyndon B. Johnson, message to Congress, November 27, 1963.

No one has been barred on account of his race from fighting or dying for America—there are no "white" or "colored" signs on the foxholes or graveyards of battle.
John F. Kennedy, message to Congress, June 19, 1963.

If you will protest courageously, and yet with dignity and Christian love, when the history books are written in future generations, the historians will have to pause and say, "There lived a great people—a black people—who injected new meaning and dignity into the veins of civilization."

MARTIN LUTHER KING, JR., speech, Montgomery, Alabama, December 31, 1955.

For years now I have heard the word "Wait!" It rings in the ear of every Negro with piercing familiarity. This "Wait" has almost always meant "Never."

MARTIN LUTHER KING, JR., "Letter from a Birmingham Jail," April 16, 1963.

When we ask Negroes to abide by the law, let us also declare that the white man does not abide by law in the ghettos. Day in and day out he violates welfare laws to deprive the poor of their meager allotments; he flagrantly violates building codes and regulations; his police make a mockery of law; he violates laws on equal employment and education and the provisions of civil services. The slums are the handiwork of a vicious system of the white society; Negroes live in them, but they do not make them, any more than a prisoner makes a prison.

MARTIN LUTHER KING, JR., The Trumpet of Conscience, 1967.

Rights that depend on the sufferance of the State are of uncertain tenure.

SUZANNE LAFOLLETTE, "What Is To Be Done," Concerning Women, 1926.

Black people cannot and will not become integrated into American society on any terms but those of self-determination and autonomy.

GERDA LERNER, Black Women in White America, 1972.

When, and if, our voters' list contains a large percentage of voters of other than Caucasian stock, then our constitutional form of government becomes impossible and unworkable.

TOM LINDER, letter to Atlanta Journal, 1948.

So far as I can see it [woman's suffrage] has made little difference beyond doubling the number of voters. There is no woman's vote as such. They divide up just about as the men do.

ALICE ROOSEVELT LONGWORTH, Crowded Hours, 1933.

The American Republic is now almost 200 years old, and in the eyes of the law women are still not equal with men. The special legislation which will remedy that situation is the Equal Rights Amendment. Its language is short and simple: *Equality of rights under the law shall not be abridged in the United States or by any state on account of sex.*

CLARE BOOTHE LUCE, Bulletin of the Baldwin School, September, 1974.

I'm the world's original gradualist. I just think ninety-odd years is gradual enough.

THURGOOD MARSHALL, reply to Eisenhower's call for blacks' patience, I.F. Stone's Weekly, May 19, 1958.

Suddenly enfranchised, hastily given the keys of all cities and all liberties, women resemble one of the new states created after a war. We have not owned our freedom long enough to know exactly how it should be used.

PHYLLIS McGINLEY, "The Honor of Being a Woman," The Province of the Heart, 1959.

There is no longer any need to shoot down Indians in order to take away their rights and lands. Legislation and the combination of three forces, our own attorneys, the Indian Claims Commission and the Indian Bureau, do the trick legally.

JOSEPHINE C. MILLS, letter, March, 1964, in Virgina Irving Armstrong, comp., I Have Spoken: American History Through the Voices of the Indians, 1971.

Only when metal has been brought to white heat can it be shaped and molded. This is what we intend to do to the South and the country, bring them to white heat and then remold them.

BOB PARRIS MOSES, Struggle, 1963.

Yet the tragic fact is that love is not the answer to hate—not in the world of politics, at any rate. Color is indeed a political rather than a human or a personal reality and if politics (which is to say power) has made it into a human and a personal reality, then only politics (which is to say power) can unmake it once again. But the way of politics is slow and bitter, and as impatience on the one side is matched by a setting of the jaw on the other, we move closer and closer to an explosion and blood may yet run in the streets.

NORMAN PODHORETZ, "My Negro Problem—and Ours," Doings and Undoings, 1963.

The equal rights of women have but just reached the region of possibilities. Men have only just left off sneering and have but just begun to consider. Every step of progress from the harem and the veil to free society and property holding has been steadily fought by the vanity, selfishness and indolence, not only of mankind but of womankind also.

THOMAS BRACKETT REED, in Samuel Walker McCall, The Life of Thomas Brackett Reed, 1914.

Where, after all, do universal human rights begin? In small places, close to home—so close and so small that they cannot be seen on any maps of the world. Yet they *are* the world of the individual person; the neighborhood he lives in; the school or college he attends; the factory, farm or office where he works. Such are the places where every man, woman and child seeks equal justice, equal opportunity, equal dignity without discrimination. Unless these rights have meaning there, they have little meaning anywhere. Without concerned citizen action to uphold them close to home, we shall look in vain for progress in the larger world.

ELEANOR ROOSEVELT, speech, "The Great Question," United Nations, 1958.

The single most impressive fact about the attempt by American women to obtain the right to vote is how long it took.

ALICE ROSSI, "Along the Suffrage Trail," *The Feminist Papers*, 1973.

Women's rights in essence is really a movement for freedom, a movement for equality, for the dignity of all women, for those who work outside the home and those who dedicate themselves with more altruism than any profession I know to being wives and mothers, cooks and chauffeurs, decorators and child psychologists and loving human beings.

JILL RUCKELSHAUS, in article by Frederic A. Birmingham, "Jill Ruckelshaus: Lady of Liberty," *Saturday Evening Post*, March 3, 1973.

The embattled gates to equal rights have indeed opened up for modern women, but I sometimes think to myself: "That is not what I meant by freedom—it is only 'social progress.'"

SONYA RUDIKOFF, "Women and Success," *Commentary*, October, 1974.

Let me say with a Georgia accent that we cannot solve this problem if it requires a diplomatic passport to claim the rights of an American citizen.

DEAN RUSK, on restaurants admitting African diplomats but refusing African-Americans, *Life*, January 1, 1962.

Everything's a milestone now. Pretty soon there'll be the first Negro that ever walked across Broadway with the sun shining, who parts his hair on the right.

NIPSEY RUSSELL, interview, *New York Post*, September 27, 1964.

There is a strong moralistic strain in the civil rights movement that would remind us that power corrupts, forgetting that the absence of power also corrupts.

BAYARD RUSTIN, "From Protest to Politics," *Commentary*, February, 1965.

The defeat of the Equal Rights Amendment is the greatest victory for women's rights since the woman's suffrage movement of 1920.

PHYLLIS SCHLAFLY, 1979, in Lois and Alan Gordon, *American Chronicle*, 1987.

Women's rights, men's rights—human rights—all are threatened by the ever-present spectre of war so destructive now of human material and moral values as to render victory indistinguishable from defeat.

ROSIKA SCHWIMMER, speech, Centennial Celebration of Seneca Falls Convention of Women's Rights, July, 1948.

The great mass of Negroes are more concerned with where they work than with where they eat; winning the right to eat at a desegregated lunch counter is small consolation to men who cannot afford the price of the meal.

CHARLES E. SILBERMAN, *Crisis in Black and White*, 1964.

Integration is vitally important not so much for Negroes as for whites, who must learn to live in a world in which they are indeed the minority.

CHARLES E. SILBERMAN, *Crisis in Black and White*, 1964.

"Civil Rights" is a term that did not evolve out of black culture, but, rather, out of American law. As such, it is a term of limitation. It speaks only to physical possibilities—necessary and treasured, of course—but not of the spirit.

ALICE WALKER, "Silver Writes," 1982, *In Search of Our Mothers' Gardens*, 1983.

I have a black, a woman, two Jews and a cripple. And we have talent.

JAMES WATT, comment on staff, speech, U.S. Chamber of Commerce, September 21, 1983.

We march because by the grace of God and the force of truth the dangerous, hampering walls of prejudice and inhuman injustices must fall.

We march because we want to make impossible a repetition of Waco, Memphis, and East St. Louis [anti-Negro riots] by arousing the conscience of the country, and to bring the murderers of our brothers, sisters, and innocent children to justice.

We march because we deem it a crime to be silent in the face of such barbaric acts.

We march because we are thoroughly opposed to Jim Crow cars, segregation, discrimination, disenfranchisement, lynching, and the host of evils that are forced on us. It is time that the spirit of Christ should be manifested in the making and execution of laws.

We march because we want our children to live in a better land and enjoy fairer conditions than have fallen to our lot.

Why We March, leaflet, 1917.

The common goal of 22 million Afro-Americans is respect as *human beings*, the God-given right to be a *human being*. Our common goal is to obtain the *human rights* that America has been denying us. We can never get civil rights in America until our *human rights* are first restored. We will never be recognized as citizens there until we are first recognized as *humans*.

MALCOLM X, "Racism: The Cancer That Is Destroying America," *Egyptian Gazette*, August 25, 1964.

I for one believe that if you give people a thorough understanding of what confronts them and the basic causes that produce it, they'll create their own program, and when the people create a program, you get action.

MALCOLM X, in John Henrik Clarke, *Malcolm X: The Man and His Time*, 1969.

The core of the civil rights problem is the matter of achieving equal opportunity for Negroes in the labor market. For it stands to reason that all our other civil rights depend on that one for fulfillment. We cannot afford better education for our children, better housing or medical care unless we have jobs.

WHITNEY M. YOUNG, JR., in Nelson A. Rockefeller, *Unity, Freedom and Peace: A Blueprint for Tomorrow*, 1968.

CRIME AND PUNISHMENT

Stripped of ethical rationalizations and philosophical pretensions, a crime is anything that a group in power chooses to prohibit.

FREDA ADLER, *Sisters in Crime*, 1975.

[Rape] is the only crime in which the victim becomes the accused.

FREDA ADLER, *Sisters in Crime*, 1975.

Americans are solicitous enough concerning the rights of the individual criminal; they need to cultivate regard for the rights of the community.

ANONYMOUS JUDGE, in Richard O'Connor, *Courtroom Warrior*, 1963.

We are men. We are not beasts. We only want to live.

ATTICA PRISON INMATES, 1971, in Lois and Alan Gordon, *American Chronicle*, 1987.

Payola is the year's new word. It doesn't sound as ugly as *bribe*, but it means the same thing.

WILLIAM ATTWOOD, *Look*, March 29, 1960.

Accomplice, n. One associated with another in a crime, having guilty knowledge and complicity, as an attorney who defends a criminal, knowing him guilty. This view of the attorney's position in the matter has not hitherto commanded the assent of attorneys, no one having offered them a fee for assenting.

AMBROSE BIERCE, *The Devil's Dictionary*, 1906.

We are incarcerating more people on a per capita basis in California than any country in the world other than South Africa or the Soviet Union.

ROSE BIRD, *Newsweek*, August 9, 1982.

Crime and the fear of crime have permeated the fabric of American life.

WARREN E. BURGER, to American Bar Association, Houston, Texas, February 8, 1981.

A far greater factor [than abolishing poverty] is the deterrent effect of swift and certain consequences: swift arrest, prompt trial, certain penalty and—at some point—finality of judgment.

WARREN E. BURGER, to American Bar Association, Houston, Texas, February 8, 1981.

They talk about me not being on the legitimate. Why, lady, nobody's on the legit., when it comes down to cases; you know that.

AL CAPONE, in Fred D. Pasley, *Al Capone: The Biography of a Self-Made Man*, 1930.

I am going to St. Petersburg, Florida, tomorrow. Let the worthy citizens of Chicago get their liquor the best they can. I'm sick of the job—it's a thankless one and full of grief. I've been spending the best years of my life as a public benefactor.

AL CAPONE, 1927, in Lois and Alan Gordon, *American Chronicle*, 1987.

Criminality and criminal actions do not always consist of breaking man's laws.

SHIRLEY CHISHOLM, testimony, House Select Commmittee on Crime, September 17, 1969.

You simply cannot hang a millionaire in America.

BOURKE COCKRAN, in Shane Leslie, *American Wonderland*, 1936.

In England there was a time when one hundred different offenses were punishable with death, and it made no difference. The English people strangely found out that so fast as they repealed the severe penalties and so fast as they did away with punishing men by death, crime decreased instead of increased; that the smaller the penalty the fewer the crimes. Hanging men in our country jails does not prevent murder. It makes murderers.

CLARENCE DARROW, speech to prisoners, Cook County Jail, 1902.

Given a child falling into a river, an old person in a burning building, and a woman fainting in the street, a band of convicts would risk their lives to give aid as quickly at least as a band of millionaires.

CLARENCE DARROW, Resist Not Evil, 1903.

I can picture them awakened in the gray light of morning, furnished a suit of clothes by the state, led to the scaffold,...black caps down over their heads,...the hangman pressing a spring....I can see them fall through space.

CLARENCE DARROW, courtroom appeal against death penalty for Leopold and Loeb, 1924, in Lois and Alan Gordon, American Chronicle, 1987.

Jails and prisons are designed to break human beings, to convert the population into specimens in a zoo—obedient to our keepers, but dangerous to each other.

ANGELA DAVIS, Angela Davis: An Autobiography, 1974.

Organized crime inevitably gravitates to cash.

DANIEL DELIGMAN, Fortune, March 2, 1987.

If you're in the contracting business in this country, you're suspect. If you're in the contracting business in New Jersey, you're indictable. If you're in the contracting business in New Jersey and are Italian, you're convicted.

RAYMOND J. DONOVAN, confirmation hearings before Senate Labor Committee, January 27, 1981.

The chief problem in any community cursed with crime is not the punishment of the criminals, but the preventing of the young from being trained to crime.

W.E.B. DU BOIS, The Souls of Black Folk, 1903.

The rod is only wrong in the wrong hands.

JOSEPH GAULD, Time, August 9, 1976.

The manufacturer or marketer of a Saturday Night Special knows or ought to know that he is making or selling a product principally to be used in criminal activity.

ELLEN GOODMAN, on Maryland State Supreme Court, "Saturday Night Snubbies," Washington Post, October, 1985.

There are two kinds of crimes: those committed by people who are caught and convicted, and those committed by people who are not. Which category a particular crime falls into is directly related to the wealth, power, and prestige of the criminal. The former category includes such crimes as purse snatching, mugging, armed robbery, and breaking and entering. The latter category includes war atrocities, embezzlement, most political actions, and budget appropriations.

DICK GREGORY, Dick Gregory's Political Primer, 1972.

A nation that represses social problems with police power will become something of an armed camp—which is not a very happy place for either the wardens or the prisoners.

MICHAEL HARRINGTON, Toward a Democratic Left, 1968.

You goddamn bastards. I hope an atom bomb falls on every one of you.

VIRGINIA HILL HAUSER, Bugsy Siegel's girlfriend, to Kefauver committee, 1950.

Only the man who has enough good in him to feel the justice of the penalty can be punished; the others can only be hurt.

WILLIAM ERNEST HOCKING, The Coming World Civilization, 1957.

I can tell you this on a stack of Bibles: prisons are archaic, brutal, unregenerative, overcrowded hell holes where the inmates are treated like animals with absolutely not one humane thought given to what they are going to do once they are released. You're an animal in a cage and you're treated like one.

JIMMY HOFFA, Hoffa: The Real Story, 1975.

We have to choose, and for my part I think it a lesser evil that some criminals should escape than that the Government should play an ignoble part.

OLIVER WENDELL HOLMES, JR., opinion, Olmstead v. United States, 1928.

A whipping never hurts so much as the thought that you are being whipped.

EDGAR W. HOWE, Country Town Sayings, 1911.

"How does a person become an outlaw, DuBois?" Elgar inquired mildly....

"One is born to the calling," DuBois answered. "Many are called, but few choose. You see, society decides which of its segments are going to be outside its borders. Society says, 'These are the legitimate channels to my rewards. They are closed to you forever.' So then the outlawed segments must seek rewards through illegitimate channels."

KRISTIN HUNTER, *The Landlord*, 1966.

America has the longest prison sentences in the West, yet the only condition long sentences demonstrably cure is heterosexuality.

BRUCE JACKSON, *New York Times*, September 12, 1968.

Question a thief and he'll laugh at you. Put a light on him, take his cigarettes away, and hit him a blow just above the kidneys where it won't leave a sign, and he'll stop laughing. Hit him enough blows and pretty soon he'll be pleading to answer questions. This isn't telling secrets and it isn't breaking a scandal. It's a fact of life. Doctors use stethoscopes and cops use force.

NORMAN KATKOV, *The Fabulous Fanny*, 1953.

You refuse to testify further?
Mr. Senator, I want to think of my health first. When I testify, I want to testify truthfully, and my mind don't function.

SENATOR ESTES KEFAUVER AND FRANK COSTELLO, Kefauver committee hearings, 1950.

I hate this "crime doesn't pay" stuff. Crime in the United States is perhaps one of the biggest businesses in the world today.

PETER KIRK, *Wall Street Journal*, February 16, 1960.

It got to the point where there were just too many quiz shows. Ratings began to drop....Some producers turned to rigging....They just couldn't afford to lose their sponsors.

HAL MARCH, "The $64,000 Question," 1959.

Behind the facades of respectability, family life and surprisingly modest homes [are] fathers who hate drugs but sell tons of heroin, gambling czars who lose heavily on the horses, murderers who take offense at off-color language around women and Runyonesque characters with funny nicknames who beat people to death with hammers.

ROBERT D. McFADDEN, "The Mafia of the 1980s: Divided and Under Siege," *New York Times*, March 11, 1987.

The study of crime begins with the knowledge of oneself.

HENRY MILLER, "The Soul of Anaesthesia," *The Air-Conditioned Nightmare*, 1945.

When is conduct a crime, and when is a crime not a crime? When Somebody Up There—a monarch, a dictator, a Pope, a legislator—so decrees.

JESSICA MITFORD, *Kind and Unusual Punishment*, 1971.

Those of us on the outside [of prisons] do not like to think of wardens and guards as our servants. Yet they are, and they are intimately locked in a deadly embrace with their human captives behind the prison walls. By extension so are we. A terrible double meaning is thus imparted to the original question of human ethics: Am I my brother's keeper?

JESSICA MITFORD, *Kind and Unusual Punishment*, 1971.

Radical and revolutionary ideologies are seeping into the prisons. Whereas formerly convicts tended to regard themselves as unfortunates whose accident of birth at the bottom of the heap was largely responsible for their plight, today many are questioning the validity of the heap.

JESSICA MITFORD, *Kind and Unusual Punishment*, 1971.

Nobody shot me.

DYING MORAN GANG MEMBER, St. Valentine's Day, 1929, in Lois and Alan Gordon, *American Chronicle*, 1987.

You have put me in here a cub, but I will come out roaring like a lion, and I will make all hell howl!

CARRY NATION, on her imprisonment, ca. 1901, in Carleton Beals, *Cyclone Carry*, 1962.

ATTICA PRISON TO BE CONVICT'S PARADISE.

HEADLINE, *New York Times*, August 2, 1931.

Money never goes to jail.

POPULAR WISDOM.

Crime is a logical extension of the sort of behavior that is often considered perfectly respectable in legitimate business.

ROBERT RICE, *The Business of Crime*, 1956.

This man [Vanzetti], although he may not actually have committed the crime...is...the enemy of our existing institutions....The defendant's ideals are cognate with crime.

WEBSTER THAYER, Sacco-Vanzetti trial, 1927, in Lois and Alan Gordon, *American Chronicle*, 1987.

[The producer] instructed me on how to answer the questions....He gave me a script to memorize....I would give almost anything I have to reverse the course of my life in the last three years.

CHARLES VAN DOREN, "The $64,000 Question," 1959.

I am innocent. I am suffering because I am a radical...an Italian...more for my family and for my beloved than for myself, but I am so convinced to be right that if you could execute me two times, and I could be reborn two other times, I would live again to do what I have done already.

BARTOLOMEO VANZETTI, 1927, in Lois and Alan Gordon, *American Chronicle*, 1987.

Our system nurtures criminals with the same care the Air Force Academy uses to turn out second lieutenants.

JO WALLACH, *Newsweek*, September 14, 1970.

Men copied the realities of their hearts when they built prisons.

RICHARD WRIGHT, *The Outsider*, 1953.

DISCRIMINATION AND RACISM

An image used to brainwash the black world. It goes along with angels who are white, Jesus was white, Miss America is white, Miss World is white, angel food cake is white, and devil's food cake is black.

MUHAMMAD ALI, on Tarzan, *The Village Voice*, June 6, 1977.

As long as you keep a person down, some part of you has to be down there to hold him down, so it means you cannot soar as you otherwise might.

MARIAN ANDERSON, interview, CBS-TV, December 30, 1957.

If growing up is painful for the Southern Black girl, being aware of her displacement is the rust on the razor that threatens the throat. It is an unnecessary insult.

MAYA ANGELOU, *I Know Why the Caged Bird Sings*, 1970.

We [Black Americans] turned the other cheek so often our heads seemed to revolve on the end of our necks like old stop-and-go signs.... We forgave as if forgiving was our talent.

MAYA ANGELOU, *The Heart of a Woman*, 1981.

Why does integration have to begin with *our* children?

ANONYMOUS, *New York Times*, 1964.

It is a great shock at the age of five or six to find that in a world of Gary Coopers you are the Indian.

JAMES BALDWIN, speech, Cambridge Union, February 17, 1965.

Racism is the new Calvinism which asserts that one group has the stigmata of superiority and the other has those of inferiority....For racism is an *ism* to which everyone in the world today is exposed; for or against, we must take sides. And the history of the future will differ according to the decision which we make.

RUTH BENEDICT, *Race: Science and Politics*, 1940.

Racism in its nationalist phase...has been a politician's plaything....It is a dangerous plaything, a sword which can be turned in any direction to condemn the enemy of the moment.

RUTH BENEDICT, *Race: Science and Politics*, 1940.

For racial discrimination to result in the exclusion from jury service of otherwise qualified groups not only violates our Constitution and the laws enacted under it but is at war with our basic concepts of a democratic society and a representative government.

HUGO BLACK, opinion, *Smith v. State of Texas*, 1940.

Black power!

BLACK MILITANT SLOGAN, ca. 1960.

Up against the wall, motherfucker!

BLACK MILITANT SLOGAN, ca. 1960.

We believe that this racist government has robbed us and now we are demanding the overdue debt of forty acres and two mules. Forty acres and two mules [were] promised 100 years ago as restitution for slave labor and mass murder of black people. We will accept the payment in currency which will be distributed to our many communities.

BLACK PANTHER PLATFORM, 1967.

No More Iranian Students Will be Permitted on These Premises Until the Hostages Are Released.

BORDELLO SIGN NEAR RENO, Nevada, 1979.

The doctrine of "separate but equal" has no place [in public education]....Separate facilities are inherently unequal.

SUPREME COURT DECISION, *Brown v. Board of Education of Topeka*, 1954.

Within the stable economy it's necessary to eliminate all forms of sexual discrimination, and to provide women for the first time in our history with economic opportunities equal to those of men.

JIMMY CARTER, speech, Women's Agenda Conference, Washington, D.C., October 2, 1976.

I believe racism has killed more people than speed, heroin, or cancer, and will continue to kill until it is no more.

ALICE CHILDRESS, *Stagebill*, May, 1972.

Racism is so universal in this country, so widespread and deep-seated, that it is invisible because it is so normal.

SHIRLEY CHISHOLM, *Unbought and Unbossed*, 1970.

I've suffered more as a woman than as a black.

SHIRLEY CHISHOLM, 1971, in Lois and Alan Gordon, *American Chronicle*, 1987.

What we're saying today is that you're either part of the solution or you're part of the problem.

ELDRIDGE CLEAVER, speech, San Francisco State, *Post Prison Writings and Speeches*, 1969.

Some of the best pretending in the world is done in front of white folks.

OSSIE DAVIS, *Purlie Victorious*, 1961.

[B]eing a star has made it possible for me to get insulted in places where the average Negro could never *hope* to go and get insulted.

SAMMY DAVIS, JR., *Yes I Can*, 1965.

We don't expect to live in [these houses]...very long. Some of the junior executives expect to become seniors...and a lot of us will be transferred all over the U.S....We want to be sure there is a good resale value.

COUPLE IN DEERFIELD, Illnois, complaining about blacks moving into neighborhood, 1960, in Lois and Alan Gordon, *American Chronicle*, 1987.

I don't want any of them here. They are a dangerous element....It makes no difference whether he is an American citizen, he is still a Japanese. American citizenship does not necessarily determine loyalty. You need not worry about the Italians at all except in certain cases. Also, the same for the Germans except in individual cases. But we must worry about the Japanese all the time until he is wiped off the map.

J.L. DEWITT, testimony to subcommittee of House Naval Affairs Committee, April 13, 1943.

[The Truman civil rights plan] wants to reduce us to the status of a mongrel, inferior race, mixed in blood, our Anglo-Saxon heritage a mockery.

F. DIXON, speech, Dixiecrat convention, 1948.

The problem of the twentieth century is the problem of the color line.

W.E.B. DU BOIS, speech, Pan-African Conference, London, England, January, 1900.

Women have made enormous strides in the last decade, but they still do not seem to understand what a power they could be if they took more interest in government on all levels. If they realized how much government affected their lives and those of their children, they could not resist having a stronger voice in the affairs of the nation, the states and their home communities. We are not a minority but we still are treated as though we were one, and a small one at that.

INDIA EDWARDS, *Pulling No Punches*, 1977.

A girl should not expect special privileges because of her sex, but neither should she "adjust" to prejudice and discrimination. She must learn to compete then, not as a woman, but as a human being.

INDIA EDWARDS, *Pulling No Punches*, 1977.

A woman is handicapped by her sex, and handicaps society, either by slavishly copying the pattern of man's advance in the professions, or by refusing to compete with man at all. But with the vision to make a new life plan of her own, she can fulfill a commitment to profession and politics, and to marriage and motherhood with equal seriousness.

INDIA EDWARDS, *Pulling No Punches*, 1977.

White folks seemed always to expect you to know those things which they'd done everything they could think of to prevent you from knowing.

RALPH ELLISON, *Invisible Man*, 1947.

The [15th] amendment nullifies sophisticated as well as simple-minded modes of discrimination.

FELIX FRANKFURTER, opinion, *Lane v. Wilson*, 1939.

We're queer, we're here, get used to it.

SLOGAN OF GAY ORGANIZATION, Fresh Air, public radio, May 24, 1991.

In the twilight of the twentieth century, the most vaunted private clubs are also in the business of business. The women excluded from membership or banned from the premises, women who aren't allowed to sit in the lobby or walk through the front door, are penalized in doing business with the boys.

ELLEN GOODMAN, "The Last Bastion Case," *Washington Post*, February, 1988.

Everybody looks on this Civil War Centennial in a different light. Up in Harlem, all it means is the 100th anniversary of separate rest rooms.... That's why the South never suffered from the Recession. Too busy building washrooms.

DICK GREGORY, *From the Back of the Bus*, 1962.

I know a Southener who owned an amusement park and almost went out of his mind—over where to put us on the merry-go-round.

DICK GREGORY, *From the Back of the Bus*, 1962.

People keep talking about the white race and the black race—and it really doesn't make sense. I played Miami last week—met a fella two shades darker than me—and his name was Ginsberg!... Took my place in two sit-in demonstrations—nobody knew the difference....Then he tried for a third lunch counter and blew the whole bit. Asked for blintzes.

DICK GREGORY, *From the Back of the Bus*, 1962.

Just being a Negro doesn't qualify you to understand the race situation any more than being sick makes you an expert on medicine.

DICK GREGORY, "...and they didn't even have what I wanted," *Nigger*, 1964.

The South stands at Armageddon.... We cannot make the slightest concession to the enemy in this dark and lamentable hour of struggle. There is no more difference in compromising the integrity of race on the playing field than in doing so in the classroom.

MARVIN GRIFFIN, on 1954 *Brown v. Board of Education*, 1955.

The laws which force segregation do not presume the inferiority of a people; they assume an inherent equalness. It is the logic of the lawmakers that if a society does not erect artificial barriers between people at every point of contact, the people might fraternize and give their attention to the genuine, shared problems of the community.

LORRAINE HANSBERRY, *A Matter of Color*, 1959.

A young white boy's badness is simply the overflowing of young animal spirits; the black boy's badness is badness, pure and simple.

LETTER FROM A BLACK MOTHER, *Independent*, September 18, 1902.

The men of our group have developed as a result of living under a ruthless system, a set of mannerisms that numb the soul. We have been made the floor mat of the world.

GEORGE JACKSON, letter to mother, March, 1966.

[W]hen we're unemployed, we're called lazy; when the whites are unemployed it's called a depression, which is the psycho-linguistics of racism.

JESSE JACKSON, interview with David Frost, *The Americans*, 1970.

This is a theatre of assault. The play that will split the heavens will be called THE DESTRUCTION OF AMERICA. The heroes will be Crazy Horse, Denmark Vesey, Patrice Lumumba.

LEROI JONES, "The Revolutionary Theatre," 1965.

It is probably true that the majority of our wild Indians have no inherited tendencies whatever toward morality or chastity, according to an enlightened standard. Chastity and morality among them must come from education and contact with the better element of the whites.

W.A. JONES, in Wayne Moquin and Charles Van Doren, eds., *Great Documents on American Indian History*, 1973.

We think short is better. We use less food and fiber. We take up less space. The short people I know don't complain about being short; they complain about things not fitting.

DIANE KEATON, co-founder of the National Association of Short Adults, *New York Times Magazine*, June 16, 1991.

It is a measure of the Negro's circumstance that, in America, the smallest things usually take him so very long, and that, by the time he wins them, they are no longer little things: they are miracles.

MURRAY KEMPTON, "George," *Part of Our Time*, 1955.

What we need in the United States is not division; what we need in the United States is not hatred; what we need in the United States is not violence or lawlessness, but love and wisdom, and compassion toward one another, and a feeling of justice towards those who still suffer within our country, whether they be white or they be black.

ROBERT F. KENNEDY, speech, Indianapolis, Indiana, April 4, 1968.

Discrimination is a hellhound that gnaws at Negroes in every waking moment of their lives to remind them that the lie of their inferiority is accepted as truth in the society dominating them.

MARTIN LUTHER KING, JR., speech, Southern Christian Leadership Conference, Atlanta, Georgia, August 16, 1967.

[I]t is necessary to understand that Black Power is a cry of disappointment. The Black Power slogan did not spring full grown from the head of some philosophical Zeus. It was born from the wounds of despair and disappointment. It is a cry of daily hurt and persistent pain.

MARTIN LUTHER KING, JR., *Where Do We Go from Here: Chaos or Community?*, 1967.

Five score years ago, a great American, in whose symbolic shadow we stand, signed the Emancipation Proclamation. This momentous decree came as a great beacon light of hope to millions of Negro slaves who had been seared in the flames of withering injustice. It came as a joyous daybreak to end the long night of captivity.

But one hundred years later, we must face the tragic fact that the Negro is still not free. One hundred years later, the life of the Negro is still sadly crippled by the manacles of segregation and the chains of discrimination. One hundred years later, the Negro lives on a lonely island of poverty in the midst of a vast ocean of material prosperity. One hundred years later, the Negro is still languishing in the corners of American society and finds himself an exile in his own land. So we have come here today to dramatize an appalling condition.

In a sense we have come to our nation's Capital to cash a check. When the architects of our republic wrote the magnificent words of the Constitution and the Declaration of Independence, they were signing a promissory note to which every American was to fall heir. This note was a promise that all men would be guaranteed the unalienable rights of life, liberty, and the pursuit of happiness.

It is obvious today that America has defaulted on this promissory note insofar as her citizens of color are concerned. Instead of honoring this sacred obligation, America has given the Negro people a bad check; a check which has come back marked "insufficient funds." But we refuse to believe that the bank of justice is bankrupt. We refuse to believe that there are insufficient funds in the great vaults of opportunity of this nation. So we have come to cash this check—a check that will give us upon demand the riches of freedom and the security of justice.

We have also come to this hallowed spot to remind America of the fierce urgency of *now*. This is no time to engage in the luxury of cooling off or to take the tranquilizing drug of gradualism. *Now* is the time to make real the promises of democracy. *Now* is the time to rise from the dark and desolate valley of segregation to the sunlit path of racial justice. *Now* is the time to open the doors of opportunity to all of God's children. *Now* is the time to lift our nation from the quicksands of racial injustice to the solid rock of brotherhood.

It would be fatal for the nation to overlook the urgency of the moment and to underestimate the determination of the Negro. This sweltering summer of the Negro's legitimate discontent will not pass until there is an invigorating autumn of freedom and equality. Nineteen sixty-three is not an end, but a beginning. Those who hope that the Negro needed to blow off steam and will now be content will have a rude awakening if the nation returns to business as usual. There will be neither rest nor tranquility in America until the Negro is granted his citizenship rights. The whirlwinds of revolt will continue to shake the foundations of our nation until the bright day of justice emerges.

But there is something that I must say to my people who stand on the warm threshold which leads into the palace of justice. In the process of gaining our rightful place we must not be guilty of wrongful deeds. Let us not seek to satisfy our thirst for freedom by drinking from the cup of bitterness and hatred. We must forever conduct our struggle on the high plane of dignity and discipline. We must not allow our creative protest to degenerate into physical violence. Again and again we must rise to the majestic heights of meeting physical force with soul force.

The marvelous new militancy which has engulfed the Negro community must not lead us to a distrust of all white people, for many of our white brothers, as evidenced by their presence here today, have come to realize that their destiny is tied up with our destiny and their freedom is inextricably bound to our freedom. We cannot walk alone.

And as we walk, we must make the pledge that we shall march ahead. We cannot turn back. There are those who are asking the devotees of civil rights, "When will you be satisfied?"

We can never be satisfied as long as the Negro is the victim of the unspeakable horrors of police brutality.

We can never be satisfied as long as our bodies, heavy with the fatigue of travel, cannot gain lodging in the motels of the highways and the hotels of the cities.

We cannot be satisfied as long as the Negro's basic mobility is from a smaller ghetto to a larger one.

We can never be satisfied as long as a Negro in Mississippi cannot vote and a Negro in New York believes he has nothing for which to vote.

No, no, we are not satisfied, and we will not be satisfied until justice rolls down like waters and righteousness like a mighty stream.

I am not unmindful that some of you have come here out of great trials and tribulations. Some of you have come fresh from narrow jail cells. Some of you have come from areas where your quest for freedom left you battered by the storms of persecution and staggered by the winds of police brutality. You have been the veterans of creative suffering. Continue to work with the faith that unearned suffering is redemptive.

Go back to Mississippi, go back to Alabama, go back to South Carolina, go back to Georgia, go back to Louisiana, go back to the slums and ghettos of our Northern cities, knowing that somehow this situation can and will be changed. Let us not wallow in the valley of despair.

I say to you today, my friends, that in spite of the difficulties and frustrations of the moment I still have a dream. It is a dream deeply rooted in the American dream.

I have a dream that one day this nation will rise up and live out the true meaning of its creed: "We hold these truths to be self-evident; that all men are created equal."

I have a dream that one day on the red hills of Georgia the sons of former slaves and the sons of former slaveowners will be able to sit down together at the table of brotherhood.

I have a dream that one day even the state of Mississippi, a desert state sweltering with the heat of injustice and oppression, will be transformed into an oasis of freedom and justice.

I have a dream that my four little children will one day live in a nation where they will not be judged by the color of their skin but by the content of their character.

I have a dream today.

I have a dream that one day the state of Alabama, whose governor's lips are presently dripping with the words of interposition and nullification, will be transformed into a situation where little black boys and black girls will be able to join hands with little white boys and white girls and walk together as sisters and brothers.

I have a dream today.

I have a dream that one day every valley shall be exalted, every hill and mountain shall be made low, the rough places will be made plain, and the crooked places will be made straight, and the glory of the Lord shall be revealed, and all flesh shall see it together.

This is our hope. This is the faith with which I return to the South. With this faith we will be able to hew out of the mountain of despair a stone of hope. With this faith we will be able to transform the jangling discords of our nation into a beautiful symphony of brotherhood.

With this faith we will be able to work together, to pray together, to struggle together, to go to jail together, to stand up for freedom together, knowing that we will be free one day.

This will be the day when all of God's children will be able to sing with new meaning, "My country 'tis of thee, sweet land of liberty, of thee I sing. Land where my fathers died, land of the Pilgrims' pride, from every mountainside, let freedom ring."

And if America is to be a great nation, this must become true. So let freedom ring from the prodigious hilltops of New Hampshire. Let freedom ring from the mighty mountains of New York. Let freedom ring from the heightening Alleghenies of Pennsylvania! Let freedom ring from the snow-capped Rockies of Colorado! Let freedom ring from the curvaceous peaks of California! But not only that; let freedom ring from Stone Mountain of Georgia! Let freedom ring from Lookout Mountain of Tennessee!

Let freedom ring from every hill and mole-hill of Mississippi. From every mountain-side, let freedom ring.

When we let freedom ring, when we let it ring from every village and every hamlet, from every state and every city, we will be able to speed up that day when all of God's children, black men and white men, Jews and Gentiles, Protestants and Catholics, will be able to join hands and sing in the words of the old Negro spiritual, "Free at last! Free at last! Thank God Almighty, we are free at last!"

MARTIN LUTHER KING, JR., speech, "I Have a Dream," Lincoln Memorial, Washington, D.C., August 28, 1963.

Two, four, six, eight,

We won't integrate.

WHITE STUDENTS' CHANT, Central High School, Little Rock, Arkansas, 1957.

Male supremacy has kept her [woman] down. It has not knocked her out.

CLARE BOOTHE LUCE, *Saturday Review/World*, August 24, 1974.

I intend to continue not to be angry or bear ill will to anyone.

AUTHERINE LUCY, on expulsion from the University of Alabama, 1956, in Lois and Alan Gordon, *American Chronicle*, 1987.

Jews are accepted socially with just enough qualification to make them aware that they do not entirely "belong."

ROBERT S. LYND AND HELEN MERRELL LYND, *Middletown: A Study in Contemporary American Culture*, 1929.

That's part of American greatness, is discrimination. Yes, sir. Inequality, I think, breeds freedom and gives a man opportunity.

LESTER MADDOX, *New York Times Magazine*, November 6, 1966.

Gentlemen: Please accept my resignation. I don't care to belong to any social organization that will accept me as a member.

GROUCHO MARX, letter of resignation to Friars Club of Beverly Hills, *The Groucho Phile*, 1976.

Has the Gestapo come to America? Have we not risen in righteous anger at Hitler's mistreatment of the Jews? Then, is it not incongruous that citi-

zen Americans of Japanese descent should be similarly mistreated and prosecuted?

MIKI MASOKA, to Tolan Committee, National Defense Migration hearings, 1942.

It is of very doubtful value to enlist the gifts of women if bringing women into fields that have been defined as male frightens the men, unsexes the women, muffles and distorts the contribution women could make, either because their presence excludes men from the occupation or because it changes the quality of the men who enter it.

MARGARET MEAD, *Male and Female*, 1948.

Eliminating the patriarchal and racist base of the existing social system requires a revolution, not a reform.

Ms., first issue, 1971.

Down in front.

MOTTO, National Association of Short Adults, *New York Times Magazine*, June 16, 1991.

[We seek] to confront with concrete action the conditions which now prevent women from enjoying equality of opportunity and freedom of choice which is their right as individual Americans and as human beings.

MANIFESTO, National Organization for Women, 1966.

Racial oppression of black people in America has done what neither class oppression or sexual oppression, with all their perniciousness, has ever done: destroyed an entire people and their culture.

ELEANOR HOLMES NORTON, in Robin Morgan, ed., *Sisterhood Is Powerful*, 1970.

I have learned that the subtle art of rejection used with finesse can be every bit as abusive as a punch in the face.

GORDON PARKS, "The Long Search for Pride," *Life*, August 16, 1963.

The white man has forever enjoyed the fruit, while the black man has patiently served it.

GORDON PARKS, "The Black Panthers and the Police," *Born Black*, 1971.

America is still a racist nation. It has not learned much from the turbulent decade just passed. We black people are still perplexed by the blood we must shed and the deaths we must die—as Americans. Some of us are born to be leaders, some to be followers. Some of us are born with great talents, some with none at all. But what seems to matter far more is that we are born black. That single fact would control our destiny above all others.

GORDON PARKS, "Papa Rage: A Visit with Eldridge Cleaver," *Born Black*, 1971.

I would say to the Negro: before demanding to be a white man socially and politically, learn to be a white man morally and intellectually—and to the white man: the black man is our brother, a younger brother, not adult, not disciplined, but tragic, pitiable, and lovable; act as his brother and be patient.

WILLIAM ALEXANDER PERCY, *Lanterns on the Levee*, 1941.

It is no longer a question of property in human flesh or of the boundary lines of slavery. Today it is subtle, complex, involved. Then it struck men, now it strikes manhood; then it chained the intellect, now it removes the fetters from the mind but sets bounds as to the sphere of its exercise.

REVERDY RANSOM, sermon on slavery, "The Martyrdom of John Brown," Boston, Massachusetts, December 2, 1909.

Nothing less than a radical reconstruction of American society is required if the Negro is to be able to take his rightful place in American life. And the reconstruction must begin not just in Oxford, Mississippi, or Birmingham, Alabama, but in New York, Philadelphia, Chicago, and other great cities of the North as well.

CHARLES E. SILBERMAN, *Crisis in Black and White*, 1964.

I knew, though I would not for years confess it aloud, that in trying to shut the Negro race away from us, we have shut ourselves away from so many good, creative, honest, deeply human things in life. I began to understand slowly at first but more and more clearly as the years passed, that the warped, distorted frame we have put around every Negro child from birth is around every white child also. Each is on a different side of the frame but each is pinioned there. And I knew that what cruelly shapes and cripples the personality of one is as cruelly shaping and crippling the personality of the other.

LILLIAN SMITH, *Killers of the Dream*, 1949.

It [Ku Klux Klan] gathers under its hood the mentally ill, the haters who have forgot what it is they hate or who dare not harm their real hate object, and also the bored and confused and ignorant. The Klan is made up of ghosts on the search for ghosts who have haunted the southern soul too long.

LILLIAN SMITH, *Killers of the Dream*, 1949.

[In 1986]...I found myself half-listening to a radio interview with a local black leader on "the state of black America." Long before...I had begun to feel that public discussions of the race issue had become virtually choreographed. Blacks were expected to speak on tones of racial entitlement, to show a modified black power assertiveness—not as strident as the sixties black power rhetoric, but certainly not as ameliorative as the integrationist tone of the civil rights era. Racism had to be offered as the greatest barrier to black progress, and blacks themselves had still to be seen primarily as racial victims. Whites, on the other hand, had both to show concern and a measure of befuddlement at how other whites could still be racist. There also had to be in whites a clear deference to the greater racial authority of blacks, whose color translated into a certain racial expertise. If there was more than one black, whites usually receded into the [background] while the black "experts" argued. This is still the standard media formula, the ideal choreography of black and white.

SHELBY STEELE, *The Content of Our Character*, 1990.

If four children had been killed in the bombing of a Berlin church by Communists, the country would be on the verge of war. But when four Senators...framed a resolution asking that the Sunday after the Birmingham bombing be set aside as a national day of mourning, they knew their fellow Senators too well even to introduce it.

I.F. STONE, on bombing of Birmingham church, "The Wasteland in the White Man's Heart," *I.F. Stone's Weekly*, September 30, 1963.

The cry of "black power" is less a programme than an incantation to deal with the crippling effects of white supremacy. The "black" affirms a lost racial pride and the "power" the virility of which the Negro has been robbed by generations of humiliation. Its swift spread testifies to the deep feelings it satisfies. It is not practical politics; it is psychological therapy.

I.F. STONE, "Why They Cry Black Power," *I.F. Stone's Weekly*, September 19, 1966.

It is impossible for any white person in the United States, no matter how sympathetic and broad, to realize what life would mean to him if his incentive to effort were suddenly snatched away. To the lack of incentive to effort, which is the awful shadow under which we live, may be traced the wreck and ruin of scores of colored people.

MARY CHURCH TERRELL, "What It Means to Be Colored in the Capital of the United States," *A Colored Woman in a White World*, 1907.

Any discrimination, like sharp turns in a road, becomes critical because of the tremendous speed at which we are traveling into the high-tech world of a service economy.

CLARENCE THOMAS, speech, Savannah State College, June 9, 1985.

How can a black man honestly sing "My Country 'Tis of Thee" when he doesn't own enough of his country in which to bury a cockroach?

MELVIN B. TOLSON, "The Death of an Infidel," *Washington Tribune*, April 2, 1938.

Today's New Negro must teach the young white man how to row his boat called the race problem. This will be difficult, for there are so many misleaders, white and black, who shout the wrong instructions from the bank. If these disillusioned and prejudiced old heads would keep their mouths shut, the young Negro and the young white man would learn the trick of moving their bodies and paddles in union.

MELVIN B. TOLSON, "A Discussion of Hogs, Dogs, Fish, and the Declaration of Independence," *Washington Tribune*, July 22, 1939.

To America's largest minority group, color is a birthmark and poverty a birthright; the Bill of Rights is a book sealed with seven seals; and the quest for a job, in prosperous times, takes on the hazard and ingenuity and sensation of a Homeric episode. The simple prerogatives and opportunities which white citizens take for granted are luscious fruit beyond the reach and grasp of black men. The Negro suffers all the disadvantages of being poor, plus the proscriptions of being black.

MELVIN B. TOLSON, "I Am Thankful for the Great Depression," *Washington Tribune*, September 30, 1939.

I draw the line in the dust and toss the gauntlet before the feet of tyranny, and I say segregation now, segregation tomorrow, segregation forever.

GEORGE C. WALLACE, inaugural address, 1963, *Life*, December 26, 1969.

To separate [black children] from others of similar age and qualifications solely because of their race generates a feeling of inferiority as to their status in the community that may affect their hearts and minds in a way unlikely ever to be undone....In the field of public education the doctrine of "separate but equal" has no place. Separate educational facilities are inherently unequal.

EARL WARREN, opinion, *Brown v. Board of Education*, Topeka, 1954.

When we are dealing with the Caucasian race [in America], we have methods that will test...loyalty. But when we deal with the Japanese, we are in an entirely different field.

EARL WARREN, on evacuating Japanese to relocation camps, 1942, in Lois and Alan Gordon, *American Chronicle*, 1987.

You tie us and then taunt us for a lack of bravery, but one day we will break the bonds. You may use our labor for two and a half centuries and then taunt us for our poverty, but let me remind you we will not always remain poor. You may withhold even the knowledge of how to read God's word and learn the way from earth to glory and then taunt us for our ignorance, but we would remind you that there is plenty of room at the top, and we are climbing.

GEORGE HENRY WHITE, speech to Congress, "Defense of the Negro Race, Charges Answered," January 29, 1901.

The attitude of the white citizens of this country toward the Negroes has undeniably had some of the unlovely characteristics of an alien imperialism, a smug racial superiority, a willingness to exploit an unprotected people....When we talk of freedom of opportunity for all nations, the mocking paradoxes in our own society become so clear that they can no longer be ignored.

WENDELL WILLKIE, *PM*, July 21, 1942.

The white people of the country, as well as I, wish to see the colored people progress, and admire the progress they have already made, and want to see them continue along independent lines. There is, however, a great prejudice against colored people....It will take one hundred years to eradicate this prejudice, and we must deal with it as practical men. Segregation is not humiliating but a benefit, and ought to be so regarded by you gentlemen. If your organization goes out and tells the colored people of the country that it is a humiliation, they will so regard it, but if you do not tell them so, and regard it rather as a benefit, they will regard it the same. The only harm that will come will be if you cause them to think it is a humiliation.

WOODROW WILSON, reply to Monroe Trotter, ca. 1913, in William Loren Katz, ed., *Eyewitness: The Negro in American History,* 1967.

Lynching is a murder. For the past four hundred years our people have been lynched physically but now it's done politically. We're lynched politically, we're lynched economically, we're lynched socially, we're lynched in every way that you can imagine.

MALCOLM X, remarks, TV program, "The Open Mind," October 15, 1961.

I think that the black man in America wants to be recognized as a human being and it's almost impossible for one who has enslaved another to bring himself to accept the person who used to pull his plow, who used to be an animal, subhuman, who used to be considered as such by him—it's almost impossible for that person in his right mind to accept that person as his equal.

MALCOLM X, remarks, TV program, "The Open Mind," October 15, 1961.

We want no integration with this wicked race that enslaved us. We want complete separation from this race of devils. But we should not be expected to leave America and go back to our own homeland empty-handed. After four hundred years of slave labor, we have some *back pay* coming, a bill owed to us that must be collected.

MALCOLM X, speech, December 1, 1963.

Racism is a human problem and a crime that is absolutely so ghastly that a person who is fighting racism is well within his rights to fight against it by any means necessary until it is eliminated.

MALCOLM X, speech, December 12, 1964.

I don't see an American dream;...I see an American nightmare....Three hundred and ten years we worked in this country without a dime in return.

MALCOLM X, 1964, in Lois and Alan Gordon, *American Chronicle*, 1987.

[A]n American Negro isn't a man—he's a walking defense mechanism.

FRANK YERBY, *Speak Now*, 1969.

DRUGS AND ALCOHOL

Of all the tyrannies which have usurped power over humanity, few have been able to enslave the mind and body as imperiously as drug addiction.

FREDA ADLER, *Sisters in Crime*, 1975.

When you stop drinking, you have to deal with this marvelous personality that started you drinking in the first place.

JIMMY BRESLIN, *Table Money*, 1986.

Pot will probably be legal in ten years. Why? Because in this audience probably every other one of you knows a law student who smokes pot, who will become a senator, who will legalize it to protect himself. But then no one will smoke it anymore. You'll see.

LENNY BRUCE, in John Cohen, ed., *The Essential Lenny Bruce*, 1967.

It is not heroin or cocaine that makes one an addict, it is the need to escape from a harsh reality. There are more television addicts, more baseball and football addicts, more movie addicts, and certainly more alcohol addicts in this country than there are narcotics addicts.

SHIRLEY CHISHOLM, testimony to House Select Committee on Crime, September 17, 1969.

The country couldn't run with prohibition. That is the industrial fact.

HENRY FORD, in Arthur Zipser and George Novack, *Who's Hooey: Nitwitticisms of the Notable*, 1932.

The athletes are doing just what society expects. Cocaine is a crime of affluence. The kid has too much money. Heroes are doing what they always did: Surrogates, fighting out the battles for the public....When I played, you fell over it. I don't think it's different than it ever was. Athletes

1. We admitted we were powerless over alcohol—that our lives had become unmanageable.

2. Came to believe that a Power greater than ourselves could restore us to sanity.

3. Made a decision to turn our will and our lives over to the care of God *as we understood Him.*

4. Made a searching and fearless moral inventory of ourselves.

5. Admitted to God, to ourselves, and to another human being the exact nature of our wrongs.

6. Were entirely ready to have God remove all these defects of character.

7. Humbly asked Him to remove our shortcomings.

8. Made a list of all persons we had harmed, and became willing to make amends to them all.

9. Made direct amends to such people wherever possible, except when to do so would injure them or others.

10. Continued to take personal inventory and when we were wrong promptly admitted it.

11. Sought through prayer and meditation to improve our conscious contact with God *as we understood Him*, praying only for knowledge of His will for us and the power to carry that out.

12. Having had a spiritual awakening as the result of these steps, we tried to carry this message to all alcoholics, and to practice these principles in all our affairs.

ALCOHOLICS ANONYMOUS, 12 Steps.

hang around with people who tell them, "The rules don't apply to you."

PETER GENT, *New York Times*, October 26, 1982.

Athletes are protected more than any group in the school system....We have a state rule that anybody caught drinking cannot participate for nine weeks. With an athlete, this rule is overlooked.

MARY ELLEN HARRIS, conference on sports and drug abuse, University of Wisconsin, 1981.

Like the Red Menace of the early 1950s, the current drug hysteria has led to a loyalty oath—this time, the urine test.

ABBIE HOFFMAN, *The Best of Abbie Hoffman*, 1987.

All dope can do for you is kill you...the long hard way. And it can kill the people you love right along with you.

BILLIE HOLIDAY, *Lady Sings the Blues*, 1956.

A great social and economic experiment, noble in motive and far-reaching in purpose.

HERBERT HOOVER, letter on prohibition to William E. Borah, February 28, 1928.

Alcoholic psychosis is nothin' more or less 'n ole D.T.'s in a dinner suit.

KIN HUBBARD, *Abe Martin's Broadcast*, 1930.

All the no-saying and no-preaching in the world will fail to keep men, and youths growing into manhood, away from John Barleycorn when John Barleycorn is everywhere accessible, and where John Barleycorn is everywhere the connotation of manliness, and daring, and great-spiritedness. The only rational thing for the twentieth century folk to do is to cover up the well.

JACK LONDON, *John Barleycorn*, 1913.

An era of chemical McCarthyism is at hand, and "guilty until proven innocent" is the new slogan.

GEORGE LUNDBERT, on drug testing, *U.S. News & World Report*, December 15, 1986.

The most important influence creating the violence in football is the high-dose amphetamine. You actually become, for the peak effect of the drug, crazy. And it's the most murderous type of crazy that we know. It is the paranoid psychotic, the killer of presidents.

ARNOLD MANDELL, *New York Daily News*, March 18, 1979.

I noticed that mannequins in windows were smiling and Elizabeth Taylor from an enormous poster advertising the film *Cleopatra* several times gestured for me to come to her.

REPORT OF PSYCHEDELIC DRUG EXPERIENCE, in R. Masters and J. Johnson, *The Varieties of Psychedelic Experience*, 1966.

We believe in the coming of His kingdom whose service is perfect freedom, because His laws, written in our members as well as in nature and in grace, are perfect, converting the soul.

We believe in the gospel of the Golden Rule, and that each man's habits of life should be an example safe and beneficent for every other man to follow.

We believe that God created both man and woman in His own image, and, therefore, we believe in one standard of purity for both men and women, and in the equal right of all to hold opinions and to express the same with equal freedom.

We believe in a living wage; in an eight-hour day; in courts of conciliation and arbitration; in justice as opposed to greed of gain; in "peace on earth and goodwill to men."

We therefore formulate and, for ourselves, adopt the following pledge, asking our sisters and brothers of a common danger and a common hope to make common cause with us in working its reasonable and helpful precepts into the practice of everyday life:

I hereby solemnly promise, *God helping me*, to abstain from all distilled, fermented, and malt liquors, including wine, beer, and cider, and to employ all proper means to discourage the use of and traffic in the same.

To conform and enforce the rationale of this pledge, we declare our purpose to educate the young; to form a better public sentiment; to reform so far as possible, by religious, ethical, and scientific means, the drinking classes; to seek the transforming power of Divine Grace for ourselves and all for whom we work, that they and we may willfully transcend no law of pure and wholesome living; and finally we pledge ourselves to labor and to pray that all of these principles, founded upon the Gospel of Christ, may be worked out into the customs of society and the laws of the land.

LEAFLET, National Woman's Christian Temperance Union, 1902.

Tolerance to my mind has been greatly overrated....I take as much pleasure in detesting the good brothers and sisters of the [Anti-Saloon] League as they have in hating me.

WESTBROOK PEGLER, in Oliver Pilat, *Pegler: Angry Man of the Press*, 1963.

Today, there is a drug and alcohol abuse epidemic in this country. And no one is safe from it—not you, not me and certainly not our children, because this epidemic has their names written on it.

NANCY REAGAN, address to nation with Ronald Reagan, September 14, 1986.

Cocaine arrived in my life with my first-round draft into the NFL in 1974. It has dominated my life....Eventually, it took control and almost killed me....Cocaine may be found in quantity throughout the NFL. It's pushed on players.... Sometimes it's pushed *by* players....Just as it controlled me, it now controls and corrupts the game, because so many players are on it.

DON REESE, *Sports Illustrated*, June 14, 1982.

I ask especially that no state shall, by law or otherwise, authorize the return of the saloon, either in its old form or in some modern guise.

FRANKLIN D. ROOSEVELT, proclamation on repeal of Eighteenth Amendment, December 5, 1933.

To pass prohibitory laws to govern localities where the sentiment does not sustain them is simply equivalent to allowing free liquor, plus lawlessness.

THEODORE ROOSEVELT, letter to William Howard Taft, July 16, 1908.

Alcohol was a threat to women, for it released men from the moral control they had learned from a diet of preaching and scolding from ministers and mothers alike.

ALICE ROSSI, *The Feminist Papers*, 1973.

The prohibition law, written for weaklings and derelicts, has divided the nation, like Gaul, into three parts—wets, drys and hypocrites.

FLORENCE SABIN, speech, February 9, 1931.

It *is* a cocaine world, fast and smug, and self-conscious—like putting your face in the photocopy

CONTRACT FOR LIFE

A Contract for Life Between Parent and Teenager

The S.A.D.D. Drinking-Driver Contract

Teenager: I agree to call you for advice and/or transportation at any hour, from any place, if I am ever in a situation where I have been drinking or a friend or date who is driving me has been drinking.

_____

Signature

_____

Date

Parent: I agree to come and get you at any hour, any place, no questions asked and no argument at that time, or I will pay for a taxi to bring you home safely. I expect we would discuss this issue at a later time.

I agree to seek safe, sober transportation home if I am ever in a situation where I have had too much to drink or a friend who is driving me has had too much to drink.

_____

Signature

_____

Date

S.A.D.D. does not condone drinking by those below the legal drinking age. S.A.D.D. encourages all young people to obey the laws of their state, including laws relating to the legal drinking age.

CONTRACT FOR LIFE, Students Against Drunk Driving, 1990.

---

machine, then making a copy of that, a copy of that, copies inside copies, echoes inside echoes, until we've lost the original.

IAN SHOALES, "Cocaine," I Gotta Go, June 12, 1982.

A Coke at snack time, a drink before dinner, a cup of coffee after dinner, a cigarette with the coffee—very relaxing. Four shots of drugs. Domesticated ones.

ADAM SMITH, Powers of Mind, 1975.

All over America at this moment pleasurable surges of self-esteem are fading. People are discovering that the principal thing one does with cocaine is run out of it.

ROBERT STONE, "A Higher Horror of the Whiteness: Cocaine's Coloring of the American Psyche," Harper's, December, 1986.

"I think this calls for a drink" has long been one of our national slogans.

JAMES THURBER, "Merry Christmas," Alarms and Diversions, 1964.

The saloon is the poor man's club.

CHARLES D. WILLIAMS, Michigan, ca. 1900.

ENVIRONMENT AND POLLUTION

We live in an environment whose principal product is garbage. The shined shoe in such a society is a hypocritial statement because it pro-motes the lie that we can thrive on garbage without being dirtied by it.

RUSSELL BAKER, "Observer," New York Times, February 22, 1968.

If the earth does grow inhospitable toward human presence, it is primarily because we have lost our sense of courtesy toward the earth and its inhabitants, our sense of gratitude, our willingness to recognize the sacred character of habitat, our capacity for the awesome, for the numinous quality of every earthly reality.

THOMAS BERRY, The Dream of the Earth, 1988.

The world to-day is sick to its thin blood for lack of elemental things, for fire before the hands, for water welling from the earth, for air, for dear earth itself underfoot.

HENRY BESTON, "The Beach," The Outermost House, 1928.

DDT is one of the safest pesticides being used.

JAMES M. BROWN, letter, American Way, June, 1970.

Those who think we're powerless to do anything about the "greenhouse effect" are forgetting about the "White House effect." As President, I intend to do something about it.

GEORGE BUSH, speech, Erie Metropark, Michigan, August 31, 1988, in Jonathan Weiner, The Next One Hundred Years, 1990.

Over increasingly large areas of the United States, spring now comes unheralded by the return of the birds, and the early mornings are strangely silent where once they were filled with the beauty of bird song.

RACHEL CARSON, *The Silent Spring,* 1962.

As crude a weapon as the cave man's club, the chemical barrage has been hurled against the fabric of life.

RACHEL CARSON, *The Silent Spring,* 1962.

Under the philosophy that now seems to guide our destinies, nothing must get in the way of the man with the spray gun.

RACHEL CARSON, *The Silent Spring,* 1962.

Viewed ecologically, the human saga is a tragic success story.

WILLIAM R. CATTON, JR., "On the Dire Destiny of Human Lemmings," in Michael Tobias, ed., *Deep Ecology,* 1985.

Sooner or later, wittingly or unwittingly, we must pay for every intrusion on the natural environment.

BARRY COMMONER, *Science and Survival,* 1966.

Air pollution is not merely a nuisance and a threat to health. It is a reminder that our most celebrated technological achievements—the automobile, the jet plane, the power plant, industry in general, and indeed the modern city itself—are, in the environment, failures.

BARRY COMMONER, *The Closing Circle: Nature, Man, and Technology,* 1972.

The environmental crisis is somber evidence of an insidious fraud hidden in the vaunted productivity and wealth of modern, technology-based society.

BARRY COMMONER, *The Closing Circle: Nature, Man, and Technology,* 1972.

Blessed be the starving blacks of Mississippi with their outdoor privies, for they are ecologically sound, and they shall inherit a nation.

WAYNE H. DAVIS, "Overpopulated America," *The New Republic,* January 10, 1970.

Contemporary public concern for protecting nature's ecological equilibrium should lead to the conferral of standing upon environmental objects to sue for their own preservation.

WILLIAM O. DOUGLAS, opinion, *Sierra Club* v. *Morton,* 1972.

If it should turn out that we have mishandled our own lives as several civilizations before us have done, it seems a pity that we should

involve the violet and the tree frog in our departure.

LOREN EISELEY, "The Lethal Factor," *The Star Thrower,* 1963.

Ruin is the destination toward which all men rush, each pursuing his own best interest in a society that believes in the freedom of the commons. Freedom in a commons brings ruin to all.

GARRETT HARDIN, "The Tragedy of the Commons," *Science,* December 13, 1968.

How can we help a foreign country to escape overpopulation? Clearly the worst thing we can do is send food....Atomic bombs would be kinder. For a few moments the misery would be acute, but it would soon come to an end for most of the people, leaving a very few survivors to suffer thereafter.

GARRETT HARDIN, "The Immorality of Being Softhearted," *Stanford Alumni Almanac,* January, 1969.

The trouble with the current emphasis on preserving "endangered species" is that, however beneficial to wildlife the campaign works out to be, it makes all animals seem like museum pieces, worth saving for sentimental considerations and as figures of speech (to "shoot a sitting duck"), but as a practical matter already dead and gone.

EDWARD HOAGLAND, "Dogs and the Tug of Life," *Red Wolves and Black Bears,* 1976.

Our conservation must be not just the classic conservation of production and development, but a creative conservation of restoration and innovation. Its concern is not with nature alone, but with the total relation between man and the world around him. Its object is not just man's welfare but the dignity of man's spirit.

LYNDON B. JOHNSON, message to Congress, February 8, 1965.

If we care about the land, it will be necessary to redefine whole economies, not just the farm economy. A complex, solid economy could certainly grow around a policy of cooperation with natural environments. Why haven't we proposed such policies—on as grand a scale as national defense—when our own species is at stake?

JANET KAUFFMAN, "Letting Go: The Virtue of Vacant Ground," in Michael Martone, ed., *A Place of Sense,* 1988.

After all, this is a world of rock and water and air. It is elemental. It is not ours.

What do we want to *do* with it? Because we are conscious creatures, the entire planet—the universe—has become a place for the pleasure of the human mind. And being human, we *must* range and speculate. We must terrify ourselves with our thinking. This is our art.

But in the dailiness of human life, in the physical world of carbon and hydrogen, oxygen and uranium, we may not range thoughtlessly or speculate endlessly to our gain. The world is not ours to use up, or blanket with our debris, or despoil.

JANET KAUFFMAN, "Letting Go: The Virtue of Vacant Ground," in Michael Martone, ed., *A Place of Sense,* 1988.

It strains belief to know that Neil Armstrong can walk on the moon, 250,000 miles away, but that he cannot swim in Lake Erie, a few miles from his Ohio home.

EDWARD M. KENNEDY, January 26, 1970, in Thomas P. Collins and Louis M. Savary, eds., *A People of Compassion,* 1972.

The earth we abuse and the living things we kill will, in the end, take their revenge; for in exploiting their presence we are diminishing our future.

MARYA MANNES, *More in Anger,* 1958.

What *right* has any citizen of a free country, whatever his foresight and shrewdness, to seize on sources of life for his own behoof that are the common heritage of all; what *right* has legislature or court to help in the seizure; and striking still more deeply, what *right* has any generation to wholly consume, much less waste, those sources of life without which the children or the children's children must starve or freeze?

W. J. McGEE, "The Conservation of Natural Resources," 1910.

Water is the most precious, limited natural resource we have in this country....But because water belongs to no one—except the people—special interests, including government polluters, use it as their private sewers.

RALPH NADER, Introduction, in David Zwick and Marcy Benstock, *Water Wasteland,* 1971.

One person's trash is another's living space.

NATIONAL ACADEMY OF SCIENCES, "Waste Management and Control," 1965.

In dealing with the environment we must learn not how to master nature but how to master ourselves, our institutions, and our technology.

RICHARD M. NIXON, message to Congress on release of *Environmental Quality: The First Annual Report of the Council on Environmental Quality,* 1970.

We have come to accept with enthusiasm the unprofessional, unappreciative, unskilled butchery of the land that goes under the name of planning.

WILLIAM L. PEREIRA, recalled on his death, *Time,* November 25, 1985.

The first great fact about conservation is that it stands for development.

GIFFORD PINCHOT, *The Fight for Conservation,* 1910.

The outgrowth of conservation, the inevitable result, is national efficiency.

GIFFORD PINCHOT, *The Fight for Conservation,* 1910.

Conservation is the application of common sense to the common problems for the common good. Since its objective is the ownership, control, development, processing, distribution, and use of the natural resources for the benefit of the people, it is by its very nature the antithesis of monopoly.

GIFFORD PINCHOT, *Breaking New Ground,* 1947.

Approximately 80% of our air pollution stems from hydrocarbons released by vegetation. So let's not go overboard in setting and enforcing tough emissions standards for man-made sources.

RONALD REAGAN, *Sierra,* September 10, 1980.

It is safe to say that the prosperity of our people depends directly on the energy and intelligence with which our natural resources are used. It is equally clear that these resources are the final basis of national power and perpetuity. Finally, it is ominously evident that these resources are in the course of rapid exhaustion.

THEODORE ROOSEVELT, speech, national conference on conservation, 1908.

We travel together, passengers on a little spaceship, dependent on its vulnerable reserves of air and soil; all committed for our safety to its security and peace; preserved from annihilation only by the care, the work and, I will say, the love we give our fragile craft.

ADLAI E. STEVENSON, in Garrett Hardin, *Exploring New Ethics for Survival,* 1972.

It goes somehow against the grain to learn that cost-benefit analyses can be done neatly on lakes, meadows, nesting gannets, even whole oceans. It is hard enough to confront the environmental options ahead, and the hard choices, but even harder when the price tags are so visible. Even the new jargon is disturbing: it hurts the spirit, somehow, to read the word *environ-*

ments, when the plural means that there are so many alternatives there to be sorted through, as in a market, and voted on.

LEWIS THOMAS, "Natural Man," *The Lives of a Cell*, 1974.

Intoxicated with the power to manipulate nature, some misguided men have produced a rationale to replace the Myth of Superabundance. It might be called the Myth of Scientific Supremacy, for it rests on the rationalization that the scientists can fix everything tomorrow.

STEWART L. UDALL, *The Quiet Crisis*, 1963.

It was a sad fact, also, that the men, women, and children of America the Beautiful became the litter champions of the world.

STEWART L. UDALL, *The Quiet Crisis*, 1963.

[T]oday the conservation movement finds itself turning back to ancient Indian land ideas, to the Indian understanding that we are not outside of nature, but of it....In recent decades we have slowly come back to some of the truths that the Indian knew from the beginning; that unborn generations have a claim on the land equal to our own; that men need to learn from nature, to keep an ear to the earth, and to replenish their spirits in frequent contacts with animals and wild land.

STUART UDALL, *The Quiet Crisis*, 1963.

Ecology has become the political substitute for the word "motherhood."

JESSE UNRUH, *Newsweek*, January 26, 1970.

We're all living in a chemical soup.

LANCE A. WALLACE, *Newsweek*, January 7, 1985.

We talk about a space race. There is a space race down here on the ground. In this race every human being is a superpower and the competition no longer stands a chance. Other species are bound to this or that patch of turf, and this planet. We feel bound to no patch of turf on Earth, bound only for the stars. We sacrifice a marsh, a bay, a park, a lake. We sacrifice a sparrow. We trade one countdown for another.

JONATHAN WEINER, *The Next One Hundred Years*, 1990.

I think man's gradual, creeping contamination of the planet, his sending up of dust into the air, his strontium additive in our bones, his discharge of industrial poisons into rivers that once flowed clear, his mixing of chemicals with fog on the east wind add up to a fantasy of such grotesque proportions as to make everything said on the subject seem pale and anemic by contrast.

E.B. WHITE, "Sootfall and Fallout," October 18, 1956, *Essays of E.B. White*, 1977.

Christianity bears a huge burden of guilt....We shall continue to have a worsening ecologic crisis until we reject the Christian axiom that nature has no reason for existence save to serve man.

LYNN WHITE, JR., "The Historical Roots of Our Economic Crisis," *Science*, March 10, 1967.

HEALTH

If you can't be good, be sanitary.

ATTRIBUTED TO AMERICAN SOLDIERS IN FRANCE DURING WORLD WAR I.

Getting a man to wear a condom isn't as simple as saying "You look better in a hat."

ANONYMOUS, *New York Times*, July 8, 1987.

When it comes to your health, I recommend frequent doses of that rare commodity among Americans—common sense.

VINCENT ASKEY, speech, Bakersfield, California, October 20, 1960.

The *healthy*, the *strong* individual, is the one who asks for help when he needs it. Whether he's got an abscess on his knee or in his soul.

RONA BARRETT, *Miss Rona: An Autobiography*, 1974.

We all basically go back to being a child when we're in a dentist's chair.

ARTHUR BENJAMIN, *Newsweek*, May 5, 1986.

If this country is to survive, the best-fed-nation myth had better be recognized for what it is: propaganda designed to produce wealth but not health.

ADELLE DAVIS, *Let's Eat Right To Keep Fit*, 1954.

The subject no longer has to be mentioned by name. Someone is sick. Someone else is feeling better now. A friend has just gone back into the hospital. Another has died. The unspoken name, of course, is AIDS.

DAVID W. DUNLAP, *New York Times*, April 23, 1985.

If the AIDS antibody test becomes a requirement for passports or visas, millions of Americans can kiss their dream vacations goodbye.

GAY RIGHTS ADVOCATE, *Boston Globe*, January, 1987.

My generation is the first in my species to have put fitness next to godliness on the scale of things. Keeping in shape has become *the* impera-

For centuries woman has gone forth with man to till the fields, to feed and clothe the nations. She has sacrificed her life to populate the earth. She has overdone her labors. She now steps forth and demands that women shall cease producing in ignorance. To do this she must have knowledge to control birth. This is the first immediate step she must take toward the goal of her freedom.

Those who are opposed to this are simply those who do not know. Anyone who like myself has worked among the people and found on one hand an ever-increasing population with its ever-increasing misery, poverty and ignorance, and on the other hand a stationary or decreasing population with its increasing wealth and higher standards of living, greater freedom, joy and happiness, cannot doubt that birth control is the liveliest issue of the day and one on which depends the future welfare of the race....

My first clear impression of life was that large families and poverty went hand in hand. I was born and brought up in a glass factory town in the western part of New York State. I was one of eleven children—so I had some personal experience of the struggles and hardships a large family endures.

When I was seventeen years old my mother died from overwork and the strain of too frequent childbearing. I was left to care for the younger children and share the bur-

dens of all. When I was old enough I entered a hospital to take up the profession of nursing.

In the hospital I found that seventy-five percent of the diseases of men and women are the result of ignorance of their sex functions. I found that every department of life was open to investigation and discussion except that shaded valley of sex. The explorer, scientist, inventor may go forth in their various fields for investigation and return to lay the fruits of their discoveries at the feet of society. But woe to him who dares explore that forbidden realm of sex. No matter how pure the motive, no matter what miseries he sought to remove, slanders, persecutions and jail await him who dares bear the light of knowledge into that cave of darkness.

So great was the ignorance of the women and girls I met concerning their own bodies that I decided to specialize in women's diseases and took up gynecological and obstetrical nursing.

A few years of this work brought me to a shocking discovery—that knowledge of the methods of controlling birth was accessible to the women of wealth while the working women were deliberately kept in ignorance of this knowledge!

I found that the women of the working class were as anxious to obtain this knowledge as their sisters of wealth, but that they were told that there are laws on the statute books against imparting it to them. And

---

tive of our middle age. The heaviest burden of guilt we carry into our forties is flab. Our sense of failure is measured by the grade on a stress test.

ELLEN GOODMAN, "105 and Still Walking," *Washington Post*, June, 1988.

The woman in question has arrived at the stage of life where dental hygienists warn, "Your teeth are fine but your gums will have to come out." The average American hygienist, a major stockholder in floss, today prescribes a salvage plan, a middle-age evening ritual that has become the new national vespers.

ELLEN GOODMAN, "Racing Time," *Washington Post*, October, 1985.

The good old days! I won't say I'm out of condition now—but I even puff going downstairs.

DICK GREGORY, *From the Back of the Bus*, 1962.

Over and over, these men cry out against the weight of so many losses—not just a lover dead, but friends and friends of friends, dozens of them, until it seems that AIDS is all there is and all there ever will be.

JANE GROSS, "AIDS: The Next Phase," *New York Times*, March 16, 1987.

There is only one thing people like that is good for them: a good night's sleep.

EDGAR WATSON HOWE, *Country Town Sayings*, 1911.

the medical profession was most religious in obeying these laws when the patient was a poor woman.

I found that the women of the working class had emphatic views on the crime of bringing children into the world to die of hunger. They would rather risk their lives through abortion than give birth to little ones they could not feed and care for.

For the laws against imparting this knowledge force these women into the hands of the filthiest midwives and the quack abortionists—unless they bear unwanted children—with the consequence that the deaths from abortions are almost wholly among the working-class women....

Is woman's health not to be considered? Is she to remain a producing machine? Is she to have time to think, to study, to care for herself? Man cannot travel to his goal alone. And until woman has knowledge to control birth she cannot get the time to think and develop. Until she has the time to think, neither the suffrage question nor the social question nor the labor question will interest her, and she will remain the drudge that she is and her husband the slave that he is just as long as they continue to supply the market with cheap labor.

Let me ask you: Has the State any more right to ravish a woman against her will by keeping her in ignorance than a man has through brute force? Has the State a better right to decide when she shall bear offspring?...

Am I to be classed as immoral because I advocate small families for the working class while Mr. Roosevelt can go up and down the length of the land shouting and urging these women to have large families and is neither arrested nor molested but considered by all society as highly moral?

But I ask you which is the more moral—to urge this class of woman to have only those children she desires and can care for, or to delude her into breeding thoughtlessly? Which is America's definition of morality?

You will agree with me that a woman should be free.

Yet no adult woman who is ignorant of the means to prevent conception can call herself free.

No woman can call herself free who cannot choose the time to be a mother or not as she sees fit. This should be woman's first demand....

Woman must be protected from incessant childbearing before she can actively participate in the social life. She must triumph over Nature's and Man's laws which have kept her in bondage. Just as man has triumphed over Nature by the use of electricity, shipbuilding, bridges, etc., so must woman triumph over the laws which have made her a childbearing machine.

MARGARET H. SANGER, "The Case for Birth Control," 1917.

AIDS has a personal message for all of us.

STEPHEN C. JOSEPH, *New York*, March 23, 1987.

Children should not grow up in America with twisted limbs or retarded minds simply because their parents cannot afford the care they need. Families should not be dumped into poverty by unnecessary illness and disability. No American should face financial disaster because of the costs of decent health. No American should give up his children's education, or exhaust his savings, or mortgage his home and future, to pay the cost of health.

EDWARD M. KENNEDY, speech, October 15, 1975, in Henry Steele Commager, ed., *Our Day and Generation*, 1979.

America doesn't need a double-standard of health—one for those who can afford it and another for those who can't.

EDWARD M. KENNEDY, speech, February 1, 1976, in Henry Steele Commager, ed., *Our Day and Generation*, 1979.

What we have today in the United States is not so much a health-care system as a disease-cure system.

EDWARD M. KENNEDY, speech, May 31, 1979, in Henry Steele Commager, ed., *Our Day and Generation*, 1979.

Within our potential system AIDS will strain America's most fundamental values. It will test the bounds of individuals' rights to privacy and liberty and the limits of government's right to overrule those rights to protect society.

RICHARD KNOX, *Boston Globe*, May 17, 1987.

If you turn your back on these people, you yourself are an animal. You may be a well-dressed animal, but you are nevertheless an animal.

EDWARD KOCH, on AIDS epidemic, State of the City Address, New York City, March 16, 1987.

What we're seeing is two things—the commodization of drugs that are well-being enhancers and the creeping redefinition of what it means to be healthy.

JOHN D. LANTOS, *New York Times*, June 16, 1991.

The doctor says i hev got me thet sickness like Tom Prescott and thet is the reeson wy i am coughin sometime....It is a terrible plague....The doctor says i will be dead in about fore months.

WEST VIRGINIA MINER, in Albert Maltz, *New Masses*, 1935.

A hospital bed is a parked taxi with the meter running.

GROUCHO MARX, *Reader's Digest*, March, 1973.

Society is going to have to realize that we're in the midst of the biggest public health crisis that has occurred in most people's lifetimes.

KENNETH H. MAYER, *Boston Globe*, May 17, 1987.

I am no expert on sex education, but I know the first lesson must be that sex makes babies; that babies get hurt and sometimes die if they are not well cared for; and that human beings stay at the animal level if they think of themselves instead of the welfare of their offspring when they breed.

INA S. MOORE, *New York Times*, May 16, 1981.

Avoid fried meats which angry up the blood. If your stomach disputes you, lie down and pacify it with cool thoughts. Keep the juices flowing by jangling around gently as you move. Go very light on the vices, such as carrying on in society. The social ramble ain't restful. Avoid running at all times. Don't look back. Someone might be gaining on you.

LEROY (SATCHEL) PAIGE, prescription for staying young, *Collier's*, June 13, 1953.

Anabolic steroids do not enhance athletic ability.

PHYSICIAN'S DESK REFERENCE WARNING, *Playboy*, February, 1978.

You can't prevent a sexually transmitted epidemic without talking about sex.

SAM PUCKETT, *New York*, March 23, 1987.

I remember in high school when a classmate began taking the pill and suddenly started to look like a balloon at the Macy's Thanksgiving parade. I remember when the women in my college dormitory gritted their teeth and had a plastic article that looked as if it had been made by Mattell placed inside their bodies. And I remember an absolutely uproarious all-female brunch where a friend described her first experience with a contraceptive device, which shot out a bathroom window into the college quadrangle. She never retrieved it. I wouldn't have, either.

ANNA QUINDLEN, *New York Times*, June 17, 1987.

Health care is being converted from a social service to an economic commodity, sold in the marketplace and distributed on the basis of who can afford to pay for it.

ARNOLD RELMAN, on takeover of public hospitals by commercial business, *New York Times*, January 25, 1985.

The real hope of the world lies in putting as painstaking thought into the business of mating as we do into other big businesses.

MARGARET SANGER, 1922, in Lois and Alan Gordon, *American Chronicle*, 1987.

There is nothing more damaging to adequate sex instruction than timidity, shame, embarrassment, or a general hyper-emotionalism regarding matters of sex. The attitude that sex is shameful, disgusting, immoral, and so on, makes it *impossible* for anyone to deal adequately with the problem.

ALEXANDER A. SCHNEIDERS, *The Child and Problems of Today*, 1952.

Illness is the night-side of life, a more onerous citizenship. Everyone who is born holds dual citizenship, in the kingdom of the well and in the kingdom of the sick. Although we all prefer to use only the good passport, sooner or later each of us is obliged, at least for a spell, to identify ourselves as citizens of that other place.

SUSAN SONTAG, *Illness as Metaphor*, 1978.

Keeping off a large weight loss is a phenomenon about as common in American medicine as an impoverished dermatologist.

CALVIN TRILLIN, *Alice, Let's Eat*, 1978.

Even mature, educated, married couples who conscientiously practice contraception not infrequently conceive a potential child. The chances that an attractive teenager, however careful, will avoid pregnancy in a decade or more of sustained sexual activity approach zero.

DAVID B. WILSON, *Boston Globe*, July 29, 1986.

LABOR

We colored people can't organize without you and you white folks can't organize without us. Aren't we all brothers and ain't God the Father of us all? We live under the same sun, eat the same food, wear the same kind of clothes, work on the same land, raise the same crop for the same landlord who oppresses and cheats us both. For a long time now the white folks and the colored folks have been fighting each other and both of us has been getting whipped all the time. We don't have nothing against one another but we got plenty against the landlord. The same chain that holds my people holds your people too. If we're chained together on the outside, we ought to stay chained together in the union. It won't do no good for us to divide because there's where the trouble has been all the time. The landlord is always betwixt us, beatin' us and starvin' us, and makin' us fight each other. There ain't but one way for us to get him where he can't help himself and that's fer us to get together and stay together.

BLACK SHARECROPPER AT SOUTHERN TENANT FARMERS' UNION MEETING, 1919, in William Loren Katz, ed., *Eyewitness: The Negro in American History,* 1967.

We don't so much want to see a female Einstein become an assistant professor. We want a woman schlemiel to get promoted as quickly as a male schlemiel.

BELLA ABZUG, 1977, in Lois and Alan Gordon, *American Chronicle,* 1987.

[This nation is becoming] a nation of hamburger stands, a country stripped of industrial capacity and meaningful work,...a service economy,...a nation of citizens busily buying and selling cheeseburgers and rootbeer floats.

AFL-CIO PUBLIC SERVICE STATEMENT, 1974.

The rights and interests of the laboring man will be protected and cared for, not by the labor agitators but by the Christian men to whom God in His infinite wisdom has given the control of the property interests of the country, and upon the successful management of which so much depends.

GEORGE F. BAER, letter to W.F. Clark, who requested Baer to end coal strike, July 17, 1902.

The prosecution of modern war rests completely upon the operation of labor in mines, mills and factories, so that labor fights there just as truly as the soldiers do in the trenches.

MARY RITTER BEARD, *A Short History of the American Labor Movement,* 1920.

Neither the common law nor the Fourteenth Amendment confers the absolute right to strike.

LOUIS D. BRANDEIS, opinion, *Dorchy v. Kansas,* 1926.

In addition to the inflation, we have stagnating productivity. People don't work the way they used to.

ARTHUR BURNS, 1975, in Lois and Alan Gordon, *American Chronicle,* 1987.

There is no right to strike against the public safety by anybody, anywhere, any time.

CALVIN COOLIDGE, telegram to Samuel Gompers regarding Boston police strike, September 14, 1919.

One of the chief arguments used in support of the policy of an open shop is that every man has an inalienable and constitutional right to work. I never found that in the Constitution.

CLARENCE DARROW, *The Railroad Trainman,* November, 1909.

Every man has the inalienable right to work.

ATTRIBUTED TO EUGENE V. DEBS.

The workers are the saviors of society, the redeemers of the race.

EUGENE V. DEBS, speech, New York City, December 10, 1905.

If the unemployed could eat plans and promises they would be able to spend the winter on the Riviera.

W.E.B. DU BOIS, "As the Crow Flies," *Crisis,* January, 1931.

We'll never recognize the United Auto Workers Union or any other union.

HENRY FORD, 1937, in Lois and Alan Gordon, *American Chronicle,* 1987.

As to the great mass of working girls and women, how much independence is gained if the narrowness and lack of freedom of the home are exchanged for the narrowness and lack of freedom of the factory, sweatshop, department store, or office?

EMMA GOLDMAN, "The Tragedy of Women's Emancipation," *Anarchism and Other Essays,* 1911.

The labor of a human being is not a commodity or article of commerce. You can't weigh the soul of a man with a bar of pig iron.

SAMUEL GOMPERS, *Seventy Years of Life and Labor,* 1925.

Adam Smith was wrong. Individuals working for their own best interests are not good for the whole country. American management and labor are only hurting each other and themselves by adopting adversarial roles. While Americans are fighting with each other, the rest of the world will walk right by us economically.

ANONYMOUS REPLY, competitiveness survey, *Harvard Business Review*, September/October, 1987.

I will die like a true-blue rebel. Don't waste any time in mourning—organize.

BIG BILL HAYWOOD, farewell telegram before death, November 18, 1915.

We are here to confederate the workers of this country into a working-class movement that shall have for its purpose the emancipation of the working class from the slave bondage of capitalism.... This organization will be formed, based and founded on the class struggle, having in view no compromise and no surrender, and but one object and one purpose and that is to bring the workers of this country into the possession of the full value of their toil.

BIG BILL HAYWOOD, to Continental Congress of the Working Class, Chicago, June 27, 1905.

There is no doubt that the most competitive manufacturers are those who have learned to produce more with fewer people.

EDWARD L. HENNESSY, JR., *New York Times*, March 13, 1988.

Work and pray, live on hay,

You'll get pie in the sky when you die.

JOE HILL, labor song, "The Preacher and the Slave," ca. 1910.

The American labor force is composed of the most uncommon collection of rugged individualists ever assembled for mutual cause. They like to do their own griping and to solve their own problems. They do not want outside help and instinctively resist it. They were never "joiners"—and that included unions.

JIMMY HOFFA, *The Trials of Jimmy Hoffa*, 1970.

In the old days all you needed was a handshake. Nowadays you need forty lawyers.

JIMMY HOFFA, *Hoffa: The Real Story*, 1975.

The working class and the employing class have nothing in common. There can be no peace so long as hunger and want are found among millions of working people and the few, who make up the employing class, have all the good things

of life. Between these two classes a struggle must go on until all the toilers come together on the political, as well as on the industrial field, and take and hold that which they produce by their labor, through an economic organization of the working class without affiliation with any political party.

PREAMBLE TO CONSTITUTION OF INDUSTRIAL WORKERS OF THE WORLD, Chicago, Illinois, June, 1905.

"Why is it?" I asked. "Why is it that so many workers live in unspeakable misery?" With their hands they have built great cities and they cannot be sure of a roof over their heads. With their hands they have opened mines and dragged forth with the strength of their bodies the buried sunshine of dead forests, and they are cold. They have gone down into the bowels of the earth for diamonds and gold, and they have no money for a loaf of bread. With their hands they erect temples and palaces and their habitation is a crowded room in a tenement. They plough and sow and fill our hands with flowers while their own are full of husks.

HELEN KELLER, *The Woman Rebel*, April, 1914.

Modern cynics and skeptics...see no harm in paying those to whom they entrust the minds of their children a smaller wage than is paid to those to whom they entrust the care of their plumbing.

JOHN F. KENNEDY, speech, 90th anniversary of Vanderbilt University, May 19, 1963.

No tin hat brigade of goose-stepping vigilantes or Bible-babbling mob of blackguarding and corporation-paid scoundrels will prevent the onward march of labor.

JOHN L. LEWIS, *Time*, September 9, 1937.

The program of the CIO has a two-fold purpose. The first is to bring security and liberty to those who work for their living. In achieving this it is our conviction that we implement the second purpose, the creation of economic and social stability. It is only upon such economic stability that a lasting democratic form of government can exist.

JOHN L. LEWIS, speech, First Constitutional Convention of Committee for Industrial Organization, November 14, 1938.

The effort to build up unions is as much the work of pioneers as the extension of civilization into the wilderness. The unions are the first feeble effort to conquer the industrial jungle for democratic life.

WALTER LIPPMANN, *Drift and Mastery*, 1914.

The working class is loyal to friends, not ideas.

NORMAN MAILER, *The Armies of the Night*, 1968.

Anyone who possesses a natural right may make use of all legitimate means to protect it, and to safeguard it from violation.

WILLIAM CARDINAL O'CONNELL, pastoral letter, November 23, 1912.

The worker has the right to refuse to work, that is, to strike, and to induce by peaceful and lawful methods others to strike with him.

WILLIAM CARDINAL O'CONNELL, pastoral letter, November 23, 1912.

When I get thinking about this dangerous union thing, this empire of the irresponsible which President Roosevelt has set up in this country, I find that I am more afraid of that than of Hitler.

WESTBROOK PEGLER, column, "Fair Enough," ca. 1943.

55 HOURS OR NOTHING!

SIGN CARRIED BY STRIKING CHILDREN, Philadelphia textile mills, 1903.

If the great laboring masses of people, black and white, are kept forever snarling over the question as to who is superior or inferior, they will…take a long time to combine for achievement of a common benefit.

ASA PHILIP RANDOLPH, "Segregation in Public Schools," *The Messenger*, June, 1924.

No labor leader can deliver the vote. If any labor leader says he can deliver the vote he is kidding you or himself. He can influence and try to mobilize his people around issues, and they will deliver the vote.

WALTER REUTHER, *The Nation*, December 3, 1952.

A living wage includes not merely decent maintenance for the present but also a reasonable provision for such future needs as sickness, invalidity, and old age.

ROMAN CATHOLIC ARCHBISHOPS AND BISHOPS OF UNITED STATES, pastoral letter, February 22, 1920.

I see an America where the workers are really free and through their great unions, undominated by any outside force or any dictator within, can take their proper place in the council tables with the owners and managers of business.

FRANKLIN D. ROOSEVELT, speech, Democratic National Convention, June 27, 1936.

It is essential that there should be organization of labor. This is an era of organization. Capital organizes and therefore labor must organize.

THEODORE ROOSEVELT, speech, Milwaukee, Wisconsin, October 14, 1912.

Where the employer and the union enjoy equal bargaining power a mediator is more often able to arrange an equitable settlement.

IRWIN ROSS, "Labor Mediators," *Harper's*, May, 1941.

I do not believe that a shorter work year will be achieved through a four-day week for most people—I am not sure that wives want their husbands underfoot that much.

GEORGE P. SHULTZ, *American Way*, 1970.

The story of women's work in gainful employments is a story of constant changes or shiftings of work and workshops, accompanied by long hours, low wages, unsanitary conditions, overwork, and the want on the part of the woman of training, skill, and vital interest in her work.

HELEN L. SUMNER, Senate report, "History of Women in Industry in the United States," 1911.

There is no difference, ethically, between killing a man instantly or slowly over-working or starving him to death.

HERBERT A. THORPE, "A Defense of Assassination," *The Woman Rebel*, July, 1914.

If you become a defender of labor, you become an enemy of capital.

MELVIN B. TOLSON, "Portrait of Jesus, the Young Radical," *Washington Tribune*, July 4, 1938.

Courtesy and respectful treatment of labor is now routine, is expected, and there is trouble if it doesn't come.

JACOB VINER, in Arthur Goodfriend, *What Is America?*, 1954.

Unemployed purchasing power means unemployed labor and unemployed labor means human want in the midst of plenty. This is the most challenging paradox of modern times.

HENRY A. WALLACE, speech, 1934.

The great struggling unknown masses of the men who are at the base of everything are the dynamic force that is lifting the levels of society. A nation is as great, and only as great, as her rank and file.

WOODROW WILSON, in W.B. Hale, comp., *The New Freedom*, 1913.

The eight-hour day now undoubtedly has the sanction of the judgment of society in its favor and should be adopted as a basis for wages even where the actual work to be done cannot be completed within eight hours.

WOODROW WILSON, speech to press, August 19, 1916.

If the so-called revolutionary labor movement must justify its actions at the bar of the very public opinion and morality that have created and sustained laws against labor, it is a wishy washy, milk-and-watery, weakneed [sic] movement at best.

EDITORIAL, *The Woman Rebel*, July, 1914.

PEACE AND DISARMAMENT

I ain't got no quarrel with those Vietcong. They never called me "nigger."

MUHAMMAD ALI, 1966, *National Enquirer*, March 25, 1980.

The point was that there were people who could destroy mankind and that they were foolish and arrogant, crazy, and must be begged not to do it. Let the enemies of life step down. Let each man now examine his heart. Without a great change of heart, I would not trust myself in a position of authority. Do I love mankind? Enough to spare it, if I should be in a position to blow it to hell? Now let us all dress in our shrouds and walk on Washington and Moscow. Let us lie down, men, women, and children, and cry, "Let life continue—we may not deserve it, but let it continue."

SAUL BELLOW, *Herzog*, 1964.

To what central cause can one attribute such enormous dissent and resistance? The power structure calls it a breakdown of law and order, but those who resist say it stems from a breakdown of law and justice. Which is to say—their conclusion is essentially the same as that of those resisting abroad. Both feel that the American power structure is, by and large, lawless, and that it must be made lawful.

DANIEL BERRIGAN, "Statement at Sentencing," *Prison Journals*, May 24, 1968.

Peace is the skillful management of conflict.

KENNETH BOULDING, "A National Peace Academy," *Beasts, Ballads, and Bouldingisms*, 1977.

War is an invention of the human mind. The human mind can invent peace with justice.

NORMAN COUSINS, *Who Speaks for Man?*, 1952.

Just as it would be stupid to plant weeds and try to harvest vegetables, so it would be stupid to encourage the lies, conscription, and murder of war, and hope to produce democracy, freedom, and brotherhood.

DAVE DELLINGER, on entering prison for refusing to serve in public service camp, 1943.

As long as armies exist, any serious conflict will lead to war. A pacifism which does not actively fight against the armament of nations is and must remain impotent.

ALBERT EINSTEIN, *The World as I See It*, 1934.

By its existence, the Peace Movement denies that governments know best; it stands for a different order of priorities: the human race comes first.

MARTHA GELLHORN, "Conclusion," *The Face of War*, 1988.

[Peace:] An idea which seems to have originated in Switzerland but has never caught hold in the United States. Supporters of this idea are frequently accused of being unpatriotic and trying to create civil disorder.

DICK GREGORY, *Dick Gregory's Political Primer*, 1972.

I would suggest that Quakers have done their share to make the country what it is…and that I had not supposed hitherto that we regretted our inability to expel them because they believe more than some of us do in the teachings of the Sermon on the Mount.

OLIVER WENDELL HOLMES, JR., opinion, on conscientious objection, *United States* v. *Schwimmer*, 1929.

There is no way to peace. Peace is the way.

A.J. MUSTE, *New York Times*, November 16, 1967.

The pacifist is as surely a traitor to his country and to humanity as is the most brutal wrongdoer.

THEODORE ROOSEVELT, speech, Pittsburgh, Pennsylvania July 27, 1917.

Defeat would be bad enough, but victory would be intolerable.

HUNTER S. THOMPSON, on dilemma of Florida police before Vietnam veterans' march on 1972 Republican National Convention, *Fear and Loathing on the Campaign Trail, '72*, 1973.

When I realize what a vast amount of time the world would have for useful and sensible tasks if each country could take its mind off "the enemy," I am appalled.

E.B. WHITE, "A Report in January," January 30, 1958, *Essays of E.B. White*, 1977.

It will be a great day when our schools get all the money they need and the air force has to hold a bake sale to buy a bomber.

WOMEN'S INTERNATIONAL LEAGUE OF PEACE AND FREEDOM, 1991.

POVERTY AND HUNGER

Private beneficence is totally inadequate to deal with the vast numbers of the city's disinherited.

JANE ADDAMS, *Twenty Years at Hull House*, 1910.

The common stock of intellectual enjoyment should not be difficult of access because of the economic position of him who would approach it.

JANE ADDAMS, *Twenty Years at Hull House*, 1910.

If you've seen one slum, you've seen them all.

SPIRO T. AGNEW, TV interview, Detroit, Michigan, October 6, 1969.

Money talks; it is the only conversation worth hearing when times are bad.

FRED ALLEN, *Much Ado About Me*, 1956.

To smash something is the ghetto's chronic need. Most of the time it is the members of the ghetto who smash each other, and themselves. But as long as the ghetto walls are standing there will always come a moment when these outlets do not work.

JAMES BALDWIN, *Notes of a Native Son*, 1955.

Anyone who has ever struggled with poverty knows how extremely expensive it is to be poor.

JAMES BALDWIN, "Fifth Avenue Uptown," *Esquire*, July, 1960.

Hunger makes a thief of any man.

PEARL S. BUCK, *The Good Earth*, 1931.

Squeamishness was never yet bred in an empty pocket.

JAMES BRANCH CABELL, *The Cream of the Jest*, 1917.

"Crisis" seems to be too mild a word to describe conditions in countless African-American communities. It is beyond crisis when in the richest nation in the world, African Americans in Harlem live shorter lives than the people of Bangladesh, one of the poorest nations of the world.

JOHNETTA B. COLE, speech, NAACP convention, Los Angeles, California, July 9, 1990.

Poverty breeds lack of self-reliance.

DANIEL DELEON, *Two Pages from Roman History*, 1903.

Just because a child's parents are poor or uneducated is no reason to deprive the child of basic human rights to health care, education, proper nutrition. Clearly we ignore the needs of black children, poor children, and handicapped children in the country.

MARIAN WRIGHT EDELMAN, in article by Margie Cassady, "Society's Push-Out Children," *Psychology Today*, June, 1975.

When society does step in to help out a poor woman attempting to raise children on her own, all that it customarily has to offer is some government-surplus cheese, a monthly allowance so small it would barely keep a yuppie male in running shoes, and the contemptuous epithet "welfare cheat." It would be far more reasonable to honor the survivors of pregnancy and childbirth with at least some respect and special benefits that we give, without a second thought, to veterans of foreign wars.

BARBARA EHRENREICH, *New York Times*, February 7, 1985.

The "discovery" of poverty at the beginning of the 1960s was something like the "discovery" of America almost five hundred years earlier. In the case of these exotic terrains, plenty of people were on the site before the discoverers ever arrived.

BARBARA EHRENREICH, *Fear of Falling*, 1990.

I used to think I was poor. Then they told me I wasn't poor, I was needy. They told me it was self-defeating to think of myself as needy, I was deprived. Then they told me underprivileged was overused. I was disadvantaged. I still don't have a dime. But I have a great vocabulary.

JULES FEIFFER, cartoon, in William Safire, *Safire's Political Dictionary*, 1965.

The children who go to bed hungry in a Harlem slum or a West Virginia mining town are not being deprived because no food can be found to give them; they are going to bed hungry because, despite all our miracles of invention and production, we have not yet found a way to make the necessities of life available to all of our citizens— including those whose failure is not lack of personal industry or initiative, but only an unwise choice of parents.

J. WILLIAM FULBRIGHT, *Old Myths and New Realities*, 1964.

It is an elementary mark of sophistication always to mistrust the man who blames on revolutionaries what should be attributed to deprivation.

JOHN KENNETH GALBRAITH, "Poverty and the Way People Behave," 1965.

The figures proved that the absolute easiest way to be poor is to be born out of wedlock to a young woman. If you need a statistic to memorize, try this one: 92.8 percent of all children in black, single, female-headed families where the mother is under thirty and did not complete high school, are in poverty.

ELLEN GOODMAN, "Celebrity Moms," *Washington Post*, May, 1985.

There are tens of millions of Americans who are beyond the welfare state. Taken as a whole there is a culture of poverty...bad health, poor housing, low levels of aspiration and high levels of mental distress. Twenty per cent of a nation, some 32,000,000.

MICHAEL HARRINGTON, *The Culture of Poverty*, 1971.

Our affluent [American] society contains those of talent and insight who are driven to prefer poverty, to choose it, rather than to submit to the desolation of an empty abundance.

MICHAEL HARRINGTON, *The Other America: Poverty in the United States*, 1962.

America has the best-dressed poverty the world has ever known....It is much easier in the United States to be decently dressed than it is to be decently housed, fed, or doctored.

MICHAEL HARRINGTON, *The Other America: Poverty in the United States*, 1962.

Poverty is expensive to maintain.

MICHAEL HARRINGTON, *The Other America: Poverty in the United States*, 1962.

Poor people know poor people, and rich people know rich people. It is one of the few things La Rouchefoucauld did not say, but then La Rouchefoucauld never lived in the Bronx.

Moss Hart, Act One, 1959.

It has been said that there is no law for starving men. This is an error. There is the law of self-preservation, stronger than all man-made laws and which all enactments and legislative decrees cannot destroy.

CATHERINE HOLT, *The Woman Rebel*, March, 1914.

We in America today are nearer to the final triumph over poverty than ever before in the history of any land. The poorhouse is vanishing from among us. We have not yet reached the goal, but given a chance to go forward with the policies of the last eight years, we shall soon, with the help of God, be within sight of the day when poverty shall be banished from this nation.

HERBERT HOOVER, speech accepting Republican presidential nomination, August 11, 1928.

Poverty is now an inhuman anachronism.

HUBERT H. HUMPHREY, *Beyond Civil Rights: A New Day of Equality*, 1968.

Poverty indeed *is* the strenuous life—without brass bands, or uniforms, or hysteric popular applause, or lies, or circumlocutions.

WILLIAM JAMES, *The Varieties of Religious Experience*, 1902.

This administration today, here and now, declares unconditional war on poverty in America. I urge this Congress and all Americans to join with me in that effort. It will not be a short or easy struggle—no single weapon or strategy will suffice—but we shall not rest until that war is won.

LYNDON B. JOHNSON, State of the Union message, January 8, 1964.

The curse of poverty has no justification in our age. It is socially as cruel and blind as the practice of cannibalism at the dawn of civilization, when men ate each other because they had not yet learned to take food from the soil or to consume the abundant animal life around them. The time has come for us to civilize ourselves by the total, direct and immediate abolition of poverty.

MARTIN LUTHER KING, JR., *Where Do We Go from Here: Chaos or Community?*, 1967.

It is obvious that relief is of the scantiest kind and in some districts entirely nonexistent. In one camp the women talked brokenheartedly of a bowel disease which they called 'Flux' that had proved fatal to some of the children and was the result of prolonged underfeeding and efforts to stay the pangs of hunger by devouring chunks of raw cabbage or anything at all which they could lay hands on.

JENNIE LEE, on Kentucky mining camp, 1932, in Lois and Alan Gordon, *American Chronicle*, 1987.

I am for lifting everyone off the social bottom. In fact, I am for doing away with the social bottom altogether.

CLARE BOOTHE LUCE, *Time*, February 14, 1964.

We shall never solve the paradox of want in the midst of plenty by doing away with plenty.

OGDEN MILLS, speech, New York City, March 21, 1934.

I should like to find out at what stage of your poverty other people realize or sense it, and pass you by as one no longer interesting or useful to them....You realize that for the first time in your rather carefree, indifferent life you are worth more dead than alive—a good deal more.

FRANK G. MOORHEAD, *Nation*, 1931.

Our place is beside the poor, behind the working man. They are our people.

GEORGE CARDINAL MUNDELEIN, speech, Chicago, Illinois, January 2, 1938.

[T]he culture of the underclass, increasingly violent and bizarre, fosters alienation. As each new social experiment fails to diminish the size of the underclass, our increasing national wealth will make it possible to bypass the problem by treating the inner city as an urban analogue of the Indian reservation.

CHARLES MURRAY, *National Review*, July 8, 1991.

The economic situation of the Negroes in America is pathological.

GUNNAR MYRDAL, *An American Dilemma*, 1944.

There is no major city in America where you cannot see homeless men sitting in parking lots holding signs that say "I will work for food."

ANN W. RICHARDS, Democratic National Convention, July 18, 1988.

Poverty is a noose that strangles humility and breeds disrespect for God and man.

WILBUR RIEGERT, in Stan Steiner, *The New Indians*, 1968.

I see one-third of a nation ill-housed, ill-clad, ill-nourished.

FRANKLIN D. ROOSEVELT, inaugural address, January 20, 1937.

O, it's plain as your hand. The poor white man and the poor black man is sittin in the same saddle today—big dudes branched em off that way. The control of a man, the controllin power, is in the hands of the rich man....That class is standin together and the poor white man is out there on the colored list—I've caught that: ways and actions a heap of times speaks louder than words.

NATE SHAW, in Theodore Rosengarten, *All God's Dangers: The Life of Nate Shaw*, 1974.

To see the Poor People's March on Washington in perspective, remember that the rich have been marching on Washington ever since the beginning of the Republic. They came in carriages and they come on jets. They don't have to put up in shanties. Their object is the same but few

respectable people are untactful enough to call it handouts.

I.F. STONE, "The Rich March on Washington All the Time," *I.F. Stone's Weekly*, May 13, 1968.

There is no excuse for poverty in a society which can spend $80 billion a year on its war machine. If national security comes first, as the spokesmen for the Pentagon tell us, then we can only reply that the clearest danger to the national security lies in the rising revolt of our black population. Our own country is becoming a Vietnam. As if in retribution for the suffering we have imposed, we are confronted by the same choices: either to satisfy the aspirations of the oppressed or to try and crush them by force.

I.F. STONE, "In Defence of the Campus Rebels," *I.F. Stone's Weekly*, May 19, 1969.

Whatever capital you divert to the support of a shiftless and good-for-nothing person is so much diverted from some other employment, and that means from somebody else.

WILLIAM GRAHAM SUMNER, *The Forgotten Men and Other Essays*, 1919.

[Two million dollars' worth of food to] all people with welfare cards, social security pension cards, food stamps, medical cards, parole or probation papers, and jail or bail release slips.

RANSOM DEMAND BY SYMBIONESE LIBERATION ARMY FOR PATTY HEARST, 1974, in Lois and Alan Gordon, *American Chronicle*, 1987.

Welfare is like a traffic accident. It can happen to anybody, but especially it happens to women.

JOHNNIE TILLMON, "Welfare Is a Women's Issue," in Francine Klagsbrun, ed., *The First Ms. Reader*, 1972.

America cannot afford to have whole areas and communities of people in such dire social and economic circumstances. Not only for her economic well-being, but for her moral well-being as well. America has given a great social and moral message to the world and demonstrated, perhaps not forcefully enough, that freedom and responsibility as an ethic is inseparable from and, in fact, the cause of the fabulous American standard of living. America has not, however, been diligent enough in promulgating this philosophy within her own borders.

CLYDE WARRIOR, testimony, National Advisory Committee on Rural Poverty, Memphis, Tennessee, 1967.

The basic cure for poverty is money.

GEORGE A. WILEY, statement to Democratic platform committee, Chicago, Illinois, 1968.

No one can love his neighbor on an empty stomach.

WOODROW WILSON, speech, New York City, May 23, 1912.

Hunger does not breed reform; it breeds madness, and all the ugly distempers that make an ordered life impossible.

WOODROW WILSON, speech to Congress, November 11, 1918.

PROSTITUTION

COYOTE—Call Off Your Old Tired Ethics.

ACRONYM, prostitutes' rights group.

What it comes down to is this: the grocer, the butcher, the baker, the merchant, the landlord, the druggist, the liquor dealer, the policeman, the doctor, the city father and the politician—these are people who make money out of prostitution, these are the real reapers of the wages of sin.

POLLY ADLER, A House Is Not a Home, 1953.

Whether our reformers admit it or not, the economic and social inferiority of women is responsible for prostitution.

EMMA GOLDMAN, "The Traffic in Women," Anarchism and Other Essays, 1911.

Monogamy and prostitution go together.

KATE MILLETT, The Prostitution Papers, 1971.

The worst part about prostitution is that you're obliged not to sell sex only, but your humanity. That's the worst part of it: that what you're selling is your human dignity. Not really so much in bed, but in accepting the agreement—in becoming a bought person.

KATE MILLETT, The Prostitution Papers, 1971.

The fact that sex is directly linked to money only through prostitution represents the devious way in which society deals with its truths.

KATE MILLETT, The Prostitution Papers, 1971.

Prostitution is really the only crime in the penal law where two people are doing a thing mutually agreed upon and yet only one, the female partner, is subject to arrest.

KATE MILLETT, The Prostitution Papers, 1971.

It is a silly question to ask a prostitute why she does it....These are the highest-paid "professional" women in America.

GAIL SHEEHY, Hustling, 1971.

This is the chief fact about a streetwalker's life. Every night she talks to a hundred potential customers. She has copfaces and plainclothesfaces to memorize, judgefaces to remember how to play, prossfaces to compete with, different faces bear directly on her life. For women it is the nearest thing to war. As in the game of war, all grasp of individual human dignity eventually slips away and all others blur into one common undistinguished face: the enemy.

GAIL SHEEHY, Hustling, 1971.

She was sitting on the stoop. When I walked by, she crossed her legs showing her thighs and winked. I walked over to her. She said: "How about it, hon?" I said: "Christ, kid, if I had any dough I'd rather eat."

M. SHULIMSON, in Albert Maltz, New Masses, 1934.

[P]rostitution continues to flourish for the simple reason that it is needed. If most men and women were forced to rely upon physical charm to attract lovers, their sexual lives would be not only meager but in a youth-worshiping country like America painfully brief.

GORE VIDAL, "Notes on Pornography," New York Review of Books, March 31, 1966.

VIOLENCE

The American Dream is, in part, responsible for a great deal of crime and violence because people feel that the country owes them not only a living but a good living.

DAVID ABRAHAMSEN, San Francisco Examiner & Chronicle, November 18, 1975.

Frustration is the wet nurse of violence.

DAVID ABRAHAMSEN, San Francisco Examiner & Chronicle, November 18, 1975.

Something curious is going on in America. Murder is a growth industry, particularly this special kind of murder, the bogeyman homicide, the sadistic slaying by a stranger who, without comprehensible motive, steps out of the shadows and savages.

JOEL ACHENBACH, Washington Post, April 14, 1991.

The serial killer has become an American Original, a romantic icon, like the cowboy.

JOEL ACHENBACH, Washington Post, April 14, 1991.

Hungry people cannot be good at learning or producing anything, except perhaps violence.

PEARL BAILEY, Pearl's Kitchen, 1973.

We're seeing a new sort of violence. It's being used not as a means to an end, but for recreational purposes, for pleasure.

ARTHUR BEISSER, on violence in sports, *Sports Illustrated*, March 1, 1976.

Violence is as American as cherry pie.

HUBERT GEROLD (H. RAP) BROWN, *Die, Nigger, Die*, 1969.

We are unalterably opposed to the presentation of the female body being stripped, bound, raped, tortured, mutilated and murdered in the name of commercial entertainment and free speech.

SUSAN BROWNMILLER, *Against Our Will: Men, Women and Rape*, 1975.

We, as a nation, have opted to be ruler of the world and all that we survey. And, my friends, however benevolent and kind we might wish to be, the violence that surrounds us in our streets and in our homes and in our world is evidence that we have succumbed to the temptation of the desert. We face a deep and profound spiritual crisis.

JOAN B. CAMPBELL, sermon, Riverside Church, New York City, April 21, 1991.

Shoot to kill.

RICHARD DALEY, 1968, in Lois and Alan Gordon, *American Chronicle*, 1987.

Not only do most people accept violence if it is perpetuated by legitimate authority, they also regard violence against certain kinds of people as inherently legitimate, no matter who commits it.

EDGAR Z. FRIEDENBERG, *New York Review of Books*, October 20, 1966.

Anybody can kill anybody.

LYNETTE (SQUEAKY) FROMME, *Time*, September 15, 1975.

A street thug and a paid killer are professionals—beasts of prey, if you will, who have disassociated themselves from the rest of humanity and can now see human beings in the same way that trout fishermen see trout.

WILLARD GAYLIN, *The Killing of Bonnie Garland*, 1982.

In the attempt to distance ourselves from violence, to seek out a safe emotional suburb far from the inner city, we have long tagged family abuse by race and class and place. But when that doesn't work, we hunt to find another difference between us and them, a line that promises to keep danger remote.

ELLEN GOODMAN, "Hedda Nussbaum: The Woman with a Punch-bag Face," *Washington Post*, December, 1988.

Violence? I don't think of it as violence. I think of it as contact. And contact is a part of life.

"MEAN JOE" GREENE, Pittsburgh Steeler, *New York Times Magazine*, November 30, 1980.

Based on some estimates, guns are statistically like rats. They outnumber our population. Not surprisingly, our output of ammunition for civilian firearms almost staggers the imagination. American industry outdoes all other nations in the production of bullets. Nearly 5 billion rounds of ammunition flow through the marketplace each year. That is enough, laid end to end, to stretch a bandoleer of ammunition three times around the equator. All of those bullets could not only wipe out the world's entire human population, but they could decimate practically most of the world's species of wildlife.

EDWARD M. KENNEDY, speech to U.S. Senate, February 17, 1971, in Thomas P. Collins and Louis M. Savary, eds., *A People of Compassion*, 1972.

Violence is an admission that one's ideas and goals cannot prevail on their own merits.

EDWARD M. KENNEDY, June 10, 1970, in Thomas P. Collins and Louis M. Savary, eds., *A People of Compassion*, 1972.

Man was born into barbarism when killing his fellow man was a normal condition of existence. He became endowed with a conscience. And he has now reached the day when violence toward another human being must become as abhorrent as eating another's flesh.

MARTIN LUTHER KING, JR., *Why We Can't Wait*, 1963.

Nonviolence is the answer to the crucial political and moral questions of our time: the need for man to overcome oppression and violence without resorting to oppression and violence. Man must evolve for all human conflict a method which rejects revenge, aggression and retaliation. The foundation of such a method is love.

MARTIN LUTHER KING, JR., Nobel Prize acceptance speech, Stockholm, Sweden, December 11, 1964.

The limitation of riots, moral questions aside, is that they cannot win and their participants know it. Hence, rioting is not revolutionary but reactionary because it invites defeat. It involves an emotional catharsis, but it must be followed by a sense of futility.

MARTIN LUTHER KING, JR., *The Trumpet of Conscience*, 1967.

When violent death comes to the prosperous suburbs, it comes clanking into the room dressed in Darth Vader's black armor, a terrible apparition born of trolls and risen from the abyss. Seen in the remote distance of the Third World, death loses its hideous visage and wears the livery of a meek and courteous statistic.

LEWIS H. LAPHAM, "Realpolitik," *Los Angeles Times*, October, 1983.

A society that presumes a norm of violence and celebrates aggression, whether in the subway, on the football field, or in the conduct of its business, cannot help making celebrities of the people who would destroy it.

LEWIS H. LAPHAM, "Citizen Goetz," *Harper's*, March, 1985.

Action, swiftness, violence, power: these are native, homegrown American qualities, derived from the vast continent that has been ours to open up, and the big prizes that have made our economy into a jungle where the law is eat or be eaten.

MAX LERNER, "Violence Without Meaning," *Actions and Passions*, 1949.

The proclivity for extraordinary violence is not just an ailment of the mind, as psychologists like to think. Nor is it only a malaise of the society, as sociologists believe. It is both of these things, but is is also a sickness of the body as distinct and definite as cancer or leprosy.

VERNON H. MARK, *Life*, August, 1984.

The eternal man in the street says the street's no place for anyone anymore.

EDITORIAL, *New York Times*, December 29, 1980.

Unnecessary, unwarranted, and inexcusable.

SCRANTON REPORT, on the Kent State shootings, 1970, in Lois and Alan Gordon, *American Chronicle*, 1987.

Apart from insuring our country's survival, there can be no higher national priority than controlling domestic violence. The first duty of government is to protect the citizen from assault. Unless it does this, all the civil rights and civil liberties in the world aren't worth a dime.

RICHARD A. VIGUERIE, *The New Right—We're Ready to Lead*, 1981.

Violence is a tool of the ignorant.

FLIP WILSON, interview, *Ebony*, April, 1968.

Sports

See also **Americans on Americans**—Sports Figures; **Ethics and Morality; The Human Condition**—Competitiveness, Courage, Fame; **Social Issues**—Drugs and Alcohol, Health, Violence; **Work**—Athletes

Sport develops not character, but characters.

ANONYMOUS, in James A. Michener, *Sports in America*, 1976.

Sports and politics do mix. Behind the scenes, the two are as inextricably interwoven as any two issues can be. I'm sure politics are involved when teams get franchises or when cities build stadiums. It is unrealistic to say you shouldn't bring politics into sports.

ARTHUR ASHE, *New York Times*, October 6, 1977.

In America it is sports that is the opiate of the masses.

RUSSELL BAKER, *New York Times*, October 3, 1967.

People are frustrated these days. The times are vexing, the inflation ever escalating, the problems of daily living overwhelming. Sports, for the masses, are a prime means of escape from those problems. It is at the playing arena that people can let their emotions loose, or at least so they think.

HOWARD COSELL, *Like It Is*, 1974.

I believe in rules. Sure I do. If there weren't any rules, how could you break them?

LEO DUROCHER, *Nice Guys Finish Last*, 1975.

"How you play the game" is for college boys. When you're playing for money, winning is the only thing that matters. Show me a good loser in professional sports, and I'll show you an idiot. Show me a sportsman, and I'll show you a player I'm looking to trade to Oakland.

LEO DUROCHER, *Nice Guys Finish Last*, 1975.

I went to two high school all-star games recently where the kids had no affiliation or stake in the game. It was a chance for them to show how good they are....Instead, the kids were like thugs. They needed to show their virility. I see that behavior in the colleges and pros. The gestures and putdowns of the opposition. It's come

to symbolize excellence. I try to tell my kids the game is for fun, not humiliation.

VIC GATTO, *New York Times*, October 27, 1982.

O, Sovereign Owners and Princely Players, masters of amortization, tax shelters, bonuses and deferred compensation, go back to work. You have been entrusted with the serious work of play, and your season of responsibility has come.

A. BARTLETT GIAMATTI, *New York Times*, June 16, 1981.

I won't mention the name of this particular team we were playing, but at half time we came in, pulled off our socks and began putting iodine on the teeth marks in our legs.

RED GRANGE, *Sunday News Magazine*, January 6, 1980.

We all played poorly. It wasn't just one guy's fault. It was a real team effort.

ARNETTE HALLMAN, *New York Daily News*, April 23, 1980.

Anyone who will tear down sports will tear down America. Sports and religion have made America what it is today.

WOODY HAYES, in Bill Bradley, *Life on the Run*, 1976.

Winning is the epitome of honesty itself.

WOODY HAYES, *New York Times*, September 26, 1977.

On a good team there are no superstars. There are great players, who show they are great players by being able to play with others, as a team. They have the ability to be superstars, but if they fit into a good team, they make sacrifices, they do the things necessary to help the team win. What the numbers are in salaries or statistics don't matter; how they play together does.

RED HOLZMAN, *New York Times*, January 23, 1977.

The apologists of athleticism have created a collection of myths to convince the public that biceps is a substitute for brains.

ROBERT M. HUTCHINS, "Gate Receipts and Glory," *The Saturday Evening Post*, December 3, 1938.

It's like Noah's wife told him. She said, "Noah, honey, it's going to stop raining one of these days."

MIKE KRUKOW, *Sports Illustrated,* May 9, 1977.

Winning isn't everything. It's the only thing.

VINCE LOMBARDI, in Jerry Kramer, *Instant Replay,* 1968.

Kid, just go down there and throw yourself on the fire.

ANDY MCDONALD, to Steve Raible, *New York Times,* November 14, 1976.

Happiness in sports is winning on the road.

AL MCGUIRE, *New York Post,* March 29, 1977.

In this country, when you finish second, no one knows your name.

FRANK MCGUIRE, in James A. Michener, *Sports in America,* 1976.

I think the public today is ready to accept a new view of sports. Grantland Rice described Notre Dame's backfield as the Four Horsemen of the Apocalypse. Hell, today they look to me like nothing more than four guys who are probably flunking algebra.

JIM MURRAY, *Newsweek,* July 1, 1968.

The arrogance of the owners and their lack of sensitivity toward their fans is accelerating. They never ask the fans what they think of the policies and rules these owners set. And the fans have a right to know the full costs they are paying, as taxpayers, for the municipal stadiums most of them can't get into, even if they could afford a ticket.

RALPH NADER, announcing new consumer group, to be called FANS (Fight to Advance the Nation's Sports), *New York Times,* September 28, 1977.

Sports becomes for [team owners] diversions, more financial success, or a tax write-off. They get great competitive advantages from the Government, either directly or indirectly, while the fan faces nothing but higher ticket prices and even higher parking, hot dog and beer prices.

WILLIAM PROXMIRE, *New York Times,* September l, 1974.

I don't communicate with players. I tell them what to do. I don't understand the meaning of communication.

PAUL RICHARDS, *New York Times,* July 11, 1976.

Win this one for the Gipper.

ATTRIBUTED TO KNUTE ROCKNE, comments to Notre Dame football team, 1921.

I myself would like to see more white athletes. I think they are overlooking a good profession. I don't think it is good for the league to have all-black teams and 95% white audiences.

TED STEPIEN, *New York Daily News,* February 1, 1981.

I'm not sure [whether] I'd rather be managing or testing bulletproof vests.

JOE TORRE, *New York Times,* May 21, 1981.

Professional sports add something to the spirit and vitality of a city. They are a reflection of the city's image of itself. I don't simply believe that; I know it. A winning team can bring a city together, and even a losing team can provide a bond of common misery.

BILL VEECK, *Thirty Tons a Day,* 1972.

I don't know what other people feel like when their team loses. But I've got a pain inside.

CHARLEY WINNER, *New York Times,* October 21, 1975.

Four centuries of oppression,...hopes,...[and] bitterness...were rising to the surface. Yes, unconsciously [the young]...imputed to the brawny image of Joe Louis all the balked dreams of revenge...AND HE HAD WON!....Here's the real dynamite that Joe Louis uncovered!

RICHARD WRIGHT, 1935, in Lois and Alan Gordon, *American Chronicle,* 1987.

BASEBALL

Kill him! He hasn't got any friends.

CRY DIRECTED AT UMPIRES, ca. 1910.

Say it ain't so, Joe.

SMALL BOY TO "SHOELESS JOE" JACKSON AFTER NEWS OF CHICAGO BLACK SOX SCANDAL, 1919, *Los Angeles Times,* October 7, 1979.

When I was 4, I learned that Santa Claus didn't exist. When I was 9, I found out my father didn't know everything. When the Dodgers left I was 20, and things have never been the same.

MARTY ADLER, on Dodgers' move from Brooklyn to Los Angeles, 1957, *American Way,* October 15, 1986.

I guess the first thing I ought to say is that I thank everybody for making this day necessary.

YOGI BERRA, on being inducted into baseball's Hall of Fame, *New York Times,* August 8, 1972.

Washington [Senators] first in war, first in peace, last in the American League.

HOWARD COSELL, *Like It Is,* 1974.

Not only that, but the Pirates were in the cellar again. They lived in the cellar, like trolls. They hadn't won a pennant since 1927. Nobody could even remember when they won ball games, the bums. They had some hitters, but no pitchers.

ANNIE DILLARD, *An American Childhood*, 1987.

The Giants is dead.

CHARLEY DRESSEN, ca. 1949.

Baseball is a game of race, creed, and color. The race is to first base. The creed is the rules of the game. The color? Well, the home team wears white uniforms, and the visiting team wears gray.

JOE GARAGIOLA, *Baseball Is a Funny Game*, 1960.

Baseball gives you every chance to be great. Then it puts every pressure on you to prove that you haven't got what it takes. It never takes away the chance, and it never eases up on the pressure.

JOE GARAGIOLA, *Baseball Is a Funny Game*, 1960.

Pitchers aren't athletes.

CHUCK HILLER, *New York Post*, October 8, 1977.

The new definition of a heathen is a man who has never played baseball.

ELBERT HUBBARD, *The Roycroft Dictionary and Book of Epigrams*, 1923.

No baseball fan has to explain his mania to any other baseball fan. They are a fraternity. It is less easy, often it is hopeless, to try to explain it to anyone else. You grow technical, and you do not make sense. You grow sentimental, and you are deemed soft in the head. How, the benighted outsider asks you with no little condescension, can you grow sentimental about a cold-blooded professional sport?

JOHN K. HUTCHENS, "Confessions of a Baseball Fan," *New York Times Magazine*, July 14, 1946.

A race track swarms with sweaty oafs intent on getting something for nothing and sullen if they fail. A fight crowd is exciting and excited, and vaguely pathologic. But a baseball crowd, excepting the stray cranks and exhibitionists, is a neighborly lot.

JOHN K. HUTCHENS, "Confessions of a Baseball Fan," *New York Times Magazine*, July 14, 1946.

I'd rather hit than have sex. To hit is to show strength....God, do I love to hit that little round sum-bitch out of the park and make 'em say "Wow!"

REGGIE JACKSON, *Sports Illustrated*, June 3, 1974.

Regardless of the verdict of juries, no player that throws a ball game, no player that entertains proposals or promises to throw a game, no player that sits in a conference with a bunch of crooked players and gamblers where the ways and means of throwing games are discussed, and does not promptly tell his club about it, will ever again play professional baseball.

KENESAW MOUNTAIN LANDIS, on Chicago Black Sox scandal, August, 1921, in Joseph Durso, *Casey*, 1967.

I had bad days on the field. But I didn't take them home with me. I left them in a bar along the way home.

BOB LEMON, *New York Times*, August 15, 1976.

Records are made to be broken.

BASEBALL SAYING, in Fred Lieb, *Baseball as I Have Known It*, 1977.

If I had had the attitude that I had to play every day to be happy, I wouldn't be here right now.... I'd rather be a swing man on a championship team than a regular on another team.

LOU PINIELLA, *New York Times*, May 11, 1978.

Listen, I was the first black manager in baseball and there was incredible pressure. I don't blame anyone else. I was too tough...I lacked patience. But we had a rough situation, too. It was my first job as a manager and I wanted to win—badly. I probably got on guys a little too hard, with the wrong tone of voice.

FRANK ROBINSON, *Sports*, August, 1981.

Ninety feet between bases is perhaps as close as man has ever gotten to perfection.

RED SMITH, "60 Minutes," CBS-TV, March, 1981.

Baseball is an allegorical play about America, a poetic, complex and subtle play of courage, fear, good luck, mistakes, patience about fate and sober self-esteem (batting average). It is impossible to understand America without a thorough knowledge of baseball.

SAUL STEINBERG, "Chronology," 1954, in Harold Rosenberg, *Saul Steinberg*, 1978.

Don't cut my throat. I may want to do that later myself.

CASEY STENGEL, 1935, after Brooklyn Dodgers lost doubleheader, in Joseph Durso, *Casey*, 1967.

I couldn'ta done it without my players.

CASEY STENGEL, *Sports Illustrated*, October 13, 1975.

Look at that guy. Can't hit, can't run, can't catch. Of course, that's why they gave him to us.

CASEY STENGEL, *New York Daily News*, April 23, 1981.

Bud: You know, strange as it may seem, they give ballplayers peculiar names nowadays. On the St. Louis team Who's on first, What's on second, I Don't Know is on third.

Lou: That's what I want to find out. I want you to tell me the names of the fellows on the St. Louis team.

Bud: I'm telling you. Who's on first, What's on second, I Don't Know is on third.

Lou: You know the fellows' names?

Bud: Yes.

Lou: Well, then, who's playin' first?

Bud: Yes.

Lou: I mean the fellow's name on first base.

Bud: Who.

Lou: The fellow's name on first base for St. Louis.

Bud: Who.

Lou: The guy on first base.

Bud: Who is on first base.

Lou: Well, what are you askin' me for?

Bud: I'm not asking you, I'm telling you. Who is on first.

Lou: I'm askin' you, who is on first?

Bud: That's the man's name.

Lou: That's whose name?

Bud: Yes.

Lou: Well, go ahead, tell me.

Bud: Who.

Lou: The guy on first.

Bud: Who.

Lou: The first baseman.

Bud: Who is on first.

Lou (a new approach): Have you got a first baseman on first?

Bud: Certainly.

Lou: Well, all I'm tryin' to find out is what's the guy's name on first base.

Bud: Oh, no, no. What is on *second* base.

Lou: I'm not askin' you who's on second.

Bud: Who's on first.

Lou: That's what I'm tryin' to find out.

Bud: Well, don't change the players around.

Lou (tension mounting): I'm not changin' anybody.

Bud: Now take it easy.

Lou: What's the guy's name on first base?

Bud: What's the guy's name on *second* base.

Lou: I'm not askin' you who's on second.

Bud: Who's on first.

Lou: I don't know.

Bud: He's on third. We're not talking about him.

Lou (imploringly): How could I get on third base?

Bud: You mentioned his name.

Lou: If I mentioned the third baseman's name, who did I say is playing third?

Bud (insistently): No, Who's playing first.

Lou: Stay offa first, will ya?

Bud: Please, now what is it you'd like to know?

Lou: What is the fellow's name on third base?

Bud: What is the fellow's name on *second* base.

Lou: I'm not asking ya who's on second.

Bud: Who's on first.

Lou: I don't know.

Bud and Lou in unison: Third base!

Lou (trying a new tack): You got an outfield?

Bud: Certainly.

Lou: St. Louis got a good outfield?

Bud: Oh, absolutely.

Lou: The left fielder's name?

Bud: Why.

Lou: I don't know. I just thought I'd ask.

Bud: Well, I just thought I'd tell you.

Lou: Then tell me who's playing left field.

Bud: Who's playing first.

Lou: Stay outa the infield!

Bud: Don't mention any names out here.

Lou (firmly): I wanta know what's the fellow's name in left field.

Bud: What is on second.

Lou: I'm not askin' you who's on second.

Bud: Who is on first.

Lou: I don't know!

Bud and Lou: Third base!

(Lou begins making noises.)

Bud: Now take it easy, man.

Lou: And the left fielder's name?

Bud: Why.

Lou: Because.

Bud: Oh, he's center field.

Lou: Wait a minute. You got a pitcher on the team?

Bud: Wouldn't this be a fine team without a pitcher?

Lou: I dunno. Tell me the pitcher's name.

Bud: Tomorrow.

Lou: You don't want to tell me today?

Bud: I'm telling you, man.

Lou: Then go ahead.

Bud: Tomorrow.

Lou: What time?

Bud: What time what?

Lou: What time tomorrow are you gonna tell me who's pitching?

Bud: Now listen, Who is not pitching. Who is on—

Lou (excitedly): I'll break your arm if you say who is on first!

Bud: Then why come up here and ask?

Lou: I want to know what's the pitcher's name!

Bud: What's on second.

Lou (resigned): I don't know.

Bud: Third base.

Lou: You gotta catcher?

Bud: Yes.

Lou: The catcher's name.

Bud: Today.

Lou: Today. And Tomorrow's pitching.

Bud: Now you've got it.

Lou: That's all. St. Louis got a couple of days on their team. That's all.

Bud: Well, I can't help that. What do you want me to do?

Lou: Gotta catcher?

Bud: Yes.

Lou: I'm a good catcher, too, you know.

Bud: I know that.

Lou: I would like to play for St. Louis.

Bud: Well, I might arrange that.

Lou: I would like to catch. Now Tomorrow's pitching on the team and I'm catching.

Bud: Yes.

Lou: Tomorrow throws the ball and the guy up bunts the ball.

Bud: Yes.

Lou: So when he bunts the ball, me, bein' a good catcher, I want to throw the guy out at first base. So I pick up the ball and throw it to who?

Bud: Now that's the first thing you've said right!

Lou: *I don't even know what I'm talking about!*

Bud: Well, that's all you have to do.

Lou: I throw it to first base.

Bud: Yes.

Lou: Now who's got it?

Bud: Naturally.

Lou: Who has it?

Bud: Naturally.

Lou: Naturally.

Bud: Naturally.

Lou: I throw the ball to Naturally.

Bud: You throw it to Who.

Lou: Naturally.

Bud: Naturally, well, say it that way.

Lou: That's what I'm saying!

Bud: Now don't get excited, don't get excited.

Lou: I throw the ball to first base.

Bud: Then who gets it.

Lou: He'd better get it!

Bud: That's it. All right now, don't get excited. Take it easy.

Lou (frenzied): Now I throw the ball to first base, whoever it is grabs the ball, so the guy runs to second.

Bud: Uh-huh.

Lou: Who picks up the ball and throws it to What. What throws it to I Don't Know. I Don't Know throws it back to Tomorrow. A triple play!

Bud: Yeah, it could be.

Lou: Another guy gets up and it's a long fly ball to center. Why? I don't know. And I don't care.

Bud: What was that?

Lou: I said, I don't care.

Bud: Oh, that's our shortstop.

Bud Abbott and Lou Costello, "Who's on First" routine, ca. 1940.

Rooting for the Yankees is like rooting for U.S. Steel.

BILL VEECK, *The Hustler's Handbook*, 1965.

Baseball is not the sport of the wealthy, it is the sport of the wage earner.

BILL VEECK, *The Hustler's Handbook*, 1965.

Baseball's unique possession, the real source of our strength, is the fan's memory of the times his daddy took him to the game to see the great players of his youth. Whether he remembers it or not, the excitement of those hours, the step they represented in his own growth and the part those afternoons—even *one* afternoon—played in his relationship with his own father is bound up in his feeling toward the local ball club and toward the game. When he takes his own son to the game, as his father once took him, there is a spanning of the generations that is warm and rich, and—if I may use the word—lovely.

BILL VEECK, *The Hustler's Handbook*, 1965.

Take me out to the ball game,

Take me out with the crowd.

Buy me some peanuts and Cracker Jack,

I don't care if I never get back.

ALBERT VON TILZER AND JACK NORWORTH, song, "Take Me Out to the Ball Game," 1908.

BASKETBALL

The dunk has come back. It's more than just a basket. It's like a slap in the face [to the defender]. You do it on the playgrounds and you try to do it again and a guy will low-bridge you. 'Cause you're hitting at his pride. A slap in the face is worse than a punch in the face.

FRED "MAD DOG" CARTER, *Basketball Digest*, April, 1977.

Nobody roots for Goliath.

WILT CHAMBERLAIN, ca. 1960, *New York Times*, November 17, 1978.

I keep both eyes on my man. The basket hasn't moved on me yet.

JULIUS ERVING, *Sports Illustrated*, March 14, 1977.

The sixth man has to be so stable a player that he can instantly pick up a tempo or reverse it. He has to be able to go in and have an immediate impact....The sixth man has to have the unique ability to be in a ball game while he is sitting on the bench.

TOM HEINSOHN, *Sports Illustrated*, March 3, 1973.

You can say something to popes, kings and presidents, but you can't talk to officials. In the next war, they ought to give everybody a whistle.

ABE LEMONS, *Sports Illustrated*, March 7, 1977.

Quigg was in front of [Wilt] Chamberlain and someone else was behind. I told the kids, "If he gets the ball, wrestle him if you have to. If they beat us I want him to do it on the foul line."

FRANK MCGUIRE, *West Coast Review of Books*, 1977.

A great basketball player, almost by definition, is someone who has grown up in a constricted world, not for lack of vision or ambition but for lack of money; his environment has been limited to home, gym, and playground, and it has forced upon him, as a developing basketball player, the discipline of having nothing else to do.

JOHN MCPHEE, *A Sense of Where You Are*, 1965.

Most of the established stars in the NBA had quirks that the refs let them get away with. For example, they tended to wink at my goal tending and the "Russell" elbow....(My strategy, which worked fairly well, was to get the referees to accept the flailing elbows as my "style" so that they wouldn't call fouls on me.)...And the referees let Bob Pettit take a whole bunch of little steps just before he shot the ball. (I always protested Pettit's steps, and one night a referee just laughed and said, "Well, maybe he was walking, but he didn't go very far.")

BILL RUSSELL, *Second Wind*, 1979.

There are things kids do in the city that they don't do anywhere else. We love court savvy. You don't teach it; you get it in the city. New York kids have court savvy.

DEAN SMITH, *New York Times*, February 13, 1978.

BOXING

Float like a butterfly, sting like a bee.

MUHAMMAD ALI, on boxing style, coined by Drew "Bundini" Brown.

Not only do I knock 'em out, I pick the round.

MUHAMMAD ALI, statement to press, December, 1962.

Ali-eee! Ali-eee! There I'll be, wearing a sheet and whispering Ali-eee. I'll be the ghost that haunts boxing, and people will say, "Ali is the real champ, and everyone else is a fake."

MUHAMMAD ALI, after being stripped of title, 1968, *Sports Illustrated*, March 18, 1971.

I'm so fast I could hit you before God gets the news.

MUHAMMAD ALI, *New York Times*, June 29, 1975.

There are no pleasures in a fight, but some of my fights have been a pleasure to win.

MUHAMMAD ALI, interview, *Playboy*, November, 1975.

I am the greatest.

MUHAMMAD ALI (CASSIUS CLAY), before the Liston fight, ca.1964 .

Honey, I just forgot to duck.

JACK DEMPSEY, after losing heavyweight title to Gene Tunney, September 23, 1926.

[Jack Sharkey's] chin was there to hit, what else could I do? A fighter must protect himself at all times, it says.

JACK DEMPSEY, *New York Daily News*, July 4, 1982.

It was like I was throwing punches at the water and the water kept hittin' back. My big aim was to keep from drownin'.

JOE FRAZIER, *Sports Illustrated*, March 5, 1973.

I want him like a hog wants slop.

JOE FRAZIER, on fighting Muhammad Ali again, *New York Times*, May 30, 1976.

I'll moider da bum.

TONY GALENTO, before fight with Joe Louis, 1939.

But my big mistake was what I said to Joe [Louis] before the fight. Some newspaper guy asked me to call Joe up and when I got him, I told him, "Hey, bum, get in shape. I'm gonna eat your eyes out for grapes." I think that made him get in shape for me.

TONY GALENTO, 1939, *New York Times*, November 9, 1978.

We wuz robbed.

JOE JACOBS, after Max Schmeling lost heavyweight title to Jack Sharkey, June 21, 1932.

It seems safe enough to put it down that heavyweight prizefights have gone the way of the tournament and the duel....We have outgrown prizefights; that's all there is to it.

Life, July 21, 1910.

He can run, but he can't hide.

JOE LOUIS, before heavyweight title fight with light-heavyweight champion Billy Conn, 1941.

Prizefighting offers a profession to men who might otherwise commit murder in the street.

NORMAN MAILER, *The Fight*, 1975.

I knew he was hurt, and that if he did get up he'd be hurt some more. When you land a good punch you can feel it in your arm, your shoulder, your hip, your toes, your toenails.

KEN NORTON, *New York Times*, May 13, 1977.

I zigged when I should have zagged.

JACK ROPER, after recovering from knockout by Joe Louis, April 17, 1939.

FOOTBALL

There is an intensity and a danger in football—as in life generally—which keep us alive and awake. It is a test of our awareness and ability. Like so much of life, it presents us with the choice of responding either with fear or with action and clarity.

JOHN BRODIE, in Rick Telander, *Joe Namath and the Other Guys*, 1976.

Football has been rousing emotions for hundreds of years in a variety of forms, all having in common the idea of moving a ball from one place to another with varying degrees of violence as the means of propulsion.

HEYWOOD HALE BROUN, *Tumultuous Merriment*, 1979.

Football is, after all, a wonderful way to get rid of aggressions without going to jail for it.

HEYWOOD HALE BROUN, *Tumultuous Merriment*, 1979.

I begin psyching up the day before. I build up in my mind the idea that the opposing team hates me and is actually going to try to hurt me, to cut off my career. So I build up this hatred and the idea that "I'm going to hurt them first." I never go out to deliberately disable someone—they have a family and kids and a career like us too. But when you play rough football, someone's going to get hurt.

ROGER BROWN, *Life*, October 13, 1967.

Pro football is like nuclear warfare. There are no winners, only survivors.

FRANK GIFFORD, *Sports Illustrated*, July 4, 1960.

Sometime, Rock, when the team's up against it, when things are going wrong and the breaks are beating the boys, tell them to go in there with all they've got and win just one for the Gipper. I don't know where I'll be then, Rock, but I'll know about it and I'll be happy.

GEORGE GIPP, 1928, to Knute Rockne, *New York Times*, January 21, 1981.

Gentlemen, you are about to go forth on the greatest mission of your lives—you are about to play Harvard in football.

TAD JONES, to Yale team, in Jerry Brondfield, *Rockne*, 1976.

I was excited. It was the longest [run] I've ever made. It's the most lonely feeling in the world breaking into daylight and knowing you still have 80 yards to go.

KENNY KING, after 1980 touchdown run of 89 yards, *New York Times*, October 14, 1980.

Does football keep you from growing up? Oh, my God, yes! One hundred percent yes! I've even heard guys who I thought had no minds at all admit that.

DAVID KNIGHT, in Rick Telander, *Joe Namath and the Other Guys*, 1976.

Game plan.

ATTRIBUTED TO VINCE LOMBARDI, ca. 1950.

There are three important things in life: family, religion, and the Green Bay Packers.

VINCE LOMBARDI, in Tom Dowling, *Coach: A Season with Lombardi*, 1970.

Football isn't a contact sport, it's a collision sport. Dancing is a contact sport.

VINCE LOMBARDI, in James A. Michener, *Sports in America*, 1976.

We chase him and chase him and when we get him, we're too tired to enjoy it. He makes for a long afternoon. Guys our size, when we do that much running we're ready for a stretcher....He gets great enjoyment out of running our tongues out.

ONE OF LOS ANGELES RAMS "FEARSOME FOURSOME," on trying to tackle quarterback Fran Tarkenton, *Life*, October 13, 1967.

The wheeze about building character is a joke. Most boys we get are 18. Their character has long since been built, usually in the home. About all we can teach a kid is how to play football.

JOHN MCKAY, 1972, *Sports Illustrated*, November 13, 1973.

We set Monday night football back 2,000 years. They beat us in every phase of the game—passing, running, kicking, special teams and coaching. They even beat us coming out of the tunnel.

JOHN MCKAY, *New York Daily News*, October 8, 1980.

Let's face it, everyone knows the name of the game is "get the quarterback."

JOE NAMATH, *News World*, September 3, 1978.

I think that's the thing I'm most proud of, coming back from the adversity of those injuries. I never played as well as I would have liked to have played, but I played for 13 seasons when my doctor thought I would play for four. And I played despite a lot of adversity.

JOE NAMATH, *New York Times*, January 25, 1978.

We are the game.

NFL PLAYERS ASSOCIATION SLOGAN DURING COLLECTIVE BARGAINING, 1982.

I don't want any hot dogs on my team. If you're a hot dog you tend to get careless in the clutch.

JOE PATERNO, *Sports Illustrated*, March 15, 1976.

For when the one Great Scorer comes
   to write against your name,
He marks—not that you won or lost—
   But how you played the game.

GRANTLAND RICE, "Alumnus Football," *The Tumult and the Shouting*, 1954.

Football is a game played with the arms, legs and shoulders but mostly from the neck up.

KNUTE ROCKNE, in Jerry Brondfield, *Rockne*, 1976.

Football is good for the country. Every American has that feeling inside him that he'd like to hit somebody. He can't do it in this kind of society. But he comes out to the ballpark and he's almost in the game. It keeps him from going soft. It's the fans' way of fighting for the country.

TOM ROUSSEL, in Tom Dowling, *Coach: A Season with Lombardi*, 1970.

Football doesn't build character. It eliminates the weak ones.

DARRELL ROYAL, in James A. Michener, *Sports in America*, 1976.

When I get a chance, I like to knock a guy's head off. Then I look into his eyes to see how he feels.

ED SHUBERT, *Sports Illustrated*, November 13, 1972.

The only true religious spirit to be discerned among large bodies of undergraduates today is in the football stadium. One of the deepest spiritual experiences I ever had was one Saturday afternoon a few years ago in the Harvard Stadium. It was just that spirit which transforms football from a form of athletics to a religion, which our universities must diffuse through wider channels.

WILLARD SPERRY, *Harper's Monthly*, November, 1928.

My idea of a good hit is when the victim wakes up on the sidelines with train whistles blowing in his head and wondering who he is and what ran over him....I never make a tackle just to bring someone down. I want to punish the man I'm going after and I want him to know that it's going to hurt every time he comes my way.

JACK TATUM, *They Call Me Assassin*, 1980.

A pacifist friend of mine used to grow gloomy every year on the weekend of the Army-Navy football game. When we'd ask what was troubling him, he would always say, "About all you can hope for is that one side or the other suffers a defeat of humiliating proportions."

CALVIN TRILLIN, "Iran May Be Iraq," *The Nation*, March 16, 1985.

[F]ootball is more to the sports follower of this country than merely a game. It is at present a religion—sometimes it seems to be almost our national religion. With fervor and reverence the college man and the non-college man, the athlete and observer approach its shrines; dutifully and faithfully they make their annual pilgrimage to the football Mecca, be it Atlanta or Urbana, Cambridge or Los Angeles, Princeton or Ann Arbor. From far and near they come, the low and the high, the humble in their sports coupes from the neighboring city, the elect in their special cars from all parts of this football-mad nation.

JOHN R. TUNIS, *Harper's Monthly*, November, 1928.

Football brings out the sociologist that lurks in some otherwise respectable citizens. They say football is a metaphor for America's sinfulness. You know: the violent seizure of real estate, sublimated Manifest Destiny, oh! bury my heart in the end zone.

GEORGE WILL, "Woody Hayes: Kulturkampf in Columbus," November 19, 1974, *The Pursuit of Happiness, and Other Sobering Thoughts*, 1978.

GOLF

Golf matches are not won on the fairways or greens. They are won on the tee—the first tee.

ANONYMOUS, in Bobby Riggs, *Court Hustler*, 1973.

Golf is not, on the whole, a game for realists. By its exactitudes of measurement it invites the attention of perfectionists.

HEYWOOD HALE BROUN, *Tumultuous Merriment*, 1979.

Did you ever consider hitting it closer to the hole?

BEN HOGAN, *Sports Illustrated*, February 3, 1975.

If you watch a game, it's fun. If you play it, it's recreation. If you work at it, it's golf.

BOB HOPE, *Reader's Digest*, October, 1958.

Putting affects the nerves more than anything. I would actually get nauseated over three-footers, and there were tournaments when I couldn't keep a meal down for four days.

BYRON NELSON, *Sports Illustrated*, April 27, 1970.

The longer you play, the better chance the better player has of winning.

JACK NICKLAUS, *New York Times*, September 20, 1977.

Golf is essentially an exercise in masochism conducted out of doors; it affords opportunity for a certain swank, it induces a sense of kinship in its victims, and it forces them to breathe fresh air, but it is, at bottom, an elaborate and addictive rite calculated to drive them crazy for hours on end and send them straight to the whiskey bottle after that.

PAUL O'NEIL, "Palmer Tightens His Grip on Golf," *Life*, June 15, 1962.

It was one of those days you dream about. Every hole seemed to be six inches wide.

TOM PURTZER, *New York Times*, February 20, 1977.

TENNIS

If you're paid before you walk on the court, what's the point in playing as if your life depended on it? Hell, if you've locked up a bundle of money from a challenge match, you might as well take a vacation the rest of the year.

ARTHUR ASHE, *Newsweek*, May 23, 1977.

I don't care who you are, you're going to choke in certain matches. You get to a point where your legs don't move and you can't take a deep breath. I've done it. Sure I have. I did it at the beginning of the fifth set against Ilie Nastase in the 1972 Open. I could feel it happening. You'd start to hit the ball about a yard wide, instead of inches.

ARTHUR ASHE, *New York Times*, September 13, 1982.

There's a different breed of cats coming out here. Instead of hoi polloi, we're now getting Johnny Six-Pack.

MIKE BLANCHARD, on behavior of fans, *New York Times*, September 7, 1977.

I hate to lose more than I like to win. I hate to see the happiness on their faces when they beat me.

JIMMY CONNORS, *New York Times*, January 24, 1977.

"Good shot," "bad luck," and "hell" are the five basic words to be used in a game of tennis, though these, of course, can be slightly amplified.

VIRGINIA GRAHAM, *Say Please*, 1949.

Inside me, I just go crazy. I mess up a backhand and tell myself, "You creep," and maybe throw my racquet to vent my emotions. Then I see one coming and visualize just where I'm going to hit it, and the shot's perfect—and I feel beautiful all over.

BILLIE JEAN KING, *Newsweek*, June 3, 1974.

OTHER

Be kind to animals: Hug a hockey player.

BUMPER STICKER

I went to a fight the other night and a hockey game broke out.

RODNEY DANGERFIELD, *Sports Illustrated*, September 4, 1978.

A race horse is a hypersensitive animal. He can sense if a jockey isn't feeling well, is upset or scared. The hands and reins the jockey uses on a horse are like a telephone people use to communicate. It's a very delicate situation between jockey and horse. A rider's attitude has a lot to do with the way a horse runs.

PATRICK DAY, *New York Post*, March 30, 1977.

In four minutes of free skating you're being judged on a whole year of practice. Not many sports put you through that, being the focal point of the entire arena. You've got to look like you're enjoying yourself and accept the judges' decision and not throw a tomato at them. It's tough.

PEGGY FLEMING, *New York Times*, June 20, 1982.

Dressing a pool player in a tuxedo is like putting whipped cream on a hot dog.

"MINNESOTA FATS," *Sports Illustrated*, March 6, 1972.

If you keep the opposition on their asses, they don't score goals.

FRED SHERO, *Sports Illustrated*, May 20, 1974.

This business of favoring the deer over the hunter is a perplexing one; some of my best friends are deerslayers, and I never wish a man bad luck. As a spectator at the annual contest between deer and man, I am in the same fix as at the Harvard-Yale game—I'm not quite sure which club I'm rooting for.

E.B. WHITE, "Home-coming," December 10, 1955, *Essays of E.B. White*, 1977.

States and Regions

ALABAMA

Audemus jura nostra defendere. (We dare to defend our rights.)

State motto.

Some day I hope an American painter will do justice to the loveliness of the masterpieces of the backwoods of Alabama.

CARL CARMER, *Stars Fell on Alabama,* 1934.

Birmingham is not like the rest of the state. It is an industrial monster sprung up in the midst of a slow-moving pastoral. It does not belong.... Birmingham is a new city in an old land.

CARL CARMER, *Stars Fell on Alabama,* 1934.

I have never once thought of work in connection with the word Mobile. *Not anybody working.* A city surrounded with shells, the empty shells of bygone fiestas. Bunting everywhere, and the friable relics of yesterday's carnival. Gaiety always in retreat, always vanishing, like clouds brushing a mirror. In the center of this glissando, Mobile itself, very prim, very proper, Southern and not Southern, listless but upright, slatternly yet respectable, bright but not wicked. Mozart for the Mandolin. Not Segovia feathering Bach. Not grace and delicacy so much as anemia. Fever coolth, Musk. Fragrant ashes.

HENRY MILLER, *The Air-Conditioned Nightmare,* 1945.

ALASKA

North to the Future.

State motto.

Thinking back to my boyhood, Alaska, for all of us...was synonymous with the gold and glamour of the Yukon and Klondike: the home of sourdoughs and Eskimos....We thought of it as the cruel Arctic region....The change in less than a century heartens us as we view the future. The future is bound to be a bright, useful one. You are no longer an Arctic frontier. You constitute a bridge to the continent of Asia and all its people.

DWIGHT D. EISENHOWER, speech, Anchorage, Alaska, June 12, 1960.

As for the hardship, it cannot be conveyed by printed page or word of mouth. No man may know who has not undergone. And those who have undergone, out of their knowledge, claim that in the making of the world God grew tired, and when He came to the last barrow load, "just dumped it anyhow," and that was how Alaska happened to be.

JACK LONDON, "Gold Hunters of the North," *Revolution and Other Essays,* 1910.

A handful of people clinging to a subcontinent.

JOHN MCPHEE, *Coming into the Country,* 1977.

Alaska is a foreign country significantly populated with Americans. Its language extends to English. Its nature is its own.

JOHN MCPHEE, *Coming into the Country,* 1977.

I had always been skeptical about this all-night-daylight business. It was my belief that it would be an inferior brand, pumped up by the Chamber of Commerce, and not really what an honest man would call daylight at all. But, as usual, I was wrong. We had actual daylight all night long. (This was in June.) True, it wasn't so light at midnight as at noon. But you could stand out in the open at midnight, anywhere on the whole mainland of Alaska, and read a newspaper with ease.

ERNIE PYLE, *Home Country,* 1947.

ARIZONA

Ditat Deus. (God enriches.)

State motto.

Land of extremes. Land of contrasts. Land of surprises. Land of contradictions. A land that is never to be fully understood but always to be loved by sons and daughters sprung from such a diversity of origins, animated by such a diversity of motives and ideals, that generations must pass before they can ever fully understand each other. That is Arizona.

FEDERAL WRITERS' PROJECT, *Arizona: The Grand Canyon State*, 1956.

Most of those old settlers told it like it was, rough and rocky. They named their towns Rim-rock, Rough Rock, Round Rock, and Wide Ruins, Skull Valley, Bitter Springs, Wolf Hole, Tomb-stone. It's a tough country. The names of Arizona towns tell you all you need to know.

CHARLES KURALT, *Dateline America*, 1979.

I don't know about you, but I am suspicious of Pleasantville, New York. I am sure that Sawmill, Arizona, is more my kind of town. Or Window Rock or Hermits Rest or Turkey Flat or Grasshopper Junction. I could settle down here, just for the pleasure of having folks back home say, "Oh, don't you know what happened to old Charles? Lives now in Jackrabbit, Arizona. Just down the road from Cowlick and Bumble Bee."

CHARLES KURALT, *Dateline America*, 1979.

ARKANSAS

Regnat populus. (Let the people rule.)

State motto.

Arkansas has its own popular motto and it is this: "I've never seen nothin', I don't know nothin', I h'ain't got nothin', and I don't want nothin." These fundamental aims the people of Arkansas have achieved in every particular. Therefore the Arkansawyers are happy, the only happy and successful people in America.

C.L. EDSON, in Ernest H. Gruening, ed., *These United States*, 1924.

I could have been born in no better place than Arkansas to see first-hand what an electric power monopoly could do to the people.

CLYDE T. ELLIS, on Arkansas Power and Light, *A Giant Step*, 1966.

There is no Sunday west of St. Louis and no God west of Fort Smith.

GLENN SHIRLEY, on Arkansas religion, "Law West of Fort Smith," 1968.

CALIFORNIA

Eureka. (I have found it.)

State motto.

It's a great place to live—if you're an orange.

FRED ALLEN, on Los Angeles and Hollywood, in Max Wilk, ed., *The Wit and Wisdom of Hollywood*, 1971.

What I like about Hollywood is that one can get along by knowing two words of English—*swell* and *lousy*.

ATTRIBUTED TO VICKI BAUM, ca. 1933.

Hollywood is like Picasso's bathroom.

CANDICE BERGEN, in article by Sheila Graham, *New York Post*, February 14, 1967.

Whatever starts in California unfortunately has an inclination to spread.

JIMMY CARTER, remark at Cabinet meeting, in Robert Shogan, *Promises to Keep: Carter's First 100 Days*, 1977.

The future always looks good in the golden land, because no one remembers the past....Here is the last stop for all those who come from somewhere else, for all those who drifted away from the cold and the past and the old ways.

JOAN DIDION, "Some Dreamers of the Golden Dream," *Slouching Towards Bethlehem*, 1968.

January 11, 1965, was a bright warm day in Southern California, the kind of day when Catalina floats on the Pacific horizon and the air smells of orange blossoms and it is a long way from the bleak and difficult East, a long way from the past.

JOAN DIDION, "Some Dreamers of the Golden Dream," *Slouching Towards Bethlehem*, 1968.

California is a place in which a boom mentality and a sense of Chekhovian loss meet in uneasy suspension; in which the mind is troubled by some buried but ineradicable suspicion that things had better work here, because here, beneath that immense bleached sky, is where we run out of continent.

JOAN DIDION, "Notes from a Native Daughter," *Slouching Towards Bethlehem*, 1968.

Going back to California is not like going back to Vermont, or Chicago; Vermont and Chicago are relative constants, against which one measures one's own change. All that is constant about the

California of my childhood is the rate at which it disappears.

Joan Didion, "Notes from a Native Daughter," *Slouching Towards Bethlehem*, 1968.

It's a mining town in lotus land.

F. Scott Fitzgerald, on Hollywood, *The Last Tycoon*, 1941.

The San Francisco fog has never been sufficiently glorified. It has neither the impenetrable yellow murkiness of the London variety nor the heavy stifling sootiness of the mist that rolls in on New York across the Hudson. The fogs are pure sea water condensed by the clean hot breath of the interior valleys and blown across the peninsula by the trade winds. They come in, not an enveloping blanket but a luminous drift, conferring a magic patina on the most commonplace structures, giving them an air of age and mystery.

Arnold Genthe, *As I Remember*, 1930.

[T]he propaganda arm of the American Dream machine, Hollywood.

Molly Haskell, *From Reverence to Rape*, 1973.

East is East, and West is San Francisco, according to Californians. Californians are a race of people; they are not merely inhabitants of a State.

O. Henry, "A Municipal Report," *Strictly Business*, 1910.

Why, with a mental equipment which allows me to tell the difference between hot and cold, I stand out in this community like a modern-day Cicero. Dropped into any other city of the world, I'd rate as a possibly adequate night watchman. And let's be fair, old pal, you yourself, a leader of public thought in Hollywood, wouldn't have sufficient mental acumen anywhere else to hold down a place in a bread line!

Anita Loos, *No Mother To Guide Her*, 1961.

Hollywood always had a streak of the totalitarian in just about everything it did.

Shirley MacLaine, *You Can Get There from Here*, 1975.

It is not that Los Angeles is altogether hideous, it is even by degrees pleasant, but for an Easterner there is never any salt in the wind; it is like Mexican cooking without chili, or Chinese egg rolls missing their mustard.

Norman Mailer, *Esquire*, November, 1960.

The land around San Juan Capistrano is the pocket where the Creator keeps all his treasures. Anything will grow there.

Frances Marion, *Westward the Dream*, 1948.

A circus without a tent.

Carey McWilliams, on Los Angeles, *Southern California Country*, 1946.

Nineteen suburbs in search of a metropolis.

H.L. Mencken, on Los Angeles, *Americana*, 1925.

If you live in Beverly Hills they don't put blinkers in your car. They figure if you're that rich you don't have to tell people where you're going.

Bette Midler, *A View from a Broad*, 1980.

A trip through a sewer in a glass-bottomed boat.

Wilson Mizner, on Hollywood, *The Incredible Mizners*, 1953.

Hollywood is a carnival where there are no concessions.

Wilson Mizner, *The Wit and Wisdom of Hollywood*, 1971.

It is hereby earnestly proposed that the U.S.A. would be much better off if that big, sprawling, incoherent, shapeless, slobbering civic idiot in the family of American communities, the City of Los Angeles, could be declared incompetent and placed in charge of a guardian like any individual mental defective.

Westbrook Pegler, *New York World Telegram*, November 22, 1938.

Hollywood is a dreary industrial town controlled by hoodlums of enormous wealth, the ethical sense of a pack of jackals, and taste so degraded that it befouled everything it touched.

S.J. Perelman, in William Cole and George Plimpton, "S.J. Perelman," *Writers at Work: The Paris Review Interviews*, 1963.

I attended a dinner the other morning given for the Old Settlers of California. No one was allowed to attend unless he had been in the State 2 and one half years.

Will Rogers, *The Illiterate Digest*, 1924.

The San Francisco Bay Area [is] the playpen of countercultures.

R.Z. Sheppard, *Time*, September 8, 1986.

A place where the inmates are in charge of the asylum.

Laurence Stallings, on Hollywood, ca. 1930.

The Mojave is a big desert and a frightening one. It's as though nature tested a man for endurance and constancy to prove whether he was good enough to get to California.

John Steinbeck, *Travels with Charley*, 1962.

On Venice Beach...I once saw a man blowing truly spectacular soap bubbles the size of watermelons—still the symbol for me of the tendency of people in Southern California to become awfully good at something that isn't terribly important.

CALVIN TRILLIN, *Travels with Alice*, 1989.

Visitors to Los Angeles, then and now, were put out because the residents of Los Angeles had the inhospitable ideal of building a city comfortable to live in, rather than a monument to astonish the eye of jaded travelers.

JESSAMYN WEST, *Hide and Seek*, 1973.

All Hollywood corrupts; and absolute Hollywood corrupts absolutely.

EDMUND WILSON, "Old Antichrist's Sayings," May, 1938, *Letters on Literature and Politics 1912–1972*, 1977.

COLORADO

Nil sine Numine. (Nothing without Providence.)
State motto.

This is the kind of country you dream of running away to when you are very young and innocently hungry, before you learn that all land is owned by somebody, that you can get arrested for swinging through trees in a loincloth, and that you were born either too late or too poor for everything you want to do.

PETER S. BEAGLE, *I See By My Outfit*, 1965.

What's good, thrilling, exciting about Colorado was produced by God—not the Denver Chamber of Commerce.

EUGENE CERVI, in Neal R. Pierce, *The Mountain States of America*, 1972.

I don't know any other American city quite so fascinatingly strange [as Denver]. Not merely because the yellow cabs are painted green or because the fourteenth step on the state capitol bears the proud plaque, ONE MILE ABOVE SEA LEVEL....The remarkable thing about Denver is its ineffable closedness; when it moves, or opens up, it is like a Chippendale molting its veneer.... It is probably the most self-sufficient, isolated, self-contained, and complacent city in the world.

JOHN GUNTHER, *Inside U.S.A.*, 1947.

Water is blood in Colorado. Touch water, and you touch everything; about water the state is as sensitive as a carbuncle.

JOHN GUNTHER, *Inside U.S.A.*, 1947.

A true note struck on a Central City piano instantly brings out the Fire Department, which arrives with hatchets and busts up the interior mechanism, occasionally stopping long enough to remove a pedal.

PHILIP HAMBURGER, *An American Notebook*, 1965.

Passing through your wonderful mountains and canyons I realize that this state is going to be more and more the playground for the entire Republic....You will see this as the real Switzerland of America.

THEODORE ROOSEVELT, speech, Colorado, 1905.

CONNECTICUT

Qui transtulit sustinet. (He who transplanted sustains.)
State motto.

The Upsons lived the way every family in America wants to live—not rich but well-to-do. They had two of everything: two addresses, the flat on Park and a house in Connecticut.

PATRICK DENNIS, *Auntie Mame*, 1955.

Liberals have always been eunuchs in the court of Connecticut.

BILL MOYERS, *Listening to America*, 1971.

Hartford is a gay combination of Life Insurance and Death, for here the former had a pioneer foundation that has brought in great accumulations of cash, while Samuel Colt's "revolver" has grown into "Browning guns" and many forms of deadly repeaters that wipe out a regiment at a discharge.

DON C. SEITZ, in Ernest H. Gruening, ed., *These United States*, 1924.

Taken as a group, they [Connecticut peddlers] were probably no less honest than itinerant salesmen are wont to be, but the point is that they were probably no more so. Aggressive, pervasive, with a foot in every American door, they gave the country at large its first clear notions of the New England character, and there are some parts of the country, one fears, that have not yet revised the opinions then formed. The word "Yankee" came to mean "Connecticut Yankee," and throughout the Old South, long before Abolition days, it came to be pronounced "Damyank."

ODELL SHEPARD, *Connecticut Past and Present*, 1939.

DELAWARE

Liberty and Independence.

State motto.

Delaware has fought and bucked, hated, reviled, admired and fawned upon, ignored and courted the Du Ponts, but in the end, it has invariably bowed to Du Pont's benevolent paternalism.

JAMES WARNER BELLAH, "Delaware," *American Panorama: East of the Mississippi*, 1960.

Know the mold—and you will understand the people of the state. Hardheaded with money. Courteous, to minimum requirements, with no urban frills. Completely self-sufficient in private living. Fine judges of good food and drink—in the castles of their own homes, which accounts for the indifferent public eating places throughout the state to this day. Honest at heart—but watch yourself carefully in all business transactions, for Delawareans are, of ancient times, close traders. Comfortably cynical in all basic philosophy. And utterly unchangeable, come hell, high water, the Du Pont overlordship, or thermonuclear reaction.

JAMES WARNER BELLAH, "Delaware," *American Panorama: East of the Mississippi*, 1960.

Wilmington, with its expressways and parking lots and all its other concrete ribbons and badges, is a tired old veteran of the industrial wars and wears a vacant stare. Block after city block where people used to live and shop is broken and empty.

CHARLES KURALT, *Dateline America*, 1979.

There are two political parties in Delaware: the DuPonts and the anti-DuPonts, with the proviso that many DuPonts are members of the anti-DuPont family.

JAMES PHELAN AND ROBERT POZEN, *The Company State*, 1973.

DISTRICT OF COLUMBIA

Justitia omnibus (Justice to all.)

District motto.

Washington is like a self-sealing tank on a military aircraft. When a bullet passes through, it closes up.

DEAN ACHESON, in Walter Isaacson and Evan Thomas, *The Wise Men*, 1986.

The more I observed Washington, the more frequently I visited it, and the more people I interviewed there, the more I understood how prophetic L'Enfant was when he laid it out as a city that goes around in circles.

JOHN MASON BROWN, *Through These Men*, 1956.

We're just simple folk with the same dreams and aspirations as anyone else....The work is no different than that done in Hartford, Connecticut, or Atlanta, Georgia. Some of us will pass laws; others will filibuster; and still others will read Bella Abzug's mail. One man in a small office might give a squadron of jets to an Arab country, and another man in a small office will sell jets to Israel.

ART BUCHWALD, *The Washington Post Guide to Washington*, 1976.

That place is contaminated: Washington, D.C. It's unhealthy. It's germ-breeding. It's a pesthole. It's oozing with pus—infected and stinking with putrefaction. And it's going to spread like an insidious plague over our entire nation if something isn't done about it. And if nothing is done and done soon, Washington, D.C. is going to be the cause of our country's downfall.

OIL EXECUTIVE, in Erskine Caldwell, *Afternoons in Mid-America*, 1976.

A show of police force worthy of a banana republic is the latest attraction on the cobbled streets of Georgetown.

FRANCIS X. CLINES, *New York Times*, April 15, 1985.

There are a number of things wrong with Washington. One of them is that everyone has been too long away from home.

ATTRIBUTED TO DWIGHT D. EISENHOWER, press conference, May 11, 1955.

A place where men praise courage and act on elaborate personal cost-benefit calculation.

JOHN KENNETH GALBRAITH, *New York Times*, April 25, 1971.

The cocktail party remains a vital Washington institution, the official intelligence system.

BARBARA HOWAR, *Laughing All the Way*, 1973.

The capital city specializes in ballooning monuments and endless corridors. It uses marble like cotton wool. It is the home of government of, for, and by the people, and of taste for the people—the big, the bland, and the banal.

ADA LOUISE HUXTABLE, "The Kennedy Center, I," September 6, 1971, *Kicked a Building Lately?*, 1976.

For all of its fancy restaurants and cafes, there's not a single good neighborhood bar in Washington, a place where people of the area—young people, old people—congregate on a casual basis and talk about things over a beer or two.

DONALD KAUL, *Washington Post*, July 5, 1981.

Washington is a city of Southern efficiency and Northern charm.

JOHN F. KENNEDY, in William Manchester, *Portrait of a President*, 1962.

Washington is, for one thing, the news capital of the world. And for another, it is a company town. Most of the interesting people in Washington either work for the government or write about it.

SALLY QUINN, *We're Going To Make You a Star*, 1975.

Washington is...a city of cocker spaniels. It's a city of people who are more interested in being petted and admired, loved, than rendering the exercise of power.

ELLIOT L. RICHARDSON, *New York Times*, July 13, 1982.

[S]urely nowhere in the world do oppression and persecution based solely on the color of the skin appear more hateful and hideous than in the capital of the United States, because the chasm between the principles upon which this Government was founded, in which it still professes to believe, and those which are daily practiced under the protection of the flag, yawns so wide and deep.

MARY CHURCH TERRELL, "What It Means to Be Colored in the Capital of the United States," 1907, *A Colored Woman in a White World*, 1940.

Things get very lonely in Washingtom sometimes. The real voice of the great people of America sometimes sounds faint and distant in that strange city. You hear politics until you wish that both parties were smothered in their own gas.

WOODROW WILSON, speech, St. Louis, Missouri, September 5, 1919.

EAST

The New England conscience...does not stop you from doing what you shouldn't—it just stops you from enjoying it.

CLEVELAND AMORY, *New York*, May 5, 1980.

Of course what the man from Mars will find out first about New England is that it is neither new nor very much like England.

JOHN GUNTHER, *Inside U.S.A.*, 1947.

The East is a montage....It is old and it is young, very green in summer, very white in winter, gregarious, withdrawn and at once both sophisticated and provincial.

PHYLLIS McGINLEY, "The East Is Home," *Woman's Home Companion*, July, 1956.

There are enough antiques for sale along the roads of New England alone to furnish the houses of a population of fifty million.

JOHN STEINBECK, *Travels with Charley*, 1962.

I wonder if anybody ever reached the age of thirty-five in New England without wanting to kill himself.

BARRETT WENDELL, *Barrett Wendell and His Letters*, 1924.

FLORIDA

In God We Trust.

State motto.

Miami Beach is where neon goes to die.

LENNY BRUCE, in article by Barbara Gordon, *Saturday Review of Books*, May 20, 1972.

Physically and socially, Florida has its own North and South, but its northern area is strictly southern and its southern area definitely northern.

FEDERAL WRITERS' PROJECT, *Florida: A Guide to the Southernmost State*, 1939.

Florida is the world's greatest amusement park.

BUDD SCHULBERG, "Florida," *American Panorama: East of the Mississippi*, 1960.

The billion-dollar-a-year tourist trade, the fusion of the Old South and the restless North is rapidly producing a new kind of state which is neither Southern nor Northern, Middle Western nor Western, yet with discernible elements of all four. In fact, Florida is to the United States today what the United States was to Europe a hundred years ago—a melting pot, a frontier, a place to improve your health or your luck.

BUDD SCHULBERG, "Florida," *American Panorama: East of the Mississippi*, 1960.

The smell of money in Florida attracts men as the smell of blood attracts a wild animal.

G.M. SHELBY, "Florida Frenzy," *Harper's*, 1926.

Miami is more American than America.

GARRY WILLS, *Nixon Agonistes*, 1970.

Florida lifted itself by non-existent bootstraps, and Miami Beach is perhaps the most obvious embodiment of this process. It was willed into being. The land was not only overpriced for the sake of things that might be built on it; it was physically nudged up out of the sea.

GARRY WILLS, *Nixon Agonistes*, 1970.

Miami is...of an unimaginable awfulness— much like other American seaside resorts but on an unprecedented scale: acres of cheap white shops, mountain ranges of white hotels. After lunch, I had a taxi drive me over to Miami Beach. It goes on for miles — thousands of hotels and houses and monotonous lines of palms. I can't imagine how people live here or why so many of them come: it all seems a great insipid vacuum — less amusing than Southern California, because there is no touch of fantasy about anything.

EDMUND WILSON, letter to Elena Wilson, November 26, 1949, *Letters on Literature and Politics 1912–1972*, 1977.

GEORGIA

Wisdom, Justice, Moderation.
State motto.

I am determined that at the end of this administration we shall be able to stand up anywhere in the world—in New York, California, or Florida— and say, "I'm a Georgian," and be proud of it.

JIMMY CARTER, inaugural address as governor of Georgia, Atlanta, Georgia, January 12, 1971.

The average Georgian votes the Democratic ticket, attends the Baptist or Methodist church, goes home to midday dinner, relies greatly on high cotton prices, and is so good a family man that he flings wide his door to even the most distant of his wife's cousins' cousins.

FEDERAL WRITERS' PROJECT, *Georgia: A Guide to Its Towns and Countryside*, 1940.

I heard it said that the "architecture" of Atlanta is rococola. The pun is bad, but what the city would be like without Coca-Cola is hard to conceive....In Atlanta alone Coca-Cola has made at least a thousand millionaires.

JOHN GUNTHER, *Inside U.S.A.*, 1947.

Savannah is a living tomb about which there still clings a sensual aura as in old Corinth.

HENRY MILLER, *The Air-Conditioned Nightmare*, 1945.

HAWAII

Ua mau ke ea o ka aina i ka pono. (The life of the land is perpetuated by righteousness.)
State motto.

War is in the very fabric of Hawaii's life, ineradicably fixed in both its emotions and its economy, dominating not only its memory but its vision of the future. There is a point at which every Honolulu conversation refers back to war.

JOAN DIDION, "Letter from Paradise, 21° 19′ N, 157° 52′ W," *Slouching Towards Bethlehem*, 1968.

The spiritual destiny of Hawaii has been shaped by a Calvinist theory of paternalism enacted by the descendants of the missionaries who had carried it there: a will to do good for unfortunates regardless of what the unfortunates thought about it.

FRANCINE DU PLESSIX GRAY, *Hawaii: The Sugar-Coated Fortress*, 1972.

The *nicest* thing about Hawaii is that when we select a beauty queen at the university we don't have just *one* beauty queen. We have a Polynesian beauty queen, a Chinese beauty queen, a Japanese beauty queen, a Filipino beauty queen, a Portuguese beauty queen, a Puerto Rico beauty queen, a Negro beauty queen, *and* a Caucasian beauty queen. Six, eight beauty queens all in a row. *That's* what I like the best about Hawaii.

THOMAS HAMILTON, in Francine du Plessix Gray, *Hawaii: The Sugar-Coated Fortress*, 1972.

IDAHO

Esto perpetua. (May she endure forever.)
State motto.

We're a user-oriented society in Idaho. And the users—the miners, loggers and grazers—all camp at the same campfire.

ERNEST DAY, in Neal R. Peirce, *The Mountain States of America*, 1972.

Idaho is torn, above all, between two other states; between the pull of Washington to the north, that of Utah in the South. Half of Idaho belongs to Spokane, I heard it said, and the other half to the Mormon church.

JOHN GUNTHER, *Inside U.S.A*, 1947.

Dice 'em, hash 'em, boil 'em, mash 'em!
Idaho, Idaho, Idaho!

FORMER IDAHO FOOTBALL CHEER, in Charles Kuralt, *Dateline America*, 1979.

There were two small hotels in Ketchum, and a group of nice cabins built around a hot-water pool. The business section consisted of one block; two grocery stores; three restaurants, one drugstore, and twelve combination saloons and gambling halls. These were called "clubs." Gambling was not legal in Idaho, and neither was liquor by the drink, but nobody in Ketchum paid any attention. Everything was wide open.

ERNIE PYLE, *Home Country*, 1947.

The state with the greatest number of millionaires per capita is Idaho, for heaven's sake.

MARTIN RUSSELL, *Rocky Mountain*, November/December, 1980.

ILLINOIS

State Sovereignty—National Union.

State motto.

Chicago is an October sort of city even in spring.

NELSON ALGREN, in article by George F. Will, *Newsweek*, August 13, 1984.

I'm a little hoarse tonight. I've been living in Chicago for the past two months, and you know how it is, yelling for help on the way home every night. Things are so tough in Chicago that at Easter time, for bunnies the little kids use porcupines.

FRED ALLEN, *Much Ado About Me*, 1956.

Its women are lovely and stubborn, its men angry and ingenious. Is there a land anywhere like southern Illinois?

BAKER BROWNELL, *The Other Illinois*, 1958.

Big plans, elaborate schemes and grand designs sort of messily bleeding into one another [have] created Chicago's reputation for rawness. But that rawness is just ambition—sometimes ambition run amuck—that has acquired a life of its own.

PAT COLANDER, "A Metropolis of No Little Plans," *New York Times*, May 5, 1985.

Chicago is a city of contradictions, of private visions haphazardly overlaid and linked together. If the city was unhappy with itself yesterday—

and invariably it was—it will reinvent itself today.

PAT COLANDER, "A Metropolis of No Little Plans," *New York Times*, May 5, 1985.

In Chicago, we may not think the Picasso presiding over the Richard J. Daley Center plaza is art, but we know it's a big Picasso and it's the city's Picasso, and when the Cubs made the play-offs, the sculpture wore a baseball cap just like everything else.

PAT COLANDER, "A Metropolis of No Little Plans," *New York Times*, May 5, 1985.

Illinois is perhaps the most American of all the states. It's the U.S.A. in a capsule. Here our virtues and our faults are most exaggerated and magnified. Here somehow the heroes seem more heroic, the villains more villainous, the buffoons more comic. Here violence is more unrestrained, and the capacity for greatness is as limitless as the sweep of the unending cornfields.

CLYDE BRION DAVIS, "Illinois," *American Panorama: East of the Mississippi*, 1960.

Although the geographic center of the United States is 500 miles to the west, Illinois is the axis of the nation, the hub and vortex of all the wonderful and eccentric hullabaloo that comprises our sweet land of liberty.

CLYDE BRION DAVIS, "Illinois," *American Panorama: East of the Mississippi*, 1960.

The hub of the continent.

FEDERAL WRITERS' PROJECT, *Illinois: A Descriptive & Historical Guide*, 1939.

There's only one thing for Chicago to do, and that's to move to a better neighborhood.

HERMAN FETZER, ca. 1930, in Robert McLaughlin, *The Heartland*, 1967.

[Chicago] is the greatest and most typically American of all cities. New York is bigger and more spectacular and can outmatch it in other superlatives, but it is a "world" city, more European in some respects than American.

JOHN GUNTHER, *Inside U.S.A*, 1947.

The last copy of the Chicago *Daily News* I picked up had three crime stories on its front page. But by comparison to the gaudy days, this is small-time stuff. Chicago is as full of crooks as a saw with teeth, but the era when they ruled the city is gone forever.

JOHN GUNTHER, *Inside U.S.A*, 1947.

New York is one of the capitals of the world and Los Angeles is a constellation of plastic, San Francisco is a lady, Boston has become Urban Renewal, Philadelphia and Baltimore and Washington wink like dull diamonds in the smog of Eastern Megalopolis, and New Orleans is unremarkable past the French Quarter. Detroit is a one-trade town, Pittsburgh has lost its golden triangle, St. Louis has become the golden arch of the corporation, and nights in Kansas City close early. The oil depletion allowance makes Houston and Dallas naught but checkerboards for this sort of game. But Chicago is a great American city. Perhaps it is the last of the great American cities.

NORMAN MAILER, *Miami and the Siege of Chicago*, 1968.

Hog Butcher for the World,

Tool Maker, Stacker of Wheat,

Player with Railroads and the Nation's
     Freight Handler;

Stormy, husky, brawling,

City of the Big Shoulders.

CARL SANDBURG, "Chicago," *Chicago Poems*, 1916.

Here is the difference between Dante, Milton, and me. They wrote about hell and never saw the place. I wrote about Chicago after looking the town over for years and years.

CARL SANDBURG, in Harry Golden, *Carl Sandburg*, 1961.

The line of the buildings stood clear-cut and black against the sky; here and there out of the mass rose the great chimneys, with the river of smoke streaming away to the end of the world. It was a study in colors now, this smoke; in the sunset light it was black and brown and gray and purple. All the sordid suggestions of the place were gone—in the twilight it was a vision of power.

UPTON SINCLAIR, *The Jungle*, 1906.

First in violence, deepest in dirt, lawless, unlovely, ill-smelling, irreverent, new; an overgrown gawk of a—village, the "tough" among cities, a spectacle for the nation.

LINCOLN STEFFENS, on Chicago, *The Shame of the Cities*, 1904.

Chicago likes audacity and is always willing to have anybody try anything once; no matter who you are, where you come from, or what you set out to do, Chicago will give you a chance. The sporting spirit is the spirit of Chicago.

LINCOLN STEFFENS, *The Autobiography of Lincoln Steffens*, 1931.

Chicago is not the most corrupt American city, it's the most theatrically corrupt.

STUDS TERKEL, "Dick Cavett Show," June 9, 1978.

INDIANA

The Crossroads of America.

State motto.

Indianans have an ability to see sin at a distance but never at their very feet. Indianapolis is shocked by vice in East Chicago; Bloomington is horrified by what goes on in Terre Haute or South Bend, and so on.

ROGER BRANIGIN, in Robert McLaughlin, *The Heartland*, 1967.

This is a most peculiar state. It may not be so dynamic nor yet so creative, sociologically, as it is fecund of things which relate to the spirit—or perhaps I had better say to poetry and the interpretative arts.

THEODORE DREISER, in Ernest H. Gruening, ed., *These United States*, 1924.

I came from Indiana, the home of more first-rate second-class men than any State in the Union.

THOMAS R. MARSHALL, *Recollections*, 1925.

[Indianapolis]...where the practice of the arts was regarded as an evasion of real life by means of parlor tricks.

KURT VONNEGUT, *Palm Sunday*, 1981.

IOWA

Our Liberties We Prize and Our Rights We Will Maintain.

State motto.

[Iowa] is top-choice America, America cut thick and prime.

HARVEY ARDEN, *National Geographic*, May, 1981.

Early March is never done well in Iowa. The snow has melted and there's a subtly variegated gray on all its surfaces, the sky, the land, the faces of the buildings.

DOUGLAS BAUER, "The Way the Country Lies," in Michael Martone, ed., *A Place of Sense*, 1988.

In those crop fields, beside this pasture, the corn is ankle-high and finger-flat, the fist-size soybean plants are Kelly green against black dirt. We had better wish them well. There's a tithe growing out there to keep the big State University moving on its earnest, complicated mission—for a cup of soybeans, your kid can triangulate a star, for an ear of corn, memorize two lines of Lermontov.

VANCE BOURJAILY, *Now Playing at Canterbury*, 1976.

There is no General Theory of Little Places into which each particular Iowa county, farm community, or religious sect can be fit. How do we talk about such places? By telling stories about them, one by one.

GARY COMSTOCK, "Grandma's Backbone, Dougie's Ankle," in Michael Martone, ed., *A Place of Sense*, 1988.

The fields have turned, yellow and light brown; central Iowa gets most of its autumn from the fields. Trees and brush trim the roadsides and fence rows vividly, but the great reaching planes of quiet colors are the fields.

HAMLIN GARLAND, *A Son of the Middle Border*, 1917.

Everybody in Des Moines is insured—against fire, flood, theft, hog cholera, death, crop failure, rickets. Name it, and Des Moines has the insurance to cover it.

PHILIP HAMBURGER, *An American Notebook*, 1965.

In Des Moines, a man's eyes will light up at the mere mention of the word "corn."

PHILIP HAMBURGER, *An American Notebook*, 1965.

Iowa is graced by absolutely marvelous people. I know you hear that all the time, but it's true. They are clean, brave, thrifty, reverent, loyal, honest and able to brush after every meal.

DONALD KAUL, *Washington Post*, July 5, 1981.

Iowa winters were very cold and I well remember seeing the coal oil frozen in the lamps in the morning.

CATHERINE ANN McLOLLUM, *Journal of American Folklore*, 1943.

[Iowa is] more a demonstration farm than a place; more some cosmic public relations project designed to prove that God's in his heaven and all's right with the world.

RICHARD RHODES, *The Inland Ground*, 1970.

KANSAS

Ad astra per aspera. (To the stars through difficulties.)

State motto.

Raise less corn and more *Hell*.

ROGER BUTTERFIELD, *The American Past*, 1957.

Kansas, in sum, is one of our finest states and lives a sane, peaceful, and prosperous life.

PEARL S. BUCK, *America*, 1971.

First in Freedom, First in Wheat.

SLOGAN, in Dwight D. Eisenhower, *Eisenhower Speaks*, 1948.

We preferred the comparatively simple but more intelligent life of Kansas to Washington. There are some intelligent people in Washington. More of 'em in Kansas.

ALFRED M. LANDON, in George Will, "Alf Landon's Little House on the Prairie," *The Pursuit of Happiness, and Other Sobering Thoughts*, 1978.

Kansas is the child of Plymouth Rock.

WILLIAM ALLEN WHITE, *Autobiography*, 1946.

KENTUCKY

United We Stand, Divided We Fall.

State motto.

We are the nation's perennial problem child.

HARRY CAUDILL, in Neal Peirce, *The Border South States*, 1975.

We have a myth our economy is based on coal. It isn't; it's based on poverty.

HARRY CAUDILL, in Neal Peirce, *The Border South States*, 1975.

Wherever a Kentuckian may be, he is more than willing to boast of the beauties and virtues of his native state. He believes without reservation that Kentucky is the garden spot of the world, and is ready to dispute with anyone who questions the claim.

FEDERAL WRITERS' PROJECT, *Kentucky: A Guide to the Bluegrass State*, 1939.

Heaven is a Kentucky of a place.

METHODIST PREACHER, in Federal Writers' Project, *Kentucky: A Guide to the Bluegrass State*, 1939.

LOUISIANA

Union, Justice, and Confidence.
State motto.

In 1803 Louisiana was an unmanned, undefended empire embracing the whole watershed of the Mississippi and comprising the present states of Louisiana, Arkansas, Oklahoma, Missouri, both Dakotas, Iowa, Nebraska, Kansas, Minnesota, Colorado, Wyoming, and Montana—a third of North America.
Alistair Cooke, *America*, 1973.

In Louisiana we don't bet on football games.... We bet on whether a politician is going to be indicted or not.
Mark Duffy, on winning wager that Edwin Edwards would be charged with fraud, *New York Times*, March 3, 1985.

New Orleans is one of the two most ingrown, self-obsessed little cities in the United States. (The other is San Francisco.)
Nora Ephron, "Richard Collin and the Spaghetti Recipe," *Esquire*, September, 1975.

Hedonistic, complacent, extravagant where amusement is concerned, soft to the point sometimes of insincerity, tolerant to the point sometimes of decadence; but always vivacious, good-natured, well dressed and well mannered—these are the characteristics of a typical New Orleanian. You might think, perhaps, that his vices outweigh his virtues; it depends on what you believe is important, but there is no denying that he is an easy fellow to get along with.
Oliver Evans, *New Orleans*, 1959.

In Louisiana the live-oak is the king of the forest, and the magnolia is its queen; and there is nothing more delightful to one who is fond of the country than to sit under them on a clear, calm spring morning like this.
Joseph Jefferson, *The Autobiography of Joseph Jefferson*, 1917.

It is a town where an architect, a gourmet, or a roué is in hog heaven.
George Sessions Perry, on New Orleans, *Cities of America*, 1947.

It some ways gaudy old New Orleans very much resembles an alluring, party-loving woman who is neither as virtuous as she might be nor as young as she looks, who has a come-hither eye, an engaging trace of accent in her speech, and a weakness for the pleasures both of the table and the couch—a *femme fatale* who has known great ecstasy and tragedy, but still laughs and loves excitement, and who, after each bout of sinning, does duly confess and perhaps partially repent.
George Sessions Perry, *Cities of America*, 1947.

As a society, we're a banana republic. What we ought to do is declare bankruptcy, secede from the union and declare ourselves a banana republic and file for foreign aid. We're just about as illiterate and just about as progressive as a Latin American country.
Kevin Reilly, Louisiana State University *Daily Reveille*, June 18, 1985.

In Louisiana they vote by electricity. It's a marvelous way to vote, but Huey [Long] runs the switchboard, so it don't matter which button the boys press, all the answers come out yes.
Will Rogers, January 29, 1935, in Donald Day, ed., *The Autobiography of Will Rogers*, 1949.

MAINE

Dirigo. (I direct.)
State motto.

As Maine goes, so goes Vermont.
James A. Farley, after 1936 presidential election, when Democrats won all states but Maine and Vermont.

There are only two things that ever make the front page in Maine papers. One is a forest fire and the other is when a New Yorker shoots a moose instead of the game warden.
Groucho Marx, letter to *Variety*, August 23, 1934, *The Groucho Phile*, 1976.

Here's to the state of Maine, the land of the bluest skies, the greenest earth, the richest air, the strongest, and what is better, the sturdiest men, the fairest, and what is best of all, the truest women under the sun.
Thomas Brackett Reed, speech, Portland, Maine, August 7, 1900.

Did you ever see a place that looks like it was built just to enjoy? Well, this whole state of Maine looks that way. If it's not a beautiful lake, it's a beautiful tree, or a pretty green hay meadow. And beautiful old time houses, with barns built right in with the kitchens.
Will Rogers, July 13, 1934, in Donald Day, ed., *The Autobiography of Will Rogers*, 1949.

Don't ever ask directions of a Maine native.... Somehow we think it is funny to misdirect people and we don't smile when we do it, but we laugh inwardly. It is our nature.

A NATIVE OF MAINE, in John Steinbeck, *Travels with Charley*, 1962.

You can certainly learn to spell "moccasin" while driving into Maine, and there is often little else to do, except steer and avoid death.

E.B. WHITE, "Home-coming," December 10, 1955, *Essays of E.B. White*, 1977.

MARYLAND

Fatti maschii, parole femine. (Manly deeds, womanly words.)

State motto.

For more than a century Baltimore was known throughout the nation under the unsavory name of "Mobtown." The title owed its origin to the speed and frequency with which the citizenry found excuse to riot.

FRANCIS F. BEIRNE, *The Amiable Baltimoreans*, 1968.

Men act while women talk....This forthright sentiment is inscribed in our Great Seal of Maryland. We got rid of it for a while but it contrived to come back in 1876. Even today the seal's sexist message is spread throughout the state from Port Tobacco to Oldtown.

CARL BODE, *Maryland*, 1978.

You have never seen, on the lap of nature, so large a burden so neatly accommodated. Baltimore sits there as some quite robust but almost unnaturally good child might sit on the green apron of its nurse, with no concomitant crease or crumple, no uncontrollable "mess," by the nursery term, to betray its temper.

HENRY JAMES, *The American Scene*, 1907.

I firmly believe that Maryland is the most improbable state in the Union.

GERALD W. JOHNSON, *America-Watching*, 1976.

America in Miniature.

THEODOR MCKELDEN, ca. 1955, in Eugene L. Meyer, *Maryland Lost and Found*, 1986.

Such is Maryland in this 146th year of the republic—a great, a rich, and a puissant state, but somehow flabby underneath, somehow dead-looking in the eyes.

H.L. MENCKEN, in Ernest H. Grueing, ed., *These United States*, 1924.

A Baltimorean is not merely John Doe, an isolated individual of *homo sapiens*, exactly like every other John Doe. He is John Doe of a certain place—of Baltimore, of a definite *house* in Baltimore.

H.L. MENCKEN, *Prejudices*, 1926.

The old charm, in truth, still survives in [Baltimore] despite the frantic efforts of the boosters and boomers who, in late years, have replaced all its ancient cobblestones with asphalt, and bedizened it with Great White Ways and suburban boulevards, and surrounded it with stinking steel plants and oil refineries, and increased its population from 400,000 to 800,000.

H.L. MENCKEN, *Prejudices*, 1926.

MASSACHUSETTS

Ense petit placidam sub libertate quietem. (By the sword we seek peace, but peace only under liberty.)

State motto.

Only Bostonians can understand Bostonians and thoroughly sympathize with the inconsequences of the Boston mind.

HENRY ADAMS, *The Education of Henry Adams*, 1907.

No doubt the Bostonian has always been noted for a certain chronic irritability—a sort of Bostonitis—which, in its primitive Puritan form, seemed due to knowing too much of his neighbors, and thinking too much of himself.

HENRY ADAMS, *The Education of Henry Adams*, 1907.

In the course of my life I have tried Boston socially on all sides: I have summered it and wintered it, tried it drunk and tried it sober; and, drunk or sober, there's nothing in it—save Boston!

CHARLES FRANCIS ADAMS, JR., *Charles Francis Adams, An Autobiography*, 1916.

I have just returned from Boston. It is the only thing to do if you find yourself up there.

FRED ALLEN, letter to Groucho Marx, June 12, 1953.

And this is good old Boston

The home of the beans and the cod

Where the Lowells talk to the Cabots

And the Cabots talk only to God.

JOHN COLLINS BOSSIDY, Holy Cross Alumni Dinner, 1910, in Neal R. Peirce, *The New England States*, 1976.

Its driving energy sparked always by independence and freedom of the spirit—can this be anywhere so strong, so fascinating, so enduring as in Massachusetts?

PEARL S. BUCK, *America*, 1971.

Have faith in Massachusetts.

CALVIN COOLIDGE, speech, Massachusetts legislature, January 7, 1914.

The society of Boston was and is quite uncivilized but refined beyond the point of civilization.

T.S. ELIOT, *Little Review*, 1918.

In proportion as Boston furnished the fundamentals for an ideally cultivated life, it is not surprising that Boston should have received her share of gibes and jests from many larger but less fortunate neighbors.

JOHN P. MARQUAND, *The Late George Apley*, 1937.

"I *hated* Boston," he tells me. "Black people in Boston have so little unity they won't even get together for a riot."

ALICE WALKER, "Lulls," January 15, 1976, *In Search of Our Mothers' Gardens*, 1983.

One feels in Boston, as one feels in no other part of the States, that the intellectual movement has ceased.

H.G. WELLS, "The Future in America," 1906.

MICHIGAN

Si quaeris peninsulam amoenam circumspice. (If you seek a pleasant peninsula, look around you).
State motto.

Michigan is perhaps the strangest state in the Union, a place where the past, the present, and the future are all tied up together in a hard knot.... It is the skyscraper, the mass-production line, and the frantic rush into what the machine will some day make all of us, and at the same time it is golden sand, blue water, green pine trees on empty hills, and a wind that comes down from the cold spaces, scented with the forests that were butchered by hard-handed men in checked flannel shirts and floppy pants. It is the North Country wedded to the force that destroyed it.

BRUCE CATTON, "Michigan," *American Panorama: East of the Mississippi*, 1960.

The only state in the union boasting a spare part.

LEONARD LANSON CLINE, in Ernest H. Gruening, ed., *These United States*, 1924.

The Michiganders were a people without identity, without community of purpose or past, without tradition. Then Ford.

LEONARD LANSON CLINE, in Ernest H. Gruening, ed., *These United States*, 1924.

The capital of the new planet—the one, I mean, which will kill itself off—is of course Detroit.

HENRY MILLER, *The Air-Conditioned Nightmare*, 1945.

You can slip up on Detroit in the dead of night, consider it from any standpoint, and it's still hell on wheels.

GEORGE SESSIONS PERRY, *Cities of America*, 1947.

On the dreary yellow Michigan waste with its gray stains of frozen water, the cars wait like horses at a pond.

EDMUND WILSON, "Detroit Motors," *New Republic*, 1931.

MIDWEST

The Midwest is exactly what one would expect from a marriage between New England puritanism and *rich* soil.

JOHN GUNTHER, *Inside U.S.A.*, 1947.

You get damn few good guys in the Middle West.

ERNEST HEMINGWAY, to Waldo Pierce, on Hemingway's month-long stay in Piggot, Arkansas, 1928.

In the Middle West, the high school is the place where the band practices.

ROBERT M. HUTCHINS, *New York Herald Tribune*, April 22, 1963.

The people who know the place only by driving through it know the flatness. They skim along a grade of least resistance. The interstate defeats their best intentions. I see them starting out, big-hearted and romantic, from the density and the variety of the East to see just how big this country is. They are well read, and they have a vision as they come out of the green hills and the vista opens up, a true vision so vast that at night as they drive there are only the farmyard lights that demonstrate plane geometry by their rearranging patterns.

MICHAEL MARTONE, "The Flatness," *A Place of Sense*, 1988.

It isn't necessary to have relatives in Kansas City to be unhappy.

GROUCHO MARX, letter to Goodman Ace, January 18, 1951.

MINNESOTA

L'étoile du nord. (The star of the north.)
State motto.

To understand Minnesota it is necessary...that one respond to youth, forgiving its occasional awkwardness and egoism for the sake of its healthy vigor, its color, its alternating self-confidence and self-distrust, its eagerness for experiment. One will not expect to find here the mellowness of cities, villages, and countrysides as in the older states.
Federal Writers' Project, *Minnesota: A State Guide,* 1938.

Where all the women are strong, all the men are good looking, and all the children above average.
Garrison Keillor, 1980s, on Lake Wobegon, fictional Minnesota town of radio show "Prairie Home Companion."

Minnesotans are just different, that's all. On the day of which I speak, with the wind-chill factor hovering at fifty-seven below, hundreds of them could be perceived through the slits of my ski mask out ice fishing on this frozen lake. It was cold out there, bitter, biting, cutting, piercing, hyperborean, marmoreal cold, and there were all these Minnesotans running around outdoors, happy as lambs in the spring.
Charles Kuralt, *Dateline America,* 1979.

The state seal shows a farmer, a waterfall, a forest, and an Indian riding into the sunset. It should be changed to ice cubes rampant on a field of white, a grinning, barefoot Swede in a Grain Belt Beer T-shirt riding a snowmobile, and a shivering visitor whose stricken breath is freezing into ice crystals.
Charles Kuralt, *Dateline America,* 1979.

"Home of the Late April Slush."
Calvin Trillin, suggested motto for Minneapolis, Minnesota, "The Motto-Maker's Art," *The Nation,* February 23, 1985.

MISSISSIPPI

Virtute es armis. (By valor and arms.)
State motto.

Mississippi begins in the lobby of a Memphis, Tennessee, hotel and extends south to the Gulf of Mexico. It is dotted with little towns concen-

tric about the ghosts of the horses and mules once tethered to the hitch-rail enclosing the county courthouse and it might almost be said to have only two directions, north and south, since until a few years ago it was impossible to travel east or west in it unless you walked or rode one of the horses or mules.
William Faulkner, "Mississippi," *American Panorama: East of the Mississippi,* 1960.

For the native Mississippian long has accepted the fact that the Delta is more than a distinct geographical unit, it is also a way of life. The word "Delta" connotes for him persons charmingly lacking in provincialism rather than wide flat fields steaming with fertility and squat plantation towns that are all alike.
Federal Writers' Project, *Mississippi: A Guide to the Magnolia State,* 1949.

We Mississippi white folk...think as our land thinks, and those who understand our simple psychology and accept our way as being complete rather than clever find us tolerant but not susceptible, easy to amuse but hard to convince. Our faith is in God, next year's crop, and the Democratic Party.
Federal Writers' Project, *Mississippi: A Guide to the Magnolia State,* 1949.

Mississippians are serenely confident that they have the most colorful history of any state. Never mind that almost all of it concerns one lost concern or another.
Bern Keating, *Fodor's South,* 1979.

A debonair disregard for the truth, lawlessness allied with righteousness, and a contempt for Negroes are the major elements which go into the making of the Mississippi mind.
William McCord, *Mississippi: The Long Hot Summer,* 1965.

When you're in Mississippi, the rest of America doesn't seem real. And when you're in the rest of America, Mississippi doesn't seem real.
Bob Parris Moses, ca. 1961, in Jack Newfield, "Amite County," *Bread and Roses Too,* 1971.

MISSOURI

Sallus populi suprema lex esto. (The welfare of the people shall be the supreme law.)
State motto.

The spare Ozark hillman, with his rabbit gun and dog, is a Missourian. So is the weathered open-country farmer; the prosperous cotton planter; the subsistence sharecropper with his stairsteps family; the drawling sawmill hand; the scientific orchardist reading his bulletins from the fruit experiment stations; the lead miner; the hustling small town merchant; the Kansas City business man; the St. Louis industrialist with one eye on Jefferson City and the other on Washington; the smiling filling station attendant who talks to everyone crossing the continent; the silent riverman who lives in a shanty boat and sees almost nobody—all are Missourians.

IRVING L. DILHARD, Federal Writers' Project, *Missouri: A Guide to the Show Me State*, 1941.

Be from Missouri, of course; but for God's sake forget it occasionally.

ELBERT HUBBARD, *The Roycroft Dictionary and Book of Epigrams*, 1923.

Of course it's not just a cow town. It's not a cow town at all. The stockyards are all but gone, just like Chicago and all the other places with cow town image problems. Kansas City's a grain town.

KANSAS CITY WOMAN, *New York Times*, November 14, 1981.

A Missourian gets used to Southerners thinking him a Yankee, a Northerner considering him a cracker, a Westerner sneering at his effete Easternness, and the Easterner taking him for a cowhand.

WILLIAM LEAST HEAT MOON, *Blue Highways*, 1982.

That peppery, independent spirit, not entirely foreign to the ornery mules who helped make Missouri famous, has surfaced again and again in Missouri history, recent decades not excepted.

NEAL R. PEIRCE, *The Great Plains States of America*, 1973.

Old, genteel St. Louis—T.S. Eliot's city—thought of itself as a slice of cultivated Europe. It seemed mystified as to how it had landed here, stranded on the wrong side of the big American river.

JONATHAN RABAN, *Old Glory*, 1981.

MONTANA

Oro y plata. (Gold and silver.)
State motto.

Montana is as big as Illinois, Michigan, and Indiana. It is bigger than Italy and Japan. To say that it is the third American state in size does not, perhaps, make its enormousness tangible; say

instead that one out of every twenty-five American square miles is Montanan.

JOHN GUNTHER, *Inside U.S.A.*, 1947.

Montana: High, Wide, and Handsome.

JOSEPH KINSEY HOWARD, book title, 1943.

Colorado is high, having more peaks within its borders than any other state. Wyoming is wide, with the breadth of the plains between the Big Horns and the Grand Tetons. California is handsome, with a splendor of success. It takes all three adjectives to describe Montana.

DONALD CULROSS PEATTIE, *The Road of a Naturalist*, 1941.

Montana seems to me to be what a small boy would think Texas is like from hearing Texans.

JOHN STEINBECK, *Travels with Charley*, 1962.

It seemed to me that the frantic bustle of America was not in Montana. Its people did not seem afraid of shadows in a John Birch Society sense. The calm of the mountains and the rolling grasslands had got into the inhabitants.

JOHN STEINBECK, *Travels with Charley*, 1962.

NEBRASKA

Equality Before the Law.
State motto.

It is this determination to remain on the land, this never-ending struggle of human strength and will against natural forces, that characterizes the Nebraska temperament.

FEDERAL WRITERS' PROJECT, *Nebraska: A Guide to the Cornhusker State*, 1939.

Here the Middle West merges with the West. The farms and small towns in the eastern half suggest the rich, more densely populated country of Iowa and Illinois. The cities have much of the fast tempo and businesslike ways that prevail in the larger cities of the Midwest. But, in western Nebraska, fields give way to the great cattle ranches of the sandhill area, life is more leisurely, and manners are more relaxed. Something of the Old West still survives.

FEDERAL WRITERS' PROJECT, *Nebraska: A Guide to the Cornhusker State*, 1939.

When an Omaha man (or boy) speaks of a steak, one expects him to pull from his pocket a series of treasured snapshots of steaks.

PHILIP HAMBURGER, *An American Notebook*, 1965.

I had visions of a dark and dusty night on the plains, and the faces of Nebraska families wandering by, with their rosy children looking at everything with awe.

JACK KEROUAC, *On the Road*, 1957.

Barns back east have weather vanes on them to show which way the wind is blowing, but out here there's no need....Farmers just look out the window to see which way the barn is leaning. Some farmers...attach a logging chain to a stout pole. They can tell the wind direction by which way the chain is blowing. They don't worry about high wind until the chain starts whipping around and links begin snapping off. Then they know it's likely the wind will come up before morning.

CHARLES KURALT, *Dateline America*, 1979.

There is no obstruction but the sky.

WRIGHT MORRIS, *Ceremony in Lone Tree*, 1960.

The Platte River is famous for being a mile wide and an inch deep, and it's both sometimes. But there's other times—like this stretch along the South Fork—when it narrowed up and deepened down and hurried along looking siltier and soupier than usual, too thick to drink and too runny to eat.

DAVID WAGONER, *Whole Hog*, 1976.

I was once driving through Nebraska's Sandhills and I met a car that struck me as being peculiar. Something about the car was distinctive. I commented to that effect to my companion, and he said that something about the car had struck him as unusual too. We talked about it for a few minutes, and then we figured out what it was that was strange about the vehicle: It was the first one we had seen in two hours of travel.

ROGER WELCH, *It's Not the End of the Earth, but You Can See It from Here*, 1990.

NEVADA

All for Our Country.

State motto.

Vegas is the most extreme and allegorical of American settlements, bizarre and beautiful in its venality and in its devotion to immediate gratification, a place the tone of which is set by mobsters and

call girls and ladies' room attendants with amyl nitrite poppers in their uniform pockets.

JOAN DIDION, "Marrying Absurd," *Slouching Towards Bethlehem*, 1968.

Look at Utah and Nevada from an airplane. They are indistinguishable. You could not possibly tell where one stops and the other begins. Yet the two states differ so enormously that they might belong to different worlds. Utah is a creature of the Mormon Church....Nevada was settled...by miners and prospectors and gamblers who found California too tame. Utah is the most staid and respectable of states; Nevada is, by common convention at least, the naughtiest.

JOHN GUNTHER, *Inside U.S.A.*, 1947.

Nevada is mostly desert, mountains, and fabulous natural resources. It is one of the friendliest states I know, and it lives on four things, mining, livestock, the divorce trade, and gambling.

JOHN GUNTHER, *Inside U.S.A.*, 1947.

Neon looks good in Nevada. The tawdriness is refined out of it in so much wide black space.

JOHN MCPHEE, *Basin and Range*, 1980.

There is very little but rock and sand, alkali-laden dry lakes, buttes and craggy mountains. The desolation of Nevada is awesome.

NEIL MORGAN, *Westward Tilt—The American West Today*, 1963.

The most insidious influence of Las Vegas is its destruction of wonder: The wonder of sex, the wonder of chance, and the wonder of oneself. Everything is settled fast in Las Vegas. Like the lava outcroppings of its desert, Nevada has become a molten overflow of the American passion for excess. It is a long way from Plymouth Rock.

NEIL MORGAN, *Westward Tilt—The American West Today*, 1963.

You can read that Nevada is the most sparsely settled state in the Union, but it takes an example to make you really feel it. There was just one telephone book for the whole state! Every phone in Nevada was listed in it, plus four counties of adjoining California. And the whole thing made a thin little volume that you could stick in your topcoat pocket.

ERNIE PYLE, 1930, in Jack Newcombe, ed., *Travels in the Americas*, 1989.

NEW HAMPSHIRE

Live Free or Die.

State motto.

If two New Hampshire men aren't a match for the devil, we might as well give the country back to the Indians.

Stephen Vincent Benét, *The Devil and Daniel Webster—13 O'clock*, 1937.

New Hampshire citizens are more gregarious and more open, less clannish and ever ready to smile, and perhaps more even-tempered than those in Vermont—generally speaking, of course.

Pearl S. Buck, *America*, 1971.

I like your nickname, the "Granite State." It shows the strength of character, firmness of principle and restraint that have long characterized New Hampshire.

Gerald R. Ford, speech, Concord, New Hampshire, April 17, 1975.

She's one of the two best states in the Union.

Vermont's the other.

Robert Frost, "New Hampshire," 1923.

Politically New Hampshire is as unproductive as an abandoned farm.

Ralph D. Paine, in Ernest H. Gruening, ed., *These United States*, 1924.

I live in New Hampshire so I can get a better view of Vermont.

Maxfield Parrish, *Vermont Life*, 1952.

Making state government responsive is a task which the people of New Hampshire have not had the political intelligence to face up to.

Former New Hampshire governor, in Neal R. Peirce, *The New England States*, 1976.

NEW JERSEY

Liberty and Prosperity.

State motto.

New Jersey has always been a useful "no man's land" between the arrogance of New York and the obstinacy of Pennsylvania. The time it takes to traverse it diagonally permits a cooling off, coming or going.

Struthers Burt, *Philadelphia: Holy Experiment*, 1945.

Like China, New Jersey absorbs the invader.

Federal Writers' Project, *New Jersey: A Guide to Its Present and Past*, 1939.

A sort of laboratory in which the best blood is prepared for other communities to thrive upon.

Woodrow Wilson, in Federal Writers' Project, *New Jersey: A Guide to Its Present and Past*, 1939.

We have always been inconvenienced by New York on the one hand and Philadelphia on the other.

Woodrow Wilson, in Federal Writers' Project, *New Jersey: A Guide to Its Present and Past*, 1939.

NEW MEXICO

It Grows as It Goes.

State motto.

Land of Enchantment.

License plate.

Four score years before the first Texas cowboy scuffed a high-heeled boot on Plymouth Rock, a Mr. Coronado of Spain was eating corn off the cob in New Mexico and mailing home postcards of five-storied Pueblo tourist courts marked "Come on over, the climb is fine."

S. Omar Baker, in John Gunther, *Inside U.S.A.*, 1947.

Space is the keynote of the land—vast, limitless stretches of plain, desert, and lofty mountains, with buttes and mesas and purple distances to rest the eye.

Federal Writers' Project, *New Mexico: A Guide to the Colorful State*, 1940.

That New Mexico, which has given life to art from ancient Indian rain dances to a story like [D.H.] Lawrence's "The Woman Who Rode Away," should also have given birth to the atomic bomb, is perhaps an irony that measures the gamut of our civilization.

John Gunther, *Inside U.S.A.*, 1947.

It looks rather like Nevada, but is higher, ruggeder, more dramatic. Half the mountains seem to have their tops blown off.

John Gunther, *Inside U.S.A.*, 1947.

There is very little to explain growth here except the power of the atom—and the charm of the land.

Neil Morgan, *Westward Tilt*, 1963.

NEW YORK

Excelsior. (Ever upward.)
State motto.

All its inhabitants ascend to heaven right after their deaths, having served their full term in hell right on Manhattan Island.
Barnard Bulletin, September 22, 1967.

When an American stays away from New York too long, something happens to him. Perhaps he becomes a little provincial, a little dead, a little afraid.
SHERWOOD ANDERSON, in Mike Marqusee and Bill Harris, *New York,* 1985.

As one comes down the Henry Hudson Parkway along the river in the dusk, New York is never real; it is always fabulous.
ANTHONY BAILEY, *The New Yorker,* July 29, 1967.

What the New Yorker calls home would seem like a couple of closets to most Americans, yet he manages not only to live there but also to grow trees and cockroaches right on the premises.
RUSSELL BAKER, *New York Times,* November 18, 1978.

All of Harlem is pervaded by a sense of congestion, rather like the insistent, maddening, claustrophobic pounding in the skull that comes from trying to breathe in a very small room with all the windows shut.
JAMES BALDWIN, *Notes of a Native Son,* 1955.

My life had begun...in the invincible and indescribable squalor of Harlem....In that ghetto I was tormented. I felt caged, like an animal. I wanted to escape. I felt if I did not get out I would slowly strangle.
JAMES BALDWIN, TV narrative, June 1, 1964.

You can take a boy out of Brooklyn, but you can never get Brooklyn out of the boy.
W.T. BALLARD, *Say Yes to Murder,* 1942.

The trouble with New York is it's so convenient to everything I can't afford.
JACK BARRY, *Reader's Digest,* December, 1952.

New York, the hussy, was taken in sin again!
THOMAS BEER, *The Mauve Decade,* 1926.

What is barely hinted at in other American cities is condensed and enlarged in New York.
SAUL BELLOW, in Mike Marqusee and Bill Harris, *New York,* 1985.

I regard it [Manhattan] as a curiosity: I don't let myself get caught in the wheels.
LUDWIG BEMELMANS, *Time,* July 2, 1951.

Everybody ought to have a lower East Side in their life.
IRVING BERLIN, *Vogue,* November 1, 1962.

Nowhere is [success] pursued more ardently than in the city of New York.
STEPHEN BIRMINGHAM, *Holiday,* March, 1961.

I like the rough impersonality of New York, where human relations are oiled by jokes, complaints, and confessions—all made with the assumption of never seeing the other person again. I like New York because there are enough competing units to make it still seem a very mobile society. I like New York because it engenders high expectations simply by its pace.
BILL BRADLEY, *Life on the Run,* 1976.

People born in Queens, raised to say that each morning they get on the subway and "go to the city," have a resentment of Manhattan, of the swiftness of its life and success of the people who live there.
JIMMY BRESLIN, *Table Money,* 1986.

The present in New York is so powerful that the past is lost.
JOHN JAY CHAPMAN, letter, 1909.

The food of the city's most celebrated dining salons, with one or perhaps two exceptions, is neither predictably elegant nor superb. More often than not it is predictably commonplace.
CRAIG CLAIBORNE, *New York Times,* September 1, 1963.

Give My Regards to Broadway.
GEORGE M. COHAN, song title, 1904.

The sensual mysticism of entire vertical being.
E.E. CUMMINGS, on New York City, quoted in *Architectural Digest,* September, 1986.

In New York City we need police officers to protect even the dead.
WILLIAM J. DEAN, on desecration of graves in Potter's Field, *Time,* August 29, 1983.

New York is full of people...with a feeling for the tangential adventure, the risky adventure, the interlude that's not likely to end in any double-ring ceremony.
JOAN DIDION, *Mademoiselle,* February, 1961.

New York is a different country. Maybe it ought to have a separate government. Everybody thinks differently, acts differently. They just don't know what the hell the rest of the United States is.

HENRY FORD, *Reader's Digest*, October, 1973.

[Hell is] New York City with all the escape hatches sealed.

JAMES R. FRAKES, *New York Times*, May 19, 1974.

New York is a city of conversations overheard, of people at the next restaurant table (micrometers away) checking your watch, of people reading the stories in your newspaper on the subway train.

WILLIAM E. GEIST, "A Quiet Sendoff at the Barbershop," *New York Times*, October 25, 1986.

New York...that unnatural city where every one is an exile, none more so than the American.

CHARLOTTE PERKINS GILMAN, *The Living of Charlotte Perkins Gilman*, 1935.

Prostitution is the only business that isn't leaving the city.

ROY GOODMAN, speech, New York Press Club, October 24, 1976.

Those lions still are rude and wild,

For while they pose as meek and mild,
  To keep their fierceness hid,

Down from their pedestals they'd leap,

As soon as New York went to sleep—
  If New York ever did!

ARTHUR GUITERMAN, on lions at entrance to New York Public Library, *The New York Public Library in Fiction, Poetry, and Children's Literature*, 1950.

It is one of the great charms of New York that at the Met one may still see bejeweled Grandes Dames, rouged like crazy, wearing what at first glance appear to be black fur stoles, but then turn out to be their enervated sons slung across their mamas' magnificent shoulders; one may still see Elderly Patricians hanging from boxes by the heels, with their opera glasses pointing like guns right *down* the décolletage of the huge soprano; one may still see swarms of Liveried Chauffeurs waiting to escort their Employers to their cars, to place fur wraps around their aged shanks, to touch their caps respectfully at the words, "Home, James, and don't spare the Rolls."

TYRONE GUTHRIE, "The 'Grand' Opera Behind Grand Opera," *New York Times Magazine*, January 5, 1958.

The city of right angles and tough, damaged people.

PETE HAMILL, *New York Daily News*, November 15, 1978.

New York was the only city in the United States that did not need a booster organization....In New York we simply assumed that we were the best—in baseball as well as intellect, in brashness and in subtlety, in everything—and it would have been unseemly to remark upon such an obvious fact.

MICHAEL HARRINGTON, *Fragments of the Century*, 1973.

The lusts of the flesh can be gratified anywhere; it is not this sort of license that distinguishes New York. It is, rather, a lust of the total ego for recognition, even for eminence. More than elsewhere, everybody here wants to be Somebody.

SYDNEY J. HARRIS, *Strictly Personal*, 1953.

The only credential [New York City] asked was the boldness to dream. For those who did, it unlocked its gates and its treasures, not caring who they were or where they came from.

MOSS HART, *Act One*, 1959.

The Yappian Way.

O. HENRY, "Modern Rural Sports," *The Gentle Grafter*, 1908.

You'd think New York people was all wise; but no. They don't get a chance to learn. Everything's too compressed. Even the hayseeds are baled hayseeds. But what else can you expect from a town that's shut off from the world by the ocean on one side and New Jersey on the other?

O. HENRY, "A Tempered Wind," *The Gentle Grafter*, 1908.

The city gave him what he demanded and then branded him with its brand....He acquired that charming insolence, that irritating completeness, the sophisticated crassness, that overbalanced poise that makes the Manhattan gentleman so delightfully small in his greatness.

O. HENRY, "The Defeat of the City," *The Voice of the City*, 1908.

It couldn't have happened anywhere but in little old New York.

O. HENRY, "A Little Local Colour," *Whirligigs*, 1910.

[Like] most native New Yorkers I was born out of town, Cedar Rapids, Iowa, to be specific.

HARRY HERSHFIELD, *New York Times*, December 5, 1965.

New York: The posthumous revenge of the Merchant of Venice.

ELBERT HUBBARD, *The Roycroft Dictionary and Book of Epigrams*, 1923.

Melting pot Harlem—Harlem of honey and chocolate and caramel and rum and vinegar and lemon and lime and gall...where the subway from the Bronx keeps right on downtown.

LANGSTON HUGHES, *Freedomways*, Summer, 1963.

We have had all the reform that we want in this city for some time to come.

JOHN F. HYLAN, speech, Civil Service Reform Association, January 10, 1918.

One of the things that amaze me is the amount of energy that's in New York. You get no energy from the earth because the earth is all covered up with cement and bricks. There's no place to walk on the earth unless you go to Central Park. The energy all comes from human beings.

PHIL JACKSON, in Bill Bradley, *Life on the Run*, 1976.

The main reason why the unlighted streets were not turned into a dark and steaming jungle was the reaction of the community....In the dark all men were the same color. In the dark our fellow man was seen more clearly than in the normal light of a New York night.

STEPHEN KENNEDY, on low crime rate during blackout, *Time*, August 31, 1959.

The world is grand, awfully big and astonishingly beautiful, frequently thrilling. But I love New York.

DOROTHY KILGALLEN, *Girl Around the World*, 1936.

To start with, there's the alien accent. "Tree" is the number between two and four. "Jeintz" is the name of the New York professional football team. A "fit" is a bottle measuring seven ounces less than a quart. This exotic tongue has no relationship to any of the approved languages at the United Nations, and is only slightly less difficult to master than Urdu.

FLETCHER KNEBEL, *Look*, March 26, 1963.

No other city in the United States can divest the visitor of so much money with so little enthusiasm. In Dallas, they take away with gusto; in New Orleans, with a bow; in San Francisco, with a wink and a grin. In New York, you're lucky if you get a grunt.

FLETCHER KNEBEL, *Look*, March 26, 1963.

New York has total depth in every area. Washington has only politics; after that, the second biggest thing is white marble.

JOHN V. LINDSAY, *Vogue*, August, 1963.

Robinson Crusoe, the self-sufficient man, could not have lived in New York City.

WALTER LIPPMANN, *Newsweek*, February 26, 1968.

New York attracts the most talented people in the world in the arts and professions. It also attracts them in other fields. Even the bums are talented.

EDMUND LOVE, *Subways Are for Sleeping*, 1957.

The ills of New York cannot be solved by money. New York will be ill until it is magnificent. For New York must be ready to show the way to the rest of Western civilization. Until it does, it will be no more than the victim of the technological revolution no matter how much money it receives in its budget.

NORMAN MAILER, *New York Times Magazine*, May 18, 1965.

Seen from the middle arch of the bridge at twilight, New York with its girdle of shifting waters and its drift of purple cloud and its quick pulsations of unstable light is a miracle of splendour and beauty that lifts up the heart like the laughter of a god.

DON MARQUIS, "The Almost Perfect State," *The Best of Don Marquis*, 1927.

Terrible things happen to young girls in New York City.

MARY MARGARET McBRIDE, *A Long Way from Missouri*, 1959.

A car is useless in New York, essential everywhere else. The same with good manners.

MIGNON McLAUGHLIN, *The Second Neurotic's Notebook*, 1966.

Every great wave of popular passion that rolls up on the prairies is dashed to spray when it strikes the hard rocks of Manhattan.

H.L. MENCKEN, *Prejudices*, 1926.

New York is not all bricks and steel....It is the place where all the aspirations of the Western World meet to form one vast master aspiration....It is the icing on the pie called Christian Civilization.

H.L. MENCKEN, *Prejudices*, 1927.

He speaks English with the flawless imperfection of a New Yorker.

GILBERT MILLSTEIN, on Andre Surmain, *Esquire*, January, 1962.

I like living here. Brooklyn has given me pleasure, has helped to educate me; has afforded me, in fact, the kind of tame excitement on which I thrive.

Marianne Moore, "Brooklyn from Clinton Hill," *A Marianne Moore Reader*, 1961.

The nation's thyroid gland.

Christopher Morley, on New York City, *New York Times*, March 2, 1970.

New York is the perfect model of a city, not the model of a perfect city.

Lewis Mumford, *My Work and Days*, 1979.

The Bronx?
No thonx.

Ogden Nash, *The New Yorker*, 1931.

That's the New York thing, isn't it. People who seem absolutely crazy going around telling you how crazy they used to be before they had therapy.

Judith Rossner, *Any Minute I Can Split*, 1972.

Every person on the streets of New York is a type. The city is one big theater where everyone is on display.

Jerry Rubin, *Growing (Up) at 37*, 1976.

Genghis Khan conquered Asia with an army only half the size of New York City's civil service.

Emanuel Savas, *New York Times Magazine*, October 8, 1972.

This city's got the right name—New York. Nothing ever gets old around here.

Ralph Stephenson, on demolition of Pennsylvania station, *New York Times*, October 29, 1963.

The thing which in the subway is called congestion is highly esteemed in the night spots as intimacy.

Simeon Strunsky, *No Mean City*, 1944.

The pneumatic noisemaker is becoming the emblematic sound of New York, the way the bells of Big Ben are the sound of London.

Horace Sutton, *Saturday Evening Post*, March 11, 1961.

The Park Avenue of poodles and polished brass; it is cab country, tip-town, grassville, a window-washer's paradise.

Gay Talese, *New York Times*, June 23, 1965.

Most of the rich people are in New York. I don't care what *Forbes* says about where they live. They're here. We've got Texas rich people and California rich people and Colorado rich people. We've got rich people with new money and rich people with old money and rich people whose money just needs to sit in the window for a few

days and ripen in the sun. There's no variety of rich people we don't have in overstock. New York has more rich people than some cities have people.

Calvin Trillin, "Invasion of the Limo-Stretchers," King Features Syndicate, April 13, 1986.

Skyscraper National Park.

Kurt Vonnegut, *Slapstick*, 1976.

A thoroughfare that begins in a graveyard and ends in a river.

Description of Wall Street.

On any person who desires such queer prizes, New York will bestow the gift of loneliness and the gift of privacy. It is this largess that accounts for the presence within the city's walls of a considerable section of the population; for the residents of Manhattan are to a large extent strangers who have pulled up stakes somewhere and come to town, seeking sanctuary or fulfillment or some greater or lesser grail. The capacity to make such dubious gifts is a mysterious quality of New York. It can destroy an individual, or it can fulfill him, depending a good deal on luck. No one should come to New York to live unless he is willing to be lucky.

E.B. White, *Here Is New York*, 1949.

Although New York often imparts a feeling of great forlornness or forsakenness, it seldom seems dead or unresourceful; and you always feel that either by shifting your location ten blocks or by reducing your fortune by five dollars you can experience rejuvenation.

E.B. White, *Here Is New York*, 1949.

New York is to the nation what the white church spire is to the village—the visible symbol of aspiration and faith, the white plume saying the way is up!

E.B. White, *Here Is New York*, 1949.

A little strip of an island with a row of well-fed folks up and down the middle, and a lot of hungry folks on each side.

Harry Leon Wilson, on Manhattan, *The Spenders*, 1902.

It was a cruel city, but it was a lovely one; a savage city, yet it had such tenderness; a bitter, harsh, and violent catacomb of stone and steel and tunneled rock, slashed savagely with light, and roaring, fighting a constant ceaseless warfare of men and machinery; and yet it was so sweetly and so delicately pulsed, as full of warmth, of passion, and of love, as it was full of hate.

THOMAS WOLFE, *The Web and the Rock*, 1939.

But now the train was slowing to a halt. Long tongues of cement now appeared, and faces, swarming figures, running forms beside the train. And all these faces, forms, and figures slowed to instancy, were held there in the alertness of expectant movement. There was a grinding screech of brakes, a slight jolt, and for a moment, utter silence. At this moment there was a terrific explosion. It was New York.

THOMAS WOLFE, *The Web and the Rock*, 1939.

NORTH CAROLINA

Esse quam videri. (To be rather than seem.)
State motto.

If God isn't a Tarheel, why is the sky Carolina blue?
BUMPER STICKER.

In my honest and unbiased judgment, the Good Lord will place the Garden of Eden in North Carolina when He restores it to earth. He will do this because He will have so few changes to make in order to achieve perfection.

SAM ERVIN, *Humor of a Country Lawyer*, 1983.

A vale of humility between two mountains of conceit.

REFERENCE TO VIRGINIA AND SOUTH CAROLINA, Federal Writers' Project, *North Carolina*, 1939.

Western North Carolina is the last of the pioneer's preserve. The frontier has passed us by but this is the last isolated section to buckle under to modern times.

JOHN PARRIS, in Neal Peirce, *The Border South States*, 1975.

North Carolina begins with the brightness of sea sands and ends with the loneliness of the Smokies reaching in chill and cloud to the sky.

OVID WILLIAMS PIERCE, in Richard Walser, *The North Carolina Miscellany*, 1962.

The people of North Carolina are like that wonderful earth....I am going to *tell the truth* about these people, but God, it is the truth about America.

THOMAS WOLFE, letter to Maxwell Perkins, ca. 1930, in Wilma Dykeman and James Stokely, *The Border States*, 1968.

NORTH DAKOTA

Liberty and Union, Now and Forever, One and Inseparable.
State motto.

I like the democracy of North Dakota, the state without a millionaire and with the fewest paupers; where rich and poor find a common meeting ground in the fight for improvements in the home state....There is something of the broadness of its prairies in the mental makeup of its people. A radical is not so radical nor a conservative so conservative in this rather free-and-easy non-eastern state.

MART CONNOLLY, in Elwyn B. Robinson, *History of North Dakota*, 1966.

A State of unbounded plains and hills and Badlands—elbow room. Superb sunsets. High winds and tumbleweed. Farms and plows and sweeping fields....Little towns crowded on Saturday night, and busy cities shipping out the products of North Dakota and supplying the needs of the producers....The sad, slow wail of a coyote on the still prairie.

FEDERAL WRITERS' PROJECT, *North Dakota: A Guide to the Northern Prairie State*, 1938.

Freely admitted is the rural character of the State, and there is seldom an attempt to cover native crudities with a veneer of eastern culture.

FEDERAL WRITERS' PROJECT, *North Dakota: A Guide to the Northern Prairie State*, 1938.

All this country is still youthful. Man has not labored long enough there to thoroughly humanize it, and often you continue to find a savor of the desert or wilderness....The long broad slope between the Rocky Mountains and the Mississippi River which includes North Dakota is destined to be in most ways an ideal farming section that for extent and fertility will be unrivaled the world over.

CLIFTON JOHNSON, *Highways and Byways of the Rocky Mountains*, 1910.

I would never have been President if it had not been for my experiences in North Dakota.

THEODORE ROOSEVELT, in Elwyn B. Robinson, *History of North Dakota*, 1966.

The children of these prairies do not grow up expecting that all the bonbons of this world are going to be fed them with a runcible spoon by pampering destiny. Here you sweat by summer and shiver by winter and work and pay for everything you get, so that by the time you are an adult you are spiritually prepared for more hard work. North Dakota life has been meant to make of you a tough fighter, a hard worker.

CARROLL E. SIMCOX, speech, University of North Dakota, 1961.

If you will take a map of the United States and fold it in the middle, eastern edge against western, and crease it sharply, right in the crease will be Fargo.…That may not be a very scientific method for finding the east-west middle of the country, but it will do.

JOHN STEINBECK, *Travels with Charley,* 1962.

OHIO

With God, All Things Are Possible.
State motto.

Ohio is the farthest west of the east and the farthest north of the south.

LOUIS BROMFIELD, in John Gunther, *Inside U.S.A.,* 1947.

Basically, Ohio is nothing more nor less than a giant carpet of agriculture studded by great cities.

JOHN GUNTHER, *Inside U.S.A.,* 1947.

I know of no other metropolis with quite so impressive a record in the practical application of good citizenship to government.

JOHN GUNTHER, on Cleveland, *Inside U.S.A.,* 1947.

"Preferable to Youngstown."

CALVIN TRILLIN, suggested motto for Akron, Ohio, "The Motto-Maker's Art," *The Nation,* February 23, 1985.

OKLAHOMA

Labor omnia vincit. (Work conquers all things.)
State motto.

[In 1889] the last big tract of Indian land was declared open for settlement, in Oklahoma. The claimants and the speculators mounted their horses and lined up like trotters waiting for a starting gun. The itchy ones jumped the gun and were ever after known as Sooners—and Oklahoma was thereafter called the Sooner State.

ALISTAIR COOKE, *America,* 1973.

"Okla-homa," he explained.…"That's Choctaw. Okla-people. Humma-red. Red People. That's

what they called it when the Indians came here to live."

EDNA FERBER, *Cimarron,* 1930.

Oil. Nothing else mattered. Oklahoma, the dry, the wind-swept, the burning, was a sea of hidden oil. The red prairies, pricked, ran black and slimy with it. The work of years was undone in a day.…Compared to that which now took place the early days following the Run in '89 were idyllic. They swarmed on Oklahoma from every state in the Union.

EDNA FERBER, *Cimarron,* 1930.

The state that Oklahoma most resembles is of course Texas, if only because it too does everything with color and originality, but tell an Oklahoman that his state is a "dependency" of Texas and he will bite your eyes out.

JOHN GUNTHER, *Inside U.S.A.,* 1947.

Tall tales come out of Oklahoma just as out of Texas. One favorite describes the "crowbar hole." This is a hole through the wall that many houses have, designed to check the weather. You shove a crowbar through the hole; if it bends, the wind velocity outside is normal; if the bar breaks off, "it is better to stay in the house."

JOHN GUNTHER, *Inside U.S.A.,* 1947.

During a single day [during the Dust Bowl disaster of 1935], I heard, fifty millions *tons* of soil were blown away. People sat in Oklahoma City, with the sky invisible for three days in a row, holding dust masks over their faces and wet towels to protect their mouths at night, while the farms blew by.

JOHN GUNTHER, *Inside U.S.A.,* 1947.

A single knoll rises out of the plain in Oklahoma, north and west of the Wichita Range. For my people, the Kiowas, it is an old landmark, and they gave it the name Rainy Mountain. The hardest weather in the world is there. Winter brings blizzards, hot tornadic winds arise in the spring, and in summer the prairie is an anvil's edge.

N. SCOTT MOMADAY, *The Way to Rainy Mountain,* 1969.

Oklahoma is one of the friendliest states in the Union. Taxi drivers open the front door, so you can ride up front. If there's just one passenger he always rides with the driver, and they talk.

ERNIE PYLE, *Home Country,* 1947.

OREGON

The Union.
State motto.

Oregon's climate is not bad enough to make anybody curse it nor good enough to make anybody love it. The winter rains just barely fail of being execrable. The summers would be divine if it were not for the smoky haze which hangs over the landscape and hides nature's miracles.

CHARLES H. CHAPMAN, in Ernest H. Gruening, ed., *These United States*, 1924.

The green damp England of Oregon.

ALISTAIR COOKE, *America*, 1973.

Packed tight in a New York City subway, I have closed my eyes and imagined I was walking the ridge high above Cougar Lake. That ridge has the majesty of a cathedral.

WILLIAM O. DOUGLAS, *Of Men and Mountains*, 1950.

Oregon was settled by New Englanders in the first instance, and has a native primness, a conservatism, much like that of New Hampshire or Vermont. It is, indeed, one of the most astonishing things in America that Portland, Oregon, should be almost indistinguishable from Portland, Maine.

JOHN GUNTHER, *Inside U.S.A.*, 1947.

Oregonians...tend to be small-townish, middle-of-the-roadish, and Waspish. They're also fairly prudish about some things. *Last Tango in Paris* is not advertised in the big family newspapers, and when the society columns mention a cocktail party, it is usually called a reception.

E.J. KAHN, JR., *The New Yorker*, February 25, 1974.

Always get the skin rash up here. And athlete's foot all the way to the ankle. The moisture. It's certainly no wonder that this area has two or three natives a month take that one-way dip—it's either drown your blasted self or rot.

KEN KESEY, *Sometimes a Great Nation*, 1963.

Welcome to Oregon. While you're here I want you to enjoy yourselves. Travel, visit, drink in the beauty of our state. But for God's sake, don't move here.

TOM MCCALL, in Neal R. Peirce, *The Pacific States of America*, 1972.

Oregon is seldom heard of. Its people believe in the Bible, and hold that all radicals should be lynched. It has no poets and no statesmen.

H.L. MENCKEN, *American Mercury*, 1925.

If any West Coast city could be said to have a monopoly on propriety and an anxiousness to "keep things as they are," it is Portland, a town of quiet old wealth, discreet culture, and cautious politics.

NEAL R. PEIRCE, *The Pacific States of America*, 1972.

Oregon...a pleasant, homogeneous, self-contained state, filled with pleasant, homogeneous, self-contained people, overwhelmingly white, Protestant, and middle class. Even the working class was middle class.

ARTHUR M. SCHLESINGER, JR., *Robert Kennedy and His Times*, 1978.

Oregon is only an idea. It is in no scientific way a reality.

PHILIP WYLIE, *Generation of Vipers*, 1942.

PENNSYLVANIA

Virtue, Liberty and Independence.
State motto.

The Pennsylvania mind, as minds go, was not complex; it reasoned little and never talked; but in practical matters it was the steadiest of all American types; perhaps the most efficient; certainly the safest.

HENRY ADAMS, *The Education of Henry Adams*, 1907.

So I remembered you, ripe country of broad-backed horses, valley of cold, sweet springs and dairies with limestone floors.

STEPHEN VINCENT BENÉT, *John Brown's Body*, 1928.

But in Philadelphia, Philadelphians feel, the Right Thing is more natural and more firmly bred in [them] than anywhere else.

STEPHEN BIRMINGHAM, *The Golden Dream*, 1978.

Pittsburgh? They call it a shot-and-beer town. Hard-working guys with stumpy legs. A team with mean-looking black uniforms. Nothing squeaky-clean about Pittsburgh. It's good boys versus bad guys.

ROCKY BLIER, on Steelers, *New York Post*, January 20, 1979.

The power of Pittsburgh speaks today in uncluttered, long straight lines. Shafts of aluminum or steel climb the sky in clarity and muscular splendor.

NORMAN COUSINS, "Notes of a Changing America," 1960.

The blood in the earth runs deep at Gettysburg, but the eye sees only an enchanted land.

NORMAN COUSINS, "Visit to Gettysburg," 1964.

Nowhere in this country, from sea to sea, does nature comfort us with such assurance of plenty, such rich and tranquil beauty as in those unsung, unpainted hills of Pennsylvania.

REBECCA HARDING DAVIS, *Bits of Gossip*, 1904.

For all the insularity of the old guard, Pittsburgh was always an open and democratic town.

ANNIE DILLARD, *An American Childhood*, 1987.

Along the river sprawled for a quarter of a mile or more the huge low length of the furnaces [mills at Pittsburgh], great black bottle-like affairs with rows of stacks and long low sheds or buildings paralleling them, sheds from which came a continuous hammering and sputtering and glow of red fire. The whole was shrouded by a pall of gray smoke, even in the bright sunlight.

THEODORE DREISER, *A Book About Myself*, 1912.

On the whole I'd rather be in Philadelphia.

ATTRIBUTED TO W.C. FIELDS, proposed inscription for his tombstone.

There is positively nothing of Independence Hall, of its fine old Georgian amplitude and decency, its large serenity and symmetry and pink and drab, and its actual emphasis of detachment from the vulgar brush of things, that is *not* charming.

HENRY JAMES, *The American Scene*, 1907.

This old city is full of joiners. There's a club on every corner. Nowhere does the outsider feel as far outside as in Philadelphia.

CHARLES KURALT, *Dateline America*, 1979.

There is no part of America where the people and the soil fit as they seem to do in Pennsylvania.

WALLACE NUTTING, *Pennsylvania Beautiful*, 1924.

Pittsburgh...a smoky beauty whose hair by day drifts gray over the darkening streets, and by night is gusts of fire flaring a lightning along the rivers....There she stands, a skyscraper city set among a Y of rivers, and all circled with workshops and mills and mines....And her gift to the world is the bone-work of civilization, steel.

JAMES OPPENHEIM, *Romantic America*, 1913.

Philadelphia, a metropolis sometimes known as the City of Brotherly Love, but more accurately as the City of Bleak November Afternoons.

S.J. PERELMAN, *Westward Ha!*, 1948.

RHODE ISLAND

Hope.

State motto.

What Newport turns out to be, then, is homiletic, a fantastically elaborate stage setting for an American morality play in which money and happiness are presented as antithetical.

JOAN DIDION, "The Seacoast of Despair," *Slouching Towards Bethlehem*, 1968.

The uniqueness of Rhode Island lies in its size; [James] Bryce wrote that it might become the first American "city-state." Everybody is packed close together; almost everybody knows everybody else. An administrator—the governor, say—is at the beck and call of anybody; he must go and see for himself in an emergency, because everything is within fifty miles of his office.

JOHN GUNTHER, *Inside U.S.A.*, 1947.

One views [Aquidneck Island] as placed there, by some refinement in the scheme of nature, just as a touchstone of taste—with a beautiful little sense to be read into it by a few persons, and nothing at all to be made of it, as to its essence, by most others.

HENRY JAMES, *The American Scene*, 1907.

There is no question of illusion or disillusion about Providence—I know what it is, and have never mentally dwelt anywhere else....Providence is part of me—I *am* Providence.

H.P. LOVECRAFT, letter to Lillian Clark, March 27, 1926, in L. Sprague De Camp, *Lovecraft: A Biography*, 1975.

Rhode Island was settled and is made up of people who found it unbearable to live anywhere else in New England.

WOODROW WILSON, speech, New York City, January 29, 1911.

SOUTH

Southerners are, of course, a mythological people....Lost by choice in dreaming of high days gone and big house burned, now we cannot even wish to escape.

JONATHAN DANIELS, *A Southerner Discovers the South*, 1938.

Isn't it fantastic that George Washington Carver found over 300 uses for the lowly peanut—but the South never had any use for George Washington Carver?

DICK GREGORY, *From the Back of the Bus*, 1962.

The South is memories, memories—it cannot help believing that yesterday was better than tomorrow can possible be. Some of the memories are extraordinarily well-packaged, it is true, but when a place has been reduced in its own estimation no amount of artful packaging can hide the gloom.

LARRY MCMURTRY, *In a Narrow Grave: Essays on Texas*, 1968.

Southerners can never resist a losing cause.

MARGARET MITCHELL, *Gone With the Wind*, 1936.

Appalachia is the only region of this country with a real culture. It came to us from the British Isles—the music, the dances, the humor, the writers—but now it's ours, and I think we'll keep it.

JESSE STUART, in Neal R. Peirce, *The Border South States*, 1975.

Storytelling and copulation are the two chief forms of amusement in the South. They're inexpensive and easy to procure.

ROBERT PENN WARREN, *Newsweek*, August 25, 1980.

What a curse some old black mother in Africa, two hundred years ago, must have put upon the South when they took her child to the slave ship, and how the curse has bitten its terrible way into the destiny...not only of the South, but of America as well.

WILLIAM ALLEN WHITE, letter to Garrison Villard, 1928.

SOUTH CAROLINA

Animis opibusque parati. (Prepared in mind and resources.)

Dum spiro spero. (While I breathe, I hope.)
State mottoes.

The South Carolinian has fire in his head, comfort in his middle, and a little lead in his feet. Proud of his past, often scornful of innovations, he is not willing to adapt unless thoroughly convinced that it is a good thing....He knows his faults, at least many of them. He will discuss them and propose remedies—but woe to the outsider who reminds him of them. The faults of his State are as personal to him as a wart on his nose.

FEDERAL WRITERS' PROJECT, *South Carolina: A Guide to the Palmetto State*, 1941.

South Carolinians are among the rare folk in the South who have no secret envy of Virginians.

FEDERAL WRITERS' PROJECT, *South Carolina: A Guide to the Palmetto State*, 1941.

We were taught to be South Carolinians, Ca-ro-li-ni-ans, mind you, and not, please God, the Tarheel slur, Calinians.

WILLIAM FRANCIS GUESS, "South Carolina," *American Panorama: East of the Mississippi*, 1960.

An old Charlestonian may think of his city first and last, his heart bound to the palm-lined Battery, where echoes linger from the blasts of guns his forebears trained on two meddling foreign powers—Great Britain and the United States.

WILLIAM FRANCIS GUESS, "South Carolina," in *American Panorama: East of the Mississippi*, 1960.

SOUTH DAKOTA

Under God the People Rule.
State motto.

Hard work is a legacy of the generations who settled the prairie, broke the soil, built the sod houses, fought the droughts and grasshoppers and penny-a-pound prices for their products. It is a legacy that even those of us who leave carry with us. All of this work has produced what may be the single largest collection of powerful hands in the world.

TOM BROKAW, in John Milton, *South Dakota: A Bicentennial History*, 1977.

I guess it's the physical and cultural remoteness of South Dakota that compels everyone to memorize almost every South Dakotan who has left the state and achieved some recognition. As a child I would pore over magazines and newspapers, looking for some sign that the rest of the world knew we existed.

TOM BROKAW, in John Milton, *South Dakota: A Bicentennial History*, 1977.

You could shoot a cue ball from the southern boundary of the state all the way to Canada and halfway to the North Pole.

HOLGER CAHILL, *The Shadow of My Hand*, 1956.

The weathered skin of the Badlands is a crumbling, friable material, an inch or more deep, not to be trusted. Climbing a dry steep slope is like walking on a surface strewn with ball bearings.

JOHN MADSON, *National Geographic*, April, 1981.

The landscape appears to be neatly geometric, especially as divided by section lines, fences, county roads, and the remnants of railroad tracks; but it is full of surprises. Coloring changes with the movement of the sun and clouds, and shadows make abstract patterns on the grasses. Variable winds bend the grass, which sometimes undulates like ocean waves and at other times stands straight up as though peering for rain.

JOHN MILTON, *South Dakota: A Bicentennial History*, 1977.

The early history of South Dakota may be viewed as a series of protest movements against external forces. The first and immediate object of attack was the status of dependency under the territorial system to which the Dakota settlements were subjected beyond the normal period of federal tutelage. The second phase of the protest movement was the dissatisfaction expressed against alleged economic exploitation by railroads, grain warehouses, and other corporate interests in the form of excessive freight and elevator charges, high interest rates, and monopolistic prices.

HERBERT S. SCHELL, *History of South Dakota*, 1961.

TENNESSEE

Tennessee—America at Its Best.

State motto.

It appears to be a very American state, this Tennessee, and inhabited by very American people.

PEARL S. BUCK, *America*, 1971.

It grew from a brawling boom town on the river to the state's largest city so hurriedly that it has hardly had time to assess itself. Energetic, clean and preoccupied with its almost incredible industrial expansion, Memphis seems—despite its Beale Street, its heavy Negro population, its Cotton carnival, and a commanding position as the deep South's cotton-trade center, more like a bustling midwestern city than the mecca of Mississippi planters.

HODDING CARTER, 1947, "Tennessee," *Holiday Magazine's American Panorama: East of the Mississippi*, 1960.

There's only one place worth living in, and that's Middle Tennessee. When I get out I'm going back there. I'm going to marry a Nashville gal. I'm going to buy some Middle Tennessee land and raise Tennessee Walking Horses and Tennessee babies. I'm going to cure Tennessee hams with Tennessee hickory, and I'm not going to drink anything but old Jack Daniels sour-mash Tennessee whiskey. And if my wife ever talks about leaving Middle Tennessee, I'll drag her clean over to the Tennessee River and drown her. Hell, I'm so homesick I could root for the University and I'm a Vanderbilt man.

HOMESICK YOUNG TENNESSEE AIRMAN, in Hodding Carter, "Tennessee," *Holiday Magazine's American Panorama: East of the Mississippi*, 1960.

Striking a vein in Nashville will bring wealth beyond dreams of avarice. And the way in which this wealth is pursued and used makes Nashville not simply *another* version of the American Dream, but today—in the America of the '70s—the funkiest dream of all.

Esquire, November, 1971.

Tennesseans' lives are unhurried. Though they may complain about weather, poor crops, bad business and politics, beneath all is a certain feeling of security. The farmer will leave his plowing, the attorney his lawsuit, the business man his accounts, for a moment's or an hour's conversation with stranger or friend. With his good-tempered easiness of manners, the Tennessean has a democratic feeling of equality. His mind, unlike his bed, does not have to be made up each morning, for his judgment and dignity proceed from himself. Whether of farm, mountain, or city, he is like the Tennessee farmer who, after hearing Martin Van Buren speak, stepped up, shook the President's hand, and invited him "to come out and r'ar around with the boys."

FEDERAL WRITERS' PROJECT, *Tennessee: A Guide to the State*, 1939.

Take of London fog 30 parts; malaria 10 parts; gas leaks 20 parts; dewdrops gathered in a brickyard at sunrise 25 parts; odor of honeysuckle 15 parts. Mix. The mixture will give you an approximate conception of a Nashville drizzle.

O. HENRY, "A Municipal Report," *Strictly Business*, 1910.

What you need for breakfast, they say in east Tennessee, is a jug of good corn liquor, a thick beefsteak, and a hound dog. Then you feed the beefsteak to the hound dog.

CHARLES KURALT, *Dateline America*, 1979.

Tennessee summer days were not made for work; in fact, many a resident had doubted that they were made at all, but that they sprang to life from the cauldrons of hell.

CARL ROWAN, *South of Freedom*, 1952.

The countryside in Tennessee has a singular mildness and charm: now in summer, below the long mountains, darkish and bluish in the distance, the wheatfields show a blond that glows under a delicate pale blue sky.

EDMUND WILSON, "Tennessee Agrarians," 1931.

Chattanooga, Tennessee: old low sordid southern brick buildings, among which a few hotels, insurance companies and banks have expanded into big modern bulks, as if by sporadic effort; business streets that suddenly lapse into nigger cabins; a surrounding wilderness of mills.

EDMUND WILSON, "The Scottsboro Freight-Car Case," 1931.

TEXAS

Friendship.
State motto.

It was part of the Texas ritual. We're rich as son-of-a-bitch stew but look how homely we are, just as plain-folksy as Grandpappy back in 1836. We know about champagne and caviar but we talk hog and hominy.

EDNA FERBER, *Giant*, 1952.

I like the story, doubtless antique, that I heard near San Antonio. A child asks a stranger where he comes from, whereupon his father rebukes him gently, "Never do that, son. If a man's from Texas, he'll tell you. If he's not, why embarrass him by asking?"

JOHN GUNTHER, *Inside U.S.A.*, 1947.

Houston has been willed on the flat, uniform prairie not by some planned ideal, but by the expediency of land investment economics, first, and later by oil and petrochemical prosperity.

ADA LOUISE HUXTABLE, "Deep in the Heart of Nowhere," February 15, 1976, *Kicked a Building Lately?*, 1976.

We have never really captured San Antonio, we Texans—somehow the Spanish have managed to hold it. We have attacked with freeways and motels, shopping centers, and now the H-bomb of boosterism, HemisFair; but happily the victory still eludes us. San Antonio has kept an ambiance that all the rest of our cities lack.

LARRY MCMURTRY, *In a Narrow Grave: Essays on Texas*, 1968.

Texas could wear Rhode Island as a watch fob.

PAT NEFF, in John Gunther, *Inside U.S.A.*, 1947.

Writers facing the problem of Texas find themselves floundering in generalities, and I am no exception. Texas is a state of mind. Texas is an obsession. Above all, Texas is a nation in every sense of the word....A Texan outside of Texas is a foreigner.

JOHN STEINBECK, *Travels with Charley*, 1962.

Like most passionate nations Texas has its own private history based on, but not limited by, facts. The tradition of the tough and versatile frontiersman is true but not exclusive. It is for the few to know that in the great old days of Virginia there were three punishments for high crimes—death, exile to Texas, and imprisonment, in that order. And some of the deportees must have descendants.

JOHN STEINBECK, *Travels with Charley*, 1962.

UTAH

Industry.
State motto.

Alaska is our biggest, buggiest, boggiest state. Texas remains our largest unfrozen state. But mountainous Utah, if ironed out flat, would take up more space on a map than either.

EDWARD ABBEY, *A Voice Crying in the Wilderness*, 1989.

Utah's loveliness is a desert loveliness, unyielding and frequently sterile.

Federal Writers' Project: *Utah: A Guide to the State*, 1941.

The fertility of the land has been outstripped by the fertility of the people.

FEDERAL WRITERS' PROJECT, *Utah: A Guide to the State*, 1941.

Even if there had been no background of Joseph Smith, Angel Moroni, and the Book of Mormon, Utahans would have been incomprehensible, misunderstood and lied about, because they set down in the book of Western history the most stubbornly cross-grained chapter it contains.... Utah has always had a way of doing things different. The rest of the country has never quite got over it.

Federal Writers' Project: *Utah: A Guide to the State*, 1941.

Moody and withdrawn, the [Great Salt Lake] unites a haunting loveliness to a raw desolateness.

DALE MORGAN, in Rick Gore article, "No Way To Run a Desert," *National Geographic*, June, 1985.

VERMONT

Freedom and Unity.

State motto.

Vermont is a country unto itself. Indeed, for fourteen years after the Declaration of Independence, the State refused to join the Union and remained an independent republic.

PEARL S. BUCK, *America*, 1971.

All in all, Vermont is a jewel state, small but precious.

PEARL S. BUCK, *America*, 1971.

I love Vermont because of her hills and valleys, her scenery and invigorating climate, but most of all, because of her indomitable people. They are a race of pioneers who have almost beggared themselves to serve others. If the spirit of liberty should vanish in other parts of the union, and support of our institutions should languish, it could all be replenished from the generous store held by the people of this brave little state of Vermont.

CALVIN COOLIDGE, speech, Bennington, Vermont, September 9, 1928.

Vermonters are really something quite special and unique....This state bows to nothing; the first legislative measure it ever passed was "to adopt the laws of God...until there is time to frame better."

JOHN GUNTHER, *Inside U.S.A.*, 1947.

There is no cure for Vermont weather. It is consistent only in its inconsistency.

NOEL PERRIN, *Third Person Rural*, 1983.

Statistics prove that no Vermonter ever left the State unless transportation was furnished in advance. She is what you call a "Hard Boiled State." The principal ingredients are Granite, Rock Salt and Republicans. The last being the hardest of the three.

WILL ROGERS, March 29, 1925, in Donald Day, ed., *The Autobiography of Will Rogers*, 1949.

VIRGINIA

Sic semper tyrannis. (Thus always to tyrants.)
State motto.

That, without any fear of succeeding, the intrepid native Virginian will dauntlessly attempt to conceal his superiority to everybody else, remains a tribal virtue which has not escaped the comment of anthropologists.

JAMES BRANCH CABELL, *Let Me Live*, 1947.

The Virginia idea, it must be clearly understood, was not what is today called the American Dream. The Virginian did not dream of a democracy, with its literal meaning of the rule of the people. His dream was to found an aristocratic republic, in which superior individuals would emerge to rule the many.

CLIFFORD DOWDEY, "Virginia," *Holiday Magazine's American Panorama: East of the Mississippi*, 1960.

They were ravished with its loveliness; a warm, soft-voiced spring-green landscape dotted with sassafrass and scarlet-colored snakewood, smelling of wild strawberries and hart's tongue.

MARSHALL FISHWICK, *Virginia: A New Look at the Old Dominion*, 1959.

Despite her veneer of pink-coated fox hunters and smiling house servants, Virginia has been for a century one of the poorest states of the Union.

MARSHALL FISHWICK, *Virginia: A New Look at the Old Dominion*, 1959.

There is the name. Virginia....It sings itself....In the sweet, undulating roll of Virginia, you catch the soft folds of the Blue Ridge Mountains in the morning mist, the giddy, gaudy green Easter Egg hills billowing around Albemarle, the lazy James embracing Richmond, the dark green tobacco fields somnolent in the Southside sun, and the long, pale green combers rolling in white thunder on Virginia Beach.

GUY FRIDDELL, *What Is It About Virginia?*, 1966.

But what I liked best [about Richmond], next to the incomparable executive mansion, is the heroic (and heroically ugly) equestrian statue of George Washington, which was cast in Munich of all places, and which now stands in Capitol

Square. The general's eyes look sternly at the state house and his finger, like a flail, points to the penitentiary!

JOHN GUNTHER, *Inside U.S.A.*, 1947.

Trammel, Virginia, looks like a Monopoly board after the players have finished their game.

KATHY KAHN, *Hillbilly Women*, 1973.

A political museum piece.

V.O. KEY, *Southern Politics*, 1949.

Urbanity, *politesse*, chivalry? Go to! It was in Virginia that they invented the device for searching for contraband whiskey in women's underwear.

H.L. MENCKEN, *Prejudices*, 1920.

Virginia reeks of tobacco. Its odor saturates her like the coat of a veteran smoker. The brown stain of tobacco juice is on every page of her history.

VIRGINIA MOORE, *Virginia Is a State of Mind*, 1943.

In South Richmond, the mouse holes, lace curtains and Sears catalogs, even the baloney sandwiches and measles epidemics, always wore a faint odor of cured tobacco.

TOM ROBBINS, *Even Cowgirls Get the Blues*, 1976.

Wouldn't it be nice if when it [Arlington Cemetery] is all full, they'd just stop having wars. I mean, like you'd just say, "Well, I'm sorry but we can't get in this war because we don't have any more room left in Arlington."

JAMES WOOTEN, *New York Times*, May 31, 1971.

WASHINGTON

Alki. (Chinook, "by and by.")
State motto.

The wildest, the most remote, and I think the most picturesque beach area of our whole coastline lies under a pounding surf along the Pacific Ocean in the state of Washington.

WILLIAM O. DOUGLAS, *My Wilderness: The Pacific West*, 1960.

Rainier, from Puget Sound, is a sight for the gods, and when one looks upon him he feels that he is in the presence of the gods.

PAUL FOUNTAIN, *The Eleven Eaglets of the West*, 1905.

The bridges—and heaven knows Seattle has them—wear necklaces of light which they reflect on the dark waters.

HARD JONES, *Seattle*, 1972.

A map of Seattle doesn't help anybody much, except to show that it rather resembles Manhattan Island in shape—and part of it is indeed an island in its peculiar way.

HARD JONES, *Seattle*, 1972.

This was a jeweled, peaceable land, with the cone of Mount Hood rising fresh-whitened to the east; with a band of blue mountains across the western horizon, shutting it off from the sea.

LUCIA MOORE, *The Wheel and the Hearth*, 1953.

Nobody expects, or even wants, a city or a corporation to act the understanding, doting father. But there is an absolute coldness, a frighteningly methodical dehumanization about the way the city of Seattle achieved its goals that makes even "survival of the fittest" seem charitable in contrast.

GERALD B. NELSON, *Seattle*, 1977.

Washington is a puzzling state. We think of it as cool, pristine and evergreen. Yet the civilization around Puget Sound is industrial, cosmopolitan, intense, wracked by economic boom and bust.

NEAL R. PEIRCE, *The Pacific States of America*, 1972.

When you pick up the [Seattle] newspapers... you realize, once and for all, that Seattle is a screwy place, because the papers keep talking Alaska this and Alaska that. Anybody knows that Alaska belongs not all over the morning papers but in geography books. Yet it turns out that Alaska is virtually an outlying ward of Seattle.

GEORGE SESSIONS PERRY, *Cities of America*, 1947.

The prairies are all right. The mountains are all right. The forests and the deserts and the clear clean air of the heights, they're all right. But what a bewitching thing is a city of the sea. It was good to be in Seattle—to hear the foghorns on the Sound, and the deep bellow of departing steamers; to feel the creeping fog all around you, the fog that softens things and makes a velvet trance out of nighttime.

ERNIE PYLE, *Home Country*, 1947.

And unapproachable the great line of the Cascades with their snow-spired sentinels Hood, Adams, Jefferson, Three Sisters, etc., and out of the Bend at 3 and then through the vast and level pinelands—somewhat reminiscent of the South.

THOMAS WOLFE, *A Western Journal*, 1938.

WEST

Out where the handclasp's a little stronger,

Out where the smile dwells a little longer,
　　That's where the West begins.

ARTHUR CHAPMAN, "Out Where the West Begins," 1917.

The achieved West had given the United States something that no people had ever had before, an internal, domestic empire.

BERNARD DE VOTO, *The Year of Decision*, 1943.

Only remember—West of the Mississippi it's a little more look, see, act. A little less rationalize, comment, talk.

F. SCOTT FITZGERALD, letter to Andrew Turnbull, Summer, 1934.

In one sense California, Oregon, and Washington are not "the West" at all. In Portland I actually heard a lady say that she was "going West" on a brief trip—and she meant Utah! People on the Pacific Coast think of themselves as belonging to the "coast"; the "West" is quite something else again.

JOHN GUNTHER, *Inside U.S.A.*, 1947.

Ahead, north to Canada and west to the Coast lay what to me is the most exciting stretch of land in America. Despite its rudeness, newness, rawness, it is not worn out, not yet filled, not yet exhausted.

LARRY MCMURTRY, *In a Narrow Grave: Essays on Texas*, 1968.

If one loves the West it is sometimes deeply moving to drive along one of its rims and sense the great spread of country that lies before one.

LARRY MCMURTRY, *In a Narrow Grave: Essays on Texas*, 1968.

The West...represented "democracy"; in it, the democratic ideals of the Revolution were more completely realized than anywhere else, and its integration into the nation was the triumph of those ideals over the residue of Old World behavior in other parts of America.

JAMES OLIVER ROBERTSON, *American Myth, American Reality*, 1980.

Where population is sparse, where the supports of conventions and of laws are withdrawn and men are thrown upon their own resources, courage becomes a fundamental and essential attribute in the individual. The Western man of the old days had little choice but to be courageous.

WALTER PRESCOTT WEBB, *The Great Plains*, 1931.

WEST VIRGINIA

Montani semper liberi. (Mountaineers are always free.)
State motto.

Almost Heaven.
BUMPER STICKER.

Here is hard-core unemployment, widespread and chronic; here is a region of shacks and hovels for housing; here are cliffs and ravines without standing room for a cow or chickens. In this region of steep mountains a person is exceptionally fortunate if he is able to hack out two or three ten-foot rows of land for potatoes or beans.

ERSKINE CALDWELL, on Mingo, McDowell, and Wyoming counties, *Around About America*, 1964.

The state is one of the most mountainous in the country; sometimes it is called the "little Switzerland" of America, and I once heard an irreverent local citizen call it the "Afghanistan of the United States."

JOHN GUNTHER, *Inside U.S.A.*, 1947.

We West Virginians are very tired of being considered inhabitants of just a dominion of the Old Dominion; we would like to make it clear that our state has been independent for ninety years. Some residents take a very strong line about this and always refer to it in conversation as "*West—By God—Virginia!*"

JOHN KNOWLES, "West Virginia," *Holiday Magazine's American Panorama: East of the Mississippi*, 1960.

On the map my state is probably the funniest-looking state in the Union; it resembles a pork chop with the narrow end splayed.

JOHN KNOWLES, "West Virginia," *Holiday Magazine's American Panorama: East of the Mississippi*, 1960.

Whether or not mountaineers were always free, they were almost always poor.

JOHN ALEXANDER WILLIAMS, *West Virginia*, 1976.

WISCONSIN

Forward.
State motto.

Wisconsin is the soul of a great people. She manifests the spirit of the conqueror, whose strength has subdued the forest, quickened the soil, harnessed the forces of Nature and multiplied production. From her abundance she serves food to the world.

FRED L. HOLMES, *Old World Wisconsin*, 1944.

Wisconsin's politics have traditionally been uproar politics—full of the yammer, the squawk, the accusing finger, the injured howl. Every voter is an amateur detective, full of zeal to get out and nip a little political iniquity in the bud.

GEORGE SESSIONS PERRY, *Cities of America*, 1947.

By cheese factories and creameries they direct the stranger in rural Wisconsin, for cheese factories and creameries are the most striking landmarks of that country. His most striking impression is that the entire landscape of southern Wisconsin is as picturesquely suggestive of dairying as the skyline of Pittsburgh is of the steel industry.

FRANK PARKER STOCKBRIDGE, "The Grand Old Man of Wisconsin," in *The World's Work*, January, 1913.

WYOMING

Equal rights.

State motto.

If anything is endemic to Wyoming it is wind. This big room of space is swept out daily, leaving a bone yard of fossils, agates, and carcasses in every stage of decay. Though it was water that initially shaped the state, wind is the meticulous gardener, raising dust and pruning the sage.

GRETEL EHRLICH, *The Solace of Open Spaces*, 1985.

Things happen suddenly in Wyoming, the change of seasons and weather; for people, the violent swings in and out of isolation. But good-naturedness is concomitant with severity.

GRETEL EHRLICH, *The Solace of Open Spaces*, 1985.

Wyoming is a land of great open spaces with plenty of elbow room....There are sections of the State where it is said you can look farther and see less than any other place in the world.

FEDERAL WRITERS' PROJECT, *Wyoming: A Guide to Its History, Highways, and People*, 1941.

Here is America high, naked, and exposed; this is a massive upland almost like Bolivia.

JOHN GUNTHER, *Inside U.S.A.*, 1947.

Time

See also **Popular Culture**—Life-styles; **Science and Technology**

Well, time wounds all heels.
ATTRIBUTED TO JANE ACE, in Goodman Ace, *The Fine Art of Hypochondria*, 1966.

Time is a great conference planning our end, and youth is only the past putting a leg forward.
DJUNA BARNES, *Nightwood*, 1937.

Time has its own dimensions, and neither the sun nor the clock can encompass them all. All we can do with the astronomical absolutes of time is note them, divide them as we please, and live by them in our daily routines. Beyond that, our own emotions, our hopes and fears, our worry and our relief, shape not only our days but our hours with only casual regard for absolute or arbitrary time.
HAL BORLAND, *New York Times*, October 28, 1962.

Time does not become sacred to us until we have lived it, until it has passed over us and taken with it a part of ourselves.
JOHN BURROUGHS, "The Spell of the Past," *Literary Values and Other Papers*, 1902.

Time touches all things with destroying hand.
CHARLES WADDELL CHESTNUTT, *The House Behind the Cedars*, 1900.

I felt time in full stream, and I felt consciousness in full stream joining it, like the rivers.
ANNIE DILLARD, *An American Childhood*, 1987.

I am long on ideas, but short on time. I expect to live to be only about a hundred.
THOMAS A. EDISON, *Golden Book*, April, 1931.

Modern man thinks he loses something—time—when he does not do things quickly; yet he does not know what to do with the time he gains—except kill it.
ERICH FROMM, *The Art of Loving*, 1956.

Without even knowing it, we are assaulted by a high note of urgency all the time. We end up pacing ourselves to the city rhythm whether or not it's our own. In time we even grow hard of hearing to the rest of the world. Like a violinist stuck next to the timpani, we may lose the ability to hear our own instrument.
ELLEN GOODMAN, "Country Music," *Washington Post*, August 1986.

Time is a circus always packing up and moving away.
BEN HECHT, *Charlie: The Improbable Life and Times of Charles MacArthur*, 1957.

Time has upset many fighting faiths.
OLIVER WENDELL HOLMES, JR., opinion, *Abrams et al. v. the United States*, 1919.

Lost time was like a run in a stocking. It always got worse.
ANNE MORROW LINDBERGH, *The Steep Ascent*, 1944.

Time is the thief you cannot banish.
PHYLLIS MCGINLEY, "Ballad of Lost Objects," *Times Three: 1932–1960*, 1960.

Time is the great legalizer, even in the field of morals.
H.L. MENCKEN, *A Book of Prefaces*, 1917.

Travel

See also **Science and Technology**—Transportation

In America there are two classes of travel—first class and with children.

ROBERT BENCHLEY, in Robert E. Drennan, *The Algonquin Wits*, 1968.

He who travels west travels not only with the sun but with history.

HAL BORLAND, *New York Times*, October 17, 1954.

I've never made the trip to or from Connecticut without its resembling the worst excesses of the French Revolution.

PAT BUCKLEY, *New York Times*, November 20, 1984.

Lovers of air travel find it exhilarating to hang poised between the illusion of immortality and the fact of death.

ALEXANDER CHASE, *Perspectives*, 1966.

It is assumed that knowing the location and price of a good hotel and having a road map is about all that is needed to get you from here to wherever you want to go. But it is easier to go to the moon than it is to enter the world of another civilization. Culture—not space—is the greatest distance between two peoples.

JAMAKE HIGHWATER, Introduction, *Fodor's Indian America*, 1975.

Drop anchor anywhere and the anchor will drag—that is, if your soul is a limitless, fathomless sea, and not a dogpond.

ELBERT HUBBARD, *The Roycroft Dictionary and Book of Epigrams*, 1923.

Someday the sun is going to shine down on me in some faraway place.

MAHALIA JACKSON, *Reader's Digest*, March, 1973.

Thanks to the interstate highway system, it is now possible to travel across the country from coast to coast without seeing anything.

CHARLES KURALT, *On the Road*, 1985.

Is there *anything* as horrible as *starting* on a trip? Once you're off, that's all right, but the last moments are earthquake and convulsion, and the feeling that you are a snail being pulled off your rock.

ANNE MORROW LINDBERGH, *Hour of Gold, Hour of Lead*, 1973.

There is nothing so good for the human soul as the discovery that there are ancient and flourishing civilized societies which have somehow managed to exist for many centuries and are still in being though they have had no help from the traveler in solving their problems.

WALTER LIPPMANN, in Ronald Steel, *Walter Lippmann and the American Century*, 1980.

[A driver] is a king on a vinyl bucket-seat throne, changing direction with the turn of a wheel, changing the climate with a flick of the button, changing the music with the switch of a dial.

ANDREW H. MALCOLM, *New York Times*, April 21, 1985.

It takes time to straighten these things out, but the big item is that we're still moving. This country began with people moving, and we've been moving ever since....As long as we keep at that I guess we'll be all right.

MARY MARGARET MCBRIDE, *America for Me*, 1941.

If you reject the food, ignore the customs, fear the religion and avoid the people, you might better stay home.

JAMES A. MICHENER, in William Safire and Leonard Safire, *Good Advice*, 1982.

I was going to stay on the three million miles of bent and narrow rural American two-lane, the roads to Podunk and Toonerville. Into the sticks, the boondocks, the burgs, backwaters, jerkwaters, the wide-spots-in-the-road, the don't-blink-or-you'll-miss-it towns. Into those places where you say, "My god! What if you lived here!" The Middle of Nowhere.

WILLIAM LEAST HEAT MOON, *Blue Highways*, 1982.

I think that to get under the surface and really appreciate the beauty of any country, one has to go there poor.

GRACE MOORE, *You're Only Human Once*, 1944.

[Travel seems] not just a way of having a good time, but something that every self-respecting citizen ought to undertake, like a high-fiber diet, say, or a deodorant.

JAN MORRIS, "It's OK To Stay at Home," *New York Times*, August 30, 1985.

Rare is the American who has not dreamed of dropping whatever he is doing and hitting the road. The dream of unrestrained movement is a distinctly American one, an inheritance bequeathed to subsequent generations by those restless souls who populated the American continent. Travel—away from here, toward a vague and distant destination—is part of our national folklore.

DAVID NICHOLS, Introduction, *Ernie's America*, January, 1989.

This ain't the Waldorf; if it was you wouldn't be here.

NOTICE FOUND IN COUNTRY HOTELS, ca. 1900.

Traveling is *seeing*; it is the implicit that we travel by.

CYNTHIA OZICK, "Enchanters at First Encounter," *New York Times*, March 17, 1985.

"Potter hates Potter, and Poet hates Poet"—so runs the wisdom of the ancients—but tourist hates tourist with a cordial Christian animosity that casts all Pagan prejudices in the shade.

AGNES REPPLIER, *Compromises*, 1904.

Movement is the magic which keeps expectations high in America.

JAMES OLIVER ROBERTSON, *American Myth, American Reality*, 1980.

See America First.

SLOGAN, ca. 1914.

The sound of a jet, an engine warming up, even the clopping of shod hooves on pavement brings on the ancient shudder, the dry mouth and vacant eye, the hot palms and the churn of stomach high up under the rib cage.

JOHN STEINBECK, *Travels with Charley*, 1962.

I sought trains; I found passengers.

PAUL THEROUX, *The Great Railway Bazaar*, 1975.

Local radio stations dissolve in static every five miles; insects detonate against the windshield. He stops and has the oil checked. The American is in his seasonal migration.

JAMES THURBER, quoted in *Time*, July 20, 1970.

The real meaning of travel, like that of a conversation by the fireside, is the discovery of oneself through contact with other people, and its condition is self-commitment in the dialogue.

PAUL TOURNIER, *The Meaning of Persons*, 1957.

Growing up tends not to cure Americans of the notion that the number of miles covered is an important gauge to the success of pleasure travel.

CALVIN TRILLIN, *Travels with Alice*, 1989.

When the whistle blew and the call stretched thin across the night, one had to believe that any journey could be sweet to the soul.

CHARLES TURNER, *The Celebrant*, 1982.

Writers and travelers are mesmerized alike by knowing of their destinations.

EUDORA WELTY, *One Writer's Beginnings*, 1984.

The only people flying to Europe will be terrorists, so it will be, "Will you be sitting in armed or unarmed?"

ROBIN WILLIAMS, *US*, November 3, 1986.

War and Peace

See also **American Society; Dreams and Ideals**—*Freedom, Patriotism, Power, Security;* **Ethics and Morality; Government and Politics**—*Foreign Policy, Parties and Elections, Political Philosophies;* **Journalism and the Media; Science and Technology**—*Military Hardware;* **Social Issues**—*Peace and Disarmament;* **Work**—*Soldiers and Police Officers*

Force complete, absolute, overpowering, was applied until the enemy's will to resist and capacity to exist as a nation were broken. This was victory.

DEAN ACHESON, *Power and Diplomacy*, 1958.

After each war there is a little less democracy to save.

BROOKS ATKINSON, "January 7," *Once Around the Sun*, 1951.

There's a consensus out that it's OK to kill when your government decides who to kill. If you kill inside the country you get in trouble. If you kill outside the country, right time, right season, latest enemy, you get a medal.

JOAN BAEZ, *Daybreak*, 1966.

Take the profit out of war.

BERNARD M. BARUCH, "Taking the Profit Out of War," *Atlantic Monthly*, January, 1926.

Let this be anchored in our minds: Peace is never long preserved by weight of metal or by an armament race. Peace can be made tranquil and secure only by understanding and agreement fortified by sanctions. We must embrace international cooperation or international disintegration.

BERNARD M. BARUCH, plan presented to U.N. Atomic Energy Commission, June 14, 1946.

Behind the black portent of the new atomic age lies a hope which, seized upon with faith, can work out salvation....Let us not deceive ourselves; we must elect world peace or world destruction.

BERNARD M. BARUCH, speech, U.N. Atomic Energy Commission, August, 1946.

If we justify war, it is because all peoples always justify the traits of which they find themselves possessed, not because war will bear an objective examination of its merits.

RUTH BENEDICT, *Patterns of Culture*, 1934.

Murder is murder, no matter how official. War is obsolete.

LEONARD BERNSTEIN, *National Review*, 1989.

Peace, n. In international affairs, a period of cheating between two periods of fighting.

AMBROSE BIERCE, *The Devil's Dictionary*, 1906.

[It is resolved] that war between nations should be outlawed as an instrument of settlement of international controversies by making it a public crime.

HIRAM BORAH, Senate resolution, 1923.

Man is stumbling blindly through a spiritual darkness while toying with the precarious secrets of life and death. The world has achieved brilliance without wisdom, power without conscience. We know more about war than we know about peace, more about killing than we know about living.

OMAR BRADLEY, speech, Boston, November 10, 1948.

We don't want any more wars, but a man is a damn fool to think there won't be any more of them.

SMEDLEY BUTLER, *New York Times*, August 21, 1931.

In wartime, the degree of patriotism is directly proportional to distance from the front.

PHILIP CAPUTO, "War Torn," *New York Times Magazine*, February 24, 1991.

All the gods are dead except the god of war.

ELDRIDGE CLEAVER, "Four Vignettes," *Soul on Ice*, 1968.

As wounded men may limp through life, so our war minds may not regain the balance of their thoughts for decades.

FRANK MOORE COLBY, "War Minds," *The Colby Essays*, 1926.

No nation ever had an army large enough to guarantee it against attack in time of peace or insure it victory in time of war.

CALVIN COOLIDGE, speech, October 6, 1925.

God and the politicians willing, the United States can declare peace upon the world, and win it.

ELY CULBERTSON, *Must We Fight Russia?*, 1946.

When Wall Street yells war, you may rest assured every pulpit in the land will yell war.

EUGENE V. DEBS, speech, Canton, Ohio, June 16, 1918.

Sooner or later every war of trade becomes a war of blood.

EUGENE V. DEBS, speech, Canton, Ohio, June 16, 1918.

The working class who fight all the battles, the working class who make the supreme sacrifices, the working class who freely shed their blood and furnish the corpses, have never yet had a voice in either declaring war or making peace. It is the ruling class that invariably does both. They alone declare war and they alone make peace.

EUGENE V. DEBS, speech, Canton, Ohio, June 16, 1918.

The more horrible a depersonalized scientific mass war becomes, the more necessary it is to find universal ideal motives to justify it.

JOHN DEWEY, *Human Nature and Conduct*, 1922.

Mankind will never win lasting peace so long as men use their full resources only in tasks of war. While we are yet at peace, let us mobilize the potentialities, particularly the moral and spiritual potentialities, which we usually reserve for war.

JOHN FOSTER DULLES, *War or Peace*, 1950.

A peaceful world is a world in which differences are tolerated, and are not eliminated by violence.

JOHN FOSTER DULLES, *War or Peace*, 1950.

I can see in my mind the day when explosives will be so explosive and guns will shoot so far that only the folks that stay at home will be killed, and life insurance agents will be advising people to go into the army.

FINLEY PETER DUNNE, *Mr. Dooley Remembers*, 1963.

To my mind, to kill in war is not a whit better than to commit ordinary murder.

ALBERT EINSTEIN, *Kaizo* (Japanese magazine), Autumn, 1952.

War creates such a strain that all the pettiness, jealousy, ambition, greed, and selfishness begin to leak out the seams of the average character. On top of this are the problems created by the enemy, by weather, by international politics, including age-old racial and nationalistic ani-mosities, by every conceivable kind of difficulty, and, finally, just by the nature of war itself.

DWIGHT D. EISENHOWER, letter to Mamie Doud Eisenhower, December 16, 1942.

I say we are going to have peace even if we have to fight for it.

DWIGHT D. EISENHOWER, speech, Frankfurt, Germany, June 10, 1945.

Men acquainted with the battlefield will not be found among the numbers that glibly talk of another war.

DWIGHT D. EISENHOWER, speech, Chicago, Illinois, June 2, 1946.

War is no longer a lively adventure or expedition into romance, matching man against man in a test of the stout-hearted. Instead, it is aimed against the cities mankind has built. Its goal is their total destruction and devastation.

DWIGHT D. EISENHOWER, speech, Edinburgh, Scotland, October 3, 1946.

The peace we seek is nothing less than the fulfillment of our whole faith among ourselves and in our dealings with others. This signifies more than the stilling of guns, easing the sorrow of war. More than an escape from death, it is a way of life. More than a haven for the weary, it is a hope for the brave.

DWIGHT D. EISENHOWER, inaugural address, January 20, 1953.

Every gun that is made, every warship launched, every rocket fired signifies, in the final sense, a theft from those who hunger and are not fed, those who are cold and are not clothed. This world in arms is not spending money alone. It is spending the sweat of its laborers, the genius of its scientists, the hopes of its children....This is not a way of life at all in any true sense. Under the cloud of threatening war, it is humanity hanging from a cross of iron.

DWIGHT D. EISENHOWER, speech, American Society of Newspaper Editors, April 16, 1953.

The war stories, instead of repelling young men, bewitch them; the suffering is alluring and promises redemption. War teases them: the wounds they are ready for are painted on and can be washed off like graffiti; they believe the wounds will give them importance. And always they are led to understand what the American world, the biggest one ever, sees as manhood: a rifle, the lieutenant lifting a hand to signal, the men opening up, never such a chorus.

GLORIA EMERSON, Prologue, *Some American Men*, 1985.

The American approach to war is that it's like football, only with guns.

DAVID EVANS, *Chicago Tribune*, June 9, 1991.

[P]eople are becoming too intelligent ever to have another big war. Statesmen have not anything like the prestige they had years ago, and what is educating the ordinary people against war is that they are mixing so much. The motor-car, radio and such things are the great "mixers"....I believe the last war was too much an educator for there ever to be another on a large scale.

HENRY FORD, *The American Scrap Book*, 1928.

What causes war is not patriotism, not that human beings are willing to die in defense of their dearest ones. It is the false doctrine, fostered by the few, that war spells gain.

HENRY FORD, "Success," *Forum*, October, 1928.

Either man is obsolete or war is.

R. BUCKMINSTER FULLER, *I Seem To Be a Verb*, 1970.

That's the worst of a war—you have to go on hearing about it so long.

SUSAN GLASPELL, *Inheritors*, 1921.

In fact, it's getting harder to differentiate between war and football. Which is reality and which is metaphor?

DANIEL GOLDEN, *Boston Globe*, January 20, 1991.

[A]ll wars are wars among thieves who are too cowardly to fight and who therefore induce the young manhood of the whole world to do the fighting for them.

EMMA GOLDMAN, "Address to the Jury," *Mother Earth*, July, 1917.

Nations do not arm for war. They arm to keep themselves from war.

BARRY M. GOLDWATER, *Why Not Victory?*, 1962.

It is ironic that the United States, so often over recent years accused of having an invincibly bloodthirsty nature, is in fact a country that almost always reveals a deep and broad streak of something akin to pacifism when it comes right down to it. We know how to talk about war only when it is a many-times-removed possibility. When it becomes a more immediate threat, the same range of reservations always emerges: there will be terrible death and destruction, it is essentially somebody else's battle to fight in the first instance, the aftermath will be worse than the present, and—sometimes, but only tangentially this time—the United States has either no right, no national interest or no moral standing that warrants intervention.

MEG GREENFIELD, *Newsweek*, January 21, 1991.

We have one foot in genesis and the other in apocalypse, and annihilation is always one immediate option.

MICHAEL HARRINGTON, *Toward a Democratic Left*, 1968.

Frankly, I'd like to see the government get out of war altogether and leave the whole field to private industry.

JOSEPH HELLER, *Catch-22*, 1961.

I did not want to read about the war. I was going to forget the war. I had made a separate peace.

ERNEST HEMINGWAY, *A Farewell to Arms*, 1929.

We in America should see that no man is ever given, no matter how gradually, or how noble and excellent the man, the power to put this country into a war which is now being prepared and brought closer each day with all the premeditation of a long-planned murder. For when you give power to an executive you do not know who will be filling that position when the time of crisis comes.

ERNEST HEMINGWAY, "Notes on the Next War: A Serious Letter," *Esquire*, September, 1935.

There are worse things than war. Cowardice,... treachery,... and simply selfishness.

ERNEST HEMINGWAY, 1937, in Lois and Alan Gordon, *American Chronicle*, 1987.

When a nation is at war many things that might be said in time of peace are such a hindrance to its effort that their utterance will not be endured so long as men fight and no court could regard them as protected by any constitutional right.

OLIVER WENDELL HOLMES, JR., opinion, *Schenck v. United States*, 1919.

I do not...think that a philosophic view of the world would regard war as absurd.

OLIVER WENDELL HOLMES, JR., opinion, *United States v. Schwimmer*, 1929.

Older men declare war. But it is youth that must fight and die. And it is youth who must inherit the tribulation, the sorrow, and the triumphs that are the aftermath of war.

HERBERT HOOVER, speech, Republican National Convention, Chicago, June 27, 1944.

Peace: A monotonous interval between fights.

ELBERT HUBBARD, *The Roycroft Dictionary and Book of Epigrams*, 1923.

So long as governments set the example of killing their enemies, private individuals will occasionally kill theirs.

ELBERT HUBBARD, *The Roycroft Dictionary and Book of Epigrams*, 1923.

War: The sure result of the existence of armed men.

ELBERT HUBBARD, *The Roycroft Dictionary and Book of Epigrams*, 1923.

That wars and rumors of wars are the great threats to political stability and to liberty needs no demonstration. Total war means total subjection of the individual to the state.

ROBERT H. JACKSON, *The Supreme Court in the American System of Government*, 1955.

What we now need to discover in the social realm is the moral equivalent of war: something heroic that will speak to men as universally as war does, and yet will be as compatible with their spiritual selves as war has proved itself to be incompatible.

WILLIAM JAMES, *The Varieties of Religious Experience*, ca. 1910.

In this age when there can be no losers in peace and no victors in war, we must recognize the obligation to match national strength with national restraint.

LYNDON B. JOHNSON, speech to Congress, November 27, 1963.

Peace is a journey of a thousand miles and it must be taken one step at a time.

LYNDON B. JOHNSON, speech, U.N. General Assembly, December 17, 1963.

No man should think that peace comes easily. Peace does not come by merely wanting it, or shouting for it, or marching down Main Street for it. Peace is built brick by brick, mortared by the stubborn effort and the total energy and imagination of able and dedicated men. And it is built in the living faith that, in the end, man can and will master his own destiny.

LYNDON B. JOHNSON, *The Vantage Point: Perspectives of the Presidency, 1963–1969*, 1971.

The only moral virtue of war is that it compels the capitalist system to look itself in the face and admit it is a fraud. It compels the present society to admit that it has no morals it will not sacrifice for gain.

HELEN KELLER, "Menace of the Militarist Program," *New York Call*, December 20, 1915.

I wonder whether even in the past total victory was not really an illusion from the standpoint of the victors. In a sense, there is not total victory short of genocide, unless it be a victory over the minds of men. But the total military victories are rarely victories over the minds of men.

GEORGE F. KENNAN, *American Diplomacy, 1900–1950*, 1951.

A war regarded as inevitable or even probable, and therefore much prepared for, has a very good chance of eventually being fought.

GEORGE F. KENNAN, *The Cloud of Danger*, 1977.

[A] nuclear disaster, spread by winds and water and fear, could well engulf the great and the small, the rich and the poor, the committed and the uncommitted alike. Mankind must put an end to war or war will put an end to mankind.

JOHN F. KENNEDY, speech, United Nations, September 25, 1961.

No man who witnessed the tragedies of the last war, no man who can imagine the unimaginable possibilities of the next war can advocate war out of irritability or frustration or impatience.

JOHN F. KENNEDY, Veterans Day Address, Arlington National Cemetery, November 11, 1961.

Peace is a daily, a weekly, a monthly process, gradually changing opinions, slowly eroding old barriers, quietly building new structures.

JOHN F. KENNEDY, speech, U.N. General Assembly, September 20, 1963.

[Man] is, perhaps, no more prone to war than he used to be and no more inclined to commit other evil deeds. But a given amount of ill will or folly will go further than it used to.

JOSEPH WOOD KRUTCH, "The Loss of Confidence," *The Measure of Man*, 1954.

Americans tend to think of foreign affairs in terms of sporting events that allow for unambiguous results. Either the team wins or it loses; the game is over within a reasonable period of time, and everybody can go back to doing something else.

LEWIS H. LAPHAM, "Brave New World," *Harper's*, March, 1991.

You may call for peace as loudly as you wish, but where there is no brotherhood there can in the end be no peace.

Max Lerner, "The Gifts of the Magi," *Actions and Passions*, 1949.

The way to prevent war is to bend every energy toward preventing it, not to proceed by the dubious indirection of preparing for it.

Max Lerner, "On Peacetime Military Training," *Actions and Passions*, 1949.

I don't think old men ought to promote wars for young men to fight. I don't like warlike old men.

Walter Lippmann, TV interview, May, 1961.

It is fatal to enter any war without the will to win it.

Douglas MacArthur, speech, Republican National Convention, July 7, 1952.

I know war as few other man now living know it, and nothing to me is more revolting. I have long advocated its complete abolition, as its very destructiveness on both friend and foe has rendered it useless as a method of settling international disputes.

Douglas MacArthur, farewell speech to Congress, April 19, 1951.

War's very object is victory, not prolonged indecision. In war there is no substitute for victory.

Douglas MacArthur, farewell speech to Congress, April 19, 1951.

The great question is: can war be outlawed? If so, it would mark the greatest advance in civilization since the Sermon on the Mount.

Douglas MacArthur, speech to American Legion, Los Angeles, January 26, 1955.

I listen vainly, but with thirsty ears, for the witching melody of faint bugles blowing reveille, of far drums beating the long roll. In my dreams I hear again the crash of guns, the rattle of musketry, the strange, mournful mutter of the battlefield.

Douglas MacArthur, speech, West Point, May 12, 1962.

Nations may make peace. It is harder for fighting men.

William Manchester, "Okinawa: The Bloodiest Battle of All," *New York Times Magazine*, June 14, 1987.

If all Americans understood the nature of battle, they might be vulnerable to truth. But the myths of warfare are embedded deep in our ancestral memories. By the time children have reached the age of awareness, they regard uniforms, decorations and Sousa marches as exalted, and those who argue otherwise are regarded as unpatriotic.

William Manchester, "Okinawa: The Bloodiest Battle of All," *New York Times Magazine*, June 14, 1987.

By education and occupation, Americans are completely unwarlike. In the last war, United States soldiers were known as the most homesick army in the world. Americans have too much to lose by war. And they know it, too; no demagogue can persuade them to the contrary.

Frederick Martin, in Arthur Goodfriend, *What Is America?*, 1954.

The dangers of atomic war are overrated. It would be hard on little, concentrated countries like England. In the United States we have lots of space.

Robert Rutherford McCormick, *Chicago Tribune*, February 23, 1950.

There is no record in history of a nation that ever gained anything valuable by being unable to defend itself.

H.L. Mencken, *Prejudices*, 1926.

War is the only sport that is genuinely amusing. And it is the only sport that has any intelligible use.

H.L. Mencken, *Prejudices*, 1926.

War may make a fool of man, but it by no means degrades him; on the contrary, it tends to exalt him, and its net effects are much like those of motherhood on women.

H.L. Mencken, *Minority Report*, 1956.

War represents a vice that mankind would like to get rid of but which it cannot do without. Man is like an alcoholic who knows that drink will destroy him but who always has a reason for drinking. So with war.

Thomas Merton, *Love and Living*, 1980.

If there is to be any peace it will come through being, not having.

Henry Miller, "The Wisdom of the Heart," *The Wisdom of the Heart*, 1941.

The immediate cause of World War III is the preparation of it.

C. Wright Mills, 1959, in Lois and Alan Gordon, *American Chronicle*, 1987.

[N]ever in history has mankind been given more reason to look forward to the future with hope. For the blast which blew nineteenth-century nationalism to pieces at Hiroshima may also have cleared the way for a new Renaissance—a new era of co-operation leading up to the twentieth-century Empire of the World.

Lynn Montross, on bombing of Hiroshima, 1946.

Democracies are indeed slow to make war, but once embarked upon a martial venture are equally slow to make peace and reluctant to make a tolerable, rather than a vindictive, peace.

Reinhold Niebuhr, *The Structure of Nations and Empires,* 1959.

There is only one threat to world peace, the one that is presented by the internationalist communist conspiracy.

Richard M. Nixon, speech, Whittier College, June 12, 1954.

Our goal will be peace. Our instrument for achieving peace will be law and justice. Our hope will be that, under these conditions, the vast energies now devoted to weapons of war will instead be used to clothe, house, and feed the entire world. This is the only goal worthy of our aspirations. Competing in this way, nobody will lose, and mankind will gain.

Richard M. Nixon, *The Challenges We Face,* 1960.

I grew out of one war and into another. My father came from leaden ships of sea, from the Pacific theater; my mother was a WAVE. I was the offspring of the great campaign against the tyrants of the 1940's, one explosion in the Baby Boom, one of millions come to replace those who had just died. My bawling came with the first throaty note of a new army in spawning. I was bred with the haste and dispatch and careless muscle-flexing of a nation giving bridle to its own good fortune and success. I was fed by the spoils of the 1945 victory.

Tim O'Brien, *If I Die in a Combat Zone, Box Me Up and Ship Me Home,* 1973.

The only war I ever approved of was the Trojan War; it was fought over a woman and the men knew what they were fighting for.

William Lyon Phelps, sermon, Riverside Church, New York City, June 25, 1933.

In moral terms, wars follow a perverse pattern: the more highfalutin the motive, the more pain inflicted on civilians.

Harrison Rainie, *U.S. News & World Report,* February 18, 1991.

Make wars unprofitable and you make them impossible.

Asa Philip Randolph, "The Cause and Remedy of Race Riots," *The Messenger,* September, 1919.

Violence seldom accomplishes permanent and desired results. Herein lies the futility of war.

Asa Philip Randolph, *The Truth About Lynching,* ca. 1922.

There can be no compromise with war; it cannot be reformed or controlled; cannot be disciplined into decency or codified into common sense, for war is the slaughter of human beings, temporarily regarded as enemies, on as large a scale as possible.

Jeannette Rankin, speech, National Council for the Prevention of War, 1929.

You can no more win a war than you can win an earthquake.

Jeannette Rankin, in Hannah Josephson, *Jeannette Rankin: First Lady in Congress,* 1974.

As a woman I can't go to war, and I refuse to send anyone else.

Jeannette Rankin, in Hannah Josephson, *Jeannette Rankin: First Lady in Congress,* 1974.

People don't start wars, governments do.

Ronald Reagan, *Time,* March 18, 1985.

War means an ugly mob-madness, crucifying the truthtellers, choking the artists, sidetracking reforms, revolutions, and the working of social forces.

John Reed, "Whose War?" *The Masses,* April, 1917.

What red-blooded American could oppose so shining a concept as victory? It would be like standing up for sin against virtue.

Matthew B. Ridgway, *The Korean War,* 1967.

It isn't enough to talk about peace. One must believe in it. And it isn't enough to believe in it. One must work at it.

Eleanor Roosevelt, Voice of America broadcast, November 11, 1951.

I have seen war. I have seen war on land and sea. I have seen blood running from the wounded. I have seen men coughing out their gassed lungs. I have seen the dead in the mud. I have seen cities destroyed....I have seen children starving. I have seen the agony of mothers and wives. I hate war.

Franklin D. Roosevelt, speech, Chautauqua, New York, August 14, 1936.

Peace, like charity, begins at home.

FRANKLIN D. ROOSEVELT, speech, Chautauqua, New York, August 14, 1936.

The epidemic of world lawlessness is spreading.... War is a contagion.

FRANKLIN D. ROOSEVELT, speech, Chicago, Illinois, October 5, 1937.

More than an end to war, we want an end to the beginnings of all wars.

FRANKLIN D. ROOSEVELT, prepared speech not delivered because of his death one day earlier, April 13, 1945.

Peace is normally a great good, and normally it coincides with righteousness, but it is righteousness and not peace which should bind the conscience of a nation as it should bind the conscience of an individual; and neither a nation nor an individual can surrender conscience to another's keeping.

THEODORE ROOSEVELT, message to Congress, December 4, 1906.

We should do all in our power to hasten the day when there shall be peace among the nations—a peace based upon justice and not upon cowardly submission to wrong.

THEODORE ROOSEVELT, message to Congress, December 4, 1906.

War is not merely justifiable, but imperative, upon honorable men, upon an honorable nation, where peace can only be obtained by the sacrifice of conscientious conviction or of national welfare.

THEODORE ROOSEVELT, message to Congress, December 4, 1906.

A just war is in the long run far better for a nation's soul than the most prosperous peace obtained by acquiescence in wrong or injustice. Moreover, though it is criminal for a nation not to prepare for war, so that it may escape the dreadful consequences of being defeated in war, yet it must always be remembered that even to be defeated in war may be far better than not to have fought at all.

THEODORE ROOSEVELT, message to Congress, December 4, 1906.

That is one universal effect of war on the imagination: time, as a moral factor, instantly changes expression and changes pace. Everyman suddenly has a vision of sudden death.

PAUL ROSENFELD, "F. Scott Fitzgerald," *Men Seen: Twenty-Four Modern Authors*, 1925.

The drum-beating martial mood of wartime is often followed by a pot-stirring and baby-rocking domestic ethos in its aftermath.

ALICE ROSSI, *The Feminist Papers*, 1973.

Even a successful war doesn't guarantee a blissful peace.

ROBERT J. SAMUELSON, *Newsweek*, March 18, 1991.

Sometime they'll give a war and nobody will come.

CARL SANDBURG, *The People, Yes*, 1936.

To call war the soil of courage and virtue is like calling debauchery the soil of love.

GEORGE SANTAYANA, *The Life of Reason*, 1905–1906.

The four great motives which move men to social activity are hunger, love, vanity, and fear of superior powers. If we search out the causes which have moved men to war we find them under each of these motives or interests.

WILLIAM GRAHAM SUMNER, "War," *War and Other Essays*, 1911.

War and revolution never produce what is wanted, but only some mixture of the old evils with new ones; what is wanted is a peaceful and rational solution of problems and situations—but that requires great statesmanship and great popular sense and virtue. In the past the work has been done by war and revolution, with haphazard results and great attendant evils.

WILLIAM GRAHAM SUMNER, "War," *War and Other Essays*, 1911.

If you want a war, nourish a doctrine. Doctrines are the most fearful tyrants to which men ever are subject, because doctrines get inside of a man's own reason and betray him against himself. Civilized men have done their fiercest fighting for doctrines.

WILLIAM GRAHAM SUMNER, "War," *War and Other Essays*, 1911.

There is no state of readiness for war; the notion calls for never-ending sacrifices.... A wiser rule would be to make up your mind soberly what you want, peace or war, and then to get ready for what you want; for what we prepare for is what we shall get.

WILLIAM GRAHAM SUMNER, "War," *War and Other Essays*, 1911.

War, undertaken for justifiable purposes, such as to punish aggression in Korea, has often had the principal results of wrecking the country intended to be saved and spreading death and destruction among an innocent civilian population.

ROBERT A. TAFT, *A Foreign Policy for Americans*, 1951.

Far from establishing liberty throughout the world, war has actually encouraged and built up the development of dictatorships and has only restored liberty in limited areas at the cost of untold hardship, of human suffering, of death and destruction beyond the conception of our fathers.

ROBERT A. TAFT, *A Foreign Policy for Americans*, 1951.

The first and most imperative necessity in war is money, for money means everything else—men, guns, ammunition.

IDA TARBELL, *The Tariff in Our Times*, 1906.

Mankind's greatest collective fear, the doomsday fear, currently seems to have fascinated an incredible variety and number of people. Prophecies of doom are nothing new. Some of mankind's oldest myths have to do with the destruction of the world by fire.... Today, much of the doomsday thinking centers on nuclear war.

EDWARD TELLER, *The Pursuit of Simplicity*, 1980.

They have not wanted *Peace* at all; they have wanted to be spared war—as though the absence of war was the same as peace.

DOROTHY THOMPSON, "On the Record," May, 1958.

The butter to be sacrificed because of the war always turns out to be the margarine of the poor.

JAMES TOBIN, speech, Social Sciences Association, Washington, D.C., December 27, 1967.

I want peace and I'm willing to fight for it.

HARRY S TRUMAN, diary entry, in Robert H. Ferrell, *Off the Record*, May 22, 1945.

I would rather have peace in the world than be President.

HARRY S TRUMAN, Christmas message, Independence, Missouri, December 24, 1948.

O Lord our God, help us to tear their soldiers to bloody shreds with our shells; help us to cover their smiling fields with the pale forms of their patriot dead; help us to drown the thunder of the guns with the shrieks of their wounded, writhing in pain.... For our sakes who adore Thee, Lord, blast their hopes, blight their lives, protract their bitter pilgrimage, make heavy their steps, water their way with tears, stain the white snow with the blood of their wounded feet!

MARK TWAIN, "The War Prayer," 1905.

In a third of a century the only people who have benefited from the constant raid on our treasury and the sacrifice of our young men have been the companies that are engaged in making instruments of war—with the connivance of those congressmen who award the contracts and those generals who, upon early retirement, go to work for those same companies.

GORE VIDAL, "The State of the Union," *Mom, the Flag, and Apple Pie*, 1976.

[A]s a peace machine, the value [of the airplane] to the world will be beyond computation. Would a declaration of war between Russia and Japan be made, if within an hour thereafter, a swiftly gliding [airplane] might take its flight from St. Petersburg and drop half a ton of dynamite over the [Japanese] war offices? Could any nation afford to war upon any other with such hazards in view?

JOHN BRISBEN WALKER, *Cosmopolitan*, March, 1904.

War is fear cloaked in courage.

WILLIAM C. WESTMORELAND, *McCall's*, December, 1966.

As the soldier prays for peace he must be prepared to cope with the hardships of war and to bear its scars.

WILLIAM C. WESTMORELAND, *A Soldier Reports*, 1976.

Wilson said that America's doughboys fought for the Fourteen Points. Roosevelt said the GI was fighting for the Four Freedoms. Johnson and Humphrey sent men out to die for the planting of dams in Vietnam. Nixon preaches a war of generosity. Each time we have fought in this century, our leaders have denied that we did it for ourselves.

GARRY WILLS, *Nixon Agonistes*, 1970.

The example of America must be the example not merely of peace because it will not fight, but of peace because peace is the healing and elevating influence of the world, and strife is not. There is such a thing as a man being too proud to fight. There is such a thing as a nation being so right that it does not need to convince others by force that it is right.

WOODROW WILSON, speech, Convention Hall, Philadelphia, Pennsylvania, May 10, 1915.

The gravity of the situation which confronts the world today necessitates my appearance before a joint session of the Congress. The foreign policy and the national security of this country are involved.

The United States has received from the Greek Government an urgent appeal for financial and economic assistance. Preliminary reports from the American Economic Mission now in Greece and reports from the American Ambassador in Greece corroborate the statement of the Greek Government that assistance is imperative if Greece is to survive as a free nation....

One of the primary objectives of the foreign policy of the United States is the creation of conditions in which we and other nations will be able to work out a way of life free from coercion. This was a fundamental issue in the war with Germany and Japan. Our victory was won over countries which sought to impose their will, and their way of life, upon other nations.

To ensure the peaceful development of nations, free from coercion, the United States has taken a leading part in establishing the United Nations. The United Nations is designed to make possible lasting freedom and independence for all its members. We shall not realize our objectives, however, unless we are willing to help free peoples to maintain their free institutions and their national integrity against aggressive movements that seek to impose on them totalitarian regimes. This is no more than a frank recognition that totalitarian regimes imposed on free peoples, by direct or indirect aggression, undermine the foundations of international peace and hence the security of the United States....

At the present moment in world history nearly every nation must choose between alternative ways of life. The choice is too often not a free one.

One way of life is based upon the will of the majority, and is distinguished by free institutions, representative government, free elections, guarantees of individual liberty, freedom of speech and religion, and freedom from political oppression.

The second way of life is based upon the will of the minority forcibly imposed upon the majority. It relies upon terror and oppression, a controlled press and radio, fixed elections, and the suppression of personal freedoms.

I believe that it must be the policy of the United States to support free peoples who are resisting attempted subjugation by armed minorities or by outside pressures.

I believe that we must assist free peoples to work out their own destinies in their own way.

Only a peace between equals can last. Only a peace the very principle of which is equality and a common participation in a common benefit. The right state of mind, the right feeling between nations, is as necessary for a lasting peace as is the just settlement of vexed questions of territory or of racial and national allegiance.

The equality of nations upon which peace must be founded if it is to last must be an equality of rights; the guarantees exchanged must neither recognize nor imply a difference between big nations and small, between those that are powerful and those that are weak.

WOODROW WILSON, speech to U.S. Senate, "Peace Without Victory," January 22, 1917.

COLD WAR

War was going on long before anybody dreamed up Communism. It's just the latest justification for self-righteousness.

JOAN BAEZ, *Daybreak*, 1966.

The biggest thing that has happened in the world in my life, in our lives, is this: By the grace of God, America won the Cold War.

GEORGE BUSH, State of the Union adress, January 28, 1992.

There is no nook or cranny in all the world into which Communist influence does not penetrate.

JOHN FOSTER DULLES, *War or Peace*, 1950.

I believe that our help should be primarily through economic and financial aid which is essential to economic stability and orderly political processes.

The world is not static, and the status quo is not sacred. But we cannot allow changes in the status quo in violation of the charter of the United Nations by such methods as coercion, or by such subterfuges as political infiltration. In helping free and independent nations to maintain their freedom, the United States will be giving effect to the principles of the charter of the United Nations.

It is necessary only to glance at a map to realize that the survival and integrity of the Greek nation are of grave importance in a much wider situation. If Greece should fall under the control of an armed minority, the effect upon its neighbor, Turkey, would be immediate and serious. Confusion and disorder might well spread throughout the entire Middle East.

Moreover, the disappearance of Greece as an independent state would have a profound effect upon those countries in Europe whose peoples are struggling against great difficulties to maintain their freedoms and their independence while they repair the damages of war.

It would be an unspeakable tragedy if these countries, which have struggled so long against overwhelming odds, should lose that victory for which they sacrificed so much. Collapse of free institutions and loss of independence would be disastrous not only for them but for the world. Discouragement and possibly failure would quickly be the lot of neighboring peoples striving to maintain their freedom and independence.

Should we fail to aid Greece and Turkey in this fateful hour, the effect will be far reaching to the West as well as to the East. We must take immediate and resolute action....

The seeds of totalitarian regimes are nurtured by misery and want. They spread and grow in the evil soil of poverty and strife. They reach their full growth when the hope of a people for a better life has died. We must keep that hope alive. The free peoples of the world look to us for support in maintaining their freedoms.

If we falter in our leadership, we may endanger the peace of the world—and we shall surely endanger the welfare of this nation.

Great responsibilities have been placed upon us by the swift movement of events. I am confident that the Congress will face these responsibilities squarely.

HARRY S TRUMAN, message to Congress, later known as Truman Doctrine, March 12, 1947.

America, when will we end the human war? Go fuck yourself with your atomic bomb.

ALLEN GINSBERG, "America," in *Howl and Other Poems*, 1956.

I am not willing to accept the idea that there are no Communists left in this country. I think if we lift enough rocks we'll find some.

BARRY M. GOLDWATER, 1959, in Lois and Alan Gordon, *American Chronicle*, 1987.

It is clear that the main element of any United States policy toward the Soviet Union must be that of a long-term, patient but firm and vigilant containment of Russian expansive tendencies.

GEORGE F. KENNAN, "The Sources of Soviet Conduct," *Foreign Affairs*, July, 1947.

Khrushchev reminds me of the tiger hunter who has picked a place on the wall to hang the tiger's skin long before he has caught the tiger. This tiger has other ideas.

JOHN F. KENNEDY, *New York Times*, December 24, 1961.

The Cold War supplied both the economic and iconographic staples of American politics, and the belief in the Soviet Union as the Land of Mordor furnished the cover story for official sleights of hand that otherwise might have been seen as dishonest, stingy, or murderous.

LEWIS H. LAPHAM, "Old Glory," *Harper's*, September, 1989.

Who is this man? He looks like an American. He dresses like an American....But...he hates American democracy. He is a fifth columnist! Don't trust him!

LEAGUE OF HUMAN RIGHTS, Freedom and Democracy, 1940.

America has won the cold war—almost without trying. America's aim, at least since 1956...has been not to win this conflict but to negotiate a truce. It won nonetheless, not on the strength of its arms or the skill of its diplomats, but by virtue of the power of the democratic ideas on which the American system is based and the failure of the Communist idea.

JOSHUA MURAVCHIK, Exporting Democracy: Fulfilling America's Destiny, 1991.

Unless the system in which you have political freedom proves that it is the most efficient in bringing about economic progress, Communism is going to gain increasing adherents throughout the world. We have to bear in mind this essential fact: the terrible poverty and misery that so many people suffer cannot continue to be endured. They know there must be a way out, and they are going to take the way that they think is the quickest and surest, in the long run.

RICHARD M. NIXON, in Earl Mazo, Richard Nixon: A Political and Personal Portrait, 1959.

[The U.S. and USSR] are like two scorpions in a bottle, each capable of killing the other but only at the risk of his own life....The atomic clock ticks faster and faster.

J. ROBERT OPPENHEIMER, 1956, in Lois and Alan Gordon, American Chronicle, 1987.

Few predictions seem more certain than this: Russia is going to surpass us in mathematics and the social sciences....

In short, unless we depart utterly from our present behavior, it is reasonable to expect that by no later than 1975 the United States will be a member of the Union of Soviet Socialist Republics.

GEORGE R. PRICE, Life, November 18, 1957.

Our anti-communism has become so totally a national obsession that it colors and dominates all our thinking, all our planning, and all our name-calling. We no longer give much thought to what is better for America, but rather what is worse for Russia. The most effective argument in official debate or personal argument is the assertion that communists favor a course of action someone is opposing.

The Progressive, October, 1951.

It is impossible to view Vietnam without taking into consideration where it fits into the gigantic chess game called the cold war. The stakes in that game are no less than our very existence, and only the president has access to all the facts necessary for each move.

RONALD REAGAN, Sincerely, Ronald Reagan, 1976.

You use whatever force is necessary to achieve the purpose, and I would like to feel that there wouldn't be a need for using armed force if we made it apparent that we have the will, if necessary, to do that.

RONALD REAGAN, in Hedrick Smith et. al., Reagan the Man, the President, 1980.

Let us never forget that there can be no second place in a contest with Russia and there can be no second chance if we lose.

H.G. RICKOVER, 1959, in Lois and Alan Gordon, American Chronicle, 1987.

THE WORLD DEMANDS

CLEMENCY FOR THE ROSENBERGS

FRENCH DEPUTIES SAY CLEMENCY

300 BRITISH SCIENTISTS SAY CLEMENCY

POPE PIUS SAYS CLEMENCY

2500 MINISTERS SAY CLEMENCY

RABBIS OF ISRAEL SAY CLEMENCY

POSTER ON BEHALF OF ETHEL AND JULIUS ROSENBERG, 1953.

We were eyeball-to-eyeball and the other fellow just blinked.

DEAN RUSK, on Cuban missile crisis, Saturday Evening Post, December 8, 1962.

I killed more people tonight than I have fingers on my hands....I enjoyed every minute of it.... They were Commies....They figure us all to be as soft as horse manure.

MICKEY SPILLANE, In a Lonely Night, 1951.

GULF WAR

Do we fear our enemies more than we love our children?

BUMPER STICKER, ca. 1991.

We're Going To War To Defend People Who Won't Let Women Drive?

BUTTON, 1991.

In effect, each [press] pool member is an unpaid employee of the Department of Defense, on whose behalf he or she prepares the news of the war for the outer world.

MALCOLM W. BROWNE, "The Military vs. the Press," *New York Times Magazine*, March 3, 1991.

Seven months ago, America and the world drew a line in the sand. We declared that the aggression against Kuwait would not stand, and tonight America and the world have kept their word.

GEORGE BUSH, address, February 27, 1991.

Halfway around the world, we are engaged in a great struggle in the skies and on the seas and sands. We know why we're there. We are Americans—part of something larger than ourselves. For two centuries, we've done the hard work of freedom. And tonight, we lead the world in facing down a threat to decency and humanity.

GEORGE BUSH, State of the Union Address, January 29, 1991.

Amidst the flurry of flags and yellow ribbons, we as Christians try to make sense of it all. One thing we know for certain: Desert storms create an illusion of strength. They blind us to history. They obscure the truth of the present, and they blur our vision of the future that God intends for God's people.

JOAN B. CAMPBELL, sermon, Riverside Church, New York City, April 21, 1991.

I don't believe for a second that defeating him [Saddam Hussein] will mean the advent of "a new world order." But I am convinced that failing to beat him will make the present world order far more perilous.

PHILIP CAPUTO, "War Torn," *New York Times Magazine*, February 24, 1991.

All wars begin in an atmosphere of innocence and optimism, and this one started with…techno-innocence, techno-optimism.

PHILIP CAPUTO, "War Torn," *New York Times Magazine*, February 24, 1991.

The networks, with their repulsive computer-generated graphics, their self-important promo spots, their maestro anchormen orchestrating live theatrical reports from around the globe, have been covering this conflict as if it were a mini-series. Order a pizza and watch a building disappear.

PHILIP CAPUTO, "War Torn," *New York Times Magazine*, February 24, 1991.

[W]ith Operation Desert Shield, our leaders are reduced to begging foreign powers for the means to support our warrior class. It does not seem to occur to us that the other great northern powers…might not have found the stakes so high or the crisis quite so threatening. It has not pene-

trated our imagination that in a world where the powerful, industrialized nation-states are at last at peace, there might be other ways to face down a pint-size Third World warrior state than with massive force of arms.

BARBARA EHRENREICH, "The Warrior Culture," *Time*, October 15, 1990.

But however you vote…let us come together after the vote with the notion that we are Americans here, not Democrats and not Republicans… without anything but the solemn cry that on this great decision day we voted as our conscience and judgment told us we should.

THOMAS S. FOLEY, during debate authorizing president to use force, January 12, 1991.

In the gulf, President Bush cannot argue that the United States is protecting other democracies, because Kuwait and Saudi Arabia are feudal societies. The other larger interest—oil—is one the President is reluctant to articulate, officials say, because many people would find the use of American troops to fight over resources mercenary. Thus, the Bush Administration falls back on the admired, but somewhat abstract, principle that aggression must never be allowed to pay.

THOMAS L. FRIEDMAN, *New York Times*, November 11, 1990.

One of the earliest casualties in America's desert war was the truth, wounded by an information directorate bent on controlling the words and images that flow from the battlefields. Political managers, who seem determined to apply the same spin control to war news that they routinely use on campaign news, have, with the acquiescence of a military haunted by Vietnam, clogged a vital artery leading to America's brain.

JOSEPH L. GALLOWAY, on press censorship, *U.S. News & World Report*, February 4, 1991.

If a bomb falls in the desert and our audio doesn't pick it up, does it still make a sound?

DANIEL GOLDEN, *Boston Globe*, January 20, 1991.

The days of delusion are dead in Baghdad. The city has finally discovered the obvious: a contest between a Third World semi-power fighting World War II and a First World superpower fighting World War III is no contest at all.

MICHAEL KELLY, *New Republic*, February 11, 1991.

[T]his is America's first real Republican war in this century.

MORTON KONDRACKE, *New Republic*, February 11, 1991.

Just two hours ago, allied air forces began an attack on military targets in Iraq and Kuwait. These attacks continue as I speak. Ground forces are not engaged.

This conflict started August 2nd when the dictator of Iraq invaded a small and helpless neighbor. Kuwait—a member of the Arab League and a member of the United Nations—was crushed; its people brutalized. Five months ago, Saddam Hussein started this cruel war against Kuwait. Tonight, the battle has been joined.

This military action, taken in accord with United Nations resolutions—and with the consent of the United States Congress—follows months of constant and virtually endless diplomatic activity on the part of the United Nations, the United States and many, many other countries....

Now the 28 countries with forces in the Gulf area have exhausted all reasonable efforts to reach a peaceful resolution, and have no choice but to drive Saddam from Kuwait by force. We will not fail.

As I report to you, air attacks are underway against military targets in Iraq. We are determined to knock out Saddam Hussein's nuclear bomb potential. We will also destroy his chemical weapons facilities. Much of Saddam's artillery and tanks will be destroyed. Our operations are designed to best protect the lives of all the coalition forces by targeting Saddam's vast military arsenal....

Our objectives are clear. Saddam Hussein's forces will leave Kuwait. The legitimate government of Kuwait will be restored to its rightful place and Kuwait will once again be free. Iraq will eventually comply with all relevant United Nations resolutions. And then, when peace is restored, it is our hope that Iraq will live as a peaceful and cooperative member of the family of nations, thus enhancing the security and stability of the Gulf.

Some may ask, why act now? Why not wait? The answer is clear: The world could wait no longer. Sanctions, though having some effect, showed no signs of accomplishing their objective. Sanctions were tried for well over five months, and we and our allies concluded that sanctions alone would not force Saddam from Kuwait.

While the world waited, Saddam Hussein systematically raped, pillaged and plundered a tiny nation, no threat to his own. He subjected the people of Kuwait to unspeakable atrocities—and among those maimed and murdered, innocent children.

While the world waited, Saddam sought to add to the chemical weapons arsenal he now possesses an infinitely more dangerous weapon of mass destruction—a nuclear weapon.

And while the world waited, while the world talked peace and withdrawal, Saddam Hussein dug in and moved massive forces into Kuwait.

While the world waited, while Saddam stalled, more damage was being done to the fragile economies of the Third World, the emerging democracies of Eastern Europe, to the entire world including to our own economy.

The United States, together with the United Nations, exhausted every means at our disposal to bring this crisis to a peaceful end.

Whatever one thinks of the policies that have led us to war in the Persian Gulf, the speed and energy of the American commitment have been remarkable....

But in six months or six years we have made no progress on a host of domestic problems. Indeed, we have made no real commitment to address them—no commitment of mind or resources.

ANTHONY LEWIS, *New York Times*, February 11, 1991.

Will there be hell to pay in the aftermath of a successful campaign against Saddam? No war begets the consequences men and women expect of it. And it would be sheer folly to speak of a postwar balance of power with any certainty. The case for resisting aggression must always be made on its own merits. We can be prudent about future consequences, cautious about excessive retribution, hopeful of the rehabilitation of

However, Saddam clearly felt that by stalling and threatening and defying the United Nations he could weaken the forces arrayed against him.

While the world waited, Saddam Hussein met every overture of peace with open contempt. While the world prayed for peace, Saddam prepared for war.

I had hoped that when the United States Congress, in historic debate, took its resolute action, Saddam would realize he could not prevail and would move out of Kuwait in accord with the United Nations resolutions. He did not do that. Instead, he remained intransigent, certain that time was on his side.

Saddam was warned over and over again to comply with the will of the United Nations. Leave Kuwait or be driven out. Saddam has arrogantly rejected all warnings. Instead he tried to make this a dispute between Iraq and the United States of America.

Well, he failed. Tonight, 28 nations—countries from five continents: Europe and Asia, Africa and the Arab League—have forces in the Gulf area standing shoulder to shoulder against Saddam Hussein. These countries had hoped the use of force could be avoided. Regrettably, we now believe that only force will make him leave.

Prior to ordering our forces into battle, I instructed military commanders to take every necessary step to prevail as quickly as possible for American and allied servicemen and women. I've told the American people before that this will not be another Vietnam. And I repeat this here tonight. Our troops will have the best possible support in the entire world, and they will not be asked to fight with one hand tied behind their back.

I'm hopeful that this fighting will not go on for long, and that casualties will be held to an absolute minimum.

This is an historic moment. We have, in this past year, made great progress in ending the long era of conflict and Cold War. We have before us the opportunity to forge, for ourselves and for future generations, a new world order—a world where the rule of law, not the law of the jungle, governs the conduct of nations.

When we are successful, and we will be, we have a real chance at this new world order—an order in which a credible United Nations can use its peacekeeping role to fulfill the promise and vision of the U.N.'s founders.

We have no argument with the people of Iraq—indeed, for the innocents caught in this conflict, I pray for their safety.

Our goal is not the conquest of Iraq—it is the liberation of Kuwait. It is my hope that somehow the Iraqi people can, even now, convince their dictator that he must lay down his arms, leave Kuwait, and let Iraq itself rejoin the family of peace-loving nations....

Tonight, as our forces fight, they and their families are in our prayers. May God bless each and every one of them, and the coalition forces at our side in the Gulf—and may He continue to bless our nation, the United States of America.

GEORGE BUSH, speech to nation, January 16, 1991.

---

the aggressor. With these principles established, war is a reasonable gamble. Were we to make the outcome of a good peace the precondition of resisting aggressors, the case for any war would be virtually impossible to sustain.

EDITORIAL, *The New Republic*, February 11, 1991.

SEND US IN TO KICK SOME OR SEND US HOME TO GET SOME.

SIGN, U.S. airfield, Saudi Arabia, *Newsweek*, January 21, 1991.

With the thunderous razzle-dazzle of a Tomahawk missile launch, America unleashed the full fury of modern warfare on the Middle East last week. The first results were spectacular and terrifying....It all seemed effortless, antiseptic and surreal: casualties were very light, at least among the attackers, and the high-tech gadgets in America's multibillion-dollar arsenal seemed to work with surgical lethality. Like a day at the office, one pilot said. This one's for you, Saddam.

Newsweek, January 28, 1991.

It was an awesome military feat, undoubtedly the most lopsided victory in the annals of war, the swiftest bit of conquering across a broad front in the history of civilization. Or is civilization not quite the right word?

DAVID NYHAN, *Boston Globe,* March 3, 1991.

Once we had taken out his eyes, we did what could best be described as the Hail Mary play in football.

H. NORMAN SCHWARZKOPF, news conference, on strategy of ground troops, Riyadh, Saudi Arabia, February 27, 1991.

As far as Saddam Hussein being a great military strategist, he is neither a strategist nor is he schooled in the operational art nor is he a tactician nor is he a general nor is he a soldier. Other than that, he's a great military man. I want you to know that.

H. NORMAN SCHWARZKOPF, news conference, Riyadh, Saudi Arabia, February 27, 1991.

To accuse our representatives of "voting on the side of Saddam Hussein" is as ridiculous as saying that those who believe Amtrak should run on time are admirers of Mussolini.

JOHN SILBER, *Boston Globe,* February 17, 1991.

KOREAN WAR

Red China is not the powerful nation seeking to dominate the world. Frankly, in the opinion of the Joint Chiefs of Staff, this strategy would involve us in the wrong war, at the wrong place, at the wrong time, and with the wrong enemy.

OMAR BRADLEY, testimony to Senate committee on desirability of widening Korean War, May 15, 1951.

If fight we must, let's go in there and shoot the works for victory with everything at our disposal.

MARK CLARK, testimony to Congress, ca. 1954, in Dean Acheson, *Power and Diplomacy,* 1958.

It is surely a curious characteristic of democracy: this amazing ability to shift gears overnight in one's ideological attitudes, depending on whether one considers one's self at war or at peace. Day before yesterday, let us say, the issues at stake between ourselves and another power were not worth the life of a single American boy. Today, nothing else counts at all; our cause is holy; the

cost is no consideration; violence must know no limitations short of unconditional surrender.

GEORGE F. KENNAN, *American Diplomacy, 1900–1950,* 1951.

[Chinese military intervention] created a new war and an entirely new situation, a situation not contemplated when our forces were committed against the North Korean invaders; a situation which called for new decisions in the diplomatic sphere to permit the realistic adjustment of military strategy. Such decisions have not been forthcoming.

DOUGLAS MACARTHUR, speech to Congress, April 19, 1951.

Of the nations of the world, Korea alone, up to now, is the sole one which has risked its all against communism. The magnificence of the courage and fortitude of the Korean people defies description.

DOUGLAS MACARTHUR, speech to Congress, April 19, 1951.

It isn't just dust that is settling in Korea, Senator, it is American blood.

DOUGLAS MACARTHUR, testimony, Senate hearing, *Time,* May 14, 1951.

It is fatal to enter any war without the will to win it.

DOUGLAS MACARTHUR, speech, Republican National Convention, July 7, 1952.

The willingness to settle for a stalemate...was all that brought peace to Korea....We had finally come to realize that military victory was not what it had been in the past—that it might even elude us forever if the means we used to achieve it brought wholesale devastation to the world or led us down the road of international immorality past the point of no return.

MATTHEW B. RIDGWAY, *The Korean War,* 1967.

This was a police action, a limited war, whatever you want to call it to stop aggression and to prevent a big war. And that's all it ever was.

HARRY S TRUMAN, in Merle Miller, *Plain Speaking: An Oral Biography of Harry S Truman,* 1974.

If we had not persuaded the United Nations to back up the free Republic of Korea, Western Europe would have gone into the hands of the Communists.

HARRY S TRUMAN, *The Autobiography of Harry S Truman,* 1980.

The attack upon Korea makes it plain that Communism has passed beyond the use of subversion to conquer independent nations and will now use armed invasion and war. Accordingly, I have ordered the Seventh Fleet to prevent any attack on Formosa.

HARRY S TRUMAN, 1950, in Lois and Alan Gordon,
American Chronicle, 1987.

MILITARY AND MILITARISM

We are evidently willing to sacrifice our own lives and the lives of millions of others, born and unborn—but not one minute of pleasure. We will have more arms, but not more taxes; we will aggrandize the military-industrial establishment, but not at the cost of self-aggrandizement. We will have defense and self-indulgence, which is to say, defense and debt. Surely not many nations before us have espoused bankruptcy and suicide as forms of self-defense.

WENDELL BERRY, 1984, "Property, Patriotism, and
National Defense," *Home Economics*, 1987.

I spent thirty-three years and four months in active military service....And during that period I spent most of my time being a high-class muscle man for big business, for Wall Street and for the bankers. In short, I was a racketeer, a gangster for capitalism....I helped make Mexico safe for American oil interests in 1914. I helped make Haiti and Cuba a decent place for the National City Bank boys to collect revenue in. I helped purify Nicaragua for the international banking house of Brown Brothers...I brought light to the Dominican Republic for American sugar interests in 1916. I helped make Honduras "right" for American fruit companies in 1903. Looking back on it, I might have given Al Capone a few hints.

SMEDLEY BUTLER, interview, *New York Times*, August,
1931.

No nation ever had an army large enough to guarantee it against attack in time of peace or insure it victory in time of war.

CALVIN COOLIDGE, speech, October 6, 1925.

We oppose militarism. It means conquest abroad and intimidation and oppression at home. It means the strong arm which has ever been fatal to free institutions. It is what millions of our citizens have fled from in Europe. It will impose upon our peace loving people a large standing army and unnecessary burden of taxation, and will be a constant menace to their liberties.

DEMOCRATIC PARTY PLATFORM PLANK, 1900.

It should not be forgotten that the atomic bombs were made in this country as a preventive measure. It was to head off its use by the Germans if they discovered it. We are in effect making the low standards of the enemy in the last war our own for the present.

ALBERT EINSTEIN, 1947, in Robert Jungk, *Brighter Than a
Thousand Suns*, 1958.

If I had known that the Germans would not succeed in constructing the atom bomb, I would never have lifted a finger.

ALBERT EINSTEIN, 1947, in Robert Jungk, *Brighter Than a
Thousand Suns*, 1958.

I think you know that I believe we must be strong militarily, but beyond a certain point military strength can become a national weakness.

DWIGHT D. EISENHOWER, October, 1960, conversation
with Norman Cousins, *Pathology of Power*, 1987.

In the councils of government, we must guard against the acquisition of unwarranted influence, whether sought or unsought, by the military-industrial complex. The potential for the disastrous rise of misplaced power exists and will persist. We must never let the weight of this combination endanger our liberties or democratic processes.

DWIGHT D. EISENHOWER, presidential farewell address,
January 17, 1961.

Militarism is the great preserver of our ideals of hardihood, and human life with no use for hardihood would be contemptible.

WILLIAM JAMES, "The Moral Equivalent of War," 1910.

Militarism...is one of the chief bulwarks of capitalism, and the day that militarism is undermined, capitalism will fail.

HELEN KELLER, *The Story of My Life*, 1903.

It is an unfortunate fact that we can secure peace only by preparing for war.

JOHN F. KENNEDY, speech, Seattle, Washington,
September 6, 1960.

A nation that continues year after year to spend more money on military defense than on programs of social uplift is approaching spiritual death.

MARTIN LUTHER KING, JR., *Where Do We Go from Here:
Chaos or Community?*, 1967.

What are we to make of terms like "nuclear exchange," "escalation," "nuclear yield," "counterforce," "megatons," or of "the window of vulnerability" or (ostensibly much better) "window of opportunity"? Quite simply, these words provide a way of talking about nuclear weapons without really talking about them. In them we find nothing about billions of human beings being incinerated or literally melted, nothing about millions of corpses. Rather, the weapons come to seem ordinary and manageable or even mildly pleasant: a "nuclear exchange" sounds something like mutual gift-giving.

ROBERT JAY LIFTON, *Indefensible Weapons*, 1982.

We may not be in the slightest danger of invasion, but if in an armed world we disarm, we shall count less and less in the councils of nations.

WALTER LIPPMANN, "A Cure for Militarism," *Metropolitan*, February, 1915.

They talk about conscription as being a democratic institution. Yes; so is a cemetery.

MEYER LONDON, speech, U.S. House of Representatives, April 25, 1917.

A warlike spirit, which alone can create and civilize a state, is absolutely essential to national defense and to national perpetuity.

DOUGLAS MACARTHUR, *Infantry Journal*, March, 1927.

I find in existence a new and heretofore unknown and dangerous concept that the members of the Armed Forces owe their primary allegiance and loyalty to those who temporarily exercise the authority of the executive branch of the government, rather than to the country and its Constitution they are sworn to defend. No proposition could be more dangerous. None could cast greater doubt on the integrity of the Armed Forces.

DOUGLAS MACARTHUR, speech, Massachusetts legislature, July 25, 1951.

While we go on developing smart bombs, we no longer are producing smart high school graduates.

LORETTA MCLAUGHLIN, *Boston Globe*, January 27, 1991.

The price of eternal vigilance is indifference.

MARSHALL MCLUHAN, *Understanding Media*, 1964.

Massive atomic deterring power can win us years of grace, years in which to wrench history from its present course and direct it toward the enshrinement of human brotherhood.

JAMES O'BRIEN MCMAHON, speech to U.S. Senate, September 18, 1951.

No matter what the atomic age brings, America will always need sailors and ships and shipborne aircraft to preserve her liberty, her communications with the free world, even her existence. If the deadly missiles with their apocalyptic warheads are ever launched at America, the Navy will still be out on blue water fighting for her, and the nation or alliance that survives will be the one that retains command of the oceans.

SAMUEL ELIOT MORISON, *The Two-Ocean War*, 1963.

The U.S. Constitution is a remarkable document—and a demanding one for those of us who choose to make our career in the military. We are required to pledge our sacred honor to a document that looks at the military...as a necessary, but undesirable, institution useful in times of crisis; and to be watched carefully at all other times.

COLIN POWELL, speech, Hofburg Palace, Vienna, Austria, January, 1990, *U.S. News & World Report*, February 4, 1991.

In setting our military goals we need first of all to recognize that most of the world's most basic woes do not lend themselves to purely military solutions.

MATTHEW B. RIDGWAY, *The Korean War*, 1967.

There is something magnificent, a contagion of enthusiasm, in the sight of a great volunteer army. The North and the South knew the thrill during our own great war. Conscription may form a great and admirable machine, but it differs from the trained army of volunteers as a body differs from a soul. But it costs a country heavy in grief, does a volunteer army; for the flower of the country goes.

MARY ROBERTS RINEHART, *Kings, Queens and Pawns*, 1915.

Our American merchant ships must be protected by our American Navy. It can never be doubted that the goods *will* be delivered by this nation, whose Navy believes in the tradition of "Damn the torpedoes; full speed ahead!"

FRANKLIN D. ROOSEVELT, Navy Day address, October 27, 1941.

In this country of ours, the man who has not raised himself to be a soldier, and the woman who has not raised her boy to be a soldier for the right, neither one of them is entitled to citizenship in the Republic.

THEODORE ROOSEVELT, speech, Camp Upton, Yaphank,
New York, November 18, 1917.

Are we so devoid of spiritual and moral force and intellectual ingenuity that we cannot possibly prevent war by any means other than military preparedness?

MARGARET CHASE SMITH, *Christian Science Monitor*,
January 15, 1952.

We are sick to death of war, defense spending and all things military. We are disgusted with and weary of the vilification that has been heaped upon us, at home as well as abroad, for our attempts to block communist enslavement in Southeast Asia. We yearn to turn away from foreign entanglements and to begin making our own house a better place to live in.

MARGARET CHASE SMITH, "It's Time To Speak Up for
National Defense," *Reader's Digest*, March, 1972.

The arms race is based on an optimistic view of technology and a pessimistic view of man. It assumes there is no limit to the ingenuity of science and no limit to the deviltry of human beings.

I.F. STONE, "Nixon and the Arms Race," *New York
Review of Books*, March 27, 1969.

It won't be until the bombs get so big that they can annihilate everything that people will really become terrified and begin to take a reasonable line in politics. Those who oppose the hydrogen bomb are behaving like ostriches if they think they are going to promote peace in that way.

EDWARD TELLER, in Robert Jungk, *Brighter Than a
Thousand Suns*, 1958.

This weapon is to be used against Japan between now and August 10th....It seems to be the most terrible thing ever discovered, but it can be made the most useful.

HARRY S TRUMAN, diary entry, July 25, 1945.

If there is one basic element in our Constitution, it is civilian control of the military.

HARRY S TRUMAN, *Memoirs*, 1955.

Maybe the answer to Selective Service is to start everyone off in the army and draft them for civilian life as needed.

BILL VAUGHAN, *Half the Battle*, 1967.

Absolute freedom of navigation upon the seas, outside territorial waters, alike in peace and in war, except as the seas may be closed in whole or in part by international action for the international convenants.

WOODROW WILSON, speech to Congress, second of
Fourteen Points, January 8, 1918.

NUCLEAR WAR

It is no longer possible to shield ourselves with arms alone against the ordeal of attack. For modern war visits destruction on the victor and vanquished alike....The way to win an atomic war is to make certain it never starts.

OMAR BRADLEY, speech, Boston, Massachusetts,
November 10, 1948.

We are now speeding inexorably towards the day when even the ingenuity of our scientists may be unable to save us from the consequences of a single rash act or a lone reckless hand upon the switch of an uninterceptible missile....Have we already gone too far in this search for peace through the accumulation of peril? Is there any way to halt this trend—or must we push on with new devices until we inevitably come to judgment before the atom?

OMAR BRADLEY, speech, Washington, D.C., November 5,
1957.

If the attack happens on July 1, say some people have paid withholding and some people have paid nothing, but you have to forgive and forget on both sides.

FEDERAL EMERGENCY MANAGEMENT AGENCY, Executive Order
11490, 1969.

Following a nuclear attack on the United States, the U.S. Postal Service plans to distribute Emergency Change of Address Cards.

FEDERAL EMERGENCY MANAGEMENT AGENCY, Executive Order
11490, 1969.

Be sure to carry your credit cards, cash, checks, stocks, insurance policies, and will. Every effort will be made to clear trans-nuclear attack checks, including those drawn on destroyed banks. You will be encouraged to buy U.S. Savings Bonds.

FEDERAL EMERGENCY MANAGEMENT AGENCY, Executive Order
11490, 1969.

Dig a hole, cover it with a couple of doors and then throw three feet of dirt on top....It's the dirt that does it....You know, dirt is just great stuff....If there are enough shovels to go around, everybody's going to make it.

THOMAS K. JONES, on how to survive nuclear war, in Robert Scheer, *With Enough Shovels: Reagan, Bush and Nuclear War*, 1981.

The question so often asked, "Would the survivors envy the dead?" may turn out to have a simple answer. No, they would be incapable of such feelings. They would not so much envy as, inwardly and outwardly, resemble the dead.

ROBERT JAY LIFTON AND KAI ERIKSON, "Nuclear War's Effect on the Mind," *New York Times*, March 15, 1982.

Advertisement before a nuclear attack:

RUN FOR YOUR LIFE!

You've always been careful when it comes to your health.

You've jogged.

You've done the marathon in under three.

You're a leader. A winner. A survivor. A runner.

So when your life depends on it you'll want running shoes that give you blast-off capability equal to the situation.

NUKES

The *Nuke* running shoe has a unique deep-waffle sole that gives you that extra spring you need to go from Ground Zero to Mile 20 in just five seconds. Break in a pair of *Nukes* today. You might be there to be glad you did.

Meet Mr. Bomb: A Practical Guide to Nuclear Extinction, 1982.

The dangers of atomic war are overrated. It would be hard on little, concentrated countries like England. In the United States we have lots of space.

ROBERT RUTHERFORD MCCORMICK, *Chicago Tribune*, February 23, 1950.

[A] nuclear war could alleviate some of the factors leading to today's ecological disturbances that are due to current high-population concentrations and heavy industrial production.

OFFICIAL OF U.S. OFFICE OF CIVIL DEFENSE, ca. 1980, in Jonathan Schell, *The Fate of the Earth*, 1982.

The premise of the private-shelter programme, as begun under Eisenhower and taken over by Kennedy, is that in the event of thermonuclear war each citizen must provide his own protection and be his own Secretary of Defence; the Defence Department, so-called, turns out to be for Offence only.

I.F. STONE, "Those Who Can't Afford Bomb Shelters— Do They Deserve To Die?" *I.F. Stone's Weekly*, October, 16, 1961.

Mankind's greatest collective fear, the doomsday fear, currently seems to have fascinated an incredible variety and number of people. Prophecies of doom are nothing new. Some of mankind's oldest myths have to do with the destruction of the world by fire....Today, much of the doomsday thinking centers on nuclear war.

EDWARD TELLER, *The Pursuit of Simplicity*, 1980.

VIETNAM WAR

The United States could well declare unilaterally that this stage of the Vietnam War is over—that we have "won" in the sense that our armed forces are in control of most of the field and no potential enemy is in a position to establish its authority over South Vietnam....It may be a far-fetched proposal, but nothing else has worked.

GEORGE D. AIKEN, October 19, 1966.

The way to get out of Vietnam is to declare victory and leave.

GEORGE D. AIKEN, quoted in *Time*, December 31, 1984.

At last there is light at the end of the tunnel.

JOSEPH ALSOP, syndicated column, September 13, 1965.

I felt sorry. I don't know why I felt sorry. John Wayne never felt sorry.

AMERICAN SOLDIER AFTER KNIFING VIETCONG SOLDIER, in Robert Jay Lifton, *Home from the War*, 1974.

The Sign of the American Chicken.

BUMPER STICKER, Vietnam War era.

Hey, hey, LBJ, how many kids did you kill today?

CHANT OF VIETNAM WAR PROTESTERS, mid–1960's.

We got in more trouble for killing water buffalo than we did for killing people. That was something I could never adjust to.

LEE CHILDRESS, in Al Santoli, *Everything We Had: An Oral History of the Vietnam War by Thirty-Three American Soldiers Who Fought It*, 1981.

Whether history will judge this war to be different or not, we cannot say. But this we can say with certainty: a government and a society that silences those who dissent is one that has lost its way. This we can say: that what is essential in a free society is that there should be an atmosphere where those who wish to dissent and even to demonstrate can do so without fear of recrimination or vilification.

HENRY STEELE COMMAGER, *Freedom and Order*, 1966.

The corner has definitely been turned toward victory in Vietnam.

DEFENSE DEPARTMENT ANNOUNCEMENT, May, 1963.

You have a row of dominoes set up, you knock over the first one, and what will happen to the last one is...that it will go over very quickly.

DWIGHT D. EISENHOWER, on strategic importance of Indochina, press conference, April 7, 1954.

If force is going to do the bidding, you must commit the amount of force necessary to bring the conflict to a successful conclusion.

DWIGHT D. EISENHOWER, remark at meeting on Vietnam with Lyndon B. Johnson, 1966.

Television showed us the war. It showed us the war in a way that was—if you chose to watch television, at least—unavoidable. You could not turn the page. You could not even switch channels: all you got was another network showing you the war.

NORA EPHRON, "Bob Haldeman and CBS," *Esquire*, July, 1975.

As I rejected amnesty, so I reject revenge. I ask all Americans who ever asked for goodness and mercy in their lives, who ever sought forgiveness for their trespasses, to join in rehabilitating all the casualties of the tragic conflict of the past.

GERALD R. FORD, on Americans who avoided draft, to Veterans of Foreign Wars, Chicago, Illinois, August 19, 1974.

General Maxwell D. Taylor...laid down in 1961 the original strategy....*The strategy has worked—* brilliantly. In a manner altogether astounding to behold....From being on the verge of losing its position in South Vietnam lock, stock, and barrel, the U.S. has driven the main enemy army to the brink of defeat. Never in modern times has there been a smoother, surer, swifter reversal in the tide of a...struggle.

"THE WAR WE'VE WON," *Fortune*, April, 1967.

The Senate must not remain silent now while the president uses the armed forces of the United States to fight an undeclared and undisclosed war in Laos.

WILLIAM FULBRIGHT, 1970, in Lois and Alan Gordon, *American Chronicle*, 1987.

The American war in Vietnam destroyed three ancient civilizations. They had survived through millennia everything history can do, which is always plenty, but they could not survive us, who understood nothing about them, nor valued them, and do not grieve for them.

MARTHA GELLHORN, "Last Words on Vietnam, 1987," *The Face of War*, 1988.

Once upon a time our traditional goal in war— and can anyone doubt that we are at war?—was victory. Once upon a time we were proud of our strength, our military power. Now we seem ashamed of it. Once upon a time the rest of the world looked to us for leadership. Now they look to us for a quick handout and a fence-straddling international posture.

BARRY M. GOLDWATER, *Why Not Victory?*, 1962.

To insist on strength...is not war-mongering. It is peace-mongering.

BARRY M. GOLDWATER, *New York Times*, August 11, 1964.

I think it is reasonable that if we must continue to fight wars, they ought to be fought by those people who really want to fight them. Since it seems to be the top half of the generation gap that is the most enthusiastic about going to war why not send the Old Folks Brigade to Vietnam—with John Wayne leading them?

DICK GREGORY, *Dick Gregory's Political Primer*, 1972.

Some people just wanted to blow it all to hell, animal, vegetable and mineral. They wanted a Vietnam they could fit into their car ashtrays.

MICHAEL HERR, *Dispatches*, 1977.

The battle against Communism must be joined in Southeast Asia with strength and determination...or the United States, inevitably, must surrender the Pacific and take up our defenses on our own shores.

LYNDON B. JOHNSON, 1961, in Stanley Karnow, *Vietnam: A History*, 1983.

We still seek no wider war.

LYNDON B. JOHNSON, statement after Gulf of Tonkin incident, August 4, 1964.

In that region there is nothing that we covet. There is nothing we seek. There is no territory or no military position or no political ambition. Our one desire and our one determination is that the people of Southeast Asia be left in peace to work out their own destinies in their own ways.

LYNDON B. JOHNSON, press conference, March 13, 1965.

No commander in chief could meet face to face with these soldiers without asking himself: What is it they are doing there?... They are there to keep aggression from succeeding. They are there to stop one nation from taking over another nation by force. They are there to help people who do not want to have an ideology pushed down their throats and imposed upon them. They are there because somewhere, and at some place, the free nations of the world must say again to the militant disciples of Asian communism: This far and no further. The time is now, and the place is Vietnam.

LYNDON B. JOHNSON, remarks, Manila, Philippines, for broadcast to American people, October 27, 1966.

I report to you that our country is challenged at home and abroad: that it is our will that is being tried and not our strength: our sense of purpose and not our ability to achieve a better America.

LYNDON B. JOHNSON, State of the Union address, January 17, 1968.

Our objective in South Vietnam has never been the annihilation of the enemy. It has been to bring about a recognition in Hanoi that its objective—taking over the South by force—could not be achieved.

LYNDON B. JOHNSON, address to nation, March 31, 1968.

I believe that a peaceful Asia is far nearer to reality because of what America has done in Vietnam.

LYNDON B. JOHNSON, address to nation, March 31, 1968.

This was a war of no fixed front. The "enemy" might be two or three divisions at one time, as at Khe Sanh, or two or three armed men sneaking into a village at night to murder the village chief. It was a war of subversion, terror, and assassination, of propaganda, economic disruption, and sabotage. It was a political war, an economic war, and a fighting war—all at the same time.

LYNDON B. JOHNSON, *The Vantage Point: Perspectives of the Presidency, 1963–1969*, 1971.

I believe there is a light at the end of what has been a long and lonely tunnel.

LYNDON B. JOHNSON, speech, September 21, 1966, in Neil Sheehan et al., *The Pentagon Papers*, 1971.

It is a selfish and shallow activism which can be bought off with a high lottery number while the killing goes on. Even if only one American boy each month is forced to go eight thousand miles to kill or be killed among an enemy he does not hate, in a war without reason, in a place we have ravished and ruined, no American of conscience can stand silent.

EDWARD M. KENNEDY, Harvard Law School Forum, September 27, 1971, in Thomas P. Collins and Louis M. Savary, eds., *A People of Compassion*, 1972.

The problem of campus violence cannot be solved by the resort to self-contained principles like the need for law and order, or the preservation of academic discipline. The problem must be seen in the larger political context of our society itself, the central fact of which is the war in Vietnam.

EDWARD M. KENNEDY, testimony to Commission on Campus Unrest, Washington, D.C., July 15, 1970, in Thomas P. Collins and Louis M. Savary, eds., *A People of Compassion*, 1972.

Pouring money, materiel and men into the jungles [of Vietnam] without at least a remote prospect of victory would be dangerously futile and self-destructive.

JOHN F. KENNEDY, speech to U.S. Senate, April 6, 1954.

Should I become President...I will not risk American lives...by permitting any other nation to drag us into the wrong war at the wrong place at the wrong time through an unwise commitment that is unwise militarily, unnecessary to our security and unsupported by our allies.

JOHN F. KENNEDY, speech, *New York Times*, October 13, 1960.

In the final analysis, it is their war. They are the ones who have to win or lose it. We can help them, we can give them equipment, we can send our men out there as advisers, but they have to win it, the people of Vietnam.

JOHN F. KENNEDY, press conference, September 3, 1963.

We have a problem in making our power credible, and Vietnam is the place.

JOHN F. KENNEDY, 1961, in Stanley Karnow, *Vietnam: A History*, 1983.

The troops will march in, the bands will play, the crowds will cheer, and in four days everyone will have forgotten. Then we will be told we have to send in more troops. It's like taking a drink. The effect wears off, and you have to take another.

JOHN F. KENNEDY, in Stanley Karnow, *Vietnam: A History*, 1983.

Can we ordain to ourselves the awful majesty of God—to decide what cities and villages are to be destroyed, who will live and who will die, and who will join the refugees wandering in a desert of our own creation?

ROBERT F. KENNEDY, speech, March 18, 1968.

I do not want—as I believe most Americans do not want—to sell out American interests, to simply withdraw, to raise the white flag of surrender. That would be unacceptable to us as a country and as a people. But I am concerned—as I believe most Americans are concerned—that the course we are following at the present time is deeply wrong. I am concerned—as I believe most Americans are concerned—that we are acting as if no other nations existed, against the judgment and desires of neutrals and our historic allies alike. I am concerned—as I believe most Americans are concerned—that our present course will not bring victory; will not bring peace; will not stop the bloodshed; and will not advance the interests of the United States or the cause of peace in the world.

I am concerned that, at the end of it all, there will only be more Americans killed; more of our treasure spilled out; and because of the bitterness and hatred on every side of this war, more hundreds of thousands of Vietnamese slaughtered; so that they may say, as Tacitus said of Rome: "They made a desert, and called it peace."

ROBERT F. KENNEDY, speech, March 18, 1968.

We are entitled to ask—we are required to ask—how many more men, how many more lives, how much more destruction will be asked, to provide the military victory that is always just around the corner, to pour into this bottomless pit of our dreams?

ROBERT F. KENNEDY, speech, March 18, 1968.

The bombs in Vietnam explode at home; they destroy the hopes and possibilities for a decent America.

MARTIN LUTHER KING, JR., *Where Do We Go from Here: Chaos or Community?*, 1967.

Somehow this madness must cease. We must stop now. I speak as a child of God and brother to the suffering poor of Vietnam. I speak for those whose land is being laid waste, whose homes are being destroyed, whose culture is being subverted. I speak for the poor in America who are paying the double price of smashed hopes at home and death and corruption in Vietnam. I speak as a citizen of the world, for the world as it stands aghast at the path we have taken. I speak as an American to the leaders of my own nation. The great initiative in this war is ours. The initiative to stop it must be ours.

MARTIN LUTHER KING, JR., *The Trumpet of Conscience*, 1967.

Vietnam presumably taught us that the United States could not serve as the world's policeman; it should also have taught us the dangers of trying to be the world's midwife to democracy when the birth is scheduled to take place under conditions of guerrilla war.

JEANE KIRKPATRICK, "Dictatorship and Double Standards," *Commentary*, November, 1979.

Psychologists or sociologists may explain some day what it is about that distant monochromatic land, of green mountains and fields merging with an azure sea, that for millennia has acted as a magnet for foreigners who sought glory there and found frustration, who believed that in its rice fields and jungles some principle was to be established and entered them only to recede in disillusion.

HENRY KISSINGER, *White House Years*, 1979.

The time has come to stop beating our heads against stone walls under the illusion that we have been appointed policeman to the human race.

WALTER LIPPMANN, *New York Herald Tribune*, February 2, 1965.

The war in Vietnam was bad for America because it was a bad war, as all wars are bad if they consist of rich boys fighting poor boys when the rich boys have an advantage in the weapons.

NORMAN MAILER, *The Armies of the Night*, 1968.

If the Devil was devoted to destroying all belief in conservative values among the intelligent and prosperous, he could not have picked a finer instrument to his purpose than the war in Vietnam.

NORMAN MAILER, *St. George and the Godfather*, 1972.

In the end, we simply cut and ran. The American national will had collapsed.

GRAHAM A. MARTIN, on 10th anniversary of fall of Saigon, *New York Times*, April 30, 1985.

Vietnam is a military problem. Vietnam is a political problem; and as the war goes on it has become more clearly a moral problem.

EUGENE J. MCCARTHY, *The Limits of Power*, 1967.

It is said that we must carry on the war in Vietnam in order to preserve and defend our national honor. Our national honor is not at stake, and should not so readily be offered. In every other great war of the century, we have had the support of what is generally accepted as the decent opinion of mankind. We do not have that today. We cannot, of course, depend only on this opinion to prove our honor; it may not be sound. But always in the past we have not only had this support, but we have used it as a kind of justification for our actions.

EUGENE J. McCARTHY, *The Limits of Power*, 1967.

We seem bent upon saving the Vietnamese from Ho Chi Minh, even if we have to kill them and demolish their country to do it....I do not intend to remain silent in the face of what I regard as a policy of madness which, sooner or later, will envelop my son and American youth by the millions for years to come.

GEORGE McGOVERN, speech to U.S. Senate, April 25, 1967.

Every senator in this chamber is partly responsible for sending 50,000 young Americans to an early grave.

GEORGE McGOVERN, 1971, in Lois and Alan Gordon, *American Chronicle*, 1987.

Vietnam was our longest, costliest, and, as it went on, our least popular war; it was also the least understood. And the more attempts were made to explain, the more puzzling it became.

MERLE MILLER, *Lyndon: An Oral Biography*, 1980.

Like robots suffering an obscure sorrow, they carried the casket of the new Unknown Soldier, the one from Vietnam. [It] was a different kind of war for the United States [in] a shattering time, a bomb that originated a world away and went off in the middle of the American mind. [Now] the prevailing note was one of acceptance and reconciliation, as if in burying the Unknown Soldier, the nation were also interring another measure of its residual bitterness.

LANCE MORROW, "War and Remembrance: A Bit of the Bitterness Is Buried Along with an Unknown Soldier," *Time*, June 11, 1984.

Vietnam arrived in the American mind like some strange, violent hallucination, just when the nation was most prosperous and ambitious, shooting spaceships at the moon. Sweet America cracked open like a geode. The bizarre catastrophe of that war shattered so much in American life (pride in country, faith in government, the idea of manhood, and the worth of the dollar, to

begin the list) that even now the damage has not yet been properly assessed.

LANCE MORROW, "Bringing the Vietnam Veterans Home," *Fishing in the Tiber*, 1988.

We did a fine job there. If it happened in World War II, they still would be telling stories about it. But it happened in Vietnam, so nobody knows about it. They don't even tell recruits about it today. Marines don't talk about Vietnam. We lost. They never talk about losing. So it's just wiped out, all of that's off the slate, it doesn't count. It makes you a little bitter.

JOHN MUIR, in Al Santoli, *Everything We Had: An Oral History of the Vietnam War*, 1981.

A memorial at once national and personal. In each sharply etched name one reads the price paid by yet another family. In the sweeping pattern of names, chronological by day of death, 1959 to 1975, one reads the price paid by the nation.

NEW YORK TIMES, editorial on Vietnam Memorial, "The Black Gash of Shame," April 14, 1985.

The official rationale for Vietnam—global anti-communism wed to the rhetoric of social reform and renamed counterinsurgency—was the heart of the mistake made by the Kennedy Administration.

JACK NEWFIELD, Introduction, *Bread and Roses Too*, 1971.

If in order to avoid further Communist expansion in Asia and particularly in Indo-China, if in order to avoid it we must take the risk by putting American boys in, I believe that the executive branch of the government has to take the politically unpopular position of facing up to it and doing it, and I personally would support such a decision.

RICHARD M. NIXON, speech, April 16, 1954.

We must never forget that if the war in Vietnam is lost...the right of free speech will be extinguished throughout the world.

RICHARD M. NIXON, *New York Times*, October 27, 1965.

What the United States wants for South Vietnam is not the important thing. What North Vietnam wants for South Vietnam is not the important thing. What is important is what the people of South Vietnam want.

RICHARD M. NIXON, address to nation, May 14, 1969.

Let me be quite blunt. Our fighting men are not going to be worn down; our mediators are not going to be talked down; and our allies are not going to be let down.

RICHARD M. NIXON, address to nation, May 14, 1969.

The defense of freedom is everybody's business—not just America's business. And it is particularly the responsibility of the people whose freedom is threatened. In the previous administration, we Americanized the war in Vietnam. In this administration, we are Vietnamizing the search for peace.

RICHARD M. NIXON, speech, November 3, 1969.

Tonight—to you, the great silent majority of my fellow Americans—I ask for your support.

RICHARD M. NIXON, speech, November 3, 1969.

My fellow Americans, we live in an age of anarchy, both abroad and at home.

RICHARD M. NIXON, TV address on incursion into Cambodia, April 30, 1970.

No event in American history is more misunderstood than the Vietnam War. It was misreported then, and it is misremembered now.

RICHARD M. NIXON, "No More Vietnams," *New York Times*, March 28, 1985.

I know that probably most of you think I'm an S.O.B., but I want you to know I understand just how you feel.

RICHARD M. NIXON, to student demonstrators, 1970, in Lois and Alan Gordon, *American Chronicle*, 1987.

If the Indochina war proves anything at all, it is the susceptibility of government to self-deluded error.

LIANE NORMAN, "Selective Conscientious Objection," *Center*, May/June, 1972.

The incredible war in Vietnam has provided the razor, the terrifying sharp cutting edge, that has finally severed the last vestiges of illusion that morality and democracy are the guiding principles of American foreign policy. The saccharine, self-righteous moralism that promises the Vietnamese a billion dollars of economic aid at the very moment we are delivering billions for economic and social destruction and political repression is rapidly losing what power it might ever have had to reassure us about the decency of our foreign policy.

PAUL POTTER, speech, Washington, D.C., April 17, 1965.

It's silly talking about how many years we will have to spend in the jungles of Vietnam when we could pave the whole country and put parking stripes on it and still be home for Christmas.

RONALD REAGAN, interview, Fresno *Bee*, October 10, 1965.

We should declare war on North Vietnam. We could pave the whole place over by noon and be home for dinner.

RONALD REAGAN, in Edmund G. Brown, *Reagan: The Political Chameleon*, 1976.

Their casualties are going up at a rate they cannot sustain....I see light at the end of the tunnel.

WALT ROSTOW, *Look*, December 12, 1967.

The Vietcong are going to collapse within weeks.

WALT ROSTOW, 1965, in Lois and Alan Gordon, *American Chronicle*, 1987.

You know, if I thought of a child dying, that's the way it was. That's war. Children die. You kill them, they kill you. Women kill you, you kill them. That's it. There's no Geneva Convention. There's no rules. There's nothing.

GAYLE SMITH, in Al Santoli, *Everything We Had: An Oral History of the Vietnam War*, 1981.

I'd rather see America save her soul than her face.

NORMAN THOMAS, to antiwar demonstrators, Washington, D.C., November 27, 1965.

Numbers have dehumanized us. Over breakfast coffee we read of 40,000 American dead in Vietnam. Instead of vomiting, we reach for the toast. Our morning rush through crowded streets is not to cry murder but to hit that trough before somebody else gobbles our share.

DALTON TRUMBO, Introduction, *Johnny Got His Gun*, 1970.

Ignorance was not a factor in the American endeavor in Vietnam pursued through five successive presidencies, although it was to become an excuse.

BARBARA TUCHMAN, *The March of Folly*, 1984.

It became necessary to destroy the town to save it.

UNIDENTIFIED U.S. ARMY MAJOR, on decision to bomb Bentre, Vietnam, February 7, 1968.

I can envision a small cottage somewhere, with a lot of writing paper, and a dog, and a fireplace and maybe enough money to give myself some Irish coffee now and then and entertain my two friends.

RICHARD VAN DE GEER, letter to friend before he was killed, May 15, 1975, officially last American to die in Vietnam War, *Time*, April 15, 1985.

American policy…has been to scrupulously respect the neutrality of the Cambodian people.…

North Vietnam, however, has not respected that neutrality.

For the past five years,…North Vietnam has occupied military sanctuaries all along the Cambodian frontier with South Vietnam.

North Vietnam in the last two weeks has stripped away all pretense of respecting the sovereignty or the neutrality of Cambodia. Thousands of their soldiers are invading the country from the sanctuaries; they are encircling the capital of Phnom Penh.…

Cambodia, as a result of this, has sent out a call to the United States, to a number of other nations, for assistance. Because if this enemy effort succeeds, Cambodia would become a vast enemy staging area and a springboard for attacks on South Vietnam along six hundred miles of frontier, a refuge where enemy troops could return from combat without fear of retaliation.…

[T]his is the decision I have made.

In cooperation with the armed forces of South Vietnam, attacks are being launched this week to clean out major enemy sanctuaries on the Cambodian-Vietnam border.…

These actions are in no way directed at the security interests of any nation. Any government that chooses to use these actions as a pretext for harming relations with the United States will be doing so on its own responsibility and on its own initiative, and we will draw the appropriate conclusions.…

We take this action not for the purpose of expanding the war into Cambodia, but for the purpose of ending the war in Vietnam and winning the just peace we all desire. We have made and we will continue to make every possible effort to end this war through negotiation at the conference table rather than through more fighting on the battlefield.

Let us look again at the record. We have stopped the bombing of North Vietnam. We have cut air operations by over 20 percent. We have announced withdrawal of over 250,000 of our men. We have offered to withdraw all of our men, if they will withdraw theirs. We have offered to negotiate all issues with only one condition—and that is that the future of South Vietnam be determined not by North Vietnam, not by the United States, but by the people of South Vietnam themselves.

The answer of the enemy has been intransigence at the conference table, belligerence in Hanoi, massive military aggression in Laos and Cambodia, and stepped-up attacks in South Vietnam designed to increase American casualties.

This attitude has become intolerable. We will not react to this threat to American lives merely by plaintive diplomatic protests. If we did, the credibility of the United States would be destroyed in every area of the world where only the power of the United States deters aggression.

Tonight I again warn the North Vietnamese that if they continue to escalate the fighting when the United States is withdrawing its forces, I shall meet my responsibility as Commander in Chief of our Armed Forces to take the action I consider necessary to defend the security of our American men.

The action that I have announced tonight puts the leaders of North Vietnam on notice that we will be patient in working for peace, we will be conciliatory at the conference table, but we will not be humiliated. We will not be defeated. We will not allow American men by the thousands to be killed by an enemy from privileged sanctuaries.

The time came long ago to end this war through peaceful negotiations. We stand ready for those negotiations. We have made major efforts, many of which must remain secret. I say tonight that all the offers and approaches made previously remain on the conference table whenever Hanoi is ready to negotiate seriously.

But if the enemy response to our most conciliatory offers for peaceful negotiation continues to be to increase its attacks and humiliate and defeat us, we shall react accordingly.

My fellow Americans, we live in an age of anarchy, both abroad and at home. We see mindless attacks on all the great institutions which have been created by free civilizations in the last five hundred years. Even here in the United States, great universities are being systematically destroyed. Small nations all over the world find themselves under attack from within and from without.

If, when the chips are down, the world's most powerful nation, the United States of America, acts like a pitiful, helpless giant, the forces of totalitarianism and anarchy will threaten free nations and free institutions throughout the world.

It is not our power but our will and character that is being tested tonight. The question all Americans must ask and answer tonight is this: Does the richest and strongest nation in the history of the world have the character to meet a direct challenge by a group which rejects every effort to win a just peace, ignores our warning, tramples on solemn agreements, violates the neutrality of an unarmed people, and uses our prisoners as hostages?

If we fail to meet this challenge, all other nations will be on notice that despite its overwhelming power the United States, when a real crisis comes, will be found wanting.

During my campaign for the Presidency, I pledged to bring Americans home from Vietnam. They are coming home.

I promised to end this war. I shall keep that promise.

I promised to win a just peace. I shall keep that promise.

We shall avoid a wider war. But we are also determined to put an end to this war....

No one is more aware than I am of the political consequences of the action I have taken. It is tempting to take the easy political path: to blame this war on previous administrations and to bring all of our men home immediately, regardless of the consequences, even though that would mean defeat for the United States; to desert 18 million South Vietnamese people who have put their trust in us and to expose them to the same slaughter and savagery which the leaders of North Vietnam inflicted on hundreds of thousands of North Vietnamese who chose freedom when the Communists took over North Vietnam in 1954; to get peace at any price now, even though I know that a peace of humiliation for the United States would lead to a bigger war or surrender later.

I have rejected all political considerations in making this decision.

Whether my party gains in November is nothing compared to the lives of 400,000 brave Americans fighting for our country and for the cause of peace and freedom in Vietnam. Whether I may be a one-term President is insignificant compared to whether by our failure to act in this crisis the United States proves itself to be unworthy to lead the forces of freedom in this critical period in world history. I would rather be a one-term president and do what I believe is right than to be a two-term president at the cost of seeing America become a second-rate power and to see this nation accept the first defeat in its proud 190-year history.

RICHARD M. NIXON, on invasion of Cambodia, April 30, 1970.

We have reached an important point when the end begins to come into view.

WILLIAM C. WESTMORELAND, speech, National Press Club, November 21, 1967.

Press and television had created an aura not of victory but of defeat, which, coupled with the vocal antiwar elements, profoundly influenced timid officials in Washington. It was like two boxers in a ring, one having the other on the ropes, close to a knock-out, when the apparent winner's second inexplicably throws in the towel.

WILLIAM C. WESTMORELAND, *A Soldier Reports*, 1976.

Even though American resolve fell short in the end, it remains a fact that few countries have ever engaged in such idealistic magnanimity; and no gain or attempted gain for human freedom can be discounted.

WILLIAM C. WESTMORELAND, *A Soldier Reports*, 1976.

Only You Can Prevent Forests.

SIGN IN ROOM OF U.S. AIRMEN SPRAYING DEFOLIANTS, in William C. Westmoreland, *A Soldier Reports*, 1976.

We have stopped losing the war.

WILLIAM C. WESTMORELAND, 1966, in Lois and Alan Gordon, *American Chronicle*, 1987.

WORLD WAR I

Come on, you sons of bitches! Do you want to live forever?

ATTRIBUTED TO U.S. MARINE, Battle of Belleau Wood, June 6, 1918.

Has there ever been danger of war between Germany and ourselves, members of the same Teutonic race? Never has it even been imagined.

ANDREW CARNEGIE, "The Baseless Fear of War," *Independent*, February 13, 1913.

The purpose of the Allies is exactly the purpose of the Central Powers, and that is the conquest and spoliation of the weaker nations that have always been the purpose of war.

EUGENE V. DEBS, speech, Canton, Ohio, June 16, 1918.

Wake up America.

AUGUSTUS P. GARDNER, speech, October 16, 1916.

I find a hundred thousand sorrows touching my heart, and there is ringing in my ears like an admonition eternal, an insistent call, "It must not be again!"

WARREN G. HARDING, speech, service for American soldiers killed in World War I, Hoboken, New Jersey, May 23, 1921.

When the war closed, the most vital of all issues both in our country and throughout the world was whether governments should continue their wartime ownership and operation of many instrumentalities of production and distribution. We were challenged with a peace-time choice between the American system of rugged individualism and a European philosophy of diametrically opposed doctrines—doctrines of paternalism and state socialism. The acceptance of these ideas would have meant the destruction of self-government through centralization of government. It would have meant the undermining of the individual initiative and enterprise through which our people have grown to unparalleled greatness.

HERBERT HOOVER, speech, New York City, October 22, 1928.

In 1917, we entered World War I civilization, in order to preserve Western civilization, specifically the civilization of Western Europe from German domination; to defend and protect our declared neutral rights, especially that of freedom of the seas; and to preserve our national honor.

EUGENE J. McCARTHY, *The Limits of Power*, 1967.

We are going into war upon the command of gold. We are going to run the risk of sacrificing millions of our countrymen's lives in order that other countrymen may coin their lifeblood into money.

We are about to do the bidding of wealth's terrible mandate.

GEORGE NORRIS, speech to Congress, April 4, 1917.

Hell, Heaven or Hoboken by Christmas.

ATTRIBUTED TO JOHN J. PERSHING, 1918.

We are fighting in the quarrel of civilization against barbarism, of liberty against tyranny. Germany has become a menace to the whole world. She is the most dangerous enemy of liberty now existing.

THEODORE ROOSEVELT, speech, Oyster Bay, Long Island, New York, April, 1917.

To most of the people it [World War I] had seemed far away, something that could never come close.

Some resented it, others seized upon it now to help break up the long monotony of everyday living—more terribly thrilling than a fire in the business district, a drowning in the river, or the discovery that the cashier of the Farmers' Bank had been embezzling. Something had come, it seemed, to shake up that placid, solid, comfortable life of home, changing things around, shifting values that had seemed to be fixed.

RUTH SUCKOW, *The Odyssey of a Nice Girl*, 1925.

It was said in the First World War that the French fought for their country, the British fought for freedom of the seas, and the Americans fought for souvenirs.

HARRY S TRUMAN, in Margaret Truman, *Harry S Truman*, 1973.

The Great War has never been for us so embedded a part of our national tradition as the Civil War or World War II. It is somehow less "ours."

BARBARA TUCHMAN, "How We Entered World War I," *New York Times Magazine*, May 5, 1967.

The Yanks are coming.

WAR CRY, 1917.

A war to end all wars.

H.G. WELLS, 1914, popularized by Woodrow Wilson.

The United States must be neutral in fact as well as in name during these days that are to try men's souls. We must be impartial in thought as well as in action, must put a curb upon our sentiments as well as upon every transaction that might be construed as a preference of one party to the struggle before another.

WOODROW WILSON, proclamation, August 18, 1914.

Our whole duty, for the present, at any rate, is summed up in this motto: "America first."

WOODROW WILSON, speech, New York City, April 20, 1915.

I am not saying this with even the slightest thought of criticism of other nations....The example of America must be the example not merely of peace because it will not fight, but of peace because peace is the healing and elevating influence of the world and strife is not. There is such a thing as a man too proud to fight.

WOODROW WILSON, speech three days after the Germans sank the *Lusitania*, Philadelphia, Pennsylvania, May, 1915.

It must be a peace without victory....Victory would mean peace forced upon the loser, a victor's terms imposed upon the vanquished. It would be accepted in humiliation, under duress, at an intolerable sacrifice, and would leave a sting, a resentment, a bitter memory upon which terms of peace would rest, not permanently, but only as upon quicksand. Only a peace between equals can last. Only a peace the very principle of which is equality and a common participation in a common benefit.

WOODROW WILSON, speech to U.S. Senate, January 22, 1917.

Since it has unhappily proved impossible to safeguard our neutral rights by diplomatic means against the unwarranted infringements they are suffering at the hands of Germany, there may be no recourse but to *armed* neutrality.

WOODROW WILSON, speech to Congress, February 26, 1917.

The world must be made safe for democracy. Its peace must be planted upon the tested foundations of political liberty. We have no selfish ends to serve. We desire no conquest, no dominion. We seek no indemnities for ourselves, no material compensation for the sacrifices we shall freely make.

WOODROW WILSON, message to Congress, April 2, 1917.

There are, it may be, many months of fiery trial and sacrifice ahead of us. It is a fearful thing to lead this great peaceful people into war, into the most terrible and disastrous of all wars, civilization itself seeming to be in the balance. But the right is more precious than peace, and we shall fight for the things which we have always carried nearest our hearts—for democracy, for the right of those who submit to authority to have a voice in their own governments, for the rights and liberties of small nations, for a universal dominion of right by such a concert of free peoples as shall bring peace and safety to all nations and make the world itself at last free.

To such a task we can dedicate our lives and our fortunes, everything that we are and everything that we have, with the pride of those who know that the day has come when America is privileged to spend her blood and her might for the principles that gave her birth and happiness and the peace which she has treasured. God helping her, she can do no other.

WOODROW WILSON, message to Congress, April 2, 1917.

The moral climax of this, the culminating and final war for human liberty, has come.

WOODROW WILSON, speech to Congress enumerating Fourteen Points, January 8, 1918.

There is...but one response possible from us: force, force to the utmost, force without stint or limit, the righteous and triumphant force which shall make right the law of the world and cast every selfish dominion down in the dust.

WOODROW WILSON, speech, Baltimore, Maryland, April 6, 1918.

WORLD WAR II

PEACE OR WAR? Which will you choose? Should we fight for England?...Let's stop the Rush toward War! Let's make America impregnable.

AMERICA FIRST COMMITTEE, 1940.

There are various theories as to what characteristics, what combination of traits, what qualities in our men won the war. This democratic heritage is highly thought of; the instinctive mechanical know-how of thousands of our young men is frequently cited; the church and Coca-Cola, baseball, and the movies all come in for their share of credit; but, speaking from my own observation of our armed forces, I should say the war was won on coffee.

ILKA CHASE, Free Admission, 1948.

While the rest of the world came out bruised and scarred and nearly destroyed, we came out with the most unbelievable machinery, tools, manpower, money. The war was fun for America.... And the rest of the world was bleeding and in pain.

PAUL EDWARDS, in Studs Terkel, The Good War, 1984.

More than any other war in history, this war has been an array of the forces of evil against those of righteousness. It had to have its leaders and it had to be won—but no matter what the sacrifice, no matter what the suffering of populations, no matter what the cost, the war had to be won.

DWIGHT D. EISENHOWER, speech, Frankfurt, Germany, June 10, 1945.

A Japanese attack on Pearl Harbor is a strategic impossibility.

GEORGE FIELDING ELIOT, "The Impossible War with Japan," September 1938.

Praise the Lord and pass the ammunition.

ATTRIBUTED TO HOWELL M. FORGY, Pearl Harbor, 1941.

Wear it up, wear it out, make it do, or do without.

HOME FRONT SAYING, 1943, in Lois and Alan Gordon, American Chronicle, 1987.

The war's over. One or two of those things, and Japan will be finished.

LESLIE R. GROVES, after first atomic bomb test, July 16, 1945.

Catch-22 says [the military authorities] have a right to do anything we can't stop them from doing.

JOSEPH HELLER, Catch-22, 1955.

Your city will be obliterated unless your government surrenders.

LEAFLETS DROPPED ON HIROSHIMA, August 5, 1945.

As long as Europe prepares for war, America must prepare for neutrality.

WALTER LIPPMANN, New York Herald Tribune, May 17, 1934.

The President of the United States ordered me to break through the Japanese lines...for the purpose, as I understand it, of organizing the American offensive against Japan, a primary object of which is the relief of the Philippines. I came through and I shall return.

DOUGLAS MACARTHUR, statement to press after arrival in Australia from Corregidor, March 20, 1942.

I have returned. By the grace of Almighty God, our forces stand again on Philippine soil.

DOUGLAS MACARTHUR, following U.S. landing on Leyte, October 20, 1944.

Given the assumption that nuclear weapons would contribute nothing to victory, the battle of Okinawa had to be fought. No one doubted the need to bring Japan to its knees. But some Americans came to hate the things we had to do, even when convinced that doing them was absolutely necessary; they had never understood the bestial, monstrous and vile means required to reach the objective—an unconditional Japanese surrender.

WILLIAM MANCHESTER, "Okinawa: The Bloodiest Battle of All," New York Times Magazine, June 14, 1987.

I feel like a fugitive from th' law of averages.

BILL MAULDIN, cartoon caption, Up Front, 1944.

Look at an infantryman's eyes and you can tell how much war he has seen.

BILL MAULDIN, cartoon caption, Up Front, 1944.

We sure liberated the hell out of this place.

AMERICAN SOLDIER, on heavily damaged French village, in Max Miller, The Far Shore, 1945.

There is one great thing you men will be able to say after this war is all over and you are at home once again. And you may thank God for it. You

Yesterday, December 7, 1941—a date which will live in infamy—the United States of America was suddenly and deliberately attacked by naval and air forces of the empire of Japan.

The United States was at peace with that nation and, at the solicitation of Japan, was still in conversation with its government and its emperor looking toward the maintenance of peace in the Pacific.

Indeed, one hour after Japanese air squadrons had commenced bombing in the American island of Oahu the Japanese ambassador to the United States and his colleague delivered to our secretary of state a formal reply to a recent American message. And, while this reply stated that it seemed useless to continue the existing diplomatic negotiations, it contained no threat or hint of war or of armed attack.

It will be recorded that the distance of Hawaii from Japan makes it obvious that the attack was deliberately planned many days or even weeks ago. During the intervening time the Japanese government has deliberately sought to deceive the United States by false statements and expressions of hope for continued peace.

The attack yesterday on the Hawaiian islands has caused severe damage to American naval and military forces. I regret to tell you that very many American lives have been lost. In addition American ships have been reported torpedoed on the high seas between San Francisco and Honolulu.

Yesterday the Japanese government also launched an attack against Malaya.

Last night Japanese forces attacked Hong Kong.

Last night Japanese forces attacked Guam.

Last night Japanese forces attacked the Philippine Islands.

Last night the Japanese attacked Wake Island.

And this morning the Japanese attacked Midway Island.

Japan has therefore undertaken a surprise offensive extending throughout the Pacific area. The facts of yesterday and today speak for themselves. The people of the United States have already formed their opinions and well understand the implications to the very life and safety of our nation.

As commander in chief of the Army and Navy I have directed that all measures be taken for our defense.

Always will our whole nation remember the character of the onslaught against us.

No matter how long it may take us to overcome this premeditated invasion, the American people in their righteous might will win through to absolute victory.

I believe that I interpret the will of the Congress and of the people when I assert that we will not only defend ourselves to the uttermost but will make it very certain that this form of treachery shall never again endanger us.

Hostilities exist. There is no blinking at the fact that our people, our territory and our interests are in grave danger.

With confidence in our armed forces, with the unbounding determination of our people, we will gain the inevitable triumph. So help us God.

I ask that the Congress declare that since the unprovoked and dastardly attack by Japan on Sunday, December 7, 1941, a state of war has existed between the United States and the Japanese empire.

FRANKLIN D. ROOSEVELT, message to Congress, December 8, 1941.

---

may be thankful that twenty years from now when you are sitting by the fireplace with your grandson on your knee and he asks you what you did in the great World War II, you won't have to cough, shift him to the other knee and say, "Well, your Granddaddy shoveled shit in Louisiana." No Sir! You can look him straight in the eye and say, "Son, your Granddaddy rode with the great Third Army and a son-of-a-bitch named George Patton."

GEORGE S. PATTON, speech to troops of Sixth Armored Division, May 31, 1944.

We are having one hell of a war.

GEORGE S. PATTON, letter to A.D. Surles, December 15, 1944.

I cannot believe that war is the best solution. No one won the last war, and no one will win the next war.

ELEANOR ROOSEVELT, letter to Harry S Truman, March 22, 1948, in Joseph P. Lash, *Eleanor: The Years Alone*, 1972.

SNAFU—Situation Normal, All Fouled Up.

SAYING.

Kilroy was here.

SOLDIERS' GRAFFITO.

Berlin does not hide its contempt for the democracies: "stupid cows" Goebbels calls them.... Today it is Madrid. Tomorrow it will be Prague. How long before it knocks at our own doors?

I.F. STONE, *The Nation*, 1937.

We turned back to look at Hiroshima. The city was hidden by that awful cloud...boiling up, mushrooming, terrible and incredibly tall.

PAUL W. TIBBETS, "How To Drop an Atom Bomb," *Saturday Evening Post*, June 8, 1946.

I was a strong rooter for the USA in World War II. I kept myself very well informed on that war, even though I was only a child. My father had told me that when the USA won that war we'd have bubble gum again. You might say I had a stake in that war. Also as soon as the USA won that war I could quit collecting newspapers for General Eisenhower. I couldn't imagine what he wanted with that many copies of the *Kansas City Star*. After a while, I began to envision General Eisenhower sitting over in Europe somewhere behind a sort of fortress of newspapers, chewing bubble gum.

CALVIN TRILLIN, "Iran May Be Iraq," *The Nation*, March 16, 1985.

This is a solemn but glorious hour. I only wish that Franklin D. Roosevelt had lived to witness this day. General Eisenhower informs me that the forces of Germany have surrendered to the United Nations. The flags of freedom fly all over Europe.

HARRY S TRUMAN, VE-Day message to nation, White House, May 8, 1945.

Sixteen hours ago an American airplane dropped one bomb on Hiroshima, an important Japanese Army base. That bomb had more power than 20,000 tons of TNT. It had more than two thousand times the blast power of the British "Grand Slam," which is the largest bomb ever yet used in the history of warfare....It is an atomic bomb. It is a harnessing of the basic power of the universe. The force from which the sun draws its powers has been loosed against those who brought war to the Far East.

HARRY S TRUMAN, message to nation, August 6, 1945.

Pearl Harbor is one of the greatest, if not the very greatest, maritime fortresses in the world. Pearl Harbor has immense reserves of fuel and food, and huge and clanging hospitals for the healing of any wounds which steel can suffer. It is the one sure sanctuary in the whole of the vast Pacific both for ships and men.

JOHN W. VANDERCOOK, *Vogue*, January 1, 1941.

Women

Whenever serious intellectuals—psychologists, sociologists, practicing physicians, Nobel Prize novelists—take time off from their normal pursuits to scrutinize and appraise the Modern American Woman they turn in unanimously dreary reports. They find her uninformed, intellectually lazy, lacking in ambition, and disgustingly docile in the presence of dominating males.

GRACE ADAMS, *Harper's*, March, 1939.

Old-fashioned ways which no longer apply to changed conditions are a snare in which the feet of women have always become readily entangled.

JANE ADDAMS, "Utilization of Women in City
Government," *Newer Ideals of Peace*, 1907.

When a woman ceases to alter the fashion of her hair, you guess that she has passed the crisis of her experience.

MARY AUSTIN, *The Land of Little Rain*, 1903.

Let me state here and now that the black woman in America can justly be described as a "slave of a slave."

FRANCES M. BEAL, "Double Jeopardy: To Be Black and
Female," in Robin Morgan, ed., *Sisterhood Is Powerful*,
1970.

If we are not to have a chance to fulfill our one potentiality—the power of loving—why were we not born men? At least we could have had an occupation then.

RUTH BENEDICT, in Margaret Mead, *An Anthropologist at
Work*, 1951.

Women in love are less ashamed than men. They have less to be ashamed of.

AMBROSE BIERCE, *The Devil's Dictionary*, 1906.

A career woman who has survived the hurdle of marriage and maternity encounters a new obstacle: the hostility of men.

CAROLINE BIRD, *Born Female*, 1968.

Femininity appears to be one of those pivotal qualities that are so important no one can define it.

CAROLINE BIRD, *Born Female*, 1968.

The things we believe in and want done will not be done until women are in elective office.

CATHERINE DRINKER BOWEN, *National Business Week*,
September, 1974.

Effeminacy is not a feminine possession any more than a masculine one. Men or women become effeminate when privilege and lack of responsibility have made them weak. The true female creature, unspoiled, is tough, persistent, and strong.

PEARL S. BUCK, speech, U.S. House of Representatives,
January 16, 1941.

Few American women, it seemed to me, simply rejoice in being what they are, and because they cannot rejoice they tend to be fretful and jealous of each other. Being self-doubtful, they achieve far less than they should. And the root of all this self-doubt, which has become a part of their very natures, is to be found in their uncertainty as human beings and this uncertainty springs from their unsatisfactory relationship to men.

PEARL S. BUCK, speech, U.S. House of Representatives,
January 16, 1941.

Women are bound by a traditionalism which they themselves maintain. Nothing else binds them except the tradition that their place is in the home, or at most only a little beyond the home in the small affairs of their own community.

PEARL S. BUCK, speech, U.S. House of Representatives,
January 16, 1941.

[Women] must be forced to realize that it is not enough to create, as blindly as beasts do, simply more life. The environment of their children today is not primarily the home. It is far more truly the world. And with the world women have had very little to do. If they refuse to come

We are here to move history forward.

We are women from every State and Territory in the Nation.

We are women of different ages, beliefs and lifestyles.

We are women of many economic, social, political, racial, ethnic, cultural, educational and religious backgrounds.

We are married, single, widowed and divorced.

We are mothers and daughters.

We are sisters.

We speak in varied accents and languages but we share the common language and experience of American women who throughout our Nation's life have been denied the opportunities, rights, privileges and responsibilities accorded to men.

For the first time in the more than 200 years of our democracy, we are gathered in a National Women's Conference, charged under Federal law to assess the status of women in our country, to measure the progress we have made, to identify the barriers that prevent us from participating fully and equally in all aspects of national life, and to make recommendations to the President and to the Congress for means by which such barriers can be removed.

We recognize the positive changes that have occurred in the lives of women since the founding of our nation. In more than a century of struggle from Seneca Falls 1848 to Houston 1977, we have progressed from being non-persons and slaves whose work and achievements were unrecognized, whose needs were ignored, and whose rights were suppressed to being citizens with freedoms and aspirations of which our ancestors could only dream.

We can vote and own property. We work in the home, in our communities and in every occupation. We are 40 percent of the labor force. We are in the arts, sciences, professions and politics. We raise children, govern States, head businesses and institutions, climb mountains, explore the ocean depths and reach toward the moon.

Our lives no longer end with the childbearing years. Our life span has increased to more than 75 years. We have become a majority of the population, 51.3 percent, and by the 21st century, we shall be an even larger majority.

But despite some gains made in the past 200 years, our dream of equality is still withheld from us and millions of women still face a daily reality of discrimination, limited opportunities and economic hardship.

Man-made barriers, laws, social customs and prejudices continue to keep a majority of women in an inferior position without full control of our lives and bodies.

From infancy throughout life, in personal and public relations, in the family, in the

---

out of their seclusion, their safety, their irresponsibility toward the policies which compel us to chaos and war, then there is no hope for the human race.

PEARL S. BUCK, speech to the House of Representatives, January 16, 1941.

No lady is ever a gentleman.

JAMES BRANCH CABELL, *Something About Eve*, 1927.

The whole aim of the woman movement has been to destroy the idea that obedience is necessary to women; to train women to such self-respect that they would not grant obedience and to train men to such comprehension of equity they would not exact it.

CARRIE CHAPMAN CATT, speech, National American Woman Suffrage Association, February, 1902.

The world taught woman nothing skillful and then said her work was valueless. It permitted her no opinions and said she did not know how to think. It forbade her to speak in public, and said the sex had no orators. It denied her the schools, and said the sex had no genius. It robbed her of every vestige of responsibility, and then called her weak. It taught her that every pleasure must come as a favor from men, and

schools, in every occupation and profession, too often we find our individuality, our capabilities, our earning powers diminished by discriminatory practices and outmoded ideas of what a woman is, what a women can do, and what a woman must be.

Increasingly, we are victims of crimes of violence in a culture that degrades us as sex objects and promotes pornography for profit.

We are poorer than men. And those of us who are minority women—blacks, Hispanic Americans, Native Americans, and Asian Americans—must overcome the double burden of discrimination based on race and sex.

We lack effective political and economic power. We have only minor and insignificant roles in making, interpreting and enforcing our laws, in running our political parties, businesses, unions, schools and institutions, in directing the media, in governing our country, in deciding issues of war or peace.

We do not seek special privileges, but we demand as a human right a full voice and role for women in determining the destiny of our world, our nation, our families and our individual lives.

We seek these rights for all women, whether or not they choose as individuals to use them.

We are part of a worldwide movement of women who believe that only by bringing women into full partnership with men and respecting our rights as half the human race can we hope to achieve a world in which the whole human race—men, women and children—can live in peace and security.

Based on the views of women who have met in every State and Territory in the past year, the National Plan of Action is presented to the President and the Congress as our recommendations for implementing Public Law 94–167.

We are entitled to and expect serious attention to our proposals.

We demand immediate and continuing action on our National Plan by Federal, State, public, and private institutions so that by 1985, the end of the International Decade for Women proclaimed by the United Nations, everything possible under the law will have been done to provide American women with full equality.

The rest will be up to the hearts, minds and moral consciences of men and women and what they do to make our society truly democratic and open to all.

We pledge ourselves with all the strength of our dedication to this struggle "to form a more perfect Union."

"Declaration of American Women," National Women's Conference, Houston, Texas, 1977.

---

when to gain it she decked herself in paint and fine feathers, as she had been taught to do, it called her vain.

Carrie Chapman Catt, speech, National American Woman Suffrage Association, February, 1902.

No woman is justified in being supported in idleness by a man. The most womanly woman today is the woman who works.

Carrie Chapman Catt, 1923, in Lois and Alan Gordon, *American Chronicle*, 1987.

A lady is one who never shows her underwear unintentionally.

Lillian Day, *Kiss and Tell*, 1931.

Some women are like Pompeii; some are like Verdun; some are like Kokomo, Ind., on a Sunday afternoon.

Benjamin De Casseres, *Fantasia Impromptu: The Adventures of an Intellectual Faun*, 1937.

No woman has ever told the truth of her life. The autobiographies of most famous women are a series of accounts of the outward existence, of petty details and anecdotes which give no realization of their real life. For the great moments of joy or agony they remain strangely silent.

Isadora Duncan, *My Life*, 1927.

[Women] must pay for everything....They do get more glory than men for comparable feats. But, also, women get more notoriety when they crash.

AMELIA EARHART, 1929, in Lois and Alan Gordon, *American Chronicle*, 1987.

The woman who doesn't want to make a home is undermining our nation.

MRS. THOMAS A. EDISON, 1930, in Lois and Alan Gordon, *American Chronicle*, 1987.

Direct thought is not an attribute of femininity. In this woman is now centuries...behind man.

THOMAS A. EDISON, "The Woman of the Future," *Good Housekeeping*, October 12, 1912.

The original idea of feminism as I first encountered it, in about 1969, was twofold: that nothing short of equality will do *and* that in a society marred by injustice and cruelty, equality will never be good enough. That idea does not lend itself to condensation into three letters of the alphabet or two-digit button inscriptions, but it is still the best idea, I believe, that women have ever had.

BARBARA EHRENREICH, "Why We Lost the ERA," *The Worst Years of Our Lives*, 1986.

The women's liberation movement at this point in history makes the American Communist Party of the 1930s look like a monolith.

NORA EPHRON, "On Never Having Been a Prom Queen," August, 1972, *Crazy Salad: Some Things about Women*, 1975.

Once I tried to explain to a fellow feminist why I liked wearing makeup: she replied by explaining why she does not. Neither of us understood a word the other said.

NORA EPHRON, "On Never Having Been a Prom Queen," August, 1972, *Crazy Salad: Some Things about Women*, 1975.

It would be practically impossible to write an accurate novel about the quality of life for single women in New York without writing a B novel, for the simple reason that life for single women in New York *is* a B novel.

NORA EPHRON, "The Girls in the Office," September, 1972, *Crazy Salad: Some Things about Women*, 1975.

[A woman must] accept herself fully as a woman [and] know...she is dependent on a man. There is no fantasy in her mind about being an independent woman, a contradiction in terms.

MARYNIA FARNHAM AND FERDINAND LUNDBERG, *Modern Woman*, 1947.

Even at this late date in our sociological evolution, women are still on trial in what remains essentially a man's world.

DIANNE FEINSTEIN, *Business Today*, Spring, 1987.

A woman can look both moral and exciting—if she also looks as if it was quite a struggle.

EDNA FERBER, *Reader's Digest*, December, 1954.

One of the most important problems to be solved in the new century is this: shall women be flowers or vegetables, ornamental or useful?

HENRY T. FINCK, *Independent*, April 11, 1901.

Let us by all means throw open to them [women] all employments in which their health, their purity, and their womanliness do not suffer; but let this be regarded, not as a special privilege and an indication of social progress, but as a necessary evil to be cured in as many cases as possible by marriage or some other way of bringing the workers back to their deserted homes.

HENRY T. FINCK, *Independent*, April 11, 1901.

Women, despite the fact that nine out of ten of them go through life with a death-bed air either of snatching-the-last-moment or with martyr-resignation, do not die tomorrow—or the next day. They have to live on to any one of the many bitter ends.

ZELDA FITZGERALD, "Eulogy on the Flapper," *Metropolitan*, June, 1922.

American women no longer know who they are.

BETTY FRIEDAN, *The Feminine Mystique*, 1963.

The original necessity for the ceaseless presence of the woman to maintain that altar fire—and it was an altar fire in very truth at one period—has passed with the means of prompt ignition; the matchbox has freed the housewife from that incessant service, but the feeling that women should stay at home is with us yet.

CHARLOTTE PERKINS GILMAN, "Two Callings," *The Home*, 1910.

Women like to sit down with trouble as if it were knitting.

ELLEN GLASGOW, *The Sheltered Life*, 1932.

True emancipation begins neither at the polls nor in courts. It begins in woman's soul.

EMMA GOLDMAN, "The Tragedy of Women's Emancipation," *Anarchism and Other Essays*, 1911.

The soldier's business is to take life. For that he is paid by the State, eulogized by political charlatans and upheld by public hysteria. But woman's function is to give life, yet neither the State nor politicians nor public opinion have ever made the slightest provision in return for the life woman has given.

EMMA GOLDMAN, "The Social Aspects of Birth Control," *Mother Earth*, April, 1916.

Somehow feminists who want to transform our culture, not just adapt to it, have to convince young women that embracing feminism does not mean embracing victimhood, that you can be for others and still be for yourself, that you can "make it" in bed and in the marketplace, that women can indeed be visible without subjugating their souls behind traditional female—or male—masks.

SUZANNE GORDON, *Boston Globe*, December 26, 1990.

What, after all, is feminism? What makes a truly liberated woman? Is feminism—as a social movement—no more than a collection of individual women who want to be equal to men in a man's world? Is the real liberated woman one who does little more than say yes to careerism, safe sex and "making it" in America's overhyped, sensationalistic, commercial culture? Or is feminism about attaining equality *and* making a difference? Is it about helping the majority of women improve their lives by transforming that culture?

SUZANNE GORDON, *Boston Globe*, December 26, 1990.

Women [in politics] are going to have to be purer than Ceasar's wife.

BETSY GOTBAUM, *Time*, September 6, 1984.

The moment we accept the theory that women must enter wage-earning occupations only when compelled to do so by poverty, that moment we degrade labor and lower the status of all women who are engaged in it.

IDA HUSTED HARPER, response to article by Henry T. Finck, *Independent*, May 16, 1901.

Nothing could be more demoralizing than the injunction to women to "regard their employment as a necessary evil to be cured in as many cases as possible by marriage." It is a sorry compliment to a man to be taken like a dose of medicine.

IDA HUSTED HARPER, response to article by Henry T. Finck, *Independent*, May 16, 1901.

It may be that in selecting a wife "men want a girl who has not rubbed off the peach bloom of innocence by exposure to a rough world," but it is not permitted all girls to stay at home and take care of their peach bloom.

IDA HUSTED HARPER, response to article by Henry T. Finck, *Independent*, May 16, 1901.

I refuse to believe that trading recipes is silly. Tuna-fish casserole is at least as real as corporate stock.

BARBARA GRIZZUTI HARRISON, "Secrets Women Tell Each Other," *McCall's*, August, 1975.

Plain women know more about men than beautiful ones do.

KATHARINE HEPBURN, in Charles Higham, *Kate*, 1975.

You can be up to your boobies in white satin, with gardenias in your hair and no sugar cane for miles, but you can still be working on a plantation.

BILLIE HOLIDAY, with William Dufty, *Lady Sings the Blues*, 1956.

Even the proudest of women are willing to accept orders when the time is ripe; and I am fully convinced that to be domineered over by the right man is a thing all good women warmly desire.

ELBERT HUBBARD, *The Roycroft Dictionary and Book of Epigrams*, 1923.

The blaming of woman for all the ills of the world is the crowning blunder of certain creeds.

ELBERT HUBBARD, *The Roycroft Dictionary and Book of Epigrams*, 1923.

When a woman works, she gets a woman's wage; but when she sins she gets a man's pay—and then some.

ELBERT HUBBARD, *The Roycroft Dictionary and Book of Epigrams*, 1923.

To know the right woman is a liberal education.

ELBERT HUBBARD, *The Roycroft Dictionary and Book of Epigrams*, 1923.

Young women with ambitions should be very crafty and cautious, lest mayhap they be caught in the soft, silken mesh of a happy marriage, and go down to oblivion, dead to the world.

ELBERT HUBBARD, *The Roycroft Dictionary and Book of Epigrams*, 1923.

A woman's duty: To look the whole world in the face with a go-to-hell look in the eyes; to have an ideal; to speak and act in defiance of convention.

INTERNATIONAL LADIES' GARMENT WORKERS' UNION, *The Woman Rebel*, March, 1914.

To conclude that women are unfitted to the task of our historic society seems to me the equivalent of closing male eyes to female facts.

LYNDON B. JOHNSON, swearing-in ceremony of women appointees, White House, April 13, 1964.

[W]omen's liberation is not a debatable issue.

JILL JOHNSTON, *Lesbian Nation*, 1973.

Women are natural guerrillas. Scheming, we nestle into the enemy's bed, avoiding open warfare, watching the options, playing the odds.

SALLY KEMPTON, "Cutting Loose," *Esquire*, July, 1970.

If people believed that women crack under pressure when men don't, they'd believe that women as a group are not as capable or as gutsy as men. I just had to win.

BILLIE JEAN KING, on tennis match with Bobby Riggs, *American Way*, June, 1974.

In those days, it didn't matter: you could be a Wimbledon champion, Phi Beta Kappa, Miss America, Nobel Peace Prize winner, but if they asked you about marriage and you didn't at least have a hot prospect ready to get down on one knee, you knew you were considered to be no more than half a woman.

BILLIE JEAN KING, *Billie Jean*, 1982.

The outer limitations to woman's progress are caused by the fact we are living in a man's culture.

OLGA KNOPF, *Women on Their Own*, 1935.

For the first time in the world's history it is possible for a nation's women in general to have or to be able to look forward to having homes and the means of furnishing them in keeping with their instinctive longings. The women of America are to be congratulated, not only in the opportunity but because of the manner in which they are responding to it. When the record is finally written this may stand as their greatest contribution.

EDITORIAL, *Ladies' Home Journal*, February, 1928.

Black women...are trained from childhood to become workers, and expect to be financially self-supporting for most of their lives. They know they will have to work, whether they are married or single; work to them, unlike to white women, is not a liberating goal, but rather an imposed lifelong necessity.

GERDA LERNER, *Black Women in White America*, 1972.

Of all the accomplishments of the American woman, the one she brings off with the most spectacular success is having babies.

Life, 1956.

The people I'm furious with are the women's liberationists. They keep getting up on soapboxes and proclaiming women are brighter than men.

That's true, but it should be kept quiet or it ruins the whole racket.

ANITA LOOS, *New York Times*, February 10, 1974.

NORA: When a man can't explain a woman's actions, the first thing he thinks about is the condition of her uterus.

CLARE BOOTHE LUCE, *Slam the Door Softly*, 1970.

Male supremacy has kept woman down. It has not knocked her out.

CLARE BOOTHE LUCE, *Saturday Review/World*, September 15, 1974.

I may be dressing like a traditional bimbo, whatever, but I'm in charge....And isn't that what feminism is all about; you know, equality for men and women? And aren't I in charge of my life, doing the things I want to do?

MADONNA, in an article by Suzanne Gordon, "Madonna the Feminist," *Boston Globe*, December 26, 1990.

Nobody objects to a woman being a good writer or sculptor or geneticist as long as she manages also to be a good wife, mother, good-looking, good-tempered, well-dressed, well-groomed, unaggressive.

MARYA MANNES, "New Bites by a Girl Gadfly," *Life*, June, 1964.

Ah, wonderful women! Just give me a comfortable couch, a dog, a good book, and a woman. Then if you can get the dog to go somewhere and read the book, I might have a little fun!

GROUCHO MARX, comedy routine performed for men and women serving in World War II, ca. 1943.

It's this no-nonsense side of women that is pleasant to deal with. They are the real sportsmen. They don't have to be constantly building up frail egos by large public performances like over-tipping the hat-check girl, speaking fluent French to the Hungarian waiter, and sending back the wine to be recooled.

PHYLLIS MCGINLEY, "Some of My Best Friends...," *The Province of the Heart*, 1959.

Women hate revolutions and revolutionists. They like men who are docile, and well-regarded at the bank, and never late at meals.

H.L. MENCKEN, *Prejudices*, 1924.

When women kiss it always reminds one of prize-fighters shaking hands.

H.L. MENCKEN, "Sententiae," *The Vintage Mencken*, 1955.

Many women do not recognize themselves as discriminated against; no better proof could be found of the totality of their conditioning.

KATE MILLETT, *Sexual Politics*, 1969.

We've been begging and pleading for equal rights and equal pay when in fact the position of women is so oppressive, one of the things we need to be most concerned about is our physical safety.

KATE MILLETT, *Miami Herald*, November 12, 1975.

I'm tired of everlasting being unnatural and never doing anything I want to do. I'm tired of acting like I don't eat more than a bird, and walking when I want to run and saying I feel faint after a waltz, when I could dance for two days and never get tired. I'm tired of saying, 'How wonderful you are!' to fool men who haven't got one-half the sense I've got and I'm tired of pretending I don't know anything, so men can tell me things and feel important while they're doing it....

MARGARET MITCHELL, *Gone With the Wind*, 1936.

A total woman caters to her man's special quirks, whether it be in salads, sex, or sports.

MARABEL MORGAN, *The Total Woman*, 1975.

Goodbye, goodbye forever, counterfeit Left, counterfeit Left, male-dominated, cracked-glass-mirror reflection of the Amerikan nightmare. Women are the real left.

ROBIN MORGAN, ca. 1960, *Sixties Papers*, 1985.

What I consider my weaknesses are feminine traits: incapacity to destroy, ineffectualness in battle.

ANAÏS NIN, diary entry, January, 1943, *The Diary of Anaïs Nin*, 1969.

Their [women's] minds, their emotions, their creative impulses have been more savagely distorted through the years than the feet of Chinese women were distorted by custom-decreed bandages.

ALICE BEAL PARSONS, *Woman's Dilemma*, 1926.

Until changing economic conditions made the thing actually happen, struggling early society would hardly have guessed that woman's road to gentility would lie through doing nothing at all.

EMILY JAMES PUTNAM, *The Lady: Studies of Certain Significant Phases of Her History*, 1910.

Women's chains have been forged by men, not by anatomy.

ESTELLE R. RAMEY, in Francine Klagsbrun, ed., *The First Ms. Reader*, 1972.

The individual woman is required...a thousand times a day to choose either to accept her appointed role and thereby rescue her good disposition out of the wreckage of her self-respect, or else follow an independent line of behavior and rescue her self-respect out of the wreckage of her good disposition.

JEANNETTE RANKIN, in Hannah Josephson, *Jeannette Rankin: First Lady in Congress*, 1974.

The pitfall of the feminist is the belief that the interests of men and women can ever be severed; that what brings suffering to the one can leave the other unscathed.

AGNES REPPLIER, *Points of Friction*, 1920.

As long as birth, metaphorically or literally, remains an experience of passively handing over our minds and our bodies to male authority and technology, other kinds of social change can only minimally change our relationship to ourselves, to power, and to the world outside our body.

ADRIENNE RICH, *Of Woman Born*, 1976.

The worser effect on both man and woman is found where woman's acceptance of insult, having grown mechanical, is eventually unconscious.

ELIZABETH ROBINS, *Ancilla's Share*, 1924.

It occurred to me when I was thirteen and wearing white gloves and Mary Janes and going to dancing school, that no one should have to dance backward all their lives.

JILL RUCKELSHAUS, speech, 1973.

The modern woman is the curse of the universe. A disaster, that's what. She thinks that before her arrival on the scene no woman ever did anything worthwhile before, no woman was ever liberated until her time, no woman really ever amounted to anything.

ADELA ROGERS ST. JOHN, in article by Merg Guswiler, "Some Are Born Great," *Los Angeles Herald-Examiner*, October 13, 1974.

The problem of birth control has arisen directly from the effort of the feminine spirit to free itself from bondage.

MARGARET SANGER, *Woman and the New Race*, 1920.

Women are too much inclined to follow in the footsteps of men, to try to think as men think, to try to solve the general problems of life as men solve them....The woman is not needed to do man's work. She is not needed to think man's thoughts....Her mission is not to enhance the masculine spirit, but to express the feminine;

hers is not to preserve a man-made world, but to create a human world by the infusion of the feminine element into all of its activities.

MARGARET SANGER, *Woman and the New Race*, 1920.

No woman can call herself free who does not own and control her body. No woman can call herself free until she can choose consciously whether she will or will not be a mother.

MARGARET SANGER, *Woman and the New Race*, 1920.

I think it's [the women's movement] an antifamily movement that is trying to make perversion acceptable as an alternate life-style.

PHYLLIS SCHLAFLY, *New York Times*, December 15, 1975.

I have a brain and a uterus, and I use both.

PAT SCHROEDER, response to question on being both mother and congresswoman, *New York Times Magazine*, 1972.

Who ever walked behind anyone to freedom? If we can't go hand in hand, I don't want to go.

HAZEL SCOTT, in article by Margo Jefferson, "Great (Hazel) Scott," *Ms.*, November, 1974.

Woman's virtue is man's greatest invention.

CORNELIA OTIS SKINNER, *Paris '90*, 1952.

Some leaders are born women.

SLOGAN, United Nations International Women's Day conference, March, 1983.

Our black brothers are our sisters.

SLOGAN, ca. 1960.

IF YOU THINK EQUALITY IS THE GOAL...YOUR STANDARDS ARE TOO LOW.

SLOGAN, ca. 1970.

Give the young women who follow you a heritage of peace instead of the world of suspicion, aggression, treason, character assassination and moral delinquency that has been thrust upon you by the older generation that has preceded you.

MARGARET CHASE SMITH, speech, Westbrook Junior College, Portland, Maine, June 7, 1953.

The failure of women to produce genius of the first rank in most of the supreme forms of human effort has been used to block the way of all women of talent and ambition for intellectual achievement in a manner that would be amusingly absurd were it not so monstrously unjust and socially harmful.

ANNA GARLIN SPENCER, *Woman's Share in Social Culture*, 1912.

No book has yet been written in praise of a woman who let her husband and children starve or suffer while she invented even the most useful things, or wrote books, or expressed herself in art, or evolved philosophic systems.

ANNA GARLIN SPENCER, *Woman's Share in Social Culture*, 1912.

Biologically and temperamentally...women were made to be concerned first and foremost with child care, husband care and home care.

BENJAMIN SPOCK, in article by Barbara S. Deckard, "Woman's Movement: Political, Socioeconomic and Psychological," *Issues*, 1979.

A liberated woman is one who has sex before marriage and a job after.

GLORIA STEINEM, *Newsweek*, March 28, 1960.

We [women] are not more moral, we are only less corrupted by power.

GLORIA STEINEM, "A New Egalitarian Life Style," *New York Times*, August 26, 1971.

I have met brave women who are exploring the outer edge of human possibility, with no history to guide them, and with a courage to make themselves vulnerable that I find moving beyond the words to express it.

GLORIA STEINEM, *Ms.*, April, 1972.

Women may be the one group that grows more radical with age.

GLORIA STEINEM, *Outrageous Acts and Everyday Rebellions*, 1983.

Women whose identity depends more on their outsides than their insides are dangerous when they begin to age.

GLORIA STEINEM, *Outrageous Acts and Everyday Rebellions*, 1983.

Women aren't supposed to work. They're supposed to be married.

JOHNNIE TILLMON, "Welfare Is a Woman's Issue," in Francine Klagsbrun, ed., *The First Ms. Reader*, 1972.

I'm the kind of woman that likes to enjoy herselves in peace.

ALICE WALKER, *The Temple of My Familiar*, 1989.

WITCH lives and laughs in every woman. She is the free part of each of us, beneath the shy smiles, the acquiescence to absurd male determination, the make-up or fresh-suffocating clothes our sick society demands. There is no "joining" WITCH. If you are a woman and dare to look within yourself, you are a WITCH. You make your own rules.

WOMEN'S INTERNATIONAL TERRORIST CONSPIRACY FROM HELL (WITCH), leaflet, ca. 1968, in Howard Zinn, *The Twentieth Century*, 1980.

Work

See also **American Society**; **Business**—Bosses and Workers; **Dreams and Ideals**—Excellence, Leisure, Risk, Security; **Economics**—Depression and Inflation; **Government and Politics**—Domestic Policy, Parties and Elections, Political Philosophies; **The Human Condition**—Ambition, Competitiveness, Creativity, Duty, Fame, Ingenuity, Success; **Life's Lessons**; **Popular Culture**; **Social Issues**—Civil Rights, Discrimination and Racism, Labor; **Sports**

Apparently we have not yet recovered manual labor from the deep distrust which centuries of slavery and the feudal system have cast upon it. To get away from menial work, to do obviously little with one's hands, is still the desirable status.

JANE ADDAMS, "Educational Methods," *Democracy and Social Ethics*, 1902.

It is easy to believe that life is long and one's gifts are vast—easy at the beginning, that is. But the limits of life grow more evident; it becomes clear that great work can be done rarely, if at all.

ALFRED ADLER, quoted in *The New Yorker*, February 19, 1972.

The price one pays for pursuing any profession, or calling, is an intimate knowledge of its ugly side.

JAMES BALDWIN, *Nobody Knows My Name: The Black Boy Looks at the White Boy*, 1961.

We can say without exaggeration that the present national ambition of the United States is unemployment. People live for quitting time, for weekends, for vacations, and for retirement....

WENDELL BERRY, 1986, "A Defense of the Family Farm," *Home Economics*, 1987.

All there is to be said for work as opposed to dancing is that it is so much easier.

HEYWOOD BROUN, *Pieces of Hate*, 1922.

Attempt the impossible in order to improve your work.

BETTE DAVIS, *Mother Goddamn*, 1974.

People don't choose their careers; they are engulfed by them.

JOHN DOS PASSOS, *New York Times*, October 25, 1959.

There is no substitute for hard work.

THOMAS A. EDISON, *Golden Book*, April, 1931.

It is not work that men object to, but the element of drudgery. We must drive out drudgery wherever we find it. We shall never be wholly civilized until we remove the treadmill from the daily job.

HENRY FORD, *My Life and Work*, 1923.

The labor of a human being is not a commodity or article of commerce. You can't weigh the soul of a man with a bar of pig-iron.

SAMUEL GOMPERS, *Seventy Years of Life and Labor*, 1925.

To love what you do and feel that it matters—how could anything be more fun?

KATHARINE GRAHAM, in article by Jane Howard, *Ms.*, October, 1974.

But it is not hard work which is dreary; it is superficial work. That is always boring in the long run, and it has always seemed strange to me that in our endless discussions about education so little stress is ever laid on the pleasure of becoming an educated person, the enormous interest it adds to life. To be able to be caught up into the world of thought—that is to be educated.

EDITH HAMILTON, *Bryn Mawr School Bulletin*, 1959.

The only jobs for which no man is qualified are human incubator and wet nurse. Likewise, the only job for which no woman is or can be qualified is sperm donor.

WILMA SCOTT HEIDE, *NOW Official Biography*, 1971.

Busy as a one-armed man with the nettle-rash pasting on wallpaper.

O. HENRY, "The Ethics of Pig," *The Gentle Grafter*, 1908.

Work is hard. Distractions are plentiful. And time is short.

ADAM HOCHSCHILD, *New York Times*, February 5, 1985.

The riders in a race do not stop short when they reach the goal. There is a little finishing canter before coming to a standstill. There is time to hear the kind voice of friends and to say to one-self: "The work is done."

Oliver Wendell Holmes, Jr., radio broadcast celebrating his 90th birthday, March 8, 1931.

I used to think that the main-spring was broken by 80, although my father kept on writing. I hope I was wrong for I am keeping on in the same way. I like it and want to produce as long as I can.

Oliver Wendell Holmes, Jr., letter to Frederick Pollock, ca. 1925, in Catherine Drinker Bowen, *Yankee from Olympus*, 1944.

I don't in a day at my desk ever once think about what my sex is. I'm thinking about my job.

Karen N. Horn, *Working Woman*, March, 1988.

It is man who sanctifies a place, and it is work that sanctifies a man.

Elbert Hubbard, *The Roycroft Dictionary and Book of Epigrams*, 1923.

Any man who has a job has a chance.

Elbert Hubbard, *The Roycroft Dictionary and Book of Epigrams*, 1923.

A man's vocation is no measure for the inner feelings nor a guarantee of his earnest desire to live right and attain the highest standards.

Jack Johnson, *Jack Johnson in the Ring and Out*, 1927.

Moccasins have no bootstraps.

Kiowa Apache, on different cultural attitudes toward work, in Stan Steiner, *The New Indians*, 1968.

I go on working for the same reason that a hen goes on laying eggs.

H.L. Mencken, in Will Durant, *On the Meaning of Life*, 1932.

Stepping up to that first morning embrace of work is intimidating.

Diane Michener, "Catching the Sun," *Working It Out*, 1977.

America is no place for an artist: to be an artist is to be a moral leper, an economic misfit, a social liability. A corn-fed hog enjoys a better life than a creative writer, painter, or musician. To be a rabbit is better still.

Henry Miller, *The Air-Conditioned Nightmare*, 1945.

When God foreclosed on Eden, he condemned Adam and Eve to go to work. Work has never recovered from that humiliation.

Lance Morrow, "What Is the Point of Working?" *Fishing in the Tiber*, 1988.

The parallel between women and Negros is the deepest truth of American life, for together they form the unpaid or underpaid labor on which America runs.

Gunnar Myrdal, *An American Dilemma*, 1944.

Farmer, laborer, clerk: That's a brief history of the United States.

John Naisbitt, *Megatrends*, 1984.

I don't pity any man who does hard work worth doing. I admire him. I pity the creature who does not work, at whichever end of the social scale he may regard himself as being.

Theodore Roosevelt, speech, Chattanooga, Tennessee, September 8, 1902.

How interesting that splendid minds cannot see the class war, how they chant the inabilities of the worker—how he needs a boss—a master or all would be chaos. How hard to realize that if we like a job—like the work or the work was at all interesting everyone would like to do things—but to expect a human man or woman to like being molded day by day into a machine is laughable.

Margaret Sanger, journal entry, November 6, 1914.

The definition of woman's work is shitwork.

Gloria Steinem, in article by John Brady, "Freelancer with No Time to Write," *Writer's Digest*, February, 1974.

My God, who *wouldn't* want a wife?

Judy Syfers, "I Want a Wife," in Francine Klagsbrun, ed., *The First Ms. Reader*, 1972.

Wages are the measure of dignity that society puts on a job.

Johnnie Tillmon, "Welfare Is a Women's Issue," in Francine Klagsbrun, ed., *The First Ms. Reader*, 1972.

Never allow your sense of self to become associated with your sense of job. If your job vanishes, your self doesn't.

Gordon Van Sauter, *Working Woman*, February, 1988.

Nothing ever comes to one, that is worth having, except as a result of hard work.

Booker T. Washington, *Up from Slavery*, 1901.

No race can prosper till it learns that there is as much dignity in tilling the field as in writing a poem.

Booker T. Washington, *Up from Slavery*, 1901.

ARCHITECTS

Architect, n. One who drafts a plan of your house, and plans a draft of your money.
AMBROSE BIERCE, *The Devil's Dictionary*, 1906.

Architects are pretty much high-class whores. We can turn down projects the way they can turn down some clients, but we've both got to say yes to someone if we want to stay in business.
PHILIP JOHNSON, *Esquire*, December, 1980.

It was hell for women architects then. They didn't want us in school or in the profession. …One thing I've never understood about this prejudice is that it's so strange in view of the fact that the drive to build has always been in women.
GERTRUDE LEMP KERBIS, in Betty Medsger, *Women at Work*, 1975.

I am an eyewitness to the ways in which people relate to themselves and to each other, and my work is a way of scooping and ladling that experience.
RICHARD NEUTRA, *Christian Science Monitor*, July 1, 1977.

The great thing about being an architect is you can walk into your dreams.
HAROLD E. WAGONER, in Father Edward Chin's tribute to Wagoner's restoration of All Saints' Church, Philadelphia, Pennsylvania, *Episcopalian*, October, 1986.

The physician can bury his mistakes, but the architect can only advise his clients to plant vines.
FRANK LLOYD WRIGHT, *New York Times Magazine*, October 4, 1953.

ARTISTS

I have noted that, barring accidents, artists whose powers wear best and last longest are those who have trained themselves to work under adversity....Great artists treasure their time with a bitter and snarling miserliness.
CATHERINE DRINKER BOWEN, speech, "The Nature of the Artist," Scripps College, April 27, 1961.

Artistic growth is, more than it is anything else, a refining of the sense of truthfulness. The stupid believe that to be truthful is easy; only the artist, the great artist, knows how difficult it is.
WILLA CATHER, *The Song of the Lark*, 1915.

Every artist undresses his subject, whether human or still life. It is his business to find essences in surfaces, and what more attractive and challenging surface than the skin around a soul?
RICHARD CORLISS, on Andrew Wyeth's studies of Helga Testorf, *Time*, August 18, 1986.

I paint to rest from the phenomena of the external world—to pronounce and to make notations of its essences with which to verify the inner eye.
MORRIS GRAVES, *Christian Science Monitor*, February 19, 1964.

An artist's originality is balanced by a corresponding conservatism, a superstitiousness, about it; which might be boiled down to "What worked before will work again."
NANCY HALE, *Mary Cassatt: A Biography of the Great American Painter*, 1975.

New artists must break a hole in the subconscious and go fishing there.
ROBERT BEVERLY HALE, *Time*, April 11, 1960.

I don't mind being miserable as long as I'm painting well.
GRACE HARTIGAN, in article by Cindy Nemser, *Art Talk*, 1975.

My aim in painting has always been the most exact transcription possible of my most intimate impression of nature.
EDWARD HOPPER, *Life*, April 17, 1950.

Scratch an artist and you surprise a child.
JAMES GIBBONS HUNEKER, *The Man and His Music*, 1900.

It seems likely that many of the young who don't wait for others to call them artists, but simply announce that they are, don't have the patience to make art.
PAULINE KAEL, *Kiss Kiss Bang Bang*, 1968.

The life of the artist is, in relation to his work, stern and lonely. He has labored hard, often amid deprivation, to perfect his skill. He has turned aside from quick success in order to strip his vision of everything secondary or cheapening. His working life is marked by intensive application and intense discipline.
JOHN F. KENNEDY, 1963, introduction to book on National Cultural Center, Washington D.C., *New York Post*, January 7, 1964.

The truth is, as everyone knows, that the great artists of the world are never puritans, and seldom ever ordinarily respectable. No virtuous man—that is, virtuous in the YMCA sense—has ever painted a picture worth looking at, or written a symphony worth hearing, or a book worth reading, and it is highly improbable that the thing has ever been done by a virtuous woman.

H.L. MENCKEN, *Prejudices*, 1919.

I don't advise any one to take it [painting] up as a business proposition, unless they really have talent, and are crippled so as to deprive them of physical labor,

Then with help they might make a living,

But with taxes and income taxes there is little money in that kind of art for the ordinary artis [sic]

But I will say that I have did remarkable for one of my years, and experience,

As for publicity, that Im [sic] too old to care for now....

GRANDMA MOSES, "How I Paint and Why," *New York Times Magazine*, May 11, 1947.

If I didn't start painting, I would have raised chickens.

GRANDMA MOSES, *Grandma Moses, My Life's History*, 1947.

I've been sculpting for many years. It's almost like breathing for me.

LOUISE NEVELSON, in Louis Botto, "Work in Progress Louise Nevelson," *Intellectual Digest*, April, 1972.

If I have sorrow or enjoyment, my works go along with me. They are not just forms as such. Somehow they have a life of their own and they reflect me.

LOUISE NEVELSON, in Louis Botto, "Work in Progress Louise Nevelson," *Intellectual Digest*, April, 1972.

I found myself saying to myself—I can't live where I want to—I can't go where I want to—I can't do what I want to. I can't even say what I want to. I decided I was a very stupid fool not to at least paint as I wanted to and say what I wanted to when I painted, as that seemed to be the only thing I could do that didn't concern anybody but myself.

GEORGIA O'KEEFFE, exhibition catalog, January, 1923, *Georgia O'Keeffe*, 1976.

It takes only a little analysis to see the pattern of neglect, exclusion, condescension, and downright exploitation in the treatment of women artists of color in this country. The double bind

of racism and sexism cramps creativity; training is almost impossible to obtain.

KAREN PETERSON AND J.J. WILSON, *Women Artists*, 1976.

I cannot convince myself that a painting is good unless it is popular. If the public dislikes one of my *Post* covers, I can't help disliking it myself.

NORMAN ROCKWELL, quoted in article by Arthur C. Danto, "Freckles for the Ages," *New York Times*, September 28, 1986.

An artist is a dreamer consenting to dream of the actual world.

GEORGE SANTAYANA, *The Life of Reason*, 1905–1906.

My sculpture grew from painting. My analogy and reference is with color. Flash reference and afterimage vision is historied in painting. I chew the fat with painters. My student days, WPA days, Romany Marie and McSorley days were with painters—Graham, Davis, Resnikoff, De Kooning, Xceron, Edgar Levy, Gorky, Stella, etc. In these early days it was Cubist talk. Theirs I suppose was the Cubist canvas, and my reference image was the Cubist construction. The lines then had not been drawn by the pedants—in Cubist talk, Mondrian and Kandinsky were included.

DAVID SMITH, "Notes on My Work," *Arts*, February, 1960.

I believe in perception as being the highest order of recognition. My faith in it comes as close to an ideal as I have. When I work, there is no consciousness of ideals—but intuition and impulse.

DAVID SMITH, "Notes on My Work," *Arts*, February, 1960.

I'd asked around 10 or 15 people for suggestions....Finally one lady friend asked the right question, "Well, what do you love most?" That's how I started painting money.

ANDY WARHOL, "Andy Warhol Inc., Portrait of the Artist as a Middle-Aged Businessman," *Manhattan Inc.*, October, 1984.

I'm like a prostitute...never off duty.

ANDREW WYETH, *Time*, August 18, 1986.

I dream a lot. I do more painting when I'm not painting. It's in the subconscious.

ANDREW WYETH, *Time*, August 18, 1986.

I don't deal in controversy. I deal in fun. It's separate from reality.

DEAN YOUNG, on continuing comic strip *Blondie* begun by Chic Young, *Newsweek*, October 1, 1984.

ATHLETES

Fighters were not supposed to be human or intelligent. Just brutes that exist to entertain and to satisfy the crowd's thirst for blood.

MUHAMMAD ALI, *The Greatest*, 1975.

It's just a job. Grass grows, birds fly, waves pound the sand. I beat people up.

MUHAMMAD ALI, *New York Times*, April 6, 1977.

There's no need for a white athlete to have another dimension, unless you're a Steve Garvey or a Bill Bradley, a Goose Gossage or a Conrad Dobler—all the fan cares about is what he does on the field. But there's a need by fans for the black athlete to be multi-dimensional because he's the most-watched personage in America. I'll bet that seven out of 10 black faces you see on television are athletes. The black athlete carries the image of the black community. He carries the cross, in a way, until blacks make inroads in other dimensions.

ARTHUR ASHE, *New York Times*, October 26, 1982.

There has never been a great athlete who died not knowing what pain is.

BILL BRADLEY, in John McPhee, *A Sense of Where You Are*, 1965.

By the end of the season, I feel like a used car.

BOB BRENLY, *American Way*, May 14, 1985.

I have found most baseball players to be afflicted with tobacco-chewing minds.

HOWARD COSELL, *Like It Is*, 1974.

Boxers have those quick, automatic, reflexive insights that enable them to decipher an opponent's vulnerabilities and to strike at them with immediacy. They can amaze you with their perception, and, even though they're in a brutal sport, with their sensitivity and concern for others.

HOWARD COSELL, *Like It Is*, 1974.

In me younger days 'twas not considhered rayspictable f'r to be an athlete. An athlete was always a man that was not sthrong enough f'r wurruk. Fractions dhruv him fr'm school an' th' vagrancy laws dhruv him to baseball.

FINLEY PETER DUNNE, *Mr. Dooley's Opinions*, 1901.

Ballplayers are a superstitious breed, nobody more than I, and while you are winning you'd murder anybody who tried to change your sweatshirt, let alone your uniform.

LEO DUROCHER, *Nice Guys Finish Last*, 1975.

The mound is a mountain. You are at the bottom trying to hit uphill. The pitcher is King Kong. The bat should have telephone wires on it, the way it feels. Somebody must have put grease in the resin. Even the spikes are complaining through your shoes; they can't find the right spot in the batter's box.

JOE GARAGIOLA, *Baseball Is a Funny Game*, 1960.

Don't read Landry's playbook all the way through. Everybody dies at the end.

PETE GENT, *Newsweek*, January 22, 1979.

Glamorous, huh? Singers can wear gowns to hide the bulges, and wigs and make-up. But our bodies are seen the way they really are. We come off the court sweating, hair dripping. Our life is showering and changing. I change clothes five times a day and wash my hair every day. It's a tough role to play, so you don't see many femmes fatales in tennis dresses.

BILLIE JEAN KING, *Sports Illustrated*, June 26, 1972.

It's really impossible for athletes to grow up. As long as you're playing, no one will let you. On the one hand, you're a child, still playing a game. And everybody around you acts like a kid, too. But on the other hand, you're a superhuman hero that everyone dreams of being. No wonder we have such a hard time understanding who we are.

BILLIE JEAN KING, *Billie Jean*, 1982.

You've got to win in sports—that's talent—but you've also got to learn to remind everybody how you did win, and how often. That comes with experience.

BILLIE JEAN KING, *Billie Jean*, 1982.

The point is—and this is necessary to understand the difference between male and female athletes—that in the arena, men take for granted the fact that they are males and concentrate on being athletes. Women never forget that they are females.

DICK LACEY, *New York Times*, December 18, 1977.

What helped me develop my quickness was fear. I think the rougher the opponent, the quicker I am.

SUGAR RAY LEONARD, *New York Times*, June 17, 1980.

In my book a tennis player is the complete athlete. He has to have the speed of a sprinter, the endurance of a marathon runner, the agility of a boxer or fencer and the gray matter of a good football quarterback. Baseball, football, basketball players are good athletes, but they don't need all these attributes to perform well.

BOBBY RIGGS, *Court Hustler*, 1973.

BUSINESSPEOPLE

Secretaries may be specially prized, and the top secretaries exceptionally well paid, because they give men who can afford to pay well the subservient, watchful and admiring attention that Victorian wives used to give their husbands.

CAROLINE BIRD, *Born Female*, 1968.

To be a manager, you have to start at the bottom, no exceptions.

HENRY BLOCK, *Inc.*, December, 1987.

Few companies would have reached the going-concern stage without the inflated confidence of their founders. Entrepreneurs tend to be like eighteen-year-old marines who believe the bullet will go right through them without hurt or harm.

DEAVER BROWN, *The Entrepreneur's Guide*, 1980.

Managing a ball club is the most vulnerable job in the world....If you don't win, you're going to be fired. If you do win, you've only put off the day you're going to be fired. And no matter what you do, you're going to be second-guessed. The manager is the only person in the ball park who has to call it right now. Everybody else can call it after it's over.

LEO DUROCHER, *Nice Guys Finish Last*, 1975.

A consultant is someone who takes your watch away to tell you what time it is.

ED FINKELSTEIN, *New York Times*, April 29, 1979.

My father always told me that all businessmen were sons of bitches, but I never believed it till now.

JOHN F. KENNEDY, on steel industry executives who increased prices, April 11, 1962, in Arthur M. Schlesinger, Jr., *A Thousand Days*, 1965.

By the time you rise through the ranks, the culture of homogenization has bred the spirit and imagination out of you.

RALPH NADER, *Best of Business Quarterly*, Winter, 1986.

Anonymity and withdrawal are part of the CEO's inventory of power. The reverse of anonymity is visibility, which brings with it an expectation of accountability. If you want to operate without accountability, you make yourself difficult to reach.

RALPH NADER, *Best of Business Quarterly*, Winter, 1986.

Bankers Are Just Like Anybody Else, Except Richer.

OGDEN NASH, poem title, *I'm a Stranger Here Myself*, 1938.

The brand of leadership we propose has a simple base of MBWA (Managing By Wandering Around). To "wander," with customers and vendors and our own people, is to be in touch with the first vibrations of the new.

TOM PETERS AND NANCY AUSTIN, *A Passion for Excellence*, 1985.

The future work of the businessman is to teach the teacher, preach to the preacher, admonish the parent, advise the doctor, justify the lawyer, superintend the statesman, fructify the farmer, stabilize the banker, harness the dreamer, and reform the reformer.

EDWARD E. PURINTON, *Independent*, April 16, 1921.

I am married to my business.

BETTY RIVERA, *Hispanic Business*, June, 1987.

Most managers were trained to be the thing they most despise—bureaucrats.

ALVIN TOFFLER, *Newsweek*, April 4, 1988.

CLERGY

He could smell a sinner five miles away on a windless day.

HELEN HAYES, *On Reflection: An Autobiography*, 1968.

As a career, the business of an orthodox preacher is about as successful as that of a celluloid dog chasing an asbestos cat through hell.

ELBERT HUBBARD, *The Roycroft Dictionary and Book of Epigrams*, 1923.

It is not easy to be a nun. It is a life of sacrifice and self-abnegation. It is a life against nature. Poverty, chastity and obedience are extremely difficult. But there are always the graces if you will pray for them. Pray that you may all become St. Johns, lovers of Christ.

KATHRYN HULME, *The Nun's Story*, 1956.

Thrust into an undesired aloofness as earthly representatives of an ideal popularly regarded as impossible of achievement by "poor, weak human nature," charged with persuading the community to adopt a way of life at variance with its current concerns, they [ministers] seize upon every opportunity which seems to offer a means of sharing in the life about them without yielding too much of the principles to which they are committed.

ROBERT S. LYND AND HELEN MERRELL LYND, *Middletown: A Study in Contemporary American Culture*, 1929.

A great preacher is a great artist. Words are his tubes of paint. Verse, his brush. The souls of men the canvas on which he portrays the truths caught in moments of inspiration. The God-man is a man of imagination.

MELVIN B. TOLSON, "Portrait of Jesus, the Young Radical," *Washington Tribune*, July 4, 1938.

EDUCATORS

No honest historian can take part with—or against—the forces he has to study. To him even the extinction of the human race should be merely a fact to be grouped with other vital statistics.

HENRY ADAMS, *The Education of Henry Adams*, 1907.

A teacher affects eternity; he can never tell where his influence stops.

HENRY ADAMS, *The Education of Henry Adams*, 1907.

Nothing is more tiresome than a superannuated pedagogue.

HENRY ADAMS, *The Education of Henry Adams*, 1907.

When will the public cease to insult the teacher's calling with empty flattery? When will men who would never for a moment encourage their own sons to enter the work of the public schools cease to tell us that education is the greatest and noblest of all human callings?

WILLIAM C. BAGLEY, *Craftsmanship in Teaching*, 1911.

The condition of the true artisan, perhaps, is most nearly akin to the gifted schoolteacher's: an all but anonymous calling that allows for mastery, even for a sort of genius, but rarely for fame, applause, or wealth, whose chief reward must be the mere superlative doing of the thing.

JOHN BARTH, "Teacher: The Making of a Good One," *Harper's*, 1986.

My belief is that the last thing a good teacher wants to do is teach outside the classroom; certainly my own vision of bliss halfway through a term is solitary confinement in a soundproof cell.

JACQUES BARZUN, *Teacher in America*, 1944.

In teaching you cannot see the fruit of a day's work. It is invisible and remains so, maybe for twenty years.

JACQUES BARZUN, *Teacher in America*, 1944.

How then do you pour a little bit of what you feel and think and know into another's mind?... To help children visualize, to convince them, the teachers use maps, charts, diagrams, they write words on the board, they gesture, admonish, orate. Hence the fatigue and hence the rule that good teaching is a matter of basal metabolism. Some teachers have the facts but not the phosphorescence of learning.

JACQUES BARZUN, *Teacher in America*, 1944.

Teaching is not a lost art, but the regard for it is a lost tradition.

JACQUES BARZUN, *Newsweek*, December 5, 1955.

I am sure it is one's duty as a teacher to try to show boys that no opinions, no tastes, no emotions are worth much unless they are one's own. I suffered acutely as a boy from the lack of being shown this.

A.C. BENSON, *The Upton Letters*, 1905.

The professors laugh at themselves, they laugh at life; they long ago abjured the bitch-goddess Success, and the best of them will fight for his scholastic ideals with a courage and persistence that would shame a soldier. The professor is not afraid of words like *truth*; in fact he is not afraid of words at all.

CATHERINE DRINKER BOWEN, *Adventures of a Biographer*, 1946.

For the educator, complacent in his ivory tower, to scorn affiliation with a cause he considers to be noble, to refuse to attempt to win disciples from the ranks of students he is in a position to influence, is unmistakably to forswear a democratic responsibility, and to earn for himself the contemptible title of dilettante and solipsist.

WILLIAM F. BUCKLEY, JR., *God and Man at Yale*, 1951.

[Many a teacher] will chill the fire in a January stove...and will furrow the brow of a happy, barefoot boy....She rings the bell, calls the roll, and hears the spelling and arithmetic with the same spirit in which she counts the linen for the wash. At best her brow wears the gloom of forced duty.

FREDERIC BURK, "The Withered Heart of the Schools,"
Educational Review, December, 1907.

Arrogance, pedantry, and dogmatism are the occupational diseases of those who spend their lives directing the intellects of the young.

HENRY SEIDEL CANBY, *Alma Mater*, 1936.

Educators can no longer assume that somebody else will do the educational job for them. With everybody going to school till adulthood, school has become the place for learning whatever one needs in order to be both human and effective.

PETER F. DRUCKER, *The Age of Discontinuity*, 1968.

Teaching is the only major occupation of man for which we have not yet developed tools that make an average person capable of competence and performance. In teaching we rely on the "naturals," the ones who somehow know how to teach. Nobody seems to know, however, what it is the "naturals" do that the rest of us do not. No one knows what they do not do that the rest of us do.

PETER F. DRUCKER, *The Age of Discontinuity*, 1968.

We have inadvertently designed a system in which being good at what you do as a teacher is not formally rewarded, while being poor at what you do is seldom corrected nor penalized.

ELLIOTT EISNER, *New York Times*, September 3, 1985.

I have never heard anyone whom I consider a good teacher claim that he or she *is* a good teacher—in the way that one might claim to be a good writer or surgeon or athlete. Self-doubt seems very much a part of the job of teaching: one can never be sure how well it is going.

JOSEPH EPSTEIN, "A Class Act," *Quest*, September, 1981.

Scholarship must be free to follow crooked paths to unexpected conclusions.

CHARLES FRANKEL, *Time*, May 14, 1979.

To regard teachers—in our entire educational system, from the primary grades to the university— as priests of our democracy is therefore not to indulge in hyperbole. It is the special task of teachers to foster those habits of open-mindedness and critical inquiry which alone make for responsible citizens, who, in turn, make possible an enlightened and effective public opinion.

FELIX FRANKFURTER, opinion, *Wieman v. Updegraff*, 1952.

Teaching is an instinctual art, mindful of potential, craving of realizations, a pausing, seamless process.

A. BARTLETT GIAMATTI, "The American Teacher," *Harper's*,
July, 1980.

Teachers are expected to reach unattainable goals with inadequate tools. The miracle is that at times they accomplish this impossible task.

HAIM G. GINOTT, *Teacher and Child*, 1972.

Good teaching is one-fourth preparation and three-fourths theatre.

GAIL GODWIN, *The Odd Woman*, 1974.

The classroom and teacher occupy the most important part, the most important position of the human fabric....In the schoolhouse we have the heart of the whole society.

HARRY GOLDEN, *So Long as You're Healthy: Teachers'
Revolution*, 1970.

A good teacher feels his way, looking for response.

PAUL GOODMAN, *Growing Up Absurd*, 1960.

A Socrates in every classroom.

A. WHITNEY GRISWOLD, on standard for Yale faculty, *Time*,
June 11, 1951.

Everyone who remembers his own educational experience remembers teachers, not methods and techniques. The teacher is the kingpin of the educational situation. He makes or breaks programs.

SIDNEY HOOK, *Education for Modern Man*, 1946.

As you look at your youngsters, be sure that your standards of promptness, of attention, of quiet, of courtesy, are realistically geared to children, not idealistically geared to angels.

JAMES L. HYMES, JR., "The Oldest Order Changeth," *NEA
Journal*, April, 1953.

A good teacher is one who helps you become who you feel yourself to be. A good teacher is also one who says something you won't understand until 10 years later.

JULIUS LESTER, "College Teachers," *Quest*, September,
1981.

The scholar digs his ivory cellar in the ruins of the past and lets the present sicken as it will.

ARCHIBALD MACLEISH, *The Irresponsibles*, 1940.

If one cannot state a matter clearly enough so that even an intelligent twelve-year-old can understand it, one should remain within the cloistered walls of the university and laboratory until one gets a better grasp of one's subject matter.

MARGARET MEAD, *Redbook,* July, 1963.

The most extraordinary thing about a really good teacher is that he or she transcends accepted educational methods. Such methods are designed to help average teachers approximate the performance of good teachers.

MARGARET MEAD, *Redbook,* September, 1972.

The teacher's life should have three periods—study until 25, investigation until 40, profession until 60, at which age I would have him retired on a double allowance.

WILLIAM OSLER, speech, Baltimore, Maryland, February 22, 1905.

What constitutes the teacher is the passion to make scholars.

GEORGE HERBERT PALMER, *The Teacher, Essays and Addresses on Education: The Ideal Teacher,* 1908.

The teacher should never lose his temper in the presence of the class. If a man, he may take refuge in profane soliloquies; if a woman, she may follow the example of one sweet-faced and apparently tranquil girl—go out in the yard and gnaw a post.

WILLIAM LYON PHELPS, *Teaching in School and College,* 1912.

Men frequently view teaching as a stepping stone to educational administration while women look to careers as classroom teachers.

CAROL POLOWY, "Sex Discrimination: The Legal Obligations of Educational Institutions," *Vital Speeches,* February 1, 1975.

The inexperienced teacher, fearing his own ignorance, is afraid to admit it. Perhaps that courage only comes when one knows to what extent ignorance is almost universal.

EZRA POUND, *ABC of Reading,* 1934.

Scholars who enter a field because of what it can do for them in career terms (rather than because of what they can do for it) often end up as members of intellectual blocs—gatekeeprs insisting on tolls being paid to their fields and their preferred factors from any intellectual traffic.

DAVID RIESMAN, *Constraint and Variety in American Education,* 1956.

You've become silly from teaching children! You give them what little sense you have, and they give you all their stupidity.

JOSEPH ROTH, *The Story of a Simple Man,* 1931.

Teachers should unmask themselves, admit into consciousness the idea that one does not need to know everything there is to know and one does not have to pretend to know everything there is to know.

ESTHER P. ROTHMAN, *Troubled Teachers,* 1977.

You don't have to talk too hard when you talk to a teacher.

J.D. SALINGER, *The Catcher in the Rye,* 1951.

A good teacher is firm and active. It is important not to confuse firmness with punishment. The two are by no means identical.

PERCIVAL M. SYMONDS, "Classroom Discipline," *Teachers College Record,* December, 1949.

A teacher should have maximal authority, and minimal power.

THOMAS SZASZ, *The Second Sin: Education,* 1973.

Good teachers are costly, but bad teachers cost more.

BOB TALBERT, *Detroit Free Press,* April 5, 1982.

I'm never going to be a movie star. But then, in all probability, Liz Taylor is never going to teach first and second grade.

MARY H. WILSON, *Newsweek,* July 4, 1976.

The business of the American teacher is to liberate American citizens to think apart and act together.

STEPHEN S. WISE, *New York Times Magazine,* March 22, 1953.

One good teacher in a lifetime may sometimes change a delinquent into a solid citizen.

PHILIP WYLIE, *Generation of Vipers,* 1942.

FARMERS AND RANCHERS

[The farmer] sees the very definitions of the land continuously changing, or at most briefly poised; he sees, in both senses, the way the country lies.

DOUGLAS BAUER, "The Way the Country Lies," in Michael Martone, ed., *A Place of Sense,* 1988.

How extraordinary. To think that the lure of the life has always been its reliability. I imagine a farmer, year after year, growing old with the ceremony, opening the earth and placing his seeds, the *sureness* of the life, until he achieves a perfectly reductive sublimity and dies on the land in the way he has lived, solemnly placed, his last seed, in his soil.

It's this certainty that farmers need, to be able to predict their clean and ordered steps toward death.

Douglas Bauer, "The Way the Country Lies," in Michael Martone, ed., *A Place of Sense*, 1988.

It was Alexandra who could always tell about what it had cost to fatten each steer, and who could guess the weight of a hog before it went on the scales closer than John Bergson himself. Lou and Oscar were industrious, but he could never teach them to use their heads about their work.

Willa Cather, *O Pioneers!*, 1913.

To herd sheep is to discover a new human gear somewhere between second and reverse—a slow, steady trot of keenness with no speed. There is no flab in these days. But the constant movement of sheep from water hole to water hole, from camp to camp, becomes a form of longing.

Gretel Ehrlich, *The Solace of Open Spaces*, 1985.

Farming looks mighty easy when your plow is a pencil and you're a thousand miles from the corn field.

Dwight D. Eisenhower, speech, Peoria, Illinois, September 25, 1956.

About the only thing that will make a Wyoming cattleman reach for his gun nowadays is to call him a "farmer." A "rancher," he wants it clearly understood, drinks only canned milk, never eats vegetables, and grows nothing but hay and whiskers.

John Gunther, *Inside U.S.A.*, 1947.

Little ol' boy in the Panhandle told me the other day you can still make a small fortune in agriculture. Problem is, you got to start with a large one.

Jim Hightower, speech, Dallas Chamber of Commerce, *New York Times*, March 9, 1986.

The only difference between a pigeon and the American farmer today is that a pigeon can still make a deposit on a John Deere.

Jim Hightower, speech, Dallas Chamber of Commerce, *New York Times*, March 9, 1986.

Real cowgirls don't identify much with Tom Robbins' nubile maids who know more about whooping cranes than cattle and would rather roll in the hay with each other than pitch it to the horses. But Robbins points out a basic truth. While the cow*boy* is our favorite American hero—the quintessential man—most of us see

the cow*girl* as a child who will grow up someday and be something else. The cowboy's female counterpart—who can ride and rope and wrangle, who understands land and stock and confronts the elements on a daily basis—is somehow missing from our folklore.

Teresa Jordan, *Cowgirls, Women of the American West*, 1982.

These [country women] are women of the American soil. They are a hardy stock. They are the roots of our country....They are not our well-advertised women of beauty and fashion.... These women represent a different mode of life. They are of *themselves* a very great American style. They live with courage and purpose, a part of our tradition.

Dorothea Lange, quoted in Anne Tucker, ed., *The Woman's Eye*, 1973.

Farmers now are members of a capital-intensive industry that values good bookwork more than backwork. So several times a year almost every farmer must seek operating credit from the college fellow in the white shirt and tie—in effect, asking financial permission to work hard on his own land.

Andrew H. Malcolm, "Murder on the Family Farm," *New York Times*, March 23, 1986.

The more experience cowboys get, the more their world can shrink. Men they once admired, diminish; knowing is the beginning of knowing too much. The bigger the country, the bigger the appetite for seeing new country. Cowboys, like anyone else, are seldom satisfied with their lives.

Kurt Markus, *Buckaroo*, 1987.

The cowboy and the farmer are genuinely inimical types: they have seldom mixed easily.

Larry McMurtry, *In a Narrow Grave: Essays on Texas*, 1968.

No one hates his job so heartily as a farmer.

H.L. Mencken, "What Is Going On in the World?" *American Mercury*, November, 1933.

[B]ut it's our land. We measured it and broke it up. We were born on it, and we got killed on it, died on it. Even if it's no good, it's still ours. That's what makes it ours—being born on it, working it, dying on it. That makes ownership, not a paper with numbers on it.

John Steinbeck, *The Grapes of Wrath*, 1939.

And all their love was thinned with money, and all their fierceness dribbled away in interest until they were no longer farmers at all, but little shopkeepers of crops, little manufacturers who must sell before they can make.

JOHN STEINBECK, *The Grapes of Wrath*, 1939.

Where industrialization of agriculture runs its full course the term "farmer" no more suggests a man with hand on the plow than "manufacturer" now means what once it did—a maker of things by hand.

PAUL S. TAYLOR, "Good-by to the Homestead Farm," *Harper's*, May, 1941.

FIRST LADIES

This was one of those terrific, pummeling White House days that can stretch and grind and use you—even I, who only live on the periphery. So what must it be like for Lyndon!

CLAUDIA "LADY BIRD" JOHNSON, diary entry, March 14, 1968, *A White House Diary*, 1970.

The first lady is, and always has been, an unpaid public servant elected by one person, her husband.

CLAUDIA "LADY BIRD" JOHNSON, *U.S. News & World Report*, March 9, 1987.

A politician ought to be born a foundling and remain a bachelor.

CLAUDIA "LADY BIRD" JOHNSON, *Time*, December 1, 1975.

The one thing I do not want to be called is First Lady. It sounds like a saddle horse.

JACQUELINE KENNEDY, in Peter Collier and David Horowitz, *The Kennedys*, 1984.

Being first lady is the hardest unpaid job in the world.

PAT NIXON, interview, Monrovia, Liberia, March 15, 1972.

I have sacrificed everything in my life that I consider precious in order to advance the political career of my husband.

PAT NIXON, in Betty Medsger, *Women at Work*, 1975.

Any lady who is first lady likes being first lady. I don't care what they say, they like it.

RICHARD M. NIXON, *Newsweek*, March 22, 1971.

Always be on time. Do as little talking as humanly possible. Remember to lean back in the parade car so everybody can see the President. Be sure not to get too fat because you'll have to sit three in the back seat.

ELEANOR ROOSEVELT, on campaign behavior for first ladies, *New York Times*, November 11, 1962.

The first ladyship is the only federal office in which the holder can neither be fired nor impeached.

WILLIAM SAFIRE, *New York Times*, March 2, 1987.

GOVERNMENT OFFICIALS AND POLITICIANS

The perfect bureaucrat is the man who manages to make no decisions and escapes all responsibility.

BROOKS ATKINSON, *Once Around the Sun*, 1951.

Politician, n. An eel in the fundamental mud upon which the superstructure of organized society is reared. When he wriggles he mistakes the agitation of his tail for the trembling of the edifice. As compared with the statesman, he suffers the disadvantage of being alive.

AMBROSE BIERCE, *The Devil's Dictionary*, 1906.

The function of a briefing paper is to prevent the ambassador from saying something dreadfully indiscreet. I sometimes think its true object is to prevent the ambassador from saying anything at all.

KINGMAN BREWSTER, speech, English-Speaking Union, Edinburgh, Scotland, September 8, 1977.

The opportunist thinks of me and today. The statesman thinks of us and tomorrow.

DWIGHT D. EISENHOWER, speech, Lafayette College, Easton, Pennsylvania, November 1, 1946.

Politics is a profession; a serious, complicated and, in its true sense, a noble one.

DWIGHT D. EISENHOWER, letter to Leonard V. Finder, January 22, 1948.

There is one thing about being president—nobody can tell you when to sit down.

DWIGHT D. EISENHOWER, "Sayings of the Week," *Observer*, August 9, 1953.

Freedom is essential to the politician. A politician must have independent means to pay ordinary bills, the mortgage, the doctor. A politician should be able to look anyone in the eye and say: "Sorry, I can't do that."

MILLICENT FENWICK, *Boston Globe*, August 6, 1982.

Politics really must be a rotten profession considering what awful moral cowards most politicians become as soon as they get a job.

MARTHA GELLHORN, "The War in China," *The Face of War*, 1988.

[Statesman:] One who cannot compromise with what he knows to be right or make political deals which will allow a form of evil or injustice to be even temporarily victorious. Usually not an elected public official. In times of crisis, the statesman flexes his mind and not his muscle.

DICK GREGORY, *Dick Gregory's Political Primer*, 1972.

[Statesmanship:] The art of uncompromising devotion to humanity, the alleviation of suffering, and the creation of a decent and peaceful environment throughout the world.

DICK GREGORY, *Dick Gregory's Political Primer*, 1972.

The biggest problem in politics is that you help some S.O.B. get what he wants and then he throws you out of the train.

MARTHA GRIFFITHS, on Michigan governor James Blanchard's decision to drop her from reelection ticket, *New York Times*, September 5, 1990.

A politician will do anything to keep his job— even become a patriot.

WILLIAM RANDOLPH HEARST, editorial, August 28, 1933.

You can't adopt politics as a profession and remain honest.

LOUIS McHENRY HOWE, speech, Columbia University, January 17, 1933.

If you're in politics and you can't tell when you walk into a room who's for you and who's against you, then you're in the wrong line of work.

LYNDON B. JOHNSON, in Booth Mooney, *The Lyndon Johnson Story*, 1964.

In politics it is difficult sometimes to decide whether the politicians are humorless hypocrites or hypocritical humorists.

FRANK RICHARDSON KENT, *Baltimore Sun*, July 24, 1932.

The public life of every political figure is a continual struggle to rescue an element of choice from the pressure of circumstance.

HENRY KISSINGER, *White House Years*, 1979.

High office teaches decision making, not substance. [It] consumes intellectual capital; it does not create it. Most high officials leave office with the perceptions and insights with which they entered; they learn how to make decisions but not what decisions to make.

HENRY KISSINGER, *White House Years*, 1979.

A woman politician [executive] learns to operate on two levels: a gender-neutral level, focussing on the issue, and a gender-sensitive level, always alert to the signals.

MADELEINE KUNIN, *The Journal of State Government*, September/October, 1987.

Politics, like theater, is one of those things where you've got to be wise enough to know when to leave.

RICHARD LAMM, *U.S. News & World Report*, January 26, 1987.

What this country needs is more unemployed politicians.

EDWARD LANGLEY, *San Francisco Chronicle*, October 24, 1980.

Politicians have the same occupational hazard as generals—focusing on the last battle and overreacting to that.

ANN F. LEWIS, *New York Times*, September 24, 1986.

The politician says: "I will give you what you want." The statesman says: "What you think you want is this. What it is possible for you to get is that. What you really want, therefore, is the following."

WALTER LIPPMANN, *A Preface to Morals*, 1929.

Successful...politicians are insecure and intimidated men. They advance politically only as they placate, appease, bribe, seduce, bamboozle or otherwise manage to manipulate the demanding and threatening elements in their constituencies.

WALTER LIPPMANN, *The Public Philosophy*, 1955.

It is the mark of the successful politician that he faces the inevitable, and then takes credit for it. Jumping the bandwagon can be made to look like leadership if the move is made dexterously enough.

CHARLES McCABE, in Edmund G. Brown, *Reagan: The Political Chameleon*, 1976.

A good [politician] is quite as unthinkable as an honest burglar.

H.L. MENCKEN, *Newsweek*, September 12, 1955.

Politics is like retail. You keep the customers you have, and then you make new ones.

BARBARA A. MIKULSKI, *Business Week*, August 11, 1986.

One has to be a lowbrow, a bit of a murderer, to be a politician, ready and willing to see people sacrificed, slaughtered, for the sake of an idea, whether a good one or a bad one.

HENRY MILLER, in George Plimpton, ed., *Writers at Work*, 1963.

The politician is…trained in the art of inexactitude. His words tend to be blunt or rounded, because if they have a cutting edge they may later return to wound him.

EDWARD R. MURROW, speech, England, October 19, 1959, in A.M. Sperber, *Murrow*, 1986.

Political success comes from a combination of hard work and breaks. But unless you have the guts to take chances when the breaks come your way, and the determination and stamina to work hard, you will never amount to much more than a political hack and a perennial "almost-ran" in your political career.

RICHARD M. NIXON, in Earl Mazo, *Richard Nixon: A Political and Personal Portrait*, 1959.

Politics is an art and a science. Politicians are, in the main, honorable, above average in their intellectual equipment, and effective in getting action on problems that less practical people only talk or write about. An individual has to be a politician before he can be a statesman.

RICHARD M. NIXON, in Earl Mazo, *Richard Nixon: A Political and Personal Portrait*, 1959.

The man who deliberately weakens his party almost invariably ends up by weakening himself.

RICHARD M. NIXON, in Earl Mazo, *Richard Nixon: A Political and Personal Portrait*, 1959.

If more politicians in this country were thinking about the next generation instead of the next election, it might be better for the United States and the world.

CLAUDE PEPPER, *Orlando Sentinel-Star*, December 29, 1946.

The politician who steals is worse than a thief. He is a fool. With the grand opportunities all around for a man with political pull, there's no excuse for stealin' a cent.

GEORGE WASHINGTON PLUNKITT, *Time*, August 22, 1955.

I had been lauded as a star in sports and had been praised in movies; in politics I found myself misrepresented, cursed, vilified, denounced, and libeled. Yet it was by far the most fascinating part of my life.

RONALD REAGAN, *Where's the Rest of Me?*, 1965.

Twelve years ago, Barbara Jordan—another Texas woman—made the keynote address to this convention. Two women in 160 years is about par for the course. But if you give us a chance, we can perform. After all, Ginger Rogers did everything that Fred Astaire did, she just did it backwards and in high heels.

ANN W. RICHARDS, Democratic National Convention, July 18, 1988.

Politics is not a vocation. It is not even an avocation. It's an incurable disease. If it ever gets in one's blood, it can never be eradicated.

JOSEPH T. ROBINSON, speech, Charlotte, North Carolina, 1928.

Politics is the best show in America. I love animals and I love politicians and I love to watch both of 'em play, either back home in their native state or after they have been captured and sent to the zoo or to Washington.

WILL ROGERS, in *New York Times* article, January 28, 1984.

Politicians cannot afford to deal in finalities and ultimate truths; they abide, by and large, by probabilities and reasonable assumptions and the law of averages.

RICHARD ROVERE, *Senator Joe McCarthy*, 1959.

Diplomats make it their business to conceal the facts.

MARGARET SANGER, *Woman and the New Race*, 1920.

Bureaucrats are the only people in the world who can say absolutely nothing and mean it.

HUGH SIDEY, *Time*, November 29, 1976.

When a bureaucrat makes a mistake and continues to make it, it usually becomes the new policy.

HUGH SIDEY, *Time*, November 29, 1976.

Make politics a sport, as they do in England, or a profession, as they do in Germany….But don't try to reform politics with the banker, the lawyer, and the drygoods merchant, for these are businessmen.

LINCOLN STEFFENS, "Great Types of Modern Business—Politics," *Ainslee's*, October, 1901.

After lots of people who go into politics have been in it for a while they find that to stay in politics they have to make all sorts of compromises to satisfy their supporters and that it becomes awfully important for them to keep their jobs because they have nowhere else to go.

ADLAI E. STEVENSON, interview, 1958.

A diplomat is a person who can tell you to go to hell in such a way that you actually look forward to the trip.

CASKIE STINNETT, *Out of the Red*, 1960.

A career politician finally smelling the White House is not much different from a bull elk in the rut. He will stop at nothing, trashing anything that gets in his way; and anything he can't handle personally he will hire out—or, failing that, make a deal. It is a difficult syndrome for most people to understand, because few of us ever come close to the kind of Ultimate Power and Achievement that the White House represents to a career politician.

HUNTER S. THOMPSON, *Fear and Loathing on the Campaign Trail, '72*, 1973.

A leader has to lead, or otherwise he has no business in politics.

HARRY S TRUMAN, in Merle Miller, *Plain Speaking: An Oral Biography of Harry S Truman*, 1974.

Defeat in itself was part and parcel of the great gambling game of politics. A man who could not accept it and try again was not of the stuff of which leaders are made.

AGNES SLIGH TURNBULL, *The Golden Journey*, 1955.

I happen to think that American politics is one of the noblest arts of mankind; and I cannot do anything else but write about it.

THEODORE H. WHITE, *New York Times*, June 22, 1965.

The best time to listen to a politician is when he's on a stump on a street corner in the rain late at night when he's exhausted. Then he doesn't lie.

THEODORE H. WHITE, *New York Times*, January 5, 1969.

Tin-horn politicians.

WILLIAM ALLEN WHITE, *Emporia Gazette*, October 25, 1901.

The American creed is that most politicians of all parties are bad, the worst ones generally being in the other party, and the good ones all dead or out of office.

WILLIAM ALLEN WHITE, *Masks in a Pageant*, 1928.

There is no indispensable man. The government will not collapse and go to pieces if any one of the gentlemen who are seeking to be entrusted with its guidance should be left at home.

WOODROW WILSON, 1912, *New York Times Magazine*, June 10, 1956.

HOMEMAKERS

The mature woman...after having raised her children has been a "chief executive officer" at home for ten years or more. No one told her whether to dust first or make the beds first—and both chores got done. Yet when she starts working, she is put under a "supervisor" who treats her as a moron who has never done anything on her own before when what she needs is a teacher and an assistant.

PETER F. DRUCKER, *Management in Turbulent Times*, 1980.

American housewives have not had their brains shot away, nor are they schizophrenic in the clinical sense. But if...the fundamental human drive is not the urge for pleasure or the satisfaction of biological needs, but the need to grow and to realize one's full potential, their comfortable, empty, purposeless days are indeed cause for a nameless terror.

BETTY FRIEDAN, *The Feminine Mystique*, 1963.

No girl child today should responsibly be brought up to be a housewife. Too much has been made of defining human personality and destiny in terms of the sex organs. After all, we share the human brain.

BETTY FRIEDAN, 1968, in Lois and Alan Gordon, *American Chronicle*, 1987.

The cocktail party or dinner party is, essentially, an affair, more refined and complex than those at which embroidery or livestock are entered in competition but for the same ultimate purpose of displaying and improving the craftsmanship or breed. The cleanliness of the house, the excellence of the garden, the taste, quality and condition of the furnishings and the taste, quality and imagination of the food and intoxicants and the deftness of their service are put on display before the critical eye of those invited to appraise them. Comparisons are made with other exhibitors. Ribbons are not awarded, but the competent administrator is duly proclaimed a good housekeeper, a gracious hostess, a clever manager or, more simply, a really good wife.

JOHN KENNETH GALBRAITH, *Annals of an Abiding Liberal*, 1979.

A human creature must do human work; and all women are no more to be contented as house servants and housekeepers than all men would be.

CHARLOTTE PERKINS GILMAN, "The Passing of Matrimony," *Harper's Bazaar*, June, 1906.

I think housework is the reason most women go to the office.

HELOISE, *Editor & Publisher*, April 27, 1963.

I believe that all women, but especially house-wives, tend to think in lists....The idea of a series of items, following one another docilely, forms the only possible reasonable approach to life if you have to live it with a home and a hus-band and children, none of whom would dream of following one another docilely.

SHIRLEY JACKSON, *Life Among the Savages*, 1953.

Time was when kitchens were big and dark, for keeping house was a gloomy business....But now! Gay colors are the order of the day. Red pots and pans! Blue gas stoves!....It is a rainbow, in which the cook sings at her work and never thinks of household tasks as drudgery.

EDITORIAL, *Ladies' Home Journal*, April, 1928.

By and large, mothers and housewives are the only workers who do not have regular time off. They are the great vacationless class.

ANNE MORROW LINDBERGH, *Gift from the Sea*, 1955.

Housework isn't bad in itself—the trouble with it is that it's inhumanly lonely.

PAT LOUD, *Pat Loud: A Woman's Story*, 1974.

When there is no private realm, rank derives only from jobs, and a person without a job, no matter how charming, amusing, educated, beau-tiful, or rich, is a person without social identifi-cation or standing. This is why women who were once proud of singlehandedly maintaining pri-vate, domestic, community, social, and cultural life for men who could manage only one job apiece, are now ashamed or defensive about being housewives.

JUDITH MARTIN, *Common Courtesy*, 1985.

To be a housewife is...a difficult, a wrenching, sometimes an ungrateful job if it is looked on only as a job. Regarded as a profession, it is the noblest as it is the most ancient of the catalogue. Let none persuade us differently or the world is lost indeed.

PHYLLIS MCGINLEY, *Sixpence in Her Shoe*, 1964.

Home life...has been robbed by the removal of *creative* work. You cannot make women contented with cooking and cleaning and *you need not try*.

ELLEN H. SWALLOW RICHARDS, ca. 1900.

It is either a very dull woman, or an unusually self-sufficient woman, who can escape being affected by the wearisome combination of high altitude, three-day sandstorms, and the lonely and tremendous reach of land and sky.

Worst of all to me was the monotony of unac-customed housework. It was often too heavy for me, and was always an uninteresting drudgery. No one can deny that the men worked hard too. But they were out of doors, usually on horseback and working with animals, and they were free to meet others interested in the same business.

It was a truly surprised and unhappy rancher who said: "I can't figure out why my wife went crazy. Why, she ain't been out of the kitchen in twenty years!"

He merely expressed the viewpoint of many another man. It had not occurred to him that woman is a gregarious animal—or should be.

DOROTHY ROSS, *Stranger to the Desert*, 1958.

Housework, if it is done right, can kill you.

JOHN SKOW, "Erma in Bomburbia," *Time*, July 2, 1984.

For a woman to get a rewarding sense of total creation by way of the multiple monotonous chores that are her daily lot would be as irra-tional as for an assembly line worker to rejoice that he had created an automobile because he tightened a bolt.

EDITH MENDEL STERN, "Women Are Household Slaves," *American Mercury*, January, 1949.

JUDGES AND LAWYERS

The trouble with lawyers is they convince them-selves that their clients are right.

CHARLES W. AINEY, letter to Eugene Gerhart, August 25, 1963.

I don't think it's useful to talk about percentages when discussing lawyer competency. It depends on one's standards for competency. If the stan-dard is that of lawyers who shouldn't be practic-ing at all, the incompetence rate is, maybe, five percent. If the standard is room for improve-ment, that would include 99 percent of all lawyers and 99.9 percent of all judges.

ANTHONY G. AMSTERDAM, *Los Angeles Times*, November 5, 1978.

The public regards lawyers with great distrust. They think lawyers are smarter than the average guy but use their intelligence deviously. Well, they're wrong; usually, they are not smarter.

F. Lee Bailey, *Los Angeles Times*, January 9, 1972.

[A lawyer's] performance in the courtroom is responsible for about 25 percent of the outcome; the remaining 75 percent depends on the facts.

Melvin Belli, *U.S. News & World Report*, September 20, 1982.

Holmes divided lawyers into kitchen knives, razors, and stings. Brandeis, he said, was a sting.

Catherine Drinker Bowen, *Yankee from Olympus*, 1944.

Lawyers better remember they are human beings, and a human being who hasn't his periods of doubts and distresses and disappointments must be a cabbage, not a human being.

Felix Frankfurter, "Proceedings in Honor of Mr. Justice Frankfurter and Distinguished Alumni," *Occasional Pamphlet*, Harvard Law School, 1960.

There is no surer way to misread any document than to read it literally.... As nearly as we can, we must put ourselves in the place of those who uttered the words, and try to divine how they would have dealt with the unforeseen situation; and, although their words are by far the most decisive evidence of what they would have done, they are by no means final.

Learned Hand, opinion, *Giuseppi v. Walling*, 1944.

Obviously, the whole purpose of a police investigation is frustrated if a suspect is entitled to have a lawyer during preliminary questioning, for any lawyer worth his fee will tell him to keep his mouth shut.

Frank S. Hogan, *New York Times*, December 2, 1965.

Law is what a judge dispenses. The judge, however, is no representative of the average man's common sense. A certain remoteness from the experiences of everyday life and a certain rigidity of viewpoint are essential to his role as judge.

Gerhart Husserl, *Journal of Social Philosophy*, July, 1940.

What most impresses us about great jurists is not their tenacious grasp of fine points, honed almost to invisibility; it is the moment when we are suddenly aware of the sweep and direction of the law, and its place in the lives of men.

Irving R. Kaufman, speech, Institute of Judicial Administration, August 26, 1969.

Never, never, never, on cross-examination ask a witness a question you don't already know the answer to, was a tenet I absorbed with my baby-food. Do it, and you'll often get an answer you

don't want, an answer that might wreck your case.

Harper Lee, *To Kill a Mockingbird*, 1960.

Lawyers as a group are no more dedicated to justice or public service than a private public utility is dedicated to giving light.

David Melinkoff, *San Francisco Examiner & Chronicle*, June 22, 1973.

Judge—a law student who marks his own examination papers.

H.L. Mencken, "Sententiae," *The Vintage Mencken*, 1955.

Lawyers are like beavers: They get in the mainstream and damn it up.

John Naisbitt, *Megatrends*, 1984.

Most lawyers who win a case advise their clients "We have won," and when justice has frowned upon their cause..."*You* have lost."

Louis Nizer, *My Life in Court*, 1960.

The difference between an office lawyer and a trial lawyer is as great as between an internist and a surgeon. Both require high talents, but the specialized skills and tools are so different that they may as well be in different professions.

Louis Nizer, *Newsweek*, December 10, 1973.

Lawyers [are] operators of the toll bridge across which anyone in search of justice has to pass.

Jane Bryant Quinn, *Newsweek*, October 9, 1978.

[The] ideal client is the very wealthy man in very great trouble.

John Sterling, "Lawyers and the Laws of Economics," *American Bar Association Journal*, April, 1960.

[T]he job of a judge is to figure out what the law says, not what he wants it to say. There is a difference between the role of a judge and that of a policy maker.... Judging requires a certain impartiality.

Clarence Thomas, conversation with Dinesh D'Souza, *Wall Street Journal*, July 2, 1991.

Next to the confrontation between two highly trained, finely honed batteries of lawyers, jungle warfare is a stately minuet.

Bill Veeck, *The Hustler's Handbook*, 1965.

An incompetent attorney can delay a trial for years or months. A competent attorney can delay one even longer.

Evelle J. Younger, *Los Angeles Times*, March 3, 1971.

PERFORMING ARTISTS

People wouldn't know a good actor if they saw one, but they can recognize a good part....If you have a good part in a hit, your whole life will change, you will become a success, and you will pay a price for that success. You will play the same part all the rest of your life under different names.

GEORGE ABBOTT, in Heywood Hale Broun, *Tumultuous Merriment*, 1979.

We are living in the machine age. For the first time in history the comedian has been compelled to supply himself with jokes and comedy material to compete with the machine. Whether he knows it or not, the comedian is on a treadmill to oblivion.

FRED ALLEN, *Treadmill to Oblivion*, 1954.

In the theater the actor has uncertainty, broken promises, constant travel and a gypsy existence. In radio, if you were successful, there was an assured season of work. The show could not close if there was nobody in the balcony. There was no travel and the actor could enjoy a permanent home. There may have been other advantages but I didn't need to know them.

FRED ALLEN, *Treadmill to Oblivion*, 1954.

An actor's popularity is fleeting. His success has the life expectancy of a small boy who is about to look into a gas tank with a lighted match.

FRED ALLEN, *Much Ado About Me*, 1956.

I am sure that if all the hours vaudeville performers spent trying to improve their acts had been donated to science, automation would have been here fifty years sooner.

FRED ALLEN, *Much Ado About Me*, 1956.

The vaudeville actor was part gypsy and part suitcase.

FRED ALLEN, *Much Ado About Me*, 1956.

It's one of the tragic ironies of the theatre that only one man in it can count on steady work—the night watchman.

TALLULAH BANKHEAD, *Tallulah*, 1952.

For an actress to be a success she must have the face of Venus, the brains of Minerva, the grace of Terpsichore, the memory of Macaulay, the figure of Juno, and the hide of a rhinoceros.

ETHEL BARRYMORE, in George Jean Nathan, *The Theatre in the Fifties*, 1953.

Audiences? No, the plural is impossible. Whether it be in Butte, Montana, or Broadway, it's an audience. The same great hulking monster with four thousand eyes and forty thousand teeth.

JOHN BARRYMORE, to playwright Ashton Stevens, April, 1906, in Gene Fowler, *Good Night, Sweet Prince*, 1943.

The Great Actor always must act. He must make a ceremony of waking up in the morning. He must sit in his room and act so that his whole body vibrates to the thrill of it. Forever he must be a poseur. Every last second of his life must be pose and posture.

LIONEL BARRYMORE, in Gene Fowler, *Good Night, Sweet Prince*, 1943.

Any little pinhead who makes one picture is a "star."

HUMPHREY BOGART, in Richard Schickel, *The Stars*, 1962.

The only thing you owe the public is a good performance.

HUMPHREY BOGART, in Max Wilk, *The Wit and Wisdom of Hollywood*, 1971.

Your audience gives you everything you need.... There is no director who can direct you like an audience.

FANNY BRICE, in Norman Katkov, *The Fabulous Fanny*, 1952.

Every actor has a natural animosity toward every other actor, present or absent, living or dead. Most Hollywood directors did not understand that, any more than they understood why an actor might be tempted to withhold the rapt devotion to the master which they considered essential to their position of command.

LOUISE BROOKS, *Lulu in Hollywood*, 1982.

There was no other occupation in the world that so closely resembled enslavement as the career of a film star.

LOUISE BROOKS, *Lulu in Hollywood*, 1982.

When I was under contract to Paramount in 1928, [I] complained about being forced to hang around Hollywood waiting to make some film. "That's what we are paying you for—your time," was the harsh comment of the front office. "You mean my life," I said to myself.

LOUISE BROOKS, *Lulu in Hollywood*, 1982.

Your true...tragedy is enacted on the stage of a man's soul, and with the man's reason as lone auditor.

JAMES BRANCH CABELL, *The Cream of the Jest*, 1917.

I'd like to think that when I sing a song, I can let you know all about the heartbreak, struggle, lies and kicks in the ass I've gotten over the years for being black and everything else, without actually saying a word about it.

RAY CHARLES, interview, *Playboy*, 1970.

The movie actor, like the sacred king of primitive tribes, is a god in captivity.

ALEXANDER CHASE, *Perspectives*, 1966.

Guts and imagination were the two things Lee Strasberg said an actor needed.

Out of work is the one thing an actor generally gets.

CHRIS CHASE, *How To Be a Movie Star, or A Terrible Beauty Is Born*, 1968.

An actor admits to no incapacity whatever. You find three-hundred-pound bald guys sidling up to a director who's looking for a romantic lead, and whispering shyly, "I work without my glasses."

CHRIS CHASE, *How To Be a Movie Star, or A Terrible Beauty Is Born*, 1968.

A good education is usually harmful to a dancer. A good calf is better than a good head.

AGNES DE MILLE, news item, February 1, 1954.

My band is my instrument.

DUKE ELLINGTON, *The New Yorker*, July, 1944.

The requirements for glamour in jazz too often include eccentricity, limited technical scope (supposedly compensated by "soul"), a personal background of social problems, and a tendency to show up for the Wednesday matinee at midnight on Thursday.

LEONARD FEATHER, *From Satchmo to Miles*, 1972.

I've got the celluloid in my blood.

W.C. FIELDS, in Robert Lewis Taylor, *W.C. Fields, His Follies and Fortunes*, 1949.

[Metro-Goldwyn-Mayer] had us working days and nights on end. They'd give us pep-up pills to keep us on our feet long after we were exhausted. Then they'd take us to the studio hospital and knock us cold with sleeping pills....Then after four hours they'd wake us up and give us the pep-up pills again so we could work another seventy-two hours in a row.

JUDY GARLAND, in Anne Edwards, *Judy Garland*, 1975.

From the very moment they enter the career of ballet, dancers are programmed in diffidence. For ballet is more than art, more than business; it is

a closed world where those in authority have almost total control over every aspect of the dancer's life.

Behind the intricate and beautiful choreography we see onstage is an even more forceful yet subtle choreography of power.

SUZANNE GORDON, *Off Balance: The Real World of Ballet*, 1983.

I think songwriters have the greatest obituaries in the world. When a songwriter dies, the minute you read the list of songs he wrote, you start to identify with him....People read the obit and they respond, "Oh, my God, he wrote *that*. I remember the first time I heard that song, I was at a dance with a girl...."

ABEL GREEN, in Max Wilk, *They're Playing Our Song*, 1973.

You can't write a good song about a whore-house unless you been in one.

WOODY GUTHRIE, *Broadside*, 1964.

An actress's life is so transitory—suddenly you're a building.

HELEN HAYES, on Broadway theater named for her, November, 1955.

It is difficult, if not impossible, for a star to occupy an inch of space without bursting seams, cramping everyone else's style and unbalancing a play. No matter how self-effacing a famous player may be, he makes an entrance as a casual neighbor and the audience interest shifts to the house next door.

HELEN HAYES, *On Reflection: An Autobiography*, 1968.

It's such a cuckoo business. And it's a business you go into because you're egocentric. It's a very embarrassing profession.

KATHARINE HEPBURN, in "Hepburn: She Is the Best," *Los Angeles Times*, November 24, 1974.

Actors are cattle.

ALFRED HITCHCOCK, *Saturday Evening Post*, May 22, 1943.

People don't understand the kind of fight it takes to record what you want to record the way you want to record it.

BILLIE HOLIDAY, with William Dufty, *Lady Sings the Blues*, 1956.

Every dancer lives on the threshold of chucking it.

JUDITH JAMISON, *New York Times Magazine*, December 5, 1976.

Any girl can be glamorous. All you have to do is stand still and look stupid.

HEDY LAMARR, in Richard Schickel, *The Stars*, 1962.

I've made so many movies playing a hooker that they don't pay me in the regular way any more. They leave it on the dresser.

SHIRLEY MACLAINE, *Out on a Limb*, 1983.

Even the ears must dance.

NATALIA MAKAROVA, *Newsweek*, May 19, 1975.

Actors begin where militia colonels, Fifth Avenue rectors and Rotary orators leave off. The most modest of them (barring, perhaps, a few unearthly traitors to the craft) matches the conceit of the solitary pretty girl on a slow ship.

H.L. MENCKEN, *Damn! A Book of Calumny*, 1918.

To play great music, you must keep your eyes on a distant star.

YEHUDI MENUHIN, *Reader's Digest*, December, 1953.

We hide ourselves in our music to reveal ourselves.

JIM MORRISON, *Today*, Winter, 1975.

I left the screen because I didn't want what happened to Chaplin to happen to me. When he discarded the little tramp, the little tramp turned around and killed him.

MARY PICKFORD, in Aljean Harmetz, *New York Times* article, March 28, 1971.

So much of our profession is taken up with pretending, with the interpretation of never-never roles, that an actor must spend at least half his waking hours in fantasy, in rehearsal or shooting. If he is only an actor, I feel, he is much like I was in *King's Row*, only half a man—no matter how great his talents.

RONALD REAGAN, *Where's the Rest of Me?*, 1965.

The performer may have a responsibility toward the composer, but the composer has none toward the performer beyond the practical one of making his music performable on some terms.

NED ROREM, *The Final Diary*, 1974.

A concert is like a bullfight—the moment of truth.

ARTUR RUBINSTEIN, in Robert Jacobson, *Reverberations*, 1974.

The worst feeling in the world is to go back into an empty hall after the audience has left. You see the work lights and the bare stage, and you can't believe there was so much happening in there just a few minutes ago. I can never be left alone after a concert. I need someone to help me come down.

MELANIE SAFKA, *Rolling Stone*, April 1, 1971.

The biggest gift that your fans can give you is just treatin' you like a human being, because anything else dehumanizes you.

BRUCE SPRINGSTEEN, *Rolling Stone*, 1984.

My only problem is finding a way to play my fortieth fallen female in a different way from my thirty-ninth.

BARBARA STANWYCK, interview with Hedda Hopper, 1953.

Leave them when you're looking good and thank God for the trust funds Mama set up.

CONSTANCE TALMADGE, in Richard Schickel, *The Stars*, 1962.

Learning to conduct is a lot like being in boot camp using live ammo.

KATE TAMARKIN, Vermont Public Radio, May 3, 1991.

Polyphony, flatted fifths, half-tones—they don't mean a thing. I just pick up my horn and play what I feel.

JACK TEAGARDEN, *New York Times*, January 16, 1964.

You got to have smelt a lot of mule manure before you can sing like a hillbilly.

HANK WILLIAMS, ca. 1940, *Look*, July 13, 1971.

SCIENTISTS AND DOCTORS

He just wanted to get that knife into me. He'd cut you if you had dandruff.

FANNY BRICE, in Norman Katkov, *The Fabulous Fanny*, 1953.

The books of the great scientists are gathering dust on the shelves of learned libraries. And rightly so. The scientist addresses an infinitesimal audience of follow composers. His message is not devoid of universality, but its universality is disembodied and anonymous. While the artist's communication is linked forever with its original form, that of the scientist is modified, amplified, fused with the ideas and results of others, and melts into the stream of knowledge and ideas which forms our culture. The scientist has in common with the artist only this: that he can find no better retreat from the world than his work and also no stronger link with the world than his work.

MAX DELBRUCK, Nobel lecture, 1969.

Science is a wonderful thing if one does not have to earn one's living at it.

ALBERT EINSTEIN, letter to California student, March 24, 1951, in Helen Dukas and Banesh Hoffman, *Albert Einstein: The Human Side*, 1979.

Bone hunting is not really a very romantic occupation. One walks day after day along miles of frequently unrewarding outcrop. One grows browner, leaner, and tougher, it is true, but one is far from the bright lights, and the prospect, barring a big strike, like a mammoth, is always to abandon camp and go on. It was really a gypsy profession, then, for those who did the field collection.

Loren Eiseley, "The Last Neanderthal," *The Star Thrower*, 1964.

Not by reason alone, but by the combustive chemistry of idea and temperament mixed, do scientists carry on.

Philip Hilts, *Scientific Temperaments: Three Lives in Contemporary Science*, 1982.

Who ever said that doctors are truthful or even intelligent? You're getting a lot if they know their profession.

Marjorie Karmel, *Thank You, Dr. Lamaze*, 1959.

[Scientists] are peeping Toms at the keyhole of eternity.

Arthur Koestler, *The Roots of Coincidence*, 1972.

The national unwillingness to call things by their right names weighs heavily on the whole of society, but on no other class in the society does the projection of the magical wish fall as vividly as it falls on doctors. The noncombatants decline to accept the limits of medicine. They expect not only perfect health but also a cure for death.

Lewis H. Lapham, speech, "The Senior Practitioner," speech at Northwestern Medical School, June, 1987.

Scientists, like game players, prefer to devise their own strategies, even though these depend on an assimilated, shared body of knowledge.

S.E. Luria, *A Slot Machine, A Broken Test Tube: An Autobiography*, 1984.

Sometimes age corrects the excessive illusions, and scientists begin to look upon their enterprises with a cooler, more existential eye. But this attitude rarely appears in [the] book. The doubts and inner struggles of scientists, unlike those of novelists, are more often converted into inner turmoil than into print.

S.E. Luria, *A Slot Machine, A Broken Test Tube: An Autobiography*, 1984.

If you know you are on the right track, if you have this inner knowledge, then nobody can turn you off...regardless of what they say.

Barbara McClintock, in Evelyn Fox Keller, "Barbara McClintock: The Overlooked Genius of Genetics," *A Passion To Know: 20 Profiles in Science*, 1985.

[After getting consistent, repeatable results from an experiment] I had no sense of elation, just of relief. It is like having a headache for ten years, and suddenly it goes away. It comes back, unfortunately, the next week, if you're crazy enough to be doing experimental science.

Mark Ptashne, in Philip Hilts, "Mark Ptashne: Molecular Mission," *A Passion To Know: 20 Profiles in Science*, 1985.

You do an experiment because your own philosophy makes you want to know the result. It's too hard, and life is too short, to spend your time doing something because someone else has said it's important. You must feel the thing yourself—feel that it will change your outlook and your way of life. You must bring it back to the human condition, the human expression—much closer to what the artist is supposed to feel.

I.I. Rabi, in Jeremy Bernstein, *Experiencing Science*, 1978.

I think physicists are the Peter Pans of the human race. They never grow up, and they keep their curiosity. Once you are sophisticated, you know too much—far too much.

I.I. Rabi, in Jeremy Bernstein, *Experiencing Science*, 1978.

Medical doctors strike me as ignorant as to how a *healthy* body works. They know how to control or repair some diseased bodies, but their medicine is often worse than the disease. And what about the pressure and competitiveness of the pharmaceutical industry and the make-profits-quick motives of the food corporations? Medical doctors put little or no emphasis on nutrition, exercise, and energy balance. They are paid when we are sick, not when we are well.

Jerry Rubin, *Growing (Up) at 37*, 1976.

A good scientist is a person in whom the childhood quality of perennial curiosity lingers on. Once he gets an answer, he has other questions.

Frederick Seitz, *Fortune*, April, 1976.

Curiosity may have killed the cat, but it has never been detrimental to the doctor.

Peter J. Steinchrohn, *More Years for the Asking*, 1940.

The great secret of doctors, known only to their wives, but still hidden from the public, is that most things get better by themselves; most things, in fact, are better in the morning.

Lewis Thomas, *New York Times*, July 4, 1976.

What good is discovery if you can't celebrate it with firecrackers?

John Wheeler, in Dennis Overbye, "John Wheeler: Messenger at the Gates of Time," *A Passion To Know: 20 Profiles in Science*, 1985.

Nothing comes harder than original thought. Even the most gifted scientist spends only a tiny fraction of his waking hours doing it, probably less than one tenth of one percent. The rest of the time his mind hugs the coast of the known, reworking old information, adding lesser data, giving reluctant attention to the ideas of others (what use can *I* make of them?), warming lazily to the memory of successful experiments, and looking for a problem—always looking for a problem, something than can be accomplished, that will lead somewhere, anywhere.

EDWARD O. WILSON, *Biophilia*, 1984.

The scientists most esteemed by their colleagues are those who are both very original and committed to the abstract ideal of truth in the midst of the clamoring demands of ego and ideology. They pass the acid test of promoting new knowledge even at the expense of losing credit for it....Their principal aim is to discover natural law marked by *elegance*, the right mix of simplicity and latent power.

EDWARD O. WILSON, *Biophilia*, 1984.

SOLDIERS AND POLICE OFFICERS

It was February, it was early in the morning, it was cold, and there was no heat. Standing around in my pelt, with the frigid drafts caressing my nates and adjacent areas, I felt like an Eskimo awaiting his turn at a public shower bath.

FRED ALLEN, description of wait for draft medical exam, *Much Ado About Me*, 1956.

The nation which forgets its defenders will be itself forgotten.

CALVIN COOLIDGE, speech, Northampton, Massachusetts, July 27, 1920.

—What You Can Do to Help the Returning Veteran

—Will He Be Changed?

—After two or three weeks he should be finished with talking, with oppressive remembering. If he still goes over the same stories, reveals the same emotions, you had best consult a psychiatrist. This condition is neurotic.

Good Housekeeping, 1945.

Sometimes I didn't know if an action took a second or an hour or if I dreamed it or what. In war more than in other life you don't really know what you're doing most of the time, you're just behaving, and afterward you can make up any kind of bullshit you want to about it, say you felt good or bad, loved it or hated it, did this or that, the right thing or the wrong thing.

MICHAEL HERR, *Dispatches*, 1977.

A soldier is a slave—he does what he is told to do—everything is provided for him—his head is a superfluity. He is only a stick used by men to strike other men; and he is often tossed to Hell without a second thought.

ELBERT HUBBARD, *The Roycroft Dictionary and Book of Epigrams*, 1923.

The power to wage war is the power to wage war successfully.

CHARLES EVANS HUGHES, *The Supreme Court of the United States*, 1928.

You have to understand something about police in whatever city and country in the world: they're tough. Reporters have a word for it: copper-hard. It's not a cause so much as an effect. You walk a beat for eight hours, with kids jeering at you, drunks clawing at you, women screaming at you, men insulting you, and nobody, not the shopkeeper, the cab driver, the bartender, the pedestrian, none of them with even a smile for you, and you get tough awful fast.

NORMAN KATKOV, *The Fabulous Fanny*, 1953.

The world has turned over many times since I took the oath on the plain at West Point, and the hopes and dreams have long since vanished. But I still remember the refrain of one of the most popular barrack ballads of that day, which proclaimed, most proudly, that "Old soldiers never die. They just fade away." And like the soldier of the ballad, I now close my military career and just fade away—an old soldier who tried to do his duty as God gave him the light to see that duty.

DOUGLAS MACARTHUR, farewell speech to Congress, April 19, 1951.

A general is just as good or just as bad as the troops under his command make him.

DOUGLAS MACARTHUR, on receiving congressional resolution of gratitude, August 16, 1962.

Wars may be fought with weapons, but they are won by men. It is the spirit of the men who follow and of the man who leads that gains the victory.

GEORGE S. PATTON, *Cavalry Journal*, September, 1933.

A pint of sweat will save a gallon of blood.

GEORGE S. PATTON, message to troops en route to North Africa, October, 1942.

You begin to feel that you can't go on forever without being hurt. I feel that I have used up all my chances. And I hate it. I don't want to be killed.

ERNIE PYLE, 1945, in Lois and Alan Gordon, *American Chronicle*, 1987.

Great horror as war itself is, every honest soldier knows that it has its moments of joy—joy in the fellowship of one's fighting comrades, joy and pride in the growth of a fighting spirit and the conviction of invincibility that shines out of the faces of well-led and well-disciplined troops; and the small but treasured joy of a warm fire and a plain hot meal at the end of a cold and difficult day.

MATTHEW B. RIDGWAY, *The Korean War*, 1967.

No man in uniform, be he private or five-star general, may decide for himself whether an order is consonant with his personal views. While the loyalty he owes his superiors is reciprocated with equal force in the loyalty owed him from above, the authority of his superiors is not open to question.

MATTHEW B. RIDGWAY, *The Korean War*, 1967.

A man who is good enough to shed his blood for his country is good enough to be given a square deal afterwards. More than that no man is entitled to, and less than that no man shall have.

THEODORE ROOSEVELT, speech, Springfield, Illinois, June 4, 1903.

Humilities are piled on a soldier…so in order that he may, when the time comes, be not too resentful of the final humility—a meaningless and dirty death.

JOHN STEINBECK, *East of Eden*, 1952.

Air power is our initial line of defense, but no one has proved to my satisfaction that we will have only world wars to be settled only by big bangs….Infantrymen at one time or another become indispensable. Nothing we have discovered or expect to discover will reduce the need for brave men to fight our battles.

MAXWELL D. TAYLOR, quoted in obituary, *New York Times*, April 21, 1987.

The core of the military profession is discipline and the essence of discipline is obedience. Since this does not come naturally to men of independent and rational mind, they must train themselves in the habit of obedience on which lives and the fortunes of battle may someday depend.

Reasonable orders are easy enough to obey; it is capricious, bureaucratic or plain idiotic demands that form the habit of discipline.

BARBARA TUCHMAN, *Stilwell and the American Experience in China: 1911–1945*, 1970.

The difficult we do immediately. The impossible takes a little longer.

MOTTO, U.S. Army Corps of Engineers, World War II.

The lines of red are lines of blood, nobly and unselfishly shed by men who loved the liberty of their fellow men more than they loved their own lives and fortunes.

WOODROW WILSON, speech, Flag Day, May 7, 1915.

Let it be your pride, therefore, to show all men everywhere not only what good soldiers you are, but also what good men you are, keeping yourselves fit and straight in everything, and pure and clean through and through. Let us set for ourselves a standard so high that it will be a glory to live up to it, and then let us live up to it and add a new laurel to the crown of America.

WOODROW WILSON, message to U.S. forces, September 4, 1917.

WRITERS

It is a sad fact about our culture that a poet can earn much more money writing or talking about his art than he can by practicing it.

W. H. AUDEN, Foreword, *The Dyer's Hand*, 1962.

Nobody loves a poet.

IRVING BABBITT, *Rousseau and Romanticism*, 1919.

I handled the first Presidential bowel movement in the history of the *New York Times*.

RUSSEL L. BAKER, in Nora Ephron, "Russell Baker," *Esquire*, April, 1976.

At this time I had decided the only thing I was fit for was to be a writer, and this notion rested solely on my suspicion that I would never be fit for real work, and that writing didn't require any.

RUSSELL BAKER, *Growing Up*, 1982.

The biggest obstacle to professional writing today is the necessity for changing a typewriter ribbon.

ROBERT BENCHLEY, "Learn To Write," *Chips Off the Old Benchley*, 1949.

When you were living a tale you did not have time to color it as it should be colored—your mind stuck on odd useless trifles—the teeth of a man you struck—the feel of an iron bar—the shape of a sail against the stars. Besides, in life you were hungry and thirsty and had to make water—things which did not happen in a tale, or, if they did, assumed heroic proportions.

STEPHEN VINCENT BENÉT, *Spanish Bayonet*, 1926.

What makes a good writer of history is a guy who is suspicious. Suspicion marks the real difference between the man who wants to write honest history and the one who'd rather write a good story.

JIM BISHOP, *New York Times*, February 5, 1955.

For your born writer, nothing is so healing as the realization that he has come upon the right word.

CATHERINE DRINKER BOWEN, *Adventures of a Biographer*, 1946.

[D]uring the actual work of creation the writer cuts himself off from all others and confronts his subject alone. He moves into a realm where he has never been before—perhaps where no one has ever been. It is a lonely place, and even a little frightening.

RACHEL CARSON, speech, American Association of University Women, June 22, 1956.

The discipline of the writer is to learn to be still and listen to what his subject has to tell him.

RACHEL CARSON, speech, American Association of University Women, June 22, 1956.

Your complete literary chap is a writing animal; and when he dies he lives a cocoon as large as a hay stack, in which every breath he has drawn is recorded in writing.

JOHN JAY CHAPMAN, *Greek Genius and Other Essays*, 1915.

In my opinion, any novelist who can't lure a reader away from a bad soap opera is wasting his time.

JOHN CHEEVER, "In Praise of Readers," *Parade*, December 28, 1980.

Most women in this business don't cover games. Ninety percent of us don't—not a good balance. The standard idea of a woman sportswriter's story is doing Steve Garvey's wife or writing a feature about Nancy Lopez. The men on the beat are always aware of that. This is why locker-room access is the heart of it all. Access is the key to covering games, and you aren't a sportswriter—you haven't paid your dues—unless you cover.

BETTY CUNIBERTI, in article by Roger Angell, *The New Yorker*, April 9, 1979.

The artistic impulse seems not to wish to produce finished work. It certainly deserts us halfway, after the idea is born; and if we go on, art is labor.

CLARENCE DAY, *This Simian World*, 1920.

But the poet's job is, after all, to translate God's poem (or is it the Fiend's?) into words.

BABETTE DEUTSCH, "Poetry at the Mid-Century," in Helen Hull, ed., *The Writer's Book*, 1950.

The poet...like the lover...is a person unable to reconcile what he knows with what he feels. His peculiarity is that he is under a certain compulsion to do so.

BABETTE DEUTSCH, "Poetry at the Mid-Century," in Helen Hull, ed., *The Writer's Book*, 1950.

Novelists, whatever else they may be besides, are also children talking to children—in the dark.

BERNARD DE VOTO, *The World of Fiction*, 1950.

Writing a book is like rearing children—willpower has very little to do with it.

ANNIE DILLARD, "To Fashion a Text," in William Zinsser, ed., *Inventing the Truth*, 1987.

The progress of an artist is a continual self-sacrifice, a continual extinction of personality.

T.S. ELIOT, "Tradition and the Individual Talent," 1917, in Walter Jackson Bate, ed., *Criticism: The Major Texts*, 1952.

Writers should know when not to intervene, for very little of any life can be tidily explained and its seams made straight.

GLORIA EMERSON, "Prologue," *Some American Men*, 1985.

I like to think of the world I created as being a kind of keystone in the universe; that, small as the keystone is, if it were ever taken away the universe itself would collapse.

WILLIAM FAULKNER, quoted in Malcolm Cowley, *A Second Flowering*, 1973.

All good writing is *swimming under water* and holding your breath.

F. SCOTT FITZGERALD, letter to daughter, ca. 1940, *The Crack-up*, 1945.

Often I think writing is a sheer paring away of oneself, leaving always something thinner, barer, more meagre.

F. SCOTT FITZGERALD, letter to daughter, April 27, 1940, *The Crack-up*, 1945.

Poetry is either something that lives like fire inside you—like music to the musician or Marxism to the Communist—or else it is nothing, an empty, formalized bore, around which pedants can endlessly drone their notes and explanations.

F. Scott Fitzgerald, letter to daughter, August 3, 1940, *The Crack-up*, 1945.

Writing free verse is like playing tennis with the net down.

Robert Frost, speech, Milton [Massachusetts] Academy, May 17, 1935.

Like a piece of ice on a hot stove a poem must ride on its own melting. A poem may be worked over once it is in being, but may not be worried into being.

Robert Frost, Introduction, *Collected Poems*, 1939.

No tears in the writer, no tears in the reader. No surprise for the writer, no surprise for the reader.

Robert Frost, "The Figure a Poem Makes," Preface, *Collected Poems*, 1939.

Originality is something that is easily exaggerated, especially by authors contemplating their own work.

John Kenneth Galbraith, *The Affluent Society*, 1976.

We are all desperately afraid of sounding like Carry Nation. I must take the risk. Any writer who wants to do his best against a deadline should stick to Coca-Cola.

John Kenneth Galbraith, *Annals of an Abiding Liberal*, 1979.

The essential tragedy and hopelessness of most human life under the conditions into which our society was swiftly hardening embittered me, called for expression, but even then I did not know that I had found my theme. I had no intention at the moment of putting it into fiction.

Hamlin Garland, *A Son of the Middle Border*, 1917.

The sense of the insanity and wickedness of this war grew in me until, for purposes of mental hygiene, I gave up trying to think or judge, and turned myself into a walking tape recorder with eyes. The way people stay half sane in war, I imagine, is to suspend a large part of their reasoning minds, lose most of their sensitivity, laugh when they get the smallest chance, and go a bit, but increasingly, crazy.

Martha Gellhorn, "The War in Finland," *The Face of War*, 1988.

The average contributor to this magazine is semiliterate; that is, he is ornate to no purpose, full of

senseless and elegant variations, and can be relied on to use three sentences where a word would do.

Wolcott Gibbs, "Theory and Practice of Editing *The New Yorker* Articles," in James Thurber, *The Years with Ross*, 1957.

The great thing is to last and get your work done and see and hear and learn and understand; and write when there is something that you know; and not before; and not too damned much after.

Ernest Hemingway, *Death in the Afternoon*, 1932.

Shells are all much the same. If they don't hit you, there's no story, and if they do, you don't have to write it.

Ernest Hemingway, dispatch for North American Newspaper Alliance, October 7, 1937.

For a true writer each book should be a new beginning where he tries again for something that is beyond attainment. He should always try for something that has never been done or that others have tried and failed. Then sometimes, with great luck, he will succeed. How simple the writing of literature would be if it were only necessary to write in another way what has been well written. It is because we have had such great writers in the past that a writer is driven far out past where he can go, out to where no one can help him.

Ernest Hemingway, speech recorded for Nobel Prize Committee, accepting Nobel Prize for literature, 1954.

A writing man is something of a black sheep, like the village fiddler. Occasionally a fiddler becomes a violinist, and is a credit to his family, but as a rule he would have done better had his tendency been toward industry and saving.

Edgar Watson Howe, *The Blessing of Business*, 1918.

The poor writers we have always with us—if we take the daily paper.

Elbert Hubbard, *The Roycroft Dictionary and Book of Epigrams*, 1923.

It is through the ghost[writer] that the great gift of knowledge which the inarticulate have for the world can be made available.

Elizabeth Janeway, in Helen Hull, ed., *The Writer's Book*, 1950.

There is always this to be said for the literary profession—like life itself, it provides its own revenges and antidotes.

Elizabeth Janeway, in Helen Hull, ed., *The Writer's Book*, 1950.

The Negro artist, because of his middle-class background, carried the artificial social burden as the "best and most intelligent" of Negroes, and usually entered into the "serious" arts to exhibit his familiarity with the social graces, i.e., as a method or means of displaying his participation in the "serious" aspects of American culture. To be a writer was to be "cultivated," in the stunted bourgeois sense of the word. It had nothing to do with the investigation of the human soul. It was, and is, a social preoccupation rather than an aesthetic one.

LeRoi Jones, "The Myth of a 'Negro Literature,'" *On Being Black*, 1970.

A good many young writers make the mistake of enclosing a stamped, self-addressed envelope, big enough for the manuscript to come back in. This is too much of a temptation to the editor.

Ring Lardner, *How To Write Short Stories*, 1924.

The moral dimension of language must be brought out. All good writers are troublemakers, all good writers are sworn enemies of complacency and dogma. The storyteller's responsibility is not to be wise; a storyteller is the person who creates an atmosphere in which wisdom can reveal itself.

Barry Lopez, Introduction, in Stephen Trimble, *Words from the Land*, 1988.

Nine-tenths of the best poetry of the world has been written by poets less than thirty years old; a great deal more than half of it has been written by poets under twenty-five.

H.L. Mencken, *Prejudices*, 1922.

You call this a script? Give me a couple of $5,000-a-week writers and I'll write it myself.

Joseph Pasternak, in Max Wilk, *The Wit and Wisdom of Hollywood*, 1971.

I loathe writing. On the other hand, I'm a great believer in money.

S.J. Perelman, interview, *Life*, 1962.

I wrote from the worm's-eye point of view.

Ernie Pyle, *Here Is Your War*, 1943.

Every misused word revenges itself forever upon a writer's reputation.

Agnes Repplier, *Points of Friction*, 1920.

I ain't no lady. I'm a newspaperwoman.

Hazel Brannon Smith, in article by T. George Harris, *Look*, November 16, 1965.

What I like in a good author is not what he says, but what he whispers.

Logan Pearsall Smith, *Afterthoughts*, 1931.

The great struggle of a writer is to learn to write as he would talk.

Attributed to Lincoln Steffens, in Justin Kaplan, *Lincoln Steffens: A Biography*, 1974.

The profession of book-writing makes horse racing seem like a solid, stable business.

John Steinbeck, Nobel Prize acceptance speech, Stockholm, Sweden, 1962.

Writers are notorious for using any reason to keep from working: over-researching, retyping, going to meetings, waxing the floors—anything.

Gloria Steinem, *Outrageous Acts and Everyday Rebellions*, 1983.

A poet looks at the world as a man looks at a woman.

Wallace Stevens, "Adagia," *Opus Posthumous*, 1957.

Your typewriter is a public trust. The sound may be the most beautiful noise you know. But it has meaning and justification only if it is a part of the gloriously discordant symphony of a free society.

Adlai E. Stevenson, speech, Washington, D.C., December 12, 1960.

There is probably some long-standing "rule" among writers, journalists, and other word-mongers that says: "When you start stealing from your own work you're in bad trouble." And it may be true.

Hunter S. Thompson, *Fear and Loathing on the Campaign Trail, '72*, 1973.

Skilled professional liars are as much in demand in politics as they are in the advertising business...and the main function of any candidate's press secretary is to make sure the press gets nothing but upbeat news.

Hunter S. Thompson, *Fear and Loathing on the Campaign Trail, '72*, 1973.

There is, of course, a certain amount of drudgery in newspaper work, just as there is in teaching classes, tunnelling into a bank, or being President of the United States. I suppose that even the most pleasurable of imaginable occupations, that of batting baseballs through the windows of the R.C.A. Building, would pale a little as the days ran on.

James Thurber, "Memoirs of a Drudge," *The Thurber Carnival*, 1945.

With sixty staring me in the face, I have developed inflammation of the sentence structure and a definite hardening of the paragraphs.

James Thurber, *New York Post*, June 30, 1955.

Certainly one knows more at forty than one did at twenty. And contrary to all American mythology, the novel is the rightful province not of the young but of the middle-aged.

Gore Vidal, "On Revising One's Own Work," *New York Times Book Review*, November 14, 1965.

To interrupt catastrophe is the artist's highest goal at a time when, like it or not, pure novelist and worldly polemicist are both in the same boat..., each bailing water since it is not (yet) man's nature to drown without a struggle.

Gore Vidal, Preface, June 6, 1968, *Reflections Upon a Sinking Ship*, 1969.

Writing saved me from the sin and *inconvenience* of violence—as it saves most writers who live in "interesting" oppressive times and are not afflicted by personal immunity.

Alice Walker, "One Child of One's Own: A Meaningful Digression Within the Work(s)," 1979, *In Search of Our Mothers' Gardens*, 1983.

Writing fiction is an interior affair. Novels and stories always will be put down little by little out of personal feeling and personal beliefs arrived at alone and at firsthand over a period of time as time is needed. To go outside and beat the drum is only to interrupt, and so finally to forget and to lose. Fiction has, and must keep, a private address.

Eudora Welty, *The Eye of the Story*, 1979.

Writing is so difficult that I often feel that writers, having had their hell on earth, will escape all punishment hereafter.

Jessamyn West, *To See the Dream*, 1956.

A writer is like a bean plant—he has his little day, and then gets stringy.

E.B. White, letter to Harold Ross, September 9, 1938.

I was interested in your remarks about the writer as poser, because, of course, all writing is both a mask and an unveiling, and the question of honesty is uppermost, particularly in the case of the essayist, who must take his trousers off without showing his genitals. (I got my training in the upper berths of Pullman cars long ago.)

E.B. White, letter to Scott Elledge, February 16, 1964.

Invariably, it is this for which I write: the joy... of an argument firmly made, like a nail straightly driven, its head flush to the plank.

George Will, "Journalism and Friendship," January 19, 1981, *The Pursuit of Virtue and Other Tory Notions*, 1982.

There is a serious profession of journalism, and it involves its own special problems. To write what you are interested in writing, and to succeed in getting editors to pay for it, is a feat that may require pretty close calculation and a good deal of ingenuity.

Edmund Wilson, *Letters on Literature and Politics 1912–1972*, 1977.

This is man: a writer of books, a putter-down of words, a painter of pictures, a maker of ten thousand philosophies. He grows passionate over ideas, he hurls scorn and mockery at another's work, he finds the one way, the true way, for himself, and calls all others false—yet in the billion books upon the shelf there is not one that can tell him how to draw a single fleeting breath in peace and comfort.

Thomas Wolfe, *You Can't Go Home Again*, 1934.

AUTHOR AND SOURCE INDEX

SUBJECT INDEX

excellence in —, 116L

fear process of re- —, 100L

first quality of good —, 319R

I.Q. disservice to creativity in —, 340L

one thing that can kill Movies, 331R

possible to get — at university, 166R

progress as nation no swifter than progress in —, 136L

"separate but equal" has no place, 158R, 393R, 400R

surest path of wisdom is liberal —, 385R

Educational, talk of — value of newspaper, 279L

Educational television, close look at gum surgery [as] sitting down to dinner, 334L

Educators, 511–513, *see also* Teacher

education too important left to —, 160L

language to add importance to unimportant, 290L

paid smaller wage than to whom entrust care of plumbing, 412R

sex in hands of — not pretty thing, 337R

unlock treasure, 168L

Effeminacy, not feminine possession, 497R

Effete

corps of impudent snobs, 109L

society [fears] its children is —, 11L

Efficiency

outgrowth of conservation is —, 406R

three-martini lunch epitome of —, 67L

Washington city of Southern —, 436L

Efficient, Americans most — people, 182R

Effort, grandness of —, 270R

Egocentric, business you go into because —, 522R

Egomania, symptoms alert diagnostician can spot, 244L

Egotism

is anesthetic dulls pain of stupidity, 244L

religion chapter in history of —, 356R

Eight-hour-day, should be adopted, 414L

Eighties, my — are passionate, 3L

Eighties (decade). *See* 1980s

Einstein, A.

even — needed help on 1040 form, 153L

if — doesn't like natural laws, 35R

Eisenhower, D.

bestowed upon golf enthusiasm withheld from ideas, 31L

better [with a putter] than with long shots, 179R

contribution to make politics boring, 33R

[distrusted] people of brilliance, 31L

don't know any more about politics, 25L

doubt if — can stand a second term, 33L

great tortoise, 31R

I Like Ike, 190R

quit collecting newspapers for —, 496L

too easily swayed, 181R

Elect, do not — wisest to represent us, 196L

Election

American — represents death, 113R

do job as if never be another —, 202R

Elections, 218–224, *see also* Campaign and political slogans; Vote

Electricity, in Louisiana vote by —, 441R

Elemental, world sick for lack of — things, 404R

Eleventh hour, at —, 265R

Eliminate, don't — problems by eliminating people, 384L

Elite, where — meet to eat, 332R

Ellington, D.

elegant and awe-inspiring, 27R

great conjurer of passion, 27R

Ellis Island, 126R

Emancipation

of working class, 412L

Proclamation but not fact, 120L, 387R

true — begins in woman's soul, 387R, 500R

Embarrass, if not from Texas why — by asking?, 458L

Emission, not go overboard in — standards, 406R

Emotion

good manners to do with —s, 320R

patriotism not short outburst of —, 134L

Empire, internal, domestic —, 461L

Employment, 79–80, *see also* Job; Labor; Unemployment; Work

capital to support shiftless diverted from other —, 417R

demoralizing to regard — as necessary evil, 501L

determination to give — to idle men, 199L

gainful — does not describe public office, 211L

open to [women] all —, but as necessary evil, 500R

Empty, days cause for nameless terror, 518R

Enchanting, no one find children as —, 351L

Enchantment, Land of —, 447R

Encroachment, insidious —, 116R

End

educational process own —, 159R

is this — of Rico?, 327R

life is — in itself, 297R

light at — of tunnel, 484R, 486L, 489R

of [Vietnam war] come into view, 492L

power not — in itself, 135L

promised to — war, 491L

want — to beginnings of all wars, 472L

war to — all wars, 493L

Endangered species, emphasis on preserving, 405R

Ends

democratic — demand democratic methods, 103L

wealth the means, people the —, 155L

Endure, love —s when lovers love many things together, 264L

End zone, bury my heart in —, 429L

Enemies, forgive —, but never forget names, 297R

Enemy, *see also* War

death not the —, 92L

don't have personal — left, 243L

how could science be — of religion?, 366L

met — and he is us, 266R

of mankind enslaves by terror, 128R

press is the —, 281L

privilege to prove world is his —, 244L

says: "I am your friend," 253L

time-consuming to have —, 255R

world his —, 244L

Energy, 376–377

in New York, 450L

science all-pervasive —, 367L

Engine, of change, 373R

Engineering, architecture begins where — ends, 51R

England, *see also* British

green damp — of Oregon, 454L

New — neither new nor like —, 436L

should we fight for —?, 494L

English language. *See* Language

Enjoy

ability to — moment, 1L

built just to —, 441R

capacity and chance to —, 4L

ice cream while on your plate, 299R

Enlarged, in New York, 448L

Enough, Had —?, 190R

Enriches, whatever — uneconomic, 154L

Enslave, few [tyrannies] — [like] drug addiction, 401R

Enslaved, *see also* Slave

impossible for one who has — to accept, 401L

want no integration with race that — us, 401L

Entertainment

electrical appliance offers more — than TV set, 335R

formula for success in —, 337L

supra-ideology of television, 335L

Entrepreneur

allowed freedom to use public, 174R

trend of Democracy toward —, 228L

use word [for] any government we do not like, 199L

Social issues, 383–420, *see also* Domestic policy; specific issues

Society, *see also* America/American headings; Civilization; Culture; Foreign views on Americans; Primitive society; Social issues

acting out a — I'd live in as orangutan, 87R

as a —, we're a banana republic, 441R

better to have — where all have something, 98L

college not founded to give — what it wants, 166L

contemporary — is repressive —, 89R

diseased, 315R

family is God's basic unit in —, 343L

first overcommunicated —, 376L

first — in which children are poorest group, 86R

free — right to be unpopular, 122R

free —'s future depends upon morality in proportion to wealth, 174R

individualism reward for full participation in —, 128L

is like air, 90R

isolated — never again be possible, 379R

is riddled with comedy, 258R

judge — by people it produces, 91R

justice accomodation of conflicting interests of —, 130L

most stable in which men and women work together, 90L

neutron bomb symbol of —'s anomalies, 378L

no guarantee that high IQ people produce better —, 261R

novelists declared enemies of their —, 58L

of Boston uncivilized but refined, 443L

permissive — acts liberal, 296L

schools petrify —, 170L

separation of religion from —, 365L

so beautifully sentimental on murder, 385L

taxes dues we pay for membership in —, 153L

user-oriented —, 437R

where freedom is possession of only savage few, 119L

which [fears] its children is effete, 11L

whole fabric of —, 295L

words hold — together, 286L

Sociology, economics without — skeletal, 143L

Socrates

in every classroom, 512R

might define [university] as conversation about wisdom, 165L

Soft, Americans too —, 12R

Soil

fifty million *tons* of — blown away, 453R

people and — fit, 455L

to call war — of courage, 472R

Solar system, lunatic asylum of —, 339R

Soldier

not raised to be — not entitled to citizenship, 482R

prepared to cope with hardships of war, 473R

Soldiers, 525–526, *see also* Military; War

Solemn, people want — ass as President, 200L

Solitary, only — know full joys of friendship, 344L

Solitude

marriage affords company and — at same time, 348L

un-American, 15L

Solution

cannot believe war best —, 496L

no — possible now, 384L

part of — or part of problem, 394L

when demand — with no costs, no —s, 144L

Solvency, matter of temperament, 147L

Somebody, everybody wants to be —, 449R

Song, *see also* Sing

blues —s of despair; gospel —s of hope, 61L

can't write good — about whorehouse unless been in one, 522R

care not who writes laws of country [if can] listen to its —s, 61L

like people, animals, plants, 62L

[popular] — is machine-made, 60L

Songwriters, have greatest obituaries, 522R

Sons of bitches. *See* SOB

Sooner, Oklahoma called — state, 453L

Sorrow, *see also* Pain; Sadness

hundred thousand —s touching my heart, 492L

no such thing as old age, only —, 4R

Sorry

John Wayne never felt —, 484R

love means never having to say you're —, 264R

Soul

art is the — of a people, 48L

begins at conception, 383R

can't weigh — with bar of pig-iron, 401R, 505R

cultivated by study/thought, 160L

feets tired, but — rested, 386R

hunger of the —, 163R

man immortal because has —, 95R

of the Negro, 99L

rather see America save her — than face, 489R

sad — can kill you, 241L

technology throws loop of wire around our —s, 373L

throw energies of his — into making something, 246R

to dispose a — to action, 238R

true emancipation begins in woman's —, 387R, 500R

Sound

accept a — is a —, 59R

moving pictures need — [like] Beethoven symphonies need lyrics, 329R

music is feeling, not —, 62L

talking picture will never supersede motion picture without —, 331L

Sour, grapes beyond reach can be *really* —, 298R

South, 455–456

bring to white heat and then remold, 388R

camp meetings and revivals —'s past/present, 359L

glowing climate for guilt, 363R

stands at Armageddon, 395L

too busy building [separate] washrooms, 394R

white — united in insistence upon segregation, 386R

South Carolina, 456

South Dakota, 456–457

Southeast Asia. *See* Vietnam War

South Korea. *See* Korean War

South Vietnam. *See* Vietnam War

Souvenirs, American fought for —, 493L

Soviet Union, *see also* Cold War; Russia; Union of Soviet Socialist Republics

choose either confrontation or cooperation, 474R

driven by fear of —, 252R

secret agreement between U.S. and —, 208L

U.S. policy toward — containment, 475L

Space, 138, *see also* Frontier

there is a — race down here on the ground, 407L

Space Age, students equipped to cope with —, 170R

Space exploration, 379–380

beaten you to moon, 181R

meaningless unless coincides with interior expansion, 381L

right stuff, 137L

Sputnik recognized crisis, 170R

Space ship, we travel together on little —, 406R

Spared, wanted to be — war, 473L

Spare part, only state boasting —, 443L

Spark, single revolutionary —, 295R

Speak

cannot — clearly cannot think cogently, 163R

please — up!, 188R, 216L

softly and carry big stick, 208L

Special, what makes [American Man] so —?, 303L

Specialization, out of hand, 373R

Spectator sport, stakes too high for government be —, 187L